Larson Boswell Kanold Stiff

Worked-Out Solution Key

The Solution Key provides step-by-step solutions for all the exercises in the student edition.

McDougal Littell
A HOUGHTON MIFFLIN COMPANY
Evanston, Illinois • Boston • Dallas

Copyright © 2001 by McDougal Littell Inc.
All rights reserved.

No part of this work may be reproduced or transmitted in any form or by any means, electronic or mechanical, including photocopying and recording, or by any information storage or retrieval system without prior written permission by McDougal Littell Inc. unless such copying is expressly permitted by federal copyright law. Address inquiries to Manager, Rights and Permissions, McDougal Littell Inc., P.O. Box 1667, Evanston, IL 60204.

ISBN: 0-618-07864-9

3456789 -DWI- 04 03 02 01

Contents

PRE-COURSE TEST

Decimals *(p. xviii)*

1.
$$\begin{array}{r} 3.400 \\ +6.005 \\ \hline 9.405 \end{array}$$

2.
$$\begin{array}{r} 27.77 \\ -18.09 \\ \hline 9.68 \end{array}$$

3.
$$\begin{array}{r} 13.67 \\ \times\ 23.7 \\ \hline 9569 \\ 41010 \\ 273400 \\ \hline 323.979 \end{array}$$

4. $9.744 \div 0.87 = 974.4 \div 87$

$$\begin{array}{r} 11.2 \\ 87\overline{)974.4} \\ 87 \\ \hline 104 \\ 87 \\ \hline 17\ 4 \\ 17\ 4 \\ \hline 0 \end{array}$$

Factors and Multiples *(p. xviii)*

5. $8 = 2^3$
$28 = 2^2 \cdot 7$
$\text{GCF} = 2^2 = 4$

6. $36 = 2^2 \cdot 3^2$
$42 = 2 \cdot 3 \cdot 7$
$\text{GCF} = 2 \cdot 3 = 6$

7. $54 = 2 \cdot 3^3$
$81 = 3^4$
$\text{GCF} = 3^3 = 27$

8. $50 = 2 \cdot 5^2$
$150 = 2 \cdot 3 \cdot 5^2$
$\text{GCF} = 2 \cdot 5^2 = 50$

9. $6 = 2 \cdot 3$
7 is prime
$\text{LCM} = 2 \cdot 3 \cdot 7 = 42$

10. $10 = 2 \cdot 5$
$15 = 3 \cdot 5$
$\text{LCM} = 2 \cdot 3 \cdot 5 = 30$

11. $24 = 2^3 \cdot 3$
$38 = 2 \cdot 19$
$\text{LCM} = 2^3 \cdot 3 \cdot 19 = 456$

12. $12 = 2^2 \cdot 3$
$36 = 2^2 \cdot 3^2$
$\text{LCM} = 2^2 \cdot 3^2 = 36$

13. 2 is prime
$10 = 2 \cdot 5$
$\text{LCD} = 2 \cdot 5 = 10$

14. $8 = 2^3$
7 is prime
$\text{LCD} = 2^3 \cdot 7 = 56$

15. $9 = 3^2$
$12 = 3 \cdot 2^2$
$\text{LCD} = 3^2 \cdot 2^2 = 36$

16. $20 = 2^2 \cdot 5$
$32 = 2^5$
$\text{LCD} = 2^5 \cdot 5 = 160$

Fractions *(p. xviii)*

17. $12, \frac{1}{12}$

18. $\frac{3}{16}, \frac{16}{3}$

19. $\frac{9}{5}, \frac{5}{9}$

20. $2\frac{1}{3} = \frac{7}{3}, \frac{3}{7}$

21. $\frac{3}{4} - \frac{1}{4} = \frac{2}{4} = \frac{1}{2}$

22. $\frac{1}{2} + \frac{1}{8} = \frac{4}{8} + \frac{1}{8} = \frac{5}{8}$

23. $\frac{6}{7} + \frac{5}{9} = \frac{54}{63} + \frac{35}{63} = \frac{89}{63}$

24. $11\frac{1}{4} - 2\frac{5}{8} = \frac{45}{4} - \frac{21}{8} = \frac{90}{8} - \frac{21}{8} = \frac{69}{8}$

25. $\frac{1}{2} \times \frac{6}{11} = \frac{6}{22} = \frac{3}{11}$

26. $\frac{7}{11} \div \frac{3}{5} = \frac{7}{11} \cdot \frac{5}{3} = \frac{35}{33}$

27. $\frac{4}{15} \div \frac{8}{3} = \frac{4}{15} \cdot \frac{3}{8} = \frac{2 \cdot 2 \cdot 3}{3 \cdot 5 \cdot 2 \cdot 2 \cdot 2} = \frac{1}{10}$

28. $4\frac{1}{8} \times \frac{2}{3} = \frac{33}{8} \cdot \frac{2}{3} = \frac{3 \cdot 11 \cdot 2}{2 \cdot 2 \cdot 2 \cdot 3} = \frac{11}{4}$

Fractions, Decimals, and Percents *(p. xviii)*

29. $7\% = 0.07 = \frac{7}{100}$

30. $26\% = 0.26 = \frac{26}{100} = \frac{13}{50}$

31. $48\% = 0.48 = \frac{48}{100} = \frac{12}{25}$

32. $84\% = 0.84 = \frac{84}{100} = \frac{21}{25}$

33. $0.08 = 8\% = \frac{8}{100} = \frac{2}{25}$

Copyright © McDougal Littell Inc.
All rights reserved.

Pre-Course Test *continued*

34. $0.15 = 15\% = \frac{15}{100} = \frac{3}{20}$

35. $0.47 = 47\% = \frac{47}{100}$

36. $0.027 = 2.7\% = \frac{27}{1000}$

37. $\frac{9}{10} = 0.9 = 90\%$

38. $\frac{4}{5} = 0.8 = 80\%$

39. $\frac{7}{8} = 0.875 = 87.5\%$

40. $\frac{11}{20} = 0.55 = 55\%$

Comparing and Ordering Numbers *(p. xix)*

41. $138 < 198$

42. $781 > 718$

43. $8.4 > 8.2$

44. $-7.88 < -4.88$

45. $\frac{5}{12} < \frac{3}{4} = \frac{9}{12}$

46. $\frac{3}{6} = \frac{1}{2} = \frac{4}{8} = \frac{1}{2}$

47. $\frac{5}{3} = 1\frac{2}{3} = 1\frac{4}{6} > 1\frac{3}{6} = 1\frac{1}{2}$

48. $16\frac{2}{3} = 16\frac{16}{24} < 16\frac{21}{24} = 16\frac{7}{8}$

49. 44, 47, 74, 77

50. 8, 80, 88, 808

51. 0.19, 0.4, 0.49, 0.9

52. $-6.5, -6, -5.4, 6.4$

53. $\frac{1}{2} = 0.5, \frac{4}{7} \approx 0.57, \frac{3}{5} = 0.6, \frac{5}{8} = 0.625$

54. $\frac{6}{13} \approx 0.46, \frac{5}{4} = 1.25, \frac{9}{7} \approx 1.29, \frac{6}{4} = 1.5$

55. $\frac{13}{11} \approx 1.18, \frac{7}{5} = 1.4, 1\frac{5}{9} \approx 1.56, 1\frac{3}{4} = 1.75$

56. $-16\frac{1}{4} = -16.25, -16\frac{1}{8} = -16.125, -15\frac{2}{3} \approx -15.67,$

$-15\frac{1}{9} \approx -15.11$

Perimeter, Area, and Volume *(p. xix)*

57. $P = 18 + 27 + 32 = 77$ ft

58. $P = (4.7)(4) = 18.8$ cm

59. $A = (13)^2 = 169$ yd^2

60. $A = (7.7)(4.5) = 34.65$ km^2

61. $V = (19)^3 = 6859$ m^3

62. $V = (5.9)(8.6)(1.2) = 60.888$ in.^{3}

Data Displays *(p.xix)*

63. bar graph or circle graph

Measures of Central Tendency *(p. xix)*

64. mean:
$(1 + 3 + 3 + 3 + 4 + 5 + 6 + 7 + 7 + 9) \div 10$
mean: 4.8
median: $(4 + 5) \div 2 = 4.5$
mode: 3

65. mean: $(17 + 22 + 36 + 47 + 51 + 58 + 65 + 80 + 85 + 89) \div 10 = 55$
median: $(51 + 58) \div 2 = 54.5$
no mode

66. mean: $(4 + 5 + 5 + 9 + 10 + 12 + 12 + 18 + 21 + 23) \div 10 = 11.9$
median: $(10 + 12) \div 2 = 11$
mode: 5, 12

67. mean: $(101 + 198 + 222 + 291 + 357 + 387 + 402 + 423 + 564 + 572) \div 10 = 351.7$
median: $(357 + 387) \div 2 = 372$
no mode

Copyright © McDougal Littell Inc.
All rights reserved.

Pre-Course Practice

Decimals *(p. xx)*

1. $14 + 7.1 = 21.1$

2. $$\begin{array}{r} 11.000 \\ -\ 0.003 \\ \hline 10.997 \end{array}$$

3. $$\begin{array}{r} 19.76 \\ +\ 48.19 \\ \hline 67.95 \end{array}$$

4. $$\begin{array}{r} 73.80 \\ -\ 6.93 \\ \hline 66.87 \end{array}$$

5. $$\begin{array}{r} 10.200 \\ 3.805 \\ 1.100 \\ \hline 15.105 \end{array}$$

6. $$\begin{array}{r} 7.20 \\ -\ 3.56 \\ \hline 3.64 \end{array}$$

7. $$\begin{array}{r} 17 \\ \times\ 3.9 \\ \hline 153 \\ 510 \\ \hline 66.3 \end{array}$$

8. $$\begin{array}{r} 6.08 \\ \times\ 3.15 \\ \hline 3040 \\ 6080 \\ 182400 \\ \hline 19.1520 \end{array}$$

9. $$\begin{array}{r} 15.2 \\ \times\ 5.02 \\ \hline 304 \\ 76000 \\ \hline 76.304 \end{array}$$

10. $$\begin{array}{r} 0.019 \\ \times\ 0.27 \\ \hline 133 \\ 380 \\ \hline 0.00513 \end{array}$$

11. $$\begin{array}{r} 45.28 \\ \times\ 16.1 \\ \hline 4528 \\ 271680 \\ 452800 \\ \hline 729.008 \end{array}$$

12. $26.01 \div 5.1 = 260.1 \div 51$
$$\begin{array}{r} 5.1 \\ 51\overline{)260.1} \\ 255 \\ \hline 5\,1 \\ 5\,1 \\ \hline 0 \end{array}$$

13. $7.03 \div 1.9 = 70.3 \div 19$
$$\begin{array}{r} 3.7 \\ 19\overline{)70.3} \\ 57 \\ \hline 13\,3 \\ 13\,3 \\ \hline 0 \end{array}$$

14. $21.84 \div 0.84 = 2184 \div 84$
$$\begin{array}{r} 26 \\ 84\overline{)2184} \\ 168 \\ \hline 504 \\ 504 \\ \hline 0 \end{array}$$

15. $0.0196 \div 0.056 = 19.6 \div 56$
$$\begin{array}{r} 0.35 \\ 56\overline{)19.60} \\ 16\,8 \\ \hline 2\,80 \\ 2\,80 \\ \hline 0 \end{array}$$

Factors and Multiples *(p. xx)*

1. 12: 1, 2, 3, 4, 6, 12
2. 41: 1, 41
3. 54: 1, 2, 3, 6, 9, 18, 27, 54
4. 126: 1, 2, 3, 6, 7, 9, 14, 18, 21, 42, 63, 126
5. $54 = 2 \cdot 3^3$
6. $60 = 2^2 \cdot 3 \cdot 5$
7. $35 = 5 \cdot 7$
8. 47 is prime
9. 16: 1, 2, 4, 8, 16
   20: 1, 2, 4, 5, 10, 20
   Common factors: 1, 2, 4
10. 24: 1, 2, 3, 4, 6, 8, 12, 24
    36: 1, 2, 3, 4, 6, 9, 12, 18, 36
    Common factors: 1, 2, 3, 4, 6, 12
11. 28: 1, 2, 4, 7, 14, 28
    42: 1, 2, 3, 6, 7, 14, 21, 42
    Common factors: 1, 2, 7, 14

Copyright © McDougal Littell Inc.
All rights reserved.

Pre-Course Practice *continued*

12. 60: 1, 2, 3, 4, 5, 6, 10, 12, 15, 20, 30, 60
72: 1, 2, 3, 4, 6, 8, 9, 12, 18, 24, 36, 72
Common factors: 1, 2, 3, 4, 6, 12

13. $8 = 2^3$
$12 = 2^2 \cdot 3$
$\text{GCF} = 2^2 = 4$

14. $10 = 2 \cdot 5$
$25 = 5^2$
$\text{GCF} = 5$

15. $15 = 3 \cdot 5$
$24 = 2^3 \cdot 3$
$\text{GCF} = 3$

16. $24 = 2^3 \cdot 3$
$30 = 2 \cdot 3 \cdot 5$
$\text{GCF} = 2 \cdot 3 = 6$

17. $36 = 2^2 \cdot 3^2$
$42 = 2 \cdot 3 \cdot 7$
$\text{GCF} = 2 \cdot 3 = 6$

18. $54 = 2 \cdot 3^3$
$81 = 3^4$
$\text{GCF} = 3^3 = 27$

19. $68 = 2^2 \cdot 17$
$82 = 2 \cdot 41$
$\text{GCF} = 2$

20. $102 = 2 \cdot 3 \cdot 17$
$214 = 2 \cdot 107$
$\text{GCF} = 2$

21. $9 = 3^2$
$12 = 2^2 \cdot 3$
$\text{LCM} = 2^2 \cdot 3^2 = 36$

22. $8 = 2^3$
5 is prime
$\text{LCM} = 2^3 \cdot 5 = 40$

23. $14 = 2 \cdot 7$
$21 = 3 \cdot 7$
$\text{LCM} = 2 \cdot 3 \cdot 7 = 42$

24. $24 = 2^3 \cdot 3$
$8 = 2^3$
$\text{LCM} = 2^3 \cdot 3 = 24$

25. $12 = 2^2 \cdot 3$
$16 = 2^4$
$\text{LCM} = 2^4 \cdot 3 = 48$

26. $70 = 2 \cdot 5 \cdot 7$
$14 = 2 \cdot 7$
$\text{LCM} = 2 \cdot 5 \cdot 7 = 70$

27. $36 = 2^2 \cdot 3^2$
$50 = 2 \cdot 5^2$
$\text{LCM} = 2^2 \cdot 3^2 \cdot 5^2 = 900$

28. $22 = 2 \cdot 11$
$30 = 2 \cdot 3 \cdot 5$
$\text{LCM} = 2 \cdot 3 \cdot 5 \cdot 11 = 330$

29. $8 = 2^3$
$6 = 2 \cdot 3$
$\text{LCM} = 2^3 \cdot 3 = 24$

30. $12 = 2^2 \cdot 3$
$8 = 2^3$
$\text{LCM} = 2^3 \cdot 3 = 24$

31. $12 = 2^2 \cdot 3$
$20 = 2^2 \cdot 5$
$\text{LCM} = 2^2 \cdot 3 \cdot 5 = 60$

32. $6 = 2 \cdot 3$
$15 = 3 \cdot 5$
$\text{LCM} = 2 \cdot 3 \cdot 5 = 30$

33. $4 = 2^2$
$28 = 2^2 \cdot 7$
$\text{LCM} = 2^2 \cdot 7 = 28$

34. 11 is prime
13 is prime
$\text{LCM} = 11 \cdot 13 = 143$

35. $6 = 2 \cdot 3$
$27 = 3^3$
$\text{LCM} = 2 \cdot 3^3 = 54$

36. $40 = 2^3 \cdot 5$
$52 = 2^2 \cdot 13$
$\text{LCM} = 2^3 \cdot 5 \cdot 13 = 520$

Fractions *(p. xxi)*

1. $8, \frac{1}{8}$

2. $\frac{1}{16}, 16$

3. $\frac{9}{5}, \frac{5}{9}$

4. $3\frac{4}{7} = \frac{25}{7}, \frac{7}{25}$

5. $\frac{7}{12} - \frac{1}{12} = \frac{6}{12} = \frac{1}{2}$

6. $\frac{1}{8} + \frac{3}{8} = \frac{4}{8} = \frac{1}{2}$

7. $\frac{9}{10} + \frac{3}{10} = \frac{12}{10} = \frac{6}{5} = 1\frac{1}{5}$

8. $\frac{5}{15} - \frac{2}{15} = \frac{3}{15} = \frac{1}{5}$

9. $\frac{1}{3} + \frac{2}{9} = \frac{3}{9} + \frac{2}{9} = \frac{5}{9}$

10. $\frac{17}{20} - \frac{3}{5} = \frac{17}{20} - \frac{12}{20} = \frac{5}{20} = \frac{1}{4}$

11. $\frac{1}{6} + \frac{5}{8} = \frac{4}{24} + \frac{15}{24} = \frac{19}{24}$

12. $1\frac{2}{3} - \frac{8}{9} = \frac{5}{3} - \frac{8}{9} = \frac{15}{9} - \frac{8}{9} = \frac{7}{9}$

13. $\frac{3}{5} \times \frac{1}{2} = \frac{3}{10}$

14. $\frac{2}{3} \times \frac{3}{8} = \frac{1}{4}$

15. $\frac{3}{5} \times 1\frac{1}{2} = \frac{3}{5} \times \frac{3}{2} = \frac{9}{10}$

16. $2\frac{2}{3} \times 3\frac{3}{8} = \frac{8}{3} \cdot \frac{27}{8} = 9$

Copyright © McDougal Littell Inc.
All rights reserved.

Pre-Course Practice *continued*

17. $\frac{2}{5} \div \frac{4}{5} = \frac{2}{5} \cdot \frac{5}{4} = \frac{1}{2}$

18. $\frac{2}{3} \div \frac{8}{9} = \frac{2}{3} \cdot \frac{9}{8} = \frac{3}{4}$

19. $5\frac{1}{4} \div \frac{7}{8} = \frac{21}{4} \cdot \frac{8}{7} = 6$

20. $4\frac{4}{5} \div 1\frac{1}{3} = \frac{24}{5} \div \frac{4}{3} = \frac{24}{5} \cdot \frac{3}{4} = \frac{18}{5} = 3\frac{3}{5}$

21. $\frac{2}{3} + \frac{5}{6} = \frac{4}{6} + \frac{5}{6} = \frac{9}{6} = \frac{3}{2} = 1\frac{1}{2}$

22. $9\frac{3}{8} - 5\frac{1}{4} = 9\frac{3}{8} - 5\frac{2}{8} = 4\frac{1}{8}$

23. $8\frac{2}{5} + 5\frac{3}{8} = 8\frac{16}{40} + 5\frac{15}{40} = 13\frac{31}{40}$

24. $\frac{4}{5} \cdot \frac{1}{4} = \frac{1}{5}$

25. $1\frac{2}{3} \div 1\frac{1}{4} = \frac{5}{3} \div \frac{5}{4} = \frac{5}{3} \cdot \frac{4}{5} = \frac{4}{3} = 1\frac{1}{3}$

26. $5\frac{3}{8} \cdot 3\frac{3}{4} = \frac{43}{8} \cdot \frac{15}{4} = \frac{645}{32} = 20\frac{5}{32}$

27. $\frac{1}{4} \div \frac{1}{5} = \frac{1}{4} \cdot \frac{5}{1} = \frac{5}{4} = 1\frac{1}{4}$

28. $1\frac{2}{3} - \frac{3}{4} = \frac{5}{3} - \frac{3}{4} = \frac{20}{12} - \frac{9}{12} = \frac{11}{12}$

Fractions, Decimals, and Percents *(p. xxi)*

1. $8\% = 0.08 = \frac{8}{100} = \frac{2}{25}$

2. $25\% = 0.25 = \frac{25}{100} = \frac{1}{4}$

3. $38\% = 0.38 = \frac{38}{100} = \frac{19}{50}$

4. $73\% = 0.73 = \frac{73}{100}$

5. $135\% = 1.35 = 1\frac{35}{100} = 1\frac{7}{20}$

6. $350\% = 3.5 = 3\frac{5}{10} = 3\frac{1}{2}$

7. $6.4\% = 0.064 = \frac{64}{1000} = \frac{8}{125}$

8. $0.15\% = 0.0015 = \frac{15}{10000} = \frac{3}{2000}$

9. $0.44 = 44\% = \frac{44}{100} = \frac{11}{25}$

10. $0.09 = 9\% = \frac{9}{100}$

11. $0.13 = 13\% = \frac{13}{100}$

12. $0.008 = 0.8\% = \frac{8}{1000} = \frac{1}{125}$

13. $1.6 = 160\% = 1\frac{6}{10} = 1\frac{3}{5}$

14. $3.04 = 304\% = 3\frac{4}{100} = 3\frac{1}{25}$

15. $6.6 = 660\% = 6\frac{60}{100} = 6\frac{3}{5}$

16. $4.75 = 475\% = 4\frac{75}{100} = 4\frac{3}{4}$

17. $\frac{3}{5} = 0.6 = 60\%$

18. $\frac{5}{8} = 0.625 = 62.5\%$

19. $\frac{17}{25} = \frac{68}{100} = 0.68 = 68\%$

20. $\frac{11}{12} \approx 0.917 = 91.7\%$

21. $5\frac{1}{5} = 5.2 = 520\%$

22. $2\frac{1}{4} = 2.25 = 225\%$

23. $3\frac{1}{16} \approx 3.063 = 306.3\%$

24. $8\frac{3}{7} \approx 8.429 = 842.9\%$

Comparing and Ordering Numbers *(p. xxii)*

1. $13{,}458 < 14{,}455$

2. $907 < 971$

3. $-8344 > -8434$

4. $-49.5 < -49.05$

5. $0.58 > 0.578$

6. $0.0394 < 0.394$

7. $\frac{75}{80} = \frac{15}{16} > \frac{9}{10} = \frac{72}{80}$

8. $\frac{13}{20} > \frac{1}{4} = \frac{5}{20}$

9. $\frac{9}{24} = \frac{3}{8}$

10. $7\frac{1}{4} = 7.25 > 7\frac{1}{5} = 7.2$

11. $-2\frac{11}{16} > -3\frac{2}{9}$

12. $18\frac{16}{24} = 18\frac{2}{3} > 18\frac{5}{8} = 18\frac{15}{24}$

13. 1075, 1507, 1705, 1775

14. 30,138; 30,831; 38,381; 38,831

15. $-0.205, -0.035, -0.019, -0.013$

16. 6.034, 6.30, 6.33, 6.34

17. $\frac{2}{7} = \frac{176}{616}, \frac{5}{11} = \frac{280}{616}, \frac{1}{2} = \frac{308}{616}, \frac{5}{8} = \frac{385}{616}$

18. $\frac{3}{7} \approx 0.43, \frac{4}{9} = 0.44, \frac{3}{4} = 0.75, \frac{4}{5} = 0.80$

Copyright © McDougal Littell Inc.
All rights reserved.

Pre-Course Practice *continued*

19. $-\frac{4}{2} = -\frac{12}{6}, -\frac{3}{2} = -\frac{9}{6}, -\frac{4}{3} = -\frac{8}{6}, -\frac{2}{3} = -\frac{4}{6}$

20. $\frac{3}{8} = 0.375, \frac{7}{9} \approx 0.78, \frac{5}{4} = 1.25, 1\frac{4}{7} \approx 1.57$

21. $\frac{7}{5} = \frac{21}{15}, 1\frac{3}{5} = \frac{8}{5} = \frac{24}{15}, \frac{5}{3} = \frac{25}{15}, 1\frac{4}{5} = \frac{9}{5} = \frac{27}{15}$

22. $14\frac{2}{3} \approx 14.67, 14\frac{5}{7} \approx 14.71, 15\frac{5}{9} \approx 15.56, 15\frac{5}{8} = 15.625$

Perimeter, Area, and Volume *(p. xxii)*

1. $P = 4(2.5) = 10$ m
2. $P = 9 + 13 + 13 = 35$ in.
3. $P = 2(6.8) + 2(4.5) = 22.6$ km
4. $P = 2(12.5) + 2(11.6) = 48.2$ cm
5. $P = 5(19) = 95$ ft
6. $A = (1.67)^2 = 2.7889$ yd^2
7. $A = (1.4)(2.8) = 3.92$ in.^{2}
8. $A = \frac{1}{2}(15)(10) = 75$ cm^2
9. $V = (34)^3 = 39{,}304$ ft^3
10. $V = 18(6)(3) = 324$ m^3
11. $V = 6.5(5.5)(2.2) = 78.65$ mm^3

Data Displays *(p. xxiii)*

1. 0 to 60 by tens: 0, 10, 20, 30, 40, 50, 60
2. 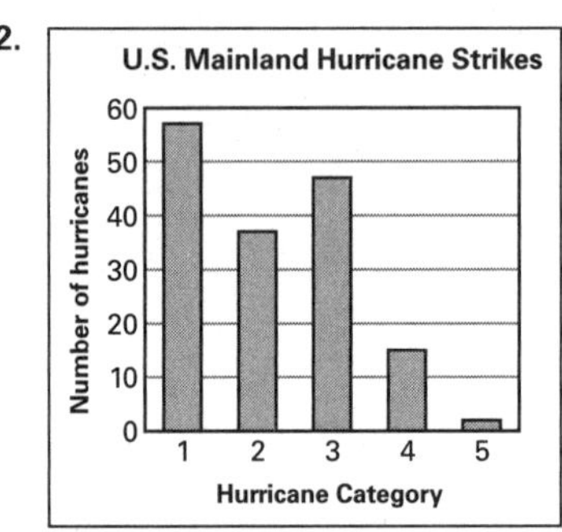

3. 0 to 25 by fives: 0, 5, 10, 15, 20, 25
4. 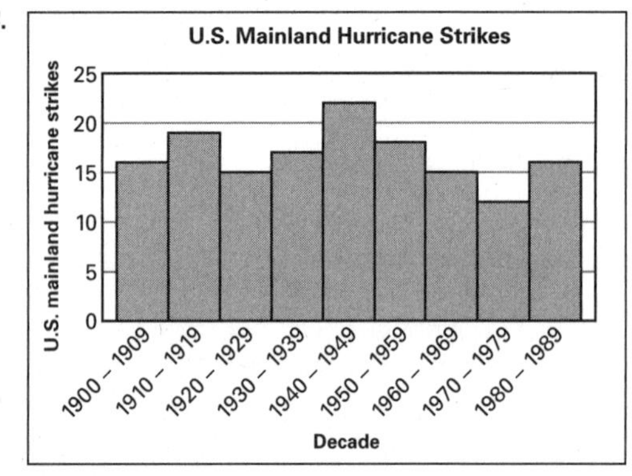

5. bar graph; 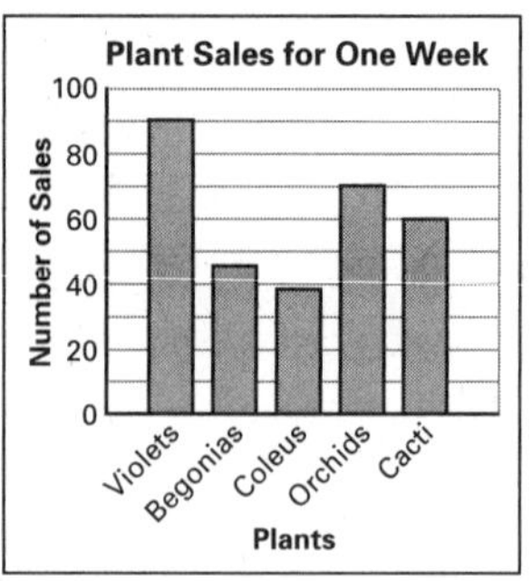

6. bar graph; 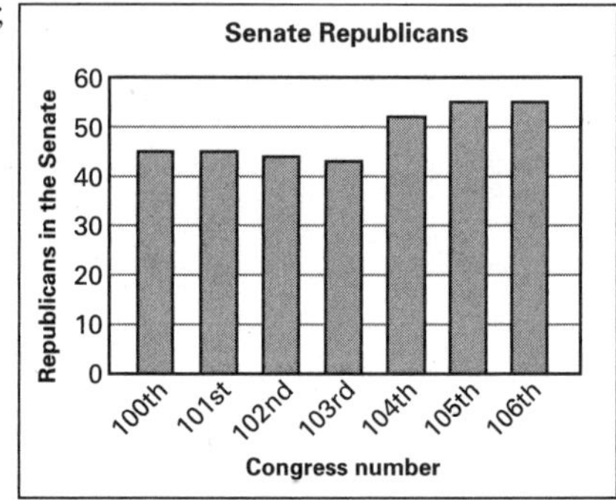

Measures of Central Tendency *(p. xxiii)*

1. mean: $(1 + 2 + 3 + 3 + 4 + 6 + 7 + 7 + 7 + 9) \div 10 = 4.9$
   median: $(4 + 6) \div 2 = 5$
   mode: 7 (occurs the most times)
2. mean: $(7 + 12 + 15 + 15 + 16 + 16 + 17 + 18 + 19 + 23) \div 10 = 15.8$
   median: $(16 + 16) \div 2 = 16$
   mode: 15, 16 (each occurs twice)
3. mean: $(10 + 27 + 32 + 39 + 48 + 58 + 59 + 73 + 86 + 89) \div 10 = 52.1$
   median: $(48 + 58) \div 2 = 53$
   no mode: each number occurs only once
4. mean: $(43 + 44 + 45 + 45 + 52 + 53 + 53 + 54 + 55 + 55) \div 10 = 49.9$
   median: $(52 + 53) \div 2 = 52.5$
   modes: 45, 53, 55 (each occurs twice)

Copyright © McDougal Littell Inc.
All rights reserved.

CHAPTER 1

Chapter Opener

Think & Discuss (p. 1)

1. \$48 **2.** \$120

Chapter Readiness Quiz (p. 2)

1. (B), $10 - 4(2)$ has no variables in the expression.

2. 7^3 is a power. (A)

3. Perimeter = sum of the length of the sides of a polygon. Perimeter $= 10 + 20 + 10 + 20 = 60$ ft (B)

4. $0.5 > \frac{1}{4}$ since $\frac{1}{4} = 0.25$ (A)

Lesson 1.1

1.1 Checkpoint (pp. 3–5)

1. $10 + x$; 10 plus x; addition

2. $13 - x$; 13 minus x; subtraction

3. $\frac{x}{16}$; x divided by 16; division

4. $24x$; 24 times x; multiplication

5. $7x = 7(3) = 21$ **6.** $5 + x = 5 + (3) = 8$

7. $\frac{12}{x} = \frac{12}{(3)} = 4$ **8.** $x - 2 = (3) - 2 = 1$

9. $d = r \cdot t$
$d = (60)(3)$
$d = 180$ mi

10. Perimeter $= 12 + 12 + 12 + 12 = 48$ in.

11. $A = \frac{1}{2} \cdot b \cdot h$

$A = \frac{1}{2} \cdot 12 \cdot 7$

$A = 42$ square meters

1.1 Guided Practice (p. 6)

1. y **2.** s **3.** b

4. r and t **5.** evaluate, value

6. 5 divided by c, division **7.** p minus 4, subtraction

8. 5 plus n, addition **9.** 8 times x , multiplication

Evaluate the variable expression when $k = 3$.

10. $11 + k = 11 + (3) = 14$

11. $k - 2 = (3) - 2 = 1$

12. $7k = 7(3) = 21$

13. $\frac{k}{33} = \frac{(3)}{33} = \frac{1}{11}$ **14.** $\frac{18}{k} = \frac{18}{(3)} = 6$

15. $18 \cdot k = 18 \cdot (3) = 54$

16. a. To find the perimeter, add the length of each side of the triangle. 6 cm + 8 cm + 10 cm = 24 cm

b. 9 in. + 15 in. + 12 in. = 36 in.

1.1 Practice and Applications (pp. 6–8)

17. $y + 8$; y plus 8 (C) **18.** $y - 8$; y minus 8 (D)

19. $\frac{y}{8}$; y divided by 8 (B) **20.** $8y$; 8 times y (A)

21. $9 + p = 9 + (11) = 20$ **22.** $\frac{1}{2} + t = \frac{1}{2} + (2) = 2\frac{1}{2}$

23. $\frac{b}{7} = \frac{14}{7} = 2$ **24.** $\frac{d}{12} = \frac{(36)}{12} = 3$

25. $(4)(n) = (4)(5) = 20$ **26.** $8a = 8(6) = 48$

27. $12 - x = 12 - (3) = 9$ **28.** $9 - y = 9 - (8) = 1$

29. $10r = 10(7) = 70$ **30.** $13c = 13(3) = 39$

31. $\frac{18}{x} = \frac{18}{3} = 6$ **32.** $\frac{63}{k} = \frac{63}{(9)} = 7$

33. $d = rt$
$d = (65)(4)$
$d = 260$ mi

34. $d = rt$
$d = (75)(2)$
$d = 150$ mi

35. $d = rt$
$d = (8)(5)$
$d = 40$ ft

36. $d = rt$; Since the rate is given in kilometers per hour, and the time is given in minutes, we must convert so that both measurements have the same units.

Convert: 30 min $= \frac{1}{2}$ h $= 0.5$ h

$d = (8)(0.5)$

$d = 4$ km

37. $d = rt$
$d = (170)(2)$
$d = 340$ mi

38. $d = rt$
$d = (450)(3)$
$d = 1350$ mi

39. $d = rt$; Since the rate and time have different units (seconds and minutes) convert one of the measurements so that it has the same units as the other measurement.
Convert: 1 min = 60 sec
$d = (4)(60)$
$d = 240$ ft

For Exercises 40–42, the perimeter is the sum of the lengths of the sides of the polygons.

40. Perimeter = 13 ft + 10 ft + 8 ft = 31 ft

41. Perimeter = 10 m + 22 m + 10 m + 22 m = 64 m

Copyright © McDougal Littell Inc.
All rights reserved.

42. Perimeter = 12 in. + 12 in. + 12 in. + 12 in. + 12 in.
= 60 in.

For Exercises 43–45, the area of the triangle is $\frac{1}{2} \cdot \text{base} \cdot \text{height}$.

43. $A = \frac{1}{2}bh$

$A = \frac{1}{2}(5)(4)$

$A = 10 \text{ m}^2$

44. $A = \frac{1}{2}bh$

$A = \frac{1}{2}(10)(6)$

$A = 30 \text{ mi}^2$

45. $A = \frac{1}{2}bh$

$A = \frac{1}{2}(4)(3)$

$A = 6 \text{ yd}^2$

46. $A = l \cdot w$

$A = (362)(275)$; to estimate, round 362 to 400, and 275 to 300.

$A \approx (400)(300)$

$A \approx 120{,}000 \text{ mi}^2$

47. Use the distance formula, $d = rt$. Since the rate is in miles per *hour*, and the time is in *minutes*, we must convert one of the measurements so that the units are the same.
Convert:

$15 \text{ min} = \frac{1}{4} \text{ h}$

$d = (500)\left(\frac{1}{4}\right)$

$d = 125 \text{ mi}$

48. $(4 \cancel{\text{h}})\left(\frac{60 \text{ mi}}{1 \cancel{\text{h}}}\right) = 240 \text{ mi}$

49. $80 \text{ mi} \div \frac{20 \text{ mi}}{1 \text{ h}} = 80 \cancel{\text{mi}} \times \frac{1 \text{ h}}{20 \cancel{\text{mi}}} = 4 \text{ h}$

1.1 Standardized Test Practice (p. 8)

50. $d = rt$

$d = (60)(6)$

$d = 360 \text{ mi}$ (C)

51. Perimeter = sum of lengths of all sides
Perimeter = 4 cm + 8 cm + 7 cm = 19 cm (H)

1.1 Mixed Review (p. 8)

52. 32.8 − 4; change 4 to 4.0 and line up the decimal points to subtract.

$$\begin{array}{r} {}^{2\,1} \\ \cancel{3}2.8 \\ -4.0 \\ \hline 28.8 \end{array}$$

53. Write the addends in column format, lining up the decimal points.

$$\begin{array}{r} {}^{1} \\ 3.98 \\ +\ 5.50 \\ \hline 9.48 \end{array}$$

54.
$$\begin{array}{r} 0.1 \\ \times\ 50 \\ \hline \end{array}$$
Multiply
$$\begin{array}{r} 1 \\ \times\ 50 \\ \hline 50 \end{array}$$
then place a decimal point one place value to the left in the answer, since there is one digit to the right of a decimal point in the factors. 5.0 = 5

55. $\left(\frac{30}{10}\right)(5) = \frac{\overset{15}{\cancel{30}}}{\underset{1}{\cancel{10}}} = \frac{\overset{1}{\cancel{5}}}{1} = 15$

56. $(60)\left(\frac{2}{12}\right) = \frac{\overset{5}{\cancel{60}}}{1} \cdot \frac{2}{\underset{1}{\cancel{12}}} = 10$

57. $\left(\frac{3}{15}\right)\left(\frac{5}{6}\right) = \frac{\overset{1}{\cancel{3}}}{\underset{3}{\cancel{15}}} \cdot \frac{\overset{1}{\cancel{5}}}{\underset{2}{\cancel{6}}} = \frac{1}{6}$

1.1 Maintaining Skills (p. 8)

To add the decimal numbers in Exercises 58–66, place the addends in column format and line up the decimal points. Use zeroes to hold the places to the right of the decimal points as needed.

58. 2.3 + 4.5
$$\begin{array}{r} 2.3 \\ +\ 4.5 \\ \hline 6.8 \end{array}$$

59. 16.8 + 7.1
$$\begin{array}{r} {}^{1} \\ 16.8 \\ +\ 7.1 \\ \hline 23.9 \end{array}$$

60. 0.09 + 0.0.5
$$\begin{array}{r} {}^{1} \\ 0.09 \\ +\ 0.05 \\ \hline 0.14 \end{array}$$

61. 1.0008 + 10.15
$$\begin{array}{r} 1.0008 \\ +\ 10.1500 \\ \hline 11.1508 \end{array}$$

62. 123.8 + 0.03
$$\begin{array}{r} 123.80 \\ +\ 0.03 \\ \hline 123.83 \end{array}$$

Copyright © McDougal Littell Inc.
All rights reserved.

63. $46 + 7.55$

$$\begin{array}{r} \overset{1}{4}6.00 \\ +\ 7.55 \\ \hline 53.55 \end{array}$$

64. $0.32 + 0.094$

$$\begin{array}{r} 0.3\overset{1}{2}0 \\ +\ 0.094 \\ \hline 0.414 \end{array}$$

65. $6.105 + 7.3$

$$\begin{array}{r} 6.105 \\ +\ 7.300 \\ \hline 13.405 \end{array}$$

66. $2.008 + 1.10199$

$$\begin{array}{r} 2.00800 \\ +\ 1.10199 \\ \hline 3.10999 \end{array}$$

Lesson 1.2

1.2 Checkpoint (pp. 9–11)

1. 3 squared $= 3^2$

2. x to the fourth power $= x^4$

3. s cubed $= s^3$

4. $(t - s)^3 = (4 - 2)^3$ Replace t with 4 and s with 2.
$= (2)^3$
$= 8$

5. $(s^2) + (t^2) = (2)^2 + (4)^2$ Replace t with 4 and s with 2.
$= 4 + 16$ Evaluate the powers.
$= 20$ Add.

6. $(t + s)^2 = (4 + 2)^2$ Replace t with 4 and s with 2.
$= (6)^2$ Evaluate the operation in the parentheses.
$= 36$ Evaluate the power.

7. $(t^2) - (s^2) = (4^2) - (2^2)$ Replace t with 4 and s with 2.
$= 16 - 4$ Evaluate the powers.
$= 12$ Subtract.

8. $(s^2) + t = (2^2) + 4$ Replace t with 4 and s with 2.
$= 4 + 4$ Evaluate the power.
$= 8$ Add.

9. $(t^2) - s = (4^2) - 2$ Replace t with 4 and s with 2.
$= 16 - 2$ Evaluate the power.
$= 14$ Subtract.

10. $A = s^2$
$A = 2^2 = 4 \text{ ft}^2$

1.2 Guided Practice (p. 12)

1. base

2. exponent

3. power

4. parentheses, brackets

5. 3^7; three to the seventh power (B)

6. 7^3; seven to the third power (C)

7. 4^6; four to the sixth power (A)

8. 6^4; six to the fourth power (D)

9. $t^2 = (3)^2 = 3 \cdot 3 = 9$

10. $1 + t^3 = 1 + (3)^3 = 1 + (3 \cdot 3 \cdot 3) = 1 + 27 = 28$

11. $4t^2 = 4(3)^2 = 4(3 \cdot 3) = 4 \cdot 9 = 36$

12. $(4t)^2 = (4 \cdot 3)^2 = (12)^2 = 12 \cdot 12 = 144$

1.2 Practice and Applications (pp. 12–14)

13. two cubed; 2^3

14. p squared; p^2

15. nine to the fifth power; 9^5

16. b to the eighth power; b^8

17. $3 \cdot 3 \cdot 3 \cdot 3 = 3^4$

18. $4x \cdot 4x \cdot 4x = (4x)^3$

19. Area of a square = side · side
$A = (5)(5) = 5^2 = 25$

20. $9^2 = 9 \cdot 9 = 81$

21. $2^4 = 2 \cdot 2 \cdot 2 \cdot 2 = 16$

22. $7^3 = 7 \cdot 7 \cdot 7 = 343$

23. $2^6 = 2 \cdot 2 \cdot 2 \cdot 2 \cdot 2 \cdot 2 = 64$

24. $5^4 = 5 \cdot 5 \cdot 5 \cdot 5 = 625$

25. $1^8 = 1 \cdot 1 \cdot 1 \cdot 1 \cdot 1 \cdot 1 \cdot 1 \cdot 1 = 1$

26. $10^3 = 10 \cdot 10 \cdot 10 = 1000$

27. $0^6 = 0 \cdot 0 \cdot 0 \cdot 0 \cdot 0 \cdot 0 = 0$

28. $w^2 = (12)^2 = 144$

29. $b^3 = (9)^3 = 729$

30. $c^4 = (3)^4 = 81$

31. $h^5 = (2)^5 = 32$

32. $n^2 = (11)^2 = 121$

33. $x^3 = (5)^3 = 125$

For Exercises 34–39, use a calculator to evaluate the powers. You may have to look at the instructions for your calculator to find what keystrokes to use.

34. $8^6 = 262{,}144$

35. $13^5 = 371{,}293$

36. $5^9 = 1{,}953{,}125$

37. $12^7 = 35{,}831{,}808$

38. $6^6 = 46{,}656$

39. $3^{12} = 531{,}441$

40. $(c + d)^2 = (4 + 5)^2 = (9)^2 = 81$

41. $(d^2) + c = (5^2) + 4 = 25 + 4 = 29$

42. $(c^3) + d = (4^3) + 5 = 64 + 5 = 69$

43. $(d^2) - (c^2) = (5^2) - (4^2) = (25) - (16) = 9$

44. $(d - c)^7 = (5 - 4)^7 = (1)^7 = 1$

45. $(d^2) - d = (5^2) - 5 = 25 - 5 = 20$

46. $2x^2 = 2(7)^2 = 2(49) = 98$

47. $6t^4 = 6(1)^4 = 6(1) = 6$

48. $7b^2 = 7(3)^2 = 7(9) = 63$

49. $(5w)^3 = (5 \cdot 5)^3 = (25)^3 = 15{,}625$

50. $(4x)^3 = (4 \cdot 1)^3 = (4)^3 = 64$

51. $(5y)^5 = (5 \cdot 2)^5 = (10)^5 = 100{,}000$

Copyright © McDougal Littell Inc.
All rights reserved.

Chapter 1 *continued*

52. The floor is square. The area of a square is side times side or side squared.
$A = s^2 = (14)^2 = 196$
196 square feet of carpet is needed.

53. The volume of a cube is the length of a side to the third power.
$V = 2^3 = 8$
The volume is 8 ft³.

54. $V = s^3 = (9.5)^3 = 857.375 \text{ in.}^3$

55. Each edge has 2 cubes. Volume $= 2^3 = 8$ cubic units.

56. Each edge has 3 cubes. Volume $= 3^3 = 27$ cubic units.

57. Each edge has 4 cubes. Volume $= 4^3 = 64$ cubic units.

58. Find the volume of the cube, then divide by 2.
Volume of container $= (6)(6)(6) = 216 \text{ in.}^3$
Since it is half full, $\frac{216}{2} = 108 \text{ in.}^3$

59. The volume of the second candle mold is $(4)^3 = 64 \text{ in.}^3$ (since it is a cube). The volume of the wax is 108 in.^3, which is more than 64 in.^3, so the second container will not hold as much melted wax as the first container.

60. *Sample answer*: A cube that is 5 inches on each side would be large enough to hold the wax. The volume of the cube is $5^3 = 125 \text{ in.}^3$ which is greater than 108 in.^3

1.2 Standardized Test Practice (p. 14)

61. $2x^2 = 2(5)^2 = 2(25) = 50$ (C)

62. 1 kiloliter $= 10^3$ liters
There are $10^3 = 1000$ liters in a kiloliter. (H)

63. Volume $= l \cdot w \cdot h$
$V = (3)(3)(3) = 27 \text{ ft}^3$ (D)

1.2 Mixed Review (p.14)

For Exercises 64–66, the perimeter is found by finding the sum of all the sides of the polygon.

64. $x + x + x + x = 3 + 3 + 3 + 3 = 12$

65. $x + x + x + x + x + x = 6x = 6(3) = 18$

66. $x + 2x + 2x = 3 + 2(3) + 2(3) = 3 + 6 + 6 = 15$

67. $9j = 9(5) = 45$

68. $6 + t = 6 + (21) = 27$

69. $\frac{b}{2} = \frac{(18)}{2} = 9$

70. $25 - n = 25 - (3) = 22$

71. $c + 4 = (24) + 4 = 28$

72. $(7)(r) = (7)(11) = 77$

73. $\frac{24}{s} = \frac{24}{(8)} = 3$

74. $3m = 3(7) = 21$

75. $d - 13 = (22) - 13 = 9$

1.2 Maintaining Skills (p.14)

76. $\frac{4}{8} = \frac{1}{2}$

77. $\frac{10}{2} = 5$

78. $\frac{15}{10} = \frac{3 \cdot \cancel{5}}{2 \cdot \cancel{5}} = \frac{3}{2}$

79. $\frac{6}{20} = \frac{3 \cdot \cancel{2}}{10 \cdot \cancel{2}} = \frac{3}{10}$

80. $\frac{8}{14} = \frac{4 \cdot \cancel{2}}{7 \cdot \cancel{2}} = \frac{4}{7}$

81. $\frac{18}{21} = \frac{6 \cdot \cancel{3}}{7 \cdot \cancel{3}} = \frac{6}{7}$

82. $\frac{8}{6} = \frac{4 \cdot \cancel{2}}{3 \cdot \cancel{2}} = \frac{4}{3}$

83. $\frac{27}{3} = 9$

84. $\frac{25}{15} = \frac{5 \cdot \cancel{5}}{3 \cdot \cancel{5}} = \frac{5}{3}$

85. $\frac{21}{7} = 3$

86. $\frac{3}{24} = \frac{1}{8}$

87. $\frac{28}{4} = 7$

88. *Sample estimate:* $3 - 1 = 2$
$$\begin{array}{r} 2.5 \\ -0.5 \\ \hline 2.0 \end{array}$$

89. *Sample estimate:* $0.3 - 0 = 0.3$
$$\begin{array}{r} {\scriptstyle 2\,1} \\ 0.\cancel{3}0 \\ -0.03 \\ \hline 0.27 \end{array}$$

90. *Sample estimate:* $10 + 5 = 15$
$$\begin{array}{r} 10.350 \\ +\ 5.301 \\ \hline 15.651 \end{array}$$

91. *Sample estimate:* $4 + 1 = 5$
$$\begin{array}{r} 3.710 \\ +\ 1.054 \\ \hline 4.764 \end{array}$$

92. *Sample estimate:* $2 - 0 = 2$
$$\begin{array}{r} {\scriptstyle 1\,1} \\ 2.1 \\ -0.2 \\ \hline 1.9 \end{array}$$

93. *Sample estimate:* $5 + 1 = 6$
$$\begin{array}{r} {\scriptstyle 1} \\ 5.175 \\ +\ 1.150 \\ \hline 6.325 \end{array}$$

Lesson 1.3

1.3 Checkpoint (pp. 15–17)

1. $2x^2 + 5 = 2(2)^2 + 5$ Replace x with 2.
$= 2(4) + 5$ Evaluate the power.
$= 8 + 5$ Multiply.
$= 13$ Add.

2. $8 - x^2 = 8 - (2)^2$ Replace x with 2.
$= 8 - 4$ Evaluate the power.
$= 4$ Subtract.

Copyright © McDougal Littell Inc.
All rights reserved.

Chapter 1 *continued*

3. $6 + 3x^3 = 6 + 3(2)^3$ Replace x with 2.
$= 6 + 3(8)$ Evaluate the power.
$= 6 + 24$ Multiply.
$= 30$ Add.

4. $20 - 4x^2 = 20 - 4(2)^2$ Replace x with 2
$= 20 - 4(4)$ Evaluate the power.
$= 20 - 16$ Multiply.
$= 4$ Subtract.

5. $4x^2 + 5 - 3 = 4(1)^2 + 5 - 3$ Replace x with 1.
$= 4(1) + 5 - 3$ Evaluate the power.
$= 4 + 5 - 3$ Multiply.
$= 9 - 3$ Add (left to right rule).
$= 6$

6. $5 - x^3 - 1 = 5 - (1)^3 - 1$ Replace x with 1.
$= 5 - 1 - 1$ Evaluate the power.
$= 4 - 1$ Subtract (left to right rule).
$= 3$

7. $\dfrac{2x}{x^2 - 1 + 5} = \dfrac{2(1)}{(1)^2 - 1 + 5}$ Replace x with 1.
$= \dfrac{2}{(1)^2 - 1 + 5}$ Simplify the numerator.
$= \dfrac{2}{1 - 1 + 5}$ Simplify the denominator, evaluate the power.
$= \dfrac{2}{0 + 5}$ Subtract (left to right rule).
$= \dfrac{2}{5}$ Add.

8. 26 points; multiply 4 by 3, then add 1, then multiply by 2.

9. 25 points; multiply 6 by 2 and then by 2 again. Divide 2 by 2, then add the quotient to the previous result.

1.3 Guided Practice (p. 18)

1. b, d, a, c (see page 15)

2. If the operations have the same priority, use the left-to-right rule.

3. $5 \cdot 6 \cdot 2 = 30 \cdot 2$ Multiply from left to right.
$= 60$

4. $16 \div 4 - 2 = 4 - 2$ Divide 16 by 4.
$= 2$ Subtract.

5. $4 + 9 - 1 = 13 - 1$ Add, then subtract (use left-to-right rule).
$= 12$

6. $2 \cdot 8^2 = 2 \cdot 64$ Evaluate the power.
$= 128$ Multiply.

7. $15 + 6 \div 3 = 15 + 2$ Divide 6 by 3.
$= 17$ Add.

8. $9 \div 3 \cdot 2 = 3 \cdot 2$ Divide, then multiply (use left to right rule).
$= 6$

9. $2 \cdot 3^2 + 5 = 2 \cdot 9 + 5$ Evaluate the power.
$= 18 + 5$ Multiply.
$= 23$ Add.

10. $2^3 \cdot 3^2 = 8 \cdot 9$ Evaluate the powers.
$= 72$ Multiply.

11. $x^2 - 5 = (3)^2 - 5$ Substitute.
$= 9 - 5$ Evaluate the power.
$= 4$ Subtract.

12. $x^3 + 5x = (3)^3 + 5(3)$ Substitute.
$= 27 + 5(3)$ Evaluate the power.
$= 27 + 15$ Multiply.
$= 42$ Add.

13. $x + 3x^4 = (3) + 3(3)^4$ Substitute.
$= (3) + 3(81)$ Evaluate the power.
$= (3) + 243$ Multiply.
$= 246$ Add.

14. $\dfrac{27}{x} - 2 + 16 = \dfrac{27}{(3)} - 2 + 16$ Divide.
$= 9 - 2 + 16$ Subtract, then add (using left-to-right rule).
$= 7 + 16$
$= 23$

15. $\dfrac{15}{x} + 2^3 - 10 = \dfrac{15}{(3)} + 2^3 - 10$ Evaluate the power.
$= \dfrac{15}{(3)} + 8 - 10$ Divide.
$= 5 + 8 - 10$ Add, then subtract (using left-to-right rule).
$= 13 - 10$
$= 3$

16. $\dfrac{24}{x} \cdot 5 = \dfrac{24}{(3)} \cdot 5$ Divide, then multiply (using the left-to-right rule).
$= 8 \cdot 5$
$= 40$

1.3 Practice and Applications (pp. 18–21)

17. $13 + 3 \cdot 7 = 13 + 21$ Multiply.
$= 34$ Add.

18. $7 + 8 \div 2 = 7 + 4$ Divide.
$= 11$ Add.

19. $2^4 - 5 \cdot 3 = 16 - 5 \cdot 3$ Evaluate the power.
$= 16 - 15$ Multiply.
$= 1$ Subtract.

20. $6^2 + 4 = 36 + 4$ Evaluate the power.
$= 40$ Add.

21. $4^3 + 9 \cdot 2 = 64 + 9 \cdot 2$ Evaluate the power.
$= 64 + 18$ Multiply.
$= 82$ Add.

22. $3 \cdot 2 + \dfrac{5}{9} = 6 + \dfrac{5}{9}$ Multiply.
$= 6\dfrac{5}{9}$ Add.

23. $6 \cdot 2p^2 = 6 \cdot 2(5)^2$ Substitute.
$= 6 \cdot 2(25)$ Evaluate the power.
$= 12(25)$ Multiply.
$= 300$ Multiply.

Copyright © McDougal Littell Inc.
All rights reserved.

24. $2g \cdot 5 = 2(4) \cdot 5$ Substitute.
$= 8 \cdot 5$ Multiply (using the left-to-right rule).
$= 40$

25. $14(n + 1) = 14(2 + 1)$ Substitute.
$= 14(3)$ Evaluate the operation in the parentheses.
$= 42$ Multiply.

26. $\frac{x}{7} + 16 = \frac{(14)}{7} + 16$ Substitute.
$= 2 + 16$ Divide.
$= 18$ Add.

27. $2^3 + 5 - 2 = 8 + 5 - 2$ Evaluate the power.
$= 13 - 2$ Add then subtract (left-to-right rule).
$= 11$

28. $4 \cdot 2 + 15 \div 3 = 8 + 5$ Multiply, then divide.
$= 13$ Add.

29. $6 \div 3 + 2 \cdot 7 = 2 + 14$ Divide and multiply.
$= 16$ Add.

30. $5 + 8 \cdot 2 - 4 = 5 + 16 - 4$ Multiply.
$= 21 - 4$ Add, then subtract (left-to-right rule).
$= 17$

31. $16 + 8 \cdot 2^2 = 16 + 8 \cdot 4$ Evaluate the power.
$= 16 + 32$ Multiply.
$= 48$ Add.

32. $2 \cdot 3^2 - 7 = 2 \cdot 9 - 7$ Evaluate the power.
$= 18 - 7$ Multiply.
$= 11$ Subtract.

33. $10 - 3 + (2 + 5) = 10 - 3 + (7)$ Evaluate the operation in the parentheses.
$= 7 + 7$ Subtract, then add (left-to-right rule).
$= 14$

34. $7 + 18 - (6 - 3) = 7 + 18 - (3)$ Evaluate the operation in the parentheses.
$= 25 - 3$ Add, then subtract (left-to-right rule).
$= 22$

35. $[(7 \cdot 4) + 3] + 15 = [(28) + 3] + 15$ Evaluate the operation in the parentheses.
$= [31] + 15$ Evaluate the operation in the brackets.
$= 46$

36. $\frac{6 \cdot 4}{4 + 3^2 - 1} = \frac{6 \cdot 4}{4 + 9 - 1}$ Evaluate the power.
$= \frac{24}{4 + 9 - 1}$ Simplify the numerator by multiplication.
$= \frac{24}{13 - 1}$ Simplify the denominator, work from left to right.
$= \frac{24}{12}$ Simplify the fraction by division.
$= 2$

37. $\frac{13 - 4}{18 - 4^2 + 1} = \frac{13 - 4}{18 - 16 + 1}$ Evaluate the power.
$= \frac{9}{18 - 16 + 1}$ Simplify the numerator.
$= \frac{9}{2 + 1}$ Simplify the denominator by subtracting then adding (left-to-right rule).
$= \frac{9}{3}$ Add.
$= 3$ Reduce the fraction.

38. $\frac{5^2 \cdot 2}{1 + 6^2 - 12} = \frac{25 \cdot 2}{1 + 36 - 12}$ Evaluate the powers.
$= \frac{50}{1 + 36 - 12}$ Multiply.
$= \frac{50}{37 - 12}$ Add, then subtract (left-to-right rule).
$= \frac{50}{25}$ Subtract.
$= 2$ Divide.

39. $\frac{21 + 9}{5^2 + 40 - 5} = \frac{21 + 9}{25 + 40 - 5}$ Evaluate the power.
$= \frac{30}{25 + 40 - 5}$ Simplify the numerator.
$= \frac{30}{65 - 5}$ Simplify the denominator, use the left-to-right rule.
$= \frac{30}{60}$ Subtract.
$= \frac{1}{2}$ Simplify the fraction.

40. $\frac{3^3 + 8 - 7}{2 \cdot 7} = \frac{27 + 8 - 7}{2 \cdot 7}$ Evaluate the power.
$= \frac{35 - 7}{2 \cdot 7}$ Simplify the numerator, use the left-to-right rule.
$= \frac{28}{2 \cdot 7}$ Simplify the numerator.
$= \frac{28}{14}$ Simplify the denominator.
$= 2$ Divide.

Copyright © McDougal Littell Inc.
All rights reserved.

41. $\dfrac{4 \cdot 2^5}{16 - 4^2 + 1} = \dfrac{4 \cdot 32}{16 - 16 + 1}$ Evaluate the powers.

$= \dfrac{128}{16 - 16 + 1}$ Simplify the numerator.

$= \dfrac{128}{0 + 1}$ Simplify the denominator, use the left-to-right rule.

$= \dfrac{128}{1} = 128$ Divide.

42. Choice B is correct because the brackets show that you simplify the numerator before dividing by the denominator.

43. $15 - 6 \div 3 \times 4 = 15 - 2 \times 4$ Divide, then multiply (left-to-right rule).

$= 15 - 8$

$= 7$ Subtract.

Calculator B has the correct answer of 7.

44. $15 - 9 \div 3 + 7 = 15 - 3 + 7$ Divide.

$= 12 + 7$ Subtract, then add (left-to-right rule).

$= 19$

Calculator A has the correct answer of 19.

45. $15 + 10 \div 5 + 4 = 15 + 2 + 4$ Divide.

$= 17 + 4$ Add (left-to-right rule).

$= 21$ Add.

Calculator A has the correct answer of 21.

46. $4 \times 3 \div 6 \div 2 = 12 \div 6 \div 2$ Multiply, then divide by 6 (left-to-right rule).

$= 2 \div 2$

$= 1$ Finally, divide by 2.

Neither calculator has the correct answer.

47. The cost of a complete uniform is \$230 + \$300 + \$40 + \$15 + \$100 + \$200.
The cost of 35 uniforms (without the discount) is 35(\$230 + \$300 + \$40 + \$15 + \$100 + \$200).
The cost with the discount is 35(\$230 + \$300 + \$40 + \$15 + \$100 + \$200) − \$2000.

48. 35(\$230 + \$300 + \$40 + \$15 + \$100 + \$200) − \$2000 = 35(\$855) − \$2000 Evaluate the operation in the parentheses.

= \$30,975 − \$2000 Multiply.

= \$28,975 Subtract.

49. Area of Shaded region = Area of outer square − Area of inner square.

$= (x)(x) - \left(\frac{1}{2}x\right)\left(\frac{1}{2}x\right)$

$= x^2 - \left(\frac{1}{2}x\right)^2$ Rewrite using powers.

$= x^2 - \frac{1}{4}x^2$ Evaluate the power.

$= \frac{3}{4}x^2$ Subtract like terms.

50. $\frac{3}{4}x^2 = \frac{3}{4}(8)^2$ Substitue.

$= \frac{3}{\cancel{4}}(\overset{16}{\cancel{64}})$ Evaluate the power.

$= 48$ Simplify.

51. Total admission price = cost for 2 adults + cost of 1 senior + cost of 3 children.
Since one child is under 4 years, there is no charge, so we will calculate the cost for 2 children.
Admission price = 2(\$7) + \$5 + 2(\$4).

52. 2(\$7) + \$5 + 2(\$4) = \$14 + \$5 + \$8 Multiply.

= \$19 + \$8 Add.

= \$27

Copyright © McDougal Littell Inc.
All rights reserved.

53. Cost of hat plus its tax plus cost of hot dog plus cost of nachos
$= 10 + (0.06)10 + 2.75 + 3.5$ Multiply.
$= 10 + 0.60 + 2.75 + 3.5$ Add.
$= 10.60 + 2.75 + 3.5$
$= 13.35 + 3.5$
$= 16.85$
You owe $16.85.

1.3 Standardized Test Practice (p. 20)

54. $4^2 - 10 \div 2 = 16 - 10 \div 2$ Evaluate the power.
$= 16 - 5$ Divide.
$= 11$ (B) Subtract.

55. $32 - x^2 + 9 = 32 - (2)^2 + 9$ Substitute 2 for x.
$= 32 - 4 + 9$ Evaluate the power.
$= 28 + 9$ Subtract, then add (left-
$= 37$ (H) to-right rule).

56. a. $3 + 3 \times 5 - 2 = 3 + 15 - 2$ Multiply.
$= 18 - 2$ Add, then subtract
$= 16$ (left-to-right rule).

b. $18 \div 6 \times 3 + 3 = 3 \times 3 + 3$ Divide, then multiply (left-to-right rule).
$= 9 + 3$
$= 12$ Add.

c. $7 + 14 \div 7 \times 4 = 7 + 2 \times 4$ Divide, then multiply (left-to-right rule).
$= 7 + 8$
$= 15$ Add.

d. $2^2 \cdot 3 - 6 \cdot 2 = 4 \cdot 3 - 6 \cdot 2$ Evaluate the power.
$= 12 - 12$ Multiply.
$= 0$ Subtract.

The expression that has a value of 12 is B.

57. $\dfrac{3^2 + 6 - 5}{2 \cdot 5} = \dfrac{9 + 6 - 5}{2 \cdot 5}$ Simplify the numerator, evaluate the power
$= \dfrac{15 - 5}{2 \cdot 5}$ Add, then subtract (left-to-right rule).
$= \dfrac{10}{2 \cdot 5}$
$= \dfrac{10}{10}$ Simplify the denominator, multiply.
$= 1$ (F) Divide.

1.3 Mixed Review (p. 21)

58. $(8)(a) = (8)(4)$ Substitute 4 for a.
$= 32$ Multiply.

59. $\dfrac{24}{x} = \dfrac{24}{(3)}$ Substitute 3 for x.
$= 8$ Divide.

60. $c + 15 = (12) + 15$ Substitute 12 for c.
$= 27$ Add.

61. $\dfrac{x}{2} \cdot x = \dfrac{\overset{9}{\cancel{(18)}}}{2} \cdot (18)$ Substitute 18 for x.
$= 162$ Multiply.

62. $9t = 9(7)$ Substitute 7 for t.
$= 63$ Multiply.

63. $25 - y = 25 - (14)$ Substitute 14 for y.
$= 11$ Subtract.

64. twelve squared $= 12^2$

65. z to the sixth power $= z^6$

66. $2b \cdot 2b \cdot 2b = (2b)^3$

67. $9t^2 = 9(3)^2$ Substitute 3 for t.
$= 9(9)$ Evaluate the power.
$= 81$ Multiply.

68. $(7h)^3 = (7 \cdot 1)^3$ Substitute 1 for h.
$= (7)^3$ Evaluate the operation in the parentheses.
$= 343$ Evaluate the power.

69. $(6w)^2 = (6 \cdot 5)^2$ Substitute 5 for w.
$= (30)^2$ Evaluate the operation in the parentheses.
$= 900$ Evaluate the power.

1.3 Maintaining Skills (p. 21)

70. 15 is composite.
Its factors are 1, 3, 5, 15.
$1 \times 15 = 15$ and $3 \times 5 = 15$

71. 9 is composite.
Its factors are 1, 3, 9.
$1 \times 9 = 9$ and $3 \times 3 = 9$

72. 13 is prime.
Its only factors are 1, 13.
$1 \times 13 = 13$

73. 38 is composite.
Its factors are 1, 2, 19, 38.
$1 \times 38 = 38$ and $2 \times 19 = 38$

74. 46 is composite.
Its factors are 1, 2, 23, 46.
$1 \times 46 = 46$ and $2 \times 23 = 46$

75. 50 is composite.
Its factors are 1, 2, 5, 10, 25, 50.
$1 \times 50 = 50$, $2 \times 25 = 50$, $5 \times 10 = 50$

76. 64 is composite.
Its factors are 1, 2, 4, 8, 16, 32, 64.
$1 \times 64 = 64$, $2 \times 32 = 64$, $4 \times 16 = 64$, $8 \times 8 = 64$

77. 29 is prime.
Its only factors are 1, 29.
$1 \times 29 = 29$

Quiz 1 *(p. 21)*

1. $6x = 6(3) = 18$

2. $42 \div x = 42 \div 3 = 14$

3. $x + 29 = 3 + 29 = 32$

4. $12 - x = 12 - 3 = 9$

Copyright © McDougal Littell Inc.
All rights reserved.

5. $5x - 10 = 5(3) - 10$ Substitute.
$= 15 - 10$ Multiply.
$= 5$ Subtract.

6. $10 + 2x = 10 + 2(3)$ Substitute.
$= 10 + 6$ Multiply.
$= 16$ Add.

7. $x^2 - 3 = 3^2 - 3$ Substitute.
$= 9 - 3$ Evaluate the power.
$= 6$ Subtract.

8. $2x^3 = 2(3)^3$ Substitute.
$= 2(27)$ Evaluate the power.
$= 54$ Multiply.

9. $(2x)^3 = (2 \cdot 3)^3$ Substitute.
$= (6)^3$ Evaluate the operation in the parentheses.
$= 216$ Evaluate the power.

10. $d = rt$
$d = (50)(4)$
$d = 200$ mi

11. $d = rt$
$d = (500)(4)$
$d = 2000$ mi

12. $d = rt$
$d = (10)(2)$
$d = 20$ mi

13. six cubed $= 6^3$

14. $4 \cdot 4 \cdot 4 \cdot 4 \cdot 4 = 4^5$

15. $5y \cdot 5y \cdot 5y = (5y)^3$

16. $3 \cdot 3 \cdot 3 = 3^3$

17. $2x \cdot 2x \cdot 2x \cdot 2x = (2x)^4$

18. eight squared $= 8^2$

19. The box is a cube, so each edge is the same length, 4 feet. The volume of a cube is $V = s^3$, or, in this case, $V = 4 \cdot 4 \cdot 4 = 64 \text{ ft}^3$.

20. $\dfrac{7 \cdot 2^2}{7 + (2^3 - 1)} = \dfrac{7 \cdot 4}{7 + (2^3 - 1)}$ Simplify the numerator, evaluate the power.
$= \dfrac{28}{7 + (2^3 - 1)}$ Multiply.
$= \dfrac{28}{7 + (8 - 1)}$ Simplify the denominator, evaluate the operation in the parentheses by first evaluating the power.
$= \dfrac{28}{7 + (7)}$ Finish evaluating the operation in the parentheses by subtracting.
$= \dfrac{28}{14}$ Add.
$= 2$ Divide.

21. $\dfrac{(3^2 - 3)}{2 \cdot 9} = \dfrac{(9 - 3)}{2 \cdot 9}$ Simplify the numerator, first evaluate the power.
$= \dfrac{6}{2 \cdot 9}$ Subtract.
$= \dfrac{6}{18}$ Simplify the denominator by multiplying.
$= \dfrac{1}{3}$ Simplify the fraction.

22. $\dfrac{6^2 - 11}{2(17 + 2 \cdot 4)} = \dfrac{36 - 11}{2(17 + 2 \cdot 4)}$ Simplify the numerator, evaluate the power.
$= \dfrac{25}{2(17 + 2 \cdot 4)}$ Subtract.
$= \dfrac{25}{2(17 + 8)}$ Simplify the denominator, evaluate the operation in the parentheses by first multiplying.
$= \dfrac{\overset{1}{\cancel{25}}}{2(\cancel{25})}$ Finish the operation in the parentheses by adding.
$= \dfrac{1}{2}$ Simplify the fraction.

1.4 Developing Concepts: Explore *(pp. 22–23)*

1.

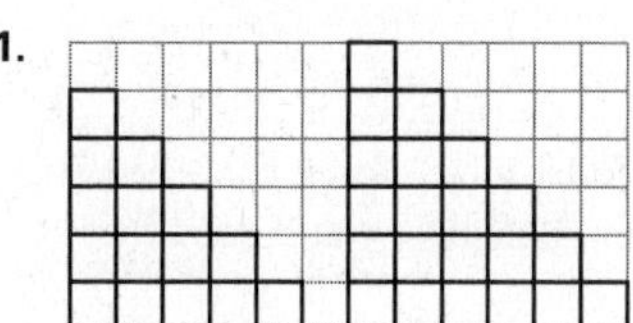

2.

Figure	*Perimeter*	*Pattern*
1	4	$4 \cdot 1$
2	8	$4 \cdot 2$
3	12	$4 \cdot 3$
4	16	$4 \cdot 4$
5	20	$4 \cdot 5$
6	24	$4 \cdot 6$

Think About It (p. 22)

1.

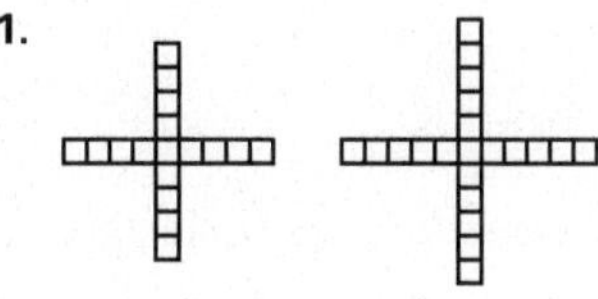

Copyright © McDougal Littell Inc.
All rights reserved.

2.

Figure	Perimeter	Pattern
1	4	$8 \cdot 1 - 4$
2	12	$8 \cdot 2 - 4$
3	20	$8 \cdot 3 - 4$
4	28	$8 \cdot 4 - 4$
5	36	$8 \cdot 5 - 4$
6	44	$8 \cdot 6 - 4$

3. Continuing the pattern, the 10th figure would have a perimeter of 76 units. The pattern is $p = 8n - 4$.

Lesson 1.4

1.4 Checkpoint (pp. 25–26)

1. $2 = 6 - x$
   $2 = 6 - (4); x = 4$

2. $x + 3 = 11$
   $(8) + 3 = 11; x = 8$

3. $\frac{x}{4} = 5$
   $\frac{(20)}{4} = 5; x = 20$

4. $14 = 2x$
   $14 = 2(7); x = 7$

5. Since the chips cost a dollar more, and you needed \$0.50 more with the less expensive chips, you'll need \$1.50 more.

6. $3n - 4 \le 8$ Replace n with 2.
   $3(2) - 4 \overset{?}{\le} 8$ Multiply.
   $6 - 4 \overset{?}{\le} 8$ Subtract.
   $2 \le 8$ True; therefore 2 is a solution.

7. $3n - 4 \le 8$ Replace n with 3.
   $3(3) - 4 \overset{?}{\le} 8$ Multiply.
   $9 - 4 \overset{?}{\le} 8$ Subtract.
   $5 \le 8$ True; therefore 3 is a solution.

8. $3n - 4 \le 8$ Replace n with 4.
   $3(4) - 4 \overset{?}{\le} 8$ Multiply.
   $12 - 4 \overset{?}{\le} 8$ Subtract.
   $8 \le 8$ True; therefore 4 is a solution.

9. $3n - 4 \le 8$ Replace n with 5.
   $3(5) - 4 \overset{?}{\le} 8$ Multiply.
   $15 - 4 \overset{?}{\le} 8$ Subtract.
   $11 \not\le 8$ False; therefore 5 is not a solution.

10. $2x \le 500$
    $2(300) \overset{?}{\le} 500$
    $600 \not\le 500$ False; Therefore 300 calories does not meet the vet's restriction.

1.4 Guided Practice (p. 27)

1. $3x + 1 = 14$ is an equation because it is a statement with an equal sign between two expressions.

2. $7y - 6$ is an expression; it is a statement only.

3. $5(y^2 + 4) - 7$ is an expression, a statement without an equal sign.

4. $5x - 1 = 3 + x$ is an equation, two expressions with an equal sign between them.

5. $3x + 2 \le 8$ is an inequality, two expressions with an inequality symbol between them.

6. $5x > 20$ is an inequality, two expressions with an inequality symbol between them.

7. An x value of 4 is a *solution* of the equation $x + 1 = 5$, because $4 + 1 = 5$. (When x is replaced by 4, the statement is true.)

8. $a + 8 = 13$ Replace a with 5.
   $5 + 8 \overset{?}{=} 13$ Add.
   $13 = 13$ True, therefore 5 is a solution.

9. $27 = 36 - 2a$ Replace a with 5.
   $27 \overset{?}{=} 36 - 2(5)$ Multiply.
   $27 \overset{?}{=} 36 - 10$ Subtract.
   $27 \ne 26$ False, therefore 5 is not a solution.

10. $a - 0 = 5$ Replace a with 5.
    $5 - 0 \overset{?}{=} 5$ Subtract.
    $5 = 5$ True; therefore 5 is a solution.

11. $2a + 1 = 11$ Replace a with 5.
    $2(5) + 1 \overset{?}{=} 11$ Multiply.
    $10 + 1 \overset{?}{=} 11$ Add.
    $11 = 11$ True; therefore 5 is a solution.

12. $6a - 5 = 15$ Replace a with 5.
    $6(5) - 5 \overset{?}{=} 15$ Multiply.
    $30 - 5 \overset{?}{=} 15$ Subtract.
    $25 \ne 15$ False; therefore 5 is not a solution.

13. $5a + 4 = 26$ Replace a with 5.
    $5(5) + 4 \overset{?}{=} 26$ Multiply.
    $25 + 4 \overset{?}{=} 26$ Add.
    $29 \ne 26$ False; therefore 5 is not a solution.

14. $45 \div a = 9$ Replace a with 5.
    $45 \div 5 \overset{?}{=} 9$ Divide.
    $9 = 9$ True; therefore 5 is a solution.

15. $a^2 + 2 = 27$ Replace a with 5.
    $5^2 + 2 \overset{?}{=} 27$ Evaluate the power.
    $25 + 2 \overset{?}{=} 27$ Add.
    $27 = 27$ True; therefore 5 is a solution.

16. $\frac{40}{a} = 8$ Replace a with 5.
    $\frac{40}{5} \overset{?}{=} 8$ Divide.
    $8 = 8$ True; therefore 5 is a solution.

17. $b + 10 > 19$ Replace b with 8.
    $8 + 10 \overset{?}{>} 19$ Add.
    $18 \not> 19$ False; therefore 8 is not a solution.

18. $14 - b \le 3$ Replace b with 8.
    $14 - 8 \overset{?}{\le} 3$ Subtract.
    $6 \not\le 3$ False; therefore 8 is not a solution.

Copyright © McDougal Littell Inc.
All rights reserved.

19. $5b > 35$ Replace b with 8.
$5(8) \overset{?}{>} 35$ Multiply.
$40 > 35$ True; therefore 8 is a solution.

20. $8 \geq 64 \div b$ Replace b with 8.
$8 \overset{?}{\geq} 64 \div 8$ Divide.
$8 \geq 8$ True; therefore 8 is a solution.

21. $3b - 24 > 0$ Replace b with 8.
$3(8) - 24 \overset{?}{>} 0$ Multiply.
$24 - 24 \overset{?}{>} 0$ Subtract.
$0 \not> 0$ False; therefore 8 is not a solution.

22. $16 \leq b^2$ Replace b with 8.
$16 \overset{?}{\leq} (8)^2$ Evaluate the power.
$16 \leq 64$ True; therefore 8 is a solution.

23. $60 > 7b + 3$ Replace b with 8.
$60 \overset{?}{>} 7(8) + 3$ Multiply.
$60 \overset{?}{>} 56 + 3$ Add.
$60 > 59$ True; therefore 8 is a solution.

24. $18 - b < 10$ Replace b with 8.
$18 - 8 \overset{?}{<} 10$ Subtract.
$10 \not< 10$ False; therefore 8 is not a solution.

25. $37 \geq 4b$ Replace b with 8.
$37 \overset{?}{\geq} 4(8)$ Multiply.
$37 \geq 32$ True; therefore 8 is a solution.

1.4 Practice and Applications (pp. 27–29)

26. $3b + 1 = 13$ Replace b with 4.
$3(4) + 1 \overset{?}{=} 13$ Multiply.
$12 + 1 \overset{?}{=} 13$ Add.
$13 = 13$ True; therefore 4 is a solution.

27. $5r - 10 = 11$ Replace r with 5.
$5(5) - 10 \overset{?}{=} 11$ Multiply.
$25 - 10 \overset{?}{=} 11$ Subtract.
$15 \neq 11$ False; therefore 5 is not a solution.

28. $4c + 2 = 10$ Replace c with 2.
$4(2) + 2 \overset{?}{=} 10$ Multiply.
$8 + 2 \overset{?}{=} 10$ Add.
$10 = 10$ True; therefore 2 is a solution.

29. $6d - 5 = 31$ Replace d with 6.
$6(6) - 5 \overset{?}{=} 31$ Multiply.
$36 - 5 \overset{?}{=} 31$ Subtract.
$31 = 31$ True; therefore 6 is a solution.

30. $5 + x^2 = 17$ Replace x with 3.
$5 + 3^2 \overset{?}{=} 17$ Evaluate the power.
$5 + 9 \overset{?}{=} 17$ Add.
$14 \neq 17$ False; therefore 3 is not a solution.

31. $2y^3 + 3 = 5$ Replace y with 1.
$2(1)^3 + 3 \overset{?}{=} 5$ Evaluate the power.
$2(1) + 3 \overset{?}{=} 5$ Multiply.
$2 + 3 \overset{?}{=} 5$ Add.
$5 = 5$ True; therefore 1 is a solution.

32. $9 + 2t = 15$ Replace t with 12.
$9 + 2(12) \overset{?}{=} 15$ Multiply.
$9 + 24 \overset{?}{=} 15$ Add.
$33 \neq 15$ False; therefore 12 is not a solution.

33. $n^2 - 5 = 20$ Replace n with 5.
$(5)^2 - 5 \overset{?}{=} 20$ Evaluate the power.
$25 - 5 \overset{?}{=} 20$ Subtract.
$20 = 20$ True; therefore 5 is a solution.

34. $x + 3 = 8; x = 5$
$5 + 3 = 8$

35. $n + 6 = 11; n = 5$
$5 + 6 = 11$

36. $p - 13 = 20; p = 33$
$33 - 13 = 20$

37. $r - 1 = 7; r = 8$
$8 - 1 = 7$

38. $3y = 12; y = 4$
$3(4) = 12$

39. $4p = 36; p = 9$
$4(9) = 36$

40. $z \div 4 = 5; z = 20$
$20 \div 4 = 5$

41. $\frac{x}{7} = 3; x = 21$
$\frac{21}{7} = 3$

42. $2b = 28; b = 14$
$2(14) = 28$

43. $11t = 22; t = 2$
$11(2) = 22$

44. $29 - d = 10; d = 19$
$29 - 19 = 10$

45. $3 + y = 8; y = 5$
$3 + 5 = 8$

46. $r + 30 = 70; r = 40$
$40 + 30 = 70$

47. $\frac{42}{x} = 7; x = 6$
$\frac{42}{6} = 7$

48. $7m = 49; m = 7$
$7(7) = 49$

49. Model D is best since the unknown number of minutes (x) plus 20 minutes to get to the gas station and fill your tank plus 15 minutes to go from the gas station to the hair stylist equals 60 minutes.
$x + 20 + 15 = 60$

50. $x + 20 + 15 = 60$
$x + 35 = 60; x = 25$
$25 + 35 = 60$

Copyright © McDougal Littell Inc.
All rights reserved.

51. $n - 2 < 6$ Replace n with 3.
$3 - 2 \overset{?}{<} 6$ Subtract.
$1 < 6$ True; therefore 3 is a solution.

52. $a - 7 \geq 15$ Replace a with 22.
$22 - 7 \overset{?}{\geq} 15$ Subtract.
$15 \geq 15$ True; therefore 22 is a solution.

53. $6 + y \leq 8$ Replace y with 3.
$6 + 3 \overset{?}{\leq} 8$ Add.
$9 \nleq 8$ False; therefore 3 is not a solution.

54. $s + 5 > 8$ Replace s with 4.
$4 + 5 \overset{?}{>} 8$ Add.
$9 > 8$ True; therefore 4 is a solution.

55. $7g \geq 47$ Replace g with 7.
$7(7) \overset{?}{\geq} 47$ Multiply.
$49 \geq 47$ True; therefore 7 is a solution.

56. $72 \div t > 6$ Replace t with 12.
$72 \div 12 \overset{?}{>} 6$ Divide.
$6 > 6$ False; therefore 12 is not a solution.

57. $3b \geq 100$ Use mental math to solve for b.
$3(34) \overset{?}{\geq} 100$ $b = 34$
$102 \geq 100$ If $b = 33$, $3(33) = 99 < 100$, so 33 is not enough.
You need to sell 34 boxes or more.

58. $20n \geq 150$ Replace n with 6.
$20(6) \overset{?}{\geq} 150$ Multiply.
$120 \ngeq 150$ False; no, you will not have enough money in 6 months.

59. Replace v with each speed to find m.

$m = \frac{v}{660}$

$m = \frac{4620}{660} = 7$ Test Aircraft

$m = \frac{1320}{660} = 2$ Supersonic

$m = \frac{660}{660} = 1$ Jet

60. a. $? + x = 18$ Replace x with 6.
$? + 6 = 18$
$12 + 6 = 18$ The missing number is 12.

b. $? \cdot x = 30$ Replace x with 6.
$? \cdot 6 = 30$
$5 \cdot 6 = 30$ The missing number is 5.

c. $\frac{?}{x} = 6$ Replace x with 6.
$\frac{?}{6} = 6$
$\frac{36}{6} = 6$ The missing number is 36.

1.4 Standardized Test Practice (p. 29)

61. $5(8 - x) = 25$
Since $5(8 - 3) = 5(5) = 25$, 3 is the solution (B).

62. $250 \geq x + 12$ Replace x with 238.
$250 \overset{?}{\geq} 238 + 12$
$250 \geq 250$ True; therefore 238 is a solution (F).

63. Since a soccer field is rectangular, its area is length times width. The width cannot be greater than 100 yards, so use 100 yards for the width. Let x = the unknown length. Their product must be less than or equal to 13,000 square yards.
$100x \leq 13{,}000$ (B)

1.4 Mixed Review (p. 29)

64. $b - 12$ Replace b with 43.
$43 - 12 = 31$

65. $12 + x$ Replace x with 4.
$12 + 4 = 16$

66. $12n$ Replace n with 4.
$12(4) = 48$

67. $\frac{y}{15}$ Replace y with 30.
$\frac{30}{15} = 2$

68. $3 \cdot 3 \cdot 3 \cdot 3 \cdot 3 = 3^5$

69. seven squared $= 7^2$

70. $y \cdot y \cdot y \cdot y = y^4$

71. $9 \cdot 9 \cdot 9 \cdot 9 \cdot 9 \cdot 9 = 9^6$

72. twelve cubed $= 12^3$

73. $8d \cdot 8d \cdot 8d = (8d)^3$

74. $9 + 12 - 4 = 21 - 4$ Add, then subtract (using
$= 17$ left-to-right rule).

75. $7 + 56 \div 8 - 2 = 7 + 7 - 2$ Divide.
$= 14 - 2$ Add, then subtract
$= 12$ (using left-to-right rule).

76. $63 \div 3 \cdot 3 = 21 \cdot 3$ Divide, then multiply (using left-
$= 63$ to-right rule).

77. $4 \cdot 2 - 5 = 8 - 5$ Multiply.
$= 3$ Subtract.

78. $3 + 13 - 6 = 16 - 6$ Add, then subtract (using
$= 10$ left-to-right rule).

79. $49 \div 7 + 2 = 7 + 2$ Divide.
$= 9$ Add.

Copyright © McDougal Littell Inc.
All rights reserved.

Chapter 1 *continued*

80. $(28 \div 4) + 3^2 = 7 + 3^2$ Evaluate the operation in the parentheses.
$= 7 + 9$ Evaluate the power.
$= 16$ Add.

81. $\frac{4^2 + 2}{2} = \frac{16 + 2}{2}$ Simplify the numerator, evaluate the power.
$= \frac{18}{2}$ Add.
$= 9$ Divide.

82. $2[(2 + 3)^2 - 10] = 2[(5)^2 - 10]$ Evaluate the operation in the parentheses.
$= 2[25 - 10]$ Evaluate the power in the brackets.
$= 2[15]$ Finish evaluating the operation in the brackets.
$= 30$ Multiply.

1.4 Maintaining Skills (p. 29)

83. 5.<u>6</u>4; 5.6
84. 0.2<u>6</u>25; 0.26
85. 0.45<u>6</u>95; 0.457
86. 15.<u>2</u>95; 15.3
87. 758.9<u>4</u>9; 758.95
88. 32.65<u>8</u>2; 32.658
89. 0.<u>3</u>25; 0.3
90. 26.9<u>6</u>; 27.0 (use the zero to hold the tenth's place.)
91. 4.0<u>9</u>65; 4.10 (use the zero to hold the hundredth's place.)

Lesson 1.5

1.5 Checkpoint (pp. 30–32)

1. 11 more than a number; $x + 11$
2. A number decreased by 10; $x - 10$
3. The quotient of 8 and a number; $\frac{8}{x}$
4. The product of 2 and a number; $2x$
5. The product of 5 and a number x is 25.
$5x = 25$
6. 10 times a number x is greater than or equal to 50.
$10x \geq 50$
7. $(\$.10)x = \$5.00$
$x = 50$ min
8. $(\$.20)x = \$4.00$
$x = 20$ min

1.5 Guided Practice (p. 33)

1. Decreased indicates subtraction.
2. $7 - n$
3. A number increased by 11; $x + 11$ (B)
4. The product of 11 and a number; $11x$ (D)
5. The difference of a number and 11; $x - 11$ (A)
6. The quotient of a number and 11; $\frac{x}{11}$ (C)
7. $x + 10 = 24$
8. $7y = 42$
9. $\frac{20}{n} \leq 2$

1.5 Practice and Applications (pp. 33–35)

10. $x - 3$
11. $10 - x$
12. $5 + x$
13. $x + 9$
14. $4x$
15. $\frac{x}{50}$
16. $15 + x$
17. $x + 18$
18. $x - 6$
19. $x - 7$
20. $x + 2 = 4$ (B)
21. $2x = 4$ (D)
22. $x - 4 = 2$ (A)
23. $\frac{x}{4} = 2$ (C)
24. $x + 20 = 30$
25. $x + 10 \geq 44$
26. $18 - x = 6$
27. $35 < 21 - x$
28. $13x > 60$
29. $7x = 56$
30. $\frac{x}{22} < 3$
31. $\frac{35}{x} = 7$
32. $x + 10 = 15$
$5 + 10 = 15; x = 5$
33. $28 - x = 18$
$28 - 10 = 18; x = 10$
34. $25x = 100$
$25(4) = 100; x = 4$
35. $\frac{49}{x} = 7$
$\frac{49}{7} = 7; x = 7$
36. Area of a rectangle is length times width.
$(3x)(x) \leq 50$
$3x^2 \leq 50$
37. $d = rt$
$110 = 55t$
$110 = 55(2); t = 2$ h
38. Each township has $6 \times 6 = 36$ mi². Each square mile = 640 acres. 36 mi² is $36 \times 640 = 23{,}040$ acres.
39. The cost of the band is $\left(\frac{\$75}{\text{h}}\right)(3\text{ h}) = \$225$. If you already have \$175, then $\$225 - \$175 = \$50$ is the amount needed.

1.5 Standardized Test Practice (p. 35)

40. $n - 4 = 10$ (A)
41. $h = m + 2$ (G)

Copyright © McDougal Littell Inc.
All rights reserved.

1.5 Mixed Review (p. 35)

42. Volume of a cube is length × width × height. In this case the volume is (10 ft)(10 ft)(10 ft) = 1000 ft^3.

43.
$8k - 2 = 30$ Replace k with 4.
$8(4) - 2 \stackrel{?}{=} 30$ Multiply.
$32 - 2 \stackrel{?}{=} 30$ Subtract.
$30 = 30$ True; therefore 4 is a solution.

44.
$15 + 2c = 5c$ Replace c with 5.
$15 + 2(5) \stackrel{?}{=} 5(5)$ Simplify both sides of the equation.
$15 + 10 \stackrel{?}{=} 25$ Add.
$25 = 25$ True; therefore 5 is a solution.

45.
$\frac{r^2}{2} = 40$ Replace r with 9.
$\frac{9^2}{2} \stackrel{?}{=} 40$ Evaluate the power.
$\frac{81}{2} \stackrel{?}{=} 40$ Divide.
$40.5 \neq 40$ False; therefore 9 is not a solution.

46.
$50 = 3w$ Replace w with 15.
$50 \stackrel{?}{=} 3(15)$ Multiply.
$50 \neq 45$ False; therefore 15 is not a solution.

1.5 Maintaining Skills (p. 35)

47. $28\% = \frac{28}{100} = 0.28$ **48.** $25\% = \frac{25}{100} = 0.25$

49. $40\% = \frac{40}{100} = 0.4$ **50.** $22\% = \frac{22}{100} = 0.22$

51. $45\% = \frac{45}{100} = 0.45$ **52.** $90\% = \frac{90}{100} = 0.9$

53. $17.4\% = \frac{17.4}{100} = 0.174$ **54.** $6.51\% = \frac{6.51}{100} = 0.0651$

Quiz 2 *(p. 35)*

1.
$10x - 5 = 35$ Replace x with 4.
$10(4) - 5 \stackrel{?}{=} 35$ Multiply.
$40 - 5 \stackrel{?}{=} 35$ Subtract.
$35 = 35$ True; therefore 4 is a solution.

2.
$\frac{x}{4} = 0$ Replace x with 4.
$\frac{4}{4} \stackrel{?}{=} 0$ Divide.
$1 \neq 0$ False; therefore 4 is not a solution.

3.
$x^2 + 5 = 21$ Replace x with 4.
$(4)^2 + 5 \stackrel{?}{=} 21$ Evaluate the power.
$16 + 5 \stackrel{?}{=} 21$ Add.
$21 = 21$ True; therefore 4 is a solution.

4.
$3a > 50$ Replace a with 20.
$3(20) \stackrel{?}{>} 50$ Multiply.
$60 > 50$ True; therefore 20 is a solution.

5.
$10 + a < 30$ Replace a with 20.
$10 + 20 \stackrel{?}{<} 30$ Add.
$30 \nless 30$ False; therefore 20 is not a solution.

6.
$40 + 3a \geq 50$ Replace a with 20.
$40 + 3(20) \stackrel{?}{\geq} 50$ Multiply.
$40 + 60 \stackrel{?}{\geq} 50$ Add.
$100 \geq 50$ True; therefore 20 is a solution.

7.
$\frac{a}{5} \leq 5$ Replace a with 20.
$\frac{20}{5} \stackrel{?}{\leq} 5$ Divide.
$4 \leq 5$ True; therefore 20 is a solution.

8.
$\frac{80}{a} \geq 5$ Replace a with 20.
$\frac{80}{20} \stackrel{?}{\geq} 5$ Divide.
$4 \ngeq 5$ False; therefore 20 is not a solution.

9.
$\frac{a}{5} - 2 \leq 5$ Replace a with 20.
$\frac{20}{5} - 2 \stackrel{?}{\leq} 5$ Divide.
$4 - 2 \stackrel{?}{\leq} 5$ Subtract.
$2 \leq 5$ True; therefore 20 is a solution.

10. The area is the length times the width.
$8x = 32$
$8(4) = 32$
The width $x = 4$ units.

11. $\frac{x}{9} < 17$

12. $10x = 50$

13. $y + 10 \geq 57$

14. $y - 6 = 15$

Lesson 1.6

1.6 Checkpoint (pp. 37–38)

1.

Verbal Model: [Width of first garden] · [Length of first garden] = [Width of second garden] · [Length of second garden]

Labels
Width of first garden = 5 (meters)
Length of first garden = 16 (meters)
Width of second garden = 8 (meters)
Length of second garden = x (meters)

Algebraic Model
$5(16) = 8(x)$ Write algebraic model.
$80 = 8x$ Simplify.
$10 = x$ Solve with mental math.

The second garden should be 10 m long.

Copyright © McDougal Littell Inc.
All rights reserved.

2. Verbal Model [Your speed] · [Time] = [Distance]

Labels Your speed = 10 (miles per hour)

Time = t (hours)

Distance = 6.2 (miles)

Algebraic Model $10t = 6.2$ Write algebraic model.

$t = 0.62$ Solve with mental math.

It will take 0.62 hours to run the last 6.2 miles.

3. Calculate your time:

The time for the first 20 miles is

$$d = rt$$
$$20 = 8t$$
$$20 \div 8 = t$$
$$2.5 = t$$

It took 2.5 hours for first 20 miles plus 0.62 hours for last 6.2 miles for a total of $2.5 + 0.62 = 3.12$ hours. Your time is faster than your friend's time.

1.6 Guided Practice (p. 39)

1. modeling **2.** verbal

3. Write a verbal model. Assign labels to the verbal model to write an algebraic model. Solve the algebraic model and answer the original question. Check that your answer is reasonable.

4. B is correct.

1.6 Practice and Applications (pp. 39–41)

5. Time to wait for subway + time to ride subway = time to get home (t).

$(15 - 3) + 8 = t$ Evaluate.

$12 + 8 = t$

$20 = t$

It will take 20 minutes to get home.

6. walking speed · time to walk home = distance to home

7. walking speed = 4 mi/h; time to walk = t; distance to home = 1 mi

8. $4t = 1$

9. $t = \frac{1}{4}$; It will take $\frac{1}{4}$ of an hour or 15 minutes to walk home.

10. Walking; although the subway ride takes much less time, you have to wait 12 minutes for the next train, so it will take 20 minutes by subway and only 15 minutes walking.

11. original length + number of days · growth rate = total length

12. original length = x (ft)
number of days = 31
growth rate = 1 (ft/day)
total length = 50 (ft)

13. $x + (1 \cdot 31) = 50$ (B)

14. $x + (1 \cdot 31) = 50$

$x + 31 = 50$

$19 + 31 = 50$

$x = 19$; 19 ft

15. $19 + 1 \cdot 31 = 19 + 31 = 50$

16. number of weeks worked · amount saved each week (\$) = price of stereo with CD (\$)

17. number of weeks worked = 8
amount saved each week = m (\$)
price of stereo with CD = 480 (\$)

18. $8m = 480$

19. $8m = 480$

$8(60) = 480$

$m = 60$; \$60

20. $8(60) = 480$

21. a. Your votes must be greater than the votes for your opponent.

$95 + x > 120 +$ (the votes that aren't yours out of 45)

$95 + x > 120 + (45 - x)$

b. If $x = 36$, the inequality is still true.

$95 + 36 \overset{?}{>} 120 + (45 - 36)$

$131 \overset{?}{>} 120 + (9)$

$131 > 129$

If x is 35, the inequality is not true.

$95 + 35 \overset{?}{>} 120 + (45 - 36)$

$130 \overset{?}{>} 120 + (10)$

$130 \not> 130$

False; it would be a tie.

1.6 Standardized Test Practice (p. 41)

22. The formula for the distance, rate, and time is $d = rt$. Choice (A) is correct.

23. The choice (J) is correct. The variable x represents the speed Jim was driving. Jim has to pay \$10 for each mile over 45 miles per hour. This can be found by subtracting 45 from Jim's speed, and multiplying by 10. This amount does not include the \$25 that all speeders are charged, so \$175 − \$25 is the amount Jim pays over the flat rate of \$25.

1.6 Mixed Review (p. 41)

24. $x^2 - 2 = 7^2 - 2$ Replace x with 7.

$= 49 - 2$ Evaluate the power.

$= 47$ Subtract.

25. $(2x)^3 = (2 \cdot 5)^3$ Replace x with 5.

$= 10^3$ Evaluate the operation in the parentheses.

$= 1000$ Evaluate the power.

Copyright © McDougal Littell Inc.
All rights reserved.

26. $(10 - x)^2 = (10 - 6)^2$ Replace x with 6.
$= (4)^2$ Evaluate the operation in the parentheses.
$= 16$ Evaluate the power.

27. $22 - 4^2 \div 2 = 22 - 16 \div 2$ Evaluate the power.
$= 22 - 8$ Divide.
$= 14$ Subtract.

28. $4 + 8 \cdot 4 - 1 = 4 + 32 - 1$ Multiply.
$= 36 - 1$ Add, then subtract (using left-to-right rule).
$= 35$

29. $2 \cdot 4 + (7 - 3) = 2 \cdot 4 + (4)$ Evaluate the operation in the parentheses.
$= 8 + 4$ Multiply.
$= 12$ Add.

30. $2x - 3 < 15$ Replace x with 9.
$2(9) - 3 \overset{?}{<} 15$ Multiply.
$18 - 3 \overset{?}{<} 15$ Subtract.
$15 \not< 15$ False; therefore 9 is not a solution.

31. $3x + 4 \leq 16$ Replace x with 4.
$3(4) + 4 \overset{?}{\leq} 16$ Multiply.
$12 + 4 \overset{?}{\leq} 16$ Add.
$16 \leq 16$ True; therefore 4 is a solution.

32. $16 + x^2 \div 4 = 17$ Replace x with 2.
$16 + 2^2 \div 4 \overset{?}{=} 17$ Evaluate the power.
$16 + 4 \div 4 \overset{?}{=} 17$ Divide.
$16 + 1 \overset{?}{=} 17$ Add.
$17 = 17$ True; therefore 2 is a solution.

33. The profit of the lemonade times the number of lemonades (l) plus the profit of the tacos times the number of tacos equals the profit.
$0.25l + 0.50(100) = 100$
$0.25l + 50 = 100$
$0.25(200) + 50 = 100;$
200 lemonades were sold.

1.6 Maintaining Skills (p. 41)

34. $\frac{3}{2}$

$\begin{array}{r} 1 \\ 2\overline{)3} \\ \underline{2} \\ 1 \end{array}$

$1\frac{1}{2}$

35. $\frac{7}{4}$

$\begin{array}{r} 1 \\ 4\overline{)7} \\ \underline{4} \\ 3 \end{array}$

$1\frac{3}{4}$

36. $\frac{11}{3}$

$\begin{array}{r} 3 \\ 3\overline{)11} \\ \underline{9} \\ 2 \end{array}$

$3\frac{2}{3}$

37. $\frac{13}{6}$

$\begin{array}{r} 2 \\ 6\overline{)13} \\ \underline{12} \\ 1 \end{array}$

$2\frac{1}{6}$

38. $\frac{16}{5}$

$\begin{array}{r} 3 \\ 5\overline{)16} \\ \underline{15} \\ 1 \end{array}$

$3\frac{1}{5}$

39. $\frac{21}{9}$

$\begin{array}{r} 2 \\ 9\overline{)21} \\ \underline{18} \\ 3 \end{array}$

$2\frac{3}{9} = 2\frac{1}{3}$

40. $\frac{18}{4}$

$\begin{array}{r} 4 \\ 4\overline{)18} \\ \underline{16} \\ 2 \end{array}$

$4\frac{2}{4} = 4\frac{1}{2}$

41. $\frac{15}{7}$

$\begin{array}{r} 2 \\ 7\overline{)15} \\ \underline{14} \\ 1 \end{array}$

$2\frac{1}{7}$

42. $\frac{30}{8}$

$\begin{array}{r} 3 \\ 8\overline{)30} \\ \underline{24} \\ 6 \end{array}$

$3\frac{6}{8} = 3\frac{3}{4}$

43. $\frac{54}{12}$

$\begin{array}{r} 4 \\ 12\overline{)54} \\ \underline{48} \\ 6 \end{array}$

$4\frac{6}{12} = 4\frac{1}{2}$

44. $\frac{84}{36}$

$\begin{array}{r} 2 \\ 36\overline{)84} \\ \underline{72} \\ 12 \end{array}$

$2\frac{12}{36} = 2\frac{1}{3}$

45. $\frac{20}{3}$

$\begin{array}{r} 6 \\ 3\overline{)20} \\ \underline{18} \\ 2 \end{array}$

$6\frac{2}{3}$

Lesson 1.7

1.7 Checkpoint (pp. 42–44)

1.

Year	1970	1975	1980	1985
Total	1136.9	1128.2	1142.0	1221.2

Year	1990	1995	2000
Total	1224.7	1274.8	1290.0

(Total = Dairy + Vegetables + Fruit)

The least consumption was in 1975 and the greatest in 2000.

2.

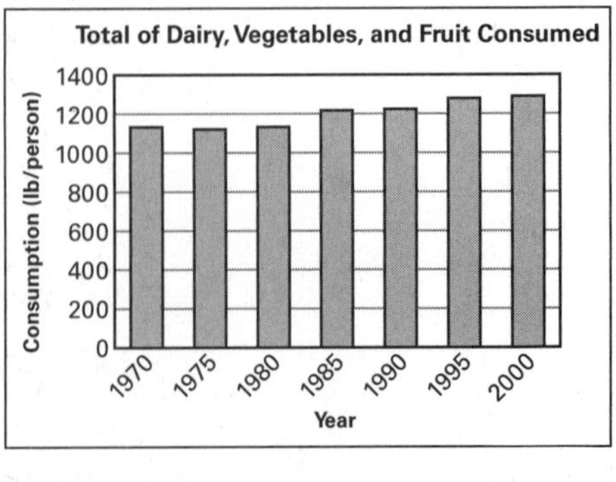

Copyright © McDougal Littell Inc.
All rights reserved.

3. 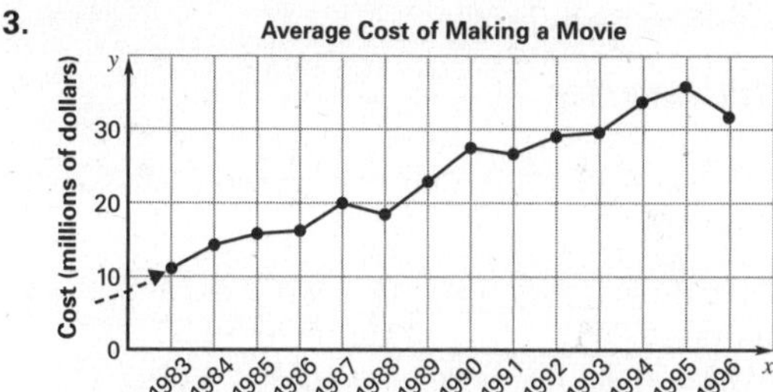

The graph with more tick marks on the vertical axis is easier to interpret because it's easier to determine the value of a given point on a line.

1.7 Guided Practice (p. 45)

1. Data are information, facts, or numbers that describe something; *Sample answer:* Height of students in your class.
2. Tables, bar graphs, line graphs
3. False; the rainfall decreases from June to July, from September to October, and from November to December.
4. True; both months average 3.4.
5. False; the greatest amount of rain is in September.

1.7 Practice and Applications (pp. 45–47)

6.

Player	1	2	3	4
Round 1	90	88	79	78
Round 2	94	84	83	80
Round 3	92	86	81	79

$(90 + 94) \div 2 = 92$
$(88 + 84) \div 2 = 86$
$(79 + 83) \div 2 = 81$
$(78 + 80) \div 2 = 79$

7. Player 4 has the lowest average. Player 1 has the highest average.

8.

Age	1980	1985	1990	1995	2000
14–19	18,199	17,732	16,697	18,922	20,500

9. The least number were enrolled in 1990; the greatest number were enrolled in 2000.
10. No; enrollment decreased from 1980 to 1985 and from 1985 to 1990. It increased from 1990 to 1995 and 1995 to 2000.
11. About 150 ft
12. No; for example, the braking distance for a car going 50 mi/h is about 3 times the braking distance of a car going 25 mi/h.
13. The braking distance at that speed is about 300 ft. You need to have time to react to any emergency and still allow time for your car to travel that distance while stopping.

14. 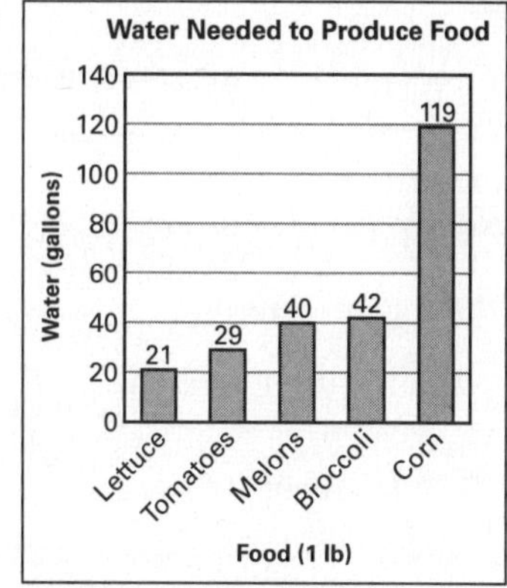

15. The 6 years from 1991 to 1996.
16. About $4.25
17. 1998

18. 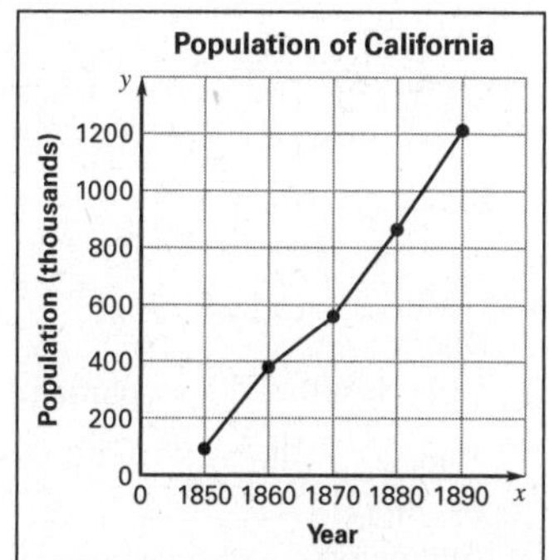

19. 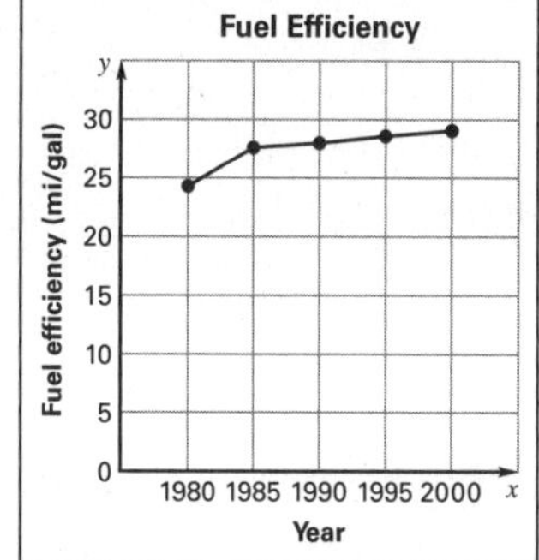

Sample answer: I chose a line graph because line graphs are useful in showing changes over time.

1.7 Standardized Test Practice (p. 47)

20. (B) The line graph is used to show changes in data over time.
21. (H) The decrease from May to June is about $140 - 95 = 45$ kWh.
22. (A) about $130 + 125 + 115 + 110 = 480$ kWh

Copyright © McDougal Littell Inc.
All rights reserved.

1.7 Mixed Review (p.47)

For Exercises 23–25, the perimeter is the total of the lengths of the sides of each polygon.

23. Perimeter $= 7 + 14 + 7 + 14 = 42$ in.
Area = length × width $= 7 \times 14 = 98$ in.^{2}

24. Perimeter $= 10 + 10 + 12 = 32$ m
Area $= \frac{1}{2}b \cdot h = \frac{1}{2}(12)(8) = 48$ m^2

25. Perimeter $= 24 + 25 + 7 = 56$ ft
Area $= \frac{1}{2}b \cdot h = \frac{1}{2}(7)(24) = 84$ ft^2

26.
$17 - x < 12$ Replace x with 5.
$17 - (5) < 12$ Subtract.
$12 \not< 12$ False; therefore 5 is not a solution.

27.
$x + 3x \geq 18$ Replace x with 5.
$(5) + 3(5) \overset{?}{\geq} 18$ Multiply.
$5 + 15 \geq 18$ Add.
$20 \geq 18$ True; therefore 5 is a solution.

28.
$5x \div 2 = 12.5$ Replace x with 5.
$5(5) \div 2 \overset{?}{=} 12.5$ Multiply, then divide (left-to-right rule).
$25 \div 2 = 12.5$ Divide.
$12.5 = 12.5$ True; therefore 5 is a solution.

29.
$2.5 > 1.2x - 3$ Replace x with 5.
$2.5 > 1.2(5) - 3$ Multiply.
$2.5 > 6 - 3$ Subtract.
$2.5 \not> 3$ False; therefore 5 is not a solution.

30.
$x^2 = 25$ Replace x with 5.
$5^2 \overset{?}{=} 25$ Evaluate the power.
$25 = 25$ True; therefore 5 is a solution.

31.
$(3x)^2 \leq 255$ Replace x with 5.
$(3 \cdot 5)^2 \leq 255$ Evaluate the operation in the parentheses.
$(15)^2 \leq 255$ Evaluate the power.
$225 \leq 255$ True; therefore 5 is a solution.

32.
$3x + 2x = 25$ Replace x with 5.
$3(5) + 2(5) \overset{?}{=} 25$ Multiply.
$15 + 10 \overset{?}{=} 25$ Add.
$25 = 25$ True; therefore 5 is a solution.

33.
$19 - 2x > 10$ Replace x with 5.
$19 - 2(5) > 10$ Multiply.
$19 - 10 > 10$ Subtract.
$9 \not> 10$ False; therefore 5 is not a solution.

34.
$16 \leq 3x + 1$ Replace x with 5.
$16 \leq 3(5) + 1$ Multiply.
$16 \leq 15 + 1$ Add.
$16 \leq 16$ True; therefore 5 is a solution.

1.7 Maintaining Skills (p. 47)

35. $71.717 < 77.117$

36. $2.6 < 2.65$ since $2.6 = 2.60 = 2\frac{60}{100}$ and $2.65 = 2\frac{65}{100}$; $\frac{60}{100} < \frac{65}{100}$

37. $0.01 > 0.0001$
$(0.0100 > 0.0001)$

38. $1.666 < 1.67$
$(1.666 < 1.670)$

39. $15.7 = 15.700$

40. $0.4321 < 0.434$
$(0.4321 < 0.4340)$

41. $0.48 > 0.479$
$(0.480 > 0.479)$

42. $3.11 > 3.09$

43. $9.54 = 9.540$

Lesson 1.8

1.8 Checkpoint (p. 50)

1.

Input d	0	20	40	60
Output p	14.7	23.6	32.5	41.4

2.

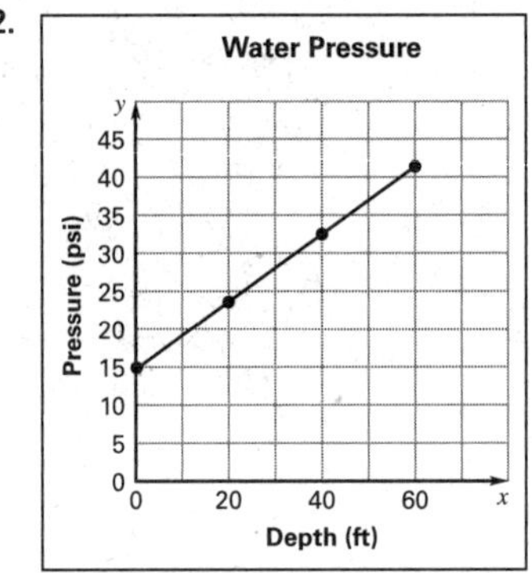

1.8 Guided Practice (p. 51)

1. input; output

2. domain

3. range

4.

Input n	1	2	3	4	5	6
Output C	77	89	101	113	125	137

5.

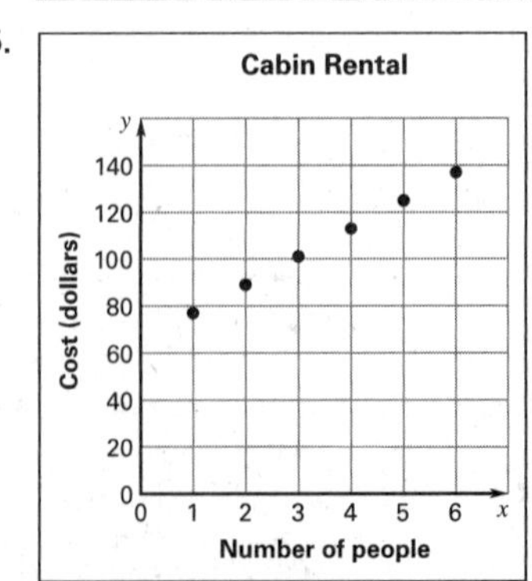

Copyright © McDougal Littell Inc.
All rights reserved.

6. The range is the set of output values: 77, 89, 101, 113, 125, 137

1.8 Practice and Applications (pp. 51–54)

7. Replace x with 0, 1, 2, 3, 4, and 5 to calculate the output for $y = 6x + 5$.

$y = 6(0) + 5$	$y = 6(1) + 5$	$y = 6(2) + 5$
$y = 0 + 5$	$y = 6 + 5$	$y = 12 + 5$
$y = 5$	$y = 11$	$y = 17$
$y = 6(3) + 5$	$y = 6(4) + 5$	$y = 6(5) + 5$
$y = 18 + 5$	$y = 24 + 5$	$y = 30 + 5$
$y = 23$	$y = 29$	$y = 35$

Input x	0	1	2	3	4	5
Output y	5	11	17	23	29	35

8. Replace x with 0, 1, 2 3, 4, and 5 to calculate the output for $y = 26 - 2x$.

$y = 26 - 2(0)$	$y = 26 - 2(1)$	$y = 26 - 2(2)$
$y = 26 - 0$	$y = 26 - 2$	$y = 26 - 4$
$y = 26$	$y = 24$	$y = 22$
$y = 26 - 2(3)$	$y = 26 - 2(4)$	$y = 26 - 2(5)$
$y = 26 - 6$	$y = 26 - 8$	$y = 26 - 10$
$y = 20$	$y = 18$	$y = 16$

Input x	0	1	2	3	4	5
Output y	26	24	22	20	18	16

9. Replace x with 0, 1, 2 3, 4, and 5 to calculate the output for $y = (x + 3) \cdot 7$.

$y = (0 + 3) \cdot 7$	$y = (1 + 3) \cdot 7$	$y = (2 + 3) \cdot 7$
$y = (3) \cdot 7$	$y = (4) \cdot 7$	$y = (5) \cdot 7$
$y = 21$	$y = 28$	$y = 35$
$y = (3 + 3) \cdot 7$	$y = (4 + 3) \cdot 7$	$y = (5 + 3) \cdot 7$
$y = (6) \cdot 7$	$y = (7) \cdot 7$	$y = (8) \cdot 7$
$y = 42$	$y = 49$	$y = 56$

Input x	0	1	2	3	4	5
Output y	21	28	35	42	49	56

10. Replace x with 0, 1, 2 3, 4, and 5 to calculate the output for $y = 85 - 15x$.

$y = 85 - 15(0)$	$y = 85 - 15(1)$	$y = 85 - 15(2)$
$y = 85 - 0$	$y = 85 - 15$	$y = 85 - 30$
$y = 85$	$y = 70$	$y = 55$
$y = 85 - 15(3)$	$y = 85 - 15(4)$	$y = 85 - 15(5)$
$y = 85 - 45$	$y = 85 - 60$	$y = 85 - 75$
$y = 40$	$y = 25$	$y = 10$

Input x	0	1	2	3	4	5
Output y	85	70	55	40	25	10

11. Replace x with 0, 1, 2 3, 4, and 5 to calculate the output for $y = 5(15 - x)$.

$y = 5(15 - 0)$	$y = 5(15 - 1)$	$y = 5(15 - 2)$
$y = 5(15)$	$y = 5(14)$	$y = 5(13)$
$y = 75$	$y = 70$	$y = 65$
$y = 5(15 - 3)$	$y = 5(15 - 4)$	$y = 5(15 - 5)$
$y = 5(12)$	$y = 5(11)$	$y = 5(10)$
$y = 60$	$y = 55$	$y = 50$

Input x	0	1	2	3	4	5
Output y	75	70	65	60	55	50

12. Replace x with 0, 1, 2 3, 4, and 5 to calculate the output for $y = 2(6x + 10)$.

$y = 2(6 \cdot 0 + 10)$	$y = 2(6 \cdot 1 + 10)$
$y = 2(0 + 10)$	$y = 2(6 + 10)$
$y = 2(10)$	$y = 2(16)$
$y = 20$	$y = 32$
$y = 2(6 \cdot 2 + 10)$	$y = 2(6 \cdot 3 + 10)$
$y = 2(12 + 10)$	$y = 2(18 + 10)$
$y = 2(22)$	$y = 2(28)$
$y = 44$	$y = 56$
$y = 2(6 \cdot 4 + 10)$	$y = 2(6 \cdot 5 + 10)$
$y = 2(24 + 10)$	$y = 2(30 + 10)$
$y = 2(34)$	$y = 2(40)$
$y = 68$	$y = 80$

Input x	0	1	2	3	4	5
Output y	20	32	44	56	68	80

13.

14.

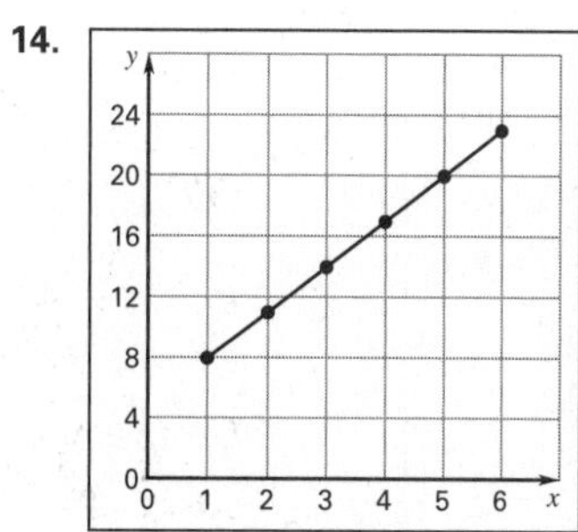

Copyright © McDougal Littell Inc.
All rights reserved.

15. $d = 0.2t$

Replace t with the values 0, 5, 10, 15, 20, 25, and 30 to calculate the output d.

$d = 0.2(0)$ $\quad d = 0$

$d = 0.2(5)$ $\quad d = 1.0$

$d = 0.2(10)$ $\quad d = 2.0$

$d = 0.2(15)$ $\quad d = 3.0$

$d = 0.2(20)$ $\quad d = 4.0$

$d = 0.2(25)$ $\quad d = 5.0$

$d = 0.2(30)$ $\quad d = 6.0$

Input x	0	5	10	15	20	25	30
Output y	0	1.0	2.0	3.0	4.0	5.0	6.0

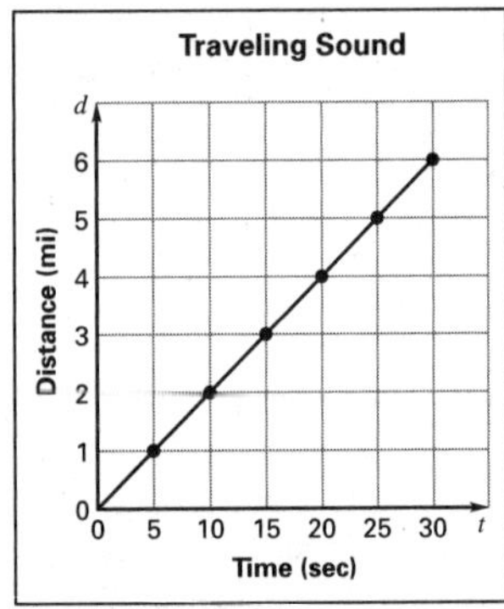

16. Yes, since there is exactly one output for each input.

17. No, since the input value 3 has two output values.

18. Yes, since there is exactly one output for each input.

19. No, since the input value 1 has two output values.

20. Use $d = 178t$; replace t with the input values 0.25, 0.50, 0.75, 1.00, 1.25, and 1.50 to calculate the output values.

$d = 178(0.25)$ $\quad d = 44.5$

$d = 178(0.50)$ $\quad d = 89$

$d = 178(0.75)$ $\quad d = 133.5$

$d = 178(1.00)$ $\quad d = 178$

$d = 178(1.25)$ $\quad d = 222.5$

$d = 178(1.50)$ $\quad d = 267$

Input x	0.25	0.50	0.75	1.00	1.25	1.5
Output y	44.5	89	133.5	178	222.5	267

21.

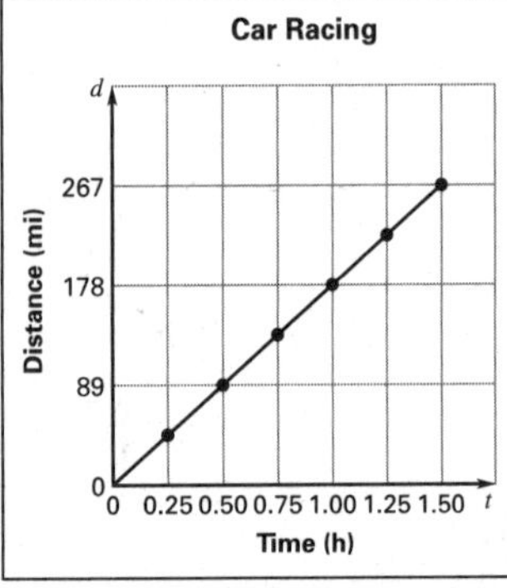

22. Since t represents time, t can be any positive number or zero. It does not make sense for t to be negative, since time cannot be negative. When $t = 0$, this means no time has passed or it represents the starting moment.

23. a. $d = rt$

$d = 11t$

b.

Input t	7	14	28
Output d	77	154	308

Replace t with the input values.

$d = 11(7)$ $\quad d = 77$

$d = 11(14)$ $\quad d = 154$

$d = 11(28)$ $\quad d = 308$

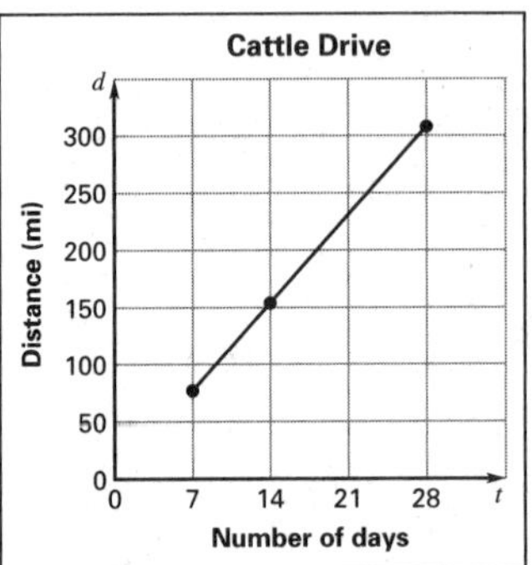

c. $d = 11t$ $\quad$ Replace d with 1100 and solve for t.

$1100 = 11t$

$1100 = 11(100)$

$t = 100$ days

24. a. Rent = cost per day times the number of days.

$R = \$90n$

Replace n with the input values to find the output values.

$R = 90(1)$ $\quad R = 90$

$R = 90(2)$ $\quad R = 180$

$R = 90(3)$ $\quad R = 270$

$R = 90(4)$ $\quad R = 360$

Number of days n	1	2	3	4
Cost of renting R	90	180	270	360

b.

Scuba Diving

Copyright © McDougal Littell Inc.
All rights reserved.

25.

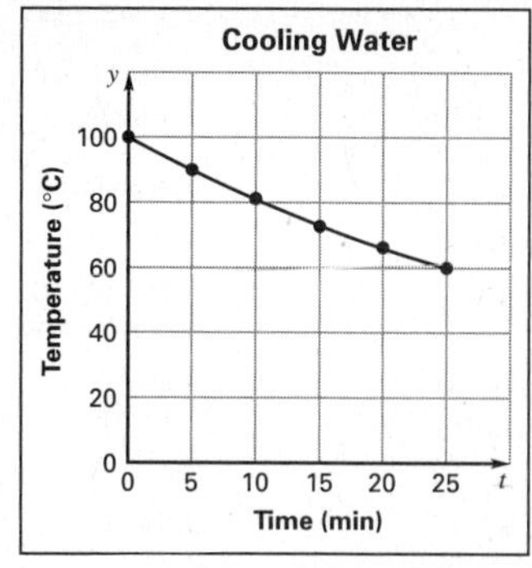

After graphing the points for the known temperatures, connect the points with a line or a curve that best fits the points.

26. Choose a few points in the domain to use as input values and calculate the range.

Input x	0	1	2	3	4
Output y	0	2	4	9	16

$y = x^2$

$y = 0^2$ $\quad y = 1^2 \quad y = 2^2$

$y = 0 \quad y = 1 \quad y = 4$

$y = 3^2 \quad y = 4^2$

$y = 9 \quad y = 16$

By observation, the output values are increasing between 0 and 16. The range is limited to $0 \le y \le 16$.

1.8 Standardized Test Practice (p. 53)

27. Table D is not a function since there are two output values for the input values of 5 and 6.

28. Choice F has an output of 27 since $j = 4a + 15 = 4(3) + 15 = 12 + 15 = 27$.

29. Choice A, $F = 50 + 25t$ is the function best represented by the graph. This can be figured out by replacing t with some input values to see if the output matches the values shown on the graph.

$F = 50 + 25(0) \quad F = 50 + 25(2) \quad F = 50 + 25(4)$

$F = 50 + 0 \quad F = 50 + 50 \quad F = 50 + 100$

$F = 50 \quad F = 100 \quad F = 150$

1.8 Mixed Review (p. 54)

30. $a + c = 3 + 5 = 8$

31. $(a + c)^2 = (3 + 5)^2 = (8)^2 = 64$

32. $a^2 + c^2 = 3^2 + 5^2 = 9 + 25 = 34$

33. $ac = 3 \cdot 5 = 15$

34. $a \cdot (c^2) = 3(5^2) = 3(25) = 75$

35. $(a^2) \cdot c = (3^2) \cdot 5 = 9 \cdot 5 = 45$

36. $9 - n$

37. $\frac{72}{x} > 7$

1.8 Maintaining Skills (p. 54)

38. $\frac{2}{9} + \frac{8}{9} = \frac{10}{9} = 1\frac{1}{9}$

39. $\frac{5}{12} + \frac{1}{12} = \frac{6}{12} = \frac{1}{2}$

40. $\frac{12}{15} + \frac{7}{15} = \frac{19}{15} = 1\frac{4}{15}$

41. $\frac{11}{3} + \frac{2}{3} = \frac{13}{3} = 4\frac{1}{3}$

42. $\frac{5}{6} + \frac{7}{6} = \frac{12}{6} = 2$

43. $\frac{2}{8} + \frac{1}{8} = \frac{3}{8}$

44. $\frac{3}{5} + \frac{1}{5} = \frac{4}{5}$

45. $\frac{3}{4} + \frac{9}{4} = \frac{12}{4} = 3$

46. $\frac{9}{14} + \frac{3}{14} = \frac{12}{14} = \frac{6}{7}$

Quiz 3 *(p. 54)*

1.

Verbal Model: [Price per can or bottle] · ([Number of cans] + [Number of bottles]) = [Amount paid]

Labels
Price per can or bottle = 5 (cents)
Number of cans = 4
Number of bottles = n
Amount paid = 50 (cents)

Algebraic Model
$5(4 + n) = 50$
$20 + 5n = 50$
$5n = 30$
$n = 6$

Jean has 6 bottles in her collection.

2.

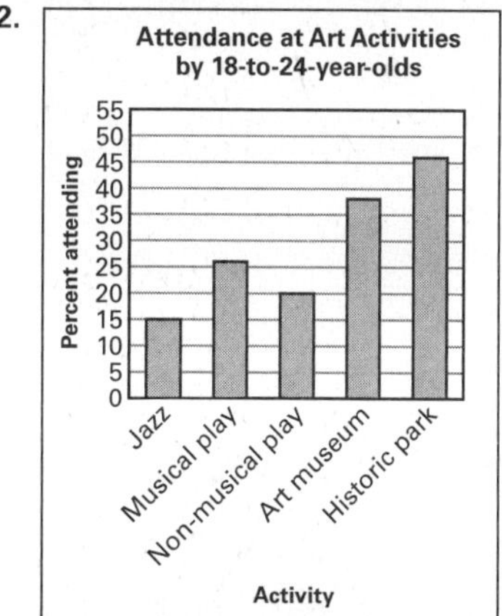

3. *Sample answer:* Attending historic parks was most popular; attending a jazz concert is about a third as popular as attending a historic park. Since the percents total more than 100%, some 18- to 24-year-olds attend more than one kind of arts activity.

Copyright © McDougal Littell Inc.
All rights reserved.

4. Replace t with the input values to calculate the output values.

$h = 200 + 25t$

$h = 200 + 25(0)$
$h = 200 + 0$
$h = 200$

$h = 200 + 25(1)$
$h = 200 + 25$
$h = 225$

$h = 200 + 25(2)$
$h = 200 + 50$
$h = 250$

$h = 200 + 25(3)$
$h = 200 + 75$
$h = 275$

$h = 200 + 25(4)$
$h = 200 + 100$
$h = 300$

Input t	0	1	2	3	4
Output h	200	225	250	275	300

5.

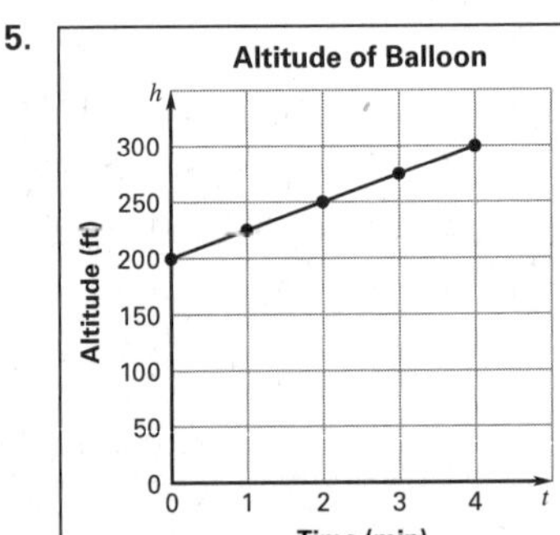

6. The range is the set of output values between 200 and 300, or $h \geq 200$ and $h \leq 300$.

Chapter 1 Summary and Review *(pp. 55–58)*

1. $a + 14 = (6) + 14$
$= 20$

2. $18x = 18(2)$
$= 36$

3. $\frac{m}{3} = \frac{18}{3}$
$= 6$

4. $\frac{15}{y} = \frac{15}{(3)} = 5$

5. $p - 12 = (22) - 12$
$= 10$

6. $5b = 5(6)$
$= 30$

7. distance = rate · time
$d = (3)(2)$
$d = 6$; 6 mi

8. distance = rate · time
$d = (2)(6)$
$d = 12$; 12 mi

9. distance = rate · time
$d = (175)(3)$
$d = 525$; 525 mi

10. Perimeter = the sum of the lengths of each side of the polygon.
Perimeter = 19 + 8 + 14 = 41 ft

11. Perimeter = the sum of the lengths of each side of the polygon.
Perimeter = 3 + 10 + 3 + 10 = 26 m

12. 8^4 **13.** 6^3 **14.** 5^5

15. $x^4 = (2)^4 = 16$

16. $(5x)^3 = (5 \cdot 5)^3$
$= (25)^3$
$= 15{,}625$

17. $6 + (b^3) = 6 + (3^3)$
$= 6 + 27$
$= 33$

18. $9 + (3 - 2) - 3^2 = 9 + (1) - 3^2$ Evaluate the operation in the parentheses.
$= 9 + (1) - 9$ Evaluate the power.
$= 10 - 9$ Add, then subtract (left-to-right rule).
$= 1$

19. $(14 - 7)^2 + 5 = (7)^2 + 5$ Evaluate the operation in the parentheses.
$= 49 + 5$ Evaluate the power.
$= 54$ Add.

20. $6 + 2^2 - (7 - 5) = 6 + 2^2 - (2)$ Evaluate the operation in the parentheses.
$= 6 + 4 - (2)$ Evaluate the power.
$= 10 - 2$ Add, then subtract (left-to-right rule).
$= 8$

21. $\frac{15 - 6}{6 + 3^2 - 12} = \frac{9}{6 + 3^2 - 12}$ Simplify the numerator.
$= \frac{9}{6 + 9 - 12}$ Simplify the denominator; evaluate the power.
$= \frac{9}{15 - 12}$ Add, then subtract (left-to-right-rule).
$= \frac{9}{3}$
$= 3$ Divide.

22. $\frac{28 + 4}{4^2} = \frac{32}{4^2}$ Simplify the numerator.
$= \frac{32}{16}$ Simplify the denominator.
$= 2$ Divide.

23. $\frac{3^3 + 7}{4 \cdot 2} = \frac{27 + 7}{4 \cdot 2}$ Simplify the numerator; evaluate the power.
$= \frac{34}{4 \cdot 2}$ Add.
$= \frac{34}{8}$ Simplify the denominator.
$= \frac{17 \cdot 2}{4 \cdot 2}$ Simplify the fraction.
$= \frac{17}{4}$

24. $2a - 3 = 2$ Replace a with 4.
$2(4) - 3 \stackrel{?}{=} 2$ Multiply.
$8 - 3 \stackrel{?}{=} 2$ Subtract.
$5 \neq 2$ False; therefore 4 is not a solution.

Copyright © McDougal Littell Inc.
All rights reserved.

25. $x^2 - x = 2$ Replace x with 2.
$2^2 - 2 \stackrel{?}{=} 2$ Evaluate the power.
$4 - 2 \stackrel{?}{=} 2$ Subtract.
$2 = 2$ True; therefore 2 is a solution.

26. $9y - 3 > 24$ Replace y with 3.
$9(3) - 3 \stackrel{?}{>} 24$ Multiply.
$27 - 3 \stackrel{?}{>} 24$ Subtract.
$24 \ngtr 24$ False; therefore 3 is not a solution.

27. $5x + 2 \stackrel{?}{\leq} 27$ Replace x with 5.
$5(5) + 2 \stackrel{?}{\leq} 24$ Multiply.
$25 + 2 \stackrel{?}{\leq} 24$ Add.
$27 \leq 27$ True; therefore 5 is a solution.

28. $w + 7 = 15$
$(8) + 7 = 15$
$w = 8$

29. $10 - r = 7$
$10 - (3) = 7$
$r = 3$

30. $4h = 32$
$4(8) = 32$
$h = 8$

31. $\frac{c}{4} = 4$
$\frac{(16)}{4} = 4$
$c = 16$

32. $16 + k = 20$
$16 + (4) = 20$
$k = 4$

33. $10g = 100$
$10(10) = 100$
$g = 10$

34. $\frac{27}{x} = 3$

35. $x + 30$ **36.** $8x > 5$ **37.** $x - 9$

38. Cost per bottle · Number of bottles = Total cost;
$0.75b = 75$
$b = 100$; 100 bottles

39.

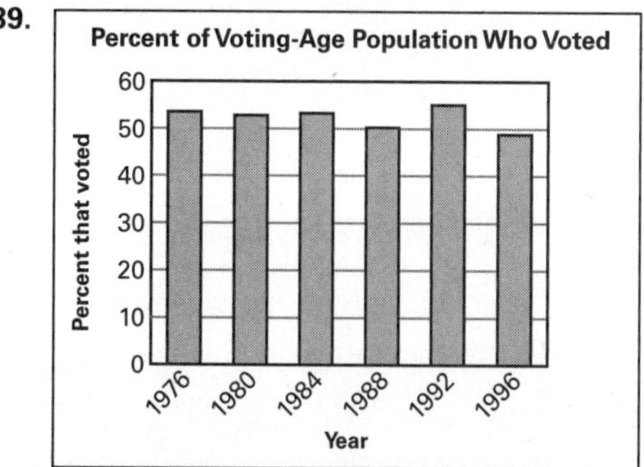

$48.9 + 55.1 < 53.5 + 53.3$
$104 < 106.8$
Yes.

40. Replace w with the input values 1, 2, 3, 4, and 5 to find the output values for P.

$P = 4(1) + 6(1)$
$P = 4 + 6$
$P = 10$

$P = 4(2) + 6(2)$
$P = 8 + 12$
$P = 20$

$P = 4(3) + 6(3)$
$P = 12 + 18$
$P = 30$

$P = 4(4) + 6(4)$
$P = 16 + 24$
$P = 40$

$P = 4(5) + 6(5)$
$P = 20 + 30$
$P = 50$

Input w	1	2	3	4	5
Output P	10	20	30	40	50

The range is the set of output values 10, 20, 30, 40, and 50.

Chapter 1 Test (p. 59)

1. $5y + x^2 = 5(3) + (5)^2$ Replace y with 3 and x with 5.
$= 5(3) + 25$ Evaluate the power.
$= 15 + 25$ Multiply.
$= 40$ Add.

2. $\frac{24}{y} - x = \frac{24}{3} - (5)$ Replace y with 3 and x with 5.
$= 8 - 5$ Divide.
$= 3$ Subtract.

3. $2y + 9x - 7 = 2(3) + 9(5) - 7$ Replace y with 3 and x with 5.
$= 6 + 45 - 7$ Multiply.
$= 51 - 7$ Add, then subtract
$= 44$ (left-to-right rule).

4. $(5y + x) \div 4 = (5 \cdot 3 + 5) \div 4$ Replace y with 3 and x with 5.
$= (15 + 5) \div 4$ Evaluate the operation in the parentheses, first multiply, then add.
$= (20) \div 4$
$= 5$ Divide.

5. $5y \cdot 5y \cdot 5y \cdot 5y = (5y)^4$

6. nine cubed $= 9^3$ **7.** six to the nth power $= 6^n$

8. $5 \cdot (4 + 6) = 5 \cdot (10) = 50$

9. $d = rt$
$100 = 35t$
If $t = 3$ hours, then $35(3) = 105$ miles, which means in three hours you would be able to go a little further than 100 miles. Yes, 3 hours is enough time.

10. $7n$ **11.** $x \geq 90$ **12.** $\frac{m}{2}$

13. $y - 3$ **14.** $8 - s = 4$ **15.** $9 < t$

16. $(2 \cdot 3)^2 \stackrel{?}{=} 2 \cdot 3^2$
$(6)^2 \stackrel{?}{=} 2 \cdot 9$
$36 \neq 18$ False.

17. $8 - 6 \stackrel{?}{=} 6 - 8$
$2 \neq -2$ False.

18. $1 + 3 = 4$ True.

Copyright © McDougal Littell Inc.
All rights reserved.

Chapter 1 *continued*

19. $x^3 = 8$ Replace x with 2.
$2^3 \stackrel{?}{=} 8$ Evaluate the power.
$8 = 8$ True.

20. $9x > x^3$ Replace x with 3.
$9(3) \stackrel{?}{>} 3^3$ Simplify each side of the inequality.
$27 \not> 27$ False.

21. $8 \leq y^2$ Replace y with 3.
$8 \stackrel{?}{\leq} 3^2$ Evaluate the power.
$8 \leq 9$ True.

22. Amount collected = cost per student times the number of students who have paid.
$\$3920 = \$35x$
$\$3920 = \$35(112)$;
112 students have paid.

23. The total cost of the material is equal to the number of flags times 0.6 square yards per flag times $2.00 per square yard.

24. Cost = 20(0.6)($2.00) = $24.00

25.

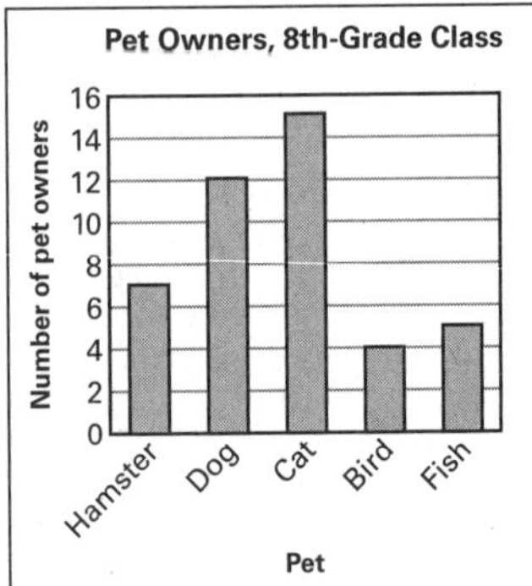

26. cat

Chapter 1 Standardized Test *(p. 60)*

1. $9 - x \geq 2$
$9 - (7) \stackrel{?}{\geq} 2$
$2 \geq 2$
Choice A

2. $[(5 \cdot 9) \div x] + 6 = [(5 \cdot 9) \div 3] + 6$ Replace x with 3.
$= [(45) \div 3] + 6$ Evaluate the operation in the parentheses.
$= [15] + 6$ Evaluate the operation in the brackets.
$= 21$ (D) Add.

3. 5 times the difference of 8 and a number $x = 5(8 - x)$.
Choice A

4. 2 more than 3 times the number of students $y = 2 + 3y$.
Choice C

5. (A) All represent functions. For each input value, there is exactly one output. (For III, the input 1 is written twice, but it has only one output, 3.)

6. The pounds of chocolate consumed per person in Switzerland is about 20.8. The pounds of chocolate consumed per person in the United States is about 11.8. The difference $20.8 - 11.8 = 9$. Choice C

7. The pounds of chocolate consumed in Norway is about 17.5. The pounds of chocolate consumed per person in the United States is about 11.8. The difference $17.5 - 11.8 = 5.7$. Choice B

Chapter 1 Maintaining Skills *(p. 61)*

1. $$\begin{array}{r} 2.3 \\ +\ 0.4 \\ \hline 2.7 \end{array}$$

2. $$\begin{array}{r} 3.5 \\ -\ 2.1 \\ \hline 1.4 \end{array}$$

3. $$\begin{array}{r} {\scriptstyle 1\ 1\ \ } \\ 8.75 \\ +\ 3.35 \\ \hline 12.10 \text{ or } 12.1 \end{array}$$

4. $$\begin{array}{r} 10.6 \\ -2.6 \\ \hline 8.0 \text{ or } 8 \end{array}$$

5. $$\begin{array}{r} 3.006 \\ +\ 2.800 \\ \hline 5.806 \end{array}$$

6. $$\begin{array}{r} {\scriptstyle 1\ 1} \\ 4.25 \\ -0.08 \\ \hline 4.17 \end{array}$$

7. $$\begin{array}{r} {\scriptstyle 1\ 1\ \ \ } \\ 3.990 \\ +\ 0.254 \\ \hline 4.244 \end{array}$$

8. $$\begin{array}{r} 6.20 \\ -0.17 \\ \hline 6.03 \end{array}$$

9. $$\begin{array}{r} 123.5 \\ +\ 32.3 \\ \hline 155.8 \end{array}$$

10. $$\begin{array}{r} {\scriptstyle 7\ 1\ } \\ 32.80 \\ -12.21 \\ \hline 20.59 \end{array}$$

11. $$\begin{array}{r} 0.09 \\ +\ 0.90 \\ \hline 0.99 \end{array}$$

12. $$\begin{array}{r} {\scriptstyle 6\ 1\ } \\ 17.0 \\ -16.5 \\ \hline 0.5 \end{array}$$

13–20.

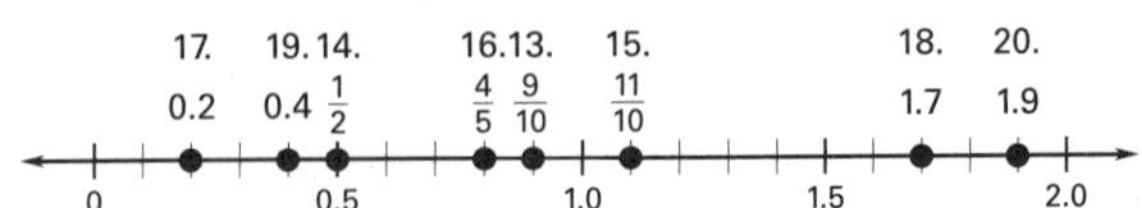

Copyright © McDougal Littell Inc.
All rights reserved.

CHAPTER 2

Chapter Opener

Think & Discuss (p. 63)

1. *Sample answer:* temperature. A negative number indicates a temperature less than 0°F. A positive number indicates a temperature greater than 0°F.

2. $\dfrac{120\text{ ft}}{15\text{ s}} = 8$ ft/s downward

   $\dfrac{160\text{ ft}}{15\text{ s}} = 10\frac{2}{3}$ ft/s upward

Chapter Readiness Quiz *(p. 64)*

1. The variable is *r*. B

2. An expression does not contain a complete equality or inequality. C

3. Convert to mixed numbers and order:

   $2\frac{3}{11}, 2\frac{5}{8}, 2\frac{2}{3}, 2\frac{3}{4}, 2\frac{5}{6}$. D

4. $9\frac{1}{6} \div 1\frac{3}{8} = \dfrac{55}{6} \div \dfrac{11}{8}$

   $= \dfrac{55}{6} \cdot \dfrac{8}{11}$

   $= \dfrac{20}{3} = 6\frac{2}{3}$; C

Lesson 2.1

2.1 Checkpoint (pp. 66–67)

1. $-6 < -2, -2 > -6$

2. $2 > -3, -3 < 2$

3. $5 < 7, 7 > 5$

4. $-3, -\frac{5}{4} = -1\frac{1}{4}, -1, 0, \frac{3}{2} = 1\frac{1}{2}, 4$

5. $-8, -3, -\frac{1}{2}, 3, 3.2, 4.5$

6. Feb. 24 (20°F > 10°F) and Feb. 25 (17°F > 10°F)

2.1 Guided Practice (p. 68)

1. negative, positive

2. whole

3.

4.

5.

6.

7. $-4 > -5$

8. $0 > -8$

9. $6.7 > -6.7$

10. $\frac{3}{2} > \frac{2}{3}$

11. $-8, -3, -2, 1, 2$

12. $-6.1, -4, 1.2, 5, 7$

13. $-9, -7, -\frac{1}{5}, \frac{5}{4} = 1\frac{1}{4}, 2$

2.1 Practice and Applications (pp. 68–70)

14.

15.

16.

17.

18.

19.

20.

21.

22.

23. $-2 < 3, 3 > -2$

24. $-6 < 4, 4 > -6$

25. $-6 < -1, -1 > -6$

26. $-7 < -5, -5 > -7$

Copyright © McDougal Littell Inc.
All rights reserved.

Chapter 2 *continued*

27. −8 −6 −4 −2 0 2 4

$-4 < 0, 0 > -4$

28. −12 −8 −4 0 4 8 12

$-8 < 8, 8 > -8$

29. −12 −8 −4 0 4 8 12

$10 < 11, 11 > 10$

30. −12 −8 −4 0 4 8

$-12 < 9, 9 > -12$

31. D **32.** B **33.** C **34.** A

35. −1.5 0.5 2.5

−3 −2 −1 0 1 2 3

36. −5.6 −0.3 2

−6 −4 −2 0 2 4 6

37. 4.2 4.4 4.6

3 4 5 6

38. $-\frac{7}{8}$ −0.5

−3 −2 −1 0 1 2 3

39. $-\frac{9}{2}$ −2.8 4.3

−6 −4 −2 0 2 4 6

40. $-\frac{7}{3}$ $\frac{3}{4}$

−4 −3 −2 −1 0 1 2

41. $-\frac{2}{3}$ $-\frac{1}{2}$ $\frac{1}{2}$

−2 −1 0 1

42. $\frac{1}{3}$ $\frac{3}{2}$ $\frac{11}{4}$

−3 −2 −1 0 1 2 3

43. $-\frac{8}{3}$ $-\frac{2}{5}$ $\frac{9}{10}$

−3 −2 −1 0 1 2 3

44. $-4, -1.8, -0.6, 0.7, 3, 4.6$

45. $-3.0, -0.3, -0.2, 0, 0.2, 2.0$

46. $-6.8, -6.2, -6.1, 6.1, 6.3, 6.7$

47. $-5.2, -5.1, -\frac{10}{4} = -2\frac{1}{2}, 3.4, 4.1, \frac{9}{2} = 4\frac{1}{2}$

48. $-5, -\frac{3}{4}, -\frac{1}{2}, \frac{1}{6}, 2, 7$

49. $-2.6, -\frac{1}{2}, 0, \frac{1}{2}, 4.8$

50. If $x > -4$, then $-4 < x$.

51. If $3 < y$, then $y > 3$.

52. 12,799 ft above sea level = 12,799 ft elevation

53. 8 ft below sea level = −8 ft elevation

54. sea level = 0 elevation

55.

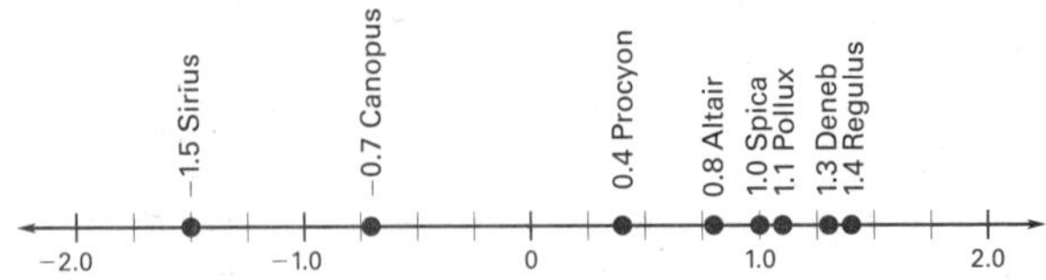

56. Altair's magnitude = 0.8. The magnitudes less than 0.8 are −0.7 (Canopus), 0.4 (Procyon), −1.5 (Sirius).

57. The magnitudes that are greater than that of Procyon (0.4) are 1.1 (Pollux), 0.8 (Altair), 1.0 (Spica), 1.4 (Regulus), and 1.3 (Deneb).

58. The least apparent magnitude is −1.5, Sirius.

59. The greatest apparent magnitude is 1.4, Regulus.

2.1 Standardized Test Practice (p.70)

60. $-9 < 5$; D

61. -10; F

62. $-1.9, -0.5, 0, 0.5, 1.8$; B

2.1 Mixed Review (p. 70)

63. 2 ft by 2 ft is a square, so its area is

$A = s^2 = 2^2 = 4 \text{ ft}^2$

64. 4 in. by 4 in. is a square, so its area is
$A = s^2 = 4^2 = 16 \text{ in.}^2$

65. Area $A = s^2 = 9^2 = 81 \text{ cm}^2$.

66. $9 - y = 1; 9 - (8) = 1; y = 8$

67. $t + 6 = 10; (4) + 6 = 10; t = 4$

68. $2a = 8; 2(4) = 8; a = 4$

69. $15 \div r = 3; 15 \div (5) = 3; r = 5$

70. $\frac{k}{2} = 8; \frac{(16)}{2} = 8; k = 16$

71. $\frac{27}{h} = 9; \frac{27}{(3)} = 9; n = 3$

72.

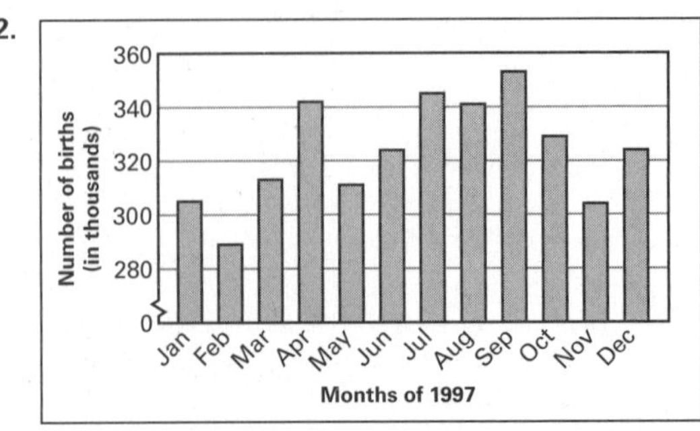

Copyright © McDougal Littell Inc.
All rights reserved.

73. Replace H with $20\% = 0.20$, $40\% = 0.40$, $60\% = 0.60$, $70\% = 0.70$, and $100\% = 1.00$.

$T = 0.08H + 64.3$
$T = 0.08(0.20) + 64.3$
$T = 0.016 + 64.3$
$T = 64.32°$
$T = 0.08(0.40) + 64.3$
$T = 0.032 + 64.3$
$T = 64.33°$
$T = 0.08(0.60) + 64.3$
$T = 0.048 + 64.3$
$T = 64.35°$
$T = 0.08(0.70) + 64.3$
$T = 0.056 + 64.3$
$T = 64.36°$
$T = 0.08(1.00) + 64.3$
$T = 0.08 + 64.3$
$T = 64.38°$

Input H	20%	40%	60%	70%	100%
Output T	64.32	64.33	64.35	64.36	64.38

74.

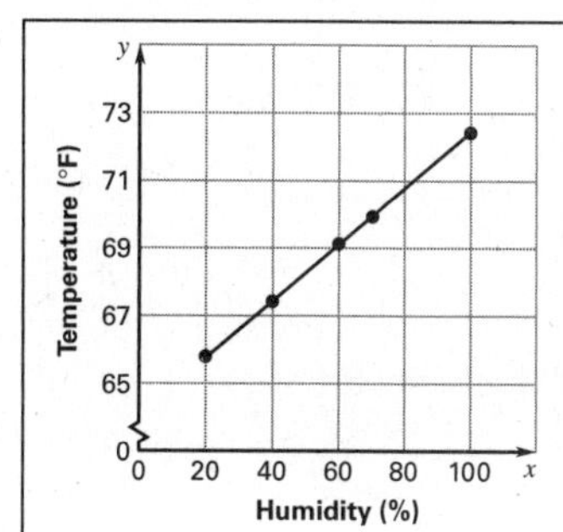

75. The range is the set of output values; $64.32 \le T \le 64.38$

2.1 Maintaining Skills (p. 70)

76. $18 = 9 \times 2 = 3 \times 3 \times 2 = 3^2 \times 2$

77. $35 = 5 \times 7$

78. 47 is prime.

79. $64 = 8 \times 8 = 2 \times 2 \times 2 \times 2 \times 2 \times 2 = 2^6$

80. $100 = 10 \times 10 = 2 \times 5 \times 2 \times 5 = 2^2 \times 5^2$

81. 101 is prime.

82. $110 = 2 \times 5 \times 11$

83. $144 = 12 \times 12 = 2 \times 6 \times 2 \times 6$
$= 2 \times 2 \times 3 \times 2 \times 2 \times 3$
$= 2^4 \times 3^2$

Lesson 2.2

2.2 Checkpoint (pp. 72–73)

1. $|-4| = 4$

2. $|0| = 0$

3. $\left|\frac{3}{2}\right| = \frac{3}{2}$

4. $-|1.7| = -1.7$
The absolute value of 1.7 is 1.7; The opposite of the absolute value of -1.7 is -1.7.

5. $|x| = -4$; The absolute value of a number is never negative.

6. $|x| = 1.5$; $|1.5| = 1.5$ and $|-1.5| = 1.5$, so $x = 1.5$ or -1.5.

7. $|x| = \frac{1}{6}$; $\left|\frac{1}{6}\right| = \frac{1}{6}$ and $\left|-\frac{1}{6}\right| = \frac{1}{6}$, so $x = \frac{1}{6}$ or $-\frac{1}{6}$.

8. Velocity indicates speed and direction. The direction is downward so the velocity is -17 ft/sec.

9. Speed is absolute value of velocity, so speed $= |-17| = 17$ ft/sec.

10. False; *Sample answer:* if $a = -4$, then $-a = -(-4) = 4$, which is positive.

11. True; if a is a negative number, its absolute value is positive, and a positive number is greater than a negative number. If a is zero or positive, its absolute value is itself.

12. False; *Sample answer:* the absolute value of -3 is 3.

2.2 Guided Practice (p. 74)

1. -2

2. 0

3. Opposite of 1 is -1.

4. Opposite of -3 is 3.

5. Opposite of -2.4 is 2.4.

6. Opposite of $\frac{1}{2}$ is $-\frac{1}{2}$.

7. $|-12| = 12$

8. $|6| = 6$

9. $-|5.1| = -5.1$

10. $\left|-\frac{1}{5}\right| = \frac{1}{5}$

11. $|x| = 8$; $|8| = 8$ and $|-8| = 8$; $x = 8$ or -8.

12. $|x| = -9$; The absolute value of a number is never negative, so there is no solution.

13. $|x| = 5.5$; $|5.5| = 5.5$ and $|-5.5| = 5.5$; $x = 5.5$ or -5.5.

14. $|x| = \frac{2}{3}$; $\left|\frac{2}{3}\right| = \frac{2}{3}$ and $\left|-\frac{2}{3}\right| = \frac{2}{3}$; $x = \frac{2}{3}$ or $-\frac{2}{3}$.

15. False; *Sample answer:* if $a = -2$, then $-(-2) = 2$, which is greater than -2.

16. True; The absolute value of a number is its distance from zero on a number line, and distance is zero or positive.

2.2 Practice and Applications (pp. 74–76)

17. Opposite of 8 is -8.

18. Opposite of -3 is 3.

19. Opposite of -10 is 10.

20. Opposite of 0 is 0.

21. Opposite of -3.8 is 3.8.

22. Opposite of 2.5 is -2.5.

23. Opposite of $-\frac{1}{9}$ is $\frac{1}{9}$.

24. Opposite of $\frac{5}{6}$ is $-\frac{5}{6}$.

25. $|7| = 7$

26. $|-4| = 4$

27. $-|3| = -3$

28. $-|-2| = -2$

29. $|-0.8| = 0.8$

30. $|-4.5| = 4.5$

Copyright © McDougal Littell Inc.
All rights reserved.

31. $\left|\frac{2}{3}\right| = \frac{2}{3}$

32. $-\left|-\frac{8}{9}\right| = -\frac{8}{9}$

33. $|x| = 4$; $|4| = 4$ and $|-4| = 4$; $x = 4$ or -4.

34. $|x| = 0$; $|0| = 0$; $x = 0$.

35. $|x| = -2$; The absolute value of a number is never negative, so there is no solution.

36. $|x| = 1$; $|1| = 1$ and $|-1| = 1$; $x = 1$ or -1.

37. $|x| = 3.7$; $|3.7| = 3.7$ and $|-3.7| = 3.7$; $x = 3.7$ or -3.7.

38. $|x| = -9.6$; The absolute value of a number is never negative, so there is no solution.

39. $|x| = \frac{11}{2}$; $\left|\frac{11}{2}\right| = \frac{11}{2}$ and $\left|\frac{-11}{2}\right| = \frac{11}{2}$; $x = \frac{11}{2}$ or $-\frac{11}{2}$.

40. $|x| = \frac{5}{6}$; $\left|\frac{5}{6}\right| = \frac{5}{6}$ and $\left|-\frac{5}{6}\right| = \frac{5}{6}$; $x = \frac{5}{6}$ or $-\frac{5}{6}$.

41. Range is $|800| + |-280| = 800 + 280 = 1080$ for Mercury.
Range is $|98| + |-190| = 98 + 190 = 288$ for Mars.

42. Range for:
Venus: $|847| - |847| = 847 - 847 = 0$
Earth: $|98| - |8| = 98 - 8 = 90$
Jupiter: $|-244| - |-244| = 244 - 244 = 0$
Saturn: $|-301| - |-301| = 301 - 301 = 0$
Uranus: $|-353| - |-353| = 353 - 353 = 0$
Neptune: $|-373| - |-373| = 373 - 373 = 0$
Pluto: $|-393| - |-393| = 393 - 393 = 0$

43. descending = negative

44. rising = positive

45. lifts = positive

46. falling = negative

47. Velocity indicates speed and direction.
Descending = negative direction; -6 ft/sec

48. Speed = absolute value of velocity.
Speed = $|-6| = 6$ ft/sec

49. Velocity indicates speed and direction.
climbs = positive direction; 400 ft/min

50. Speed = absolute value of velocity.
Speed = $|400| = 400$ ft/min

51. False; the opposite of $-a$ is a. If $-a = 5$, then $a = -5$, which is negative.

52. True; The absolute value of any number is greater than or equal to zero.

53. True; The absolute value of any number is greater than or equal to zero.

54. Always true; the absolute value of a number is its distance away from zero on a number line. The distance that a number is from zero is equal to the distance its opposite is from zero, only on the opposite side of zero on the number line.

55. This is only true when $x = 0$, since $-|0| = -0 = 0$ and $|0| = 0$. For any other number x, $-|x| = -x$ and $|x| = x$; $-x \neq x$ when $x \neq 0$.

2.2 Standardized Test Practice (p. 76)

56. Opposite of 5 is -5; D

57. $-|-2| = -2$; G

58. $|x| = 18$; $|18| = 18$ and $|-18| = 18$, so $x = 18$ and -18; C

59. Velocity indicates speed and direction; descends = negative direction; -3 m/sec; H

2.2 Mixed Review (p. 76)

60. $x + 3 = (2) + 3 = 5$

61. $a - 7 = (10) - 7 = 3$

62. $3y = 3(0) = 0$

63. $(t)(5) = (15)(5) = 75$

64. $\frac{z}{2} = \frac{(8)}{2} = 4$

65. $\frac{9}{p} = \frac{9}{(3)} = 3$

66. $x - 5 = 8$

67. $x + 8 = 17$

68. $\frac{15}{n} \geq 3$

69. $9y < 6$

70. 

$-7 < 7, 7 > -7$

71.

$-6 < -2, -2 > -6$

72. 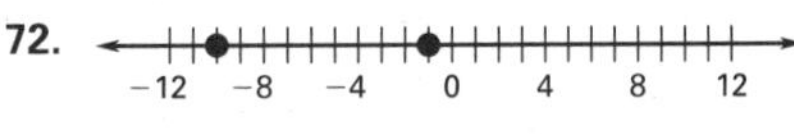

$-10 < -1, -1 > -10$

73.

$-3 < 0.4, 0.4 > -3$

74.

$-3.3 < 2.2, 2.2 > -3.3$

75.

$-10 < -\frac{1}{10}, -\frac{1}{10} > -10$

2.2 Maintaining Skills (p. 76)

76. $\frac{3}{4} - \frac{1}{4} = \frac{2}{4} = \frac{1 \cdot 2}{2 \cdot 2} = \frac{1}{2}$

77. $\frac{7}{9} - \frac{2}{9} = \frac{5}{9}$

Copyright © McDougal Littell Inc.
All rights reserved.

78. $\frac{7}{10} - \frac{3}{10} = \frac{4}{10} = \frac{2 \cdot 2}{2 \cdot 5} = \frac{2}{5}$

79. $\frac{14}{15} - \frac{4}{15} = \frac{10}{15} = \frac{2 \cdot 5}{3 \cdot 5} = \frac{2}{3}$

80. $\frac{25}{27} - \frac{16}{27} = \frac{9}{27} = \frac{1 \cdot 9}{3 \cdot 9} = \frac{1}{3}$

81. $\frac{41}{44} - \frac{19}{44} = \frac{22}{44} = \frac{22 \cdot 1}{22 \cdot 2} = \frac{1}{2}$

Lesson 2.3

2.3 Developing Concepts: Explore *(p. 77)*

3. $-8 + 3 = -5$

Think About It (p. 77)

1.

2 + 4 = 6

$2 + 4 = 6$

2.

−1 + −5 = −6

$-1 + -5 = -6$

3.

3 + −3 = 0

$3 + -3 = 0$

4. $3 + 3 = 6$

3 + 3 = 6

5. $-4 + (-2) = -6$

−4 + (−2) = −6

6. $-3 + 2 = -1$

7. $5 + (-2) = 3$

+ + +
+ +

8. The sum of two positive integers is *always* a positive integer. (Combining positive algebra tiles with more positive tiles results in a larger pile of positive algebra tiles.)

9. The sum of two negative integers is *never* a positive integer. (Combining negative algebra tiles with more negative tiles results in a larger pile of negative algebra tiles.)

10. The sum of a positive integer and a negative integer is *sometimes* a negative integer. (If a small number of positive algebra tiles are combined with a larger number of negative tiles, there will be negative tiles left over after the "zero pairs" are formed.)

2.3 Checkpoint (pp. 78–80)

1. $-4 + 5 = 1$

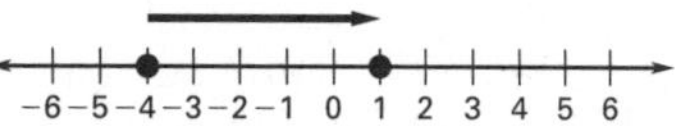

2. $-1 + (-2) = -3$

3. $4 + (-5) = -1$

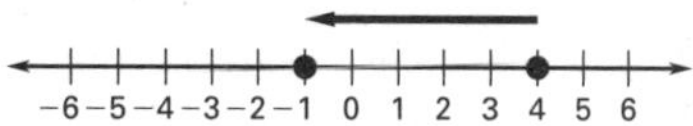

4. $0 + (-4) = -4$

5. $-3 + (-7)$; Add -3 and -7, which have the same sign.
1. *Add* their absolute values; $3 + 7 = 10$
2. *Attach* the common (negative) sign; $-(10) = -10$
Answer: $-3 + (-7) = -10$

6. $-1 + 3$; Add -1 and 3, which have different signs.
1. *Subtract* their absolute values; $3 - 1 = 2$
2. *Attach* the sign of the number with the larger absolute value; $+(2) = 2$
Answer: $-1 + 3 = 2$

7. $8 + (-3)$; Add 8 and -3, which have different signs.
1. *Subtract* their absolute values; $8 - 3 = 5$
2. *Attach* the sign of the number with the largest absolute value; $+(5) = 5$
Answer: $8 + (-3) = 5$

8. $2 + 3$; Add 2 and 3, which have the same sign.
1. *Add* their absolute values; $2 + 3 = 5$
2. *Attach* the common (positive) sign; $+(5) = 5$
Answer: $2 + 3 = 5$

9. $-7 + 11 + 7$

$= -7 + 7 + 11$	Commutative property
$= (-7 + 7) + 11$	Associative property
$= 0 + 11$	Inverse property
$= 11$	Identity property

10. $-5 + 1 + 2$

$= -5 + (1 + 2)$	Associative property
$= -5 + 3$	Add 1 and 2.
$= -2$	Add -5 and 3.

Copyright © McDougal Littell Inc.
All rights reserved.

11. $3 + \left(-\frac{1}{3}\right) + \left(-\frac{2}{3}\right)$ — Associative property

$= 3 + \left[\left(-\frac{1}{3}\right) + \left(-\frac{2}{3}\right)\right]$ — Add $\left(-\frac{1}{3}\right)$ and $\left(-\frac{2}{3}\right)$.

$= 3 + \left(-\frac{3}{3}\right)$ — Simplify $\left(-\frac{3}{3}\right)$.

$= 3 + (-1)$ — Add 3 and -1.

$= 2$

12. $(-13,143) + (-6,783) + (-4,735) = -24{,}661$; a loss of \$24,661

13. $(-4,735) + (3,825) + (7,613) = 6{,}703$; a profit of \$6,703

2.3 Guided Practice (p. 81)

1. Commutative property (order does not change the sum); $5 + (-9) = -9 + 5$; B
2. Associative property (grouping does not change the sum); $5 + (4 + 9) = (5 + 4) + 9$; D
3. Identity property (sum of a number and 0 is the number); $-8 + 0 = -8$ A
4. Inverse property (sum of a number and its opposite is 0); $-8 + 8 = 0$; C
5. Start at -5; move 9 units to the right; end at 4.

   $-5 + 9 = 4$

6. $-2\ -1\ 0\ 1\ 2\ 3\ 4\ 5\ 6\ 7\ 8\ 9\ 10$

   $7 + (-3) = 4$

7. 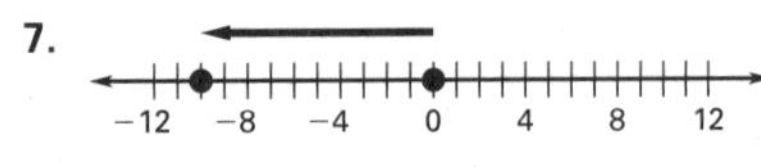

   $0 + (-10) = -10$

8. $-8\ -7\ -6\ -5\ -4\ -3\ -2\ -1\ 0\ 1\ 2\ 3\ 4$

   $-7 + 3 = -4$

9. $12 + (-5)$; Add 12 and -5, which have different signs.
   1. *Subtract* their absolute values; $12 - 5 = 7$
   2. *Attach* the sign of the number with larger absolute value; $+(7) = 7$

   Answer: $12 + (-5) = 7$

10. $-4 + 5$; Add -4 and 5, which have different signs.
    1. *Subtract* their absolute values; $5 - 4 = 1$
    2. *Attach* the sign of the number with larger absolute value; $+(1) = 1$

    Answer: $-4 + 5 = 1$

11. $-7 + (-3)$; Add -7 and -3, which have the same sign.
    1. *Add* their absolute values; $7 + 3 = 10$
    2. *Attach* the common (negative) sign; $-(10) = -10$

    Answer: $-7 + -3 = -10$

12. $-4 + 3 + (-2)$

$= (-4 + 3) + (-2)$ — Associative property

$= -1 + -2$ — Add -4 and 3.

$= -3$ — Add 1 and -2.

13. $5 + (-5) + 7$

$= [5 + (-5)] + 7$ — Associative property

$= [0] + 7$ — Inverse property

$= 7$ — Identity property

14. $-3 + 0 + 7$

$= (-3 + 0) + 7$ — Associative property

$= -3 + 7$ — Identity property

$= 4$ — Add -3 and 7.

2.3 Practice and Applications (pp. 81–83)

15. $-1 + (-2) = -3$; C
16. $3 + (-5) = -2$; A
17. $-2 + 2 = 0$; B
18. $-8\ -7\ -6\ -5\ -4\ -3\ -2\ -1\ 0\ 1\ 2\ 3\ 4$

    $-6 + 2 = -4$

19. $-8\ -7\ -6\ -5\ -4\ -3\ -2\ -1\ 0\ 1\ 2\ 3\ 4$

    $2 + (-8) = -6$

20. $-8\ -7\ -6\ -5\ -4\ -3\ -2\ -1\ 0\ 1\ 2\ 3\ 4$

    $-3 + (-3) = -6$

21. $-12\ -10\ -8\ -6\ -4\ -2\ 0$

    $-4 + (-7) = -11$

22. $-6\ -5\ -4\ -3\ -2\ -1\ 0\ 1\ 2\ 3\ 4\ 5\ 6$

    $-4 + 5 = 1$

23. $-6\ -5\ -4\ -3\ -2\ -1\ 0\ 1\ 2\ 3\ 4\ 5\ 6$

    $3 + (-7) = -4$

24. $-12\ -10\ -8\ -6\ -4\ -2\ 0$

    $-10 + 1 = -9$

25. 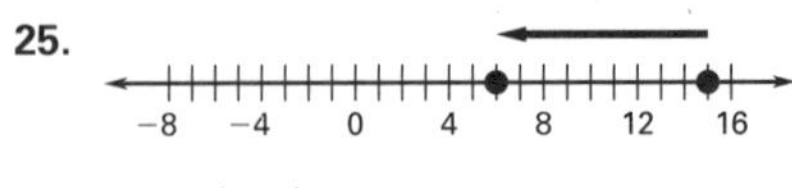

    $15 + (-9) = 6$

26. $-20\ -16\ -12\ -8\ -4\ 0\ 4$

    $-12 + (-5) = -17$

Copyright © McDougal Littell Inc.
All rights reserved.

27. $9 + (-2)$
1. *Subtract* absolute values; $9 - 2 = 7$
2. *Attach* sign of number with larger absolute value; $+(7) = 7$
Answer: $9 + (-2) = 7$

28. $-6 + (-11)$
1. *Add* absolute values; $6 + 11 = 17$
2. *Attach* common (negative) sign: $-(17) = -17$
Answer: $-6 + (-11) = -17$

29. $-7 + (-4)$
1. *Add* absolute values; $7 + 4 = 11$
2. *Attach* common (negative) sign; $-(11) = -11$
Answer: $-7 + (-4) = -11$

30. $-5 + 2$
1. *Subtract* absolute values; $5 - 2 = 3$
2. *Attach* sign of number with larger absolute value; $-(3) = -3$
Answer: $-5 + 2 = -3$

31. $8 + (-5)$
1. *Subtract* absolute values; $8 - 5 = 3$
2. *Attach* sign of number with larger absolute value; $+(3) = 3$
Answer: $8 + (-5) = 3$

32. $-6 + (-3)$
1. *Add* absolute values; $6 + 3 = 9$
2. *Attach* common (negative) sign: $-(9) = -9$
Answer: $-6 + (-3) = -9$

33. $-10 + (-21)$
1. *Add* absolute values; $10 + 21 = 31$
2. *Attach* common (negative) sign: $-(31) = -31$
Answer: $-10 + (-21) = -31$

34. $49 + (-58)$
1. *Subtract* absolute values; $58 - 49 = 9$
2. *Attach* sign of number with larger absolute value; $-(9) = -9$
Answer: $49 + (-58) = -9$

35. $-62 + 27$
1. *Subtract* absolute values; $62 - 27 = 35$
2. *Attach* sign of number with larger absolute value; $-(35) = -35$
Answer: $-62 + 27 = -35$

36. $-16 + 0 = -16$; identity property (sum of 0 and a number is the number)

37. $-3 + (-5) = -5 + (-3)$; commutative property (order does not change the sum)

38. $(-4 + 3) + 5 = -4 + (3 + 5)$; associative property (the way numbers are grouped does not change the sum)

39. $16 + (-16) = 0$; inverse property (the sum of a number and its opposite is 0)

40. "only one real number" = *unique* number (closure property)

41. $6 + 10 + (-6)$
$= 6 + (-6) + 10$ Commutative property
$= 0 + 10$ Associative property
$= 10$ Inverse property
Identity property

42. $7 + (-2) + (-9)$
$= [7 + (-2)] + (-9)$ Associative property
$= 5 + (-9)$ Add 7 and -2.
$= -4$ Add 5 and -9.

43. $8 + (-4) + (-4)$
$= 8 + [(-4) + (-4)]$ Associative property
$= 8 + (-8)$ Add -4 and -4.
$= 0$ Inverse property

44. $-24.5 + 6 + 8$
$= -24.5 + (6 + 8)$ Associative property
$= -24.5 + 14$ Add $6 + 8$.
$= -10.5$ Add -24.5 and 14.

45. $5.4 + 2.6 + (-3)$
$= (5.4 + 2.6) + (-3)$ Associative property
$= 8 + (-3)$ Add 5.4 and 2.6.
$= 5$ Add 8 and -3.

46. $2.2 + (-2.2) + (2.2)$
$= [2.2 + (-2.2)] + 2.2$ Associative property
$= 0 + 2.2$ Inverse property
$= 2.2$ Identity property

47. $4 + \frac{1}{10} + \left(-\frac{1}{10}\right)$
$= 4 + \left[\frac{1}{10} + \left(-\frac{1}{10}\right)\right]$ Associative property
$= 4 + 0$ Inverse property
$= 4$ Identity property

48. $9 + (-4) + \left(-\frac{1}{2}\right)$
$= [9 + (-4)] + \left(-\frac{1}{2}\right)$
$= 5 + \left(-\frac{1}{2}\right)$
$= 4\frac{1}{2}$

49. $\frac{1}{7} + (-2) + \left(-\frac{5}{7}\right)$
$= \frac{1}{7} + \left(-\frac{5}{7}\right) + (-2)$
$= -\frac{4}{7} + -2$
$= -2\frac{4}{7}$

50. $-2.95 + 5.76 + (-88.6) = -85.79$

51. $10.97 + (-51.14) + (-40.97) = -81.14$

52. $20.37 + 190.8 + (-85.13) = 126.04$

Copyright © McDougal Littell Inc.
All rights reserved.

53. $300.3 + (-22.24) + 78.713 = 356.773$

54. Add the profits and losses.

$3{,}515 + 5{,}674 + (-8{,}993) + (-907) = -711$;
A negative sign indicates a loss of \$711.

55. Let -1 represent each *birdie*,
let -2 represent each *eagle*,
let 1 represent each *bogey*, and
let 0 represent each *par*.
Find the sum of the birdies, pars, bogeys, and eagles.

$-1 + 0 + -1 + 0 + -2 + 1 + 1 + 1 + -1 = -2$;
two strokes under par.

56. True: *Sample answers:*
1. $-(5 + 3) = -(8) = -8$ and

$-(5) + (-3) = -5 + (-3) = -8$
2. $-(-6 + 2) = -(-4) = 4$ and

$-(-6) + -(2) = 6 + (-2) = 4$

2.3 Standardized Test Practice (p. 82)

57. Add the money earned (positive number) to the money spent (negative number) for each month.
January: $1676 + (-1427) = 249$
March: $1851 + (-1556) = 295$
May: $1921 + (-1602) = 319$
June: $1667 + (-1989) = -322$
The most money was saved in May, \$319; C

58. Add the money earned (positive number) to the money spent (negative number) for each month.
January: $1676 + (-1427) = 249$
February: $1554 + (-1771) = -217$
April: $1567 + (-1874) = -307$
June: $1667 + (-1989) = -322$
The money spent most exceeded the money earned in June, $-\$322$; J

2.3 Mixed Review (p. 83)

59. four squared $= 4^2$

60. k to the ninth power $= k^9$

61. x cubed $= x^3$

62. $15 - 5 + 5^2$ Evaluate the power.
$= 15 - 5 + 25$ Subtract, then add (left-to-right rule).
$= 10 + 25$
$= 35$

63. $18 \cdot 2 - 1 \cdot 3$ Multiply.
$= 36 - 3$ Subtract.
$= 33$

64. $1 + 3 \cdot 5 - 8$ Multiply.
$= 1 + 15 - 8$ Add, then subtract (left-to-right rule).
$= 16 - 8$
$= 8$

65. $2(9 - 6 - 1)$ Evaluate the operation in the parentheses.
$= 2(3 - 1)$ Subtract (left-to-right rule).
$= 2(2)$ Multiply.
$= 4$

66. $10 - (3 + 2) + 4$ Evaluate the operation in the parentheses.
$= 10 - (5) + 4$ Subtract, then add (left-to-right rule).
$= 5 + 4$
$= 9$

67. $2 \cdot (6 + 10) - 8$ Evaluate the operation in the parentheses.
$= 2 \cdot (16) - 8$ Multiply.
$= 32 - 8$ Subtract.
$= 24$

68. $x + 5 = 10$ Replace x with 7.
$(7) + 5 = 10$ Add.
$12 = 10$ False; therefore 7 is not a solution

69. $7y - 15 = 6$ Replace y with 3.
$7(3) - 15 = 6$ Multiply.
$21 - 15 = 6$ Subtract.
$6 = 6$ True; therefore 3 is a solution.

70. $17 - 3w = 2$ Replace w with 5.
$17 - 3(5) = 2$ Multiply.
$17 - 15 = 2$ Subtract.
$2 = 2$ True; therefore 5 is a solution.

71. $a^2 - 3 = 5$ Replace a with 4.
$(4)^2 - 3 = 5$ Evaluate the power.
$16 - 3 = 5$ Subtract.
$13 = 5$ False; therefore 4 is not a solution.

72. $1 + p^3 = 9$ Replace p with 2.
$1 + 2^3 = 9$ Evaluate the power.
$1 + 8 = 9$ Add.
$9 = 9$ True; therefore 2 is a solution.

73. $2n^2 + 10 = 14$ Replace n with 1.
$2(1)^2 + 10 = 14$ Evaluate the power.
$2(1) + 10 = 14$ Multiply.
$2 + 10 = 14$ Add.
$12 = 14$ False; therefore 1 is not a solution.

2.3 Maintaining Skills (p. 83)

74. Round 422 to 400.
Round 451 to 500.
$400 + 500 = 900$

75. Round 8362 to 8400.
Round 941 to 900.
$8400 + 900 = 9300$

76. Round 27 to 0.
Round 159 to 200.
$0 + 200 = 200$

Copyright © McDougal Littell Inc.
All rights reserved.

77. Round 675 to 700.
Round 589 to 600.
$700 - 600 = 100$

78. Round 1084 to 1100.
Round 179 to 200.
$1100 - 200 = 900$

79. Round 3615 to 3600.
Round 663 to 700.
$3600 - 700 = 2900$

Quiz 1 *(p. 83)*

1. 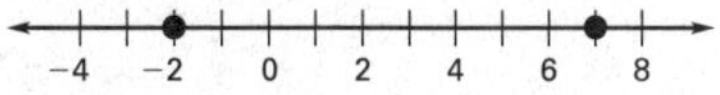 −4 −2 0 2 4 6 8

$-2 < 7, 7 > -2$

2. 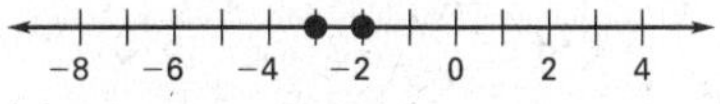 −8 −6 −4 −2 0 2 4

$-3 < -2, -2 > -3$

3. 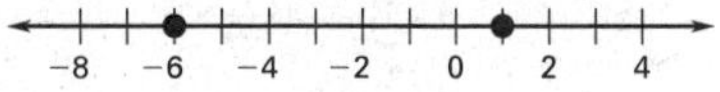 −8 −6 −4 −2 0 2 4

$-6 < 1, 1 > -6$

4. $-10, -8, -3, 2, 9$

5. $-7, -5.2, 3.3, 5, 7.1$

6. $-1, -\frac{2}{5}, 0, \frac{1}{10}, 2$

7. $|5| = 5$

8. $|-13| = 13$

9. $-|0.56| = -(0.56) = -0.56$

10. $|x| = -10$; no solution; the absolute value of a number is never negative.

11. $|x| = 2.7$; $|2.7| = 2.7$ and $|-2.7| = 2.7$, so $x = 2.7$ and -2.7

12. $|x| = \frac{3}{5}$; $\left|\frac{3}{5}\right| = \frac{3}{5}$ and $\left|-\frac{3}{5}\right| = \frac{3}{5}$, so $x = \frac{3}{5}$ and $-\frac{3}{5}$

13. $-6 + (-7) = -13$

14. $4 + (-10) = -6$

15. $-5 + 9 = 4$

16. $$\begin{aligned}-5 + 1 + (-3) &= (-5 + 1) + (-3)\\ &= -4 + -3\\ &= -7\end{aligned}$$

17. $$\begin{aligned}-6 + 2.9 + 1.1 &= -6 + (2.9 + 1.1)\\ &= -6 + 4\\ &= -2\end{aligned}$$

18. $$\begin{aligned}\frac{1}{5} + 0 + \left(-\frac{1}{5}\right) &= \frac{1}{5} + -\frac{1}{5} + 0\\ &= \left(\frac{1}{5} + -\frac{1}{5}\right) + 0\\ &= 0 + 0\\ &= 0\end{aligned}$$

19. Let gains be represented by positive numbers and losses by negative numbers. Add the gains and losses.

$5 + 2 + (-12) + 15 = 10$
The result is a 10 yard gain, so yes, the team scored a touchdown.

Lesson 2.4

2.4 Developing Concepts: Explore *(p. 84)*

4. $3 - 6 = -3$

Think About It (p. 84)

1. 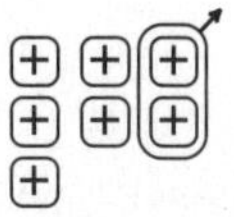 $7 - 2 = 5$

2. 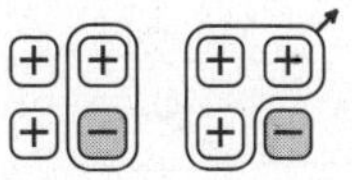 $2 - 3 = -1$

3. 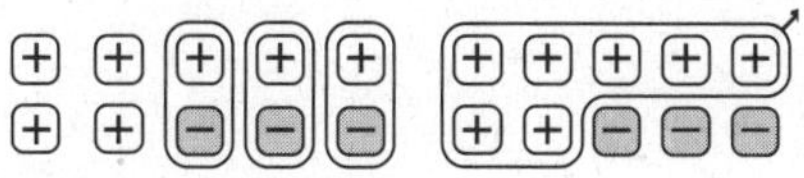 $4 - 7 = -3$

4. 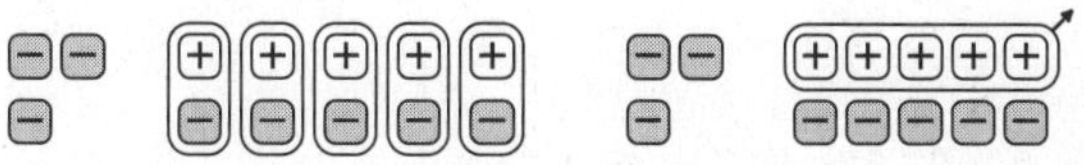 $-3 - 5 = -8$

5. 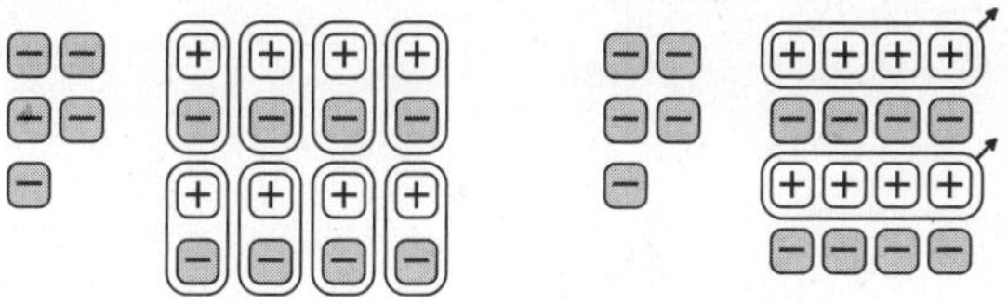 $-5 - 8 = -13$

6. 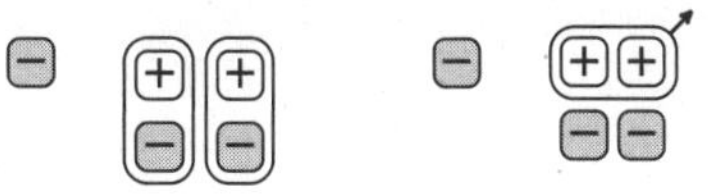 $-1 - 2 = -3$

7. 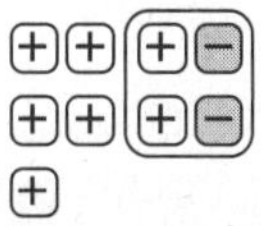 $7 + (-2) = 5$

8. 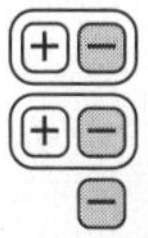 $2 + (-3) = -1$

9. 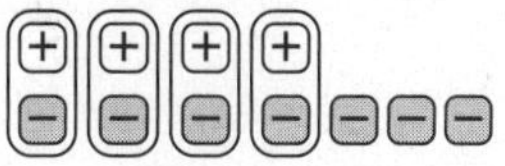 $4 + (-7) = -3$

10. 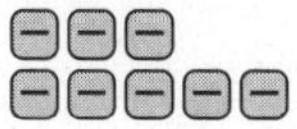 $-3 + (-5) = -8$

Copyright © McDougal Littell Inc.
All rights reserved.

Chapter 2 *continued*

11. 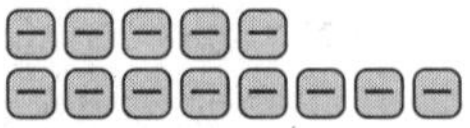 $-5 + (-8) = -13$

12.  $-1 + (-2) = -3$

13. True; removing positive tiles is the same as adding the same amount of negative tiles to make "zero pairs."

14. False; if the number you are subtracting from is a positive number that is larger than the amount you are subtracting, the answer will still be positive (i.e., $5 - 4 = 1$).

Think About It (p. 85)

1. 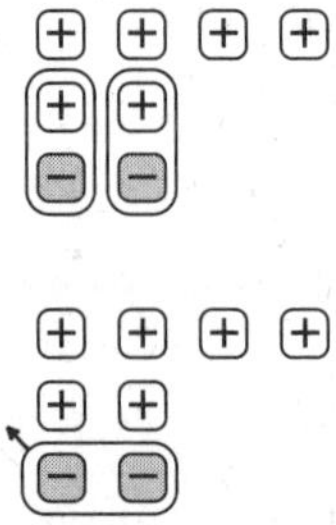 $4 - (-2) = 6$

2. 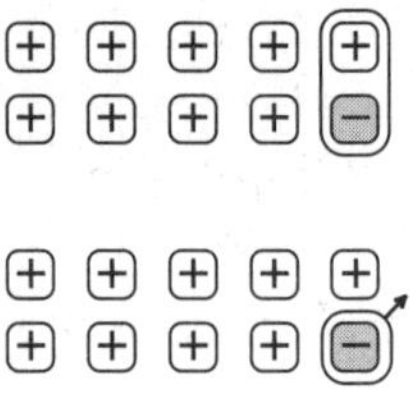 $8 - (-1) = 9$

3. 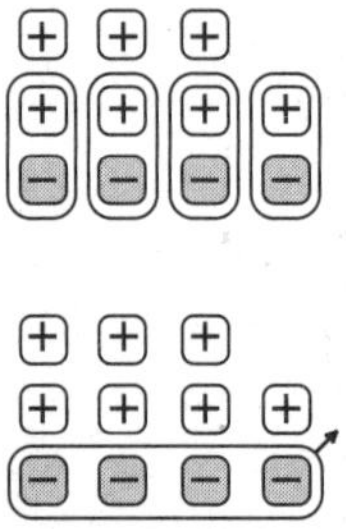 $3 - (-4) = 7$

4. 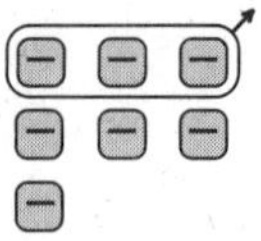 $-7 - (-3) = -4$

5. 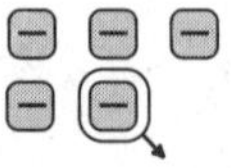 $-5 - (-1) = -4$

6. 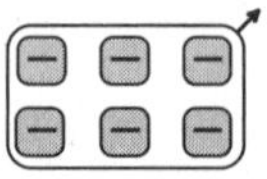 $-6 - (-6) = 0$

7.  $4 + 2 = 6$

8. 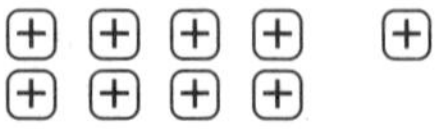 $8 + 1 = 9$

9.  $3 + 4 = 7$

10. 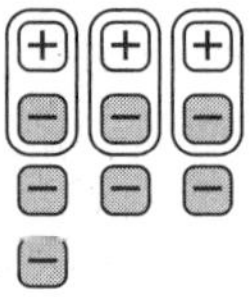 $-7 + 3 = -4$

11. 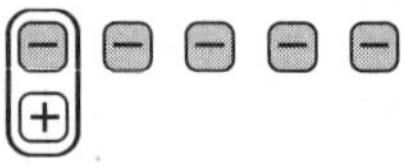 $-5 + 1 = -4$

12. 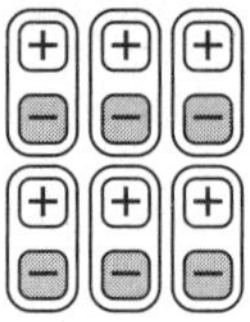 $-6 + 6 = 0$

13. True; removing a negative tile is the same as adding a positive tile to make a "zero pair."

14. False; $5 - (-4) = 9$; when subtracting a negative integer, the difference will be negative only if the number you subtract from is less than the subtrahend.

2.4 Checkpoint (pp. 87–88)

1. $-3 - 5$
$= -3 + (-5)$ Add the opposite of 5.
$= -8$ Use rules of addition.

2. $12.7 - 10$
$= 12.7 + (-10)$ Add the opposite of 10.
$= 2.7$ Use rules of addition.

3. $1 - (-2) - 6$
$= 1 + 2 + (-6)$ Add the opposites of -2 and 6.
$= -3$ Use rules of addition.

Copyright © McDougal Littell Inc.
All rights reserved.

4. $7 - \frac{2}{3} - \frac{5}{3}$

$= 7 + \left(-\frac{2}{3}\right) + \left(-\frac{5}{3}\right)$ Add the opposites of $\frac{2}{3}$ and $\frac{5}{3}$.

$= 4\frac{2}{3}$ Use the rules of addition.

5.

Input	*Function*	*Output*
$x = -3$	$y = 4 - (-3)$	$y = 7$
$x = -1$	$y = 4 - (-1)$	$y = 5$
$x = 1$	$y = 4 - (1)$	$y = 3$
$x = 3$	$y = 4 - (3)$	$y = 1$

6. $x - 3 = x + (-3)$; Use subtraction rule to rewrite the difference as a sum.
The terms are x and -3.

7. $-2 - 5x = -2 + (-5x)$; Use subtraction rule to rewrite the difference as a sum.
The terms are -2 and $-5x$.

8. $-4 + 6x$
The terms are -4 and $6x$.

9. $7x + 2$
The terms are $7x$ and 2.

10. Subtract each day's closing price from the closing price for the previous day.

Date	*Closing Price*	*Change*
Nov. 11	47.44	$47.44 - 46.75 = 0.69$
Nov. 12	47.31	$47.31 - 47.44 = -0.13$
Nov. 13	47.75	$47.75 - 47.31 = 0.44$
Nov. 14	48.75	$48.75 - 47.75 = 1.00$

2.4 Guided Practice (p. 89)

1. terms

2. No; $-7x$ is the term.

3. $-2 - 5 = -7$

4. $4 - 5 = 4 + (-5) = -1$

5. $0 - (-7) = 0 + 7 = 7$

6. $-2 - 8.7 = -2 + (-8.7) = -10.7$

7. $2 - (-3) - 6 = 2 + 3 + (-6) = -1$

8. $-3 - 2 - (-5) = -3 + (-2) + 5 = 0$

9. $6 - 2 - \frac{1}{2} = 6 + (-2) + \left(-\frac{1}{2}\right) = 3\frac{1}{2}$

10.

Input	*Function*	*Output*
$x = -5$	$y = 10 - (-5)$	$y = 15$
$x = -1$	$y = 10 - (-1)$	$y = 11$
$x = 1$	$y = 10 - (1)$	$y = 9$
$x = 5$	$y = 10 - (5)$	$y = 5$

11. $12 - 5x = 12 + (-5x)$
Terms: $12, -5x$

12. $5w - 8 = 5w + (-8)$
Terms: $5w, -8$

13. $-12y + 6$
Terms: $-12y, 6$

2.4 Practice and Applications (pp. 89–91)

14. $4 - 9 = 4 + (-9) = -5$

15. $6 - (-3) = 6 + 3 = 9$

16. $-8 - (-5) = -8 + 5 = -3$

17. $-2 - 9 = -2 + (-9) = -11$

18. $-10 - 5 = -10 + (-5) = -15$

19. $25 - (-14) = 25 + 14 = 39$

20. $-10 - (-42) = -10 + 42 = 32$

21. $95 - 59 = 95 + (-59) = 36$

22. $-3 - 1.7 = -3 + (-1.7) = -4.7$

23. $5.4 - (-3.8) = 5.4 + 3.8 = 9.2$

24. $9.6 - 6.5 = 9.6 + (-6.5) = 3.1$

25. $-2.2 - (-1) = -2.2 + 1 = -1.2$

26. $\frac{4}{3} - \frac{7}{3} = \frac{4}{3} + \left(-\frac{7}{3}\right) = -\frac{3}{3} = -1$

27. $\frac{3}{4} - \left(-\frac{9}{4}\right) = \frac{3}{4} + \frac{9}{4} = \frac{12}{4} = 3$

28. $-\frac{5}{8} - \left(-\frac{3}{8}\right) = -\frac{5}{8} + \frac{3}{8} = -\frac{2}{8} = -\frac{1}{4}$

29. $-4 - \frac{1}{2} = -4 + \left(-\frac{1}{2}\right) = -4\frac{1}{2}$

30. $-1 - 5 - 8 = -1 + (-5) + (-8) = -14$

31. $2 - (-4) - 7 = 2 + 4 + (-7) = -1$

32. $4 - (-3) - (-5) = 4 + 3 + 5 = 12$

33. $46 - 17 - (-2) = 46 + (-17) + 2 = 31$

34. $-15 - 16 - 81 = -15 + (-16) + (-81) = -112$

35. $11 - (-23) - 77 = 11 + 23 + (-77) = -43$

36. $-8 - 3.1 - 6.2 = -8 + (-3.1) + (-6.2) = -17.3$

37. $2.3 - (-9.5) - 1.6 = 2.3 + 9.5 + (-1.6) = 10.2$

38. $8.4 - 5.2 - (-4.7) = 8.4 + (-5.2) + 4.7 = 7.9$

39. $\frac{5}{7} - \frac{4}{7} - \left(-\frac{6}{7}\right) = \frac{5}{7} + \left(-\frac{4}{7}\right) + \frac{6}{7} = \frac{7}{7} = 1$

40. $-\frac{4}{9} - \frac{2}{9} - \frac{5}{9} = -\frac{4}{9} + \left(-\frac{2}{9}\right) + \left(-\frac{5}{9}\right)$

$= -\frac{11}{9}$

$= -1\frac{2}{9}$

Copyright © McDougal Littell Inc.
All rights reserved.

41. $\frac{7}{10} - \left(-\frac{3}{10}\right) - \left(-\frac{1}{10}\right) = \frac{7}{10} + \frac{3}{10} + \frac{1}{10}$
$= \frac{11}{10}$
$= 1\frac{1}{10}$

42.

Input	*Function*	*Output*
$x = -2$	$y = (-2) - 8$	$y = -10$
$x = -1$	$y = (-1) - 8$	$y = -9$
$x = 0$	$y = (0) - 8$	$y = -8$
$x = 1$	$y = (1) - 8$	$y = -7$

43.

Input	*Function*	*Output*
$x = -2$	$y = 12 - (-2)$	$y = 14$
$x = -1$	$y = 12 - (-1)$	$y = 13$
$x = 0$	$y = 12 - (0)$	$y = 12$
$x = 1$	$y = 12 - (1)$	$y = 11$

44.

Input	*Function*	*Output*
$x = -2$	$y = -(-2) - (-5)$	$y = 7$
$x = -1$	$y = -(-1) - (-5)$	$y = 6$
$x = 0$	$y = -(0) - (-5)$	$y = 5$
$x = 1$	$y = -(1) - (-5)$	$y = 4$

45.

Input	*Function*	*Output*
$x = -2$	$y = -8.5 - (-2)$	$y = -6.5$
$x = -1$	$y = -8.5 - (-1)$	$y = -7.5$
$x = 0$	$y = -8.5 - (0)$	$y = -8.5$
$x = 1$	$y = -8.5 - (1)$	$y = -9.5$

46.

Input	*Function*	*Output*
$x = -2$	$y = -(-2) - 12.1$	$y = -10.1$
$x = -1$	$y = -(-1) - 12.1$	$y = -11.1$
$x = 0$	$y = -(0) - 12.1$	$y = -12.1$
$x = 1$	$y = -(1) - 12.1$	$y = -13.1$

47.

Input	*Function*	*Output*
$x = -2$	$y = (-2) - \frac{1}{2}$	$y = -2\frac{1}{2}$
$x = -1$	$y = (-1) - \frac{1}{2}$	$y = -1\frac{1}{2}$
$x = 0$	$y = (0) - \frac{1}{2}$	$y = -\frac{1}{2}$
$x = 1$	$y = (1) - \frac{1}{2}$	$y = \frac{1}{2}$

48. $-4 - y = -4 + (-y)$
Terms: $-4, -y$

49. $-x - 7 = -x + (-7)$
Terms: $-x, -7$

50. $-3x + 6$
Terms: $-3x, 6$

51. $9 - 28x = 9 + (-28x)$
Terms: $9, -28x$

52. $-10 + 4b$
Terms: $-10, 4b$

53. $a - 5 = a + (-5)$
Terms: $a, -5$

54.

Date	*Closing Price*	*Change*
Sept. 12	103.19	103.19 − 101.31 = 1.88
Sept. 13	105.75	105.75 − 103.19 = 2.56
Sept. 14	104.44	104.44 − 105.75 = −1.31
Sept. 15	102.19	102.19 − 104.44 = −2.25

55. The submarine rose up.
$-450 - (-725) = -450 + 725 = 275$ ft

56. $3741 - 11042 = -7301$ ft
$3079 - 3741 = -662$ ft
$1196 - 3079 = -1883$ ft
$1273 - 1196 = 77$ ft
$-38 - 1273 = -1311$ ft
$7983 - (-38) = 8021$ ft

57. $-7301 - 662 - 1883 + 77 - 1311 + 8021 = -3059$

58. True; $8 - (-6) = 8 + 6 = 14$
(Subtraction rule). Subtracting a negative number is the same as adding its opposite (positive). Adding two positive numbers always results in a positive number.

59. True; $-4 - 2 = -6$.
Subtracting a positive number is the same as adding its opposite (a negative number). The sum of two negative numbers is always negative.

2.4 Standardized Test Practice (p. 91)

60. $5 - \left(-\frac{1}{3}\right) + \frac{2}{3} = 5 + \frac{1}{3} + \frac{2}{3}$
$= 5 + \left(\frac{1}{3} + \frac{2}{3}\right)$
$= 5 + \frac{3}{3}$
$= 5 + 1 = 6$
D

61. $x - 7$
$= -(-1) - 7$ Replace x with -1.
$= 1 + (-7)$ Subtraction rule
$= -6$
G

62. $-12x - 2y + 1 = -12x + (-2y) + 1$
Terms: $-12x, -2y, 1$
$2y$ is not a term; B

63. $-100 + (-300) = -400$; F

Copyright © McDougal Littell Inc.
All rights reserved.

2.4 Mixed Review (p. 91)

64. $9 - 2 \cdot 2 - 3$
$= 9 - 4 - 3$ Multiply.
$= 5 - 3$ Subtract (left-to-right rule).
$= 2$

65. $1 \cdot 10 + 5 \cdot 5$
$= 10 + 25$ Multiply.
$= 35$ Add.

66. $8^2 + 6 - 7$
$= 64 + 6 - 7$ Evaluate the power.
$= 70 - 7$ Add, then subtract.
$= 63$ (left-to-right rule).

67. $4 \cdot 2^3 + 9$
$= 4 \cdot 8 + 9$ Evaluate the power.
$= 32 + 9$ Multiply.
$= 41$ Add.

68. $4 \cdot (12 \div 6) - 5$
$= 4 \cdot (2) - 5$ Evaluate the operation in the parentheses.
$= 8 - 5$ Multiply.
$= 3$ Subtract.

69. $(10 - 2) \cdot 7 + 8$
$= (8) \cdot 7 + 8$ Evaluate the operation in the parentheses.
$= 56 + 8$ Multiply.
$= 64$ Add.

70. $3.54 + 2.24 = 5.78$ million participants in 1994–95; false

71. $3.71 + 2.24$ is about $4 + 2 = 6$ million participants; true

72. −2 0 2 4 6 8 10

73.

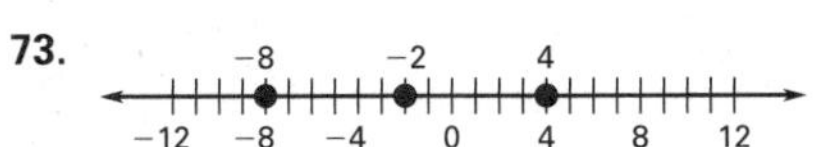

74. −12 −8 −4 0 4 8 12

75. −4.3 2 6.5
−4 −2 0 2 4 6

76. −9.1 0.5
−12 −8 −4 0 4 8 12

77.

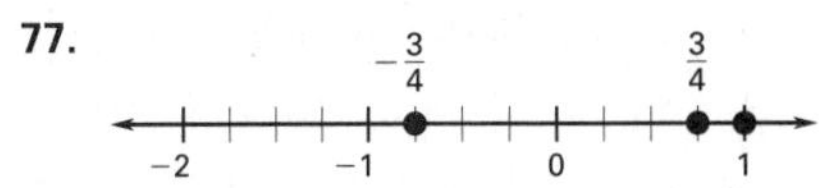

2.4 Maintaining Skills (p. 91)

78. $5 \times 0.25 = 1.25$
$25 \times 5 = 125$

79. $0.1 \times 0.4 = 0.04$
$1 \times 4 = 4$

80. $0.004 \times 4.2 = 0.0168$
$42 \times 4 = 168$

81. $1.69 \times 0.02 = 0.0338$
$169 \times 2 = 338$

82. $3.6 \times 0.3 = 1.08$
$36 \times 3 = 108$

83. $9.4 \times 2.04 = 19.176$
204×94: $816 + 18360 = 19176$

2.5 Developing Concepts: Explore *(p. 92)*

1.

Product	Equivalent Sum	Solution
3(–3)	–3 + (–3) + (–3)	–9
2(–5)	–5 + (–5)	–10
4(–2)	–2 + (–2) + (–2) + (–2)	–8

2.

Product	Use definition of opposites	Use result from Step 1	Solution
–3(–3)	–(3)(–3)	–(–9)	9
–2(–5)	–(2)(–5)	–(–10)	10
–4(–2)	–(4)(–2)	–(–8)	8

Think About It (p. 92)

1. $3(2) = 2 + 2 + 2 = 6$

2. $4(5) = 5 + 5 + 5 + 5 = 20$

3. $2(-6) = -6 + (-6) = -12$

4. $5(-3) = -3 + (-3) + (-3) + (-3) + (-3) = -15$

5. $-2(6) = -(2)(6) = -(6 + 6) = -(12) = -12$

6. $-3(4) = -(3)(4) = -(4 + 4 + 4) = -(12) = -12$

7. $-5(-5) = -(5)(-5)$
$= -[(-5) + (-5) + (-5) + (-5) + (-5)]$
$= -[-25]$
$= 25$

8. $-4(-3) = -(4)(-3)$
$= -[-3 + (-3) + (-3) + (-3)]$
$= -[-12]$
$= 12$

9. always **10.** never **11.** never

Lesson 2.5

2.5 Checkpoint (pp. 93–95)

1. $3(-5) = -15$; one negative factor = negative product

2. $-2(4)(5) = -40$; one negative factor = negative product

3. $-\frac{1}{3}(-3)(-2) = -2$; three negative factors = negative product

Copyright © McDougal Littell Inc.
All rights reserved.

4. $(-2)^3 = -8$; three negative factors = negative product

5. $8(-t) = -8t$; one negative factor = negative product

6. $-x(-x)(-x)(-x) = x^4$; four negative factors = positive product

7. $-7(-b)^3 = 7b^3$; four negative factors = positive product

8. $-9(x)(-2)$
$= 18x$ two negative factors = positive product
$= 18(-2)$ Replace x with -2.
$= -36$ one negative factor = negative product

9. $3(4)(-x)$
$= -12x$ one negative factor = negative product
$= -12(-2)$ Replace x with -2.
$= 24$ two negative factors = positive product

10. $3(-x)^3$
$= -3x^3$ three negative factors = negative product
$= -3(-2)^3$ Replace x with -2.
$= 24$ four negative factors = positive product

11. $7(x^2)(-5)$
$= -35x^2$ one negative factor = negative product
$= -35(-2)^2$ Replace x with -2.
$= -140$ three negative factors = negative product

12. $4.5(-15) = -67.5$ ft

2.5 Guided Practice (p. 96)

1. commutative property (order does not change product); $4(-2) = (-2)4$; B

2. associative property (the way factors are grouped does not change the product); $-7(5 \cdot 2) = (-7 \cdot 5) \cdot 2$; E

3. identity property (product of 1 and a number is the number); $1 \cdot (-15) = -15$; D

4. property of zero (product of a number and zero is zero); $0 \cdot 8 = 0$; C

5. property of a negative one (the product of a number and negative one is the opposite of the number); $-1 \cdot 9 = -9$; A

6. $9(-1) = -9$

7. $-5(7) = -35$

8. $-4(-6) = 24$

9. $(-1)^5 = -1$

10. $-3(-6)(a) = 18a$

11. $5(-t)(-t)(-t)(-t) = 5t^4$

12. $6(-x)^3 = -6x^3$

13. $2(-5)(-x)$
$= 10x$ Replace x with 4.
$= 10(4)$
$= 40$

14. $6(-2)(x)$
$= -12x$ Replace x with -3.
$= -12(-3)$
$= 36$

2.5 Practice and Applications (pp. 96–98)

15. an even number × an even number = an even number (Yes, the set is closed.)

16. an odd number + an odd number ≠ an odd number (No, the set is not closed.) For example, $3 + 5 = 8$, an even number

17. $-7(4) = -28$; one negative factor

18. $5(-5) = -25$; one negative factor

19. $-6.3(2) = -12.6$; one negative factor

20. $-7(-1.2) = 8.4$; two negative factors

21. $-\frac{1}{2}\left(\frac{8}{3}\right) = -\frac{4}{3}$; one negative factor

22. $-12\left(-\frac{1}{4}\right) = 3$; two negative factors

23. $(-6)^3 = -216$; three negative factors

24. $(-4)^4 = 256$; four negative factors

25. $-(7)^2 = -49$; opposite of a positive product

26. $-2(-5)(7) = 70$; two negative factors

27. $6(9)(-1) = -54$; one negative factor

28. $-5(-4)(-8) = -160$; three negative factors

29. $2.7(-6)(-6) = 97.2$; two negative factors

30. $-3.3(-1)(-1.5) = -4.95$; three negative factors

31. $15\left(-\frac{2}{15}\right)\left(\frac{3}{4}\right) = -\frac{3}{2}$; one negative factor

32. $-3(-y) = 3y$; two negative factors

33. $7(-x) = -7x$; one negative factor

34. $-2(k) = -2k$; one negative factor

35. $5(-a)(-a)(-a) = -5a^3$; three negative factors

36. $-8(z)(z) = -8z^2$; one negative factor

37. $-2(5)(-r)(-r) = -10r^2$; three negative factors

38. $(-b)^3 = -b^3$; three negative factors

39. $-2(-x)^2 = -2x^2$; two negative factors

40. $-(-y)^4 = -y^4$; opposite of a positive number

41. $-8(d) = -8(6) = -48$

42. $3(-4)(n) = -12n = -12(-2) = 24$

43. $-3(-a)(-a) = -3a^2 = -3(-7)^2 = -3(49) = -147$

44. $9(-2)(-r)^3 = 18r^3$
$= 18(2)^3$
$= 18(8)$
$= 144$

45. $-4.1(-5)(h) = 20.5h = 20.5(2) = 41$

Copyright © McDougal Littell Inc.
All rights reserved.

9. $-(4 - 2x) = -1(4) - (-1)(2x)$
$= -4 - (-2x)$
$= -4 + 2x$ or $2x - 4$

10. $(4 - m)(-2) = 4(-2) - m(-2)$
$= -8 - (-2m)$
$= -8 + 2m$ or $2m - 8$

11. $3(1.25) = 3(1 + 0.25)$
$= 3(1) + 3(0.25)$
$= 3 + 0.75$
$= 3.75$; \$3.75

2.6 Guided Practice (p. 103)

1. $2(x + 3)$
$= 2(x) + 2(3)$ Distribute 2 to each item.
$= 2x + 6$ Multiply.

2. $(x + 4)5$
$= x(5) + 4(5)$ Distribute 5 to each item.
$= 5x + 20$ Multiply.

3. $7(x - 3)$
$= 7(x) - 7(3)$ Distribute 7 to each term.
$= 7x - 21$ Multiply.

4. $(x - 6)4$
$= x(4) - 6(4)$ Distribute 4 to each term.
$= 4x - 24$ Multiply.

5. $12(x + 5)$; $12x + 60$

6. $12(x + 5) = 12x + 60$

7. $3(x + 2) = 3(x) + 3(2) = 3x + 6$; D

8. $(x + 3)(-2) = x(-2) + 3(-2)$
$= -2x + (-6)$ or $-2x - 6$; C

9. $-3(x - 2) = -3(x) - (-3)(2)$
$= -3x - (-6)$
$= -3x + 6$; B

10. $(3 - x)2 = 3(2) - x(2) = 6 - 2x$; A

11. $4(1.15) = 4(1 + 0.15)$
$= 4(1) + 4(0.15)$
$= 4 + 0.6$
$= 4.6$

12. $9(1.95) = 9(2 - 0.05)$
$= 9(2) - 9(0.05)$
$= 18 - 0.45$
$= 17.55$

2.6 Practice and Applications (pp. 103–106)

13. $3(4 + x) = 12 + 3x$

14. $7(2 + x) = 14 + 7x$

15. $(x + 5)(11) = 11x + 55$

16. $9(2x + 4) = 18x + 36$

17. $3(x + 4) = 3(x) + 3(4) = 3x + 12$

18. $5(w + 6) = 5(w) + 5(6) = 5w + 30$

19. $7(1 + t) = 7(1) + 7(t) = 7 + 7t$

20. $(y + 4)5 = y(5) + 4(5) = 5y + 20$

21. $(2 + u)6 = 2(6) + u(6) = 12 + 6u$

22. $(x + 8)7 = x(7) + 8(7) = 7x + 56$

23. $2(2y + 1) = 2(2y) + 2(1) = 4y + 2$

24. $(3x + 7)4 = 3x(4) + 7(4) = 12x + 28$

25. $3(4 + 6a) = 3(4) + 3(6a) = 12 + 18a$

26. $(9 + 3n)2 = 9(2) + 3n(2) = 18 + 6n$

27. $(x + 2)1.3 = x(1.3) + 2(1.3) = 1.3x + 2.6$

28. $\frac{1}{5}(10 + 15r) = \frac{1}{5}(10) + \frac{1}{5}(15r) = 2 + 3r$

29. $5(y - 2) = 5(y) - 5(2) = 5y - 10$

30. $2(x - 3) = 2(x) - 2(3) = 2x - 6$

31. $9(7 - a) = 9(7) - 9(a) = 63 - 9a$

32. $(x - 2)2 = x(2) - 2(2) = 2x - 4$

33. $(7 - m)4 = 7(4) - m(4) = 28 - 4m$

34. $(n - 7)2 = n(2) - 7(2) = 2n - 14$

35. $10(1 - 3t) = 10(1) - 10(3t) = 10 - 30t$

36. $7(6w - 1) = 7(6w) - 7(1) = 42w - 7$

37. $(3x - 3)6 = 3x(6) - 3(6) = 18x - 18$

38. $(9 - 5a)4 = 9(4) - 5a(4) = 36 - 20a$

39. $(-3.1u - 0.8)3 = -3.1u(3) - 0.8(3) = -9.3u - 2.4$

40. $5\left(\frac{1}{10}x - \frac{2}{15}\right) = 5\left(\frac{1}{10}x\right) - 5\left(\frac{2}{15}\right) = \frac{1}{2}x - \frac{2}{3}$

41. $-3(r + 8) = -3(r) + (-3)(8)$
$= -3r + (-24)$
$= -3r - 24$

42. $-2(x - 6) = -2(x) - (-2)(6) = -2x + 12$

43. $-(1 + s) = -1(1) + (-1)(s) = -1 - s$

44. $(2 + t)(-2) = 2(-2) + t(-2)$
$= -4 + (-2t)$
$= -4 - 2t$

45. $(y + 9)(-1) = y(-1) + 9(-1)$
$= -y + -9$
$= -y - 9$

46. $(x - 4)(-3) = x(-3) - 4(-3)$
$= -3x - (-12)$
$= -3x + 12$

47. $-6(4a + 3) = -6(4a) + (-6)(3)$
$= -24a + (-18)$
$= -24a - 18$

48. $(9x + 1)(-7) = 9x(-7) + 1(-7) = -63x - 7$

49. $-(6y - 5) = -1(6y) - (-1)(5)$
$= -6y - (-5)$
$= -6y + 5$

50. $(3d - 8)(-5) = 3d(-5) - 8(-5)$
$= -15d - (-40)$
$= -15d + 40$

Copyright © McDougal Littell Inc.
All rights reserved.

51. $(2.3 - 7w)(-6) = 2.3(-6) - 7w(-6)$
$= -13.8 - (-42w)$
$= -13.8 + 42w$

52. $-\frac{3}{8}(x + 24) = -\frac{3}{8}(x) + \left(-\frac{3}{8}\right)(24)$
$= \left(-\frac{3}{8}\right)x + (-9)$
$= -\frac{3}{8}x - 9$

53. forgot to distribute 9 to 5;
$9(3 - 5) = 9(3) - 9(5)$
$= 27 - 45$
$= -18$

54. dropped the negative sign in front of the 8;
$-2(7 - 8) = -2(7) - (-2)(8)$
$= -14 - (-16)$
$= -14 + 16$
$= 2$

55. $4(6.11) = 4(6 + 0.11)$
$= 4(6) + 4(0.11)$
$= 24 + 0.44$
$= 24.44$

56. $10(7.25) = 10(7 + 0.25)$
$= 10(7) + 10(0.25)$
$= 70 + 2.50$
$= 72.50$

57. $3(9.20) = 3(9 + 0.20)$
$= 3(9) + 3(0.20)$
$= 27 + 0.60$
$= 27.60$

58. $7(5.98) = 7(6 - 0.02)$
$= 7(6) - 7(0.02)$
$= 42 - 0.14$
$= 41.86$

59. $2(2.90) = 2(3 - 0.10)$
$= 2(3) - 2(0.10)$
$= 6 - 0.20$
$= 5.80$

60. $6(8.75) = 6(9 - 0.25)$
$= 6(9) - 6(0.25)$
$= 54 - 1.50$
$= 52.50$

61. $-3(4.10) = -3(4 + 0.10)$
$= -3(4) + (-3)(0.10)$
$= -12 + (-0.30)$
$= -12.30$

62. $-9(1.02) = -9(1 + 0.02)$
$= -9(1) + (-9)(0.02)$
$= -9 + (-0.18)$
$= -9.18$

63. $-2(11.05) = -2(11 + 0.05)$
$= -2(11) + (-2)(0.05)$
$= -22 + (-0.10)$
$= -22.10$

64. $-8(2.80) = -8(3 - 0.20)$
$= -8(3) - (-8)(0.20)$
$= -24 - (-1.60)$
$= -24 + 1.60$
$= -22.40$

65. $-5(10.99) = -5(11 - 0.01)$
$= -5(11) - (-5)(0.01)$
$= -55 - (-0.05)$
$= -55 + 0.05$
$= -54.95$

66. $-4(5.95) = -4(6 - 0.05)$
$= -4(6) - (-4)(0.05)$
$= -24 - (-0.20)$
$= -24 + 0.20$
$= -23.80$

67. $4(4.99) = 4(5 - 0.01)$
$= 4(5) - 4(0.01)$
$= 20 - 0.04$
$= 19.96$; \$19.96

68. $7(1.05) = 7(1 + 0.05)$
$= 7(1) + 7(0.05)$
$= 7 + 0.35$
$= 7.35$; \$7.35

69. $5(2.09) = 5(2 + 0.09)$
$= 5(2) + 5(0.09)$
$= 10 + 0.45$
$= 10.45$; \$10.45

70. $2(4.95) = 2(5 - 0.05)$
$= 2(5) - 2(0.05)$
$= 10 - 0.10$
$= 9.90$; \$9.90

71. $200(x + 225)$; $200x + 45{,}000$

72. $200(x + 225) = 200x + 45{,}000$

73. $200(75 + 225) = 200(300) = 60{,}000 \text{ yd}^2$
Check:
$200(75) + 45{,}000 = 15{,}000 + 45{,}000 = 60{,}000 \text{ yd}^2$

2.6 Standardized Test Practice (p. 105)

74. $(x + 7)3 = x(3) + 7(3) = 3x + 21$; D

75. $6(x - 2) = 6(x) - 6(2) = 6x - 12$; G

76. $(5 - x)(-17) = 5(-17) - x(-17)$
$= -85 - (-17x)$
$= -85 + 17x$; D

77. $5(20 - 0.01)$; G

2.6 Mixed Review (p. 106)

78. $\frac{10 \cdot 8}{4^2 \cdot 4} = \frac{80}{16 \cdot 4} = \frac{80}{64} = \frac{16 \cdot 5}{16 \cdot 4} = \frac{5}{4}$

79. $\frac{6^2 - 12}{3^2 + 1} = \frac{36 - 12}{9 + 1} = \frac{24}{10} = \frac{2 \cdot 12}{2 \cdot 5} = \frac{12}{5}$

Copyright © McDougal Littell Inc.
All rights reserved.

80. $\frac{75 - 5^2}{13 + 3 \cdot 4} = \frac{75 - 25}{13 + 12} = \frac{50}{25} = \frac{25 \cdot 2}{25 \cdot 1} = 2$

81. $\frac{3 \cdot 7 + 9}{2^4 + 5 - 11} = \frac{21 + 9}{16 + 5 - 11} = \frac{30}{21 - 11} = \frac{30}{10} = 3$

82. $\frac{4 \cdot 2 + 5^3}{3^2 - 2} = \frac{4 \cdot 2 + 125}{9 - 2} = \frac{8 + 125}{7} = \frac{133}{7} = 19$

83. $\frac{6 + 7^2}{3^3 - 9 - 7} = \frac{6 + 49}{27 - 9 - 7} = \frac{55}{18 - 7} = \frac{55}{11} = 5$

84. Commutative property of addition (order does not change the sum).

85. Identity property of addition (The sum of zero and a number is the number).

86. Property of opposites (the sum of opposites is zero).

87. Associative property of addition (the way numbers are grouped does not change the sum).

88. $6 - 7 = -1$ 89. $9 - (-3) = 9 + 3 = 12$

90. $4 - 8 - 3 = 4 + (-8) + (-3) = -4 + (-3) = -7$

91. $6 - (-8) - 11 = 6 + 8 + (-11)$
$= 14 + (-11)$
$= 3$

92. $7.2 - 9 - 8.5 = 7.2 + (-9) + (-8.5)$
$= 7.2 + (-8.5) + (-9)$
$= -1.3 + (-9)$
$= -10.3$

93. $\frac{1}{3} - \frac{2}{3} - 1 = \frac{1}{3} + \left(-\frac{2}{3}\right) + (-1)$
$= \left(-\frac{1}{3}\right) + (-1)$
$= -1\frac{1}{3}$

2.6 Maintaining Skills (p. 106)

94. $0.14 = \frac{14}{100} = \frac{2 \cdot 7}{2 \cdot 50} = \frac{7}{50}$

95. $0.25 = \frac{25}{100} = \frac{1 \cdot 25}{4 \cdot 25} = \frac{1}{4}$

96. $0.34 = \frac{34}{100} = \frac{2 \cdot 17}{2 \cdot 50} = \frac{17}{50}$

97. $0.50 = \frac{50}{100} = \frac{1 \cdot 50}{2 \cdot 50} = \frac{1}{2}$

98. $0.75 = \frac{75}{100} = \frac{3 \cdot 25}{4 \cdot 25} = \frac{3}{4}$

99. $0.82 = \frac{82}{100} = \frac{2 \cdot 41}{2 \cdot 50} = \frac{41}{50}$

100. $0.90 = \frac{90}{100} = \frac{9 \cdot 10}{10 \cdot 10} = \frac{9}{10}$

101. $0.96 = \frac{96}{100} = \frac{4 \cdot 24}{4 \cdot 25} = \frac{24}{25}$

Quiz 2 (p. 106)

1.

Input	*Function*	*Output*
$x = -3$	$y = (-3) - 12$	$y = -15$
$x = -1$	$y = (-1) - 12$	$y = -13$
$x = 1$	$y = (1) - 12$	$y = -11$
$x = 3$	$y = (3) - 12$	$y = -9$

2.

Input	*Function*	*Output*
$x = -3$	$y = 27 - (-3)$	$y = 30$
$x = -1$	$y = 27 - (-1)$	$y = 28$
$x = 1$	$y = 27 - (1)$	$y = 26$
$x = 3$	$y = 27 - (3)$	$y = 24$

3.

Input	*Function*	*Output*
$x = -3$	$y = (-3) - \frac{1}{4}$	$y = -3\frac{1}{4}$
$x = -1$	$y = (-1) - \frac{1}{4}$	$y = -1\frac{1}{4}$
$x = 1$	$y = (1) - \frac{1}{4}$	$y = \frac{3}{4}$
$x = 3$	$y = (3) - \frac{1}{4}$	$y = 2\frac{3}{4}$

4. $2x - 9 = 2x + (-9)$; terms: $2x, -9$

5. $8 - x = 8 + (-x)$; terms: $8, -x$

6. $-10x + 4$; terms: $-10x, 4$

7. $19.88 - 19.63 = 0.25$
$20.00 - 19.88 = 0.12$
$19.88 - 20.00 = -0.12$
$19.75 - 19.88 = -0.13$

8. $-7(9) = -63$

9. $-5(-6) = 30$

10. $35(-80) = -2800$

11. $-1.8(-6) = 10.8$

12. $-15\left(\frac{1}{5}\right) = -3$

13. $-10(-3)(9) = 270$

14. $(x + 2)11 = x(11) + 2(11) = 11x + 22$

15. $5(12 - y) = 5(12) - 5(y) = 60 - 5y$

16. $-4(3a - 4) = -4(3a) - (-4)(4)$
$= -12a - (-16)$
$= -12a + 16$

17. $2(24.95) = 2(25 - 0.05)$
$= 2(25) - 2(0.05)$
$= 50 - 0.10$
$= 49.90$; \$49.90

Copyright © McDougal Littell Inc.
All rights reserved.

Lesson 2.7

2.7 Checkpoint (pp. 107–109)

1. $-5x^2 - x + 8 + 6x - 10$ Rewrite as a sum.
$= -5x^2 + (-x) + 8 + 6x + (-10)$
Like terms: $-x$ and $6x$, 8 and -10

2. $-3x^2 + 2x + x^2 - 4 + 7x$ Rewrite as a sum.
$= -3x^2 + 2x + x^2 + (-4) + 7x$
Like terms: $-3x^2$ and x^2, $2x$ and $7x$

3. $5x - 2x$
$= (5 - 2)x$ Distributive property
$= 3x$ Subtract coefficients.

4. $8m - m - 3m + 5$
$= (8 - 1 - 3)m + 5$ Distributive property
$= 4m + 5$ Subtract coefficients.

5. $-x^2 + 5x + x^2$
$= -x^2 + x^2 + 5x$ Group like terms.
$= (-1 + 1)x^2 + 5x$ Distributive property
$= 0x^2 + 5x$ Add coefficients.
$= 0 + 5x$ Property of zero
$= 5x$ Identity property

6. $3(y + 2) - 4y$
$= 3(y) + 3(2) - 4y$ Distributive property
$= 3y + 6 + (-4y)$ Multiply; rewrite as a sum.
$= 3y + (-4y) + 6$ Group like terms.
$= (3 + -4)y + 6$ Distributive property
$= -y + 6$ Add coefficients.

7. $9x - 4(2x - 1)$
$= 9x + (-4)(2x + (-1))$ Rewrite as a sum.
$= 9x + (-4)(2x) + (-4)(-1)$ Distributive property
$= 9x + (-8x) + 4$ Multiply.
$= (9 + (-8))x + 4$ Distributive property
$= (1)x + 4$ Add coefficients.
$= x + 4$ Identity property of multiplication

8.
$-(z + 2) - 2(1 - z)$
$= -1(z + 2) + (-2)(1 + (-z))$ Rewrite as a sum.
$= (-1)z + (-1)(2) + (-2)(1) + (-2)(-z)$ Distributive property
$= -z + (-2) + (-2) + 2z$ Multiply.
$= -z + 2z + (-2) + (-2)$ Group like terms.
$= (-1 + 2)z + (-4)$ Combine like terms.
$= z - 4$

9. $d = 0.4t + 0.06(45 - t)$
$= 0.4t + 0.06(45) - 0.06(t)$ Distributive property
$= 0.4t - 0.06t + 2.7$ Multiply.
$= 0.34t + 2.7$ Combine like terms.

10. Replace t with 30.
$d = 0.34(30) + 2.7$ Multiply.
$d = 10.2 + 2.7$ Add.
$d = 12.9$ miles (or about 13 miles)

2.7 Guided Practice (p. 110)

1. The coefficient of $7x^2$ is 7.
The coefficient of $-5x$ is -5.

2. Rewrite as a sum:
$-6 - 3x^2 + 3x - 4x + 9x^2$
$= -6 + (-3)x^2 + 3x + (-4)x + 9x^2$.
Like terms: $-3x^2$ and $9x^2$, $3x$ and $-4x$

3. $5r + r = (5 + 1)r = 6r$

4. $w - 3w = (1 - 3)w = -2w$

5. $-4k - 8 + 4k = -4k + (-8) + 4k$
$= -4k + 4k + (-8)$
$= (-4 + 4)k + (-8)$
$= 0k + (-8)$
$= 0 + (-8)$
$= -8$

6. $12 - 10m + m - 3 = 12 + (-10m) + m + (-3)$
$= -10m + m + 12 + (-3)$
$= (-10 + 1)m + 12 + (-3)$
$= -9m + 9$ or $9 - 9m$

7. $2a^2 + 3a + 2a^2 - 5 = 2a^2 + 2a^2 + 3a - 5$
$= (2 + 2)a^2 + 3a - 5$
$= 4a^2 + 3a - 5$

8. $8 - 4t - 6t^2$; already simplified

9. $14f + 4(f + 1) = 14f + 4(f) + 4(1)$
$= 14f + 4f + 4$
$= (14 + 4)f + 4$
$= 18f + 4$

10. $21g - 2(g - 4) = 21g + (-2)(g - 4)$
$= 21g + (-2)g - (-2)(4)$
$= (21 + (-2))g - (-8)$
$= 19g + 8$

11. $-5(2m + 4) - m = -5(2m) + (-5)(4) + (-m)$
$= -10m + (-20) + (-m)$
$= -10m + (-m) + (-20)$
$= (-10 + -1)m + (-20)$
$= (-11)m + (-20)$
$= -11m - 20$

12. $7(3a + 2) + 5 = 7(3a) + 7(2) + 5$
$= 21a + 14 + 5$
$= 21a + 19$

13. $5(x - 7) + 4(x + 2) = 5(x) - 5(7) + 4(x) + 4(2)$
$= 5x - 35 + 4x + 8$
$= 5x + (-35) + 4x + 8$
$= 5x + 4x + (-35) + 8$
$= (5 + 4)x + (-27)$
$= 9x + (-27)$ or $9x - 27$

Copyright © McDougal Littell Inc.
All rights reserved.

14. $2(4t - 1) - 4(1 - t)$
$= 2(4t) - 2(1) + (-4)(1) - (-4)t$
$= 8t - 2 + (-4) + 4t$
$= 8t + 4t + (-2) + (-4)$
$= (8 + 4)t + (-6)$
$= 12t - 6$

2.7 Practice and Applications (pp. 110–112)

15. $3a + 5a$
like terms: $3a$ and $5a$

16. $5s^2 - 10s^2 = 5s^2 + (-10s^2)$
like terms: $5s^2$ and $-10s^2$

17. $m + 8 + 6m$
like terms: m and $6m$

18. $2p + 1 + 2p + 5$
like terms: $2p$ and $2p$, 1 and 5

19. $-6w - 12 - 3w + 2w^2$
like terms: $-6w$ and $-3w$

20. $3x^2 + 4x + 8x - 7x^2$
like terms: $3x^2$ and $-7x^2$, $4x$ and $8x$

21. $-12m + 5m = (-12 + 5)m = -7m$

22. $4y - 3y = (4 - 3)y = 1y = y$

23. $3c - 5 - c = 3c + (-5) + (-c)$
$= 3c + (-c) + (-5)$
$= (3 + (-1))c + (-5)$
$= 2c - 5$

24. $5 - h + 2 = 5 + 2 - h$
$= 7 - h$

25. $r + 2r + 3r - 7 = (1 + 2 + 3)r - 7$
$= 6r - 7$

26. $8 + 2z + 4 + 3z = 2z + 3z + 8 + 4$
$= (2 + 3)z + 12$
$= 5z + 12$

27. $2n - 3 - n^2$; already simplified

28. $6a - 2a^2 + 4a - a^2 = 6a + (-2)a^2 + 4a + (-a^2)$
$= 6a + 4a + (-2)a^2 + (-a^2)$
$= (6 + 4)a + (-2 + (-1))a^2$
$= 10a + (-3)a^2$ or $10a - 3a^2$

29. $p^2 + 4p + 5p^2 - 2 = p^2 + 5p^2 + 4p - 2$
$= (1 + 5)p^2 + 4p - 2$
$= 6p^2 + 4p - 2$

30. $-10(b - 1) + 4b = -10(b) - (-10)(1) + 4b$
$= -10b + 10 + 4b$
$= (-10 + 4)b + 10$
$= -6b + 10$

31. $9 - 4(9 + y) = 9 + (-4)(9 + y)$
$- 9 + (\ 4)(9) + (-4)y$
$= 9 + (-36) + (-4y)$
$= -27 + (-4y)$ or $-27 - 4y$

32. $6(4 + f) - 8f = 6(4) + 6(f) + (-8)f$
$= 24 + 6f + (-8)f$
$= 24 + (6 + (-8))f$
$= 24 - 2f$

33. $1 - 2(6 + 3r) = 1 + (-2)(6) + (-2)(3r)$
$= 1 + (-12) + (-6r)$
$= -11 + (-6r)$ or $-11 - 6r$

34. $-5(2 + 7x) - 3x = -5(2) + (-5)(7x) - 3x$
$= -10 + (-35)x - 3x$
$= -10 + (-35 - 3)x$
$= -10 + (-38)x$ or $-10 - 38x$

35. $5(2m + 5) - 6 = 5(2m) + 5(5) - 6$
$= 10m + 25 - 6$
$= 10m + 19$

36. $3(4p + 3) + 4(p - 1) = 3(4p) + 3(3) + 4(p) - 4(1)$
$= 12p + 9 + 4p - 4$
$= 12p + 4p + 9 - 4$
$= (12 + 4)p + 5$
$= 16p + 5$

37. $9(c + 3) - 7(c - 3)$
$= 9(c + 3) + (-7)(c - 3)$
$= 9(c) + 9(3) + (-7)(c) - (-7)(3)$
$= 9c + 27 + (-7c) + 21$
$= 9c + (-7c) + 27 + 21$
$= (9 + (-7))c + 48$
$= 2c + 48$

38. $4(x + 2) - (x + 2) = 4(x) + 4(2) - x - 2$
$= 4x + 8 - x - 2$
$= 4x - x + 8 - 2$
$= (4 - 1)x + 6$
$= 3x + 6$

39. 7 is not a like term with $3x$ and $-2x$
$3x + 7 - 2x = 3x - 2x + 7$
$= (3 - 2)x + 7$
$= 1x + 7$
$= x + 7$

40. distribute $3(x - 2)$ before combining like terms:
$3(x - 2) + 5x = 3(x) - 3(2) + 5x$
$= 3x - 6 + 5x$
$= 3x + 5x - 6$
$= (3 + 5)x - 6$
$= 8x - 6$

41. $(x - 7) + x + (x - 7) + x$
$= x + (-7) + x + x + (-7) + x$
$= x + x + x + x + (-7) + (-7)$
$= 4x + (-14)$ or $4x - 14$

42. $(x - 2) + (x + 11) + (2x + 3)$
$= x + (-2) + x + 11 + 2x + 3$
$= x + x + 2x + (-2) + 11 + 3$
$= (1 + 1 + 2)x + 12$
$= 4x + 12$

Copyright © McDougal Littell Inc.
All rights reserved.

43. $2(x + 2) + (x + 4) + 2(x + 2) + (x + 4)$
$= 2(x) + 2(2) + x + 4 + 2(x) + 2(2) + x + 4$
$= 2x + 4 + x + 4 + 2x + 4 + x + 4$
$= 2x + x + 2x + x + 4 + 4 + 4 + 4$
$= (2 + 1 + 2 + 1)x + 16$
$= 6x + 16$

44. $(x + 2) + 9(x - 2) + 2(x - 2)$
$= x + 2 + 9(x) - 9(2) + 2x - 2(2)$
$= x + 2 + 9x - 18 + 2x - 4$
$= x + 9x + 2x + (2 - 18 - 4)$
$= (1 + 9 + 2)x + (-20)$
$= 12x + (-20)$ or $12x - 20$

45. $W = 90.25(150 - n) + 114n$; A

46. $W = 90.25(150) - 90.25(n) + 114n$
$W = 13{,}537.50 - 90.25n + 114n$
$W = 13{,}537.50 + (-90.25 + 114)n$
$W = 13{,}537.50 + 23.75n$
or
$W = 23.75n + 13{,}537.50$

47. Replace n with 90
$W = 23.75(90) + 13{,}537.50$
$W = 2137.50 + 13{,}537.50$
$W = 15{,}675$ tons

48. $T = 15c + 60(8 - c)$

49. $T = 15c + 60(8) - 60(c)$
$T = 15c + 480 - 60c$
$T = 15c + 480 + (-60c)$
$T = 15c + (-60c) + 480$
$T = (15 + (-60))c + 480$
$T = -45c + 480$

50. Replace c with 5
$T = -45(5) + 480$
$T = -225 + 480$
$T = 255$ lb

51. $x + 20 + 0.06(x + 20)$
$= x + 20 + 0.06(x) + 0.06(20)$
$= x + 20 + 0.06x + 1.2$
$= x + 0.06x + 20 + 1.2$
$= (1 + 0.06)x + 20 + 1.2$
$= 1.06x + 21.2$

52. Replace x with 35:
$1.06(35) + 21.2 \stackrel{?}{\leq} 58$
$37.1 + 21.2 \stackrel{?}{\leq} 58$
$58.3 \neq 58.$
No, you would need \$.30. Alternatively, solve for x:
$1.06x + 21.2 \leq 58$
$1.06x \leq 36.80$
$x \leq 34.72.$
The price of the jeans must be less than or equal to \$34.72.

53. $-x(8 - x) + 2x = -(2)(8 - 2) + 2(2)$
$= -2(8) - (-2)(2) + 4$
$= -16 + 4 + 4$
$= -8$
$-x(8 - x) + 2x = -x(8) - (-x)(x) + 2x$
$= -8x + x^2 + 2x$
$= -8x + 2x + x^2$
$= -(8 + 2)x + x^2$
$= -6x + x^2$
Now replace x with 2.
$= -6(2) + (2)^2$
$= -12 + 4$
$= -8$

54. $6(-x - 3) - x(9 + x)$
$= 6(-4 - 3) - 4(9 + 4)$
$= 6(-7) - 4(13)$
$= -42 - 52$
$= -94$
$6(-x - 3) - x(9 + x)$
$= 6(-x) - 6(3) + (-x)(9) + (-x)(x)$
$= -6x + (-18) + (-9x) + (-x^2)$
$= -6x + (-9x) + (-18) + (-x^2)$
$= (-6 + (-9))x + (-18) - x^2$
$= -15x + (-18) - x^2$
Now replace x with 4.
$= -15(4) + (-18) - (4)^2$
$= -15(4) + (-18) - 16$
$= -60 + (-18) - 16$
$= -78 - 16$
$= -94$

2.7 Standardized Test Practice (p. 112)

55. $5 + 13d - 3d^2$ Rewrite as a sum.
$= 5 + 13d + (-3d^2)$
coefficient of d^2-term is -3; A

56. $3x - 9 + 2x^2$ has no like terms, therefore is simplified; G

57. $2x - 3x^2 - x = 2x - x - 3x^2$
$= (2 - 1)x - 3x^2$
$= 1x - 3x^2$
$= x - 3x^2$; C

58. $-4(y + 2) - 5y = -4(y) + (-4)(2) - 5y$
$= -4y + (-8) - 5y$
$= -4y - 5y + (-8)$
$= (-4 - 5)y - 8$
$= -9y - 8$; F

2.7 Mixed Review (p. 112)

59. about 35%

60. 1996: about 65%
1997: about 78%

78% − 65% = 13%
about 13%

61. $-1 + 10 = 9$

62. $8 + (-4) = 4$

Copyright © McDougal Littell Inc.
All rights reserved.

63. $-3 + (-3) = -6$

64. $6.5 + (-3.4) = 3.1$

65. $-9.7 + (-4.4) = -14.1$

66. $-\frac{1}{4} + \frac{7}{4} = \frac{6}{4} = \frac{3}{2}$

67. $9(-4)(x) = 9(-4)(5)$
$= -36(5)$
$= -180$

68. $-5(6)(a) = -30(a) = -30(-2) = 60$

69. $-3(t)(t) = -3(-1)(-1) = -3$

70. $7(2)(-w)(-w) = 7(2)(-6)(-6) = 504$

71. $-8.3(-1.2)(p) = -8.3(-1.2)(3)$
$= 9.96(3)$
$= 29.88$

72. $-\frac{10}{3}\left(\frac{12}{2}\right)(d) = -\frac{10}{3}\left(\frac{12}{2}\right)(-4) = 80$

2.7 Maintaining Skills (p. 112)

73. $\frac{2}{10}, \frac{4}{10}, \frac{5}{10}, \frac{6}{10}, \frac{9}{10}$

74. $\frac{3}{8}, \frac{3}{7}, \frac{3}{5}, \frac{3}{3}, \frac{3}{2}$

75. $\frac{1}{4} = \frac{2}{8}, \frac{3}{8}, \frac{4}{8}, \frac{3}{4} = \frac{6}{8}, \frac{7}{8}$

76. $\frac{1}{5} = \frac{2}{10}, \frac{3}{10}, \frac{1}{2} = \frac{5}{10}, \frac{7}{10}, \frac{4}{5} = \frac{8}{10}$

77. $\frac{2}{6}, \frac{4}{6}, \frac{3}{4}, \frac{2}{2}, \frac{5}{2}$

$\frac{2}{6} = \frac{1}{3} = 0.\overline{3}; \frac{2}{2} = 1; \frac{4}{6} = \frac{2}{3} = 0.\overline{6}; \frac{5}{2} = 2.5; \frac{3}{4} = 0.75$

78. $\frac{1}{7}, \frac{3}{14}, \frac{2}{5}, \frac{1}{2}, \frac{8}{10}$

$\frac{1}{7} \approx 0.14; \frac{1}{2} = 0.5; \frac{3}{14} \approx 0.21; \frac{8}{10} = 0.8; \frac{2}{5} = 0.4$

79. $\frac{3}{8}, \frac{8}{8}, 1\frac{2}{8}, \frac{12}{8} = 1\frac{4}{8}, 2\frac{1}{8}$

80. $4\frac{2}{9}, 4\frac{4}{6}, 5\frac{1}{9}, 5\frac{1}{2}, 5\frac{2}{3};$

$4\frac{2}{9} = 4.\overline{2}; 5\frac{1}{2} = 5.5; 4\frac{4}{6} = 4.\overline{6}; 5\frac{2}{3} = 5.\overline{6}$

$5\frac{1}{9} = 5.\overline{1}$

81. $\frac{11}{15}, \frac{4}{5}, \frac{5}{6}, 2\frac{2}{3}, 2\frac{7}{10}$

$\frac{11}{15} = 0.7\overline{3}; 2\frac{2}{3} = 2.\overline{6}; \frac{4}{5} = 0.8; 2\frac{7}{10} = 2.7; \frac{5}{6} = 0.8\overline{3}$

Lesson 2.8

2.8 Checkpoint (pp. 114–115)

1. $8 \div (-4) = -2$

2. $-5 \div \left(-2\frac{1}{2}\right) = -5 \div \left(-\frac{5}{2}\right) = -5 \cdot \left(-\frac{2}{5}\right) = 2$

3. $\frac{-\frac{3}{4}}{3} = -\frac{3}{4} \div 3 = -\frac{3}{4} \cdot \frac{1}{3} = -\frac{1}{4}$

4. $\frac{3}{-\frac{3}{4}} = 3 \div \left(-\frac{3}{4}\right) = 3 \cdot \left(-\frac{4}{3}\right) = -4$

5. $\frac{-y}{2x + 1} = \frac{-(-5)}{2(2) + 1}$ Rewrite as division.
$= -(-5) \div [2(2) + 1]$
$= 5 \div [4 + 1]$
$= 5 \div 5 = 1$

6. $\frac{24 - 8x}{-4} = (24 - 8x) \div (-4)$ Rewrite as division.
$= (24 - 8x) \cdot \left(-\frac{1}{4}\right)$ Multiply by reciprocal.
$= 24\left(-\frac{1}{4}\right) - 8x\left(-\frac{1}{4}\right)$ Distribute.
$= -6 - (-2x)$ Multiply.
$= -6 + 2x$

7. If x is replaced with 2, the denominator is $(2) - 2 = 0$ and the function is undefined. The domain is the set of all real numbers except 2.

8. If x is replaced with 8, the denominator is $8 - (8) = 0$ and the function is undefined. The domain is the set of all real numbers except 8.

9. The domain is the set of all real numbers.

10. If x is replaced by 0, the denominator is 0 and the function is undefined. The domain is the set of all real numbers except 0.

2.8 Guided Practice (p. 116)

1. reciprocal

2. quotient

3. $32, \frac{1}{32}$

4. $-7, -\frac{1}{7}$

5. $-\frac{1}{5}, -5$

6. $4\frac{2}{3} = \frac{14}{3}, \frac{3}{14}$

7. $-12 \div 3 = -4$

8. $-7 \div \left(-\frac{1}{2}\right) = -7 \cdot (-2) = 14$

9. $\frac{1}{5} \div \left(-\frac{1}{10}\right) = \frac{1}{5} \cdot (-10) = -2$

10. $-8 \div 2\frac{2}{3} = -8 \div \frac{8}{3} = -8 \cdot \frac{3}{8} = -3$

11. $\frac{a - 4}{b} = (a - 4) \div b$
$= (-2 - 4) \div (-3)$
$= -6 \div (-3)$
$= 2$

Copyright © McDougal Littell Inc.
All rights reserved.

12. $\dfrac{36 - 12x}{-6}$

$= (36 - 12x) \div (-6)$ Rewrite as division.

$= (36 - 12x) \cdot \left(-\dfrac{1}{6}\right)$ Multiply by reciprocal.

$= (36)\left(-\dfrac{1}{6}\right) - 12x\left(-\dfrac{1}{6}\right)$ Distribute.

$= -6 - (-2)x$ Multiply.

$= -6 + 2x$ or $2x - 6$

13. If x is replaced by 4, then the denominator is $(4) - 4 = 0$ and the function is undefined. The domain is all real numbers except 4.

14. The domain is all real numbers.

15. If x is replaced by 0, the denominator is $7(0) = 0$ and the function is undefined. The domain is all real numbers except 0.

16. If x is replaced by -2, the denominator is $(-2) + 2 = 0$ and the function is undefined. The domain is all real numbers except -2.

2.8 Practice and Applications (pp. 116–118)

17. Multiply by the reciprocal:

$-9 \div \dfrac{1}{3} = -9 \cdot 3 = -27$

18. Multiply by the reciprocal of divisor, not dividend:

$\dfrac{2}{5} \div -\dfrac{8}{15} = \dfrac{2}{5} \cdot \dfrac{-15}{8} = -\dfrac{3}{4}$

19. $9 \div (-3) = -3$

20. $-10 \div (-5) = 2$

21. $-4 \div 4 = -1$

22. $8 \div (-2) = -4$

23. $-45 \div 9 = -5$

24. $-24 \div 4 = -6$

25. $-50 \div (-25) = 2$

26. $-51 \div 17 = -3$

27. $6 \div \left(-\dfrac{1}{2}\right) = 6 \cdot (-2) = -12$

28. $-9 \div \left(-\dfrac{3}{4}\right) = -9 \cdot \left(-\dfrac{4}{3}\right) = 12$

29. $-7 \div 8\dfrac{2}{5} = -7 \div \dfrac{42}{5} = -7 \cdot \dfrac{5}{42} = -\dfrac{5}{6}$

30. $54 \div \left(-2\dfrac{4}{7}\right) = 54 \div \left(-\dfrac{18}{7}\right)$

$= 54 \cdot \left(-\dfrac{7}{18}\right)$

$= -21$

31. $\dfrac{-6}{-\frac{1}{2}} = -6 \div \left(-\dfrac{1}{2}\right) = -6 \cdot (-2) = 12$

32. $\dfrac{3}{-\frac{5}{6}} = 3 \div \left(-\dfrac{5}{6}\right) = 3 \cdot \left(-\dfrac{6}{5}\right) = -\dfrac{18}{5}$

33. $\dfrac{-18}{\frac{3}{8}} = -18 \div \dfrac{3}{8} = -18 \cdot \dfrac{8}{3} = -48$

34. $\dfrac{-20}{-\frac{3}{5}} = -20 \div \left(-\dfrac{3}{5}\right) = -20 \cdot \left(-\dfrac{5}{3}\right) = \dfrac{100}{3}$

35. $\dfrac{\frac{1}{3}}{-3} = \dfrac{1}{3} \div (-3) = \dfrac{1}{3} \cdot \left(-\dfrac{1}{3}\right) = -\dfrac{1}{9}$

36. $\dfrac{-\frac{8}{9}}{-2} = -\dfrac{8}{9} \div (-2) = -\dfrac{8}{9} \cdot \left(-\dfrac{1}{2}\right) = \dfrac{4}{9}$

37. $\dfrac{-\frac{21}{2}}{7} = -\dfrac{21}{2} \div 7 = -\dfrac{21}{2} \cdot \dfrac{1}{7} = -\dfrac{3}{2}$

38. $\dfrac{-\frac{12}{5}}{-8} = -\dfrac{12}{5} \div (-8) = -\dfrac{12}{5} \cdot \left(-\dfrac{1}{8}\right) = \dfrac{3}{10}$

39. $\dfrac{x - 5}{6} = \dfrac{(3) - 5}{6} = \dfrac{-2}{6} = -\dfrac{1}{3}$

40. $\dfrac{3r - 3}{11} = \dfrac{3(-10) - 3}{11} = \dfrac{-30 - 3}{11} = \dfrac{-33}{11} = -3$

41. $\dfrac{3a - b}{a} = \dfrac{3(-3) - (3)}{(-3)}$

$= \dfrac{-9 - 3}{-3}$

$= \dfrac{-12}{-3}$

$= 4$

42. $\dfrac{2 - 4x}{y} = \dfrac{2 - 4(2)}{\frac{1}{2}}$

$= \dfrac{2 - 8}{\frac{1}{2}}$

$= \dfrac{-6}{\frac{1}{2}}$

$= -6 \div \dfrac{1}{2} = -6 \cdot 2 = -12$

43. $\dfrac{18x - 9}{3} = (18x - 9) \div 3$

$= (18x - 9) \cdot \dfrac{1}{3}$

$= 18x\left(\dfrac{1}{3}\right) - 9\left(\dfrac{1}{3}\right)$

$= 6x - 3$

44. $\dfrac{22r + 10}{-2} = (22r + 10) \div (-2)$

$= (22r + 10) \cdot \left(-\dfrac{1}{2}\right)$

$= 22r\left(-\dfrac{1}{2}\right) + 10\left(-\dfrac{1}{2}\right)$

$= -11r + 5$

45. $\dfrac{-56 + h}{-8}$; Already simplified since there is no coefficient (other than 1) on the h term.

Copyright © McDougal Littell Inc.
All rights reserved.

46. $\frac{45 - 5n}{5} = (45 - 5n) \div 5$
$= (45 - 5n) \cdot \frac{1}{5}$
$= 45\left(\frac{1}{5}\right) - 5n\left(\frac{1}{5}\right)$
$= 9 - n$

47. $\frac{-44 - 8t}{-4} = (-44 - 8t) \div (-4)$
$= (-44 - 8t) \cdot -\frac{1}{4}$
$= -44\left(-\frac{1}{4}\right) - 8t\left(-\frac{1}{4}\right)$
$= 11 + 2t$

48. $\frac{60y - 108}{12} = (60y - 108) \div 12$
$= (60y - 108) \cdot \frac{1}{12}$
$= 60y\left(\frac{1}{12}\right) - 108\left(\frac{1}{12}\right)$
$= 5y - 9$

49. If x is replaced by -2, the denominator is $(-2) + 2 = 0$ and the function is undefined. The domain is all real numbers except -2.

50. If x is replaced by 0, the denominator is $3(0) = 0$ and the function is undefined. The domain is all real numbers except 0.

51. The domain is all real numbers.

52. If x is replaced by 7, the denominator is $7 - (7) = 0$ and the function is undefined. The domain is all real numbers except 7.

53. Velocity $= \frac{-21 \text{ m}}{2 \text{ sec}} = -10.5$ m/sec

54. Velocity $= \frac{-20{,}000 \text{ ft}}{25 \text{ min}} = -800$ ft/min

2.8 Standardized Test Practice (p. 117)

55. D; *Sample answer:* The reciprocal of $\frac{1}{2}$ is 2, which is greater than 1.

2.8 Mixed Review (p. 118)

56. $x + 17 = 25$
$(8) + 17 = 25$
$x = 8$

57. $a - 5 = 19$
$(24) - 5 = 19$
$a = 24$

58. $34 - n = 17$
$34 - (17) = 17$
$n = 17$

59. $2b = 10$
$2(5) = 10$
$b = 5$

60. $y \div 4 = 6$
$(24) \div 4 = 6$
$y = 24$

61. $\frac{60}{x} = 6$
$\frac{60}{(10)} = 6$
$x = 10$

62. $9 = x - 21$ **63.** $2x \ge 7$ **64.** $\frac{x}{-6} = 3$

65. $-8 - 4 - 9 = -8 + (-4) + (-9) = -21$

66. $12 - (-8) - 5 = 12 + 8 - 5 = 15$

67. $-6.3 - 4.1 - 9.5 = -6.3 + (-4.1) + (-9.5)$
$= -10.4 + (-9.5)$
$= -19.9$

68. $1.4 - 6.2 - 9.1 = 1.4 + (-6.2) + (-9.1)$
$= 1.4 + (-15.3)$
$= -13.9$

69. $5 - \frac{1}{2} - \frac{1}{4} = 5 + \left(-\frac{1}{2}\right) + \left(-\frac{1}{4}\right)$
$= 5 + \left(-\frac{2}{4}\right) + \left(-\frac{1}{4}\right)$
$= 5 + \left(-\frac{3}{4}\right)$
$= 4\frac{1}{4}$ or $\frac{17}{4}$

70. $-\frac{2}{3} - \frac{1}{6} - \left(-\frac{5}{9}\right)$
$= \left(-\frac{2}{3} \cdot \frac{6}{6}\right) + \left(-\frac{1}{6} \cdot \frac{3}{3}\right) + \left(\frac{5}{9} \cdot \frac{2}{2}\right)$
$= -\frac{12}{18} + \left(-\frac{3}{18}\right) + \frac{10}{18}$
$= -\frac{5}{18}$

2.8 Maintaining Skills (p. 118)

71. $-3 < 3$ **72.** $5 > -6$

73. $-8 < 9$ **74.** $-7 < -4$

75. $0 > -2$ **76.** $-1 = -1$

77. $-6 < 2$ **78.** $-4 > -5$

Quiz 3 *(p. 118)*

1. Like terms: $3x$ and $-7x$
2. Like terms: $6a$ and $9a$, -5 and 10
3. Like terms: $-5p$ and $-p$
4. $-17t - 9t = (-17 - 9)t = -26t$

Copyright © McDougal Littell Inc.
All rights reserved.

5. $5 + 3d - d + 2 = 3d - d + 5 + 2$
$= (3 - 1)d + 7$
$= 2d + 7$ or $7 + 2d$

6. $6g^2 - 8g - 5g^2 = 6g^2 - 5g^2 - 8g$
$= (6 - 5)g^2 - 8g$
$= 1g^2 - 8g$
$= g^2 - 8g$

7. $3(a + 1) - 7 = 3(a) + 3(1) - 7$
$= 3a + 3 - 7$
$= 3a - 4$

8. $-2(4 - p) + p - 1 = -2(4) - (-2)p + p - 1$
$= -8 + 2p + p - 1$
$= -8 - 1 + 2p + p$
$= -9 + (2 + 1)p$
$= -9 + 3p$ or $3p - 9$

9. $-(w - 7) - 2(1 + w)$
$= -1(w) - (-1)(7) + (-2)(1) + (-2)(w)$
$= -w + 7 + (-2) + (-2w)$
$= -w + (-2w) + 7 + (-2)$
$= (-1 + -2)w + 5$
$= (-3)w + 5$ or $5 - 3w$

10. $15 \div (-3) = -5$

11. $-144 \div (-9) = 16$

12. $-12 \div \frac{3}{8} = -12 \cdot \frac{8}{3} = -32$

13. $-28 \div \left(-2\frac{4}{7}\right) = -28 \div \left(-\frac{18}{7}\right)$
$= -28 \cdot \left(-\frac{7}{18}\right)$
$= \frac{98}{9}$

14. $\frac{-36}{\frac{2}{3}} = -36 \div \frac{2}{3} = -36 \cdot \frac{3}{2} = -54$

15. $\frac{-\frac{1}{4}}{-2} = -\frac{1}{4} \div (-2) = -\frac{1}{4} \cdot \left(-\frac{1}{2}\right) = \frac{1}{8}$

16. $\frac{20 - 8x}{4} = (20 - 8x) \div 4$
$= (20 - 8x) \cdot \frac{1}{4}$
$= 20\left(\frac{1}{4}\right) - 8x\left(\frac{1}{4}\right)$
$= 5 - 2x$

17. Already simplified since the term 1 is not divisible by 3.

18. $\frac{-15x + 10}{-5} = (-15x + 10) \div (-5)$
$= (-15x + 10) \cdot \left(-\frac{1}{5}\right)$
$= -15x\left(-\frac{1}{5}\right) + 10\left(-\frac{1}{5}\right)$
$= 3x - 2$

19. If x is replaced by -2, the denominator is $2 + (-2) = 0$ and the function is undefined. The domain is all real numbers except -2.

20. The domain is all real numbers.

21. If x is replaced with 0, the denominator is 0, and the function is undefined. The domain is all real numbers except 0.

Chapter 2 Extension

Checkpoint (p. 119)

1. Each term is 3 more than the previous term. The next three terms are $15 + 3 = 18$, $18 + 3 = 21$, and $21 + 3 = 24$.

2. The pattern is $1^2 = 1$, $2^2 = 4$, $3^2 = 9$, $4^2 = 16$, etc. So the 7th term is $7^2 = 49$, the 8th term is $8^2 = 64$, and the 9th term is $9^2 = 81$.

Exercises (p. 120)

1. The conclusion is based on observations, so it is based on inductive reasoning.

2. The conclusion is based on a mathematical fact, so it is based on deductive reasoning.

3. This conclusion is based on several observations, and so it is based on inductive reasoning.

4. Sample answer: $1^2 \not> 1$

5. By observation it looks like the pattern is $2^0 = 1$, $2^1 = 2$, $2^3 = 8$, etc. So the 7th term is $2^6 = 64$, the 8th term is $2^7 = 128$, and the 9th term is $2^8 = 256$. Another way to find the next term is to double the previous term.

6. $(x + 2) + (-2)$

$= x + [2 + (-2)]$	Associative property
$= x + 0$	Property of opposites
$= x$	Identity property of addition

7. *Sample answer:* Inductive reasoning: You see your neighbor walking his dog every morning at 7:00 A.M. for 14 consecutive days. You conclude that your neighbor walks his dog every morning. Deductive reasoning: The commuter train to Boston leaves Worcester every morning at 6:15 A.M. It is
6:20 A.M. You conclude that the train has left.

Chapter 2 Summary and Review *(pp. 121–124)*

1. $-6, -4, -3, 1, 2, 5$

2. $-2, -1.9, 3.1, 4.3, 5, 5.3$

3. $-2, -1, -\frac{1}{2}, \frac{2}{3}, 1, 4, 6$

4. $|3| = 3$

5. $|-5| = 5$

6. $-|100| = -(100) = -100$

7. $-|-45| = -(45) = -45$

8. $|-3.2| = 3.2$

9. $-|-9.1| = -(9.1) = -9.1$

10. $-\left|\frac{1}{9}\right| = -\frac{1}{9}$

11. $\left|3\frac{1}{2}\right| = 3\frac{1}{2}$

Copyright © McDougal Littell Inc.
All rights reserved.

12. $9 + (-10) + (-3) = 9 + [(-10) + (-3)]$
$= 9 + (-13)$
$= -4$

13. $-35 + 41 + (-18) = -35 + (-18) + 41$
$= [-35 + (-18)] + 41$
$= -53 + 41$
$= -12$

14. $-2.5 + 6 + (-3) = -2.5 + (-3) + 6$
$= [-2.5 + (-3)] + 6$
$= -5.5 + 6$
$= 0.5$

15. $2.4 + (-3.4) + 6 = [2.4 + 6] + (-3.4)$
$= 8.4 + (-3.4)$
$= 5$

16. $9 + (-3) + \frac{1}{4} = [9 + (-3)] + \frac{1}{4}$
$= 6 + \frac{1}{4}$
$= 6\frac{1}{4}$

17. $\frac{1}{3} + (-8) + \left(-\frac{1}{3}\right) = \left[\frac{1}{3} + \left(-\frac{1}{3}\right)\right] + (-8)$
$= 0 + (-8)$
$= -8$

18. $-2 - 7 - (-8) = -2 + (-7) + 8$
$= [-2 + (-7)] + 8$
$= -9 + 8$
$= -1$

19. $18 - 14 - (-15) = 18 + (-14) + 15$
$= [18 + (-14)] + 15$
$= 4 + 15$
$= 19$

20. $2 - 1.5 - 4 = 2 + (-1.5) + (-4)$
$= 2 + [-1.5 + (-4)]$
$= 2 + (-5.5)$
$= -3.5$

21. $-5.7 - (-3.1) - 8.6 = -5.7 + 3.1 + (-8.6)$
$= [-5.7 + (-8.6)] + 3.1$
$= -14.3 + 3.1$
$= -11.2$

22. $-7 - \frac{3}{8} - 13 = -7 + \left(-\frac{3}{8}\right) + (-13)$
$= [-7 + (-13)] + \left(-\frac{3}{8}\right)$
$= -20 + \left(-\frac{3}{8}\right)$
$= -20\frac{3}{8}$

23. $-3 - \left(-\frac{1}{4}\right) - \frac{1}{2} = -3 + \frac{1}{4} + \left(-\frac{1}{2}\right)$
$= -3 + \left[\frac{1}{4} + \left(-\frac{1}{2}\right)\right]$
$= -3 + \left(-\frac{1}{4}\right)$
$= -3\frac{1}{4}$

24. $-3(12) = -36$; one negative factor = negative product

25. $-40(-15) = 600$; two negative factors = positive product

26. $-7(-6)(-2) = -84$; three negative factors = negative product

27. $-14(-0.3) = 4.2$; two negative factors = positive product

28. $-3.2(10)(-2) = 64$; two negative factors = positive product

29. $24\left(-\frac{7}{12}\right) = -14$; one negative factor = negative product

30. $-5(-x) = 5x$; two negative factors = positive product

31. $3(-f) = -3f$; one negative factor = negative product

32. $10(-a)(-a)(-a) = -10a^3$; three negative factors = negative product

33. $-6(2)(t)(t) = -12t^2$; one negative factor = negative product

34. $(-y)^3 = -y^3$; three negative factors = negative product

35. $-81(-b)^2 = -81b^2$; three negative factors = negative product

36. $5(x + 12) = 5(x) + 5(12) = 5x + 60$

37. $(y + 6)9 = y(9) + 6(9) = 9y + 54$

38. $10(z - 1) = 10(z) - 10(1) = 10z - 10$

39. $(3 - w)2 = 3(2) - w(2) = 6 - 2w$

40. $-2(x + 13) = -2(x) + (-2)(13) = -2x - 26$

41. $(t + 11)(-3) = t(-3) + 11(-3) = -3t - 33$

42. $-8(m - 7) = -8(m) - (-8)(7) = -8m + 56$

43. $(x - 10)(-6) = x(-6) - 10(-6) = -6x + 60$

44. $-2.5(s - 5) = -2.5(s) - (-2.5)(5) = -2.5s + 12.5$

45. $3a + 6a = (3 + 6)a = 9a$

46. $2x^2 + 9x^2 + 4 = (2 + 9)x^2 + 4$
$= 11x^2 + 4$

47. $4 + f - 1 = 4 + (-1) + f$
$= 3 + f$

48. $3(d + 1) - 2 = 3(d) + 3(1) - 2$
$= 3d + 3 - 2$
$= 3d + 1$

Copyright © McDougal Littell Inc.
All rights reserved.

49. $6t - 2(t - 1) = 6t + (-2)(t - 1)$
$= 6t + (-2)(t) - (-2)(1)$
$= 6t + (-2)t + 2$
$= [6 + (-2)]t + 2$
$= 4t + 2$

50. $2(x + 3) + 3(2x - 5) = 2(x) + 2(3) + 3(2x) - 3(5)$
$= 2x + 6 + 6x - 15$
$= 2x + 6x + 6 - 15$
$= (2 + 6)x - 9$
$= 8x - 9$

51. $8 \div (-2) = -4$

52. $-7 \div 7 = -1$

53. $-5 \div \left(-\frac{1}{2}\right) = -5 \cdot (-2) = 10$

54. $-10 \div \left(-\frac{3}{7}\right) = -10 \cdot \left(-\frac{7}{3}\right) = \frac{70}{3}$ or $23\frac{1}{3}$

55. $\frac{1}{2} \div \left(-\frac{3}{4}\right) = \frac{1}{2} \cdot \left(-\frac{4}{3}\right) = -\frac{2}{3}$

56. $\left(-\frac{3}{7}\right) \div \left(-\frac{9}{14}\right) = \left(-\frac{3}{7}\right) \cdot \left(-\frac{14}{9}\right) = \frac{2}{3}$

57. $12 \div \left(-1\frac{1}{3}\right) = 12 \div \left(-\frac{4}{3}\right) = 12 \cdot \left(-\frac{3}{4}\right) = -9$

58. $-63 \div 4\frac{1}{5} = -63 \div \frac{21}{5} = -63 \cdot \frac{5}{21} = -15$

Chapter Test *(p. 125)*

1. $-9, -5, -2, 3, 4, 9$

2. $-6.4, -4, -2.7, 3.1, 5, 8$

3. $-5, -\frac{5}{2}, -\frac{5}{4}, \frac{3}{4}, 2, 3$

4. $5, -5$

5. $-4, 4$

6. $9.2, -9.2$

7. $-\frac{5}{6}, \frac{5}{6}$

8. $|8| = 8$

9. $|-17| = 17$

10. $-|4.5| = -(4.5) = -4.5$

11. $-\left|-\frac{1}{4}\right| = -\left(\frac{1}{4}\right) = -\frac{1}{4}$

12. $4 + (-9) = -5$

13. $-25 + 31 = 6$

14. $9 + (-10) + 2 = 9 + 2 + (-10)$
$= (9 + 2) + (-10)$
$= 11 + (-10)$
$= 1$

15. $7 + 6.5 + (-3.5) = 7 + [6.5 + (-3.5)]$
$= 7 + 3$
$= 10$

16. Let losses be negative numbers and profits be positive numbers. Add the losses and profits.
$2{,}190 + 1{,}527 + (-2{,}502) + (-267) = 948$;
a profit of $948

17. $-6 - 8 = -6 + (-8) = -14$

18. $15 - (-15) = 15 + 15 = 30$

19. $6 - (-4) - (-3) = 6 + 4 + 3 = 13$

20. $-2.47 - (-3.97) - 2 = -2.47 + 3.97 + (-2)$
$= [-2.47 + (-2)] + 3.97$
$= -4.47 + 3.97$
$= -0.50$ or -0.5

21. $-6(4) = -24$

22. $-8(-100) = 800$

23. $-9(8)(-5) = 360$

24. $-3(15)\left(-\frac{7}{15}\right) = 21$

25. $-8(-x) = 8x$

26. $5(-w)(-w) = 5w^2$

27. $8(-4)(a)(a)(a) = -32a^3$

28. $-15(-z)^2 = -15z^2$

29. $-44(4.5) = -198$ ft

30. $(a + 11)9 = a(9) + 11(9) = 9a + 99$

31. $8(4 - x) = 8(4) - 8(x) = 32 - 8x$

32. $(6 + y)(-12) = 6(-12) + y(-12) = -72 - 12y$

33. $(-5)(3 - z) = -5(3) - (-5)(z) = -15 + 5z$

34. $t^2 - 9 + t^2 = t^2 + t^2 - 9$
$= (1 + 1)t^2 - 9$
$= 2t^2 - 9$

35. $14p + 2(5 - p) = 14p + 2(5) - 2(p)$
$= 14p + 10 + (-2p)$
$= 14p + (-2p) + 10$
$= [14 + (-2)]p + 10$
$= 12p + 10$

36. $-9(y + 11) + 6 = -9(y) + (-9)(11) + 6$
$= -9y + (-99) + 6$
$= -9y + (-93)$
$= -9y - 93$

37. $2(a + 3) - 5(a - 4)$
$= 2(a) + 2(3) + (-5)a - (-5)(4)$
$= 2a + 6 + (-5a) + 20$
$= [2a + (-5a)] + (6 + 20)$
$= [2 + (-5)]a + 26$
$= -3a + 26$

38. $t(0.5) + 0.06(17 - t) =$ total distance
Simplify, then replace t with 10.
$0.5t + 0.06(17) - 0.06(t) = 0.5t + 1.02 - 0.06t$
$= 0.5t - 0.06t + 1.02$
$= (0.5 - 0.06)t + 1.02$
$= 0.44t + 1.02$
$= 0.44(10) + 1.02$
$= 4.4 + 1.02$
$= 5.42$ or about 5.4 miles

39. $-36 \div (-4) = 9$

40. $-56 \div \left(-\frac{7}{8}\right) = -56 \cdot \left(-\frac{8}{7}\right) = 64$

41. $-\frac{3}{8} \div \frac{1}{2} = -\frac{3}{8} \cdot 2 = -\frac{3}{4}$

Copyright © McDougal Littell Inc.
All rights reserved.

42. $39 \div \left(1\frac{3}{10}\right) = 39 \div \left(-\frac{13}{10}\right)$
$= 39 \cdot \left(-\frac{10}{13}\right)$
$= -30$

Chapter Standardized Test *(p. 126)*

1. C; $\frac{1}{4} = 0.25 < \frac{1}{3} = 0.\bar{3}$

2. A; -3

3. $|x| = 10$
$|10| = 10$ and $|-10| = 10$
$x = -10$ and 10; D

4. $-9 + 3 + (-4) = -6 + (-4) = -10$; B

5. $-4 - 6 - (-10) = -4 + (-6) + 10$
$= -10 + 10$
$= 0$; B

6. $-x - 13 = -(9) - 13 = -9 + (-13) = -22$; A

7. $26.75 - 26.81 = -0.06$; B

8. $\left(-\frac{1}{2}\right)\left(-\frac{2}{3}\right) = \frac{1}{3}$; C

9. $(-2)(4)(-n)^3 = (-2)(4)(-3)^3$
$= (-2)(4)(-27)$
$= 216$; D

10. $(4 - a)(-3) = 4(-3) - a(-3) = -12 + 3a$; C

11. $3(25 - 0.01)$; D

12. $6(x + 3) - 2(4 - x)$
$= 6(x) + 6(3) + (-2)(4) - (-2)(x)$
$= 6x + 18 + (-8) + 2x$
$= 6x + 2x + 18 + (-8)$
$= (6 + 2)x + 10$
$= 8x + 10$; D

13. $\frac{4p + q}{p} = \frac{4(-2) + (-3)}{(-2)}$
$= \frac{-8 + (-3)}{-2}$
$= \frac{-11}{-2} = \frac{11}{2}$; D

Maintaining Skills *(p. 127)*

1. Area $= s^2 = 5^2 = 25$ square units

2. Area $= \ell \times w = 8 \times 4 = 32$ square units

3. Area $= s^2 = 10^2 = 100$ square units

4. Area $= \frac{1}{2}bh = \frac{1}{2}(4)(4) = 8$ square units

5.

Book Type	Fiction	Nonfiction	Other
Number	549	103	348

First find the total number of books:
$549 + 103 + 348 = 1000$
Write fractions comparing the number of each type to the total number of books, then multiply by 360°.

$\frac{549}{1000} \cdot 360° = 197.64 \cdot \approx 198°$

$\frac{103}{1000} \cdot 360° = 37.08 \approx 37°$

$\frac{348}{1000} \cdot 360° = 125.28° \approx 125°$

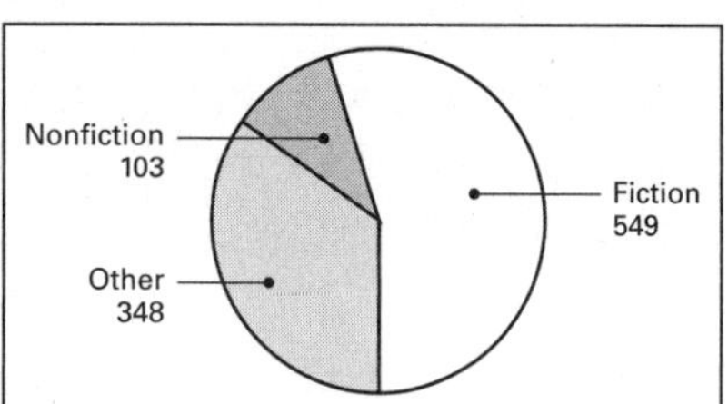

Copyright © McDougal Littell Inc.
All rights reserved.

Chapter 3

Chapter Opener

Think & Discuss (p. 129)

1. $d = rt$

Flying rate (miles per hour)	*Time (hours)*	*Distance (miles)*
30	1	30
30	$\frac{1}{2}$	15
30	$\frac{1}{6}$	5

2. 1 hour = 60 minutes

3. $\frac{1}{2}$ hour $= \frac{1}{2} \cdot 60 = 30$ minutes

4. $\frac{1}{6}$ hour $= \frac{1}{6} \cdot 60 = 10$ minutes

5. 30 miles per hour $\cdot \frac{1}{30}$ hour = 1 mile

$\frac{1}{30}$ hour $= \frac{1}{30} \cdot 60 = 2$ minutes

It will take an eagle 2 minutes to fly 1 mile.

Chapter Readiness Quiz (p. 130)

1. D **2.** D **3.** C **4.** B **5.** *C*

Lesson 3.1

3.1 Developing Concepts: Explore *(p. 131)*

3. $x = -7$; You used subtraction to solve the equation.

Think & Discuss (p. 131)

1. $x + 4 = 6$

$x = 2$

2. $x + 3 = 8$

$x = 5$

3. $x + 7 = -1$

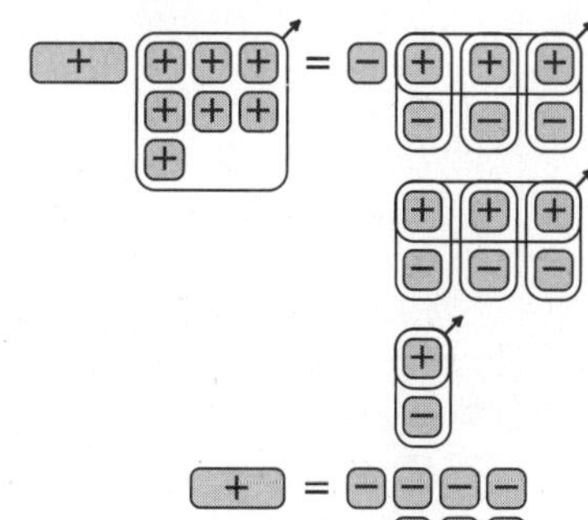

$x = -8$

4. $x + 2 = -7$

$x = -9$

5. $x - 3 = 2$

$x = 5$

6. $x - 1 = 5$

$x = 6$

Copyright © McDougal Littell Inc.
All rights reserved.

7. $x - 7 = 1$

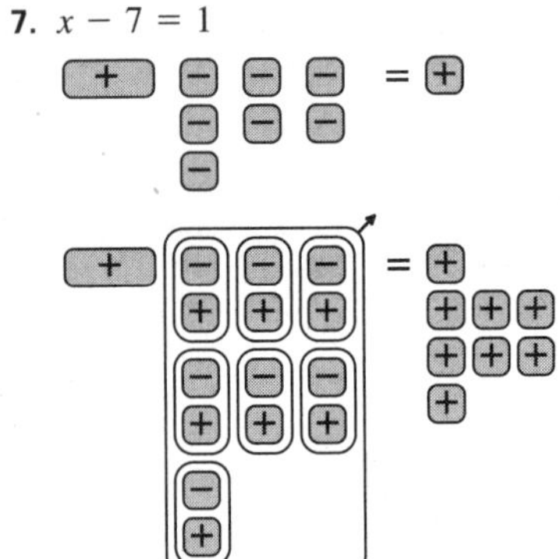

$x = 8$

8. $x - 2 = -6$

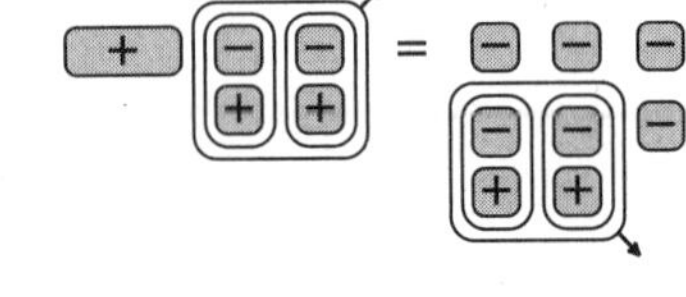

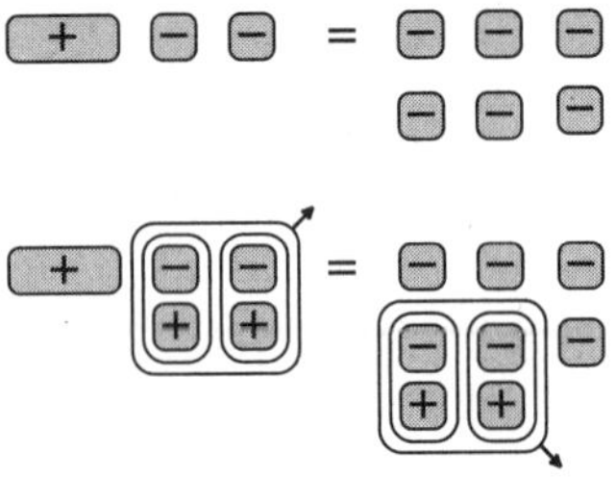

$x = -4$

9. $x - 4 = -3$

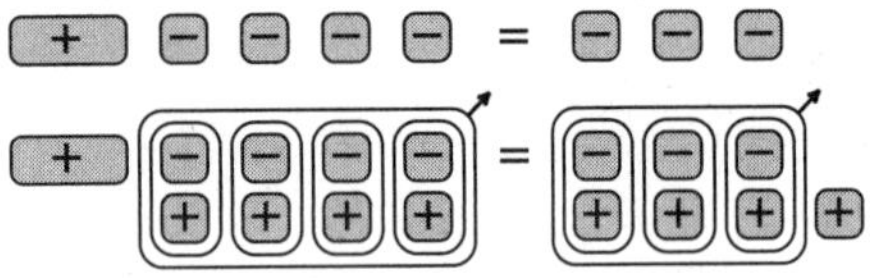

$x = 1$

10. No; the student must subtract 3 from both sides of the equation:

$x + 3 = -4$

$x + 3 - 3 = -4 - 3$

$x = -7$

Lesson 3.1

3.1 Checkpoint (p. 133)

1.

$-2 = x - 4$	Write original equation.
$-2 + 4 = x - 4 + 4$	Add 4 to each side to undo the subtraction.
$2 = x$	Simplify both sides.

Check:

$-2 = x - 4$	Write original equation.
$-2 \stackrel{?}{=} 2 - 4$	Substitute 2 for x.
$-2 = -2$	Solution is correct.

2.

$x - (-9) = 6$	Write original equation.
$x + 9 = 6$	Use subtraction rule to simplify.
$x + 9 - 9 = 6 - 9$	Subtract 9 from each side to undo addition.
$x = -3$	Simplify both sides.

Check:

$x - (-9) = 6$	Write original equation.
$-3 - (-9) \stackrel{?}{=} 6$	Substitute -3 for x.
$-3 + 9 = 6$	Use subtraction rule to simplify.
$6 = 6$	Solution is correct.

3.

$y + 5 = -1$	Write original equation.
$y + 5 - 5 = -1 - 5$	Subtract 5 from each side to undo addition.
$y = -6$	Simplify both sides.

Check:

$y + 5 = -1$	Write original equation.
$-6 + 5 \stackrel{?}{=} -1$	Substitute -6 for y.
$-1 = -1$	Solution is correct.

4.

$t - 7 = 30$	Write original equation.
$t - 7 + 7 = 30 + 7$	Add 7 to each side to undo subtraction.
$t = 37$	Simplify both sides.

Check:

$t - 7 = 30$	Write original equation.
$37 - 7 \stackrel{?}{=} 30$	Substitute 37 for t.
$30 = 30$	Solution is correct.

5.

$-8 = x + 14$	Write original equation.
$-8 - 14 = x + 14 - 14$	Subtract 14 from each side to undo addition.
$-22 = x$	Simplify both sides.

Check:

$-8 = x + 14$	Write original equation.
$-8 \stackrel{?}{=} -22 + 14$	Substitute -22 for x.
$-8 = -8$	Solution is correct.

6.

$3 = x - (-11)$	Write original equation.
$3 = x + 11$	Use subtraction rule to simplify.
$3 - 11 = x + 11 - 11$	Subtract 11 from each side to undo addition.
$-8 = x$	Simplify both sides.

Check:

$3 = x - (-11)$	Write original equation.
$3 = x + 11$	Use subtraction rule to simplify.
$3 \stackrel{?}{=} -8 + 11$	Substitute -8 for x.
$3 = 3$	Solution is correct.

7. Temperature on Jan. 24 = Temperature on Jan. 23 − Degrees Fallen

8. $-56 = 44 - T$

9.

$-56 = 44 - T$	Write original equation.
$-56 - 44 = 44 - T - 44$	Subtract 44 from each side.
$-100 = -T$	Simplify both sides.
$100 = T$	T is the opposite of -100.

$T = 100°$

Copyright © McDougal Littell Inc.
All rights reserved.

Chapter 3 *continued*

3.1 Guided Practice (p. 135)

1. equivalent

2. inverse

3. not linear; exponent of variable a is 2, not 1

4. linear; exponent of variable y is 1

5. linear; exponent of variable r is 1

6. not linear; exponent of variable x is 2, not 1

7.
$$\begin{aligned} r + 3 &= 2 \\ r + 3 - 3 &= 2 - 3 \\ r &= -1 \end{aligned}$$

8.
$$\begin{aligned} 9 &= x - 4 \\ 9 + 4 &= x - 4 + 4 \\ 13 &= x \end{aligned}$$

9.
$$\begin{aligned} 7 + c &= -10 \\ 7 + c - 7 &= -10 - 7 \\ c &= -17 \end{aligned}$$

10.
$$\begin{aligned} -1 &= t - 6 \\ -1 + 6 &= t - 6 + 6 \\ 5 &= t \end{aligned}$$

11.
$$\begin{aligned} 4 + x &= 8 \\ 4 + x - 4 &= 8 - 4 \\ x &= 4 \end{aligned}$$

12.
$$\begin{aligned} x + 4 - 3 &= 9 \\ x + 1 &= 9 \\ x + 1 - 1 &= 9 - 1 \\ x &= 8 \end{aligned}$$

13.
$$\begin{aligned} r - (-2) &= 5 \\ r + 2 &= 5 \\ r + 2 - 2 &= 5 - 2 \\ r &= 3 \end{aligned}$$

14.
$$\begin{aligned} -1 &= d - (-12) \\ -1 &= d + 12 \\ -1 - 12 &= d + 12 - 12 \\ -13 &= d \end{aligned}$$

15.
$$\begin{aligned} 6 - (-y) &= 3 \\ 6 + y &= 3 \\ 6 + y - 6 &= 3 - 6 \\ y &= -3 \end{aligned}$$

16. *Sample answer:* $M - 4.50 = 7.50$

17. *Sample answer:* addition

18.
$$\begin{aligned} M - 4.50 &= 7.50 \\ M - 4.50 + 4.50 &= 7.50 + 4.50 \\ M &= 12 \end{aligned}$$
You started with \$12 in your pocket.

3.1 Practice and Applications (pp. 135–137)

19. subtract 28

20. subtract 17

21. add 3

22. add 15

23. subtract -12

24. add -2

25.
$$\begin{aligned} x + 9 &= 18 \\ x + 9 - 9 &= 18 - 9 \\ x &= 9 \end{aligned}$$

26.
$$\begin{aligned} m - 20 &= 45 \\ m - 20 + 20 &= 45 + 20 \\ m &= 65 \end{aligned}$$

27.
$$\begin{aligned} x - 8 &= -13 \\ x - 8 + 8 &= -13 + 8 \\ x &= -5 \end{aligned}$$

28.
$$\begin{aligned} 4 + x &= 7 \\ 4 + x - 4 &= 7 - 4 \\ x &= 3 \end{aligned}$$

29.
$$\begin{aligned} x + 5 &= 15 \\ x + 5 - 5 &= 15 - 5 \\ x &= 10 \end{aligned}$$

30.
$$\begin{aligned} 11 &= r - 4 \\ 11 + 4 &= r - 4 + 4 \\ 15 &= r \end{aligned}$$

31.
$$\begin{aligned} t - 2 &= 6 \\ t - 2 + 2 &= 6 + 2 \\ t &= 8 \end{aligned}$$

32.
$$\begin{aligned} -9 &= 2 + y \\ -9 - 2 &= 2 + y - 2 \\ -11 &= y \end{aligned}$$

33.
$$\begin{aligned} n - 5 &= -9 \\ n - 5 + 5 &= -9 + 5 \\ n &= -4 \end{aligned}$$

34.
$$\begin{aligned} y + 12 &= -12 \\ y + 12 - 12 &= -12 - 12 \\ y &= -24 \end{aligned}$$

35.
$$\begin{aligned} y - 12 &= 12 \\ y - 12 + 12 &= 12 + 12 \\ y &= 24 \end{aligned}$$

36.
$$\begin{aligned} a - 3 &= -2 \\ a - 3 + 3 &= -2 + 3 \\ a &= 1 \end{aligned}$$

37.
$$\begin{aligned} t - 5 &= -20 \\ t - 5 + 5 &= -20 + 5 \\ t &= -15 \end{aligned}$$

38.
$$\begin{aligned} x + 7 &= -14 \\ x + 7 - 7 &= -14 - 7 \\ x &= -21 \end{aligned}$$

39.
$$\begin{aligned} 34 + x &= 10 \\ 34 + x - 34 &= 10 - 34 \\ x &= -24 \end{aligned}$$

Copyright © McDougal Littell Inc.
All rights reserved.

40. $\frac{1}{3} + x = \frac{2}{3}$

$\frac{1}{3} + x - \frac{1}{3} = \frac{2}{3} - \frac{1}{3}$

$x = \frac{1}{3}$

41. $\frac{2}{5} = a - \frac{1}{5}$

$\frac{2}{5} + \frac{1}{5} = a - \frac{1}{5} + \frac{1}{5}$

$\frac{3}{5} = a$

42. $r + \frac{3}{4} = \frac{1}{4}$

$r + \frac{3}{4} - \frac{3}{4} = \frac{1}{4} - \frac{3}{4}$

$r = -\frac{2}{4} = -\frac{1}{2}$

43. $t - (-4) = 4$

$t + 4 = 4$

$t + 4 - 4 = 4 - 4$

$t = 0$

44. $6 = y - (-11)$

$6 = y + 11$

$6 - 11 = y + 11 - 11$

$-5 = y$

45. $x - (-8) = 13$

$x + 8 = 13$

$x + 8 - 8 = 13 - 8$

$x = 5$

46. $r - (-7) = -16$

$r + 7 = -16$

$r + 7 - 7 = -16 - 7$

$r = -23$

47. $19 - (-y) = 25$

$19 + y = 25$

$19 + y - 19 = 25 - 19$

$y = 6$

48. $2 - (-b) = -6$

$2 + b = -6$

$2 + b - 2 = -6 - 2$

$b = -8$

49. $x + 5 - 2 = 6$

$x + 3 = 6$

$x + 3 - 3 = 6 - 3$

$x = 3$

50. $12 - 5 = n + 7$

$7 = n + 7$

$7 - 7 = n + 7 - 7$

$0 = n$

51. $-3 = a + (-4)$

$-3 = a - 4$

$-3 + 4 = a - 4 + 4$

$1 = a$

52. $3 + x + 4 = 12$

$x + 7 = 12$

$x + 7 - 7 = 12 - 7$

$x = 5$ ft

53. $x + 15 + 8 = 43$

$x + 23 = 43$

$x + 23 - 23 = 43 - 23$

$x = 20$ cm

54. C;

$15 + 7 = x$

$22 = x$; 22 CDs

55. B;

$15 - x = 7$

$15 - x - 15 = 7 - 15$

$-x = -8$

$x = 8$; 8 members

56. A;

$x + 15 = 7$

$x + 15 - 15 = 7 - 15$

$x = -8$; 8° below zero

57. $43{,}368 + x = 49{,}831$

$43{,}368 + x - 43{,}368 = 49{,}831 - 43{,}368$

$x = 6463$ seats

58. $x + 418 = 4218$

$x + 418 - 418 = 4218 - 418$

$x = 3800$ acres

59. $4218 + 3800 + 2764 - 248 = x$

$10{,}534 = x$

10,534 acres

60. A;

$53 - x = 47$

$53 - x - 53 = 47 - 53$

$-x = -6$

$x = 6$

$6

61. $-7 = x - (-2)$ Original equation

$-7 = x + 2$ Simplify with subtraction rule.

$-9 = x$ Subtract 2 from both sides.

62. $x + 4 - 6 + 1 - 8 - 3 + 1 - 6 = 0$

$x + 4 + (-6) + 1 + (-8) + (-3) + 1 + (-6) = 0$

$x - 17 = 0$

$x - 17 + 17 = 0 + 17$

$x = 17$

17th floor

3.1 Standardized Test Practice (p. 137)

63. A; $x + 7 = 24$

64. G; $x^2 = 10$ is not linear since the exponent of the variable x is 2, not 1.

Copyright © McDougal Littell Inc.
All rights reserved.

3.1 Mixed Review (p. 137)

65. $5x = 160$

66. $\frac{t}{6} = 48$

67. $36 - k = 15$

68. $\frac{y}{3} = 12$

69. $4(x + 2) = 4(x) + 4(2) = 4x + 8$

70. $7(3 - 2y) = 7(3) - 7(2y) = 21 - 14y$

71. $-5(y + 4) = -5(y) + (-5)4 = -5y - 20$

72. $(3x + 8)(-2) = 3x(-2) + 8(-2) = -6x - 16$

73. $-2(x - 6) = -2(x) - (-2)(6) = -2x + 12$

74. $3(8 - 7x) = 3(8) - 3(7x) = 24 - 21x$

3.1 Maintaining Skills (p.137)

75. $\frac{2}{3} \cdot \frac{6}{7} = \frac{4}{7}$

76. $\frac{3}{8} \cdot \frac{4}{9} = \frac{1}{6}$

77. $\frac{1}{10} \cdot \frac{15}{16} = \frac{3}{32}$

78. $\frac{7}{8} \cdot \frac{1}{2} = \frac{7}{16}$

79. $\frac{3}{4} \cdot \frac{16}{21} = \frac{4}{7}$

80. $\frac{6}{7} \cdot \frac{3}{5} = \frac{18}{35}$

81. $\frac{7}{22} \cdot \frac{22}{7} = 1$

82. $\frac{3}{16} \cdot \frac{4}{4} = \frac{3}{16}$

Lesson 3.2

3.2 Checkpoint (pp. 139–140)

1. $60 = 5x$ Write original equation.
$\frac{60}{5} = \frac{5x}{5}$ Divide each side by 5 to undo multiplication.
$12 = x$ Simplify.
Check:
$60 = 5x$ Write original equation.
$60 \stackrel{?}{=} 5(12)$ Substitute 12 for x.
$60 = 60$ Solution is correct.

2. $\frac{r}{3} = 11$ Write original equation.
$3\left(\frac{r}{3}\right) = 3(11)$ Multiply each side by 3 to undo the division.
$r = 33$ Simplify.
Check:
$\frac{r}{3} = 11$ Write original equation.
$\frac{33}{3} \stackrel{?}{=} 11$ Substitute 33 for r.
$11 = 11$ Solution is correct.

3. $\frac{n}{4} = -2$ Write original equation.
$4\left(\frac{n}{4}\right) = 4(-2)$ Multiply each side by 4 to undo division.
$n = -8$ Simplify.
Check:
$\frac{n}{4} = -2$ Write original equation.
$\frac{(-8)}{4} \stackrel{?}{=} -2$ Substitute -8 for n.
$-2 = -2$ Solution is correct.

4. $-3x = -9$ Write original equation.
$\frac{-3x}{-3} = \frac{-9}{-3}$ Divide by -3 to undo division.
$x = 3$ Simplify.
Check:
$-3x = -9$ Write original equation.
$-3(3) \stackrel{?}{=} -9$ Substitute 3 for x.
$-9 - 9$ Solution is correct.

5. $6 = \frac{3}{4}x$ Write original equation.
$\frac{4}{3}(6) = \frac{4}{3}\left(\frac{3}{4}x\right)$ Multiply each side by the reciprocal, $\frac{4}{3}$.
$8 = x$ Simplify.
Check:
$6 = \frac{3}{4}x$ Write original equation.
$6 \stackrel{?}{=} \frac{3}{4}(8)$ Substitute 8 for x.
$6 = 6$ Solution is correct.

6. $12 = -\frac{4}{5}y$ Multiply each side by the reciprocal, $-\frac{5}{4}$.
$-\frac{5}{4}(12) = -\frac{5}{4}\left(-\frac{4}{5}y\right)$
$-15 = y$ Simplify.
Check:
$12 = -\frac{4}{5}y$ Write original equation.
$12 \stackrel{?}{=} -\frac{4}{5}(-15)$ Substitute -15 for y.
$12 = 12$ Solution is correct.

Copyright © McDougal Littell Inc.
All rights reserved.

7. $\frac{3}{5}x = 24$ Write original equation.

$\frac{5}{3}\left(\frac{3}{5}x\right) = \frac{5}{3}(24)$ Multiply each side by the reciprocal, $\frac{5}{3}$.

$x = 40$ Simplify.

Check:

$\frac{3}{5}x = 24$ Write original equation.

Substitute 40 for x.

$\frac{3}{5}(40) \stackrel{?}{=} 24$ Solution is correct.

$24 = 24$

8. $-6 = \frac{2}{7}m$ Write original equation.

$\frac{7}{2}(-6) = \frac{7}{2}\left(\frac{2}{7}\right)m$ Multiply each side by the reciprocal, $\frac{7}{2}$.

$-21 = m$ Simplify.

Check:

$-6 = \frac{2}{7}m$ Write original equation.

$-6 \stackrel{?}{=} \frac{2}{7}(-21)$ Substitute -21 for m.

$-6 = -6$ Solution is correct.

9. $8 \cdot y = 129{,}600$

10. $8 \cdot y = 129{,}600$ Write original equation.

$\frac{8y}{8} = \frac{129{,}600}{8}$ Division property of equality.

$y = 16{,}200$ hours

3.2 Guided Practice (p. 141)

1. addition and subtraction, multiplication and division

2. C; If $a = b$, then $a + c = b + c$.

3. A; If $a = b$, then $ca = cb$.

4. D; If $a = b$ and $c \neq 0$, then $\frac{a}{c} = \frac{b}{c}$.

5. B; If $a = b$, then $a - c = b - c$.

6. $3x = 18$

$\frac{3x}{3} = \frac{18}{3}$

$x = 6$

Check:

$3x = 18$

$3(6) \stackrel{?}{=} 18$

$18 = 18$

7. $19m = -19$

$\frac{19m}{19} = -\frac{19}{19}$

$m = -1$

Check:

$19m = -19$

$19(-1) \stackrel{?}{=} -19$

$-19 = -19$

8. $-5x = 3$

$\frac{-5x}{-5} = -\frac{3}{5}$

$x = -\frac{3}{5}$

Check:

$-5x = 3$

$-5\left(-\frac{3}{5}\right) \stackrel{?}{=} 3$

$3 = 3$

9. $\frac{y}{4} = 8$

$4\left(\frac{y}{4}\right) = 4(8)$

$y = 32$

Check:

$\frac{y}{4} = 8$

$\frac{(32)}{4} \stackrel{?}{=} 8$

$8 = 8$

10. $\frac{r}{-5} = 20$

$-5\left(\frac{r}{-5}\right) = -5(20)$

$r = -100$

Check:

$\frac{r}{-5} = 20$

$\frac{(-100)}{-5} \stackrel{?}{=} 20$

$20 = 20$

11. $\frac{b}{-7} = -4$

$-7\left(\frac{b}{-7}\right) = -7(-4)$

$b = 28$

Check:

$\frac{b}{-7} = -4$

$\frac{(28)}{-7} \stackrel{?}{=} -4$

$-4 = -4$

12. $\frac{3}{8}t = 6$

$\frac{8}{3}\left(\frac{3}{8}t\right) = \frac{8}{3}(6)$

$t = 16$

Check:

$\frac{3}{8}t = 6$

$\frac{3}{8}(16) \stackrel{?}{=} 6$

$6 = 6$

Copyright © McDougal Littell Inc.
All rights reserved.

13. $4 = -\frac{2}{3}x$

$-\frac{3}{2}(4) = -\frac{3}{2}\left(-\frac{2}{3}x\right)$

$-6 = x$

Check:

$4 = -\frac{2}{3}x$

$4 = -\frac{2}{3}(-6)$

$4 = 4$

14. $\frac{4}{5}t = 0$

$\frac{5}{4}\left(\frac{4}{5}t\right) = \frac{5}{4}(0)$

$t = 0$

Check:

$\frac{4}{5}t = 0$

$\frac{4}{5}(0) = 0$

$0 = 0$

15. $630 = r(10.5)$

$\frac{630}{10.5} = \frac{r(10.5)}{10.5}$

$60 = r$

60 mi/h

3.2 Practice and Applications (pp. 141–143)

16. multiply by 6

17. divide by 5

18. divide by $\frac{2}{3}$ $\left(\text{or multiply by } \frac{3}{2}\right)$

19. divide by -4

20. multiply by -3

21. multiply by 7

22. $3r = 21$

$\frac{3r}{3} = \frac{21}{3}$

$r = 7$

23. $7y = -56$

$\frac{7y}{7} = -\frac{56}{7}$

$y = -8$

24. $18 = -2a$

$\frac{18}{-2} = \frac{-2a}{-2}$

$-9 = a$

25. $-4n = 24$

$\frac{-4n}{-4} = \frac{24}{-4}$

$n = -6$

26. $8x = 3$

$\frac{8x}{8} = \frac{3}{8}$

$x = \frac{3}{8}$

27. $10x = 110$

$\frac{10x}{10} = \frac{110}{10}$

$x = 11$

28. $30b = 5$

$\frac{30b}{30} = \frac{5}{30}$

$b = \frac{1}{6}$

29. $-10x = -9$

$\frac{-10x}{-10} = \frac{-9}{-10}$

$x = \frac{9}{10}$

30. $288 = 16u$

$\frac{288}{16} = \frac{16u}{16}$

$18 = u$

31. $\frac{x}{2} = -5$

$2\left(\frac{x}{2}\right) = 2(-5)$

$x = -10$

32. $\frac{t}{4} = -4$

$4\left(\frac{t}{4}\right) = 4(-4)$

$t = -16$

33. $6 = \frac{d}{5}$

$5(6) = 5\left(\frac{d}{5}\right)$

$30 = d$

34. $\frac{m}{-4} = -\frac{3}{4}$

$-4\left(\frac{m}{-4}\right) = -4\left(-\frac{3}{4}\right)$

$m = 3$

35. $\frac{y}{7} = 12$

$7\left(\frac{y}{7}\right) = 7(12)$

$y = 84$

36. $-\frac{h}{3} = -16$

$-3\left(-\frac{h}{3}\right) = -3(-16)$

$h = 48$

Copyright © McDougal Littell Inc.
All rights reserved.

37. $\frac{3}{4}k = 1$

$\frac{4}{3}\left(\frac{3}{4}k\right) = \frac{4}{3}(1)$

$k = \frac{4}{3}$

38. $-\frac{2}{5}y = 4$

$-\frac{5}{2}\left(-\frac{2}{5}y\right) = -\frac{5}{2}(4)$

$y = -10$

39. $0 = \frac{7}{8}x$

$\frac{8}{7}(0) = \frac{8}{7}\left(\frac{7}{8}x\right)$

$0 = x$

40. $-\frac{1}{3}y = 6$

$-3\left(-\frac{1}{3}y\right) = -3(6)$

$y = -18$

41. $10 = \frac{5}{6}x$

$\frac{6}{5}(10) = \frac{6}{5}\left(\frac{5}{6}x\right)$

$12 = x$

42. $\frac{5}{8}m = -20$

$\frac{8}{5}\left(\frac{5}{8}m\right) = \frac{8}{5}(-20)$

$m = -32$

43. $12 = \frac{2}{3}x$

$\frac{3}{2}(12) = \frac{3}{2}\left(\frac{2}{3}x\right)$

$18 = x$

44. $\frac{3}{7}x = 6$

$\frac{7}{3}\left(\frac{3}{7}x\right) = \frac{7}{3}(6)$

$x = 14$

45. $-\frac{4}{5}x = 36$

$-\frac{5}{4}\left(-\frac{4}{5}x\right) = -\frac{5}{4}(36)$

$x = -45$

46. Multiply both sides of the equation by $\frac{5}{2}$.

$\frac{2}{5}x = 10$

$\frac{5}{2}\left(\frac{2}{5}x\right) = \frac{5}{2}(10)$

$x = 25$

47. Multiply by $-\frac{4}{3}$.

$-\frac{3}{4}x = 6$

$-\frac{4}{3}\left(-\frac{3}{4}x\right) = -\frac{4}{3}(6)$

$x = -8$

48. $\frac{x}{12} = 45$

$12\left(\frac{x}{12}\right) = 12(45)$

$x = 540$ peanuts

49. $\frac{3}{8} \cdot p = 3.30$

$\frac{8}{3}\left(\frac{3}{8} \cdot p\right) = \frac{8}{3}(3.30)$

$p = 8.80$; \$8.80

50. A;

$\frac{x}{4} = 37$

$4\left(\frac{x}{4}\right) = 4(37)$

$x = 148$ pounds

51. $52x = 676$

$\frac{52x}{52} = \frac{676}{52}$

$x = 13$ pieces per week

52. $\frac{t}{5} = 9$

$5\left(\frac{t}{5}\right) = 5(9)$

$t = 45$; 45 sec

53. $3x + 2x + 3x + 2x = 220$

$10x = 220$

$\frac{10x}{10} = \frac{220}{10}$

$x = 22$

width: $3(x) = 3(22) = 66$ ft

length: $2(x) = 2(22) = 44$ ft

3.2 Standardized Test Practice (p. 143)

54. B; Divide by -8

55. F;

$-\frac{5}{7}x = -2$

$-\frac{7}{5}\left(-\frac{5}{7}x\right) = -\frac{7}{5}(-2)$

$x = \frac{14}{5}$

Copyright © McDougal Littell Inc.
All rights reserved.

56. *D*

I:

$$\frac{3}{5}x = 3$$
$$\frac{5}{3}\left(\frac{3}{5}x\right) = \frac{5}{3}(3)$$
$$x = 5$$

II:

$$\frac{x}{5} = 2$$
$$5\left(\frac{x}{5}\right) = 5(2)$$
$$x = 10$$

III:

$$2x = 10$$
$$\frac{2x}{2} = \frac{10}{2}$$
$$x = 5$$

IV:

$$-x = -5$$
$$x = 5$$

3.2 Mixed Review (p. 143)

57. $15 - 8x + 12 = 15 + 12 - 8x$
$= 27 - 8x$

58. $4y - 9 + 3y = 4y + 3y - 9$
$= (4 + 3)y - 9$
$= 7y - 9$

59. $5x + 6 - 7x = 5x + (-7x) + 6$
$= [5 + (-7)]x + 6$
$= -2x + 6$

60. $-2(x + 8) + 36 = -2(x) + (-2)(8) + 36$
$= -2x + (-16) + 36$
$= -2x + 20$

61. $5(y + 3) + 7y = 5(y) + 5(3) + 7y$
$= 5y + 15 + 7y$
$= 5y + 7y + 15$
$= (5 + 7)y + 15$
$= 12y + 15$

62. $3(y - 10) - 5y = 3(y) - 3(10) - 5y$
$= 3y + (-30) + (-5y)$
$= 3y + (-5y) + (-30)$
$= [3 + (-5)]y - 30$
$= -2y - 30$

63. $4 + y = 12$
$4 + y - 4 = 12 - 4$
$y = 8$

64. $t - 2 = 1$
$t - 2 + 2 = 1 + 2$
$t = 3$

65. $-14 = r + 5$
$-14 - 5 = r + 5 - 5$
$-19 = r$

66. $-6 + x = -15$
$-6 + x + 6 = -15 + 6$
$x = -9$

67. $x - (-6) = 8$
$x + 6 = 8$
$x + 6 - 6 = 8 - 6$
$x = 2$

68. $a - (-9) = -2$
$a + 9 = -2$
$a + 9 - 9 = -2 - 9$
$a = -11$

69. A;
$x + 6 = 24$
$x + 6 - 6 = 24 - 6$
$x = 18$

3.2 Maintaining Skills (p. 143)

70. $5 = 5$
$35 = 5 \cdot 7$
$\text{GCF} = 5$

71. $30 = 2 \cdot 3 \cdot 5$
$40 = 2^3 \cdot 5$
$\text{GCF} = 2 \cdot 5 = 10$

72. $12 = 2^2 \cdot 3$
$22 = 2 \cdot 11$
$\text{GCF} = 2$

73. $10 = 2 \cdot 5$
$25 = 5 \cdot 5$
$\text{GCF} = 5$

74. $17 = 17$
$51 = 3 \cdot 17$
$\text{GCF} = 17$

75. $27 = 3^3$
$36 = 2^2 \cdot 3^2$
$\text{GCF} = 3^2 = 9$

76. $14 = 2 \cdot 7$
$42 = 2 \cdot 3 \cdot 7$
$\text{GCF} = 2 \cdot 7 = 14$

77. $9 = 3^2$
$24 = 2^3 \cdot 3$
$\text{GCF} = 3$

78. $21 = 3 \cdot 7$
$49 = 7^2$
$\text{GCF} = 7$

Copyright © McDougal Littell Inc.
All rights reserved.

Lesson 3.3

3.3 Checkpoint (pp. 144–146)

1.

$6x - 15 = 9$	Write original equation.
$6x - 15 + 15 = 9 + 15$	Add 15 to each side to undo subtraction.
$6x = 24$	Simplify.
$\frac{6x}{6} = \frac{24}{6}$	Divide each side by 6 to undo multiplication.
$x = 4$	Simplify.

Check:

$6x - 15 = 9$	Write original equation.
$6(4) - 15 \stackrel{?}{=} 9$	Substitute 4 for x.
$24 - 15 \stackrel{?}{=} 9$	Multiply.
$9 = 9$	Solution is correct.

2.

$7x - 4 = -11$	Write original equation.
$7x - 4 + 4 = -11 + 4$	Add 4 to each side to undo subtraction.
$7x = -7$	Simplify.
$\frac{7x}{7} = \frac{-7}{7}$	Divide each side by 7 to undo multiplication.
$x = -1$	Simplify.

Check:

$7x - 4 = -11$	Write original equation.
$7(-1) - 4 = -11$	Substitute -1 for x.
$-7 - 4 = -11$	Multiply.
$-11 = -11$	Solution is correct.

3.

$2y + 5 = 1$	Write original equation.
$2y + 5 - 5 = 1 - 5$	Subtract 5 from each side to undo addition.
$2y = -4$	Simplify.
$\frac{2y}{2} = \frac{-4}{2}$	Divide each side by 2 to undo multiplication.
$y = -2$	Simplify.

Check:

$2y + 5 = 1$	Write original equation.
$2y + 5 = 1$	Substitute -2 for x.
$2(-2) + 5 \stackrel{?}{=} 1$	Multiply.
$-4 + 5 \stackrel{?}{=} 1$	Solution is correct.
$1 = 1$	

4.

$$174 = 24 + 30d$$
$$174 - 24 = 24 + 30d - 24$$
$$150 = 30d$$
$$\frac{150}{30} = \frac{30d}{30}$$
$5 = d$; 5 km

5.

$$6(x + 2) = 15$$
$$6x + 12 = 15$$
$$6x + 12 - 12 = 15 - 12$$
$$6x = 3$$
$$\frac{6x}{6} = \frac{3}{6}$$
$$x = \frac{1}{2}$$

Check:

$$6(x + 2) = 15$$
$$6\left(\frac{1}{2} + 2\right) \stackrel{?}{=} 15$$
$$6\left(\frac{5}{2}\right) \stackrel{?}{=} 15$$
$$15 = 15$$

6.

$$8 - 4(x + 1) = 8$$
$$8 - 4(x + 1) - 8 = 8 - 8$$
$$-4(x + 1) = 0$$
$$\frac{-4(x + 1)}{-4} = \frac{0}{-4}$$
$$x + 1 = 0$$
$$x + 1 - 1 = 0 - 1$$
$$x = -1$$

Check:

$$8 - 4(x + 1) = 8$$
$$8 - 4(-1 + 1) \stackrel{?}{=} 8$$
$$8 - 4(0) \stackrel{?}{=} 8$$
$$8 - 0 \stackrel{?}{=} 8$$
$$8 = 8$$

7.

$$3m + 2(m - 5) = 10$$
$$3m + 2(m) - 2(5) = 10$$
$$3m + 2m - 10 = 10$$
$$(3 + 2)m - 10 = 10$$
$$5m - 10 = 10$$
$$5m - 10 + 10 = 10 + 10$$
$$5m = 20$$
$$\frac{5m}{5} = \frac{20}{5}$$
$$m = 4$$

Check:

$$3m + 2(m - 5) = 10$$
$$3(4) + 2(4 - 5) \stackrel{?}{=} 10$$
$$3(4) + 2(-1) \stackrel{?}{=} 10$$
$$12 + (-2) \stackrel{?}{=} 10$$
$$10 = 10$$

Copyright © McDougal Littell Inc.
All rights reserved.

8. $6 = \frac{3}{4}(x + 7)$ Write original equation.

$\frac{4}{3}(6) = \frac{4}{3}\left(\frac{3}{4}\right)(x + 7)$ Multiply each side by $\frac{4}{3}$, the reciprocal of $\frac{3}{4}$.

$8 = x + 7$ Simplify.

$8 - 7 = x + 7 - 7$ Subtract 7 from each side.

$1 = x$ Simplify.

Check:

$6 = \frac{3}{4}(x + 7)$ Write original equation.

$6 = \frac{3}{4}(1 + 7)$ Substitute 1 for x.

$6 = \frac{3}{4}(8)$ Evaluate the operation in the parentheses.

$6 = 6$ Solution is correct.

9. $\frac{4}{5}(x - 2) = 8$ Write original equation.

$\frac{5}{4}\left(\frac{4}{5}\right)(x - 2) = \frac{5}{4}(8)$ Multiply each side by $\frac{5}{4}$, the reciprocal of $\frac{4}{5}$.

$x - 2 = 10$ Simplify.

$x - 2 + 2 = 10 + 2$ Add 2 to each side.

$x = 12$ Simplify.

Check:

$\frac{4}{5}(x - 2) = 8$ Write original equation.

$\frac{4}{5}(12 - 2) \stackrel{?}{=} 8$ Substitute 12 for x.

$\frac{4}{5}(10) \stackrel{?}{=} 8$ Evaluate the operation in the parentheses.

$8 = 8$ Solution is correct.

10. $-\frac{3}{5}(x + 1) = 9$ Write original equation.

$-\frac{5}{3}\left(-\frac{3}{5}\right)(x + 1) = -\frac{5}{3}(9)$ Multiply each side by $-\frac{5}{3}$, the reciprocal.

$x + 1 = -15$ Simplify.

$x + 1 - 1 = -15 - 1$ Subtract 1 from each side.

$x = -16$ Simplify.

Check:

$-\frac{3}{5}(x + 1) = 9$ Write original equation.

$-\frac{3}{5}(-16 + 1) \stackrel{?}{=} 9$ Substitute -16 for x.

$-\frac{3}{5}(-15) \stackrel{?}{=} 9$ Evaluate the operation in the parentheses.

$9 = 9$ Solution is correct.

3.3 Guided Practice (p. 146)

1. like terms: $5x$ and x

2. like terms: $8x$ and $-4x$

3. like terms: $2t$ and $-6t$, t^2 and $6t^2$

4. Distribute:

$$\begin{aligned} 4x + 2(x + 1) &= 4x + 2(x) + 2(1) \\ &= 4x + 2x + 2 \end{aligned}$$

like terms: $4x$ and $2x$

5. Distribute:

$$\begin{aligned} 3 - m + 2(m - 2) &= 3 - m + 2(m) - 2(2) \\ &= 3 + (-m) + 2m + (-4) \end{aligned}$$

like terms: $-m$ and $2m$, 3 and -4

6. Distribute:

$$\begin{aligned} 8 - 3(x + 4) + 3x &= 8 + (-3)x + (-3)(4) + 3x \\ &= 8 + (-3x) + (-12) + 3x \end{aligned}$$

like terms: $-3x$ and $3x$, 8 and -12

7.
$$\begin{aligned} 4x + 3 &= 11 \\ 4x + 3 - 3 &= 11 - 3 \\ 4x &= 8 \\ \frac{4x}{4} &= \frac{8}{4} \\ x &= 2 \end{aligned}$$

8.
$$\begin{aligned} 7y - 3 &= 25 \\ 7y - 3 + 3 &= 25 + 3 \\ 7y &= 28 \\ \frac{7y}{7} &= \frac{28}{7} \\ y &= 4 \end{aligned}$$

9.
$$\begin{aligned} 2x - 9 &= -11 \\ 2x - 9 + 9 &= -11 + 9 \\ 2x &= -2 \\ \frac{2x}{2} &= \frac{-2}{2} \\ x &= -1 \end{aligned}$$

10.
$$\begin{aligned} 3r - r + 15 &= 41 \\ (3 - 1)r + 15 &= 41 \\ 2r + 15 &= 41 \\ 2r + 15 - 15 &= 41 - 15 \\ 2r &= 26 \\ \frac{2r}{2} &= \frac{26}{2} \\ r &= 13 \end{aligned}$$

11.
$$\begin{aligned} 13 &= 12t - 5 - 3t \\ 13 &= 12t - 3t - 5 \\ 13 &= (12 - 3)t - 5 \\ 13 &= 9t - 5 \\ 13 + 5 &= 9t - 5 + 5 \\ 18 &= 9t \\ \frac{18}{9} &= \frac{9t}{9} \\ 2 &= t \end{aligned}$$

Copyright © McDougal Littell Inc.
All rights reserved.

12. $$\begin{aligned} -8 + 5a - 2 &= 20 \\ 5a - 10 &= 20 \\ 5a - 10 + 10 &= 20 + 10 \\ 5a &= 30 \\ \frac{5a}{5} &= \frac{30}{5} \\ a &= 6 \end{aligned}$$

13. $$\begin{aligned} 5(d - 7) &= 90 \\ \frac{5(d - 7)}{5} &= \frac{90}{5} \\ d - 7 &= 18 \\ d - 7 + 7 &= 18 + 7 \\ d &= 25 \end{aligned}$$

14. $$\begin{aligned} 3(8 + b) &= 27 \\ \frac{3(8 + b)}{3} &= \frac{27}{3} \\ 8 + b &= 9 \\ 8 + b - 8 &= 9 - 8 \\ b &= 1 \end{aligned}$$

15. $$\begin{aligned} -4(x + 6) &= 12 \\ \frac{-4(x + 6)}{-4} &= \frac{12}{-4} \\ x + 6 &= -3 \\ x + 6 - 6 &= -3 - 6 \\ x &= -9 \end{aligned}$$

16. $$\begin{aligned} \frac{3}{4}(x + 6) &= 12 \\ \frac{4}{3}\left(\frac{3}{4}\right)(x + 6) &= \frac{4}{3}(12) \\ x + 6 &= 16 \\ x + 6 - 6 &= 16 - 6 \\ x &= 10 \end{aligned}$$

17. $$\begin{aligned} \frac{1}{3}(x - 1) &= 6 \\ 3\left(\frac{1}{3}\right)(x - 1) &= 3(6) \\ x - 1 &= 18 \\ x - 1 + 1 &= 18 + 1 \\ x &= 19 \end{aligned}$$

18. $$\begin{aligned} \frac{2}{3}(x + 8) &= 8 \\ \frac{3}{2}\left(\frac{2}{3}\right)(x + 8) &= \frac{3}{2}(8) \\ x + 8 &= 12 \\ x + 8 - 8 &= 12 - 8 \\ x &= 4 \end{aligned}$$

3.3 Practice and Applications (pp. 147–149)

19. $$\begin{aligned} 48 &= 11n + 26 \\ 48 - 26 &= 11n + 26 - 26 \\ 22 &= 11n \\ \frac{22}{11} &= \frac{11n}{11} \\ 2 &= n \end{aligned}$$

20. $$\begin{aligned} 2x + 7 &= 15 \\ 2x + 7 - 7 &= 15 - 7 \\ 2x &= 8 \\ \frac{2x}{2} &= \frac{8}{2} \\ x &= 4 \end{aligned}$$

21. $$\begin{aligned} 5p - 16 &= 54 \\ 5p - 16 + 16 &= 54 + 16 \\ 5p &= 70 \\ \frac{5p}{5} &= \frac{70}{5} \\ p &= 14 \end{aligned}$$

22. $$\begin{aligned} 3g - 1 &= 8 \\ 3g - 1 + 1 &= 8 + 1 \\ 3g &= 9 \\ \frac{3g}{3} &= \frac{9}{3} \\ g &= 3 \end{aligned}$$

23. $$\begin{aligned} 3y + 5 &= 11 \\ 3y + 5 - 5 &= 11 - 5 \\ 3y &= 6 \\ \frac{3y}{3} &= \frac{6}{3} \\ y &= 2 \end{aligned}$$

24. $$\begin{aligned} 7t - 9 &= 19 \\ 7t - 9 + 9 &= 19 + 9 \\ 7t &= 28 \\ \frac{7t}{7} &= \frac{28}{7} \\ t &= 4 \end{aligned}$$

25. $$\begin{aligned} 4a + 9a &= 39 \\ (4 + 9)a &= 39 \\ 13a &= 39 \\ \frac{13a}{13} &= \frac{39}{13} \\ a &= 3 \end{aligned}$$

26. $$\begin{aligned} 5w + 2w &= 77 \\ (5 + 2)w &= 77 \\ 7w &= 77 \\ \frac{7w}{7} &= \frac{77}{7} \\ w &= 11 \end{aligned}$$

27. $$\begin{aligned} 8n - 3n - 4 &= 21 \\ (8 - 3)n - 4 &= 21 \\ 5n - 4 &= 21 \\ 5n - 4 + 4 &= 21 + 4 \\ 5n &= 25 \\ \frac{5n}{5} &= \frac{25}{5} \\ n &= 5 \end{aligned}$$

Copyright © McDougal Littell Inc.
All rights reserved.

28. $$\begin{aligned} 22x - 12x &= 60 \\ (22 - 12)x &= 60 \\ 10x &= 60 \\ \frac{10x}{10} &= \frac{60}{10} \\ x &= 6 \end{aligned}$$

29. $$\begin{aligned} 4c + (-7c) &= 9 \\ [4 + (-7)]c &= 9 \\ -3c &= 9 \\ \frac{-3c}{-3} &= \frac{9}{-3} \\ c &= -3 \end{aligned}$$

30. $$\begin{aligned} 9t - 15t &= -18 \\ (9 - 15)t &= -18 \\ -6t &= -18 \\ \frac{-6t}{-6} &= \frac{-18}{-6} \\ t &= 3 \end{aligned}$$

31. $$\begin{aligned} 5(6 + j) &= 45 \\ 5(6) + 5(j) &= 45 \\ 30 + 5j &= 45 \\ 30 + 5j - 30 &= 45 - 30 \\ 5j &= 15 \\ \frac{5j}{5} &= \frac{15}{5} \\ j &= 3 \end{aligned}$$

32. $$\begin{aligned} 3(k - 2) &= 18 \\ 3(k) - 3(2) &= 18 \\ 3k - 6 &= 18 \\ 3k - 6 + 6 &= 18 + 6 \\ 3k &= 24 \\ \frac{3k}{3} &= \frac{24}{3} \\ k &= 8 \end{aligned}$$

33. $$\begin{aligned} -2(4 - m) &= 10 \\ -2(4) - (-2)m &= 10 \\ -8 + 2m &= 10 \\ -8 + 2m + 8 &= 10 + 8 \\ 2m &= 18 \\ \frac{2m}{2} &= \frac{18}{2} \\ m &= 9 \end{aligned}$$

34. $$\begin{aligned} x + 4(x + 3) &= 17 \\ x + 4(x) + 4(3) &= 17 \\ x + 4x + 12 &= 17 \\ (1 + 4)x + 12 &= 17 \\ 5x + 12 &= 17 \\ 5x + 12 - 12 &= 17 - 12 \\ 5x &= 5 \\ \frac{5x}{5} &= \frac{5}{5} \\ x &= 1 \end{aligned}$$

35. $$\begin{aligned} 8y - (8 + 6y) &= 20 \\ 8y + (-1)(8) + (-1)(6y) &= 20 \\ 8y + (-8) + (-6y) &= 20 \\ 8y + (-6y) - 8 &= 20 \\ (8 - 6)y - 8 &= 20 \\ 2y - 8 &= 20 \\ 2y - 8 + 8 &= 20 + 8 \\ 2y &= 28 \\ \frac{2y}{2} &= \frac{28}{2} \\ y &= 14 \end{aligned}$$

36. $$\begin{aligned} x - 2(3x - 2) &= -6 \\ x + (-2)(3x) - (-2)(2) &= -6 \\ x + (-6x) + 4 &= -6 \\ [1 + (-6)]x + 4 &= -6 \\ -5x + 4 &= -6 \\ -5x + 4 - 4 &= -6 - 4 \\ -5x &= -10 \\ \frac{-5x}{-5} &= \frac{-10}{-5} \\ x &= 2 \end{aligned}$$

37. $$\begin{aligned} \frac{3}{4}(x + 9) &= 15 \\ \frac{4}{3}\left(\frac{3}{4}\right)(x + 9) &= \frac{4}{3}(15) \\ x + 9 &= 20 \\ x + 9 - 9 &= 20 - 9 \\ x &= 11 \end{aligned}$$

38. $$\begin{aligned} \frac{1}{4}(t + 10) &= 5 \\ 4\left(\frac{1}{4}\right)(t + 10) &= 4(5) \\ t + 10 &= 20 \\ t + 10 - 10 &= 20 - 10 \\ t &= 10 \end{aligned}$$

39. $$\begin{aligned} \frac{2}{3}(x + 3) &= 6 \\ \frac{3}{2}\left(\frac{2}{3}\right)(x + 3) &= \frac{3}{2}(6) \\ x + 3 &= 9 \\ x + 3 - 3 &= 9 - 3 \\ x &= 6 \end{aligned}$$

40. did not distribute the 2 over the -3

$$\begin{aligned} 2(x - 3) &= 5 \\ 2(x) - 2(3) &= 5 \\ 2x - 6 &= 5 \\ 2x - 6 + 6 &= 5 + 6 \\ 2x &= 11 \\ \frac{2x}{2} &= \frac{11}{2} \\ x &= 5\frac{1}{2} \end{aligned}$$

Copyright © McDougal Littell Inc.
All rights reserved.

41. 5 and $3x$ are not like terms, $3x$ cannot be subtracted from 5.

$$5 - 3x = 10$$
$$5 - 3x - 5 = 10 - 5$$
$$-3x = 5$$
$$\frac{-3x}{-3} = \frac{5}{-3}$$
$$x = -\frac{5}{3}$$

42. Multiply right-hand side of equation by 4, do not divide by 4.

$$\frac{1}{4}(x - 2) = 8$$
$$4\left(\frac{1}{4}\right)(x - 2) = 4(8)$$
$$x - 2 = 32$$
$$x - 2 + 2 = 32 + 2$$
$$x = 34$$

43.

Solution Step	*Explanation*
$\frac{5x}{2} + 3 = 6$	Original equation
$\frac{5x}{2} = 3$	Subtraction property of equality
$5x = 6$	Multiplication property of equality
$x = \frac{6}{5}$	Division property of equality

44. C;

$$4x - 400 = 100$$
$$4x - 400 + 400 = 100 + 400$$
$$4x = 500$$
$$\frac{4x}{4} = \frac{500}{4}$$
$$x = 125 \text{ people}$$

45.

$$90 + 65m = 1000$$
$$90 + 65m - 90 = 1000 - 90$$
$$65m = 910$$
$$\frac{65m}{65} = \frac{910}{65}$$
$$m = 14 \text{ months}$$

46.

$$d = \frac{n}{2} + 26$$
$$50 = \frac{n}{2} + 26 \qquad \text{Substitute 50 for } d.$$
$$50 - 26 = \frac{n}{2} + 26 - 26$$
$$24 = \frac{n}{2}$$
$$2(24) = 2\left(\frac{n}{2}\right)$$
$$48 = n$$

48 pounds per square inch

47.

$$4(2y + 1) - 6y = 18$$
$$4(2y) + 4(1) - 6y = 18$$
$$8y + 4 - 6y = 18$$
$$(8 - 6)y + 4 = 18$$
$$2y + 4 = 18$$
$$2y + 4 - 4 = 18 - 4$$
$$2y = 14$$
$$\frac{2y}{2} = \frac{14}{2}$$
$$y = 7$$

48.

$$22x + 2(3x + 5) = 66$$
$$22x + 2(3x) + 2(5) = 66$$
$$22x + 6x + 10 = 66$$
$$(22 + 6)x + 10 = 66$$
$$28x + 10 = 66$$
$$28x + 10 - 10 = 66 - 10$$
$$28x = 56$$
$$\frac{28x}{28} = \frac{56}{28}$$
$$x = 2$$

49.

$$6x + 3(x + 4) = 15$$
$$6x + 3(x) + 3(4) = 15$$
$$6x + 3x + 12 = 15$$
$$(6 + 3)x + 12 = 15$$
$$9x + 12 = 15$$
$$9x + 12 - 12 = 15 - 12$$
$$9x = 3$$
$$\frac{9x}{9} = \frac{3}{9}$$
$$x = \frac{1}{3}$$

50.

$$7 - (2 - g) = -4$$
$$7 + (-1)(2) - (-1)(g) = -4$$
$$7 - 2 + g = -4$$
$$5 + g = -4$$
$$5 + g - 5 = -4 - 5$$
$$g = -9$$

51.

$$-x + (5x - 7) = -5$$
$$-x + 5x - 7 = -5$$
$$(-1 + 5)x - 7 = -5$$
$$4x - 7 = -5$$
$$4x - 7 + 7 = -5 + 7$$
$$4x = 2$$
$$\frac{4x}{4} = \frac{2}{4}$$
$$x = \frac{1}{2}$$

Copyright © McDougal Littell Inc.
All rights reserved.

Chapter 3 *continued*

52.
$$\begin{aligned} 5a - (2a - 1) &= -2 \\ 5a + (-1)(2a) - (-1)(1) &= -2 \\ 5a - 2a + 1 &= -2 \\ (5 - 2)a + 1 &= -2 \\ 3a + 1 &= -2 \\ 3a + 1 - 1 &= -2 - 1 \\ 3a &= -3 \\ \frac{3a}{3} &= \frac{-3}{3} \\ a &= -1 \end{aligned}$$

3.3 Standardized Test Practice (p. 148)

53. D;

Check:
$$\begin{aligned} 9x - 5x - 19 &= 21 \\ 9(10) - 5(10) - 19 &\stackrel{?}{=} 21 \\ 90 - 50 - 19 &\stackrel{?}{=} 21 \\ 40 - 19 &\stackrel{?}{=} 21 \\ 21 &= 21 \end{aligned}$$

54. H; $34x + 339 = 458$

3.3 Mixed Review (p. 149)

55. a^6 **56.** x^5 **57.** 4^3 **58.** 5^2

59. t^3 **60.** $(3x)^5$

61. $5 + 8 - 3 = 13 - 3 = 10$

62. $32 \cdot 4 + 8 = 128 + 8 = 136$

63. $5 \cdot (12 - 4) + 7 = 5 \cdot (8) + 7 = 40 + 7 = 47$

64. $-6 \div 3 - 4 \cdot 5 = -2 - 20 = -22$

65.
$$\begin{aligned} 2 - 8 \div -\frac{2}{3} &= 2 - 8 \cdot \left(-\frac{3}{2}\right) \\ &= 2 - (-12) \\ &= 2 + 12 = 14 \end{aligned}$$

66.
$$\begin{aligned} \frac{(3-6)^2 + 6}{-5} &= [(3-6)^2 + 6] \div (-5) \\ &= [(-3)^2 + 6] \div (-5) \\ &= [9 + 6] \div (-5) \\ &= 15 \div (-5) \\ &= -3 \end{aligned}$$

3.3 Maintaining Skills (p. 149)

67. $\frac{1}{4} = 0.25 < 0.35$

68. $1.5 > \frac{5}{5} = 1$ **69.** $0.30 < \frac{2}{3} = 0.\bar{6}$

70. $\frac{8}{5} = 1.6$ **71.** $\frac{17}{2} = 8.5 < 9.5$

72. $0 = \frac{0}{7}$ **73.** $2.7 < \frac{14}{5} = 2.8$

74. $\frac{6}{8} = 0.75$

Quiz 1 *(p. 149)*

1.
$$\begin{aligned} x - 14 &= 7 \\ x - 14 + 14 &= 7 + 14 \\ x &= 21 \end{aligned}$$

2.
$$\begin{aligned} y + 8 &= -9 \\ y + 8 - 8 &= -9 - 8 \\ y &= -17 \end{aligned}$$

3.
$$\begin{aligned} 5 &= m - (-12) \\ 5 &= m + 12 \\ 5 - 12 &= m + 12 - 12 \\ -7 &= m \end{aligned}$$

4.
$$\begin{aligned} 10x &= -10 \\ \frac{10x}{10} &= -\frac{10}{10} \\ x &= -1 \end{aligned}$$

5.
$$\begin{aligned} 47 &= \frac{x}{6} \\ 6(47) &= 6\left(\frac{x}{6}\right) \\ 282 &= x \end{aligned}$$

6.
$$\begin{aligned} 3 &= \frac{3}{5}x \\ \frac{5}{3}(3) &= \frac{5}{3}\left(\frac{3}{5}x\right) \\ 5 &= x \end{aligned}$$

7. B;
$$\begin{aligned} x + 4 &= 91 \\ x + 4 - 4 &= 91 - 4 \\ x &= 87 \end{aligned}$$

8.
$$\begin{aligned} 6x &= 72 \\ \frac{6x}{6} &= \frac{72}{6} \\ x &= 12; \$12 \end{aligned}$$

9.
$$\begin{aligned} 2x - 5 &= 13 \\ 2x - 5 + 5 &= 13 + 5 \\ 2x &= 18 \\ \frac{2x}{2} &= \frac{18}{2} \\ x &= 9 \end{aligned}$$

10.
$$\begin{aligned} 12 + 9x &= 30 \\ 12 + 9x - 12 &= 30 - 12 \\ 9x &= 18 \\ \frac{9x}{9} &= \frac{18}{9} \\ x &= 2 \end{aligned}$$

Copyright © McDougal Littell Inc.
All rights reserved.

11.
$$\begin{aligned} 8n - 10 - 12n &= -18 \\ 8n - 12n - 10 &= -18 \\ (8 - 12)n - 10 &= -18 \\ -4n - 10 &= -18 \\ -4n - 10 + 10 &= -18 + 10 \\ -4n &= -8 \\ \frac{-4n}{-4} &= \frac{-8}{-4} \\ n &= 2 \end{aligned}$$

12.
$$\begin{aligned} 6(5y - 3) + 2 &= 14 \\ 6(5y) - 6(3) + 2 &= 14 \\ 30y - 18 + 2 &= 14 \\ 30y - 16 &= 14 \\ 30y - 16 + 16 &= 14 + 16 \\ 30y &= 30 \\ \frac{30y}{30} &= \frac{30}{30} \\ y &= 1 \end{aligned}$$

13.
$$\begin{aligned} 7x - 8(x + 3) &= 1 \\ 7x + (-8)(x) + (-8)(3) &= 1 \\ 7x - 8x - 24 &= 1 \\ (7 - 8)x - 24 &= 1 \\ -1x - 24 &= 1 \\ -x - 24 + 24 &= 1 + 24 \\ -x &= 25 \\ x &= -25 \end{aligned}$$

14.
$$\begin{aligned} \frac{2}{3}(x + 1) &= 10 \\ \frac{3}{2}\left(\frac{2}{3}\right)(x + 1) &= \frac{3}{2}(10) \\ x + 1 &= 15 \\ x + 1 - 1 &= 15 - 1 \\ x &= 14 \end{aligned}$$

15.
$$\begin{aligned} 2m + 12 &= 30 \\ 2m + 12 - 12 &= 30 - 12 \\ 2m &= 18 \\ \frac{2m}{2} &= \frac{18}{2} \\ m &= 9 \end{aligned}$$

9 min

Lesson 3.4

3.4 Developing Concepts: Explore *(p. 150)*

2. $2x + 5 = 9$
3. $2x = 4$
4. $x = 2$

Think About It (p. 150)

1. $4x + 4 = 3x + 7$

$x = 3$

2. $2x + 3 = 6 + x$

$x = 3$

3. $6x + 5 = 3x + 14$

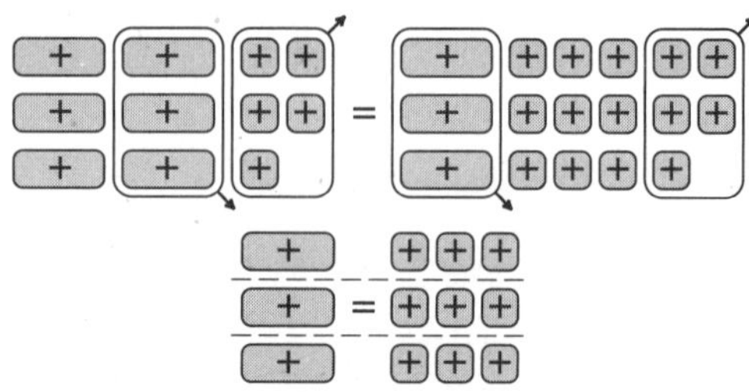

$x = 3$

4. $5x + 2 = 10 + x$

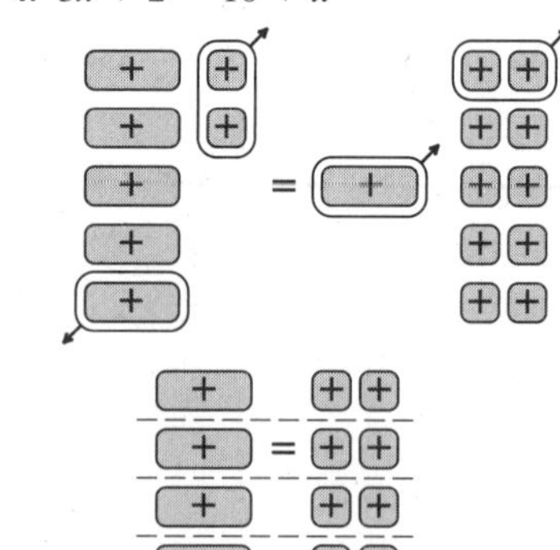

$x = 2$

5. $8x + 3 = 7x + 3$

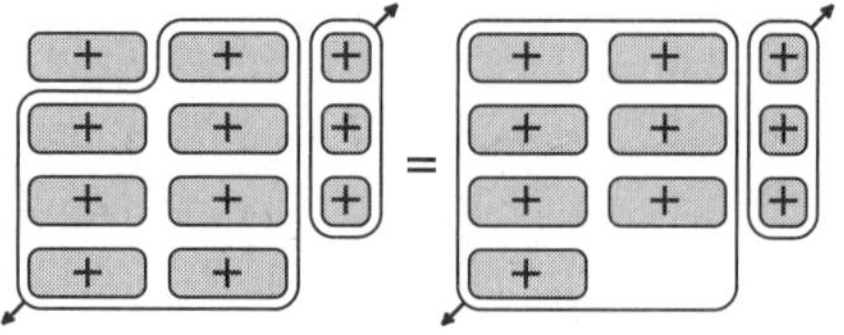

$x = 0$

6. $x + 9 = 1 + 3x$

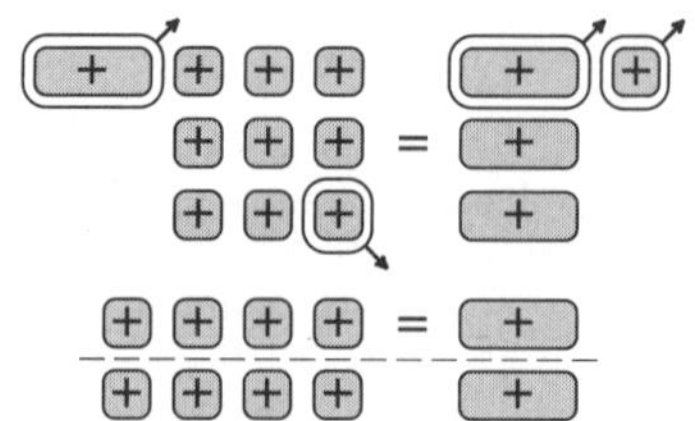

$x = 4$

7.

$2x + 2 = x + 4$	Original equation.
$x + 2 = 4$	Remove (subtract) x from each side.
$x = 2$	Remove (subtract) 2 from each side.

Copyright © McDougal Littell Inc.
All rights reserved.

3.4 Checkpoint (pp. 152–153)

1. $34 - 3x = 14x$ Write original equation.
$34 - 3x + 3x = 14x + 3x$ Add $3x$ to both sides.
$34 = 17x$ Combine like terms.
$\frac{34}{17} = \frac{17x}{17}$ Divide each side by 17.
$2 = x$ Simplify.

Check:
$34 - 3x = 14x$ Write original equation.
$34 - 3(2) \stackrel{?}{=} 14(2)$ Substitute 2 for x.
$34 - 6 \stackrel{?}{=} 28$ Multiply.
$28 = 28$ Solution is correct.

2. $5y - 2 = y + 10$ Write original equation.
$5y - 2 - y = y + 10 - y$ Subtract y from both sides.
$4y - 2 = 10$ Combine like terms.
$4y - 2 + 2 = 10 + 2$ Add 2 to both sides.
$4y = 12$ Simplify.
$\frac{4y}{4} = \frac{12}{4}$ Divide both sides by 4.
$y = 3$ Simplify.

Check:
$5y - 2 = y + 10$ Write original equation.
$5(3) - 2 = (3) + 10$ Substitute 3 for y.
$15 - 2 = 3 + 10$ Multiply.
$13 = 13$ Solution is correct.

3. $-6x + 4 = -8x$ Write original equation.
$-6x + 4 + 8x = -8x + 8x$ Add $8x$ to both sides.
$2x + 4 = 0$ Combine like terms.
$2x + 4 - 4 = 0 - 4$ Subtract 4 from both sides.
$2x = -4$ Simplify.
$\frac{2x}{2} = \frac{-4}{2}$ Divide both sides by 2.
$x = -2$ Simplify.

Check:
$-6x + 4 = -8x$ Write original equation.
$-6(-2) + 4 \stackrel{?}{=} -8(-2)$ Substitute -2 for x.
$12 + 4 \stackrel{?}{=} 16$ Multiply.
$16 = 16$ Solution is correct.

4. $5x - 3x + 4 = 3x + 8$ Write original equation.
$2x + 4 = 3x + 8$ Combine like terms.
$2x + 4 - 2x = 3x + 8 - 2x$ Subtract $2x$ from each side.
$4 = x + 8$ Combine like terms.
$4 - 8 = x + 8 - 8$ Subtract 8 from each side.
$-4 = x$ Simplify.

Check:
$5x - 3x + 4 = 3x + 8$ Write original equation.
$5(-4) - 3(-4) + 4 \stackrel{?}{=} 3(-4) + 8$ Substitute -4 for x.
$-20 + 12 + 4 \stackrel{?}{=} -12 + 8$ Multiply.
$-4 = -4$ Solution is correct.

5. $6x + 3 = 8 + 7x + 2x$ Write original equation.
$6x + 3 = 8 + 9x$ Combine like terms.
$6x + 3 - 6x = 8 + 9x - 6x$ Subtract $6x$ from each side.
$3 = 8 + 3x$ Combine like terms.
$3 - 8 = 8 + 3x - 8$ Subtract 8 from each side.
$-5 = 3x$ Simplify.
$\frac{-5}{3} = \frac{3x}{3}$ Divide each side by 3.
$-\frac{5}{3} = x$ Simplify.

Check:
$6x + 3 = 8 + 7x + 2x$
$6\left(-\frac{5}{3}\right) + 3 \stackrel{?}{=} 8 + 7\left(-\frac{5}{3}\right) + 2\left(-\frac{5}{3}\right)$
$-10 + 3 \stackrel{?}{=} 8 + \left[\left(-\frac{35}{3}\right) + \left(-\frac{10}{3}\right)\right]$
$-7 \stackrel{?}{=} 8 - \frac{45}{3}$
$-7 \stackrel{?}{=} 8 - 15$
$-7 = -7$

6. $2(x + 4) = 2x + 8$ Write original equation.
$2x + 8 = 2x + 8$ Use distributive property.
$2x + 8 - 2x = 2x + 8 - 2x$ Subtract $2x$ from each side.
$8 = 8$ Combine like terms.

Answer: The equation $8 = 8$ is always true, so all values of x are solutions. The original equation is an identity.

7. $2(x + 4) = x - 8$ Write original equation.
$2x + 8 = x - 8$ Use distributive property.
$2x + 8 - x = x - 8 - x$ Subtract x from each side.
$x + 8 = -8$ Combine like terms.
$x + 8 - 8 = -8 - 8$ Subtract 8 from each side.
$x = -16$ Simplify both sides.

Answer: The solution is -16. The original equation has one solution.

8. $2(x + 4) = 2x - 8$ Write original equation.
$2x + 8 = 2x - 8$ Use distributive property.
$2x + 8 - 2x = 2x - 8 - 2x$ Subtract $2x$ from each side.
$8 \neq -8$ Combine like terms.

Answer: The equation $8 = -8$ is never true no matter what value of x. The original equation has no solution.

9. $2(x + 4) = x + 8$ Write original equation.
$2x + 8 = x + 8$ Use distributive property.
$2x + 8 - x = x + 8 - x$ Subtract x from each side.
$x + 8 = 8$ Combine like terms.
$x + 8 - 8 = 8 - 8$ Subtract 8 from each side.
$x = 0$ Simplify both sides.

Answer: The solution is 0. The original equation has one solution.

Copyright © McDougal Littell Inc.
All rights reserved.

3.4 Guided Practice (p. 154)

1. identity

2.
$$\begin{aligned} -2(4-x) &= 2x-8 \\ -8+2x &= 2x-8 \\ -8+2x-2x &= 2x-8-2x \\ -8 &= -8 \end{aligned}$$
Yes, the equation is true for all values of x.

3. coefficient of $3y$ is 3.

4. coefficient of $3x$ is 3
coefficient of $8x$ is 8

5. coefficient of $4x$ is 4
coefficient of $-2x$ is -2

6. coefficient of $5x$ is 5
coefficient of $-4x$ is -4
coefficient of $-x$ is -1

7. coefficient of $5m$ is 5
coefficient of $-7m$ is -7

8. Distribute the 2: $2(x+1) = 2x+2$.
The coefficient of $2x$ is 2.

9.
$$\begin{aligned} 7x+3 &= 2x-2 \\ 7x+3-2x &= 2x-2-2x \\ 5x+3 &= -2 \\ 5x+3-3 &= -2-3 \\ 5x &= -5 \\ \frac{5x}{5} &= \frac{-5}{5} \\ x &= -1 \end{aligned}$$
one solution

10.
$$\begin{aligned} 5(x-5) &= 5x+24 \\ 5x-25 &= 5x+24 \\ 5x-25-5x &= 5x+24-5x \\ -25 &\neq 24 \end{aligned}$$
no solution

11.
$$\begin{aligned} 12-5a &= -2a-9 \\ 12-5a+5a &= -2a-9+5a \\ 12 &= 3a-9 \\ 12+9 &= 3a-9+9 \\ 21 &= 3a \\ \frac{21}{3} &= \frac{3a}{3} \\ 7 &= a \end{aligned}$$
one solution

12.
$$\begin{aligned} 3(4c+7) &= 12c \\ 12c+21 &= 12c \\ 12c+21-12c &= 12c-12c \\ 21 &\neq 0 \end{aligned}$$
no solution

13.
$$\begin{aligned} x-2x+3 &= 3-x \\ -x+3 &= 3-x \\ -x+3+x &= 3-x+x \\ 3 &= 3 \end{aligned}$$
identity

14.
$$\begin{aligned} 6y-3y+6 &= 5y-4 \\ 3y+6 &= 5y-4 \\ 3y+6-3y &= 5y-4-3y \\ 6 &= 2y-4 \\ 6+4 &= 2y-4+4 \\ 10 &= 2y \\ \frac{10}{2} &= \frac{2y}{2} \\ 5 &= y \end{aligned}$$
one solution

15. B; $3x + 20 = 5x$

16.
$$\begin{aligned} 3x+20 &= 5x \\ 3x+20-3x &= 5x-3x \\ 20 &= 2x \\ \frac{20}{2} &= \frac{2x}{2} \\ 10 &= x \end{aligned}$$
10 pies

3.4 Practice and Applications (pp. 154–156)

17. $x + 2 = 3x - 4$ Subtract x from each side.

18. $5t + 12 = 2t$ Subtract $2t$ from each side.

19. $2x - 7 = -8x + 13$ Add $8x$ to each side.

20. $-4x = -9 + 5x$ Add $4x$ to each side.

21.
$$\begin{aligned} 15-2y &= 3y \\ 15-2y+2y &= 3y+2y \\ 15 &= 5y \\ \frac{15}{5} &= \frac{5y}{5} \\ 3 &= y \end{aligned}$$

22.
$$\begin{aligned} 2p-9 &= 5p+12 \\ 2p-9-2p &= 5p+12-2p \\ -9 &= 3p+12 \\ -9-12 &= 3p+12-12 \\ -21 &= 3p \\ \frac{-21}{3} &= \frac{3p}{3} \\ -7 &= p \end{aligned}$$

23.
$$\begin{aligned} 5x-16 &= 14-5x \\ 5x-16+5x &= 14-5x+5x \\ 10x-16 &= 14 \\ 10x-16+16 &= 14+16 \\ 10x &= 30 \\ \frac{10x}{10} &= \frac{30}{10} \\ x &= 3 \end{aligned}$$

24.
$$\begin{aligned} -3g+9 &= 15g-9 \\ -3g+9+3g &= 15g-9+3g \\ 9 &= 18g-9 \\ 9+9 &= 18g-9+9 \\ 18 &= 18g \\ \frac{18}{18} &= \frac{18g}{18} \\ 1 &= g \end{aligned}$$

Copyright © McDougal Littell Inc.
All rights reserved.

25.
$$\begin{aligned} 11x - 21 &= 17 - 8x \\ 11x - 21 + 8x &= 17 - 8x + 8x \\ 19x - 21 &= 17 \\ 19x - 21 + 21 &= 17 + 21 \\ 19x &= 38 \\ \frac{19x}{19} &= \frac{38}{19} \\ x &= 2 \end{aligned}$$

26.
$$\begin{aligned} 4x + 27 &= 3x + 34 \\ 4x + 27 - 3x &= 3x + 34 - 3x \\ x + 27 &= 34 \\ x + 27 - 27 &= 34 - 27 \\ x &= 7 \end{aligned}$$

27.
$$\begin{aligned} 5x - 4x &= -6x + 3 \\ x &= -6x + 3 \\ x + 6x &= -6x + 3 + 6x \\ 7x &= 3 \\ \frac{7x}{7} &= \frac{3}{7} \\ x &= \frac{3}{7} \end{aligned}$$

28.
$$\begin{aligned} 10y &= 2y - 6y + 7 \\ 10y &= -4y + 7 \\ 10y + 4y &= -4y + 7 + 4y \\ 14y &= 7 \\ \frac{14y}{14} &= \frac{7}{14} \\ y &= \frac{1}{2} \end{aligned}$$

29.
$$\begin{aligned} r - 2 + 3r &= 6 + 5r \\ 4r - 2 &= 6 + 5r \\ 4r - 2 - 4r &= 6 + 5r - 4r \\ -2 &= 6 + r \\ -2 - 6 &= 6 + r - 6 \\ -8 &= r \end{aligned}$$

30.
$$\begin{aligned} 4 + 6x - 9x &= 3x \\ 4 - 3x &= 3x \\ 4 - 3x + 3x &= 3x + 3x \\ 4 &= 6x \\ \frac{4}{6} &= \frac{6x}{6} \\ \frac{2}{3} &= x \end{aligned}$$

31.
$$\begin{aligned} 2t - 3t + 8 &= 3t - 8 \\ -t + 8 &= 3t - 8 \\ -t + 8 + t &= 3t - 8 + t \\ 8 &= 4t - 8 \\ 8 + 8 &= 4t - 8 + 8 \\ 16 &= 4t \\ \frac{16}{4} &= \frac{4t}{4} \\ 4 &= t \end{aligned}$$

32.
$$\begin{aligned} 13x + 8 + 8x &= -9x - 22 \\ 21x + 8 &= -9x - 22 \\ 21x + 8 + 9x &= -9x - 22 + 9x \\ 30x + 8 &= -22 \\ 30x + 8 - 8 &= -22 - 8 \\ 30x &= -30 \\ \frac{30x}{30} &= -\frac{30}{30} \\ x &= -1 \end{aligned}$$

33.
$$\begin{aligned} -x + 6 - 5x &= 14 - 2x \\ -6x + 6 &= 14 - 2x \\ -6x + 6 + 6x &= 14 - 2x + 6x \\ 6 &= 14 + 4x \\ 6 - 14 &= 14 + 4x - 14 \\ -8 &= 4x \\ -\frac{8}{4} &= \frac{4x}{4} \\ -2 &= x \end{aligned}$$

34.
$$\begin{aligned} 5x - 3x + 4 &= 3x + 8 \\ 2x + 4 &= 3x + 8 \\ 2x + 4 - 2x &= 3x + 8 - 2x \\ 4 &= x + 8 \\ 4 - 8 &= x + 8 - 8 \\ -4 &= x \end{aligned}$$

35. Error: $3x - 12x = -9x$, not $9x$.
$$\begin{aligned} 3x &= 12x + 45 \\ 3x - 3x &= 12x + 45 - 3x \\ 0 &= 9x + 45 \\ 0 - 45 &= 9x \\ -45 &= 9x \\ -\frac{45}{9} &= \frac{9x}{9} \\ -5 &= x \end{aligned}$$

36. Error: Add $3c$ to $5c$ instead of subtracting $3c$.
$$\begin{aligned} 4c - 6 + c &= 4 - 3c \\ 5c - 6 &= 4 - 3c \\ 5c - 6 + 3c &= 4 - 3c + 3c \\ 8c - 6 &= 4 \\ 8c - 6 + 6 &= 4 + 6 \\ 8c &= 10 \\ \frac{8c}{8} &= \frac{10}{8} \\ c &= \frac{5}{4} \end{aligned}$$

37.
$$\begin{aligned} 8c - 4 &= 20 - 4c \\ 8c - 4 + 4c &= 20 - 4c + 4c \\ 12c - 4 &= 20 \\ 12c - 4 + 4 &= 20 + 4 \\ 12c &= 24 \\ \frac{12c}{12} &= \frac{24}{12} \\ c &= 2 \end{aligned}$$

one solution

Copyright © McDougal Littell Inc.
All rights reserved.

38.
$$\begin{aligned} 24 - 6r &= 6(4 - r) \\ 24 - 6r &= 24 - 6r \\ 24 - 6r + 6r &= 24 - 6r + 6r \\ 24 &= 24 \end{aligned}$$
identity

39.
$$\begin{aligned} -7 + 4m &= 6m - 5 \\ -7 + 4m - 4m &= 6m - 5 - 4m \\ -7 &= 2m - 5 \\ -7 + 5 &= 2m - 5 + 5 \\ -2 &= 2m \\ \frac{-2}{2} &= \frac{2m}{2} \\ -1 &= m \end{aligned}$$
one solution

40.
$$\begin{aligned} 6m - 5 &= 7m + 7 - m \\ 6m - 5 &= 6m + 7 \\ 6m - 5 - 6m &= 6m + 7 - 6m \\ -5 &\neq 7 \end{aligned}$$
no solution

41.
$$\begin{aligned} 3x - 7 &= 2x + 8 + 4x \\ 3x - 7 &= 6x + 8 \\ 3x - 7 - 3x &= 6x + 8 - 3x \\ -7 &= 3x + 8 \\ -7 - 8 &= 3x + 8 - 8 \\ -15 &= 3x \\ -\frac{15}{3} &= \frac{3x}{3} \\ -5 &= x \end{aligned}$$
one solution

42.
$$\begin{aligned} 6 + 3c &= -c - 6 \\ 6 + 3c + c &= -c - 6 + c \\ 6 + 4c &= -6 \\ 6 + 4c - 6 &= -6 - 6 \\ 4c &= -12 \\ \frac{4c}{4} &= -\frac{12}{4} \\ c &= -3 \end{aligned}$$
one solution

43. $8 + 6a = 6a - 1$
Subtracting $6a$ from each side would leave $8 = -1$;
no solution

44. $6a + 8 = 2a$; one solution

45. $8 + 6a = 2a + 8$; one solution

46. $8 + 6a = 6a + 8$; The expressions are equivalent; identity

47.
$$\begin{aligned} 8t &= 3(t + 55) \\ 8t &= 3t + 165 \\ 5t &= 165 \\ t &= 33 \end{aligned}$$
33 hours downstream $+(33 + 55)$ hours upstream
$= 121$ hours

48.
$$\begin{aligned} 90t &= 100 + 70t \\ 20t &= 100 \\ t &= 5 \text{ seconds} \end{aligned}$$

49.
$$\begin{aligned} 90t &= 500 + 70t \\ 20t &= 500 \\ t &= 25 \text{ seconds} \end{aligned}$$
It would take 25 seconds to catch up to the gazelle at top speed, but the cheetah would only last for 20 seconds at top speed, so the gazelle is safe.

50.
$$\begin{aligned} 2(2x + 3) &= -6(x + 9) \\ 4x + 6 &= -6x - 54 \\ 4x + 6 + 6x &= -6x - 54 + 6x \\ 10x + 6 &= -54 \\ 10x &= -60 \\ x &= -6 \end{aligned}$$

51.
$$\begin{aligned} 7 - (-4t) &= 4t - 14 - 21t \\ 7 + 4t &= -17t - 14 \\ 7 + 21t &= -14 \\ 21t &= -21 \\ t &= -1 \end{aligned}$$

52.
$$\begin{aligned} -\frac{3}{4}x + 5 &= \frac{1}{4}x - 3 \\ 5 &= x - 3 \\ 8 &= x \end{aligned}$$

53.
$$\begin{aligned} 7 - \frac{1}{3}x &= \frac{2}{3}x + 4 \\ 7 &= x + 4 \\ 3 &= x \end{aligned}$$

3.4 Standardized Test Practice (p. 156)

54. I.
$$\begin{aligned} 3x - 4x + 18 &= 5x \\ -x + 18 &= 5x \\ 18 &= 6x \\ 3 &= x \end{aligned}$$
II.
$$\begin{aligned} 4 + 6x &= 8x - 2 \\ 4 &= 2x - 2 \\ 6 &= 2x \\ 3 &= x \end{aligned}$$
III.
$$\begin{aligned} 2x - 8 &= 7 - x \\ 3x - 8 &= 7 \\ 3x &= 15 \\ x &= 5 \end{aligned}$$
I and II are equivalent; A

55. H;
$$\begin{aligned} 6j - 4 &= 4j + 4 \\ 6(4) - 4 &\stackrel{?}{=} 4(4) + 4 \\ 24 - 4 &\stackrel{?}{=} 16 + 4 \\ 20 &= 20 \end{aligned}$$

56.
$$\begin{aligned} 15x + 6 - x &= 16x + 6 - 2x \\ 14x + 6 &= 14x + 6 \\ 6 &= 6 \end{aligned}$$
identity; D

Copyright © McDougal Littell Inc.
All rights reserved.

Chapter 3 *continued*

3.4 Mixed Review (p. 156)

57. $d = rt$
$d = 48(3) = 144$ miles

58. $7 \cdot y = 7(8) = 56$

59. $x - 5 = 13 - 5 = 8$

60. $\frac{x}{4} = \frac{56}{4} = 14$

61. $x^3 = 6^3 = 216$

62. $4t^2 = 4(3)^2 = 4(9) = 36$

63. $(3x)^2 = (3 \cdot 4)^2 = (12)^2 = 144$

64. $(10 + 6) \div 2 - 3 = 16 \div 2 - 3 = 8 - 3 = 5$

65. $8 + 4 \div (3 - 1) = 8 + 4 \div 2 = 8 + 2 = 10$

66. $14 - 2 \cdot 5 - 3 = 14 - 10 - 3 = 4 - 3 = 1$

67. yes; $49.99 + 2.99 = \$52.98$, which is less than \$53.00

68. $3 + (-4) = -1$

69. $-6 + 2 = -4$

70. $-11 + (-8) = -19$

71. $5 + 16 + (-9) = 21 + (-9) = 12$

72. $8 + (-7) + (-10) = 1 + (-10) = -9$

73. $-22 + (-5) + 4 = -27 + 4 = -23$

74. $15x = 255$
$x = 17$

75. $236x = 0$
$x = 0$

76. $\frac{1}{5}x = 9$
$x = 45$

77. $\frac{2}{3}x = 60$
$x = \frac{3}{2}(60)$
$x = 90$

3.4 Maintaining Skills (p. 156)

78. $15 \div 0.05 = 300$
$5\overline{)1500}$ = 300

79. $4 \div 0.002 = 2000$
$2\overline{)4000}$ = 2000

80. $20 \div 0.4 = 50$
$4\overline{)200}$ = 50

81. $8.1 \div 0.9 = 9$
$9\overline{)81}$ = 9

82. $0.72 \div 0.3 = 2.4$
$3\overline{)7.2}$ = 2.4

83. $6.4 \div 0.8 = 8$
$8\overline{)64}$ = 8

84. $46.2 \div 0.02 = 2{,}310$
$2\overline{)4620}$ = 2310

85. $39.1 \div 0.01 = 3{,}910$
$1\overline{)3910}$ = 3910

86. $23.4 \div 0.04 = 585$
$4\overline{)2340}$ = 585
20
34
32
20
20

Lesson 3.5

3.5 Checkpoint (pp. 158–159)

1.

$6(x + 3) + 3x = 3(x - 2)$	Write original equation.
$6x + 18 + 3x = 3x - 6$	Use distributive property.
$9x + 18 = 3x - 6$	Combine like terms.
$6x + 18 = -6$	Subtract $3x$ from each side.
$6x = -24$	Subtract 18 from each side.
$x = -4$	Divide each side by 6.

2.

$4x + (2 - x) = -3(x + 2)$	Write original equation.
$4x + 2 - x = -3x - 6$	Use distributive property.
$3x + 2 = -3x - 6$	Combine like terms.
$6x + 2 = -6$	Add $3x$ to both sides.
$6x = -8$	Subtract 2 from each side.
$x = -\frac{8}{6}$	Divide each side by 6.
$x = -\frac{4}{3}$	Simplify.

3.

$-2(4x + 2) = -2(x + 3) + 9$	Write original equation.
$-8x - 4 = -2x - 6 + 9$	Use distributive property.
$-8x - 4 = -2x + 3$	Combine like terms.
$-4 = 6x + 3$	Add $8x$ to each side.
$-7 = 6x$	Subtract 3 from each side.
$-\frac{7}{6} = x$	Divide each side by 6.

Copyright © McDougal Littell Inc.
All rights reserved.

4. $\frac{1}{3}(3y - 12) = 6 - 2(y - 1)$ Write original equation.
$y - 4 = 6 - 2y + 2$ Use distributive property.
$y - 4 = 8 - 2y$ Combine like terms.
$3y - 4 = 8$ Add $2y$ to each side.
$3y = 12$ Add 4 to each side.
$y = 4$ Divide each side by 3.

5. $8x = 3x + 50$
$5x = 50$
$x = 10$
If you rent a video game 10 times, the cost will be equal. If you rent it less than 10 times, it would cost less renting at the video store. If you rent it more than 10 times, it would cost less renting at the video game club.

3.5 Guided Practice (p. 160)

1. subtraction
2. addition
3. division
4. multiplication
5. $3(2 + 5) = 3(2) + 5$;
false; the 5 also should be multiplied by 3.
6. $(2 + 5)3 = 2(3) + 5(3)$; true
7. $8(6 - 4) = 8(6) - 8(4)$; true
8. $(6 - 4)8 = 6 - 4(8)$; false; the 6 also should be multiplied by 8.
9. $-2(4 + 3) = -8 + 6$; false; should be -6
10. $-2(4 - 3) = -8 + 6$; true
11. $2(x - 1) = 3(x + 1)$
$2x - 2 = 3x + 3$
$-2 = x + 3$
$-5 = x$
Check:
$2(x - 1) = 3(x + 1)$
$2(-5 - 1) \stackrel{?}{=} 3(-5 + 1)$
$2(-6) \stackrel{?}{=} 3(-4)$
$-12 = -12$

12. $3(x + 2) = 4(5 + x)$
$3x + 6 = 20 + 4x$
$6 = 20 + x$
$-14 = x$
Check:
$3(x + 2) = 4(5 + x)$
$3(-14 + 2) \stackrel{?}{=} 4(5 + -14)$
$3(-12) \stackrel{?}{=} 4(-9)$
$-36 = -36$

13. $6(8 + 3a) = -2(a - 4)$
$48 + 18a = -2a + 8$
$48 + 20a = 8$
$20a = -40$
$a = -2$
Check:
$6(8 + 3a) = -2(a - 4)$
$6(8 + 3 \cdot (-2)) \stackrel{?}{=} -2(-2 - 4)$
$6(8 - 6) \stackrel{?}{=} -2(-2 - 4)$
$6(2) \stackrel{?}{=} -2(-6)$
$12 = 12$

14. $8(4 - r) + r = -6(3 + r)$
$32 - 8r + r = -18 - 6r$
$32 - 7r = -18 - 6r$
$32 = -18 + r$
$50 = r$
Check:
$8(4 - r) + r = -6(3 + r)$
$8(4 - 50) + 50 \stackrel{?}{=} -6(3 + 50)$
$8(-46) + 50 \stackrel{?}{=} -6(53)$
$-368 + 50 \stackrel{?}{=} -318$
$-318 = -318$

15. $-4(m + 6) + 2m = 3(m + 2)$
$-4m - 24 + 2m = 3m + 6$
$-2m - 24 = 3m + 6$
$-24 = 5m + 6$
$-30 = 5m$
$-6 = m$
Check:
$-4(m + 6) + 2m = 3(m + 2)$
$-4(-6 + 6) + 2(-6) \stackrel{?}{=} 3(-6 + 2)$
$-4(0) + 2(-6) \stackrel{?}{=} 3(-4)$
$-12 = -12$

16. $7(c - 7) + 4c = -2(c + 5)$
$7c - 49 + 4c = -2c - 10$
$11c - 49 = -2c - 10$
$13c - 49 = -10$
$13c = 39$
$c = 3$
Check:
$7(c - 7) + 4c = -2(c + 5)$
$7(3 - 7) + 4(3) \stackrel{?}{=} -2(3 + 5)$
$7(-4) + 4(3) \stackrel{?}{=} -2(8)$
$-28 + 12 \stackrel{?}{=} -16$
$-16 = -16$

Copyright © McDougal Littell Inc.
All rights reserved.

17. $\frac{3}{8}(16x - 8) = 9 - 5(x - 2)$

$6x - 3 = 9 - 5x + 10$
$6x - 3 = 19 - 5x$
$11x - 3 = 19$
$11x = 22$
$x = 2$

Check:

$\frac{3}{8}(16x - 8) = 9 - 5(x - 2)$

$\frac{3}{8}(16 \cdot 2 - 8) \stackrel{?}{=} 9 - 5(2 - 2)$

$\frac{3}{8}(24) \stackrel{?}{=} 9 - 0$

$9 = 9$

18. $\frac{1}{5}(25 - 5k) = 21 - 3(k - 4)$

$5 - k = 21 - 3k + 12$
$5 - k = 33 - 3k$
$5 + 2k = 33$
$2k = 28$
$k = 14$

Check:

$\frac{1}{5}(25 - 5k) = 21 - 3(k - 4)$

$\frac{1}{5}(25 - 5 \cdot 14) \stackrel{?}{=} 21 - 3(14 - 4)$

$\frac{1}{5}(-45) \stackrel{?}{=} 21 - 3(10)$

$-9 \stackrel{?}{=} 21 - 30$
$-9 = -9$

3.5 Practice and Applications (pp. 160–162)

19. $3(x + 6) = 5(x - 4)$
$3x + 18 = 5x - 20$
$18 = 2x - 20$
$38 = 2x$
$19 = x$

20. $7(6 - y) = -3(y - 2)$
$42 - 7y = -3y + 6$
$42 = 4y + 6$
$36 = 4y$
$9 = y$

21. $5(x + 2) = x + 6(x - 3)$
$5x + 10 = x + 6x - 18$
$5x + 10 = 7x - 18$
$10 = 2x - 18$
$28 = 2x$
$14 = x$

22. $8(x + 5) = 7(x + 8)$
$8x + 40 = 7x + 56$
$x + 40 = 56$
$x = 16$

23. $24y - 2(6 - y) = 6(3y + 2)$
$24y - 12 + 2y = 18y + 12$
$26y - 12 = 18y + 12$
$8y - 12 = 12$
$8y = 24$
$y = 3$

24. $7(b + 2) - 4b = 2(b + 10)$
$7b + 14 - 4b = 2b + 20$
$3b + 14 = 2b + 20$
$b + 14 = 20$
$b = 6$

25. $4(m + 3) - 2m = 3(m - 3)$
$4m + 12 - 2m = 3m - 9$
$2m + 12 = 3m - 9$
$12 = m - 9$
$21 = m$

26. $2(a + 4) = 2(a - 4) + 4a$
$2a + 8 = 2a - 8 + 4a$
$2a + 8 = 6a - 8$
$8 = 4a - 8$
$16 = 4a$
$4 = a$

27. $4 + 5(3 - x) = 4(8 + 2x)$
$4 + 15 - 5x = 32 + 8x$
$19 - 5x = 32 + 8x$
$19 = 32 + 13x$
$-13 = 13x$
$-1 = x$

28. $5(-x + 2) = -3(7x + 2) + 8x$
$-5x + 10 = -21 - 6 + 8x$
$-5x + 10 = -13x - 6$
$8x + 10 = -6$
$8x = -16$
$x = -2$

29. $10(2x + 4) = -(-8 - 9x) + 3x$
$20x + 40 = 8 + 9x + 3x$
$20x + 40 = 8 + 12x$
$8x + 40 = 8$
$8x = -32$
$x = -4$

30. $9(t - 4) - 2t = 5(t - 2)$
$9t - 36 - 2t = 5t - 10$
$7t - 36 = 5t - 10$
$2t - 36 = -10$
$2t = 26$
$t = 13$

31. $3(x + 2) = \frac{1}{4}(12x + 4) - 5x$

$3x + 6 = 3x + 1 - 5x$
$3x + 6 = -2x + 1$
$5x + 6 = 1$
$5x = -5$
$x = -1$

Copyright © McDougal Littell Inc.
All rights reserved.

32. $\frac{2}{5}(10x + 25) = -10 - 4(x + 3)$
$$4x + 10 = -10 - 4x - 12$$
$$4x + 10 = -22 - 4x$$
$$8x + 10 = -22$$
$$8x = -32$$
$$x = -4$$

33. $\frac{1}{2}(8n - 2) = -(-8 + 9n) - 5n$
$$4n - 1 = 8 - 9n - 5n$$
$$4n - 1 = 8 - 14n$$
$$18n - 1 = 8$$
$$18n = 9$$
$$n = \frac{1}{2}$$

34. $2(8 - 4x) = \frac{1}{3}(33 - 18x) + 3$
$$16 - 8x = 11 - 6x + 3$$
$$16 - 8x = 14 - 6x$$
$$16 = 14 + 2x$$
$$2 = 2x$$
$$1 = x$$

35. $\frac{3}{4}(24 - 20t) + 9t = 2(5t + 1)$
$$18 - 15t + 9t = 10t + 2$$
$$18 - 6t = 10t + 2$$
$$18 = 16t + 2$$
$$16 = 16t$$
$$1 = t$$

36. $\frac{2}{3}(9n - 6) = 4(n + 1)$
$$6n - 4 = 4n + 4$$
$$2n - 4 = 4$$
$$2n = 8$$
$$n = 4$$

37.

$3(x - 4) + 2x = 6 - x$	Write the original equation.
$3x - 12 + 2x = 6 - x$	Use the distributive property.
$5x - 12 = 6 - x$	Combine like terms.
$6x - 12 = 6$	Add x to each side.
$6x = 18$	Add 12 to each side.
$x = 3$	Divide each side by 6.

38. Error: $-8(-t - 4) = 8t + 32$
$$-\frac{2}{3}(24t - 27) = -8(-t - 4) - 6$$
$$-16t + 18 = 8t + 32 - 6$$
$$-16t + 18 = 8t + 26$$
$$-24t + 18 = 26$$
$$-24t = 8$$
$$t = -\frac{1}{3}$$

39. Error: $-4(3 - n) = -12 + 4n$
$$-4(3 - n) = 8(4n - 3)$$
$$-12 + 4n = 32n - 24$$
$$-12 = 28n - 24$$
$$12 = 28n$$
$$\frac{3}{7} = n$$

40. $20 + 3n = 5n$
$$20 = 2n$$
$$10 = n$$
If you use the computer center more than 10 times, it will cost less to become a member. The cost is the same, member or non-member, if you use the center 10 times exactly.

41. B; $12 + 7x = 15 + 4x$

42. Studio A: $12 + 7x = 12 + 7(2) = \$26$
Studio B: $15 + 4x = 15 + 4(2) = \$23$
Studio B would charge less.

43. C;
$$(16 + 8)x = 450 + 6x$$
$$24x = 450 + 6x$$
$$18x = 450$$
$$x = 25$$
You will need to use the gym more than 25 times to justify the cost of the yearly fee.

44. $-3(7 - 3n) + 2n = 5(2n - 4)$
$$-21 + 9n + 2n = 10n - 20$$
$$-21 + 11n = 10n - 20$$
$$-21 + n = -20$$
$$n = 1$$

45. $4x + 3(x - 2) = -5(x - 4) - x$
$$4x + 3x - 6 = -5x + 20 - x$$
$$7x - 6 = -6x + 20$$
$$13x - 6 = 20$$
$$13x = 26$$
$$x = 2$$

46. $-7 + 8(5 - 3q) = 3(7 - 9q)$
$$-7 + 40 - 24q = 21 - 27q$$
$$33 - 24q = 21 - 27q$$
$$33 + 3q = 21$$
$$3q = -12$$
$$q = -4$$

47. $y + 2(y - 6) = -(2y - 14) + 49$
$$y + 2y - 12 = -2y + 14 + 49$$
$$3y - 12 = -2y + 63$$
$$5y - 12 = 63$$
$$5y = 75$$
$$y = 15$$

48. $\frac{1}{3}(3x - 12) = 6 - 2(x - 1)$
$$x - 4 = 6 - 2x + 2$$
$$x - 4 = 8 - 2x$$
$$3x - 4 = 8$$
$$3x = 12$$
$$x = 4$$

Copyright © McDougal Littell Inc.
All rights reserved.

49. $2(6 - 2x) = -9x - \frac{1}{2}(-4x + 6)$

$$\begin{aligned} 12 - 4x &= -9x + 2x - 3 \\ 12 - 4x &= -7x - 3 \\ 12 + 3x &= -3 \\ 3x &= -15 \\ x &= -5 \end{aligned}$$

50. $x + 300{,}000 + 400{,}000 + 800{,}000 = 4\frac{3}{4}x$

$$\begin{aligned} x + 1{,}500{,}000 &= 4\tfrac{3}{4}x \\ 1{,}500{,}000 &= 3\tfrac{3}{4}x \\ 1{,}500{,}000 &= \tfrac{15}{4}x \\ \tfrac{4}{15}(1{,}500{,}000) &= \tfrac{4}{15}\left(\tfrac{15}{4}x\right) \\ 4(100{,}000) &= x \\ 400{,}000 &= x \end{aligned}$$

400,000 km

51. Jupiter to Io = 400,000 km
Jupiter to Europa = 300,000 + 400,000 = 700,000 km
Jupiter to Ganymede = 700,000 + 400,000 = 1,100,000 km
Jupiter to Callisto
= 1,100,000 + 800,000 = 1,900,000 km

3.5 Standardized Test Practice (p. 162)

52. B; Subtract 6 from each side.

53. H; $\frac{1}{3}(7x + 5) = 3x - 5$

$$\begin{aligned} \tfrac{7}{3}x + \tfrac{5}{3} &= 3x - 5 \\ 2\tfrac{1}{3}x + 1\tfrac{2}{3} &= 3x - 5 \\ 1\tfrac{2}{3} &= \tfrac{2}{3}x - 5 \\ 6\tfrac{2}{3} &= \tfrac{2}{3}x \\ \tfrac{20}{3} &= \tfrac{2}{3}x \\ \tfrac{3}{2}\left(\tfrac{20}{3}\right) &= \tfrac{3}{2}\left(\tfrac{2}{3}x\right) \\ 10 &= x \end{aligned}$$

3.5 Mixed Review (p. 162)

54. $6(-6) = -36$; one negative factor = negative product

55. $-3(-12) = 36$; two negative factors = positive product

56. $-8(-5) = 40$; two negative factors = positive product

57. $11(-7) = -77$; one negative factor = negative product

58. $h + 7 - 6h = -5h + 7$

59. $3w^2 + 2w - 3w = 3w^2 - w$

60. $ab + 4a - b$; already simplified

61. $3s + 5t - 2s + 6t = s + 11t$

62. $x - y + 2xy$; already simplified

63. $-8m - m^2 + 2m = -6m - m^2$

3.5 Maintaining Skills (p. 162)

64. $\begin{array}{r} 11.9 \\ -\ 1.2 \\ \hline 10.7 \end{array}$

65. $\begin{array}{r} 15.75 \\ -\ 4.25 \\ \hline 11.50 \end{array}$ or 11.5

66. $\begin{array}{r} 3.6 \\ -\ 0.5 \\ \hline 3.1 \end{array}$

67. $\begin{array}{r} 12.44 \\ -\ 6.02 \\ \hline 6.42 \end{array}$

68. $\begin{array}{r} 22.87 \\ -\ 2.99 \\ \hline 19.88 \end{array}$

69. $\begin{array}{r} 56.32 \\ -\ 33.83 \\ \hline 22.49 \end{array}$

Lesson 3.6

3.6 Checkpoint (pp. 163–165)

1. $24x + 43 = 66$

$$\begin{aligned} 24x &= 23 \\ x &= \tfrac{23}{24} \\ x &\approx 0.958\overline{3} \\ x &\approx 0.96 \end{aligned}$$

2. $-42x + 28 = 87$

$$\begin{aligned} -42x &= 59 \\ x &= -\tfrac{59}{42} \\ x &\approx -1.4047 \\ x &\approx -1.40 \end{aligned}$$

3. $22x - 39x = 19$

$$\begin{aligned} -17x &= 19 \\ x &= \tfrac{19}{-17} \\ x &\approx -1.1176 \\ x &\approx -1.12 \end{aligned}$$

4. $2.4x - 0.9 = 12.4$

$$\begin{aligned} 2.4x &= 13.3 \\ x &= \tfrac{13.3}{2.4} \\ x &\approx 5.541\overline{6} \\ x &\approx 5.5 \end{aligned}$$

Copyright © McDougal Littell Inc.
All rights reserved.

5. $1.13y - 25.34 = 0.26y$
$0.87y - 25.34 = 0$
$0.87y = 25.34$
$y = \frac{25.34}{0.87}$
$y \approx 29.1264$
$y \approx 29.1$

6. $14.7 + 2.3x = 4.06$
$2.3x = -10.64$
$x = \frac{-10.64}{2.3}$
$x \approx -4.62608$
$x \approx -4.6$

7. $3.25n - 4.71 = 0.52n$
$2.73n - 4.71 = 0$
$2.73n = 4.71$
$n = \frac{4.71}{2.73}$
$n \approx 1.72527$
$n \approx 1.7$

8. $x + 0.07x = 25$
$1.07x = 25$
$x = \frac{25}{1.07}$
$x \approx 23.36$; \$23.36

3.6 Guided Practice (p. 166)

1. *Sample answer:* Sharing the cost of a meal may not divide evenly.

2. B; $x \approx 0.46$ shows that the answer is not exactly 0.46.

3. is equal to

4. is approximately equal to

5. does it equal?

6. does not equal or is unequal to

7. $23.4459 \approx 23.4$

8. $108.2135 \approx 108.2$

9. $-13.8953 \approx -13.9$

10. $62.9788 \approx 63.0$

11. $56.068 \approx 56.1$

12. $0.555 \approx 0.6$

13. $8.839 \approx 8.8$

14. $-75.1234 \approx -75.1$

15. $2.2x = 15$
$x = \frac{15}{2.2}$
$x \approx 6.82$
Check:
$2.2x = 15$
$2.2(6.82) \stackrel{?}{\approx} 15$
$15.004 \approx 15$

16. $14 - 9x = 37$
$-9x = 23$
$x = \frac{23}{-9}$
$x \approx -2.56$
Check:
$14 - 9x = 37$
$14 - 9(-2.56) \stackrel{?}{\approx} 37$
$37.04 \approx 37$

17. $3(3t - 14) = -4$
$9t - 42 = -4$
$9t = 38$
$t = \frac{38}{9}$
$t \approx 4.22$
Check:
$3(3t - 14) = -4$
$3[3(4.22) - 14] \stackrel{?}{\approx} -4$
$-4.02 \approx -4$

18. $2.69 - 3.64x = 23.78x$
$2.69 = 27.42x$
$\frac{2.69}{27.42} = x$
$0.10 \approx x$
Check:
$2.69 - 3.64x = 23.78x$
$2.69 - 3.64(0.10) \stackrel{?}{\approx} 23.78(0.10)$
$2.326 \approx 2.378$

19. $13.80 = x + 0.15x$
$13.80 = 1.15x$
$\frac{13.80}{1.15} = x$
$12 = x$; \$12

3.6 Practice and Applications (pp. 166–169)

20. $13x - 7 = 27$
$13x = 34$
$x = \frac{34}{13}$
$x \approx 2.62$
Check:
$13x - 7 = 27$
$13(2.62) - 7 \stackrel{?}{\approx} 27$
$27.06 \approx 27$

21. $38 = -14 + 9a$
$52 = 9a$
$\frac{52}{9} = a$
$5.78 \approx a$
Check:
$38 = -14 + 9a$
$38 \stackrel{?}{\approx} -14 + 9(5.78)$
$38 \approx 38.02$

Copyright © McDougal Littell Inc.
All rights reserved.

Chapter 3 *continued*

22. $$\begin{aligned} 17x - 33 &= 114 \\ 17x &= 147 \\ x &= \frac{147}{17} \\ x &\approx 8.65 \end{aligned}$$

Check:

$$\begin{aligned} 17x - 33 &= 114 \\ 17(8.65) - 33 &\stackrel{?}{\approx} 114 \\ 114.05 &\approx 114 \end{aligned}$$

23. $$\begin{aligned} -7x + 32 &= -21 \\ -7x &= -53 \\ x &= \frac{53}{7} \\ x &\approx 7.57 \end{aligned}$$

Check:

$$\begin{aligned} -7x + 32 &= -21 \\ -7(7.57) + 32 &\stackrel{?}{\approx} -21 \\ -20.99 &\approx -21 \end{aligned}$$

24. $$\begin{aligned} -7x + 17 &= -6 \\ -7x &= -23 \\ x &= \frac{23}{7} \\ x &\approx 3.29 \end{aligned}$$

Check:

$$\begin{aligned} -7x + 17 &= -6 \\ -7(3.29) + 17 &\stackrel{?}{\approx} -6 \\ -6.03 &\approx -6 \end{aligned}$$

25. $$\begin{aligned} 18 - 3y &= 5 \\ -3y &= -13 \\ y &= \frac{13}{3} \\ y &\approx 4.33 \end{aligned}$$

Check:

$$\begin{aligned} 18 - 3y &= 5 \\ 18 - 3(4.33) &\stackrel{?}{\approx} 5 \\ 5.01 &\approx 5 \end{aligned}$$

26. $$\begin{aligned} 99 &= 21t + 56 \\ 43 &= 21t \\ \frac{43}{21} &= t \\ 2.05 &\approx t \end{aligned}$$

Check:

$$\begin{aligned} 99 &= 21t + 56 \\ 99 &\stackrel{?}{\approx} 21(2.05) + 56 \\ 99 &\approx 99.05 \end{aligned}$$

27. $$\begin{aligned} -35m + 75 &= 48 \\ -35m &= -27 \\ m &= \frac{27}{35} \\ m &\approx 0.77 \end{aligned}$$

Check:

$$\begin{aligned} 35m + 75 &= 48 \\ -35(0.77) + 75 &\stackrel{?}{\approx} 48 \\ 48.05 &\approx 48 \end{aligned}$$

28. $$\begin{aligned} -16x - 18 &= 3 \\ -16x &= 21 \\ x &= -\frac{21}{16} \\ x &\approx -1.31 \end{aligned}$$

Check:

$$\begin{aligned} -16x - 18 &= 3 \\ -16(-1.31) - 18 &\stackrel{?}{\approx} 3 \\ 2.96 &\approx 3 \end{aligned}$$

29. $$\begin{aligned} 42 &= 23x - 9 \\ 51 &= 23x \\ \frac{51}{23} &= x \\ 2.22 &\approx x \end{aligned}$$

Check:

$$\begin{aligned} 42 &= 23x - 9 \\ 42 &\stackrel{?}{\approx} 23(2.22) - 9 \\ 42 &\approx 42.06 \end{aligned}$$

30. $$\begin{aligned} 9.47x &= 7.45x - 8.81 \\ 2.02x &= -8.81 \\ x &\approx -4.36 \end{aligned}$$

31. $$\begin{aligned} 39.21x + 2.65 &= 42.03x \\ 2.65 &= 2.82x \\ 0.94 &\approx x \end{aligned}$$

32. $$\begin{aligned} 12.67 + 42.35x &= 5.34x \\ 12.67 + 37.01x &= 0 \\ 37.01x &= -12.67 \\ x &\approx -0.34 \end{aligned}$$

33. $$\begin{aligned} 4.65x - 4.79 &= -6.84x \\ 11.49x - 4.79 &= 0 \\ 11.49x &= 4.79 \\ x &\approx 0.42 \end{aligned}$$

34. $$\begin{aligned} 7.87 - 9.65x &= 8.52x - 3.21 \\ 7.87 &= 18.17x - 3.21 \\ 11.08 &= 18.17x \\ 0.61 &\approx x \end{aligned}$$

35. $$\begin{aligned} 8.79x - 6.54 &= 6.48 + 13.75x \\ -6.54 &= 6.48 + 4.96x \\ -13.02 &= 4.96x \\ -2.63 &\approx x \end{aligned}$$

36. B; about 2.4 kg shows the answer is not exact, but an approximation.

37. $m = 150 + 0.38x$

38. $$\begin{aligned} m &= 150 + 0.38x \\ 300 &= 150 + 0.38x \\ 150 &= 0.38x \\ \$395 &\approx x \end{aligned}$$

39. $$\begin{aligned} 2.5x + 0.7 &= 4.6 - 1.3x \\ 25x + 7 &= 46 - 13x \\ 38x + 7 &= 46 \\ 38x &= 39 \\ x &\approx 1.0 \end{aligned}$$

Copyright © McDougal Littell Inc.
All rights reserved.

40. $1.1x + 3.2 = 0.2x - 1.4$
$11x + 32 = 2x - 14$
$9x + 32 = -14$
$9x = -46$
$x \approx -5.1$

41. $3.35x + 2.29 = 8.61$
$100(3.35x + 2.29) = 100(8.61)$
$335x + 229 = 861$
$335x = 632$
$x \approx 1.9$

42. $0.625y - 0.184 = 2.506y$
$1000(0.625y - 0.184) = 1000(2.506y)$
$625y - 184 = 2506y$
$-184 = 1881y$
$-0.1 \approx y$

43. $162 + 30 = 71n$
where n is the number of buses needed

44. $162 + 30 = 71n$
$192 = 71n$
$2.7 \approx n$
Three buses will be needed since seven-tenths of a bus is impractical.

45. Round up to 3. If you round down to 2, some of the passengers will have to be left behind.

3.6 Standardized Test Practice (p. 168)

46. C; $10^3 = 1000$

47. F;
$7.2x + 5.6 = -8.4 - 3.7x$
$10.9x + 5.6 = -8.4$
$10.9x = -14$
$x \approx -1.28$ (nearest hundredth)

48. B; $42.5r = 8.7$

49. $42.5r = 8.7$
$r \approx 0.2$
F

3.6 Mixed Review (pp. 168–169)

50. $-225.00 + 310.25 = 85.25$
The amount increased by $85.25.

51. Total withdrawn is the sum of the negative amounts:
$-225.00 + (-72.45) + (-400.00) = -697.45$
$697.45 withdrawn in June

52. Total change is sum of all deposits and withdrawals:
$-225.00 + 310.25 + 152.33 + (-72.45) + (-400.00)$
$= -\$234.87$

53.

Input	*Function*	*Output*
$t = 2$	$A = 8 + 5(2)$	$A = 18$
$t = 3$	$A = 8 + 5(3)$	$A = 23$
$t = 4$	$A = 8 + 5(4)$	$A = 28$
$t = 5$	$A = 8 + 5(5)$	$A = 33$
$t = 6$	$A = 8 + 5(6)$	$A = 38$

54. $8, -8$

55. $-3, 3$

56. $0.2, -0.2$

57. $\frac{4}{5}, -\frac{4}{5}$

58. $7.5, -7.5$

59. $5.6, -5.6$

60. $-4.9, 4.9$

61. $-16, 16$

3.6 Maintaining Skills (p. 169)

62. $1\frac{2}{7} + 2\frac{3}{7} = 3\frac{5}{7}$

63. $4\frac{7}{8} + 9\frac{1}{8} = 13\frac{8}{8} = 14$

64. $3\frac{5}{12} + 2\frac{5}{12} = 5\frac{10}{12} - 5\frac{5}{6}$

65. $5\frac{3}{14} + 8\frac{9}{14} = 13\frac{12}{14} = 13\frac{6}{7}$

66. $6\frac{21}{40} + 10\frac{9}{40} = 16\frac{30}{40} = 16\frac{3}{4}$

67. $9\frac{12}{16} + 15\frac{13}{16} = 24\frac{25}{16} = 25\frac{9}{16}$

68. $3\frac{8}{11} + 5\frac{3}{11} = 8\frac{11}{11} = 9$

69. $8\frac{1}{3} + 2\frac{2}{3} = 10\frac{3}{3} = 11$

70. $6\frac{7}{10} + 7\frac{5}{10} = 13\frac{12}{10} = 14\frac{2}{10} = 14\frac{1}{5}$

Quiz 2 *(p. 169)*

1. $27 - y = 7 - y$
$27 \neq 7$; no solution

2. $18 + 5n = 8n$
$18 = 3n$
$6 = n$; one solution

3. $-4(x + 4) = -2(2x + 8)$
$-4x - 16 = -4x - 16$
$-16 = -16$; identity

4. $\frac{1}{8}(64r + 32) = \frac{1}{2}(16r - 8)$
$8r + 4 = 8r - 4$
$4 \neq -4$; no solution

Copyright © McDougal Littell Inc.
All rights reserved.

5. $$\begin{aligned} 2y + 5 &= -y - 4 \\ 3y + 5 &= -4 \\ 3y &= -9 \\ y &= -3 \end{aligned}$$

6. $$\begin{aligned} 13m &= 15m + 14 \\ 0 &= 2m + 14 \\ -14 &= 2m \\ -7 &= m \end{aligned}$$

7. $$\begin{aligned} 8x - 3 - 5x &= 2x + 7 \\ 3x - 3 &= 2x + 7 \\ x - 3 &= 7 \\ x &= 10 \end{aligned}$$

8. $$\begin{aligned} 9 - 4x &= 6x + 2 - 3x \\ 9 - 4x &= 3x + 2 \\ 9 &= 7x + 2 \\ 7 &= 7x \\ 1 &= x \end{aligned}$$

9. $$\begin{aligned} 5 + 4(x - 1) &= 3(2 + x) \\ 5 + 4x - 4 &= 6 + 3x \\ 4x + 1 &= 6 + 3x \\ x + 1 &= 6 \\ x &= 5 \end{aligned}$$

10. $$\begin{aligned} -3(4 - r) + 4r &= 2(4 + r) \\ -12 + 3r + 4r &= 8 + 2r \\ -12 + 7r &= 8 + 2r \\ -12 + 5r &= 8 \\ 5r &= 20 \\ r &= 4 \end{aligned}$$

11. $$\begin{aligned} 8n + 4(-5 - 7n) &= -2(n + 1) \\ 8n - 20 - 28n &= -2n - 2 \\ -20n - 20 &= -2n - 2 \\ -20 &= 18n - 2 \\ -18 &= 18n \\ -1 &= n \end{aligned}$$

12. $$\begin{aligned} x - 5(x + 2) &= x + 3(3 - 2x) \\ x - 5x - 10 &= x + 9 - 6x \\ -4x - 10 &= -5x + 9 \\ x - 10 &= 9 \\ x &= 19 \end{aligned}$$

13. $$\begin{aligned} \frac{1}{2}(2k - 4) &= 3(k + 2) - 3k \\ k - 2 &= 3k + 6 - 3k \\ k - 2 &= 6 \\ k &= 8 \end{aligned}$$

14. $$\begin{aligned} \frac{1}{3}(6x - 3) &= 6(2 + x) - 5x \\ 2x - 1 &= 12 + 6x - 5x \\ 2x - 1 &= 12 + x \\ x - 1 &= 12 \\ x &= 13 \end{aligned}$$

15. $$\begin{aligned} 10t &= 7t + 28 \\ 3t &= 28 \\ t &= \frac{28}{3} \\ t &= 9\frac{1}{3} \text{ hrs} \end{aligned}$$

If you use the bike for $9\frac{1}{3}$ hours you will be charged for 10 hours, and the costs will be equivalent. You need to rent the bike for at least 10 hours to justify the cost of the helmet.

16. $$\begin{aligned} 7x + 19 &= 11 \\ 7x &= -8 \\ x &= -\frac{8}{7} \approx -1.14 \end{aligned}$$

17. $$\begin{aligned} -13c + 51c &= -26 \\ 38c &= -26 \\ c &= -\frac{26}{38} \approx -0.68 \end{aligned}$$

18. $$\begin{aligned} 3.6y + 7.5 &= 8.2y \\ 7.5 &= 4.6y \\ \frac{7.5}{4.6} &= y \\ y &\approx 1.63 \end{aligned}$$

19. $$\begin{aligned} 18y - 8 &= 4y - 3 \\ 14y - 8 &= -3 \\ 14y &= 5 \\ y &= \frac{5}{14} \approx 0.36 \end{aligned}$$

20. $$\begin{aligned} 2.24x - 33.52 &= 8.91x \\ -33.52 &= 6.67x \\ -\frac{33.52}{6.67} &= x \\ x &\approx -5.03 \end{aligned}$$

21. $$\begin{aligned} 3.2x - 4.9 &= 8.4x + 6.7 \\ -4.9 &= 5.2x + 6.7 \\ -11.6 &= 5.2x \\ -\frac{11.6}{5.2} &= x \\ x &\approx -2.23 \end{aligned}$$

22. $\frac{39}{5} = 7\frac{4}{5}$; It's impractical to give $\frac{4}{5}$ of a card, so you should give each friend 7 cards and keep the leftovers.

3.6 Using a Graphing Calculator: Try These *(p. 170)*

1. $Y_1 = 19.65x + 2.2(x - 6.05)$
$Y_2 = 255.65$

X	Y1	Y2
12.0	248.89	255.65
12.1	251.08	255.65
12.2	253.26	255.65
12.3	255.45	255.65
12.4	257.63	255.65
12.5	259.82	255.65
12.6	262.00	255.65

L1(1)=6

$x = 12.3$

Copyright © McDougal Littell Inc.
All rights reserved.

2. $Y_1 = 16.2(3.1 - x) - 31.55x$
$Y_2 = -19.5$

X	Y1	Y2
1.0	2.470	-19.5
1.1	-2.305	-19.5
1.2	-7.080	-19.5
1.3	-11.86	-19.5
1.4	-16.63	-19.5
1.5	-21.41	-19.5
1.6	-26.18	-19.5

X=1.5

$x = 1.5$

3. $Y_1 = 3.56x + 2.43$
$Y_2 = 6.17x - 11.40$

X	Y1	Y2
5.0	20.230	19.450
5.1	20.586	20.067
5.2	20.942	20.684
5.3	21.298	21.301
5.4	21.654	21.918
5.5	22.010	22.535
5.6	22.366	23.152

X=5.3

$x = 5.3$

4. $Y_1 = 3.5(x - 5.6) + 0.03x$
$Y_2 = 4.2x - 25.5$

X	Y1	Y2
8.3	9.699	9.36
8.4	10.052	9.78
8.5	10.405	10.20
8.6	10.758	10.62
8.7	11.111	11.04
8.8	11.464	11.46
8.9	11.817	11.88

X=8.8

$x = 8.8$

Lesson 3.7

3.7 Checkpoint (pp. 172–173)

1. $A = \frac{1}{2}bh$ Write original formula.
$2A = bh$ Multiply each side by 2.
$\frac{2A}{b} = h$ Divide each side by b.

2. $\frac{2A}{b} = h$

$\frac{2(25)}{10} = h$ Substitute the given values into the new formula.
$5 = h$; 5 in.

3. $d = rt$ Write original formula.
$\frac{d}{r} = t$ Divide each side by r.

4. $\frac{d}{r} = t$

$\frac{40{,}000{,}000}{50{,}000} = t$ Substitute the given values into the new formula.
$800 = t$; 800 days

3.7 Guided Practice (p. 174)

1. equation

2. solve

3. $r - s = t$ Write original formula.
$r = t + s$ Add s to each side.

4. $ax + b = c$ Write original formula.
$b = c - ax$ Subtract ax from each side.

5. $3y = x$ Write original formula.
$y = \frac{x}{3}$ Divide each side by 3.

6. $2j + 5 = k$ Write original formula.
$2j = k - 5$ Subtract 5 from each side.
$j = \frac{k - 5}{2}$

7. $x = \frac{1}{2}(y + 4)$ Write original formula.
$2x = y + 4$ Multiply each side by 2.
$2x - 4 = y$ Subtract 4 from each side.

8. $6(s - 1) = t$ Write original formula.
$6s - 6 = t$ Use distributive property.
$6s = t + 6$ Add 6 to each side.
$s = \frac{t + 6}{6}$ Divide each side by 6.

9. $A = \ell w$
$\frac{A}{\ell} = w$

10. $w = \frac{A}{\ell}$
$w = \frac{104}{13} = 8$ in.

3.7 Practice and Applications (pp. 174–176)

11. $F = \frac{9}{5}C + 32$
$F - 32 = \frac{9}{5}C$
$\frac{5}{9}(F - 32) = C$

12. $C = \frac{5}{9}(98.6 - 32)$
$C = \frac{5}{9}(66.6)$
$C = 37°$

13. $A = \ell w$
$\frac{A}{\ell} = w$; $w = \frac{36}{9} = 4$

Copyright © McDougal Littell Inc.
All rights reserved.

14. $A = \frac{1}{2}bh$

$2A = bh$

$\frac{2A}{b} = h$

$h = \frac{2(24)}{8} = 6$

15. $A = \ell w$

$\frac{A}{w} = \ell$

$\ell = \frac{112}{7} = 16$

16. $A = \frac{1}{2}bh$

$2A = bh$

$\frac{2A}{h} = b$

$b = \frac{2(22)}{4} = \frac{44}{4} = 11$

17. $P = 2\ell + 2w$

$P - 2\ell = 2w$

$\frac{P - 2\ell}{2} = w$

$w = \frac{18 - 2(6)}{2} = \frac{6}{2} = 3$

$A = \ell \cdot w$

$A = (6)(3) = 18 \text{ cm}^2$

18. $d = \frac{m}{v}$

$vd = m$

$v = \frac{m}{d}$

19. $v = \frac{m}{d}$

$v = \frac{4.0}{0.24} \approx 16.67 \text{ cm}^3$

20. B; $t = \frac{2475}{440}$

21. $t = \frac{2475}{440} \approx 6$ min.

22. $P = 64d + 2112$

$P - 2112 = 64d$

$\frac{(P - 2112)}{64} = d$

23. $d = \frac{P - 2112}{64} = \frac{4032 - 2112}{64} = 30$ ft

24.

$P = a + b + c$	Original equation
$P - b = a + c$	Subtract b from each side.
$P - b - c = a$	Subtract c from each side.

3.7 Standardized Test Practice (p. 176)

25. $d = rt$

$\frac{d}{r} = t$

$t = \frac{205}{55} \approx 4$ h; D

26. $C = \frac{5}{9}(F - 32)$

$\frac{9}{5}C = F - 32$

$\frac{9}{5}C + 32 = F$

$F = \frac{9}{5}(25) + 32$

$= 45 + 32 = 77°F$; J

3.7 Mixed Review (p. 176)

27. $x - 8 < 5$

$12 - 8 \stackrel{?}{<} 5$

$4 < 5$; 4 is a solution

28. $4 + k \geq 32$

$4 + 30 \stackrel{?}{\geq} 32$

$34 \geq 32$; 30 is a solution

29. $9a > 54$

$9(5) \stackrel{?}{>} 54$

$45 \not> 54$; 5 is not a solution

30. $t + 17 < 46$

$21 + 17 \stackrel{?}{<} 46$

$38 < 46$; 21 is a solution

31. $12x \leq 70$

$12(6) \stackrel{?}{\leq} 70$

$72 \not\leq 70$; 6 is not a solution

32. $y - 33 \geq 51$

$84 - 33 \stackrel{?}{\geq} 51$

$51 \geq 51$; 84 is a solution

33. $6x < 35$

$6(6) \stackrel{?}{<} 35$

$36 \not< 35$; 6 is not a solution

34. $14 - y > 12$

$14 - 4 \stackrel{?}{>} 12$

$10 \not> 12$; 4 is not a solution

35. $42 + x \leq 65$

$42 + 23 \stackrel{?}{\leq} 65$

$65 \leq 65$; 23 is a solution

36. Pro-sports (44%)

37. 28%

38. $31\% = \frac{31}{100}$; 31

Copyright © McDougal Littell Inc.
All rights reserved.

3.7 Maintaining Skills (p. 176)

39. $\frac{21}{49} = \frac{3 \cdot 7}{7 \cdot 7} = \frac{3}{7}$

40. $\frac{50}{85} = \frac{10 \cdot 5}{17 \cdot 5} = \frac{10}{17}$

41. $\frac{16}{72} = \frac{8 \cdot 2}{8 \cdot 9} = \frac{2}{9}$

42. $\frac{48}{64} = \frac{8 \cdot 6}{8 \cdot 8} = \frac{6}{8} = \frac{3}{4}$

43. $\frac{16}{32} = \frac{1}{2}$

44. $\frac{36}{48} = \frac{12 \cdot 3}{12 \cdot 4} = \frac{3}{4}$

45. $\frac{28}{32} = \frac{7 \cdot 4}{8 \cdot 4} = \frac{7}{8}$

46. $\frac{9}{27} = \frac{1}{3}$

Lesson 3.8

3.8 Checkpoint (pp. 177–179)

1. Won: 8

Lost: $15 - 8 = 7$

Ratio: $\frac{8}{7}$

2. $\frac{1200 \text{ miles}}{4 \text{ hours}} = 300 \text{ mi/h}$

3. $\frac{\$45}{3 \text{ lawns}} = \frac{\$15}{\text{lawn}}$

4. $8 \text{ pounds} \times \frac{16 \text{ ounces}}{1 \text{ pound}} = 128 \text{ ounces}$

5. $84 \text{ days} \times \frac{1 \text{ week}}{7 \text{ days}} = 12 \text{ weeks}$

6. $d = \left(19\frac{\text{mi}}{\text{gal}}\right)(13 \text{ gal}) = 247 \text{ miles}$

7. $\$140 \text{ U.S. dollars} \times \frac{1.466 \text{ Canadian dollars}}{\text{U.S. dollar}} =$

$205 Canadian

3.8 Guided Practice (p. 180)

1. ratio

2. different

3. one

4. unit analysis

5. $\frac{36}{45} = \frac{9 \cdot 4}{9 \cdot 5} = \frac{4}{5}$

6. $\frac{12}{10} = \frac{2 \cdot 6}{2 \cdot 5} = \frac{6}{5}$

7. $\frac{14}{21} = \frac{2 \cdot 7}{3 \cdot 7} = \frac{2}{3}$

8. $\frac{77}{55} = \frac{11 \cdot 7}{11 \cdot 5} = \frac{7}{5}$

9. $\frac{2 \text{ miles}}{40 \text{ min}} = 0.05 \text{ mi/min}$

10. $\frac{\$1.50}{24 \text{ teabags}} = \$.06/\text{teabag}$

11. $\frac{10.5 \text{ miles}}{\text{gallon}} \times 22 \text{ gallons} = 231 \text{ miles}$

3.8 Practice and Applications (pp. 180–182)

12. $\frac{5}{10} = \frac{5 \cdot 1}{5 \cdot 2} = \frac{1}{2}$

13. $\frac{30}{120} = \frac{3 \cdot 10}{12 \cdot 10} = \frac{3}{12} = \frac{3 \cdot 1}{3 \cdot 4} = \frac{1}{4}$

14. $\frac{8}{136} = \frac{8 \cdot 1}{8 \cdot 17} = \frac{1}{17}$

15. $\frac{60}{100} = \frac{6}{10} = \frac{2 \cdot 3}{2 \cdot 5} = \frac{3}{5}$

16. $\frac{6}{8} = \frac{2 \cdot 3}{2 \cdot 4} = \frac{3}{4}$

17. $\frac{66}{18} = \frac{6 \cdot 11}{6 \cdot 3} = \frac{11}{3}$

18. $\frac{15}{20} = \frac{5 \cdot 3}{5 \cdot 4} = \frac{3}{4}$

19. $\frac{28}{35} = \frac{4 \cdot 7}{5 \cdot 7} = \frac{4}{5}$

20. $\frac{\text{passes completed}}{\text{passes thrown}}; \frac{15}{30} = \frac{15 \cdot 1}{15 \cdot 2} = \frac{1}{2}$

21. $\frac{\text{first teeth}}{\text{permanent teeth}}; \frac{20}{32} = \frac{4 \cdot 5}{4 \cdot 8} = \frac{5}{8}$

22. $\frac{\$126}{18 \text{ h}} - \$7/\text{h}$

23. $\frac{45 \text{ mi}}{3 \text{ days}} = 15 \text{ mi/day}$

24. $\frac{\$3}{5 \text{ containers}} = \$.60/\text{container}$

25. $\frac{\$2}{5 \text{ cans}} = \$.40/\text{can}$

26. $\frac{440 \text{ g}}{8 \text{ servings}} = 55 \text{ g/serving}$

27. $\frac{20 \text{ oz}}{2.5 \text{ servings}} = 8 \text{ oz/serving}$

28. Average: $\frac{2 + 3 + 4 + 3}{4} = \frac{12}{4} = 3$ books/month

29. $\frac{50 \text{ mi}}{1 \text{ h}} \cdot 2 \text{ h} = 100 \text{ mi}$

30. 108 in.; $\frac{1 \text{ ft}}{12 \text{ in.}} = 9 \text{ ft}$

31. $720 \text{ sec} \cdot \frac{1 \text{ min}}{60 \text{ sec}} = 12 \text{ min}$; A

32. $60 \text{ eggs} \cdot \frac{1 \text{ doz}}{12 \text{ eggs}} = 5 \text{ doz}$

33. $2 \text{ yr} \cdot \frac{12 \text{ months}}{1 \text{ yr}} = 24 \text{ months}$

34. $168 \text{ days} \cdot \frac{1 \text{ week}}{7 \text{ days}} = 24 \text{ weeks}$

35. $1270 \text{ min} \cdot \frac{1 \text{ h}}{60 \text{ min}} = 21.2 \text{ h}$

36. $100 \text{ yds} \cdot \frac{3 \text{ ft}}{\text{yd}} = 300 \text{ ft}$

37. $2000 \text{ m} \cdot \frac{\text{km}}{1000 \text{ m}} = 2 \text{ km}$

Copyright © McDougal Littell Inc.
All rights reserved.

38. $\dfrac{(9 + 10 + 12 + 15 + 18)\text{ mi}}{(30 + 30 + 35 + 45 + 45)\text{ min}} = \dfrac{64\text{ mi}}{185\text{ min}}$

$\approx 0.35\text{ mi/min}$

39. $\dfrac{64\text{ mi}}{185\text{ min}} \cdot \dfrac{60\text{ min}}{1\text{ h}} \approx 21\text{ mi/h}$

40. $\dfrac{30\text{ mi}}{\text{h}} \cdot \dfrac{1\text{ h}}{60\text{ min}} = 0.5\text{ mi/min}$

41. $6\text{ mi} \cdot \dfrac{\text{min}}{0.5\text{ mi}} = 12\text{ min}$

42. $\$325 \cdot \dfrac{9.242\text{ pesos}}{\$} \approx 3004\text{ pesos}$

43. $840\text{ pesos} \cdot \dfrac{\$}{9.242\text{ pesos}} \approx \$91$

3.8 Standardized Test Practice (p. 182)

44. Blue marbles: $28 - 6 = 22$

$\dfrac{6}{22} = \dfrac{2 \cdot 3}{2 \cdot 11} = \dfrac{3}{11}$; D

45. $\dfrac{m\text{ mi}}{2\text{ hr}}$ or $\dfrac{m}{2}$; J

46. $154\text{ mi} \cdot \dfrac{\text{gal}}{22\text{ mi}} \cdot 2 = 14\text{ gal}$; B

47. $\$90\text{ Canadian} \cdot \dfrac{\text{U.S.}}{1.466\text{ Canadian}} = \$61\text{ U.S.}$; F

3.8 Mixed Review (p. 182)

48.

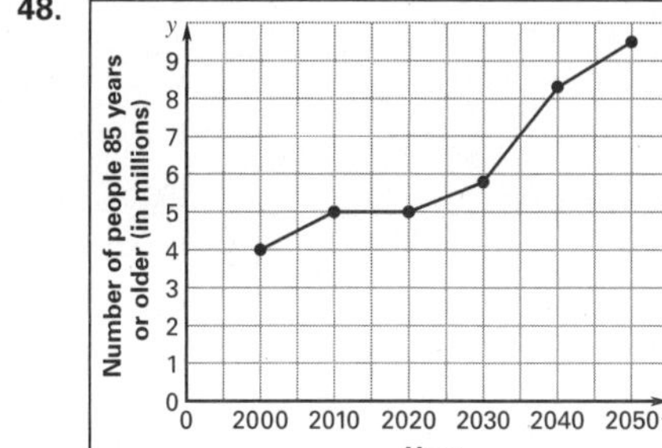

49. −6 −4 −2 0 2 4 6

$4 > -3;\ -3 < 4$

50. −6 −4 −2 0 2 4 6

$-5 < -2;\ -2 > -5$

51. −8 −6 −4 −2 0 2 4

$-6 < 3;\ 3 > -6$

52. $-7a - 9 = 6$

$-7a = 15$

$a = -\dfrac{15}{7} \approx -2.14$

Check:

$-7a - 9 = 6$

$-7(-2.14) - 9 \overset{?}{\approx} 6$

$5.98 \approx 6$

53. $10 - 3x = 4x$

$10 = 7x$

$1.43 \approx \dfrac{10}{7} = x$

Check:

$10 - 3x = 4x$

$10 - 3(1.43) \overset{?}{\approx} 4(1.43)$

$5.71 \approx 5.72$

54. $5x + 14 = -x$

$6x + 14 = 0$

$6x = -14$

$x = -\dfrac{14}{6} = -\dfrac{7}{3} \approx -2.33$

Check:

$5x + 14 = -x$

$5(-2.33) + 14 \overset{?}{\approx} -(-2.33)$

$2.35 \approx 2.33$

55. $A = \ell \cdot w$

$\dfrac{A}{\ell} = w$

$w = \dfrac{9000}{120} = 75\text{ ft}$

3.8 Maintaining Skills (p. 182)

56. $\dfrac{3}{4}, \dfrac{2}{5}$

$4 = 2^2$

5 is prime

$\text{LCD} = 2^2 \cdot 5 = 20$

57. $\dfrac{2}{9}, \dfrac{3}{18}$

$9 = 3^2$

$18 = 2 \cdot 3^2$

$\text{LCD} = 2 \cdot 3^2 = 18$

58. $\dfrac{5}{6}, \dfrac{8}{30}$; LCD = 30

59. $\dfrac{2}{3}, \dfrac{4}{7}$; $\text{LCD} = 3 \cdot 7 = 21$

60. $\dfrac{1}{16}, \dfrac{9}{20}$

$16 = 2^4$

$20 = 2^2 \cdot 5$

$\text{LCD} = 2^4 \cdot 5 = 80$

61. $\dfrac{14}{54}, \dfrac{31}{81}$

$54 = 2 \cdot 3^3$

$81 = 3^4$

$\text{LCD} = 2 \cdot 3^4 = 162$

Copyright © McDougal Littell Inc.
All rights reserved.

62. $\frac{3}{64}, \frac{17}{24}$
$64 = 2^6$
$24 = 2^3 \cdot 3$
$\text{LCD} = 2^6 \cdot 3 = 192$

63. $\frac{8}{49}, \frac{59}{70}$
$49 = 7^2$
$70 = 2 \cdot 5 \cdot 7$
$\text{LCD} = 2 \cdot 5 \cdot 7^2 = 490$

Lesson 3.9

3.9 Checkpoint (pp. 184–185)

1. $a = p \cdot b$
$a = (15\%)(100 \text{ meters})$
$a = 0.15(100) = 15 \text{ meters}$

2. $12 = 0.60b$
$20 = b$

3. $8 = p(20)$
$0.40 = p$
$40\% = p$

4. $20 = p(8)$
$2.5 = p$
$250\% = p$

5. $D = p \cdot R$
$D = 0.10(\$80) = \$8$ (discount)
Sale Price: $80 - 8 = \$72$

3.9 Guided Practice (p. 186)

1. $16 = (0.10)(160)$ or $(0.1)(160)$

2. 160 **3.** $0.15b = 12$ **4.** $99 = p(212)$

5. $a = 0.06(27)$ **6.** $13 = 0.45b$

7. $35 = p(20)$
$1.75 = p$
$175\% = p$

8. $(12\%)5 = a$
$(0.12)5 = a$
$0.6 = a$

9. $18 = 0.25b$
$72 = b$

10. $24 = 1.20b$
$20 = b$

11. $a = 0.06(10)$

12. $a = 0.06(10) = 0.6 = \$0.60$

3.9 Practice and Applications (pp. 186–188)

13. $a = (0.39)(50)$; B
39% of 50 is what number?

14. $39 = p(50)$; C
\$39 is what percent of \$50?

15. $39 = 0.50b$; A
39 is 50% of what number?

16. $a = 0.35(750) = \$262.50$

17. $a = 0.25(80) = 20$

18. $d = 0.24(710) = 170.4$ mi

19. $\ell = 0.14(220) = 30.8$ ft

20. $a = 0.08(800) = 64$ tons

21. $a = 2.00(5) = 10$

22. $52 = 0.125b$
$416 = b$

23. $42 = 0.50\ell$
$84 \text{ ft} = \ell$

24. $0.45d = 135$
$d = 300$ mi

25. $0.02b = 20$
$b = \$1000$

26. $30 = 0.20b$
$150 \text{ g} = b$

27. $90 = 0.45b$
$200 = b$

28. $3 = p(40)$
$0.075 = p$
$7.5\% = p$

29. $240 = p(50)$
$4.8 = p$
$480\% = p$

30. $55 = p(20)$
$2.75 = p$
$275\% = p$

31. $18 = p(60)$
$0.3 = p$
$30\% = p$

32. $9 = p(60)$
$0.15 = p$
$15\% = p$

33. $80 = p(400)$
$0.2 = p$
$20\% = p$

34. Area of large rectangle: $60 \cdot 40 = 2400$
Area of small square: $20 \cdot 20 = 400$
Area of blue region: $2400 - 400 = 2000$
Area of yellow region: $= 400$
Blue:
$2000 = p(2400)$
$0.8\overline{3} = p$
$83.3\% \approx p$
Yellow:
$400 = p(2400)$
$0.1\overline{6} = p$ or 16.7%

Copyright © McDougal Littell Inc.
All rights reserved.

35. A: 30%(60) = \$18 discount
Cost = \$60 − \$18 = \$42
B: 20%(60) = \$12 discount
Sale price = \$60 − \$12 = \$48

10%(48) = \$4.80 additional discount
Final price: \$48 − \$4.80 = \$43.20
The coat costs \$42 at Store A and \$43.20 at Store B. You will not save money at Store B.

36. Total votes: 180 + 72 + 39 + 12 = 303
Lincoln:
$180 = p(303)$
$59\% \approx p$
Breckenridge:
$72 = p(303)$
$24\% \approx p$
Bell:
$39 = p(303)$
$13\% \approx p$
Douglas:
$12 = p(303)$
$4\% \approx p$

37. $735 = p(3500)$
$21\% = p$

38. $630 = p(3500)$
$18\% \approx p$

39. $945 = p(3500)$
$27\% = p$

40. greater than

41. $a = 300\%b$, so
$a = 3.00b$ or $a = 3b$
Sample answer: 30 is 300% of 10
$30 = 3(10)$

3.9 Standardized Test Practice (p. 188)

42. D; $x = (0.25)(120)$

43. $a = 0.20(35) = 7$; \$7; H

3.9 Mixed Review (p. 188)

44. $x + 18 = 45$; $x = 27$

45. $21x = 105$; $x = 5$

46. $|9| = 9$

47. $|-32| = 32$

48. $-|5| = -(5) = -5$

49. $-|-16| = -(16) = -16$

3.9 Maintaining Skills (p. 188)

50. 1013, 1031, 1103, 1130, 1301

51. 217, 270, 2017, 2170, 2701

52. 23.25, 23.4, 23.45, 23.5, 23.53

53. 5.09, 5.1, 5.19, 5.9, 5.91

Quiz 3 *(p. 188)*

1. $d = rt$
$\frac{d}{r} = t$

2. $A = \frac{1}{2}bh$
$2A = bh$
$\frac{2A}{b} = h$

3. $d = \frac{m}{v}$
$vd = m$
$v = \frac{m}{d}$

4. $7 \text{ weeks} \cdot \frac{7 \text{ days}}{1 \text{ week}} = 49 \text{ days}$

5. $108 \text{ in.} \cdot \frac{1 \text{ ft}}{12 \text{ in.}} = 9 \text{ ft}$

6. $\frac{20 \text{ students}}{1 \text{ classroom}} \cdot \frac{15 \text{ classrooms}}{1 \text{ school}} = \frac{300 \text{ students}}{\text{school}}$

7. $\frac{24 \text{ h}}{1 \text{ day}} \cdot 10 \text{ days} = 240 \text{ h}$

8. discount = \$23 − \$17.25 = \$5.75

9. $5.75 = p(23)$
$0.25 = p$
$25\% = p$

Chapter Summary and Review *(pp. 189–192)*

1. $y - 15 = -4$
$y - 15 + 15 = -4 + 15$
$y = 11$
Check:
$y - 15 = -4$
$11 - 15 \stackrel{?}{=} -4$
$-4 = -4$

2. $7 + x = -3$
$7 + x - 7 = -3 - 7$
$x = -10$
Check:
$7 + x = -3$
$7 + (-10) \stackrel{?}{=} -3$
$-3 = -3$

3. $t - (-10) = 2$
$t + 10 = 2$
$t + 10 - 10 = 2 - 10$
$t = -8$
Check:
$t - (-10) = 2$
$-8 - (-10) \stackrel{?}{=} 2$
$-8 + 10 \stackrel{?}{=} 2$
$2 = 2$

Copyright © McDougal Littell Inc.
All rights reserved.

4. $81 = 3t$
$\frac{81}{3} = \frac{3t}{3}$
$27 = t$
Check:
$81 = 3t$
$81 \stackrel{?}{=} 3(27)$
$81 = 81$

5. $-6x = 54$
$\frac{-6x}{-6} = \frac{54}{-6}$
$x = -9$
Check:
$-6(x) = 54$
$-6(-9) \stackrel{?}{=} 54$
$54 = 54$

6. $\frac{x}{4} = -16$
$4\left(\frac{x}{4}\right) = 4(-16)$
$x = -64$
Check:
$\frac{x}{4} = -16$
$\frac{-64}{4} \stackrel{?}{=} -16$
$-16 = -16$

7. $26 + 9x = -1$
$26 + 9x - 26 = -1 - 26$
$9x = -27$
$\frac{9x}{9} = \frac{-27}{9}$
$x = -3$

8. $-32 = 4c - 12$
$-32 + 12 = 4c - 12 + 12$
$-20 = 4c$
$\frac{-20}{4} = \frac{4c}{4}$
$-5 = c$

9. $9r - 2 - 6r = 1$
$3r - 2 = 1$
$3r - 2 + 2 = 1 + 2$
$3r = 3$
$\frac{3r}{3} = \frac{3}{3}$
$r = 1$

10. $-2(4 - x) - 7 = 5$
$-8 + 2x - 7 = 5$
$2x - 15 = 5$
$2x - 15 + 15 = 5 + 15$
$2x = 20$
$\frac{2x}{2} = \frac{20}{2}$
$x = 10$

11. $n + 3(1 + 2n) = 17$
$n + 3 + 6n = 17$
$7n + 3 = 17$
$7n + 3 - 3 = 17 - 3$
$7n = 14$
$\frac{7n}{7} = \frac{14}{7}$
$n = 2$

12. $\frac{3}{4}(x + 8) = 9$
$\frac{4}{3}\left(\frac{3}{4}\right)(x + 8) = \frac{4}{3}(9)$
$x + 8 = 12$
$x + 8 - 8 = 12 - 8$
$x = 4$

13. $24 - 3x = 9x$
$24 = 12x$
$2 = x$; one solution

14. $15x - 23 = 15x$
$-23 \neq 0$; no solution

15. $2m - 9 = 6 - m$
$3m - 9 = 6$
$3m = 15$
$m = 5$; one solution

16. $36 - 4d = 4(9 - d)$
$36 - 4d = 36 - 4d$
$36 = 36$; identity

17. $12 + 11h = -18 - 4h$
$12 + 15h = -18$
$15h = -30$
$h = -2$; one solution

18. $2x + 18 + 4x = -2x + 10$
$6x + 18 = -2x + 10$
$8x + 18 = 10$
$8x = -8$
$x = -1$; one solution

19. $12 + n = 6 + 2n$
$12 = 6 + n$
$6 = n$; 6 weeks

20. $3x - 4 = 3$
$3x = 7$
$x = \frac{7}{3} \approx 2.33$

21. $5x - 9 = 18x - 23$
$-9 = 13x - 23$
$14 = 13x$
$1.08 \approx \frac{14}{13} = x$

22. $13.7t - 4.7 = 9.9 + 8.1t$
$5.6t - 4.7 = 9.9$
$5.6t = 14.6$
$t = \frac{14.6}{5.6} \approx 2.61$

Copyright © McDougal Littell Inc.
All rights reserved.

23. $V = \ell wh$

$\frac{V}{wh} = \ell$

24. $d = \frac{m}{v}$

$dv = m$

25. $P = a + b + c$

$P - a - c = b$

26. $\frac{340 \text{ mi}}{20 \text{ gal}} = 17 \text{ mi/gal}$

27. $5 \text{ gal} \times \frac{17 \text{ mi}}{1 \text{ gal}} = 85 \text{ mi}$

28. $5 = p(20)$

$25\% = p$

Chapter Test *(p. 193)*

1. $x + 3 = 8$

$x = 5$

Check:

$x + 3 = 8$

$5 + 3 \stackrel{?}{=} 8$

$8 = 8$

2. $19 = a - 4$

$23 = a$

Check:

$19 = a - 4$

$19 \stackrel{?}{=} 23 - 4$

$19 = 19$

3. $-2y = -18$

$y = 9$

Check:

$-2y = -18$

$-2(9) \stackrel{?}{=} -18$

$-18 = -18$

4. $22 = 3p - 5$

$27 = 3p$

$9 = p$

Check:

$22 = 3p - 5$

$22 \stackrel{?}{=} 3(9) - 5$

$22 = 22$

5. $r - (-7) = 14$

$r + 7 = 14$

$r = 7$

Check:

$r - (-7) = 14$

$7 - (-7) \stackrel{?}{=} 14$

$14 = 14$

6. $\frac{x}{2} = -6$

$x = -12$

Check:

$\frac{x}{2} = -6$

$-\frac{12}{2} \stackrel{?}{=} -6$

$-6 = -6$

7. $\frac{5}{3}(9 + w) = -10$

$\frac{3}{5}\left(\frac{5}{3}\right)(9 + w) = \frac{3}{5}(-10)$

$9 + w = -6$

$w = -15$

Check:

$\frac{5}{3}(9 + w) = -10$

$\frac{5}{3}(9 - 15) \stackrel{?}{=} -10$

$\frac{5}{3}(-6) \stackrel{?}{=} -10$

$-10 = -10$

8. $-\frac{3}{4}x - 2 = -8$

$-\frac{3}{4}x = -6$

$-\frac{4}{3}\left(-\frac{3}{4}\right)x = -\frac{4}{3}(-6)$

$x = 8$

Check:

$-\frac{3}{4}x - 2 \stackrel{?}{=} -8$

$-\frac{3}{4}(8) - 2 \stackrel{?}{=} -8$

$-6 - 2 = -8$

$-8 = -8$

9. $14 - 5t = 3t$

$14 = 8t$

$\frac{14}{8} = t$

$\frac{7}{4} = t$; one solution

10. $6x - 9 = 10x + 7$

$-9 = 4x + 7$

$-16 = 4x$

$-4 = x$; one solution

11. $-3(x - 2) = 6 - 3x$

$-3x + 6 = 6 - 3x$

$6 = 6$; identity

Copyright © McDougal Littell Inc.
All rights reserved.

12. $$\begin{aligned} \frac{3}{4}(9x + 12) &= 15x \\ \frac{4}{3}\left(\frac{3}{4}\right)(9x + 2) &= \frac{4}{3}(15x) \\ 9x + 2 &= 20x \\ 2 &= 11x \\ \frac{2}{11} &= x\text{; one solution} \end{aligned}$$

13. $$\begin{aligned} 24y - (5y + 6) &= 27y + 3 \\ 24y - 5y - 6 &= 27y + 3 \\ 19y - 6 &= 27y + 3 \\ -6 &= 8y + 3 \\ -9 &= 8y \\ -\frac{9}{8} &= y\text{; one solution} \end{aligned}$$

14. $$\begin{aligned} -5r - 6 + 4r &= -r + 2 \\ -r - 6 &= -r + 2 \\ -6 &\neq 2\text{; no solution} \end{aligned}$$

15. $$\begin{aligned} 26 + 9p &= 58p \\ 26 &= 49p \\ 0.53 \approx \frac{26}{49} &= p \end{aligned}$$

16. $$\begin{aligned} -34 &= 8x - 15 \\ -19 &= 8x \\ -2.38 \approx -\frac{19}{8} &= x \end{aligned}$$

17. $$\begin{aligned} 15x - 18 &= 37 \\ 15x &= 55 \\ x &= \frac{55}{15} \approx 3.67 \end{aligned}$$

18. $$\begin{aligned} 13.2k + 4.3 &= 2.7k \\ 10.5k + 4.3 &= 0 \\ 10.5k &= -4.3 \\ k &= -\frac{4.3}{10.5} \approx -0.41 \end{aligned}$$

19. $$\begin{aligned} 42.6x - 29.4 &= -3.5x \\ 46.1x - 29.4 &= 0 \\ 46.1x &= 29.4 \\ x &= \frac{29.4}{46.1} \approx 0.64 \end{aligned}$$

20. $$\begin{aligned} 3.82 + 1.25x &= 5.91 \\ 1.25x &= 2.09 \\ x &= \frac{2.09}{1.25} \approx 1.67 \end{aligned}$$

21. $$\begin{aligned} A &= \ell w \\ \frac{A}{w} &= \ell \end{aligned}$$

22. $$\begin{aligned} \frac{9}{5}C + 32 &= F \\ \frac{9}{5}C &= F - 32 \\ C &= \frac{5}{9}(F - 32) \end{aligned}$$

23. $$\begin{aligned} A &= \frac{1}{2}bh \\ 2A &= bh \\ \frac{2A}{b} &= h \end{aligned}$$

24. $98 \text{ days} \times \frac{1 \text{ week}}{7 \text{ days}} = 14 \text{ weeks}$

25. $37 \text{ h} \times \frac{60 \text{ min}}{1 \text{ h}} = 2220 \text{ min}$

26. $15 \text{ yd} \times \frac{3 \text{ ft}}{1 \text{ yd}} = 45 \text{ ft}$

27. $a = 0.30(650) = 195$

28. $$\begin{aligned} 36 &= 0.15(b) \\ \$240 &= b \end{aligned}$$

29. $$\begin{aligned} 4 &= p(20) \\ 20\% &= p \end{aligned}$$

30. $$\begin{aligned} a &= 0.45(200) \\ a &= 90 \text{ lb} \end{aligned}$$

31. C; $12x = 72$

32. $$\begin{aligned} 8 + 3e &= 26 \\ 3e &= 18 \\ e &= 6 \text{ errands} \end{aligned}$$

33. $\$175 \text{ U.S.} \times \frac{1.466 \text{ Canadian}}{\text{U.S.}} = \$257 \text{ Canadian}$

Chapter Standardized Test *(p. 194)*

1. $$\begin{aligned} 4 - x &= -5 \\ -x &= -9 \\ x &= 9\text{; D} \end{aligned}$$

2. Multiply each side by $\frac{5}{3}$; D

3. $$\begin{aligned} x + x + 3x + 3x &= 40 \\ 8x &= 40 \\ x &= 5 \text{ cm; B} \end{aligned}$$

4. $$\begin{aligned} 9x - 4(3x - 2) &= 4 \\ 9x - 12x + 8 &= 4 \\ -3x + 8 &= 4 \\ -3x &= -4 \\ x &= \frac{4}{3}\text{; C} \end{aligned}$$

5. $$\begin{aligned} \frac{1}{3}(27x + 18) &= 12 \\ 9x + 6 &= 12 \\ 9x &= 6 \\ x &= \frac{6}{9} = \frac{2}{3}\text{; B} \end{aligned}$$

6. $$\begin{aligned} -2y + 3(4 - y) &= 12 - 5y \\ -2y + 12 - 3y &= 12 - 5y \\ -5y + 12 &= 12 - 5y \\ 12 &= 12 \end{aligned}$$

identity; D

Copyright © McDougal Littell Inc.
All rights reserved.

7. $0.75t = 12$
$t = 16$; C

8. $13.6y - 14.8 = 4.1y - 6.3$
$9.5y - 14.8 = -6.3$
$9.5y = 8.5$
$y = \frac{8.5}{9.5} \approx 0.9$; D

9. $C = \frac{5}{9}(F - 32)$
$\frac{9}{5}C = F - 32$
$\frac{9}{5}C + 32 = F$
$\frac{9}{5}(10°) + 32 = F$
$18 + 32 = F$
$50° = F$; D

10. $\frac{108 \text{ envelopes}}{45 \text{ min}} \times \frac{60 \text{ min}}{1 \text{ h}} \times 2 \text{ h}$
$= 288$ envelopes
D

11. $a = 0.26(250)$
$a = 65$ m
B

Maintaining Skills *(p. 195)*

1.

Wind Chill at 40° F
Temperature (°F): 0, 9, 11, 13
Wind speed (mi/h): 0, 25, 30, 35, 40

2.

Input r	0	2	4
Output C	100	118	136

Input	*Function*	*Output*
$r = 0$	$C = 100 + 9(0)$	$C = 100$
$r = 2$	$C = 100 + 9(2)$	$C = 118$
$r = 4$	$C = 100 + 9(4)$	$C = 136$

Chapters 1–3 Cumulative Practice *(pp. 196–197)*

1. $20 - 4y = 20 - 4(3) = 20 - 12 = 8$

2. $\frac{x}{4} + 12 = \frac{8}{4} + 12 = 2 + 12 = 14$

3. $x^2 - 8 = (7)^2 - 8 = 49 - 8 = 41$

4. $(6 + x) + 3x = (6 + 6) + 3(6) = 12 + 18 = 30$

5. $(3t)^3 = (3 \cdot 2)^3 = 6^3 = 216$

6. $8x^2 = 8(4)^2 = 8(16) = 128$

7. $9 \div 3 + 2 = 3 + 2 = 5$

8. $-5 + 3 \cdot 8 - 6 = -5 + 24 - 6 = 19 - 6 = 13$

9. $\frac{4 \cdot 9}{3} - 5 = \frac{36}{3} - 5 = 12 - 5 = 7$

10. $20 - (-3) - 8 = 20 + 3 - 8 = 23 - 8 = 15$

11. $2 \cdot 35 + (-13) = 70 - 13 = 57$

12. $[(6 \cdot 4) + 5] - 7 = [24 + 5] - 7 = 29 - 7 = 22$

13. $4 + 2x = 12$
$4 + 2(2) \stackrel{?}{=} 12$
$4 + 4 \stackrel{?}{=} 12$
$8 \neq 12$; not a solution

14. $6x - 5 = 13$
$6(3) - 5 \stackrel{?}{=} 13$
$18 - 5 \stackrel{?}{=} 13$
$13 = 13$; is a solution

15. $3y + 7 = 31$
$3(8) + 7 \stackrel{?}{=} 31$
$24 + 7 \stackrel{?}{=} 31$
$31 = 31$; is a solution

16. $x - 4 < 6$
$9 - 4 \stackrel{?}{<} 6$
$5 < 6$; is a solution

17. $5m + 3 > 8$
$5(1) + 3 \stackrel{?}{>} 8$
$8 \not> 8$; is not a solution

18. $9 \le 22 - 4x$
$9 \le 22 - 4(3)$
$9 \le 22 - 12$
$9 \le 10$; is a solution

19. $x^3 - 8$

20. $2x - 4 = 10$

21. $-3x < 12$

22. $x + 15 \ge 30$

23.

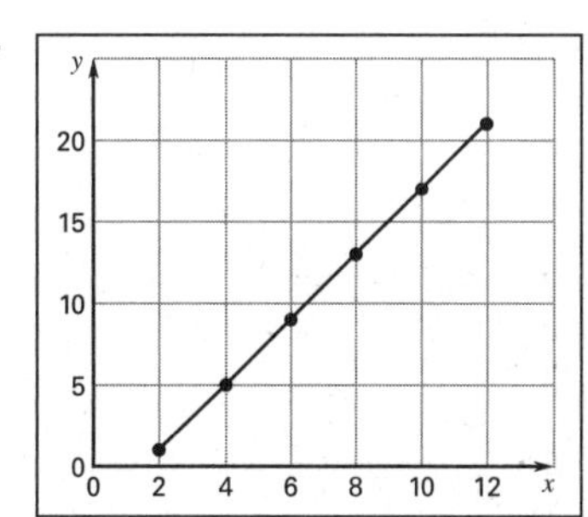

24. $0 < 6$

25. $-9 < -8$

26. $-1.5 < -1$

27. $\frac{5}{4} > \frac{4}{5}$

28. $-2.1 < 1.2$

29. $-109 < -101$

30. $2 > -3$

31. $-6 < 9$

Copyright © McDougal Littell Inc.
All rights reserved.

32. $-4(x)(6) = -24x$ **33.** $5(-y)^3 = -5y^3$

34. $8(-3)(-x)(-x) = -24x^2$

35. $-(4 - 2t) = -4 + 2t$

36. $-2(x + 3) - 1 = -2x - 6 - 1 = -2x - 7$

37. $(6x - 9)\frac{2}{3} = 6x\left(\frac{2}{3}\right) - 9\left(\frac{2}{3}\right) = 4x - 6$

38. $3 + 6(x - 4) = 3 + 6x - 24 = 6x - 21$

39. $5(9x + 5) - 2x = 45x + 25 - 2x = 43x + 25$

40. $d = -6t$

41. $d = -6(5) = -30$ ft; negative; downward velocity is negative

42. $15(x + 6)$; $15x + 90$

43. $15(x + 6) = 15(x) + 15(6) = 15x + 90$

44.
$$x + 11 = 19$$
$$x = 8$$

45.
$$x - (-7) = -2$$
$$x + 7 = -2$$
$$x = -9$$

46.
$$9b = 135$$
$$b = 15$$

47.
$$35 = 3c - 19$$
$$54 = 3c$$
$$18 = c$$

48.
$$\frac{p}{2} - 9 = -1$$
$$\frac{p}{2} = 8$$
$$p = 16$$

49.
$$4(2x - 9) = 6(10x - 6)$$
$$8x - 36 = 60x - 36$$
$$-36 = 52x - 36$$
$$0 = 52x$$
$$0 = x$$

50.
$$3(q - 12) = 5q + 2$$
$$3q - 36 = 5q + 2$$
$$-36 = 2q + 2$$
$$-38 = 2q$$
$$-19 = q$$

51.
$$\frac{3}{4}(2x + 5) = 6$$
$$\frac{4}{3}\left(\frac{3}{4}\right)(2x + 5) = \frac{4}{3}(6)$$
$$2x + 5 = 8$$
$$2x = 3$$
$$x = \frac{3}{2}$$

52.
$$9(2p + 1) - 3p = 4p - 6$$
$$18p + 9 - 3p = 4p - 6$$
$$15p + 9 = 4p - 6$$
$$11p + 9 = -6$$
$$11p = -15$$
$$p = -\frac{15}{11}$$

53.
$$3(50) + 2n = 750$$
$$150 + 2n = 750$$
$$2n = 600$$
$$n = 300 \text{ rolls}$$

54.
$$8x - 5 = 24$$
$$8x = 29$$
$$x = \frac{29}{8} \approx 3.63$$

55.
$$70 = 9 - 3x$$
$$61 = -3x$$
$$-20.33 \approx \frac{61}{-3} = x$$

56.
$$-3.46y = -5.78$$
$$y = \frac{-5.78}{-3.46} \approx 1.67$$

57.
$$4.17n + 3.29 = 2.74n$$
$$1.43n + 3.29 = 0$$
$$1.43n = -3.29$$
$$n = -\frac{3.29}{1.43} \approx -2.30$$

58.
$$2.4(0.3 + x) = 8.7$$
$$0.72 + 2.4x = 8.7$$
$$2.4x = 7.98$$
$$x = \frac{7.98}{2.4} \approx 3.33$$

59.
$$23.5a + 12.5 = 9.3a - 4.8$$
$$14.2a + 12.5 = -4.8$$
$$14.2a = -17.3$$
$$a = -\frac{17.3}{14.2} \approx -1.22$$

60.
$$A = \frac{1}{2}bh$$
$$2A = bh$$
$$\frac{2A}{b} = h$$

61.
$$h = \frac{2A}{b}$$
$$h = \frac{2(120)}{24} = \frac{240}{24} = 10 \text{ cm}$$

62. $t = 6$ h
$d = 66{,}660 - 66{,}300 = 360$ mi
$d = rt$
$\frac{d}{t} = r$; $r = \frac{360 \text{ mi}}{6 \text{ h}} = 60$ mi/h

63. discount: $a = 0.30(65) = \$19.50$
Sale price: $\$65 - \$19.50 = \$45.50$

Copyright © McDougal Littell Inc.
All rights reserved.

Chapters 1–3 Project *(pp. 198–199)*

1. *Sample answer:* a change of clothes, change for breaking large bills

2. Total expenses:
$20(1.47) + 8(2.99) + 8(1.99) + 20(0.99) + 6(0.79)$
$= \$93.78$

3.

Input	*Function*	*Output*
$x = 20$	$y = 4(20)$	$y = 80$
$x = 40$	$y = 4(40)$	$y = 160$
$x = 60$	$y = 4(60)$	$y = 240$
$x = 80$	$y = 4(80)$	$y = 320$
$x = 100$	$y = 4(100)$	$y = 400$

Cars washed	20	40	60	80	100
Income earned	\$80	\$160	\$240	\$320	\$400

4.

Input	*Function*	*Output*
$x = 20$	$y = 6(20)$	$y = \$120$
$x = 40$	$y = 6(40)$	$y = \$240$
$x = 60$	$y = 6(60)$	$y = \$360$
$x = 80$	$y = 6(80)$	$y = \$480$
$x = 100$	$y = 6(100)$	$y = \$600$

Cars washed/vacuumed	20	40	60	80	100
Income earned	\$120	\$240	\$360	\$480	\$600

5. $60(4) + 40(6) = 240 + 240 = \$480$

6. Profit: $\$480 - \$93.78 = \$386.22$

7. $I = 4x + 6y$

8. $P = 4x + 6y - 93.78$

Copyright © McDougal Littell Inc.
All rights reserved.

CHAPTER 4

Chapter Opener

Think & Discuss (p. 201)

1. *Sample answer:* Water flowing over a waterfall or down a river; the greater the gradient (steepness), the more power is generated. A steep landscape is difficult for building houses.
2. *Sample answer:* **(2)** is steeper than **(1)**

Chapter Readiness Quiz *(p. 202)*

1. B
2. $\frac{-3-(-1)}{2} = \frac{-3+1}{2} = \frac{-2}{2} = -1$, B
3. $[2(5)]^2 = [10]^2 = 100$, D

Lesson 4.1

4.1 Checkpoint (pp. 203–205)

1. $A(3, 0)$, $B(2, 3)$, $C(-3, 1)$, $D(-2, -2)$

2–5.

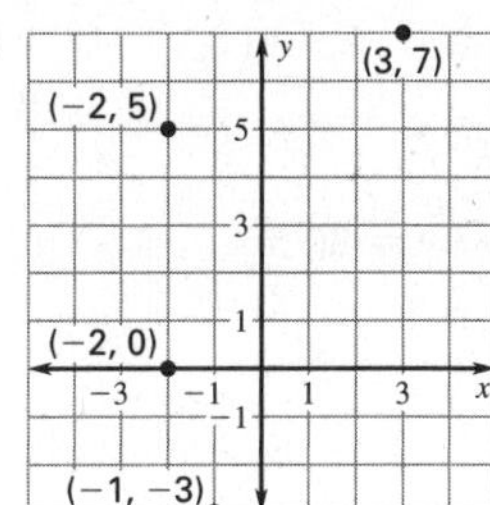

6. III
7. none; it is on the x-axis.
8. IV
9. II

10.

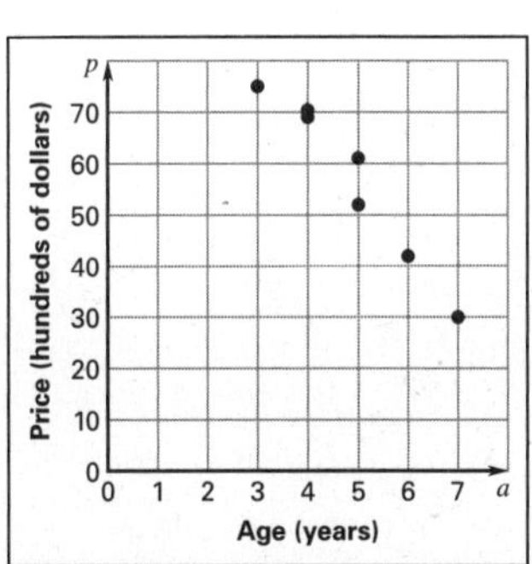

Price decreases as age increases.

4.1 Guided Practice (p. 206)

1. ordered pair
2. 5
3. quadrants

4.

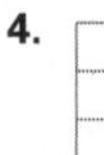

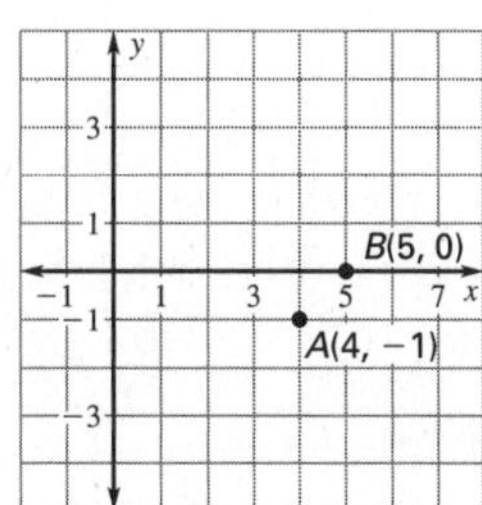

5.

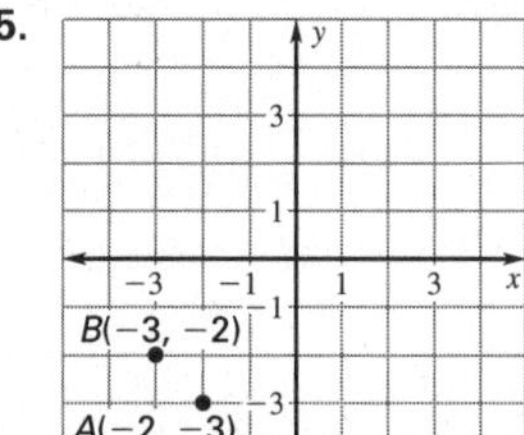

6. never
7. always
8. always
9. always

4.1 Practice and Applications (pp. 206–207)

10. $A(-3, 2)$, $B(-1, -2)$, $C(2, 0)$, $D(2, 3)$
11. $A(2, 4)$, $B(0, -1)$, $C(-1, 0)$, $D(-2, -1)$
12. $A(-3, 0)$, $B(-4, -3)$, $C(0, 2)$, $D(1, -2)$

13.

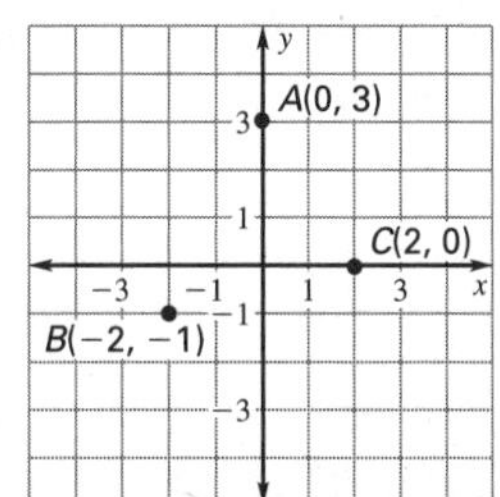

14.

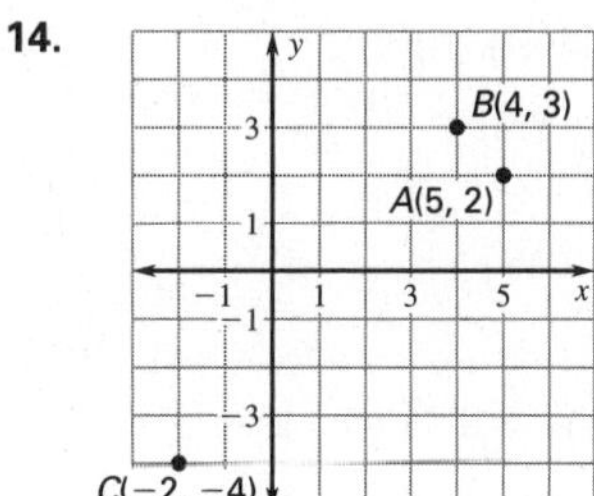

Copyright © McDougal Littell Inc.
All rights reserved.

15.

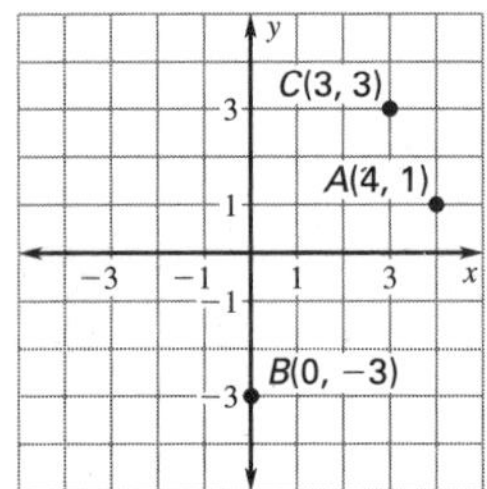

16.

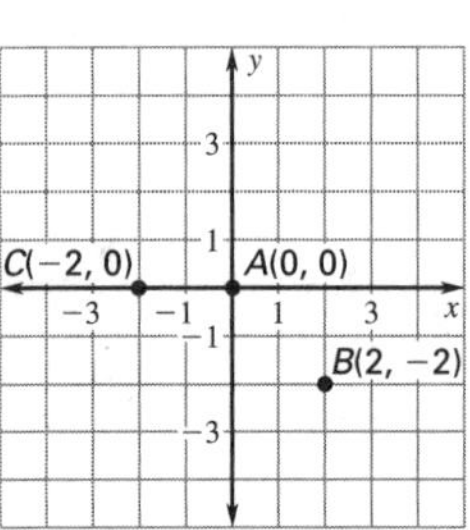

17.

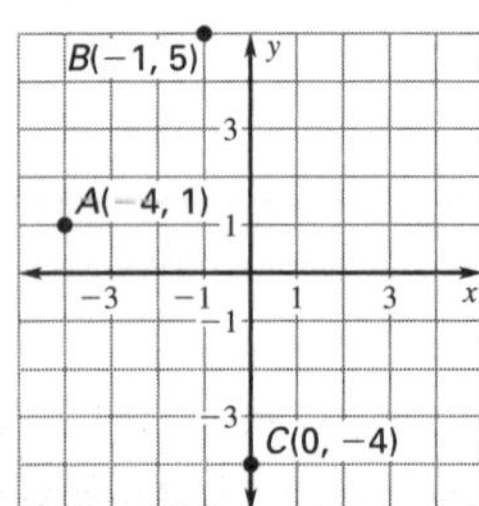

18.

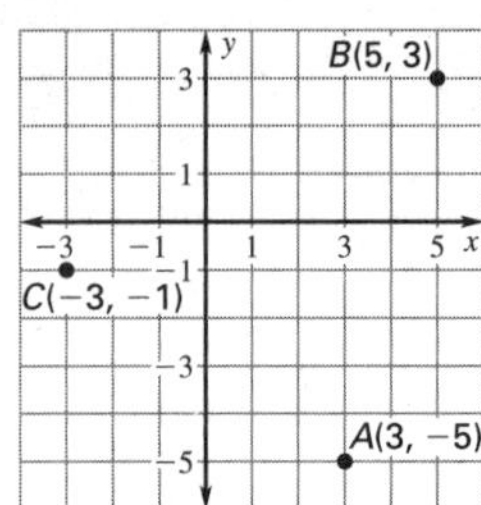

19. $(5, -3)$, positive x, negative y, IV

20. $(-2, 7)$, negative x, positive y, II

21. $(6, 17)$, positive x, positive y, I

22. $(14, -5)$, positive x, negative y, IV

23. $(-4, -2)$, negative x, negative y, III

24. $(3, 9)$, positive x, positive y, I

25. $(-5, -2)$, negative x, negative y, III

26. $(-5, 6)$, negative x, positive y, II

27. horizontal: pounds
vertical: inches

28. about (4000, 220)

29. C; length tends to increase as weight increases.

30. W: weight $= 2010$
G: gas mileage $= 29$

31. Gas mileage decreases as weight increases.

32. The greater the length of the car, the less the gas mileage will be, since the weight increases as the length increases.

33.

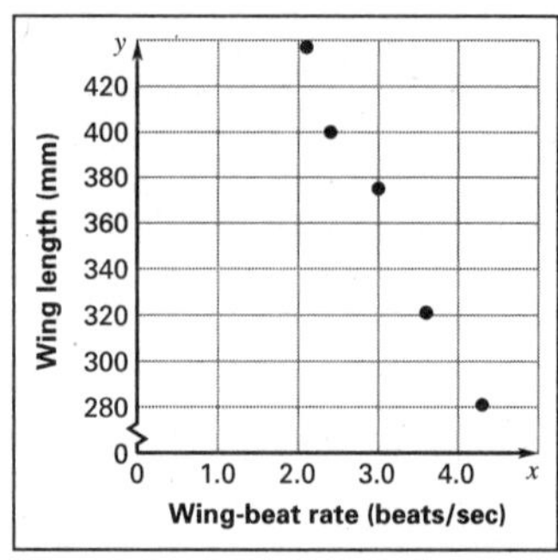

34. slowest: 2.1
fastest: 4.3
slowest is farthest left; fastest is farthest right.

35. As wing-beat rate increases, wing length decreases.

4.1 Standardized Test Practice (p. 208)

36. $(-7, 3)$, B

37. Quadrant III, H

38. $(8, -7)$, D

39. y-axis, G

4.1 Mixed Review (p. 208)

40. $3(2) + 9 = 6 + 9 = 15$

41. $13 - (4 + 2) = 13 - 6 = 7$

42. $4.2(3) + 17.9 = 12.6 + 17.9 = 30.5$

43. $-(-2) - (-1) = 2 + 1 = 3$

44. $4^2 - 3 = 16 - 3 = 13$

45. $12 + 3^3 = 12 + 27 = 39$

46. $1.5^5 + 10 = 7.59375 + 10$
$= 17.59375$

47. $\dfrac{2^2 + 3^2}{2 - 3} = \dfrac{4 + 9}{-1} = \dfrac{13}{-1} = -13$

48. 2.6

49. 1.07

50. $\dfrac{9}{10}$

51. $\dfrac{2}{3}$

52. $3x - 6 = 0$
$3x = 6$
$x = \dfrac{6}{3} = 2$

53. $6x + 5 = 35$
$6x = 30$
$x = \dfrac{30}{6} = 5$

54. $x + 1 = -3$
$x = -3 - 1$
$x = -4$

Copyright © McDougal Littell Inc.
All rights reserved.

55. $a - 3 = -2$
$a = -2 + 3$
$a = 1$

56. $\frac{1}{2}x - 1 = -1$
$\frac{1}{2}x = 0$
$x = 2 \cdot 0$
$x = 0$

57. $\frac{1}{5}r + 3 = 4$
$\frac{1}{5}r = 1$
$r = 1 \cdot 5$
$r = 5$

4.1 Maintaining Skills (p. 208)

58. $7\frac{4}{9} - 4\frac{1}{9} = 7 - 4 + \frac{4}{9} - \frac{1}{9} = 3 + \frac{3}{9} = 3 + \frac{1}{3} = 3\frac{1}{3}$

59. $3\frac{2}{3} - 1\frac{1}{3} = 3 - 1 + \frac{2}{3} - \frac{1}{3} = 2 + \frac{1}{3} = 2\frac{1}{3}$

60. $8\frac{3}{4} - 7\frac{3}{4} = 8 - 7 + \frac{3}{4} - \frac{3}{4} = 1 + 0 = 1$

61. $9\frac{8}{15} - 2\frac{4}{15} = 9 - 2 + \frac{8}{15} - \frac{4}{15} = 7 + \frac{4}{15} = 7\frac{4}{15}$

62. $8\frac{9}{13} - 5\frac{2}{13} = 8 - 5 + \frac{9}{13} - \frac{2}{13} = 3 + \frac{7}{13} = 3\frac{7}{13}$

63. $6\frac{7}{11} - 6\frac{2}{11} = 6 - 6 + \frac{7}{11} - \frac{2}{11} = 0 + \frac{5}{11} = \frac{5}{11}$

64. $17\frac{5}{8} - 10\frac{3}{8} = 17 - 10 + \frac{5}{8} - \frac{3}{8} = 7 + \frac{2}{8}$
$= 7 + \frac{1}{4} = 7\frac{1}{4}$

65. $12\frac{17}{21} - 7\frac{2}{21} = 12 - 7 + \frac{17}{21} - \frac{2}{21} = 5 + \frac{15}{21}$
$= 5 + \frac{5}{7} = 5\frac{5}{7}$

66. $18\frac{9}{4} - 3\frac{3}{14} = 18 - 3 + \frac{9}{14} - \frac{3}{14} = 15 + \frac{6}{14}$
$= 15 + \frac{3}{7} = 15\frac{3}{7}$

4.2 Developing Concepts: Explore *(p. 209)*

1. $8 + 4(1) = 8 + 4 = 12$
2. D is a solution; $-4 + 4(4) = -4 + 16 = 12$
   E is not a solution; $-1 + 4(2) = -1 + 8 \neq 12$
   F is not a solution; $2 + 4(1) = 2 + 4 \neq 12$
   G is a solution; $4 + 4(2) = 4 + 8 = 12$
3. The solutions of $x + 4y = 12$ lie on a line.

Think About It (p. 209)

1.

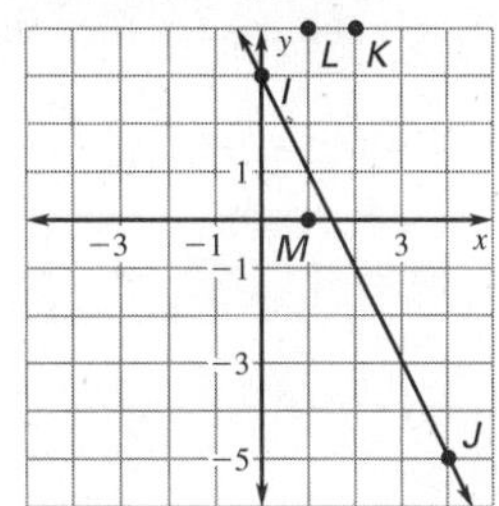

K: $2(2) + 4 \neq 3$, not a solution
L: $2(1) + 4 \neq 3$, not a solution
M: $2(1) + 0 \neq 3$, not a solution

2.

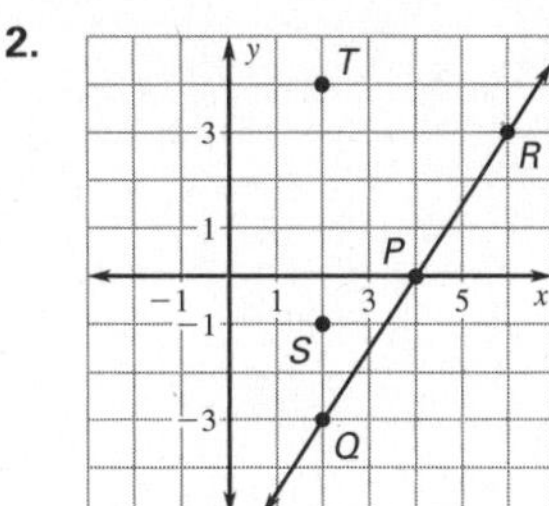

R: $3(6) - 2(3) = 12$, solution
S: $3(2) - 2(-1) \neq 12$, not a solution
T: $3(2) - 2(4) \neq 12$, not a solution

3. Solutions to a linear equation fall on the graph of the equation.

Lesson 4.2

4.2 Checkpoint (pp. 210–212)

1. a. $2(-3) + (7) = 1$
$-6 + 7 = 1$
$1 = 1$
solution

b. $2(3) + (-7) = 1$
$6 - 7 = 1$
$-1 \neq 1$
not solution

c. $2\left(\frac{1}{2}\right) + (0) = 1$
$1 + 0 = 1$
$1 = 1$
solution

d. $2\left(\frac{5}{2}\right) + (-6) = 1$
$5 - 6 = 1$
$-1 \neq 1$
not solution

2.

$2x - y = 7$	Write original equation.
$-y = -2x + 7$	Subtract $2x$ from each side.
$y = 2x - 7$	Opposite of y is the opposite of each term on the right side.

3.

$6x + 3y = 18$	Write original equation.
$3y = -6x + 18$	Subtract $6x$ from each side.
$y = \frac{-6x}{3} + \frac{18}{3}$	Divide each side by 3.
$y = -2x + 6$	Simplify.

4.

$4y - 3x = -28$	Write original equation.
$4y = 3x - 28$	Add $3x$ to each side.
$y = \frac{3x}{4} - \frac{28}{4}$	Divide each side by 4.
$y = \frac{3}{4}x - 7$	Simplify.

Copyright © McDougal Littell Inc.
All rights reserved.

5. $y = -2x + 1$
Sample answer: Substitute 0, -1, and 2 for x, then find the corresponding y-values.

$y = -2(0) + 1$
$y = 0 + 1$
$y = 1$
$(0, 1)$

$y = -2(-1) + 1$
$y = 2 + 1$
$y = 3$
$(-1, 3)$

$y = -2(2) + 1$
$y = -4 + 1$
$y = -3$
$(2, -3)$

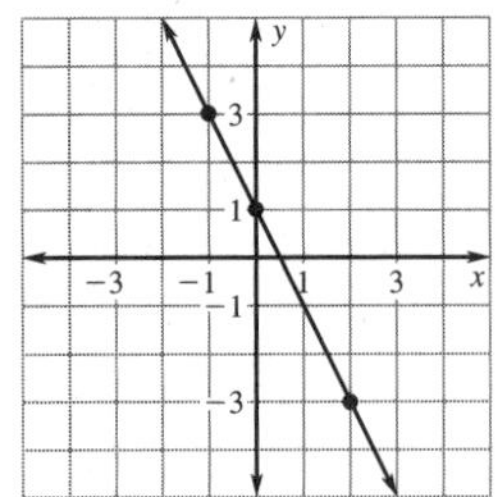

6. $x - y = 7$
Sample answer:

$x - y = 7$	Rewrite in function form.
$-y = -x + 7$	Subtract x from each side.
$y = x - 7$	Opposite of y is the opposite of each term on the right side.

Substitute 0, -1, and 1 for x, then find the corresponding y-values.

$y = 0 - 7$
$y = -7$
$(0, -7)$

$y = -1 - 7$
$y = -8$
$(-1, -8)$

$y = 1 - 7$
$y = -6$
$(1, -6)$

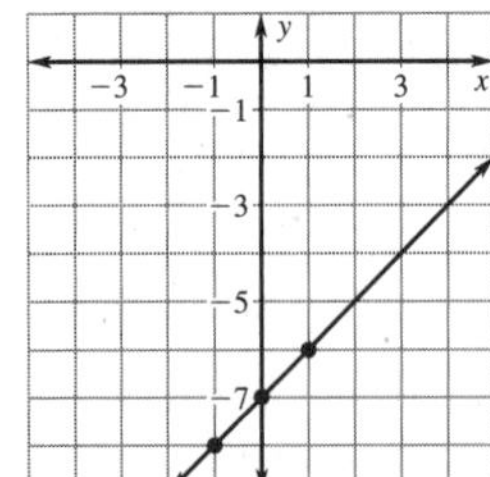

7. $4x + y = -3$ Rewrite in function form.
$y = -4x - 3$ Subtract $4x$ from each side.

Sample answer: Substitute -2, -1, and 0 for x, then find the corresponding y-values.

$y = -4(-2) - 3$
$y = 8 - 3$
$y = 5$
$(-2, 5)$

$y = -4(-1) - 3$
$y = 4 - 3$
$y = 1$
$(-1, 1)$

$y = -4(0) - 3$
$y = 0 - 3$
$y = -3$
$(0, -3)$

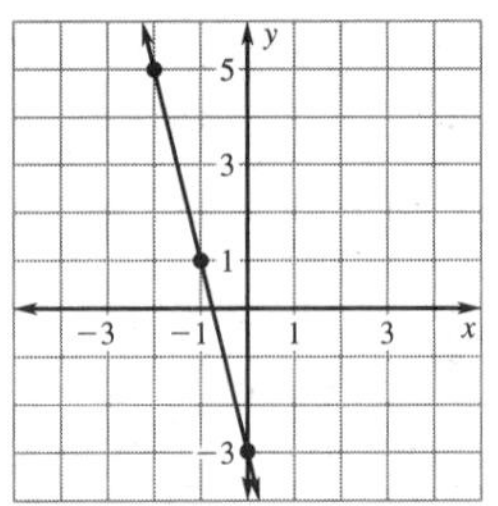

4.2 Guided Practice (p. 213)

1. solution **2.** function

3. $x - y = -7$ Write original equation.
$-3 - 4 \stackrel{?}{=} -7$ Substitute -3 for x and 4 for y.
$-7 = -7$ $(-3, 4)$ is a solution.

4. $x + y = 10$ Write original equation.
$2 + (-12) \stackrel{?}{=} 10$ Substitute 2 for x and -12 for y.
$-10 \neq 10$ $(2, -12)$ is not a solution.

5. $4x - y = 23$ Write original equation.
$4(5) - (-3) \stackrel{?}{=} 23$ Substitute 5 for x and -3 for y.
$23 = 23$ $(5, -3)$ is a solution.

6. $5x + 3y = -8$ Write original equation.
$5(2) + 3(-4) \stackrel{?}{=} -8$ Substitute 2 for x and -4 for y.
$-2 \neq -8$ $(2, -4)$ is not a solution.

7. $x + y = -2$ Write original equation.
$y = -x - 2$ Subtract x from each side.

8. $x + 3y = 9$ Write original equation.
$3y = -x + 9$ Subtract x from each side.
$y = \frac{-x}{3} + \frac{9}{3}$ Divide each side by 3.
$y = \left(-\frac{1}{3}\right)x + 3$ Simplify.

9. $4x + 2 + 2y = 10$ Write original equation.
$4x + 2y = 8$ Subtract 2 from each side
$2y = -4x + 8$ Subtract $4x$ from each side.
$y = \frac{-4x}{2} + \frac{8}{2}$ Divide each side by 2.
$y = -2x + 4$ Simplify.

10. $y = 4x - 1$
Sample answer: Substitute 0, -1, and 1 for x, then find the corresponding values of y.

x-values	*function*	*y-values*	*ordered pairs*
$x = 0$	$y = 4(0) - 1$	$y = -1$	$(0, -1)$
$x = -1$	$y = 4(-1) - 1$	$y = -5$	$(-1, -5)$
$x = 1$	$y = 4(1) - 1$	$y = 3$	$(1, 3)$

Copyright © McDougal Littell Inc.
All rights reserved.

11. $y = 5x + 7$

Sample answer: Substitute 0, -1, and 1 for x, then find the corresponding values of y.

x-values	*function*	*y-values*	*ordered pairs*
$x = 0$	$y = 5(0) + 7$	$y = 7$	(0, 7)
$x = -1$	$y = 5(-1) + 7$	$y = 2$	$(-1, 2)$
$x = 1$	$y = 5(1) + 7$	$y = 12$	(1, 12)

12. $y = \frac{1}{2}x + 3$

Sample answer: Substitute 0, -2, and 2 for x, then find the corresponding values of y.

x-values	*function*	*y-values*	*ordered pairs*
$x = 0$	$y = \frac{1}{2}(0) + 3$	$y = 3$	(0, 3)
$x = -2$	$y = \frac{1}{2}(-2) + 3$	$y = 2$	$(-2, 2)$
$x = 2$	$y = \frac{1}{2}(2) + 3$	$y = 4$	(2, 4)

13. *Sample table*: $y = x - 4$

x	-2	-1	0	1	2
y	-6	-5	-4	-3	-2

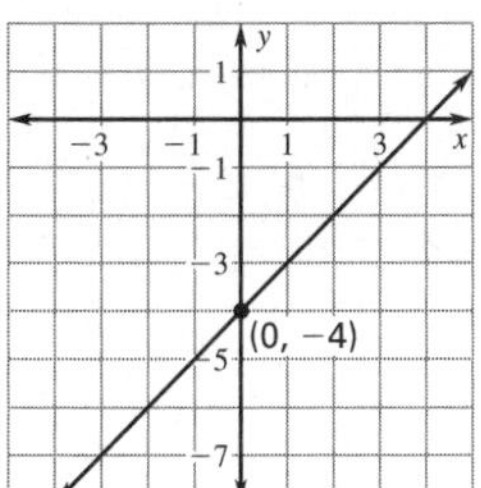

14. *Sample table*: $y = x + 5$

x	-2	-1	0	1	2
y	3	4	5	6	7

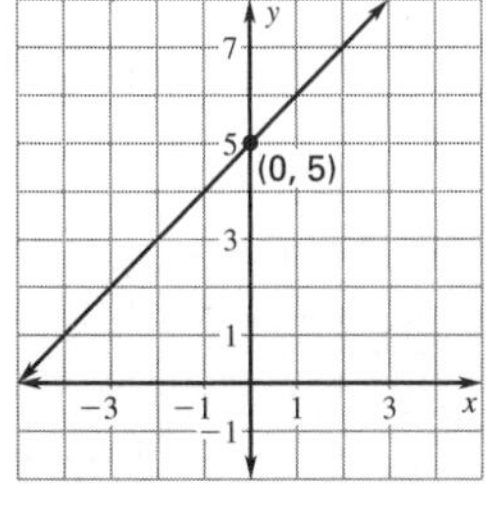

15. *Sample table:*

$x + y = 6$ Rewrite in function form.

$y = -x + 6$ Subtract x from each side.

x	-2	-1	0	1	2
y	8	7	6	5	4

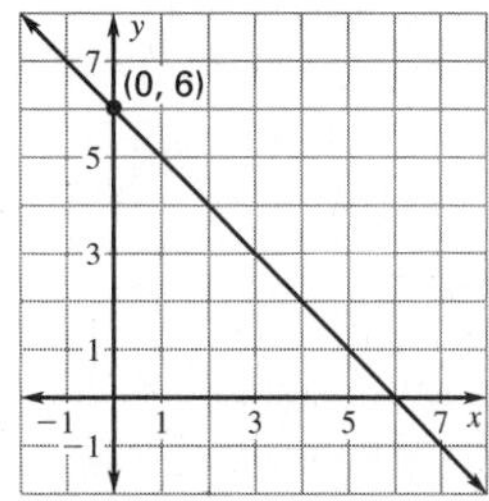

4.2 Practice and Applications (pp. 213–215)

16. $y = 2x + 1$ Write original equation.
$11 \stackrel{?}{=} 2(5) + 1$ Substitute 5 for x and 11 for y.
$11 = 11$ (5, 11) is a solution.

17. $y = 5 - 3x$ Write original equation.
$0 \stackrel{?}{=} 5 - 3(2)$ Substitute 2 for x and 0 for y.
$0 \neq -1$ (2, 0) is not a solution.

18. $2y - 4x = 8$ Write original equation.
$2(8) - 4(-2) \stackrel{?}{=} 8$ Substitute -2 for x and 8 for y.
$24 \neq 8$ $(-2, 8)$ is not a solution.

19. $5x - 8y = 15$ Write original equation.
$5(3) - 8(0) \stackrel{?}{=} 15$ Substitute 3 for x and 0 for y.
$15 \neq 15$ (3, 0) is a solution.

20. $6y - 3x = -9$ Write original equation.
$6(-1) - 3(1) \stackrel{?}{=} -9$ Substitute 1 for x and -1 for y.
$-9 = -9$ $(1, -1)$ is a solution.

21. $-2x - 9y = 7$ Write original equation.
$-2(-1) - 9(-1) \stackrel{?}{=} 7$ Substitute -1 for x and -1 for y.
$11 \neq 7$ $(-1, -1)$ is not a solution.

22. $-3x + y = 12$ Original equation.
$y = 3x + 12$ Add $3x$ to each side.

23. $2x + 3y = 6$ Original equation.
$3y = -2x + 6$ Subtract $2x$ from each side.
$y = \frac{-2x}{3} + \frac{6}{3}$ Divide each side by 3.
$y = \left(-\frac{2}{3}\right)x + 2$ Simplify.

24. $x + 4y = 4$ Original equation.
$4y = -x + 4$ Subtract x from each side.
$y = \frac{-x}{4} + \frac{4}{4}$ Divide each side by 4.
$y = \left(-\frac{1}{4}\right)x + 1$ Simplify.

Copyright © McDougal Littell Inc.
All rights reserved.

25.
$$\begin{aligned} 5x + 5y &= 19 && \text{Original equation.}\\ 5y &= -5x + 19 && \text{Subtract } 5x \text{ from each side.}\\ y &= \frac{-5x}{5} + \frac{19}{5} && \text{Divide each side by 5.}\\ y &= -x + \frac{19}{5} && \text{Simplify.} \end{aligned}$$

26.
$$\begin{aligned} 5y - 2x &= 15 && \text{Original equation.}\\ 5y &= 2x + 15 && \text{Add } 2x \text{ to each side.}\\ y &= \frac{2x}{5} + \frac{15}{5} && \text{Divide each side by 5.}\\ y &= \frac{2}{5}x + 3 && \text{Simplify.} \end{aligned}$$

27.
$$\begin{aligned} -x - y &= 5 && \text{Original equation.}\\ -y &= x + 5 && \text{Add } x \text{ to each side.}\\ y &= -x - 5 && \text{Opposite of } y \text{ equals the opposite of the terms on the right side.} \end{aligned}$$

28.
$$\begin{aligned} 2x + 5y &= -15 && \text{Original equation.}\\ 5y &= -2x - 15 && \text{Subtract } 2x \text{ from each side.}\\ y &= \frac{-2x}{5} - \frac{15}{5} && \text{Divide each side by 5.}\\ y &= \left(-\frac{2}{5}\right)x - 3 && \text{Simplify.} \end{aligned}$$

29.
$$\begin{aligned} 3x + 2y &= -3 && \text{Original equation.}\\ 2y &= -3x - 3 && \text{Subtract } 3x \text{ from each side.}\\ y &= \frac{-3x}{2} - \frac{3}{2} && \text{Divide each side by 2.}\\ y &= \left(-\frac{3}{2}\right)x - \frac{3}{2} && \text{Simplify.} \end{aligned}$$

30.
$$\begin{aligned} 4x - y &= 18 && \text{Original equation.}\\ -y &= -4x + 18 && \text{Subtract } 4x \text{ from each side.}\\ y &= 4x - 18 && \text{Opposite of } y \text{ equals opposite of the terms on the right side.} \end{aligned}$$

31. $y = 3x - 5$
Sample answer: Let $x = 0$, 1, and -1.

x	*function*	*y*	*ordered pairs*
0	$y = 3(0) - 5$	-5	$(0, -5)$
1	$y = 3(1) - 5$	-2	$(1, -2)$
-1	$y = 3(-1) - 5$	-8	$(-1, -8)$

32. $y = 7 - 4x$
Sample answer: Let $x = 0$, 1, and -1.

x	*function*	*y*	*ordered pairs*
0	$y = 7 - 4(0)$	7	$(0, 7)$
1	$y = 7 - 4(1)$	3	$(1, 3)$
-1	$y = 7 - 4(-1)$	11	$(-1, 11)$

33. $y = -2x - 6$
Sample answer: Let $x = 0$, 1, and -1.

x	*function*	*y*	*ordered pairs*
0	$y = -2(0) - 6$	-6	$(0, -6)$
1	$y = -2(1) - 6$	-8	$(1, -8)$
-1	$y = -2(-1) - 6$	-4	$(-1, -4)$

34.
$$\begin{aligned} x + 2y &= 8 && \text{Rewrite in function form.}\\ 2y &= -x + 8 && \text{Subtract } x \text{ from each side.}\\ y &= \frac{-x}{2} + \frac{8}{2} && \text{Divide each side by 2.}\\ y &= \left(-\frac{1}{2}\right)x + 4 && \text{Simplify.} \end{aligned}$$

Sample answer: Let $x = 0$, 2, and -2.

x	*function*	*y*	*ordered pairs*
0	$y = \left(-\frac{1}{2}\right)(0) + 4$	4	$(0, 4)$
2	$y = \left(-\frac{1}{2}\right)(2) + 4$	3	$(2, 3)$
-2	$y = \left(-\frac{1}{2}\right)(-2) + 4$	5	$(-2, 5)$

35.
$$\begin{aligned} 2x + 3y &= 9 && \text{Rewrite in function form.}\\ 3y &= -2x + 9 && \text{Subtract } 2x \text{ from each side.}\\ y &= \frac{-2x}{3} + \frac{9}{3} && \text{Divide each side by 3.}\\ y &= \left(-\frac{2}{3}\right)x + 3 && \text{Simplify.} \end{aligned}$$

Sample answer: Let $x = 0$, 3, and -3.

x	*function*	*y*	*ordered pairs*
0	$y = \left(-\frac{2}{3}\right)(0) + 3$	3	$(0, 3)$
3	$y = \left(-\frac{2}{3}\right)(3) + 3$	1	$(3, 1)$
-3	$y = \left(-\frac{2}{3}\right)(-3) + 3$	5	$(-3, 5)$

36.
$$\begin{aligned} 3x - 5y &= 15 && \text{Rewrite in function form.}\\ -5y &= -3x + 15 && \text{Subtract } 3x \text{ from each side.}\\ y &= \frac{-3x}{-5} + \frac{15}{-5} && \text{Divide each side by } -5.\\ y &= \left(\frac{3}{5}\right)x - 3 && \text{Simplify.} \end{aligned}$$

Sample answer: Let $x = 0$, 5, and 1.

x	*function*	*y*	*ordered pairs*
0	$y = \left(\frac{3}{5}\right)(0) - 3$	-3	$(0, -3)$
5	$y = \left(\frac{3}{5}\right)(5) - 3$	0	$(5, 0)$
1	$y = \left(\frac{3}{5}\right)(1) - 3$	$-2\frac{2}{5}$	$\left(1, -2\frac{2}{5}\right)$

Copyright © McDougal Littell Inc.
All rights reserved.

37. $5x + 2y = 10$ Rewrite in function form.

$2y = -5x + 10$ Subtract $5x$ from each side.

$y = \frac{-5x}{2} + \frac{10}{2}$ Divide each side by 2.

$y = \left(-\frac{5}{2}\right)x + 5$ Simplify.

Sample answer: Let $x = 0$, 2, and 4.

x	*function*	y	*ordered pairs*
0	$y = \left(-\frac{5}{2}\right)(0) + 5$	5	(0, 5)
2	$y = \left(-\frac{5}{2}\right)(2) + 5$	0	(2, 0)
4	$y = \left(-\frac{5}{2}\right)(4) + 5$	−5	(4, −5)

38. $y - 3x = 9$ Rewrite in function form.

$y = 3x + 9$ Add $3x$ to each side.

Sample answer: Let $x = 0$, 1, and −1.

x	*function*	y	*ordered pairs*
0	$y = 3(0) + 9$	9	(0, 9)
1	$y = 3(1) + 9$	12	(1, 12)
−1	$y = 3(-1) + 9$	6	(−1, 6)

39. $-5x - 3y = 12$ Rewrite in function form.

$-3y = 5x + 12$ Add $5x$ to each side.

$y = \frac{5x}{-3} + \frac{12}{-3}$ Divide each side by −3.

$y = \left(-\frac{5}{3}\right)x - 4$ Simplify.

Sample answer: Let $x = 0$, 1, and 3.

x	*function*	y	*ordered pairs*
0	$y = \left(-\frac{5}{3}\right)(0) - 4$	−4	(0, −4)
1	$y = \left(-\frac{5}{3}\right)(1) - 4$	$-5\frac{2}{3}$	$\left(1, -5\frac{2}{3}\right)$ or $\left(1, -\frac{17}{3}\right)$
3	$y = \left(-\frac{5}{3}\right)(3) - 4$	−9	(3, −9)

40. *Sample table:* $y = 3x + 3$

x	−2	−1	0	1	2
y	−3	0	3	6	9

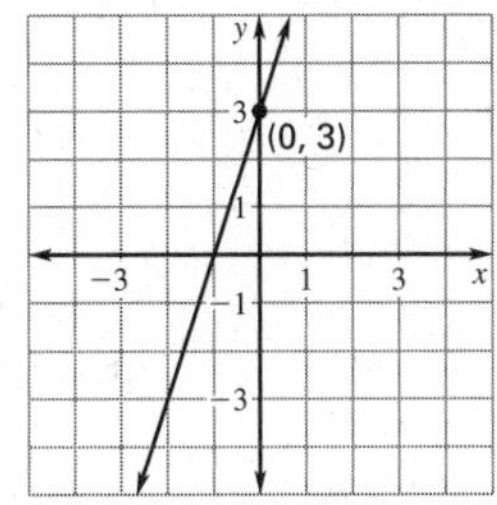

41. *Sample table:* $y = 4x + 2$

x	−2	−1	0	1	2
y	−6	−2	2	6	10

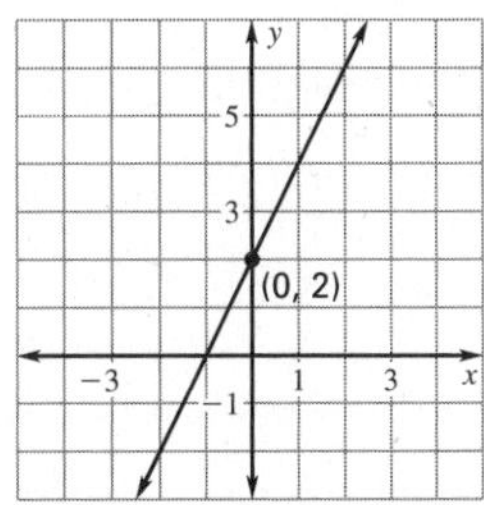

42. *Sample table:* $y = 3x - 4$

x	−2	−1	0	1	2
y	−10	−7	−4	−1	2

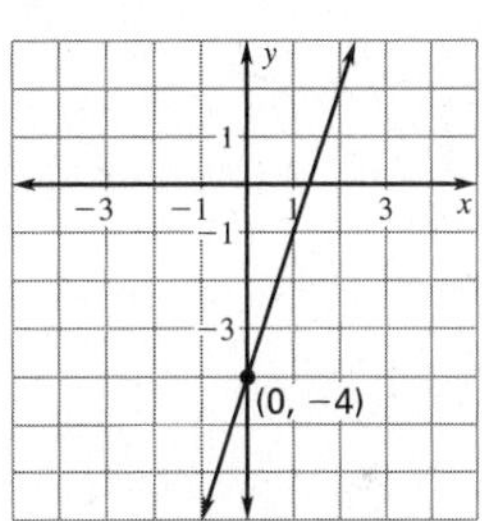

43. *Sample table:*

$y - 5x = -2$

$y = 5x - 2$

x	−2	−1	0	1	2
y	−12	−7	−2	3	8

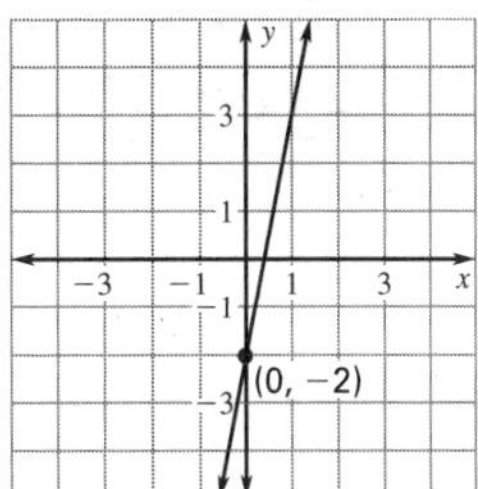

Copyright © McDougal Littell Inc.
All rights reserved.

44. *Sample table:*

$x + y = 1$

$y = -x + 1$

x	−2	−1	0	1	2
y	3	2	1	0	−1

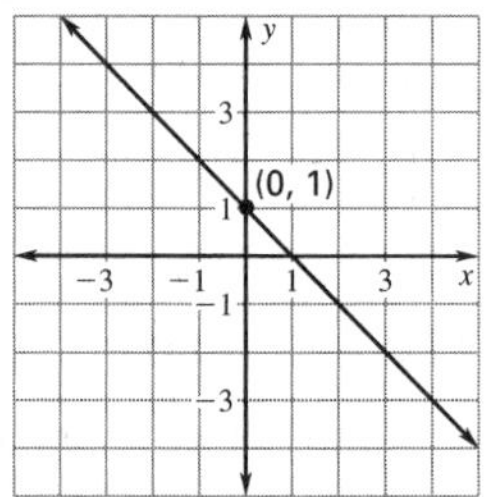

45. *Sample table:*

$2x + y = 3$

$y = -2x + 3$

x	−2	−1	0	1	2
y	7	5	3	1	−1

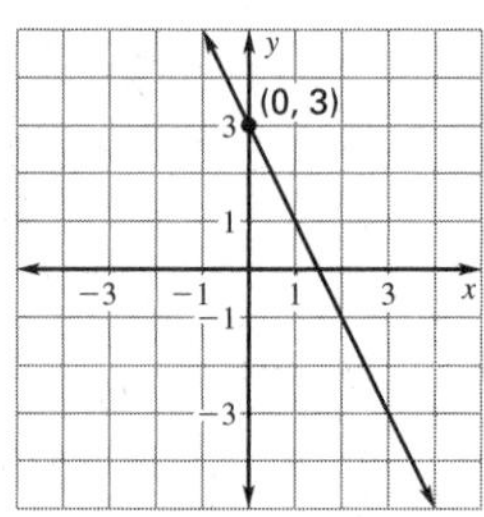

46. *Sample table:*

$y - 4x = -1$

$y = 4x - 1$

x	−2	−1	0	1	2
y	−9	−5	−1	3	7

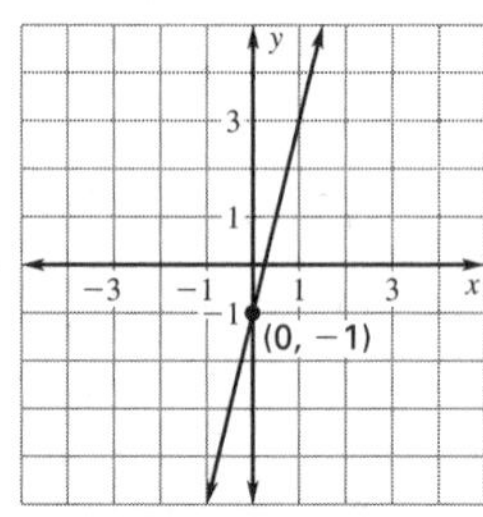

47. *Sample table:*

$x + 4y = 48$

$4y = -x + 48$

$y = \left(-\frac{1}{4}\right)x + 12$

x	−4	−2	0	2	4
y	13	$12\frac{1}{2}$	12	$11\frac{1}{2}$	11

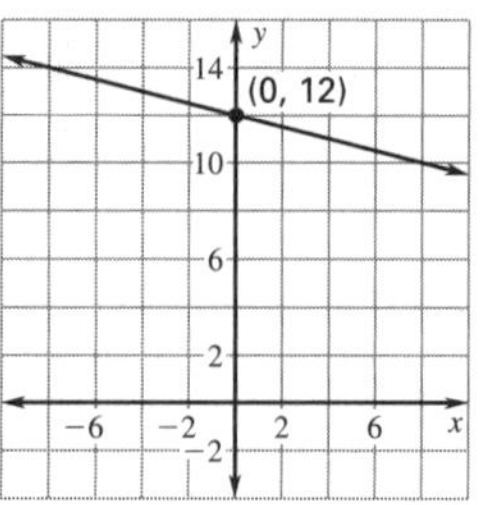

48. *Sample table:*

$5x + 5y = 25$

$5y = -5x + 25$

$y = -x + 5$

x	−2	−1	0	1	2
y	7	6	5	4	3

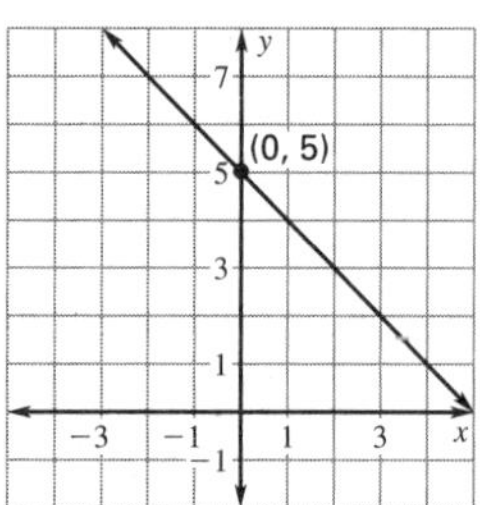

49. Calories burned while running · Running time + Calories burned while swimming · Swimming time = Total calories burned

Calories burned while running = 7.1 (cal/min)
Running time = x (min)
Calories burned while swimming = 10.1 (cal/min)
Swimming time = y (min)
Total calories burned = 800 (cal)

$7.1x + 10.1y = 800$

50.

x	20	40	60	80
y	65	51	37	23

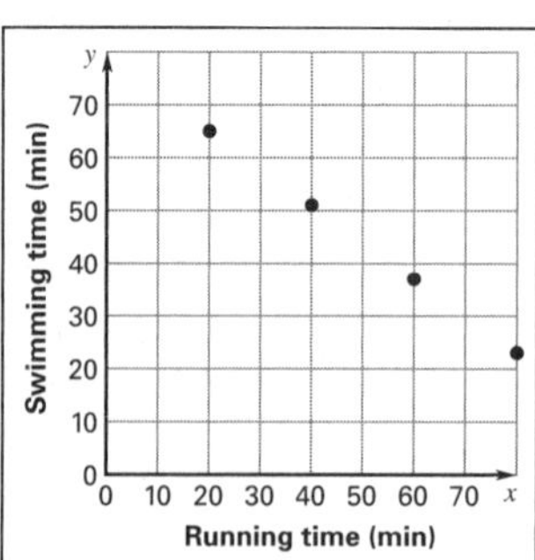

Copyright © McDougal Littell Inc.
All rights reserved.

51. $7.1x + 10.1y = 800$ Original equation.
$7.1(45) + 10.1y = 800$ Substitute 45 for x (running time)
$319.5 + 10.1y = 800$ Multiply.
$10.1y = 480.5$ Subtract 319.5 from each side.
$y \approx 47.6$ or about 48 minutes

52. 

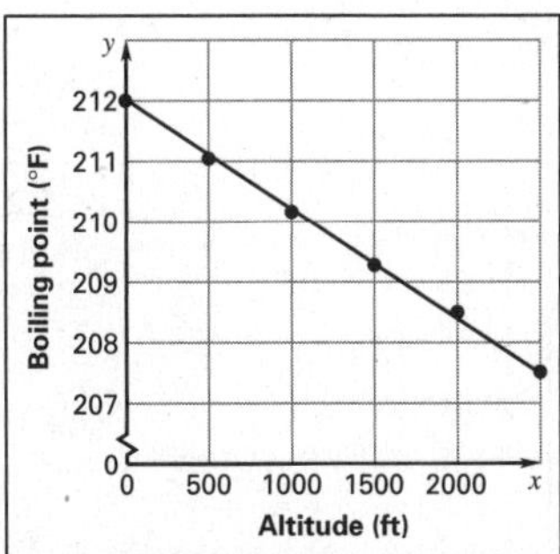

53. The boiling temperature of water decreases as altitude increases.

54. $h = 6.76t + 14.9$

t	0	1	2	3	4	5	6
h	14.9	21.66	28.42	35.18	41.94	48.7	55.46

55.

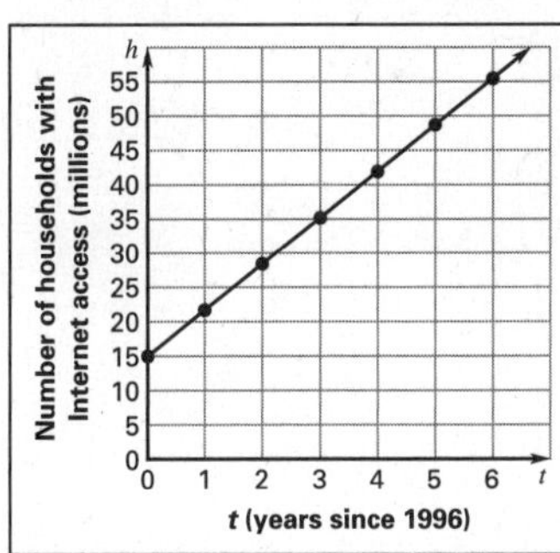

56. *Sample answer:* The graph indicates that with each year more households are obtaining Internet access. Since the world population is finite, this trend cannot continue indefinitely.

4.2 Standardized Test Practice (p. 215)

57. D; $-3(8) + (19) \stackrel{?}{=} -5$

58. H

$-2x + 5y = 10$ Original equation.
$5y = 2x + 10$ Add $2x$ to each side.
$y = \frac{2x}{5} + \frac{10}{5}$ Divide each side by 5.
$y = \frac{2}{5}x + 2$ Simplify.

59. Select 2 points on the line and test them to see if they are solutions.
Sample answer: Test (0, 3) and (−6, 0).
D; $-(0) + 2(3) \stackrel{?}{=} 6$
and $-(-6) + 2(0) \stackrel{?}{=} 6$

4.2 Mixed Review (p. 215)

60. $5 + 2 + (-3) = 7 + (-3) = 4$

61. $-6 + (-14) + 8 = -20 + 8 = -12$

62. $-18 + (-10) + (-1) = -28 + (-1) = -29$

63. $-\frac{1}{3} + 6 + \frac{1}{3} = \left(-\frac{1}{3} + \frac{1}{3}\right) + 6 = 0 + 6 = 6$

64. $3a - 5b - 7a + 2b = -4a - 3b$

65. $-6x + 2y - 8x + 4y = -14x + 6y$

66. $n^2 + 3m - 9m - 3n^2 = -2n^2 - 6m$

67. $-4r - 5t^3 + 2r - 7r = -9r - 5t^3$ or $-5t^3 - 9r$

68. $2c^2 - 4c + 8c^2 - 4c^3 = -4c^3 + 10c^2 - 4c$

69. $-3k^3 - 5k + h + 5k = -3k^3 + h$

70. $-2z = -26$
$z = 13$

71. $\frac{2}{3}t = -10$
$t = \frac{3}{2}(-10)$
$t = -15$

72. $6c = -96$
$c = \frac{-96}{6} = -16$

73. $-\frac{p}{7} = -9$
$p = (-7)(-9) = 63$

4.2 Maintaining Skills (p. 215)

74. $0.15 = 15\%$ **75.** $0.63 = 63\%$

76. $0.5 = 50\%$ **77.** $0.02 = 2\%$

78. $0.005 = 0.5\%$ **79.** $1.27 = 127\%$

80. $3 = 300\%$ **81.** $8.6 = 860\%$

Lesson 4.3

4.3 Checkpoint (pp. 216–218)

1.

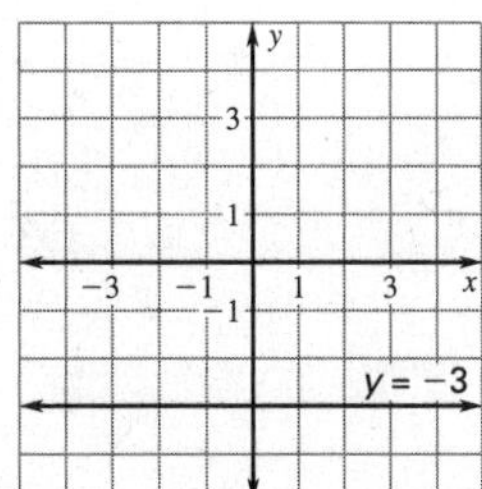

Copyright © McDougal Littell Inc.
All rights reserved.

2. 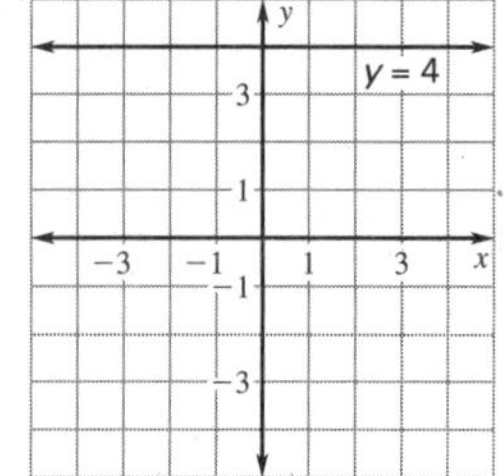

3. 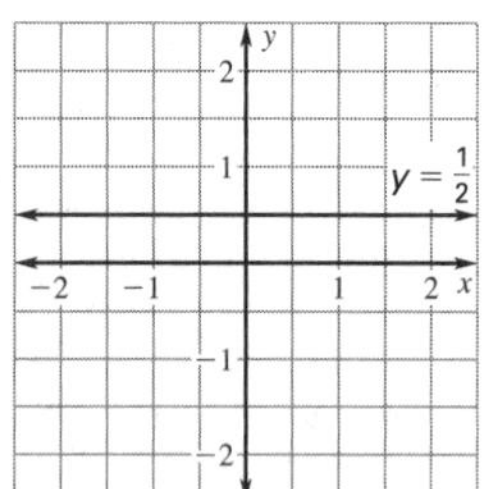

4. 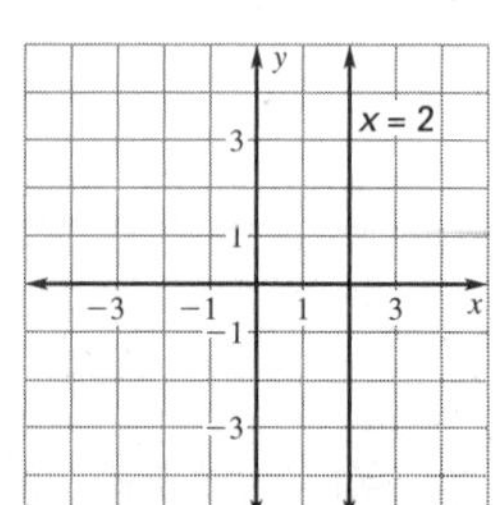

5. 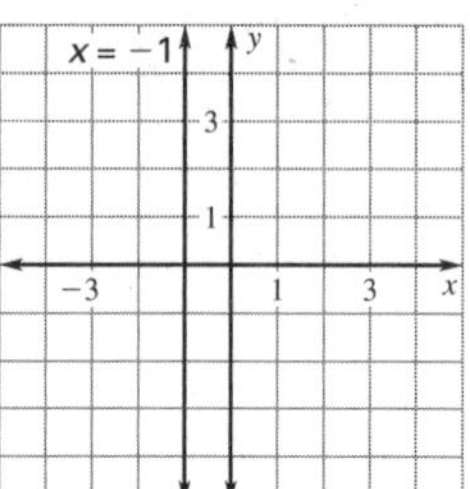

6. 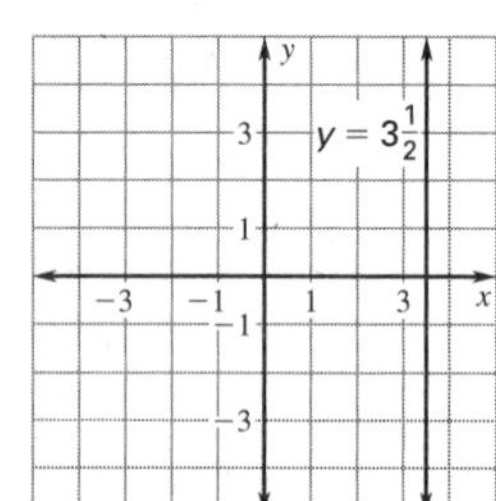

7. $y = -2$

8. $x = 4$

9. $H = 8364$;
domain: all values of t years from 1980 to present
range: 8364

4.3 Guided Practice (p. 219)

1. horizontal
2. vertical
3. constant
4. 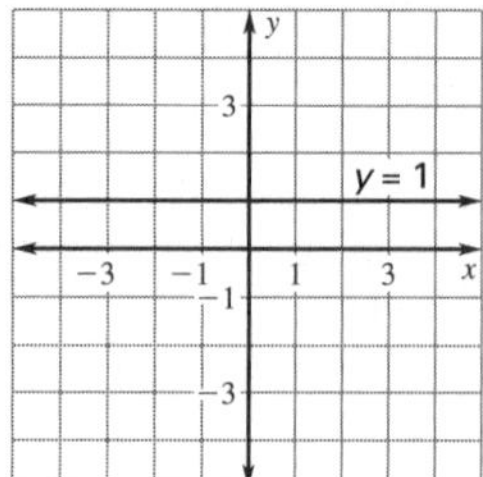

5. 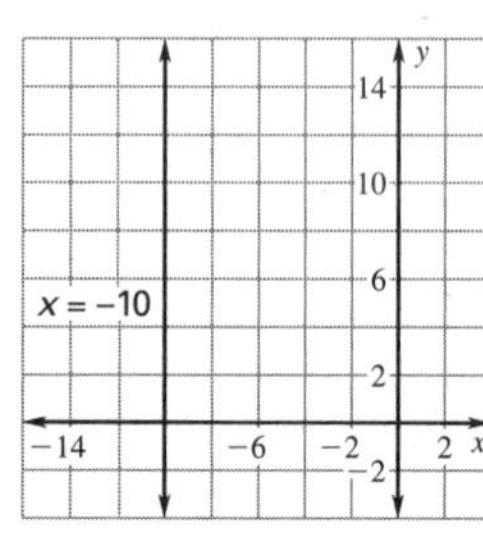

6. 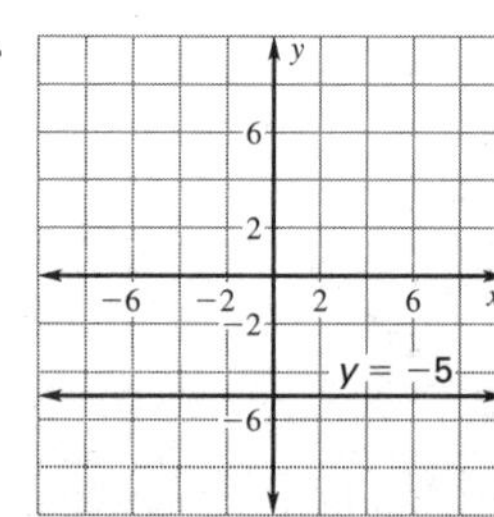

7. 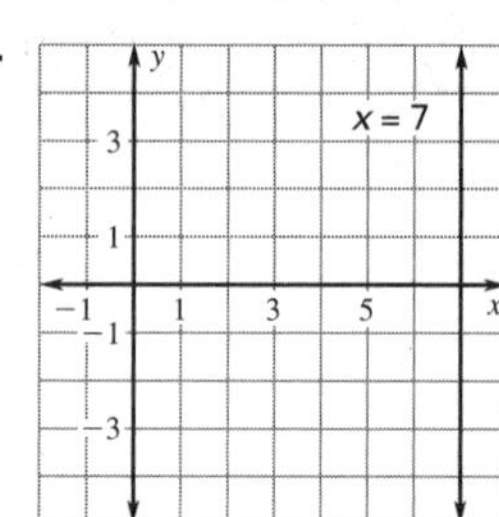

8. $y = -3$ (horizontal line)
9. $x = 3$ (vertical line)
10. always
11. sometimes
12. never (It's always vertical.)
13. always

4.3 Practice and Applications (pp. 219–220)

14. $y = -2$
(–2, –2) is a solution since its y-value is –2.

15. $y = 3$
(3, –3) is not a solution since its y-value is not 3.

16. $y = 0$
(0, 1) is not a solution since its y-value is not 0.

17. $x = 5$
(–5, –5) is not a solution since its x-value is not 5.

Copyright © McDougal Littell Inc.
All rights reserved.

18. $x = 9$
Choose any ordered pairs with x-values of 9.
Sample answers: (9, 0), (9, 1), (9, 2)

19. $x = \frac{1}{2}$

Choose any ordered pairs with x-values of $\frac{1}{2}$.

Sample answers: $\left(\frac{1}{2}, 0\right), \left(\frac{1}{2}, 2\right), \left(\frac{1}{2}, -2\right)$

20. $y = 10$
Choose any ordered pairs with y-values of 10.
Sample answers: (0, 10), (1, 10), (5, 10)

21. $y = -5$
Choose any ordered pairs with y-values of -5.
Sample answers: (0, -5), (3, -5), (-3, -5)

22. $x = -10$
Choose any ordered pairs with x-values of -10.
Sample answers: (-10, 0), (-10, 1), (-10, 2)

23. $y = 7$
Choose any ordered pairs with y-values of 7.
Sample answers: (0, 7), (-2, 7), (-3, 7)

24.

25.

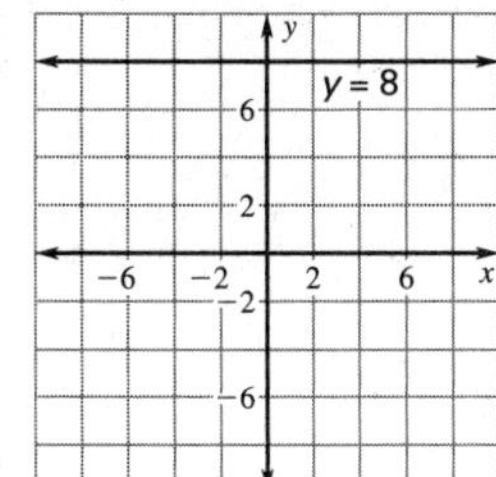

26.

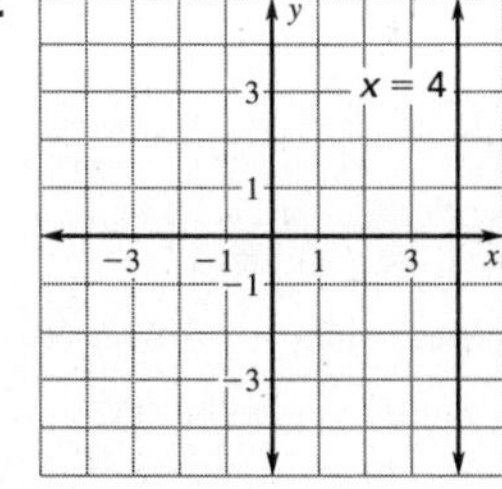

27.

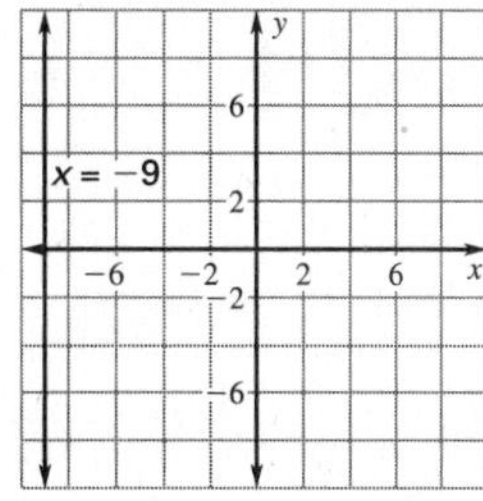

28.

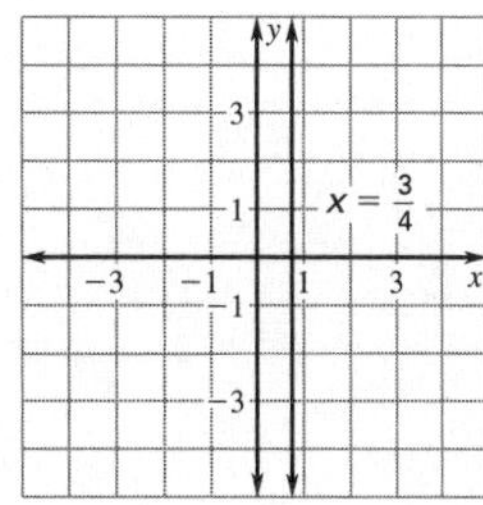

29.

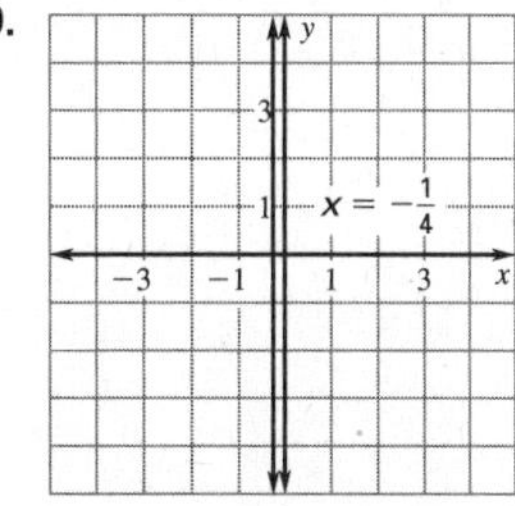

30. $y = 2$ (horizontal line)

31. $x = -4$ (vertical line)

32. $y = -1$ (horizontal line)

33. a. $H = 110$; domain: 0–5; range: 110

b. $H = 160$; domain: 0–10; range: 160

34. a. $T = 80$; domain: 0–100; range: 80

b. $T = 54$; domain: 0–100; range: 54

4.3 Standardized Test Practice (p. 221)

35. C; the y-value is -3, not 3.

36. F; the y-value of (3, 5) is 5.

4.3 Mixed Review (p. 221)

37. $17 - 6 + 4 - 8 = 11 + 4 - 8 = 15 - 8 = 7$

38. $6 + 9 \div 3 + 3 = 6 + 3 + 3 = 9 + 3 = 12$

39. $4 \cdot 5 - 2 \cdot 6 = 20 - 12 = 8$

40. $9 \cdot 6 \div 3 \cdot 18 = 54 \div 3 \cdot 18 = 18 \cdot 18 = 324$

41. $22 - 8 \div 2 \cdot 3 = 22 - 4 \cdot 3 = 22 - 12 = 10$

42. $0.75 \div 2.5 \cdot 2 + 1 = 0.3 \cdot 2 + 1 - 0.6 + 1 = 1.6$

Copyright © McDougal Littell Inc.
All rights reserved.

43. $r - (-4) = 9$
$r + 4 = 9$
$r = 5$

44. $-8 - (-c) = 10$
$-8 + c = 10$
$c = 18$

45. $15 - (-b) = 30$
$15 + b = 30$
$b = 15$

4.3 Maintaining Skills (p. 215)

46. $\frac{2}{3}, \frac{7}{8}$

LCD $= 3 \cdot 8 = 24; \frac{2}{3} \cdot \frac{8}{8} = \frac{16}{24}; \frac{7}{8} \cdot \frac{3}{3} = \frac{21}{24}$

47. $\frac{5}{7}, \frac{2}{3}$

LCD $= 7 \cdot 3 = 21; \frac{5}{7} \cdot \frac{3}{3} = \frac{15}{21}; \frac{2}{3} \cdot \frac{7}{7} = \frac{14}{21}$

48. $\frac{1}{2}, \frac{3}{7}$

LCD $= 2 \cdot 7 = 14; \frac{1}{2} \cdot \frac{7}{7} = \frac{7}{14}; \frac{3}{7} \cdot \frac{2}{2} = \frac{6}{14}$

49. $\frac{5}{7}, \frac{4}{21}$

LCD $= 21$, since 21 is divisible by 7.

$\frac{5}{7} \cdot \frac{3}{3} = \frac{15}{21}; \frac{4}{21}$

50. $\frac{8}{9}, \frac{7}{12}$

LCD: $3 \cdot 3 = 9$
$2 \cdot 2 \cdot 3 = 12$
$3 \cdot 3 \cdot 2 \cdot 2 = 36$
$\frac{8}{9} \cdot \frac{4}{4} = \frac{32}{36}; \frac{7}{12} \cdot \frac{3}{3} = \frac{21}{36}$

51. $\frac{12}{13}, \frac{5}{26}$

LCD $= 26$, since 26 is divisible by 13.
$\frac{12}{13} \cdot \frac{2}{2} = \frac{24}{26}; \frac{5}{26}$

52. $\frac{7}{18}, \frac{2}{15}$

LCD: $3 \cdot 3 \cdot 2 = 18$
$3 \cdot 5 = 15$
$3 \cdot 3 \cdot 2 \cdot 5 = 90$
$\frac{7}{18} \cdot \frac{5}{5} = \frac{35}{90}; \frac{2}{15} \cdot \frac{6}{6} = \frac{12}{90}$

53. $\frac{3}{20}, \frac{7}{15}$

LCD: $2 \cdot 2 \cdot 5 = 20$
$3 \cdot 5 = 15$
$2 \cdot 2 \cdot 3 \cdot 5 = 60$
$\frac{3}{20} \cdot \frac{3}{3} = \frac{9}{60}; \frac{7}{15} \cdot \frac{4}{4} = \frac{28}{60}$

Quiz 1 *(p. 221)*

1.

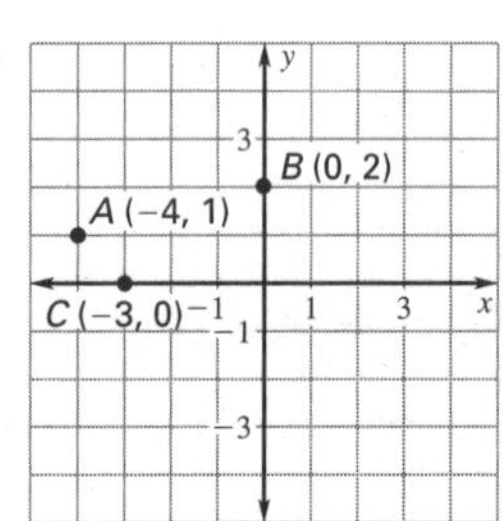

2.

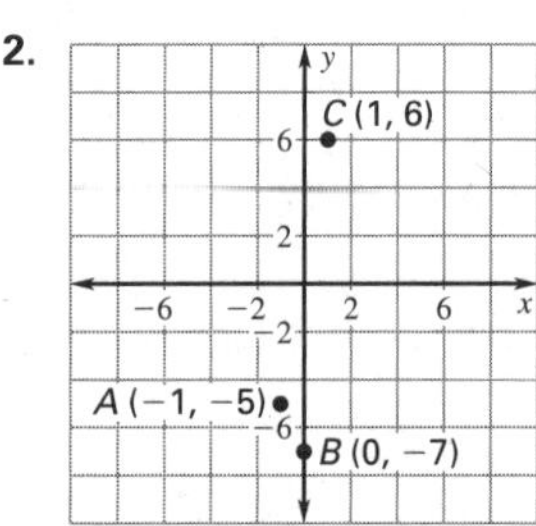

3.

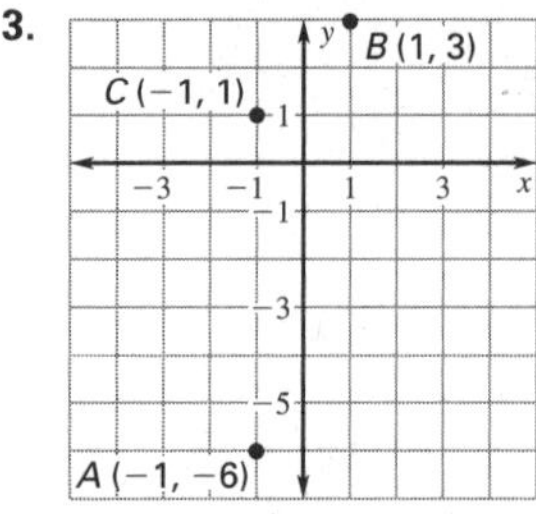

4.

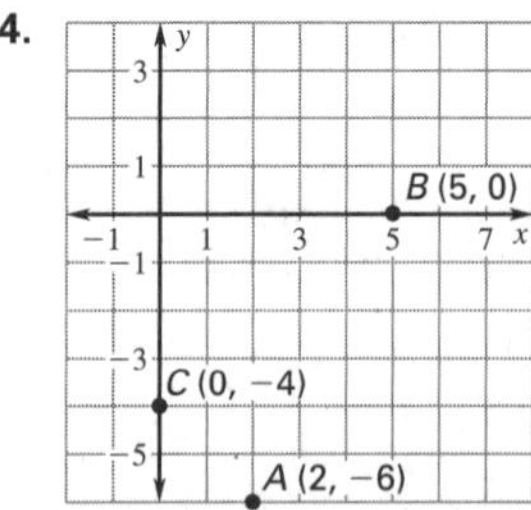

5. (6, 8) has positive x-value, positive y-value: I

6. $(-4, -15)$ has negative x-value, negative y-value: III

7. $(5, -9)$ has positive x-value, negative y-value: IV

8. $(-3, 3)$ has negative x-value, positive y-value: II

9.

$2x + y = 0$	Original equation.
$y = -2x + 0$	Subtract $2x$ from each side.
$y = -2x$	Simplify.

Copyright © McDougal Littell Inc.
All rights reserved.

10. $5x - 2y = 20$ Original equation.

$-2y = -5x + 20$ Subtract $5x$ from each side.

$y = \frac{-5x}{-2} + \frac{20}{-2}$ Divide each side by -2.

$y = \frac{5}{2}x - 10$ Simplify.

11. $-4x - 8y = 32$ Original equation.

$-8y = 4x + 32$ Add $4x$ to each side.

$y = \frac{4x}{-8} + \frac{32}{-8}$ Divide each side by -8.

$y = -\frac{1}{2}x - 4$ Simplify.

12. $y = 2x - 6$

Sample answers: Let $x = 0, 1, 2$.

$y = 2(0) - 6$ $\quad$ $y = 2(1) - 6$

$y = -6$ $\quad$ $y = -4$

$(0, -6)$ $\quad$ $(1, -4)$

$y = 2(2) - 6$

$y = -2$

$(2, -2)$

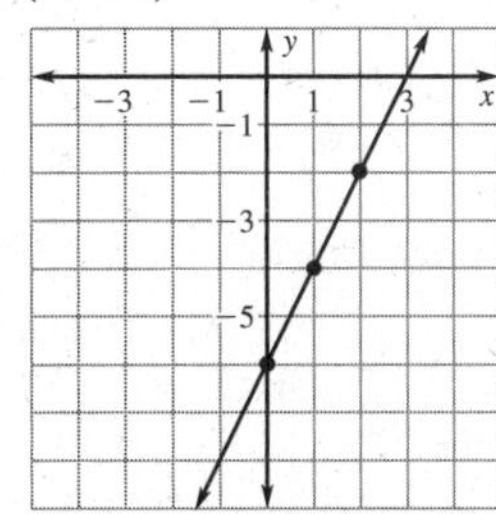

13. $y = 4x + 1$

Sample answers: Let $x = 0, 1, -1$.

$y = 4(0) + 1$ $\quad$ $y = 4(1) + 1$

$y = 1$ $\quad$ $y = 5$

$(0, 1)$ $\quad$ $(1, 5)$

$y = 4(-1) + 1$

$y = -3$

$(-1, -3)$

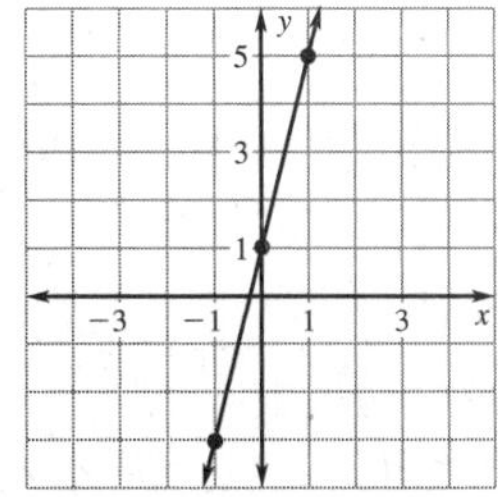

14. $y = 2(-3x + 1)$

Sample answers: Let $x = 0, 1, -1$.

$y = 2(-3 \cdot 0 + 1)$ $\quad$ $y = 2(-3 \cdot 1 + 1)$

$y = 2(1) = 2$ $\quad$ $y = 2(-2) = -4$

$(0, 2)$ $\quad$ $(1, -4)$

$y = 2[-3 \cdot (-1) + 1]$

$y = 2(4) = 8$

$(-1, 8)$

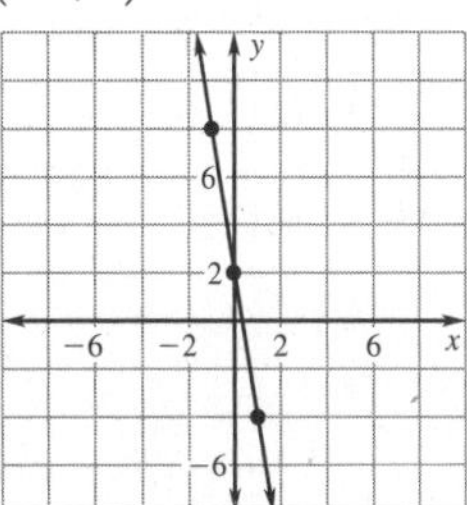

15. $y = -3(x - 4)$

Sample answers: Let $x = 0, 3, 6$.

$y = -3(0 - 4)$ $\quad$ $y = -3(3 - 4)$

$y = -3(-4) = 12$ $\quad$ $y = -3(-1) = 3$

$(0, 12)$ $\quad$ $(3, 3)$

$y = -3(6 - 4)$

$y = -3(2) = -6$

$(6, -6)$

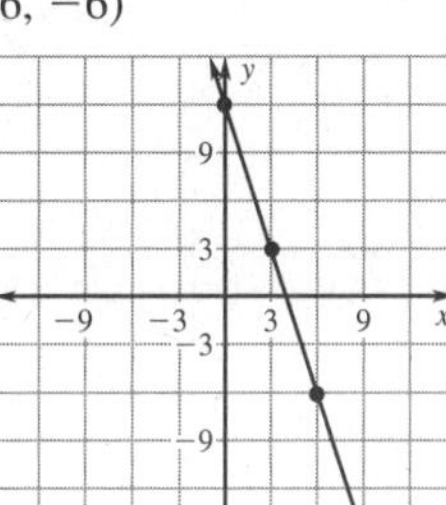

16. $10x + y = 5$ Rewrite in function form.

$y = -10x + 5$

Sample answers: Let $x = 0, 1, 2$

$y = -10(0) + 5$ $\quad$ $y = -10(1) + 5$

$y = 5$ $\quad$ $y = -5$

$(0, 5)$ $\quad$ $(1, -5)$

$y = -10(2) + 5$

$y = -15$

$(2, -15)$

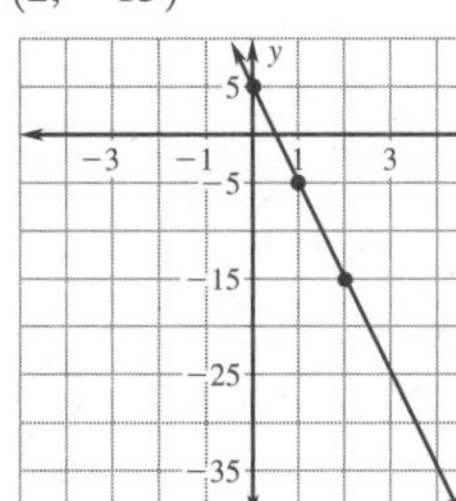

Copyright © McDougal Littell Inc.
All rights reserved.

17. $6 = 8x - 3y$ Rewrite in function form.

$3y = 8x - 6$ Add $3y$ and subtract 6 from each side.

$y = \frac{8x}{3} - \frac{6}{3}$ Divide each side by 3.

$y = \frac{8}{3}x - 2$ Simplify.

Sample answers: Let $x = 0, 3, -3$.

$y = \frac{8}{3}(0) - 2$ $y = \frac{8}{3}(3) - 2$

$y = -2; (0, -2)$ $y = 6; (3, 6)$

$y = \frac{8}{3}(-3) - 2$

$y = -10; (-3, -10)$

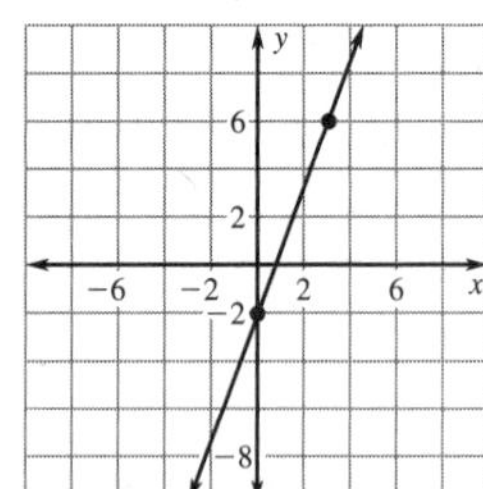

18.

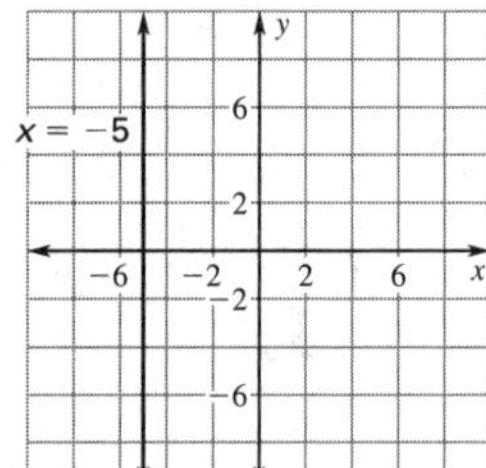

19.

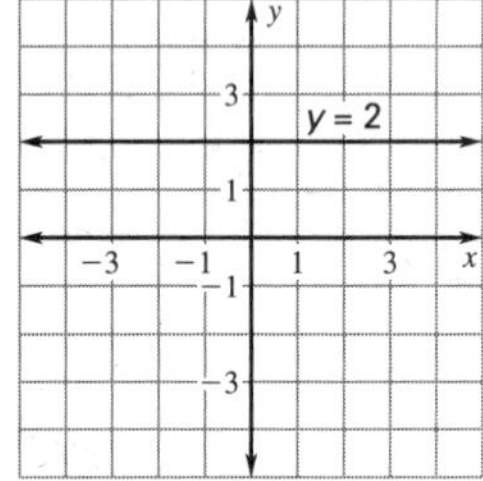

20.

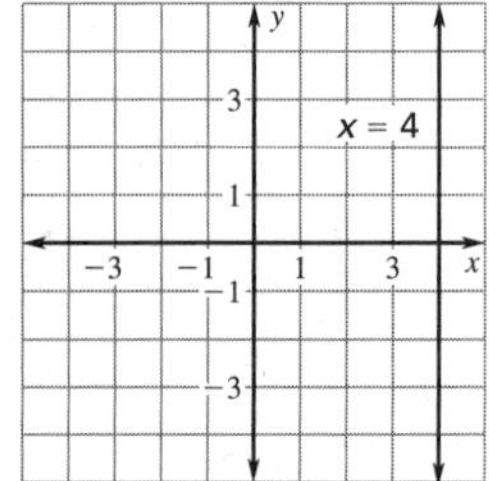

Lesson 4.4

4.4 Checkpoint (pp. 223–224)

1. $3x - 4y = 12$ Original equation.

$3x - 4(0) = 12$ Substitute 0 for y.

$3x = 12$ Multiply.

$x = 4$ Divide each side by 3.

x-intercept: 4

2. $3x - 4y = 12$ Original equation.

$3(0) - 4y = 12$ Substitute 0 for x.

$-4y = 12$ Multiply.

$y = -3$ Divide each side by –4.

y-intercept: -3

3. $3x - 6y = 18$ Original equation.

$3x - 6(0) = 18$ Substitute 0 for y.

$3x = 18$ Multiply.

$x = 6$ Divide each side by 3.

x-intercept: 6

$3x - 6y = 18$ Original equation.

$3(0) - 6y = 18$ Substitute 0 for x.

$-6y = 18$ Multiply.

$y = -3$ Divide each side by -6.

y-intercept: -3

4. $4x - 5y = 20$ Original equation.

$4x - 5(0) = 20$ Substitute 0 for y.

$4x = 20$ Multiply.

$x = 5$ Divide each side by 4.

x-intercept: 5

$4x - 5y - 20$ Original equation.

$4(0) - 5y = 20$ Substitute 0 for x.

$-5y = 20$ Multiply.

$y = -4$ Divide each side by -5.

y-intercept: -4

5. $y = -2x + 50$ Original equation.

$0 = -2x + 50$ Substitute 0 for y.

$2x = 50$ Add $2x$ to each side.

$x = 25$ Divide each side by 2.

x-intercept: 25

$y = -2x + 50$ Original equation.

$y = -2(0) + 50$ Substitute 0 for x.

$y = 50$ Simplify.

y-intercept: 50

6. $2x + 5y = 10$ Original equation.

$2x + 5(0) = 10$ Substitute 0 for y.

$2x = 10$ Multiply.

$x = 5$ Divide each side by 2.

x-intercept: 5

$2x + 5y = 10$ Original equation.

$2(0) + 5y = 10$ Substitute 0 for x.

$5y = 10$ Multiply.

$y = 2$ Divide each side by 5.

y-intercept: 2

Copyright © McDougal Littell Inc.
All rights reserved.

7. $x - 6y = 6$ Original equation.
$x - 6(0) = 6$ Substitute 0 for y.
$x = 6$ Simplify.
x-intercept: 6

$x - 6y = 6$ Original equation.
$0 - 6y = 6$ Substitute 0 for x.
$-6y = 6$ Simplify.
$y = -1$ Divide each side by –6.
y-intercept: -1

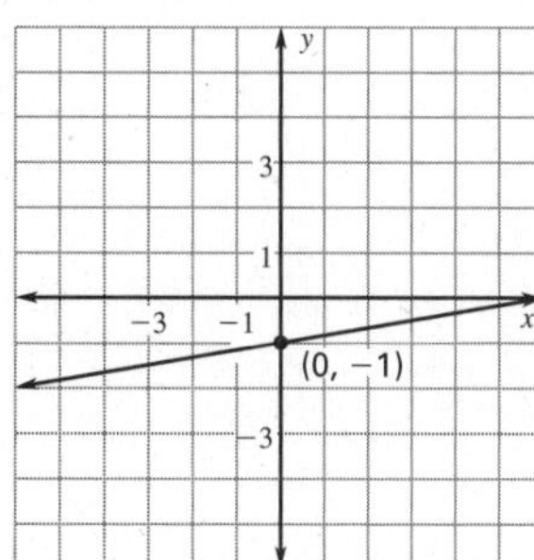

8. $12x - 4y = 96$ Original equation.
$12x - 4(0) = 96$ Substitute 0 for y.
$12x = 96$ Multiply.
$x = 8$ Divide each side by 12.
x-intercept: 8

$12x - 4y = 96$ Original equation.
$12(0) - 4y = 96$ Substitute 0 for x.
$-4y = 96$ Multiply.
$y = -24$ Divide each side by -4.
y-intercept: -24

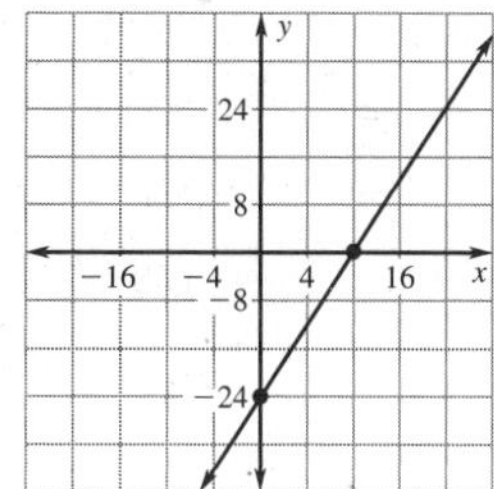

4.4 Guided Practice (p. 225)

1. 3 **2.** 5

3. $5x + 4y = 30$
$5x + 4(0) = 30$
$5x = 30$
$x = 6$
x-intercept: 6

4. $y = 2x + 20$
$0 = 2x + 20$
$-2x = 20$
$x = -10$
x-intercept: -10

5. $-7x - 3y = 21$
$-7x - 3(0) = 21$
$-7x = 21$
$x = -3$
x-intercept: -3

6. $6x + 3y = 51$
$6(0) + 3y = 51$
$3y = 51$
$y = 17$
y-intercept: 17

7. $-2x - 8y = 16$
$-2(0) - 8y = 16$
$-8y = 16$
$y = -2$
y-intercept: -2

8. $10x - y = -5$
$10(0) - y = -5$
$-y = -5$
$y = 5$
y-intercept: 5

9. $y = x + 2$
$0 = x + 2$
$-x = 2$
$x = -2$
x-intercept: -2

$y = x + 2$
$y = 0 + 2$
$y = 2$
y-intercept: 2

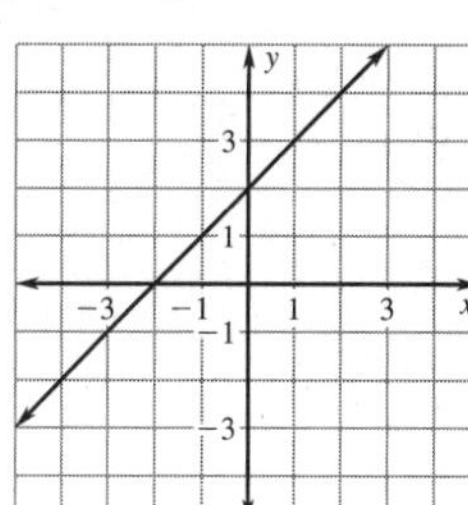

Copyright © McDougal Littell Inc.
All rights reserved.

10. $y - 2x = 3$
$0 - 2x = 3$
$-2x = 3$
$x = -\frac{3}{2}$
x-intercept: $-\frac{3}{2}$

$y - 2x = 3$
$y - 2(0) = 3$
$y = 3$
y-intercept: 3

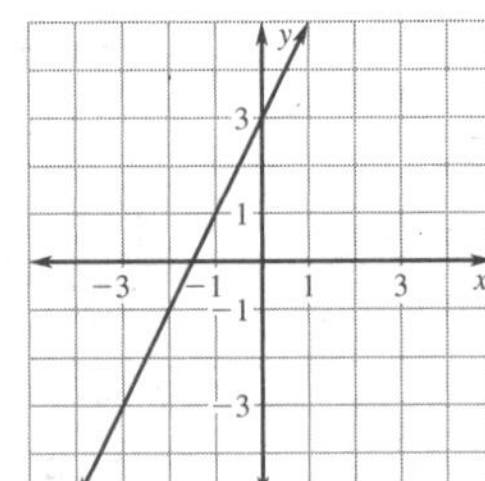

11. $2x - y - 4$
$2x - 0 = 4$
$2x = 4$
$x = 2$
x-intercept: 2

$2x - y = 4$
$2(0) - y = 4$
$-y = 4$
$y = -4$
y-intercept: -4

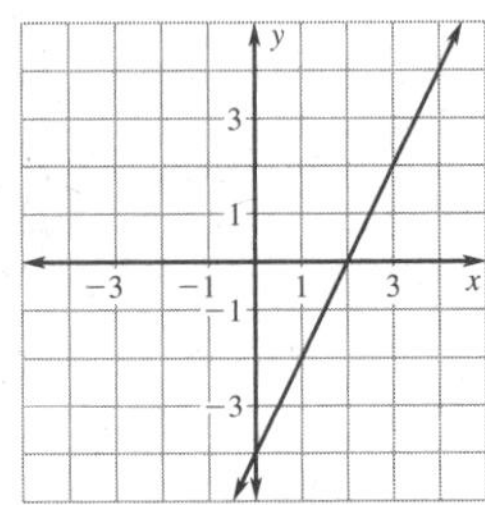

12. $3y = -6x + 3$
$3(0) = -6x + 3$
$0 = -6x + 3$
$6x = 3$
$x = \frac{1}{2}$
x-intercept: $\frac{1}{2}$

$3y = -6x + 3$
$3y = -6(0) + 3$
$3y = 3$
$y = 1$
y-intercept: 1

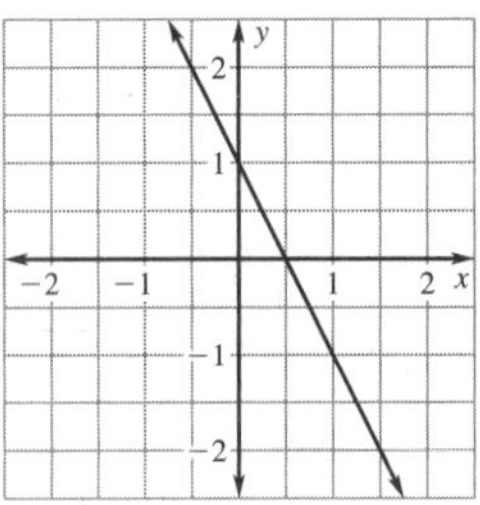

13. $5y = 5x + 15$
$5(0) = 5x + 15$
$0 = 5x + 15$
$-5x = 15$
$x = -3$
x-intercept: -3

$5y = 5x + 15$
$5y = 5(0) + 15$
$5y = 15$
$y = 3$
y-intercept: 3

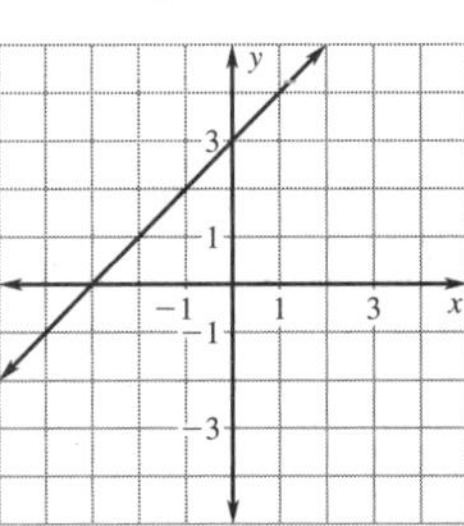

14. $x - y = 1$
$x - 0 = 1$
$x = 1$
x-intercept: 1

$x - y = 1$
$0 - y = 1$
$-y = 1$
$y = -1$
y-intercept: -1

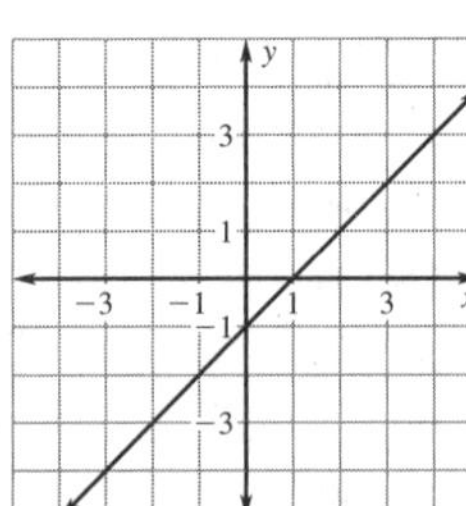

4.4 Practice and Applications (pp. 225–227)

15. x-intercept: 2
y-intercept: 3

16. x-intercept: -2
y-intercept: 4

17. x-intercept: -4
y-intercept: -1

Copyright © McDougal Littell Inc.
All rights reserved.

Chapter 4 *continued*

18. $x - 2y = 4$
$x - 2(0) = 4$
$x = 4$
x-intercept: 4

19. $x + 4y = -2$
$x + 4(0) = -2$
$x = -2$
x-intercept: -2

20. $2x - 3y = 6$
$2x - 3(0) = 6$
$2x = 6$
$x = 3$
x-intercept: 3

21. $5x + 6y = 95$
$5x + 6(0) = 95$
$5x = 95$
$x = 19$
x-intercept: 19

22. $-6x - 4y = 42$
$-6x - 4(0) = 42$
$-6x = 42$
$x = -7$
x-intercept: -7

23. $9x - 4y = 54$
$9x - 4(0) = 54$
$9x = 54$
$x = 6$
x-intercept: 6

24. $-x - 5y = 12$
$-x - 5(0) = 12$
$-x = 12$
$x = -12$
x-intercept: -12

25. $2x + 6y = -24$
$2x + 6(0) = -24$
$2x = -24$
$x = -12$
x-intercept: -12

26. $-13x - y = 39$
$-13x - 0 = 39$
$-13x = 39$
$x = -3$
x-intercept: -3

27. $y = 4x - 2$
$y = 4(0) - 2$
$y = -2$
y-intercept: -2

28. $y = -3x + 7$
$y = -3(0) + 7$
$y = 7$
y-intercept: 7

29. $y = 13x + 26$
$y = 13(0) + 26$
$y = 26$
y-intercept: 26

30. $y = 6x - 24$
$y = 6(0) - 24$
$y = -24$
y-intercept: -24

31. $3x - 4y = 16$
$3(0) - 4y = 16$
$-4y = 16$
$y = -4$
y-intercept: -4

32. $2x - 17y = -51$
$2(0) - 17y = -51$
$-17y = -51$
$y = 3$
y-intercept: 3

33.

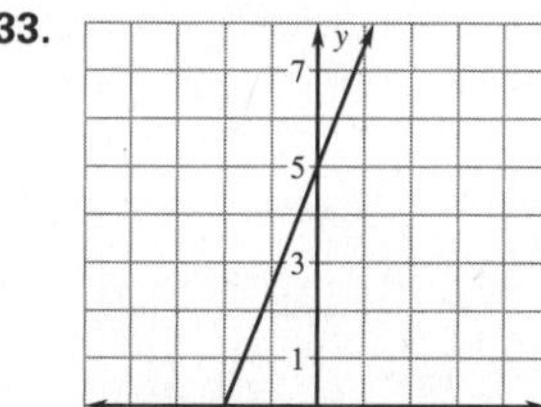

34.

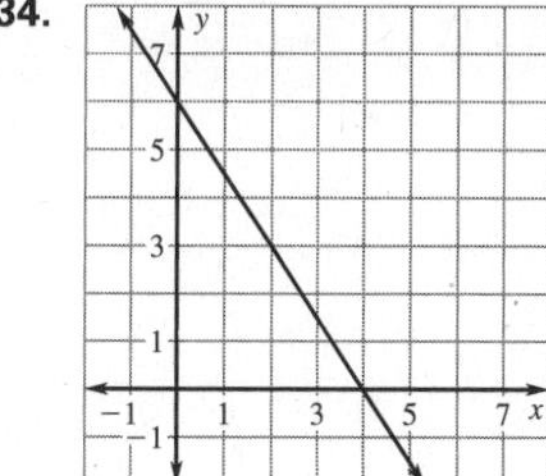

35.

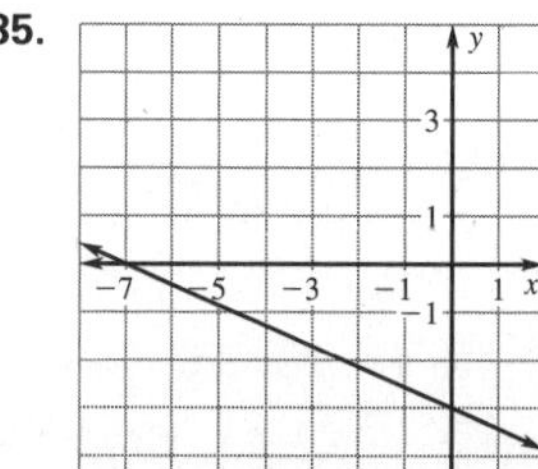

36. $y = 4x - 2$
$0 = 4x - 2$
$-4x = -2$
$x = \frac{1}{2}$ (x-intercept)

$y = 4x - 2$
$y = 4(0) - 2$
$y = -2$ (y-intercept)

B

Copyright © McDougal Littell Inc.
All rights reserved.

37. $y = 4x + 2$

$0 = 4x + 2$

$-4x = 2$

$x = -\frac{1}{2}$ (*x*-intercept)

$y = 4x + 2$

$y = 4(0) + 2$

$y = 2$ (*y*-intercept)

C

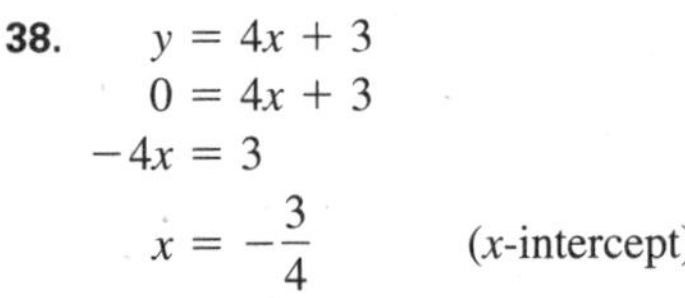

38. $y = 4x + 3$

$0 = 4x + 3$

$-4x = 3$

$x = -\frac{3}{4}$ (*x*-intercept)

$y = 4x + 3$

$y = 4(0) + 3$

$y = 3$ (*y*-intercept)

A

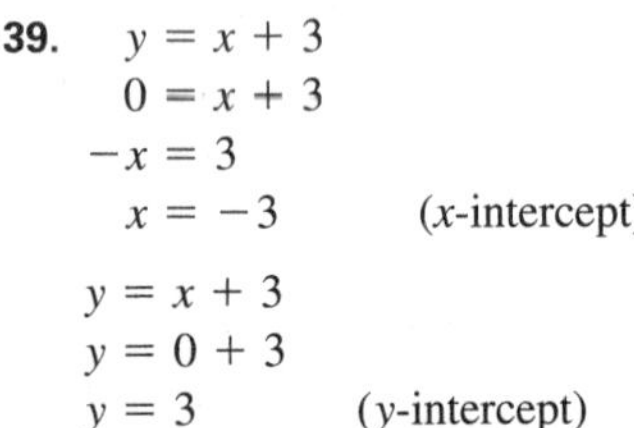

39. $y = x + 3$

$0 = x + 3$

$-x = 3$

$x = -3$ (*x*-intercept)

$y = x + 3$

$y = 0 + 3$

$y = 3$ (*y*-intercept)

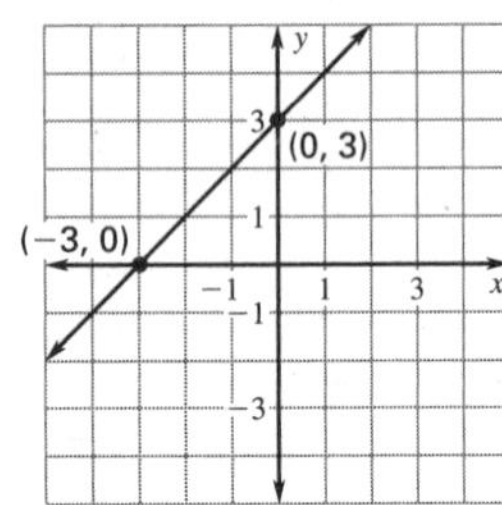

40. $y = x + 9$

$0 = x + 9$

$-x = 9$

$x = -9$ (*x*-intercept)

$y = x + 9$

$y = 0 + 9$

$y = 9$ (*y*-intercept)

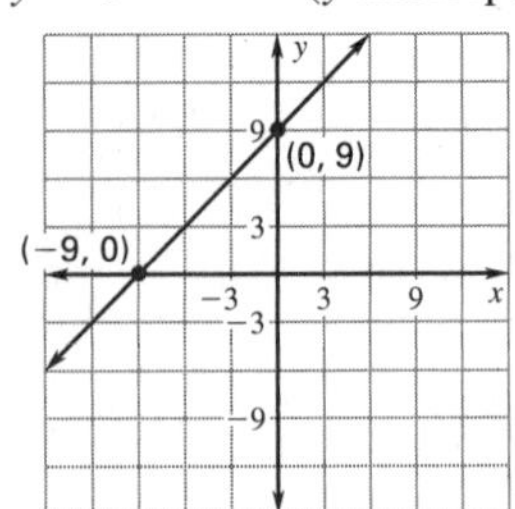

41. $y = -4 + 2x$

$0 = -4 + 2x$

$-2x = -4$

$x = 2$ (*x*-intercept)

$y = -4 + 2x$

$y = -4 + 2(0)$

$y = -4$ (*y*-intercept)

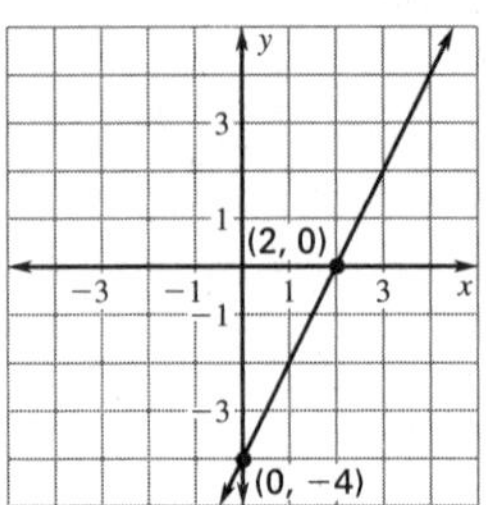

42. $y = 2 - x$

$0 = 2 - x$

$x = 2$ (*x*-intercept)

$y = 2 - x$

$y = 2 - 0$

$y = 2$ (*y*-intercept)

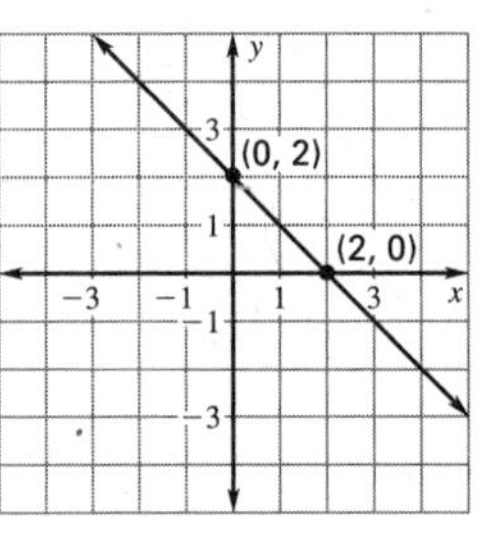

43. $y = -3x + 9$

$0 = -3x + 9$

$3x = 9$

$x = 3$ (*x*-intercept)

$y = -3x + 9$

$y = -3(0) + 9$

$y = 9$ (*y*-intercept)

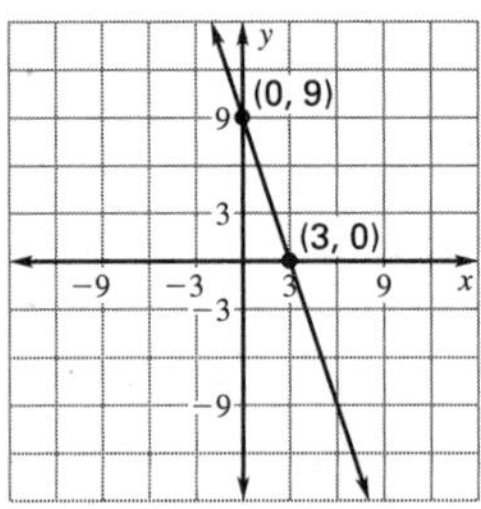

44. $y = 4x - 6$

$0 = 4x - 6$

$-4x = -6$

$x = \frac{3}{2}$ (*x*-intercept)

$y = 4x - 6$

$y = 4(0) - 6$

$y = -6$ (*y*-intercept)

Copyright © McDougal Littell Inc.
All rights reserved.

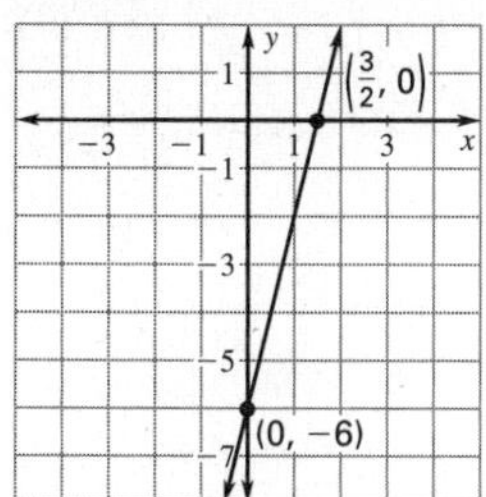

45. $36x + 4y = 44$

$36x + 4(0) = 44$

$36x = 44$

$x = \frac{44}{36} = \frac{4 \cdot 11}{4 \cdot 9} = \frac{11}{9}$ (x-intercept)

$36x + 4y = 44$

$36(0) + 4y = 44$

$4y = 44$

$y = 11$ (y-intercept)

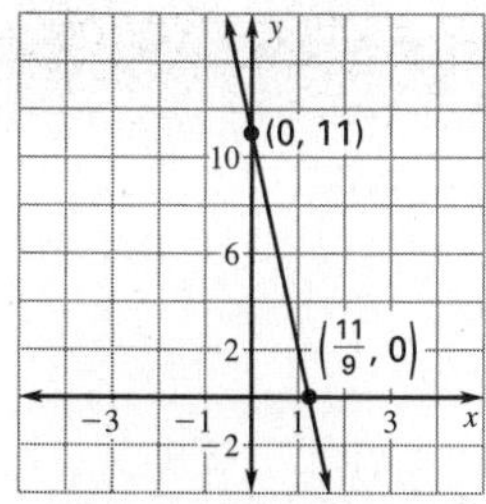

46. $y = 10x + 50$

$0 = 10x + 50$

$-10x = 50$

$x = -5$ (x-intercept)

$y = 10x + 50$

$y = 10(0) + 50$

$y = 50$ (y-intercept)

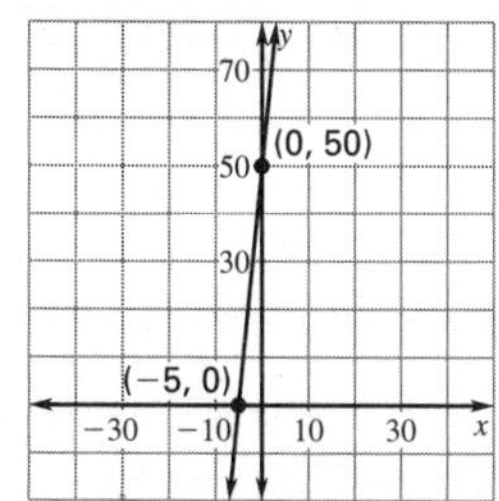

47. $-9x + y = 36$

$-9x + 0 = 36$

$-9x = 36$

$x = -4$ (x-intercept)

$-9x + y = 36$

$-9(0) + y = 36$

$y = 36$ (y-intercept)

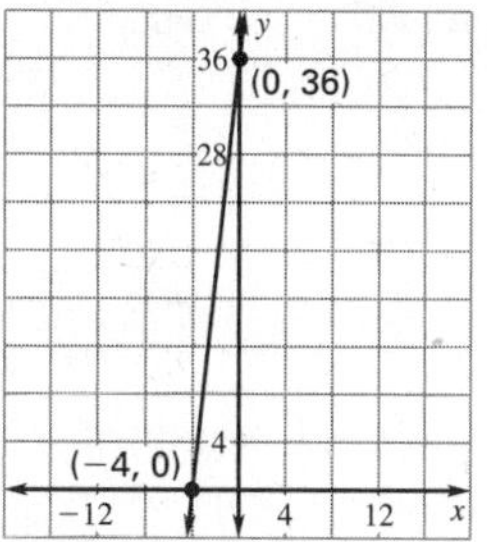

48. $2x + y = 15$

$2x + 0 = 15$

$2x = 15$

$x = \frac{15}{2}$ or $7\frac{1}{2}$ (x-intercept)

$2x + y = 15$

$2(0) + y = 15$

$y = 15$ (y-intercept)

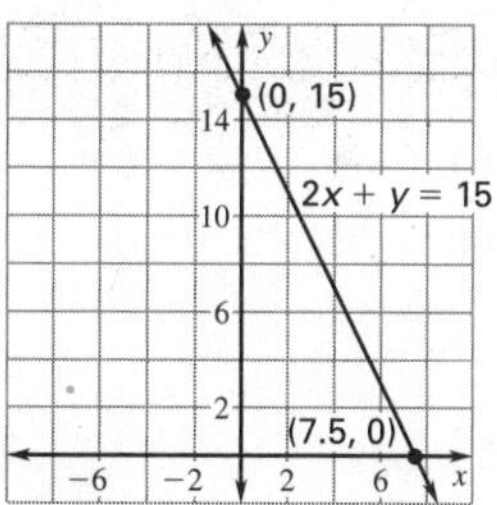

49. x-intercept: 7.5 (see Ex. 48)
If students get in free, the adult ticket price needs to be \$7.50.

50. y-intercept: 15 (see Ex. 48)
If adults get in free, the student ticket price needs to be \$15.

51. *Sample answer*: From the graph (Ex. 48), it must be at least \$6.

52. $y = -6.6x + 229$

$y = -6.6(0) + 229$

$y = 229$ (y-intercept)

Number of railroad employees in 1989 (in thousands)

53. $x = 1995 - 1989 = 6$

$y = -6.6x + 229$

$y = -6.6(6) + 229$

$y = 189.4$

About 189,000 people.

54. *Sample answer*: No, the model would eventually predict a negative number of employees.

Copyright © McDougal Littell Inc.
All rights reserved.

4.4 Standardized Test Practice (p. 227)

55. $3x + y = -9$
$3x + 0 = -9$
$3x = -9$
$x = -3$; A

56. $2x - 3y = 12$
$2(0) - 3y = 12$
$-3y = 12$
$y = -4$; F

4.4 Mixed Review (p. 227)

57. $5 - 9 = -4$

58. $17 - (-6) = 17 + 6 = 23$

59. $|8| - 13 = 8 - 13 = -5$

60. $7 - |-8| = 7 - 8 = -1$

61. $-\frac{2}{3} - \left(-\frac{7}{3}\right) = -\frac{2}{3} + \frac{7}{3} = \frac{5}{3}$

62. $-4 - (-5) = -4 + 5 = 1$

63. $-8 - 9 = -17$

64. $13.8 - 6.9 = 6.9$

65. $54 \div 9 = 6$

66. $-72 \div 8 = -9$

67. $26 \div (-13) = -2$

68. $-1 \div 8 = -\frac{1}{8} = -0.125$

69. $12 \div \left(-\frac{1}{5}\right) = 12 \cdot (-5) = -60$

70. $3 \div \frac{1}{4} = 3 \cdot 4 = 12$

71. $\frac{1}{8} \div \frac{1}{2} = \frac{1}{8} \cdot 2 = \frac{1}{4}$

72. $-20 \div \left(\frac{25}{2}\right) = -20 \cdot \left(\frac{2}{25}\right) = -\frac{40}{25} = -\frac{8}{5}$

73. B; $12x + 24 = 60$

74. $.298 ≈ $.30

75. $1.649 ≈ $1.65

76. $.484 ≈ $.48

77. $8.357 ≈ $8.36

78. $7.134 ≈ $7.13

79. $3.152 ≈ $3.15

80. $.005 ≈ $.01

81. $5.109 ≈ $5.11

Think About It *(p. 228)*

1. As the run increases, the slope decreases.
2. As the rise increases, the slope increases.
3. Rise equals run when the slope equals 1.

Lesson 4.5

4.5 Checkpoint (pp. 230–232)

1. $m = \frac{4 - 5}{1 - 3} = \frac{-1}{-2} = \frac{1}{2}$

2. $m = \frac{3 - 0}{4 - 2} = \frac{3}{2}$

3. $m = \frac{3 - 7}{1 - 2} = \frac{-4}{-1} = 4$

4. $m = \frac{5 - 4}{-1 - 2} = -\frac{1}{3}$

5. $m = \frac{7 - 9}{4 - 0} = \frac{-2}{4} = -\frac{1}{2}$

6. $m = \frac{-3 - 1}{1 - (-2)} = -\frac{4}{3}$

7. $m = \frac{4 - 4}{2 - 4} = \frac{0}{-2} = 0$

8. $m = \frac{4 - 1}{1 - 1} = \frac{3}{0}$; undefined

9. $m = \frac{4 - 2}{2 - 4} = \frac{2}{-2} = -1$ (negative)

4.5 Guided Practice (p. 233)

1. 15 ft

2. 25 ft

3. slope $= \frac{\text{rise}}{\text{run}} = \frac{15}{25} = \frac{3}{5}$

4.

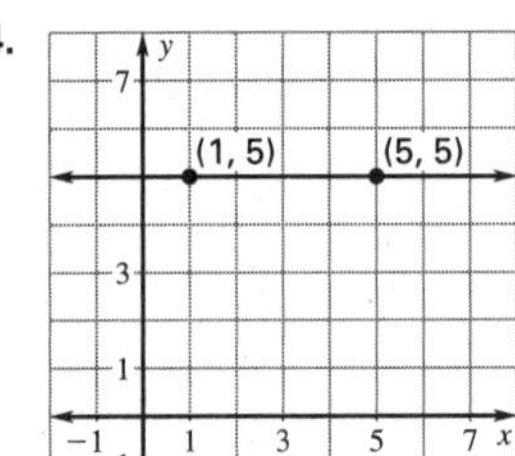

zero

5.

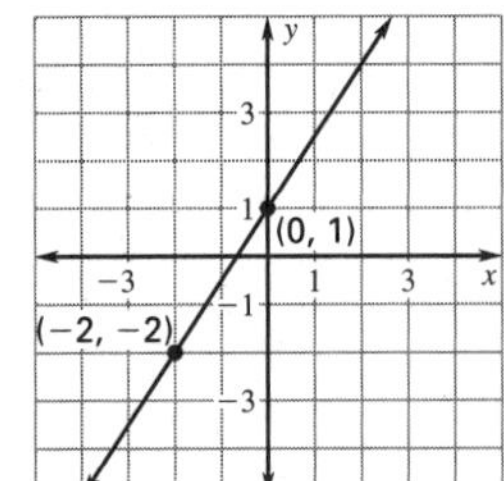

positive

6.

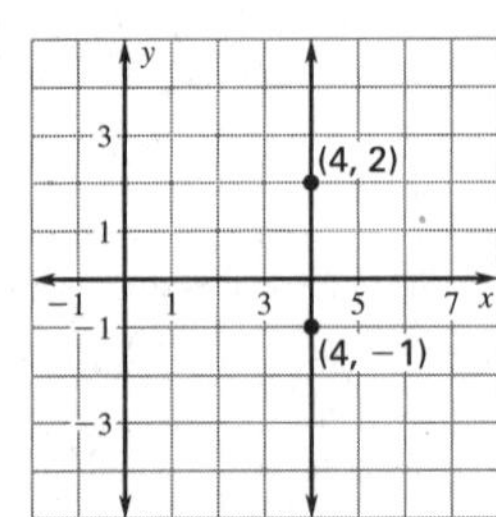

undefined

Copyright © McDougal Littell Inc.
All rights reserved.

7. 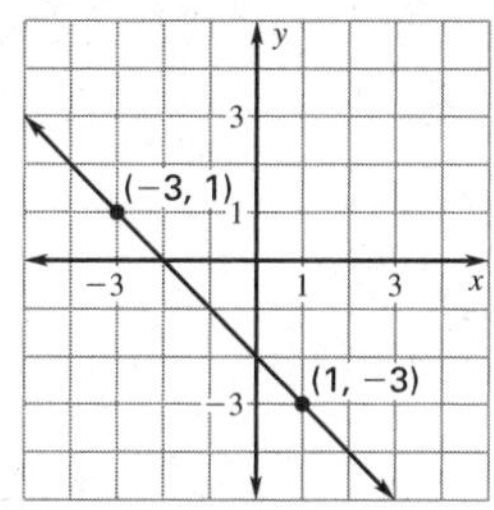

negative

8. 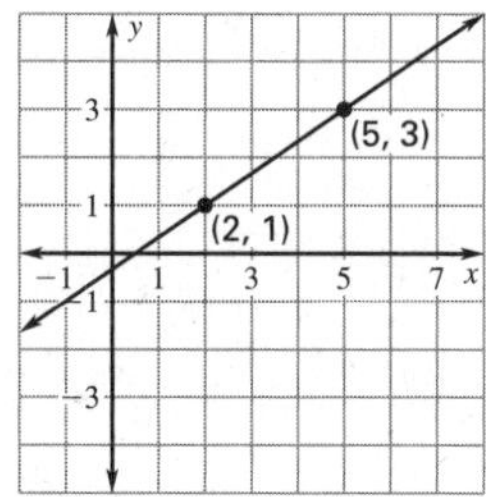

positive

9. 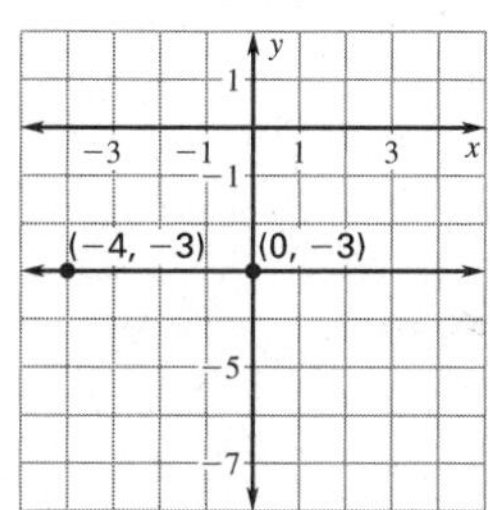

zero

10. $m = \dfrac{5 - 0}{2 - (-3)} = \dfrac{5}{5} = 1$

11. $m = \dfrac{2 - (-1)}{3 - 3} = \dfrac{3}{0}$; undefined

12. $m = \dfrac{1 - 4}{1 - (-2)} = \dfrac{-3}{3} = -1$

4.5 Practice and Applications (pp. 233–235)

13. 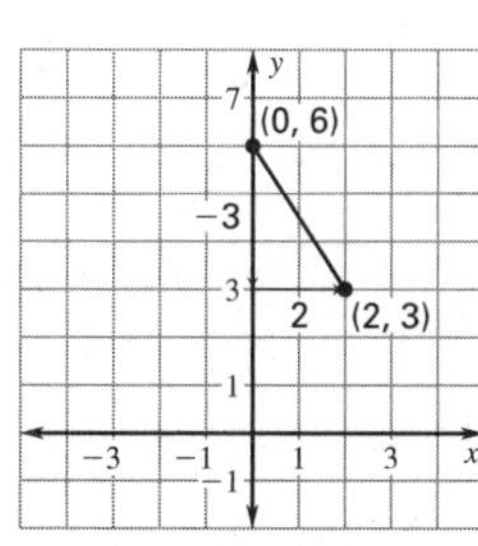

$m = \dfrac{\text{rise}}{\text{run}} = \dfrac{-3}{2} = -\dfrac{3}{2}$

14. 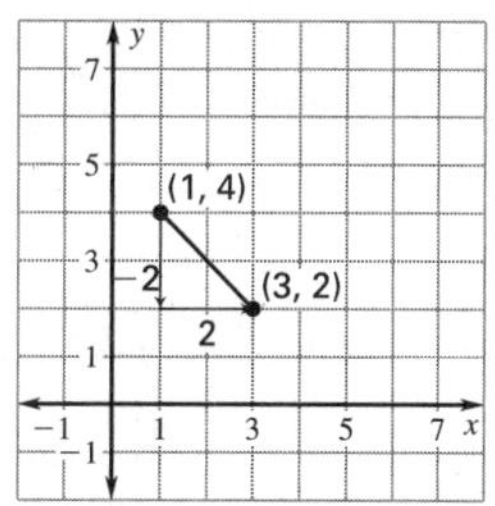

$m = \dfrac{\text{rise}}{\text{run}} = \dfrac{-2}{2} = -1$

15. 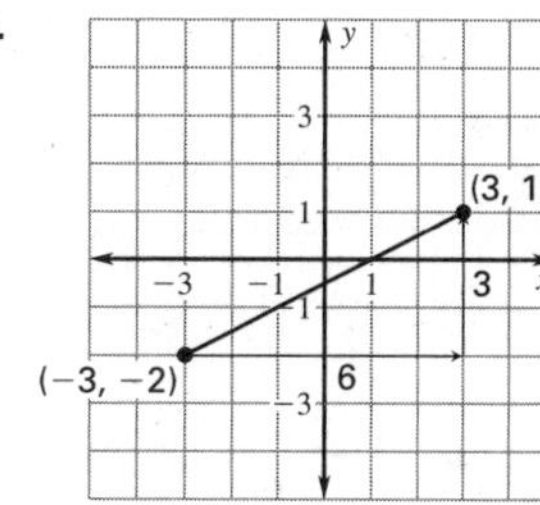

$m = \dfrac{\text{rise}}{\text{run}} = \dfrac{3}{6} = \dfrac{1}{2}$

16. 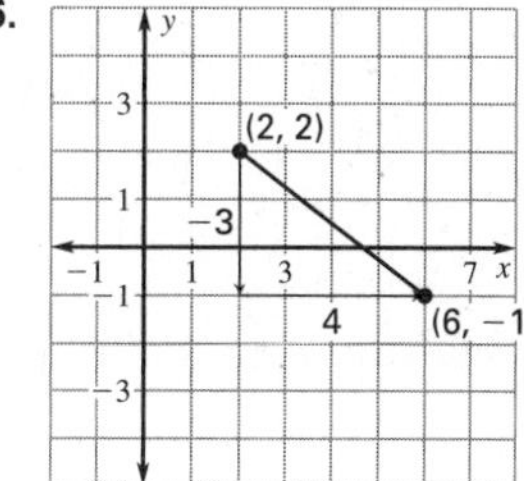

$m = \dfrac{\text{rise}}{\text{run}} = \dfrac{-3}{4} = -\dfrac{3}{4}$

17. 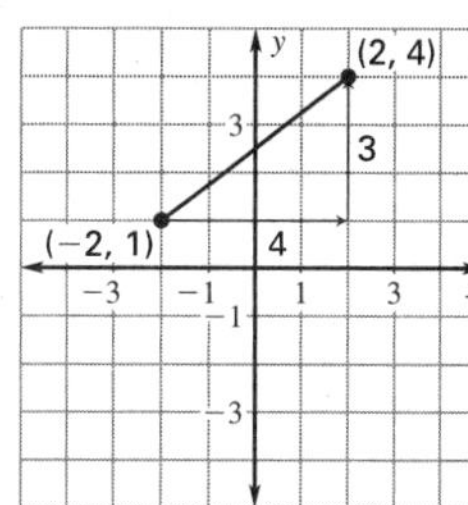

$m = \dfrac{\text{rise}}{\text{run}} = \dfrac{3}{4}$

18. 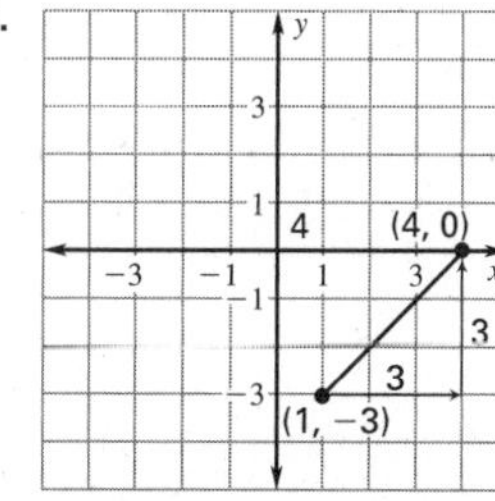

$m = \dfrac{\text{rise}}{\text{run}} = \dfrac{3}{3} = 1$

Copyright © McDougal Littell Inc.
All rights reserved.

19. $m = \frac{\text{rise}}{\text{run}} = \frac{-3}{3} = -1$ **20.** $m = \frac{\text{rise}}{\text{run}} = \frac{0}{5} = 0$

21. $m = \frac{\text{rise}}{\text{run}} = \frac{4}{4} = 1$

22. No; for example, the slope for (3, 3) and (6, 2) is $\frac{2-3}{6-3} = \frac{-1}{3} = -\frac{1}{3}$.

23. $m = \frac{5-3}{8-4} = \frac{2}{4} = \frac{1}{2}$ **24.** $m = \frac{6-4}{1-(-2)} = \frac{2}{3}$

25. $m = \frac{7-8}{7-3} = \frac{-1}{4} = -\frac{1}{4}$

26. $m = \frac{4-(-4)}{9-3} = \frac{8}{6} = \frac{4}{3}$

27. $m = \frac{8-5}{-5-(-3)} = \frac{3}{-2} = -\frac{3}{2}$

28. $m = \frac{-4-(-7)}{-4-(-6)} = \frac{-4+7}{-4+6} = \frac{3}{2}$

29. $m = \frac{7-4}{-5-0} = \frac{3}{-5}$; neither

30. $m = \frac{6-2}{1-1} = \frac{4}{0}$; undefined

31. $m = \frac{2-2}{9-6} = \frac{0}{3} = 0$

32. $m = \frac{-8-(-8)}{3-5} = \frac{0}{-2} = 0$

33. $m = \frac{1-7}{14-8} = \frac{-6}{6} = -1$; neither

34. $m = \frac{5-10}{3-3} = \frac{-5}{0}$; undefined

35. $m = \frac{\text{rise}}{\text{run}} = \frac{72}{48} = \frac{3 \times 24}{2 \times 24} = \frac{3}{2}$

36.

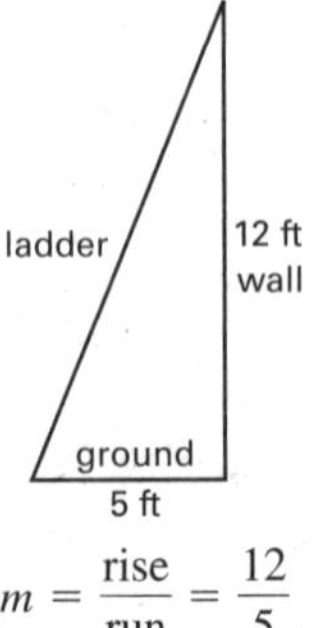

$m = \frac{\text{rise}}{\text{run}} = \frac{12}{5}$

37. *Sample answer*:

Slope from A to B: $\frac{1}{2}$

Slope from B to E: $\frac{3}{6} = \frac{1}{2}$

Slope from C to D: $\frac{1}{2}$

The slope is $\frac{1}{2}$ between each set of points.

38. slope

39. 

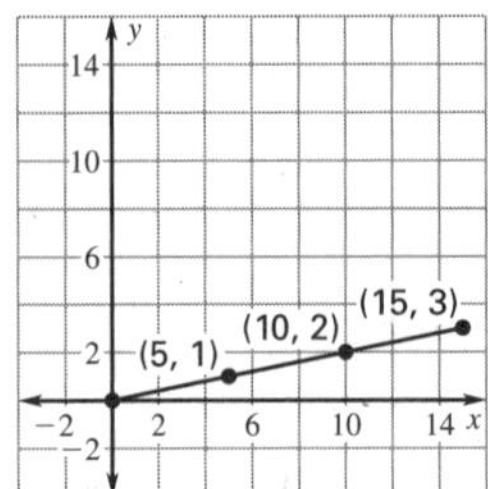

$m = \frac{\text{rise}}{\text{run}} = \frac{1}{5}$; it represents how the rise changes with respect to the run.

40. $\frac{\text{rise}}{\text{run}} = \frac{1}{5} = \frac{y}{20}$

$y = 4$; 4 ft off the ground.

41. $\frac{\text{vertical rise}}{\text{horizontal run}} = \frac{1\frac{1}{2}}{25} = \frac{\frac{3}{2}}{25} = \frac{3}{2} \div 25 = \frac{3}{2} \times \frac{1}{25} = \frac{3}{50}$

$= \frac{6}{100} = 6\%$

42. $\frac{\text{vertical rise}}{\text{horizontal run}} = \frac{70}{1000} = \frac{7}{100} = 7\%$

4.5 Standardized Test Practice (p. 235)

43. C; $m = \frac{5-3}{11-4} = \frac{2}{7}$

44. H; undefined

4.5 Mixed Review (p. 235)

45. $x + 7 = 12$
$x = 5$

46. $x - 3 = 11$
$x = 14$

47. $x - (-2) = 6$
$x + 2 = 6$
$x = 4$

48. $5y = 10x - 5$
$y = \frac{10x}{5} - \frac{5}{5}$
$y = 2x - 1$

49. $\frac{1}{3}y = \frac{2}{3}x + 3$
$y = 3\left(\frac{2}{3}x\right) + 3(3)$
$y = 2x + 9$

50. $-4x + y = 11$
$y = 4x + 11$

Copyright © McDougal Littell Inc.
All rights reserved.

51. $-8x + 2y = 10$

$$2y = 8x + 10$$

$$y = \frac{8x}{2} + \frac{10}{2}$$

$$y = 4x + 5$$

52. $-3x + 6y = 12$

$$6y = 3x + 12$$

$$y = \frac{3x}{6} + \frac{12}{6}$$

$$y = \frac{1}{2}x + 2$$

53. $x + \frac{2}{5}y = -1$

$$\frac{2}{5}y = -x - 1$$

$$y = \frac{5}{2}(-x) - \frac{5}{2}(1)$$

$$y = -\frac{5}{2}x - \frac{5}{2}$$

4.5 Maintaining Skills (p. 235)

54. $1.3 - 2.7 \stackrel{?}{=} 1.4$

$$-1.4 \neq 1.4$$

false

55. $\frac{1.8}{1.8} - 1 \stackrel{?}{=} 0$

$$1 - 1 \stackrel{?}{=} 0$$

$$0 = 0$$

true

56. $\left(\frac{2.7}{0.3} + 1\right) \div 10 \stackrel{?}{=} 0$

$$(9 + 1) \div 10 \stackrel{?}{=} 0$$

$$10 \div 10 \stackrel{?}{=} 0$$

$$1 \neq 0$$

false

57. $14.4 + 0.14 \stackrel{?}{=} 2.88$

$$14.54 \neq 2.88$$

false

58. $(7.8)(1.5) + 4.6 \stackrel{?}{=} 16.3$

$$11.7 + 4.6 \stackrel{?}{=} 16.3$$

$$16.3 = 16.3$$

true

59. $12 + 0 \cdot 7.18 \stackrel{?}{=} 12$

$$12 + 0 \stackrel{?}{=} 12$$

$$12 = 12$$

true

Lesson 4.6

4.6 Checkpoint (pp. 236–238)

1. $x = 2, y = 6$

$y = kx$ Write model for direct variation.

$6 = k(2)$ Substitute 2 for x and 6 for y.

$3 = k$ Divide each side by 2.

Answer: An equation that relates x and y is $y = 3x$.

2. $x = 3, y = 21$

$y = kx$ Write model for direct variation.

$21 = k(3)$ Substitute 3 for x and 21 for y.

$7 = k$ Divide each side by 3.

Answer: An equation that relates x and y is $y = 7x$.

3. $x = 8, y = 96$

$y = kx$ Write model for direct variation.

$96 = k(8)$ Substitute 8 for x and 96 for y.

$12 = k$ Divide each side by 8.

Answer: An equation that relates x and y is $y = 12x$.

4.

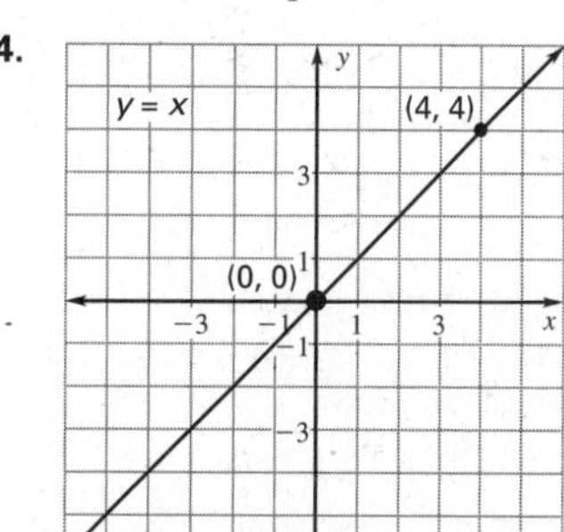

5.

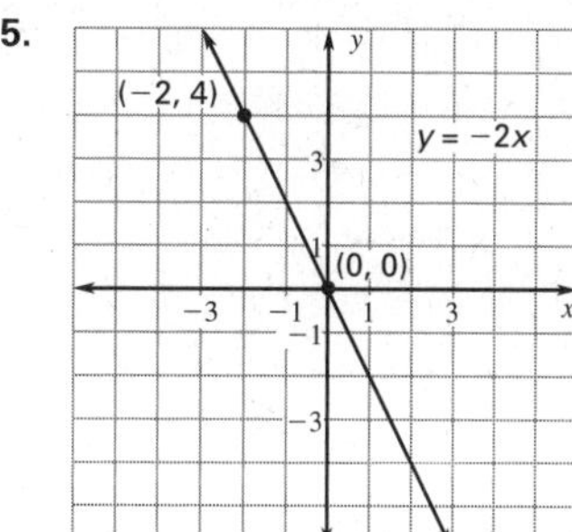

6.

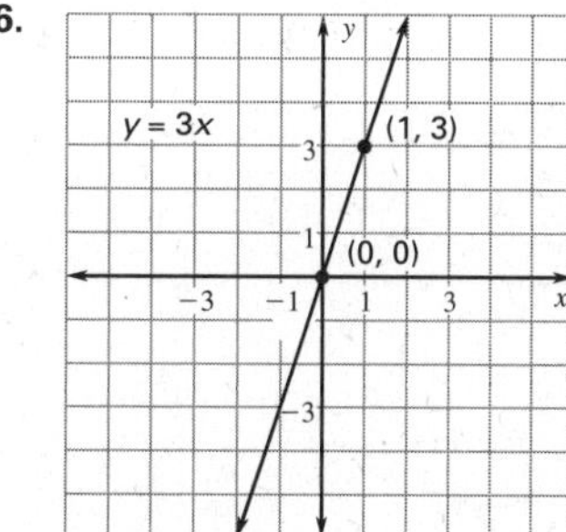

7. $T = 0.90B$ Substitute 4.5 for T.

$$4.5 = 0.90B$$

$$\frac{4.5}{0.9} = B$$

$$5 = B$$

5 ft

Copyright © McDougal Littell Inc.
All rights reserved.

4.6 Guided Practice (p. 239)

1. Two quantities vary directly when they have a constant ratio k, such as $y = kx$ or $\frac{y}{x} = k$.

2. the origin

3. $y = kx$ Equation of direct variation.
$3 = k(27)$ Substitute 3 for y, 27 for x.
$\frac{1}{9} = k$ Divide each side by 27.

4. $y = kx$ Equation of direct variation.
$8 = k(32)$ Substitute 8 for y, 32 for x.
$\frac{1}{4} = k$ Divide each side by 32.

5. $r = ks$ Equation of direct variation.
$5 = k(35)$ Substitute 5 for r, 35 for s.
$\frac{1}{7} = k$ Divide each side by 35.

6. $y = kx$ Equation of direct variation.
$2 = k(1)$ Substitute 2 for y, 1 for x.
$2 = k$ Constant of variation.
$y = 2x$ Equation that relates x and y.

7. $y = kx$ Equation of direct variation.
$25 = k(5)$ Substitute 25 for y, 5 for x.
$5 = k$ Constant of variation.
$y = 5x$ Equation that relates x and y.

8. $y = kx$ Equation of direct variation.
$36 = k(3)$ Substitute 36 for y, 3 for x.
$12 = k$ Constant of variation.
$y = 12x$ Equation that relates x and y.

9. 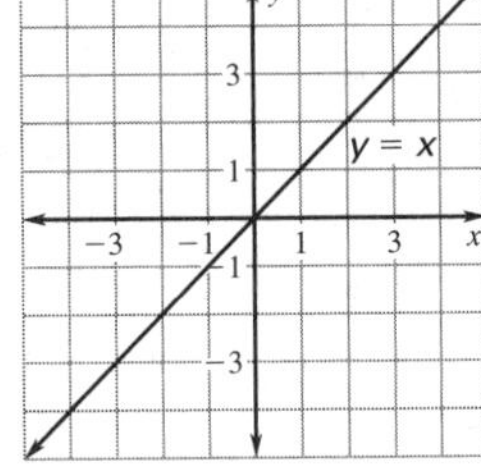

10. 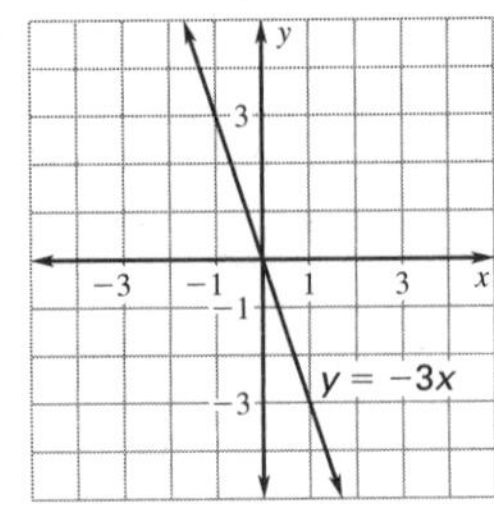

11. 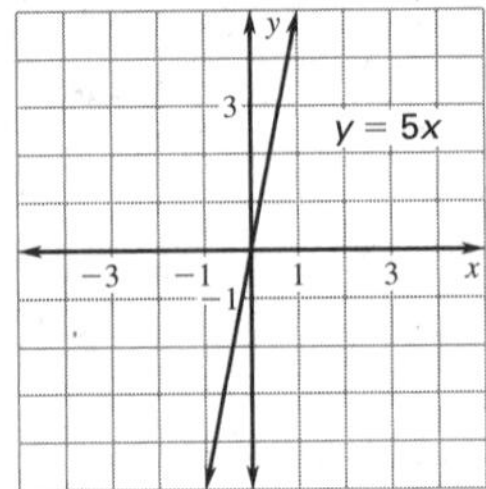

4.6 Practice and Applications (pp. 239–240)

12. $y = kx$
$54 = k(6)$
$9 = k$ (constant of variation)

13. $y = kx$
$72 = k(6)$
$12 = k$ (constant of variation)

14. $h = km$
$112 = k(12)$
$\frac{112}{12} = k$
$\frac{28}{3} = k$ (constant of variation)

15. $W = km$
$150 = k(6)$
$25 = k$ (constant of variation)

16. $y = kx$
$12 = k(4)$
$3 = k$
$y = 3x$ Equation that relates x and y.

17. $y = kx$
$35 = k(7)$
$5 = k$
$y = 5x$ Equation that relates x and y.

18. $y = kx$
$48 = k(12)$
$4 = k$
$y = 4x$ Equation that relates x and y.

19. $y = kx$
$90 = k(15)$
$6 = k$
$y = 6x$ Equation that relates x and y.

20. $y = kx$
$11 = k(22)$
$\frac{1}{2} = k$
$y = \left(\frac{1}{2}\right)x$ Equation that relates x and y.

21. $y = kx$
$-3 = k(9)$
$-\frac{1}{3} = k$
$y = -\left(\frac{1}{3}\right)x$ Equation that relates x and y.

Copyright © McDougal Littell Inc.
All rights reserved.

22. $y = kx$
$-1 = k(-1)$
$1 = k$
$y = x$ Equation that relates x and y.

23. $y = kx$
$40 = k(-4)$
$-10 = k$
$y = -10x$ Equation that relates x and y.

24. $y = kx$
$-56 = k(8)$
$-7 = k$
$y = -7x$ Equation that relates x and y.

25. Yes, direct variation; the constant is 14.

26. Yes, direct variation; the constant is π (≈ 3.14).

27.

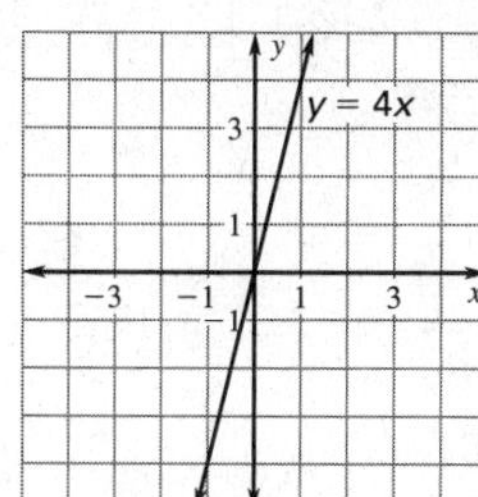

28.

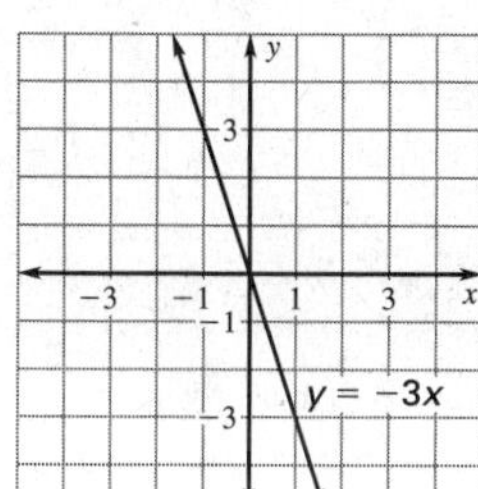

29.

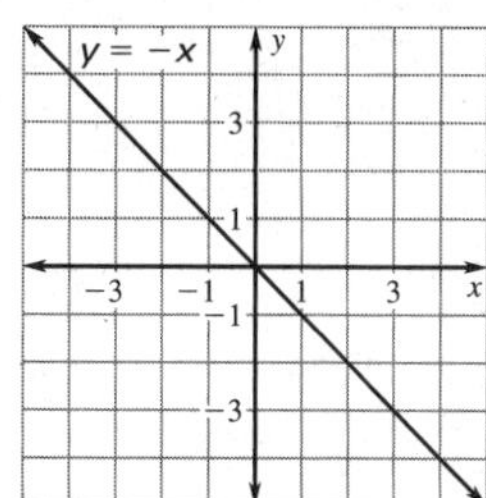

30.

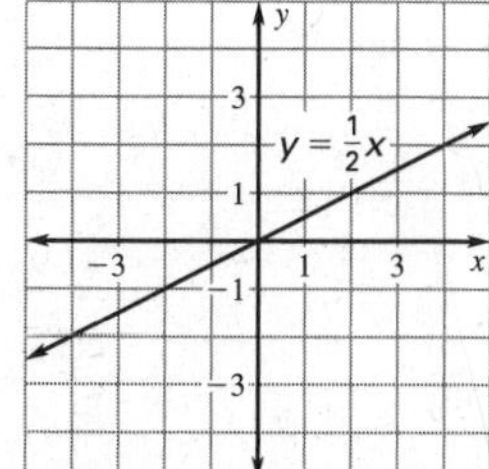

31. Yes; the line goes through the origin.

32. Yes; the line goes through the origin.

33. No; the line does not pass through the origin.

34. Let E = weight on Earth, M = weight on the moon, and k = constant of variation.
Solve for k:
$E = kM$
$360 = k(60)$
$6 = k$
$E = 6M$ (Equation that relates E and M.)
Tereshkova's weight on Earth:
$E = 6(54) = 324$ lb

35. Let w = number of words typed, t = time spent typing, and k = constant of variation.
$w = kt$
$275 = k(5)$
$55 = k$
$w = 55t$ (Equation that relates w and t.)
$935 = 55t$
$17 = t$
17 minutes to type 935 words.

36.

Violin Family	*Bass*	*Cello*	*Viola*	*Violin*
Total length, t (in.)	72	47	26	23
Body length, b (in.)	44	30	?	14
Ratio of t to b $\left(\frac{t}{b}\right)$	$\frac{18}{11} \approx 1.6$	1.6	?	1.6

$t = 1.6b$

37. Viola:
$t = 1.6b$
$26 = 1.6b$
$16.25 = b$
About 16 in.

4.6 Standardized Test Practice (p. 240)

38. $3x = y$; constant is 3; A

39. $y = kx$
$24 = k(4)$
$6 = k$
$y = 6x$; J

4.6 Mixed Review (p. 241)

40. $7x + 30 = -5$
$7x = -35$
$x = -5$

41. $4y = 26 - 9y$
$13y = 26$
$y = 2$

42. $2(w - 2) = 2$
$2w - 4 = 2$
$2w = 6$
$w = 3$

Copyright © McDougal Littell Inc.
All rights reserved.

43. $9x + 65 = -4x$
$13x + 65 = 0$
$13x = -65$
$x = -5$

44. $55 - 5y = 9y + 27$
$55 = 14y + 27$
$28 = 14y$
$2 = y$

45. $7a - 3 = 4(a - 3)$
$7a - 3 = 4a - 12$
$3a - 3 = -12$
$3a = -9$
$a = -3$

46. $15 = 7(x - y) + 3x$
$15 = 7x - 7y + 3x$
$15 = 10x - 7y$
$15 + 7y = 10x$
$7y = 10x - 15$
$y = \frac{10}{7}x - \frac{15}{7}$

47. $3x + 12 = 5(x + y)$
$3x + 12 = 5x + 5y$
$-2x + 12 = 5y$
$-\frac{2}{5}x + \frac{12}{5} = y$

48. $\$152.25 = k(21)$
$7.25 = k$
$7.25/h

49. $x - y = 10$
$5 - (-5) \stackrel{?}{=} 10$
$5 + 5 \stackrel{?}{=} 10$
$10 = 10$
a solution

50. $3x - 6y = -2$
$3(-4) - 6(-2) \stackrel{?}{=} -2$
$-12 + 12 \stackrel{?}{=} -2$
$0 \neq -2$
not a solution

51. $5x + 6y = -1$
$5(1) + 6(-1) \stackrel{?}{=} -1$
$5 - 6 \stackrel{?}{=} -1$
$-1 = -1$
a solution

52. $-4x - 3y = -8$
$-4(-4) - 3(2) \stackrel{?}{=} -8$
$16 - 6 \stackrel{?}{=} -8$
$10 \neq -8$
not a solution

53. $3x + 4y = 36$
$3(4) + 4(6) \stackrel{?}{=} 36$
$12 + 24 \stackrel{?}{=} 36$
$36 = 36$
a solution

54. $5x - 3y = 47$
$5(2) - 3(9) \stackrel{?}{=} 47$
$10 - 27 \stackrel{?}{=} 47$
$-17 \neq 47$
not a solution

4.6 Maintaining Skills (p. 241)

55. $2 \cdot 3 \cdot 11 = 6 \cdot 11 = 66$

56. $3 \cdot 5 \cdot 7 = 15 \cdot 7 = 105$

57. $2^3 \cdot 7 = 8 \cdot 7 = 56$

58. $5^3 \cdot 7 \cdot 11 = 125 \cdot 7 \cdot 11 = 875 \cdot 11 = 9{,}625$

59. $2 \cdot 3 \cdot 5 \cdot 7 \cdot 17 = 6 \cdot 5 \cdot 7 \cdot 17 = 30 \cdot 7 \cdot 17$
$= 210 \cdot 17 = 3{,}570$

60. $2^6 \cdot 3 \cdot 5^6 = 64 \cdot 3 \cdot 15{,}625 = 3{,}000{,}000$

Quiz 2 ***(p. 241)***

1. $y = 3x + 6$
$0 = 3x + 6$
$-6 = 3x$
$-2 = x$ (x-intercept)

$y = 3x + 6$
$y = 3(0) + 6$
$y = 6$ (y-intercept)

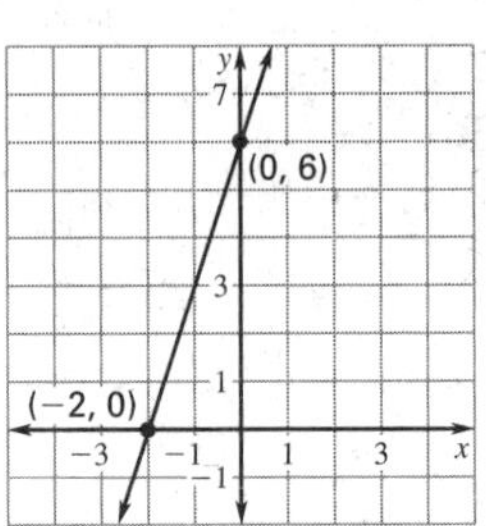

2. $y - 8x = -16$
$0 - 8x = -16$
$-8x = -16$
$x = 2$ (x-intercept)

$y - 8(0) = -16$
$y = -16$ (y-intercept)

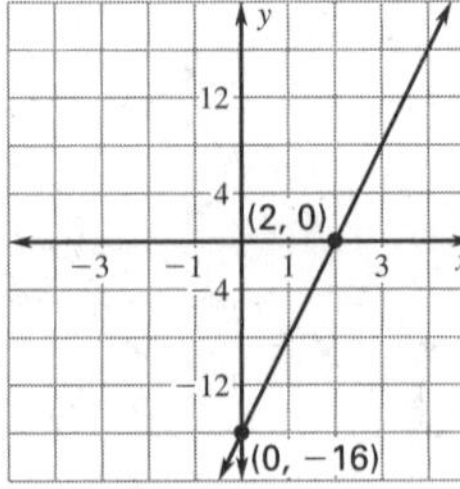

3. $x - y = 10$
$x - 0 = 10$
$x = 10$ (x-intercept)

Copyright © McDougal Littell Inc.
All rights reserved.

$x - y = 10$
$0 - y = 10$
$-y = 10$
$y = -10$ (*y*-intercept)

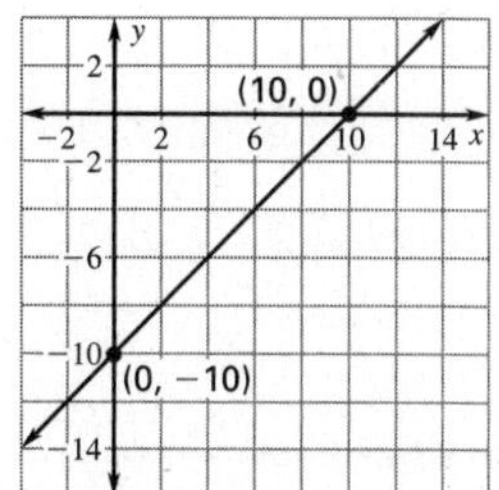

4. $2x - y = 5$
$2x - 0 = 5$
$2x = 5$
$x = \frac{5}{2}$ or $2\frac{1}{2}$ (*x*-intercept)

$2x - y = 5$
$2(0) - y = 5$
$-y = 5$
$y = -5$ (*y*-intercept)

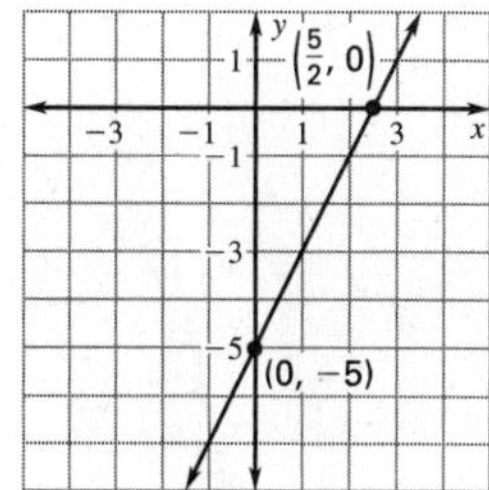

5. $4x + 2y = 20$
$4x + 2(0) = 20$
$4x = 20$
$x = 5$ (*x*-intercept)

$4x + 2y = 20$
$4(0) + 2y = 20$
$2y = 20$
$y = 10$ (*y*-intercept)

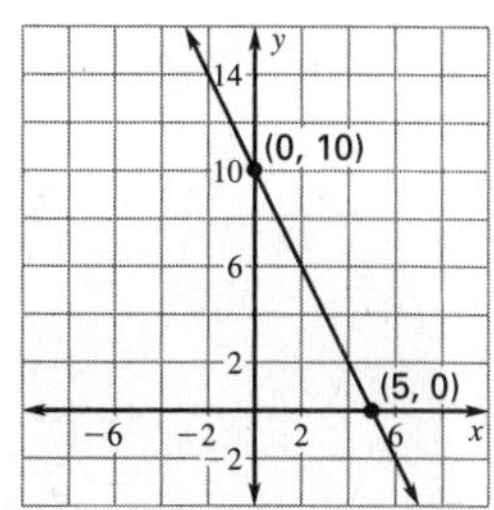

6. $x - 2y = 8$
$x - 2(0) = 8$
$x = 8$ (*x*-intercept)

$x - 2y = 8$
$0 - 2y = 8$
$-2y = 8$
$y = -4$ (*y*-intercept)

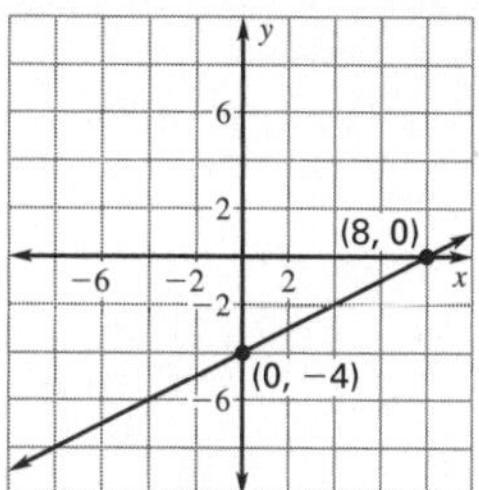

7. $m = \frac{2 - 0}{5 - 0} = \frac{2}{5}$

8. $m = \frac{-5 - (-3)}{-4 - 1} = \frac{-5 + 3}{-5} = \frac{-2}{-5} = \frac{2}{5}$

9. $m = \frac{-4 - 3}{-6 - 3} = \frac{-7}{-9} = \frac{7}{9}$

10. $m = \frac{-2 - 2}{-5 - (-3)} = \frac{-4}{-5 + 3} = \frac{-4}{-2} = 2$

11. $m = \frac{-4 - (-4)}{5 - 0} = \frac{-4 + 4}{5} = \frac{0}{5} = 0$

12. $m = \frac{6 - (-2)}{-7 - 1} = \frac{6 + 2}{-8} = \frac{8}{-8} = -1$

13. $y = kx$
$9 = k(3)$
$3 = k$
$y = 3x$

14. $y = kx$
$40 = k(5)$
$8 = k$
$y = 8x$

15. $y = kx$
$60 = k(15)$
$4 = k$
$y = 4x$

16.

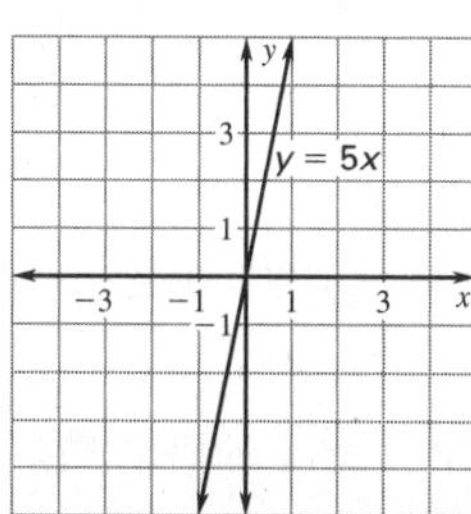

17.

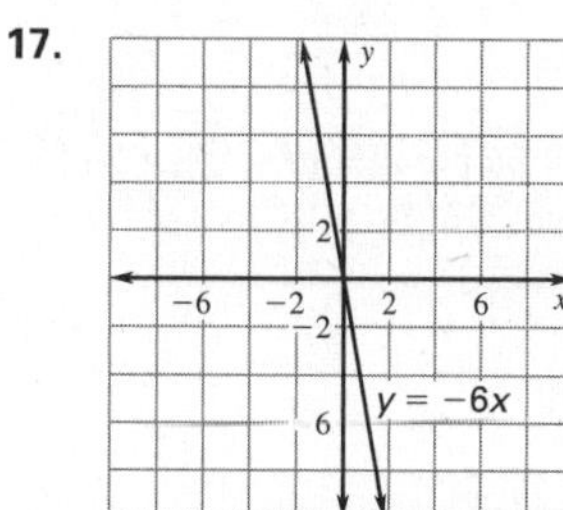

Copyright © McDougal Littell Inc.
All rights reserved.

18.

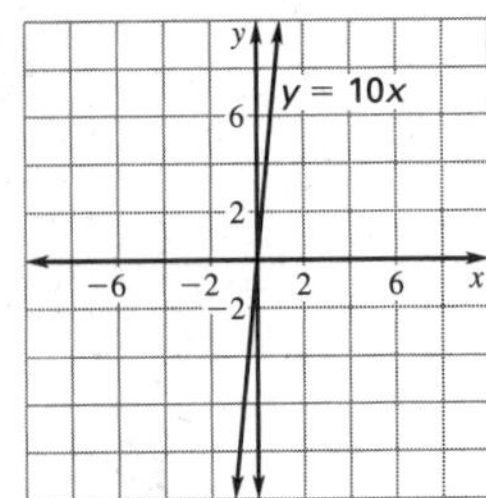

19. $b = kt$

$4200 = k(2)$

$2100 = k$

$b = 2100t$

$b = 2100(5) = 10{,}500$ bolts in 5 hours

4.7 Developing Concepts: Explore *(p. 242)*

1.

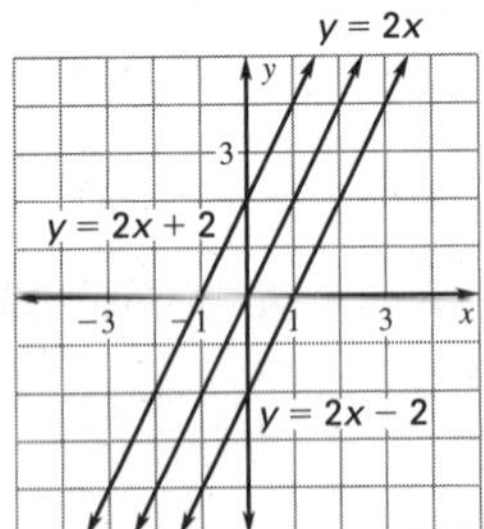

The lines are parallel.

2. Slope of $y = 2x$ is 2; crosses the axis at 0; slope of $y = 2x + 2$ is 2; crosses the axis at 2; slope of $y = 2x - 2$ is 2; crosses the axis at -2. All the equations have the same slope. The place where they cross the axis is the constant term.

3.

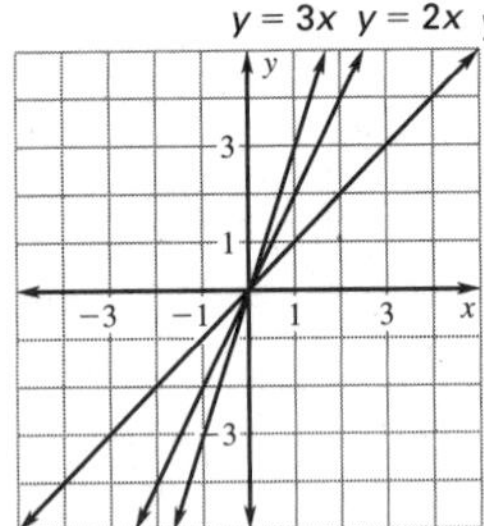

The lines intersect at (0, 0).

4. Slope of $y = x$ is 1; slope of $y = 2x$ is 2; slope of $y = 3x$ is 3. Each line crosses the y-axis at (0, 0).

Think About It (p. 242)

1. *Sample answer:* The line will be parallel to $y = 2x$ and $y = 2x + 2$, and its y-intercept will be 5.

2.

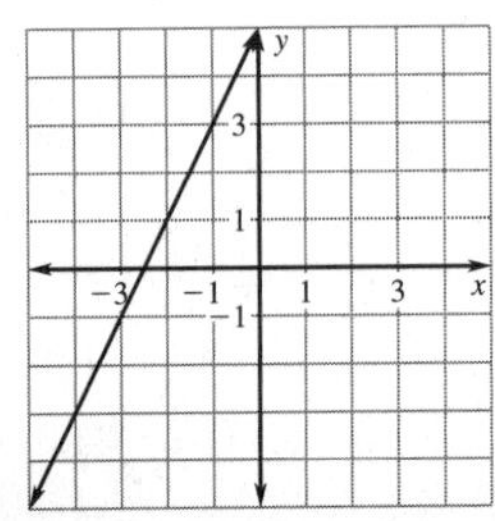

3. *Sample answer*: The graph of $y = 5x$ will have a slope of 5 and pass through the origin.

4.

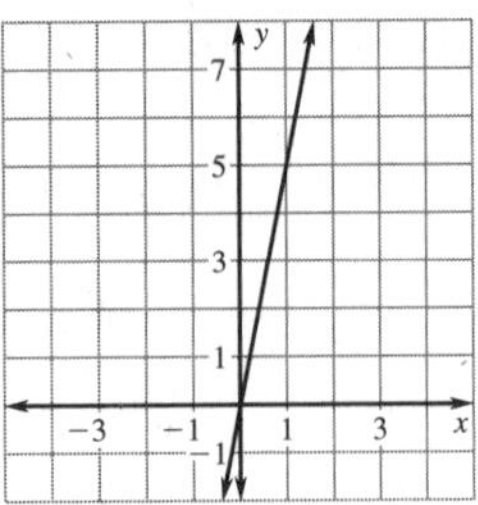

5. m gives the slope; b gives the y-intercept

Lesson 4.7

4.7 Checkpoint (pp. 244–245)

1. slope: -2

y-intercept: 3

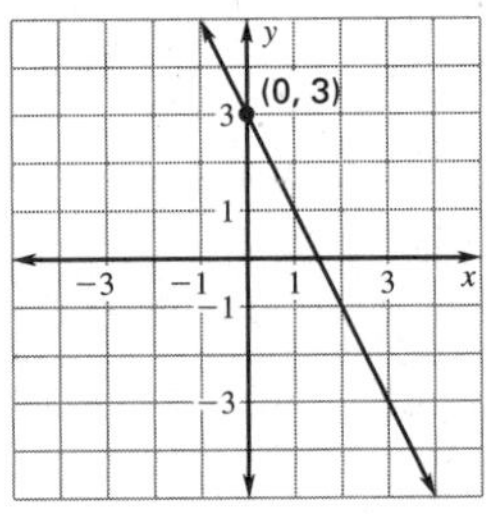

2. slope: 4

y-intercept: -5

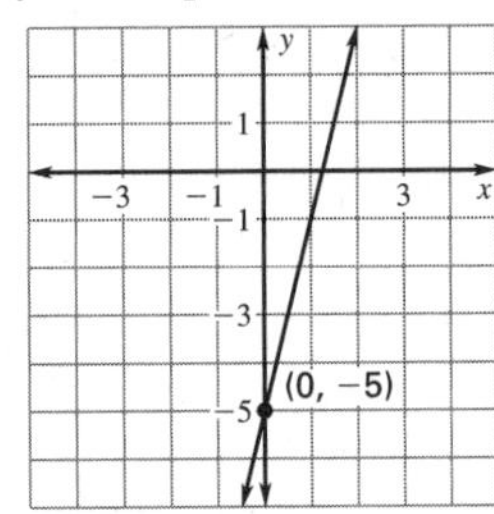

3. slope: $-\frac{2}{3}$

y-intercept: 2

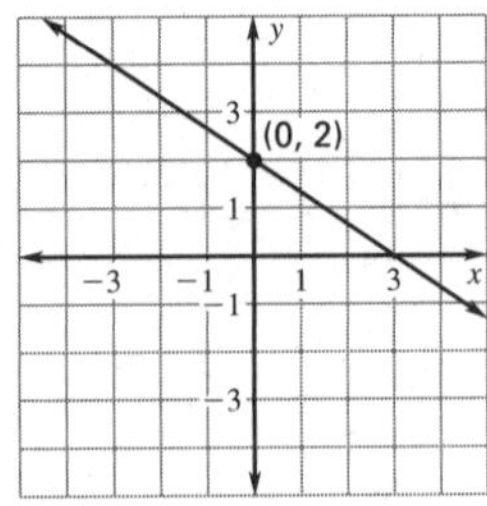

4. $y = 1.9x + 350$

$y = 1.9(60) + 350$

$y = 464$

\$464.00

Copyright © McDougal Littell Inc.
All rights reserved.

5. slope of line *a*:
$3x + 2y = 6$
$2y = -3x + 6$
$y = -\frac{3}{2}x + 3$
slope $= -\frac{3}{2}$
slope of line *b*:
$3x - 2y = 6$
$-2y = -3x + 6$
$y = \frac{3}{2}x - 3$
slope $= \frac{3}{2}$
slope of line *c*:
$6x + 4y = 6$
$4y = -6x + 6$
$y = -\frac{3}{2}x + \frac{3}{2}$
slope $= -\frac{3}{2}$
Lines *a* and *c* have slopes of $-\frac{3}{2}$ and therefore are parallel.

4.7 Guided Practice (p. 246)

1. -7
2. slope, *y*-intercepts
3. $y = 2x + 1$
$m = 2; b = 1$
4. $y = 8.5x$
$m = 8.5; b = 0$
5. $5x - y = 3$
$-y = -5x + 3$
$y = 5x - 3$
$m = 5; b = -3$
6. $y - x = 3$
$y = x + 3$
$m = 1; b = 3$
7. $y + x = 15$
$y = -x + 15$
$m = -1; b = 15$
8. $y = \frac{1}{2}x + 6$
$m = \frac{1}{2}; b = 6$
9. slope: $\frac{4}{2} = 2$
y-intercept: -2
equation: $y = 2x - 2$; B
10. $y = x + 2$ slope: 1 $\quad$ $y = x - 4$ slope: 1
Yes; the slopes are the same.

4.7 Practice and Applications (pp. 246–248)

11. $-x + y = 9$
$y = x + 9$
12. $3x + y = -11$
$y = -3x - 11$
13. $10x - 5y = 50$
$-5y = -10x + 50$
$y = \frac{-10x}{-5} + \frac{50}{-5}$
$y = 2x - 10$
14. $y - 4x = 9$
$y = 4x + 9$
15. $2y + 12 = x$
$2y = x - 12$
$y = \left(\frac{1}{2}\right)x - 6$
16. $3x - 6y = 18$
$-6y = -3x + 18$
$y = \frac{-3x}{-6} + \frac{18}{-6}$
$y = \left(\frac{1}{2}\right)x - 3$
17. $y = 6x + 4$
$m = 6; b = 4$
18. $y = 3x - 7$
$m = 3; b = -7$
19. $y = 2x - 9$
$m = 2; b = -9$
20. $y = \frac{1}{4}x - 3$
$m = \frac{1}{4}; b = -3$
21. $y - 9x = 0$
$y = 9x + 0$
$m = 9; b = 0$
22. $y = -2$
$m = 0; b = -2$
23. $12x + 4y = 24$
$4y = -12x + 24$
$y = -3x + 6$
$m = -3; b = 6$
24. $3x + 4y = 16$
$4y = -3x + 16$
$y = -\frac{3}{4}x + 4$
$m = -\frac{3}{4}; b = 4$
25. $7y - 14x = 28$
$7y = 14x + 28$
$y = 2x + 4$
$m = 2; b = 4$

Copyright © McDougal Littell Inc.
All rights reserved.

26. $y = x + 3; m = 1; b = 3$

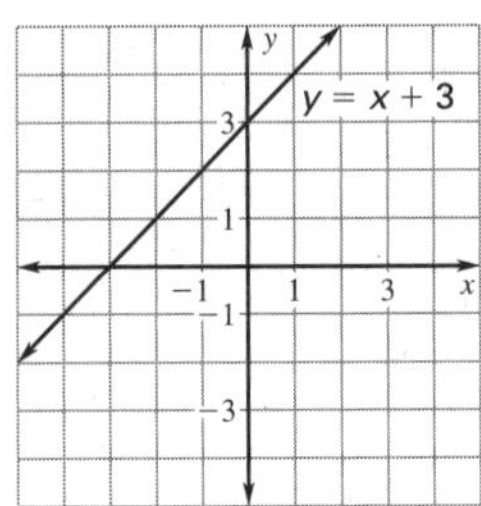

27. $y = 2x - 1; m = 2; b = -1$

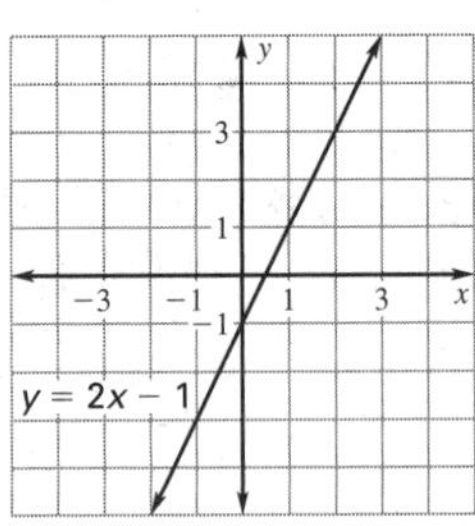

28. $y = x + 5; m = 1; b = 5$

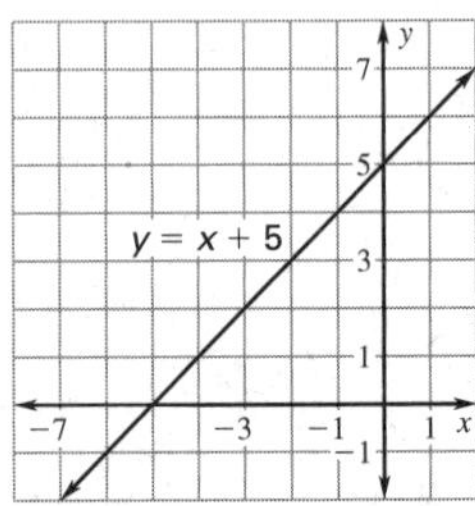

29. $y = -x + 4; m = -1; b = 4$

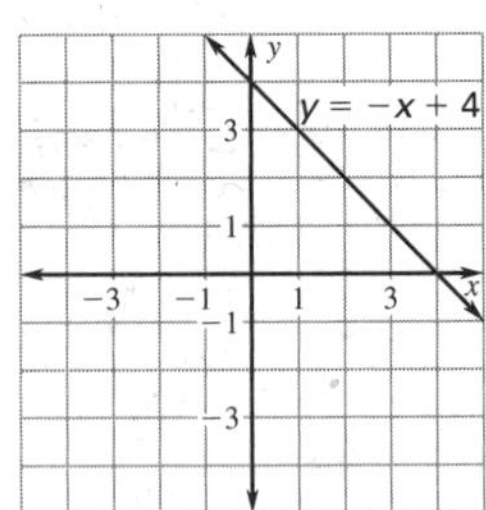

30. $y = 6 - x$

$y = -x + 6; m = -1; b = 6$

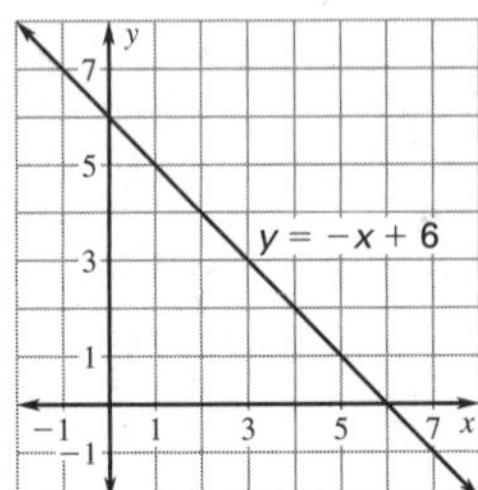

31. $y = 3x + 7; m = 3; b = 7$

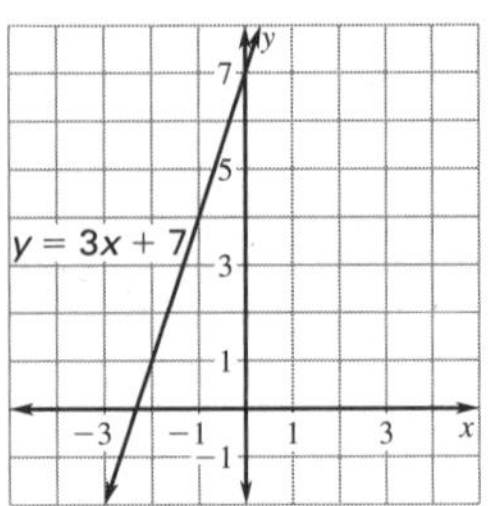

32. $y = 4x + 4; m = 4; b = 4$

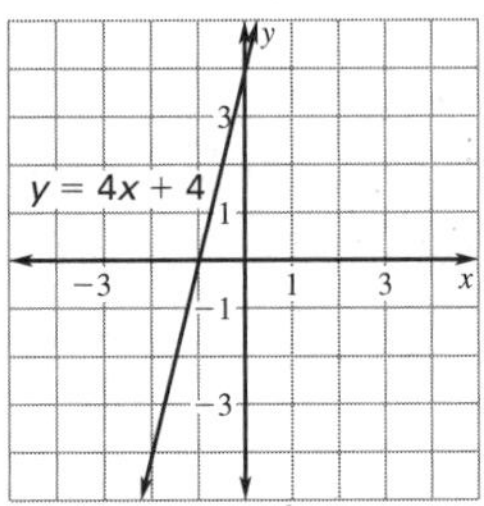

33. $y = x + 9; m = 1; b = 9$

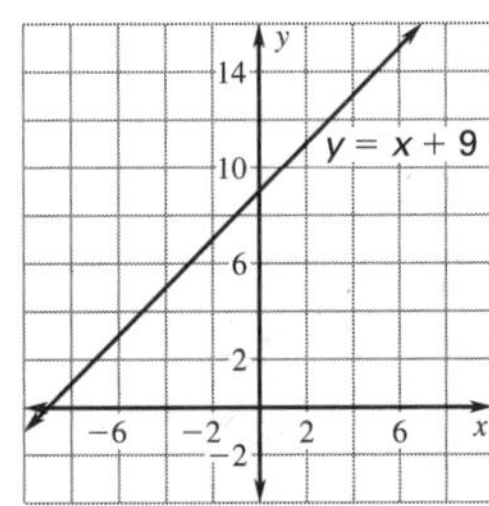

34. $y = \frac{2}{3}x; m = \frac{2}{3}; b = 0$

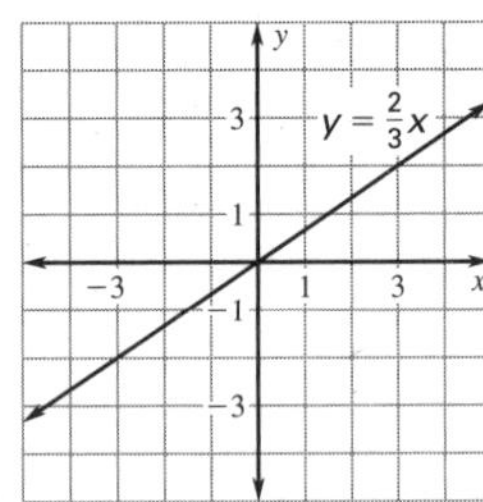

35. $x + y = 0$

$y = -x$

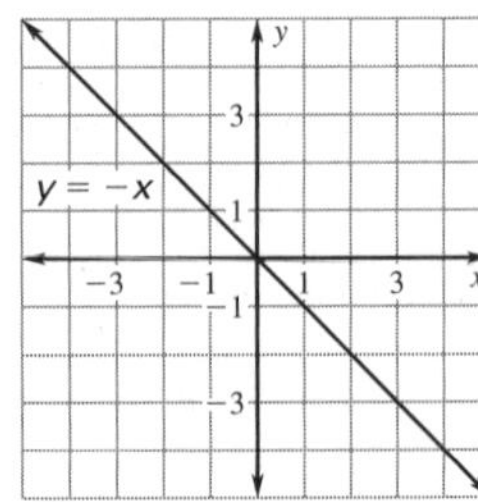

Copyright © McDougal Littell Inc.
All rights reserved.

36. $3x - 6y = 9$

$$-6y = -3x + 9$$

$$y = \frac{-3x}{-6} + \frac{9}{-6}$$

$$y = \frac{1}{2}x - \frac{3}{2}$$

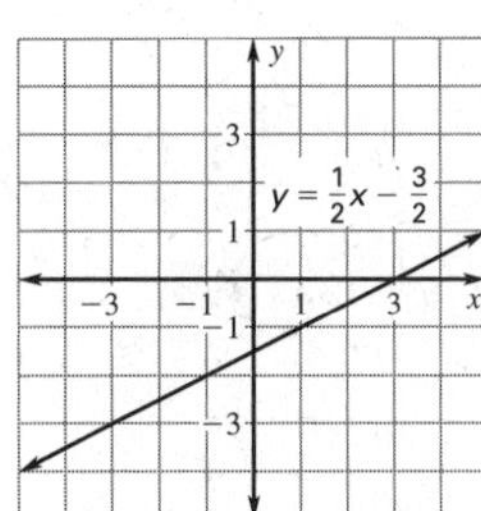

37. $4x + 5y = 15$

$$5y = -4x + 15$$

$$y = -\frac{4}{5}x + 3$$

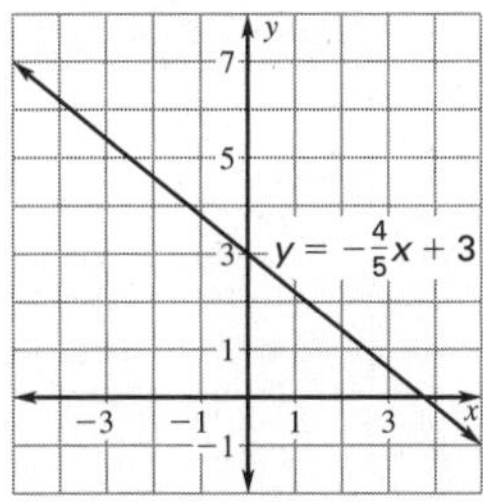

38. $4x - y - 3 = 0$

$$-y = -4x + 3$$

$$y = 4x - 3$$

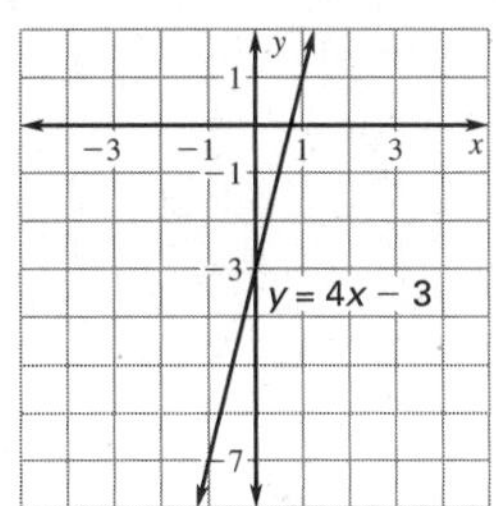

39. $x - y + 4 = 0$

$$-y = -x - 4$$

$$y = x + 4$$

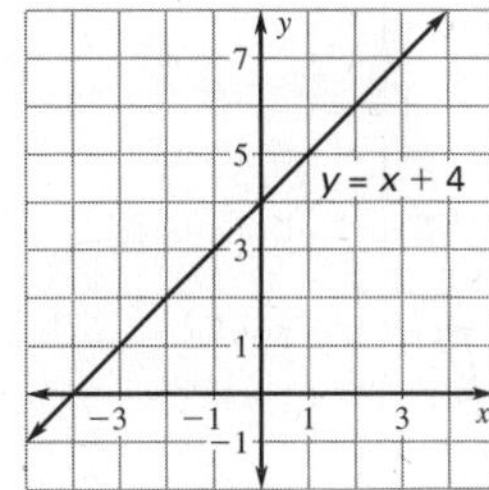

40. $2x - 3y - 6 = 0$

$$-3y = -2x + 6$$

$$y = \frac{2}{3}x - 2$$

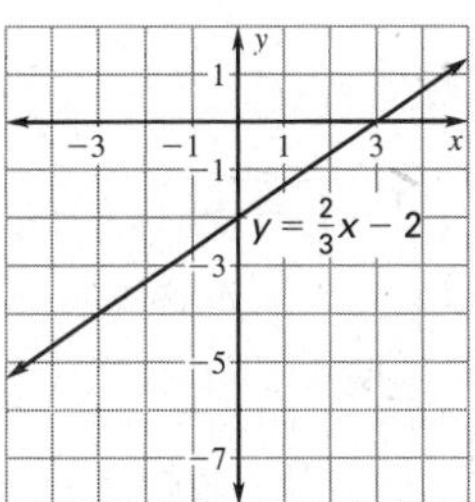

41. $5x + 15 + 5y = 10x$

$$5y = 5x - 15$$

$$y = x - 3$$

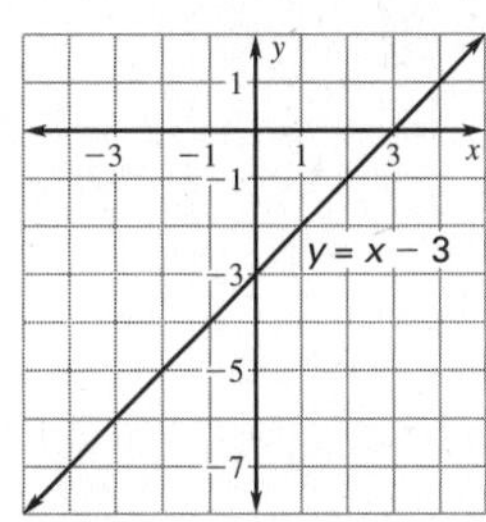

42. $2x + 2y - 4 = x + 5$

$$2y = -x + 9$$

$$y = -\frac{1}{2}x + \frac{9}{2}$$

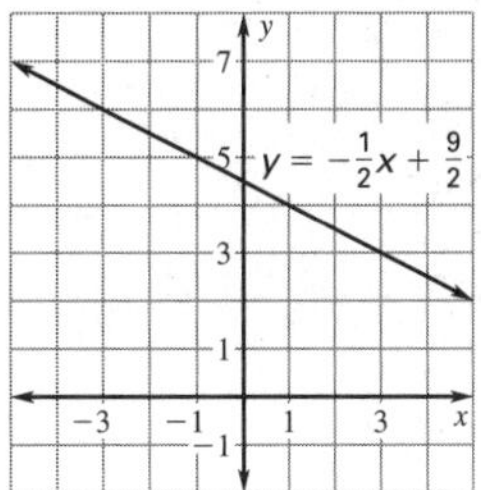

43. slope $= \frac{1}{2}$; y-intercept = 1; B

44. slope $= \frac{1}{2}$; y-intercept $= -1$; C

45. slope = 1; y-intercept = 2; A

46. $m = 1$; $b = 1$

47. $m = -\frac{4}{3}$; $b = 4$

48. $m = \frac{3}{2}$; $b = -2$

49. slope of a: -3
slope of b: $y = -3x - 4$; -3
parallel; same slope

Copyright © McDougal Littell Inc.
All rights reserved.

50. slope of *a*: $2x - 12 = y$; $m = 2$
slope of *b*: $y = 10 + 2x$ or $y = 2x + 10$
$m = 2$
parallel; same slope

51. slope of *a*: 1
slope of *b*:
$x - y = -1$
$-y = -x - 1$
$y = x + 1$
$m = 1$
parallel; same slope

52. slope of *a*:
$2x - 5y = -3$
$-5y = -2x - 3$
$y = \frac{-2x}{-5} - \frac{3}{-5}$
$y = \frac{2}{5}x + \frac{3}{5}$
$m = \frac{2}{5}$
slope of *b*:
$5x + 2y = 6$
$2y = -5x + 6$
$y = -\frac{5}{2}x + 3$
$m = -\frac{5}{2}$
not parallel; different slopes

53. slope of *a*:
$y + 6x - 8 = 0$
$y = -6x + 8$
$m = -6$
slope of *b*:
$2y = 12x - 4$
$y = 6x - 2$
$m = 6$
not parallel; different slopes

54. slope of *a*:
$3y - 4x = 3$
$3y = 4x + 3$
$y = \frac{4}{3}x + 1$
$m = \frac{4}{3}$
slope of *b*:
$3y = -4x + 9$
$y = -\frac{4}{3}x + 3$
$m = -\frac{4}{3}$
not parallel; different slopes

55. slope 1: $\frac{\text{rise}}{\text{run}} = \frac{45}{350} = \frac{5 \cdot 9}{5 \cdot 70} = \frac{9}{70}$
slope 2: $\frac{\text{rise}}{\text{run}} = \frac{50}{350} = \frac{1}{7}$

56. $y = \frac{1}{2}x + 6$
$m = \frac{1}{2}$; $b = 6$

57. The slope indicates the constant rate at which the snow was falling. The *y*-intercept indicates the amount of snow already on the ground.

58.
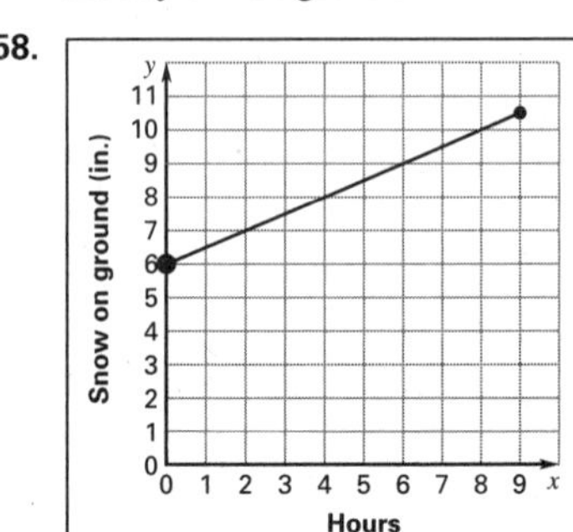

59. The slope of 30 indicates the amount of money saved each month. The *y*-intercept 50 indicates the amount already in the savings account.

60.
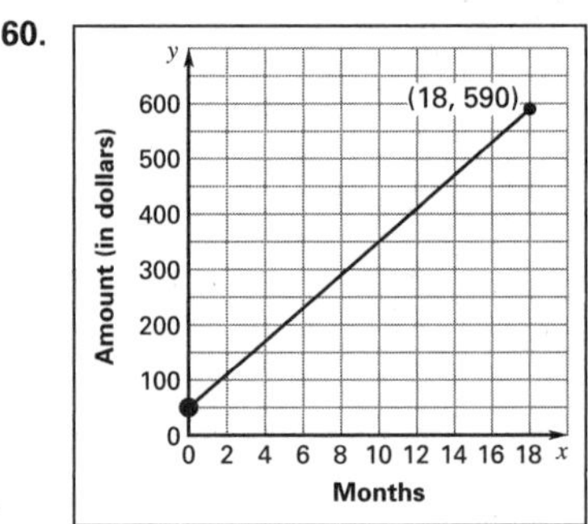

$590

61. $c = 0.15t + 0.87$

t	1	2	3	4	5	6
c	0.87	1.02	1.17	1.32	1.47	1.62

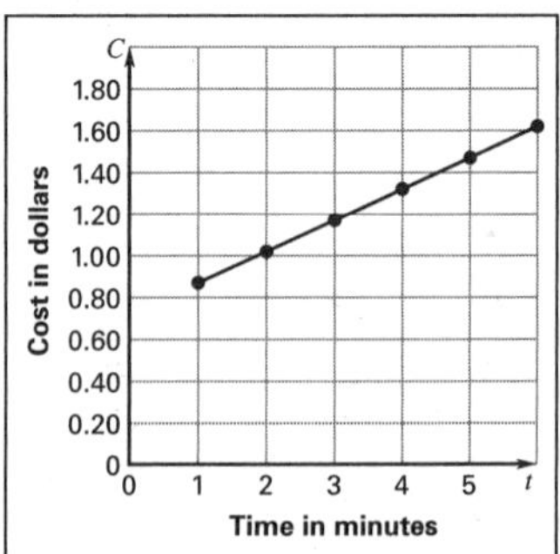

62. $m = 0.15$; cost per minute

Copyright © McDougal Littell Inc.
All rights reserved.

63. slope of *a*:
$-2x + y = 10$
$y = 2x + 10$
$m = 2$
slope of *b*:
$-6x + 3y = 13$
$3y = 6x + 13$
$y = 2x + \frac{13}{3}$
$m = 2$
slope of *c*:
$-2x - y = 6$
$-y = 2x + 6$
$y = -2x - 6$
$m = -2$
Lines *a* and *b* are parallel.

64. Parallel to $y = 4x - 5$ means the slope is 4; $b = 3$
$y = 4x + 3$

65. slope of $\overline{BA}$: $\frac{-4}{1}$

slope of $\overline{CD}$: $\frac{-4}{1}$

slope of $\overline{BC}$: $\frac{1}{2}$

slope of $\overline{AD}$: $\frac{1}{2}$

The figure is a parallelogram since its opposite sides are parallel.

66. slope of $\overline{BA}$: $\frac{-4}{1}$

slope of $\overline{CD}$: $\frac{-4}{1}$

slope of $\overline{BC}$: $\frac{2}{5}$

slope of $\overline{AD}$: $\frac{2}{5}$

The figure is a parallelogram since its opposite sides are parallel.

4.7 Standardized Test Practice (p. 249)

67. $y + 8 = 0$
$y = -8$ or $y = 0x - 8$; $m = 0$; C

68. $6x - 9y + 45 = 0$
$-9y = -6x - 45$
$y = \frac{-6x}{-9} - \frac{45}{-9}$
$y = \frac{2}{3}x + 5$; H

69. $16x - 32y = 160$
$-32y = -16x + 160$
$y = \frac{-16x}{-32} + \frac{160}{-32}$
$y = \frac{1}{2}x - 5$

$m = \frac{1}{2}$

B; parallel line also has slope of $\frac{1}{2}$.

4.7 Mixed Review (p. 249)

70. $x + 6 = 14$
$x = 8$

71. $9 - y = 4$
$-y = -5$
$y = 5$

72. $7b = 21$
$b = 3$

73. $\frac{a}{4} = 3$
$a = 12$

74. $\frac{1}{3}h - 2 = 1$
$\frac{1}{3}h = 3$
$h = 9$

75. $3x - 12 = 6$
$3x = 18$
$x = 6$

76. $2(v + 1) = 4$
$2v + 2 = 4$
$2v = 2$
$v = 1$

77. $3(x - 1) = -18$
$3x - 3 = -18$
$3x = -15$
$x = -5$

78. $5(w - 5) = 25$
$5w - 25 = 25$
$5w = 50$
$w = 10$

Copyright © McDougal Littell Inc.
All rights reserved.

79.

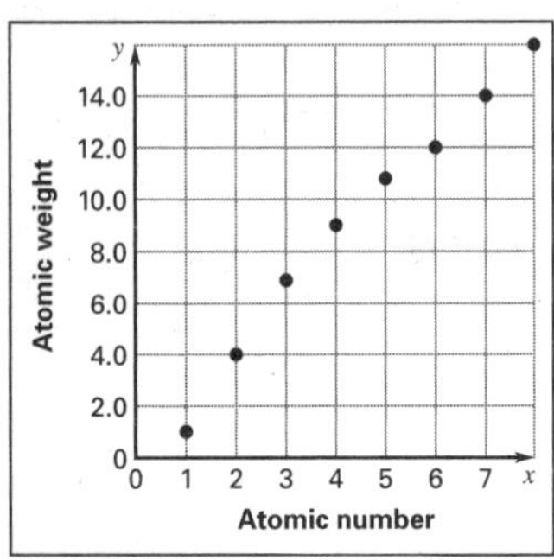

Atomic weight ≈ 2 × Atomic number

80. A; $(c - 8) + c = 32$

4.7 Maintaining Skills (p. 249)

81. $\frac{1}{8} + \frac{1}{5} = \frac{1}{8} \cdot \frac{5}{5} + \frac{1}{5} \cdot \frac{8}{8} = \frac{5}{40} + \frac{8}{40} = \frac{13}{40}$

82. $\frac{2}{3} + \frac{4}{5} = \frac{2}{3} \cdot \frac{5}{5} + \frac{4}{5} \cdot \frac{3}{3} = \frac{10}{15} + \frac{12}{15} = \frac{22}{15} = 1\frac{7}{5}$

83. $\frac{3}{4} + \frac{8}{9} = \frac{3}{4} \cdot \frac{9}{9} + \frac{8}{9} \cdot \frac{4}{4} = \frac{27}{36} + \frac{32}{36} = \frac{59}{36} = 1\frac{23}{36}$

84. $\frac{9}{11} + \frac{10}{33} = \frac{9}{11} \cdot \frac{3}{3} + \frac{10}{33} = \frac{27}{33} + \frac{10}{33} = \frac{37}{33} = 1\frac{4}{33}$

85. $\frac{6}{7} + \frac{3}{8} = \frac{6}{7} \cdot \frac{8}{8} + \frac{3}{8} \cdot \frac{7}{7} = \frac{48}{56} + \frac{21}{56} = \frac{69}{56} = 1\frac{13}{56}$

86. $\frac{1}{4} + \frac{5}{6} = \frac{1}{4} \cdot \frac{3}{3} + \frac{5}{6} \cdot \frac{2}{2} = \frac{3}{12} + \frac{10}{12} = \frac{13}{12} = 1\frac{1}{12}$

87. $\frac{2}{3} + \frac{8}{21} = \frac{2}{3} \cdot \frac{7}{7} + \frac{8}{21} = \frac{14}{21} + \frac{8}{21} = \frac{22}{21} = 1\frac{1}{21}$

88. $\frac{19}{24} + \frac{11}{12} = \frac{19}{24} + \frac{11}{12} \cdot \frac{2}{2} = \frac{19}{24} + \frac{22}{24} = \frac{41}{24} = 1\frac{17}{24}$

Developing Concepts: Try These *(p. 251)*

1.

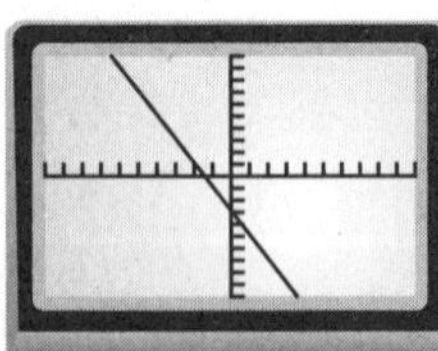

2.

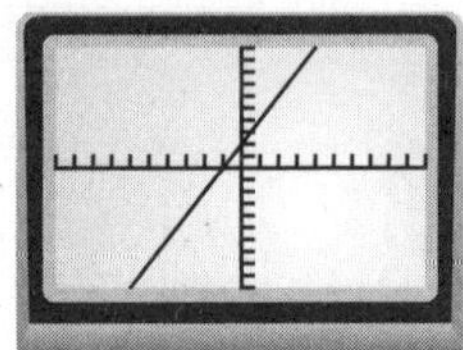

3. $x + 2y = -1$

$y = -\frac{1}{2}x - \frac{1}{2}$

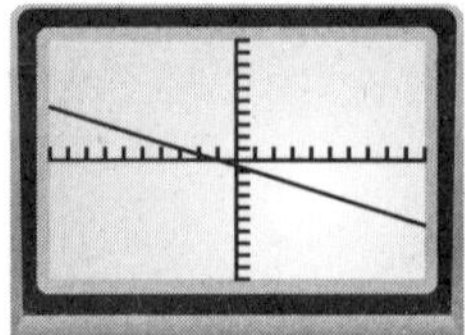

4. $x - 3y = 3$

$y = \frac{1}{3}x - 1$

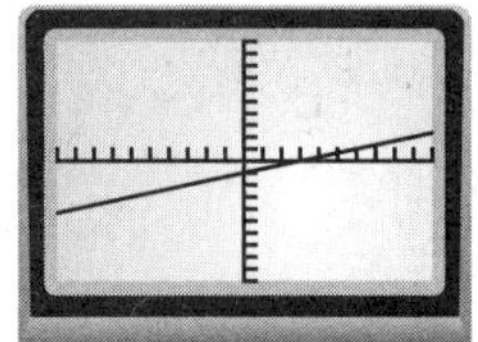

5.

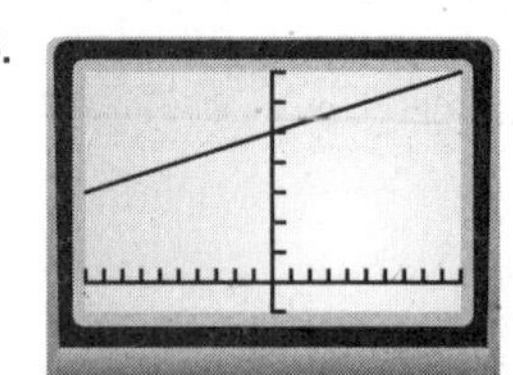

6.

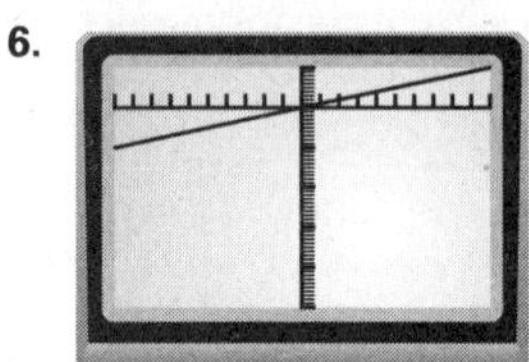

7.

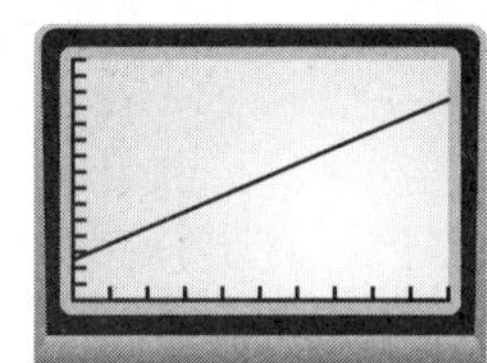

8. Xmin = −100, Xmax = 500, Xscl = 50,
Ymin = −500, Ymax = 200, Yscl = 50

9. Xmin = −6, Xmax = 6, Xscl = 1,
Ymin = −800, Ymax = 800, Yscl = 120

10. Xmin = −20, Xmax = 50, Xscl = 10,
Ymin = −20,000, Ymax = 80,000, Yscl = 5000

Lesson 4.8

4.8 Checkpoint (pp. 253–254)

1. A vertical line can be found that intersects the graph. Therefore, the graph does not represent a function.

2. Any vertical line will intersect the graph at only one point. Therefore, the graph represents a function.

Copyright © McDougal Littell Inc.
All rights reserved.

3. $f(2) = 4(2) + 5 = 13$

4. $g(-3) = (-3)^2 = 9$

5.

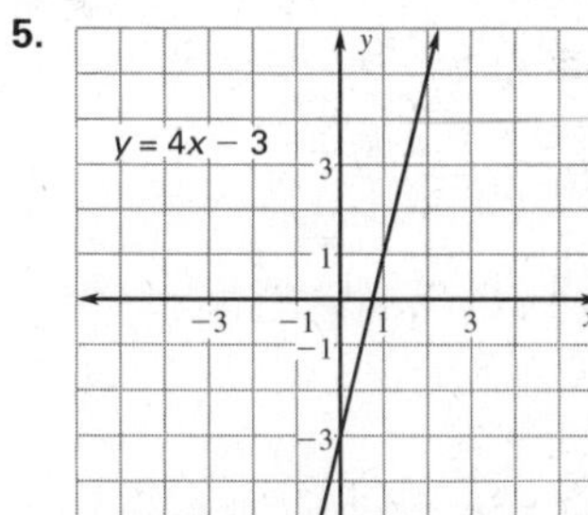

6.

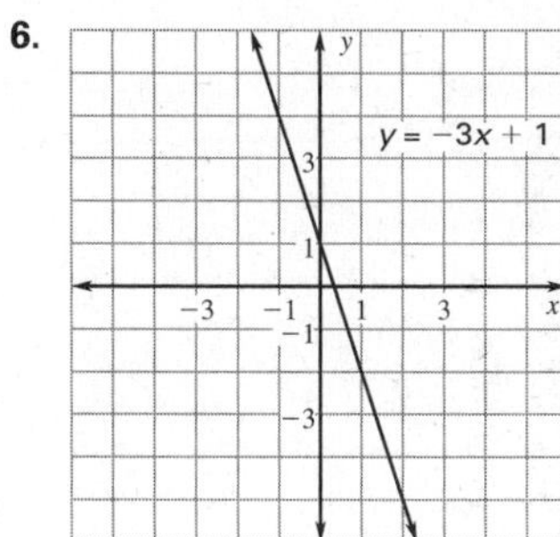

7.

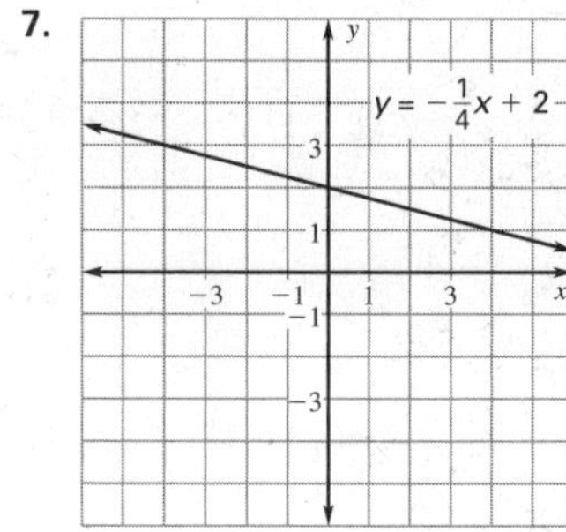

4.8 Guided Practice (p. 255)

1. ordered pairs

2. linear

3. $f(4) = -5(4) - 2 = -22$

4. $f(0) = -5(0) - 2 = -2$

5. $f(-2) = -5(-2) - 2 = 8$

6. $f\left(-\frac{1}{5}\right) = -5\left(-\frac{1}{5}\right) - 2 = -1$

7. The relation is a function. The domain is 10, 20, 30, 40, and 50. The range is 100, 200, 300, 400, and 500.

8. The relation is not a function.

9. The relation is not a function.

10. The graph represents a function since it passes the vertical line test.

11. The graph does not represent a function since it fails the vertical line test.

12. The graph does not represent a function since it fails the vertical line test.

4.8 Practice and Applications (pp. 255–257)

13. function; for every input there is exactly one output.
domain: 1, 2, 3, 4;
range: 2, 3, 4, 5

14. function; for every input there is exactly one output.
domain: 1, 2, 3, 4;
range: 0

15. not a function; for an input of 10 there are two outputs.

16. function; for every input there is exactly one output.
domain: 0, 1, 2, 3;
range: 2, 4, 6, 8

17. function; for every input there is exactly one output.
domain: 0, 2, 3, 4;
range: 1, 2, 3, 4

18. function; for every input there is exactly one output.
domain: 1, 3, 5, 7;
range: 1, 2, 3

19. function; passes vertical line test

20. not a function; crosses y-axis (a vertical line) 3 times

21. function; passes vertical line test

22. not a function; crosses y-axis (a vertical line) 3 times

23. function; passes vertical line test

24. not a function; touches y-axis (a vertical line) twice

25. $f(x) = 3x$
$f(2) = 3(2) = 6$
$f(0) = 3(0) = 0$
$f(-2) = 3(-2) = -6$

26. $g(x) = x + 4$
$g(2) = 2 + 4 = 6$
$g(0) = 0 + 4 = 4$
$g(-2) = -2 + 4 = 2$

27. $h(x) = 3x - 5$
$h(2) = 3(2) - 5 = 1$
$h(0) = 3(0) - 5 = -5$
$h(-2) = 3(-2) - 5 = -11$

28. $g(x) = -x - 6$
$g(2) = -(2) - 6 = -8$
$g(0) = -(0) - 6 = -6$
$g(-2) = -(-2) - 6 = -4$

29. $f(x) = 5x + 1$
$f(2) = 5(2) + 1 = 11$
$f(0) = 5(0) + 1 = 1$
$f(-2) = 5(-2) + 1 = -9$

30. $f(x) = -x - 3$
$f(2) = -(2) - 3 = -5$
$f(0) = -(0) - 3 = -3$
$f(-2) = -(-2) - 3 = -1$

31. $h(x) = 8x + 7$
$h(2) = 8(2) + 7 = 23$
$h(0) = 8(0) + 7 = 7$
$h(-2) = 8(-2) + 7 = -9$

Copyright © McDougal Littell Inc.
All rights reserved.

32. $f(x) = -4x + 15$
$f(2) = -4(2) + 15 = 7$
$f(0) = -4(0) + 15 = 15$
$f(-2) = -4(-2) + 15 = 23$

33. $g(x) = 5x - 6$
$g(2) = 5(2) - 6 = 4$
$g(0) = 5(0) - 6 = -6$
$g(-2) = 5(-2) - 6 = -16$

34. $f(x) = 3x - 2$; $m = 3$; $b = -2$; B

35. $f(x) = 2x + 2$; $m = 2$; $b = 2$; C

36. $f(x) = \frac{1}{2}x - 2$; $m = \frac{1}{2}$; $b = -2$; A

37.

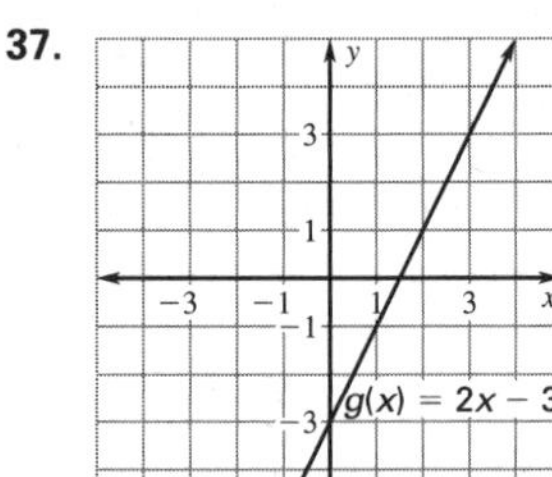

38.

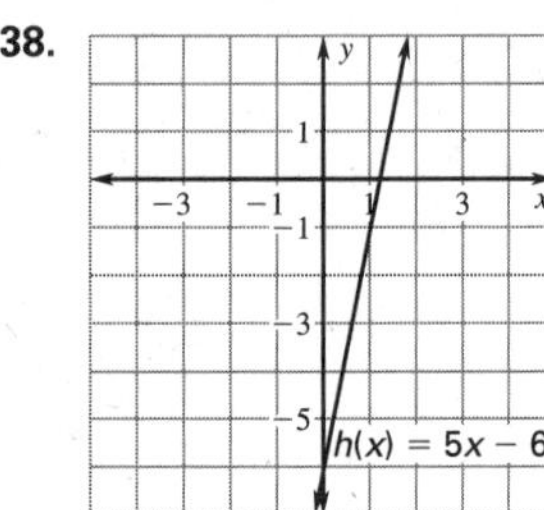

39.

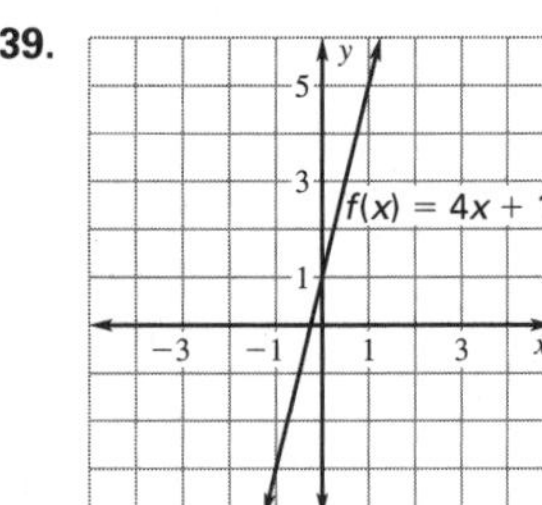

40.

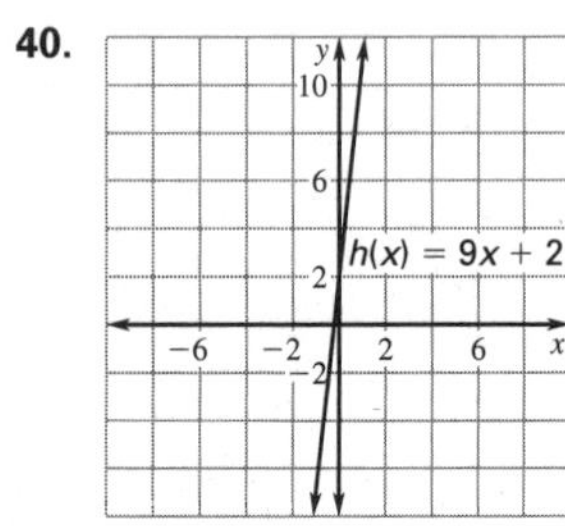

41.

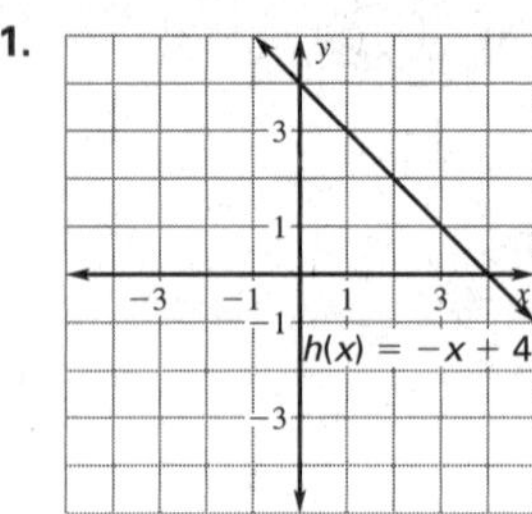

42.

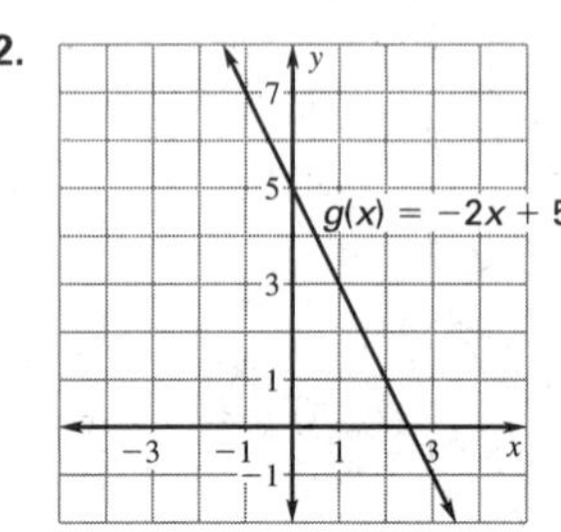

43.

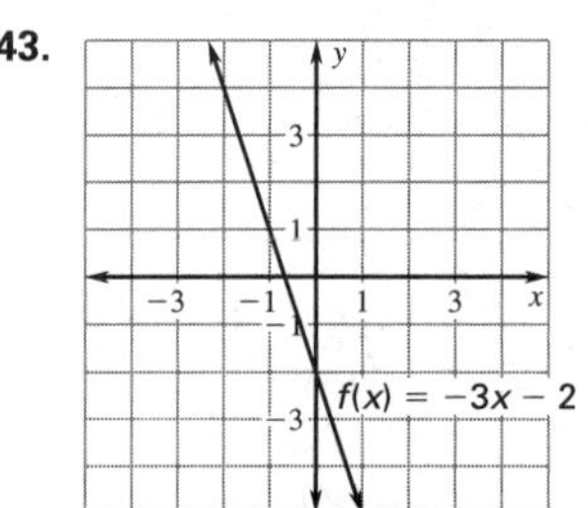

44.

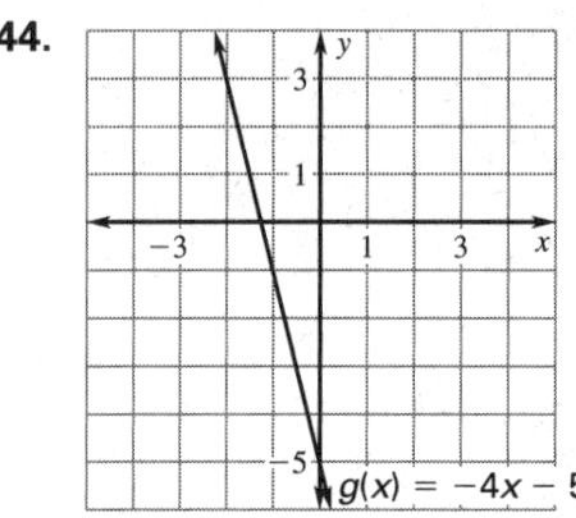

45.

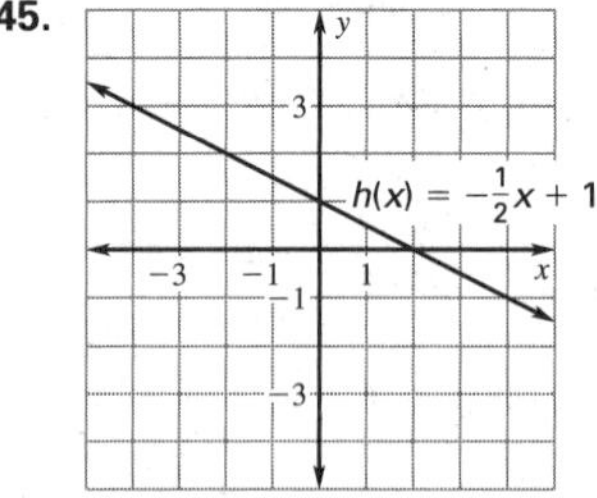

46. $f(2) = -3$; $(2, -3)$
$f(-2) = 5$; $(-2, 5)$
$m = \frac{-3 - 5}{2 - (-2)} = \frac{-8}{4} = -2$

47. $f(0) = 4$; $(0, 4)$
$f(4) = 0$; $(4, 0)$
$m = \frac{4 - 0}{0 - 4} = \frac{4}{-4} = -1$

Copyright © McDougal Littell Inc.
All rights reserved.

48. $f(-3) = -9; (-3, -9)$
$f(3) = 9; (3, 9)$
$m = \frac{-9 - 9}{-3 - 3} = \frac{-18}{-6} = 3$

49. $f(6) = -1; (6, -1)$
$f(3) = 8; (3, 8)$
$m = \frac{-1 - 8}{6 - 3} = \frac{-9}{3} = -3$

50. a function (there is a unique value of y for each value of x); domain: 1, 2, 3, 4; range: 3, 6, 9, 12

51. not a function (-2 has more than one y-value)

52. not a function (3 has more than one y-value)

53. a function (there is a unique value of y for each value of x); domain: -2, 0, 1, 2; range: -2, 0, 1, 2

54. Yes, the points closely resemble a line with a constant slope and there is only one attendance for each year.

55.

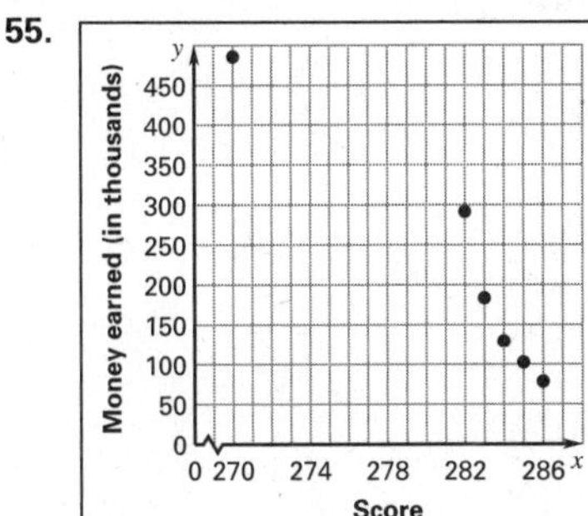

Yes, money earned is a function of the score since there is a unique amount given for each score.
domain: 270, 282, 283, 284, 285, 286
range: 486,000; 291,600; 183,600; 129,600; 102,600; 78,570

56. $d = rt$; find r
$2000 = r(40)$
$50 = r$
$d = 50t$

57. $d = 50t$
$d = 50(30) = 1500$ mi

58.

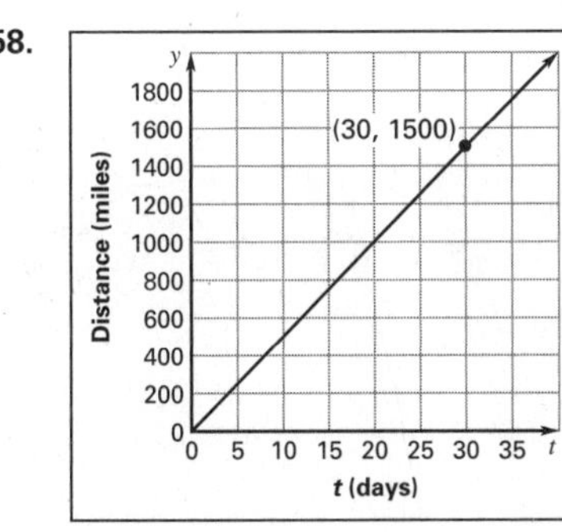

59. $d = rt$; find r
$25 = r(4.25)$
$5.88 \approx r$
$d = f(t)$; $f(t) \approx 5.88t$

4.8 Standardized Test Practice (p. 257)

60. $3x = y + 5$
$y = -3x + 5$
$f(x) = -3x + 5$; B

61. $f(x) = -x + 8$
$f(-2) = -(-2) + 8 = 2 + 8 = 10$; G

4.8 Mixed Review (p. 258)

62. $4x + 8 = 24$
$4x = 16$
$x = 4$

Check: $4x + 8 = 24$
$4(4) + 8 \stackrel{?}{=} 24$
$24 = 24$

63. $3n = 5n - 12$
$0 = 2n - 12$
$12 = 2n$
$6 = n$

Check: $3n = 5n - 12$
$3(6) \stackrel{?}{=} 5(6) - 12$
$18 = 18$

64. $9 - 5z = -8z$
$9 = -3z$
$-3 = z$

Check: $9 - 5z = -8z$
$9 - 5(-3) \stackrel{?}{=} -8(-3)$
$24 = 24$

65. $-5y + 6 = 4y + 3$
$6 = 9y + 3$
$3 = 9y$
$\frac{1}{3} = y$

Check: $-5y + 6 = 4y + 3$
$-5\left(\frac{1}{3}\right) + 6 \stackrel{?}{=} 4\left(\frac{1}{3}\right) + 3$
$-\frac{5}{3} + 6 \stackrel{?}{=} \frac{4}{3} + 3$
$4\frac{1}{3} = 4\frac{1}{3}$

66. $3b + 8 = 9b - 7$
$8 = 6b - 7$
$15 = 6b$
$\frac{15}{6} = \frac{5}{2} = b$

Check: $3b + 8 = 9b - 7$
$3\left(\frac{5}{2}\right) + 8 \stackrel{?}{=} 9\left(\frac{5}{2}\right) - 7$
$\frac{15}{2} + 8 \stackrel{?}{=} \frac{45}{2} - 7$
$7\frac{1}{2} + 8 \stackrel{?}{=} 22\frac{1}{2} - 7$
$15\frac{1}{2} = 15\frac{1}{2}$

Copyright © McDougal Littell Inc.
All rights reserved.

67. $-7q - 13 = 4 - 7q$
$-13 \neq 4$
no solution

68. $m = \frac{1-3}{2-0} = \frac{-2}{2} = -1$

69. $m = \frac{1-(-3)}{-2-2} = \frac{4}{-4} = -1$

70. $m = \frac{3-(-3)}{-3-(-1)} = \frac{6}{-2} = -3$

71. $m = \frac{-4-4}{4-2} = \frac{-8}{2} = -4$

72. $m = \frac{0-6}{8-0} = \frac{-6}{8} = -\frac{3}{4}$

73. $m = \frac{1-1}{6-4} = \frac{0}{2} = 0$

74. $m = \frac{0-(-6)}{8-0} = \frac{6}{8} = \frac{3}{4}$

75. $m = \frac{5-2}{-3-2} = \frac{3}{-5} = -\frac{3}{5}$

76. $m = \frac{5-0}{4-0} = \frac{5}{4}$

4.8 Maintaining Skills (p. 258)

77. $\frac{7}{14} = \frac{1}{2}$ **78.** $\frac{12}{36} = \frac{1}{3}$ **79.** $\frac{8}{12} = \frac{2}{3}$

Quiz 3 ***(p. 258)***

1. $y - 4 = 3x$
$y = 3x + 4; m = 3; b = 4$

2. $x = -y + 2$
$0 = -y - x + 2$
$y = -x + 2; m = -1; b = 2$

3. $2x + y = 6$
$y = -2x + 6; m = -2; b = 6$

4. $5x + 8y = 32$
$8y = -5x + 32$
$y = -\frac{5}{8}x + 4$
$m = -\frac{5}{8}; b = 4$

5. $4x - 3y = 24$
$-3y = -4x + 24$
$y = \frac{4}{3}x - 8$
$m = \frac{4}{3}; b = -8$

6. $-27 + 9y + 18 = 0$
$-9 + 9y = 0$
$9y = 9$
$y = 1$
$m = 0; b = 1$

7. $2x + 4y = 8$
$y = -\frac{1}{2}x + 2$

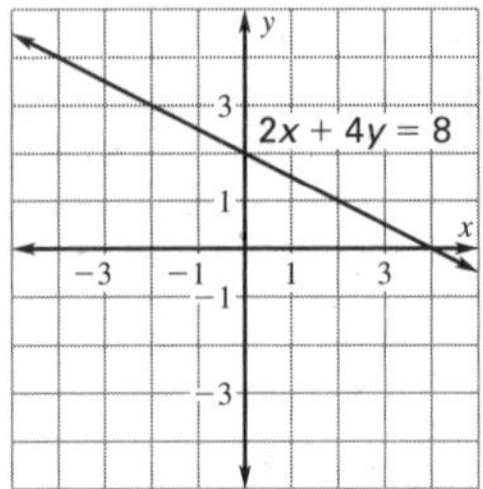

8. $-6x - 3y = 21$
$y = -2x - 7$

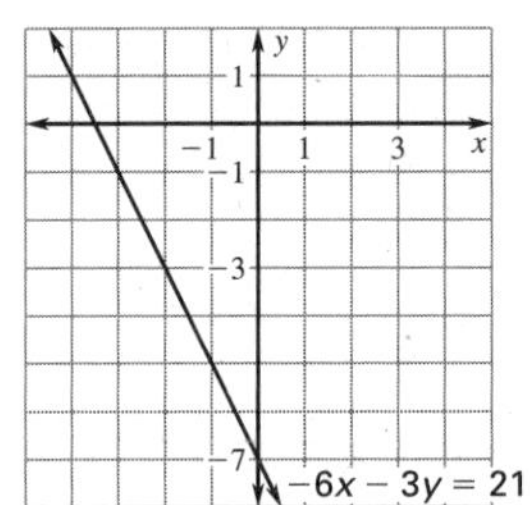

9. $-5x + y = 0$
$y = 5x$

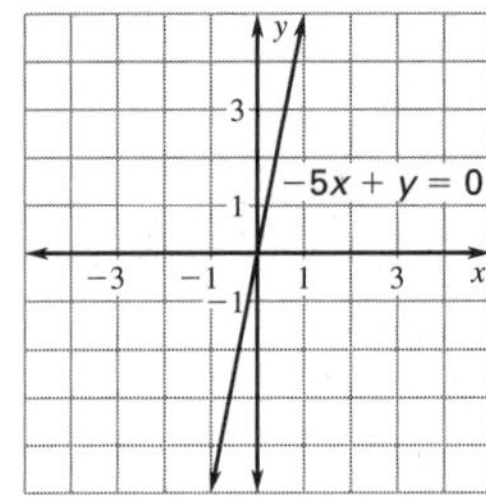

10. slope of a: -7
slope of b: $y - 7x = 10$
$y = 7x + 10; m = 7$
not parallel (different slopes)

11. slope of a: $4x - 8y + 6 = 0$
$-8y = -4x - 6$
$y = \frac{1}{2}x + \frac{3}{4}; m = \frac{1}{2}$
slope of b: $-12x + 6y = 2$
$6y = 12x + 2$
$y = 2x + \frac{1}{3}; m = 2$
not parallel (different slopes)

12. $h(x) = -8x$
$h(3) = -8(3) = -24$
$h(0) = -8(0) = 0$
$h(-4) = -8(-4) = 32$

13. $g(x) = 5x - 9$
$g(3) = 5(3) - 9 = 15 - 9 = 6$
$g(0) = 5(0) - 9 = -9$
$g(-4) = 5(-4) - 9 = -20 - 9 = -29$

Copyright © McDougal Littell Inc.
All rights reserved.

14. $f(x) = -4x + 3$
$f(3) = -4(3) + 3 = -9$
$f(0) = -4(0) + 3 = 3$
$f(-4) = -4(-4) + 3 = 19$

15. $g(x) = -3x - 12$
$g(3) = -3(3) - 12 = -21$
$g(0) = -3(0) - 12 = -12$
$g(-4) = -3(-4) - 12 = 0$

16. $h(x) = 1.4x$
$h(3) = 1.4(3) = 4.2$
$h(0) = 1.4(0) = 0$
$h(-4) = 1.4(-4) = -5.6$

17. $f(x) = \frac{1}{4}x$
$f(3) = \frac{1}{4}(3) = \frac{3}{4}$
$f(0) = \frac{1}{4}(0) = 0$
$f(-4) = \frac{1}{4}(-4) = -1$

18.
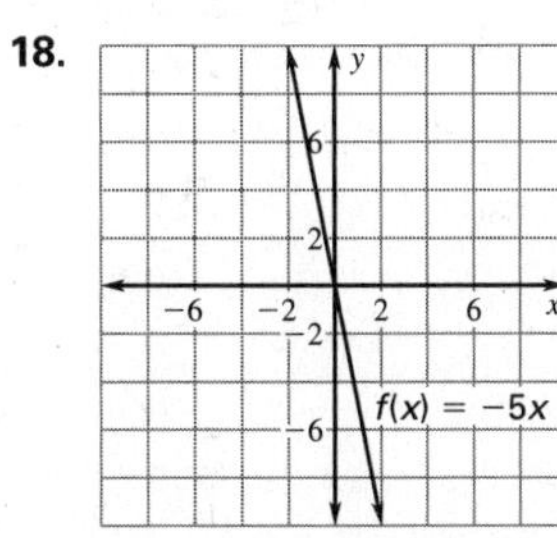

19.
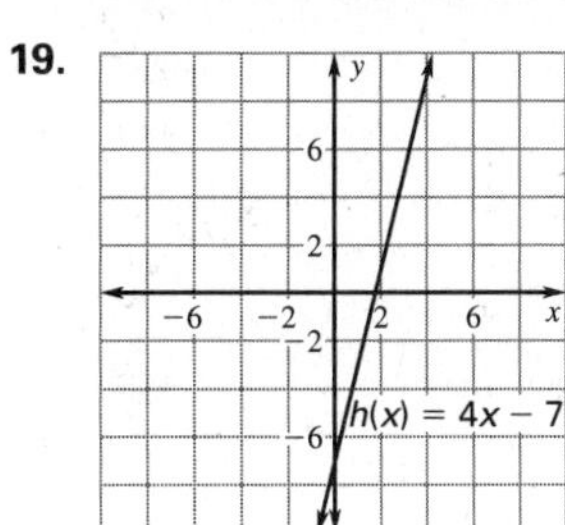

20.
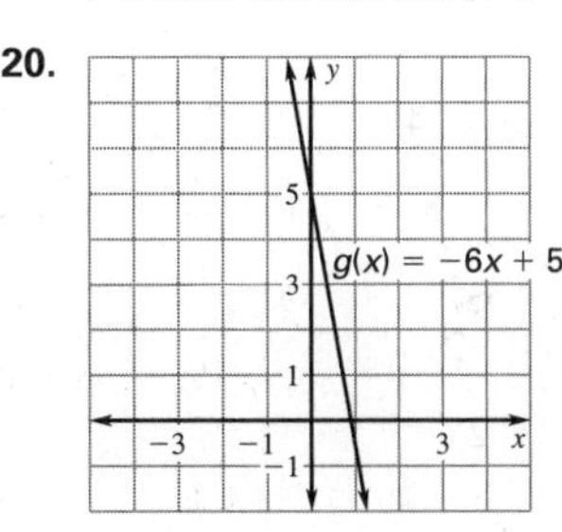

Chapter Summary and Review *(pp. 259–262)*

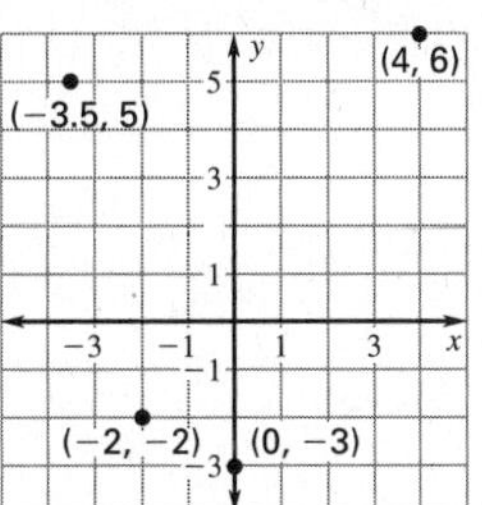

1. Quadrant I

2. Negative y-axis

3. Quadrant II

4. Quadrant III

5.
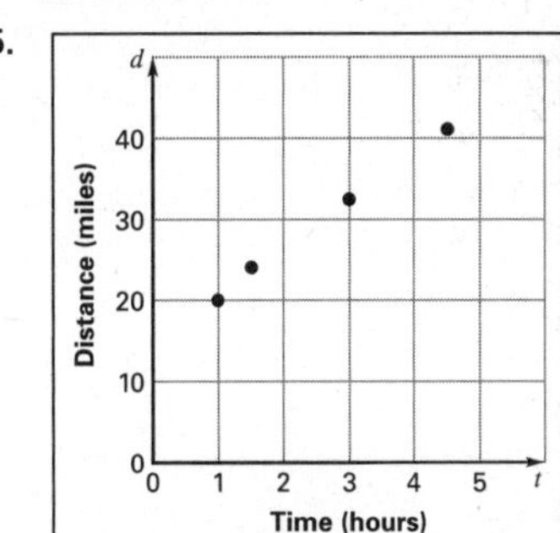

6.
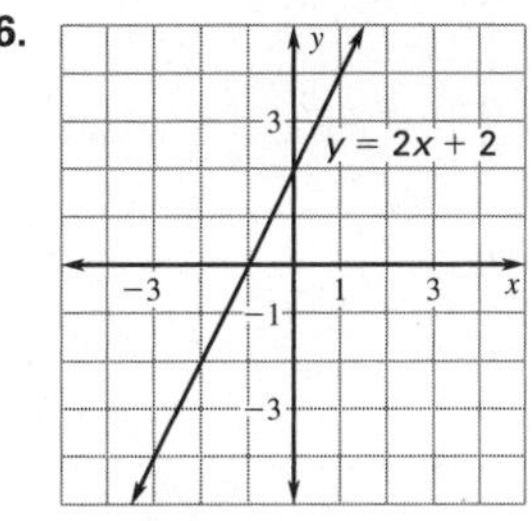

7.
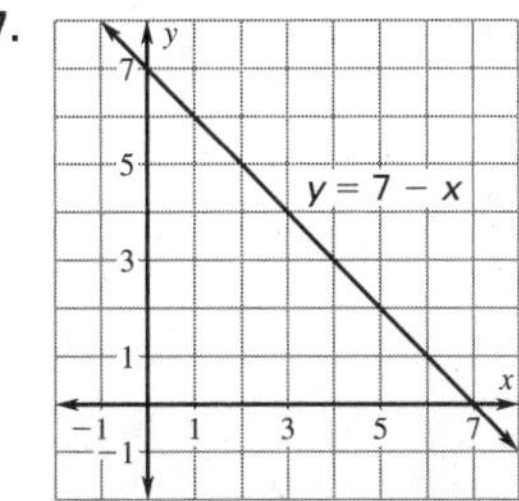

8.
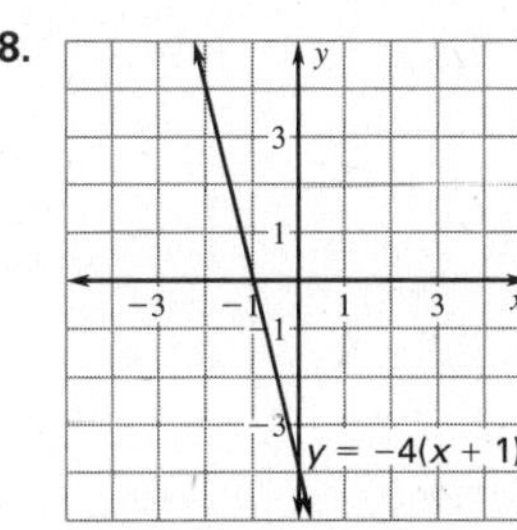

Copyright © McDougal Littell Inc.
All rights reserved.

Chapter 4 *continued*

9. $x - 10 = 2y$

$y = \frac{1}{2}x - 5$

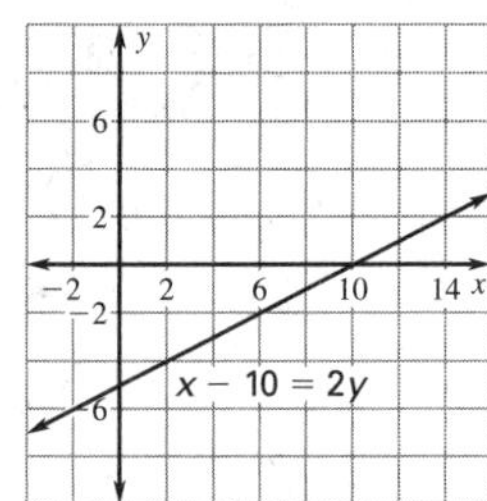

10. 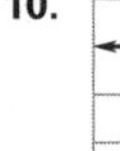

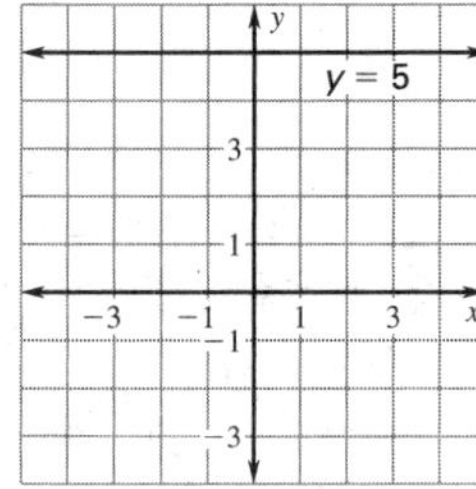

11.

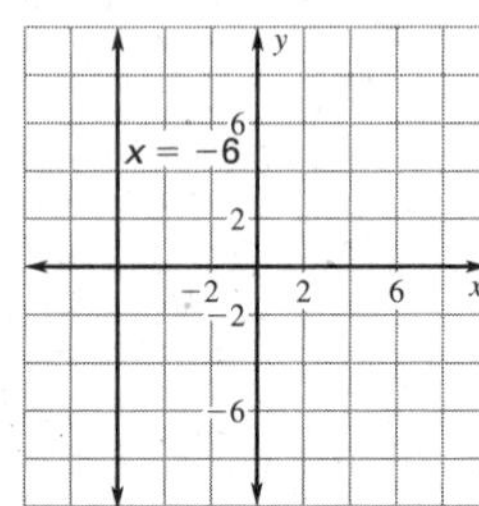

12.

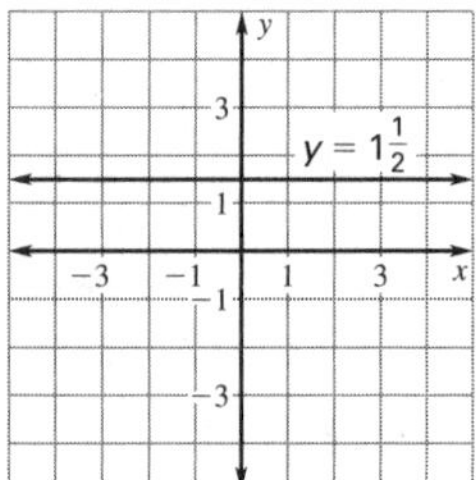

13.

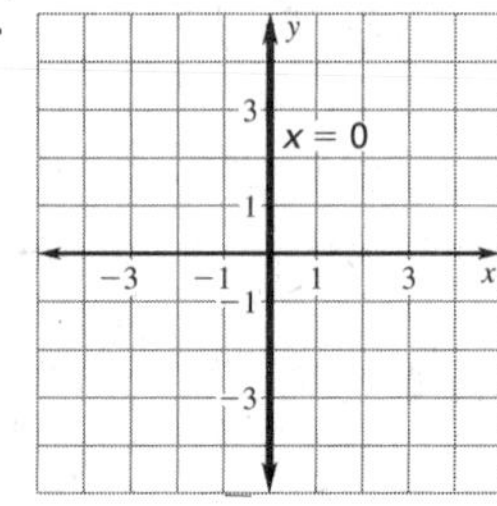

14.

$$-x + 4y = 8$$
$$-x + 4(0) = 8$$
$$-x = 8$$
$$x = -8 \quad (x\text{-intercept})$$
$$-x + 4y = 8$$
$$-(0) + 4y = 8$$
$$4y = 8$$
$$y = 2 \quad (y\text{-intercept})$$

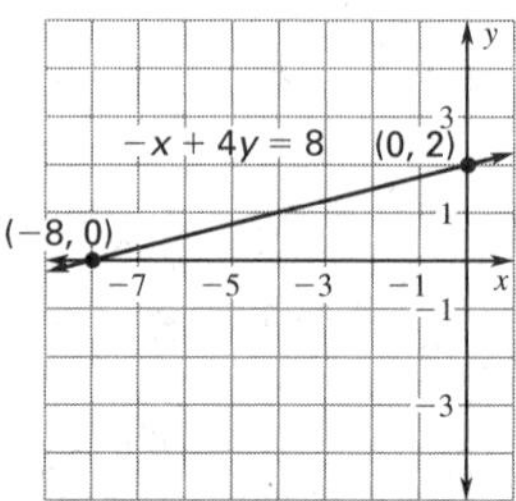

15.

$$3x + 5y = 15$$
$$3x + 5(0) = 15$$
$$3x = 15$$
$$x = 5 \quad (x\text{-intercept})$$
$$3x + 5y = 15$$
$$3(0) + 5y = 15$$
$$5y = 15$$
$$y = 3 \quad (y\text{-intercept})$$

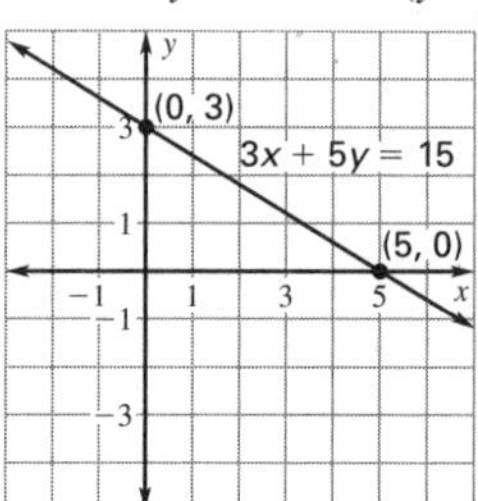

16.

$$4x - 5y = -20$$
$$4x - 5(0) = -20$$
$$4x = -20$$
$$x = -5 \quad (x\text{-intercept})$$
$$4x - 5y = -20$$
$$4(0) - 5y = -20$$
$$-5y = -20$$
$$y = 4 \quad (y\text{-intercept})$$

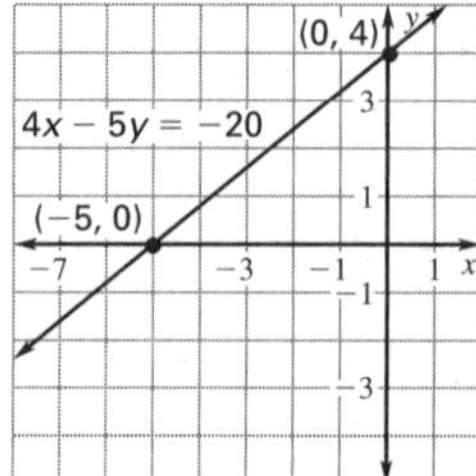

Copyright © McDougal Littell Inc.
All rights reserved.

Chapter 4 *continued*

17. $2x + 3y = 10$
$2x + 3(0) = 10$
$2x = 10$
$x = 5$ (x-intercept)
$2x + 3y = 10$
$2(0) + 3y = 10$
$3y = 10$
$y = \frac{10}{3}$ or $3\frac{1}{3}$ (y-intercept)

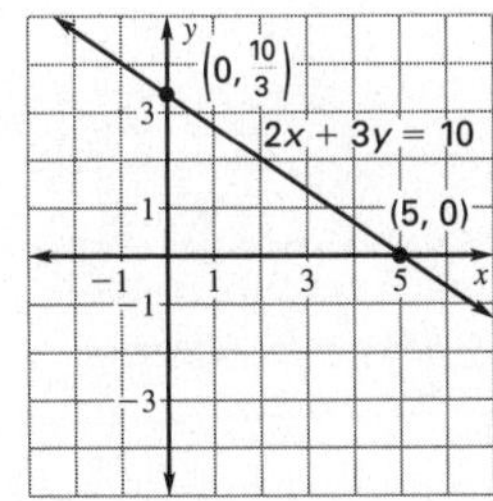

18. $m = \frac{4 - (-1)}{3 - 2} = \frac{5}{1} = 5$

19. $m = \frac{8 - 8}{-1 - 0} = \frac{0}{-1} = 0$

20. $m = \frac{0 - 4}{5 - 2} = \frac{-4}{3} = -\frac{4}{3}$

21. $m = \frac{-2 - 4}{3 - 3} = \frac{-6}{0}$; undefined

22. $y = kx$
$35 = k(7)$
$5 = k$
$y = 5x$

23. $y = kx$
$-4 = k(12)$
$-\frac{1}{3} = k$
$y = -\left(\frac{1}{3}\right)x$

24. $y = kx$
$-16 = k(4)$
$-4 = k$
$y = -4x$

25. $y = kx$
$10.5 = k(3)$
$3.5 = k$
$y = 3.5x$

26. $d = rt$
$168 = r(4)$
$42 = r$
$d = 42t$ (equation that relates d and t)
$d = 42(7) = 294$ mi in 7 hours

27. $2x + y = 6$
$y = -2x + 6$

28. $y - 4x = -1$
$y = 4x - 1$

29. $2x - 3y = 12$
$-3y = -2x + 12$
$y = \left(\frac{2}{3}\right)x - 4$

30. $5y - 2x = -10$
$5y = 2x - 10$
$y = \left(\frac{2}{5}\right)x - 2$

31. $y = -x - 2$

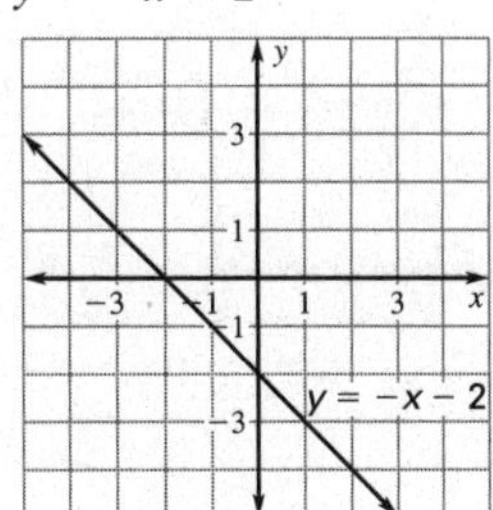

32. $y - 5x = 0$
$y = 5x$

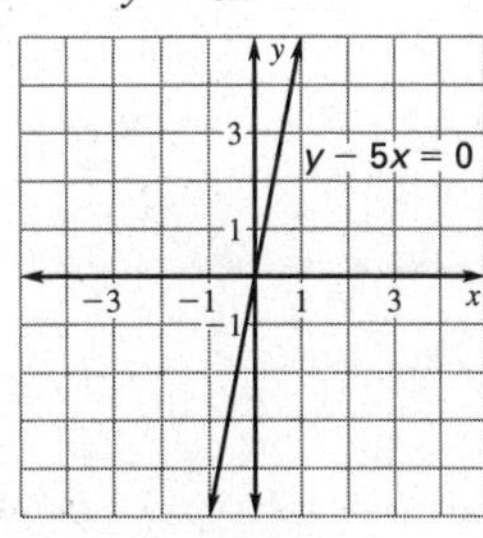

33. $x - 4y = 12$
$-4y = -x + 12$
$y = \left(\frac{1}{4}\right)x - 3$

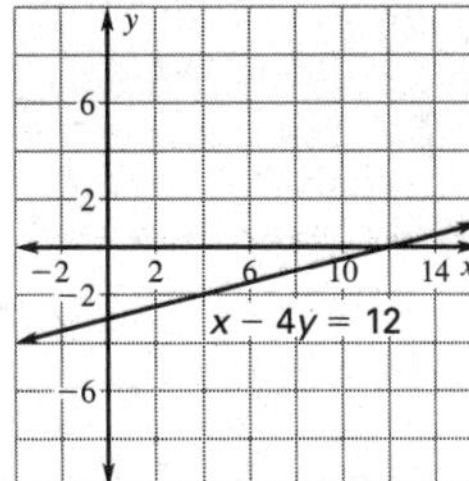

34. $-x + 6y = -24$
$6y = x - 24$
$y = \left(\frac{1}{6}\right)x - 4$

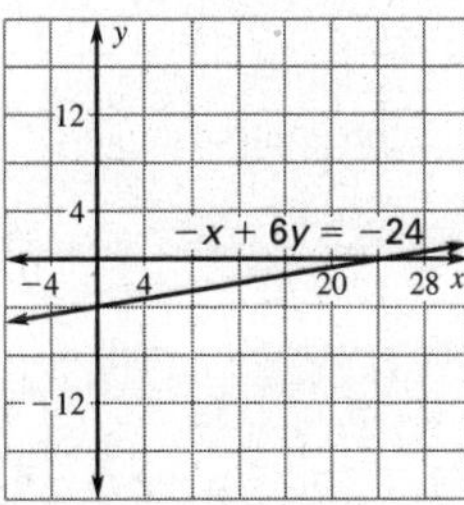

Copyright © McDougal Littell Inc.
All rights reserved.

Chapter 4 *continued*

35. $f(x) = x - 7$

$f(-2) = (-2) - 7 = -9$

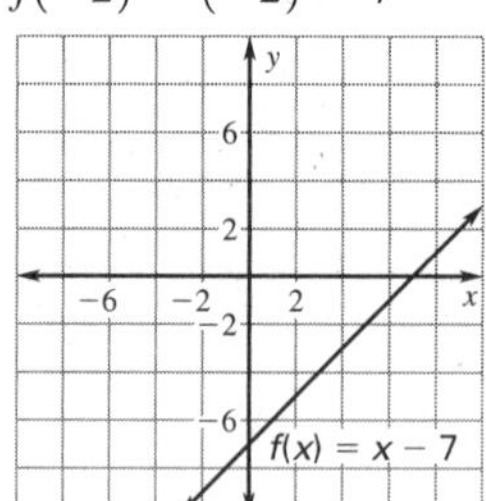

36. $f(x) = -x + 4$

$f(4) = -(4) + 4 = 0$

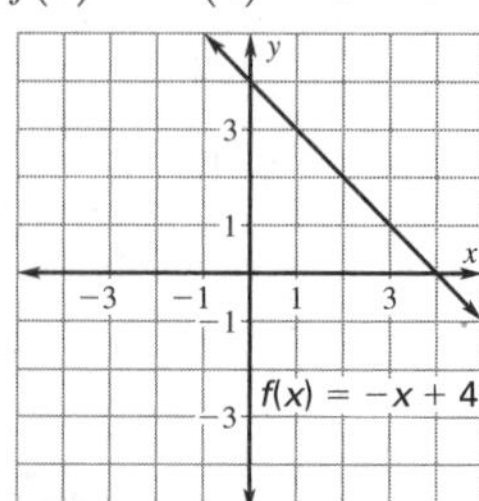

37. $f(x) = 2x - 5$

$f(8) = 2(8) - 5 = 16 - 5 = 11$

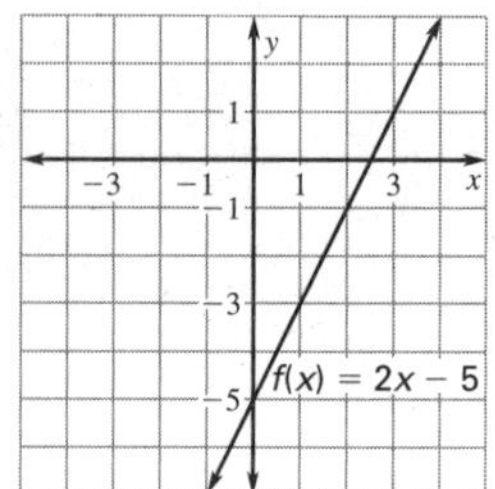

38. $f(x) = \frac{1}{4}x + 3$

$f(-24) = \frac{1}{4}(-24) + 3 = -6 + 3 = -3$

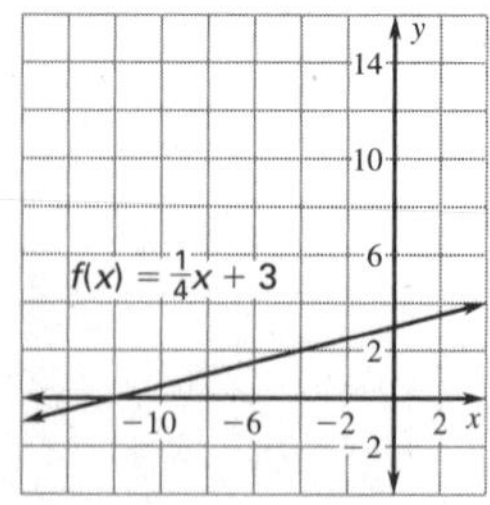

39. a function (each input has exactly one output); domain: $-1, 0, 1$; range: 2, 4, 6

40. not a function (0 has more than one output)

41. a function (each input has exactly one output); domain: $-2, 0, 2$; range: 6

42. a function (there is exactly one y-value for each x-value); domain: $-2, -1, 0, 1, 2, 3, 4$; range: $-3, -2, -1, 0, 1, 2, 3$

Chapter Test *(p. 263)*

1.

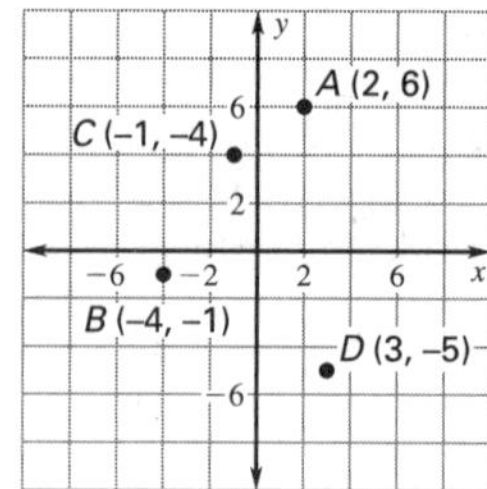

2.

D(4, 6)
A(−5, 1)
B(0, 3)
C(−1, −5)

3.

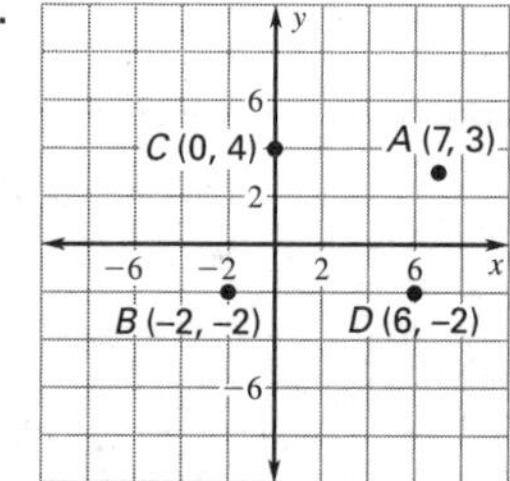

4.

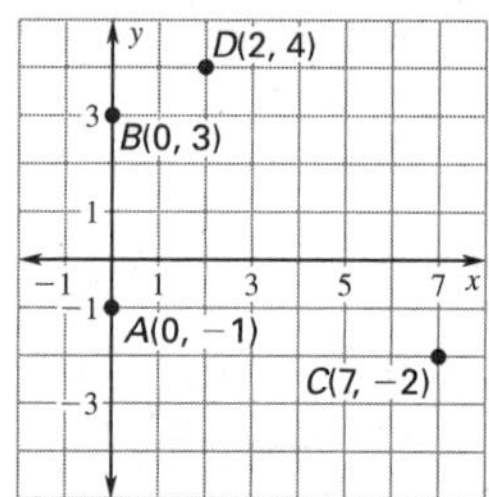

5. IV; positive x-value, negative y-value

6. II; negative x-value, positive y-value

7. III; negative x and y-values

8. positive x-axis

9. $y = -x + 3$

Sample table:

x	−2	−1	0	1	2
y	5	4	3	2	1

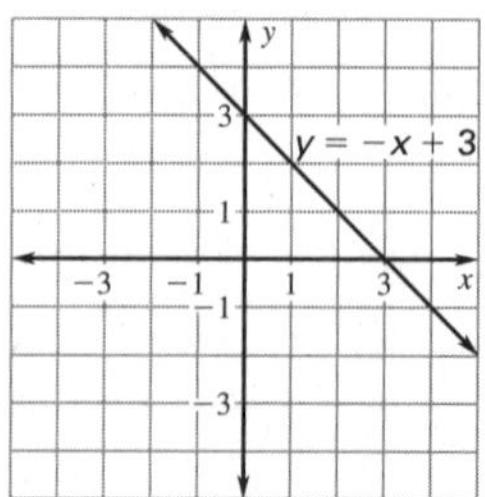

Copyright © McDougal Littell Inc.
All rights reserved.

10. $y = 4$

Sample table:

x	−2	−1	0	1	2
y	4	4	4	4	4

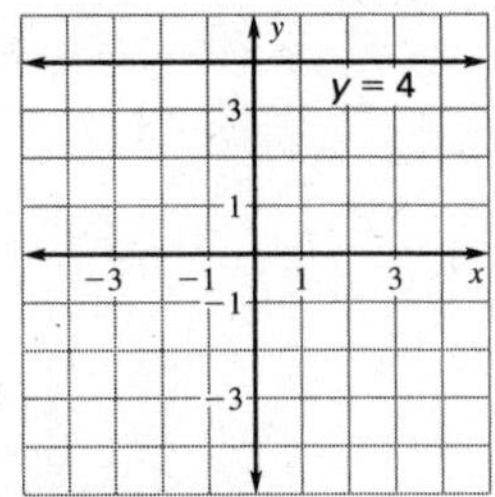

11. $y = -(5 - x)$

Sample table:

x	−2	−1	0	1	2
y	−7	−6	−5	−4	−3

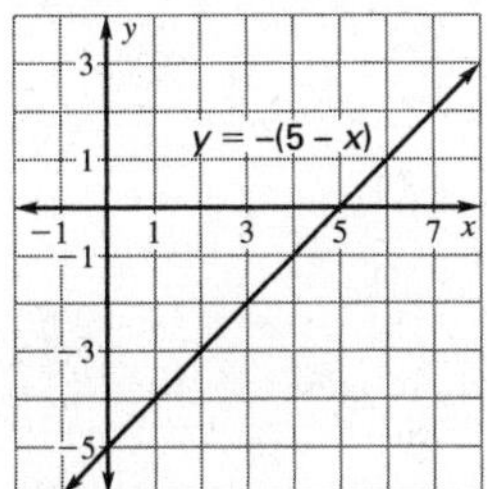

12. $x = 6$

Sample table:

x	6	6	6	6	6
y	2	1	0	−1	−2

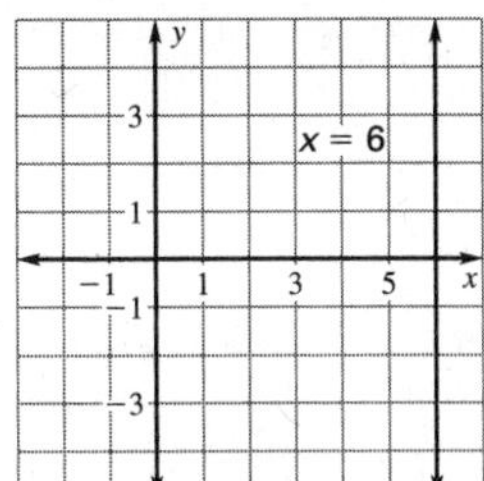

13.

y = 3x

14.

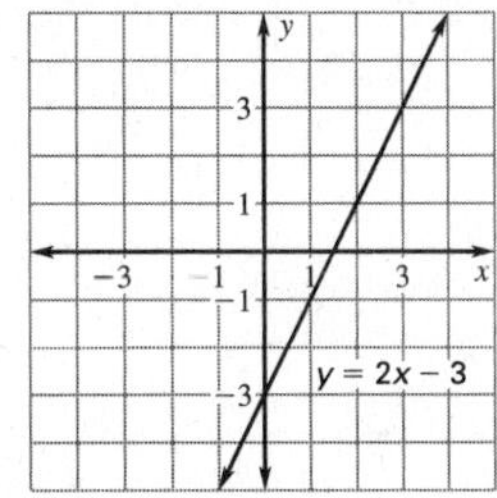

15. $2x + y - 11 = 0$

$y = -2x + 11$

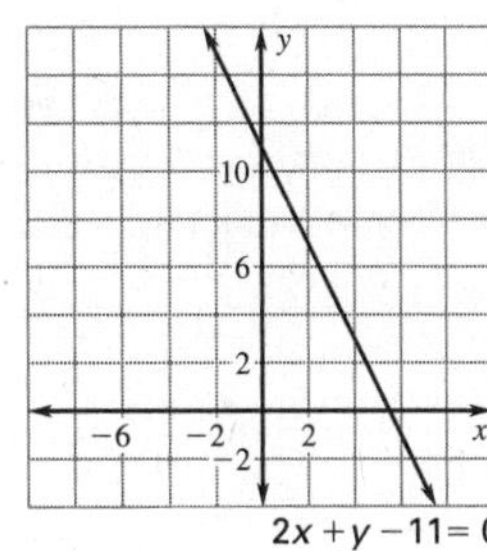

16. $y - 4x = 1$

$y = 4x + 1$

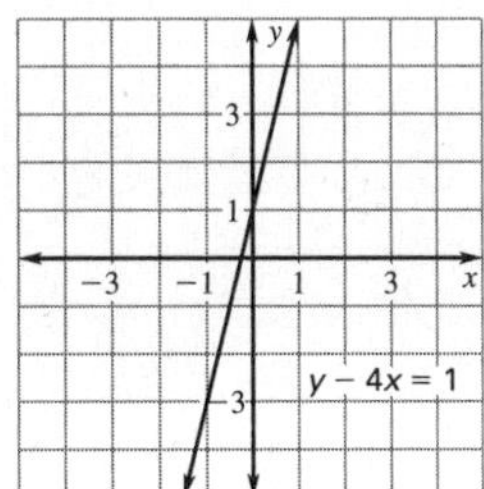

17. $m = \dfrac{-6 - 1}{-2 - 0} = \dfrac{-7}{-2} = \dfrac{7}{2}$

18. $m = \dfrac{-7 - (-1)}{5 - (-4)} = \dfrac{-6}{9} = -\dfrac{2}{3}$

19. $m = \dfrac{-2 - 5}{2 - (-3)} = \dfrac{-7}{5} = -\dfrac{7}{5}$

20. $m = \dfrac{1 - 1}{2 - (-3)} = \dfrac{0}{5} = 0$

21.
$y = kx$
$-2 = k(-2)$
$1 = k$
$y = 1x$ or $y = x$

22.
$y = kx$
$28 = k(2)$
$14 = k$
$y = 14x$

23.
$y = kx$
$15 = k(-3)$
$-5 = k$
$y = -5x$

Copyright © McDougal Littell Inc.
All rights reserved.

24. $y = kx$
$39 = k(13)$
$3 = k$
$y = 3x$

25. $-7x - y = -49$
$-y = 7x - 49$
$y = -7x + 49$

26. $18 - y - 4x = 0$
$-y = 4x - 18$
$y = -4x + 18$

27. $\frac{2}{3}x + y - 9 = 0$
$y = -\left(\frac{2}{3}\right)x + 9$

28. $x - 2y = 10$
$-2y = -x + 10$
$y = \left(\frac{1}{2}\right)x - 5$

29. $y = 4x + 3;\ m = 4$
$y = -4x - 5;\ m = -4$
not parallel; different slopes

30. $10y + 20 = 6x$
$10y = 6x - 20$
$y = \frac{3}{5}x - 2$
$m = \frac{3}{5}$
$5y = 3x + 35$
$y = \frac{3}{5}x + 7$
$m = \frac{3}{5}$
parallel; same slope

31. $f(x) = 6x$
$f(3) = 6(3) = 18$
$f(0) = 6(0) = 0$
$f(-4) = 6(-4) = -24$

32. $g(x) = 3x + 8$
$g(3) = 3(3) + 8 = 17$
$g(0) = 3(0) + 8 = 8$
$g(-4) = 3(-4) + 8 = -4$

33. $f(x) = -(x - 2)$
$f(3) = -(3 - 2) = -1$
$f(0) = -(0 - 2) = 2$
$f(-4) = -(-4 - 2) = 6$

34. a function (each foot length has exactly one shoe size)
domain: $9\frac{1}{4}, 9\frac{1}{2}, 9\frac{5}{8}, 9\frac{3}{4}, 9\frac{5}{16}, 10\frac{1}{4}, 10\frac{1}{2}$
range: $6\frac{1}{2}, 7, 8, 9\frac{1}{2}$

Chapter Standardized Test *(p. 264)*

1. D
$-9(2) + 2(0) = -18$
and
$-9(0) + 2(-9) = -18$

2. $-4(0) - \frac{1}{2}y = 10$
$-\frac{1}{2}y = 10$
$y = -20$; A

3. $3x - 4y = 20$
$-4y = -3x + 20$
$y = \frac{3}{4}x - 5$; C

4. $m = \frac{1 - 2}{2 - 1} = \frac{-1}{1} = -1$; D

5. $m = \frac{\text{rise}}{\text{run}} = \frac{3}{5}$; C

6. $5x - y = -2$
$-y = -5x - 2$
$y = 5x + 2$
$m = 5$; B

7. $(-1, -12)$; D

8. $-13x - 0 = -65$
$-13x = -65$
$x = \frac{-65}{-13} = 5$; A

9. $(-4, -5)$; B

Maintaining Skills *(p. 268)*

1. $\frac{1}{4} \div \frac{1}{2} = \frac{1}{4} \cdot \frac{2}{1} = \frac{2}{4} = \frac{1}{2}$

2. $\frac{1}{15} \div \frac{2}{5} = \frac{1}{15} \cdot \frac{5}{2} = \frac{5}{30} = \frac{1}{6}$

3. $\frac{1}{12} \div \frac{3}{4} = \frac{1}{12} \cdot \frac{4}{3} = \frac{4}{36} = \frac{1}{9}$

4. $\frac{5}{12} \div \frac{15}{16} = \frac{5}{12} \cdot \frac{16}{15} = \frac{5 \cdot 16}{12 \cdot 15} = \frac{1 \cdot 4}{3 \cdot 3} = \frac{4}{9}$

5. $\frac{3}{10} \div \frac{6}{25} = \frac{3}{10} \cdot \frac{25}{6} = \frac{3 \cdot 25}{10 \cdot 6} = \frac{1 \cdot 5}{2 \cdot 2} = \frac{5}{4}$

6. $\frac{4}{9} \div \frac{8}{27} = \frac{4}{9} \cdot \frac{27}{8} = \frac{4 \cdot 27}{9 \cdot 8} = \frac{1 \cdot 3}{1 \cdot 2} = \frac{3}{2}$

7. $\frac{3}{10} \div 3 = \frac{3}{10} \cdot \frac{1}{3} = \frac{1}{10}$

8. $\frac{16}{21} \div 4 = \frac{16}{21} \cdot \frac{1}{4} = \frac{16 \cdot 1}{21 \cdot 4} = \frac{4 \cdot 1}{21 \cdot 1} = \frac{4}{21}$

9. $4 - 8 \div 2 = 4 - 4 = 0$

10. $2^2 \cdot 3 - 3 = 4 \cdot 3 - 3 = 12 - 3 = 9$

11. $2(3 - 4) - (-3)^2 = 2(-1) - 9 = -2 - 9 = -11$

Copyright © McDougal Littell Inc.
All rights reserved.

12. $2^2 + 4[16 \div (3 - 5)] = 2^2 + 4[16 \div (-2)]$
$= 4 + 4[-8]$
$= 4 - 32$
$= -28$

13. $3 - 2[8 - (3 - 2)] = 3 - 2[8 - 1]$
$= 3 - 2[7]$
$= 3 - 14$
$= -11$

14. $6 + \dfrac{16 - 4}{2^2 + 2} - 2 = 6 + \dfrac{12}{4 + 2} - 2$
$= 6 + \dfrac{12}{6} - 2$
$= 6 + 2 - 2$
$= 6$

Copyright © McDougal Littell Inc.
All rights reserved.

Chapter 5

Think and Discuss (p. 267)

1. about 900 years
2. about 5700 years

Chapter Readiness Quiz (p. 268)

1. (C) x-intercept: -2; y-intercept: -6
2. $4(x + 8) = 20x$
   $4x + 32 = 20x$
   $32 = 16x$
   $2 = x$; (C)
3. (B) $(-4, -1)$

Lesson 5.1

5.1 Checkpoint (p. 269–271)

1. $y = mx + b$ Substitute: $m = -2, b = 7$
   $y = -2x + 7$
2. $y = mx + b$
   $y = \frac{2}{5}x + (-6)$ Substitute: $m = \frac{2}{5}; b = -6$
   $y = \frac{2}{5}x - 6$ Simplify.
3. $y = mx + b$ Write slope-intercept form.
   $(-3, 0); (0, 2)$ Choose two points on the line.
   $m = \frac{2 - 0}{0 - (-3)} = \frac{2}{3}$ Find the slope.
   y-intercept: 2 The line crosses y-axis at 2.
   $y = \frac{2}{3}x + 2$ Substitute: $m = \frac{2}{3}; b = 2$
4. $y = mx + b$ Write slope-intercept form.
   $(-2, -2)\ (2, 2)$ Choose two points on the line.
   $m = \frac{2 - (-2)}{2 - (-2)} = \frac{4}{4} = 1$ Find the slope.
   y-intercept: 0 The line crosses y-axis at 0.
   $y = (1)x + 0$ Substitute: $m = 1, b = 0$
   $y = x$ Simplify
5. $y = mx + b$ Write slope-intercept form.
   $(0, -3); (2, 1)$ Choose two points on the line.
   $m = \frac{1 - (-3)}{2 - 0} = \frac{4}{2} = 2$ Find the slope.
   y-intercept: -3 The line crosses the y-axis at -3.
   $y = 2x + (-3)$ Substitute: $m = 2, b = -3$
   $y = 2x - 3$ Simplify
6. $y = mx + b$ Write slope-intercept form.
   $(0, 1); (4, -2)$ Choose two points on the line.
   $m = \frac{-2 - 1}{4 - 0} = \frac{-3}{4} = -\frac{3}{4}$ Find the slope.
   y-intercept: 1 The line crosses y-axis at 1.
   $y = -\frac{3}{4}x + 1$ Substitute: $m = -\frac{3}{4}; b = 1$
7. $y = mx + b$ Write slope-intercept form.
   $(-2, 3); (2, -3)$ Choose two points on the line.
   $m = \frac{-3 - 3}{2 - (-2)} = \frac{-6}{4} = -\frac{3}{2}$ Find the slope.
   y-intercept: 0 The line crosses y-axis at 0.
   $y = -\frac{3}{2}x + 0$ Substitute: $m = -\frac{3}{2}; b = 0$
   $y = -\frac{3}{2}x$ Simplify.
8. $y = mx + b$ Write slope-intercept form.
   $(-3, 0); (0, -1)$ Choose two points on the line.
   $m = \frac{-1 - 0}{0 - (-3)} = \frac{-1}{3} = -\frac{1}{3}$ Find the slope.
   y-intercept: -1 The line crosses y-axis at -1.
   $y = -\frac{1}{3}x + (-1)$ Substitute: $m = -\frac{1}{3}; b = -1$
   $y = -\frac{1}{3}x - 1$ Simplify.

5.1 Guided Practice (p. 272)

1. slope-intercept form
2. $m = -4$
3. $b = -3$
4. yes; $m = -8, b = -11$
5. no
6. no
7. $m = 1; b = 0$
   $y = mx + b$
   $y = (1)x + 0$
   $y = x$
8. $m = -7; b = -2$
   $y = mx + b$
   $y = -7x + (-2)$
   $y = -7x - 2$
9. $m = -1; b = 3$
   $y = mx + b$
   $y = (-1)x + 3$
   $y = -x + 3$
10. $m = 0; b = 4$
    $y = mx + b$
    $y = (0)x + 4$
    $y = 4$
11. $m = 5; b = 5$
    $y = mx + b$
    $y = 5x + 5$
12. $m = 14; b = -6$
    $y = mx + b$
    $y = 14x + (-6)$
    $y = 14x - 6$

Copyright © McDougal Littell Inc.
All rights reserved.

5.1 Practice and Applications (p. 272–274)

13. $m = 3, b = 2$
$y = mx + b$
$y = 3x + 2$

14. $m = 1, b = -1$
$y = (1)x + (-1)$
$y = x - 1$

15. $m = 0, b = 6$
$y = (0)x + 6$
$y = 6$

16. $m = 10, b = 0$
$y = 10x + 0$
$y = 10x$

17. $m = \frac{2}{5}, b = 7$
$y = \frac{2}{5}x + 7$

18. $m = -4, b = -\frac{3}{7}$
$y = -4 + \left(-\frac{3}{7}\right)$
$y = -4x - \frac{3}{7}$

19. $m = -1, b = -\frac{2}{5}$
$y = (-1) + \left(-\frac{2}{5}\right)$
$y = -x - \frac{2}{5}$

20. $m = 0, b = 0$
$y = (0)x + 0$
$y = 0$

21. $m = -\frac{1}{5}, b = \frac{2}{3}$
$y = -\frac{1}{5}x + \frac{2}{3}$

22. $(0, -2), (1, 1)$ Choose two points on the line.
$m = \frac{1 - (-2)}{1 - 0} = \frac{3}{1} = 3$ Find the slope.
y-intercept: -2 The line crosses y-axis at -2.

23. $(-2, 2), (2, 0)$ Choose two points on the line.
$m = \frac{0 - 2}{2 - (-2)} = \frac{-2}{4} = -\frac{1}{2}$ Find the slope.
y-intercept: 1 The line crosses y-axis at 1.

24. $(-3, 3), (0, -1)$ Choose two points on the line.
$m = \frac{-1 - 3}{0 - (-3)} = \frac{-4}{3} = -\frac{4}{3}$ Find the slope.
y-intercept: -1 The line crosses y-axis at -1.

25. $(-2, -1)$ $(0, 2)$ Choose two points on the line.
$m = \frac{2 - (-1)}{0 - (-2)} = \frac{3}{2}$ Find the slope.
y-intercept: 2 The line crosses y-axis at 2.

26. $(2, 3)$ $(0, -2)$ Choose two points on the line.
$m = \frac{-2 - 3}{0 - 2} = \frac{-5}{-2} = \frac{5}{2}$ Find the slope.
y-intercept: -2 The line crosses y-axis at -2.

27. $(-3, 1), (0, -1)$ Choose two points on the line.
$m = \frac{-1 - 1}{0 - (-3)} = \frac{-2}{3} = -\frac{2}{3}$ Find the slope.
y-intercept: -1 The line crosses y-axis at -1.

5.1 Practice and Applications (cont.) p. 273

28. $(0, 1), (1, 2)$ Choose two points on the line.
$m = \frac{2 - 1}{1 - 0} = \frac{1}{1} = 1$ Find the slope.
y-intercept: 1 Line crosses y-axis at 1.
$y = mx + b$ Write slope-intercept form.
$y = (1)x + 1$ Substitute: $m = 1, b = 1$
$y = x + 1$ Simplify.

29. $(-1, 2), (0, -1)$ Choose two points on the line.
$m = \frac{-1 - 2}{0 - (-1)} = \frac{-3}{1} = -3$ Find the slope.
y-intercept: -1 Line crosses y-axis at -1.
$y = mx + b$ Write slope-intercept form.
$y = -3x + (-1)$ Substitute: $m = -3, b = -1$
$y = -3x - 1$ Simplify.

30. $(0, -1), (2, 4)$ Choose two points on the line.
$m = \frac{4 - (-1)}{2 - 0} = \frac{5}{2}$ Find the slope.
y-intercept: -1 Line crosses y-axis at -1.
$y = mx + b$ Write slope-intercept form.
$y = \frac{5}{2}x + (-1)$ Substitute: $m = \frac{5}{2}, b = -1$
$y = \frac{5}{2}x - 1$ Simplify.

31. $(-2, 3), (1, 0)$ Choose two points on the line.
$m = \frac{0 - 3}{1 - (-2)} = \frac{-3}{3} = -1$ Find the slope.
y-intercept: 1 Line crosses y-axis at 1.
$y = mx + b$ Write slope-intercept form.
$y = (-1)x + 1$ Substitute: $m = -1, b = 1$
$y = -x + 1$ Simplify.

32. $(0, 4), (2, 1)$ Choose two points on the line.
$m = \frac{1 - 4}{2 - 0} = \frac{-3}{2} = -\frac{3}{2}$ Find the slope.
y-intercept: 4 Line crosses y-axis at 4.
$y = mx + b$ Write slope-intercept form.
$y = \left(-\frac{3}{2}\right)x + 4$ Substitute: $m = -\frac{3}{2}, b = 4$

33. $(0, -1), (1, 1)$ Choose two points on the line.
$m = \frac{1 - (-1)}{1 - 0} = \frac{2}{1} = 2$ Find the slope.
y-intercept: -1 Line crosses y-axis at -1
$y = mx + b$ Write slope-intercept form.
$y = 2x + (-1)$ Substitute: $m = -2, b = -1$
$y = 2x - 1$ Simplify.

Copyright © McDougal Littell Inc.
All rights reserved.

34. y-intercept: 2
Slope: Choose two points on the line (0, 2), (2, 0)
$m = \frac{0 - 2}{2 - 0} = \frac{-2}{2} = -1$
$y = (-1)x + 2 = -x + 2$ **(B)**

35. y-intercept: -2
Slope: Choose two points on the line (0, -2), (2, 0)
$m = \frac{0 - (-2)}{2 - 0} = \frac{2}{2} = 1$
$y = (1)x + (-2)$
$y = x - 2$ **(C)**

36. y-intercept: 2
Slope: Choose two points on the line (-2, 0), (0, 2)
$m = \frac{2 - 0}{0 - (-2)} = \frac{2}{2} = 1$
$y = (1)x + 2 = x + 2$ **(A)**

37. y-intercept: 0
Slope: Choose two points on the line (-1,-1), (1, 1)
$m = \frac{1 - (-1)}{1 - (-1)} = \frac{2}{2} = 1$
$y = (1)x + 0 = x$ **(F)**

38. y-intercept: 1
Slope: 0 (horizontal line)
$y = (0)x + 1 = 1$ **(E)**

39. y-intercept: 1
Slope: Choose two points on the line (-1, 0), (0, 1)
$m = \frac{1 - 0}{0 - (-1)} = \frac{1}{1} = 1$
$y = (1)x + 1 = x + 1$ **(D)**

40. Use the points that are shown to find the slope:
(9, 13.4), (32, 13.0)
$m = \frac{13.0 - 13.4}{32 - 9} = \frac{-0.4}{23} \approx -0.017 \approx -0.02$
$b = 13.64$ (given)
$y = -0.02x + 13.64$

41. $y = -0.02x + 13.64$
Write equation
1984 is (1984 $-$1960) or 24 years past 1960. Use 24 for x-value.
$y = -0.02(24) + 13.64 = 13.16$ sec

42. 2004 is (2004 $-$ 1960) or 44 years past 1960. Use 44 for the x-value. It looks like the time would be about 12.76 seconds.

43. *Sample answer*: The prediction may be unrealistic because athletes may be unable to continue the downward trend.

44. Choose two points on the top line: (2, 4), (0, 3)
$m = \frac{3 - 4}{0 - 2} = \frac{-1}{-2} = \frac{1}{2}; b = 3$
top line: $y = \frac{1}{2}x + 3$
Choose two points on the middle line: (-2, 0), (2, 2)
$m = \frac{2 - 0}{2 - (-2)} = \frac{2}{4} = \frac{1}{2}; b = 1$
middle line: $y = \frac{1}{2}x + 1$
Choose two points on the lower line: (-2, -3), (2, -1)
$m = \frac{-1 - (-3)}{2 - (-2)} = \frac{2}{4} = \frac{1}{2}; b = -2$
bottom line: $y = \frac{1}{2}x - 2$

45. All three lines have the same slope, $\frac{1}{2}$.

46. $m = \frac{1}{2}, b = -1$
$y = \frac{1}{2}x - 1$

47. Find the slopes between the points:
$m = \frac{63.64 - 0}{0 - (-63.64)} = \frac{63.64}{63.64} = 1; b = 63.64$
$y = (1)x + 63.64$
$y = x + 63.64$
$m = \frac{0 - (-63.64)}{63.64 - 0} = \frac{63.64}{63.64} = 1; b = -63.64$
$y = (1)x + (-63.64)$
$y = x - 63.64$
$m = \frac{0 - (-63.64)}{-63.64 - 0} = \frac{63.64}{-63.64} = -1;$
$b = -63.64$
$y = (-1)x + (-63.64)$
$y = -x - 63.64$

48. *Sample answer*: All three equations have slopes of 1 or -1 and y-intercepts of 63.64 or -63.64.

49. $m = -1$ (downward slopes are negative)
$b = 63.64$
$y = -x + 63.64$

50. Slope: Choose two points on the line (0, 2), $\left(\frac{1}{2}, 0\right)$
$m = \frac{0 - 2}{\frac{1}{2} - 0} = \frac{-2}{\frac{1}{2}} = -2 \cdot \frac{2}{1} = -4; b = 2$
$y = -4x + 2$

51. $y = -4x + 2$ Substitute $\frac{3}{8}$ for x.
$y = -4\left(\frac{3}{8}\right) + 2$
$y = -\frac{3}{2} + 2 = \frac{1}{2}$ mile

Copyright © McDougal Littell Inc.
All rights reserved.

52. $b = 32$ (given)
Use the two points indicated to find the slope:
(1.5, 50), (4, 80)
$m = \dfrac{80 - 50}{4 - 1.5} = \dfrac{30}{2.5} = 12$
$y = 12x + 32$

53. $y - 12x + 32$
Substitute 5 for x: $y = 12(5) + 32$
$y = 92$ minutes

5.1 Standardized Test Practice (p. 275)

54. $b = 17.4$
Slope: $\dfrac{0.22}{1} = 0.22$
(C) $y = 0.22x + 17.4$

55. 2011 is 1 year after 2010.
When $x = 1$, $y = 17.62$ million **(H)**

5.1 Mixed Review (p. 275)

56. $\dfrac{3x}{x + y} = \dfrac{3(-3)}{-3 + 6} = \dfrac{-9}{3} = -3$

57. $\dfrac{x}{x + 2} = \dfrac{-3}{-3 + 2} = \dfrac{-3}{-1} = 3$

58. $x \cdot y = -3 \cdot 6 = -18$

59. $\dfrac{2x}{y} = \dfrac{2(-3)}{6} = \dfrac{-6}{6} = -1$

60. $x^2y = (-3)^2(6) = 9(6) = 54$

61. $\dfrac{-8x}{-4y} = \dfrac{-8(-3)}{-4(6)} = \dfrac{24}{-24} = -1$

62. $y = 6x + 3$
Sample answers: Let $x = 0, 1, 2$
$y = 6(0) + 3 = 3$ (0, 3)
$y = 6(1) + 3 = 9$ (1, 9)
$y = 6(2) + 3 = 15$ (2, 15)

63. $y = -x - 4$
Sample answers: Let $x = -1, 0, 1$
$y = -(-1) - 4 = -3$ (−1, −3)
$y = -(0) - 4 = -4$ (0, −4)
$y = -(1) - 4 = -5$ (1, −5)

64. $y = \dfrac{1}{2}x$
Sample answers: Let $x = 0, 4, 6$
$y = \dfrac{1}{2}(0) = 0$ (0, 0)
$y = \dfrac{1}{2}(4) = 2$ (4, 2)
$y = \dfrac{1}{2}(6) = 3$ (6, 3)

65. $y = -5x + 7$
Sample answers: Let $x = 0, -1, 1$
$y = -5(0) + 7 = 7$ (0, 7)
$y = -5(-1) + 7 = 12$ (−1, 12)
$y = -5(1) + 7 = 2$ (1, 2)

66. $x + y = 1$
$y = -x + 1$ Change to function form.
Sample answers: Let $x = -1, 0, 1$
$y = -(-1) + 1 = 2$ (−1, 2)
$y = -(0) + 1 = 1$ (0, 1)
$y = -(1) + 1 = 0$ (1, 0)

67. $x + 3y = 9$
$3y = -x + 9$
$y = -\dfrac{1}{3}x + 3$ Change to function form.
Sample answers: Let $x = -3, 0, 3$
$y = -\dfrac{1}{3}(-3) + 3 = 4$ (−3, 4)
$y = -\dfrac{1}{3}(0) + 3 = 3$ (0, 3)
$y = -\dfrac{1}{3}(3) + 3 = 2$ (3, 2)

68. $y + 2x = 2$ Original equation
$y = -2x + 2$ Slope-intercept form
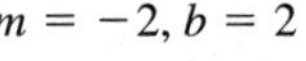
$m = -2, b = 2$

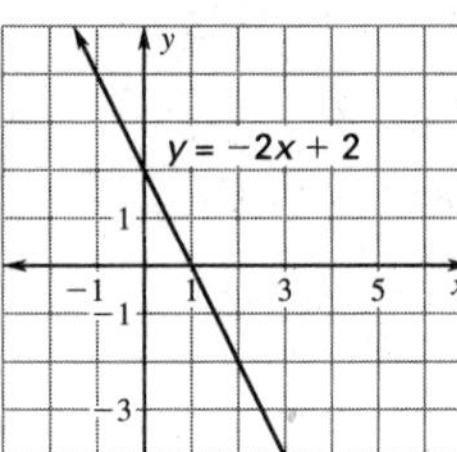

69. $3x - y = -5$ Original equation
$-y = -3x - 5$
$y = 3x + 5$ Slope-intercept form
$m = 3, b = 5$

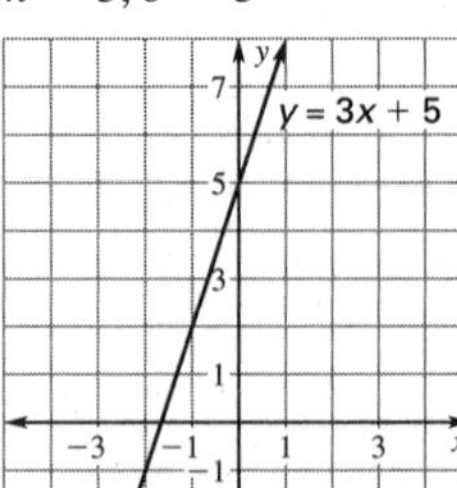

Copyright © McDougal Littell Inc.
All rights reserved.

70. $9x + 3y = 15$ Original equation
$3y = -9x + 15$
$y = -3x + 5$ Slope-intercept form
$m = -3, b = 5$

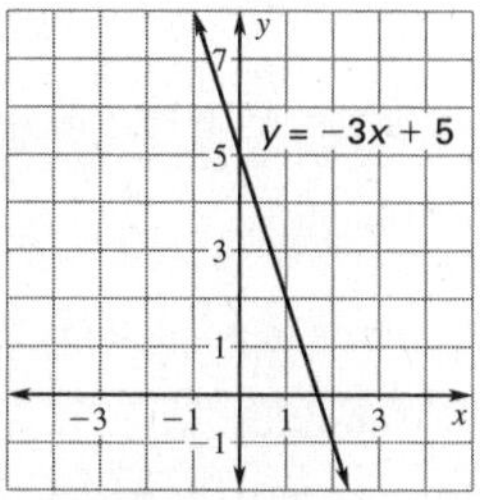

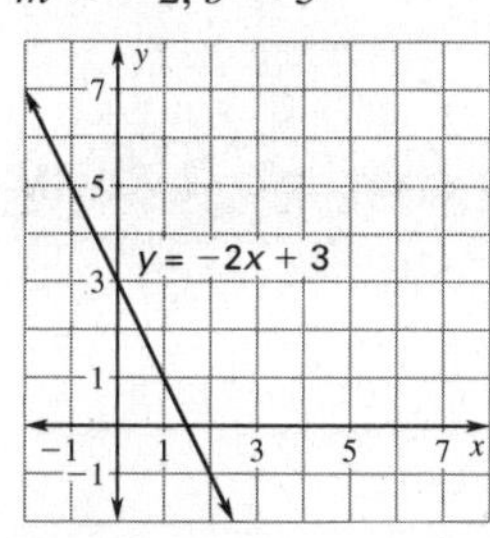

71. $4x + 2y = 6$ Original equation
$2y = -4x + 6$
$y = -2x + 3$ Slope-intercept form
$m = -2, b = 3$

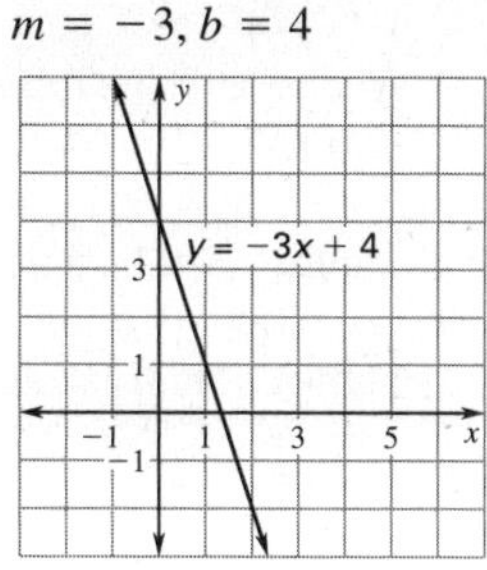

72. $4y + 12x = 16$ Original equation
$4y = -12x + 16$
$y = -3x + 4$ Slope-intercept form
$m = -3, b = 4$

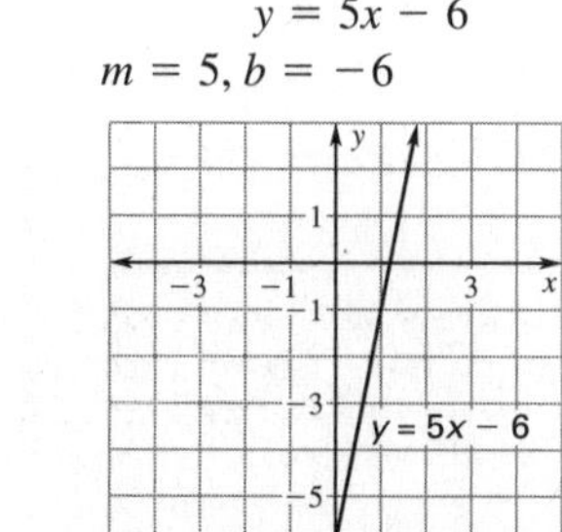

73. $25x - 5y = 30$ Original equation
$-5y = -25x + 30$
$y = 5x - 6$ Slope-intercept form
$m = 5, b = -6$

y = 5x − 6

5.1 Maintaining Skills (p. 275)

74. $50\% = \frac{50}{100} = \frac{1}{2}$

75. $75\% = \frac{75}{100} = \frac{25 \cdot 3}{25 \cdot 4} = \frac{3}{4}$

76. $1\% = \frac{1}{100}$

77. $62\% = \frac{62}{100} = \frac{2 \cdot 31}{2 \cdot 50} = \frac{31}{50}$

78. $100\% = \frac{100}{100} = 1$

79. $0.5\% = \frac{0.5}{100} = \frac{\frac{1}{2}}{100} = \frac{1}{2} \div 100 = \frac{1}{2} \cdot \frac{1}{100} = \frac{1}{200}$

80. $5\% = \frac{5}{100} = \frac{1}{20}$

81. $128\% = \frac{128}{100} = 1\frac{28}{100} = 1\frac{14}{50} = 1\frac{7}{25}$

82. $501\% = \frac{501}{100} = 5\frac{1}{100}$

83. $6\% = \frac{6}{100} = \frac{3}{50}$

5.2 Developing Concepts: Explore *(p. 276)*

3. The rise is the difference of the y-coordinates, or $y - 1$. The run is the difference of the x-coordinates, or $x - 2$.

Think About It (p. 276)

1. $-\frac{5}{2} = \frac{y - 3}{x - 2}$

$-\frac{5}{2}(x - 2) = y - 3$

2. $\frac{4}{3} = \frac{y - (-2)}{x - (-4)}$

$= \frac{y + 2}{x + 4}$

$\frac{4}{3}(x + 4) = y + 2$

Developing Concepts: Explore *(p. 277)*

3. The rise is the difference of the y-coordinates, or $y - y_1$. The run is the difference of the x-coordinates, or $x - x_1$.

Think About It (p. 277)

1. $m = \frac{\text{rise}}{\text{run}} = \frac{1}{1} = 1$

$m = \frac{y - y_1}{x - x_1}$

$1 = \frac{y - (-3)}{x - 3}$

$1 = \frac{y + 3}{x - 3}$

$y + 3 = 1(x - 3)$

2. $m = \frac{\text{rise}}{\text{run}} = -\frac{5}{2}$

$m = \frac{y - y_1}{x - x_1}$

$-\frac{5}{2} = \frac{y - 3}{x - 2}$

$y - 3 = -\frac{5}{2}(x - 2)$

Copyright © McDougal Littell Inc.
All rights reserved.

3. $m = \frac{\text{rise}}{\text{run}} = \frac{3}{1} = 3$

$m = \frac{y - y_1}{x - x_1}$

$3 = \frac{y - (-1)}{x - 2}$

$3 = \frac{y + 1}{x - 2}$

$y + 1 = 3(x - 2)$

4. $m = \frac{y - y_1}{x - x_1}$

$5 = \frac{y - 2}{x - 3}$

$y - 2 = 5(x - 3)$

5. $m = \frac{y - y_1}{x - x_1}$

$\frac{2}{3} = \frac{y - 7}{x - 12}$

$y - 7 = \frac{2}{3}(x - 12)$

6. $m = \frac{y - y_1}{x - x_1}$

$-\frac{1}{4} = \frac{y - 0}{x - (-10)}$

$-\frac{1}{4} = \frac{y}{x + 10}$

$y - 0 = -\frac{1}{4}(x + 10)$

Lesson 5.2

5.2 Checkpoint (p. 278–280)

1. From the graph find $m = -\frac{1}{2}$.

$y - y_1 = m(x - x_1)$ Write point-slope form.

$y - 0 = -\frac{1}{2}(x - 0)$ Substitute: $-\frac{1}{2}$ for m, 0 for x_1, and 0 for y_1.

$y = -\frac{1}{2}x$

2. From the graph find $m = \frac{1}{2}$.

$y - y_1 = m(x - x_1)$ Write point-slope form.

$y - 2 = \frac{1}{2}(x - 3)$ Substitute: $m = \frac{1}{2}, x_1 = 3, y_1 = 2$

3. From the graph find $m = -\frac{2}{3}$.

$y - y_1 = m(x - x_1)$ Write point-slope form.

$y - 1 = -\frac{2}{3}(x - (-3))$ Substitute: $m = -\frac{2}{3}, x_1 = -3, y_1 = 1$

$y - 1 = -\frac{2}{3}(x + 3)$ Simplify.

4. $y - y_1 = m(x - x_1)$ Write in point-slope form.

$y - 2 = \frac{1}{2}(x - 2)$ Substitute: $m = \frac{1}{2}, x_1 = 2, y_1 = 2$

5. $y - y_1 = m(x - x_1)$ Write in point-slope form.

$y - 4 = 3(x - 2)$ Substitute: $m = 3, x_1 = 2, y_1 = 4$

$y - 4 = 3x - 6$ Distribute the 3.

$y = 3x - 2$ Add 4 to each side.

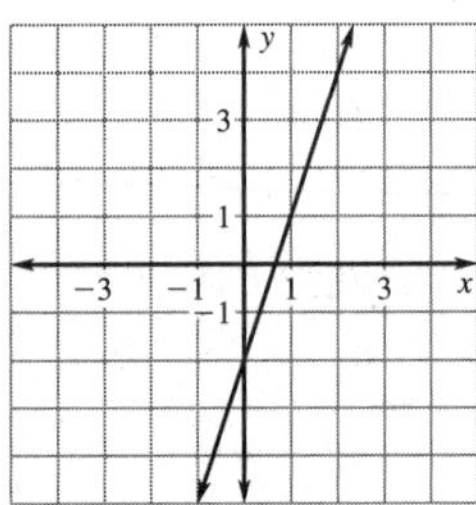

6. Slope of original line is $m = -2$.
Slope of parallel line is $m = -2$.

$y - y_1 = m(x - x_1)$ Write point-slope form.

$y - (-2) = -2(x - 3)$ Substitute: $m = -2, x_1 = 3, y_1 = -2$

$y + 2 = -2x + 6$ Simplify; distribute the -2.

$y = -2x + 4$ Subtract 2 from each side.

5.2 Guided practice (p. 281)

1. $y - y_1 = m(x - x_1)$

2. $(2, -1), m = 3$

$y - y_1 = m(x - x_1)$

$y - (-1) = 3(x - 2)$

$y + 1 = 3(x - 2)$

3. $(3, 4), m = 4$

$y - y_1 = m(x - x_1)$

$y - 4 = 4(x - 3)$

4. $(-5, -7), m = -2$

$y - y_1 = m(x - x_1)$

$y - (-7) = -2(x - (-5))$

$y + 7 = -2(x + 5)$

5. $m = \frac{1}{2}$

$y - y_1 = m(x - x_1)$

$y - 4 = \frac{1}{2}(x - 3)$

Copyright © McDougal Littell Inc.
All rights reserved.

6. $m = \frac{2}{3}$

$$y - y_1 = m(x - x_1)$$
$$y - (-5) = \frac{2}{3}(x - 1)$$
$$y + 5 = \frac{2}{3}(x - 1)$$

7. $m = \frac{3}{1} = 3$

$$y - y_1 = m(x - x_1)$$
$$y - 2 = 3(x - 2)$$

8. $(-4, 2), m = 2$

$$y - y_1 = m(x - x_1)$$
$$y - 2 = 2(x - (-4))$$
$$y - 2 = 2(x + 4)$$
$$y - 2 = 2x + 8$$
$$y = 2x + 10$$

9. $(-1, -3), m = \frac{1}{2}$

$$y - y_1 = m(x - x_1)$$
$$y - (-3) = \frac{1}{2}(x - (-1))$$
$$y + 3 = \frac{1}{2}(x + 1)$$
$$y + 3 = \frac{1}{2}x + \frac{1}{2}$$
$$y = \frac{1}{2}x - 2\frac{1}{2} \quad \text{or}$$
$$y = \frac{1}{2}x - \frac{5}{2}$$

10. $(2, -3), m = 0$

$$y - y_1 = m(x - x_1)$$
$$y - (-3) = 0(x - 2)$$
$$y + 3 = 0$$
$$y = -3$$

11. $m = 1$ original line
$m = 1$ parallel line

$$y - y_1 = m(x - x_1)$$
$$y - (-1) = 1(x - (-1))$$
$$y + 1 = x + 1$$
$$y = x$$

12. $m = -3$ original line
$m = -3$ parallel line

$$y - y_1 = m(x - x_1)$$
$$y - 4 = -3(x - 2)$$
$$y - 4 = -3x + 6$$
$$y = -3x + 10$$

13. $m = \frac{1}{4}$ original line

$m = \frac{1}{4}$ parallel line

$$y - y_1 = m(x - x_1)$$
$$y - 3 = \frac{1}{4}(x - 3)$$
$$y - 3 = \frac{1}{4}x - \frac{3}{4}$$
$$y = \frac{1}{4}x + 2\frac{1}{4} \quad \text{or}$$
$$y = \frac{1}{4}x + \frac{9}{4}$$

5.2 Practice and Applications (p. 281–283)

14. $m = -\frac{2}{3}$

$$y - y_1 = m(x - x_1)$$
$$y - 2 = -\frac{2}{3}(x - (-2))$$
$$y - 2 = -\frac{2}{3}(x + 2)$$

15. $m = \frac{1}{2}$

$$y - y_1 = m(x - x_1)$$
$$y - 2 = \frac{1}{2}(x - 1)$$

16. $m = \frac{2}{3}$

$$y - y_1 = m(x - x_1)$$
$$y - 1 = \frac{2}{3}(x - 1)$$

17. $m = \frac{1}{3}$

$$y - y_1 = m(x - x_1)$$
$$y - (-3) = \frac{1}{3}(x - (-1))$$
$$y + 3 = \frac{1}{3}(x + 1)$$

18. $m = -\frac{3}{2}$

$$y - y_1 = m(x - x_1)$$
$$y - 2 = -\frac{3}{2}(x - 3)$$

19. $m = \frac{-1}{1} = -1$

$$y - y_1 = m(x - x_1)$$
$$y - (-4) = (-1)(x - 4)$$
$$y + 4 = -(x - 4)$$

20.

$$y - y_1 = m(x - x_1)$$
$$y - (-3) = 4(x - (-1))$$
$$y + 3 = 4(x + 1)$$

Copyright © McDougal Littell Inc.
All rights reserved.

21. $y - y_1 = m(x - x_1)$
$y - 2 = -5(x - (-6))$
$y - 2 = -5(x + 6)$

22. $y - y_1 = m(x - x_1)$
$y - 0 = 2(x - (-10))$
$y = 2(x + 10)$

23. $y - y_1 = m(x - x_1)$
$y - (-2) = 2(x - (-8))$
$y + 2 = 2(x + 8)$

24. $y - y_1 = m(x - x_1)$
$y - 3 = -6(x - (-4))$
$y - 3 = -6(x + 4)$

25. $y - y_1 = m(x - x_1)$
$y - 4 = 6(x - (-3))$
$y - 4 = 6(x + 3)$

26. $y - y_1 = m(x - x_1)$
$y - 2 = -7(x - 12)$ Point-slope form
$y - 2 = -7x + 84$
$y = -7x + 86$ Slope-intercept form

27. $y - y_1 = m(x - x_1)$
$y - (-1) = 0(x - 8)$
$y + 1 = 0(x - 8)$ Point-slope form
$y + 1 = 0$
$y = -1$ Slope-intercept form

28. $y - y_1 = m(x - x_1)$
$y - (-12) = -11(x - 5)$
$y + 12 = -11(x - 5)$ Point-slope form
$y + 12 = -11x + 55$
$y = -11x + 43$ Slope-intercept form

29. $y - y_1 = m(x - x_1)$
$y - 4 = 2(x - 1)$ Point-slope form
$y - 4 = 2x - 2$
$y = 2x + 2$ Slope-intercept form

30. $y - y_1 = m(x - x_1)$
$y - 4 = 3(x - (-2))$
$y - 4 = 3(x + 2)$ Point-slope form
$y - 4 = 3x + 6$
$y = 3x + 10$ Slope-intercept form

31. $y - y_1 = m(x - x_1)$
$y - (-5) = -2(x - (-5))$
$y + 5 = -2(x + 5)$ Point-slope form
$y + 5 = -2x - 10$
$y = -2x - 15$ Slope-intercept form

32. $y - y_1 = m(x - x_1)$
$y - 2 = \frac{1}{2}(x - 6)$ Point-slope form
$y - 2 = \frac{1}{2}x - 3$
$y = \frac{1}{2}x - 1$ Slope-intercept form

33. $y - y_1 = m(x - x_1)$
$y - 1 = \frac{-1}{3}(x - (-1))$
$y - 1 = -\frac{1}{3}(x + 1)$ Point-slope form
$y - 1 = -\frac{1}{3}x - \frac{1}{3}$
$y = -\frac{1}{3}x + \frac{2}{3}$ Slope-intercept form

34. $y - y_1 = m(x - x_1)$
$y - (-2) = \frac{1}{4}(x - 4)$
$y + 2 = \frac{1}{4}(x - 4)$ Point-slope form
$y + 2 = \frac{1}{4}x - 1$
$y = \frac{1}{4}x - 3$ Slope-intercept form

35. $m = 2$ for both lines
$y - y_1 = m(x - x_1)$
$y - 4 = 2(x - 3)$
$y - 4 = 2x - 6$
$y = 2x - 2$

36. $m = \frac{-3}{5}$ for both lines
$y - y_1 = m(x - x_1)$
$y - 7 = \frac{-3}{5}(x - (-2))$
$y - 7 = \frac{-3}{5}(x + 2)$
$y - 7 = -\frac{3}{5}x - \frac{6}{5}$
$y = -\frac{3}{5}x + 5\frac{4}{5}$ or
$y = -\frac{3}{5}x + \frac{29}{5}$

37. $m = \frac{1}{3}$ for both lines
$y - y_1 = m(x - x_1)$
$y - (-4) = \frac{1}{3}(x - (-4))$
$y + 4 = \frac{1}{3}(x + 4)$
$y = \frac{1}{3}x - 2\frac{2}{3}$ or
$y = \frac{1}{3}x - \frac{8}{3}$

38. $m = 7$ for both lines
$y - y_1 = m(x - x_1)$
$y - 0 = 7(x - 8)$
$y = 7x - 56$

Copyright © McDougal Littell Inc.
All rights reserved.

39. $m = -9$ for both lines

$$\begin{aligned} y - y_1 &= m(x - x_1) \\ y - (-5) &= -9(x - 0) \\ y + 5 &= -9x + 0 \\ y &= -9x - 5 \end{aligned}$$

40. $m = \frac{1}{2}$ for both lines

$$\begin{aligned} y - y_1 &= m(x - x_1) \\ y - (-10) &= \frac{1}{2}(x - 8) \\ y + 10 &= \frac{1}{2}x - 4 \\ y &= \frac{1}{2}x - 14 \end{aligned}$$

41. Find slope by looking at rise to run ratio of any two points:

$$m = \frac{2}{1} = 2$$

$$\begin{aligned} y - y_1 &= m(x - x_1) \\ y - (-1) &= 2(x - 0) \\ y + 1 &= 2x \\ y &= 2x - 1 \end{aligned}$$

42. Find slope by looking at rise to run ratio of any two points:

$$m = \frac{2}{3}$$

$$\begin{aligned} y - y_1 &= m(x - x_1) \\ y - 3 &= \frac{2}{3}(x - 3) \\ y - 3 &= \frac{2}{3}x - 2 \\ y &= \frac{2}{3}x + 1 \end{aligned}$$

43. Find slope by looking at rise to run ratio of any two points:

$$m = \frac{-1}{1} = -1$$

$$\begin{aligned} y - y_1 &= m(x - x_1) \\ y - (-1) &= -1(x - (-3)) \\ y + 1 &= -(x + 3) \\ y + 1 &= -x - 3 \\ y &= -x - 4 \end{aligned}$$

44.

$$\begin{aligned} y - y_1 &= m(x - x_1) \\ y - 32.5 &= 0.455(x - 40) && \text{Point-slope form} \\ y - 32.5 &= 0.455x - 18.2 \\ y &= 0.455x + 14.3 && \text{Slope-intercept form} \end{aligned}$$

45. $y = 0.455x + 14.3$ Substitute: $x = 90$

$y = 0.455(90) + 14.3$

$y = 55.25$ psi

46. rate of increase $\approx$ 11 million per year (so $m = 11$).
In 1993 Americans took 413 million trips, we can get the point $1993 - 1988 = 5$ (5,413) from this information.

$$\begin{aligned} y - y_1 &= m(x - x_1) \\ y - 413 &= 11(x - 5) \\ y - 413 &= 11x - 55 \\ y &= 11x + 358 \end{aligned}$$

47. $1996 - 1988 = 8 \quad (x = 8)$

$y = 11x + 358$

$y = 11(8) + 358 = 446$ million trips

48. $2005 - 1988 = 17 \quad (x = 17)$

$y = 11x + 358$

$y = 11(17) + 358 = 545$ million trips

5.2 Standardized Test Practice (p. 283)

49. **(D)** $y + 4 = 3\left(x - \frac{3}{2}\right)$

50. $m = \frac{3}{1} = 3$

$y - y_1 = m(x - x_1)$

$y - 3 = 3(x - 0)$ **(F)**

51. $m = \frac{2}{1} = 2$ for both lines

$$\begin{aligned} y - y_1 &= m(x - x_1) \\ y - 1 &= 2(x - (-1)) \\ y - 1 &= 2(x + 1) \\ y - 1 &= 2x + 2 \\ y &= 2x + 3 \end{aligned}$$ **(D)**

5.2 Mixed Review (p. 284)

52. $2x < 24$

$2(8) \overset{?}{<} 24$

$16 < 24$ yes

53. $7y + 6 > 10$

$7(3) + 6 \overset{?}{>} 10$

$27 > 10$ yes

54. $16p - 9 \geq 71$

$16(5) - 9 \overset{?}{\geq} 71$

$71 \geq 71$ yes

55. $12a \leq a - 9$

$12(-2) \overset{?}{\leq} (-2) - 9$

$-24 \leq -11$ yes

56. $4x \leq 28$

$4(7) \overset{?}{\leq} 28$

$28 \leq 28$ yes

57. $6c - 4 > 14$

$6(3) - 4 \overset{?}{>} 14$

$14 \not> 14$ no

Copyright © McDougal Littell Inc.
All rights reserved.

58.

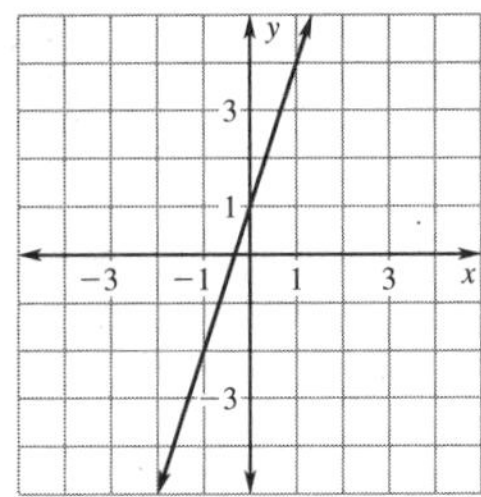

59.

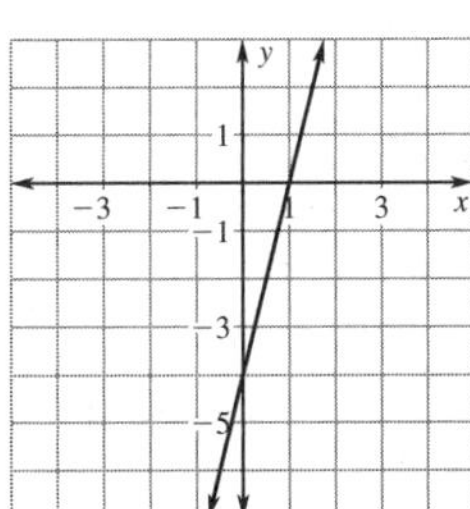

60.

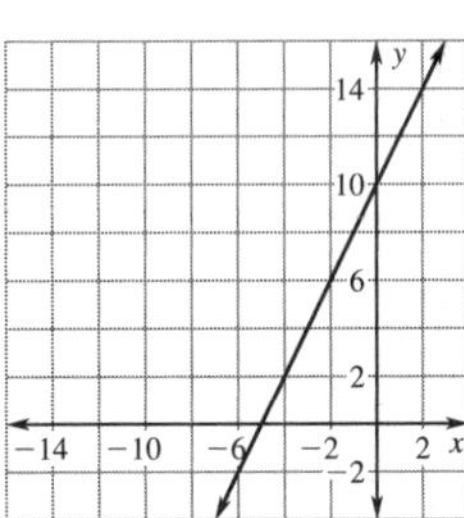

61.

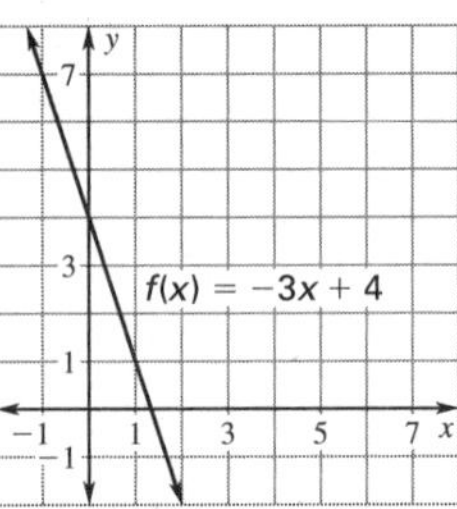

62.

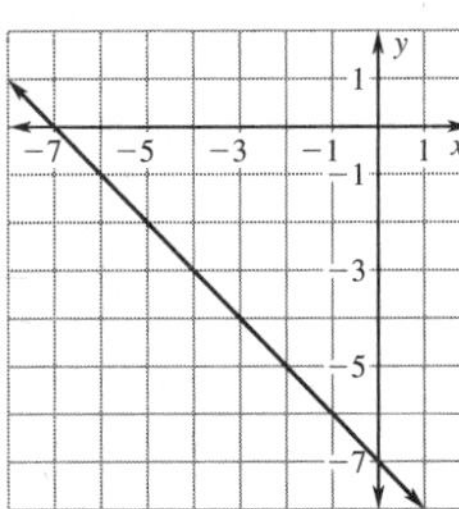

63.

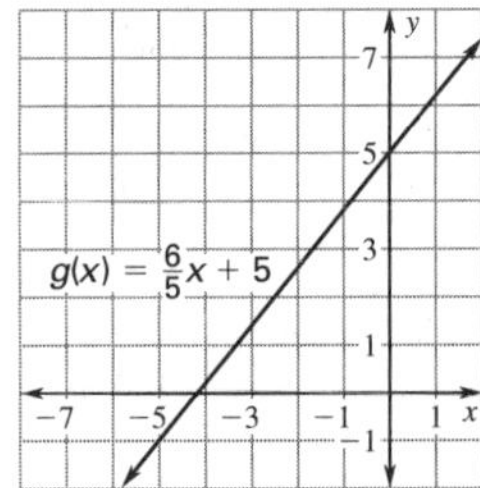

5.2 Maintaining Skills (p. 284)

64. $\frac{5}{6} - \frac{1}{2} = \frac{5}{6} - \frac{3}{6} = \frac{2}{6} = \frac{1}{3}$

65. $\frac{1}{3} - \frac{1}{18} = \frac{1}{3} \cdot \frac{6}{6} - \frac{1}{18} = \frac{6}{18} - \frac{1}{18} = \frac{5}{18}$

66. $\frac{7}{8} - \frac{2}{3} = \frac{7}{8} \cdot \frac{3}{3} - \frac{2}{3} \cdot \frac{8}{8} = \frac{21}{24} - \frac{16}{24} = \frac{5}{24}$

67. $\frac{1}{2} - \frac{1}{5} = \frac{1}{2} \cdot \frac{5}{5} - \frac{1}{5} \cdot \frac{2}{2} = \frac{5}{10} - \frac{2}{10} = \frac{3}{10}$

68. $\frac{8}{9} - \frac{1}{3} = \frac{8}{9} - \frac{1}{3} \cdot \frac{3}{3} = \frac{8}{9} - \frac{3}{9} = \frac{5}{9}$

69. $\frac{5}{7} - \frac{2}{3} = \frac{5}{7} \cdot \frac{3}{3} - \frac{2}{3} \cdot \frac{7}{7} = \frac{15}{21} - \frac{14}{21} = \frac{1}{21}$

70. $\frac{3}{5} - \frac{1}{2} = \frac{3}{5} \cdot \frac{2}{2} - \frac{1}{2} \cdot \frac{5}{5} = \frac{6}{10} - \frac{5}{10} = \frac{1}{10}$

71. $\frac{3}{4} - \frac{1}{3} = \frac{3}{4} \cdot \frac{3}{3} - \frac{1}{3} \cdot \frac{4}{4} = \frac{9}{12} - \frac{4}{12} = \frac{5}{12}$

Quiz 1 *(p. 284)*

1. $y = mx + b$ $\quad m = -2; b = 1$
$y = -2x + 1$

2. $y = mx + b$ $\quad m = 5; b = 0$
$y = 5x + 0$
$y = 5x$

3. $b = 1;$
Choose two points to find slope:
$(0, 1), (3, -1)$
$m = \frac{-1 - 1}{3 - 0} = \frac{-2}{3} = -\frac{2}{3}$
$y = mx + b$
$y = -\frac{2}{3}x + 1$

4. $b = -2$
Choose two points to find the slope:
$(0, -2), (2, 0)$
$m = \frac{0 - (-2)}{2 - 0} = \frac{2}{2} = 1$
$y = mx + b$
$y = (1)x + (-2)$
$y = x - 2$

5. $b = 3$
Choose any two points to find the slope:
$(-2, -1), (0, 3)$
$m = \frac{3 - (-1)}{0 - (-2)} = \frac{4}{2} = 2$
$y = mx + b$
$y = 2x + 3$

6. $y - y_1 = m(x - x_1)$
$y - 7 = -2(x - 7)$

Copyright © McDougal Littell Inc.
All rights reserved.

7. $y - y_1 = m(x - x_1)$
$y - (-2) = 3(x - (-8))$
$y + 2 = 3(x + 8)$

8. $y - y_1 = m(x - x_1)$
$y - 0 = \frac{-1}{2}(x - 0)$
$y = -\frac{1}{2}x$

9. $y - y_1 = m(x - x_1)$
$y - 3 = 1(x - 2)$
$y - 3 = x - 2$
$y = x + 1$

10. $y - y_1 = m(x - x_1)$
$y - 4 = 0(x - (-6))$
$y - 4 = 0$
$y = 4$

11. $y - y_1 = m(x - x_1)$
$y - (-4) = -4(x - 1)$
$y + 4 = -4x + 4$
$y = -4x + 0$
$y = -4x$

12. $m = 4$ for both lines
$y - y_1 = m(x - x_1)$
$y - 0 = 4(x - 1)$
$y = 4x - 4$

13. $m = -\frac{1}{3}$ for both lines
$y - y_1 = m(x - x_1)$
$y - (-3) = -\frac{1}{3}(x - (-3))$
$y + 3 = -\frac{1}{3}(x + 3)$
$y + 3 = -\frac{1}{3}x - 1$
$y = -\frac{1}{3}x - 4$

14. $m = -2$ for both lines
$y - y_1 = m(x - x_1)$
$y - 5 = -2(x - 0)$
$y - 5 = -2x + 0$
$y = -2x + 5$

15. $m = \frac{3}{7}$ for both lines
$y - y_1 = m(x - x_1)$
$y - (-1) = \frac{3}{7}(x - 2)$
$y + 1 = \frac{3}{7}x - \frac{6}{7}$
$y = \frac{3}{7}x - 1\frac{6}{7}$ or
$y = \frac{3}{7}x - \frac{13}{7}$

Lesson 5.3

5.3 Checkpoints (p. 285–287)

1. $m = \frac{4 - 1}{10 - 0} = \frac{3}{10}$
$b = 1$
$y = \frac{3}{10}x + 1$

2. $m = \frac{7 - 3}{4 - 2} = \frac{4}{2} = 2$
$y - y_1 = m(x - x_1)$ Choose a point to use: (2, 3)
$y - 3 = 2(x - 2)$
$y - 3 = 2x - 4$
$y = 2x - 1$

3. $m = \frac{2 - 5}{2 - (-4)} = \frac{-3}{6} = -\frac{1}{2}$
$y - y_1 = m(x - x_1)$ Choose a point to use: (2, 2)
$y - 2 = -\frac{1}{2}(x - 2)$
$y - 2 = -\frac{1}{2}x + 1$
$y = -\frac{1}{2}x + 3$

4. $m = \frac{-4 - (-1)}{4 - 1} = \frac{-3}{3} = -1$ Choose a point to use: (1, −1)
$y - (-1) = -1(x - 1)$
$y + 1 = -x + 1$
$y = -x + 0$
$y = -x$

5. $m = \frac{5 - 3}{4 - 0} = \frac{2}{4} = \frac{1}{2}$; $b = 3$
$y = mx + b$ Use slope-intercept since b is known
$y = \frac{1}{2}x + 3$

6. $m = \frac{-3 - 2}{2 - 1} = \frac{-5}{1} = -5$
$y - y_1 = m(x - x_1)$ Use point-slope since b is not known.
$y - 2 = -5(x - 1)$ Choose a point to use: (1, 2)
$y - 2 = -5x + 5$
$y = -5x + 7$

5.3 Guided Practice, (p. 288)

1. point-slope form

2. $y = mx + b$

3. $\frac{2 - (-2)}{0 - 3} = \frac{4}{-3} = -\frac{4}{3}$; $b = 2$
$y = mx + b$ Use slope-intercept since b is known
$y = -\frac{4}{3}x + 2$

Copyright © McDougal Littell Inc.
All rights reserved.

4. $m = \dfrac{1-0}{2-0} = \dfrac{1}{2}; b = 0$

$y = mx + b$ Use slope-intercept since b is known

$y = \dfrac{1}{2}x + 0$

$y = \dfrac{1}{2}x$

5. $m = \dfrac{-2-3}{-1-2} = \dfrac{-5}{-3} = \dfrac{5}{3}$

$y - y_1 = m(x - x_1)$ Use point-slope since b is unknown.

$y - 3 = \dfrac{5}{3}(x - 2)$ Choose a point to use: (2, 3)

$y - 3 = \dfrac{5}{3}x - \dfrac{10}{3}$

$y - 3 + \dfrac{9}{3} = \dfrac{5}{3}x - \dfrac{10}{3} + \dfrac{9}{3}$

$y = \dfrac{5}{3}x - \dfrac{1}{3}$

6. $m = \dfrac{5-1}{2-(-1)} = \dfrac{4}{3}$

$y - y_1 = m(x - x_1)$

$y - 1 = \dfrac{4}{3}(x - (-1))$

$y - 1 = \dfrac{4}{3}(x + 1)$

$y - 1 = \dfrac{4}{3}x + \dfrac{4}{3}$

$y = \dfrac{4}{3}x + \dfrac{4}{3} + \dfrac{3}{3}$

$y = \dfrac{4}{3}x + \dfrac{7}{3}$

7. $m = \dfrac{4-(-2)}{-6-3} = \dfrac{6}{-9} = -\dfrac{2}{3}$

$y - y_1 = m(x - x_1)$

$y - (-2) = -\dfrac{2}{3}(x - 3)$

$y + 2 = -\dfrac{2}{3}x + 2$

$y = -\dfrac{2}{3}x$

8. $m = \dfrac{6-3}{1-4} = \dfrac{3}{-3} = -1$

$y - y_1 = m(x - x_1)$

$y - 3 = -1(x - 4)$

$y - 3 = -x + 4$

$y = -x + 7$

5.3 Practice and Applications (p. 288–290)

9. $m = \dfrac{4-3}{0-2} = \dfrac{1}{-2} = -\dfrac{1}{2}$

$y - y_1 = m(x - x_1)$

$y - 3 = -\dfrac{1}{2}(x - 2)$ or

$y - 4 = -\dfrac{1}{2}(x - 0)$

$y - 4 = -\dfrac{1}{2}x$

10. $m = \dfrac{-5-0}{-6-0} = \dfrac{-5}{-6} = \dfrac{5}{6}$

$y - y_1 = m(x - x_1)$

$y - 0 = \dfrac{5}{6}(x - 0)$

$y = \dfrac{5}{6}x$ or

$y - (-5) = \dfrac{5}{6}(x - (-6))$

$y + 5 = \dfrac{5}{6}(x + 6)$

11. $m = \dfrac{4-(-10)}{12-0} = \dfrac{14}{12} = \dfrac{7}{6}$

$y - y_1 = m(x - x_1)$

$y - (-10) = \dfrac{7}{6}(x - 0)$

$y + 10 = \dfrac{7}{6}x$ or

$y - 4 = \dfrac{7}{6}(x - 12)$

12. $m = \dfrac{7-9}{8-0} = \dfrac{-2}{8} = -\dfrac{1}{4}$

$y - y_1 = m(x - x_1)$

$y - 9 = -\dfrac{1}{4}(x - 0)$

$y - 9 = -\dfrac{1}{4}x$ or

$y - 7 = -\dfrac{1}{4}(x - 8)$

13. $m = \dfrac{2-1}{0-1} = \dfrac{1}{-1} = -1$

$y - y_1 = m(x - x_1)$

$y - 1 = -1(x - 1)$

$y - 1 = -(x - 1)$ or

$y - 2 = -1(x - 0)$

$y - 2 = -x$

Copyright © McDougal Littell Inc.
All rights reserved.

14. $m = \frac{1-2}{0-(-7)} = \frac{-1}{7} = -\frac{1}{7}$

$y - y_1 = m(x - x_1)$

$y - 2 = -\frac{1}{7}(x - (-7))$

$y - 2 = -\frac{1}{7}(x + 7)$ or

$y - 1 = -\frac{1}{7}(x - 0)$

$y - 1 = -\frac{1}{7}x$

15. $m = \frac{1-6}{-13-(-8)} = \frac{-5}{-5} = 1$

$y - y_1 = m(x - x_1)$

$y - 6 = 1(x - (-8))$

$y - 6 = x + 8$ or

$y - 1 = 1(x - (-13))$

$y - 1 = x + 13$

16. $m = \frac{6-(-2)}{17-11} = \frac{8}{6} = \frac{4}{3}$

$y - y_1 = m(x - x_1)$

$y - (-2) = \frac{4}{3}(x - 11)$

$y + 2 = \frac{4}{3}(x - 11)$ or

$y - 6 = \frac{4}{3}(x - 17)$

17. $m = \frac{5-5}{4-(-4)} = \frac{0}{8} = 0$

$y - y_1 = m(x - x_1)$

$y - 5 = 0(x - (-4))$

$y - 5 = 0$ or

$y - 5 = 0(x - 4)$

$y - 5 = 0$

18. $m = \frac{-3}{1} = -3$

$b = -3$

$y = -3x - 3$

19. $m = \frac{15}{4}$

$b = 16$

$y = \frac{15}{4}x + 16$

20. $m = \frac{4}{4} = 1$

$b = 4$

$y = (1)x + 4 = x + 4$

21. $m = \frac{4}{1} = 4$

$b = 1$

$y = 4x + 1$

22. $m = \frac{1}{2}; b = \frac{1}{2}$

$y = \frac{1}{2}x + \frac{1}{2}$

23. $m = 0; b = 2$

$y = (0)x + 2$

$y = 2$

24. $m = \frac{-7-7}{2-(-5)} = \frac{-14}{7} = -2$

$y - y_1 = m(x - x_1)$

$y - 7 = -2(x - (-5))$

$y - 7 = -2(x + 5)$

$y - 7 = -2x - 10$

$y = -2x - 3$

25. $m = \frac{6-0}{-2-2} = \frac{6}{-4} = -\frac{3}{2}$

$y - y_1 = m(x - x_1)$

$y - 0 = -\frac{3}{2}(x - 2)$

$y = -\frac{3}{2}x + 3$

26. $m = \frac{4-(-5)}{3-1} = \frac{9}{2}$

$y - y_1 = m(x - x_1)$

$y - 4 = \frac{9}{2}(x - 3)$

$y - 4 = \frac{9}{2}x - \frac{27}{2}$

$y = \frac{9}{2}x - \frac{27}{2} + \frac{8}{2}$

$y = \frac{9}{2}x - \frac{19}{2}$

27. $m = \frac{6-(-2)}{2-(-1)} = \frac{8}{3}$

$y - y_1 = m(x - x_1)$

$y - (-2) = \frac{8}{3}(x - (-1))$

$y + 2 = \frac{8}{3}(x + 1)$

$y = \frac{8}{3}x + \frac{8}{3} - \frac{6}{3}$

$y = \frac{8}{3}x + \frac{2}{3}$

28. $m = \frac{-4-4}{-1-1} = \frac{-8}{-2} = 4$

$y - y_1 = m(x - x_1)$

$y - 4 = 4(x - 1)$

$y - 4 = 4x - 4$

$y = 4x$

Copyright © McDougal Littell Inc.
All rights reserved.

29. $m = \dfrac{7 - (-3)}{-3 - 2} = \dfrac{10}{-5} = -2$

$y - y_1 = m(x - x_1)$

$y - (-3) = -2(x - 2)$

$y + 3 = -2x + 4$

$y = -2x + 1$

30. $m = \dfrac{-7 - 2}{-7 - 2} = \dfrac{-9}{-9} = 1$

$y - y_1 = m(x - x_1)$

$y - (-7) = 1(x - (-7))$

$y + 7 = x + 7$

$y = x$

31. $m = \dfrac{8 - (-4)}{2 - 6} = \dfrac{12}{-4} = -3$

$y - y_1 = m(x - x_1)$

$y - 8 = -3(x - 2)$

$y - 8 = -3x + 6$

$y = -3x + 14$

32. $m = \dfrac{4 - 1}{7 - 1} = \dfrac{3}{6} = \dfrac{1}{2}$

$y - y_1 = m(x - x_1)$

$y - 1 = \dfrac{1}{2}(x - 1)$

$y - 1 = \dfrac{1}{2}x - \dfrac{1}{2}$

$y = \dfrac{1}{2}x + \dfrac{1}{2}$

33. point-slope form

$m = \dfrac{2 - (-4)}{4 - (-2)} = \dfrac{6}{6} = 1$

$y - 2 = 1(x - 4)$

$y - 2 = x - 4$

$y = x - 2$

34. slope-intercept form

$m = \dfrac{0 - (-3)}{5 - 0} = \dfrac{3}{5}; b = -3$

$y = \dfrac{3}{5}x - 3$

35. point-slope form

$m = \dfrac{3 - (-1)}{4 - (-1)} = \dfrac{4}{5}$

$y - 3 = \dfrac{4}{5}(x - 4)$

$y - 3 = \dfrac{4}{5}x - \dfrac{16}{5}$

$y = \dfrac{4}{5}x - \dfrac{1}{5}$

36. $m = \dfrac{12.5 - 2.5}{0 - 150} = \dfrac{10}{-150} = -\dfrac{1}{15}; b = 12.5$

$y = -\dfrac{1}{15}x + 12.5$

37. $m = \dfrac{60 - (-70)}{0 - 15} = \dfrac{130}{-15} = -\dfrac{26}{3}$

$b = 60$

$y = -\dfrac{26}{3}x + 60$

38. $m = \dfrac{50 - (-90)}{50 - 38} = \dfrac{140}{12} = \dfrac{35}{3}$

$y - y_1 = m(x - x_1)$

$y - 50 = \dfrac{35}{3}(x - 50)$

$y - 50 = \dfrac{35}{3}x - \dfrac{1750}{3}$

$y = \dfrac{35}{3}x - \dfrac{1750}{3} + \dfrac{150}{3}$

$y = \dfrac{35}{3}x - \dfrac{1600}{3}$

39. $\dfrac{35}{3}$ is steeper than $\dfrac{-26}{3}$;

it is steeper than on the French side.

40. $m = \dfrac{340 - 352}{15 - 35} = \dfrac{-12}{-20} = \dfrac{3}{5} = 0.6$

$y - y_1 = m(x - x_1)$

$y - 340 = 0.6(x - 15)$

$y - 340 = 0.6x - 9$

$y = 0.6x + 331$

5.3 Standardized Test Practice (p. 290)

41. $m = \dfrac{-2 - 4}{-5 - 7} = \dfrac{-6}{-12} = \dfrac{1}{2}$

$y - y_1 = m(x - x_1)$

$y - 4 = \dfrac{1}{2}(x - 7)$

$y - 4 = \dfrac{1}{2}x - \dfrac{7}{2}$

$y = \dfrac{1}{2}x + \dfrac{1}{2}$ **(D)**

42. $m = \dfrac{3 - 2}{4 - (-1)} = \dfrac{1}{5}$

$y - y_1 = m(x - x_1)$

$y - 3 = \dfrac{1}{5}(x - 4)$

$y - 3 = \dfrac{1}{5}x - \dfrac{4}{5}$

$y = \dfrac{1}{5}x + 2\dfrac{1}{5}$ or

$y = \dfrac{1}{5}x + \dfrac{11}{5}$ **(J)**

5.3 Mixed Review (p. 290)

43. $4x - 11 = -31$

$4x = -20$

$x = -5$

Copyright © McDougal Littell Inc.
All rights reserved.

44. $5x - 7 + x = 19$
$6x - 7 = 19$
$6x = 26$
$x = \frac{26}{6} = \frac{13}{3}$

45. $7y = 9y - 8$
$-2y = -8$
$y = 4$

46. $20x = 3x + 17$
$17x = 17$
$x = 1$

47. $3p + 10 = 5p - 7$
$10 = 2p - 7$
$17 = 2p$
$\frac{17}{2} = p$

48. $12x + 10 = 2x + 5$
$10x + 10 = 5$
$10x = -5$
$x = -\frac{1}{2}$

49. Slope $= \frac{8}{24} = \frac{1}{3}$

5.3 Maintaining Skills (p. 290)

50. $2\frac{5}{12} + 1\frac{1}{6} = 2\frac{5}{12} + 1\frac{2}{12} = 3\frac{7}{12}$

51. $5\frac{2}{3} + 2\frac{1}{8} = 5\frac{16}{24} + 2\frac{3}{24} = 7\frac{19}{24}$

52. $3 + \frac{2}{7} = 3\frac{2}{7}$

53. $3\frac{1}{8} + 5\frac{5}{6} = 3\frac{3}{24} + 5\frac{20}{24} = 8\frac{23}{24}$

54. $1\frac{1}{4} + 2\frac{5}{8} = 1\frac{2}{8} + 2\frac{5}{8} = 3\frac{7}{8}$

55. $17\frac{1}{3} + 9\frac{1}{2} = 17\frac{2}{6} + 9\frac{3}{6} = 26\frac{5}{6}$

56. $7\frac{3}{16} + 3\frac{19}{20} = 7\frac{15}{80} + 3\frac{76}{80} = 10\frac{91}{80} = 11\frac{11}{80}$

57. $1\frac{2}{9} + 5\frac{13}{18} = 1\frac{4}{18} + 5\frac{13}{18} = 6\frac{17}{18}$

58. $2\frac{3}{4} + 20\frac{1}{5} = 2\frac{15}{20} + 20\frac{4}{20} = 22\frac{19}{20}$

Lesson 5.4

5.4 Checkpoint (p. 291–293)

1. $y = -x + 5$ Original equation
$x + y = 5$ Add x to each side.

2. $y = -\frac{1}{2}x + 7$ Original equation
$2y = -x + 14$ Multiply each side by 2 to clear the equation of fractions.
$x + 2y = 14$ Add x to each side.

3. $y = \frac{2}{3}x + 4$ Original equation
$3y = 2x + 12$ Multiply each side by 3 to clear the equation of fractions.
$-2x + 3y = 12$ Subtract $2x$ from each side.

4. $y - y_1 = m(x - x_1)$ Write point-slope form.
$y - (-5) = -3(x - 3)$ Substitute: $m = -3$, $x = 3$, $y = -5$
$y + 5 = -3x + 9$ Simplify.
$3x + y + 5 = 9$ Add $3x$ to each side;
$3x + y = 4$ Subtract 5 from each side.

5. $m = \frac{0 - 5}{2 - 0} = \frac{-5}{2} = -\frac{5}{2}$; $b = 5$
$y = mx + b$ Slope-intercept form
$y = -\frac{5}{2}x + 5$ Substitute $m = -\frac{5}{2}$, $b = 5$
$2y = -5x + 10$ Multiply each side by 2 to clear the equation of fractions.
$5x + 2y = 10$ Add $5x$ to each side.

6. Each point on this vertical line has an x-coordinate of -1. $x = -1$

7. Each point on this horizontal line has a y-coordinate of 1. $y = 1$

5.4 Guided Practice (p. 294)

1. Slope-intercept form; $m =$ the slope; $b =$ the y-intercept

2. Standard form; *Sample answer*: $2x + 3y = -6$

3. $y = 2x - 9$ Original equation
$-2x + y = -9$ Subtract $2x$ from each side.

4. $y = \frac{1}{2}x + 8$ Original equation
$2y = x + 16$ Multiply each side by 2.
$-x + 2y = 16$ Subtract x from each side.

5. $y = \frac{3}{4}x$ Original equation
$4y = 3x$ Multiply each side by 4.
$-3x + 4y = 0$ or Subtract $3x$ from each side.
$3x - 4y = 0$ Multiply each side by -1.

6. $y - y_1 = m(x - x_1)$
$y - 4 = -4(x - 3)$
$y - 4 = -4x + 12$
$y = -4x + 16$
$4x + y = 16$

Copyright © McDougal Littell Inc.
All rights reserved.

7.
$$y - y_1 = m(x - x_1)$$
$$y - (-2) = 5(x - 1)$$
$$y + 2 = 5x - 5$$
$$-5x + y = -7$$

8.
$$y - y_1 = m(x - x_1)$$
$$y - (-5) = 3(x - (-2))$$
$$y + 5 = 3(x + 2)$$
$$y + 5 = 3x + 6$$
$$-3x + y + 5 = 6$$
$$-3x + y = 1$$ or
$$3x - y = -1$$ Multiply each side by -1.

9. $m = \frac{-2 - 1}{4 - 3} = \frac{-3}{1} = -3$
$$y - y_1 = m(x - x_1)$$
$$y - 1 = -3(x - 3)$$
$$y - 1 = -3x + 9$$
$$y = -3x + 10$$
$$3x + y = 10$$

10. $m = \frac{-5 - 6}{1 - 1} = \frac{-11}{0}$; undefined

All x-values are 1, so $x = 1$.

11. $m = \frac{3 - 0}{0 - 5} = \frac{3}{-5} = -\frac{3}{5}$
$$y - y_1 = m(x - x_1)$$
$$y - 0 = \frac{-3}{5}(x - 5)$$
$$y = \frac{-3}{5}x + 3$$
$$5y = -3x + 15$$
$$3x + 5y = 15$$

12. $y = 2$ **13.** $x = -2$ **14.** $y = -4$

5.4 Practice and Applications (p. 294–296)

15.
$$y = -5x + 2$$
$$5x + y = 2$$

16.
$$y = 3x - 8$$
$$-3x + y = -8$$ or
$$3x - y = 8$$

17.
$$y = -9 + 4x$$
$$-4x + y = -9$$ or
$$4x - y = 9$$

18.
$$y = \frac{2}{3}x$$
$$3y = 2x$$
$$-2x + 3y = 0$$ or
$$2x - 3y = 0$$

19.
$$y = \frac{-3}{8}x$$
$$8y = -3x$$
$$3x + 8y = 0$$

20.
$$y = 9x + \frac{1}{2}$$
$$2y = 18x + 1$$
$$-18x + 2y = 1$$ or
$$18x - 2y = -1$$

21.
$$y - 3 = 2(x - (-8))$$
$$y - 3 = 2(x + 8)$$
$$y - 3 = 2x + 16$$
$$y = 2x + 19$$
$$-2x + y = 19$$ or
$$2x - y = -19$$

22.
$$y - 7 = -4(x - (-2))$$
$$y - 7 = -4(x + 2)$$
$$y - 7 = -4x - 8$$
$$y = -4x - 1$$
$$4x + y = -1$$

23.
$$y - 4 = -3(x - (-1))$$
$$y - 4 = -3(x + 1)$$
$$y - 4 = -3x - 3$$
$$y = -3x + 1$$
$$3x + y = 1$$

24.
$$y - (-7) = -1(x - (-6))$$
$$y + 7 = -1(x + 6)$$
$$y + 7 = -x - 6$$
$$y = -x - 13$$
$$x + y = -13$$

25.
$$y - (-2) = 5(x - 3)$$
$$y + 2 = 5x - 15$$
$$y = 5x - 17$$
$$-5x + y = -17$$ or
$$5x - y = 17$$

26.
$$y - 6 = 0(x - 10)$$
$$y - 6 = 0$$
$$y = 6$$

27.
$$y - 9 = \frac{2}{5}(x - 2)$$
$$y - 9 = \frac{2}{5}x - \frac{4}{5}$$
$$5y - 45 = 2x - 4$$
$$5y = 2x + 41$$
$$-2x + 5y = 41$$
$$2x - 5y = -41$$

28.
$$y - (-8) = \frac{1}{2}(x - 5)$$
$$y + 8 = \frac{1}{2}x - \frac{5}{2}$$
$$2y + 16 = x - 5$$
$$2y = x - 21$$
$$-x + 2y = -21$$
$$x - 2y = 21$$

Copyright © McDougal Littell Inc.
All rights reserved.

29. $y - 3 = -\frac{1}{3}(x - 7)$

$y - 3 = -\frac{1}{3}x + \frac{7}{3}$

$3y - 9 = -x + 7$

$3y = -x + 16$

$x + 3y = 16$

30. $m = \frac{5 - 0}{0 - 4} = \frac{5}{-4} = -\frac{5}{4}$

$y - 0 = -\frac{5}{4}(x - 4)$

$y = -\frac{5}{4}x + 5$

$4y = -5x + 20$

$5x + 4y = 20$

31. $m = \frac{2 - 0}{0 - (-3)} = \frac{2}{3}$

$y - 0 = \frac{2}{3}(x - (-3))$

$y = \frac{2}{3}(x + 3)$

$y = \frac{2}{3}x + 2$

$3y = 2x + 6$

$-2x + 3y = 6$ or

$2x - 3y = -6$

32. $m = \frac{0 - 0}{2 - 0} = \frac{0}{2} = 0; y = 0$

33. $m = \frac{-1 - 1}{1 - 0} = \frac{-2}{1} = -2$

$y - 1 = -2(x - 0)$

$y - 1 = -2x$

$2x + y = 1$

34. $m = \frac{-5 - 0}{0 - (-4)} = \frac{-5}{4} = -\frac{5}{4}$

$y - 0 = -\frac{5}{4}(x - (-4))$

$y = -\frac{5}{4}(x + 4)$

$y = -\frac{5}{4}x - 5$

$4y = -5x - 20$

$5x + 4y = -20$

35. $m = \frac{-5 - 1}{2 - (-4)} = \frac{-6}{6} = -1$

$y - 1 = -1(x - (-4))$

$y - 1 = -(x + 4)$

$y - 1 = -x - 4$

$y = -x - 3$

$x + y = -3$

36. $m = \frac{2 - (-2)}{-3 - 9} = \frac{4}{-12} = -\frac{1}{3}$

$y - 2 = -\frac{1}{3}(x - (-3))$

$y - 2 = -\frac{1}{3}(x + 3)$

$y - 2 = -\frac{1}{3}x - 1$

$y = -\frac{1}{3}x + 1$

$3y = -x + 3$

$x + 3y = 3$

37. $m = \frac{2 - 3}{7 - (-3)} = \frac{-1}{10}$

$y - 2 = -\frac{1}{10}(x - 7)$

$y - 2 = -\frac{1}{10}x + \frac{7}{10}$

$10y - 20 = -x + 7$

$10y = -x + 27$

$x + 10y = 27$

38. $m = \frac{-1 - (-7)}{5 - 4} = \frac{6}{1} = 6$

$y - (-7) = 6(x - 4)$

$y + 7 = 6x - 24$

$y = 6x - 31$

$-6x + y = -31$

$6x - y = 31$

39. $y = -2$

40. $x = -3$

41. $x = 4$

42. $y = 0$

43. $x = -3\frac{1}{2}$

44. $y = 1\frac{1}{2}$

45. $x = 9$

46. $b = 9; m = -1$

$y = -x + 9$

$x + y = 9$

47. $y = 10$

48. $b = 10; m = -1$

$y = -x + 10$

$x + y = 10$

49. $b = 4; m = -1$

$y = x + 4$

$-x + y = 4$

50. $y = 1$

51. $b = 7; m = -1$

$y = -x + 7$

$x + y = 7$

52. $b = -1; m = \frac{2}{1} = 2$

$y = 2x - 1$

$-2x + y = -1$ or

$2x - y = 1$

Copyright © McDougal Littell Inc.
All rights reserved.

53. Choose two points on the line: $(-2, 0)$, $(1, -4)$

$$m = \frac{-4 - 0}{1 - (-2)} = \frac{-4}{3}$$
$$y - y_1 = m(x - x_1)$$
$$y - 0 = \frac{-4}{3}(x - (-2))$$
$$y = \frac{-4}{3}(x + 2)$$
$$y = \frac{-4}{3}x - \frac{8}{3}$$
$$3y = -4x - 8$$
$$4x + 3y = -8$$

54. $m = \frac{-2}{4} = -\frac{1}{2}$; $b = 2$

$$y = -\frac{1}{2}x + 2$$
$$2y = -x + 4$$
$$x + 2y = 4$$

55. $y = \frac{1}{3}x - 2$

$3y = x - 6$ Error: multiply each side by 3, not just the right side.

56. $y - 4 = -3[x - (-6)]$

$$y - 4 = -3(x + 6)$$
$$y - 4 = -3x - 18$$
$$y = -3x - 14$$

Error: $x - (-6) = x + 6$ (not $x - 6$)

57.

58.

Pounds of thistle seed, x	0	3	6	9	12
Pounds of dark oil sunflower seeds, y	16	12	8	4	0

59. $\frac{x}{a} + \frac{y}{b} = 1$ Intercept form

$\frac{x}{2} + \frac{y}{3} = 1$ Substitute 2 for a and 3 for b

60.

$$\frac{x}{2} + \frac{y}{3} = 1$$

$6\left(\frac{x}{2}\right) + 6\left(\frac{y}{3}\right) = 6(1)$ Multiply each side by 6 to clear the fractions.

$$3x + 2y = 6$$

5.4 Standardized Test Practice (p. 296)

61. $b = 1$.

Find slope: Choose the points $(0, 1)$, $(2, 4)$

$$m = \frac{4 - 1}{2 - 0} = \frac{3}{2}$$
$$y = mx + b$$
$$y = \frac{3}{2}x + 1$$
$$2y = 3x + 2$$

$-3x + 2y = 2$ **(A)**

62.

$$y - y_1 = m(x - x_1)$$
$$y - (-4) = 2(x - (-1))$$
$$y + 4 = 2(x + 1)$$
$$y + 4 = 2x + 2$$
$$y = 2x - 2$$

$-2x + y = -2$ **(F)**

5.4 Mixed Review (p. 297)

63. $8 + y = 3$

$$y = -5$$

64. $y - 9 = 2$

$$y = 11$$

65. $6(q + 22) = -120$

$$6q + 132 = -120$$
$$6q = -252$$
$$q = -42$$

66. $2(x + 5) = 18$

$$2x + 10 = 18$$
$$2x = 8$$
$$x = 4$$

67. $7 - 2a = -14$

$$-2a = -21$$

$a = \frac{21}{2}$ or 10.5

68. $-2 + 4c = 19$

$$4c = 21$$

$c = \frac{21}{4}$ or 5.25

69. $y = x + 5$

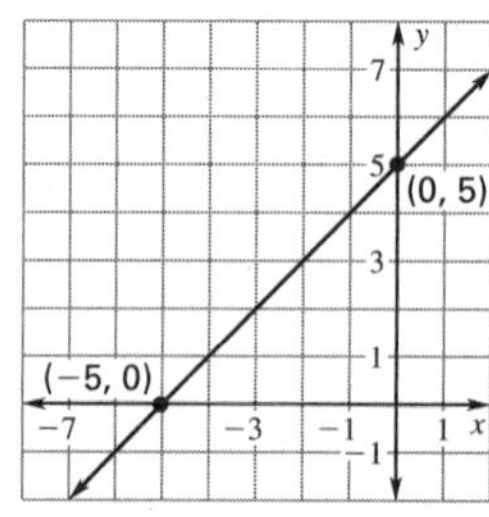

Sample table:

x	−2	−1	0	1	2
y	3	4	5	6	7

Copyright © McDougal Littell Inc.
All rights reserved.

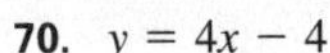

70. $y = 4x - 4$

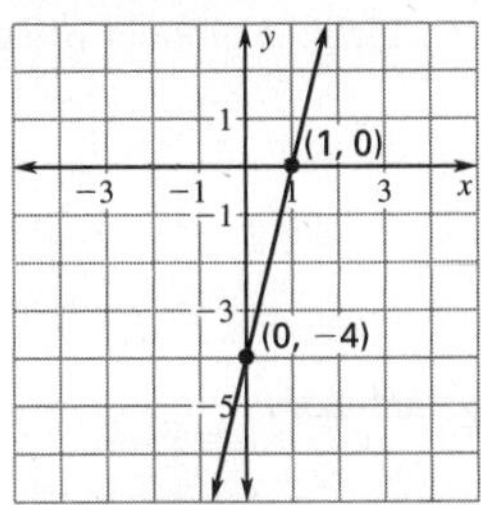

Sample table:

x	-2	-1	0	1	2
y	-12	-8	-4	0	4

71. $y = -x + 8$

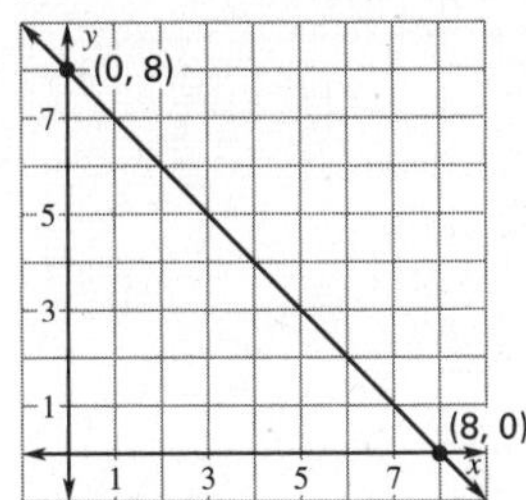

Sample table:

x	-2	-1	0	1	2
y	10	9	8	7	6

5.4 Maintaining Skills (p. 297)

72. $14.76 ≈ $15

73. $908.23 ≈ $908

74. $4,573.70 ≈ $4,574

75. $14,098.15 ≈ $14,098

76. $99.99 ≈ $100

77. $0.05 ≈ $0

78. $0.51 ≈ $1

79. $12,345.67 ≈ $12,346

Quiz 2 *(p. 297)*

1. $m = \dfrac{-2 - (-3)}{5 - 10} = \dfrac{1}{-5} = -\dfrac{1}{5}$

$$y - y_1 = m(x - x_1)$$
$$y - (-3) = -\frac{1}{5}(x - 10)$$
$$y + 3 = -\frac{1}{5}x + 2$$
$$y = -\frac{1}{5}x - 1$$

2. $m = \dfrac{5 - 2}{7 - 6} = \dfrac{3}{1} = 3$

$$y - y_1 = m(x - x_1)$$
$$y - 2 = 3(x - 6)$$
$$y - 2 = 3x - 18$$
$$y = 3x - 16$$

3. $m = \dfrac{4 - 4}{-7 - 4} = \dfrac{0}{-11} = 0$

$$y - y_1 = m(x - x_1)$$
$$y - 4 = 0(x - 4)$$
$$y - 4 = 0$$
$$y = 4$$

4. $m = \dfrac{-1 - 3}{1 - 0} = \dfrac{-4}{1} = -4;\ b = 3$

$$y = mx + b$$
$$y = -4x + 3$$

5. $m = \dfrac{0 - (-1)}{1 - (-2)} = \dfrac{1}{3}$

$$y - y_1 = m(x - x_1)$$
$$y - 0 = \frac{1}{3}(x - 1)$$
$$y = \frac{1}{3}x - \frac{1}{3}$$

6.
$$y = -3x + 9$$
$$3x + y = 9$$

7.
$$y = \frac{1}{2}x + 4$$
$$2y = x + 8$$
$$-x + 2y = 8$$

8.
$$y = \frac{2}{5}x - 1$$
$$5y = 2x - 5$$
$$-2x + 5y = -5$$

9.
$$y - y_1 = m(x - x_1)$$
$$y - 8 = 2(x - 6)$$
$$y - 8 = 2x - 12$$
$$y = 2x - 4$$
$$-2x + y = -4 \quad \text{or}$$
$$2x - y = 4$$

10.
$$y - y_1 = m(x - x_1)$$
$$y - 1 = -\frac{1}{2}(x - 4)$$
$$y - 1 = -\frac{1}{2}x + 2$$
$$y = -\frac{1}{2}x + 3$$
$$2y = -x + 6$$
$$x + 2y = 6$$

11.
$$y - y_1 = m(x - x_1)$$
$$y - 5 = \frac{2}{5}(x - 1)$$
$$y - 5 = \frac{2}{5}x - \frac{2}{5}$$
$$5y - 25 = 2x - 2$$
$$5y = 2x + 23$$
$$-2x + 5y = 23 \quad \text{or}$$
$$2x - 5y = -23$$

Copyright © McDougal Littell Inc.
All rights reserved.

12. $b = 2; m = \frac{\text{rise}}{\text{run}} = \frac{2}{1} = 2$

$y = mx + b$
$y = 2x + 2$
$-2x + y = 2$ or
$2x - y = -2$

13. $b = 1; m = \frac{\text{rise}}{\text{run}} = \frac{-1}{2}$

$y = mx + b$
$y = -\frac{1}{2}x + 1$
$2y = -x + 2$
$x + 2y = 2$

14. $y = 3$

Lesson 5.5

5.5 Checkpoint (p. 298–300)

1. one known point:
1994 is 1994 − 1985 = 9 years after 1985.
(9, 1300)
Slope = rate = 25
$y - y_1 = m(x - x_1)$
$y - 1300 = 25(x - 9)$
$y - 1300 = 25x - 225$
$y = 25x + 1075$ change x to t
$y = 25t + 1075$ where $t = 0$ represents 1985 and y is the attendance in millions.

2. 2005 is 2005 − 1985 = 20 years past 1985.
$y = 25t + 1075$
$y = 25(20) + 1075$ Substitute 20 for t.
$y = 1575$ million

3. Graph $y = 25t + 1075$

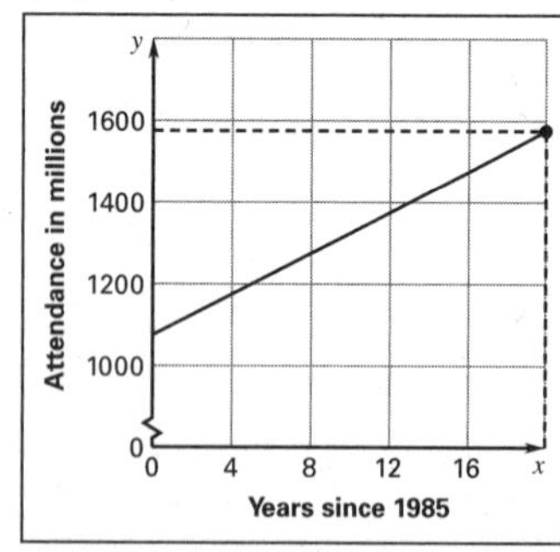

Sample answer: about 1600 million

4. Let x = amount of pounds in pasta salad.
Let y = amount of pounds of potato salad.
$4x + 5y = 60$

5.5 Guided Practice (p. 301)

1. linear model **2.** rate of change

3. y-intercept: 12.5 **(C)**
Slope: 1.5 = amount paid for each unit produced per hour

4. y-intercept: 100 **(A)**
Slope: −10 = the amount by which the amount owed decreases each week.

5. y-intercept: 20 **(B)**
Slope: 0.32 = the amount paid per day for each mile driven.

5.5 Practice and Applications (p. 301–303)

6. Slope: \$70,000 per year; 70,000
Known point: 1998 − 1990 = 8
(8, \$2,000,000)
$y - y_1 = m(x - x_1)$
$y - 2{,}000{,}000 = 70{,}000(x - 8)$
$y - 2{,}000{,}000 = 70{,}000x - 560{,}000$
$y = 70{,}000x + 1{,}440{,}000$

7. Slope: 124

8. y-intercept: 0

9. $y = mx + b$
$y = 124t + 0$
$y = 124t$

10. $y = 124t$
$y = 124(3) = 372$
(no, has not reached 400 ft)

11. $400 = 124t$
$3.22 \approx t$; about 3.2 hours

12. Slope: 28

13. y-intercept: 10

14. $y = mx + b$
$y = 28x + 10$

15.

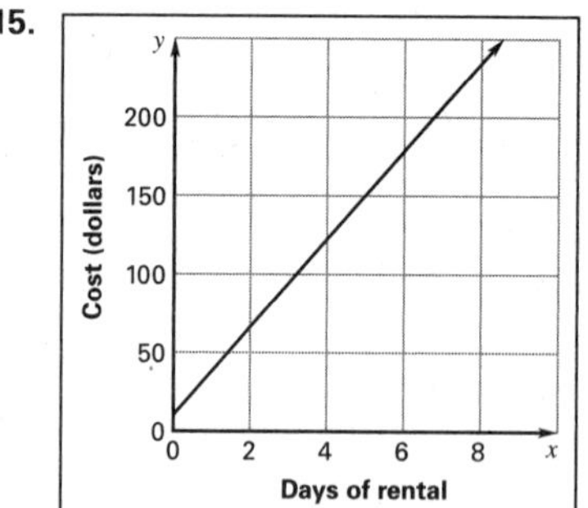

16. $y = 28x + 10$
$y = 28(3) + 10 = \$94.00$

17. $66 = 28x + 10$
$56 = 28x$
$2 = x$; 2 days

18. Slope: 2.2

19. 1995 is 1 year past 1994: (1, 48.9)

20. $y - y_1 = m(x - x_1)$
$C - 48.9 = 2.2(t - 1)$
$C - 48.9 = 2.2t - 2.2$
$C = 2.2t + 46.7$

Copyright © McDougal Littell Inc.
All rights reserved.

21. 2003 is 2003 − 1994 = 9 years past 1994.
$C = 2.2(9) + 46.7$
$C = 66.5;$ about 67 cents

22.

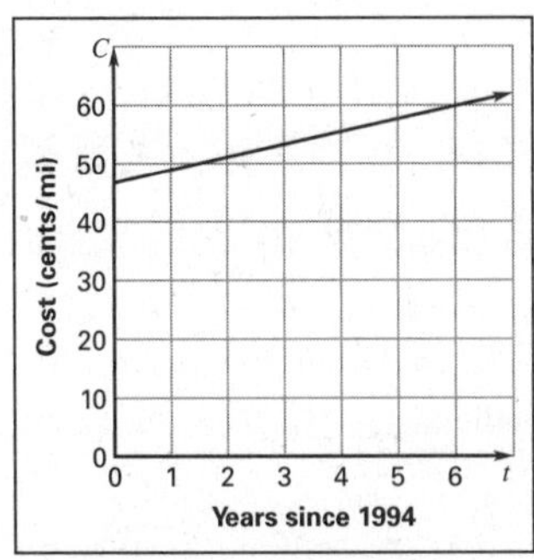

23. *Sample answer*: about 51 cents

24. Cost of student ticket = 5 (dollars);
Cost of a non-student ticket = 7 (dollars);
total cost = 315 (dollars).

25. $5x + 7y = 315$

26.

Number of student tickets, x	7	14	28	35	56	63
Number of non-student tickets, y	40	35	25	20	5	0

27. $2x + y = 102$

28. $y = -2x + 102$

29.

Number of field goals, x	20	25	30	35	40
Number of free throws, y	62	52	42	32	22

30.

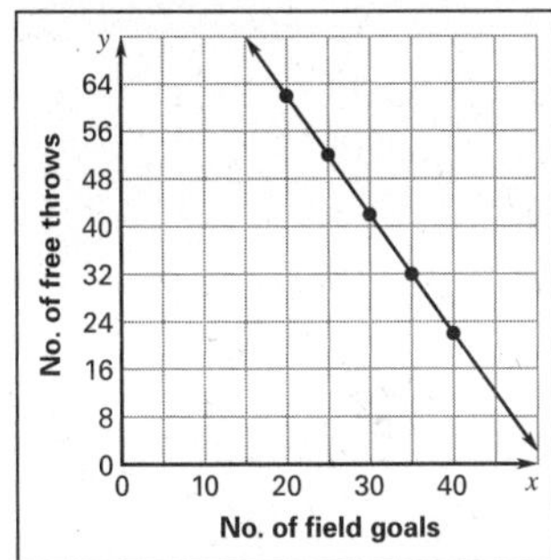

31. $2C + 1.25B = 10$

32.

Pounds of cauliflower, C	0	1	2	3	4	5
Pounds of broccoli, B	8	6.4	4.8	3.2	1.6	0

33. *Sample answer*: 4500 years

34. $y - \frac{6}{7}x + 285.7$

$y = \frac{6}{7}(5000) + 285.7$

$y \approx 4571$ years

5.5 Standardized Test Practice (p. 304)

35. **(B)** $10x + 5y = 30$

36. **(J)** $x + 2y = 84$

5.5 Mixed Review (p. 304)

37. $6 - 3 \cdot 2 = 6 - 6 = 0$

38. $12 \div 3 - 3 \cdot 1 = 4 - 3 = 1$

39. $4^2 - 6 \cdot (4 + 7) = 4^2 - 6 \cdot (11)$
$= 16 - 6 \cdot 11$
$= 16 - 66$
$= -50$

40. $5 \text{ days} \times \frac{24 \text{ hours}}{\text{day}} = 120$ hours

41. $36 \text{ inches} \times \frac{\text{foot}}{12 \text{ inches}} = 3$ feet

42. $12 \text{ years} \times \frac{12 \text{ months}}{1 \text{ year}} = 144$ months

43. $\frac{3}{7}$; *Sample answer*: The slope is the rise divided by the run of the ramp.

44. $y = mx + b$
$y = 0(x) + 7$
$y = 7$

45. $y = mx + b$
$y = -2x + 3$

46. $y = mx + b$
$y = \frac{1}{2}x + 0$
$y = \frac{1}{2}x$

47. $m = \frac{5 - (-3)}{6 - 0} = \frac{8}{6} = \frac{4}{3}$
$y - y_1 = m(x - x_1)$
$y - (-3) = \frac{4}{3}(x - 0)$
$y + 3 = \frac{4}{3}x$
$y = \frac{4}{3}x - 3$

48. $m = \frac{0 - 4}{-3 - 7} = \frac{-4}{-10} = \frac{2}{5}$
$y - y_1 = m(x - x_1)$
$y - 4 = \frac{2}{5}(x - 7)$
$y - 4 = \frac{2}{5}x - \frac{14}{5}$
$y = \frac{2}{5}x - \frac{14}{5} + \frac{20}{5}$
$y = \frac{2}{5}x + \frac{6}{5}$

Copyright © McDougal Littell Inc.
All rights reserved.

49. $m = \frac{2-2}{8-5} = \frac{0}{3} = 0$

$y - y_1 = m(x - x_1)$
$y - 2 = 0(x - 5)$
$y - 2 = 0$
$y = 2$

5.5 Maintaining Skills (p. 304)

50. $25\% = 0.25$

51. $0.3 > 3\% = 0.03$

52. $0.01 = 1\%$

53. $0.065 < 65\% = 0.65$

54. $12\% < 1.2 = 120\%$

55. $160\% = 1.6$

56. $0.017 < 17\% = 0.17$

57. $5\% = 0.05$

58. $0.889 < 89\% = 0.89$

5.6 Developing Concepts: Explore *(p. 305)*

3. $-\frac{3}{2}$

4. -1

Think About It *(p. 305)*

1. Slope of original line: $m = 1$
Slope of $\perp$ Line: $m = -1$
Product: $1 \cdot (-1) = -1$

2. Slope of original line: $m = -\frac{1}{2}$

Slope of $\perp$ Line: $m = 2$

Product: $-\frac{1}{2}(2) = -1$

3. Slope of original line:$m = \frac{3}{4}$

Slope of $\perp$ Line: $\frac{-4}{3}$

Product: $\frac{3}{4}\left(-\frac{4}{3}\right) = -1$

4. The product of the slopes of two perpendicular lines is always -1.

Lesson 5.6

5.6 Checkpoint (p. 306–308)

1. $y = 3x + 2; m = 3$
$y = -3x - 1; m = -3$
$3(-3) = -9 \neq -1;$ no

2. $y = \frac{3}{2}x + 1; m = \frac{3}{2}$

$y = -\frac{2}{3}x + 1; m = -\frac{2}{3}$

$\frac{3}{2} \cdot \left(-\frac{2}{3}\right) = -1;$ yes

3. $m = \frac{3-6}{1-3} = \frac{-3}{-2} = \frac{3}{2}$

$y - y_1 = m(x - x_1)$
$y - 3 = \frac{3}{2}(x - 1)$
$y - 3 = \frac{3}{2}x - \frac{3}{2}$
$y = \frac{3}{2}x + \frac{3}{2}$

product of slopes: $\frac{3}{2} \cdot \left(-\frac{2}{3}\right) = -1$,
so the lines are perpendicular.

4. $m = \frac{0-2}{0-1} = \frac{-2}{-1} = 2$

$y - y_1 = m(x - x_1)$
$y - 0 = 2(x - 0)$
$y = 2x$

product of slopes: $2\left(-\frac{1}{2}\right) = -1$,
so the lines are perpendicular.

5. the slope is -3,
$y - y_1 = m(x - x_1)$
$y - 4 = -3(x - 4)$
$y - 4 = -3x + 12$
$y = -3x + 16$

5.6 Guided Practice (p. 309)

1. right

2. $\frac{7}{5}$

3. $\frac{1}{5}(-5) = -1;$ yes

4. $-4\left(\frac{1}{4}\right) = -1;$ yes

5. $\frac{3}{8}\left(\frac{8}{3}\right) = 1 \neq -1;$ no

6. yes (Horizontal and vertical lines are perpendicular to each other.)

7. $m = \frac{6-0}{3-(-3)} = \frac{6}{6} = 1$

$y - y_1 = m(x - x_1)$
$y - 0 = 1(x - (-3))$
$y = x + 3$
$1(-1) = -1;$ lines are perpendicular

8. $m = \frac{2-(-4)}{-2-(-4)} = \frac{6}{2} = 3$

$y - y_1 = m(x - x_1)$
$y - (-4) = 3(x - (-4))$
$y + 4 = 3(x + 4)$
$y + 4 = 3x + 12$
$y = 3x + 8$

$3\left(-\frac{1}{3}\right) = -1;$ lines are perpendicular

Copyright © McDougal Littell Inc.
All rights reserved.

9. $m = 2$

$y - y_1 = m(x - x_1)$

$y - 2 = 2(x - 5)$

$y - 2 = 2x - 10$

$y = 2x - 8$

10. $m = \frac{1}{2}$

$y - y_1 = m(x - x_1)$

$y - 0 = \frac{1}{2}(x - 6)$

$y = \frac{1}{2}x - 3$

5.6 Practice and Applications (p. 309–311)

11. $1(1) = 1 \neq -1$; no

12. $-\frac{1}{3}(-3) = 1 \neq -1$; no

13. $\frac{1}{2}(-2) = -1$; yes

14. $\frac{3}{5}\left(-\frac{5}{3}\right) = -1$; yes

15. Change to slope-intercept form:

$4y = -7x - 16$

$y = -\frac{7}{4}x - 4$

$\frac{4}{7}\left(-\frac{7}{4}\right) = -1$; yes

16. yes (Horizontal and vertical lines are perpendicular.)

17. $y = -x - 2$; $y = x - 3$

$-1(1) = -1$; yes

18. $y = 2x + 2$; $y = -x$

$2(-1) = -2 \neq -1$; no

19. $y = -3$; $x = -2$; yes

20. $\frac{5 - (-1)}{8 - 5} = \frac{6}{3} = 2$

$y - y_1 = m(x - x_1)$

$y - 5 = 2(x - 8)$

$y - 5 = 2x - 16$

$y = 2x - 11$

$2\left(-\frac{1}{2}\right) = -1$; lines are perpendicular

21. $m = \frac{-2 - (-3)}{-2 - 1} = \frac{1}{-3}$

$y - y_1 = m(x - x_1)$

$y - (-2) = -\frac{1}{3}(x - (-2))$

$y + 2 = -\frac{1}{3}(x + 2)$

$y + 2 = -\frac{1}{3}x - \frac{2}{3}$

$y = -\frac{1}{3}x - \frac{2}{3} - \frac{6}{3}$

$y = -\frac{1}{3}x - \frac{8}{3}$

$\left(-\frac{1}{3}\right)(3) = -1$; lines are perpendicular

22. $m = \frac{0 - 6}{3 - (-3)} = \frac{-6}{6} = -1$

$y - y_1 = m(x - x_1)$

$y - 0 = -1(x - 3)$

$y = -x + 3$

$(-1)(1) = -1$; lines are perpendicular

23. $m = \frac{-7 - 5}{4 - 7} = \frac{-12}{-3} = 4$

$y - y_1 = m(x - x_1)$

$y - (-7) = 4(x - 4)$

$y + 7 = 4x - 16$

$y = 4x - 23$

$(4)\left(-\frac{1}{4}\right) = -1$; lines are perpendicular

24. $m = \frac{9 - 9}{9 - 1} = \frac{0}{8} = 0$

$y - 9 = 0(x - 1)$

$y - 9 = 0$

$y = 9$

lines are perpendicular (horizontal and vertical)

25. $m = \frac{0 - (-4)}{0 - (-6)} = \frac{4}{6} = \frac{2}{3}$

$y - y_1 = m(x - x_1)$

$y - 0 = \frac{2}{3}(x - 0)$

$y = \frac{2}{3}x$

$\frac{2}{3}\left(-\frac{3}{2}\right) = -1$; lines are perpendicular

26. $m = -\frac{1}{2}$

$y - y_1 = m(x - x_1)$

$y - 1 = -\frac{1}{2}(x - 1)$

$y - 1 = -\frac{1}{2}x + \frac{1}{2}$

$y = -\frac{1}{2}x + \frac{3}{2}$

Copyright © McDougal Littell Inc.
All rights reserved.

27. $m = -1$

$$y - y_1 = m(x - x_1)$$
$$y - (-3) = -1(x - 1)$$
$$y + 3 = -x + 1$$
$$y = -x - 2$$

28. $m = \frac{3}{2}$

$$y - y_1 = m(x - x_1)$$
$$y - 2 = \frac{3}{2}(x - 3)$$
$$y - 2 = \frac{3}{2}x - \frac{9}{2}$$
$$y = \frac{3}{2}x - \frac{5}{2}$$

29. $m = 1$

$$y - y_1 = m(x - x_1)$$
$$y - (-1) = 1(x - 0)$$
$$y + 1 = x$$
$$y = x - 1$$

30. $x = -2$

31. $m = -2$

$$y - y_1 = m(x - x_1)$$
$$y - (-1) = -2(x - 3)$$
$$y + 1 = -2x + 6$$
$$y = -2x + 5$$

32. $m = 2$

$$y - y_1 = m(x - x_1)$$
$$y - 6 = 2(x - 2)$$
$$y - 6 = 2x - 4$$
$$y = 2x + 2$$

33. $m = -\frac{8}{7}$

$$y - y_1 = m(x - x_1)$$
$$y - 3 = -\frac{8}{7}(x - 0)$$
$$y - 3 = -\frac{8}{7}x$$
$$y = -\frac{8}{7}x + 3$$

34. $m = 4$

$$y - y_1 = m(x - x_1)$$
$$y - 0 = 4(x - 0)$$
$$y = 4x$$

35. $x = -2$

36. $m = \frac{1}{2}$

$$y - y_1 = m(x - x_1)$$
$$y - (-1) = \frac{1}{2}(x - (-3))$$
$$y + 1 = \frac{1}{2}(x + 3)$$
$$y + 1 = \frac{1}{2}x + \frac{3}{2}$$
$$y = \frac{1}{2}x + \frac{1}{2}$$

37. $m = -\frac{3}{2}$

$$y - y_1 = m(x - x_1)$$
$$y - (-1) = -\frac{3}{2}(x - 2)$$
$$y + 1 = -\frac{3}{2}x + 3$$
$$y = -\frac{3}{2}x + 2$$

38. $m = -1$

$$y - y_1 = m(x - x_1)$$
$$y - 0 = -1(x - 5)$$
$$y = -x + 5$$

39. $m = \frac{1}{4}$

$$y - y_1 = m(x - x_1)$$
$$y - (-7) = \frac{1}{4}(x - (-4))$$
$$y + 7 = \frac{1}{4}(x + 4)$$
$$y + 7 = \frac{1}{4}x + 1$$
$$y = \frac{1}{4}x - 6$$

40. always

41. always

42. never

43. always

44. $y = 1$

45. old water pipe:

$$m = \frac{-1 - 3}{-3 - 0} = \frac{-4}{-3} = \frac{4}{3}$$
$$y - 3 = \frac{4}{3}(x - 0)$$
$$y - 3 = \frac{4}{3}x$$
$$y = \frac{4}{3}x + 3$$

new water pipe:

$$m = -\frac{3}{4}$$
$$y - 0 = -\frac{3}{4}(x - 2)$$
$$y = -\frac{3}{4}x + \frac{3}{2}$$

Copyright © McDougal Littell Inc.
All rights reserved.

46. $m = \frac{16 - 0}{0 - 12} = \frac{16}{-12} = -\frac{4}{3}$

$m = \frac{25 - 16}{12 - 0} = \frac{9}{12} = \frac{3}{4}$

$-\frac{4}{3}\left(\frac{3}{4}\right) = -1$; yes, a line through the first and second points is perpendicular to a line through the second and third points.

$m = \frac{25 - 0}{12 - 12} = \frac{25}{0}$; undefined

A line through the first and third points is neither parallel nor perpendicular to the other two lines.

5.6 Standardized Test Practice (p. 311)

47. p: $m = \frac{4 - 0}{6 - 4} = \frac{4}{2} = 2$

q: $m = \frac{4 - 4}{6 - 0} = \frac{0}{6} = 0$ (horizontal)

r: $m = \frac{0 - 4}{0 - 0}$; undefined (vertical)

(C) q and r are perpendicular

48. **(J)** $\frac{3}{2}\left(\frac{2}{3}\right) = 1 \neq -1$

5.6 Mixed Review (p. 312)

49. $2k - 8 - 8k = -6k - 8$

50. $-5c + 10 + 8c - 3 = 3c + 7$

51. $12x + 12y - 6x + 2 = 6x + 12y + 2$

52. $4x - 11 = -31$

$4x = -20$

$x = -5$

53. $5x - 7 + x = 19$

$6x - 7 = 19$

$6x = 26$

$x = \frac{26}{6} = \frac{13}{3}$

54. $2x - 6 = 20$

$2x = 26$

$x = \frac{26}{2} = 13$

55. horizontal

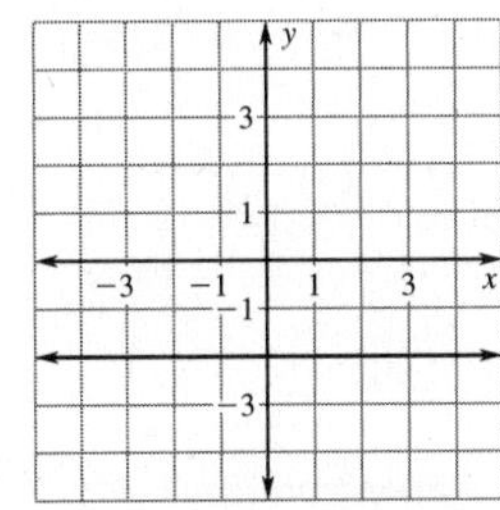

56. vertical

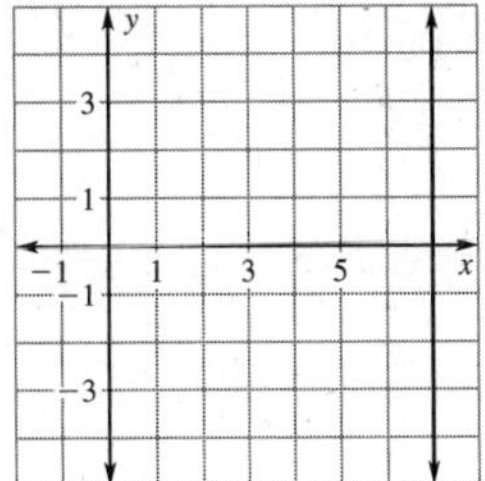

57. vertical

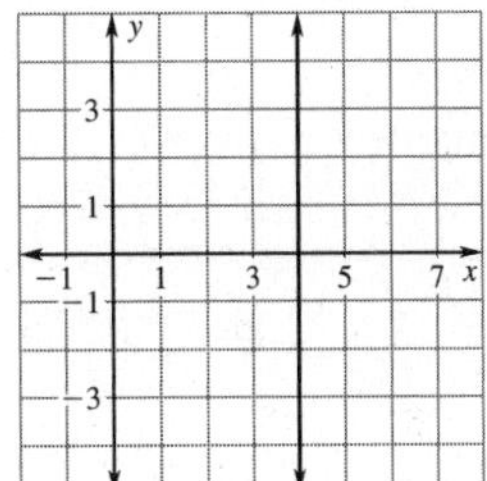

58. horizontal

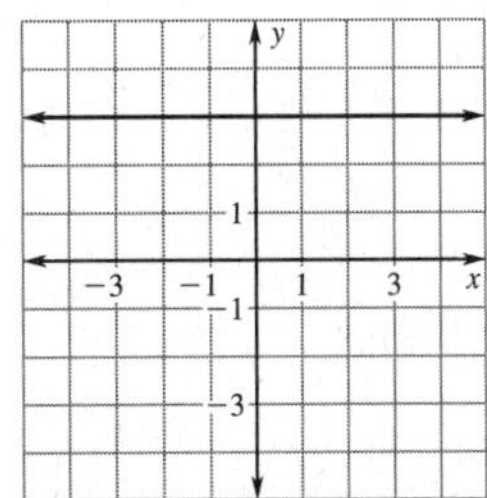

5.6 Maintaining Skills (p. 312)

59. $\frac{3}{5} \div \frac{6}{7} = \frac{3}{5} \cdot \frac{7}{6} = \frac{7}{10}$

60. $\frac{4}{5} \div \frac{3}{10} = \frac{4}{5} \cdot \frac{10}{3} = \frac{8}{3} = 2\frac{2}{3}$

61. $\frac{4}{9} \div \frac{2}{3} = \frac{4}{9} \cdot \frac{3}{2} = \frac{6}{9} = \frac{2}{3}$

62. $\frac{5}{8} \div \frac{7}{3} = \frac{5}{8} \cdot \frac{3}{7} = \frac{15}{56}$

63. $\frac{4}{9} \div \frac{9}{6} = \frac{4}{\cancel{9}_3} \cdot \frac{\cancel{6}^2}{9} = \frac{8}{27}$

64. $1\frac{4}{5} \div 2\frac{1}{2} = \frac{9}{5} \div \frac{5}{2} = \frac{9}{5} \cdot \frac{2}{5} = \frac{18}{25}$

65. $2\frac{1}{3} \div \frac{1}{3} = \frac{7}{3} \div \frac{1}{3} = \frac{7}{3} \cdot \frac{3}{1} = 7$

66. $1\frac{1}{8} \div \frac{5}{6} = \frac{9}{8} \cdot \frac{6}{5} = \frac{27}{20} = 1\frac{7}{20}$

67. $\frac{7}{8} \div \frac{13}{8} = \frac{7}{8} \cdot \frac{8}{13} = \frac{7}{13}$

68. $3\frac{3}{4} \div \frac{5}{4} = \frac{15}{4} \cdot \frac{4}{5} = 3$

Copyright © McDougal Littell Inc.
All rights reserved.

Chapter 5 *continued*

69. $\frac{2}{7} \div 3 = \frac{2}{7} \cdot \frac{1}{3} = \frac{2}{21}$

70. $5\frac{7}{10} \div 5 = \frac{57}{10} \cdot \frac{1}{5} = \frac{57}{50} = 1\frac{7}{50}$

Quiz 3 *(p. 312)*

1. $7x + 3y = 42$

2. $7x + 3y = 42$

$3y = -7x + 42$

$y = -\frac{7}{3}x + 14$

Number of touchdowns, x	0	3	6
Number of field goals, y	14	7	0

3.

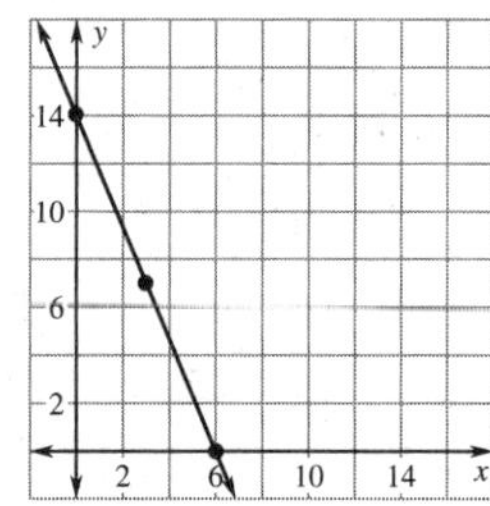

4. $\frac{1}{2}(-2) = -1$; yes

5. $1(-1) = -1$; yes

6. $m = \frac{1 - 6}{0 - 5} = \frac{-5}{-5} = 1$

$y - 6 = 1(x - 5)$

$y - 6 = x - 5$

$y = x + 1$

$(1)(-1) = -1$; lines are perpendicular

7. $m = \frac{-4 - 0}{0 - (-3)} = \frac{-4}{3} = -\frac{4}{3}$

$y - 0 = -\frac{4}{3}(x - (-3))$

$y = -\frac{4}{3}(x + 3)$

$y = -\frac{4}{3}x - 4$

$\left(-\frac{4}{3}\right)\left(\frac{3}{4}\right) = -1$; lines are perpendicular

8. $m = -2$

$y - 7 = -2(x - 2)$

$y - 7 = -2x + 4$

$y = -2x + 11$

Chapter 5 Summary and Review *(p. 313–316)*

1. $y = mx + b$

$y = 6x + (-4)$

$y = 6x - 4$

2. $y = mx + b$

$y = 1(x) + \frac{1}{2}$

$y = x + \frac{1}{2}$

3. $y = mx + b$

$y = -8x + 8$

4. $y = mx + b$

$y = 12x + \frac{5}{6}$

5. $y = mx + b$

$y = \frac{3}{2}x + 0$

$y = \frac{3}{2}x$

6. $y = mx + b$

$y = 0 \cdot x + 10$

$y = 10$

7. $b = -2$; $m = \frac{2}{1} = 2$

$y = 2x - 2$

8. $b = 1$; $m = -\frac{1}{2}$

$y = -\frac{1}{2}x + 1$

9. $b = -4$; $m = \frac{-1}{1} = -1$

$y = -x - 4$

10. $m = \frac{2}{1} = 2$

$y - 4 = 2(x - 1)$ point-slope form

$y - 4 = 2x - 2$

$y = 2x + 2$ slope-intercept form

11. $m = \frac{5}{2}$

$y - (-1) = \frac{5}{2}(x - (-3))$

$y + 1 = \frac{5}{2}(x + 3)$ point-slope form

$y + 1 = \frac{5}{2}x + \frac{15}{2}$

$y = \frac{5}{2}x + \frac{13}{2}$

12. $m = -\frac{3}{2}$

$y - 0 = -\frac{3}{2}(x - 2)$

$y = -\frac{3}{2}(x - 2)$ point-slope form

$y = -\frac{3}{2}x + 3$ slope-intercept form

Copyright © McDougal Littell Inc.
All rights reserved.

13. $m = 5$ (same slope)

$$y - 3 = 5(x - (-2))$$
$$y - 3 = 5(x + 2) \quad \text{or}$$
$$y - 3 = 5x + 10$$
$$y = 5x + 13$$

14. $m = \dfrac{-9 - 2}{4 - (-3)} = \dfrac{-11}{7}$

$$y - (-9) = -\frac{11}{7}(x - 4)$$
$$y + 9 = -\frac{11}{7}x + \frac{44}{7}$$
$$y = -\frac{11}{7}x + \frac{44}{7} - \frac{63}{7}$$
$$y = -\frac{11}{7}x - \frac{19}{7}$$

15. $m = \dfrac{-1 - 8}{-2 - 1} = \dfrac{-9}{-3} = 3$

$$y - 8 = 3(x - 1)$$
$$y - 8 = 3x - 3$$
$$y = 3x + 5$$

16. $m = \dfrac{2 - 5}{-8 - 2} = \dfrac{-3}{-10} = \dfrac{3}{10}$

$$y - 5 = \frac{3}{10}(x - 2)$$
$$y - 5 = \frac{3}{10}x - \frac{6}{10}$$
$$y = \frac{3}{10}x - \frac{3}{5} + \frac{25}{5}$$
$$y = \frac{3}{10}x + \frac{22}{5}$$

17. $m = \dfrac{-4 - 4}{2 - 1} = \dfrac{-8}{1} = -8$

$$y - 4 = -8(x - 1)$$
$$y - 4 = -8x + 8$$
$$y = -8x + 12$$

18. $m = \dfrac{8 - 8}{2 - 0} = \dfrac{0}{2} = 0$

$$y - 8 = 0(x - 0)$$
$$y - 8 = 0$$
$$y = 8$$

19. $m = \dfrac{16 - (-16)}{9 - (-9)} = \dfrac{32}{18} = \dfrac{16}{9}$

$$y - 16 = \frac{16}{9}(x - 9)$$
$$y - 16 = \frac{16}{9}x - 16$$
$$y = \frac{16}{9}x$$

20. $y - (-1) = 3(x - (-2))$

$$y + 1 = 3(x + 2)$$
$$y + 1 = 3x + 6$$
$$y = 3x + 5$$
$$-3x + y = 5 \quad \text{or}$$
$$3x - y = -5$$

21. $y - (-1) = 0(x - 6)$

$$y + 1 = 0$$
$$y = -1$$

22. $y - 3 = -4(x - 2)$

$$y - 3 = -4x + 8$$
$$y = -4x + 11$$
$$4x + y = 11$$

23. $y = 7; x = -1$

24. $y = 11; x = 9$

25. $y = -6; x = -8$

26. $m = \dfrac{10 - 0}{3 - (-1)} = \dfrac{10}{4} = \dfrac{5}{2}$

$$y - 0 = \frac{5}{2}(x - (-1))$$
$$y = \frac{5}{2}(x + 1)$$
$$y = \frac{5}{2}x + \frac{5}{2}$$
$$2y = 5x + 5$$
$$-5x + 2y = 5 \quad \text{or}$$
$$5x - 2y = -5$$

27. $m = \dfrac{7 - 5}{0 - 1} = \dfrac{2}{-1} = -2$

$$y - 7 = -2(x - 0)$$
$$y - 7 = -2x$$
$$y = -2x + 7$$
$$2x + y = 7$$

28. $m = \dfrac{-6 - 9}{-2 - 4} = \dfrac{-15}{-6} = \dfrac{5}{2}$

$$y - 9 = \frac{5}{2}(x - 4)$$
$$y - 9 = \frac{5}{2}x - 10$$
$$y = \frac{5}{2}x - 1$$
$$2y = 5x - 2$$
$$-5x + 2y = -2 \quad \text{or}$$
$$5x - 2y = 2$$

29. $P = 1{,}502{,}400 - 1200t$

$2006 - 1995 = 11$ (let $t = 11$)

$P = 1{,}502{,}400 - 1200(11)$

$P = \$1{,}489{,}200$

30. $6l + 4s = 36$

31.

Number of small posters, s	0	3	6	9
Number of large posters, l	6	4	2	0

32. $-\dfrac{7}{8}\left(-\dfrac{8}{7}\right) = 1 \neq -1$; no

Copyright © McDougal Littell Inc.
All rights reserved.

33. $5x + 10y = 3$

$10y = -5x + 3$

$y = -\frac{1}{2}x + \frac{3}{10}$

$-\frac{1}{2}(2) = -1$; yes

34. $m = -\frac{7}{5}$

$y - (-6) = -\frac{7}{5}(x - 4)$

$y + 6 = -\frac{7}{5}x + \frac{28}{5}$

$y = -\frac{7}{5}x + \frac{28}{5} - \frac{30}{5}$

$y = -\frac{7}{5}x - \frac{2}{5}$

35. $m = -2$

$y - 0 = -2(x - 0)$

$y = -2x$

36. $m = -\frac{1}{3}$

$y - 1 = -\frac{1}{3}(x - (-2))$

$y - 1 = -\frac{1}{3}(x + 2)$

$y - 1 = -\frac{1}{3}(x) + \left(-\frac{2}{3}\right)$

$y = -\frac{1}{3}x + \frac{1}{3}$

Chapter 5 Test *(p. 317)*

1. $y = 2x - 1$

2. $y = -\frac{1}{4}x + 3$

3. $y = 61x + 9$

4. $y = \frac{1}{4}x - 3$

5. $y = -3x + 3$

6. $y = 0 \cdot x + 4$

$y = 4$

7. $y - 6 = 2(x - 2)$

$y - 6 = 2x - 4$

$y = 2x + 2$

8. $y - (-9) = -5(x - 3)$

$y + 9 = 5 + 15$

$y = -5x + 6$

9. $y - (-6) = -3(x - (-5))$

$y + 6 = -3(x + 5)$

$y + 6 = -3x - 15$

$y = -3x - 21$

10. $y - 8 = -4(x - 1)$

$y - 8 = -4x + 4$

$y = -4x + 12$

11. $y - (-2) = \frac{1}{2}(x - 4)$

$y + 2 = \frac{1}{2}x - 2$

$y = \frac{1}{2}x - 4$

12. $y - (-5) = 8\left(x - \frac{1}{3}\right)$

$y + 5 = 8x - \frac{8}{3}$

$y = 8x - \frac{23}{3}$

13. $m = \frac{-1 - 2}{4 - (-3)} = \frac{-3}{7}$

$y - 2 = -\frac{3}{7}(x - (-3))$

$y - 2 = -\frac{3}{7}(x + 3)$

$y - 2 = -\frac{3}{7}x - \frac{9}{7}$

$y = -\frac{3}{7}x + \frac{5}{7}$

14. $m = \frac{-4 - 2}{8 - 6} = \frac{-6}{2} = -3$

$y - 2 = -3(x - 6)$

$y - 2 = -3x + 18$

$y = -3x + 20$

15. $m = \frac{4 - 5}{2 - (-2)} = \frac{-1}{4} = -\frac{1}{4}$

$y - 5 = -\frac{1}{4}(x - (-2))$

$y - 5 = -\frac{1}{4}x - \frac{1}{2}$

$y = -\frac{1}{4}x + \frac{9}{2}$

16. $m = \frac{0 - (-8)}{-1 - (-2)} = \frac{8}{1} = 8$

$y - 0 = 8(x - (-1))$

$y = 8(x + 1)$

$y = 8x + 8$

17. $m = \frac{4 - 2}{2 - (-5)} = \frac{2}{7}$

$y - 2 = \frac{2}{7}(x - (-5))$

$y - 2 = \frac{2}{7}(x + 5)$

$y - 2 = \frac{2}{7}x + \frac{10}{7}$

$y = \frac{2}{7}x + \frac{24}{7}$

Copyright © McDougal Littell Inc.
All rights reserved.

18. $m = \dfrac{-9 - (-1)}{1 - 9} = \dfrac{-8}{-8} = 1$

$y - (-9) = 1(x - 1)$
$y + 9 = x - 1$
$y = x - 10$

19. $-8y = 20 + \frac{2}{5}x$
$-40y = 100 + 2x$
$-2x - 40y = 100$ or
$2x + 40y = -100$

20. $5y = 25x$
$25x - 5y = 0$

21. $-2y + \frac{1}{2}x = 4$
$-4y + x = 8$
$x - 4y = 8$

22. $m = \frac{1}{5}$

$y - 5 = \frac{1}{5}(x - 3)$
$y - 5 = \frac{1}{5}x - \frac{3}{5}$
$y = \frac{1}{5}x + \frac{22}{5}$

23. $m = -1$
$y - (-2) = -1(x - (-2))$
$y + 2 = -x - 2$
$y = -x - 4$

24. $m = \frac{1}{3}$

$y - (-4) = \frac{1}{3}(x - 9)$
$y + 4 = \frac{1}{3}x - 3$
$y = \frac{1}{3}x - 7$

25. $m = -2$
$y - 0 = -2(x - 0)$
$y = -2x$

26. $m = \frac{3}{2}$

$y - 3 = \frac{3}{2}(x - (-7))$
$y - 3 = \frac{3}{2}(x + 7)$
$y - 3 = \frac{3}{2}x + \frac{21}{2}$
$y = \frac{3}{2}x + \frac{27}{2}$

27. $m = -4$
$y - 4 = -4(x - 4)$
$y - 4 = -4x + 16$
$y = -4x + 20$

28. $15x + 25y = 315$

29. $15x + 25y = 315$
$25y = -15x + 315$
$y = -\frac{3}{5}x + \frac{63}{5}$

Number of student tickets, x	1	6	11	16	21
Number of non-student tickets, y	12	9	6	3	0

30.

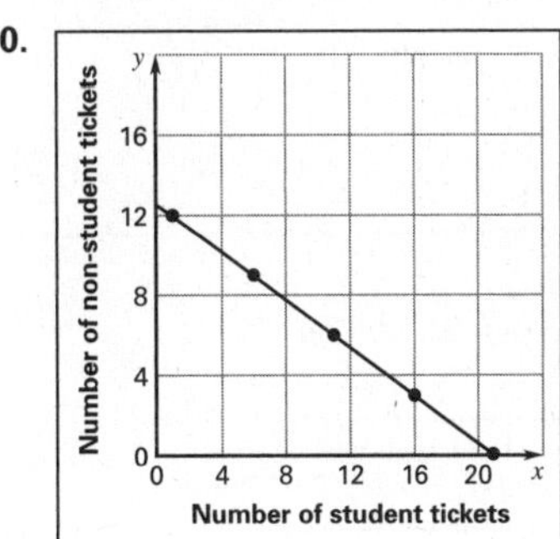

Chapter 5 Standardized Test *(p. 318)*

1. $y = 2x + \frac{2}{7}$ **(B)**

2. $y - (-5) = \frac{1}{2}(x - 4)$
$y + 5 = \frac{1}{2}x - 2$
$y = \frac{1}{2}x - 7$ **(D)**

3. $m = -2$ (same slope)
$y = -2x - \frac{3}{4}$ **(B)**

4. $m = \dfrac{4 - (-4)}{6 - 8} = \dfrac{8}{-2} = -4$
$y - 4 = -4(x - 6)$
$y - 4 = -4x + 24$
$y = -4x + 28$ **(B)**

5. (0, 5), (3, 0)
$m - \dfrac{5 - 0}{0 - 3} = \dfrac{5}{-3}$
$y - 5 = -\frac{5}{3}(x - 0)$
$y - 5 = -\frac{5}{3}x$
$y = -\frac{5}{3}x + 5$ **(C)**

6. **(D)** $-2x + y = -5$

Copyright © McDougal Littell Inc.
All rights reserved.

Chapter 5 *continued*

7. $y - 1 = -2(x - (-6))$
$y - 1 = -2(x + 6)$
$y - 1 = -2x - 12$
$y = -2x - 11$
$2x + y = -11$ **(C)**

8. $m = -\frac{1}{2}$

$y - 6 = -\frac{1}{2}(x + 5)$

$y - 6 = -\frac{1}{2}(x - (-5))$

$y - 6 = -\frac{1}{2}x - \frac{5}{2}$

$y = -\frac{1}{2}x + \frac{7}{2}$ **(D)**

Chapter 5 Maintaining Skills *(p. 319)*

1. −21 −14 −7 0 7 14 21 28

2.
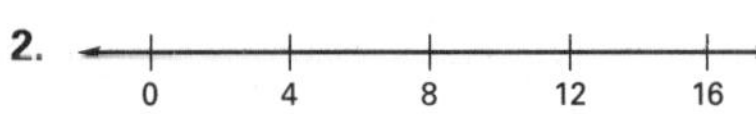

3.
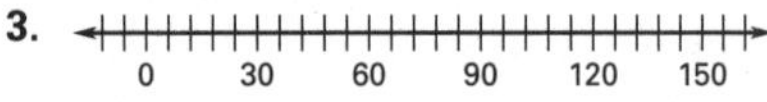

4.
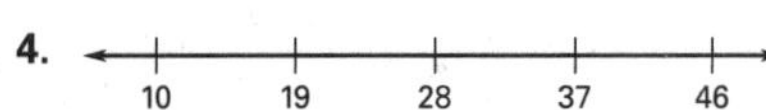

5. $0.033 < 0.0332$

6. $0.005 > 0.0045$

7. $0.0292 > 0.029$

8. $0.006 > 0.00576$

9. $0.01278 > 0.01$

10. $0.007 < 0.065$

11. $0.01 > 0.001$

12. $0.0005 < 0.003$

13. $0.0548 > 0.00549$

Copyright © McDougal Littell Inc.
All rights reserved.

CHAPTER 6

Chapter Opener *(p. 321)*

Think and Discuss (p. 321)

1. flute: 250-2300 hertz
   clarinet: 150-1800 hertz
   saxophone: 200-1350 hertz
2. flute

Chapter Readiness Quiz (p. 322)

1. C; $5a + 1 = 11$ is an "equality" (equation).
2. B;
$$\begin{aligned} 3x - 2 &\le 13 \\ 3(5) - 2 &\le 13 \\ 15 - 2 &\le 13 \\ 13 &\le 13 \end{aligned}$$
3. C;
$$\begin{aligned} 6x + 8 &= 36 + 2x \\ 6(7) + 8 &= 36 + 2(7) \\ 42 + 8 &= 36 + 14 \\ 50 &= 50 \end{aligned}$$
4. B; $y = x - 1$; $m = 1$, $b = -1$

Lesson 6.1

6.1 Checkpoint (pp. 323–325)

1. all real numbers greater than 1

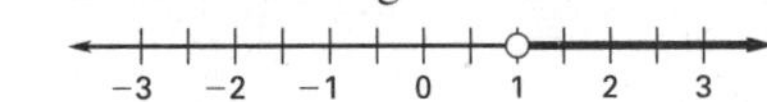

2. all real numbers greater than or equal to -1

3. all real numbers less than zero

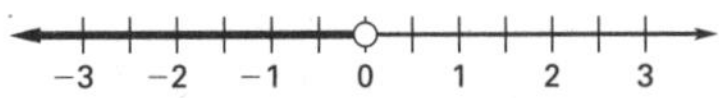

4. all real numbers less than or equal to 4

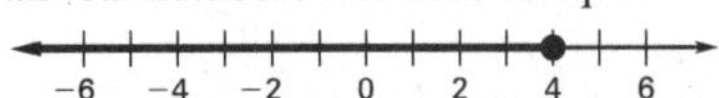

5.
$$\begin{aligned} x + 4 &< 7 && \text{Original inequality} \\ x + 4 - 4 &< 7 - 4 && \text{Subtract 4 from each side.} \\ x &< 3 && \text{Simplify.} \end{aligned}$$

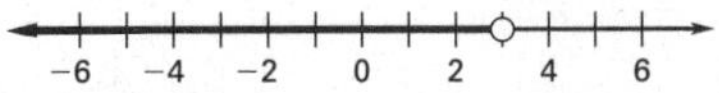

6.
$$\begin{aligned} n + 6 &\ge 2 && \text{Original inequality} \\ n + 6 - 6 &\ge 2 - 6 && \text{Subtract 6 from each side.} \\ n &\ge -4 && \text{Simplify.} \end{aligned}$$

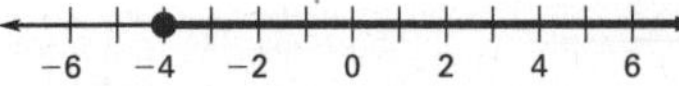

7.
$$\begin{aligned} 5 &> a + 5 && \text{Original inequality} \\ 5 - 5 &> a + 5 - 5 && \text{Subtract 5 from each side.} \\ 0 &> a \text{ or } a < 0 \end{aligned}$$

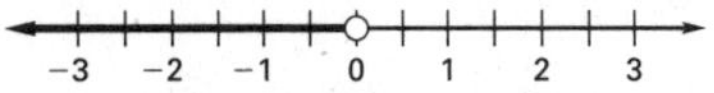

8.
$$\begin{aligned} x - 5 &\ge 2 && \text{Original inequality} \\ x - 5 + 5 &\ge 2 + 5 && \text{Add 5 to each side.} \\ x &\ge 7 && \text{Simplify.} \end{aligned}$$

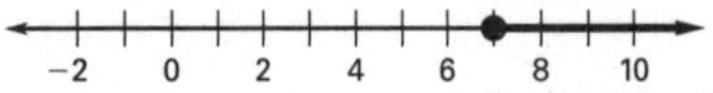

9.
$$\begin{aligned} p - 1 &\le -4 && \text{Original inequality} \\ p - 1 + 1 &\le -4 + 1 && \text{Add 1 to each side.} \\ p &\le -3 && \text{Simplify.} \end{aligned}$$

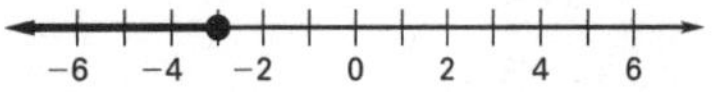

10.
$$\begin{aligned} -3 &< y - 2 && \text{Original inequality} \\ -3 + 2 &< y - 2 + 2 && \text{Add 2 to each side.} \\ -1 &< y && \text{Simplify.} \end{aligned}$$

11. $d \ge 8.8$

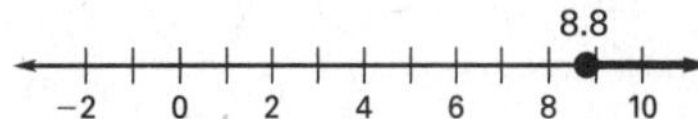

12. $d > 1600$

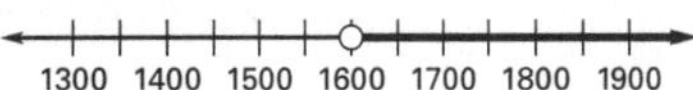

6.1 Guided Practice (p. 326)

1. It is a set of points on a number line representing all real numbers greater than or equal to a.
2. The solution to $x - 6 > 10$ is $x > 16$. It is the result of adding 6 to each side of the original inequality.
3. open
4. open
5. solid
6. open
7. solid
8. solid
9. left
10. right
11. left
12. left
13. $-6 > r - 5$ or $r - 5 < -6$; left
14. right

6.1 Practice and Applications (pp. 326–328)

15. all real numbers less than 8
16. all real numbers less than or equal to -3
17. all real numbers greater than or equal to 21
18. all real numbers greater than 0
19. 3 is greater than -3; a solution

Copyright © McDougal Littell Inc.
All rights reserved.

20. -3 is not greater than -3; not a solution

21. 0 is greater than -3; a solution

22. -1 is greater than -3; a solution

23. D | **24.** A

25. F | **26.** B

27. C | **28.** E

29. subtract 11 | **30.** add 2

31. subtract 6 | **32.** add 4

33. add 3 | **34.** subtract 17

35. $d + 4 \le 6; d \le 2$; D | **36.** $x - 3 > 2; x > 5$; C

37. $q + 12 \ge 4; q \ge -8$; B

38. $h + 6 \le -2; h \le -8$; F

39. $s - 5 \ge -5; s \ge 0$; A

40. $v - 3 < 2; v < 5$; E

41. $x + 6 < 8; x < 2$;

42. $-5 < 4 + f; -9 < f$ or $f > -9$;

43. $-4 + f < 20; f < 24$;

44. $8 + w \le -9; w \le -17$;

45. $p - 12 \ge -1; p \ge 11$;

46. $-2 > b - 5; 3 > b$ or $b < 3$;

47. $-8 \le x - 14; 6 \le x$ or $x \ge 6$;

48. $m + 7 \ge -10; m \ge -17$;

49. $-6 > c - 4; -2 > c$ or $c < -2$;

50. $-2 + z < 0; z < 2$;

51. $-10 > a - 6; -4 > a$ or $a < -4$;

52. $5 + r \ge -5; r \ge -10$;

53. $x - 5 \ge 7; x \ge 12$;

54. $14 \le 8 + n; 6 \le n$;

55. $c + 11 < 25; c < 14$;

56. a. $r > \frac{40}{7}$;

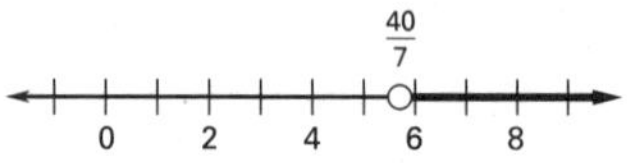

b. No; a human's capability to run at increasing speeds is limited to some finite amount.

57. rate $= \frac{5 \text{ km}}{45 \text{ min}} = \frac{1 \text{ km}}{9 \text{ min}}; r > \frac{1}{9}$

58. $p > -38.87$

59. $d > 16.3$;

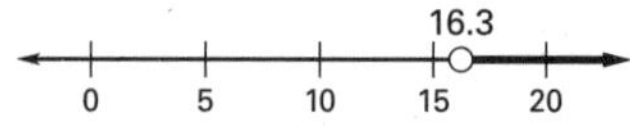

60. $w < 1324$;

61. Subtract 4 from each side.

$$x + 4 < 1$$
$$x + 4 - 4 < 1 - 4$$
$$x < -3$$

62. Add 10 to each side.

$$-9 \ge -10 + b$$
$$-9 + 10 \ge -10 + 10 + b$$
$$1 \ge b$$

6.1 Standardized Test Practice (p. 328)

63. C; The dot on its graph is solid.

64. F; 12 is not a solution.

$$-5 + t < 7$$
$$-5 + 12 \overset{?}{\le} 7$$
$$7 \not< 7$$

6.1 Mixed Review (p. 328)

65. $4x - 3 = 21$

$$4x = 24$$
$$x = 6$$

66. $-5x + 10 = 30$

$$-5x = 20$$
$$x = -4$$

Copyright © McDougal Littell Inc.
All rights reserved.

67. $-3s - 2 = -44$
$-3s = -42$
$s = 14$

68. $\frac{1}{3}x + 5 = -4$
$\frac{1}{3}x = -9$
$x = -27$

69. $\frac{1}{2}(a + 4) = 18$
$\frac{1}{2}a + 2 = 18$
$\frac{1}{2}a = 16$
$a = 32$

70. $\frac{3}{5}(x - 5) = 6$
$\frac{3}{5}x - 3 = 6$
$\frac{3}{5}x = 9$
$x = \frac{5}{3}(9) = 15$

71. $n + 2n + 5 = 14$
$3n + 5 = 14$
$3n = 9$
$n = 3$

72. $3(x - 6) = 12$
$3x - 18 = 12$
$3x = 30$
$x = 10$

73. $9 = -3(x - 2)$
$9 = -3x + 6$
$3 = -3x$
$-1 = x$

74. $d = rt$; Find r (rate) by solving the equation $d = rt$ for r.
$r = \frac{d}{t}$
Now substitute one of the ordered pairs from the table to find r.
$r = \frac{0.60}{5} = 0.12$
So the model is $d = 0.12t$.

75. $(1, 2), (4, -1)$;
$m = \frac{-1 - 2}{4 - 1} = \frac{-3}{3} = -1$;
$y - y_1 = m(x - x_1)$
$y - 2 = -1(x - 1)$
$y - 2 = -x + 1$
$y = -x + 3$

76. $(2, 0), (-4, -3)$;
$m = \frac{-3 - 0}{-4 - 2} = \frac{-3}{-6} = \frac{1}{2}$;
$y - y_1 = m(x - x_1)$
$y - 0 = \frac{1}{2}(x - 2)$
$y = \frac{1}{2}x - 1$

77. $(1, 1), (-3, 5)$;
$m = \frac{5 - 1}{-3 - 1} = \frac{4}{-4} = -1$;
$y - y_1 = m(x - x_1)$
$y - 1 = -1(x - 1)$
$y - 1 = -x + 1$
$y = -x + 2$

78. $(-1, 4), (2, 4)$;
$m = \frac{4 - 4}{2 - (-1)} = \frac{0}{3} = 0$;
$y - y_1 = m(x - x_1)$
$y - 4 = 0(x - (-1))$
$y - 4 = 0$
$y = 4$

79. $(-1, -3), (2, 3)$;
$m = \frac{3 - (-3)}{2 - (-1)} = \frac{6}{3} = 2$;
$y - y_1 = m(x - x_1)$
$y - (-3) = 2(x - (-1))$
$y + 3 = 2(x + 1)$
$y + 3 = 2x + 2$
$y = 2x - 1$

80. $(8, 1), (5, -2)$;
$m = \frac{-2 - 1}{5 - 8} = \frac{-3}{-3} = 1$;
$y - y_1 = m(x - x_1)$
$y - 1 = 1(x - 8)$
$y - 1 = x - 8$
$y = x - 7$

81. $(-2, 4), (4, 2)$;
$m = \frac{2 - 4}{4 - (-2)} = \frac{-2}{6} = -\frac{1}{3}$;
$y - y_1 = m(x - x_1)$
$y - 4 = -\frac{1}{3}(x - (-2))$
$y - 4 = -\frac{1}{3}(x + 2)$
$y - 4 = -\frac{1}{3}x - \frac{2}{3}$
$y = -\frac{1}{3}x - \frac{2}{3} + \frac{12}{3}$
$y = -\frac{1}{3}x + \frac{10}{3}$

Copyright © McDougal Littell Inc.
All rights reserved.

Chapter 6 *continued*

82. $(1, -5), (6, 5);$

$$m = \frac{5 - (-5)}{6 - 1} = \frac{10}{5} = 2;$$

$$\begin{aligned} y - y_1 &= m(x - x_1) \\ y - (-5) &= 2(x - 1) \\ y + 5 &= 2x - 2 \\ y &= 2x - 7 \end{aligned}$$

83. $(-3, 6), (2, 8);$

$$m = \frac{8 - 6}{2 - (-3)} = \frac{2}{5};$$

$$\begin{aligned} y - y_1 &= m(x - x_1) \\ y - 8 &= \frac{2}{5}(x - 2) \\ y - 8 &= \frac{2}{5}x - \frac{4}{5} \\ y &= \frac{2}{5}x - \frac{4}{5} + \frac{40}{5} \\ y &= \frac{2}{5}x + \frac{36}{5} \end{aligned}$$

6.1 Maintaining Skills (p. 328)

84. $\frac{4}{5}, \frac{5}{4}$

85. $-\frac{1}{3}, -3$

86. $\frac{24}{25}, \frac{25}{24}$

87. $-\frac{7}{32}, -\frac{32}{7}$

88. $\frac{2}{5}, \frac{5}{2}$

89. $-\frac{8}{15}, -\frac{15}{8}$

90. $3, \frac{1}{3}$

91. $-1, -1$

92. $4, \frac{1}{4}$

93. $9, \frac{1}{9}$

94. $-\frac{8}{11}, -\frac{11}{8}$

95. $\frac{5}{8}, \frac{8}{5}$

Lesson 6.2

6.2 Developing Concepts: Think About It (p. 329)

1. $4 < 9$ Original inequality
$4 + 7 \overset{?}{<} 9$ Add 7 to each side.
$11 < 16$ Simplify.
No; do not reverse the inequality when adding 7.

2. $15 > 12$ Original inequality
$15 - (-5) \overset{?}{>} 12 - (-5)$ Subtract -5 from each side.
$20 > 17$ Simplify.

No; do not reverse the inequality when subtracting -5.

3. $4 > -3$ Original inequality
$5(4) \overset{?}{>} 5(-3)$ Multiply each side by 5.
$20 > -15$ Simplify.

No; do not reverse the inequality when multiplying by 5.

4. $1 < 8$ Original inequality
$-10(1) \overset{?}{<} -10(8)$ Multiply each side by -10.
$-10 \not< -80$ Simplify.

Yes; reverse the inequality when multiplying by -10.

5. $-6 < 2$ Original inequality
$\frac{-6}{-3} \overset{?}{<} \frac{2}{-3}$ Divide each side by -3.
$2 \not< -\frac{2}{3}$ Simplify.

Yes; reverse the inequality when dividing by -3.

6. $0 < 8$ Original inequality
$\frac{0}{2} \overset{?}{<} \frac{8}{2}$ Divide each side by 2.
$0 < 4$ Simplify.

No; do not reverse the inequality when dividing by 2.

7.

	a positive number	*a negative number*
Add	no	no
Subtract	no	no
Multiply by	no	yes
Divide by	no	yes

6.2 Checkpoint (pp. 331–332)

1. $\frac{k}{4} < \frac{1}{2}$ Original inequality
$4\left(\frac{k}{4}\right) < 4\left(\frac{1}{2}\right)$ Multiply each side by 4.
$k < 2$ Simplify.

2. $18 \le 2k$ Original inequality
$\frac{18}{2} \le \frac{2k}{2}$ Divide each side by 2.
$9 \le k$ Simplify.

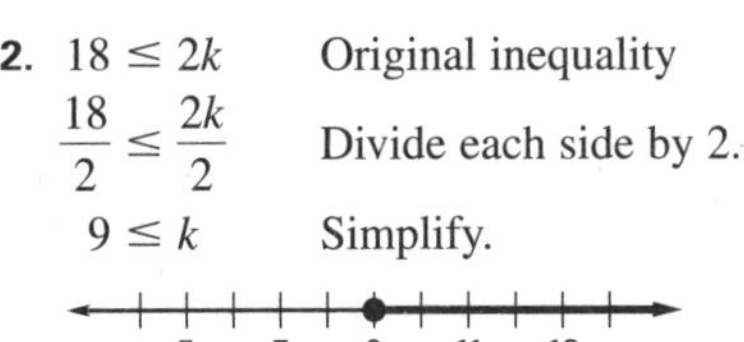

3. $6 < \frac{t}{5}$ Original inequality
$(5)(6) < 5\left(\frac{t}{5}\right)$ Multiply each side by 5.
$30 < t$ Simplify.

4. $-21 < 3y$ Original inequality
$\frac{-21}{3} < \frac{3y}{3}$ Divide each side by 3.
$-7 < y$ Simplify.

Copyright © McDougal Littell Inc.
All rights reserved.

5. $-\frac{1}{5}p > 1$ Original inequality

$-5\left(-\frac{1}{5}p\right) < -5(1)$ Multiply each side by -5 and reverse the inequality.

$p < -5$ Simplify.

6. $-\frac{2}{3}x < -5$ Original inequality

$-\frac{3}{2}\left(-\frac{2}{3}x\right) > -\frac{3}{2}(-5)$ Multiply each side by the reciprocal, $-\frac{3}{2}$, and reverse the inequality.

$1x > \frac{15}{2}$

$x > 7.5$ Simplify.

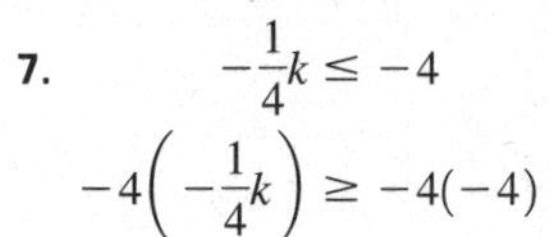

7. $-\frac{1}{4}k \leq -4$ Original inequality

$-4\left(-\frac{1}{4}k\right) \geq -4(-4)$ Multiply each side by -4 and reverse the inequality.

$k \geq 16$ Simplify.

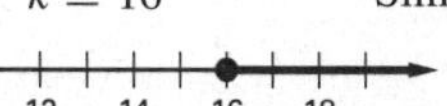

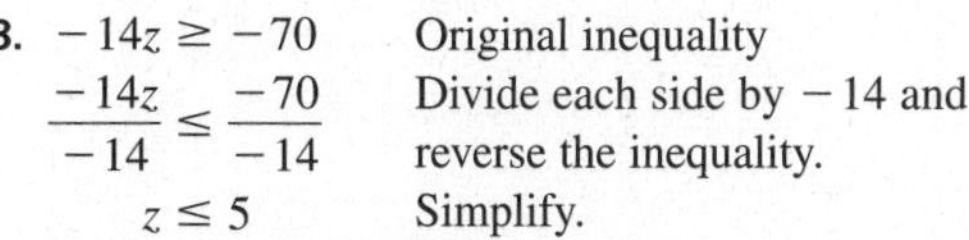

8. $-14z \geq -70$ Original inequality

$\frac{-14z}{-14} \leq \frac{-70}{-14}$ Divide each side by -14 and reverse the inequality.

$z \leq 5$ Simplify.

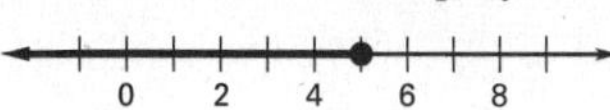

9. $-24 \leq 6t$ Original inequality

$\frac{-24}{6} \leq \frac{6t}{6}$ Divide each side by 6.

$-4 \leq t$ Simplify.

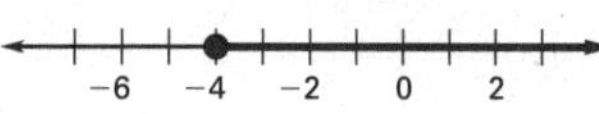

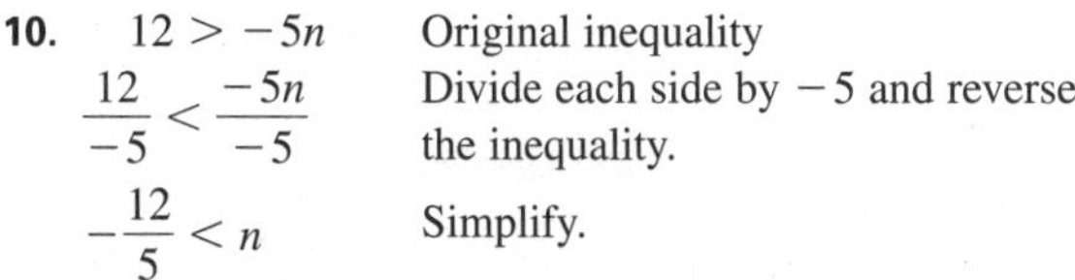

10. $12 > -5n$ Original inequality

$\frac{12}{-5} < \frac{-5n}{-5}$ Divide each side by -5 and reverse the inequality.

$-\frac{12}{5} < n$ Simplify.

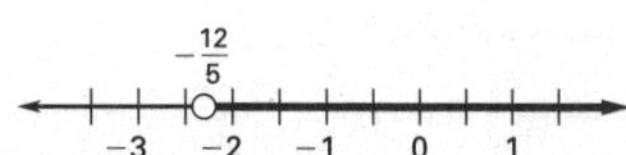

6.2 Guided Practice (p. 333)

1. *Sample answer:* To "reverse the inequality" means to change the direction of the inequality sign. For example, a "greater-than" sign would become a "less-than" sign.
2. No; $-x < 2$ is the same as $2 > -x$.
3. Multiply by 5; do not reverse
4. Multiply by 2; do not reverse
5. Divide by 4; do not reverse
6. Divide by 8; do not reverse
7. Multiply by -6; reverse
8. Multiply by -1; reverse
9. $-k \geq 42$
   $-1(-k) \leq -1(42)$
   $k \leq -42$
   This is not equivalent to $k \geq -42$. When multiplying each side by -1, the inequality is reversed.
10. $-\frac{2}{3} \leq -g$
    $-1\left(-\frac{2}{3}\right) \geq -1(-g)$
    $\frac{2}{3} \geq g$
    This is equivalent to $g \leq \frac{2}{3}$.
11. $4 > -\frac{1}{7}c$
    $-7(4) < -7\left(-\frac{1}{7}\right)c$
    $-28 < c$
    This is equivalent to $c > -28$.
12. $5z < -75$
    $\frac{5z}{5} < \frac{-75}{5}$
    $z < -15$
    This is not equivalent to $z > -15$. When dividing each side by 5, the inequality is not reversed.
13. $-11x \geq 33$
    $\frac{-11x}{-11} \leq \frac{33}{-11}$
    $x \leq -3$
    This is not equivalent to $x \geq -3$. When dividing each side by -11, the inequality is reversed.
14. $-\frac{w}{3} \leq -5$
    $-3\left(-\frac{w}{3}\right) \geq -3(-5)$
    $w \geq 15$
    This is equivalent to $w \geq 15$.

6.2 Practice and Applications (pp. 333–335)

15. Multiply by 3; do not reverse
16. Divide by 9; do not reverse
17. Multiply by 2; do not reverse
18. Divide by 2; do not reverse
19. Divide by -7; reverse
20. Multiply by -3; reverse
21. Divide by -3; reverse
22. Multiply by -6; reverse

Copyright © McDougal Littell Inc.
All rights reserved.

23. $-\frac{z}{6} \le -1$

$-6\left(-\frac{z}{6}\right) \ge -6(-1)$

$z \ge 6$

The graph of this solution is shown.

24. $-\frac{1}{3}z \le 2$

$-3\left(-\frac{1}{3}z\right) \ge -3(2)$

$z \ge -6$

The graph of this solution is not shown.

25. $5z \ge 30$

$\frac{5z}{5} \ge \frac{30}{5}$

$z \ge 6$

The graph of this solution is shown.

26. $2z \ge 12$

$\frac{2z}{2} \ge \frac{12}{2}$

$z \ge 6$

The graph of this solution is shown.

27. $12y > -24$

$\frac{12y}{12} > \frac{-24}{12}$

$y > -2$

$y > -2$ is not equivalent to $y < -2$. The inequality is not reversed when dividing by 12.

28. $-\frac{1}{8}m \ge -3$

$-8\left(-\frac{1}{8}m\right) \le -8(-3)$

$m \le 24$

$m \le 24$ is not equivalent to $m \ge 24$. When multiplying by -8, the inequality is reversed.

29. $15 < -b$

$-1(15) > -1(-b)$

$-15 > b$

equivalent

30. $\frac{1}{3}n < 3(-2)$

$3\left(\frac{1}{3}n\right) < 3(-2)$

$n < -6$

$n < -6$ is not equivalent to $n > -6$. When multiplying by 3, the inequality is not reversed.

31. $8 \le -\frac{1}{2}m$

$-2(8) \ge -2\left(-\frac{1}{2}m\right)$

$-16 \ge m$

equivalent

32. $20b \ge -2$

$\frac{20b}{20} \ge -\frac{2}{20}$

$b \ge -\frac{1}{10}$

$b \ge -\frac{1}{10}$ is not equivalent to $b \le -\frac{1}{10}$. When dividing by 20, the inequality is not reversed.

33. Reverse the inequality sign when dividing by -3; $x \le -5$

34. $0(-2) = 0$; $x \ge 0$

35. $15p < 60$

$\frac{15p}{15} < \frac{60}{15}$

$p < 4$

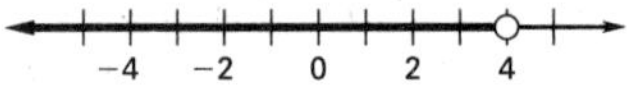

36. $6k > -120$

$\frac{6k}{6} > \frac{-120}{6}$

$k > -20$

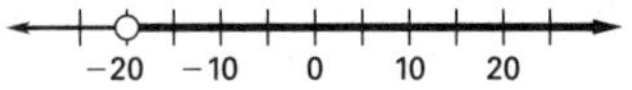

37. $\frac{2}{3}j \le -12$

$\frac{3}{2}\left(\frac{2}{3}j\right) \le \frac{3}{2}(-12)$

$j \le -18$

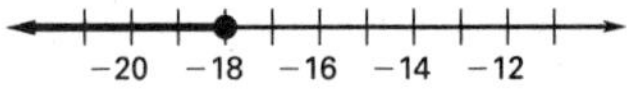

38. $-a > -100$

$-1(-a) < -1(-100)$

$a < 100$

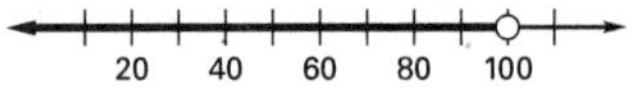

39. $-\frac{1}{5}n < 12$

$-5\left(-\frac{1}{5}n\right) > -5(12)$

$n > -60$

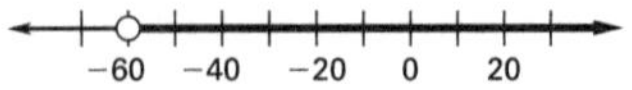

40. $20y \ge 50$

$\frac{20y}{20} \ge \frac{50}{20}$

$y \ge \frac{5}{2}$ or 2.5

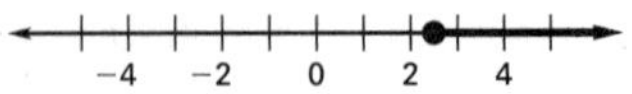

Copyright © McDougal Littell Inc.
All rights reserved.

41. $11 \geq -\frac{1}{3}m$

$-3(11) \leq -3\left(-\frac{1}{3}m\right)$

$-33 \leq m$ or $m \geq -33$

−34 −32 −30 −28 −26

42. $-18x \geq 9$

$-\frac{1}{18}(-18x) \leq -\frac{1}{18}(9)$

$x \leq -\frac{1}{2}$

−2 −1 0 1 2

43. $-\frac{a}{10} \leq -2$

$-10\left(-\frac{a}{10}\right) \geq -10(-2)$

$a \geq 20$

−10 0 10 20 30

44. $\frac{3}{4}z \geq 24$

$\frac{4}{3}\left(\frac{3}{4}z\right) \geq \frac{4}{3}(24)$

$z \geq 32$

26 28 30 32 34

45. $-12r \geq -18$

$\frac{-12r}{-12} \leq \frac{-18}{-12}$

$r \leq \frac{3}{2}$

−2 −1 0 1 2

46. $-4f \leq 14$

$\frac{-4f}{-4} \geq \frac{14}{-4}$

$f \geq -\frac{7}{2}$ or -3.5

−4 −2 0 2 4

47. $10 > 1.999d$

$10 > 2d$

$5 > d$

Round 1.999 to 2.

48. $\frac{1}{2}r \leq -50.1155$

$\frac{1}{2}r \leq -50$

$r \leq -100$

Round −50.1155 to −50.

49. $-\frac{1}{3}a \geq 5.91$

$-\frac{1}{3}a \geq 6$

$-3\left(-\frac{1}{3}a\right) \leq -3(6)$

$a \leq -18$

Round 5.91 to 6.

50. sometimes;
If x is 3, then $k(3)$ is positive.
If x is -2, then $k(-2)$ is negative.
If x is 0, then $k(0)$ is zero.

51. always

52. sometimes;
If x is -2, then $k(-2)$ is positive.
If x is 3, then $k(3)$ is negative.
If x is 0, then $k(0)$ is zero.

53. never

54. $5p \leq 25$
$p \leq 5$; 5 or less posters

55. $20n \geq 25{,}000$
$n \geq 1250$ tickets

56. $5l > 75$
$l > 15$
If Aisha takes more than 15 lessons, she should buy skates.

57. $0.85r < 27.00$
$r < 31.76$; 31 rides or less

58. $\frac{4}{x} \geq 2$;

Case 1: If x is greater than zero (positive)

$x\left(\frac{4}{x}\right) \geq x(2)$

$4 \geq 2x$

$\frac{4}{2} \geq \frac{2x}{2}$

$2 \geq x$ or $x \leq 2$

Case 2: If x is less than zero (negative)

$x\left(\frac{4}{x}\right) \leq x(2)$

$4 \leq 2x$

$\frac{4}{2} \leq \frac{2x}{2}$

$2 \leq x$ or $x \geq 2$

This is never true when x is a negative number.
Case 3: If $x = 0$, then the inequality is undefined.
There are no values of x to make Case 2 true; to satisfy Case 1, $x \leq 2$ and $x > 0$; and to satisfy Case 3, $x \neq 0$. We conclude $0 < x \leq 2$ (x must be greater than zero, but less than or equal to 2).

Copyright © McDougal Littell Inc.
All rights reserved.

6.2 Standardized Test Practice (p. 335)

59. A;
$3x \geq 9$
$x \geq 3$

60. F;
$3 \geq -k$
$-3 \leq k$ is not equivalent to $k \leq -3$

61. D;
$-5x \leq -10$
$x \geq 2$

6.2 Mixed Review (p. 335)

62. $12 - 19 = -7$

63. $-6 - 8 = -14$

64. $3 - (-1) = 3 + 1 = 4$

65. $-7 - (-7) = -7 + 7 = 0$

66. $-9 - 9 = -18$

67. $0 - (-2) = 0 + 2 = 2$

68. $52 \div (-26) = -2$

69. $-8 \div 2 = -4$

70. $-10 \div (-2) = 5$

71. $-3 \div \frac{1}{9} = -3 \cdot 9 = -27$

72. $23 \div \left(-\frac{1}{2}\right) = 23 \cdot (-2) = -46$

73. $-15 \div \left(-1\frac{2}{3}\right) = -15 \div \left(-\frac{5}{3}\right)$
$= -15 \cdot \left(-\frac{3}{5}\right)$
$= 9$

74. $2(x + 5) = 5(x - 1)$
$2x + 10 = 5x - 5$
$2x = 5x - 15$
$-3x = -15$
$x = 5$
Check:
$2(x + 5) = 5(x - 1)$
$2(5 + 5) \stackrel{?}{=} 5(5 - 1)$
$2(10) \stackrel{?}{=} 5(4)$
$20 = 20$

75. $-4(y + 3) = -(6 - 2y)$
$-4y - 12 = -6 + 2y$
$-12 = -6 + 6y$
$-6 = 6y$
$-1 = y$
Check:
$-4(y + 3) = -(6 - 2y)$
$-4(-1 + 3) \stackrel{?}{=} -[6 - 2(-1)]$
$-4(2) \stackrel{?}{=} -[6 - (-2)]$
$-8 \stackrel{?}{=} -[6 + 2]$
$-8 = -8$

76. $8 - (c + 7) = 6(11 - c)$
$8 - c - 7 = 66 - 6c$
$1 - c = 66 - 6c$
$1 - c + c = 66 - 6c + c$
$1 = 66 - 5c$
$-65 = -5c$
$13 = c$
Check:
$8 - (c + 7) = 6(11 - c)$
$8 - (13 + 7) \stackrel{?}{=} 6(11 - 13)$
$8 - (20) \stackrel{?}{=} 6(-2)$
$-12 = -12$

77. $3(-x - 2) = 2x + 2(4 + x)$
$-3x - 6 = 2x + 8 + 2x$
$-3x - 6 = 4x + 8$
$-6 = 7x + 8$
$-14 = 7x$
$-2 = x$
Check:
$3(-x - 2) = 2x + 2(4 + x)$
$3[-(-2) - 2] \stackrel{?}{=} 2(-2) + 2[(4 + (-2)]$
$3[2 - 2] \stackrel{?}{=} -4 + 2[2]$
$3[0] \stackrel{?}{=} -4 + 4$
$0 = 0$

78. $d = \frac{m}{v}; dv = m$

79. $A = \frac{1}{2}bh; 2A = bh; \frac{2A}{h} = b$

80. $P = a + b + c; P - a - b = c$

81. $A(4, -2), B(2, 1), C(-3, -3), D(0, 0)$

6.2 Maintaining Skills (p. 335)

82. 98: 1, 2, 7, 14, 49, 98

83. 140: 1, 2, 4, 5, 7, 10, 14, 20, 28, 35, 70, 140

84. 114: 1, 2, 3, 6, 19, 38, 57, 114

85. 144: 1, 2, 3, 4, 6, 8, 9, 12, 16, 18, 24, 36, 48, 72, 144

86. 289: 1, 17, 289

87. 425: 1, 5, 17, 25, 85, 425

88. 1064: 1, 2, 4, 7, 8, 14, 19, 28, 38, 56, 76, 133, 152, 266, 532, 1064

89. 2223: 1, 3, 9, 13, 19, 39, 57, 117, 171, 247, 741, 2223

90. 5480: 1, 2, 4, 5, 8, 10, 20, 40, 137, 274, 548, 685, 1096, 1370, 2740, 5480

Copyright © McDougal Littell Inc.
All rights reserved.

Lesson 6.3

6.3 Checkpoint (pp. 336–338)

1. $3x - 5 > 4$ Original inequality
$3x > 9$ Add 5 to each side.
$x > 3$ Divide each side by 3.

2. $10 - n \leq 5$ Original inequality
$-n \leq -5$ Subtract 10 from each side.
$n \geq 5$ Multiply each side by -1 and reverse the inequality.

3. $3(n - 4) \geq 6$ Original inequality
$3n - 12 \geq 6$ Use distributive property.
$3n \geq 18$ Add 12 to each side.
$n \geq 6$ Divide each side by 3.

4. $-2(x + 1) < 2$ Original inequality
$-2x - 2 < 2$ Use distributive property.
$-2x < 4$ Add 2 to each side.
$x > -2$ Divide each side by -2 and reverse the inequality.

5. $5n - 21 < 8n$ Original inequality
$-21 < 3n$ Subtract $5n$ from each side.
$-7 < n$ or $n > -7$ Divide each side by 3.

6. $-3z + 15 > 2z$ Original inequality
$15 > 5z$ Add $3z$ to each side.
$3 > z$ or $z < 3$ Divide each side by 5.

7. $x + 3 \geq 2x - 4$ Original inequality
$3 \geq x - 4$ Subtract x from each side.
$7 \geq x$ or $x \leq 7$ Add 4 to each side.

8. $4y - 3 < -y + 12$ Original inequality
$5y - 3 < 12$ Add y to each side.
$5y < 15$ Add 3 to each side.
$y < 3$ Divide each side by 5.

9. **a.** $2x$

b. $0.50x$ or $0.5x$

c. $0.5x + 12$

d. income − cost = profit
$2x - (0.5x + 12) = 2x - 0.5x - 12 = 1.5x - 12$

10. $1.5x - 12 \geq 300$
$1.5x \geq 312$
$x \geq 208$
You must sell at least 208 candles.

6.3 Guided Practice (p. 339)

1. One must first subtract 6 and then divide by 3 to solve the inequality.

2. Subtract 2 and divide by -3, reversing the inequality, to isolate the variable y.

3. $d + 2 > -1$ not multi-step; subtract 2 from each side.

4. $\frac{3}{4}a < 0$ not multi-step; multiply each side by the reciprocal $\frac{4}{3}$.

5. $-4x \geq -12$ not multi-step; divide each side by -4 and reverse the inequality.

6. $4y - 3 < 13$ multi-step; add 3 to each side then divide each side by 4.

7. $5x + 12 \leq 62$ multi-step; subtract 12 from each side then divide each side by 5.

8. $10 - c \geq 6$ multi-step; subtract 10 from each side then multiply each side by -1 and reverse the inequality.

9. $\frac{1}{2}b + 2 > 6$ multi-step; subtract 2 from each side then multiply each side by 2.

10. $3m + 2 \leq 7m$ multi-step; subtract $3m$ from each side then divide each side by 4.

11. $2w - 1 > 6w + 2$ multi-step; subtract $2w$ from each side, subtract 2 from each side, then divide each side by 4.

6.3 Practice and Applications (pp. 339–341)

12. $4x - 3 \geq 21$
$4x - 3 + 3 \geq 21 + 3$
$\frac{4x}{4} \geq \frac{24}{4}$
$x \geq 6$

13. $7 < 14 - k$
$7 - 14 < 14 - k - 14$
$-7 < -k$
$-1(-7) > -1(-k)$
$7 > k$

14. $7a - 4 < 17$; add 4, divide by 7.

15. $11 - 2n > -5$; subtract 11, divide by -2, reverse the inequality.

16. $\frac{3}{4}x + 5 > -15$; subtract 5, multiply by $\frac{4}{3}$.

17. $22 + 3b \leq -2$; subtract 22, divide by 3.

18. $\frac{4}{3}t + 5 > \frac{1}{3}t$; subtract $\frac{1}{3}t$, subtract 5.

19. $6(z - 2) < 15$; divide by 6, add 2; or distribute 6, add 12, divide by 6.

20. $x + 5 > -13$
$x > -18$

21. $-6 + 5x < 19$
$5x < 25$
$x < 5$

22. $4x - 1 \leq -17$
$4x \leq -16$
$x \leq -4$

23. $-5 \leq 6x - 12$
$7 \leq 6x$
$\frac{7}{6} \leq x$

Copyright © McDougal Littell Inc.
All rights reserved.

24. $-17 > 5x - 2$
$-15 > 5x$
$-3 > x$

25. $15 + x \geq 7$
$x \geq -8$

26. $-x + 9 \geq 14$
$-x \geq 5$
$x \leq -5$

27. $7 - 3x \leq 16$
$-3x \leq 9$
$x \geq -3$

28. $12 > -2x - 6$
$18 > -2x$
$-9 < x$

29. $3x + 9 > 6$
$3x > -3$
$x > -1$
C

30. $-3x - 9 > 6$
$-3x > 15$
$x < -5$
B

31. $-3(x - 3) > 6$
$x - 3 < -2$
$x < 1$
A
or
$-3(x - 3) > 6$
$-3x + 9 > 6$
$-3x > -3$
$x < 1$
A

32. $2(x - 4) \geq 3$
$x - 4 \geq \frac{3}{2}$
$x \geq \frac{3}{2} + \frac{8}{2}$
$x \geq \frac{11}{2}$ or 5.5

33. $\frac{1}{2}(x - 8) < 2$
$x - 8 < 4$
$x < 12$

34. $-(2x + 4) > 6$
$2x + 4 < -6$
$2x < -10$
$x < -5$

35. $15 \leq \frac{3}{2}(x + 4)$
$\frac{2}{3}(15) \leq x + 4$
$10 \leq x + 4$
$6 \leq x$

36. $-x - 4 > 3x - 2$
$-4 > 4x - 2$
$-2 > 4x$
$-\frac{1}{2} > x$

37. $6 + x \leq -4x + 1$
$6 + 5x \leq 1$
$5x \leq -5$
$x \leq -1$

38. $2x + 10 \geq 7x + 7$
$-5x + 10 \geq 7$
$-5x \geq -3$
$x \leq \frac{3}{5}$

39. $9 - 3x > 5(-x + 2)$
$9 - 3x > -5x + 10$
$9 + 2x > 10$
$2x > 1$
$x > \frac{1}{2}$

40. $-3(x + 3) < 4x - 7$
$-3x - 9 < 4x - 7$
$-9 < 7x - 7$
$-2 < 7x$
$-\frac{2}{7} < x$

41. $6(x + 2) > 3x - 2$
$6x + 12 > 3x - 2$
$3x + 12 > -2$
$3x > -14$
$x > -\frac{14}{3}$ or $-4\frac{2}{3}$

42. Add 4 to each side in the second line.
$6x - 4 \geq 2x - 8$
$6x \geq 2x - 4$
$4x \geq -4$
$x \geq -1$

43. In line 2, distribute the 4 over -1 and distribute the 3 over 1.
$4(f - 1) < 3(2f + 1)$
$4f - 4 < 6f + 3$
$-7 < 2f$
$-\frac{7}{2} < f$ or $f > -\frac{7}{2}$

44. Price per ticket · Number of tickets + Admission price ≤ Amount of $ you have
$1.25 \cdot n + 5 \leq 25$

45. $1.25n + 5 \leq 25$
$1.25n \leq 20$
$n \leq 16$
You may purchase up to 16 tickets.

46. Amount of $ you have ≥ cost of cheese pizza + cost of each topping · number of toppings

47. $18.50 \geq 14 + 0.75t$

Copyright © McDougal Littell Inc.
All rights reserved.

48. $18.50 \geq 14 + 0.75t$
$4.50 \geq 0.75t$
$6 \geq t$ or $t \leq 6$
You may purchase up to 6 additional toppings.

49. $x + x + 9 + 9 > 26$
$2x + 18 > 26$
$2x > 8$
$x > 4$ m

50. $x + x + x + x \leq 25$
$4x \leq 25$
$x \leq \frac{25}{4}$ or $6\frac{1}{4}$ m

51. $A = \frac{1}{2}bh$
$\frac{1}{2}(8)(x) < 12$
$4x < 12$
$x < 3$ ft

52. $A = \frac{1}{2}bh$
$\frac{1}{2}(24)(x) > 144$
$12x > 144$
$x > 12$ in.

6.3 Standardized Test Practice (p. 341)

53. $2x - 10 > 3(-x + 5)$
$2x - 10 > -3x + 15$
$5x - 10 > 15$
$5x > 25$
$x > 5$
C

54. F; -10
$4(x + 2) > 3x - 1$
$4(-10 + 2) \overset{?}{\geq} 3(-10) - 1$
$4(-8) \overset{?}{\geq} -30 - 1$
$-32 \not> -31$

6.3 Mixed Review (p. 341)

55. $(a + 4) - 8 = (7 + 4) - 8 = 11 - 8 = 3$

56. $3x + 2 = 3(-4) + 2 = -12 + 2 = -10$

57. $b^3 - 5 = 2^3 - 5 = 8 - 5 = 3$

58. $2(r + s) = 2(2 + 4) = 2(6) = 12$

59. $h = 4 + a$

60. $c > 2s$

61. $42.99 + 14.50 + 29.99 - 10 = \$77.48$

6.3 Maintaining Skills (p. 341)

62. $2\frac{1}{10} = \frac{21}{10}$

63. $1\frac{2}{7} = \frac{9}{7}$

64. $20\frac{6}{7} = \frac{146}{7}$

65. $3\frac{3}{4} = \frac{15}{4}$

Quiz 1 *(p. 341)*

1.
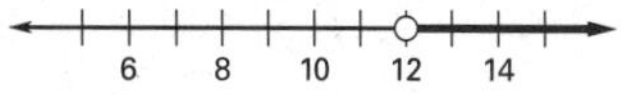

2.
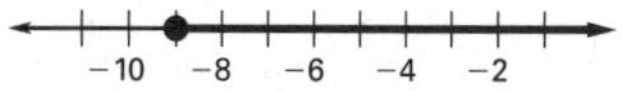

3.
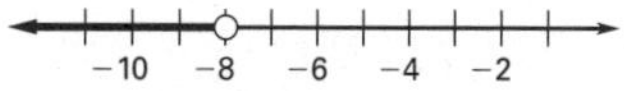

4. $a + 2 < 7; a < 5$
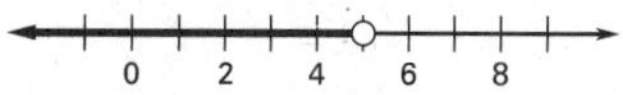

5. $-3 + m \leq -11; m \leq -8$
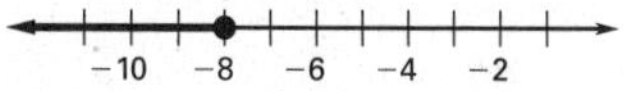

6. $-13 > b - 1; -12 > b$
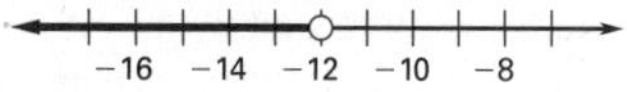

7. $\frac{1}{3}z \geq -7; z \geq -21$
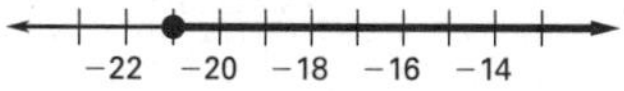

8. $-\frac{3}{4}x \leq -27; x \geq -\frac{4}{3}(-27); x \geq 36$
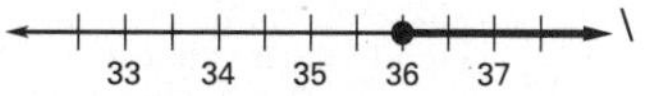

9. $105 > -15k; -7 < k$
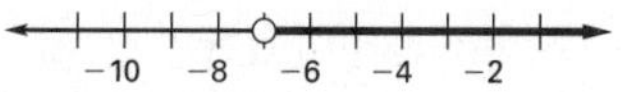

10. $h \geq 52$

11. $180 > 20x; 9 > x$; less than 9 plays (8 or less plays)

12. $5 \leq -\frac{x}{2} + 4$
$1 \leq -\frac{x}{2}$
$-2 \geq x$

13. $-4x + 2 \geq 14$
$-4x \geq 12$
$x \leq -3$

14. $-x - 4 > 3x - 12$
$-4 > 4x - 12$
$8 > 4x$
$2 > x$ or $x < 2$

15. $-(-x + 8) > -10$
$x - 8 > -10$
$x > -2$

16. $-10 \leq -2(2x - 9)$
$-10 \leq -4x + 18$
$-28 \leq -4x$
$7 \geq x$

17. $x + 3 \leq 2(x - 7)$
$x + 3 \leq 2x - 14$
$3 \leq x - 14$
$17 \leq x$

Copyright © McDougal Littell Inc.
All rights reserved.

Chapter 6 *continued*

Lesson 6.4

6.4 Checkpoint (pp. 342–344)

1. $-2 < y < 0$;
   y is greater than -2 and less than 0.

2. $7 \le t < 8$;
   t is greater than or equal to 7 and less than 8.

3. $4 \le n \le 11$;
   n is greater than or equal to 4 and less than or equal to 11.

4.
$-1 < x + 3 < 7$	Original inequality
$-1 < x + 3$ and $x + 3 < 7$	Separate inequality.
$-4 < x$ and $x < 4$	Subtract 3 from each side.
$-4 < x < 4$	Write compound inequality.

or

$-1 < x + 3 < 7$	Original inequality
$-1 - 3 < x + 3 - 3 < 7 - 3$	Subtract 3 from each expression.
$-4 < x < 4$	Simplify.

5.
$-6 \le 3x \le 12$	Original inequality
$-6 \le 3x$ and $3x \le 12$	Separate inequality.
$-2 \le x$ and $x \le 4$	Divide each side by 3.
$-2 \le x \le 4$	Write compound inequality.

or

$-6 \le 3x \le 12$	Original inequality
$-\frac{6}{3} \le \frac{3x}{3} \le \frac{12}{3}$	Divide each expression by 3.
$-2 \le x \le 4$	Simplify.

6.
$0 < x - 4 \le 12$	Original inequality
$0 < x - 4$ and $x - 4 \le 12$	Separate inequality.
$4 < x$ and $x \le 16$	Add 4 to each side.
$4 < x \le 16$	Write compound inequality.

or

$0 < x - 4 \le 12$	Original inequality
$0 + 4 < x - 4 + 4 \le 12 + 4$	Add 4 to each expression.
$4 < x \le 16$	Simplify.

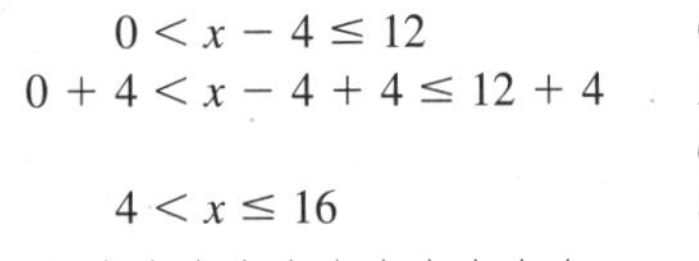

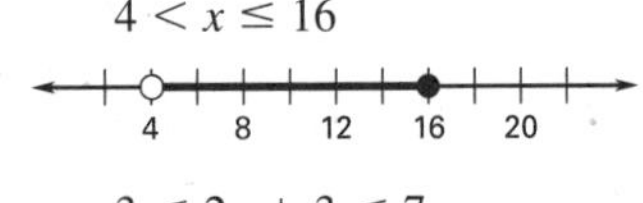

7.
$3 \le 2x + 3 \le 7$	Original inequality
$3 - 3 \le 2x + 3 - 3 \le 7 - 3$	Subtract 3 from each expression.
$0 \le 2x \le 4$	Simplify.
$\frac{0}{2} \le \frac{2x}{2} \le \frac{4}{2}$	Divide each expression by 2.
$0 \le x \le 2$	Simplify.

8.
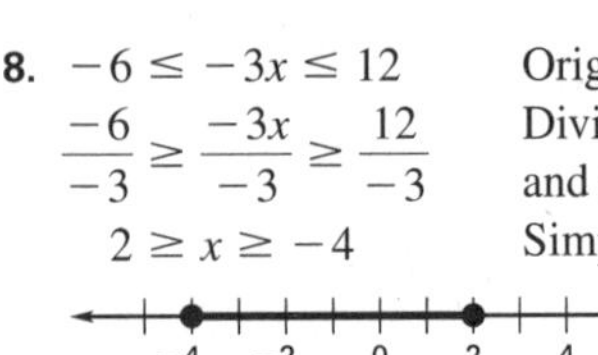

$-6 \le -3x \le 12$	Original inequality
$\frac{-6}{-3} \ge \frac{-3x}{-3} \ge \frac{12}{-3}$	Divide each expression by -3 and reverse both inequalities.
$2 \ge x \ge -4$	Simplify.

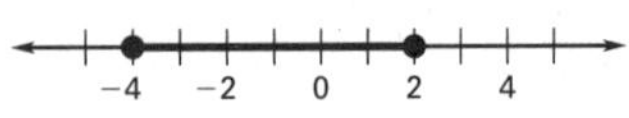

9.
$-3 \le -4 - x \le 2$	Original inequality
$-3 + 4 \le -4 - x + 4 \le 2 + 4$	Add 4 to each expression.
$1 \le -x \le 6$	Simplify.
$-1(1) \ge -1(-x) \ge -1(6)$	Multiply each expression by -1 and reverse both inequalities.
$-1 \ge x \ge -6$	Simplify.

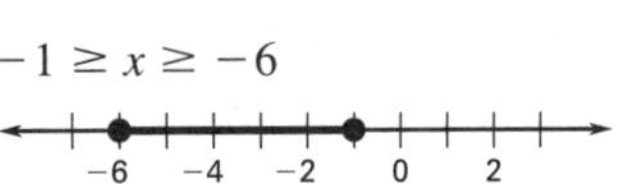

6.4 Guided Practice (p. 345)

1. and, or
2. You are "putting together" the two inequalities $3 \le x$ and $x < 9$.
3. $-1 \le x < 3$; A
4. $-1 < x$ and $x \le 3$; $-1 < x \le 3$; B
5. $4 + x$ is greater than 7 and is less than 8.
6. $2x + 3$ is greater than -1 and is less than or equal to 13.
7. $-8 - x$ is greater than or equal to 4 and is less than 7.
8. $2 < x < 5$
9. $-4 \le x \le 4$
10. $-1 \le x < 7$

6.4 Practice and Applications (pp. 345–347)

11. $-23 \le x \le -7$;
    x is greater than or equal to -23 and is less than or equal to -7.
12. $0 < x < 18$; x is greater than 0 and is less than 18.
13. $-4 \le x < 19$; x is greater than or equal to -4 and is less than 19.
14. $-4 \le x \le 0$
15. $2 < x < 3$
16. $-7 < x \le -3$
17. $-2 \le x < 2$
18. $-6 < x < -1$
19. $0 \le x < 5$
20. $1 < x \le 8$

Copyright © McDougal Littell Inc.
All rights reserved.

21. $-4 < x \leq -2$

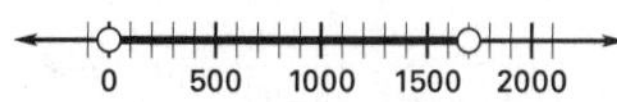

22. $10 \leq d \leq 16$

23. $85 \leq f \leq 1100$

24. $10{,}000 \leq f \leq 120{,}000$

25. $15 \leq f \leq 50{,}000$

26. $150 \leq f \leq 150{,}000$

27. $85{,}000 \leq c \leq 2{,}600{,}000$

28. $0 < l < 1700$

29. $6 < x - 6 \leq 8;\ 12 < x \leq 14$

30. $-5 < x - 3 < 6;\ -2 < x < 9$

31. $0 \leq x + 9 < 17;\ -9 \leq x < 8$

32. $-14 < 7x < 21;\ -2 < x < 3$

33. $-4 \leq 2x < 18;\ -2 \leq x < 9$

34. $4 < x - 7 < 15;\ 11 < x < 22$

35. $-3 \leq 2x + 5 \leq 11$
$-8 \leq 2x \leq 6$
$-4 \leq x \leq 3$

36. $7 \leq 3x - 8 < 19$
$15 \leq 3x < 27$
$5 \leq x < 9$

37. $10 < 3x - 2 < 19$
$12 < 3x < 21$
$4 < x < 7$

38. $0 < 12x + 6 \leq 18$
$-6 < 12x \leq 12$
$-\frac{1}{2} < x \leq 1$

39. $-7 \leq 3 - x < 5$
$-10 \leq -x < 2$
$10 \geq x > -2$

40. $-25 < -5x < 0;\ 5 > x > 0$

41. $42 < -3x \leq 48;\ -14 > x \geq -16$

42. $-5 < -6 - x < 3$
$1 < -x < 9$
$-1 > x > -9$

43. $-3 \leq 5 - 2x < 1$
$-8 \leq -2x < -4$
$4 \geq x > 2$

44. $-7 \leq -1 - 6x \leq 11$
$-6 \leq -6x \leq 12$
$1 \geq x \geq -2$

45. $-13 \leq 2 - 5x < -3$
$-15 \leq -5x < -5$
$3 \geq x > 1$

46. $-44 \leq 1 - 9x < 55$
$-45 \leq -9x < 54$
$5 \geq x > -6$

47. There is no number x such that x is greater than 3 and less than 1.

48. $-2 \leq x \leq 3$; D

49. J; $-5 > -x > -2;\ 5 < x < 2$

50. $k + 5 = 2 + 5 = 7$

51. $6a = 6(4) = 24$

52. $m - 20 = 30 - 20 = 10$

53. $\frac{x}{15} = \frac{30}{15} = 2$

54. $5z = 5(3.3) = 16.5$

55. $5p = 5(4) = 20$

56. $4 - n = 4 - 3 = 1$

Copyright © McDougal Littell Inc.
All rights reserved.

57. $\frac{t}{3} = \frac{-18}{3} = -6$

58. $2x = 2(3) = 6$

59. $x + 17 = 9; x = -8$

60. $-8 = x + 2; -10 = x$

61. $x - 4 = 12; x = 16$

62. $x - (-9) = 15; x + 9 = 15; x = 6$

63. $\frac{x}{2} = -6; x = -12$

64. $-3x = -27; x = 9$

65. $4x = -28; x = -7$

66. $-\frac{3}{4}x = 21; -\frac{4}{3}\left(-\frac{3}{4}x\right) = -\frac{4}{3}(21); x = -28$

67. $7x > 4x + 75; 3x > 75; x > 25$; more than 25 times

68. $P = 2.6t + 249$

69. 1995 is 5 years past 1990, so $t = 5$
$p = 2.6t + 249$
$p = 2.6(5) + 249$
$p = 262$; 262 million people

70. $\frac{1}{4} = \frac{1}{4} \cdot \frac{25}{25} = \frac{25}{100} = 25\%$

71. $\frac{3}{8}$; $0.375 = 37.5\%$

$$\begin{array}{r} 0.375 \\ 8\overline{)3.0} \\ \underline{2\,4} \\ 60 \\ \underline{56} \\ 40 \\ \underline{40} \\ 0 \end{array}$$

72. $\frac{4}{10} = \frac{4}{10} \cdot \frac{10}{10} = \frac{40}{100} = 40\%$

73. $\frac{1}{3}$; $0.\bar{3} = 0.33\bar{3} \approx 33\frac{1}{3}\%$

$$\begin{array}{r} 0.\bar{3} \\ 3\overline{)1.0} \\ \underline{9} \\ 1\,0 \end{array}$$

74. $\frac{37}{50} = \frac{37}{50} \cdot \frac{2}{2} = \frac{74}{100} = 74\%$

75. $\frac{3}{4} = \frac{3}{4} \cdot \frac{25}{25} = \frac{75}{100} = 75\%$

76. $\frac{3}{20} = \frac{3}{20} \cdot \frac{5}{5} = \frac{15}{100} = 15\%$

77. $\frac{21}{25} = \frac{21}{25} \cdot \frac{4}{4} = \frac{84}{100} = 84\%$

Lesson 6.5

6.5 Checkpoint (pp. 348–350)

1. x is less than 0 or x is greater than 5.
2. x is less than or equal to -10 or x is greater than or equal to 10.
3. x is less than 2 or x is greater than or equal to 3.
4. $x \le -3$ or $x > 0$; two parts
5. $x < 3$ or $x > 6$; two parts
6. $-2 < x < 7$; one part
7. $x < -5$ or $x > -4$
   $-5 \not< -5$ $-5 \not> -4$
   Not a solution
8. $x \le -3$ or $x > 0$
   $-5 \le -3$ $-5 \not> 0$
   Since -5 is less than -3, it is a solution.
9. $x - 4 < -8$ or $x + 3 > 5$
   $x < -4$ $x > 2$
10. $2x + 3 \le 1$ or $3x - 5 > 1$
    $2x \le -2$ $3x > 6$
    $x \le -1$ $x > 2$
11. velocity $= -32t + 64$
    $-32t + 64 > 32$ or $-32t + 64 < -64$
    $-32t > -32$ $-32t < -128$
    $t < 1$ $t > 4$

6.5 Guided Practice (p. 351)

1. The graph of a compound inequality with *or* has two separate parts, while a compound inequality with *and* has one shared part.
2. C; $x \le -2$ or $x \ge 1$
3. B; $1 < x$ or $x \le -2$
4. D; $x < -2$ or $1 \le x$
5. A; $x < 1$ or $x > 2$
6. x is less than or equal to -25 or x is greater than 7.
7. x is less than 10 or x is greater than 13.
8. x is less than -9 or x is greater than 3.
9. $x < -6$ or $x > -1$

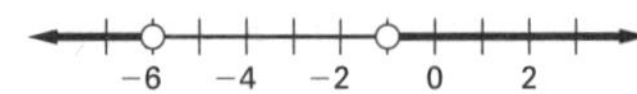

10. $x < 0$ or $x \ge 5$

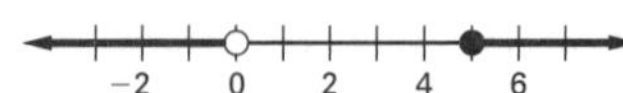

Copyright © McDougal Littell Inc.
All rights reserved.

Chapter 6 *continued*

6.5 Practice and Applications (pp. 351–353)

11. x is less than or equal to 15 or x is greater than or equal to 31.

12. x is less than 0 or x is greater than 16.

13. x is greater than 11 or x is less than or equal to -7.

14. $x \le -4$ or $x \ge 4$

15. $x \le -3$ or $x > 0$

16. $x \le -1$ or $x > 1$

17. $x \le 7$ or $x \ge 8$

18. $x < -6$ or $x > 2$

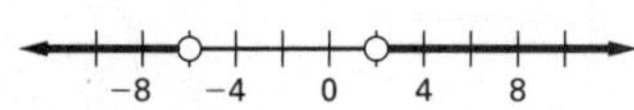

19. $x > 7$ or $x < 0$

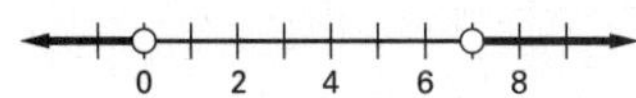

20. $x < 3$ or $x > 10$

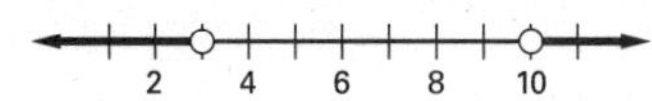

21. $x - 1 \le -3$ or $x + 3 > 8$

$x \le -2$ $\qquad$ $x > 5$

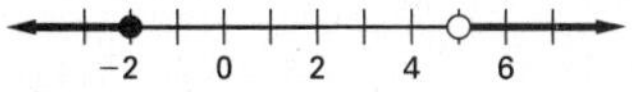

22. $-12 > 8x$ or $4x \ge 6$

$-\frac{12}{8} > x$ $\qquad$ $x \ge \frac{6}{4}$

$-\frac{3}{2} > x$ $\qquad$ $x \ge \frac{3}{2}$

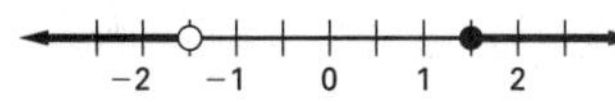

23. $x + 3 \ge 2$ or $12x \le -48$

$x \ge -1$ $\qquad$ $x \le -4$

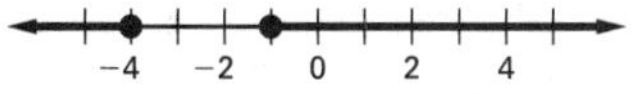

24. $-22 > 11x$ or $4 + x > 4$

$-2 > x$ $\qquad$ $x > 0$

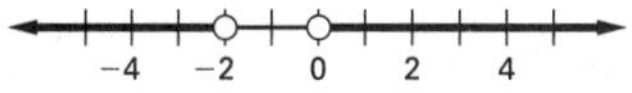

25. $7x < -42$ or $x + 5 \ge 3$

$x < -6$ $\qquad$ $x \ge -2$

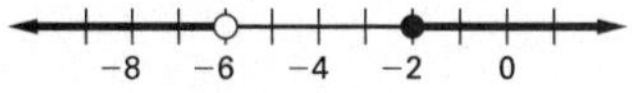

26. $5 + x \ge 20$ or $3x \le -9$

$x \ge 15$ $\qquad$ $x \le -3$

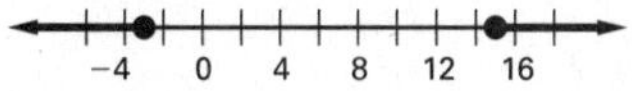

27. $x - 4 < -12$ or $2x \ge 12$

$x < -8$ $\qquad$ $x \ge 6$

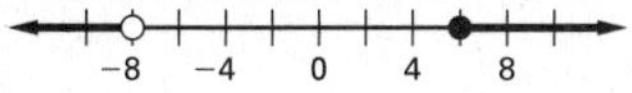

28. $-3x \le 15$ or $5 + x < -11$

$x \ge -5$ $\qquad$ $x < -16$

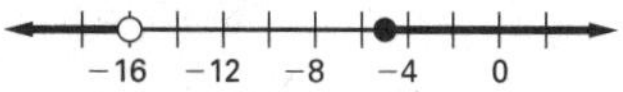

29. $x - 7 < 3$ or $2x > 24$

$x < 10$ $\qquad$ $x > 12$

$x = 8$ is a solution since $8 < 10$.

30. $5x \ge -15$ or $x + 4 < -1$

$x \ge -3$ $\qquad$ $x < -5$

$x = -4$ is not a solution since -4 is not greater than or equal to -3 and -4 is not less than -5.

31. $-2x \ge 6$ or $2x + 1 > 5$

$x \le -3$ $\qquad$ $2x > 4$

$x \le -3$ $\qquad$ $x > 2$

$x = 0$ is not a solution since 0 is not less than or equal to -3 and 0 is not greater than 2.

32. $3x < -21$ or $4x - 8 \ge 0$

$x < -7$ $\qquad$ $4x \ge 8$

$x < -7$ $\qquad$ $x \ge 2$

$x = 3$ is a solution since 3 is greater than 2.

33. $x + 10 < 8$ or $3x - 7 \ge 5$

$x < -2$ $\qquad$ $3x \ge 12$

$x < -2$ $\qquad$ $x \ge 4$

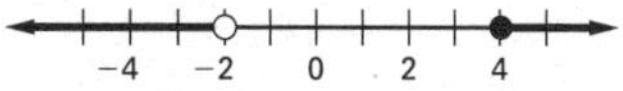

34. $-8x > 24$ or $2x - 5 > 17$

$x < -3$ $\qquad$ $2x > 22$

$x < -3$ $\qquad$ $x > 11$

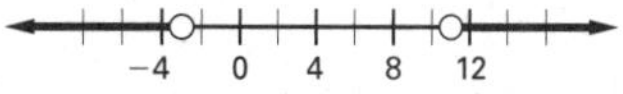

35. $2x + 1 > 13$ or $-18 > 7x + 3$

$2x > 12$ $\qquad$ $-21 > 7x$

$x > 6$ $\qquad$ $-3 > x$

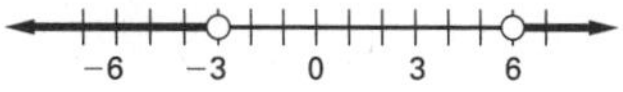

36. $6 + 2x > 20$ or $8 + x \le 0$

$2x > 14$ $\qquad$ $x \le -8$

$x > 7$ $\qquad$ $x \le -8$

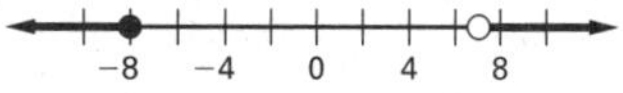

37. $2x + 7 < 3$ or $5x + 5 \ge 10$

$2x < -4$ $\qquad$ $5x \ge 5$

$x < -2$ $\qquad$ $x \ge 1$

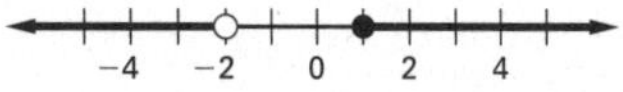

38. $3x + 8 > 17$ or $2x + 5 \le 7$

$3x > 9$ $\qquad$ $2x \le 2$

$x > 3$ $\qquad$ $x \le 1$

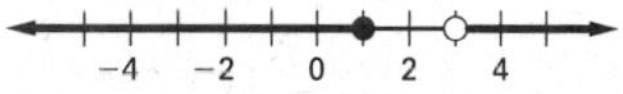

Copyright © McDougal Littell Inc.
All rights reserved.

39. $3x + 5 < -19$ or $4x + 7 \geq -1$

$3x < -24$ $\quad$ $4x \geq -8$

$x < -8$ $\quad$ $x \geq -2$

40. $1 - 5x \leq -14$ or $-3x - 2 \geq 7$

$-5x \leq -15$ $\quad$ $-3x \geq 9$

$x \geq 3$ $\quad$ $x \leq -3$

41. $v = 4t - 4$

t	0	0.5	1	1.5	2
v	−4	−2	0	2	4

The yo-yo returns back up at the same speed it had initially. It is at rest (speed is zero) half way through the cycle.

42. $4t - 4 > 2$ or $4t - 4 < -2$

$4t > 6$ $\quad$ $4t < 2$

$t > \frac{3}{2} = 1.5$ $\quad$ $t < \frac{1}{2} = 0.5$

43. $t \leq 32$ or $t \geq 212$

44. $5 \leq a < 11$

45. $y < 11$ or $y \geq 65$

46. all real numbers

6.5 Standardized Test Practice (p. 353)

47. $x \leq -4$ or $x > 0$; A

48. H;

$-2(6) \overset{?}{\geq} 18$ or $3(6) + 8 \overset{?}{>} 26$

$-12 \not\geq 18$ $\quad$ $18 + 8 \overset{?}{>} 26$

$26 \not> 26$

6.5 Mixed Review (p. 353)

49.

x	0	1	2	3	4
y	2	5	8	11	14

$y = 3x + 2$

50.

x	0	1	2	3	4
y	1	−1	−3	−5	−7

$y = -2x + 1$

51.

x	0	1	2	3	4
y	5	4	3	2	1

$y = 5 - x$

52.

x	0	1	2	3	4
y	−3	−1	1	3	5

$y = 2x - 3$

53.

x	0	1	2	3	4
y	−4	−2	0	2	4

$y = 2x - 4$

54.

x	0	1	2	3	4
y	−1	2	5	8	11

$y = 3x - 1$

55.

56.

57.

58. $1.2x - 1.7 = 4.5$

$1.2x = 6.2$

$x \approx 5.17$

59. $1.3 + 4.4x = 6.6$

$4.4x = 5.3$

$x \approx 1.20$

60. $3.6x - 8.5 = 12.4$

$3.6x = 20.9$

$x \approx 5.81$

61. $2.3x + 3.2 = 18.5$

$2.3x = 15.3$

$x \approx 6.65$

62. $2.56 - 6.54x = -5.21 - 3.25x$

$2.56 - 3.29x = -5.21$

$-3.29x = -7.77$

$x \approx 2.36$

63. $2.32x + 6.56 = 3.74 - 7.43x$

$9.75x + 6.56 = 3.74$

$9.75x = -2.82$

$x \approx -0.29$

64. $x + 6 > -6$

$x > -12$

65. $16 < x + 7$

$9 < x$

66. $9 \geq -15 + x$

$24 \geq x$

67. $x - 10 \geq 15$

$x \geq 25$

Copyright © McDougal Littell Inc.
All rights reserved.

68. $2 \le x - 7$
$9 \le x$

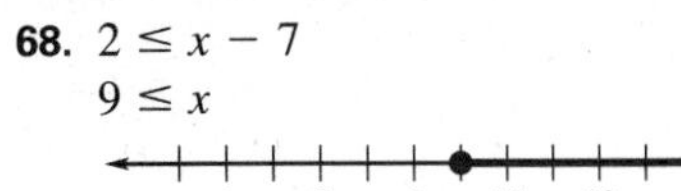

69. $-3x \le -15$
$x \ge 5$

70. $6x > -54$
$x > -9$

71. $-\frac{1}{4}x > 2$
$x < -8$

72. $\frac{3}{4}x \le 6$
$x \le \frac{4}{3}(6)$
$x \le 8$

6.5 Maintaining Skills (p. 353)

73. $\frac{1}{3}(84) = 28$

74. $\frac{1}{5}(375) = 75$

75. $\frac{1}{4}(884) = 221$

76. $\frac{1}{7}(21{,}000) = 3{,}000$

77. $\frac{1}{3}(84{,}000) = 28{,}000$

78. $\frac{1}{20}(72{,}000) = 3{,}600$

79. $\frac{1}{15}(81{,}000) = 5{,}400$

80. $\frac{1}{9}(31{,}500) = 3{,}500$

81. $\frac{1}{11}(121{,}000) = 11{,}000$

6.6 Developing Concepts: Think About It *(p. 354)*

1. *Sample answer:* In Step 2 you are using a number line to count off the distance of 2 between x and 3. In Step 1 you are finding the values of x which make $|x - 3| = 2$ true, which is the same.

2. $|x| = 5$; -5 and 5 are 5 units from 0.

3. $|x - 2| = 4$; -2 and 6 are 4 units from 0.

4. $|x + 2| = |x - (-2)| = 3$
-5 and 1 are 3 units from -2.

Lesson 6.6

6.6 Checkpoint (pp. 355–357)

1. $|x| = 6$; $x = 6$ or $x = -6$

2. $|x| = 0$; $x = 0$

3. $|x| = -6$; no solution

4. $|x + 3| = 5$;
$x + 3 = 5$ or $x + 3 = -5$
$x = 2$ $\quad x = -8$
Check: $|2 + 3| = |5| = 5$; $|-8 + 3| = |-5| = 5$

5. $|x - 3| = 5$
$x - 3 = 5$ or $x - 3 = -5$
$x = 8$ $\quad x = -2$
Check: $|8 - 3| = |5| = 5$; $|-2 - 3| = |-5| = 5$

6. $|4x - 2| = 6$
$4x - 2 = 6$ or $4x - 2 = -6$
$4x = 8$ $\quad 4x = -4$
$x = 2$ $\quad x = -1$
Check: $|4(2) - 2| = |8 - 2| = |6| = 6$;
$|4(-1) - 2| = |-4 - 2| = |-6| = 6$

7. $|3x - 2| = 0$
$3x - 2 = 0$
$3x = 2$
$x = \frac{2}{3}$
Check: $\left|3\left(\frac{2}{3}\right) - 2\right| = |2 - 2| = |0| = 0$

8. $|x + 1| + 2 = 4$
$|x + 1| = 2$
$x + 1 = 2$ or $x + 1 = -2$
$x = 1$ $\quad x = -3$
Check: $|1 + 1| + 2 = |2| + 2 = 2 + 2 = 4$;
$|-3 + 1| + 2 = |-2| + 2 = 2 + 2 = 4$

9. $|2x - 8| - 3 = 5$
$|2x - 8| = 8$
$2x - 8 = 8$ or $2x - 8 = -8$
$2x = 16$ $\quad 2x = 0$
$x = 8$ $\quad x = 0$
Check:
$|2(8) - 8| - 3 = |16 - 8| - 3 = |8| - 3 = 8 - 3 = 5$;
$|2(0) - 8| - 3 = |0 - 8| - 3 = |-8| - 3 = 8 - 3 = 5$

10. Midpoint of 4 and 12 is 8; distance to midpoint is 4;
$|x - 8| = 4$

6.6 Guided Practice (p. 358)

1. Since $|-2|$ is 2, the algebraic equation is $x + 2 = 5$.

2. A; $x - 7 = 13$; $x = 20$, and
C; $x - 7 = -13$; $x = -6$

3. two

4. none

5. none

6. one; $|x| = 0$; $x = 0$

7. $x - 4 = 10$; $x - 4 = -10$

8. $2x - 3 = 8$; $2x - 3 = -8$

9. $|3x + 2| - 1 = 5$
$|3x + 2| = 6$
$3x + 2 = 6$; $3x + 2 = -6$

Copyright © McDougal Littell Inc.
All rights reserved.

6.6 Practice and Applications (pp. 358–360)

10. $|x| = 36$
$x = 36$ or $x = -36$

11. $|x| = 9$
$x = -9$ or $x = 9$

12. no solution

13. no solution

14. $|x| = 10$
$x = 10$ or $x = -10$

15. $|x| = 100$
$x = 100$ or $x = -100$

16. $|x + 1| = 3$
$x + 1 = 3$ or $x + 1 = -3$
$x = 2$ $\quad$ $x = -4$
Check: $|2 + 1| = |3| = 3$; $|-4 + 1| = |-3| = 3$

17. $|x - 2| = 5$
$x - 2 = 5$ or $x - 2 = -5$
$x = 7$ $\quad$ $x = -3$
Check: $|7 - 2| = |5| = 5$; $|-3 - 2| = |-5| = 5$

18. $|4x| = 16$
$4x = 16$ or $4x = -16$
$x = 4$ $\quad$ $x = -4$
Check: $|4(4)| = |16| = 16$; $|4(-4)| = |-16| = 16$

19. $|3x| = 36$
$3x = 36$ or $3x = -36$
$x = 12$ $\quad$ $x = -12$
Check: $|3(12)| = |36| = 36$; $|3(-12)| = |-36| = 36$

20. $|x + 8| = 9$
$x + 8 = 9$ or $x + 8 = -9$
$x = 1$ $\quad$ $x = -17$
Check: $|1 + 8| = |9| = 9$; $|-17 + 8| = |-9| = 9$

21. $|x - 4| = 6$
$x - 4 = 6$ or $x - 4 = -6$
$x = 10$ $\quad$ $x = -2$
Check: $|10 - 4| = |6| = 6$; $|-2 - 4| = |-6| = 6$

22. $|x + 6| = -7$; no solution

23. $|8x| = 28$
$8x = 28$ or $8x = -28$
$x = 3.5$ $\quad$ $x = -3.5$
Check: $|8(3.5)| = |28| = 28$; $|8(-3.5)| = |-28| = 28$

24. $|x + 5| = 65$
$x + 5 = 65$ or $x + 5 = -65$
$x = 60$ $\quad$ $x = -70$
Check:
$|60 + 5| = |65| = 65$; $|-70 + 5| = |-65| = 65$

25. $|x - 3| = 7$
$x - 3 = 7$ or $x - 3 = -7$
$x = 10$ $\quad$ $x = -4$
Check: $|10 - 3| = |7| = 7$; $|-4 - 3| = |-7| = 7$

26. $|15 + x| = 3$
$15 + x = 3$ or $15 + x = -3$
$x = -12$ $\quad$ $x = -18$
Check:
$|15 + (-12)| = |3| = 3$; $|15 + (-18)| = |-3| = 3$

27. $\left|\frac{1}{2}x\right| = 9$
$\frac{1}{2}x = 9$ or $\frac{1}{2}x = -9$
$x = 18$ $\quad$ $x = -18$
Check: $\left|\frac{1}{2}(18)\right| = |9| = 9$; $\left|\frac{1}{2}(-18)\right| = |-9| = 9$

28. always

29. always

30. sometimes; if $p = 0$ there is one solution; if $p < 0$ there are no solutions.

31. always

32. $|6x - 4| = 2$
$6x - 4 = 2$ or $6x - 4 = -2$
$6x = 6$ $\quad$ $6x = 2$
$x = 1$ $\quad$ $x = \frac{1}{3}$
Check: $|6(1) - 4| = |6 - 4| = |2| = 2$;
$\left|6\left(\frac{1}{3}\right) - 4\right| = |2 - 4| = |-2| = 2$

33. $|4x - 2| = 22$
$4x - 2 = 22$ or $4x - 2 = -22$
$4x = 24$ $\quad$ $4x = -20$
$x = 6$ $\quad$ $x = -5$
Check: $|4(6) - 2| = |24 - 2| = |22| = 22$;
$|4(-5) - 2| = |-20 - 2| = |-22| = 22$

34. $|3x + 5| = 22$
$3x + 5 = 22$ or $3x + 5 = -22$
$3x = 17$ $\quad$ $3x = -27$
$x = \frac{17}{3}$ $\quad$ $x = -9$
Check: $\left|3\left(\frac{17}{3}\right) + 5\right| = |17 + 5| = |22| = 22$;
$|3(-9) + 5| = |-27 + 5| = |-22| = 22$

35. $|2x + 5| = 3$
$2x + 5 = 3$ or $2x + 5 = -3$
$2x = -2$ $\quad$ $2x = -8$
$x = -1$ $\quad$ $x = -4$
Check: $|2(-1) + 5| = |-2 + 5| = |3| = 3$;
$|2(-4) + 5| = |-8 + 5| = |-3| = 3$

36. $|6x - 3| = 39$
$6x - 3 = 39$ or $6x - 3 = -39$
$6x = 42$ $\quad$ $6x = -36$
$x = 7$ $\quad$ $x = -6$
Check: $|6(7) - 3| = |42 - 3| = |39| = 39$;
$|6(-6) - 3| = |-36 - 3| = |-39| = 39$

Copyright © McDougal Littell Inc.
All rights reserved.

37. $|2x - 7| = 9$

$2x - 7 = 9$ or $2x - 7 = -9$

$2x = 16$ $\quad$ $2x = -2$

$x = 8$ $\quad$ $x = -1$

Check: $|2(8) - 7| = |16 - 7| = |9| = 9;$

$|2(-1) - 7| = |-2 - 7| = |-9| = 9$

38. $|5 - 4x| - 3 = 4$

$|5 - 4x| = 7$

$5 - 4x = 7$ or $5 - 4x = -7$

$-4x = 2$ $\quad$ $-4x = -12$

$x = -\frac{1}{2}$ $\quad$ $x = 3$

Check:

$\left|5 - 4\left(-\frac{1}{2}\right)\right| - 3 = |5 + 2| - 3$

$= |7| - 3$

$= 7 - 3 = 4;$

$|5 - 4(3)| - 3 = |5 - 12| - 3 = |-7| - 3 = 7 - 3 = 4$

39. $|2x - 4| - 8 = 10$

$|2x - 4| = 18$

$2x - 4 = 18$ or $2x - 4 = -18$

$2x = 22$ $\quad$ $2x = -14$

$x = 11$ $\quad$ $x = -7$

Check: $|2(11) - 4| - 8 = |18| - 8 = 18 - 8 = 10;$

$|2(-7) - 4| - 8 = |-18| - 8 = 18 - 8 = 10$

40. $|5x - 4| + 3 = 19$

$|5x - 4| = 16$

$5x - 4 = 16$ or $5x - 4 = -16$

$5x = 20$ $\quad$ $5x = -12$

$x = 4$ $\quad$ $x = -\frac{12}{5}$

Check: $|5(4) - 4| + 3 = |16| + 3 = 16 + 3 = 19;$

$\left|5\left(-\frac{12}{5}\right) - 4\right| + 3 = |-16| + 3 = 16 + 3 = 19$

41. $|x + 2| = 6$; -8 and 4 are 6 units from -2.
A

42. $|x - 6| = 2$; 4 and 8 are 2 units from 6.
C

43. $|x - 2| = 6$; -4 and 8 are 6 units from 2.
B

44. Midpoint of 8 and 18 is $\frac{8 + 18}{2} = 13$; distance from 8 to 13 is 5; $|x - 13| = 5$

45. Midpoint of -6 and 10 is $\frac{-6 + 10}{2} = 2$; distance from -6 to 2 is 8; $|x - 2| = 8$

46. Midpoint of 2 and 9 is $\frac{2 + 9}{2} = 5.5$; distance from 2 to 5.5 is 3.5; $|x - 5.5| = 3.5$, or clear the equation of fractions by multiplying each side by 2; $|2x - 11| = 7$

47.

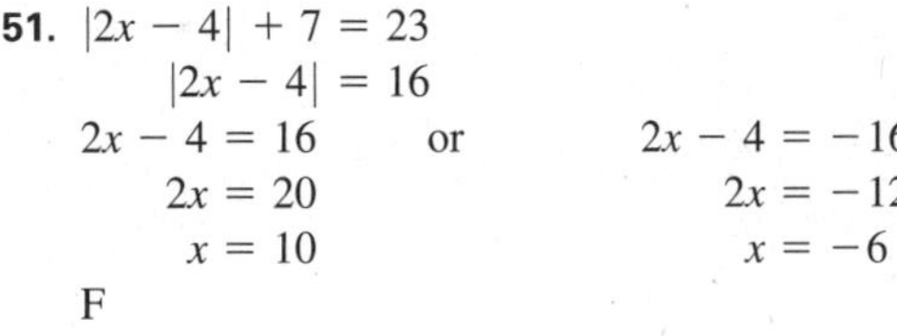

Midpoint: $\frac{91.4 + 94.5}{2} = \frac{185.9}{2} = 92.95$ million miles

distance from minimum to midpoint:

$92.95 - 91.4 = 1.55$ million miles

distance from maximum to midpoint:

$94.5 - 92.95 = 1.55$ million miles

48. $|x - 92.95| = 1.55$

49. Midpoint of 20,320 and -282 is $\frac{20{,}320 + (-282)}{2} = 10{,}019$; distance from maximum point to midpoint is $20{,}320 - 10{,}019 = 10{,}301$.

Equation: $|x - 10{,}019| = 10{,}301$

6.6 Standardized Test Practice (p. 360)

50. $|x| - 5 = 6$

$|x| = 11$

$x = 11$ or $x = -11$

D

51. $|2x - 4| + 7 = 23$

$|2x - 4| = 16$

$2x - 4 = 16$ or $2x - 4 = -16$

$2x = 20$ $\quad$ $2x = -12$

$x = 10$ $\quad$ $x = -6$

F

6.6 Mixed Review (p. 360)

52. $x = -1$

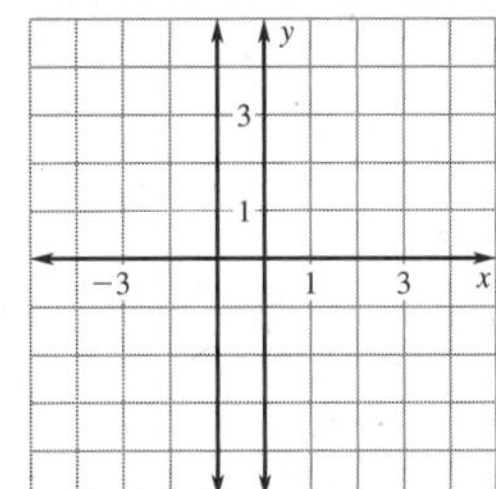

53. $3y = 15$

$y = 5$

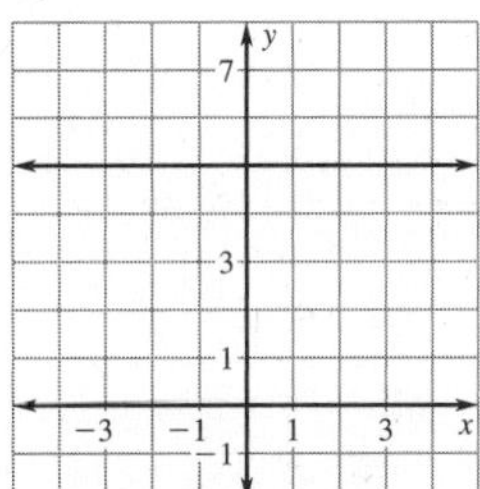

Copyright © McDougal Littell Inc.
All rights reserved.

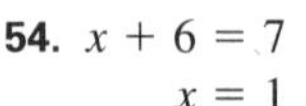

54. $x + 6 = 7$
$x = 1$

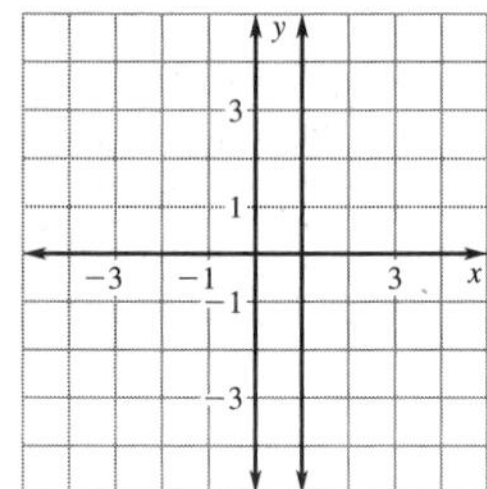

55. $5x + y = 20$
$y = -5x + 20$

56. $3x - y = 21$
$-y = -3x + 21$
$y = 3x - 21$

57. $12x = 3y + 36$
$12x - 36 = 3y$
$4x - 12 = y$ or $y = 4x - 12$

58. $y - y_1 = m(x - x_1)$
$y - 4 = 3(x - 0)$
$y - 4 = 3x$
$y = 3x + 4$

59. $y - y_1 = m(x - x_1)$
$y - (-5) = -2(x - 2)$
$y + 5 = -2x + 4$
$y = -2x - 1$

60. $y - y_1 = m(x - x_1)$
$y - 1 = 2(x - (-3))$
$y - 1 = 2(x + 3)$
$y - 1 = 2x + 6$
$y = 2x + 7$

6.6 Maintaining Skills (p. 360)

61. 48,000 **62.** 47,509.1 **63.** 47,500

64. 47,509.126 **65.** 47,509.13 **66.** 47,509

Quiz 2 *(p. 360)*

1. $-5 < x - 8 < 4$
$3 < x < 12$

2. $-10 < 2x + 8 \le 22$
$-18 < 2x \le 14$
$-9 < x \le 7$

3. $-10 \le -4x - 18 \le -2$
$8 \le -4x \le 16$
$-2 \ge x \ge -4$

4. $5x > 25$ or $2x + 9 < -1$
$x > 5$ $2x < -10$
$x > 5$ $x < -5$

5. $-3 > x + 6$ or $-x < 4$
$-9 > x$ $x > -4$

6. $2 - x < -3$ or $2x + 14 < 12$
$-x < -5$ $2x < -2$
$x > 5$ $x < -1$

7. $-128.6 < T < 136$

8. $|x| = 14$
$x = 14$ or $x = -14$

9. $|x| = -43$; no solution

10. $|x - 9| = 24$
$x - 9 = 24$ or $x - 9 = -24$
$x = 33$ $x = -15$

11. $|x + 15| = 6$
$x + 15 = 6$ or $x + 15 = -6$
$x = -9$ $x = -21$

12. $|3x - 18| = 36$
$3x - 18 = 36$ or $3x - 18 = -36$
$3x = 54$ $3x = -18$
$x = 18$ $x = -6$

13. $|5x + 10| + 15 = 60$
$|5x + 10| = 45$
$5x + 10 = 45$ or $5x + 10 = -45$
$5x = 35$ $5x = -55$
$x = 7$ $x = -11$

14. Midpoint of -3 and 18 is $\frac{-3 + 18}{2} = 7.5$; distance from maximum to midpoint is $18 - 7.5 = 10.5$;
$|x - 7.5| = 10.5$ or $|2x - 15| = 21$

Lesson 6.7

6.7 Checkpoint (pp. 362–363)

1. $|x| \le 6$ Original inequality
$x \le 6$ and $x \ge -6$ Related inequalities
$-6 \le x \le 6$ Write compound inequality.

2. $|x - 2| < 5$ Original inequality
$-5 < x - 2 < 5$ Related inequality
$-5 + 2 < x < 5 + 2$ Add 2 to each expression.
$-3 < x < 7$

3. $|x + 1| \le 4$ Original inequality
$-4 \le x + 1 \le 4$ Related inequality
$-5 \le x \le 3$

Copyright © McDougal Littell Inc.
All rights reserved.

Chapter 6 *continued*

4. $|3x| > 9$ Original inequality

$3x > 9$ or $3x < -9$ Related inequalities

$x > 3$ or $x < -3$

5. $|x - 2| \geq 7$ Original inequality

$x - 2 \geq 7$ or $x - 2 \leq -7$ Related inequalities

$x \geq 9$ or $x \leq -5$

6. $|x - 3| > 12$ Original inequality

$x - 3 > 12$ or $x - 3 < -12$ Related inequalities

$x > 15$ or $x < -9$

7. $|3x - 2| > 4$

$3x - 2 > 4$ or $3x - 2 < -4$

$3x > 6$ $\qquad$ $3x < -2$

$x > 2$ $\qquad$ $x < -\frac{2}{3}$

8. $|-32t + 64| > 48$

$-32t + 64 > 48$ or $-32t + 64 < -48$

$-32t > -16$ $\qquad$ $-32t < -112$

$t < \frac{1}{2} = 0.5$ $\qquad$ $t > 3.5$

6.7 Guided Practice (p. 364)

1. C $\qquad$ **2.** A $\qquad$ **3.** B

4. $x - 8 > 5$ or $x - 8 < -5$; (D, B)

5. $|x + 6| < 4$

$|-10 + 6| \overset{?}{<} 4$

$|-4| = 4 \not< 4$

Not a solution

6. $|x - 2| > 9$

$|7 - 2| \overset{?}{>} 9$

$|5| = 5 \not> 9$

Not a solution

7. $|5x - 2| \geq 8$

$|5(3) - 2| = |15 - 2| = |13| = 13 \geq 8$

Solution

6.7 Practice and Applications (pp. 364–366)

8. $|x| \geq 7$

$x \geq 7$ or $x \leq -7$

9. $|x| > 1$

$x > 1$ or $x < -1$

10. $|x - 16| < 10$

$x - 16 < 10$ and $x - 16 > -10$

11. $|x - 1| \leq 9$

$x - 1 \leq 9$ and $x - 1 \geq -9$

12. $|7x - 3| < 2$

$7x - 3 < 2$ and $7x - 3 > -2$

13. $|10 + 7x| \geq 11$

$10 + 7x \geq 11$ or $10 + 7x \leq -11$

14. $|x| \geq 3$

$x \geq 3$ or $x \leq -3$

15. $|x| < 15$

$-15 < x < 15$

16. $|x| \geq 5$

$x \geq 5$ or $x \leq -5$

17. $|x + 5| > 1$

$x + 5 > 1$ or $x + 5 < -1$

$x > -4$ $\qquad$ $x < -6$

18. $|8x| > 20$

$8x > 20$ or $8x < -20$

$x > \frac{5}{2}$ $\qquad$ $x < -\frac{5}{2}$

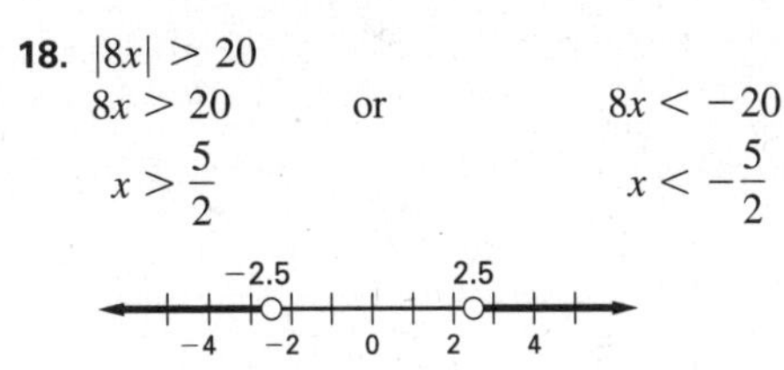

19. $|x - 10| \geq 20$

$x - 10 \geq 20$ or $x - 10 \leq -20$

$x \geq 30$ $\qquad$ $x \leq -10$

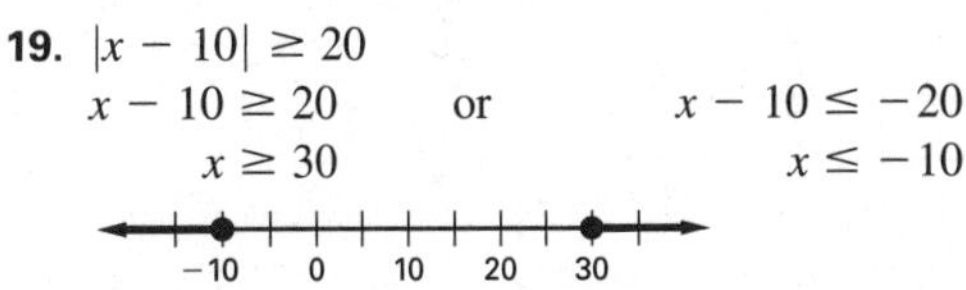

20. $|7x| \leq 49$

$-49 \leq 7x \leq 49$

$-7 \leq x \leq 7$

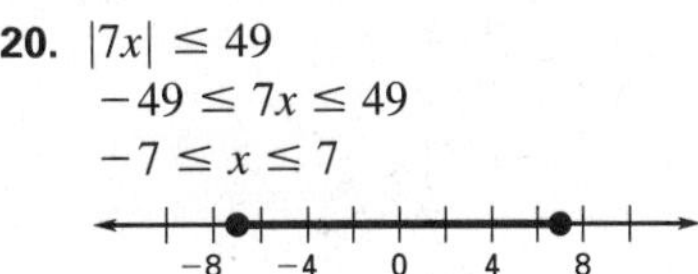

21. $|x - 4| > 8$

$x - 4 > 8$ or $x - 4 < -8$

$x > 12$ $\qquad$ $x < -4$

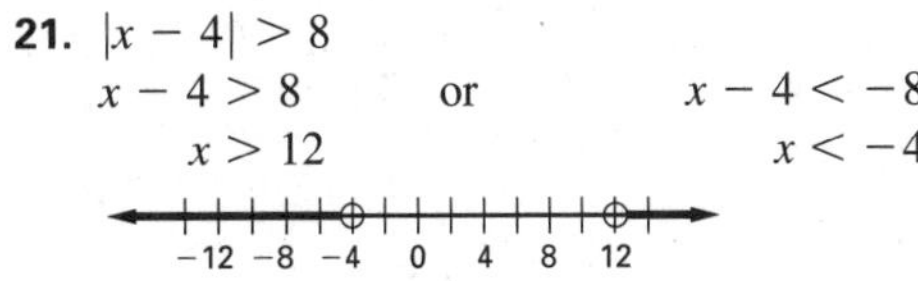

22. $|x + 3| < 8$

$-8 < x + 3 < 8$

$-11 < x < 5$

23. $|-3 + x| < 18$

$-18 < -3 + x < 18$

$-15 < x < 21$

24. $|10 + x| \leq 13$

$-13 \leq 10 + x \leq 13$

$-23 \leq x \leq 3$

Copyright © McDougal Littell Inc.
All rights reserved.

25. $|9 + x| \le 7$
$-7 \le 9 + x \le 7$
$-16 \le x \le -2$

26. always

27. never;
$-4 < x - 5 < 4$
$1 < x < 9$

28. sometimes;
$|x - 7| > 9$
$x - 7 > 9$ or $x - 7 < -9$
$x > 16$ $x < -2$

29. always;
$|x + 7| < 6$
$-6 < x + 7 < 6$
$-13 < x < -1$

30. $|2x - 9| \le 11$
$-11 \le 2x - 9 \le 11$
$-2 \le 2x \le 20$
$-1 \le x \le 10$

Test one value from each region:
$-2;\ |2(-2) - 9| = |-13| = 13 \not\le 11$
$0;\ |2(0) - 9| = |-9| = 9 \le 11$
$12;\ |2(12) - 9| = |15| = 15 \not\le 11$

31. $|4x + 2| < 6$
$-6 < 4x + 2 < 6$
$-8 < 4x < 4$
$-2 < x < 1$

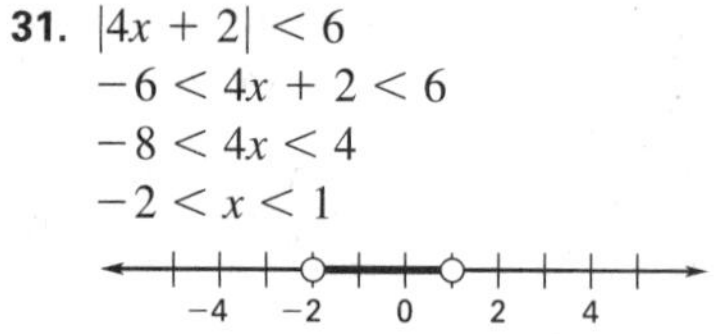

Test one value from each region:
$-3;\ |4(-3) + 2| = |-10| = 10 \not< 6$
$0;\ |4(0) + 2| = |2| = 2 < 6$
$2;\ |4(2) + 2| = |10| = 10 \not< 6$

32. $|32x - 16| > 32$
$32x - 16 > 32$ or $32x - 16 < -32$
$32x > 48$ $32x < -16$
$x > \frac{3}{2}$ $x < -\frac{1}{2}$

Test one value from each region:
$2;\ |32(2) - 16| = |48| = 48 > 32$
$0;\ |32(0) - 16| = |16| = 16 \not> 32$
$-1;\ |32(-1) - 16| = |-48| = 48 > 32$

33. $|2x + 7| > 23$
$2x + 7 > 23$ or $2x + 7 < -23$
$2x > 16$ $2x < -30$
$x > 8$ $x < -15$

Test one value from each region:
$10;\ |2(10) + 7| = |27| = 27 > 23$
$0;\ |2(0) + 7| = |7| = 7 \not> 23$
$-16;\ |2(-16) + 7| = |-25| = 25 > 23$

34. $|8x - 10| \ge 6$
$8x - 10 \ge 6$ or $8x - 10 \le -6$
$8x \ge 16$ $8x \le 4$
$x \ge 2$ $x \le \frac{1}{2}$

Test one value from each region:
$-1;\ |8(-1) - 10| = |-18| = 18 \ge 6$
$1;\ |8(1) - 10| = |-2| = 2 \not\ge 6$
$3;\ |8(3) - 10| = |14| = 14 \ge 6$

35. $|4x - 3| < 7$
$-7 < 4x - 3 < 7$
$-4 < 4x < 10$
$-1 < x < \frac{5}{2}$

Test one value from each region:
$-2;\ |4(-2) - 3| = |-11| = 11 \not< 7$
$0;\ |4(0) - 3| = |-3| = 3 < 7$
$3;\ |4(3) - 3| = |9| = 9 \not< 7$

36. $|x + 2| - 5 \ge 8$
$|x + 2| \ge 13$
$x + 2 \ge 13$ or $x + 2 \le -13$
$x \ge 11$ $x \le -15$

Test one value from each region:
$-16;\ |-16 + 2| - 5 = |-14| - 5 = 14 - 5 = 9 \ge 8$
$0;\ |0 + 2| - 5 = |2| - 5 = 2 - 5 = -3 \not\ge 8$
$12;\ |12 + 2| - 5 = |14| - 5 = 14 - 5 = 9 \ge 8$

Copyright © McDougal Littell Inc.
All rights reserved.

Chapter 6 *continued*

37. $|10 + 8x| - 2 > 16$

$|10 + 8x| > 18$

$10 + 8x > 18$ or $10 + 8x < -18$

$8x > 8$ $\quad$ $8x < -28$

$x > 1$ $\quad$ $x < -\frac{7}{2}$

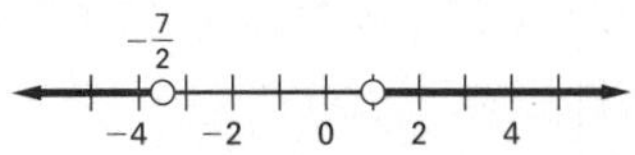

Test one value from each region:

$2;\ |10 + 8(2)| - 2 = |26| - 2 = 26 - 2 = 24 > 16$

$0;\ |10 + 8(0)| - 2 = |10| - 2 = 10 - 2 = 8 \ngtr 16$

$-4;\ |10 + 8(-4)| - 2 = |-22| - 2 = 22 - 2 = 20 > 16$

38. $|-4 + 2x| + 5 \le 23$

$|-4 + 2x| \le 18$

$-18 \le -4 + 2x \le 18$

$-14 \le 2x \le 22$

$-7 \le x \le 11$

Test one value from each region:

$-8;\ |-4 + 2(-8)| + 5 = |-20| + 5 = 25 \nleq 23$

$0;\ |-4 + 2(0)| + 5 = |-4| + 5 = 9 \le 23$

$12;\ |-4 + 2(12)| + 5 = |20| + 5 = 25 \nleq 23$

39. $|5x - 15| - 4 \ge 21$

$|5x - 15| \ge 25$

$5x - 15 \ge 25$ or $5x - 15 \le -25$

$5x \ge 40$ $\quad$ $5x \le -10$

$x \ge 8$ $\quad$ $x \le -2$

Test one value from each region:

$9;\ |5(9) - 15| - 4 = |30| - 4 = 26 \ge 21$

$0;\ |5(0) - 15| - 4 = |-15| - 4 = 11 \ngeq 21$

$-3;\ |5(-3) - 15| - 4 = |-30| - 4 = 26 \ge 21$

40. $|3x + 2| - 5 < 0$

$|3x + 2| < 5$

$-5 < 3x + 2 < 5$

$-7 < 3x < 3$

$-\frac{7}{3} < x < 1$

Test one value from each region:

$-3;\ |3(-3) + 2| - 5 = |-7| - 5 = 2 \nless 0$

$0;\ |3(0) + 2| - 5 = |2| - 5 = -3 < 0$

$2;\ |3(2) + 2| - 5 = |8| - 5 = 3 \nless 0$

41. $|3x - 9| - 2 \le 7$

$|3x - 9| \le 9$

$-9 \le 3x - 9 \le 9$

$0 \le 3x \le 18$

$0 \le x \le 6$

Test one value from each region:

$-1;\ |3(-1) - 9| - 2 = |-12| - 2 = 10 \nleq 7$

$2;\ |3(2) - 9| - 2 = |-3| - 2 = 1 \le 7$

$7;\ |3(7) - 9| - 2 = |12| - 2 = 10 \nleq 7$

42. $|-32t + 96| > 32$

$-32t + 96 > 32$ or $-32t + 96 < -32$

$-32t > -64$ $\quad$ $-32t < -128$

$t < 2$ $\quad$ $t > 4$

43. $|-32t + 160| > 64$

$-32t + 160 > 64$ or $-32t + 160 < -64$

$-32t > -96$ $\quad$ $-32t < -224$

$t < 3$ $\quad$ $t > 7$

44. $|w - 455| < 23$

$-23 < w - 455 < 23$

$432 < w < 478$

Blue

45. $|w - 600| < 5$

$-5 < w - 600 < 5$

$595 < w < 605$

Orange

46. $|w - 643| < 38$

$-38 < w - 643 < 38$

$605 < w < 681$

Orange-red

47. $|x - 2| > x + 4$

$x - 2 > x + 4$

$-2 \ngtr 4$

or

$x - 2 < -(x + 4)$

$x - 2 < -x - 4$

$2x - 2 < -4$

$2x < -2$

$x < -1$

6.7 Standardized Test Practice (p. 366)

48. $|2x + 3| > 17$

$|2(10.5) + 3| = |24| = 24 > 17$; D

49. $|2x + 1| < 3$

$-3 < 2x + 1 < 3$

$-4 < 2x < 2$

$-2 < x < 1$

H

6.7 Mixed Reivew (p. 366)

50. $y = \frac{x}{8}$; domain is all real numbers.

Copyright © McDougal Littell Inc.
All rights reserved.

51. $y = \dfrac{1}{x - 4}$; If $x = 4$, the denominator is zero and the function is undefined. The domain is all real numbers except 4.

52. $y = \dfrac{7}{x + 1}$; If $x = -1$, the denominator is zero and the function is undefined. The domain is all real numbers except -1.

53. $55 \text{ C.D.} \times \dfrac{1 \text{ U.S.D.}}{1.466 \text{ C.D.}} \approx \$38$

54. $195 \text{ U.S.D.} \times \dfrac{9.242 \text{ pesos}}{1 \text{ U.S.D.}} \approx 1802 \text{ pesos}$

55. $x = -12$;
Sample answers: $(-12, 0), (-12, 3), (-12, -4)$

56. $y = 4$;
Sample answers: $(0, 4), (1, 4), (-2, 4)$

57. $x = \dfrac{2}{3}$;

Sample answers: $\left(\dfrac{2}{3}, 0\right), \left(\dfrac{2}{3}, 1\right), \left(\dfrac{2}{3}, 5\right)$

58. function **59.** function

60. not a function; for $x > 0$, there are 2 values of y.

61. not a function; for $x < 3$, there are 2 values of y.

6.7 Maintaining Skills (p. 366)

62. $6\frac{2}{3} - 5\frac{2}{9} = 6\frac{6}{9} - 5\frac{2}{9} = 1\frac{4}{9}$

63. $8\frac{5}{6} - 3\frac{2}{9} = 8\frac{15}{18} - 3\frac{4}{18} = 5\frac{11}{18}$

64. $2\frac{2}{5} - 1\frac{3}{10} = 2\frac{4}{10} - 1\frac{3}{10} = 1\frac{1}{10}$

65. $15\frac{17}{18} - 4\frac{2}{3} = 15\frac{17}{18} - 4\frac{12}{18} = 11\frac{5}{18}$

66. $7\frac{7}{9} - 3\frac{5}{7} = 7\frac{49}{63} - 3\frac{45}{63} = 4\frac{4}{63}$

67. $19\frac{9}{12} - \frac{3}{8} = 19\frac{3}{4} - \frac{3}{8} = 19\frac{6}{8} - \frac{3}{8} = 19\frac{3}{8}$

Lesson 6.8

6.8 Checkpoint (pp. 368–369)

1. $x \geq -1$

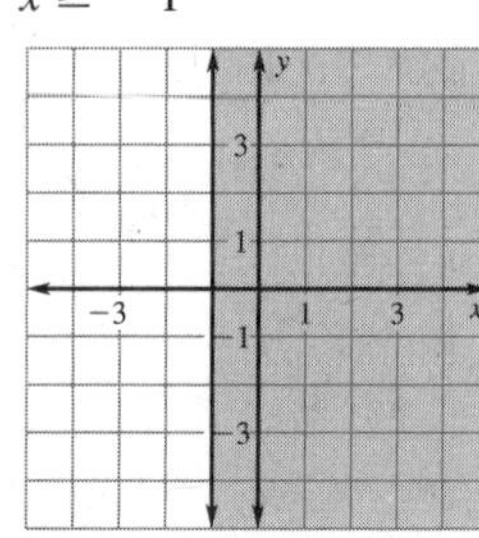

Test (0, 0): $0 \geq -1$; the origin is in the shaded region.

2. $x < 4$

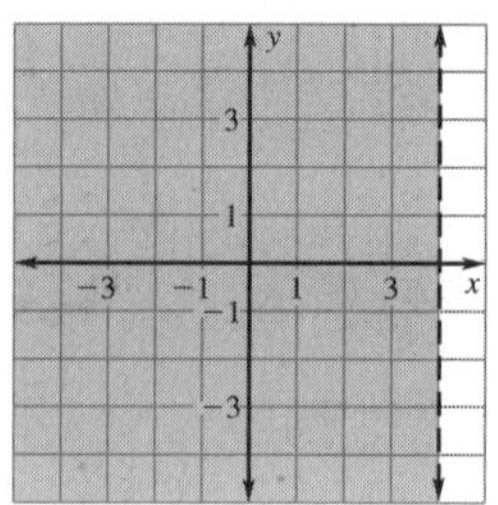

Test (0, 0): $0 < 4$; the origin is in the shaded region.

3. $y > -3$

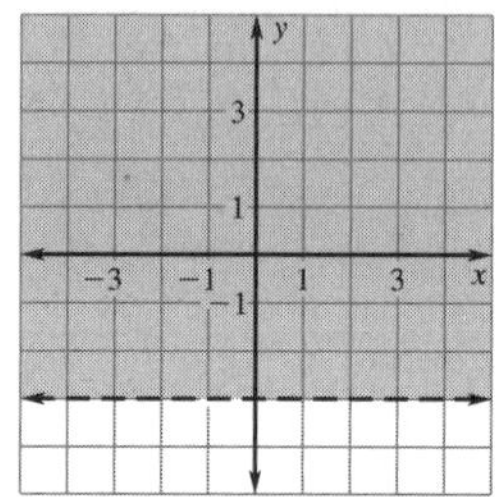

Test (0, 0): $0 > -3$; the origin is in the shaded region.

4. $y \leq 2$

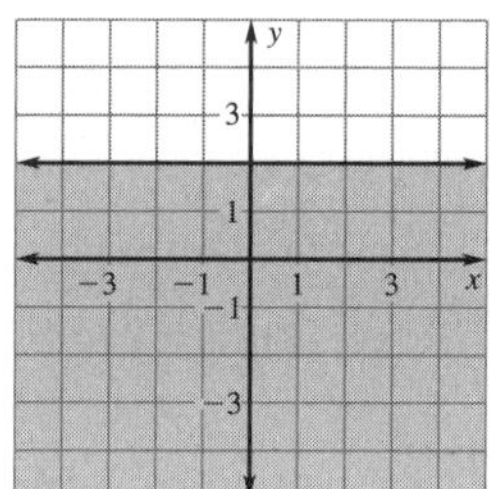

Test (0, 0): $0 \leq 2$; the origin is in the shaded region.

5. $2x + y > -1$
$y > -2x - 1$

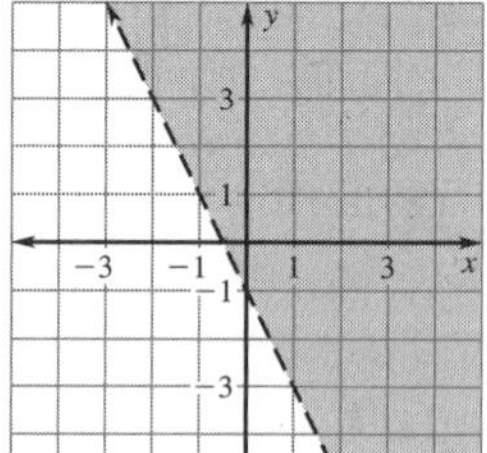

Test (0, 0):
$2(0) + 0 \overset{?}{>} -1$
$0 > -1$;
the origin is in the shaded region.

Copyright © McDougal Littell Inc.
All rights reserved.

Chapter 6 *continued*

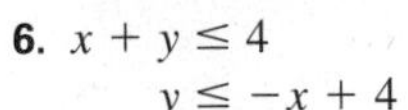

6. $x + y \le 4$
$y \le -x + 4$

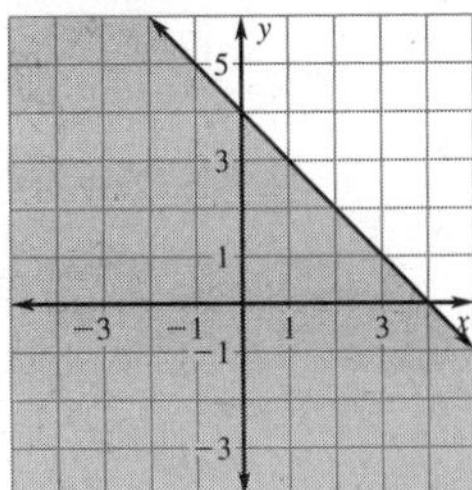

Test (0, 0):
$0 + 0 \stackrel{?}{\le} 4$
$0 \le 4;$
the origin is in the shaded region.

7. $3x - y \le 4$
$-y \le -3x + 4$
$y \ge 3x - 4$

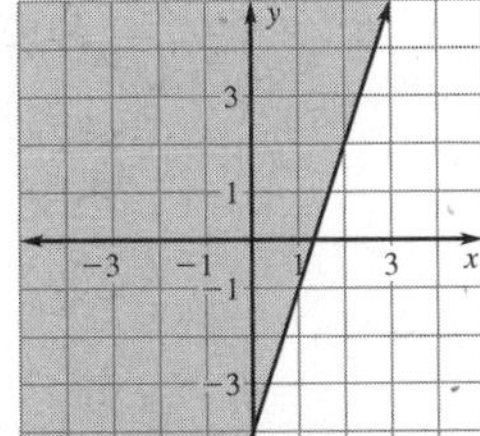

Test (0, 0):
$3(0) - 0 \stackrel{?}{\le} 4$
$0 \le -4;$
the origin is in the shaded region.

6.8 Guided Practice (p. 370)

1. Sample answer: $2x - y \ge 6$
2. $5(2) + (-3) \stackrel{?}{>} 10$
$7 \not> 10$
not a solution
3. The graph of $x > 0$ includes the half-plane to the right of the y-axis, but does not include the y-axis itself.
4. D
$x - y \le 4$
$-y \le -x + 4$
$y \ge x - 4$
slope $= 1$, y-intercept $= -4$
Test (0, 0): $0 - 0 \le 4$; true
5. B; $(2, -3)$ does not lie in the shaded region.
6. below
7. to the right
8. $0 \not< -2$; not a solution
9. $0 > -2$; a solution
10. $0 + 0 \ge -1$; a solution
11. $0 + 0 \stackrel{?}{\le} -2$
$0 \not\le -2$
not a solution
12. $3(0) - 0 \stackrel{?}{<} 3$
$0 < 3$
a solution
13. $0 - 3(0) \stackrel{?}{\ge} 12$
$0 \not\ge 12$
not a solution

6.8 Practice and Applications (pp. 370–373)

14. $x + y > -3$
$0 + 0 \stackrel{?}{>} 4$
$0 > -3$
(0, 0) is a solution.
$-6 + 3 \stackrel{?}{>} -3$
$-3 \not> -3$
$(-6, 3)$ is not a solution.
15. $2x + 2y \le 0$
$2(0) + 2(0) \stackrel{?}{\le} 0$
$0 \le 0$
(0, 0) is a solution.
$2(-1) + 2(-1) \stackrel{?}{\le} 0$
$-4 \le 0$
$(-1, -1)$ is a solution.
16. $2x + 5y \ge 10$
$2(0) + 5(0) \stackrel{?}{\ge} 10$
$0 \not\ge 10$
(0, 0) is not a solution.
$2(1) + 5(2) \stackrel{?}{\ge} 10$
$12 \ge 10$
(1, 2) is a solution.
17. $3x - 2y < 2$
$3(0) - 2(0) \stackrel{?}{<} 2$
$0 < 2$
(0, 0) is a solution.
$3(2) - 2(0) \stackrel{?}{<} 2$
$6 \not< 2$
(2, 0) is not a solution.
18. $y - 2x > 5$
$0 - 2(0) \stackrel{?}{>} 5$
$0 \not> 5$
(0, 0) is not a solution.
$1 - 2(8) \stackrel{?}{>} 5$
$-15 \not> 5$
(8, 1) is not a solution.
19. $5x + 4y \ge 6$
$5(0) + 4(0) \stackrel{?}{\ge} 6$
$0 \not\ge 6$
(0, 0) is not a solution.
$5(2) + 4(-4) \stackrel{?}{\ge} 6$
$-6 \not\ge 6$
$(2, -4)$ is not a solution.
20. B
21. C
22. A

Copyright © McDougal Littell Inc.
All rights reserved.

Chapter 6 *continued*

23. solid **24.** dashed **25.** dashed

26. $x + y > -15$
$y = -x - 15$
dashed

27. $x - y \leq 0$
$-y \leq -x$
$y = x$
solid

28. $4x + y < 9$
$y = -4x + 9$
dashed

29. $x - 2y \geq 16$
$-2y \geq -x + 16$
$y = \frac{1}{2}x - 8$
solid

30. $6x + 3y > 9$
$3y > -6x + 9$
$y = -2x + 3$
dashed

31. $-4x - 2y < 6$
$-2y < 4x + 6$
$y = -2x - 3$
dashed

32. $2x - y \leq 1$
$-y \leq -2x + 1$
$y = 2x - 1$

33. solid

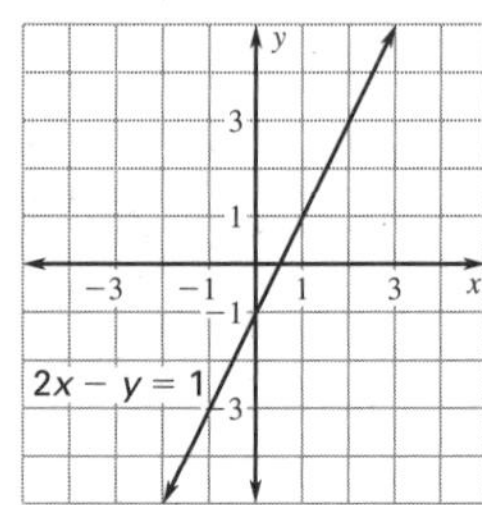

34. Test (0, 0):
$2(0) - 0 \overset{?}{\leq} 1$
$0 \leq 1$
(0, 0) is a solution.

35. $y \geq 2x - 1$

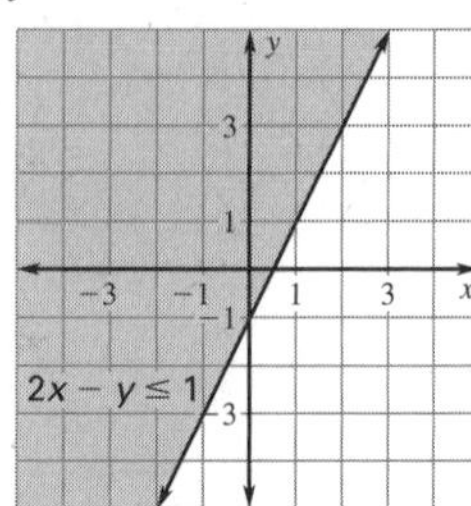

36. $x \geq -4$

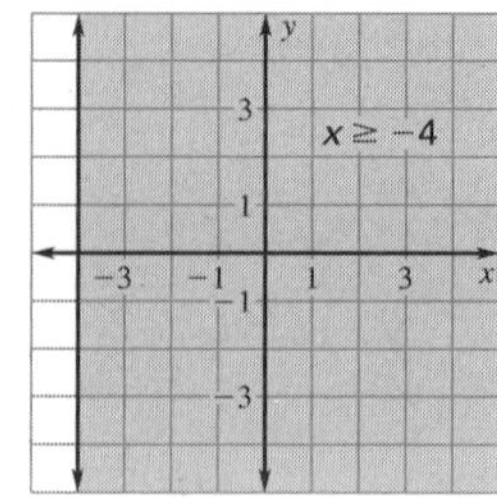

37. $x \leq 5$

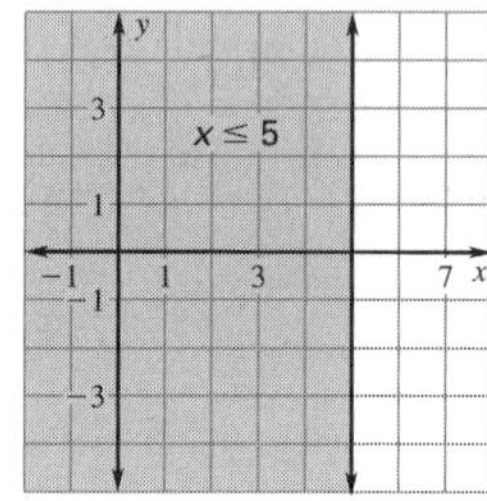

38. $y > -1$

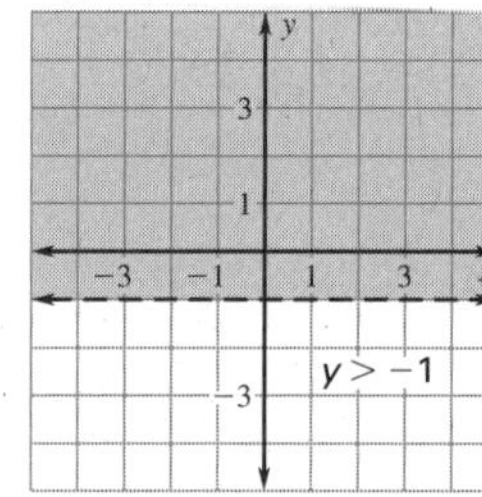

39. $x - 3 > -2$
$x > 1$

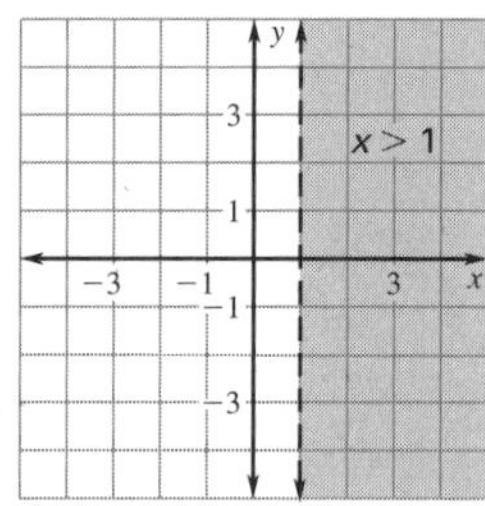

40. $y + 6 \leq 5$
$y \leq -1$

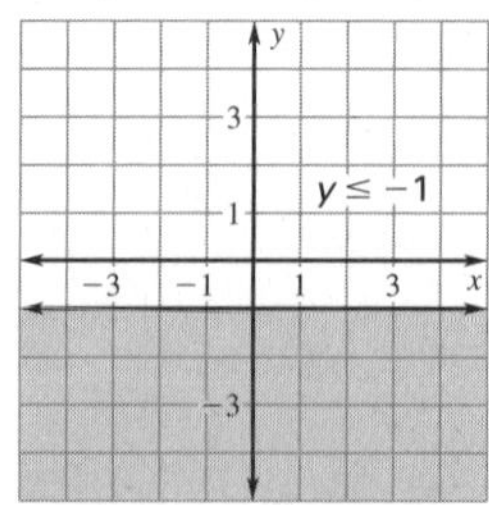

Copyright © McDougal Littell Inc.
All rights reserved.

41. $6y < 24$

$y < 4$

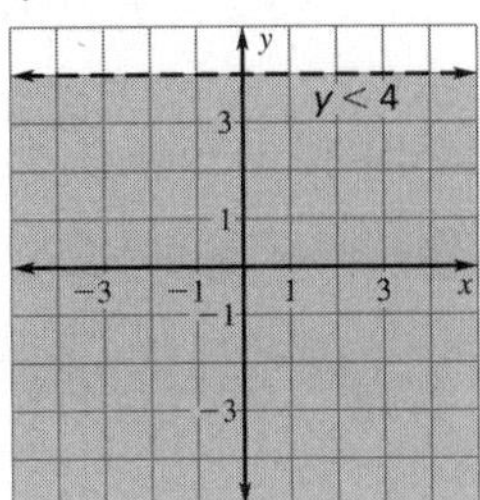

42. $3x + y \geq 9$

$y \geq -3x + 9$

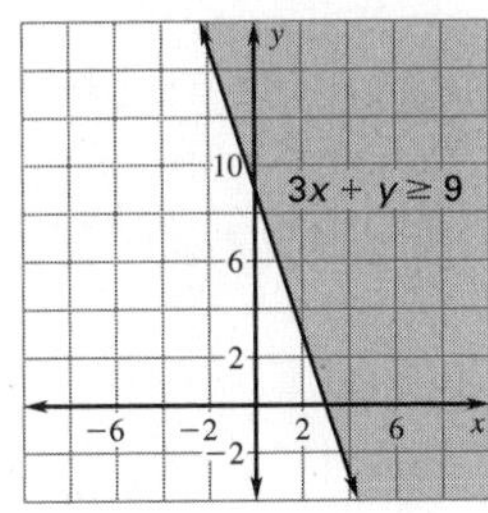

43. $y + 4x \geq -1$

$y \geq -4x - 1$

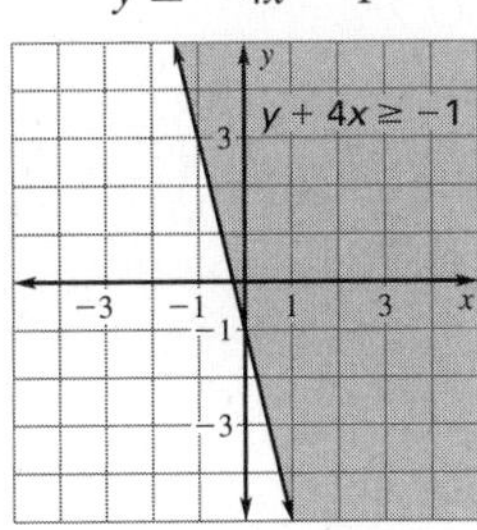

44. $x + y > -8$

$y > -x - 8$

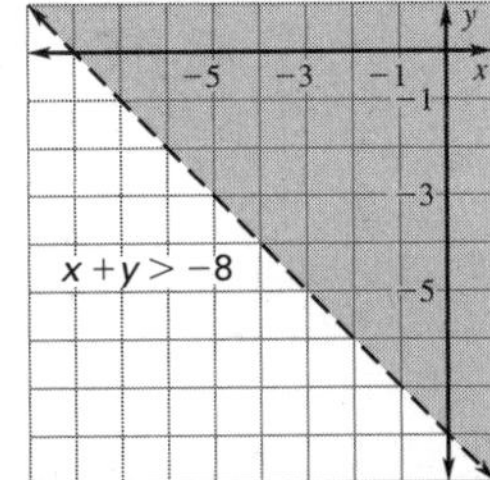

45. $x + 2y < -10$

$2y < -x - 10$

$y < -\frac{1}{2}x - 5$

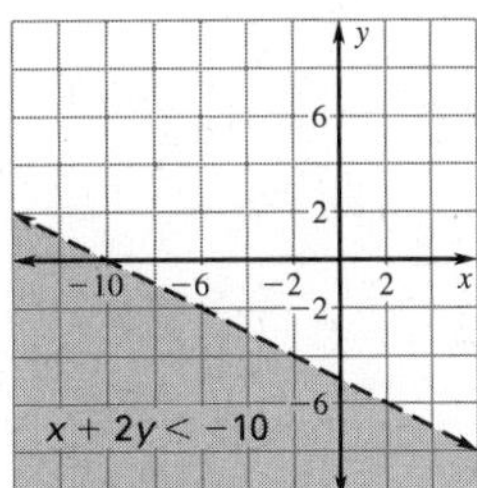

46. $x + 6y \leq 12$

$6y \leq -x + 12$

$y \leq -\frac{1}{6}x + 2$

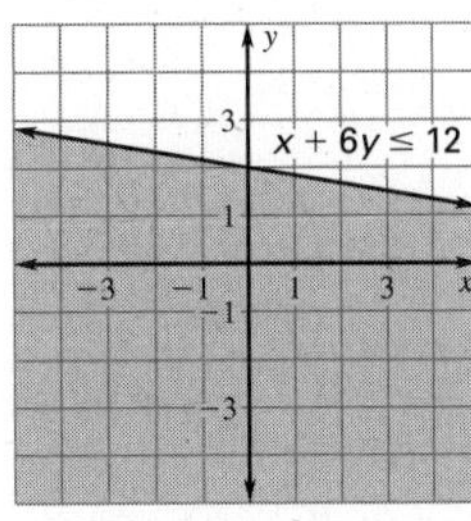

47. $4x + 3y < 24$

$3y < -4x + 24$

$y < -\frac{4}{3}x + 8$

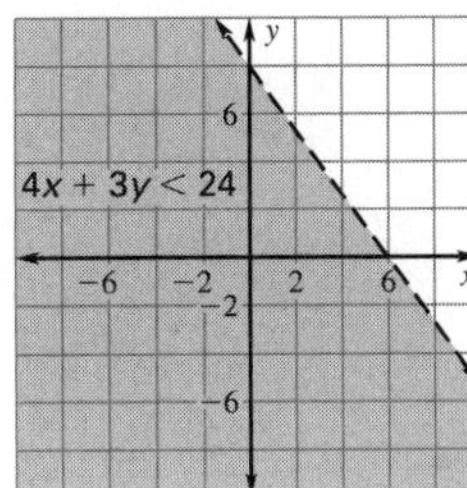

48. $2x - y > 6$

$-y > -2x + 6$

$y < 2x - 6$

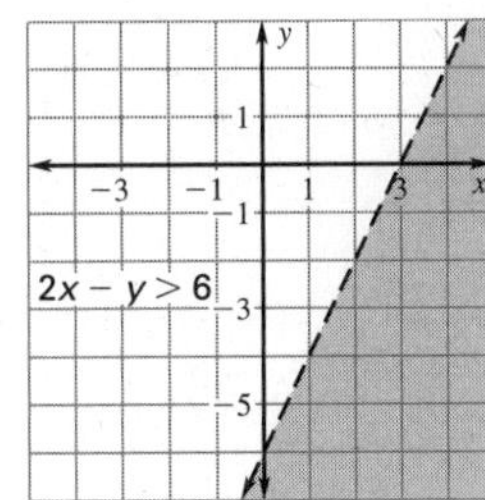

Copyright © McDougal Littell Inc.
All rights reserved.

49. $-y + x \le 11$
$-y \le -x + 11$
$y \ge x - 11$

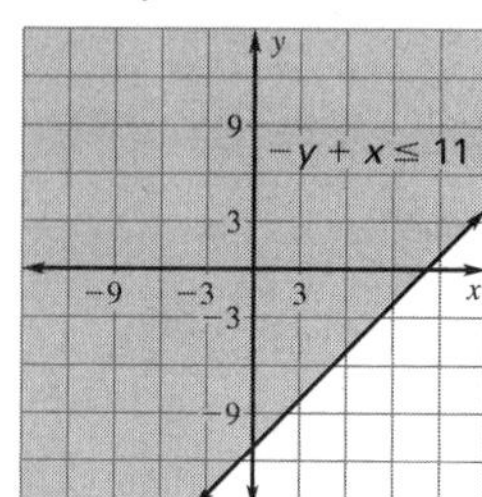

50. $-x - y < 3$
$-y < x + 3$
$y > -x - 3$

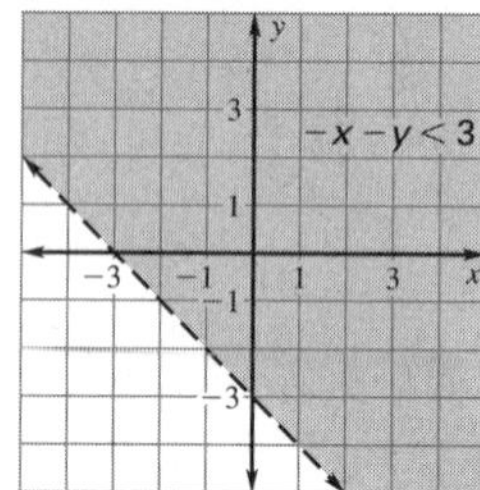

51. *Sample answer:*
(1, 3);
$123(1) + 75(3) + 195 \overset{?}{>} 500$
$543 > 500$
(3, 1);
$123(3) + 75(1) + 195 \overset{?}{>} 500$
$639 > 500$
(2, 2);
$123(2) + 75(2) + 195 \overset{?}{>} 500$
$591 > 500$

52. *Sample answer:*
(2, 2);
$102(2) + 150(2) + 41 \overset{?}{>} 500$
$545 > 500$
(1, 3);
$102(1) + 150(3) + 41 \overset{?}{>} 500$
$593 > 500$
(4, 1);
$102(4) + 150(1) + 41 \overset{?}{>} 500$
$599 > 500$

53. $y \le -2x + 3200$

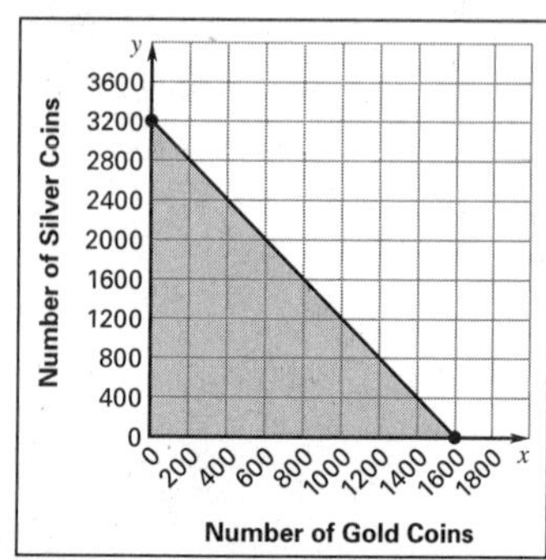

54. *Sample answer:* (1000, 1200), 1000 gold coins and 1200 silver coins; (600, 1500), 600 gold coins and 1500 silver coins.

6.8 Standardized Test Practice (p. 372)

55. D; $(2, -1)$ lies in the shaded region.

56. J; $2y - 6x > -4$; dashed line;
Test (0, 0); $2(0) - 6(0) = 0 > -4$

6.8 Mixed Review (p. 373)

57. $\frac{16 + 11 + 18}{3} = \frac{45}{3} = 15$

58. $\frac{20 + 15 + 22 + 19}{4} = \frac{76}{4} = 19$

59. $\frac{37 + 65 + 89 + 72 + 82}{5} = \frac{345}{5} = 69$

60.
$$F = \frac{9}{5}C + 32$$
$$F - 32 = \frac{9}{5}C$$
$$\frac{5}{9}(F - 32) = C$$
$$\frac{5}{9}F - \frac{160}{9} = C$$

61. $C = \frac{5}{9}(86) - \frac{160}{9}$
$C = \frac{430}{9} - \frac{160}{9} = \frac{270}{9} = 30°\text{C}$

62. $m = -5, b = 2$

63. $m = \frac{1}{2}, b = -2$

64. $5x - 5y = 1$
$-5y = -5x + 1$
$y = x - \frac{1}{5}$
$m = 1, b = -\frac{1}{5}$

65. $6x + 2y = 14$
$2y = -6x + 14$
$y = -3x + 7$
$m = -3, b = 7$

66. $y = -2; m = 0, b = -2$

67. $y = 5; m = 0, b = 5$

Copyright © McDougal Littell Inc.
All rights reserved.

6.8 Maintaining Skills (p. 373)

68. $\frac{9}{25} = \frac{36}{100} = 36\%$

69. $\frac{24 + 4 + 20 + 4}{100} = \frac{52}{100} = 52\%$

70. $\frac{8.5}{25} = \frac{34}{100} = 34\%$

Quiz 3 *(p. 373)*

1. $|x| \geq 18$

$x \geq 18$ or $x \leq -18$

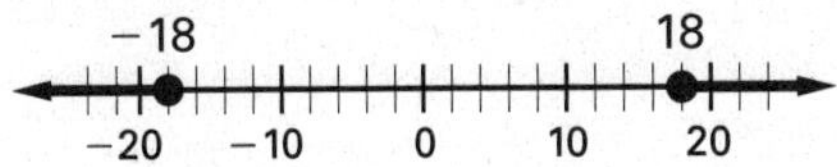

2. $|x - 4| > 1$

$x - 4 > 1$ or $x - 4 < -1$

$x > 5$ $\quad$ $x < 3$

3. $|x + 7| < 2$

$-2 < x + 7 < 2$

$-9 < x < -5$

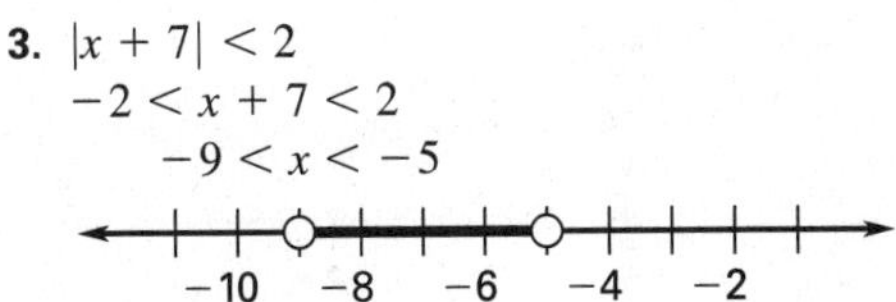

4. $|3x - 12| \leq 9$

$-9 \leq 3x - 12 \leq 9$

$3 \leq 3x \leq 21$

$1 \leq x \leq 7$

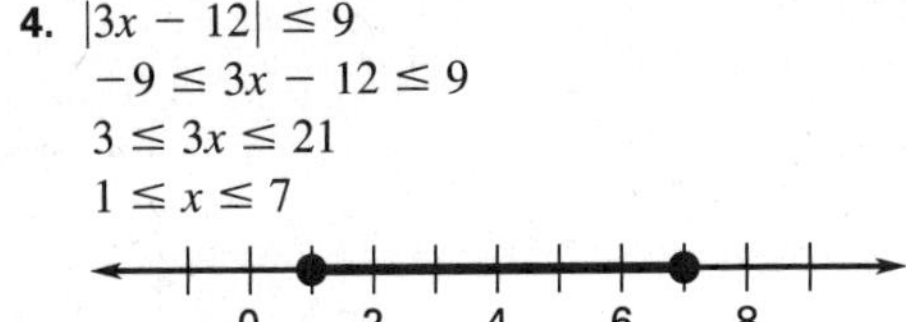

5. $|2x + 7| \leq 25$

$-25 \leq 2x + 7 \leq 25$

$-32 \leq 2x \leq 18$

$-16 \leq x \leq 9$

6. $|4x + 2| - 5 > 17$

$|4x + 2| > 22$

$4x + 2 > 22$ or $4x + 2 < -22$

$4x > 20$ $\quad$ $4x < -24$

$x > 5$ $\quad$ $x < -6$

7. $s = |-32t + 48|$

$|-32t + 48| > 24$

$-32t + 48 > 24$

$-32t > -24$

$t < \frac{3}{4} = 0.75$

or

$-32t + 48 < -24$

$-32t < -72$

$t > 2.25$

8. $x + y \leq 4$

$0 + -1 \overset{?}{\leq} 4$

$-1 \leq 4$

$(0, -1)$ is a solution.

$2 + 2 \overset{?}{\leq} 4$

$4 \leq 4$

(2, 2) is a solution.

9. $y - 3x > 0$

$0 - 3(0) \overset{?}{>} 0$

$0 \not> 0$

(0, 0) is not a solution.

$1 - 3(-4) \overset{?}{>} 0$

$13 > 0$

$(-4, 1)$ is a solution.

10. $-2x + 5y \geq 5$

$-2(2) + 5(1) \overset{?}{\geq} 5$

$1 \not\geq 5$

(2, 1) is not a solution.

$-2(-1) + 5(2) \overset{?}{\geq} 5$

$12 \geq 5$

$(-1, 2)$ is a solution.

11. $-x - 2y < 4$

$-(1) - 2(-1) \overset{?}{<} 4$

$1 < 4$

$(1, -1)$ is a solution.

$-(2) - 2(-3) \overset{?}{<} 4$

$4 \not< 4$

$(2, -3)$ is not a solution.

12. $x \leq -4$

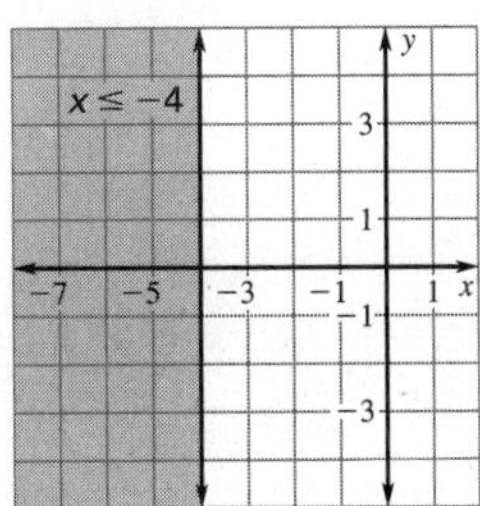

Copyright © McDougal Littell Inc.
All rights reserved.

13. $y \geq 3$

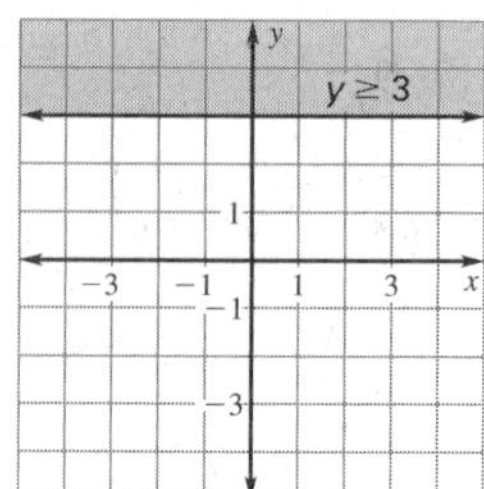

14. $y - 5x > 0$

$y > 5x$

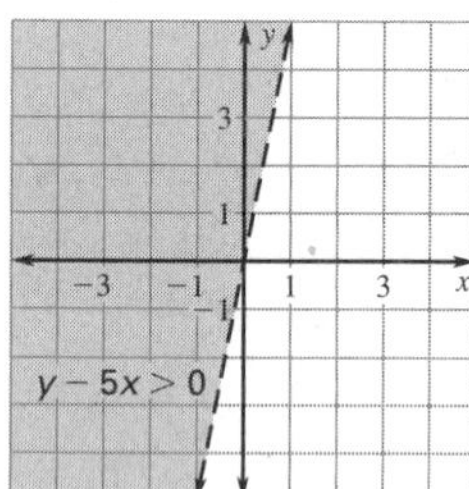

15. $y < -2x$

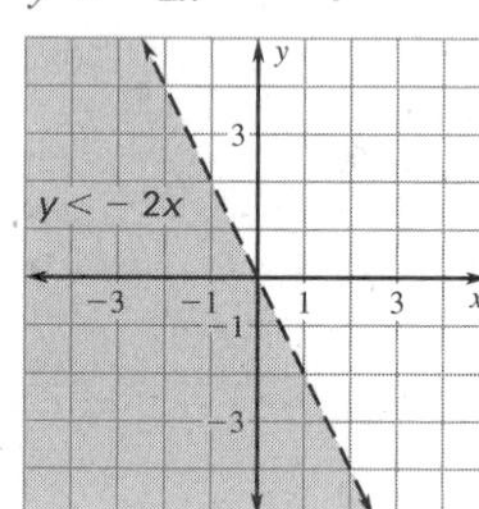

16. $3x + y > 1$

$y > -3x + 1$

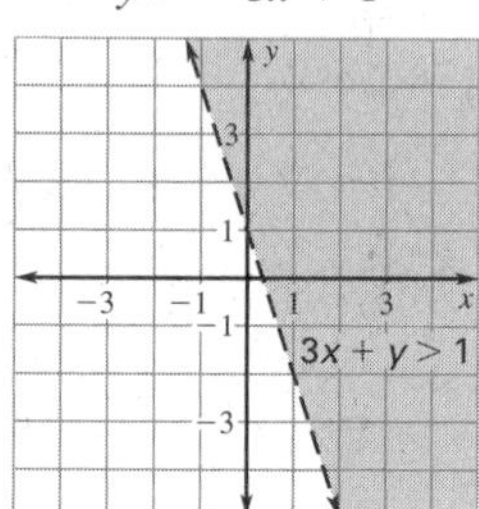

17. $2x - y \geq 5$

$-y \geq -2x + 5$

$y \leq 2x - 5$

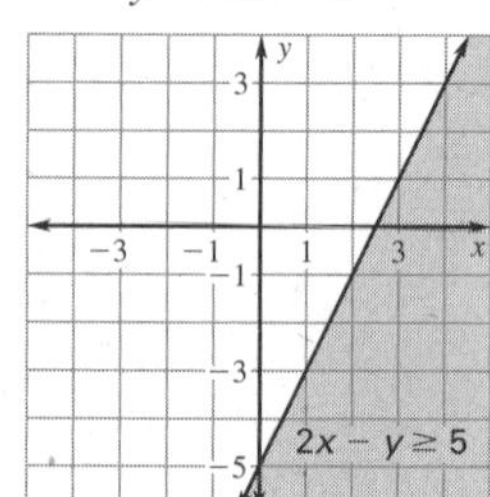

6.8 Using a Graphing Calculator: Try These

(p. 374)

1. $y < -2x - 3$

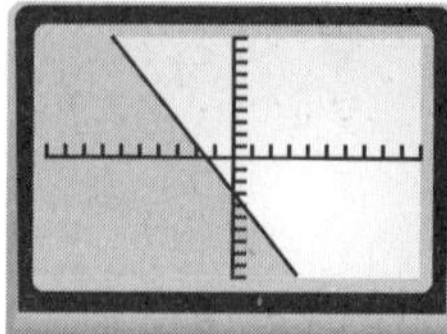

2. $y > 2x + 2$

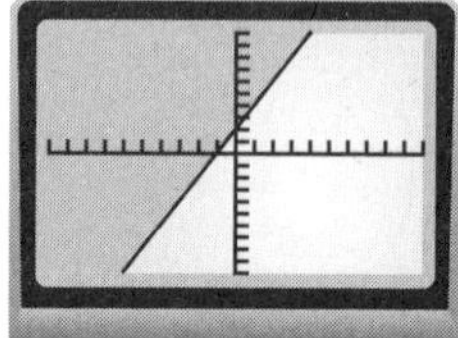

3. $x + 2y \leq -1$

$2y \leq -x - 1$

$y \leq -\frac{1}{2}x - \frac{1}{2}$

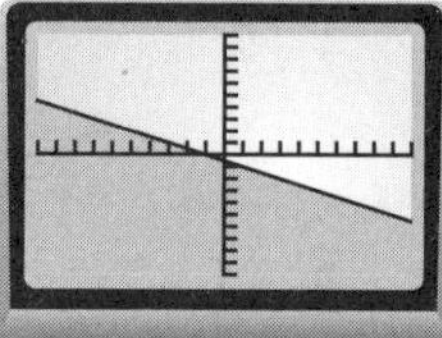

4. $x - 3y \geq 3$

$-3y \geq -x + 3$

$y \leq \frac{1}{3}x - 1$

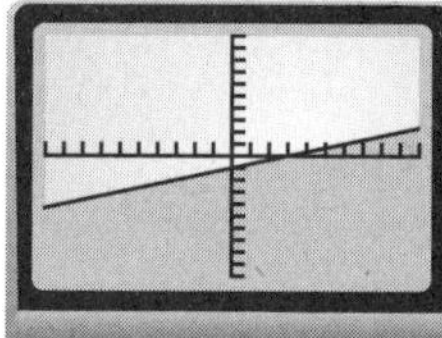

5. $y > 0.5x + 2$

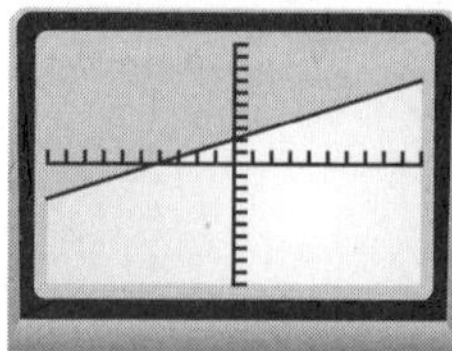

6. $y < 3x - 3.2$

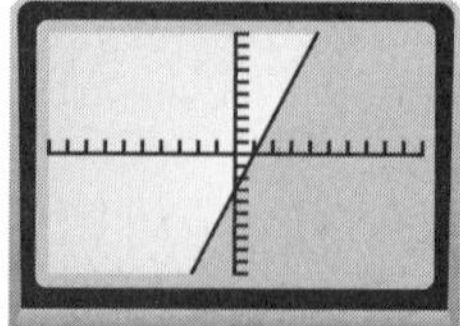

Copyright © McDougal Littell Inc.
All rights reserved.

7. $\frac{3}{4}x + y \geq 1$

$y \geq -\frac{3}{4}x + 1$

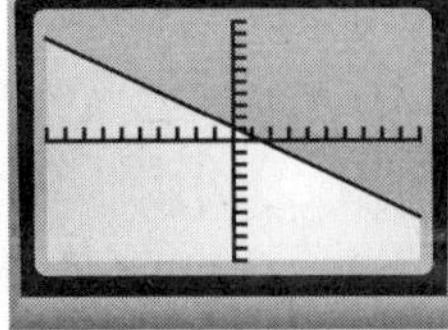

8. $\frac{x}{2} - 2y \leq 2$

$-2y \leq -\frac{x}{2} + 2$

$y \geq \frac{x}{4} - 1$

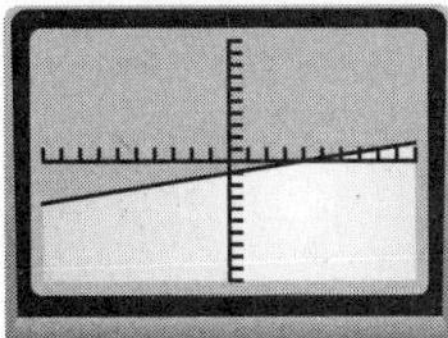

9. $y < x + 25$

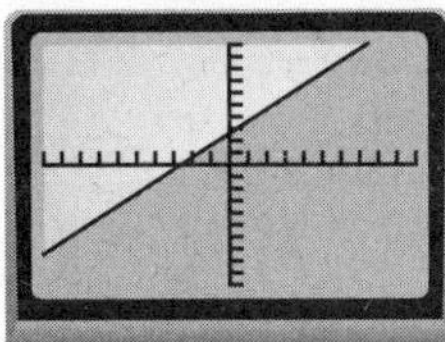

10. $y > -x + 25$

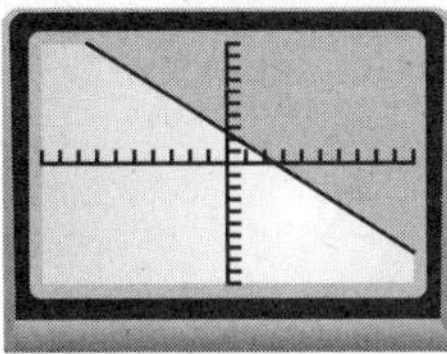

11. $y \leq 0.1x$

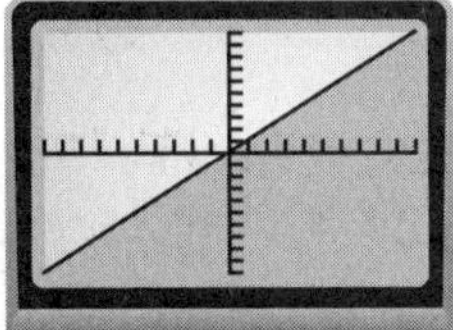

12. $y \geq 100x$

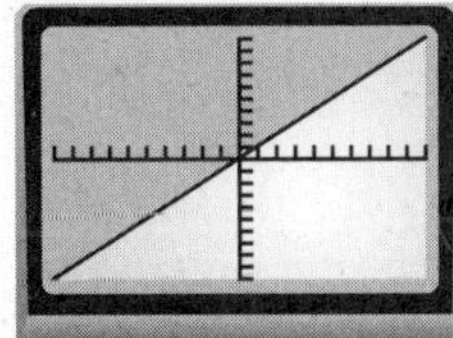

13. $y > x$

14. $y < x + 2$

Chapter Summary and Review *(pp. 375–378)*

1. $x - 5 \leq -3$

$x \leq 2$

2. $a + 6 > 28$

$a > 22$

3. $-8 < -10 + x$

$2 < x$ or $x > 2$

4. $7 + z \geq 20$

$z \geq 13$

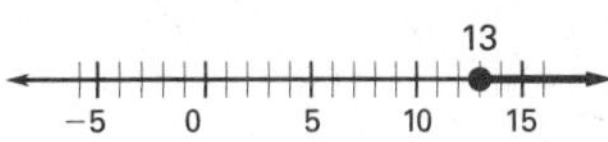

5. $64 < 8x$

$8 < x$

6. $-6k > -30$

$k < 5$

7. $-81 \geq -3p$

$27 \leq p$

8. $-81 > 9r$

$-9 > r$

9. $-\frac{3}{2}n \geq 9$

$n \leq -\frac{2}{3}(9)$

$n \leq -6$

10. $3 < \frac{x}{5}$

$15 < x$

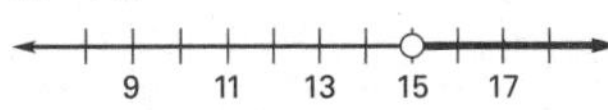

11. $\frac{t}{14} \leq 4$

$t \leq 56$

Copyright © McDougal Littell Inc.
All rights reserved.

Chapter 6 *continued*

12. $-\frac{1}{6}y \geq 3$

$y \leq -18$

−20 −18 −16 −14 −12

13. $6x - 8 \geq 4$

$6x \geq 12$

$x \geq 2$

14. $10 - 3x < -5$

$-3x < -15$

$x > 5$

15. $4x - 9 \geq 11$

$4x \geq 20$

$x \geq 5$

16. $5(x - 2) \leq 10$

$5x - 10 \leq 10$

$5x \leq 20$

$x \leq 4$

17. $-3(x - 1) > 4$

$-3x + 3 > 4$

$-3x > 1$

$x < -\frac{1}{3}$

18. $\frac{1}{4}(x + 8) < 1$

$\frac{1}{4}x + 2 < 1$

$\frac{1}{4}x < -1$

$x < -4$

19. $5 - 8x \leq -3x$

$5 \leq 5x$

$1 \leq x$ or $x \geq 1$

20. $5x > 12 + x$

$4x > 12$

$x > 3$

21. $3x - 9 \leq 2x + 4$

$x - 9 \leq 4$

$x \leq 13$

22. $9 < x + 1 < 13$

$8 < x < 12$

6 8 10 12 14

23. $-3 \leq 3x \leq 15$

$-1 \leq x \leq 5$

−2 0 2 4 6

24. $-1 \leq x - 2 < 3$

$1 \leq x < 5$

0 2 4 6 8

25. $1 < 2x - 3 < 5$

$4 < 2x < 8$

$2 < x < 4$

−4 −2 0 2 4

26. $0 < 4 - x \leq 5$

$-4 < -x \leq 1$

$4 > x \geq -1$

−4 −2 0 2 4

27. $-7 < 3 - \frac{1}{4}x \leq 1$

$-10 < -\frac{1}{4}x \leq -2$

$40 > x \geq 8$ or $8 \leq x < 40$

0 10 20 30 40

28. $x > 4$ or $3x \leq -9$

$x > 4$ $x \leq -3$

−4 −2 0 2 4

29. $2x \leq -10$ or $x + 3 > 1$

$x \leq -5$ $x > -2$

−6 −4 −2 0 2

30. $x - 7 \geq 0$ or $3 + x < -2$

$x \geq 7$ $x < -5$

−8 −4 0 4 8

31. $6x - 2 \leq 4$ or $3x > 21$

$6x \leq 6$ $x > 7$

$x \leq 1$ $x > 7$

0 2 4 6 8

32. $3x + 2 \leq -7$ or $2x + 1 \geq 9$

$3x \leq -9$ $2x \geq 8$

$x \leq -3$ $x \geq 4$

−4 −2 0 2 4

33. $\frac{1}{4}x < \frac{1}{2}$ or $3x - 6 > 24$

$x < 2$ $3x > 30$

$x < 2$ $x > 10$

−4 0 4 8 12

34. $|x| = 13$; $x = 13$ or $x = -13$

35. $|x| = -7$; no solution

Copyright © McDougal Littell Inc.
All rights reserved.

36. $|x - 1| = 6$

$x - 1 = 6$ or $x - 1 = -6$

$x = 7$ $\quad$ $x = -5$

Check: $|7 - 1| = |6| = 6$; $|-5 - 1| = |-6| = 6$

37. $|3x| = 27$

$3x = 27$ or $3x = -27$

$x = 9$ $\quad$ $x = -9$

Check: $|3(9)| = |27| = 27$; $|3(-9)| = |-27| = 27$

38. $|2x - 3| = 1$

$2x - 3 = 1$ or $2x - 3 = -1$

$2x = 4$ $\quad$ $2x = 2$

$x = 2$ $\quad$ $x = 1$

Check: $|2(2) - 3| = |1| = 1$; $|2(1) - 3| = |-1| = 1$

39. $|6x - 1| + 5 = 2$

$|6x - 1| = -3$

no solution

40. midpoint of 9 and 21: $\frac{9 + 21}{2} = 15$;

distance from maximum to midpoint: $21 - 15 = 6$

equation: $|x - 15| = 6$

41. $|x| \le 2$

$-2 \le x \le 2$

-4 -2 0 2 4

Test one value from each region:

-3; $|-3| = 3 \not\le 2$

0; $|0| = 0 \le 2$

3; $|3| = 3 \not\le 2$

42. $|6x| > 24$

$6x > 24$ or $6x < -24$

$x > 4$ $\quad$ $x < -4$

-4 -2 0 2 4

Test one value from each region:

-5; $|6(-5)| = |-30| = 30 > 24$

0; $|6(0)| = |0| = 0 \not> 24$

5; $|6(5)| = |30| = 30 > 24$

43. $|x - 10| \le 8$

$-8 \le x - 10 \le 8$

$2 \le x \le 18$

0 4 8 12 16 20

Test one value from each region:

1; $|1 - 10| = |-9| = 9 \not\le 8$

6; $|6 - 10| = |-4| = 4 \le 8$

19; $|19 - 10| = |9| = 9 \not\le 8$

44. $|4x + 8| \ge 20$

$4x + 8 \ge 20$ or $4x + 8 \le -20$

$4x \ge 12$ $\quad$ $4x \le -28$

$x \ge 3$ $\quad$ $x \le -7$

-8 -4 0 4 8

Test one value from each region:

4; $|4(4) + 8| = |24| = 24 \ge 20$

0; $|4(0) + 8| = |8| = 8 \not\ge 20$

-8; $|4(-8) + 8| = |-24| = 24 \ge 20$

45. $|2x - 2| < 8$

$-8 < 2x - 2 < 8$

$-6 < 2x < 10$

$-3 < x < 5$

-6 -4 -2 0 2 4 6

Test one value from each region:

-4; $|2(-4) - 2| = |-10| = 10 \not< 8$

0; $|2(0) - 2| = |-2| = 2 < 8$

6; $|2(6) - 2| = |10| = 10 \not< 8$

46. $|5x + 3| > 2$

$5x + 3 > 2$ or $5x + 3 < -2$

$5x > -1$ $\quad$ $5x < -5$

$x > -\frac{1}{5}$ $\quad$ $x < -1$

-1 $\quad$ $-\frac{1}{5}$

-1 0 1

Test one value from each region:

-2; $|5(-2) + 3| = |-7| = 7 > 2$

$-\frac{2}{5}$; $\left|5\left(-\frac{2}{5}\right) + 3\right| = |1| = 1 \not> 2$

0; $|5(0) + 3| = |3| = 3 > 2$

47. $|x - 4| - 5 < 1$

$|x - 4| < 6$

$-6 < x - 4 < 6$

$-2 < x < 10$

-4 0 4 8 12

Test one value from each region:

-3; $|-3 - 4| - 5 = |-7| - 5 = 7 - 5 = 2 \not< 1$

0; $|0 - 4| - 5 = |-4| - 5 = 4 - 5 = -1 < 1$

11; $|11 - 4| - 5 = |7| - 5 = 7 - 5 = 2 \not< 1$

48. $|3x| + 2 \le 11$

$|3x| \le 9$

$-9 \le 3x \le 9$

$-3 \le x \le 3$

-4 -2 0 2 4

Test one value from each region:

-4; $|3(-4)| + 2 = |-12| + 2 = 12 + 2 = 14 \not\le 11$

0; $|3(0)| + 2 = |0| + 2 = 2 \le 11$

4; $|3(4)| + 2 = |12| + 2 = 12 + 2 = 14 \not\le 11$

Copyright © McDougal Littell Inc.
All rights reserved.

49. $|2x + 1| - 5 > 7$

$|2x + 1| > 12$

$2x + 1 > 12$ or $2x + 1 < -12$

$2x > 11$ $\qquad$ $2x < -13$

$x > \frac{11}{2}$ $\qquad$ $x < -\frac{13}{2}$

$-\frac{13}{2}$ $\quad$ $\frac{11}{2}$

−6 −4 −2 0 2 4 6

Test one value from each region:

$6; |2(6) + 1| - 5 = |13| - 5 = 8 > 7$

$0; |2(0) + 1| - 5 = |1| - 5 = -4 \not> 7$

$-7; |2(-7) + 1| - 5 = |-13| - 5 = 8 > 7$

50. $y > -5$

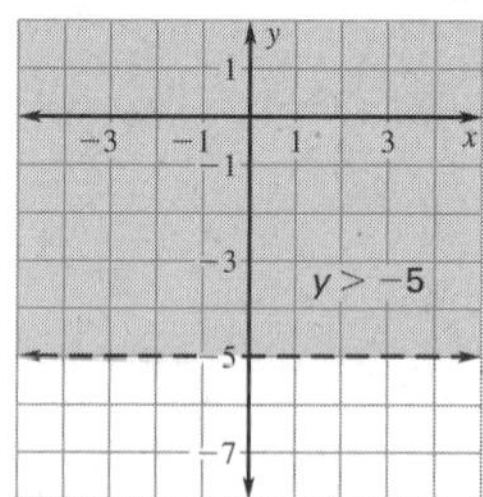

51. $x < 2$

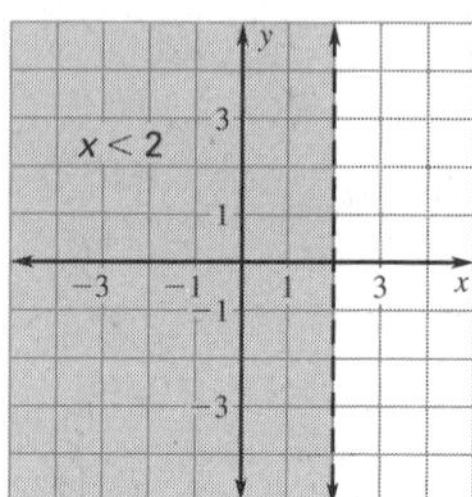

52. $-2x + y \geq 4$

$y \geq 2x + 4$

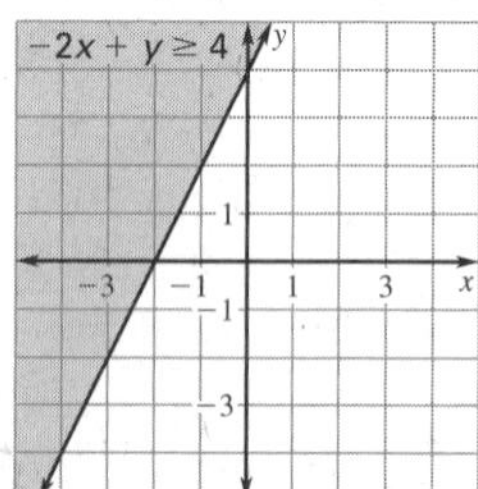

Test a point: (0, 0)

$-2(0) + 0 \overset{?}{\geq} 4$

$0 \not\geq 4$

53. $x - 3y \geq 3$

$-3y \geq -x + 3$

$y \leq \frac{1}{3}x - 1$

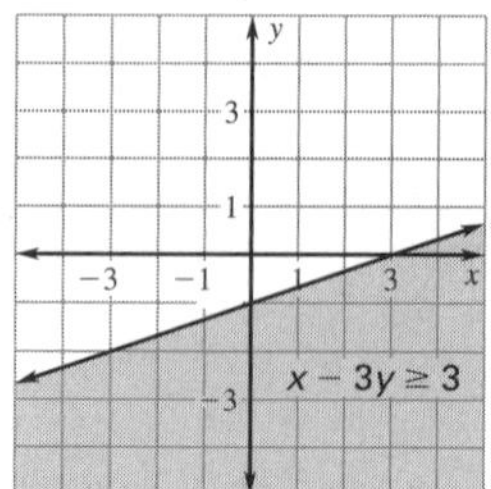

Test a point: (0, 0)

$0 - 3(0) \overset{?}{\geq} 3$

$0 \not\geq 3$

54. $2y - 6x \geq -2$

$2y \geq 6x - 2$

$y \geq 3x - 1$

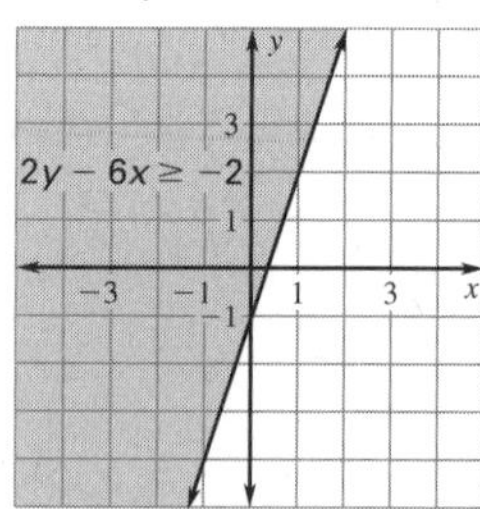

Test a point: (0, 0)

$2(0) - 6(0) \overset{?}{\geq} -2$

$0 \geq -2$

55. $3x + 6y < 12$

$6y < -3x + 12$

$y < -\frac{1}{2}x + 2$

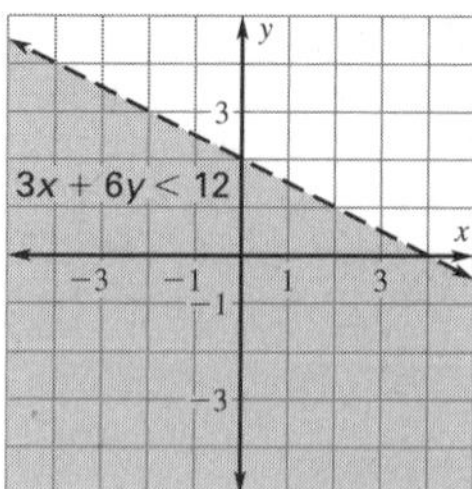

Test a point: (0, 0)

$3(0) + 6(0) \overset{?}{<} 12$

$0 < 12$

Chapter Test *(p. 379)*

1. $x - 3 < 10$

$x < 13$

11 12 13 14 15

Copyright © McDougal Littell Inc.
All rights reserved.

Chapter 6 *continued*

2. $-6 > x + 5$

$-11 > x$ or $x < -11$

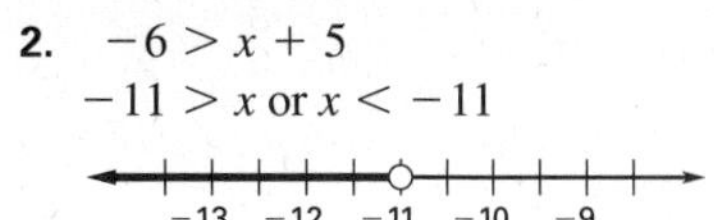

3. $-5 + x \geq 1$

$x \geq 6$

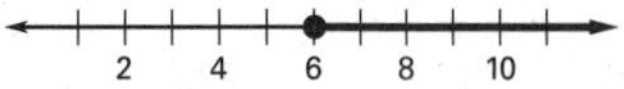

4. $\frac{1}{4}x \leq 2$

$x \leq 8$

5. $-3x < 21$

$x > -7$

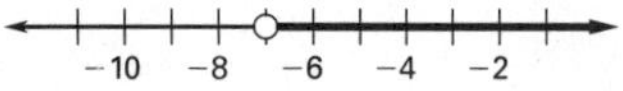

6. $-\frac{1}{2}x < 3$

$x > -6$

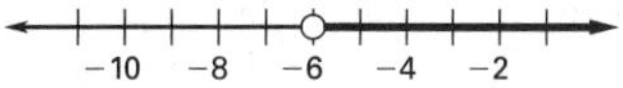

7. $6 - x > 15$

$-x > 9$

$x < -9$

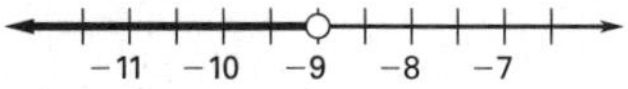

8. $3x + 2 \leq 35$

$3x \leq 33$

$x \leq 11$

9. $\frac{2}{3}x + 1 > 7$

$\frac{2}{3}x > 6$

$x > \frac{3}{2}(6)$

$x > 9$

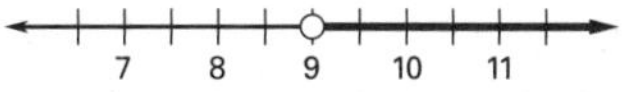

10. $2(x + 1) \geq 6$

$2x + 2 \geq 6$

$2x \geq 4$

$x \geq 2$

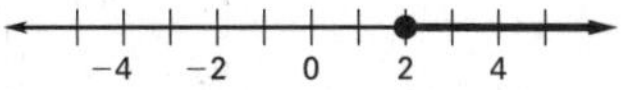

11. $3x + 5 \leq 2x - 1$

$x + 5 \leq -1$

$x \leq -6$

12. $-2(x + 4) > 3x + 17$

$-2x - 8 > 3x + 17$

$-8 > 5x + 17$

$-25 > 5x$

$-5 > x$ or $x < -5$

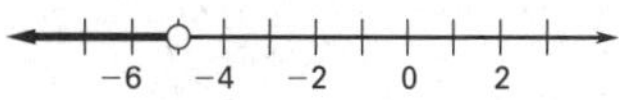

13. $-15 \leq 5x < 20$

$-3 \leq x < 4$

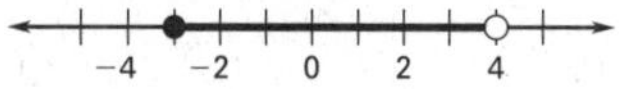

14. $-3 \leq x + 5 \leq 7$

$-8 \leq x \leq 2$

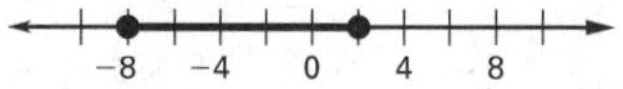

15. $-5 < 3x - 4 < 17$

$-1 < 3x < 21$

$-\frac{1}{3} < x < 7$

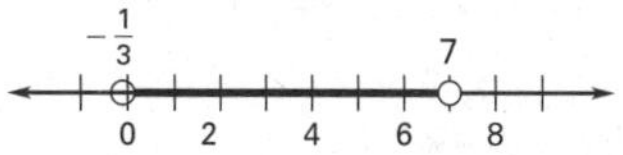

16. $-17 \leq 3x + 1 < 25$

$-18 \leq 3x < 24$

$-6 \leq x < 8$

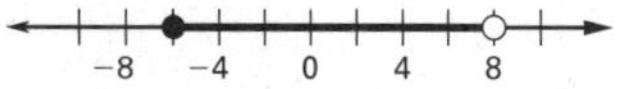

17. $x - 2 > 8$ or $x + 1 \leq 7$

$x > 10$ $x \leq 6$

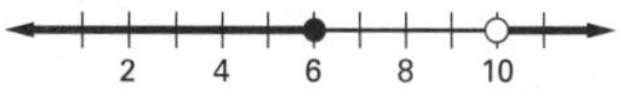

18. $-\frac{1}{2}x < -3$ or $2x < -12$

$x > 6$ $x < -6$

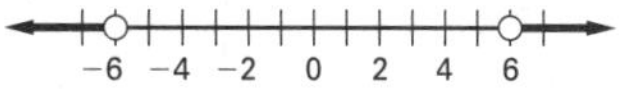

19. $x < -2$ or $3x - 5 > 1$

$x < -2$ $3x > 6$

$x < -2$ $x > 2$

20. $8x - 11 < 5$ or $4x - 7 > 13$

$8x < 16$ $4x > 20$

$x < 2$ $x > 5$

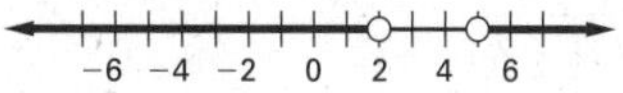

21. $6x + 9 \geq 21$ or $9x - 5 \leq 4$

$6x \geq 12$ $9x \leq 9$

$x \geq 2$ $x \leq 1$

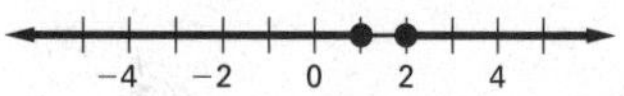

Copyright © McDougal Littell Inc.
All rights reserved.

22. $12 \le w \le 33$

23. $|x + 7| = 11$

$x + 7 = 11$ or $x + 7 = -11$

$x = 4$ $\quad$ $x = -18$

Check: $|4 + 7| = |11| = 11$; $|-18 + 7| = |-11| = 11$

24. $|3x + 4| = 16$

$3x + 4 = 16$ or $3x + 4 = -16$

$3x = 12$ $\quad$ $3x = -20$

$x = 4$ $\quad$ $x = -\frac{20}{3}$

Check: $|3(4) + 4| = |16| = 16$;

$\left|3\left(-\frac{20}{3}\right) + 4\right| = |-16| = 16$

25. $|x - 8| - 3 = 10$

$|x - 8| = 13$

$x - 8 = 13$ or $x - 8 = -13$

$x = 21$ $\quad$ $x = -5$

Check: $|21 - 8| - 3 = |13| - 3 = 10$;

$|-5 - 8| - 3 = |-13| - 3 = 13 - 3 = 10$

26. midpoint of 1 and 5 is 3; distance from 5 to 3 is 2; equation: $|x - 3| = 2$

27. midpoint of -8 and -4 is -6; distance from -8 to -6 is 2; equation: $|x - (-6)| = 2$; $|x + 6| = 2$

28. midpoint of -1 and 9 is 4; distance from 9 to 4 is 5. equation: $|x - 4| = 5$

29. $|2x| > 14$

$2x > 14$ or $2x < -14$

$x > 7$ $\quad$ $x < -7$

−8 −4 0 4 8

Test one value from each region:

8; $|2(8)| = |16| = 16 > 14$

0; $|2(0)| = |0| = 0 \not> 14$;

-8; $|2(-8)| = |-16| = 16 > 14$

30. $|4x + 5| \le 1$

$-1 \le 4x + 5 \le 1$

$-6 \le 4x \le -4$

$-\frac{3}{2} \le x \le -1$

−2 −1 0 1 2

Test one value from each region:

-2; $|4(-2) + 5| = |-3| = 3 \not\le 1$

$-\frac{5}{4}$; $\left|4\left(-\frac{5}{4}\right) + 5\right| = |0| = 0 \le 1$

0; $|4(0) + 5| = |5| = 5 \not\le 1$

31. $|3x - 9| + 6 < 18$

$|3x - 9| < 12$

$-12 < 3x - 9 < 12$

$-3 < 3x < 21$

$-1 < x < 7$

−4 −2 0 2 4 6 8

Test one value from each region:

-2; $|3(-2) - 9| + 6 = |-15| + 6 = 21 \not< 18$

0; $|3(0) - 9| + 6 = |-9| + 6 = 15 < 18$

8; $|3(8) - 9| + 6 = |15| + 6 = 21 \not< 18$

32. $x > -1$

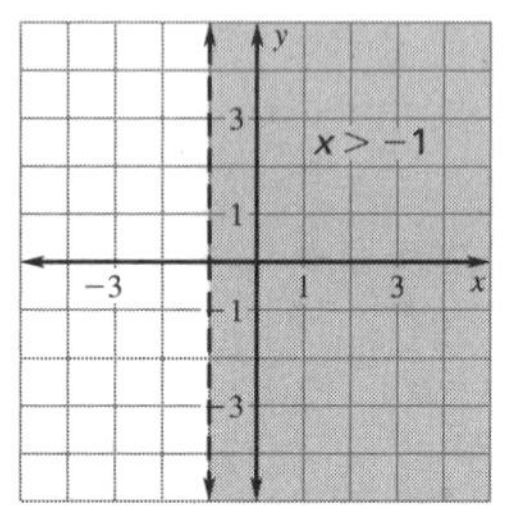

33. $y > 5$

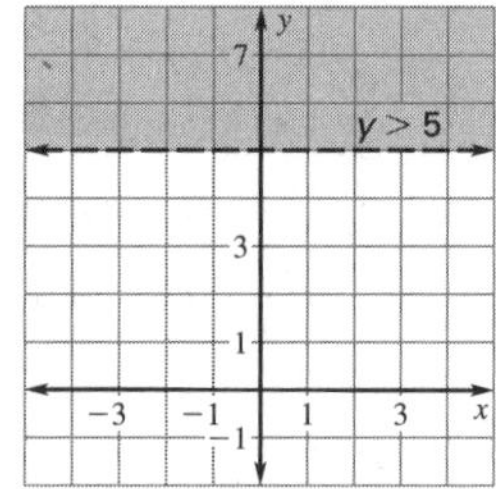

34. $y \ge 3x - 3$

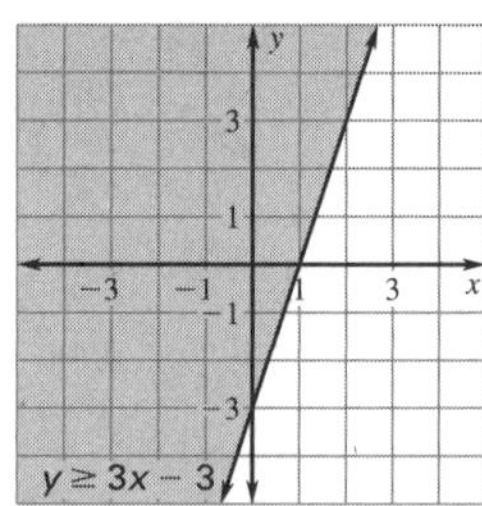

Test a point: (0, 0)

$0 \overset{?}{\ge} 3(0) - 3$

$0 \ge -3$

Copyright © McDougal Littell Inc.
All rights reserved.

35. $x + y \le 1$

$y \le -x + 1$

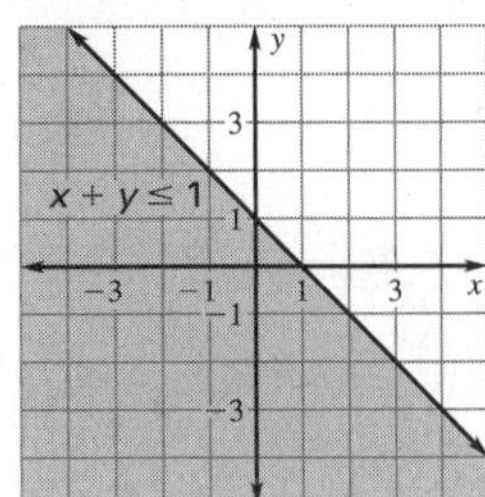

Test a point: (0, 0)

$0 + 0 \overset{?}{\le} 1$

$0 \le 1$

36. $x + 2y > 6$

$2y > -x + 6$

$y > -\frac{1}{2}x + 3$

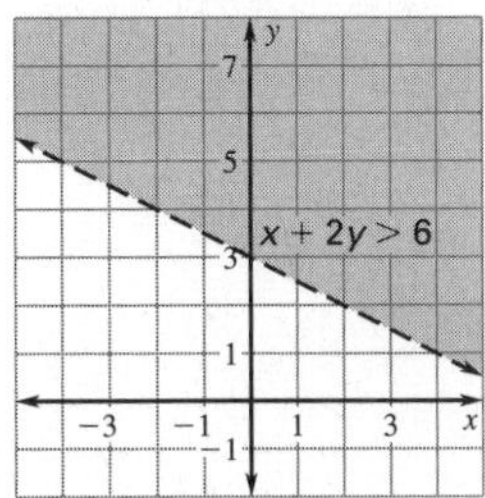

Test a point: (0, 0)

$0 + 2(0) \overset{?}{>} 6$

$0 \not> 6$

37. $3x + 4y \ge 12$

$4y \ge -3x + 12$

$y \ge -\frac{3}{4}x + 3$

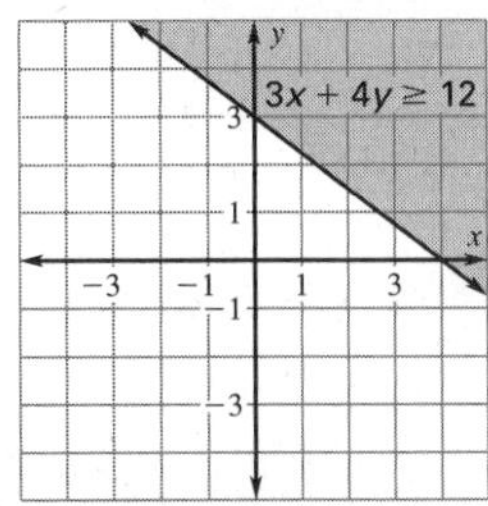

Test a point: (0, 0)

$3(0) + 4(0) \overset{?}{\ge} 12$

$0 \not\ge 12$

38. Let x be the number of sandwiches.
Let y be the number of drinks.

$2x + y < 100$; $y < -2x + 100$

Test a point: (0, 0)

$2(0) + 0 \overset{?}{<} 100$

$0 < 100$

39. *Sample answers:* (20, 50) means 20 sandwiches and 50 drinks; (30, 30) means 30 sandwiches and 30 drinks.

Chapter Standardized Test *(p. 380)*

1. $x + 5 < 12$

$x < 7$

D

2. $5x < 10$

$x < 2$

D

3. $2 - 3x \ge -4$

$-3x \ge -6$

$x \le 2$

B

4. $-3x + 4 \le x - 2$

$-4x + 4 \le -2$

$-4x \le -6$

$x \ge \frac{3}{2}$

D

5. $-4 \le x - 1 \le 5$

$-3 \le x \le 6$

A; -4

6. $-3x + 2 > 11$ or $5x + 1 > 6$

$-3x > 9$ $\quad 5x > 5$

$x < -3$ $\quad x > 1$

A

7. $|x - 7| + 5 = 17$

$|x - 7| = 12$

$x - 7 = 12$ or $x - 7 = -12$

$x = 19$ $\quad x = -5$

D

Copyright © McDougal Littell Inc.
All rights reserved.

8. $|2x - 10| \geq 6$

$2x - 10 \geq 6$ or $2x - 10 \leq -6$

$2x \geq 16$ $\qquad$ $2x \leq 4$

$x \geq 8$ $\qquad$ $x \leq 2$

C

9. B

$2x + y > 4$

$y > -2x + 4$

$m = -2; b = 4$

Test a point: (0, 0)

$2(0) + 0 \overset{?}{>} 4$

$0 \not> 4$

(0, 0) is not a solution.

Maintaining Skills *(p. 381)*

1. $5x + 5y = 5(5) + 5(9) = 25 + 45 = 70$

2. $9y + x = 9(9) + 5 = 81 + 5 = 86$

3. $2x + 3y = 2(5) + 3(9) = 10 + 27 = 37$

4. $7y + 3x = 7(9) + 3(5) = 63 + 15 = 78$

5. $12x + y = 12(5) + (9) = 60 + 9 = 69$

6. $4y + 4x = 4(9) + 4(5) = 36 + 20 = 56$

7. $3x + 4y = 3(5) + 4(9) = 15 + 36 = 51$

8. $6y + 2x = 6(9) + 2(5) = 54 + 10 = 64$

9. $-6 + (-11) = -(|-6| + |-11|)$
$= -(6 + 11)$
$= -17$

10. $-4 + (-10) = -(|-4| + |-10|)$
$= -(4 + 10)$
$= -14$

11. $8 + (-1) = |8| - |-1| = 8 - 1 = 7$

12. $-9 + (-9) = -(|-9| + |-9|) = -(9 + 9) = -18$

13. $-21 + 24 = |24| - |-21| = 24 - 21 = 3$

14. $-11 + 9 = -(|-11| - |9|) = -(11 - 9) = -2$

15. $15 + (-8) = |15| - |-8| = 15 - 8 = 7$

16. $30 + (-16) = |30| - |-16| = 30 - 16 = 14$

Chapters 1–6 Cumulative Practice *(pp. 382–383)*

1. $x + 8 = -1 + 8 = 7$

2. $3x - 2 = 3(7) - 2 = 21 - 2 = 19$

3. $x(4 + x) = 5(4 + 5) = 5(9) = 45$

4. $3(x - 5) = 3(1 - 5) = 3(-4) = -12$

5. $\dfrac{x + 8}{x} = \dfrac{4 + 8}{4} = \dfrac{12}{4} = 3$

6. $x^3 - 3x + 1 = 2^3 - 3(2) + 1 = 8 - 6 + 1 = 3$

7. $C = 65 + n$

n	0	1	2	3	4	5	6
C	65	66	67	68	69	70	71

8. $-|3| = -(3) = -3$

9. $|-2.5| = 2.5$

10. $-15 + 7 = -8$

11. $2 + (-6) + (-14) = -18$

12. $-8 - 12 = -20$

13. $3.1 - (-3.3) - 1.8 = 3.1 + 3.3 - 1.8 = 4.6$

14. velocity $= -800$ ft/min; speed $= 800$ ft/min

15. $|-33| + |50| = 83°F$

16. $4(a - 4) = 4a - 16$

17. $3(6 + x) = 18 + 3x$

18. $(5 + n)2 = 10 + 2n$

19. $(3 - t)(-5) = -15 + 5t$

20. $20x - 17x = 3x$

21. $4b + 7 + 7b = 11b + 7$

22. $5x - 3(x - 9) = 5x - 3x + 27 = 2x + 27$

23. $4(y + 1) + 2(y + 1) = 4y + 4 + 2y + 2$
$= 6y + 6$

24. $x + 4 = -1; x = -5$

25. $-3 = n - (-15)$
$-3 = n + 15$
$-18 = n$

26. $6b = -36; b = -6$

27. $\dfrac{x}{4} = 6; x = 24$

28. $3x + 4 = 13$
$3x = 9$
$x = 3$

29. $5x + 2 = -18$
$5x = -20$
$x = -4$

30. $6 + \dfrac{2}{3}x = 14$
$\dfrac{2}{3}x = 8$
$x = \dfrac{3}{2}(8)$
$x = 12$

31. $2x + 7x - 15 = 75$
$9x - 15 = 75$
$9x = 90$
$x = 10$

32. $5(x - 2) = 15$
$5x - 10 = 15$
$5x = 25$
$x = 5$

Copyright © McDougal Littell Inc.
All rights reserved.

33. $\frac{1}{3}(x - 15) = 20$

$\frac{1}{3}x - 5 = 20$

$\frac{1}{3}x = 25$

$x = 75$

34. $x - 8 = 3(x - 4)$

$x - 8 = 3x - 12$

$-8 = 2x - 12$

$4 = 2x$

$2 = x$

35. $-(x - 6) = 4x + 1$

$-x + 6 = 4x + 1$

$6 = 5x + 1$

$5 = 5x$

$1 = x$

36. $d = \frac{m}{v}$

$vd = m$

$v = \frac{m}{d}$

37. $v = \frac{m}{d}$

$v = \frac{3 \text{ gm}}{0.24 \text{ gm/cm}^3} = 12.5 \text{ cm}^3$

38. $\frac{\$1}{2 \text{ cans}} = \$0.50\text{/can}$

39. $\frac{156 \text{ miles}}{3 \text{ hours}} = 52 \text{ mi/hr}$

40. $\frac{\$480}{40 \text{ hours}} = \$12\text{/hour}$

41. $\frac{125 \text{ feet}}{5 \text{ seconds}} = 25 \text{ ft/sec}$

42.

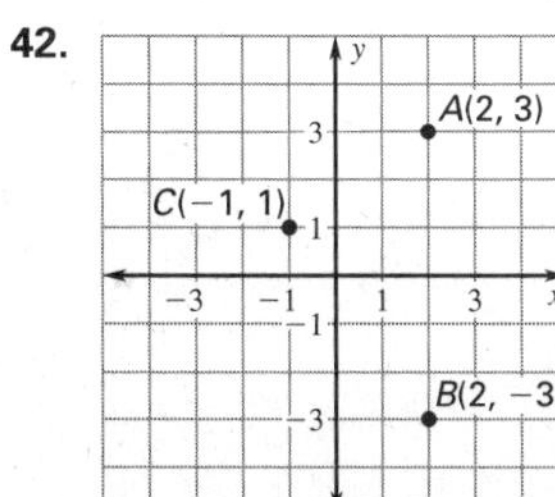

43.

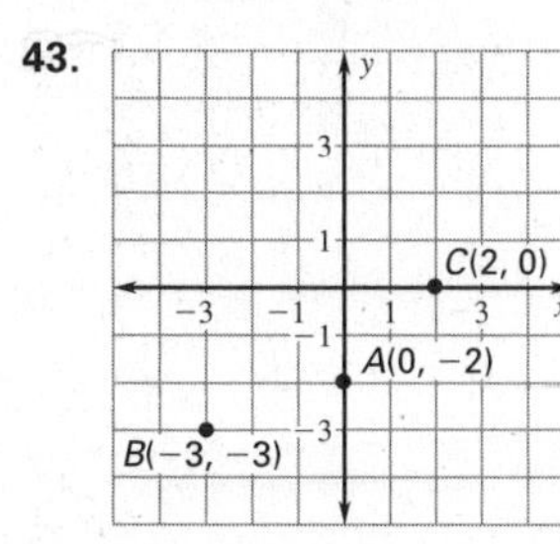

44.

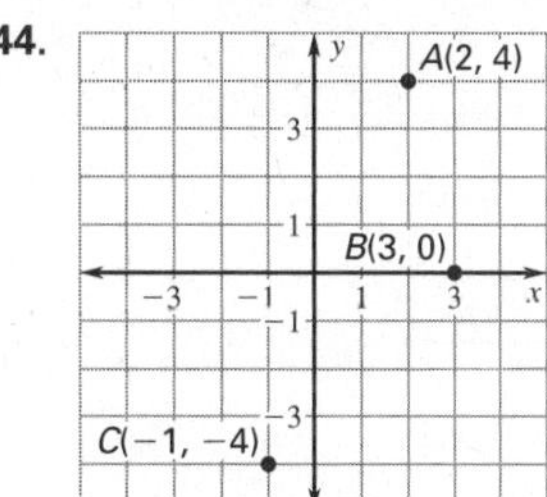

45.

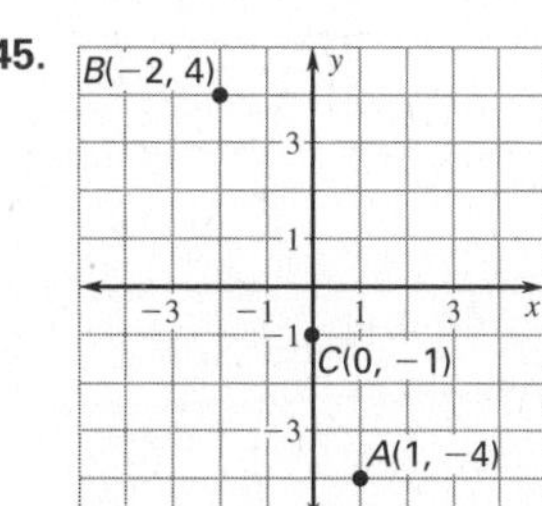

46.

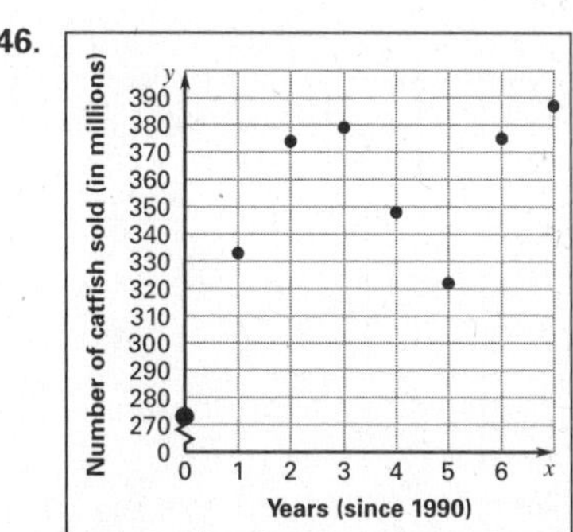

47. Sample answer: The number of catfish sold increased from 1990 to 1993, decreased from 1993 to 1995, then increased again from 1995 to 1997.

48. $x + y = 0$

$y = -x$

Sample table:

x	−2	−1	0	1	2
y	2	1	0	−1	−2

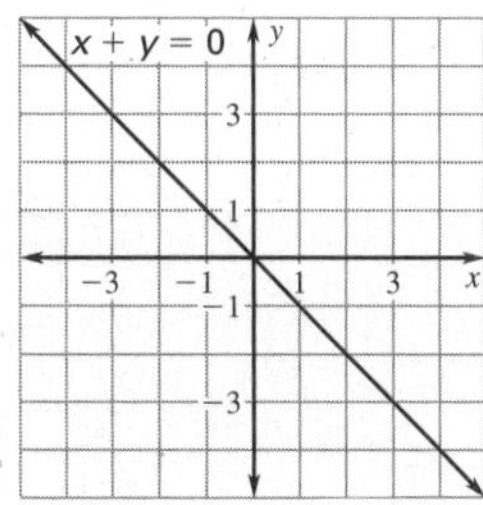

Copyright © McDougal Littell Inc.
All rights reserved.

49. $2x + y = 12$
$y = -2x + 12$

Sample table:

x	-2	-1	0	1	2
y	16	14	12	10	8

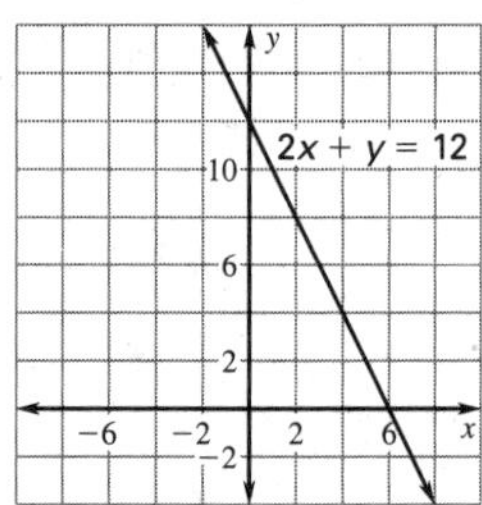

50. $x - y = 8$
$-y = -x + 8$
$y = x - 8$

Sample table:

x	-2	-1	0	1	2
y	-10	-9	-8	-7	-6

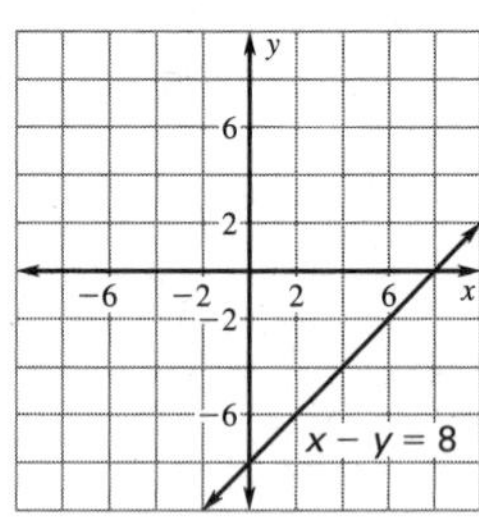

51. $x - y = 4$
$-y = -x + 4$
$y = x - 4$

Sample table:

x	-2	-1	0	1	2
y	-6	-5	-4	-3	-2

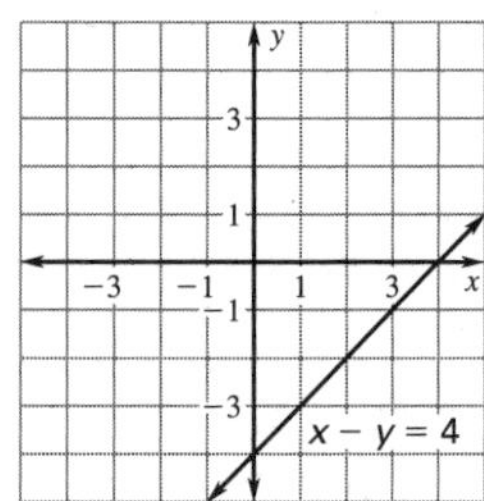

52. $2x - y = -1$
$-y = -2x - 1$
$y = 2x + 1$

Sample table:

x	-2	-1	0	1	2
y	-3	-1	1	3	5

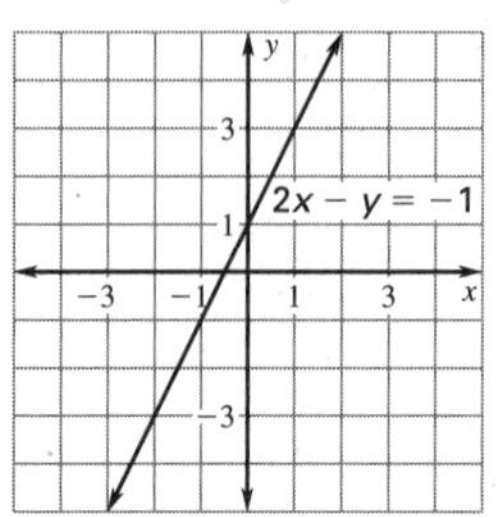

53. $x + 2y = 4$
$2y = -x + 4$
$y = -\frac{1}{2}x + 2$

Sample table:

x	-2	-1	0	1	2
y	3	2.5	2	1.5	1

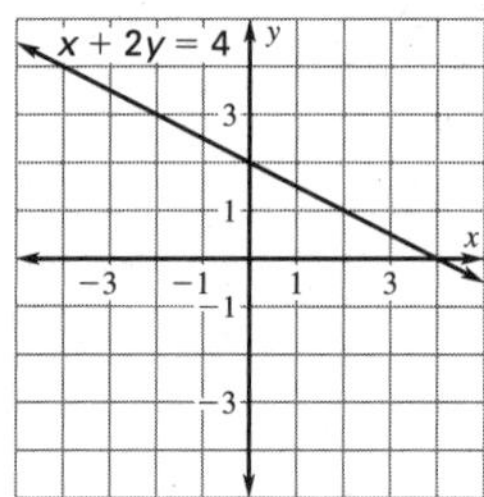

54. $y = x - 3$

55. $y = -2x + 5$

56. $y = 0x + 0; y = 0$

57. $y = 4x + 1$

58. $y - y_1 = m(x - x_1)$
$y - 1 = 2(x - (-1))$
$y - 1 = 2(x + 1)$
$y - 1 = 2x + 2$
$y = 2x + 3$

59. $y - y_1 = m(x - x_1)$
$y - 1 = 1(x - 0)$
$y - 1 = x$
$y = x + 1$

60. $y - y_1 = m(x - x_1)$
$y - 3 = 0(x - 3)$
$y - 3 = 0$
$y = 3$

61. $y - y_1 = m(x - x_1)$
$y - (-1) = \frac{1}{4}(x - 3)$
$y + 1 = \frac{1}{4}x - \frac{3}{4}$
$y = \frac{1}{4}x - \frac{7}{4}$

Copyright © McDougal Littell Inc.
All rights reserved.

62. $y - y_1 = m(x - x_1)$
$y - 6 = -5(x - (-3))$
$y - 6 = -5(x + 3)$
$y - 6 = -5x - 15$
$y = -5x - 9$

63. $y - y_1 = m(x - x_1)$
$y - 2 = -3(x - (-2))$
$y - 2 = -3(x + 2)$
$y - 2 = -3x - 6$
$y = -3x - 4$

64. $m = \frac{-2 - 0}{0 - 2} = \frac{-2}{-2} = 1;$
$y - 0 = 1(x - 2)$ or $y - (-2) = 1(x - 0)$
$y = x - 2$ $\quad y + 2 = x$

65. $m = \frac{6 - 4}{3 - 1} = \frac{2}{2} = 1;$
$y - 4 = 1(x - 1)$ or $y - 6 = 1(x - 3)$
$y - 4 = x - 1$ $\quad y - 6 = x - 3$

66. $m = \frac{2 - 10}{3 - 1} = \frac{-8}{2} = -4;$
$y - 10 = -4(x - 1)$ or $y - 2 = -4(x - 3)$

67. $m = \frac{1 - (-7)}{-2 - (-1)} = \frac{8}{-1} = -8;$
$y - (-7) = -8(x - (-1))$
$y + 7 = -8(x + 1)$
or
$y - 1 = -8(x - (-2))$
$y - 1 = -8(x + 2)$

68. $m = \frac{4 - 3}{2 - 0} = \frac{1}{2};$
$y - 3 = \frac{1}{2}(x - 0)$ or $y - 4 = \frac{1}{2}(x - 2)$
$y - 3 = \frac{1}{2}x$

69. $m = \frac{10 - 7}{8 - 4} = \frac{3}{4};$
$y - 7 = \frac{3}{4}(x - 4)$ or $y - 10 = \frac{3}{4}(x - 8)$

70. $-6 \le x + 12$
$-18 \le x$ or $x \ge -18$

71. $6 > 3x$
$2 > x$ or $x < 2$

72. $-\frac{x}{6} \ge 8$
$x \le -48$

73. $-4 - 5x \le 31$
$-5x \le 35$
$x \ge -7$

74. $-4x + 3 > -21$
$-4x > -24$
$x < 6$

75. $-x + 2 < 2(x - 5)$
$-x + 2 < 2x - 10$
$2 < 3x - 10$
$12 < 3x$
$4 < x$ or $x > 4$

76. $-3 \le x + 1 < 7$
$-4 \le x < 6$

77. $-4 \le -2x \le 10$
$2 \ge x \ge -5$ or $-5 \le x \le 2$

78. $2x > 10$ or $x + 1 < 3$
$x > 5$ $\quad x < 2$

79. $x + 3 > 7$ or $2x + 3 \le -1$
$x > 4$ $\quad 2x \le -4$
$x \le -2$

80. $|x - 8| > 10$
$x - 8 > 10$ or $x - 8 < -10$
$x > 18$ $\quad x < -2$

81. $|2x + 5| \le 7$
$-7 \le 2x + 5 \le 7$
$-12 \le 2x \le 2$
$-6 \le x \le 1$

Copyright © McDougal Littell Inc.
All rights reserved.

CHAPTER 7

Chapter Opener

7.1 Think & Discuss (p. 387)

1. 6,100,000
2. 4,400,000

7.1 Chapter Readiness Quiz (p. 388)

1. C; the term has an exponent of more than 1
2. B;
   $5(2x + 4) \stackrel{?}{=} 2(10 + 5x)$
   $10x + 20 \stackrel{?}{=} 20 + 10x$
   $10x + 20 = 10x + 20$
3. A; $2x + 6(x + 1) = -2$
   $2x + 6x + 6 = -2$
   $8x + 6 = -2$
   $8x = -8$
   $x = -1$
4. D; $7y - 8x > 56$
   A (0, 8): $7(8) - 8(0) \stackrel{?}{>} 56$
   $56 \not> 56$
   B (0, 0): $7(0) - 8(0) \stackrel{?}{>} 56$
   $0 \not> 56$
   C (−6, 1): $7(1) - 8(-6) \stackrel{?}{>} 56$
   $7 + 48 \stackrel{?}{>} 56$
   $55 \not> 56$
   D (−7, 2): $7(2) - 8(-7) \stackrel{?}{>} 56$
   $14 + 56 \stackrel{?}{>} 56$
   $70 > 56$

Lesson 7.1

7.1 Checkpoint (pp. 390–391)

1. $x + y = 4$
   $y = -x + 4; m = -1; b = 4$
   $2x + y = 5$
   $y = -2x + 5; m = -2; b = 5$

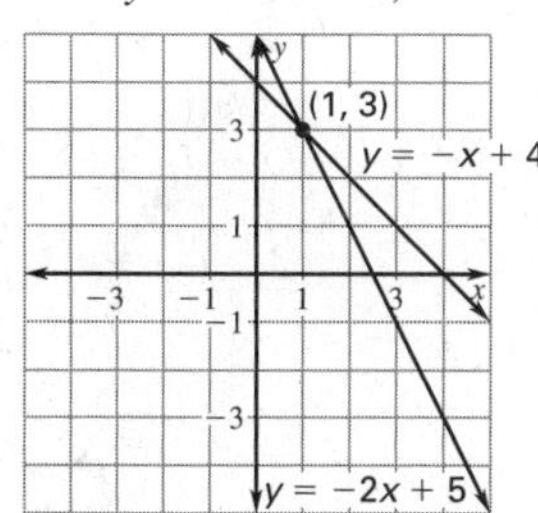

Test (1, 3)

Equation 1	Equation 2
$x + y = 4$	$2x + y = 5$
$1 + 3 \stackrel{?}{=} 4$	$2(1) + 3 \stackrel{?}{=} 5$
$4 = 4$	$5 = 5$

(1, 3) is the solution.

2. $x - y = 5$
   $-y = -x + 5$
   $y = x - 5;\ m = 1; b = -5$
   $2x + 3y = 0$
   $3y = -2x$
   $y = -\frac{2}{3}x; m = -\frac{2}{3}; b = 0$

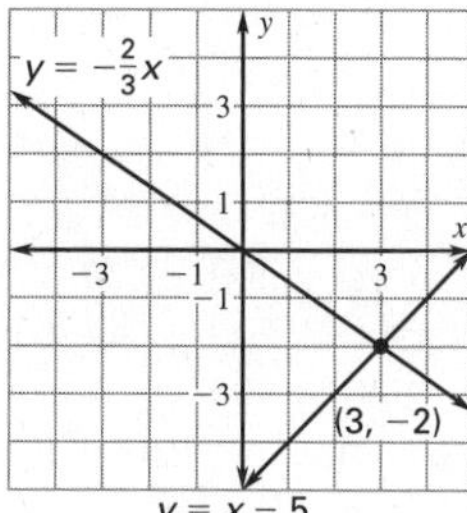

Test (3, −2)

Equation 1	Equation 2
$x - y = 5$	$2x + 3y = 0$
$3 - (-2) \stackrel{?}{=} 5$	$2(3) + 3(-2) \stackrel{?}{=} 0$
$5 = 5$	$0 = 0$

(3, −2) is the solution.

3. $x - y = -2$
   $-y = -x - 2$
   $y = x + 2;\ m = 1; b = 2$
   $x + y = -4$
   $y = -x - 4; m = -1; b = -4$

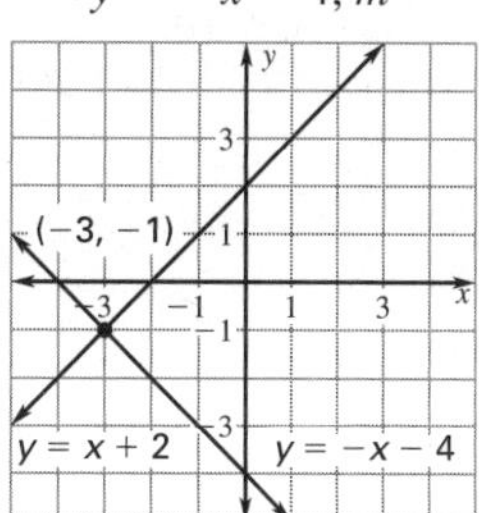

Test (−3, −1)

Equation 1	Equation 2
$x - y = -2$	$x + y = -4$
$-3 - (-1) \stackrel{?}{=} -2$	$-3 + (-1) \stackrel{?}{=} -4$
$-2 = -2$	$-4 = -4$

(−3, −1) is the solution.

Copyright © McDougal Littell Inc.
All rights reserved.

Chapter 7 *continued*

4. Science: $v = 400 + 25t$
Spanish: $v = 500 + 20t$

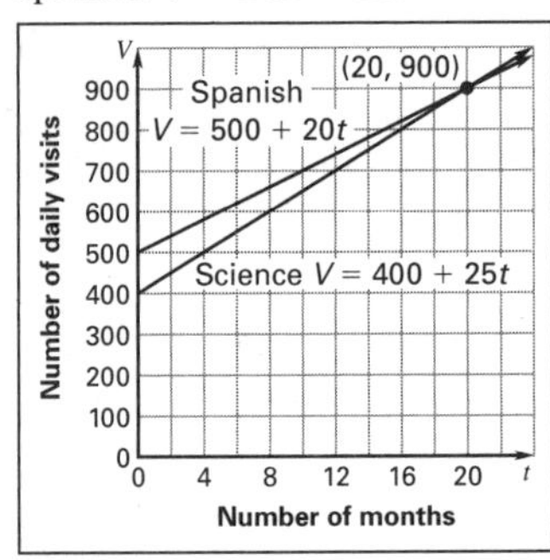

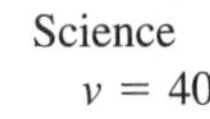

Test (20, 900)

Science	Spanish
$v = 400 + 25t$	$v = 500 + 20t$
$900 \stackrel{?}{=} 400 + 25(20)$	$900 \stackrel{?}{=} 500 + 20(20)$
$900 = 900$	$900 = 900$

(20, 900) is the solution; same number of visits will occur at 20 months

7.1 Guided Practice (p. 392)

1. To solve a system of equations graphically means to find the ordered pair (a, b) that represents the intersection of the two graphed equations.

2. (0, 2) is the point of intersection
Test:

$y = -x + 2$	$y = x + 2$
$2 \stackrel{?}{=} -(0) + 2$	$2 \stackrel{?}{=} 0 + 2$
$2 = 2$	$2 = 2$

3. $-x + y = -2$ $2x + y = 10$
$y = x - 2$ $y = -2x + 10$

4.

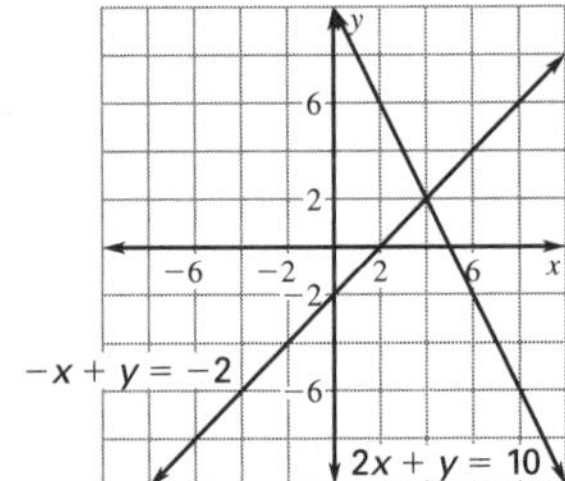

5. (4, 2)

6. $-x + y = -2$ $2x + y = 10$
$-4 + 2 \stackrel{?}{=} -2$ $2(4) + 2 \stackrel{?}{=} 10$
$-2 = -2$ $10 = 10$
(4, 2) is the solution.

7.1 Practice and Applications (pp. 392–394)

7. $3x - 2y = 11$ $-x + 6y = 7$
$3(5) - 2(2) \stackrel{?}{=} 11$ $-5 + 6(2) \stackrel{?}{=} 7$
$11 = 11$ $7 = 7$
(5, 2) is the solution.

8. $6x - 3y = -15$ $2x + y = -3$
$6(-2) - 3(1) \stackrel{?}{=} -15$ $2(-2) + 1 \stackrel{?}{=} -3$
$-15 = -15$ $-3 = -3$
$(-2, 1)$ is the solution.

9. $x + 3y = 15$ $4x + y = 6$
$3 + 3(-6) \stackrel{?}{=} 15$ $4(3) + (-6) \stackrel{?}{=} 6$
$-15 \neq 15$ $6 = 6$
$(3, -6)$ is not the solution.

10. $-5x + y = 19$ $x - 7y = 3$
$-5(-4) + (-1) \stackrel{?}{=} 19$ $-4 - 7(-1) \stackrel{?}{=} 3$
$19 = 19$ $3 = 3$
$(-4, -1)$ is the solution.

11. $-15x + 7y = 1$ $3x - y = 1$
$-15(3) + 7(5) \stackrel{?}{=} 1$ $3(3) - 5 \stackrel{?}{=} 1$
$-10 \neq 1$ $4 \neq 1$
(3, 5) is not the solution.

12. $-2x + y = 11$ $-x - 9y = -15$
$-2(6) + 1 \stackrel{?}{=} 11$ $-6 - 9(1) \stackrel{?}{=} -15$
$-11 \neq 11$ $-15 = -15$
(6, 1) is not the solution.

13. (4, 5); the solution
$-x + 2y = 6$ $x + 4y = 24$
$-(4) + 2(5) \stackrel{?}{=} 6$ $4 + 4(5) \stackrel{?}{=} 24$
$6 = 6$ $24 = 24$

14. $(-2, -2)$; the solution
$2x - y = -2$ $4x - y = -6$
$2(-2) - (-2) \stackrel{?}{=} -2$ $4(-2) - (-2) \stackrel{?}{=} -6$
$-2 = -2$ $-6 = -6$

15. (3, 0); the solution
$x + y = 3$ $-2x + y = -6$
$3 + 0 \stackrel{?}{=} 3$ $-2(3) + 0 = -6$
$3 = 3$ $-6 = -6$

16. (1, 2)
$y = -x + 3$ $y = x + 1$
$2 \stackrel{?}{=} -(1) + 3$ $2 \stackrel{?}{=} 1 + 1$
$2 = 2$ $2 = 2$

17. $(6, -6)$
$y = -6$ $x = 6$
$-6 = -6$ $6 = 6$

18. $\left(\frac{8}{5}, -\frac{4}{5}\right)$
$y = 2x - 4$ $2y = -x$
$-\frac{4}{5} \stackrel{?}{=} 2\left(\frac{8}{5}\right) - 4$ $2\left(-\frac{4}{5}\right) \stackrel{?}{=} -\frac{8}{5}$
$-\frac{4}{5} \stackrel{?}{=} \frac{16}{5} - \frac{20}{5}$ $-\frac{8}{5} = -\frac{8}{5}$
$-\frac{4}{5} = -\frac{4}{5}$

19. $(-3, -5)$
$2x - 3y = 9$ $x = -3$
$2(-3) - 3(-5) \stackrel{?}{=} 9$ $-3 = -3$
$9 = 9$

Copyright © McDougal Littell Inc.
All rights reserved.

20. $(16, -16)$

$5x + 4y = 16$ $y = -16$

$5(16) + 4(-16) \stackrel{?}{=} 16$ $-16 = -16$

$16 = 16$

21. $(-4, -5)$

$x - y = 1$ $5x - 4y = 0$

$-4 - (-5) \stackrel{?}{=} 1$ $5(-4) - 4(-5) \stackrel{?}{=} 0$

$1 = 1$ $0 = 0$

22. $(3, 1)$

$3x + 6y = 15$ $-2x + 3y = -3$

$3(3) + 6(1) \stackrel{?}{=} 15$ $-2(3) + 3(1) \stackrel{?}{=} -3$

$15 = 15$ $-3 = -3$

23. $(1, 4)$

$y = -2x + 6$ $y = 2x + 2$

$4 \stackrel{?}{=} -2(1) + 6$ $4 \stackrel{?}{=} 2(1) + 2$

$4 = 4$ $4 = 4$

24. $(0, 9)$

$5x + 6y = 54$ $-x + y = 9$

$5(0) + 6(9) \stackrel{?}{=} 54$ $-0 + 9 \stackrel{?}{=} 9$

$54 = 54$ $9 = 9$

25. 125,000 miles

26.

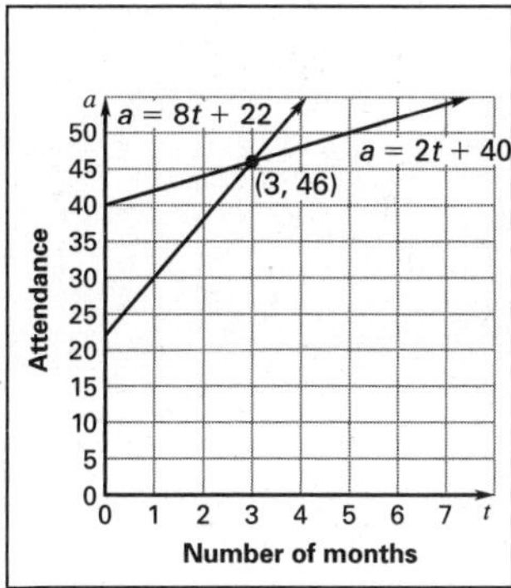

3 months

27.

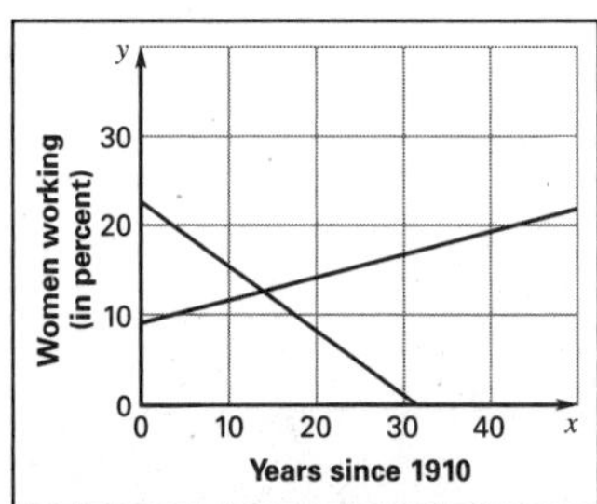

14 years

28. $y = 25 + 3x$ (me)

$y = 40 + 2x$ (sister)

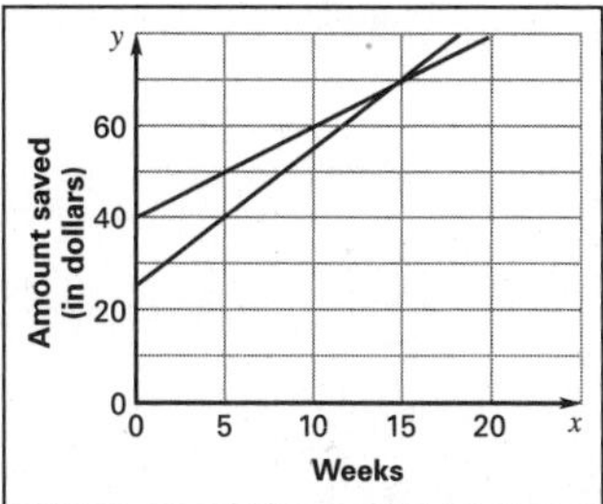

15 weeks

29. a. Since $(x + 2)$ and $(3x - 4)$ both equal y, the two expressions can be set equal to each other, and then one can solve for x.

b. $(3, 5)$

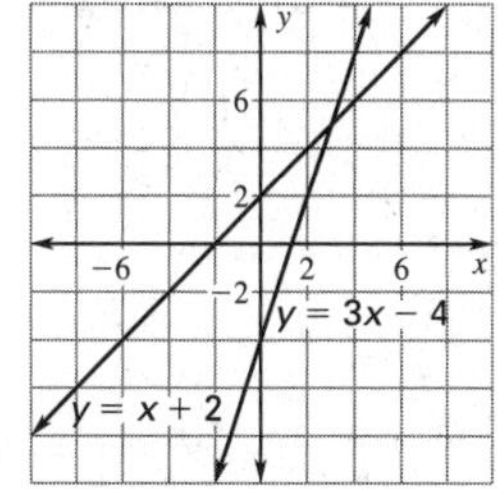

c. $x + 2 = 3x - 4$

$3 + 2 \stackrel{?}{=} 3(3) - 4$

$5 = 5$

7.1 Standardized Test Practice (p. 394)

30. D $(3, 0)$

$x + y = 3$

$3 + 0 \stackrel{?}{=} 3$

$3 = 3$

$2x + y = 6$

$2(3) + 0 \stackrel{?}{=} 6$

$6 = 6$

31. Graphed: (1) $b = 1, m = -\frac{1}{2}$

$y = -\frac{1}{2}x + 1$ Slope-intercept form

$2y = -x + 2$

$x + 2y = 2$ Standard form

(2) $b = 0, m = \frac{1}{2}$

$y = \frac{1}{2}x + 0$ Slope-intercept form

$2y = x$

$-x + 2y = 0$

$x - 2y = 0$ Standard form

G

Copyright © McDougal Littell Inc.
All rights reserved.

Chapter 7 *continued*

7.1 Mixed Review (p. 394)

32. $3x + 7 = -2$
$3x = -9$
$x = -3$

33. $15 - 2a = 7$
$-2a = -8$
$a = 4$

34. $2y + 3y = 5$
$5y = 5$
$y = 1$

35. $21 = 7(w - 2)$
$21 = 7w - 14$
$35 = 7w$
$5 = w$

36. $-2(t - 5) = 26$
$-2t + 10 = 26$
$-2t = 16$
$t = -8$

37. $4(2x + 3) = -4$
$8x + 12 = -4$
$8x = -16$
$x = -2$

38. $(3, 0), m = -4$
$y - 0 = -4(x - 3)$
$y = -4x + 12$

39. $(-4, 3), m = 1$
$y - 3 = 1[x - (-4)]$
$y - 3 = x + 4$
$y = x + 7$

40. $(1, -5), m = 4$
$y - (-5) = 4(x - 1)$
$y + 5 = 4x - 4$
$y = 4x - 9$

41. $(-4, -1), m = -2$
$y - (-1) = -2[x - (-4)]$
$y + 1 = -2(x + 4)$
$y + 1 = -2x - 8$
$y = -2x - 9$

42. $(2, 3), m = 2$
$y - 3 = 2(x - 2)$
$y - 3 = 2x - 4$
$y = 2x - 1$

43. $(-1, 5), m = -3$
$y - 5 = -3[x - (-1)]$
$y - 5 = -3(x + 1)$
$y - 5 = -3x - 3$
$y = -3x + 2$

44. $x < 4260$

4060 4160 4260 4360 4460

7.1 Maintaining Skills (p. 394)

45. $3.71 + 1.054 = 4.764$

$$\begin{array}{r} 3.710 \\ +\ 1.054 \\ \hline 4.764 \end{array}$$

46. $10.35 + 5.301 = 15.651$

$$\begin{array}{r} 10.350 \\ +\ 5.301 \\ \hline 15.651 \end{array}$$

47. $2.5 - 0.5 = 2$

$$\begin{array}{r} 2.5 \\ -\ 0.5 \\ \hline 2.0 \end{array}$$ or 2

48. $(2.1)(0.2) = 0.42$

$$\begin{array}{r} 2.1 \\ \times\ 0.2 \\ \hline 0.42 \end{array}$$

49. $\dfrac{0.3}{0.03} = 10 \quad 0.03\overline{)0.3} \quad 3\overline{)30}$ (quotient 10)

50. $\dfrac{5.175}{1.15} \times \dfrac{1000}{1000} = \dfrac{5175}{1150} = 4.5$

$$\begin{array}{r} 4\,5 \\ 1150\overline{)5175.0} \\ 4600 \\ \hline 575\,0 \\ 575\,0 \\ \hline 0 \end{array}$$

7.1 Technology: Try These *(p. 395)*

1. $(-3.5, 2.5)$

$y = x + 6$	$y = -x - 1$
$2.5 \stackrel{?}{=} -3.5 + 6$	$2.5 \stackrel{?}{=} -(-3.5) - 1$
$2.5 = 2.5$	$2.5 = 2.5$

2. $(-2.5, 5.5)$

$y = -3x - 2$	$y = x + 8$
$5.5 \stackrel{?}{=} -3(-2.5) - 2$	$5.5 \stackrel{?}{=} -2.5 + 8$
$5.5 = 5.5$	$5.5 = 5.5$

3. $(-0.8, -2.05)$

$y = -0.25x - 2.25$	$y = x - 1.25$
$-2.05 \stackrel{?}{=} -0.25(-0.8) - 2.25$	$-2.05 \stackrel{?}{=} -0.8 - 1.25$
$-2.05 = -2.05$	$-2.05 = -2.05$

4. $(23, 10.59)$

$y = 1.33x - 20$	$y = 0.83x - 8.5$
$10.59 \stackrel{?}{=} 1.33(23) - 20$	$10.59 \stackrel{?}{=} 0.83(23) - 8.5$
$10.59 = 10.59$	$10.59 = 10.59$

Copyright © McDougal Littell Inc.
All rights reserved.

Lesson 7.2

7.2 Checkpoint (pp. 397–398)

1. Solve for y in the first equation because it is easy to isolate y.
2. Solve for x in the first equation because it is easy to isolate x.
3. Solve for x in the first or second equation because it is easy to isolate x in either equation.
4. Number of Adults + Number of Children = Total Number Admitted
   $x + y = 675$
   Price for Adults · Number of Adults + Price per Child · Number of Children = Total Amount Collected
   $7x + 5y = 4275$

   Solve: Rewrite first equation, isolate x
   $x = -y + 675$
   $7x + 5y = 4275$ Substitute $-y + 675$ for x.
   $7(-y + 675) + 5y = 4275$
   $-7y + 4725 + 5y = 4275$
   $-2y = -450$
   $y = 225$
   Substitute 225 for y in the first equation to find x.
   $x + 225 = 675$
   $x = 450$
   225 children and 450 adults

7.2 Guided Practice (p. 399)

1. Step 1: Solve one equation for one of the variables.
   Step 2: Substitute the expression from Step 1 into the other equation and solve for the other variable.
   Step 3: Substitute the value from Step 2 into the revised equation from Step 1 and solve.
   Step 4: Check the solution in each of the original equations.
2. Solve for the variable that is easiest to isolate, usually this will be a variable with a coefficient of 1 or -1.
3. Equation 2; it has a coefficient of -1.
4. $5x - y = 3$
   $-y = -5x + 3$
   $y = 5x - 3$
5. $3x + 2(5x - 3) = 7$
   $3x + 10x - 6 = 7$
   $13x - 6 = 7$
   $13x = 13$
   $x = 1$
6. $y = 5(1) - 3$
   $y = 2$
   Solution: (1, 2)
   Check:
   $3(1) + 2(2) \stackrel{?}{=} 7$ $\quad$ $5(1) - 2 \stackrel{?}{=} 3$
   $7 = 7$ $\quad$ $3 = 3$
7. Step 1:
   $3x + y = 3$ Solve equation 1 for y.
   $y = -3x + 3$

   Step 2:
   $7x + 2y = 1$ Substitute $-3x + 3$ for y.
   $7x + 2(-3x + 3) = 1$ Solve for x.
   $7x - 6x + 6 = 1$
   $x + 6 = 1$
   $x = -5$

   Step 3:
   $y = -3(-5) + 3$ Substitute -5 for x into the revised equation from Step 1.
   $y = 18$ Simplify.
   Solution: $(-5, 18)$

   Step 4: Check solution by substituting $(-5, 18)$ into both original equations.
   $3(-5) + 18 \stackrel{?}{=} 3$
   $3 = 3$

   $7(-5) + 2(18) \stackrel{?}{=} 1$
   $1 = 1$
8. Step 1:
   $-x + y = 1$ Solve equation for y.
   $y = x + 1$

   Step 2:
   $2x + y = 4$ Substitute $x + 1$ for y and solve for x.
   $2x + (x + 1) = 4$
   $3x + 1 = 4$
   $3x = 3$
   $x = 1$

   Step 3:
   $y = (1) + 1$ Substitute 1 for x in the revised equation from Step 1.
   $y = 2$ Simplify.

   Solution: (1, 2)
   Step 4: Check solution y substituting (1, 2) into both original equations.
   $2(1) + (2) \stackrel{?}{=} 4$
   $4 = 4$

   $-(1) + (2) \stackrel{?}{=} 1$
   $1 = 1$
9. Step 1:
   $5y = 15$ Solve equation 2 for y.
   $y = 3$

   Step 2:
   $3x - y = 0$ Substitute 3 for y in equation 1 and solve for x.
   $3x - 3 = 0$
   $3x = 3$
   $x = 1$

   Solution: (1, 3)
   Step 3: Check solution by substituting (1, 3) into both original equations.
   $3(1) - (3) \stackrel{?}{=} 0$ $\quad$ $5(3) \stackrel{?}{=} 15$
   $0 = 0$ $\quad$ $15 = 15$

Copyright © McDougal Littell Inc.
All rights reserved.

7.2 Practice and Applications (pp. 399–400)

10. Equation 2; y has a coefficient of -1, no constant

11. Equation 2; m has a coefficient of 1, no constant

12. Equation 2; d has a coefficient of -1

13. Equation 2; x and y have coefficients of 1.

14. Equation 2; a has a coefficient of 1 and b has a coefficient of -1.

15. Equation 2; x has a coefficient of 1.

16. **(1)** $y = x - 4$
(2) $4x + (x - 4) = 26$
$5x - 4 = 26$
$5x = 30$
$x = 6$
(3) $y = (6) - 4$
$y = 2$
Solution: (6, 2)
(4) Check:
$2 \stackrel{?}{=} 6 - 4$
$2 = 2$

$4(6) + 2 \stackrel{?}{=} 26$
$26 = 26$

17. **(1)** $S = t + 4$
(2) $2t + (t + 4) = 19$
$3t + 4 = 19$
$3t = 15$
$t = 5$
(3) $S = (5) + 4$
$S = 9$
Solution: (9, 5)
(4) Check:
$9 \stackrel{?}{=} 5 + 4$
$9 = 9$

$2(5) + 9 \stackrel{?}{=} 19$
$19 = 19$

18. **(1)** $4c + d = 20$
$d = -4c + 20$
(2) $2c - (-4c + 20) = -2$
$2c + 4c - 20 = -2$
$6c - 20 = -2$
$6c = 18$
$c = 3$
(3) $d = -4(3) + 20$
$d = 8$
Solution: (3, 8)
(4) Check:
$2(3) - 8 \stackrel{?}{=} -2$ $\quad$ $4(3) + 8 \stackrel{?}{=} 20$
$-2 = -2$ $\quad$ $20 = 20$

19. **(1)** $2a = 8$
$a = 4$
(2) $(4) + b = 2$
$b = -2$
Solution (4, -2)
(3) Check:
$2(4) \stackrel{?}{=} 8$ $\quad$ $4 + (-2) \stackrel{?}{=} 2$
$8 = 8$ $\quad$ $2 = 2$

20. **(1)** $y = x + 7$
(2) $2x + 3(x + 7) = 31$
$2x + 3x + 21 = 31$
$5x + 21 = 31$
$5x = 10$
$x = 2$
(3) $y = (2) + 7$
$y = 9$
Solution: (2, 9)
(4) Check:
$2(2) + 3(9) \stackrel{?}{=} 31$ $\quad$ $9 \stackrel{?}{=} 2 + 7$
$31 = 31$ $\quad$ $9 = 9$

21. **(1)** $p + q = 4$
$p = -q + 4$
(2) $4(-q + 4) + q = 1$
$-4q + 16 + q = 1$
$-3q + 16 = 1$
$-3q = -15$
$q = 5$
(3) $p = -(5) + 4$
$p = -1$
Solution: (-1, 5)
(4) Check:
$(-1) + (5) \stackrel{?}{=} 4$ $\quad$ $4(-1) + 5 \stackrel{?}{=} 1$
$4 = 4$ $\quad$ $1 = 1$

22. **(1)** $x - 2y = -25$
$x = 2y - 25$
(2) $3(2y - 25) - y = 0$
$6y - 75 - y = 0$
$5y - 75 = 0$
$5y = 75$
$y = 15$
(3) $x = 2(15) - 25$
$x = 5$
Solution (5, 15)
(4) Check:
$(5) - 2(15) \stackrel{?}{=} -25$ $\quad$ $3(5) - 15 \stackrel{?}{=} 0$
$-25 = -25$ $\quad$ $0 = 0$

23. **(1)** $u - v = 0$
$u = v$
(2) $7(v) + v = 0$
$8v = 0$
$v = 0$
(3) $u = 0$
Solution: (0, 0)
(4) Check:
$0 - 0 \stackrel{?}{=} 0$ $\quad$ $7(0) + 0 \stackrel{?}{=} 0$
$0 = 0$ $\quad$ $0 = 0$

Copyright © McDougal Littell Inc.
All rights reserved.

24. **(1)** $x - y = 0$

$x = y$

(2) $12(y) - 5y = -21$

$7y = -21$

$y = -3$

(3) $x = -3$

Solution: $(-3, -3)$

(4) Check:

$(-3) - (-3) \stackrel{?}{=} 0$ $\quad$ $12(-3) - 5(-3) \stackrel{?}{=} -21$

$0 = 0$ $\quad$ $-21 = -21$

25. **(1)** $m + 2n = 1$

$m = -2n + 1$

(2) $5(-2n + 1) + 3n = -23$

$-10n + 5 + 3n = -23$

$-7n + 5 = -23$

$-7n = -28$

$n = 4$

(3) $m = -2(4) + 1$

$m = -7$

Solution: $(-7, 4)$

(4) Check:

$(-7) + 2(4) \stackrel{?}{=} 1$ $\quad$ $5(-7) + 3(4) \stackrel{?}{=} -23$

$1 = 1$ $\quad$ $-23 = -23$

26. **(1)** $x + 4 = 16$

$x = 12$

(2) $(12) - y = -5$

$-y = -17$

$y = 17$

Solution: $(12, 17)$

(3) Check:

$(12) - (17) \stackrel{?}{=} -5$ $\quad$ $(12) + 4 \stackrel{?}{=} 16$

$-5 = -5$ $\quad$ $16 = 16$

27. **(1)** $-3w + z = 4$

$z = 3w + 4$

(2) $-9w + 5(3w + 4) = -1$

$-9w + 15w + 20 = -1$

$6w + 20 = -1$

$6w = -21$

$w = -\frac{7}{2}$

(3) $z = 3\left(-\frac{7}{2}\right) + 4$

$z = -\frac{21}{2} + \frac{8}{2}$

$z = -\frac{13}{2}$

Solution: $\left(-\frac{7}{2}, -\frac{13}{2}\right)$

(4) Check:

$-3\left(-\frac{7}{2}\right) + \left(-\frac{13}{2}\right) \stackrel{?}{=} 4$

$\frac{21}{2} - \frac{13}{2} \stackrel{?}{=} 4$

$\frac{8}{2} \stackrel{?}{=} 4$

$4 = 4$

$-9\left(-\frac{7}{2}\right) + 5\left(-\frac{13}{2}\right) \stackrel{?}{=} 1$

$\frac{63}{2} - \frac{65}{2} \stackrel{?}{=} -1$

$-\frac{2}{2} \stackrel{?}{=} -1$

$-1 = -1$

28. Let x = number of student admissions

Let y = number of general admissions

$x + y = 525$

$4x + 6y = 2876$

(1) $x + y = 525$

$x = -y + 525$

(2) $4(-y + 525) + 6y = 2876$

$-4y + 2100 + 6y = 2876$

$2100 + 2y = 2876$

$2y = 776$

$y = 388$

(3) $x = -(388) + 525$

$x = 137$

Solution: 137 students, 388 general admissions

29. Let p = number of softballs for pony-league

Let j = number of softballs for junior league

$j + p = 80$

$4j + 3.5p = 305$

(1) $j = -p + 80$

(2) $4(-p + 80) + 3.5p = 305$

$-4p + 320 + 3.5p = 305$

$320 - 0.5p = 305$

$-0.5p = -15$

$p = 30$

(3) $j = -(30) + 80$

$j = 50$

Solution: 30 for pony-league (11-inch), 50 for junior league (12-inch)

30. $2l + 2w = 40$

$l = 4w$

(1) $l = 4w$

(2) $2(4w) + 2w = 40$

$8w + 2w = 40$

$10w = 40$

$w = 4$

(3) $l = 4(4)$

$l = 16$

Solution: width is 4 cm, length is 16 cm

Copyright © McDougal Littell Inc.
All rights reserved.

31. Let A = ABC stock
Let X = XYZ stock
$A = 3X$
$A + X = 4500$
(1) $A = 3X$
(2) $(3X) + X = 4500$
$4X = 4500$
$X = 1125$
(3) $A = 3(1125)$
$A = 3375$

Solution: \$3375 in ABC, \$1125 in XYZ.

32. Let a = meters uphill
Let b = meters downhill

$a + b = 2200$

$\frac{a}{200} + \frac{b}{250} = 10$

33. **(1)** $a + b = 2200$
$a = -b + 2200$
(2) $\frac{(-b + 2200)}{200} + \frac{b}{250} = 10$ Multiply each side by 1000 to clear the fractions.
$5(-b + 2200) + 4(b) = 10{,}000$
$-5b + 11{,}000 + 4b = 10{,}000$
$11{,}000 - b = 10{,}000$
$-b = -1000$
$b = 1000$
(3) $a = -(1000) + 2200$
$a = 1200$
Solution: 1200 meters uphill, 1000 meters downhill

34. Error: After solving for y using equation 1, the y-value needs to be substituted into equation 2, not back into equation 1. The response of $9 = 9$ indicates an identity.

(1) $3x + y = 9$
$y = -3x + 9$
(2) $-2x + (-3x + 9) = 4$
$-5x + 9 = 4$
$-5x = -5$
$x = 1$
(3) $y = -3(1) + 9$
$y = 6$

Solution: (1, 6)

7.2 Standardized Test Practice (p. 401)

35. **(B)**
$6 + 6 \stackrel{?}{=} 12$
$12 = 12$
$3(6) - 2(6) \stackrel{?}{=} 6$
$6 = 6$

36. **(H)**
$2x - y = -1$
$-y = -2x - 1$
$y = 2x + 1$

37. **(D)**
$5(8) + 2(30) \stackrel{?}{=} 100$
$40 + 60 \stackrel{?}{=} 100$
$100 = 100$

7.2 Mixed Review (p. 401)

38. $4g + 3 + 2g - 3 = 6g$

39. $3x + 2 - (5x + 2)$
$= 3x + 2 - 5x - 2 = -2x$

40. $6(2 - m) - 3m - 12$
$= 12 - 6m - 3m - 12 = -9m$

41. $4(3a + 5) + 3(-4a + 2)$
$= 12a + 20 + (-12a) + 6 = 26$

42. $6x + y = 0$
$y = -6x$; $m = -6$, $b = 0$

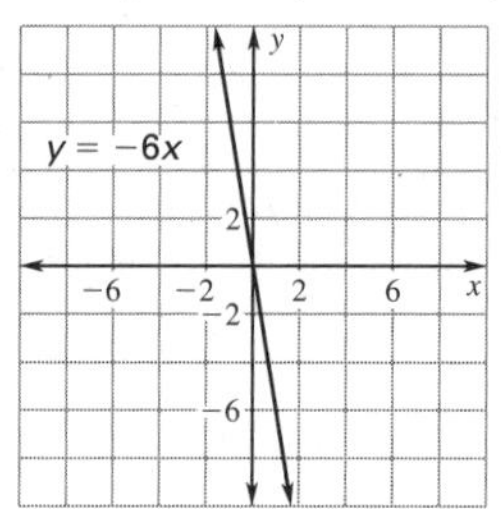

43. $8x - 4y = 16$
$-4y = -8x + 16$
$y = 2x - 4$; $m = 2$, $b = -4$

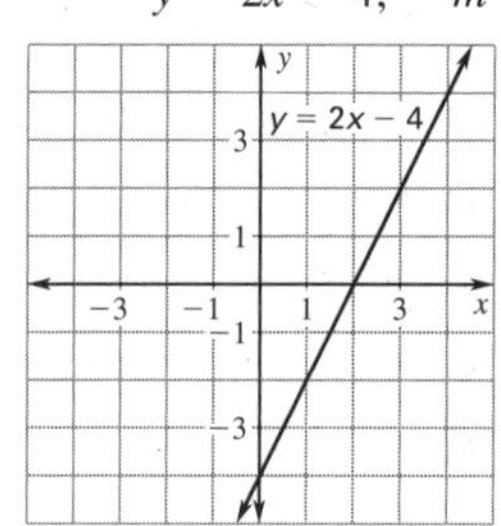

44. $3x + y = -5$
$y = -3x - 5$; $m = -3$, $b = -5$

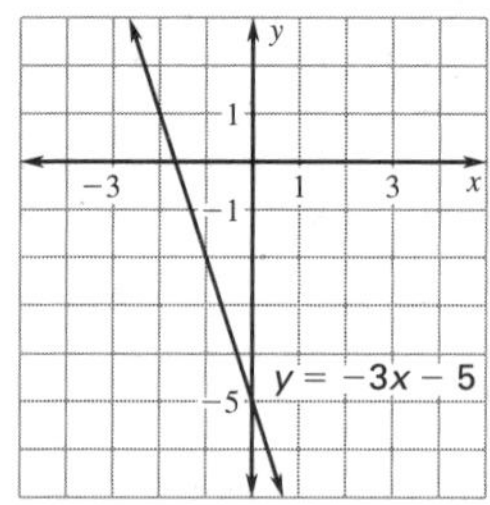

45. $5x + 3y = 3$
$3y = -5x + 3$
$y = -\frac{5}{3}x + 1$; $m = -\frac{5}{3}$, $b = 1$

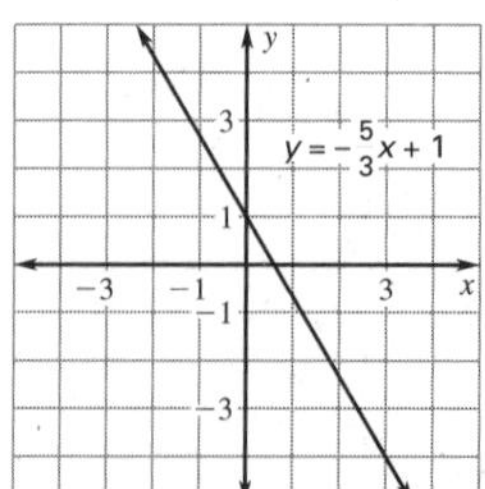

Copyright © McDougal Littell Inc.
All rights reserved.

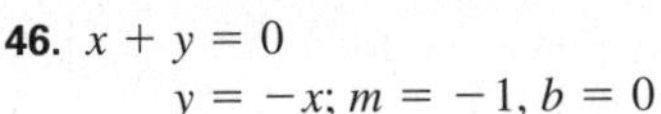

46. $x + y = 0$

$y = -x; m = -1, b = 0$

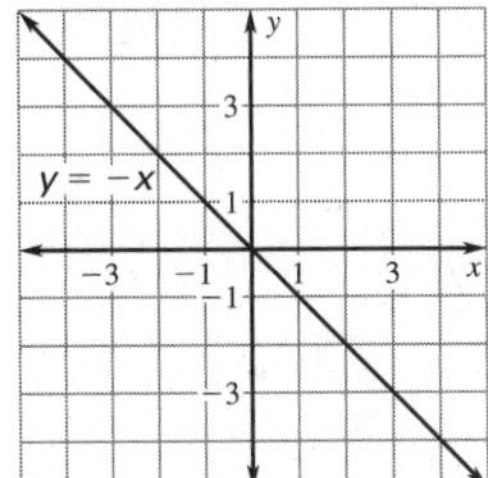

47. $y = -4; m = 0, b = -4$

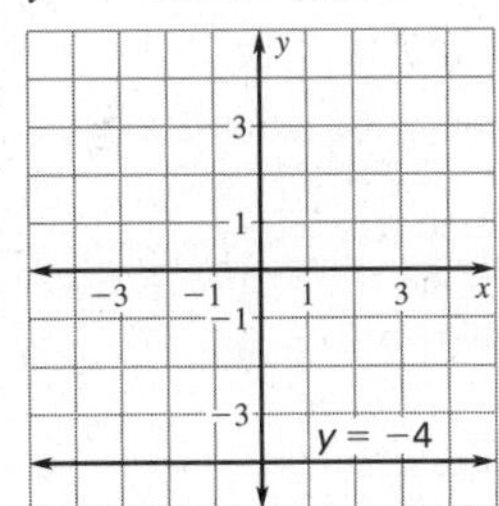

48. $5 < -x \le 1$

$5 > x \ge -1$ or $-1 \le x < 5$

49. $-14 \le x + 5 \le 14$

$-19 \le x \le 9$

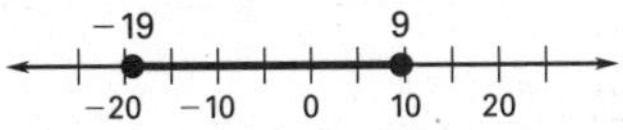

50. $-2 < -3x + 1 < 10$

$-3 < -3x < 9$

$1 > x > -3$ or $-3 < x < 1$

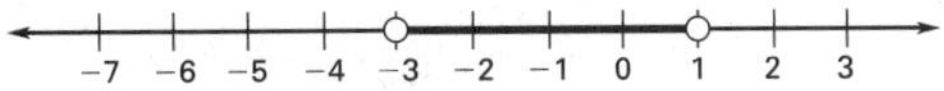

51. $x + 6 < 7$ or $4x > 12$

$x < 1$ or $x > 3$

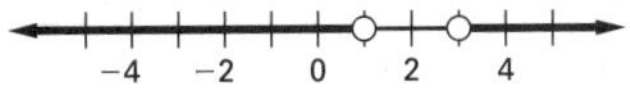

52. $3x - 2 \ge 4$ or $5 - x > 9$

$3x \ge 6$ $\quad -x > 4$

$x \ge 2$ $\quad x < -4$

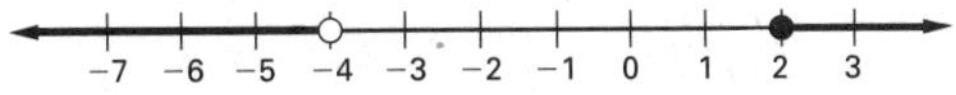

7.2 Maintaining Skills (p. 401)

53. 3: 1, 3
21: 1, 3, 7, 21
Common factors: 1, 3

54. 4: 1, 2, 4
28: 1, 2, 4, 7, 14, 28
Common factors: 1, 2, 4

55. 21: 1, 3, 7, 21
27: 1, 3, 9, 27
Common factors: 1, 3

56. 10: 1, 2, 5, 10
50: 1, 2, 5, 10, 25, 50
Common factors: 1, 2, 5, 10

57. 12: 1, 2, 3, 4, 6, 12
30: 1, 2, 3, 5, 6, 10, 15, 30
Common factors: 1, 2, 3, 6

58. 18: 1, 2, 3, 6, 9, 18
96: 1, 2, 3, 4, 6, 8, 12, 16, 24, 32, 48, 96
Common factors: 1, 2, 3, 6

59. 78: 1, 2, 3, 6, 13, 26, 39, 78
105: 1, 3, 5, 7, 15, 21, 35, 105
Common factors: 1, 3

60. 84: 1, 2, 3, 4, 6, 7, 12, 14, 21, 28, 42, 84
154: 1, 2, 7, 11, 14, 22, 77, 154
Common factors: 1, 2, 7, 14

Lesson 7.3

7.3 Checkpoint (pp. 402–404)

1.

$3x + 2y = 7$	Write equation 1.
$-3x + 4y = 5$	Write equation 2.
$6y = 12$	Add equations.
$y = 2$	Solve for y.
$3x + 2(2) = 7$	Substitute 2 for y in either equation.
$3x + 4 = 7$	Solve for x.
$3x = 3$	
$x = 1$	

Solution: (1, 2)

Check:

$3(1) + 2(2) \stackrel{?}{=} 7$

$7 = 7$

$-3(1) + 4(2) \stackrel{?}{=} 5$

$5 = 5$

2.

$4x - 2y = 2$	Write equation 1.
$3x + 2y = 12$	Write equation 2.
$7x = 14$	Add equations.
$x = 2$	Solve for x.
$4(2) - 2y = 2$	Substitute 2 for x in either equation.
$8 - 2y = 2$	Solve for y.
$-2y = -6$	
$y = 3$	

Solution: (2, 3)

Check:

$4(2) - 2(3) \stackrel{?}{=} 2$

$2 = 2$

$3(2) + 2(3) \stackrel{?}{=} 12$

$12 = 12$

Copyright © McDougal Littell Inc.
All rights reserved.

3. $5x + 2y = -4$ Write equation 1.
$-5x + 3y = 19$ Write equation 2.
$5y = 15$ Add equations.
$y = 3$ Solve for y.

$5(x) + 2(3) = -4$ Substitute 3 for y in either equation.
$5x + 6 = -4$ Solve for x.
$5x = -10$
$x = -2$
Solution: $(-2, 3)$
Check:
$5(-2) + 2(3) \stackrel{?}{=} -4$
$-4 = -4$
$-5(-2) + 3(3) \stackrel{?}{=} 19$
$19 = 19$

4. $2x - 3y = 4$ Equation 1
$-4x + 5y = -8$ Equation 2

$4x - 6y = 8$ Multiply equation 1 by 2.
$-4x + 5y = -8$ Add equation 2.
$-y = 0$ Solve for y.
$y = 0$
$2x - 3(0) = 4$ Substitute 0 for y in either equation.
$2x = 4$ Solve for x.
$x = 2$
Solution: $(2, 0)$
Check:
$2(2) - 3(0) \stackrel{?}{=} 4$
$4 = 4$
$-4(2) + 5(0) \stackrel{?}{=} -8$
$-8 = -8$

5. $3x + 4y = 6$ Equation 1
$2x - 5y = -19$ Equation 2

$15x + 20y = 30$ Multiply equation 1 by 5.
$8x - 20y = -76$ Multiply equation 2 by 4.
$23x = -46$ Add the new equations.
$x = -2$ Solve for x.

$3(-2) + 4y = 6$ Substitute -2 for x.
$-6 + 4y = 6$ Solve for y.
$4y = 12$
$y = 3$
Solution: $(-2, 3)$
Check:
$3(-2) + 4(3) \stackrel{?}{=} 6$
$6 = 6$
$2(-2) - 5(3) \stackrel{?}{=} -19$
$-19 = -19$

6. $6x + 2y = 2$ Equation 1
$-3x + 3y = -9$ Equation 2

$6x + 2y = 2$ Equation 1
$-6x + 6y = -18$ Multiply equation 2 by 2.
$8y = -16$ Add equations.
$y = -2$ Solve for y.

$6x + 2(-2) = 2$ Substitute -2 for y.
$6x - 4 = 2$ Solve for x.
$6x = 6$
$x = 1$
Solution: $(1, -2)$
Check:
$6(1) + 2(-2) \stackrel{?}{=} 2$
$2 = 2$
$-3(1) + 3(-2) \stackrel{?}{=} -9$
$-9 = -9$

7. $2x + 5y = -11$ Equation 1
$5y = 3x - 21$ Equation 2

$2x + 5y = -11$
$-3x + 5y = -21$ Rearrange equation 2.

$2x + 5y = -11$
$3x - 5y = 21$ Multiply equation 2 by -1.
$5x = 10$ Add equations.
$x = 2$ Solve for x.

$2(2) + 5y = -11$ Substitute 2 for x.
$4 + 5y = -11$ Solve for y.
$5y = -15$
$y = -3$
Solution: $(2. -3)$
Check:
$2(2) + 5(-3) \stackrel{?}{=} -11$
$-11 = -11$
$5(-3) \stackrel{?}{=} 3(2) - 21$
$-15 = -15$

8. $-13 = 4x - 3y$ Equation 1
$5x + 2y = 1$ Equation 2

$4x - 3y = -13$ Rearrange equation 1.
$5x + 2y = 1$
$8x - 6y = -26$ Multiply equation 1 by 2.
$15x + 6y = 3$ Multiply equation 2 by 3.
$23x = -23$ Add equations.
$x = -1$ Solve for x.

$5(-1) + 2y = 1$ Substitute -1 for x.
$-5 + 2y = 1$ Solve for y.
$2y = 6$
$y = 3$
Solution: $(-1, 3)$
Check:
$-13 \stackrel{?}{=} 4(-1) - 3(3)$
$-13 = -13$
$5(-1) + 2(3) \stackrel{?}{=} 1$
$1 = 1$

9. $4x + 7y = -9$ Equation 1
$3x = 3y + 18$ Equation 2

$4x + 7y = -9$
$3x - 3y = 18$ Rearrange equation 2.

$12x + 21y = -27$ Multiply equation 1 by 3.
$21x - 21y = 126$ Multiply equation 2 by 7.
$33x = 99$ Add equations.
$x = 3$

Copyright © McDougal Littell Inc.
All rights reserved.

$4(3) + 7y = -9$ Substitute 3 for x.
$12 + 7y = -9$ Solve for y.
$7y = -21$
$y = -3$
Solution: $(3, -3)$
Check:
$4(3) + 7(-3) \stackrel{?}{=} -9$
$-9 = -9$
$3(3) \stackrel{?}{=} 3(-3) + 18$
$9 = 9$

7.3 Guided Practice (p. 405)

1. Multiply one or both equations by a number so that the coefficients of the same variable are opposites.

2. Multiply the first equation by -5 to obtain $-5x - 5y = -5$.

$-5x - 5y = -5$
$5x + 4y = 14$
$-y = 9$ Add equations.
$y = -9$ Solve for y.

$x + (-9) = 1$ Substitute -9 for y.
$x = 10$ Solve for x.
Solution: $(10, -9)$

3. Error: $9x + 7x = 16x$ and $24 + 8 = 32$.
$9x + 3y = 24$ Multiply equation 1 by 3.
$7x - 3y = 8$ Equation 2
$16x = 32$ Add equations.
$x = 2$ Solve for x.

$3(2) + y = 8$ Substitute 2 for x.
$6 + y = 8$ Solve for y.
$y = 2$
Solution: $(2, 2)$

4. Add the equations to eliminate the y-terms and solve for x.
$x + 3y = 6$ Equation 1
$x - 3y = 12$ Equation 2
$2x = 18$ Add equations.
$x = 9$ Solve for x.

$9 + 3y = 6$ Substitute 9 for x.
$3y = -3$ Solve for y.
$y = -1$
Solution: $(9, -1)$

5. *Sample answer*: Multiply equation 2 by -4, then add and solve for x.
$3x - 4y = 7$ Equation 1
$-8x + 4y = -12$ Multiply equation 2 by -4.
$-5x = -5$ Add equations.
$x = 1$ Solve for x.

$2(1) - y = 3$ Substitute 1 for x.
$2 - y = 3$ Solve for y.
$-y = 1$
$y = -1$
Solution: $(1, -1)$

6. Arrange the equations with like terms in columns, then add the equations to solve for y.
$-2x + 2y = -2$ Rearrange equation 1.
$2x + 3y = 12$ Equation 2.
$5y = 10$ Add equations.
$y = 2$ Solve for y.

$2(2) = 2x - 2$ Substitute 2 for y.
$4 = 2x - 2$ Solve for x.
$6 = 2x$
$3 = x$
Solution: $(3, 2)$

7.3 Practice and Applications (pp. 405–407)

7. $x + y = 4$
$x - y = -10$
$2x = -6$
$x = -3$
$-3 + y = 4$
$y = 7$
Solution: $(-3, 7)$
Check:
$-3 + 7 \stackrel{?}{=} 4$
$4 = 4$
$-3 - 7 \stackrel{?}{=} -10$
$-10 = -10$

8. $a - b = 8$
$a + b = 20$
$2a = 28$
$a = 14$
$14 - b = 8$
$-b = -6$
$b = 6$
Solution: $(14, 6)$
Check:
$14 - 6 \stackrel{?}{=} 8$
$8 = 8$
$14 + 6 \stackrel{?}{=} 20$
$20 = 20$

9. $2x + y = 4$
$x - y = 2$
$3x = 6$
$x = 2$
$2 - y = 2$
$-y = 0$
$y = 0$
Solution: $(2, 0)$
Check:
$2(2) + 0 \stackrel{?}{=} 4$
$4 = 4$
$2 - 0 \stackrel{?}{=} 2$
$2 = 2$

Copyright © McDougal Littell Inc.
All rights reserved.

10.
$$\begin{aligned} m + 3n &= 2 \\ -m + 2n &= 3 \\ \hline 5n &= 5 \\ n &= 1 \\ m + 3(1) &= 2 \\ m + 3 &= 2 \\ m &= -1 \end{aligned}$$
Solution: $(-1, 1)$

Check:
$$\begin{aligned} -1 + 3(1) &\stackrel{?}{=} 2 \\ 2 &= 2 \\ -(-1) + 2(1) &\stackrel{?}{=} 3 \\ 3 &= 3 \end{aligned}$$

11.
$$\begin{aligned} p + 4q &= 23 \\ -p + q &= 2 \\ \hline 5q &= 25 \\ q &= 5 \\ p + 4(5) &= 23 \\ p + 20 &= 23 \\ p &= 3 \end{aligned}$$
Solution: $(3, 5)$

Check:
$$\begin{aligned} 3 + 4(5) &\stackrel{?}{=} 23 \\ 23 &= 23 \\ -(3) + 5 &\stackrel{?}{=} 2 \\ 2 &= 2 \end{aligned}$$

12.
$$\begin{aligned} 3v - 2w &= 1 \\ 2v + 2w &= 4 \\ \hline 5v \qquad &= 5 \\ v &= 1 \\ 3(1) - 2w &= 1 \\ 3 - 2w &= 1 \\ -2w &= -2 \\ w &= 1 \end{aligned}$$
Solution: $(1, 1)$

Check:
$$\begin{aligned} 3(1) - 2(1) &\stackrel{?}{=} 1 \\ 1 &= 1 \\ 2(1) + 2(1) &\stackrel{?}{=} 4 \\ 4 &= 4 \end{aligned}$$

13.
$$\begin{aligned} g + 2h &= 4 \\ -g - h &= 2 \\ \hline h &= 6 \\ -g - (6) &= 2 \\ -g &= 8 \\ g &= -8 \end{aligned}$$
Solution: $(-8, 6)$

Check:
$$\begin{aligned} -8 + 2(6) &\stackrel{?}{=} 4 \\ 4 &= 4 \\ -(-8) - (6) &\stackrel{?}{=} 2 \\ 2 &= 2 \end{aligned}$$

14.
$$\begin{aligned} 13x - 5y &= 8 \\ 3x + 5y &= 8 \\ \hline 16x \qquad &= 16 \\ x &= 1 \\ 3(1) + 5y &= 8 \\ 3 + 5y &= 8 \\ 5y &= 5 \\ y &= 1 \end{aligned}$$
Solution: $(1, 1)$

Check:
$$\begin{aligned} 13(1) - 5(1) &\stackrel{?}{=} 8 \\ 8 &= 8 \\ 3(1) + 5(1) &\stackrel{?}{=} 8 \\ 8 &= 8 \end{aligned}$$

15.
$$\begin{aligned} x + 3y &= 3 \\ -x - 6y &= -3 \quad \text{Multiply by } -1. \\ \hline -3y &= 0 \\ y &= 0 \\ x + 3(0) &= 3 \\ x &= 3 \end{aligned}$$
Solution: $(3, 0)$

Check:
$$\begin{aligned} 3 + 3(0) &\stackrel{?}{=} 3 \\ 3 &= 3 \\ -3 - 6(0) &\stackrel{?}{=} -3 \\ -3 &= -3 \end{aligned}$$

16.
$$\begin{aligned} v - w &= -5 \\ -v - 2w &= -4 \quad \text{Multiply by } -1. \\ \hline -3w &= -9 \\ w &= 3 \\ v - 3 &= -5 \\ v &= -2 \end{aligned}$$
Solution: $(-2, 3)$

Check:
$$\begin{aligned} -2 - (3) &\stackrel{?}{=} -5 \\ -5 &= -5 \\ -2 + 2(3) &\stackrel{?}{=} 4 \\ 4 &= 4 \end{aligned}$$

17.
$$\begin{aligned} 4g - 6h &= 0 \quad \text{Multiply by 2.} \\ -9g + 6h &= -15 \quad \text{Multiply by } -3. \\ \hline -5g \qquad &= -15 \\ g &= 3 \\ 2(3) - 3h &= 0 \\ 6 - 3h &= 0 \\ -3h &= -6 \\ h &= 2 \end{aligned}$$
Solution: $(3, 2)$

Check:
$$\begin{aligned} 2(3) - 3(2) &\stackrel{?}{=} 0 \\ 0 &= 0 \\ 3(3) - 2(2) &\stackrel{?}{=} 5 \\ 5 &= 5 \end{aligned}$$

Copyright © McDougal Littell Inc.
All rights reserved.

18. $3x - 3y = 0$ Multiply by 3.
$$\begin{array}{r} 3x - 3y = 0 \\ \underline{-3x - y = 2} \\ -4y = 2 \end{array}$$
$$y = -\frac{1}{2}$$
$$x - \left(-\frac{1}{2}\right) = 0$$
$$x + \frac{1}{2} = 0$$
$$x = -\frac{1}{2}$$
Solution: $\left(-\frac{1}{2}, -\frac{1}{2}\right)$

Check:
$$-\frac{1}{2} - \left(-\frac{1}{2}\right) \stackrel{?}{=} 0$$
$$0 = 0$$
$$-3\left(-\frac{1}{2}\right) - \left(-\frac{1}{2}\right) \stackrel{?}{=} 2$$
$$\frac{3}{2} + \frac{1}{2} \stackrel{?}{=} 2$$
$$2 = 2$$

19. Multiply by 3. Multiply by −2.
$$\begin{array}{r} 6a + 18z = 12 \\ \underline{-6a + 14z = -12} \\ 32z = 0 \end{array}$$
$$z = 0$$
$$2a + 6(0) = 4$$
$$2a = 4$$
$$a = 2$$
Solution: (2, 0)

Check:
$$2(2) + 6(0) \stackrel{?}{=} 4$$
$$4 = 4$$
$$3(2) - 7(0) \stackrel{?}{=} 6$$
$$6 = 6$$

20. Multiply by 4. Multiply by −5.
$$\begin{array}{r} 20e + 16f = 36 \\ \underline{-20e - 25f = -45} \\ -9f = -9 \end{array}$$
$$f = 1$$
$$5e + 4(1) = 9$$
$$5e + 4 = 9$$
$$5e = 5$$
$$e = 1$$
Solution: (1, 1)

Check:
$$5(1) + 4(1) \stackrel{?}{=} 9$$
$$9 = 9$$
$$4(1) + 5(1) \stackrel{?}{=} 9$$
$$9 = 9$$

21. Multiply by −1.
$$\begin{array}{r} 2p - q = 2 \\ \underline{-2p - 3q = -22} \\ -4q = -20 \end{array}$$
$$q = 5$$
$$2p - 5 = 2$$
$$2p = 7$$
$$p = \frac{7}{2}$$
Solution: $\left(\frac{7}{2}, 5\right)$

Check:
$$2\left(\frac{7}{2}\right) - 5 \stackrel{?}{=} 2$$
$$2 = 2$$
$$2\left(\frac{7}{2}\right) + 3(5) \stackrel{?}{=} 22$$
$$22 = 22$$

22. Multiply by −3.
$$\begin{array}{r} 9m - 3n = 20 \\ \underline{-9m - 18n = -6} \\ -21n = 14 \end{array}$$
$$n = -\frac{2}{3}$$
$$3m + 6\left(-\frac{2}{3}\right) = 2$$
$$3m - 4 = 2$$
$$3m = 6$$
$$m = 2$$
Solution: $\left(2, -\frac{2}{3}\right)$

Check:
$$9(2) - 3\left(-\frac{2}{3}\right) \stackrel{?}{=} 20$$
$$18 + 2 \stackrel{?}{=} 20$$
$$20 = 20$$
$$3(2) + 6\left(-\frac{2}{3}\right) \stackrel{?}{=} 2$$
$$6 - 4 \stackrel{?}{=} 2$$
$$2 = 2$$

23. Rearrange equation 2.
$$\begin{array}{r} x - 3y = 30 \\ \underline{x + 3y = 12} \\ 2x \quad\quad = 42 \end{array}$$
$$x = 21$$
$$21 - 3y = 30$$
$$-3y = 9$$
$$y = -3$$
Solution: (21, −3)

Check:
$$21 - 3(-3) \stackrel{?}{=} 30$$
$$30 = 30$$
$$3(-3) + 21 \stackrel{?}{=} 12$$
$$12 = 12$$

Copyright © McDougal Littell Inc.
All rights reserved.

24. $3b + 2c = 46$
$-3b - 15c = -33$ Rearrange and multiply by -3.
$-13c = 13$
$c = -1$

$3b + 2(-1) = 46$
$3b - 2 = 46$
$3b = 48$
$b = 16$
Solution: $(16, -1)$

Check:
$3(16) + 2(-1) \stackrel{?}{=} 46$
$48 - 2 \stackrel{?}{=} 46$
$46 = 46$
$5(-1) + 16 \stackrel{?}{=} 11$
$-5 + 16 \stackrel{?}{=} 11$
$11 = 11$

25. $-x + y = -9$ Rearrange.
$x + 8y = 0$
$9y = -9$
$y = -1$

$-1 = x - 9$
$8 = x$
Solution: $(8, -1)$

Check:
$-1 \stackrel{?}{=} 8 - 9$
$-1 = -1$
$8 + 8(-1) \stackrel{?}{=} 0$
$0 = 0$

26. $m - 3n = 0$ Rearrange.
$-m - 10n = -13$ Multiply by -1.
$-13n = -13$
$n = 1$

$m = 3(1)$
$m = 3$
Solution: $(3, 1)$

Check:
$3 \stackrel{?}{=} 3(1)$
$3 = 3$
$3 + 10(1) \stackrel{?}{=} 13$
$13 = 13$

27. $5p + 2q = 7$ Rearrange.
$8p - 2q = 32$ Rearrange and multiply by 2.
$13p = 39$
$p = 3$

$4(3) - 16 = q$
$12 - 16 = q$
$-4 = q$
Solution: $(3, -4)$

Check:
$2(-4) \stackrel{?}{=} 7 - 5(3)$
$-8 = -8$
$4(3) - 16 \stackrel{?}{=} -4$
$-4 = -4$

28. $u + 2v = 150$ Rearrange.
$2u + v = 150$ Rearrange.
$-2u - 4v = -300$ Multiply by -2.
$2u + v = 150$
$-3v = -150$
$v = 50$

$2u = 150 - 50$
$2u = 100$
$u = 50$
Solution: $(50, 50)$

Check:
$2(50) \stackrel{?}{=} 150 - 50$
$100 = 100$
$2(50) \stackrel{?}{=} 150 - 50$
$100 = 100$

29. $g - 10h = 43$
$-g + 5h = 18$ Rearrange.
$-5h = 61$
$h = -\frac{61}{5}$

$18 = -g + 5\left(-\frac{61}{5}\right)$
$18 = -g - 61$
$79 = -g$
$-79 = g$
Solution: $\left(-79, -\frac{61}{5}\right)$

Check:
$-79 - 10\left(-\frac{61}{5}\right) \stackrel{?}{=} 43$
$-79 + 122 \stackrel{?}{=} 43$
$43 = 43$
$18 \stackrel{?}{=} -(-79) + 5\left(-\frac{61}{5}\right)$
$18 \stackrel{?}{=} 79 - 61$
$18 = 18$

30. $5s + 8t = 70$
$-5s + 8t = -60$ Rearrange; multiply by -1.
$16t = 10$
$t = \frac{5}{8}$

$5s + 8\left(\frac{5}{8}\right) = 70$
$5s + 5 = 70$
$5s = 65$
$s = 13$
Solution: $\left(13, \frac{5}{8}\right)$

Copyright © McDougal Littell Inc.
All rights reserved.

Check:

$5(13) + 8\left(\frac{5}{8}\right) \stackrel{?}{=} 70$

$65 + 5 \stackrel{?}{=} 70$

$70 = 70$

$60 \stackrel{?}{=} 5(13) - 8\left(\frac{5}{8}\right)$

$60 \stackrel{?}{=} 65 - 5$

$60 = 60$

31. $x + 2y = 5$

$10x - 2y = 6$ Multiply by 2.

$11x = 11$

$x = 1$

$1 + 2y = 5$

$2y = 4$

$y = 2$

Solution: (1, 2)

Check:

$1 + 2(2) \stackrel{?}{=} 5$

$5 = 5$

$5(1) - 2 \stackrel{?}{=} 3$

$3 = 3$

32. $3p + q = 2$ Rearrange.

$2p - q = 3$ Rearrange.

$5 = 5$

$p = 1$

$3(1) + q = 2$

$q = -1$

Solution: $(1, -1)$

Check:

$-3(1) + 2 \stackrel{?}{=} -1$

$-1 = -1$

$-(-1) + 2(1) \stackrel{?}{=} 3$

$3 = 3$

33. $r + t = 1$ Rearrange.

$2r - t = 2$

$3r = 3$

$r = 1$

$1 + t = 1$

$t = 0$

Solution: (1, 0)

Check:

$0 + 1 \stackrel{?}{=} 1$

$1 = 1$

$2(1) - 0 \stackrel{?}{=} 2$

$2 = 2$

34. $3g + 4h = 24$ Rearrange.

$g - 2h = -2$ Rearrange.

$3g + 4h = 24$

$2g - 4h = -4$ Multiply by 2.

$5g = 20$

$g = 4$

$-2 + 2h = 4$

$2h = 6$

$h = 3$

Solution: (4, 3)

Check:

$3(4) - 24 \stackrel{?}{=} -4(3)$

$12 - 24 \stackrel{?}{=} -12$

$-12 = -12$

$-2 + 2(3) \stackrel{?}{=} 4$

$-2 + 6 \stackrel{?}{=} 4$

$4 = 4$

35. $x - 3y = -1$ Rearrange.

$2x + 3y = 7$ Rearrange.

$3x = 6$

$x = 2$

$2 - 3y = -1$

$-3y = -3$

$y = 1$

Solution: (2, 1)

Check:

$2 + 1 \stackrel{?}{=} 3(1)$

$3 = 3$

$2(2) \stackrel{?}{=} 7 - 3(1)$

$4 = 4$

36. $4a + b = 0$ Rearrange.

$a - b = 5$

$5a = 5$

$a = 1$

$1 - b = 5$

$-b = 4$

$b = -4$

Solution: $(1, -4)$

Check:

$4(1) \stackrel{?}{=} -(-4)$

$4 = 4$

$1 - (-4) \stackrel{?}{=} 5$

$5 = 5$

37. $2m - 4n = 4$ Rearrange.

$-2m + 2n = -4$ Rearrange; multiply by -2.

$-2n = 0$

$n = 0$

$m - 2 = 0$

$m = 2$

Solution: (2, 0)

Check:

$2(2) - 4 \stackrel{?}{=} 4(0)$

$0 = 0$

$2 - 2 \stackrel{?}{=} 0$

$0 = 0$

Copyright © McDougal Littell Inc.
All rights reserved.

38. $3y = -5x + 15$
$-3y = -9x + 27$ Multiply by 3.
$0 = -14x + 42$
$14x = 42$
$x = 3$

$-y = -3(3) + 9$
$-y = 0$
$y = 0$
Solution: (3, 0)

Check:
$3(0) \stackrel{?}{=} -5(3) + 15$
$0 = 0$
$-(0) \stackrel{?}{=} -3(3) + 9$
$0 = 0$

39. $3j + 5k = 19$
$-3j + 6k = 3$ Multiply by -3.
$11k = 22$
$k = 2$

$3j + 5(2) = 19$
$3j + 10 = 19$
$3j = 9$
$j = 3$
Solution: (3, 2)

Check:
$3(3) + 5(2) \stackrel{?}{=} 19$
$9 + 10 \stackrel{?}{=} 19$
$19 = 19$
$3 - 2(2) \stackrel{?}{=} -1$
$3 - 4 \stackrel{?}{=} -1$
$-1 = -1$

40. $6x + 2y = 5$
$-8x - 2y = -3$ Multiply by -1.
$-2x = 2$
$x = -1$

$6(-1) + 2y = 5$
$-6 + 2y = 5$
$2y = 11$
$y = \frac{11}{2}$

Solution: $\left(-1, \frac{11}{2}\right)$

Check:
$6(-1) + 2\left(\frac{11}{2}\right) \stackrel{?}{=} 5$
$-6 + 11 \stackrel{?}{=} 5$
$5 = 5$
$8(-1) + 2\left(\frac{11}{2}\right) \stackrel{?}{=} 3$
$-8 + 11 \stackrel{?}{=} 3$
$3 = 3$

41. $6x + 14y = 12$ Multiply by 2.
$-6x - 27y = -12$ Multiply by -3.
$-13y = 0$
$y = 0$

$3x + 7(0) = 6$
$3x = 6$
$x = 2$
Solution: (2, 0)
Check:
$3(2) + 7(0) \stackrel{?}{=} 6$
$6 = 6$
$2(2) + 9(0) \stackrel{?}{=} 4$
$4 = 4$

42. $5y = -4x + 20$ Rearrange.
$4y = -20x + 16$
$-25y = 20x - 100$ Multiply by -5.
$4y = -20x + 16$
$-21y = -84$
$y = 4$

$5(4) = -4x + 20$
$20 = -4x + 20$
$0 = -4x$
$0 = x$
Solution: (0, 4)

Check:
$5(4) - 20 \stackrel{?}{=} -4(0)$
$0 = 0$
$4(4) \stackrel{?}{=} -20(0) + 16$
$16 = 16$

43. Gold Volume + Copper Volume = 4 cm^3
Gold Density · Gold Volume +
Copper Density · Copper Volume = 46 gm
Let G = gold volume.
Let C = copper volume.

$G + C = 4$
$19G + 9C = 46$

$-9G - 9C = -36$ Multiply by -9.
$19G + 9C = 46$
$10G = 10$
$G = 1$

$1 + C = 4$
$C = 3$
Solution: 3 cm^3 of copper

Copyright © McDougal Littell Inc.
All rights reserved.

44. $7y = 9x$

$y = -3x + 12$

$$\begin{aligned} 7y &= 9x \\ -7y &= 21x - 84 \quad \text{Multiply by } -7. \\ \hline 0 &= 30x - 84 \\ 84 &= 30x \\ \frac{84}{30} &= x \\ \frac{2 \cdot 6 \cdot 7}{6 \cdot 5} &= x \\ \frac{14}{5} &= x \end{aligned}$$

$$7y = 9\left(\frac{14}{5}\right)$$

$$7y = \frac{126}{5}$$

$$y = \frac{126}{35} = \frac{18}{5}$$

Solution: $\left(\frac{14}{5}, \frac{18}{5}\right)$

45.

$$\begin{aligned} 0 &= \frac{9y}{7} - \frac{8y}{6} + 720 \\ -720 &= \frac{9y}{7} - \frac{8y}{6} \\ -720 &= \frac{9y}{7} \cdot \frac{6}{6} - \frac{8y}{6} \cdot \frac{7}{7} \\ -720 &= \frac{54y}{42} - \frac{56y}{42} \\ -720 &= \frac{-2y}{42} = -\frac{y}{21} \\ 21(720) &= y \\ 15{,}120 &= y \end{aligned}$$

$$x = \frac{9(15{,}120)}{7} + 560$$

$$x = 20{,}000$$

20,000 rolls of cotton; 15,120 men

46. $3x + 2y + z = 42$ Equation 1.

$2y + z + 12 = 3x$ Equation 2.

$x - 3y = 0$ Equation 3.

$x = 3y$ Rearrange equation 3.

$3(3y) + 2y + z = 4$ Substitute $3y$ for x in equation 1.

$9y + 2y + z = 42$

$11y + z = 42$ Simplify. [Equation 4]

$3x + 2y + z = 42$ Equation 1.

$-3x + 2y + z = -12$ Rearrange equation 2.

$4y + 2z = 30$ Add equations. [Equation 5]

$-22y - 2z = -84$ Multiply equation 4 by -2.

$4y + 2z = 30$ Equation 5.

$-18y = -54$ Add equations.

$y = 3$ Solve for y.

$x = 3(3)$ Substitute 3 for y in equation 3.

$x = 9$ Solve for x.

$3(9) + 2(3) + z = 42$ Substitute 9 for x, 3 for y in equation 1 and solve for z.

$27 + 6 + z = 42$

$33 + z = 42$

$z = 9$

Solution: (9, 3, 9)

7.3 Standardized Test Practice (p. 407)

47. $x + y = 4$

$x - 2y = 10$

$$\begin{aligned} -x - y &= -4 \quad \text{Multiply by } -1. \\ x - 2y &= 10 \\ \hline -3y &= 6 \\ y &= -2 \end{aligned}$$

$x + (-2) = 4$

$x = 6$

Solution: $(6, -2)$; A

48. $3x + 5y = -8$

$x - 2y = 1$

$$\begin{aligned} 3x + 5y &= -8 \\ -3x + 6y &= -3 \quad \text{Multiply by } -3. \\ \hline 11y &= -11 \\ y &= -1 \end{aligned}$$

$x - 2(-1) = 1$

$x + 2 = 1$

$x = -1$

Solution: $(-1, -1)$; H

7.3 Mixed Review (p. 408)

49. $y - 4 = 3[x - (-2)]$

$y - 4 = 3(x + 2)$

$y - 4 = 3x + 6$

$y = 3x + 10$

50. $y - 1 = 5(x - 5)$

$y - 1 = 5x - 25$

$y = 5x - 24$

51. $y - 3 = -3(x - 9)$

$y - 3 = -3x + 27$

$y = -3x + 30$

52. $m = \frac{2 - (-1)}{4 - (-2)} = \frac{3}{6} = \frac{1}{2}$

$y - (-1) = \frac{1}{2}[x - (-2)]$

$y + 1 = \frac{1}{2}(x + 2)$

$y + 1 = \frac{1}{2}x + 1$

$y = \frac{1}{2}x$

53. $m = \frac{1 - 5}{2 - 6} = \frac{-4}{-4} = 1$

$y - 1 = 1(x - 2)$

$y - 1 = x - 2$

$y = x - 1$

Copyright © McDougal Littell Inc.
All rights reserved.

54. $m = \frac{-3-(-5)}{-1-4} = -\frac{2}{5}$

$y - (-5) = -\frac{2}{5}(x-4)$

$y + 5 = -\frac{2}{5}x + \frac{8}{5}$

$y = -\frac{2}{5}x + \frac{8}{5} - \frac{25}{5}$

$y = -\frac{2}{5}x - \frac{17}{5}$

55. $3(1) - 2(3) \overset{?}{<} 2$

$3 - 6 \overset{?}{<} 2$

$-3 < 2$

(1, 3) is a solution.

$3(2) - 2(0) \overset{?}{<} 2$

$6 - 2 \overset{?}{<} 2$

$4 \not< 2$

(2, 0) is not a solution.

56. $5(-2) + 4(4) \overset{?}{\geq} 6$

$-10 + 16 \overset{?}{\geq} 6$

$6 \geq 6$

(−2, 4) is a solution.

$5(5) + 4(5) \overset{?}{\geq} 6$

$25 + 20 \overset{?}{\geq} 6$

$45 \geq 6$

(5, 5) is a solution.

57. $-6x - 5y = 28$

$x - 2y = 1$

$x = 2y + 1$

$-6(2y + 1) - 5y = 28$

$-12y - 6 - 5y = 28$

$-17y - 6 = 28$

$-17y = 34$

$y = -2$

$x = 2(-2) + 1$

$x = -4 + 1$

$x = -3$

Solution: (−3, −2)

58. $m + 2n = 1$

$m = -2n + 1$

$5m - 4n = -23$

$5(-2n + 1) - 4n = -23$

$-10n + 5 - 4n = -23$

$-14n + 5 = -23$

$-14n = -28$

$n = 2$

$m = -2(2) + 1$

$m = -3$

Solution: (−3, 2)

59. $g - 5h = 20$

$g = 5h + 20$

$4g + 3h = 34$

$4(5h + 20) + 3h = 34$

$20h + 80 + 3h = 34$

$23h + 80 = 34$

$23h = -46$

$h = -2$

$g = 5(-2) + 20$

$g = 10$

Solution: (10, −2)

7.3 Maintaining Skills (p. 408)

60. $\frac{1}{4} \cdot \frac{3}{3} = \frac{3}{12}$ (true)

61. $\frac{5}{7} \cdot \frac{5}{5} = \frac{25}{35}$ (true)

62. $\frac{3}{7} \cdot \frac{2}{2} = \frac{6}{14}$ $\left(\text{not } \frac{6}{16}\text{; false}\right)$

63. $\frac{2}{11} \cdot \frac{5}{5} = \frac{10}{55}$ (true)

64. $\frac{9}{7} \cdot \frac{2}{2} = \frac{18}{14}$ $\left(\text{not } \frac{18}{15}\text{; false}\right)$

65. $\frac{250}{350} = \frac{50(5)}{50(7)} = \frac{5}{7}$ $\left(\text{not } \frac{2}{3}\text{; false}\right)$

Quiz 1 *(p. 408)*

1. (3, −4)

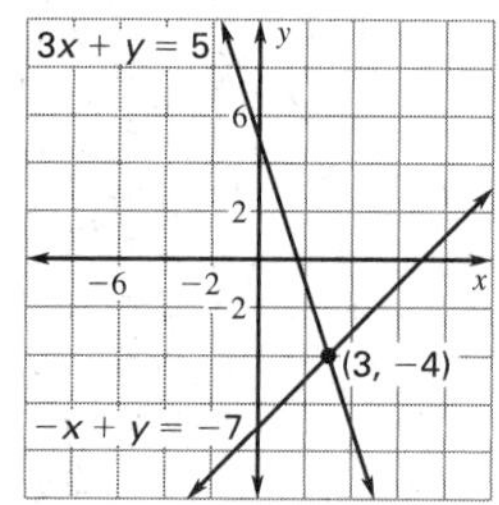

Check:

$3(3) + (-4) \overset{?}{=} 5$

$9 - 4 \overset{?}{=} 5$

$5 = 5$

$-(3) + (-4) \overset{?}{=} -7$

$-7 = -7$

Copyright © McDougal Littell Inc.
All rights reserved.

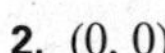

2. (0, 0)

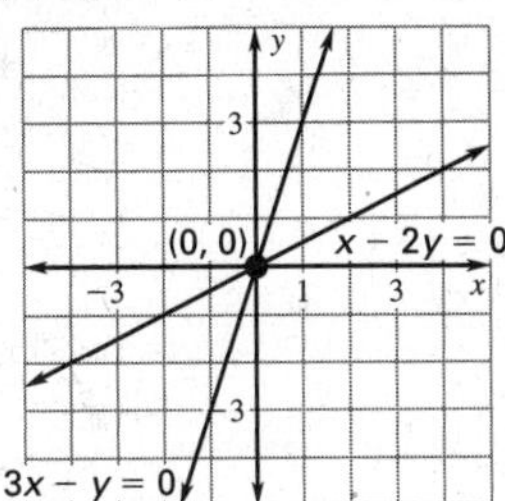

Check:

$0 - 2(0) \stackrel{?}{=} 0$

$0 = 0$

$3(0) - 0 \stackrel{?}{=} 0$

$0 = 0$

3. (6, 8)

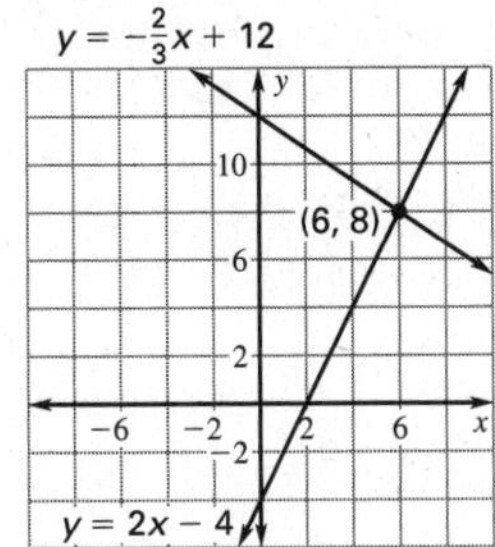

Check:

$2(6) + 3(8) \stackrel{?}{=} 36$

$12 + 24 \stackrel{?}{=} 36$

$36 = 36$

$-2(6) + 8 \stackrel{?}{=} -4$

$-12 + 8 \stackrel{?}{=} -4$

$-4 = -4$

4. $4x + 3y = 31$

$y = 2x + 7$

$4x + 3(2x + 7) = 31$

$4x + 6x + 21 = 31$

$10x + 21 = 31$

$10x = 10$

$x = 1$

$y = 2(1) + 7$

$y = 9$

Solution: (1, 9)

5. $-12x + y = 15$

$3x + 2y = 3$

Solve equation 1 for y:

$y = 12x + 15$

$3x + 2(12x + 15) = 3$

$3x + 24x + 30 = 3$

$27x + 30 = 3$

$27x = -27$

$x = -1$

$y = 12(-1) + 15$

$y = 3$

Solution: (−1, 3)

6. $x + 2y = 14$

$x = -2y + 14$

$2x + 3y = 18$

$2(-2y + 14) + 3y = 18$

$-4y + 28 + 3y = 18$

$28 - y = 18$

$-y = -10$

$y = 10$

$x = -2(10) + 14$

$x = -20 + 14$

$x = -6$

Solution: (−6, 10)

7. $2x + 3y = 36$

$2x - y = 4$

$2x + 3y = 36$

$-2x + y = -4$ Multiply by −1.

$4y = 32$

$y = 8$

$2x - 8 = 4$

$2x = 12$

$x = 6$

Solution: (6, 8)

8. $x + 7y = 12$

$3x - 5y = 10$

$-3x - 21y = -36$ Multiply by −3.

$3x - 5y = 10$

$-26y = -26$

$y = 1$

$x + 7(1) = 12$

$x + 7 = 12$

$x = 5$

Solution: (5, 1)

9. $3x - 5y = -4$

$-9x + 7y = 8$

$9x - 15y = -12$ Multiply by 3.

$-9x + 7y = 8$

$-8y = -4$

$y = \frac{1}{2}$

$3x - 5\frac{1}{2} = -4$

$3x - \frac{5}{2} = -4$

$3x = -\frac{8}{2} + \frac{5}{2}$

$3x = -\frac{3}{2}$

$x = -\frac{1}{2}$

Solution: $\left(-\frac{1}{2}, \frac{1}{2}\right)$

Copyright © McDougal Littell Inc.
All rights reserved.

10. *Sample answer*: linear combinations

$2x + 3y = 1$

$4x - 2y = 10$

$-4x - 6y = -2$ Multiply by -2.

$4x - 2y = 10$

$-8y = 8$

$y = -1$

$2x + 3(-1) = 1$

$2x - 3 = 1$

$2x = 4$

$x = 2$

Solution: $(2, -1)$

11. *Sample answer*: substitution

$x - 3y = -3$

$x = 3y - 3$

$(3y - 3) + 18y = 18$

$21y - 3 = 18$

$21y = 21$

$y = 1$

$x = 3(1) - 3$

$x = 0$

Solution: $(0, 1)$

12. *Sample answer*: linear combinations

$5x - 3y = 7$

$x + 3y = 5$

$6x = 12$

$x = 2$

$2 + 3y = 5$

$3y = 3$

$y = 1$

Solution: $(2, 1)$

13. Let x = number of discs bought at \$10.50.
Let y = number of discs bought at \$8.50.

$x + y = 10$ Equation 1

$10.5x + 8.5y = 93$ Equation 2

$y = -x + 10$

$10.5x + 8.5(-x + 10) = 93$

$10.5x - 8.5x + 85 = 93$

$2x + 85 = 93$

$2x = 8$

$x = 4$

$y = -4 + 10$

$y = 6$

Solution: 4 discs at \$10.50 each, 6 discs at \$8.50 each.

Lesson 7.4

7.4 Checkpoint (p. 410)

1. Number of A-pairs + Number of B-pairs = Total number sold

A + B = 32

Price of A-pairs · Number of A-pairs + Price of B-pairs · Number of B-pairs = Total Cost

30A + 35B = 1050

Sample answer: Since coefficients of A and B in equation 1 are 1, use substitution:

$A = -B + 32$

$30(-B + 32) + 35B = 1050$

$-30B + 960 + 35B = 1050$

$960 + 5B = 1050$

$5B = 90$

$B = 18$

$A = -18 + 32$

$A = 14$

Solution: 14 pairs of Brand A and 18 pairs of Brand B.

2. Number of pounds of peanuts + Number of pounds of cashews = Total number of pounds of mixture

$p + c = 10$

Price per pound of peanuts · Number of pounds of peanuts + Price per pound of cashews · Number of pounds of cashews = Price per pound of mixture · Total number of pounds of mixture.

$3.60p + 7.90c = 5.32(10)$ or $3.6p + 7.9c = 53.2$

Sample answer: Use substitution since the coefficients of p and c in equation 1 are 1.

$p = -c + 10$

$3.6(-c + 10) + 7.9c = 53.2$

$-3.6c + 36 + 7.9c = 53.2$

$36 + 4.3c = 53.2$

$4.3c = 17.2$

$c = 4$

$p = -4 + 10 = 6$

Solution: 6 pounds of peanuts and 4 pounds of cashews are in the mixture.

7.4 Guided Practice (p. 412)

1. *Sample answer*: A jar containing a certain number of nickels and dimes equals a certain sum of money. A system of linear combinations could be used to find how many of each coin are in the jar.

2. *Sample answer*: substitution; coefficients of x and y in equation 1 are 1.

$x = -y + 300$

$(-y + 300) + 3y = 18$

$2y + 300 = 18$

$2y = -282$

$y = -141$

$x = -(-141) + 300$

$x = 441$

Solution: $(441, -141)$

Copyright © McDougal Littell Inc.
All rights reserved.

3. *Sample answer*: linear combinations; multiply equation 2 by 3 and equation 1 by -2 to get opposite coefficients for x-term.

$$\begin{aligned} -6x - 10y &= -50 \\ 6x - 18y &= 36 \\ \hline -28y &= -14 \\ y &= \frac{1}{2} \text{ or } 0.5 \end{aligned}$$

$$\begin{aligned} 2x - 6\left(\frac{1}{2}\right) &= 12 \\ 2x - 3 &= 12 \\ 2x &= 15 \\ x &= \frac{15}{2} \text{ or } 7.5 \end{aligned}$$

Solution: (7.5, 0.5)

4. *Sample answer*: linear combinations; multiply equation 2 by -1.

$$\begin{aligned} 2x + y &= 0 \\ -x - y &= -5 \\ \hline x &= -5 \\ -5 + y &= 5 \\ y &= 10 \end{aligned}$$

Solutions: $(-5, 10)$

5. $y = 30{,}000 + 0.01x$
$y = 24{,}000 + 0.02x$

$$\begin{aligned} 24{,}000 + 0.02x &= 30{,}000 + 0.01x \\ 24{,}000 + 0.01x &= 30{,}000 \\ 0.01x &= 6{,}000 \\ x &= 600{,}000 \end{aligned}$$

$$\begin{aligned} y &= 30{,}000 + 0.01(600{,}000) \\ y &= 30{,}000 + 6{,}000 \\ y &= 36{,}000 \end{aligned}$$

Solution: \$600,000 worth of merchandise to earn \$36,000 in each job.

6. $q + d = 16$ or $d + q = 16$

7. $25q + 10d = 265$

8. $q = -d + 16$

$$\begin{aligned} 25(-d + 16) + 10d &= 265 \\ -25d + 400 + 10d &= 265 \\ -15d + 400 &= 265 \\ -15d &= -135 \\ d &= 9 \end{aligned}$$

$q = -9 + 16$
$q = 7$
Solution: 9 dimes and 7 quarters

7.4 Practice and Applications (pp. 412–414)

9. Substitution: (*Sample answer*)

$$\begin{aligned} x + y &= 2 \\ x &= -y + 2 \end{aligned}$$

$$\begin{aligned} 6(-y + 2) + y &= 2 \\ -6y + 12 + y &= 2 \\ -5y + 12 &= 2 \\ -5y &= -10 \\ y &= 2 \end{aligned}$$

$x = -2 + 2$
$x = 0$
Solution: (0, 2)

Linear combinations: (*Sample answer*)

$$\begin{aligned} x + y &= 2 \\ -6x - y &= -2 \\ \hline -5x &= 0 \\ x &= 0 \end{aligned}$$ Multiply equation 2 by -1.

$$\begin{aligned} 0 + y &= 2 \\ y &= 2 \end{aligned}$$

Solution: (0, 2)

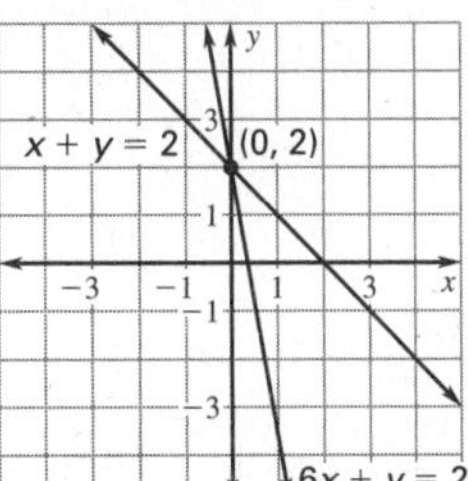

10. Substitution: (*Sample answer*)

$$\begin{aligned} x - y &= 1 \\ x &= y + 1 \end{aligned}$$

$$\begin{aligned} (y + 1) + y &= 5 \\ 2y + 1 &= 5 \\ 2y &= 4 \\ y &= 2 \end{aligned}$$

$x = 2 + 1$
$x = 3$
Solution: (3, 2)

Linear combinations: (*Sample answer*)

$$\begin{aligned} x - y &= 1 \\ x + y &= 5 \\ \hline 2x &= 6 \\ x &= 3 \end{aligned}$$

$$\begin{aligned} 3 - y &= 1 \\ -y &= -2 \\ y &= 2 \end{aligned}$$

Solution: (3, 2)

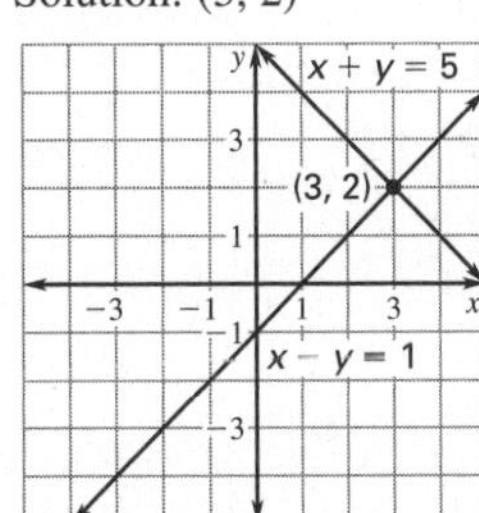

Copyright © McDougal Littell Inc.
All rights reserved.

11. Substitution: (*Sample answer*)

$-x + y = 3$
$y = x + 3$

$3x - (x + 3) = 3$
$3x - x - 3 = 3$
$2x - 3 = 3$
$2x = 6$
$x = 3$

$y = 3 + 3$
$y = 6$
Solution: (3, 6)

Linear combinations: (*Sample answer*)

$3x - y = 3$
$-x + y = 3$
$2x \quad = 6$
$x = 3$

$3(3) - y = 3$
$9 - y = 3$
$-y = -6$
$y = 6$
Solution: (3, 6)

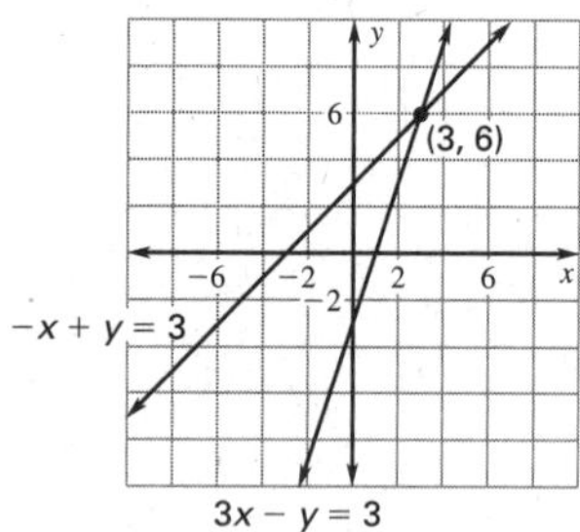

12. Addition; *y* can be easily eliminated by addition.

13. Multiplication and addition; no variable can be easily isolated.

14. Substitution; *x* can be easily solved for in equation 1.

15. Substitution; Equation 2 can be solved for *x* or *y*.

16. Multiplication and addition; no variable can be easily isolated.

17. Substitution; equations 1 or 2 can be solved for *x*.

18. *Sample answer*: Addition; *y* can be easily eliminated by addition.

$2x + y = 5$
$x - y = 1$
$3x \quad = 6$
$x = 2$

$2 - y = 1$
$-y = -1$
$y = 1$
Solution: (2, 1)

19. *Sample answer*: Multiplication and addition; *y* can be eliminated easily by multiplying equation 1 by 3.

$6x - 3y = 9$
$4x + 3y = 21$
$10x \quad = 30$
$x = 3$

$4(3) + 3y = 21$
$12 + 3y = 21$
$3y = 9$
$y = 3$
Solution: (3, 3)

20. *Sample answer*: Addition; *y* can be easily eliminated.

$x - 2y = 4$
$6x + 2y = 10$
$7x \quad = 14$
$x = 2$

$2 - 2y = 4$
$-2y = 2$
$y = -1$
Solution: (2, −1)

21. *Sample answer*: Multiplication and addition; No variable can be easily isolated.

Multiply equation 1 by 2:
$6x + 12y = 16$
$-6x + 3y = 2$
$15y = 18$
$y = \frac{6}{5}$

$3x + 6\left(\frac{6}{5}\right) = 8$

$3x + \frac{36}{5} = 8$

$3x = \frac{40}{5} - \frac{36}{5}$

$3x = \frac{4}{5}$

$x = \frac{4}{15}$

Solution: $\left(\frac{4}{15}, \frac{6}{5}\right)$

22. *Sample answer*: Substitution; equation 1 can be easily solved for *x* or *y*.

$x = -y$

$3(-y) + 2y = 1$
$-3y + 2y = 1$
$-y = 1$
$y = -1$

$x = -(-1)$
$x = 1$
Solution: (1, −1)

Copyright © McDougal Littell Inc.
All rights reserved.

23. *Sample answer*: Substitution; equation 2 can be easily solved for y.

$$3x + y = -5$$
$$y = -3x - 5$$

$$\begin{aligned} 2x - 3(-3x - 5) &= -7 \\ 2x + 9x + 15 &= -7 \\ 11x + 15 &= -7 \\ 11x &= -22 \\ x &= -2 \end{aligned}$$

$y = -3(-2) - 5$
$y = 1$
Solution: $(-2, 1)$

24. *Sample answer*: Multiplication and addition; Multiply equation 2 by 4 to eliminate x.

$$\begin{aligned} 8x + 4y &= 8 \\ -8x + 12y &= 48 \\ \hline 16y &= 56 \\ y &= \frac{7}{2} \end{aligned}$$

$$\begin{aligned} -2x + 3\left(\frac{7}{2}\right) &= 12 \\ -2x + \frac{21}{2} &= 12 \\ -2x &= \frac{24}{2} - \frac{21}{2} \\ -2x &= \frac{3}{2} \\ x &= -\frac{3}{4} \end{aligned}$$

Solution: $\left(-\frac{3}{4}, \frac{7}{2}\right)$

25. *Sample answer*: Substitution; Solve equation 1 for x.
$x = -2y + 1$

$$\begin{aligned} 5(-2y + 1) - 4y &= -23 \\ -10y + 5 - 4y &= -23 \\ -14y + 5 &= -23 \\ -14y &= -28 \\ y &= 2 \end{aligned}$$

$x = -2(2) + 1$
$x = -3$
Solution: $(-3, 2)$

26. *Sample answer*; Addition; y can be easily eliminated by addition.

$$\begin{aligned} 6x - y &= 18 \\ 8x + y &= 24 \\ \hline 14x \quad &= 42 \\ x &= 3 \end{aligned}$$

$$\begin{aligned} 8(3) + y &= 24 \\ 24 + y &= 24 \\ y &= 0 \end{aligned}$$

Solution: $(3, 0)$

27. *A*;
$x + y = 7$
$x + 3y = 19$

28. *C*;
$x + y = 5$
$3x + 5y = 19$

29. *B*;
$x + y = 7$
$x + 5y = 19$

30. Let x = time spent jogging.
Let y = time spent sprinting.

$x + y = 1.5$
$4x + 6y = 7$

$$\begin{aligned} x &= -y + 1.5 \\ 4(-y + 1.5) + 6y &= 7 \\ -4y + 6 + 6y &= 7 \\ 6 + 2y &= 7 \\ 2y &= 1 \\ y &= \frac{1}{2} \text{ or } 0.5 \end{aligned}$$

$x = -(0.5) + 1.5$
$x = 1$
Solution: 1 hour jogging; 0.5 hours sprinting

31. Number of broccoli plants + Number of pea plants = Total number of plants

$b + p = 13$
$b = -p + 13$

Space needed per plant · Number of broccoli plants + Space needed per plant · Number of pea plants = Total space available

$12b + 6p = 120$

$$\begin{aligned} 12(-p + 13) + 6p &= 120 \\ -12p + 156 + 6p &= 120 \\ 156 - 6p &= 120 \\ -6p &= -36 \\ p &= 6 \end{aligned}$$

$b = -6 + 13$
$b = 7$
Solution: 6 pea plants, 7 broccoli plants

32. $m = \frac{10500 - 6200}{25 - 0} = \frac{4300}{25} = 172$

$y - 6200 = 172(x - 0)$
$y - 6200 = 172x$
$y = 172x + 6200$ Houses needed

$m = \frac{6500 - 6100}{0 - 25} = \frac{400}{-25} = -16$

$y - 6500 = -16(x - 0)$
$y - 6500 = -16x$
$y = -16x + 6500$ Houses available

Copyright © McDougal Littell Inc.
All rights reserved.

33. $y = 172x + 6200$
$y = -16x + 6500$

$$\begin{aligned} y &= 172x + 6200 \\ -y &= \ \ 16x - 6500 \\ \hline 0 &= 188x - 300 \end{aligned}$$

$300 = 188x$

$1\frac{28}{47} = x$

$1.6 \approx x$

$y = 172\left(1\frac{28}{47}\right) + 6200$

$y \approx 6474$

Solution: (1.6, 6474)

34. Let x = number of years of growth.
Let y = height of the trees.

spruce tree: $y = 4x + 14$
hemlock tree: $y = 6x + 8$

$4x + 14 = 6x + 8$
$14 = 2x + 8$
$6 = 2x$
$3 = x$
$y = 6(3) + 8$
$y = 18 + 8$
$y = 26$

Solution: In 3 years each tree will be 26 inches tall.

35. Distance drive at 55 mph + Distance driven at 40 mph = Total distance driven

$x + y = 135$

Distance driven at 55 mph/Rate + Distance driven at 40 mph/Rate = Total time driven

Unit analysis: $\frac{\text{mi}}{\text{mi/h}} = \cancel{\text{mi}} \cdot \frac{\text{h}}{\cancel{\text{mi}}} = \text{h (time)}$

$\frac{x}{55} + \frac{y}{40} = 3$

Multiply by LCD to clear fractions:
LCD = $11 \cdot 8 \cdot 5 = 440$

$440\left(\frac{x}{55} + \frac{y}{40}\right) = 440(3)$

$8x + 11y = 1320$

Substitute: $x = -y + 135$
$8(-y + 135) + 11y = 1320$
$-8y + 1080 + 11y = 1320$
$3y + 1080 = 1320$
$3y = 240$
$y = 80$
$x = -80 + 135$
$x = 55$

Solution: 55 miles were driven at 55 miles per hour;
time driven at $\frac{55 \text{ mi}}{\text{h}} = \frac{55 \text{ mi}}{55 \text{ mi/h}} = 1$ h;
80 miles were driven at 40 miles per hour;
$\frac{80 \text{ mi}}{40 \text{ mi/h}} = 2$ h;
1 hour at 55 mi/h; 2 hours at 40 mi/h.

36. $2a = g$
$4b = a + g$
$a + 2b = p$

$$\begin{aligned} p + 2b &= a + 2b + 2b \\ &= a + 4b \\ &= a + a + g \\ &= 2a + g \\ &= 2a + 2a \\ &= 4a \end{aligned}$$

4 apples will balance the scale in the last diagram.

7.4 Standardized Test Practice (p. 414)

37. C;
$2t + 2e = 4.80$
$3t + e = 4.00$

38. $e = -3t + 4$
$2t + 2(-3t + 4) = 4.8$
$2t + (-6t) + 8 = 4.8$
$-4t + 8 = 4.8$
$-4t = -3.2$
$t = 0.8$
$e = -3(0.8) + 4$
$e = 1.6$

Solution: t = \$.80; e = \$1.60 G

7.4 Mixed Review (p. 414)

39. line a:
$m = 4$
line b:
$2y - 8x = -3$
$2y = 8x - 3$
$y = 4x - \frac{3}{2}; m = 4$

parallel; same slope

40. line a:
$4y + 5x = 1$
$4y = -5x + 1$
$y = -\frac{5}{4}x + \frac{1}{4}; m = -\frac{5}{4}$

line b:
$10x + 2y = 2$
$2y = -10x + 2$
$y = -5x + 1; m = -5$

not parallel; different slopes

41. line a:
$3x + 9y + 2 = 0$
$9y = -3x - 2$
$y = -\frac{1}{3}x - \frac{2}{9}; m = -\frac{1}{3}$

line b:
$2y = -6x + 3$
$y = -3x + \frac{3}{2}; m = -3$

not parallel; different slope

Copyright © McDougal Littell Inc.
All rights reserved.

42. line a:

$4y - 1 = 5$

$4y = 6$

$y = \frac{3}{2}; m = 0$

line b:

$6y + 2 = 8$

$6y = 6$

$y = 1; m = 0$

parallel; same slope

43.

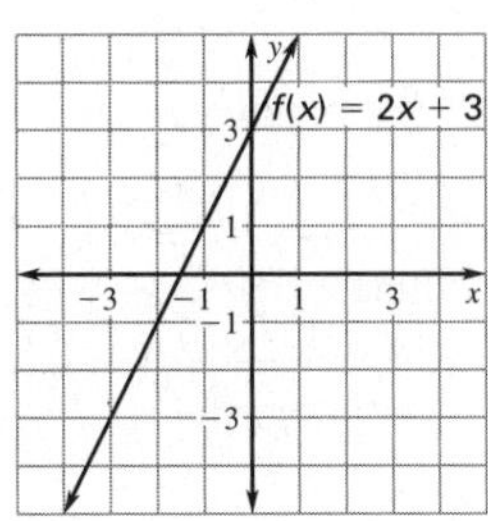

44.

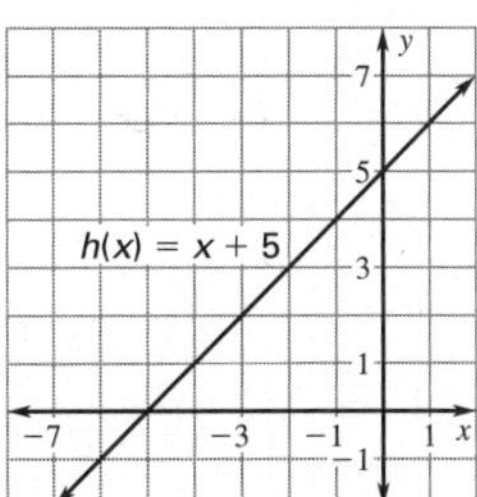

45.

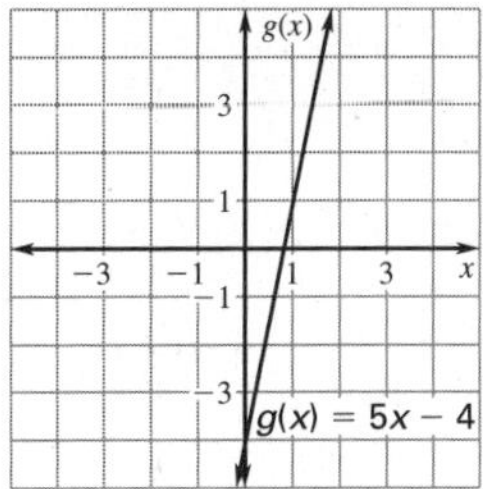

46.

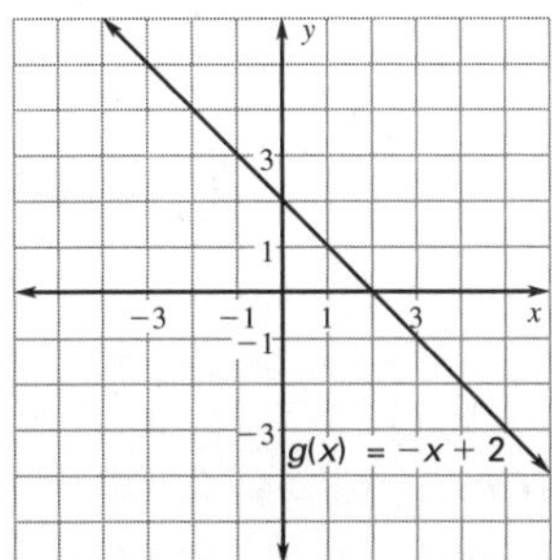

47.

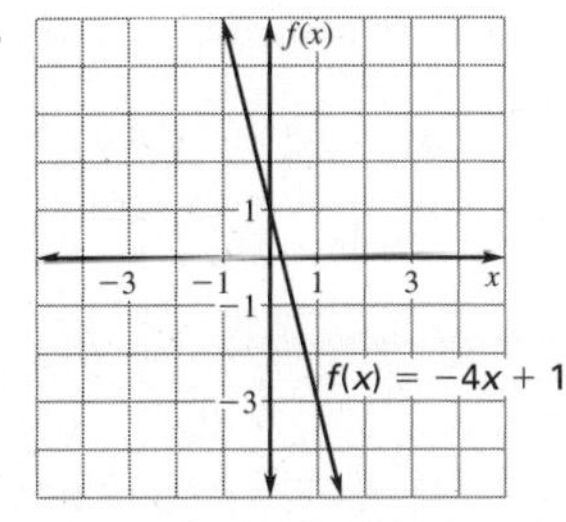

48.

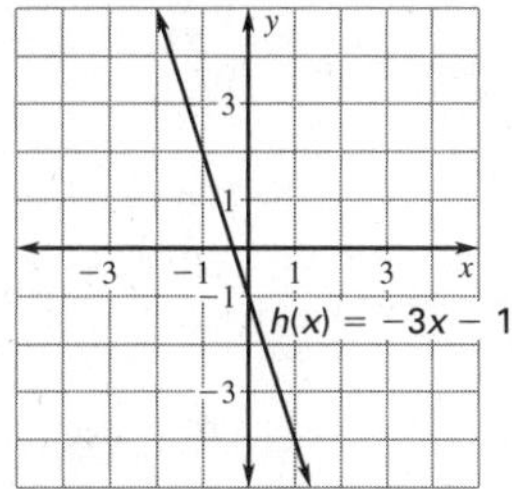

7.4 Maintaining Skills (p. 414)

49. $\frac{9}{15} + \frac{3}{5} = \frac{9}{15} + \frac{9}{15} = \frac{18}{15} = \frac{6}{5} = 1\frac{1}{5}$

50. $\frac{1}{12} + \frac{1}{2} = \frac{1}{12} + \frac{6}{12} = \frac{7}{12}$

51. $\frac{3}{8} + \frac{7}{9} = \frac{27}{72} + \frac{56}{72} = \frac{83}{72} = 1\frac{11}{72}$

52. $\frac{3}{7} + \frac{2}{5} = \frac{15}{35} + \frac{14}{35} = \frac{29}{35}$

53. $\frac{1}{10} + \frac{2}{3} = \frac{3}{30} + \frac{20}{30} = \frac{23}{30}$

54. $\frac{3}{4} + \frac{1}{6} = \frac{9}{12} + \frac{2}{12} = \frac{11}{12}$

55. $\frac{17}{32} + \frac{1}{4} = \frac{17}{32} + \frac{8}{32} = \frac{25}{32}$

56. $\frac{19}{20} + \frac{7}{8} = \frac{38}{40} + \frac{35}{40} = \frac{73}{40} = 1\frac{33}{40}$

7.5 Developing Concepts: Explore *(p. 415)*

1. a.

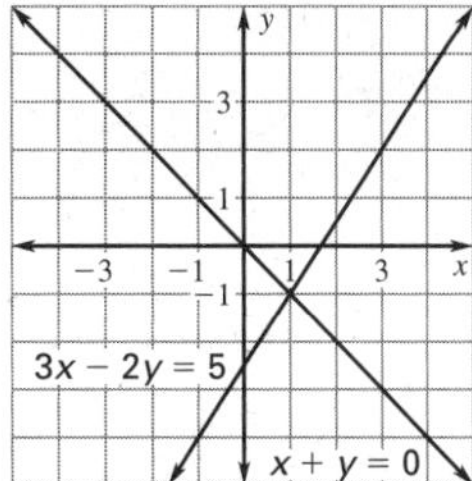

b.

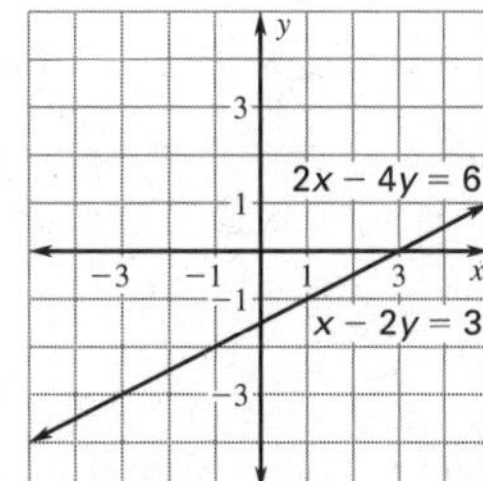

Copyright © McDougal Littell Inc.
All rights reserved.

c. 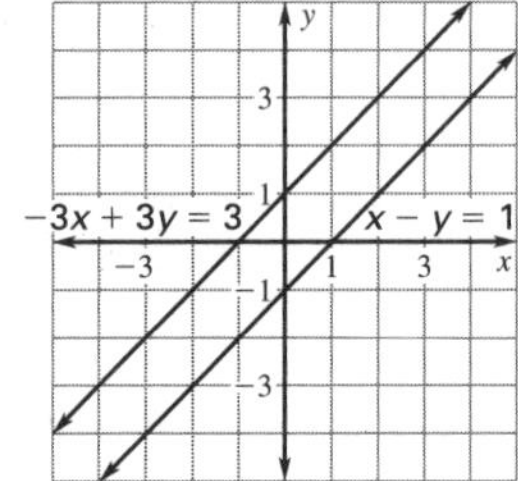

2. a. different slopes, different y-intercepts; the lines intersect at one point.

b. same line

c. same slope, different y-intercepts; lines are parallel.

3. a. $y = -x, y = \frac{3}{2}x - \frac{5}{2}$

b. $y = \frac{1}{2}x - \frac{3}{2}, y = \frac{1}{2}x - \frac{3}{2}$

c. $y = x - 1, y = x + 1$

4. a. Both equations have different values for slope and y-intercepts.

b. The equations are the same.

c. Both equations have the same value for slope but different values for the y-intercepts.

7.5 Think About It (p. 415)

1. a. Step 1: 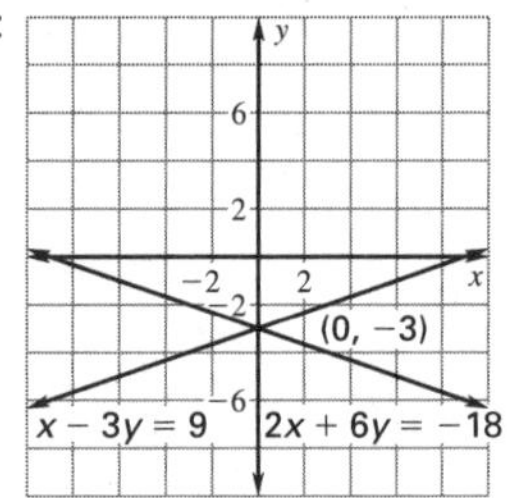

Step 2: Slopes are same "steepness" but one is negative and the other is positive; intersect at one point.

Step 3:

$x - 3y = 9$ line 1

$-3y = -x + 9$

$y = \frac{1}{3}x - 3$

$2x + 6y = -18$ line 2

$6y = -2x - 18$

$y = -\frac{1}{3}x - 3$

Step 4: Slopes are same "steepness" but one is negative and the other is positive; both equations have different slopes and same y-intercept; they intersect at the y-intercept.

b. Step 1: 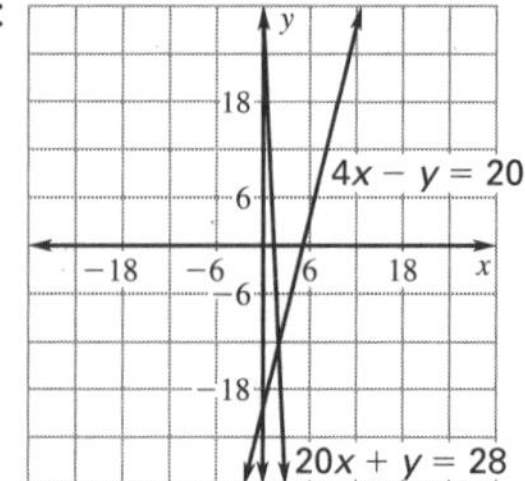

Step 2: different slopes; they intersect at one point.

Step 3:

$4x - y = 20$ line 1

$-y = -4x + 20$

$y = 4x - 20$ $m = 4; b = 20$

$20x + y = 28$ line 2

$y = -20x + 28$ $m = -20; b = 28$

Step 4: different slopes; different y-intercepts; they intersect at one point.

c. Step 1: 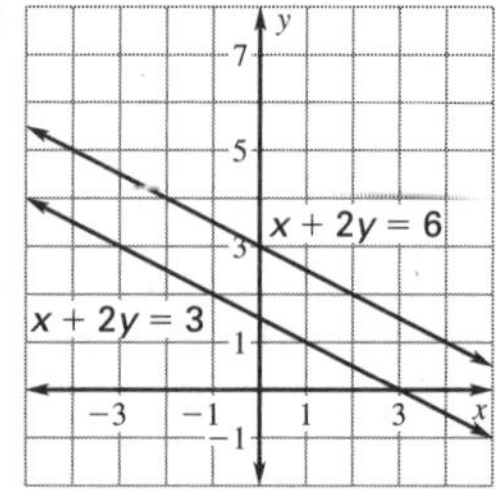

Step 2: same slope; parallel; different y-intercepts

Step 3:

$x + 2y = 3$ line 1

$2y = -x + 3$

$y = -\frac{1}{2}x + \frac{3}{2}$ $m = -\frac{1}{2}; b = \frac{3}{2}$

$x + 2y = 6$ line 2

$2y = -x + 6$

$y = -\frac{1}{2}x + 3$ $m = -\frac{1}{2}; b = 3$

Step 4: same slope; parallel; different y-intercepts

2. $y = -\frac{1}{2}x + 4; y = -\frac{1}{2}x - 4$

3. $y = \frac{1}{3}x + 1$; *Sample answer*: $3y = x + 3$

4. $y = 2; y = 4x - 2$

5. infinitely many solutions; they are the same line.

6. no solution; the lines are parallel and do not intersect.

7. exactly one solution; since they are not parallel, they must intersect at one point.

Copyright © McDougal Littell Inc.
All rights reserved.

7.5 Explore (p. 416)

1 a.
$$x + y = 0$$
$$x = -y$$
$$3x - 2y = 5$$
$$3(-y) - 2y = 5$$
$$-5y = 5$$
$$y = -1$$
$$x = -(-1)$$
$$x = 1$$
Solution: $(1, -1)$

b.
$$2x - 4y = 6$$
$$x - 2y = 3$$
$$x = 2y + 3$$
$$2(2y + 3) - 4y = 6$$
$$4y + 6 - 4y = 6$$
$$6 = 6$$
identity

c.
$$x - y = 1$$
$$x = y + 1$$
$$-3x + 3y = 3$$
$$-3(y + 1) + 3y = 3$$
$$-3y - 3 + 3y = 3$$
$$-3 \neq 3$$
no solution

2. The two lines intersect at $(1, -1)$

3. The solution is an identity; this indicates the two lines are the same line.

4. There is no solution, so the two lines are parallel.

7.5 Think About It (p. 416)

1. no solution
$$y = -\frac{1}{2}x + 4$$
$$y = -\frac{1}{2}x - 4$$
$$-\frac{1}{2}x + 4 = -\frac{1}{2}x - 4$$
$4 \neq 4$; no solution

2. infinitely many solutions
$$y = \frac{1}{3}x + 1$$
$$3y = x + 3$$
$$3\left(\frac{1}{3}x + 1\right) = x + 3$$
$$x + 3 = x + 3$$
$3 = 3$; true; infinitely many solutions

3. exactly one solution
$$y = 2$$
$$y = 4x - 2$$
$$2 = 4x - 2$$
$$4 = 4x$$
$$x = 1$$
Solution: $(1, 2)$ point of intersection

4.
$$2x - y = 3$$
$$-4x + 2y = 0$$

$4x - 2y = 6$ Multiply by 2
$-4x + 2y = 0$
$0 \neq 6$; no solution; the lines are parallel

5.
$$2x + y = 5$$
$$x - 3y = -1$$
$$y = -2x + 5$$
$$x - 3(-2x + 5) = -1$$
$$x + 6x - 15 = -1$$
$$7x - 15 = -1$$
$$7x = 14$$
$$x = 2$$
$$y = -2(2) + 5$$
$$y = 1$$
Solution: $(2, 1)$; the lines intersect at $(2, 1)$

6.
$$x + 3y = 2$$
$$2x + 6y = 4$$

$-2x - 6y = -4$ Multiply by -2.
$2x + 6y = 4$
$0 = 0$; infinitely many solutions; same line

7. *Sample answer*: There will be exactly one solution if the two lines have different slopes. There will be infinitely many solutions if the two lines are the same, that is, they have the same slope and the same y-intercept. There will be no solution if the two lines are parallel.

Lesson 7.5

7.5 Checkpoint (pp. 417–419)

1. $x = -3y + 4$ Rewrite equation 1.
$2(-3y + 4) + 6y = 4$ Substitute $(-3y + 4)$ for x.
$-6y + 8 + 6y = 4$
$8 \neq 4$; no solution; lines are parallel

2. $x - 2y = 4$
$-x + 2y = -4$ Add the equations.
$0 = 0$; true; infinitely many solutions; same line

3. $x + y = 3$ Equation 1.
$-2x - 2y = -6$ Multiply by -2.
$2x + 2y = 4$ Add equation 2.
$0 \neq -2$ no solution

4. $x + y = 3$ Equation 1.
$-2x - 2y = -6$ Multiply by -2.
$2x + 2y = 6$ Add equation 2.
$0 = 0$ infinitely many solutions

5. $x + y = 3$ Equation 1.
$-x - y = -3$ Multiply by -1.
$x + 2y = 4$ Add equation 2.
$y = 1$
$x + 1 = 3$
$x = 2$
Solution: $(2, 1)$; one solution

Copyright © McDougal Littell Inc.
All rights reserved.

7.5 Guided Practice (p. 420)

1. parallel lines

Sample answer:

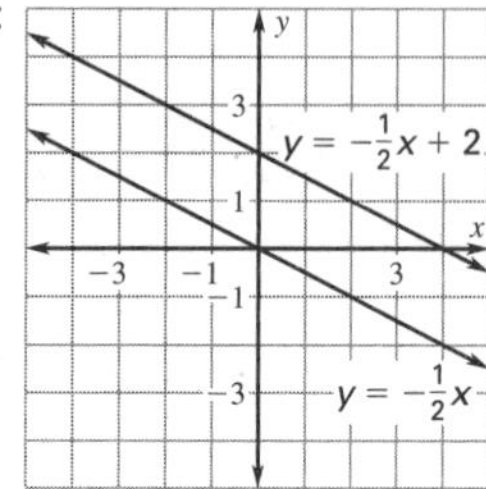

2. same line

Sample answer:

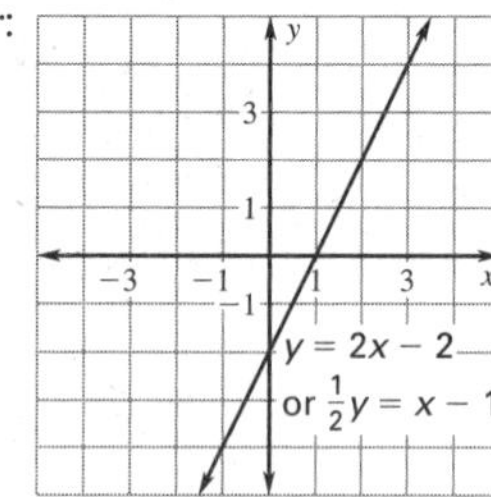

3. lines intersect at one point

Sample answer:

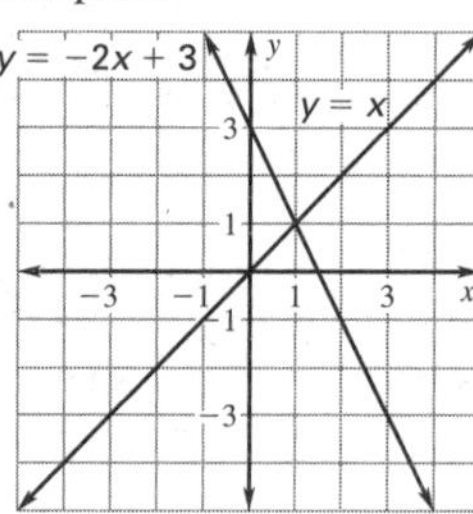

4.

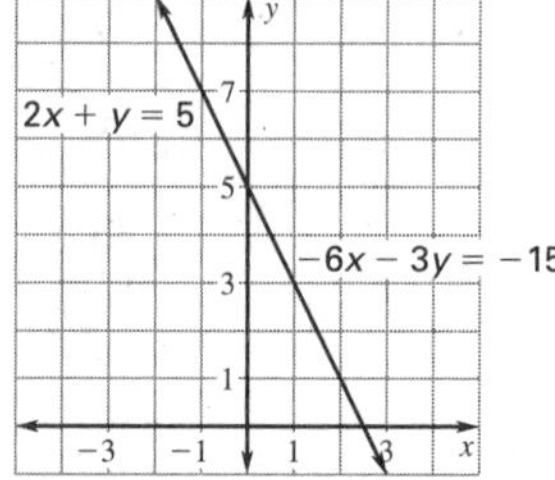

line 1:

$2x + y = 5$

$y = -2x + 5$

line 2:

$-6x - 3y = -15$

$-3y = 6x - 15$

$y = -2x + 5$

infinitely many solutions; the two equations are identical

5.

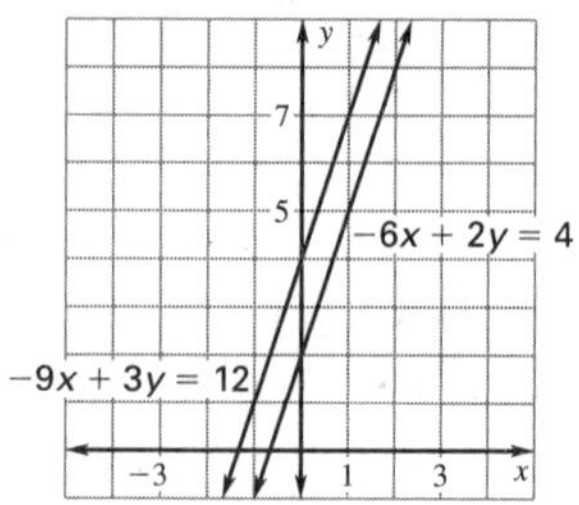

line 1:

$-6x + 2y = 4$

$2y = 6x + 4$

$y = 3x + 2$

line 2:

$-9x + 3y = 12$

$3y = 9x + 12$

$y = 3x + 4$

no solution; the two equations represent parallel lines

6.

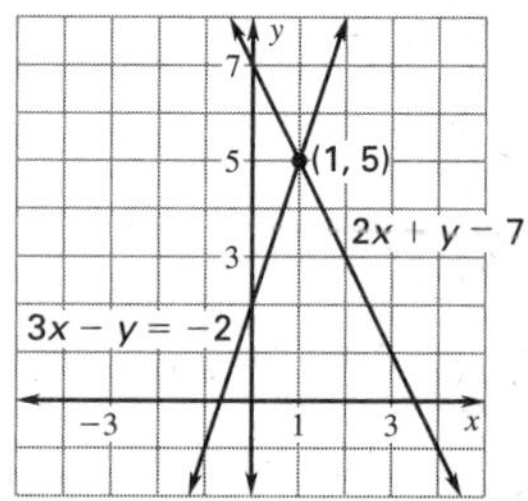

line 1:

$2x + y = 7$

$y = -2x + 7$

line 2:

$3x - y = -2$

$-y = -3x - 2$

$y = 3x + 2$

$3x + 2 = -2x + 7$

$5x + 2 = 7$

$5x = 5$

$x = 1$

$y = -2(1) + 7$

$y = 5$

one solution; (1, 5); the two equations represent lines which intersect at one point.

7. $-x + y = 7$

$y = x + 7$

$2x - 2(x + 7) = -18$

$2x - 2x - 14 = -18$

$-14 \neq -18$; no solution

8. $-4x + y = -8$

$y = 4x - 8$

$-12x + 3(4x - 8) = -24$

$-12x + 12x - 24 = -24$

$-24 = -24$; infinitely many solutions

Copyright © McDougal Littell Inc.
All rights reserved.

9. $-4x + y = -8$

$y = 4x - 8$

$2x - 2(4x - 8) = -14$

$2x - 8x + 16 = -14$

$-6x + 16 = -14$

$-6x = -30$

$x = 5$

$y = 4(5) - 8$

$y = 12$

one solution: (5, 12)

7.5 Practice and Applications (pp. 420–421)

10. $-2x + 4y = 1$

$4y = 2x + 1$

$y = \frac{1}{2}x + \frac{1}{4}$

$3x - 6y = 9$

$-6y = -3x + 9$

$y = \frac{1}{2}x - \frac{3}{2}$

E; no solution

11. $2x - 2y = 4$

$-2y = -2x + 4$

$y = x - 2$

$-x + y = -2$

$y = x - 2$

D; infinitely many solutions

12. $2x + y = 4$

$y = -2x + 4$

$-4x - 2y = -8$

$-2y = 4x - 8$

$y = -2x + 4$

F; infinitely many solutions

13. $-x + y = 1$

$y = x + 1$

$x - y = 1$

$-y = -x + 1$

$y = x - 1$

B; no solution

14. $5x + 3y = 17$

$3y = -5x + 17$

$y = -\frac{5}{3}x + \frac{17}{3}$

$x - 3y = -2$

$-3y = -x - 2$

$y = \frac{1}{3}x + \frac{2}{3}$

A; one solution

15. $x - y = 0$

$x = y$ or

$y = x$

$5x - 2y = 6$

$-2y = -5x + 6$

$y = \frac{5}{2}x - 3$

C; one solution

16. The two lines have different slopes and will intersect at one point, even though that point does not appear on the graph.

17.

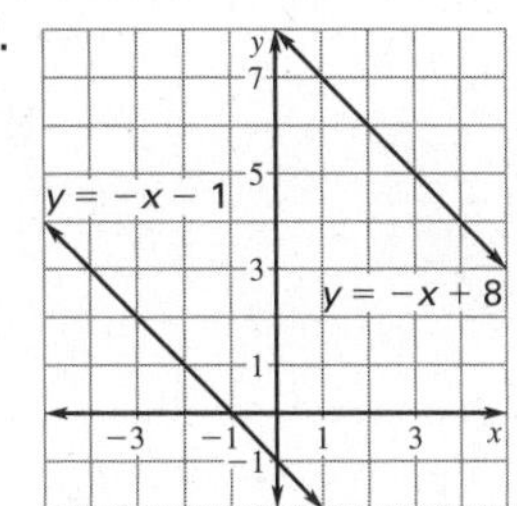

$y = -x + 8$; $y = -x - 1$; no solution

18.

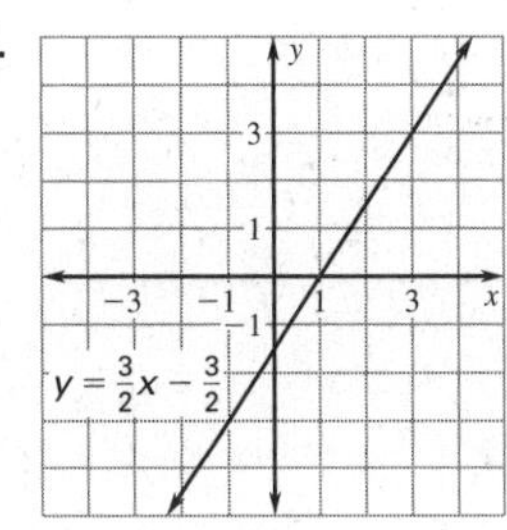

line 1:

$3x - 2y = 3$

$-2y = -3x + 3$

$y = \frac{3}{2}x - \frac{3}{2}$

line 2:

$-6x + 4y = -6$

$4y = 6x - 6$

$y = \frac{3}{2}x - \frac{3}{2}$

infinitely many solutions

Copyright © McDougal Littell Inc.
All rights reserved.

19. 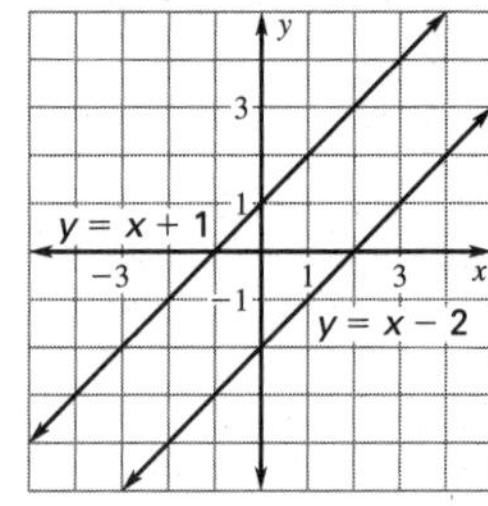

line 1:
$x - y = 2$
$-y = -x + 2$
$y = x - 2$
line 2:
$-2x + 2y = 2$
$2y = 2x + 2$
$y = x + 1$
no solution

20. 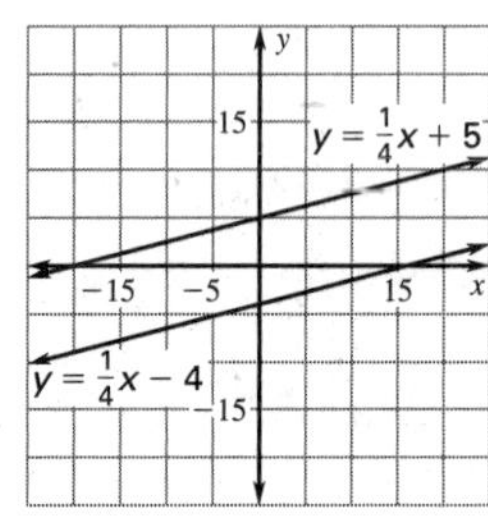

line 1:
$-x + 4y = 20$
$4y = x + 20$
$y = \frac{1}{4}x + 5$
line 2:
$3x - 12y = 48$
$-12y = -3x + 48$
$y = \frac{1}{4}x - 4$
no solution

21. 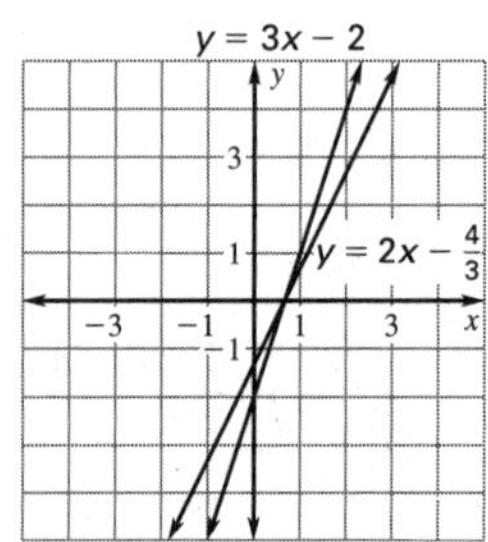

line 1:
$6x - 2y = 4$
$-2y = -6x + 4$
$y = 3x - 2$
line 2:
$12x - 6y = 8$
$-6y = -12x + 8$
$y = 2x - \frac{4}{3}$
one solution; $\left(\frac{2}{3}, 0\right)$

22. 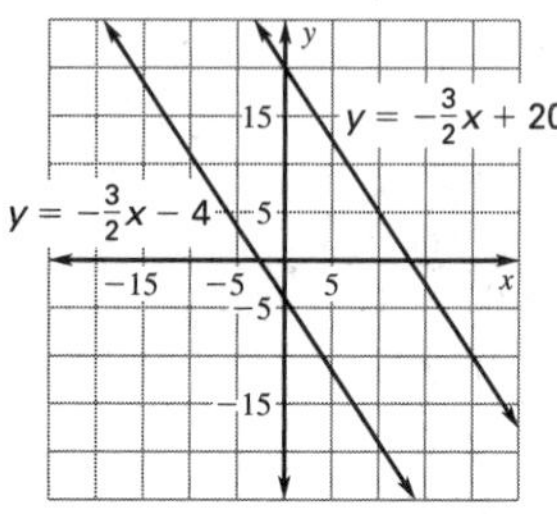

line 1:
$3x + 2y = 40$
$2y = -3x + 40$
$y = -\frac{3}{2}x + 20$
line 2:
$-3x - 2y = 8$
$-2y = 3x + 8$
$y = -\frac{3}{2}x - 4$
no solution

23. $x - y = 2$ Multiply equation 1 by 4;
$4x - 4y = 8$ Same as equation 2;
infinitely many solutions

24. $-7x + 7y = 7$
$2x - 2y = -18$

$-14x + 14y = 14$ Multiply by 2.
$14x - 14y = -126$ Multiply by 7.
$0 \neq -112$ no solution; the lines are parallel

25. $4x + 4y = -8$
$2x + 2y = -4$

$4x + 4y = -8$
$-4x - 4y = 8$ Multiply by -2.
$0 = 0$ infinitely many solutions; same line

Copyright © McDougal Littell Inc.
All rights reserved.

26. $2x + y = -4$
$4x - 2y = 8$

$y = -2x - 4$

$4x - 2(-2x - 4) = 8$
$4x + 4x + 8 = 8$
$8x + 8 = 8$
$8x = 0$
$x = 0$
$y = -2(0) - 4$
$y = -4$
one solution: $(0, -4)$; lines intersect at $(0, -4)$

27. $15x - 5y = -20$
$-3x + y = 4$

$15x - 5y = -20$
$-15x + 5y = 20$ Multiply by 5.
$0 = 0$ infinitely many solutions; same line

28. $-6x + 2y = -2$
$-4x - y = 8$

$-6x + 2y = -2$
$-8x - 2y = 16$ Multiply by 2.
$-14x = 14$
$x = -1$

$-4(-1) - y = 8$
$4 - y = 8$
$-y = 4$
$y = -4$
one solution: $(-1, -4)$; lines intersect at $(-1, -4)$

29. $2x + y = -1$
$y = -2x - 1$
$-6x - 3(-2x - 1) = -15$
$-6x + 6x + 3 = -15$
$3 \neq 15$; no solution; parallel lines

30. $6g + 6s = 48$ Multiply by $\frac{1}{6}$.

$4g + 8s = 40$ Multiply by $-\frac{1}{4}$.

$g + s = 8$
$-g - 2s = -10$
$-s = -2$
$s = 2$
$g + 2 = 8$
$g = 6$
Solution: The generator rents for \$6 per hour and the saw rents for \$2 per hour.

31. $40s + 6l = 9.6$
$20s + 3l = 4.8$ Multiply by -2.

$40s + 6l = 9.6$
$-40s - 6l = -9.6$
$0 = 0$; infinitely many solutions; we cannot find the weight

32. Let p = number of sheets of oak paneling.
Let t = number of sheets of shower tile board

$4p + 2t = 99.62$ Multiply by -3.
$12p + 6t = 298.86$

$-12p - 6t = -298.86$
$12p + 6t = 298.86$
$0 = 0$; infinitely many solutions; no, we cannot find cost

33. $8p + t = 139.69$
$t = -8p + 139.69$ Solve for t.
$4p + 2t = 99.62$ Substitute.
$4p + 2(-8p + 139.69) = 99.62$
$4p - 16p + 279.38 = 99.62$
$-12p + 279.38 = 99.62$
$-12p = -179.76$
$p = 14.98$
\$14.98 for each oak panel.

34. $6x - 9y = n$
$-2x + 3y = 3$ Multiply by 3.
$6x - 9y = n$
$-6x + 9y = 9$
$0 = 0$
$n + 9 = 0$
$n = -9$

35. *Sample answer*: $n = 5$; generally $n \neq -9$

7.5 Standardized Test Practice (p. 422)

36. C; III **37.** G; II

7.5 Mixed Review (p. 422)

38. $m = \frac{220 - 110}{3 - 1} = \frac{110}{2} = 55$; It represents the rate at which you climb, 55 ft/h.

39. 80 ft remain; $d = rt$; $80 = 55t$; $t = \frac{80}{55} = 1.45 \text{ h} \approx 1 \text{ h } 27$ min; 1 h 27 min after 3:00 P.M. is 4:27 P.M.

40.

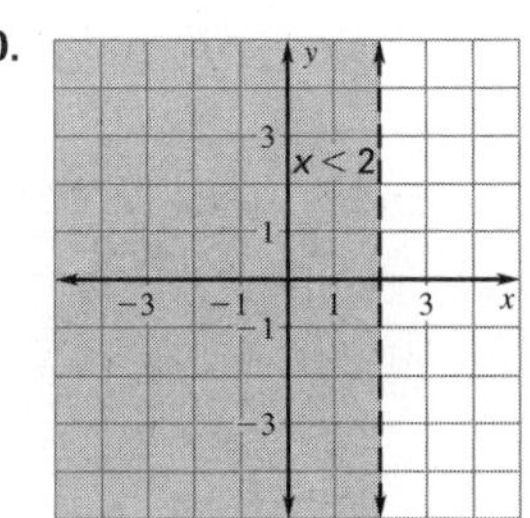

Copyright © McDougal Littell Inc.
All rights reserved.

Chapter 7 *continued*

41. 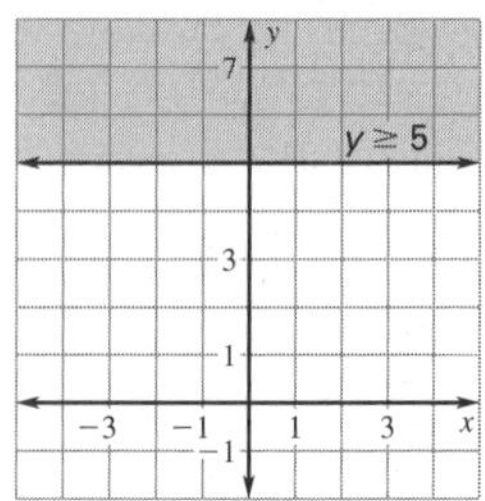

42. 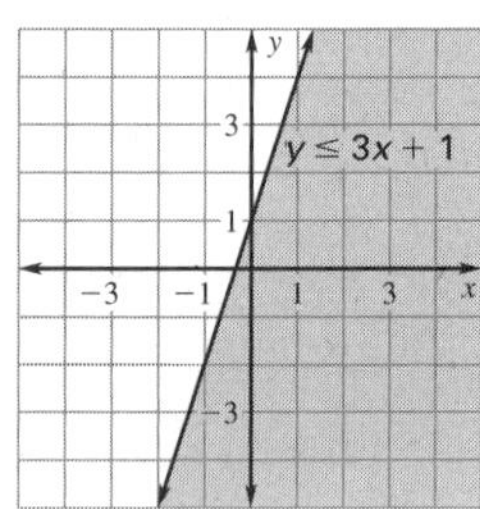

43. 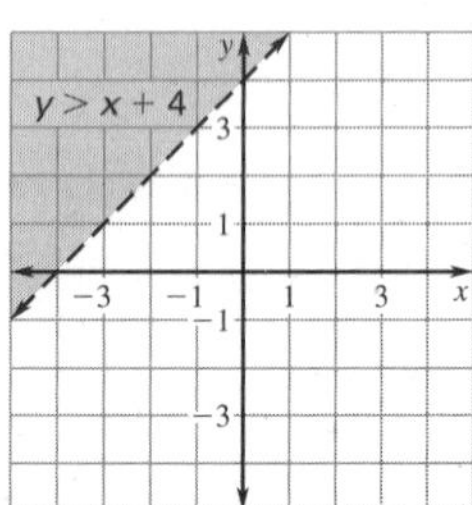

44. 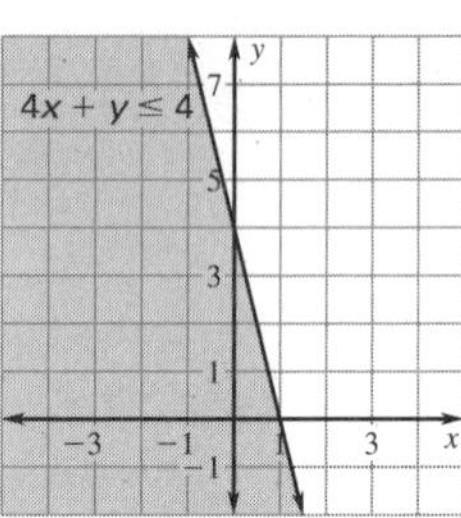

$y \leq -4x + 4$

45. 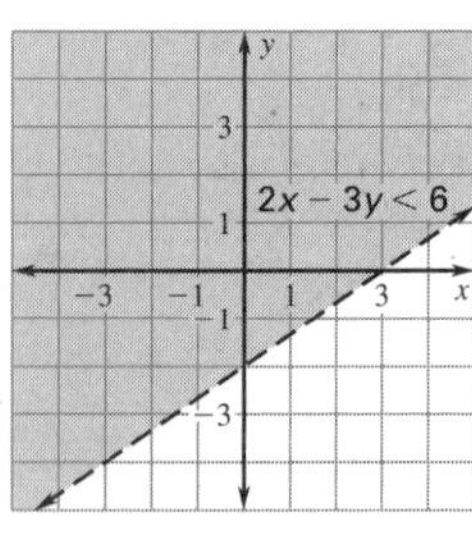

$-3y < -2x + 6;\ y > \frac{2}{3}x - 2$

7.5 Maintaining Skills (p. 422)

46. Estimate: 8

$A = \frac{1}{2}bh$

$A = \frac{1}{2}(4)(4) = 8$

47. Estimate: 20

$A = \pi r^2$

$A = \pi(2.5)^2 = 6.25\pi \approx 19.6$

48. Estimate: 25

$A = s^2$

$A = 5^2 = 25$

49. Estimate: 20

$A = b \cdot h$

$A = 4(5) = 20$

7.6 Developing Concepts: Explore *(p. 423)*

1. 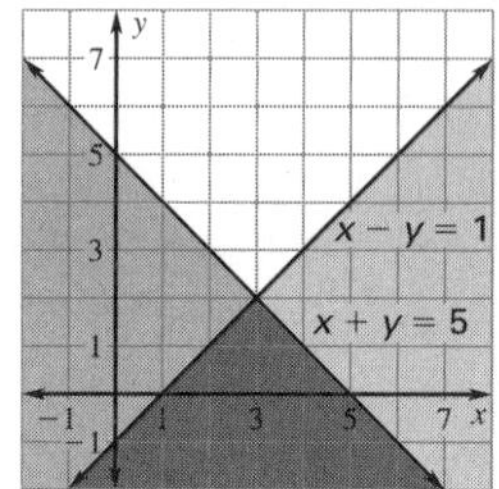

2–3. See graph above.

4. *Sample answer:* A point is a solution of both inequalities if it is on or below both lines.

7.6 Think About It (p. 423)

1. 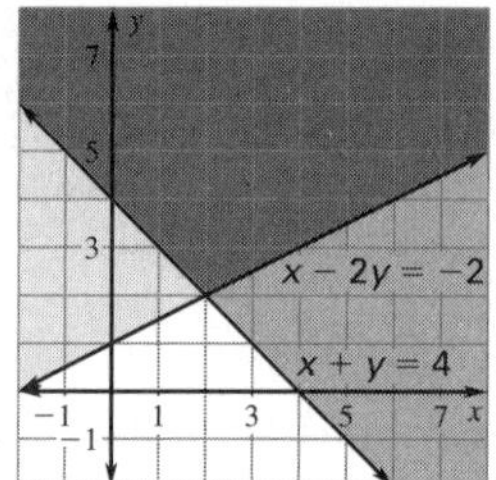

The solution is the set of points in between and on the boundaries of the two lines at the top.

2. 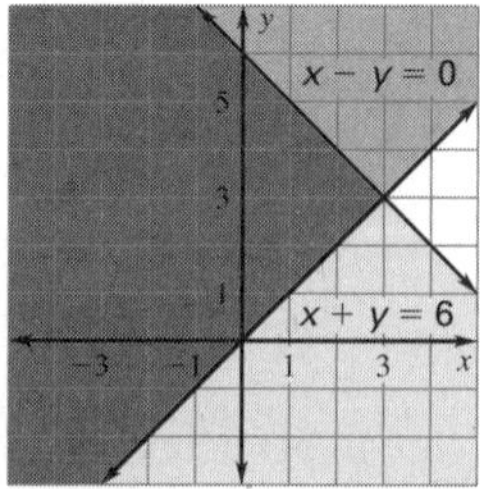

The solution is the set of points in between and on the boundaries of the two lines to the left of the graph.

Copyright © McDougal Littell Inc.
All rights reserved.

3.

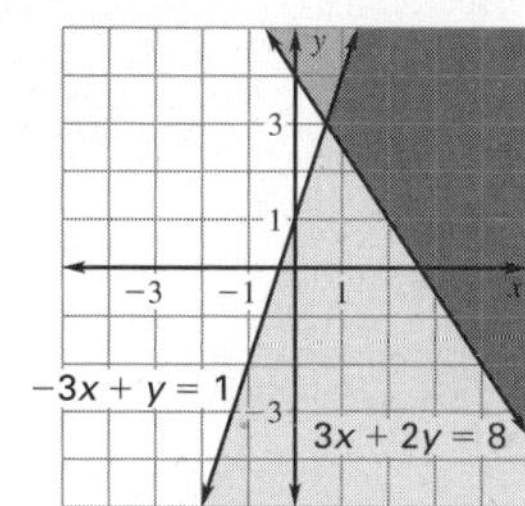

$3x + 2y \geq 8$

$2y \geq -3x + 8$

$y \geq -\frac{3}{2}x + 4$

$-3x + y \leq 1$

$y \leq 3x + 1$

The solution is the set of points in between and on the boundaries of the two lines at the right of the graph.

4.

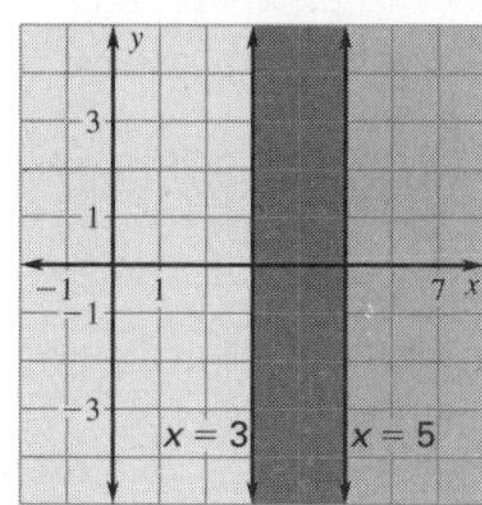

The solution is the set of points in between and including the two vertical lines.

5.

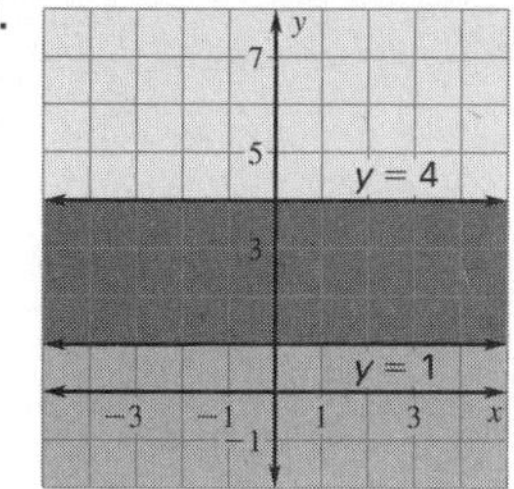

The solution is the set of points in between and including the two hoizontal lines.

6.

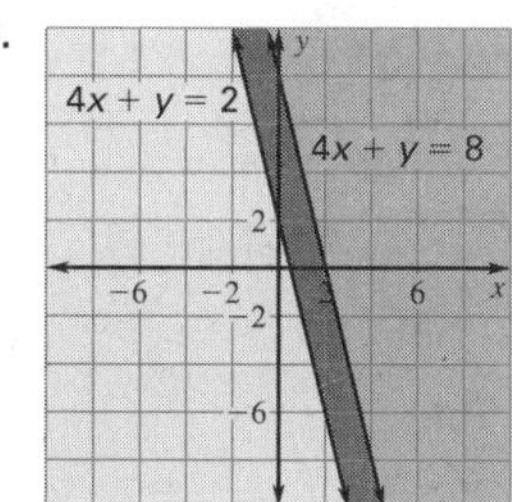

$y \geq -4x + 2$; $y \leq -4x + 8$

The solution is the set of points in between and including the two parallel lines.

7. The solution is a horizontal strip when it is the set of points between two horizontal lines. The solution is a vertical strip when it is the set of points between two vertical lines.

8. A system has no solution when the boundary lines are parallel and the graphs are nonintersecting regions on opposite sides of the lines.

9. A half-plane could be a solution when both boundary lines are parallel to the x-axis or y-axis and the intersection of the solutions is to one side of both lines.

10. If the boundary lines intersect at one point, the solution could be the set of points in one of the four "v's" formed by the lines. If the lines are parallel, the solution could be the set of points in between the two lines, or the system could be the region shaded to one side of one of the lines.

Lesson 7.6

Lesson 7.6 Checkpoint (pp. 425–426)

1.

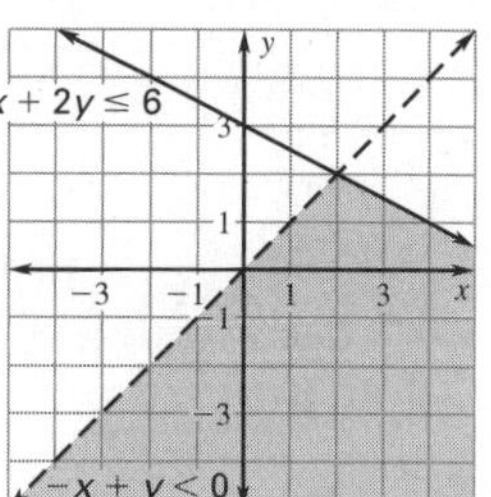

2.

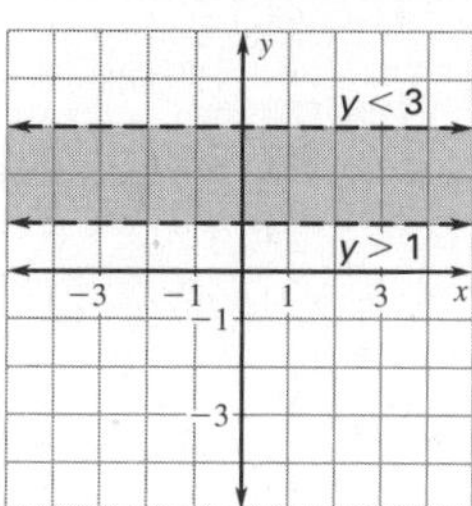

3.

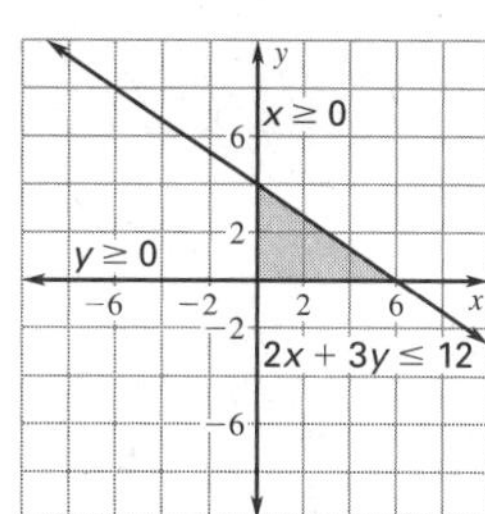

4. $y > x$, $y \leq 2$

5. $x > -1$, $x < 2$

7.6 Guided Practice (p. 427)

1. False; it is the set of ordered pairs which are solutions to both of the inequalities in the system.

2.

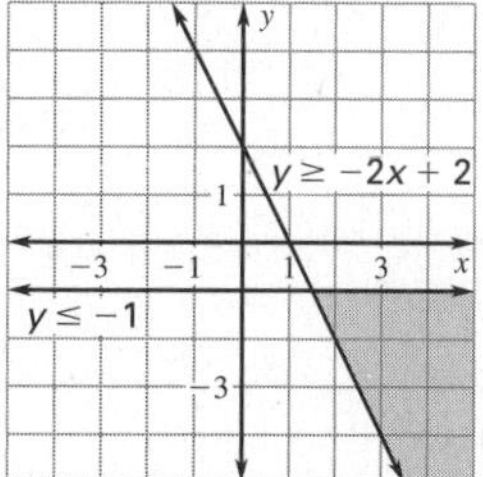

Copyright © McDougal Littell Inc.
All rights reserved.

3.

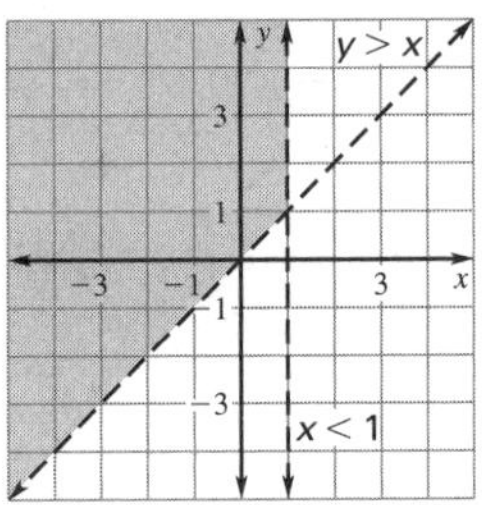

4.

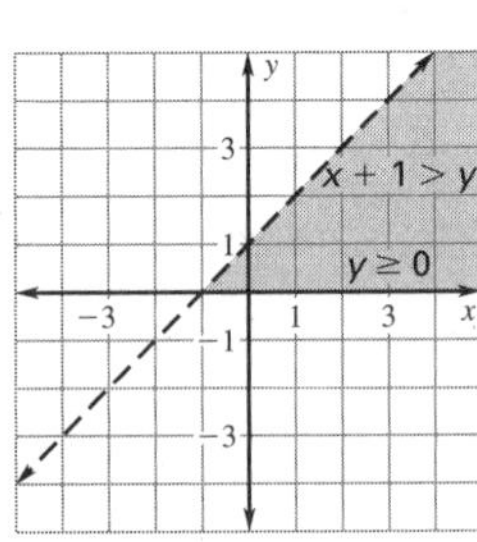

$y < x + 1; y \geq 0$

5. The student graphed $y \geq 1$ instead of $y > -1$; graphed $x \leq 2$ instead of $x \geq 2$; graphed $y \leq x - 4$ instead of $y > x - 4$.

6.

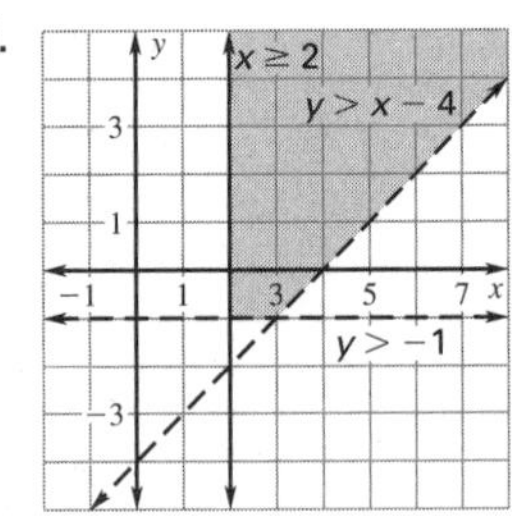

7. $y \leq -x; x > -2$

8. $y \leq 2; y > -3$

7.6 Practice and Applications (pp. 427–429)

9. *C* $y \leq -2x + 4; y \geq -2x - 4$

10. *A* $y < -2x + 4; y \leq 2x + 4$

11. *B* $y \geq -2x - 4; y > \frac{1}{2}x - 2$

12.

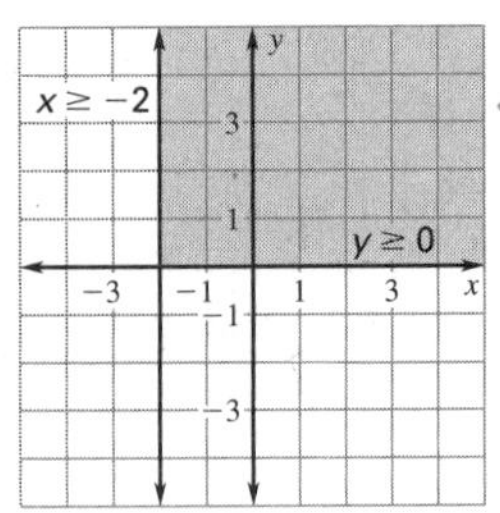

13.

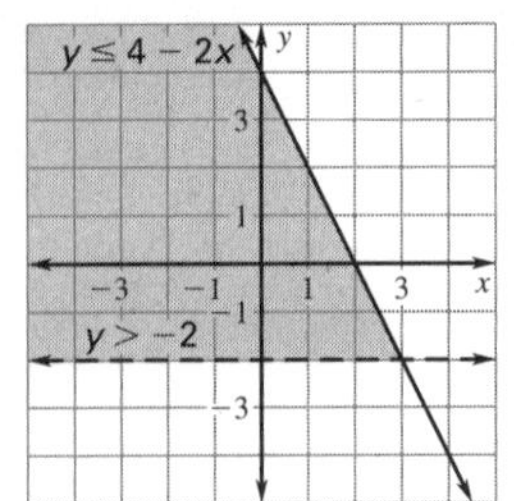

14.

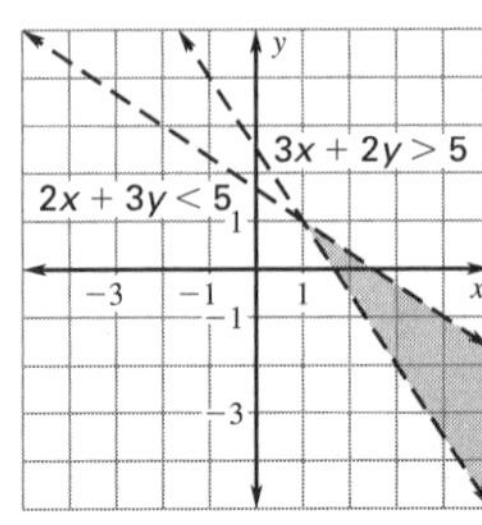

15.

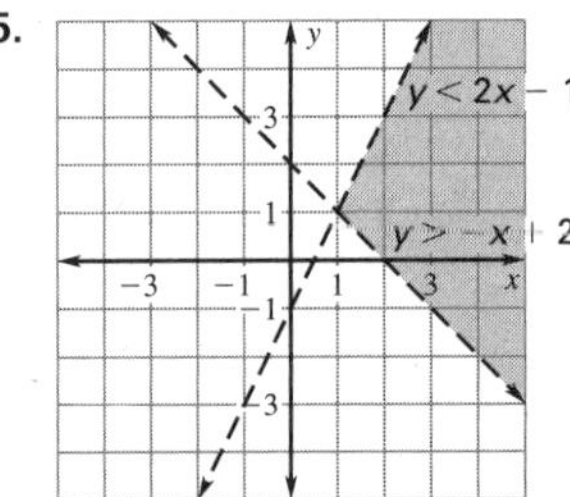

16.

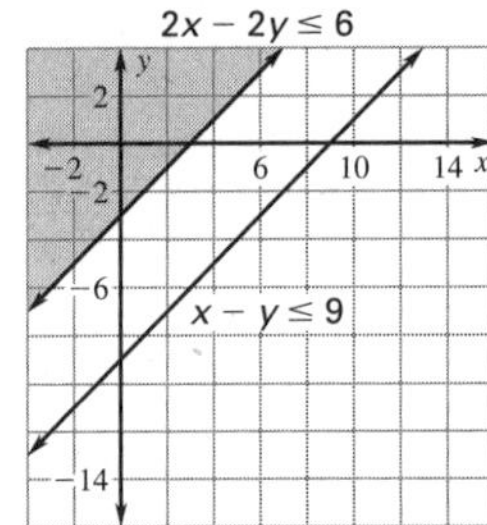

17.

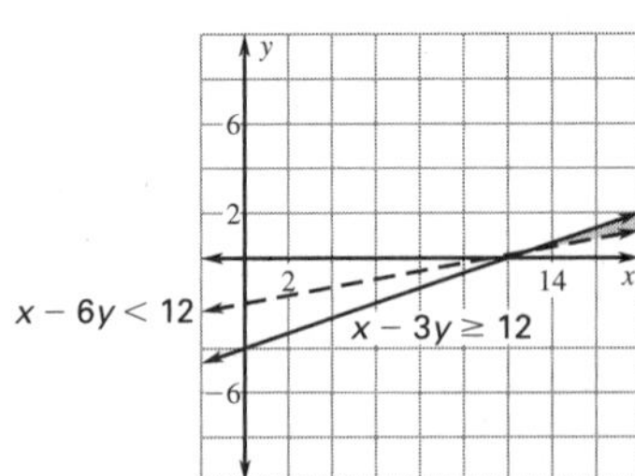

18.

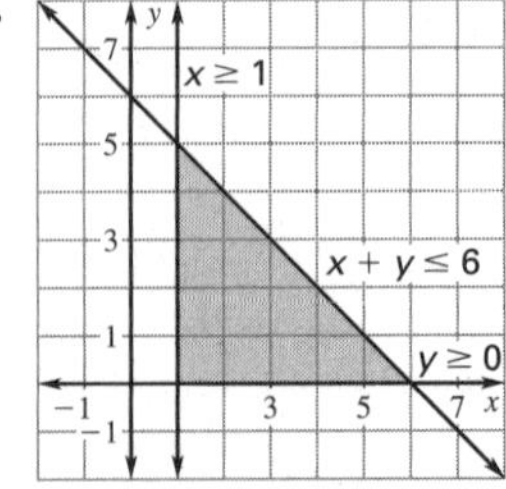

Copyright © McDougal Littell Inc.
All rights reserved.

19.

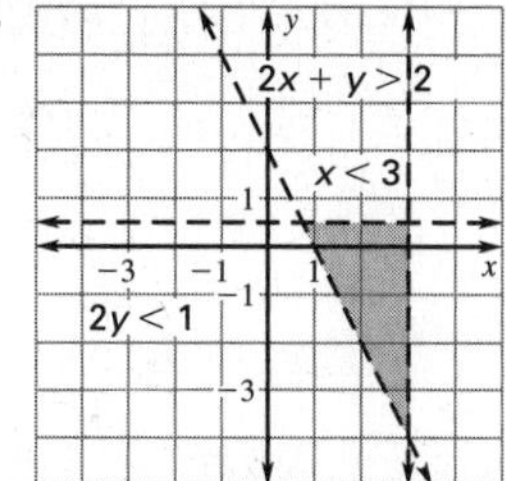

20.

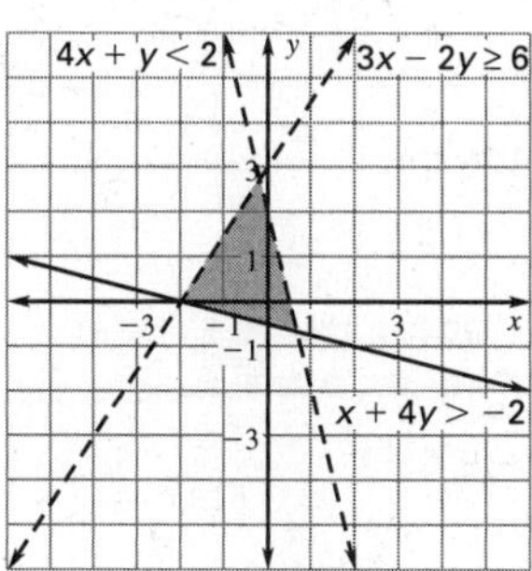

21.

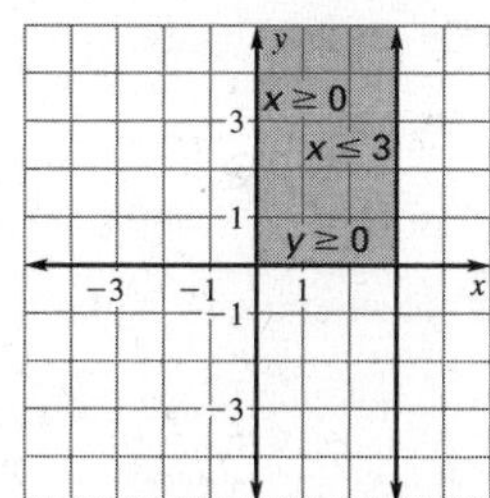

22.

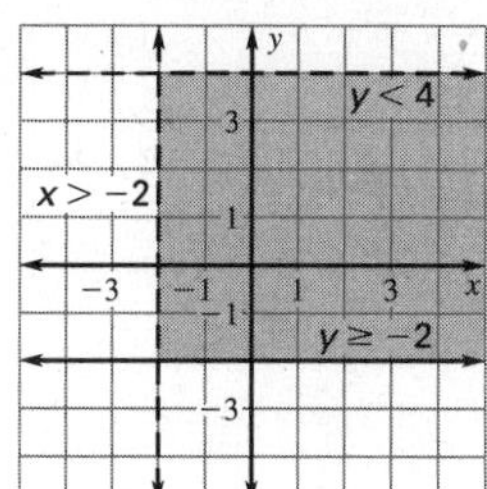

23.

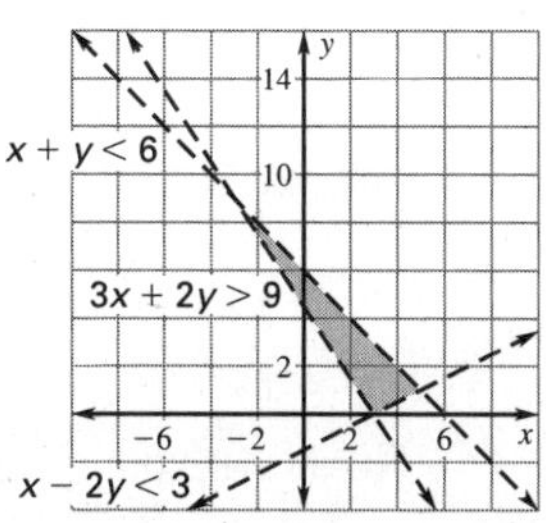

24. $y \le -\frac{5}{2}x + 4$ or $5x + 2y \le 8$;

$y > -\frac{1}{2}x - 2$ or $x + 2y > -4$

25. $y \le \frac{1}{2}x + 2$ or $2y - x \le 4$;

$y \ge \frac{1}{2}x - 2$ or $2y - x \ge -4$

26. $y \le -\frac{1}{2}x + 2$ or $x + 2y \le 4$

$y < \frac{1}{2}x + 2$ or $-x + 2y < 4$

27.

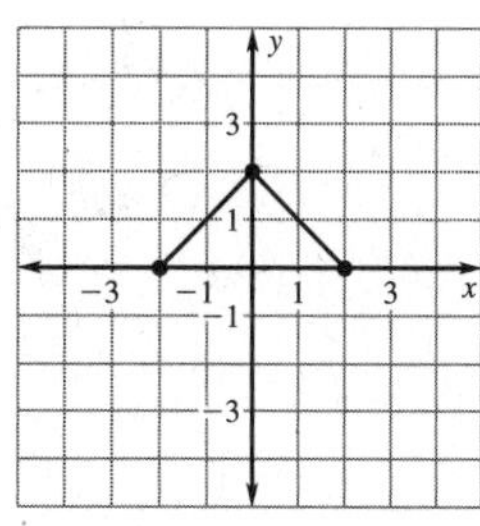

$y \ge 0$
$y \le -x + 2$
$y \le x + 2$

28.

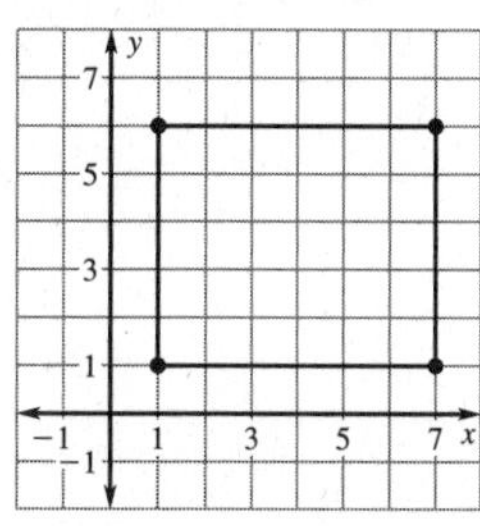

$y \ge 1$
$y \le 6$
$x \ge 1$
$x \le 7$

29.

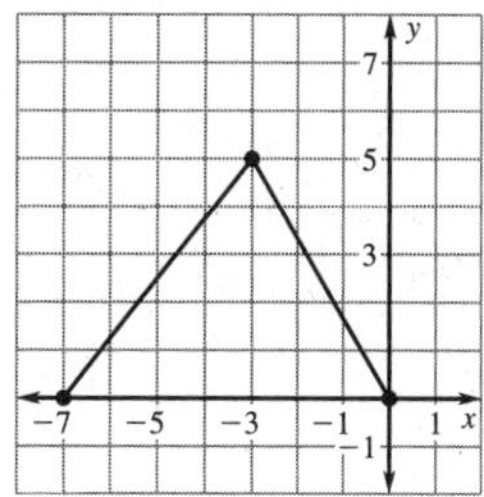

$3y \le -5x$; $y \ge 0$; $4y \le 5x - 5$

for 3rd line: $m = \dfrac{5 - 0}{-3 - (-7)} = \dfrac{5}{4}$

$$y - 5 = \frac{5}{4}[x - (-3)]$$
$$y - 5 = \frac{5}{4}x + \frac{15}{4}$$
$$y = \frac{5}{4}x + \frac{15}{4} + \frac{20}{4}$$
$$y = \frac{5}{4}x + \frac{35}{4} \text{ or } 4y \le 5x + 35$$

Copyright © McDougal Littell Inc.
All rights reserved.

30.

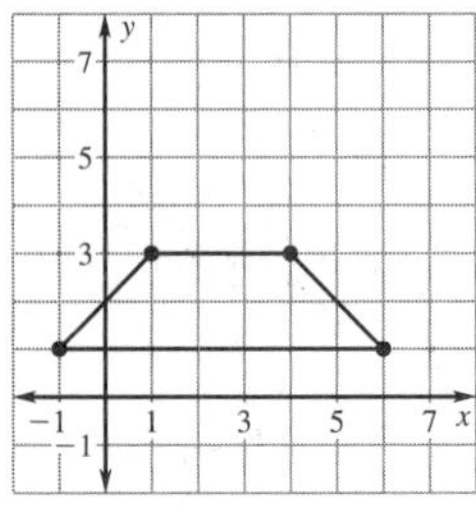

$y \le x + 2;\ y \le 3;\ y \ge 1;\ y \le -x + 7$

To find the y-intercept for a line through (6, 1) and (4, 3):

$$m = \frac{1 - 3}{6 - 4} = \frac{-2}{2} = -1$$

$$y - 1 = -1(x - 6)$$
$$y - 1 = -x + 6$$
$$y = -x + 7$$

31. $b + c \ge 240$
$b < c$
$5b + 3c \le 1200$

32.

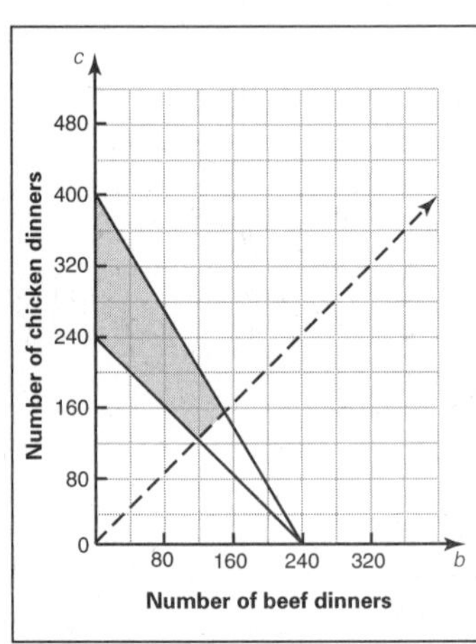

33. Quadrant I; *Sample answer*: Both b and c must be positive, since you can't have negative pounds of beef or chicken.

34. $1000m + 3500l \le 10{,}000;\ m \ge 3;\ l \ge 1$

35.

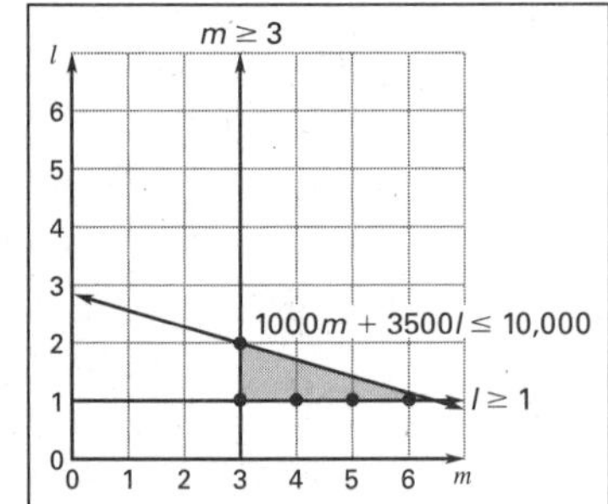

36. (3, 1) and (4, 1)

37. $b + c \le 20$
$5b + 6c \ge 90$

38. $c \le -b + 20$

$$c \ge -\frac{5}{6}b + 15$$

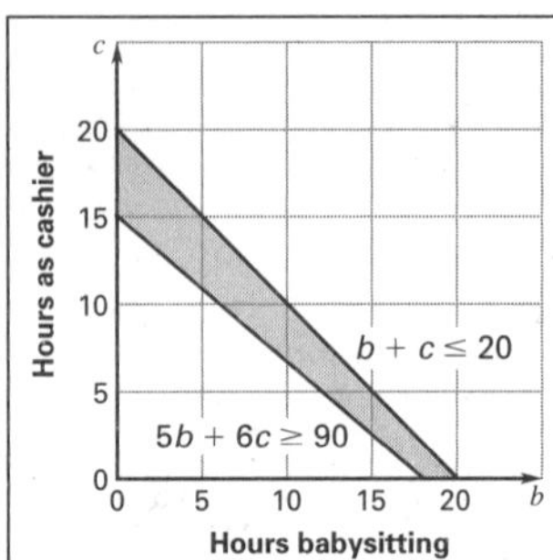

39. *Sample answer*: 5 hours babysitting and 15 hours as a cashier; 15 hours babysitting and 5 as a cashier.

40. $y \le 8;\ x \ge 0;\ y \ge x + 4$

41. $y \ge 0;\ x \ge 0;\ y \le -x + 4$

42. *Sample answer*: The area of the oak tree region is half of the area of the larger region. This can be seen by sketching the lines $y = 4$ and $x = 4$ to divide the large square into fourths. The oak trees are planted in one half of each of the fourths. Since the total area of the larger region is $8 \times 8 = 64$, the area of the oak region is $\frac{1}{2}(64) = 32$ square units.

7.6 Standardized Test Practice (p. 429)

43. $A;\ y < 3x - 1;\ y \ge -2x + 4$

44. J; (4, 2)

$2 \le 4 + 2 \qquad 2 + 4 > 4$
$2 \le 6 \qquad 6 > 4$

7.6 Mixed Review (p. 430)

45. $3^5 = 243$

46. $8^2 - 17 = 64 - 17 = 47$

47. $5^3 + 12 = 125 + 12 = 137$

48. $2(3^3 - 20) = 2(27 - 20) = 2(7) = 14$

49. $2^6 - 3 + 1 = 64 - 3 + 1 = 61 + 1 = 62$

50. $5 \cdot 2 + 4^2 = 5 \cdot 2 + 16 = 10 + 16 = 26$

51. $(x + y)^2 = (5 + 2)^2 = 7^2 = 49$

52. $(b - c)^2 = (2 - 1)^2 = 1^2 = 1$

53. $g - h^2 = 4 - 8^2 = 4 - 64 = -60$

54. $x^2 + z = 8^2 + 12 = 64 + 12 = 76$

Copyright © McDougal Littell Inc.
All rights reserved.

55. $x + y = 68$
$5x + 2y = 250$

$y = -x + 68$

$$\begin{aligned} 5x + 2(-x + 68) &= 250 \\ 5x - 2x + 136 &= 250 \\ 3x + 136 &= 250 \\ 3x &= 114 \\ x &= 38 \end{aligned}$$

$y = -38 + 68$
$y = 30$
Solution: 38 5-point questions and 30 2-point questions.

7.6 Maintaining Skills (p. 430)

56. $\frac{22}{5} = 4.4$

$$\begin{array}{r} 4.4 \\ 5\overline{)22.0} \\ \underline{20} \\ 2\,0 \\ \underline{2\,0} \\ 0 \end{array}$$

57. $\frac{37}{4} = 9.25$

$$\begin{array}{r} 9.25 \\ 4\overline{)37.00} \\ \underline{36} \\ 1\,0 \\ \underline{8} \\ 20 \\ \underline{20} \\ 0 \end{array}$$

58. $\frac{51}{12} = 4.25$

$$\begin{array}{r} 4.25 \\ 12\overline{)51.00} \\ \underline{48} \\ 3\,0 \\ \underline{2\,4} \\ 60 \\ \underline{60} \\ 0 \end{array}$$

59. $\frac{56}{20} = 2.8$

$$\begin{array}{r} 2.8 \\ 20\overline{)56.0} \\ \underline{40} \\ 16\,0 \\ \underline{16\,0} \\ 0 \end{array}$$

60. $1\frac{1}{2} = 1.5$

$$\begin{array}{r} 0.5 \\ 2\overline{)1.0} \\ \underline{1\,0} \\ 0 \end{array}$$

61. $3\frac{4}{5} = 3.8$

$$\begin{array}{r} 0.8 \\ 5\overline{)4.0} \\ \underline{4\,0} \\ 0 \end{array}$$

62. $4\frac{1}{4} = 4.25$

$$\begin{array}{r} 0.25 \\ 4\overline{)1.00} \\ \underline{8} \\ 20 \\ \underline{20} \\ 0 \end{array}$$

63. $6\frac{7}{8} = 6.875$

$$\begin{array}{r} 0.875 \\ 8\overline{)7.000} \\ \underline{6\,4} \\ 60 \\ \underline{56} \\ 40 \\ \underline{40} \\ 0 \end{array}$$

Quiz 2 *(p. 430)*

1. $2l + 2w = 22$ Rectangle

$\frac{1}{2}l + w + 5 = 12$ Triangle

$\frac{1}{2}l + w = 7$

$$\begin{aligned} 2l + 2w &= 22 \\ -2l - 4w &= -28 \quad \text{Multiply by } -4. \\ \hline -2w &= -6 \\ w &= 3 \end{aligned}$$

$$\begin{aligned} 2l + 2(3) &= 22 \\ 2l + 6 &= 22 \\ 2l &= 16 \\ l &= 8 \end{aligned}$$

Solution: $l = 8$ ft; $w = 3$ ft

Copyright © McDougal Littell Inc.
All rights reserved.

2. $12R + 18P = 44.46$
$P = R + 0.22$

$12R + 18(R + 0.22) = 44.46$
$12R + 18R + 3.96 = 44.46$
$30R + 3.96 = 44.46$
$30R = 40.50$
$R = 1.35$
$P = 1.35 + 0.22 = 1.57$
Premium costs \$1.57/gal; Regular costs \$1.35/gal

3. $3x + 2y = 12$
$9x + 6y = 18$

$-9x - 6y = -36$ Multiply equation 1 by -3.
$9x + 6y = 18$
$0 \neq -18$; no solution

4. $x + y = 1$
$x = -y + 1$

$4(-y + 1) + 8y = 8$
$-4y + 4 + 8y = 8$
$4 + 4y = 8$
$4y = 4$
$y = 1$
$x = -1 + 1$
$x = 0$
one solution: (0, 1)

5. $-4x + 11y = 44$
$4x - 11y = -44$
$0 = 0$; infinitely many solutions

6.

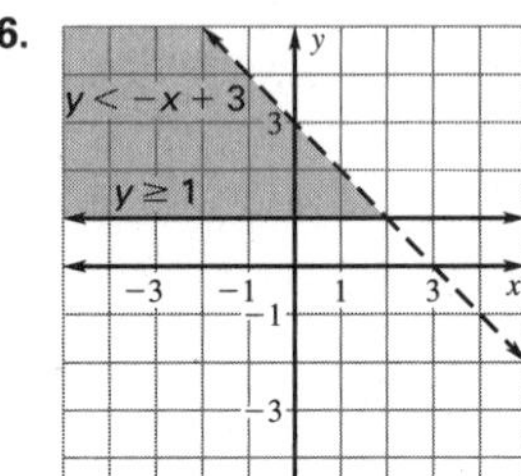

7.

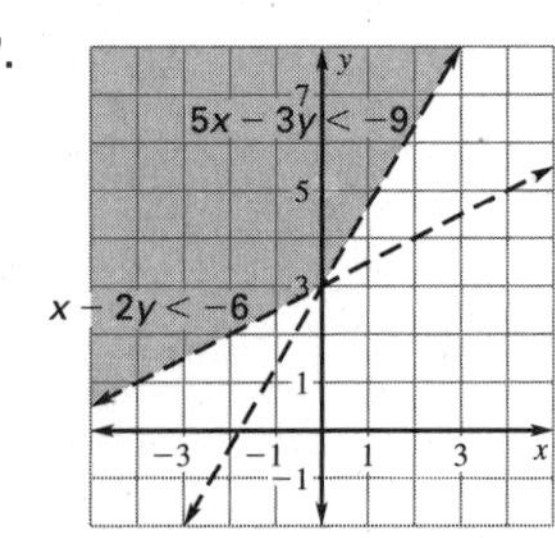

8.

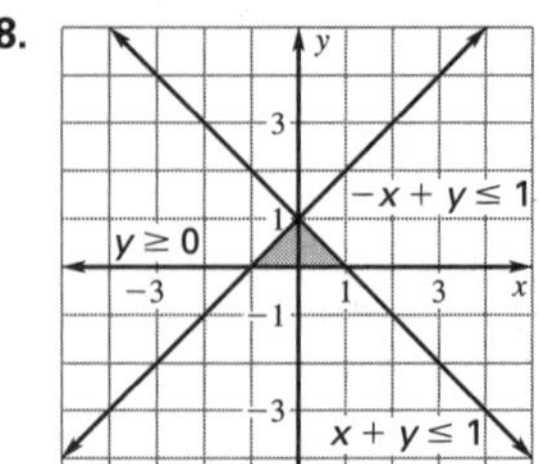

9. $y \leq -\frac{1}{2}x + 2$ or $x + 2y \leq 4$
$y \geq x - 1$ or $-x + y \geq -1$

Chapter Summary and Review *(pp. 431–434)*

1.

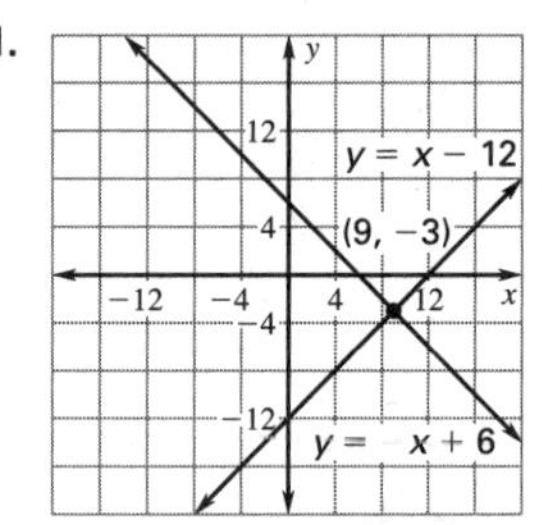

$y = -x + 6$; $y = x - 12$
$x + y = 6$
$x - y = 12$
$2x = 18$
$x = 9$
$y = 9 - 12$
$y = -3$
Solution: (9, −3)

2.

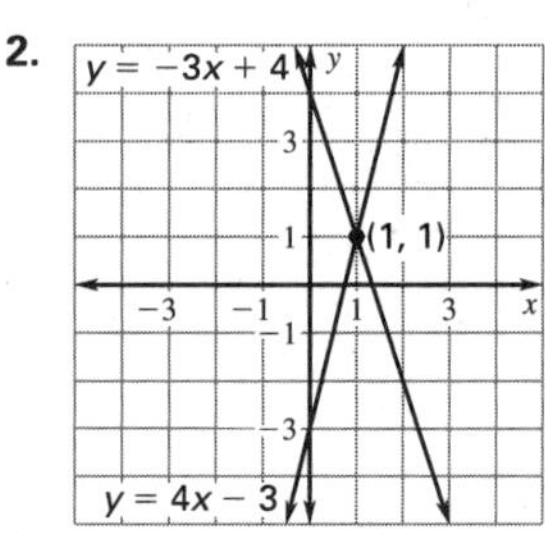

$4x - y = 3$ or $y = 4x - 3$
$3x + y = 4$ or $y = -3x + 4$
$7x = 7$
$x = 1$
$y = 4(1) - 3$
$y = 1$
one solution: (1, 1)

Copyright © McDougal Littell Inc.
All rights reserved.

3.

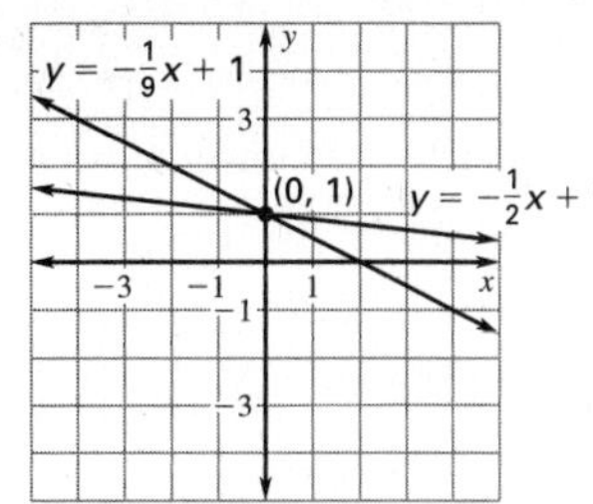

$x + 9y = 9$ or $y = -\frac{1}{9}x + 1;$

$3x + 6y = 6$ or $y = -\frac{1}{2}x + 1$

$x = -9y + 9$
$3(-9y + 9) + 6y = 6$
$-27y + 27 + 6y = 6$
$27 - 21y = 6$
$-21y = -21$
$y = 1$
$x = -9(1) + 9$
$x = 0$
one solution: (0, 1)

4.

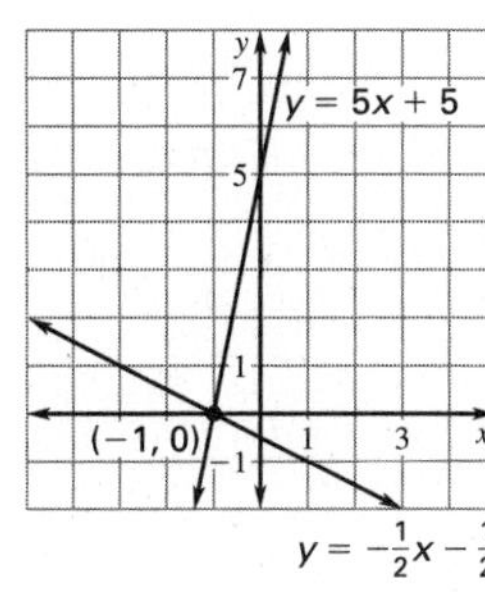

$5x - y = -5$ or $y = 5x + 5$

$3x + 6y = -3$ or $y = -\frac{1}{2}x - \frac{1}{2}$

$3x + 6(5x + 5) = -3$
$3x + 30x + 30 = -3$
$33x + 30 = -3$
$33x = -33$
$x = -1$
$y = 5(-1) + 5$
$y = 0$
one solution: $(-1, 0)$

5.

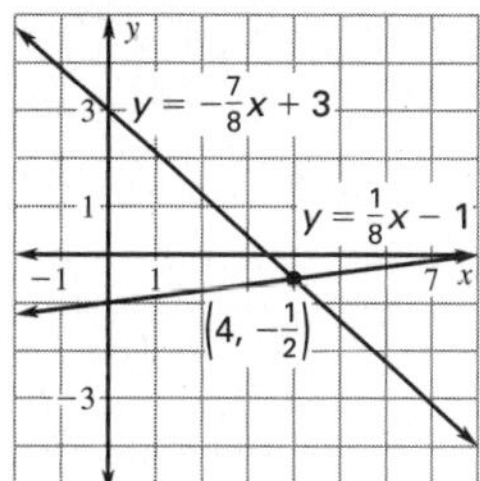

$7x + 8y = 24$ or $y = -\frac{7}{8}x + 3$

$x - 8y = 8$ or $y = \frac{1}{8}x - 1$

$8x = 32$
$x = 4$

$y = \frac{1}{8}(4) - 1$

$y = \frac{1}{2} - 1$

$y = -\frac{1}{2}$

one solution: $\left(4, -\frac{1}{2}\right)$

6.

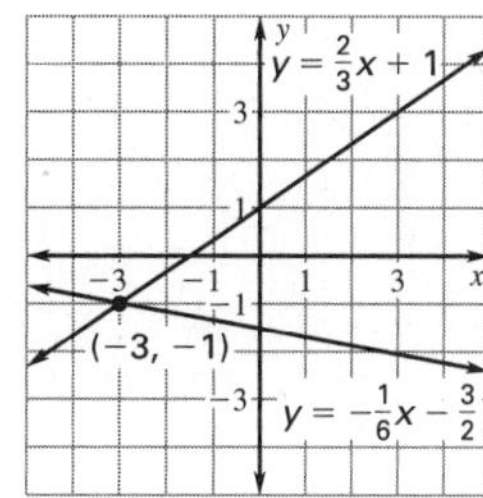

$2x - 3y = -3$ or $y = \frac{2}{3}x + 1;$

$x + 6y = -9$ or $y = -\frac{1}{6}x - \frac{3}{2}$

$x = -6y - 9$
$2(-6y - 9) - 3y = -3$
$-12y - 18 - 3y = -3$
$-15y - 18 = -3$
$-15y = 15$
$y = -1$
$x = -6(-1) - 9$
$x = -3$
one solution: $(-3, -1)$

Copyright © McDougal Littell Inc.
All rights reserved.

7. $x + 3y = 9$

$$x = -3y + 9$$
$$4(-3y + 9) - 2y = -6$$
$$-12y + 36 - 2y = -6$$
$$-14y + 36 = -6$$
$$-14y = -42$$
$$y = 3$$
$$x = -3(3) + 9$$
$$x = 0$$

Solution: $(0, 3)$

8. $7x + y = -8$

$$y = -7x - 8$$
$$-2x - 5(-7x - 8) = 7$$
$$-2x + 35x + 40 = 7$$
$$33x + 40 = 7$$
$$33x = -33$$
$$x = -1$$
$$y = -7(-1) - 8$$
$$y = -1$$

Solution: $(-1, -1)$

9. $4x + y = 4$

$$y = -4x + 4$$
$$4x - 3(-4x + 4) = -2$$
$$4x + 12x - 12 = -2$$
$$16x - 12 = -2$$
$$16x = 10$$
$$x = \frac{5}{8}$$
$$y = -4\left(\frac{5}{8}\right) + 4$$
$$y = -\frac{5}{2} + \frac{8}{2} = \frac{3}{2}$$

Solution: $\left(\frac{5}{8}, \frac{3}{2}\right)$

10. $-x + 3y = 24$

$$3y - 24 = x$$
$$5(3y - 24) + 8y = -5$$
$$15y - 120 + 8y = -5$$
$$23y - 120 = -5$$
$$23y = 115$$
$$y = 5$$
$$x = 3(5) - 24$$
$$x = -9$$

Solution: $(-9, 5)$

11. $2x + 6y = 1$

$$2x = -6y + 1$$
$$x = -3y + \frac{1}{2}$$
$$4\left(-3y + \frac{1}{2}\right) + 9y = 2$$
$$-12y + 2 + 9y = 2$$
$$-3y + 2 = 2$$
$$-3y = 0$$
$$y = 0$$
$$x = -3(0) + \frac{1}{2}$$
$$x = \frac{1}{2}$$

Solution: $\left(\frac{1}{2}, 0\right)$

12. $9x + 6y = 3$

$$6y = -9x + 3$$
$$y = -\frac{3}{2}x + \frac{1}{2}$$
$$3x - 7\left(-\frac{3}{2}x + \frac{1}{2}\right) = -26$$
$$3x + \frac{21}{2}x - \frac{7}{2} = -26$$

Multiply by 2 to clear the fractions.

$$6x + 21x - 7 = -52$$
$$27x - 7 = -52$$
$$27x = -45$$
$$x = -\frac{5}{3}$$
$$y = -\frac{3}{2}\left(-\frac{5}{3}\right) + \frac{1}{2}$$
$$y = \frac{5}{2} + \frac{1}{2} = \frac{6}{2} = 3$$

Solution: $\left(-\frac{5}{3}, 3\right)$

13. $-4x - 6y = 7$

$$x + 5y = 8$$
$$-4x - 6y = 7$$
$$4x + 20y = 32 \quad \text{Multiply by 4.}$$
$$14y = 39$$
$$y = \frac{39}{14}$$
$$x + 5\left(\frac{39}{14}\right) = 8$$
$$x + \frac{195}{14} = 8$$
$$x = \frac{112}{14} - \frac{195}{14} = -\frac{83}{14}$$

Solution: $\left(-\frac{83}{14}, \frac{39}{14}\right)$

Copyright © McDougal Littell Inc.
All rights reserved.

14. $2x + y = 0$
$5x - 4y = 26$
$8x + 4y = 0$ Multiply by 4.
$\underline{5x - 4y = 26}$
$13x = 26$
$x = 2$
$2(2) + y = 0$
$4 + y = 0$
$y = -4$
Solution: $(2, -4)$

15. $3x + 5y = -16$
$-2x + 6y = -36$
$6x + 10y = -32$ Multiply by 2.
$\underline{-6x + 18y = -108}$ Multiply by 3.
$28y = -140$
$y = -5$
$3x + 5(-5) = -16$
$3x - 25 = -16$
$3x = 9$
$x = 3$
Solution: $(3, -5)$

16. $9x + 6y = 3$
$3y + 6x = 18$
$9x + 6y = 3$
$\underline{-12x - 6y = -36}$ Multiply by -2; rearrange.
$-3x = -33$
$x = 11$
$3y + 6(11) = 18$
$3y + 66 = 18$
$3y = -48$
$y = -16$
Solution: $(11, -16)$

17. $2 - 7x = 9y$ or $-7x - 9y = -2$
$2y - 4x = 6$ or $-4x + 2y = 6$
$28x + 36y = 8$ Multiply by -4.
$\underline{-28x + 14y = 42}$ Multiply by 7.
$50y = 50$
$y = 1$
$2(1) - 4x = 6$
$2 - 4x = 6$
$-4x = 4$
$x = -1$
Solution: $(-1, 1)$

18. $4x - 9y = 1$
$25x + 6y = 4$
$8x - 18y = 2$ Multiply by 2.
$\underline{75x + 18y = 12}$ Multiply by 3.
$83x = 14$
$x = \frac{14}{83}$
$4\left(\frac{14}{83}\right) - 9y = 1$
$\frac{56}{83} - 9y = 1$
$-9y = \frac{83}{83} - \frac{56}{83} = \frac{27}{83}$
$y = \frac{27}{83} \cdot -\frac{1}{9}$
$y = -\frac{3}{83}$
Solution: $\left(\frac{14}{83}, -\frac{3}{83}\right)$

19. Let n = number of new releases.
Let r = number of regular movies.

$n + r = 5$
$3n + 2r = 13$
$-2n - 2r = -10$ Multiply by -2.
$\underline{3n + 2r = 13}$
$n = 3$
$3 + r = 5$
$r = 2$
Solution: 2 regular movies; 3 new releases

20. *Sample answer*: Addition
$-2x - 6y = -12$
$\underline{2x + 6y = 12}$
$0 = 0$; infinitely many solutions

21. *Sample answer*: Addition
$2x - 3y = 1$
$\underline{-2x + 3y = 1}$
$0 \neq 2$; no solution

22. *Sample answer*: Multiply equation 1 by 2, multiply equation 2 by -5, add equations.

$-6x + 5y = 18$ Equation 1.
$7x + 2y = 26$ Equation 2.
$-12x + 10y = 36$
$\underline{-35x - 10y = -130}$
$-47x = -94$
$x = 2$
$-6(2) + 5y = 18$
$-12 + 5y = 18$
$5y = 30$
$y = 6$
one solution: $(2, 6)$

Copyright © McDougal Littell Inc.
All rights reserved.

23.

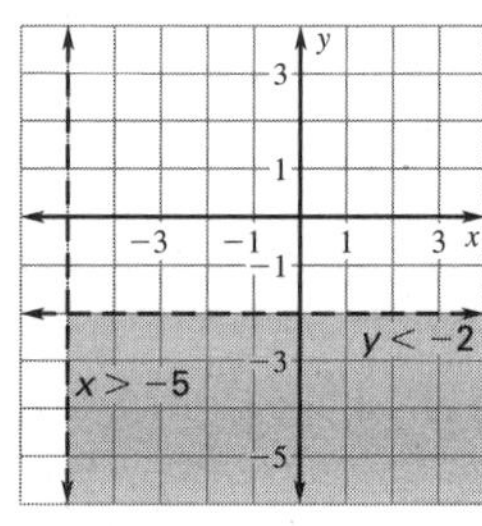

24. $2x - 10y > 8$ or $y < \frac{1}{5}x - \frac{4}{5}$

$x - 5y < 12$ $y > \frac{1}{5}x - \frac{12}{5}$

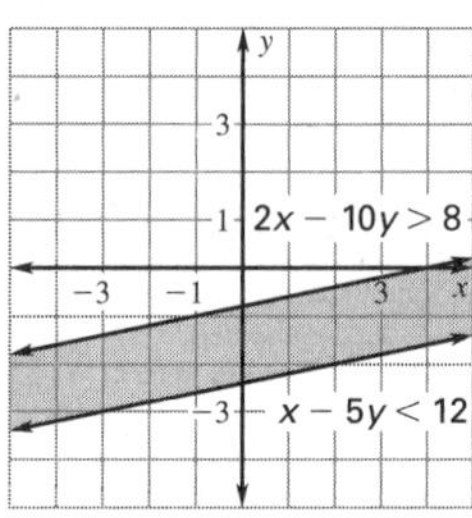

25. $-x + 3y \le 15$ or $y \le \frac{1}{3}x + 5$

$9x \ge 27$ $x \ge 3$

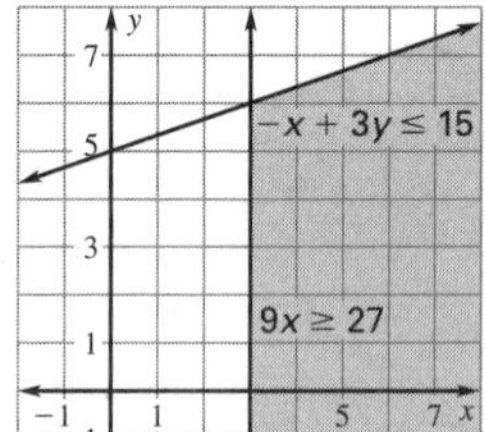

26.

$x < 5$

$y > -2$

$x + 2y > -4$ or $y > -\frac{1}{2}x - 2$

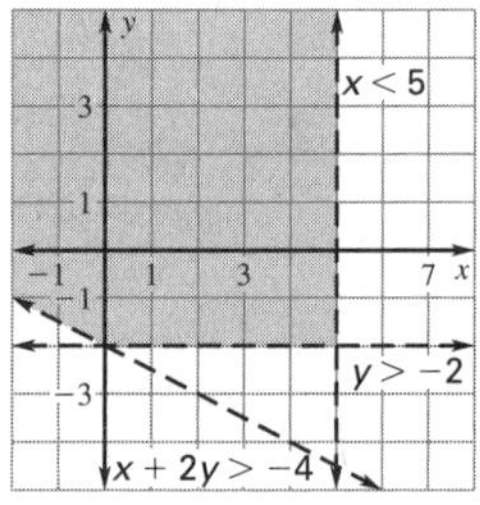

27. $x + y < 8$ or $y < -x + 8$

$x - y < 0$ $y > x$

$y \ge 4$

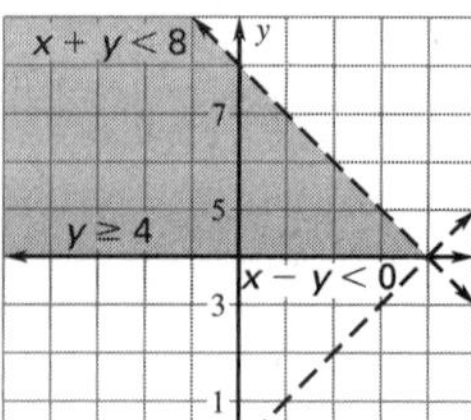

28. $7y \ge -49$ or $y \ge -7$

$-7x + y \ge -14$ $y \ge 7x - 14$

$x + y \le 10$ $y \le -x + 10$

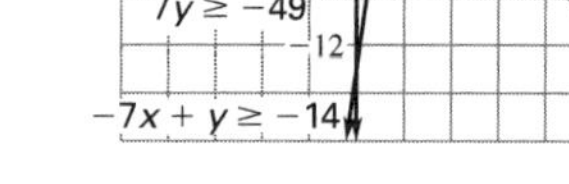

Chapter Test *(p. 435)*

1. $y = 2x - 3$

$-y = 2x - 1$ or $y = -2x + 1$

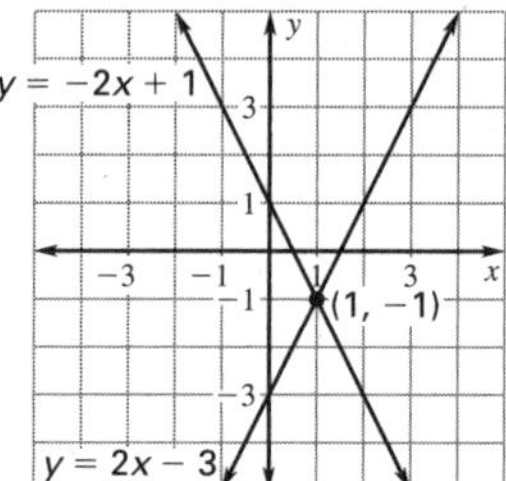

$2x - 3 = -2x + 1$

$4x - 3 = 1$

$4x = 4$

$x = 1$

$y = 2(1) - 3$

$y = -1$

Solution: $(1, -1)$

Copyright © McDougal Littell Inc.
All rights reserved.

2. $6x + 2y = 16$
$-2x + y = -2$
or
$y = -3x + 8$
$y = 2x - 2$

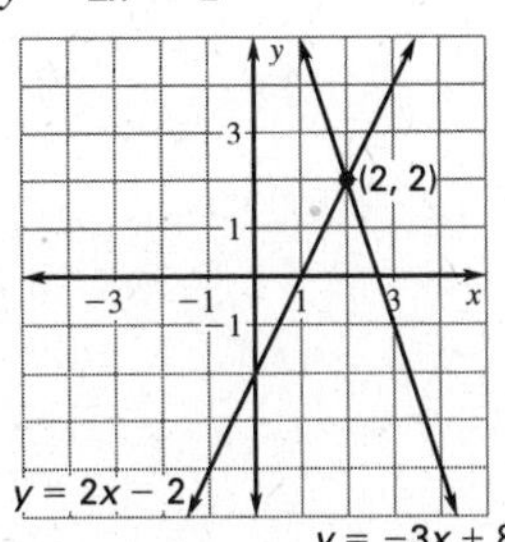

$y = 2x - 2$
$6x + 2(2x - 2) = 16$
$6x + 4x - 4 = 16$
$10x - 4 = 16$
$10x = 20$
$x = 2$
$y = 2(2) - 2$
$y = 2$
Solution: (2, 2)

3. $4x - y = 10$
$-2x + 4y = 16$
or
$y = 4x - 10$
$y = \frac{1}{2}x + 4$

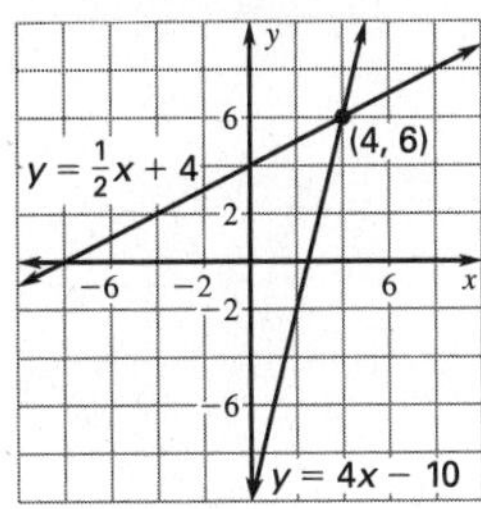

$-2x + 4(4x - 10) = 16$
$-2x + 16x - 40 = 16$
$14x - 40 = 16$
$14x = 56$
$x = 4$
$y = 4(4) - 10$
$y = 16 - 10 = 6$
Solution: (4, 6)

4. $x = -y - 5$
$-4(-y - 5) + 7y = -2$
$4y + 20 + 7y = -2$
$11y + 20 = -2$
$11y = -22$
$y = -2$
$x = -(-2) - 5$
$x = -3$
Solution: $(-3, -2)$

5. $x - 6y = -19$
$x = 6y - 19$
$7(6y - 19) + 4y = 5$
$42y - 133 + 4y = 5$
$-133 + 46y = 5$
$46y = 138$
$y = 3$
$x = 6(3) - 19$
$x = 18 - 19 = -1$
Solution: $(-1, 3)$

6. $-2x - y = 1$
$-2x - 1 = y$
$-3x + 6(-2x - 1) = 24$
$-3x - 12x - 6 = 24$
$-15x - 6 = 24$
$-15x = 30$
$x = -2$
$y = -2(-2) - 1$
$y = 3$
Solution: $(-2, 3)$

7. $6x + 7y = 5$
$4x - 2y = -10$

$12x + 14y = 10$ Multiply by 2.
$-12x + 6y = 30$ Multiply by -3.
$20y = 40$
$y = 2$
$6x + 7(2) = 5$
$6x + 14 = 5$
$6x = -9$
$x = -\frac{3}{2}$
Solution: $\left(-\frac{3}{2}, 2\right)$

8. $-7x + 2y = -5$
$10x - 2y = 6$
$3x = 1$
$x = \frac{1}{3}$
$-7\left(\frac{1}{3}\right) + 2y = -5$
$-\frac{7}{3} + 2y = -5$
$2y = -\frac{15}{3} + \frac{7}{3} = -\frac{8}{3}$
$y = -\frac{8}{3} \cdot \frac{1}{2} = -\frac{4}{3}$
Solution: $\left(\frac{1}{3}, -\frac{4}{3}\right)$

Copyright © McDougal Littell Inc.
All rights reserved.

9. $-3x + 3y = 12$
$4x + 2y = 20$

$6x - 6y = -24$ Multiply by -2.
$12x + 6y = 60$ Multiply by 3.
$18x = 36$
$x = 2$
$4(2) + 2y = 20$
$8 + 2y = 20$
$2y = 12$
$y = 6$
Solution: (2, 6)

10. Let x = number of bags of oyster shell grit.
Let y = number of bags of sunflower seeds.

$x + y = 6$ or $y = -x + 6$
$4x + 5y = 28$
$4x + 5(-x + 6) = 28$
$4x - 5x + 30 = 28$
$-x + 30 = 28$
$-x = -2$
$x = 2$
$y = -(2) + 6 = 4$
Solution: 2 bags of oyster shell grit and 4 bags of sunflower seeds.

11. $8x + 4y = -4$
$2x - y = -3$

Sample answer: Substitution
$2x + 3 = y$
$8x + 4(2x + 3) = -4$
$8x + 8x + 12 = -4$
$16x + 12 = -4$
$16x = -16$
$x = -1$
$y = 2(-1) + 3 = 1$
one solution: $(-1, 1)$

12. $-6x + 3y = -6$
$2x + 6y = 30$

$12x - 6y = 12$ Multiply by -2.
$2x + 6y = 30$
$14x = 42$
$x = 3$
$2(3) + 6y = 30$
$6 + 6y = 30$
$6y = 24$
$y = 4$
one solution: (3, 4)

13. $-3x + y = -18$
$3x - y = -16$
$0 \neq 34$; no solution

14. $3x + y = 8$ or $y = -3x + 8$
$4x + 6y = 6$
$4x + 6(-3x + 8) = 6$
$4x - 18x + 48 = 6$
$-14x + 48 = 6$
$-14x = -42$
$x = 3$
$y = -3(3) + 8$
$y = -1$
one solution: $(3, -1)$

15. $3x - 4y = 8$
$9x - 12y = 24$

$3x - 4y = 8$
$-3x + 4y = -8$ Multiply by $-\frac{1}{3}$.
$0 = 0$; infinitely many solutions

16. $6x + y = 12$ or $y = -6x + 12$
$-4x - 2y = 0$

$-4x - 2(-6x + 12) = 0$
$-4x + 12x - 24 = 0$
$8x - 24 = 0$
$8x = 24$
$x = 3$
$y = -6(3) + 12$
$y = -18 + 12 = -6$
one solution: $(3, -6)$

17.

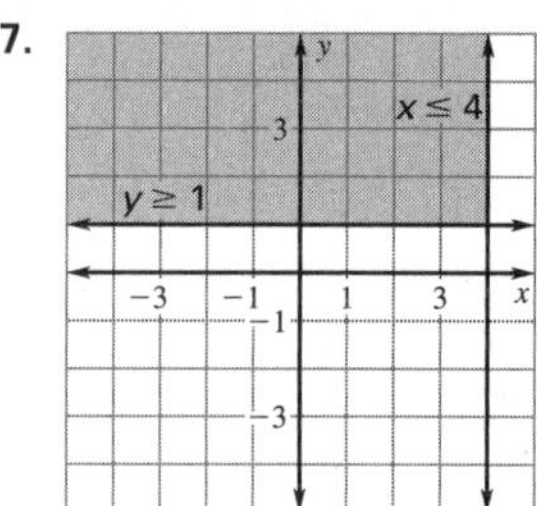

18. $-3x + 2y > 3$ or $y > \frac{3}{2}x + \frac{3}{2}$;
$x + 4y < -2$ $y < -\frac{1}{4}x - \frac{1}{2}$

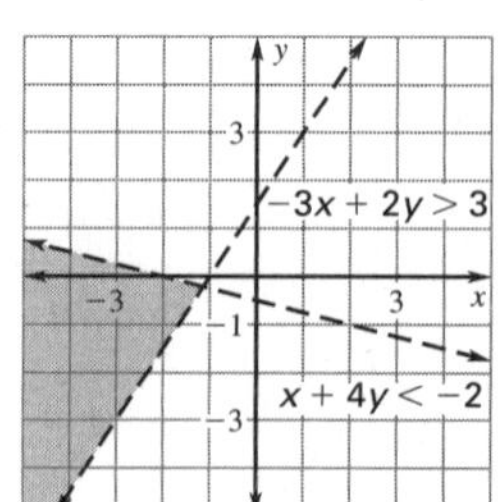

Copyright © McDougal Littell Inc.
All rights reserved.

19. $2x - 3y \le 12$ or $y \ge \frac{2}{3}x - 4$

$-x - 3y \ge -6$ $\quad y \le -\frac{1}{3}x + 2$

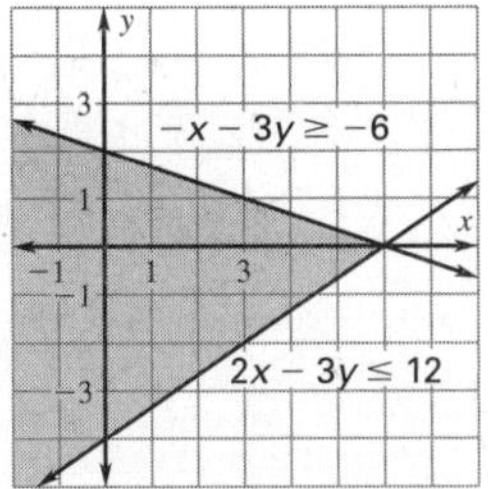

20.

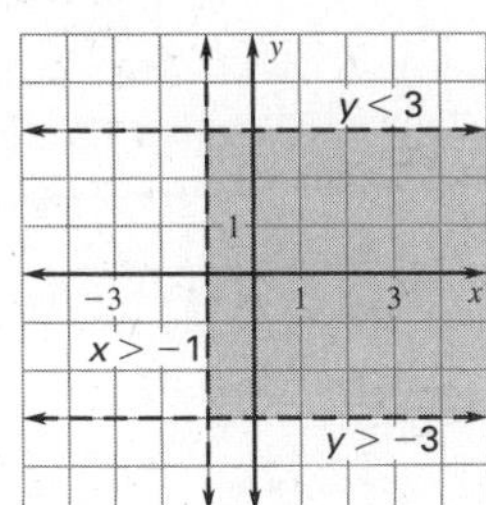

21.

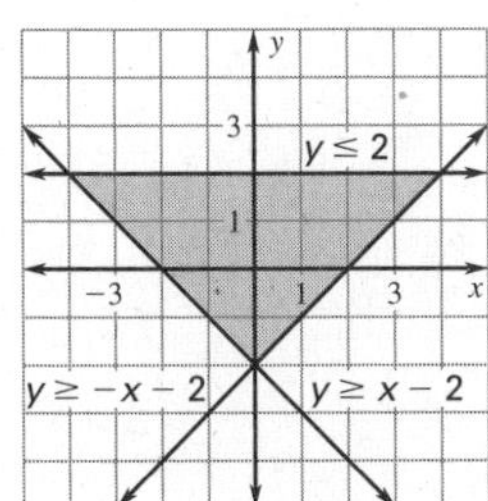

22.

23. $x > -3.5;\ y \le 2$

24. $x < 1;\ y > x - 2$

25. $y < x;\ y \le -x$

Chapter Standardized Test *(p. 436)*

1. $C\ (-1, -3)$

2. A

$3 + 4 \stackrel{?}{=} 7$ $\qquad 3 + 2(4) \stackrel{?}{=} 11$

$7 = 7$ $\qquad 11 = 11$

3. $D\ (5, 1)$

$-2(5) + 7(1) \stackrel{?}{=} -3$ $\qquad 5 - 7(1) \stackrel{?}{=} -2$

$-3 = -3$ $\qquad -2 = -2$

4. $C\ (4, 5)$

$5(4) - 6(5) \stackrel{?}{=} -10$

$20 - 30 \stackrel{?}{=} -10$

$-10 = -10$

$-15(4) + 14(5) \stackrel{?}{=} 10$

$-60 + 70 \stackrel{?}{=} 10$

$10 = 10$

5. Let x = number of times on a Ferris wheel.
Let y = number of time on roller coaster.

$x + y = 12$ or $y = -x + 12$

$3x + 5y = 50$

$3x + 5(-x + 12) = 50$

$3x - 5x + 60 = 50$

$-2x + 60 = 50$

$-2x = -10$

$x = 5$

$y = -5 + 12 = 7$

(B) You rode the roller coaster 7 times.

6. $4x - 2y = 6$

$2x - y = 3$

$4x - 2y = 6$

$-4x + 2y = -6$ $\quad$ Multiply by -2.

$0 = 0$

(C) infinitely many solutions

7. $5x + 2y = 11$

$10x + 4y = 11$

$-10x + (-4y) = -22$ $\quad$ Multiply by -2.

$10x + \quad 4y = 11$

$0 \ne -11$

(C) no solution

8. $C\ (-1, -6)$

$-6 < -(-1)$ $\qquad -6 < -1$

$-6 < 1$

9. A

$y \le 2x + 1$

$2y < -3x$ or $y < -\frac{3}{2}x$

Maintaining Skills *(p. 437)*

1. Volume = Area of base × height
$V = (5 \cdot 5) \cdot 5 = 125$ units^3

2. Volume = Area of base × height
$V = (5 \cdot 4) \cdot 1 = 20$ units^3

3. Volume = Area of base × height
$V = \left(\frac{1}{2}bh\right) \cdot 3 = \left(\frac{1}{2} \cdot 3 \cdot 2\right) \cdot 3$
$= (3)(3) = 9$ units^3

4. Volume = Area of base × height
$V = (\pi r^2) \cdot 10 = \pi(8^2) \cdot 10$
$= \pi(64)(10) = 640\pi$ units^3

5. $47\% = \frac{47}{100} = 0.47$

Copyright © McDougal Littell Inc.
All rights reserved.

6. $4\% = \frac{4}{100} = 0.04$

7. $3.5\% = \frac{3.5}{100} = 0.035$

8. $120\% = \frac{120}{100} = 1.20 = 1.2$

9. $0.61 = 0.61 \times 100\% = 61\%$

10. $0.07 = 0.07 \times 100\% = 7\%$

11. $2 = 2 \times 100\% = 200\%$

12. $0.025 = 0.025 \times 100\% = 2.5\%$

Copyright © McDougal Littell Inc.
All rights reserved.

CHAPTER 8

Chapter Opener *(p. 439)*

1.

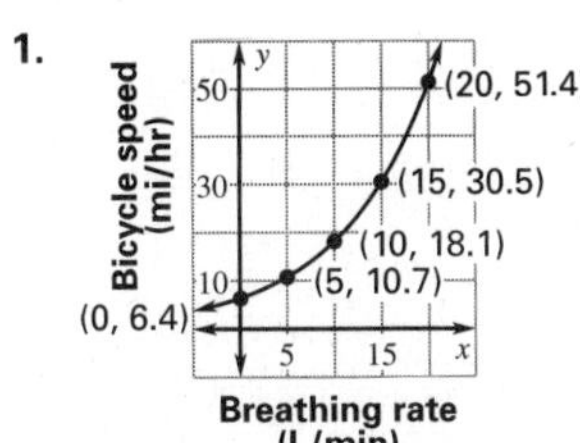

2. It increases by different amounts but by the same percent (about 59%).

Increase in Speed	*Air Intake Increase*	*Percent Increase*
0 to 5	$10.7 - 6.4 = 4.3$	$\frac{6.4}{10.7} \times 100 = 59.8\%$
5 to 10	$18.1 - 10.7 = 7.4$	$\frac{10.7}{18.1} \times 100 = 59.1\%$
10 to 15	$30.5 - 18.1 = 12.4$	$\frac{18.1}{30.5} \times 100 = 59.3\%$
15 to 20	$51.4 - 30.5 = 20.9$	$\frac{30.5}{51.4} = 59.3\%$

Chapter Readiness Quiz (p. 440)

1. base; A
2. exponent; C
3. $(3x)^2 = (3 \cdot 2)^2 = (6)^2 = 36$; D
4. $\frac{x^3}{y} = \frac{4^3}{2} = \frac{64}{2} = 32$; D
5. $\frac{\$123.75}{15 \text{ hours}} = \frac{\$8.25}{\text{hour}}$; A

8.1 Developing Concepts: Think About It *(p. 441)*

1. $6^3 \cdot 6^2 = (6 \cdot 6 \cdot 6)(6 \cdot 6) = 6^5$
2. $2 \cdot 2^4 = (2)(2 \cdot 2 \cdot 2 \cdot 2) = 2^5$
3. $a^4 \cdot a^6 = (a \cdot a \cdot a \cdot a)(a \cdot a \cdot a \cdot a \cdot a \cdot a) = a^{10}$
4. $x^2 \cdot x^7 = (x \cdot x)(x \cdot x \cdot x \cdot x \cdot x \cdot x \cdot x) = x^9$
5. $a^m \cdot a^n = a^{m+n}$

8.1 Developing Concepts: Think About It *(p. 442)*

1. $(4^2)^3 = (4^2)(4^2)(4^2) = 4^6$ 2. $(5^4)^2 = (5^4)(5^4) = 5^8$
3. $(d^3)^3 = (d^3)(d^3)(d^3) = d^9$
4. $(n^3)^4 = (n^3)(n^3)(n^3)(n^3) = n^{12}$
5. $(a^m)^n = a^{m \cdot n}$

8.1 Developing Concepts: Think About It *(p. 442)*

1. $(2 \cdot 6)^3 = (2 \cdot 6)(2 \cdot 6)(2 \cdot 6) = 2^3 \cdot 6^3$
2. $(3 \cdot 4)^5 = (3 \cdot 4)(3 \cdot 4)(3 \cdot 4)(3 \cdot 4)(3 \cdot 4) = 3^5 \cdot 4^5$
3. $(a \cdot b)^2 = (a \cdot b)(a \cdot b) = a^2b^2$
4. $(x \cdot y)^4 = (x \cdot y)(x \cdot y)(x \cdot y)(x \cdot y) = x^4y^4$
5. $(a \cdot b)^m = a^mb^m$

Lesson 8.1

8.1 Checkpoint (pp. 443–445)

1. $4^2 \cdot 4^3 = 4^{2+3} = 4^5$
2. $(-3)^2(-3) = (-3)^2 \cdot (-3)^1 = (-3)^{2+1} = (-3)^3$
3. $a \cdot a^7 = a^1 \cdot a^7 = a^{1+7} = a^8$
4. $n^5 \cdot n^2 \cdot n^3 = n^{5+2+3} = n^{10}$
5. $(4^4)^3 = 4^{4 \cdot 3} = 4^{12}$
6. $[(-3)^5]^2 = (-3)^{5 \cdot 2} = (-3)^{10}$
7. $(n^4)^5 = n^{4 \cdot 5} = n^{20}$
8. $(x^3)^3 = x^{3 \cdot 3} = x^9$
9. $(2 \cdot 4)^3 = 2^3 \cdot 4^3 = 8 \cdot 64 = 512$
10. $(-3 \cdot 5)^2 = (-3)^2 \cdot 5^2 = 9 \cdot 25 = 225$
11. $(2w)^6 = 2^6 \cdot w^6 = 64w^6$
12. $(7a)^2 = 7^2 \cdot a^2 = 49a^2$
13. $(4x^3)^4 = 4^4 \cdot x^{3 \cdot 4} = 4^4 \cdot x^{12} = 256x^{12}$
14. $(-3a^4)^2 = (-3)^2 \cdot a^{4 \cdot 2} = 9a^8$
15. $9 \cdot (9z^5)^2 = 9 \cdot 9^2 \cdot z^{5 \cdot 2} = 9^3 \cdot z^{10} = 729z^{10}$
16. $(n^2)^3 \cdot n^7 = n^{2 \cdot 3}n^7 = n^6 \cdot n^7 = n^{6+7} = n^{13}$
17. $\frac{\pi r^2}{\pi(3r)^2} = \frac{\pi r^2}{\pi \cdot 3^2 \cdot r^2} = \frac{1}{3^2} = \frac{1}{9}$ or 1 to 9

8.1 Guided Practice (p. 446)

1. B; $4^3 \cdot 4^5 = 4^{3+5}$; Product of Powers
2. C; $(2^4)^4 = 2^{4 \cdot 4}$; Power of a power
3. A; $(3 \cdot 6)^2 = 3^2 \cdot 6^2$; Power of a product
4. $2^2 \cdot 2^3 = 2^{2+3} = 2^5$
5. $(-5)^4 \cdot (-5)^2 = (-5)^{4+2} = (-5)^6$
6. $a^4 \cdot a^6 = a^{4+6} = a^{10}$
7. $(2^4)^3 = 2^{4 \cdot 3} = 2^{12}$
8. $(4^3)^3 = 4^{3 \cdot 3} = 4^9$
9. $(y^4)^5 = y^{4 \cdot 5} = y^{20}$
10. $(3 \cdot 4)^3 = 3^3 \cdot 4^3 = 27 \cdot 64 = 1728$

Copyright © McDougal Littell Inc.
All rights reserved.

11. $(2n)^4 = 2^4 \cdot n^4 = 16n^4$

12. $(3pq)^3 = 3^3 \cdot p^3 \cdot q^3 = 27p^3q^3$

8.1 Practice and Applications (pp. 446–448)

13. $3^2 \cdot 3^5 = 3^7$

14. $5^1 \cdot 5^8 = 5^9$

15. $4^{10} \cdot 4^8 = 4^{18}$

16. $x^3 \cdot x^2 = x^5$

17. $r^7 \cdot r^7 = r^{14}$

18. $a^2 \cdot a^3 = a^5$

19. $4^3 \cdot 4^6 = 4^{3+6} = 4^9$

20. $8^9 \cdot 8^5 = 8^{9+5} = 8^{14}$

21. $(-2)^3 \cdot (-2)^3 = (-2)^{3+3} = (-2)^6$

22. $b \cdot b^4 = b^{1+4} = b^5$

23. $x^6 \cdot x^3 = x^{6+3} = x^9$

24. $t^3 \cdot t^2 = t^{3+2} = t^5$

25. $(5^3)^3 = 5^9$

26. $(2^2)^4 = 2^8$

27. $[(-9)^4]^3 = (-9)^{12}$

28. $(a^2)^5 = a^{10}$

29. $(x^3)^3 = x^9$

30. $(p^2)^6 = p^{12}$

31. $(2^3)^2 = 2^{3 \cdot 2} = 2^6$

32. $(7^4)^2 = 7^{4 \cdot 2} = 7^8$

33. $[(-4)^5]^3 = (-4)^{5 \cdot 3} = (-4)^{15}$

34. $(t^5)^6 = t^{5 \cdot 6} = t^{30}$

35. $(c^8)^{10} = c^{8 \cdot 10} = c^{80}$

36. $(x^3)^2 = x^{3 \cdot 2} = x^6$

37. $(3 \cdot 7)^2 = 3^2 \cdot 7^2 = 9 \cdot 49 = 441$

38. $(4 \cdot 9)^3 = 4^3 \cdot 9^3 = 64 \cdot 729 = 46{,}656$

39. $(-4 \cdot 6)^2 = (-4)^2 \cdot 6^2 = 16 \cdot 36 = 576$

40. $(5x)^3 = 5^3 \cdot x^3 = 125x^3$

41. $(-2d)^6 = (-2)^6 \cdot d^6 = 64d^6$

42. $(ab)^2 = a^2 \cdot b^2 = a^2b^2$

43. $(2mn)^6 = 2^6 \cdot m^6 \cdot n^6 = 64m^6n^6$

44. $(10xy)^2 = 10^2 \cdot x^2 \cdot y^2 = 100x^2y^2$

45. $(-rst)^5 = (-r)^5 \cdot s^5 \cdot t^5 = -r^5 \cdot s^5 \cdot t^5$

46. $(5 \cdot 6)^4 = 5^4 \cdot 6^4 > 5 \cdot 6^4$

47. $5^2 \cdot 5^3 < (5 \cdot 5)^6 = 5^6 \cdot 5^6$

48. $(3 \cdot 2)^6 = 3^6 \cdot 2^6 < (3^2)^6 = 3^{12}$

49. $4^2 \cdot 4^8 = 4^{10} < (4 \cdot 4)^{10} = 4^{10} \cdot 4^{10} = 4^{20}$

50. $7^3 \cdot 7^4 = 7^7 < (7 \cdot 7)^4 = 7^4 \cdot 7^4 = 7^8$

51. $(6 \cdot 3)^3 = 6^3 \cdot 3^3 > 6 \cdot 3 \cdot 3 = 6 \cdot 3^2$

52. $(3b)^3 \cdot b = 3^3 \cdot b^3 \cdot b = 27b^4$

53. $-4x \cdot (x^3)^2 = -4x \cdot x^6 = -4x^7$

54. $(5a^4)^2 = 5^2 \cdot a^8 = 25a^8$

55. $(r^2s^3)^4 = r^{2 \cdot 4}s^{3 \cdot 4} = r^8s^{12}$

56. $(6z^4)^2 \cdot z^3 = 6^2 \cdot z^{4 \cdot 2} \cdot z^3$
$= 36z^8 \cdot z^3$
$= 36z^{8+3}$
$= 36z^{11}$

57. $2x^3 \cdot (-3x)^2 = 2x^3 \cdot (-3)^2 \cdot x^2$
$= 2 \cdot x^{3+2} \cdot 9$
$= 18x^5$

58. $4x \cdot (-x \cdot x^3)^2 = 4x \cdot (-x)^2 \cdot x^{3 \cdot 2}$
$= 4x \cdot x^2 \cdot x^6$
$= 4x^{1+2+6}$
$= 4x^9$

59. $(abc^2)^3 \cdot ab = a^3 \cdot b^3 \cdot c^{2 \cdot 3} \cdot a \cdot b$
$= a^{3+1}b^{3+1}c^6$
$= a^4b^4c^6$

60. $(5y^2)^3 \cdot (y^3)^2 = 5^3 \cdot y^{2 \cdot 3} \cdot y^{3 \cdot 2}$
$= 125y^6 \cdot y^6$
$= 125y^{6+6}$
$= 125y^{12}$

61. $V = \frac{4}{3}\pi r^3$ Volume of a sphere
$V = \frac{4}{3}\pi(3a)^3$ Substitute $3a$ for r.
$= \frac{4}{3}\pi(3^3) \cdot a^3$
$= \frac{4}{3}\pi(27)a^3$
$= 36\pi a^3 \approx 113.1a^3$

62. $V = \frac{1}{3}\pi r^2h$ Volume of a cone
$V = \frac{1}{3}\pi(2b^2)^2 \cdot 24$ Substitute $2b^2$ for r and 24 for h.
$= \frac{1}{3}\pi(2^2)b^{2 \cdot 2} \cdot 24$
$= \frac{1}{3}\pi(4)b^4 \cdot 24$
$= \frac{1}{3}(4)(24)\pi b^4$
$= 32\pi b^4 \approx 100.5b^4$

63. $w = 0.015s^3$ Formula for generated power
$w_1 = 0.015(20)^3$ Substitute 20 for s.
$w_2 = 0.015(10)^3$ Substitute 10 for s.
Ratio:
$\frac{0.015(20)^3}{0.015(10)^3} = \frac{20^3}{10^3}$
$= \frac{(2 \cdot 10)^3}{10^3}$
$= \frac{2^3 \cdot 10^3}{10^3}$
$= 2^3$
$= 8$
Ratio: 8 to 1

Copyright © McDougal Littell Inc.
All rights reserved.

64. $w = 0.015s^3$ Formula for generated power
$w_1 = 0.015(5)^3$ Substitute 5 for s.
$w_2 = 0.015(10)^3$ Substitute 10 for s.

Ratio:
$$\frac{0.015(5)^3}{0.015(10)^3} = \frac{5^3}{10^3} = \frac{5^3}{(2 \cdot 5)^3} = \frac{5^3}{2^3 \cdot 5^3} = \frac{1}{2^3} = \frac{1}{8}$$
Ratio: $\frac{1}{8}$ or 1 to 8

65. $2^1 = 2$; Day 1
$2^2 = 4$; Day 2
$2^3 = 8$; Day 3

66. 2^n; Day n

67. $2^{30} = 1{,}073{,}741{,}824$ pennies

68. $10,737,418.24

69. $(b^3)^2 = b^3 \cdot b^3 = b \cdot b \cdot b \cdot b \cdot b \cdot b = b^6$

8.1 Standardized Test Practice (p. 448)

70. $5^2 \cdot 5^4 = 5^{2+4} = 5^6$; A

71. $(2^3)^2 = 2^{3 \cdot 2} = 2^6 = 64$; J

72. $(4 \cdot 6)^2 = 4^2 \cdot 6^2 = 16 \cdot 36 = 576$; D

73. $(3x^2y)^3 = 3^3x^{2 \cdot 3}y^3 = 27x^6y^3$; J

8.1 Mixed Review (p. 448)

74. $b^2 = 8^2 = 64$

75. $(5 \cdot y)^4 = (5 \cdot 2)^4 = 5^4 \cdot 2^4 = 625 \cdot 16 = 10{,}000$

76. $\frac{1}{2}n^3 = \frac{1}{2}(-2)^3 = \frac{1}{2}(-8) = -4$

77. $\frac{1}{y^2} = \frac{1}{5^2} = \frac{1}{25}$

78. $\frac{24}{x^3} = \frac{24}{2^3} = \frac{24}{8} = 3$

79. $\frac{45}{a^2} = \frac{45}{2^2} = \frac{45}{4}$

80. $y = x + 2$
Sample answer:

x	−2	−1	0	1	2
y	0	1	2	3	4

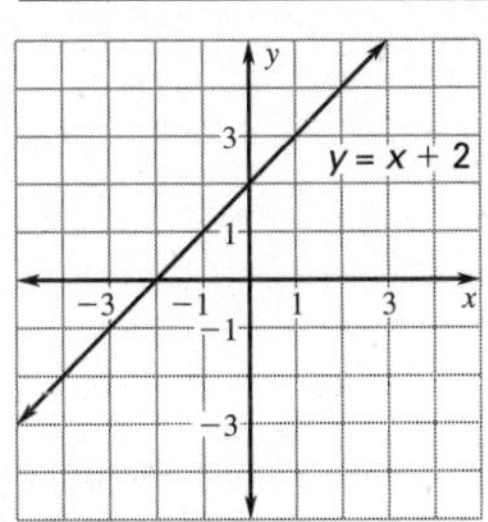

81. $y = -(x - 4)$
Sample answer:

x	−2	−1	0	1	2
y	6	5	4	3	2

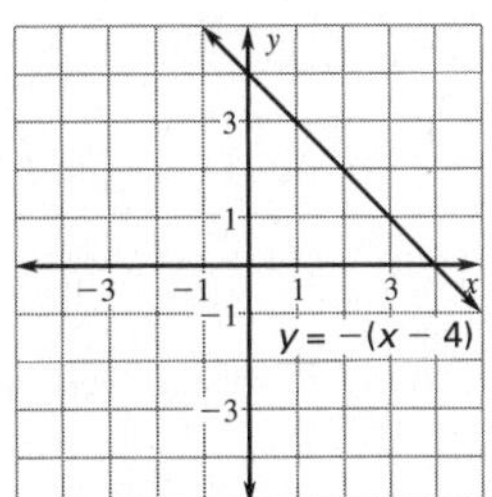

82. $y = \frac{1}{2}x - 5$
Sample answer:

x	−2	−1	0	1	2
y	−6	$-5\frac{1}{2}$	−5	$-4\frac{1}{2}$	−4

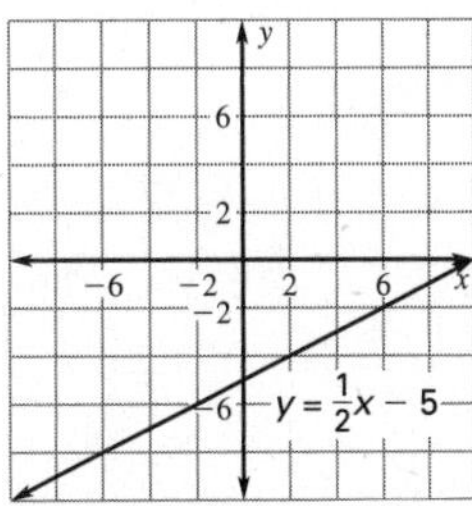

83. $y = \frac{3}{4}x + 2$
Sample answer:

x	−4	−2	0	2	4
y	−1	$\frac{1}{2}$	2	$3\frac{1}{2}$	5

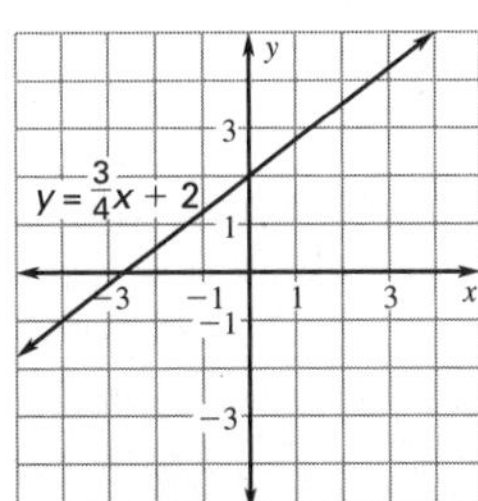

Copyright © McDougal Littell Inc.
All rights reserved.

84. $y = 2$

Sample answer:

x	-2	-1	0	1	2
y	2	2	2	2	2

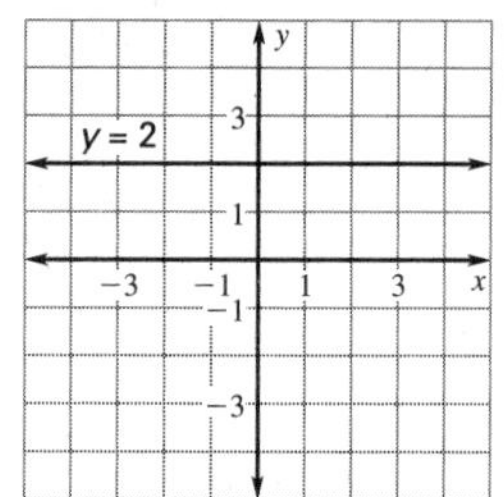

85. $x = -3$

Sample answer:

x	-3	-3	-3	-3	-3
y	-2	-1	0	1	2

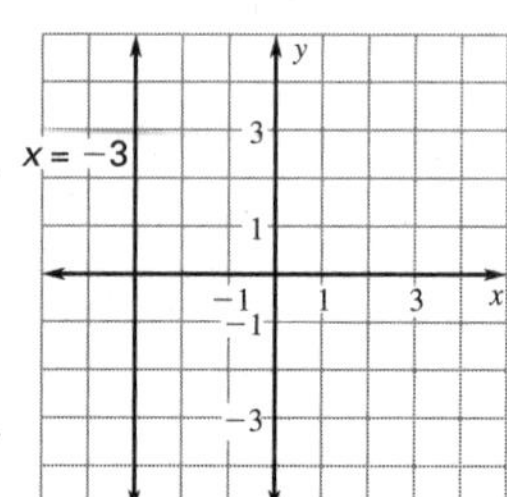

86. $-x - 2 < -5$
$-x < -3$
$x > 3$

87. $3 - x > -4$
$-x > -7$
$x < 7$

88. $7 + 3x \geq -2$
$3x \geq -9$
$x \geq -3$

89. $6x - 10 \leq -4$
$6x \leq 6$
$x \leq 1$

90. $2 < 2x + 7$
$-5 < 2x$
$-\frac{5}{2} < x$ or $x > -\frac{5}{2}$

91. $9 - 4x \leq 2$
$-4x \leq -7$
$x \geq \frac{7}{4}$

8.1 Maintaining Skills (p. 448)

92. false; $6 \times 5 = 30$ and $10 \times 3 = 30$; 30

93. true

94. true

95. false; $10 \times 1 = 10$ and $10 \times 3 = 30$; 10

96. false; $45 = 3^2 \cdot 5$; $82 = 2 \cdot 41$
$\text{LCM} = 2 \cdot 3^2 \cdot 5 \cdot 41 = 3690$

97. false;
Factors of 45: 1, 3, 5, 9, 15, 45
Factors of 82: 1, 2, 41, 82
GCF = 1

Lesson 8.2

8.2 Checkpoint (pp. 450–451)

1. $\left(\frac{1}{8}\right)^0 = 1$

2. $(-9)^{-2} = \frac{1}{(-9)^2} = \frac{1}{81}$

3. $\frac{1}{2^{-3}} = 2^3 = 8$

4. $\frac{1}{(-5)^{-2}} = (-5)^2 = 25$

5. $4^2 \cdot 4^{-3} = 4^{2+(-3)} = 4^{-1} = \frac{1}{4^1} = \frac{1}{4}$

6. $(3^{-1})^{-2} = 3^{-1(-2)} = 3^2 = 9$

7. $(2 \cdot 5)^{-2} = \frac{1}{(2 \cdot 5)^2} = \frac{1}{2^2 \cdot 5^2} = \frac{1}{4 \cdot 25} = \frac{1}{100}$

8. $7^{-3} \approx 0.0029$

9. $6^{-2} \cdot 6^{-1} \approx 0.0046$

10. $(3^3)^{-2} = 3^{-6} \approx 0.0014$

11. $2x^{-3}y^3 = 2 \cdot \frac{1}{x^3} \cdot y^3 = \frac{2y^3}{x^3}$

12. $\frac{3}{x^{-2}} = 3x^2$

13. $(5b)^{-3} = \frac{1}{(5b)^3} = \frac{1}{5^3 \cdot b^3} = \frac{1}{125b^3}$

8.2 Guided Practice (p. 452)

1. False; any non-zero number raised to the zero power equals 1.

2. True; this is the definition of negative exponents.

3. $6^0 = 1$

4. $3^{-1} = \frac{1}{3}$

5. $\frac{1}{4^{-3}} = 4^3 = 64$

6. $\frac{1}{(-2)^{-1}} = (-2)^1 = -2$

7. $2^{-4} \cdot 2^5 = 2^{-4+5} = 2^1 = 2$

8. $(3^4)^{-1} = \frac{1}{(3^4)^1} = \frac{1}{3^4} = \frac{1}{81}$

9. $(4 \cdot 1)^{-2} = \frac{1}{(4 \cdot 1)^2} = \frac{1}{4^2 \cdot 1^2} = \frac{1}{16 \cdot 1} = \frac{1}{16}$

10. $(9^{-1})^2 = 9^{-1 \cdot 2} = 9^{-2} = \frac{1}{9^2} = \frac{1}{81}$

11. $5^{-4} = 0.0016$

12. $7^{-1} \cdot 7^{-3} = 7^{-1+(-3)} = 7^{-4} \approx 0.0004$

13. $(8^2)^{-1} = 8^{-2} \approx 0.0156$

14. $(3 \cdot 4)^{-3} = 12^{-3} \approx 0.0006$

Copyright © McDougal Littell Inc.
All rights reserved.

15. $m^{-2} = \frac{1}{m^2}$

16. $a^5b^{-8} = a^5 \cdot \frac{1}{b^8} = \frac{a^5}{b^8}$

17. $\frac{3}{c^{-5}} = 3 \cdot c^5 = 3c^5$

18. $(2x)^{-3} = \frac{1}{(2x)^3} = \frac{1}{2^3 \cdot x^3} = \frac{1}{8x^3}$

8.2 Practice and Applications (pp. 452–454)

19.

x	2	5	6
x^{-1}	$\frac{1}{2}$	$\frac{1}{5}$	$\frac{1}{6}$

20.

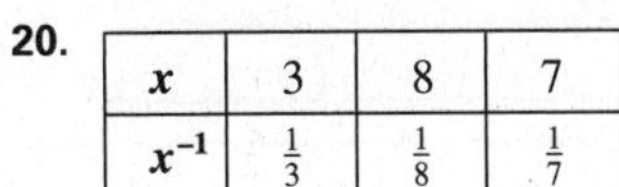

x	3	8	7
x^{-1}	$\frac{1}{3}$	$\frac{1}{8}$	$\frac{1}{7}$

21. $3^0 = 1$

22. $(-5)^0 = 1$

23. $4^{-2} = \frac{1}{4^2} = \frac{1}{16}$

24. $9^{-1} = \frac{1}{9}$

25. $(-7)^{-3} = \frac{1}{(-7)^3} = -\frac{1}{343}$

26. $\frac{1}{10^{-1}} = 10^1 = 10$

27. $\frac{1}{4^{-4}} = 4^4 = 256$

28. $\frac{1}{(-8)^{-2}} = (-8)^2 = 64$

29. $2^{-3} \cdot 2^0 = 2^{-3} \cdot 1 = \frac{1}{2^3} = \frac{1}{8}$

30. $10^{-5} \cdot 10^7 = 10^{-5+7} = 10^2 = 100$

31. $6^2 \cdot 6^{-4} = 6^{2+(-4)} = 6^{-2} = \frac{1}{6^2} = \frac{1}{36}$

32. $4^{-1} \cdot 4^{-1} = 4^{-1+(-1)} = 4^{-2} = \frac{1}{4^2} = \frac{1}{16}$

33. $(4^{-1})^{-3} = 4^{(-1)(-3)} = 4^3 = 64$

34. $(5^{-2})^2 = 5^{-4} = \frac{1}{5^4} = \frac{1}{625}$

35. $(3^2)^{-1} = 3^{-2} = \frac{1}{3^2} = \frac{1}{9}$

36. $[(-8)^{-2}]^{-1} = (-8)^{-2(-1)} = (-8)^2 = 64$

37. $(10 \cdot 2)^{-2} = \frac{1}{(10 \cdot 2)^2} = \frac{1}{10^2 \cdot 2^2} = \frac{1}{100 \cdot 4} = \frac{1}{400}$

38. $(1 \cdot 7)^{-3} = \frac{1}{(7)^3} = \frac{1}{343}$

39. $(-2 \cdot 2)^{-2} = \frac{1}{(-2 \cdot 2)^2} = \frac{1}{(-2)^2 \cdot 2^2} = \frac{1}{4 \cdot 4} = \frac{1}{16}$

40. $[4 \cdot (-3)]^{-1} = \frac{1}{4 \cdot (-3)} = -\frac{1}{12}$

41. $2^{-5} \approx 0.0313$

42. $11^{-2} \approx 0.0083$

43. $5^{-1} \cdot 5^{-3} = 5^{-1+(-3)} = 5^{-4} = 0.0016$

44. $9^{-4} \cdot 9^2 = 9^{-4+2} = 9^{-2} \approx 0.0123$

45. $(4^2)^{-1} = 4^{-2} = 0.0625$

46. $(3^{-3})^2 = 3^{-6} \approx 0.0014$

47. $(2 \cdot 7)^{-1} = 14^{-1} \approx 0.0714$

48. $(8 \cdot 3)^{-2} = 24^{-2} \approx 0.0017$

49. Error: The 5 should not be raised to a negative power.

$5x^{-3} = 5 \cdot \frac{1}{x^3} = \frac{5}{x^3}$

50. Error: Remove the negative sign from a^{-2} when rewriting in fraction form.

$a^{-2}b^3 = \frac{1}{a^2}b^3 = \frac{b^3}{a^2}$

51. $x^{-5} = \frac{1}{x^5}$

52. $3x^{-4} = \frac{3}{x^4}$

53. $x^{-2}y^4 = \frac{y^4}{x^2}$

54. $8x^{-1}y^{-6} = \frac{8}{xy^6}$

55. $\frac{1}{x^{-2}} = x^2$

56. $\frac{2}{x^{-5}} = 2x^5$

57. $\frac{y^4}{x^{-10}} = x^{10}y^4$

58. $\frac{9x^{-3}}{y^{-1}} = \frac{9y}{x^3}$

59. $(4x)^{-3} = \frac{1}{(4x)^3} = \frac{1}{4^3x^3} = \frac{1}{64x^3}$

60. $(3xy)^{-2} = \frac{1}{(3xy)^2} = \frac{1}{3^2x^2y^2} = \frac{1}{9x^2y^2}$

61. $(6x^{-3})^3 = 6^3 \cdot x^{-9} = \frac{6^3}{x^9} = \frac{216}{x^9}$

62. $\frac{1}{(4x)^{-5}} = (4x)^5 = 4^5x^5 = 1024x^5$

63. In 1800, $y = 0$.

$P = 5.31(1.03)^0$

$= 5.31(1)$

$= 5.31$

about 5.31 million people

64. In 1776, $y = 1776 - 1800 = -24$

$P = 5.31(1.03)^{-24}$

$\approx 5.31(0.4919)$

≈ 2.61

about 2.61 million people

65. Figure 1: $\frac{1}{2}$

Figure 2: $\frac{1}{2}$ of $\frac{1}{2} = \frac{1}{2} \cdot \frac{1}{2} = \frac{1}{4}$

Figure 3: $\frac{1}{2}$ of $\frac{1}{4} = \frac{1}{2} \cdot \frac{1}{4} = \frac{1}{8}$

Figure 4: $\frac{1}{2}$ of $\frac{1}{8} = \frac{1}{2} \cdot \frac{1}{8} = \frac{1}{16}$

Copyright © McDougal Littell Inc.
All rights reserved.

66. $\frac{1}{2} = \frac{1}{2^1} = 2^{-1}$; Figure 1

$\frac{1}{4} = \frac{1}{2^2} = 2^{-2}$; Figure 2

$\frac{1}{8} = \frac{1}{2^3} = 2^{-3}$; Figure 3

$\frac{1}{16} = \frac{1}{2^4} = 2^{-4}$; Figure 4

67. Pattern $= 2^{-(\text{Figure \#})}$
Figure 10: 2^{-10}

8.2 Standardized Test Practice (p. 454)

68. $\frac{1}{8} = \frac{1}{2^3} = 2^{-3}$; C

69. $(4^{-1})^{-2} = 4^{-1(-2)} = 4^2 = 16$; H

70. $3 \cdot 3^{-5} = 3^{1+(-5)} = 3^{-4} = \frac{1}{3^4} = \frac{1}{81}$; A

71. $\frac{3x^{-2}}{y^3z^{-1}} = \frac{3z}{y^3x^2}$ or $\frac{3z}{x^2y^3}$; G

8.2 Mixed Review (p. 454)

72. $\frac{6 \cdot 5}{1 + 7 \cdot 2} = \frac{30}{1 + 14} = \frac{30}{15} = 2$

73. $\frac{8 \cdot 8}{10 + 3 \cdot 2} = \frac{64}{10 + 6} = \frac{64}{16} = 4$

74. $\frac{2 \cdot 4^2}{1 + 3^2 - 2} = \frac{2 \cdot 16}{1 + 9 - 2} = \frac{32}{10 - 2} = \frac{32}{8} = 4$

75. $\frac{9 + 3^3 - 4}{8 \cdot 2} = \frac{9 + 27 - 4}{8 \cdot 2}$

$= \frac{9 + 27 - 4}{16}$

$= \frac{36 - 4}{16}$

$= \frac{32}{16}$

$= 2$

76. $\frac{(5 - 3)^2}{2 \cdot (6 - 2)} = \frac{(2)^2}{2 \cdot (4)} = \frac{4}{2 \cdot 4} = \frac{1}{2}$

77. $\frac{2 \cdot 3^4}{20 - 4^2 + 8} = \frac{2 \cdot 81}{20 - 16 + 8}$

$= \frac{162}{20 - 16 + 8}$

$= \frac{162}{4 + 8}$

$= \frac{162}{12} = 13.5$

78. $x + 1 = 6$
$x = 5$

79. $-2 = 7 + x$
$-9 = x$

80. $15 = x - (-4)$
$15 = x + 4$
$11 = x$

81. $10 = x - 5$
$15 = x$

82. $-3 + x = -8$
$x = -5$

83. $x - (-6) = -9$
$x + 6 = -9$
$x = -15$

84. $|x - 3| > 4$
$(x - 3) > 4$ or $(x - 3) < -4$
$x > 7$ $\quad$ $x < -1$

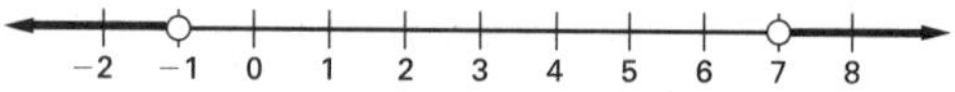

Test a point from each region of the graph.
Sample answer: Test $x = 8, 0, -2$
$|8 - 3| = |5| = 5 > 4$
$|0 - 3| = |-3| = 3 \not> 4$
$|-2 - 3| = |-5| = 5 > 4$

85. $|x + 9| < 4$
$-4 < x + 9 < 4$
$-13 < x < -5$

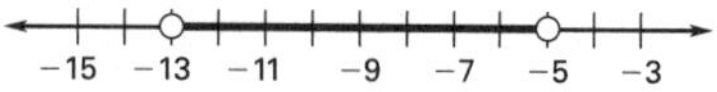

Test a point from each region of the graph.
Sample answer: Test $x = -14, -7, -4$
$|-14 + 9| = |-5| = 5 \not< 4$
$|-7 + 9| = |2| = 2 < 4$
$|-4 + 9| = |5| = 5 \not< 4$

86. $|3x + 2| \geq 10$
$3x + 2 \geq 10$ or $3x + 2 \leq -10$
$3x \geq 8$ $\quad$ $3x \leq -12$
$x \geq \frac{8}{3} = 2\frac{2}{3}$ $\quad$ $x \leq -4$

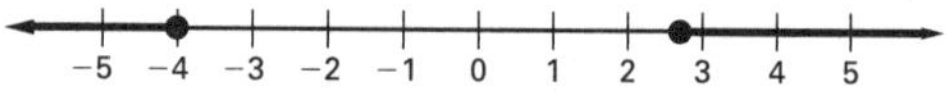

Test a point from each region of the graph.
Sample answer: Test $x = 3, 0, -5$
$|3 \cdot 3 + 2| = |11| = 11 \geq 10$
$|3 \cdot 0 + 2| = |2| = 2 \not\geq 10$
$|3(-5) + 2| = |-13| = 13 \geq 10$

87. $|5 + 2x| \leq 7$
$-7 \leq 5 + 2x \leq 7$
$-12 \leq 2x \leq 2$
$-6 \leq x \leq 1$

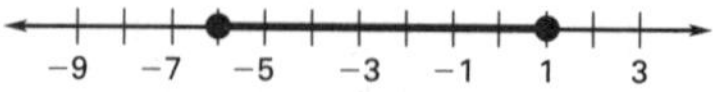

Test a point from each region of the graph.
Sample answer: Test $x = -7, 0, 2$
$|5 + 2(-7)| = |-9| = 9 \not\leq 7$
$|5 + 2(0)| = |5| = 5 \leq 7$
$|5 + 2(2)| = |9| = 9 \not\leq 7$

Copyright © McDougal Littell Inc.
All rights reserved.

88. $|x + 2| + 6 < 15$

$|x + 2| < 9$

$-9 < x + 2 < 9$

$-11 < x < 7$

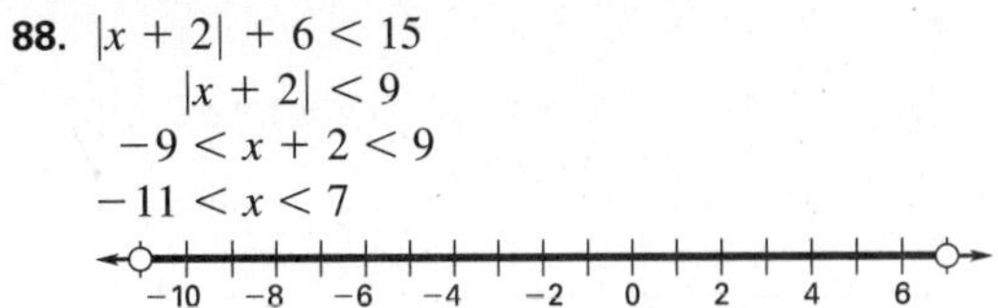

Test a point from each region of the graph.

Sample answer: Test $x = -12, 0, 8$

$|-12 + 2| + 6 = |-10| + 6 = 10 + 6 = 16 \not< 15$

$|0 + 2| + 6 = |2| + 6 = 2 + 6 = 8 < 15$

$|8 + 2| + 6 = |10| + 6 = 10 + 6 = 16 \not< 15$

89. $|3x + 7| - 5 > 8$

$|3x + 7| > 13$

$3x + 7 > 13$ or $3x + 7 < -13$

$3x > 6$ $\quad 3x < -20$

$x > 2$ $\quad x < -\frac{20}{3} = -6\frac{2}{3}$

$-\frac{20}{3}$ 2

−6 −4 −2 0 2

Test a point from each region of the graph.

Sample answer: Test $x = 3, 0, -7$

$|3(3) + 7| - 5 = |16| - 5 = 16 - 5 = 11 > 8$

$|3(0) + 7| - 5 = |7| - 5 = 7 - 5 = 2 \not> 8$

$|3(-7) + 7| - 5 = |-14| - 5 = 14 - 5 = 9 > 8$

90. $4x + y = 5$

$y = -4x + 5$

$2x - y = -2$

$2x - (-4x + 5) = -2$

$2x + 4x - 5 = -2$

$6x - 5 = -2$

$6x = 3$

$x = \frac{1}{2}$

$y = -4\left(\frac{1}{2}\right) + 5 = -2 + 5 = 3$

Solution: $\left(\frac{1}{2}, 3\right)$

91. $-3x + y = 4$

$y = 3x + 4$

$-9x + 5y = 10$

$-9 + 5(3x + 4) = 10$

$-9x + 15x + 20 = 10$

$6x + 20 = 10$

$6x = -10$

$x = -\frac{5}{3}$

$y = 3\left(-\frac{5}{3}\right) + 4 = -5 + 4 = -1$

Solution: $\left(-\frac{5}{3}, -1\right)$

92. $x - 2y = 0$

$x = 2y$

$x + 4y = 30$

$2y + 4y = 30$

$6y = 30$

$y = 5$

$x = 2(5) = 10$

Solution: $(10, 5)$

93. $x + y = 5$

$x = -y + 5$

$2x - 3y = 10$

$2(-y + 5) - 3y = 10$

$-2y + 10 - 3y = 10$

$10 - 5y = 10$

$-5y = 0$

$y = 0$

$x = -(0) + 5 = 5$

Solution: $(5, 0)$

94. $-x - 5y = 84$

$-x = 5y + 84$

$x = -5y - 84$

$x + 15y = 6$

$(-5y - 84) + 15y = 6$

$-84 + 10y = 6$

$10y = 90$

$y = 9$

$x = -5(9) - 84 = -45 - 84 = -129$

Solution: $(-129, 9)$

95. $4x - y = 5$

$y = 4x - 5$

$2x + 4y = 16$

$2x + 4(4x - 5) = 16$

$2x + 16x - 20 = 16$

$18x - 20 = 16$

$18x = 36$

$x = 2$

$y = 4(2) - 5 = 8 - 5 = 3$

Solution: $(2, 3)$

Sample answers are given for Exercises 96–103.

8.2 Maintaining Skills (p. 454)

96–103. Sample answers are given.

96. $\frac{1}{4} = \frac{2}{8} = \frac{3}{12} = \frac{4}{16}$

97. $\frac{3}{5} = \frac{6}{10} = \frac{9}{15} = \frac{12}{20}$

98. $\frac{5}{6} = \frac{10}{12} = \frac{15}{18} = \frac{20}{24}$

99. $\frac{1}{8} = \frac{2}{16} = \frac{3}{24} = \frac{4}{32}$

100. $\frac{2}{3} = \frac{4}{6} = \frac{6}{9} = \frac{8}{12}$

101. $\frac{15}{16} = \frac{30}{32} = \frac{45}{48} = \frac{60}{64}$

102. $\frac{5}{32} = \frac{10}{64} = \frac{15}{96} = \frac{20}{128}$

103. $\frac{25}{32} = \frac{50}{64} = \frac{75}{96} = \frac{100}{128}$

Copyright © McDougal Littell Inc.
All rights reserved.

Chapter 8 *continued*

Lesson 8.3

8.3 Checkpoint (pp. 455–457)

1.

x	$y = 3^x$	y
-2	$3^{-2} = \frac{1}{3^2}$	$\frac{1}{9}$
-1	$3^{-1} = \frac{1}{3}$	$\frac{1}{3}$
0	3^0	1
1	3^1	3
2	3^2	9
3	3^3	27

2. $y = 2\left(\frac{1}{3}\right)^x = 2(3^{-1})^x = 2(3^{-x})$

x	$y = 2\left(\frac{1}{3}\right)^x$	y
-2	$2(3^{-(-2)}) = 2(3^2) = 2 \cdot 9$	18
-1	$2(3^{-(-1)}) = 2(3^1) = 2 \cdot 3$	6
0	$2(3^{-(0)}) = 2(3^0) = 2 \cdot 1$	2
1	$2(3^{-1}) = 2\left(\frac{1}{3}\right)$	$\frac{2}{3}$
2	$2(3^{-2}) = 2\left(\frac{1}{3^2}\right) = \frac{2}{3^2}$	$\frac{2}{9}$
3	$2(3^{-3}) = 2\left(\frac{1}{3^3}\right) = \frac{2}{3^3}$	$\frac{2}{27}$

3.

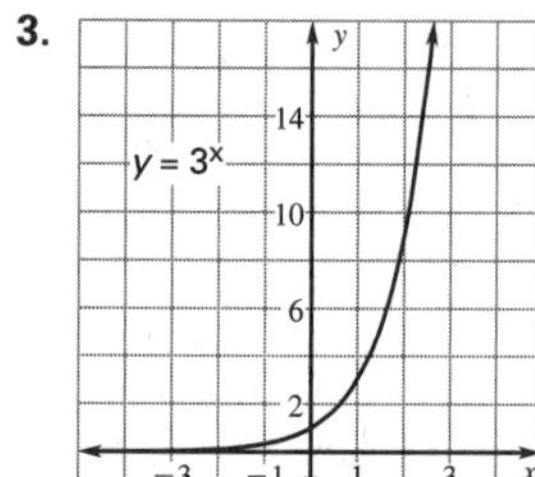

Domain: all real numbers
Range: all positive real numbers

4.

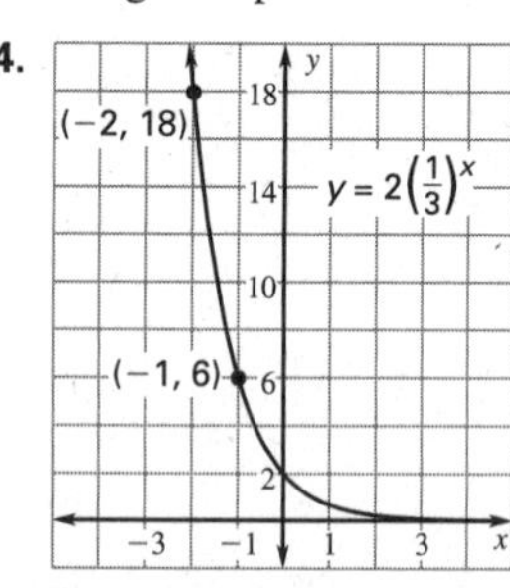

Domain: all real numbers
Range: all positive real numbers

8.3 Guided Practice (p. 458)

1. A function that is in the form of $y = ab^x$ where $b > 0$ and $b \neq 1$, and x is the variable.

2.

x	-2	-1	0	1	2	3
$y = 4^x$	$\frac{1}{16}$	$\frac{1}{4}$	1	4	16	64

3.

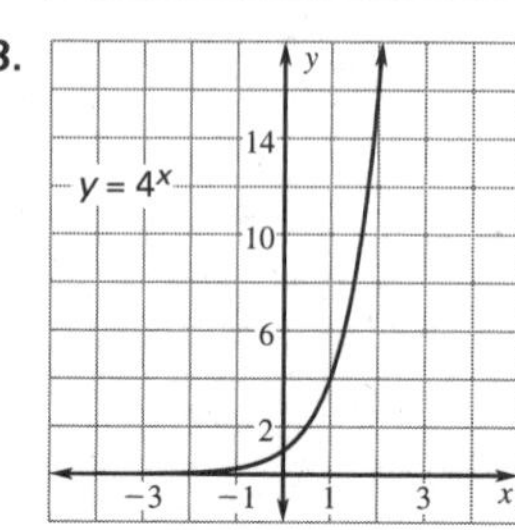

4. $y = 3\left(\frac{1}{4}\right)^x$

x	-2	-1	0	1	2	3
y	48	12	3	$\frac{3}{4}$	$\frac{3}{16}$	$\frac{3}{64}$

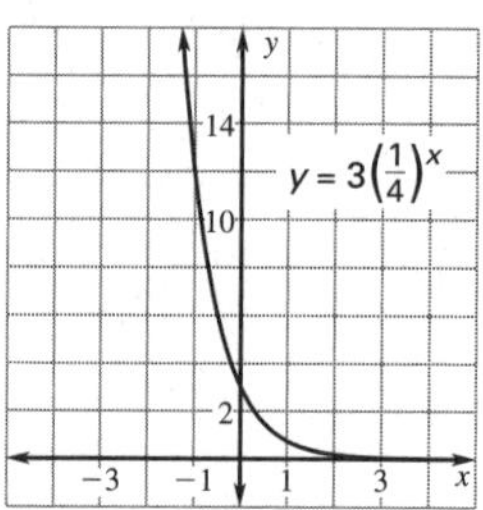

5. Domain: all real numbers
Range: all positive real numbers

6. Domain: all real numbers
Range: all negative real numbers

8.3 Practice and Applications (pp. 458–460)

7. yes; $2^0 = 1$

8. yes; $5^0 = 1$

9. no; $2(3)^0 = 2(1) = 2 \neq 1$

10. no; $5(7)^0 = 5(1) = 5 \neq 1$

11. yes; $\left(\frac{1}{8}\right)^0 = 1$

12. yes; $\left(\frac{3}{4}\right)^0 = 1$

13. no; $7\left(\frac{1}{5}\right)^0 = 7(1) = 7 \neq 1$

14. no; $4\left(\frac{4}{9}\right)^0 = 4(1) = 4 \neq 1$

Copyright © McDougal Littell Inc.
All rights reserved.

15. $y = 3^x$

x	*Function*	y
-2	$3^{-2} = \frac{1}{3^2}$	$\frac{1}{9}$
-1	$3^{-1} = \frac{1}{3}$	$\frac{1}{3}$
0	$3^0 = 1$	1
1	3^1	3
2	3^2	9
3	3^3	27

16. $y = 8^x$

x	*Function*	y
-2	$8^{-2} = \frac{1}{8^2}$	$\frac{1}{64}$
-1	$8^{-1} = \frac{1}{8}$	$\frac{1}{8}$
0	8^0	1
1	8^1	8
2	8^2	64
3	8^3	512

17. $y = 5(4)^x$

x	*Function*	y
-2	$5(4)^{-2} = \frac{5}{4^2}$	$\frac{5}{16}$
-1	$5(4)^{-1} = \frac{5}{4}$	$\frac{5}{4}$
0	$5(4)^0 = 5(1)$	5
1	$5(4)^1 = 5 \cdot 4$	20
2	$5(4)^2 = 5 \cdot 16$	80
3	$5(4)^3 = 5 \cdot 64$	320

18. $y = 3(5)^x$

x	*Function*	y
-2	$3(5)^{-2} = \frac{3}{5^2}$	$\frac{3}{25}$
-1	$3(5)^{-1} = \frac{3}{5^1}$	$\frac{3}{5}$
0	$3(5)^0 = 3(1)$	3
1	$3(5)^1 = 3(5)$	15
2	$3(5)^2 = 3(25)$	75
3	$3(5)^3 = 3(125)$	375

19. $y = \left(\frac{1}{6}\right)^x = (6^{-1})^x = 6^{-x}$

x	*Function*	y
-2	$6^{-(-2)} = 6^2$	36
-1	$6^{-(-1)} = 6^1$	6
0	$6^{-(0)} = 6^0$	1
1	$6^{-(1)} = \frac{1}{6}$	$\frac{1}{6}$
2	$6^{-(2)} = \frac{1}{6^2}$	$\frac{1}{36}$
3	$6^{-(3)} = \frac{1}{6^3}$	$\frac{1}{216}$

20. $y = \left(\frac{2}{3}\right)^x$

x	*Function*	y
-2	$\left(\frac{2}{3}\right)^{-2} = \left(\frac{3}{2}\right)^2 = \frac{3^2}{2^2}$	$\frac{9}{4}$
-1	$\left(\frac{2}{3}\right)^{-1} = \left(\frac{3}{2}\right)^1$	$\frac{3}{2}$
0	$\left(\frac{2}{3}\right)^0$	1
1	$\left(\frac{2}{3}\right)^1$	$\frac{2}{3}$
2	$\left(\frac{2}{3}\right)^2 = \frac{2^2}{3^2}$	$\frac{4}{9}$
3	$\left(\frac{2}{3}\right)^3 = \frac{2^3}{3^3}$	$\frac{8}{27}$

21. $y = 2\left(\frac{1}{7}\right)^x = 2(7^{-1})^x = 2(7^{-x})$

x	*Function*	y
-2	$2(7^{-(-2)}) = 2(7^2) = 2 \cdot 49$	98
-1	$2(7^{-(-1)}) = 2(7^1) = 2 \cdot 7$	14
0	$2(7^{-(0)}) = 2(7^0) = 2 \cdot 1$	2
1	$2(7^{-(1)}) = 2\left(\frac{1}{7}\right)$	$\frac{2}{7}$
2	$2(7^{-(2)}) = 2\left(\frac{1}{7^2}\right) = 2\left(\frac{1}{49}\right)$	$\frac{2}{49}$
3	$2(7^{-(-3)}) = 2\left(\frac{1}{7^2}\right) = 2\left(\frac{1}{343}\right)$	$\frac{2}{343}$

Copyright © McDougal Littell Inc.
All rights reserved.

22. $y = 5\left(\frac{4}{5}\right)^x$

x	*Function*	y
-2	$5\left(\frac{4}{5}\right)^{-2} = 5\left(\frac{5}{4}\right)^2 = 5\left(\frac{5^2}{4^2}\right) = \frac{5^3}{4^2}$	$\frac{125}{16}$
-1	$5\left(\frac{4}{5}\right)^{-1} = 5\left(\frac{5}{4}\right) = \frac{25}{4}$	$\frac{25}{4}$
0	$5\left(\frac{4}{5}\right)^0 = 5(1)$	5
1	$5\left(\frac{4}{5}\right)^1 = 5\left(\frac{4}{5}\right)$	4
2	$5\left(\frac{4}{5}\right)^2 = 5\left(\frac{4^2}{5^2}\right) = \frac{4^2}{5}$	$\frac{16}{5}$
3	$5\left(\frac{4}{5}\right)^3 = 5\left(\frac{4^3}{5^3}\right) = \frac{4^3}{5^2}$	$\frac{64}{25}$

23. $y = 5^x = 5^{2.5} \approx 55.90$

24. $y = 9^x = 9^{2.5} = 243$

25. $y = 8(2)^x = 8(2)^{2.5} \approx 45.25$

26. $y = 3(4)^x = 3(4)^{2.5} = 96$

27. $y = \left(\frac{1}{9}\right)^x = \left(\frac{1}{9}\right)^{2.5} \approx 0.00$

28. $y = \left(\frac{5}{8}\right)^x = \left(\frac{5}{8}\right)^{2.5} \approx 0.31$

29. $y = 6\left(\frac{1}{2}\right)^x = 6\left(\frac{1}{2}\right)^{2.5} \approx 1.06$

30. $y = -\left(\frac{3}{5}\right)^x = -\left(\frac{3}{5}\right)^{2.5} \approx -0.28$

31. Let $x = 1$; solve for y.

$y = 3^x = 3^1 = 3$; $(1, 3)$
The graph with the point $(1, 3)$ is B.

32. Let $x = 1$; solve for y.

$y = 2^x = 2^1 = 2$; $(1, 2)$
The graph with the point $(1, 2)$ is C.

33. Let $x = 1$; solve for y.

$y = 9^x = 9^1 = 9$; $(1, 9)$
The graph with the point $(1, 9)$ is A.

34. $y = 4^x$

x	-2	-1	0	1	2	3
y	$\frac{1}{16}$	$\frac{1}{4}$	1	4	16	64

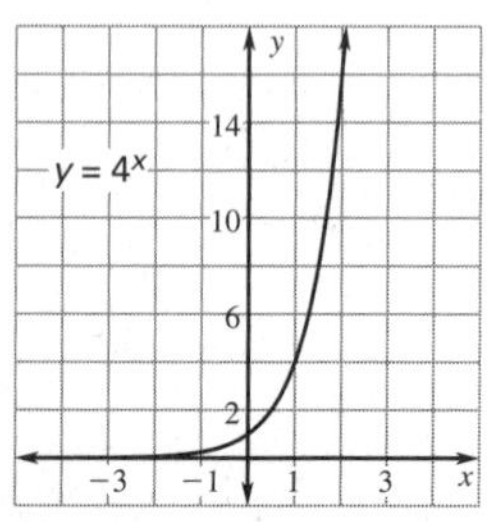

35. $y = -7^x$

x	-2	-1	0	1	2	3
y	$-\frac{1}{49}$	$-\frac{1}{7}$	-1	-7	-49	-343

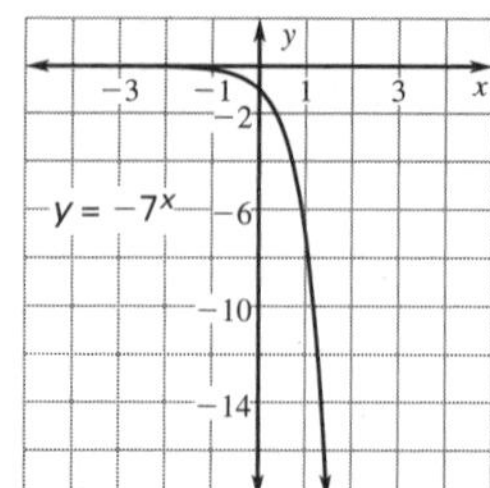

36. $y = 4(2)^x$

x	-2	-1	0	1	2	3
y	1	2	4	8	16	32

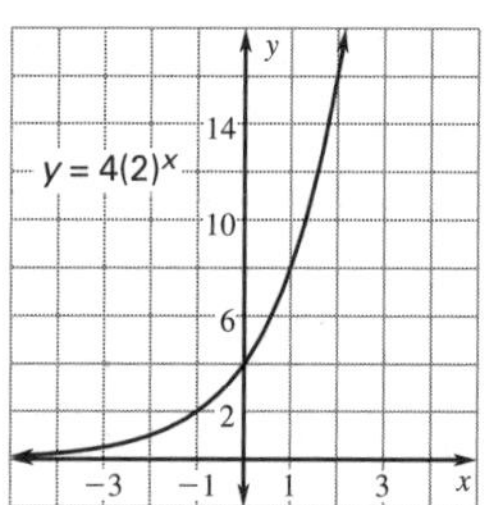

37. $y = -3(8)^x$

x	-2	-1	0	1	2	3
y	$-\frac{3}{64}$	$-\frac{3}{8}$	-3	-24	-192	-1536

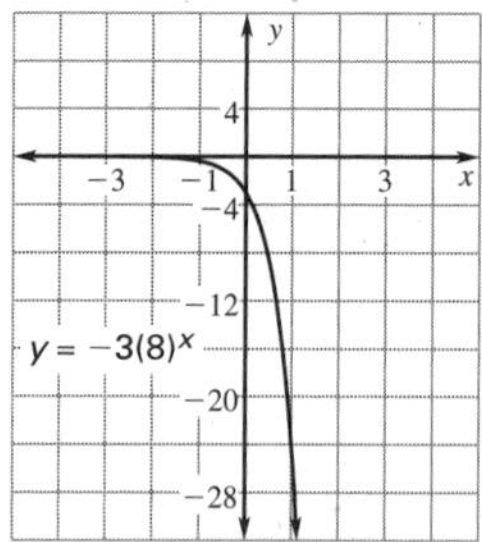

38. $y = \left(\frac{1}{2}\right)^x$

x	-2	-1	0	1	2	3
y	4	2	1	$\frac{1}{2}$	$\frac{1}{4}$	$\frac{1}{8}$

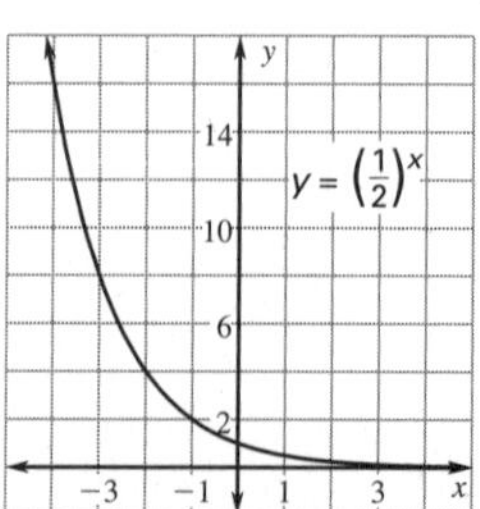

Copyright © McDougal Littell Inc.
All rights reserved.

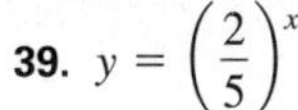

39. $y = \left(\frac{2}{5}\right)^x$

x	-2	-1	0	1	2	3
y	$\frac{25}{4}$	$\frac{5}{2}$	1	$\frac{2}{5}$	$\frac{4}{25}$	$\frac{8}{125}$

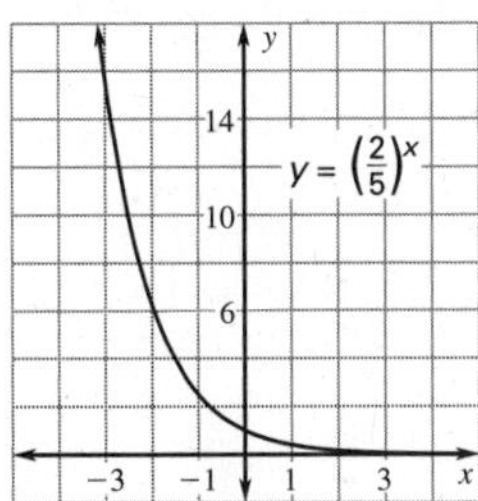

40. $y = -5\left(\frac{1}{5}\right)^x$

$= -5(5^{-1})^x$

$= -5(5^{-x})$

$= -5^1 \cdot 5^{-x}$

$= -5^{1+(-x)} = -5^{1-x}$

x	*Function*	y
-2	$-5^{-1-(-2)} = -5^{1+2} = -5^3$	-125
-1	$-5^{1-(-1)} = -5^{1+1} = -5^2$	-25
0	$-5^{1-(0)} = -5^1$	-5
1	$-5^{1-1} = -5^0 = -(1)$	-1
2	$-5^{1-2} = -5^{-1} = -\frac{1}{5}$	$-\frac{1}{5}$
3	$-5^{1-3} = -5^{-2} = -\frac{1}{5^2}$	$-\frac{1}{25}$

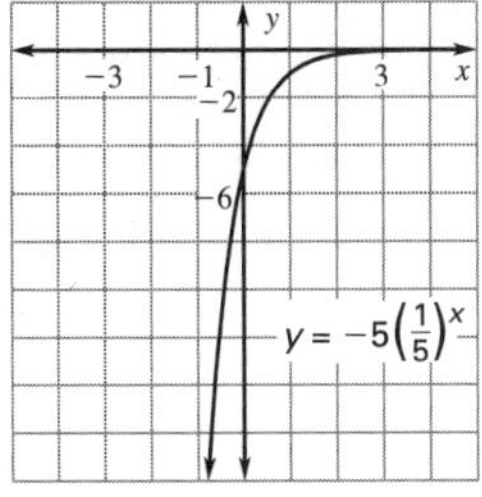

41. $y = 2\left(\frac{2}{3}\right)^x$

x	*Function*	y
-2	$2\left(\frac{2}{3}\right)^{-2} = 2\left(\frac{3}{2}\right)^2 = 2\left(\frac{3^2}{2^2}\right) = \frac{3^2}{2}$	$\frac{9}{2}$
-1	$2\left(\frac{2}{3}\right)^{-1} = 2\left(\frac{3}{2}\right) = 3$	3
0	$2\left(\frac{2}{3}\right)^0 = 2(1)$	2
1	$2\left(\frac{2}{3}\right)^1 = \frac{4}{3}$	$\frac{4}{3}$
2	$2\left(\frac{2}{3}\right)^2 = 2\left(\frac{2^2}{3^2}\right) = \frac{2^3}{3^2}$	$\frac{8}{9}$
3	$2\left(\frac{2}{3}\right)^3 = 2\left(\frac{2^3}{3^3}\right) = \frac{2^4}{3^3}$	$\frac{16}{27}$

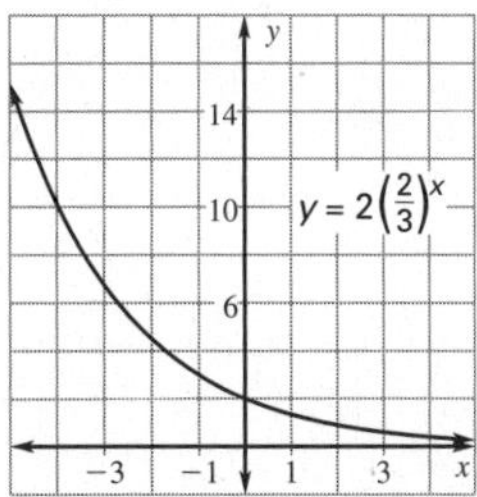

42. Domain: all real numbers
Range: all positive real numbers

43. Domain: all real numbers
Range: all negative real numbers

44. Domain: all real numbers
Range: all positive real numbers

45. Domain: all real numbers
Range: all negative real numbers

46. Domain: all real numbers
Range: all positive real numbers

47. Domain: all real numbers
Range: all positive real numbers

48. Domain: all real numbers
Range: all negative real numbers

49. Domain: all real numbers
Range: all positive real numbers

50. $S = 38{,}000(1.05)^t$

Year	t	*Function*	S
1995	-5	$38{,}000(1.05)^{-5}$	29,774
2000	0	$38{,}000(1.05)^0$	38,000
2005	5	$38{,}000(1.05)^5$	48,499
2010	10	$38{,}000(1.05)^{10}$	61,898

Copyright © McDougal Littell Inc.
All rights reserved.

50. ***continued***

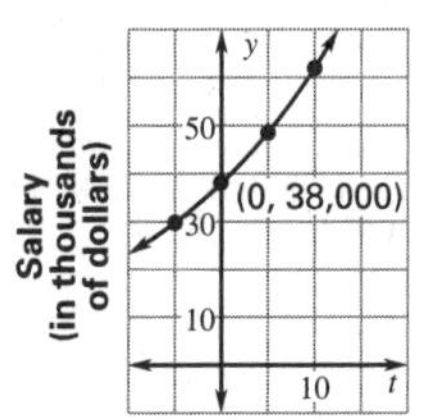

51. $U = 135(1.5)^t$

Year	*t*	*Function*	*U*
1995	-5	$135(1.5)^{-5}$	17.8
2000	0	$135(1.5)^0$	135
2005	5	$135(1.5)^5$	1025.2
2010	10	$135(1.5)^{10}$	7784.8

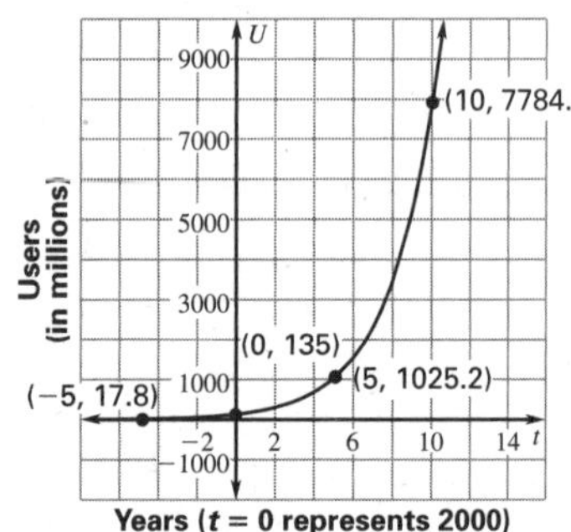

52. $y = a^x$ graphs have the common point $(0, 1)$;

$y = 2(a)^x$ have the common point $(0, 2)$ since $y = 2(a)^0 = 2 \cdot 1 = 2$.

8.3 Standardized Test Practice (p. 459)

53. When $x = 0$, $y = 2$ matches B or D;
When $x = 1$, $y = 4$ matches B.
The answer is $y = 2(2)^x$; B

54. When $x = 0$, $y = 1$ matches F or H;
When $x = -1$, $y = 2$ matches H.

$$y = \left(\frac{1}{2}\right)^x = \left(\frac{1}{2}\right)^{-1} = \left(\frac{2}{1}\right) = 2.$$

The answer is $y = \left(\frac{1}{2}\right)^x$; H

8.3 Mixed Review (p. 460)

55. $8x + 9 = 12$
$8x = 3$
$x = \frac{3}{8} \approx 0.38$
Check: $8(0.38) + 9 = 12.04 \approx 12$

56. $3y - 5 = 11$
$3y = 16$
$y = \frac{16}{3} \approx 5.33$
Check: $3(5.33) - 5 = 10.99 \approx 11$

57. $13t + 8 = 2$
$13t = -6$
$t = -\frac{6}{13} \approx -0.46$
Check: $13(-0.46) + 8 = 2.02 \approx 2$

58. $14 - 6r = -17$
$-6r = -31$
$r = \frac{31}{6} \approx 5.17$
Check: $14 - 6(5.17) = -17.02 \approx -17$

59. $11k + 12 = -9$
$11k = -21$
$k = -\frac{21}{11} \approx -1.91$
Check: $11(-1.91) + 12 = -9.01 \approx -9$

60. $-7x - 7 = -6$
$-7x = 1$
$x = -\frac{1}{7} \approx -0.14$
Check: $-7(-0.14) - 7 = -6.02 \approx -6$

61. $y = -8x + 4$
$8x + y = 4$

62. $y = 5x - 2$
$-5x + y = -2$ or $5x - y = 2$

63. $y = \frac{7}{8}x$
$8y = 7x$
$-7x + 8y = 0$ or $7x - 8y = 0$

64. $y = -\frac{2}{5}x$
$5y = -2x$
$2x + 5y = 0$

65. $y = -\frac{3}{16}x + \frac{9}{16}$
$16y = -3x + 9$
$3x + 16y = 9$

66. $y = \frac{1}{10}x - \frac{9}{10}$
$10y = x - 9$
$-x + 10y = -9$ or $x - 10y = 9$

Copyright © McDougal Littell Inc.
All rights reserved.

67. $2x - 2y = 4$

$-2y = -2x + 4$

$y = x - 2; m = 1; b = -2$

$x + 3y = 9$

$3y = -x + 9$

$y = -\frac{1}{3}x + 3; m = -\frac{1}{3}; b = 3$

one solution

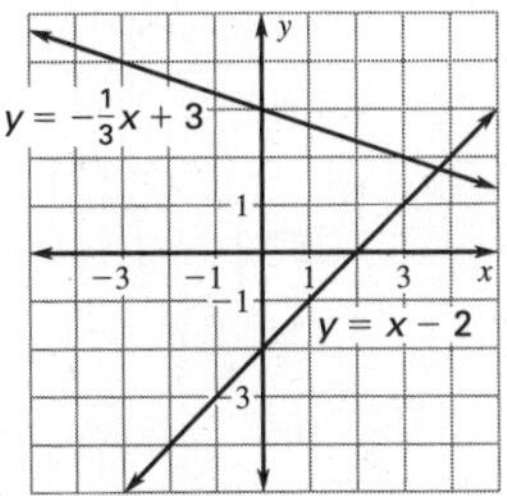

68. $-x + y = -1$

$y = x - 1; m = 1; b = -1$

$2x + 3y = 12$

$3y = -2x + 12$

$y = -\frac{2}{3}x + 4; m = -\frac{2}{3}; b = 4$

one solution

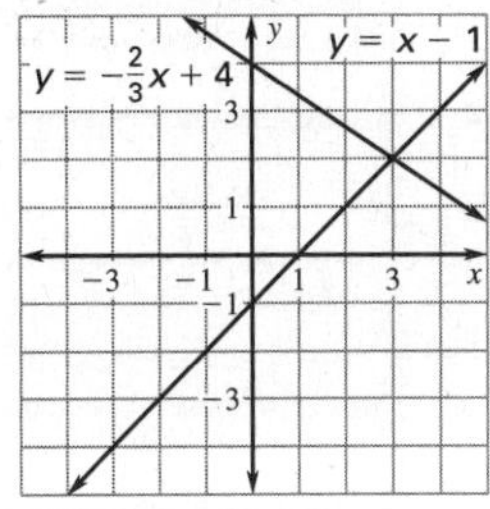

69. $6x + 2y = 3$

$2y = -6x + 3$

$y = -3x + \frac{3}{2}; m = -3; b = \frac{3}{2}$

$3x + y = -2$

$y = -3x - 2; m = -3; b = -2$

no solution

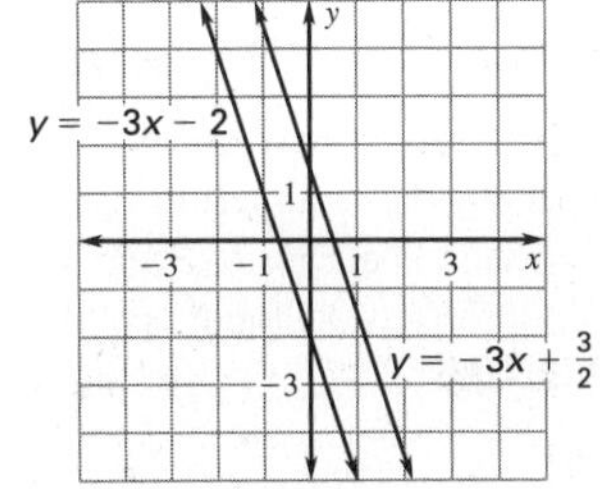

70. $x + y = 0$

$y = -x; m = -1; b = 0$

$x + 2y = 6$

$2y = -x + 6$

$y = -\frac{1}{2}x + 3; m = -\frac{1}{2}; b = 3$

one solution

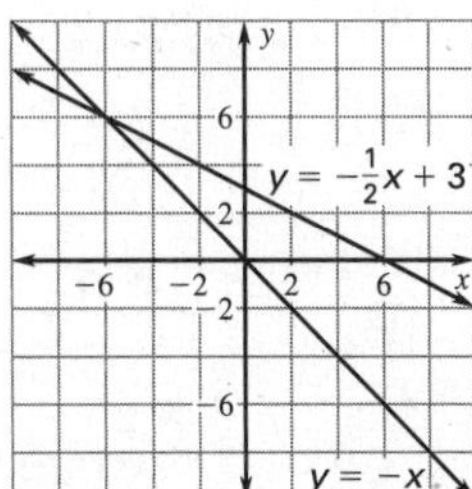

71. $4x - y = -2$

$-y = -4x - 2$

$y = 4x + 2; m = 4; b = 2$

$-12x + 3y = 6$

$3y = 12x + 6$

$y = 4x + 2; m = 4; b = 2$

infinitely many solutions (same line)

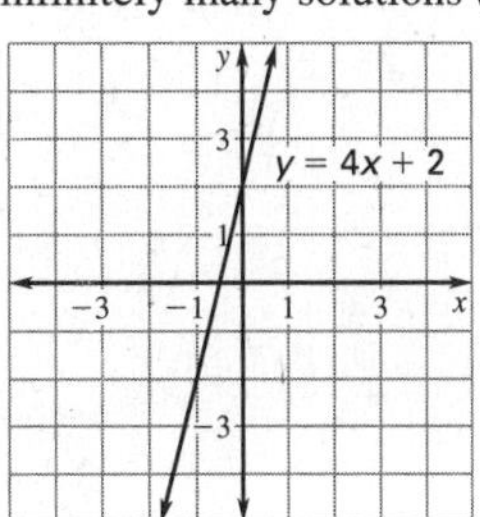

72. $-x + 3y = 3$

$3y = x + 3$

$y = \frac{1}{3}x + 1; m = \frac{1}{3}; b = 1$

$2x - y = -8$

$-y = -2x - 8$

$y = 2x + 8; m = 2; b = 8$

one solution

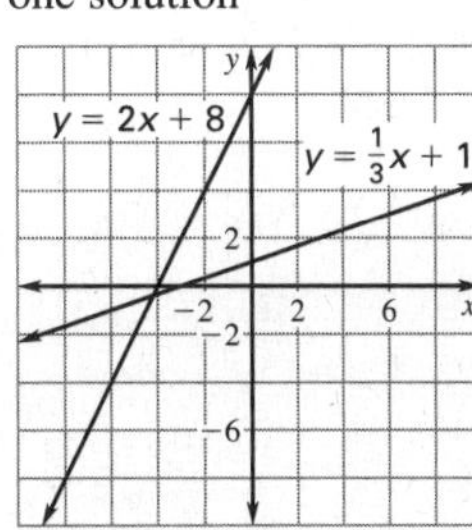

8.3 Maintaining Skills (p. 460)

73. $-5, -4, 6$

74. $\frac{4}{8} = \frac{1}{2} = 0.5, \frac{3}{5} = 0.6, \frac{5}{7} \approx 0.7$

75. $-3\frac{4}{5}, -2\frac{3}{4}, -2\frac{1}{5}$

Copyright © McDougal Littell Inc.
All rights reserved.

76. $-6.9, -6.57, -6.56$

77. $3.001, 3.01, 3.25$

78. $7.09, 7.9, 7.99$

Quiz 1 *(p. 460)*

1. $3^4 \cdot 3^6 = 3^{10} = 59{,}049$
2. $(2^3)^2 = 2^6 = 64$
3. $(8 \cdot 5)^2 = 8^2 \cdot 5^2 = 64 \cdot 25 = 1600$
4. $6^{-7} \cdot 6^9 = 6^2 = 36$
5. $(5^2)^{-1} = 5^{-2} = \frac{1}{5^2} = \frac{1}{25}$
6. $(4 \cdot 9)^0 = 1$
7. $r^5 \cdot r^8 = r^{13}$
8. $(k^4)^2 = k^8$
9. $(3d)^2 = 3^2d^2 = 9d^2$
10. $2x^{-3}y^{-9} = \frac{2}{x^3y^9}$
11. $\frac{1}{5a^{-10}b^{-12}} = \frac{a^{10}b^{12}}{5}$
12. $(mn)^{-7} = \frac{1}{m^7n^7}$
13. In 1994, $t = -6$
    $A = 1600(1.08)^{-6} \approx 1008$; about \$1008
    In 2004, $t = 4$
    $A = 1600(1.08)^4 \approx 2177$; about \$2177
14. $y = 10^x$

x	-2	-1	0	1	2	3
y	$\frac{1}{100}$	$\frac{1}{10}$	1	10	100	1000

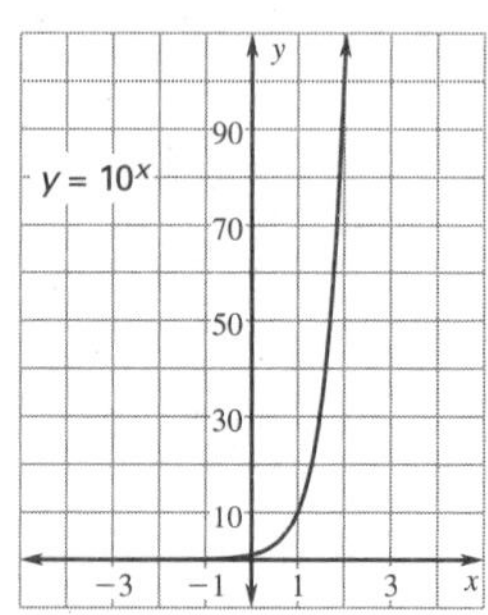

15. $y = 3(2)^x$

x	-2	-1	0	1	2	3
y	$\frac{3}{4}$	$\frac{3}{2}$	3	6	12	24

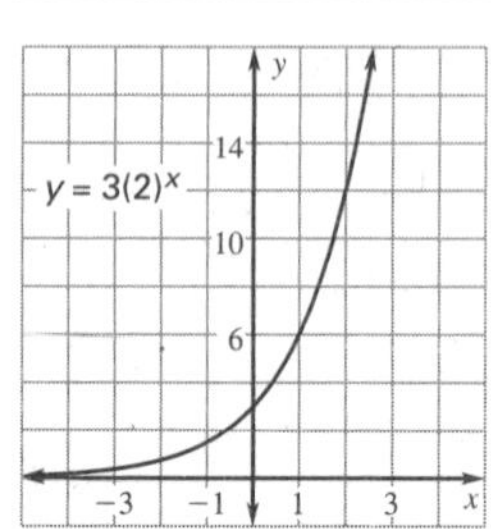

16. $y = 4\left(\frac{2}{3}\right)^x$

x	-2	-1	0	1	2	3
y	9	6	4	$\frac{8}{3}$	$\frac{16}{9}$	$\frac{32}{27}$

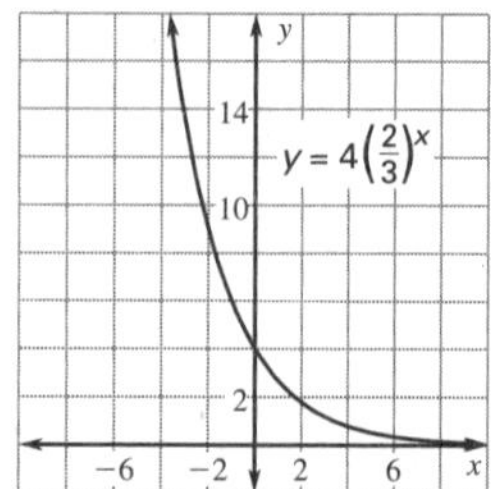

8.3 Using a Graphing Calculator: Try These
(p. 461)

1.
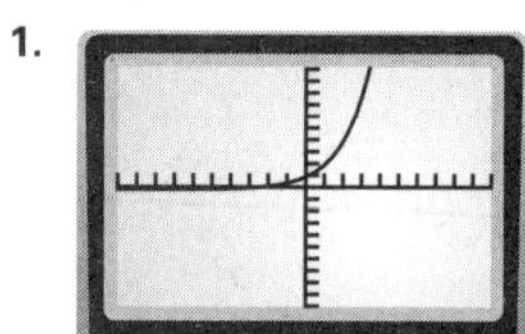

2.
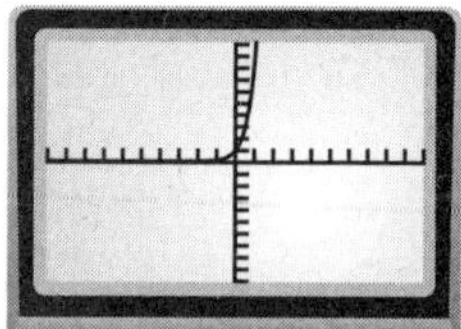

3.
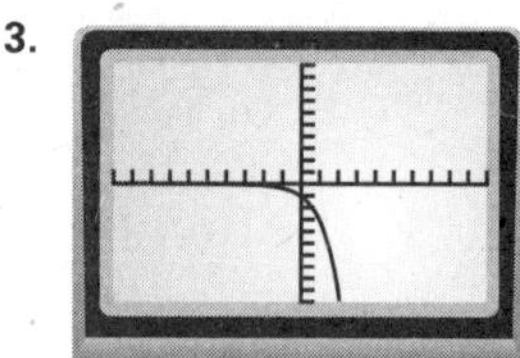

4.
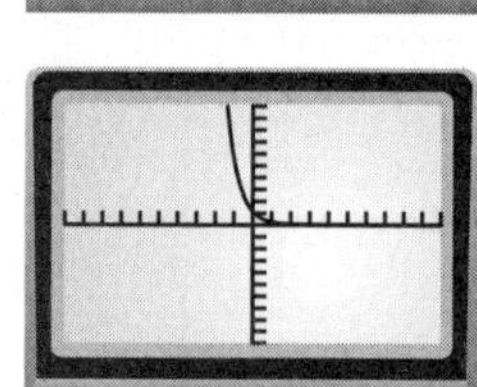

5.
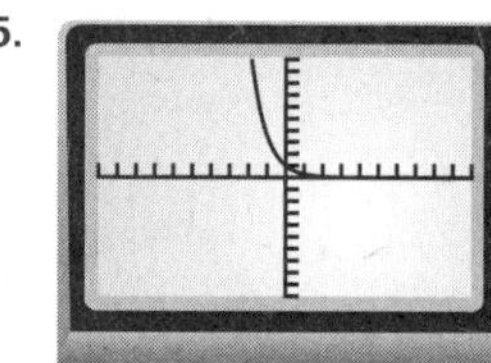

6.
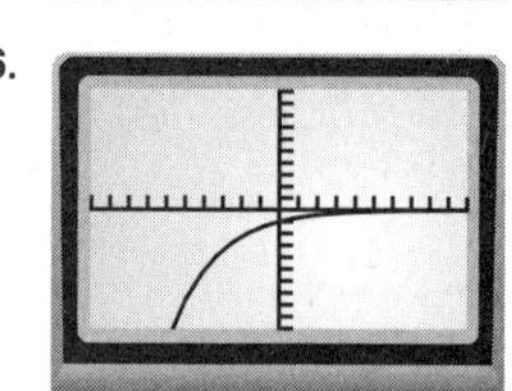

7. The graph of $y = a^x$ is increasing from left to right, contains the point (0, 1); the range is all positive real numbers. The graph of $y = -a^x$ looks like the graph of $y = a^x$ reflected over the x-axis.
8. The graph of $y = a^x$ is decreasing from left to right, contains the point (0, 1); the range is all positive real numbers. The graph of $y = -a^x$ looks like the graph of $y = a^x$ reflected over the x-axis.

Lesson 8.4

8.4 Checkpoint (pp. 462–464)

1. $\frac{8^4}{8^6} = 8^{4-6} = 8^{-2} = \frac{1}{8^2} = \frac{1}{64}$
2. $\frac{(-3)^3}{(-3)^2} = (-3)^{3-2} = (-3)^1 = -3$

Copyright © McDougal Littell Inc.
All rights reserved.

3. $\frac{x^4}{x^4} = x^{4-4} = x^0 = 1$ (where $x \neq 0$)

4. $\frac{a^9}{a^5} = a^{9-5} = a^4$

5. $\left(\frac{5}{4}\right)^3 = \frac{5^3}{4^3} = \frac{125}{64}$

6. $\left(-\frac{x}{2}\right)^4 = \frac{(-x)^4}{2^4} = \frac{(-x)^4}{16} = \frac{x^4}{16}$

7. $\left(\frac{3}{5}\right)^{-2} = \frac{3^{-2}}{5^{-2}} = \frac{5^2}{3^2} = \frac{25}{9}$

8. $\left(\frac{1}{x}\right)^{-5} = x^5$

9. $\frac{3xy^4}{x^3} \cdot \frac{y}{xy^3} = \frac{3xy^5}{x^4y^3}$
$= 3x^{-3}y^2$
$= \frac{3y^2}{x^3}$

10. $\left(\frac{5x}{y^3}\right)^3 = \frac{5^3x^3}{y^{3 \cdot 3}} = \frac{5^3x^3}{y^9} = \frac{125x^3}{y^9}$

11. $\frac{y^{-2}}{x^2} \cdot \left(\frac{x^4}{y}\right)^{-1} = \frac{1}{x^2 \cdot y^2} \cdot \frac{x^{-4}}{y^{-1}}$
$= \frac{1}{x^2y^2} \cdot \frac{y}{x^4}$
$= \frac{y}{x^{2+4}y^2}$
$= \frac{y^{1-2}}{x^6}$
$= \frac{y^{-1}}{x^6} = \frac{1}{x^6y}$

8.4 Guided Practice (p. 465)

1. B; Quotient of powers; $\frac{4^3}{4^5} = 4^{3-5}$

2. A; Power of a quotient; $\left(\frac{3}{6}\right)^2 = \frac{3^2}{6^2}$

3. $\frac{5^4}{5^1} = 5^{4-1} = 5^3 = 125$

4. $\frac{7^6}{7^9} = 7^{6-9} = 7^{-3} = \frac{1}{7^3} = \frac{1}{343}$

5. $\frac{(-2)^8}{(-2)^3} = (-2)^{8-3} = (-2)^5 = -32$

6. $\frac{5^3 \cdot 5^5}{5^9} = \frac{5^8}{5^9} = 5^{8-9} = 5^{-1} = \frac{1}{5}$

7. $\frac{x^{12}}{x^9} = x^{12-9} = x^3$

8. $\frac{a^5}{a^2} = a^{5-2} = a^3$

9. $\frac{m^5}{m^{11}} = m^{5-11} = m^{-6} = \frac{1}{m^6}$

10. $\frac{x^7 \cdot x}{x^2} = \frac{x^8}{x^2} = x^{8-2} = x^6$

11. $\left(\frac{1}{2}\right)^5 = \frac{1^5}{2^5} = \frac{1}{32}$

12. $\left(\frac{3}{5}\right)^3 = \frac{3^3}{5^3} = \frac{27}{125}$

13. $\left(\frac{-4}{3}\right)^4 = \frac{(-4)^4}{3^4} = \frac{256}{81}$

14. $\left(\frac{5}{4}\right)^{-3} = \frac{5^{-3}}{4^{-3}} = \frac{4^3}{5^3} = \frac{64}{125}$

15. $\left(\frac{-5}{m}\right)^2 = \frac{(-5)^2}{m^2} = \frac{25}{m^2}$

16. $\left(\frac{x}{y}\right)^6 = \frac{x^6}{y^6}$

17. $\left(\frac{m^3}{n^5}\right)^2 = \frac{m^{3 \cdot 2}}{n^{5 \cdot 2}} = \frac{m^6}{n^{10}}$

18. $\left(\frac{a^6}{b^9}\right)^{-5} = \frac{a^{-30}}{b^{-45}} = \frac{b^{45}}{a^{30}}$

8.4 Practice and Applications (pp. 465–468)

19. $\frac{3^9}{3^5} = 3^4$

20. $\frac{7^6}{7^2} = 7^4$

21. $\frac{9^5}{9^{11}} = 9^{-6}$

22. $\frac{x^5}{x^3} = x^2$

23. $\frac{a^{10}}{a^4} = a^6$

24. $\frac{w^4}{w} = w^3$

25. $\frac{5^6}{5^3} = 5^{6-3} = 5^3 = 125$

26. $\frac{8^2}{8^3} = 8^{2-3} = 8^{-1} = \frac{1}{8}$

27. $\frac{(-3)^6}{(-3)^6} = (-3)^{6-6} = (-3)^0 = 1$

28. $\frac{6^3 \cdot 6^2}{6^5} = \frac{6^5}{6^5} = 6^{5-5} = 6^0 = 1$

29. $\frac{x^4}{x^5} = x^{4-5} = x^{-1} = \frac{1}{x}$

30. $x^3 \cdot \frac{1}{x^2} = x^{3-2} = x^1 = x$

31. $\frac{1}{x^8} \cdot x^5 = x^{5-8} = x^{-3} = \frac{1}{x^3}$

32. $\frac{x^3 \cdot x^5}{x^2} = \frac{x^8}{x^2} = x^{8-2} = x^6$

33. $\left(\frac{1}{6}\right)^4 = \frac{1}{6^4} = \frac{1}{1296}$

34. $\left(\frac{-3}{5}\right)^2 = \frac{9}{25}$

35. $\left(\frac{2}{7}\right)^3 = \frac{8}{343}$

36. $\left(\frac{x}{y}\right)^{-2} = \frac{y^2}{x^2}$

37. $\left(\frac{a^2}{b}\right)^5 = \frac{a^{10}}{b^5}$

38. $\left(\frac{m^3}{n^2}\right)^4 = \frac{m^{12}}{n^8}$

39. $\left(\frac{1}{5}\right)^4 = \frac{1}{625}$

40. $\left(\frac{3}{4}\right)^2 = \frac{9}{16}$

41. $\left(-\frac{2}{3}\right)^3 = -\frac{8}{27}$

42. $\left(\frac{9}{6}\right)^{-1} = \frac{6}{9} = \frac{2}{3}$

43. $\left(\frac{3}{x}\right)^4 = \frac{81}{x^4}$

44. $\left(-\frac{x}{2}\right)^3 = -\frac{x^3}{8}$

45. $\left(\frac{x}{y}\right)^5 = \frac{x^5}{y^5}$

46. $\left(\frac{8}{x}\right)^{-2} = \frac{x^2}{64}$

Copyright © McDougal Littell Inc.
All rights reserved.

47. Raise the 6 to the power of 3;

$$\left(\frac{6a}{b^2}\right)^3 = \frac{6^3a^3}{b^{2\cdot3}} = \frac{216a^3}{b^6}$$

48. Subtract the y-exponents;

$$\frac{5x^2}{y^4} \cdot xy^3 = \frac{5x^3y^3}{y^4} = 5x^3y^{-1} = \frac{5x^3}{y}$$

49. $$\frac{4x^3y^3}{2xy} \cdot \frac{5xy^2}{2y} = \frac{20x^4y^5}{4xy^2} = 5x^3y^3$$

50. $$\frac{16x^3y}{-4xy^3} \cdot \frac{-2xy}{x} = \frac{-32x^4y^2}{-4x^2y^3} = 8x^2y^{-1} = \frac{8x^2}{y}$$

51. $$\frac{36a^8b^2}{ab} \cdot \frac{ab^2}{6} = \frac{36a^9b^4}{6ab} = 6a^8b^3$$

52. $$\left(\frac{2m^3n^4}{3mn}\right)^3 = \frac{2^3m^{3\cdot3}n^{4\cdot3}}{3^3m^3n^3} = \frac{8m^9n^{12}}{27m^3n^3} = \frac{8m^6n^9}{27}$$

53. $$\frac{6x^2y^2}{xy^3} \cdot \frac{(4x^2y)^2}{xy^2} = \frac{6x^2y^2 \cdot 4^2x^4y^2}{x^2y^5} = \frac{6 \cdot 16 \cdot x^6y^4}{x^2y^5} = 96x^4y^{-1} = \frac{96x^4}{y}$$

54. $$\frac{16x^5y^8}{x^7y^4} \cdot \left(\frac{x^3y^2}{8xy}\right)^4 = \frac{16x^5y^8}{x^7y^4} \cdot \frac{x^{12}y^8}{8^4x^4y^4} = \frac{16x^{17}y^{16}}{4096x^{11}y^8} = \frac{x^6y^8}{256}$$

55. $$\frac{x^2}{xy^{-4}} \cdot \frac{2x^{-3}y^4}{3xy^{-1}} = xy^4 \cdot \frac{2x^{-4}y^5}{3} = xy^4 \cdot \frac{2y^5}{3x^4} = \frac{2xy^9}{3x^4} = \frac{2x^{-3}y^9}{3} = \frac{2y^9}{3x^3}$$

56. $$\frac{5x^{-3}y^2}{x^5y^{-1}} \cdot \frac{(2xy^3)^{-2}}{xy} = 5x^{-8}y^3 \cdot \frac{2^{-2}x^{-2}y^{-6}}{xy} = \frac{5x^{-10}y^{-3}}{2^2xy} = \frac{5x^{-11}y^{-4}}{4} = \frac{5}{4x^{11}y^4}$$

57. $$\frac{4xy}{2x^{-1}y^{-3}} \cdot \left(\frac{2xy^2}{3xy}\right)^{-2} = \frac{4x^2y^4}{2} \cdot \frac{2^{-2}x^{-2}y^{-4}}{3^{-2}x^{-2}y^{-2}} = 2x^2y^4 \cdot \frac{3^2x^2y^2}{2^2x^2y^4} = \frac{2 \cdot 9 \cdot x^4y^6}{4 \cdot x^2 \cdot y^4} = \frac{9x^2y^2}{2}$$

58. In 1998, $t = 4$; in 1995, $t = 1$.

$$\frac{\text{1998 sales}}{\text{1995 sales}} = \frac{3723(\frac{6}{5})^4}{3723(\frac{6}{5})^1} = \left(\frac{6}{5}\right)^{4-1} = \left(\frac{6}{5}\right)^3 = \frac{6^3}{5^3} = \frac{216}{125} = 1.728$$

59. In 1985, $t = 5$; in 1990, $t = 10$.

$$\frac{\text{1985 salaries}}{\text{1990 salaries}} = \frac{136(1.18)^5}{136(1.18)^{10}} = (1.18)^{5-10} = (1.18)^{-5} \approx 0.437$$

60. $$\frac{\text{Weight of 5 yr old}}{\text{Weight of 2 yr old}} = \frac{1.21(1.42)^5}{1.21(1.42)^2} = (1.42)^{5-2} = (1.42)^3 \approx 2.863$$

61. $S = 200\left(\frac{4}{5}\right)^n$

Weeks n	0	1	2	3	4	5	6
Words S	200	160	128	102	82	66	52

62.

$a^0 = a^{n-n}$	Substitution property of equality
$= \frac{a^n}{a^n}$	Quotient of powers property
$= 1$	Canceling a common factor

63.

$a^{-n} = a^{n-2n}$	Substitution property of equality
$= \frac{a^n}{a^{2n}}$	Quotient of powers property
$= \frac{a^n}{a^n \cdot a^n}$	Product of powers property
$= \frac{1}{a^n}$	Canceling a common factor

64. 1 sheet: 0.0032 in.
Doubled once; 2 sheets: 2(0.0032) in.
Doubled twice; 4 sheets: $2[2(0.0032) \text{ in.}] = 2^2(0.0032)$
Doubled 3 times; 8 sheets: $2[2^2(0.0032)] = 2^3(0.0032)$
Doubled 25 times;
thickness $= 2^{25}(0.0032) \approx 107{,}374.18$ in. ≈ 8948 ft

Copyright © McDougal Littell Inc.
All rights reserved.

8.4 Standardized Test Practice (p. 468)

65. B; $\frac{x^{-9}}{x^{-3}} = x^{-9-(-3)} = x^{-6} = \frac{1}{x^6}$

66. J; $\left(\frac{2}{9}\right)^{-3} = \frac{2^{-3}}{9^{-3}} = \frac{9^3}{2^3} = \frac{729}{8}$

67. D; $\frac{4x^3y}{18x^2} \cdot \frac{9}{16x^2y} = \frac{36x^3y}{288x^4y} = \frac{x^{-1}}{8} = \frac{1}{8x}$

68. G; $\frac{x^{-2}}{y^{-3}} \cdot \left(\frac{x}{y}\right)^{-1} = \frac{y^3}{x^2} \cdot \frac{y}{x} = \frac{y^4}{x^3}$

8.4 Mixed Review (p. 468)

69. $10^5 = 100{,}000$

70. $10^1 = 10$

71. $10^0 = 1$

72. $10^{-4} = \frac{1}{10^4} = \frac{1}{10{,}000} = 0.0001$

73. $m = \frac{6-2}{4-(-4)} = \frac{4}{8} = \frac{1}{2}$

$y - 6 = \frac{1}{2}(x - 4)$

$y - 6 = \frac{1}{2}x - 2$

$y = \frac{1}{2}x + 4$

74. $m = \frac{3-(-5)}{0-(-4)} = \frac{8}{4} = 2$

$y - 3 = 2(x - 0)$

$y - 3 = 2x$

$y = 2x + 3$

75. $m = \frac{-11-(-7)}{3-(-1)} = \frac{-4}{4} = -1$

$y - (-7) = -1[x - (-1)]$

$y + 7 = -1(x + 1)$

$y + 7 = -x - 1$

$y = -x - 8$

76. $m = \frac{-3-9}{1-3} = \frac{-12}{-2} = 6$

$y - 9 = 6(x - 3)$

$y - 9 = 6x - 18$

$y = 6x - 9$

77. $m = \frac{7-(-2)}{-4-5} = \frac{9}{-9} = -1$

$y - (-2) = -1(x - 5)$

$y + 2 = -x + 5$

$y = -x + 3$

78. $m = \frac{-2-8}{-4-1} = \frac{-10}{-5} = 2$

$y - 8 = 2(x - 1)$

$y - 8 = 2x - 2$

$y = 2x + 6$

79. $2(-3) + 4(2) \stackrel{?}{=} 2$

$-6 + 8 \stackrel{?}{=} 2$

$2 = 2$

$-(-3) + 5(2) \stackrel{?}{=} 13$

$3 + 10 \stackrel{?}{=} 13$

$13 = 13$

A solution

80. $3(3) - 4(1) \stackrel{?}{=} 5$

$9 - 4 \stackrel{?}{=} 5$

$5 = 5$

$3 + 6(1) \stackrel{?}{=} 8$

$3 + 6 \stackrel{?}{=} 8$

$9 \neq 8$

Not a solution

81. $8(1) + 4(-1) \stackrel{?}{=} 6$

$8 - 4 \stackrel{?}{=} 6$

$4 \neq 6$

Not a solution

82. $4 - 5(-1) \stackrel{?}{=} 9$

$4 + 5 \stackrel{?}{=} 9$

$9 = 9$

$3(4) + 5(-1) \stackrel{?}{=} 11$

$12 - 5 \stackrel{?}{=} 11$

$7 \neq 11$

Not a solution

83. $x - y = 4$

$\underline{x + y = 12}$

$2x = 16$

$x = 8$

$8 + y = 12$

$y = 4$

Solution: (8, 4)

Check:

$8 - 4 \stackrel{?}{=} 4$ $\quad$ $8 + 4 \stackrel{?}{=} 12$

$4 = 4$ $\quad$ $12 = 12$

84. $-p + 2q = 12$

$\underline{p + 6q = 20}$

$8q = 32$

$q = 4$

$p + 6(4) = 20$

$p + 24 = 20$

$p = -4$

Solution: $(-4, 4)$

Check:

$-(-4) + 2(4) \stackrel{?}{=} 12$ $\quad$ $-4 + 6(4) \stackrel{?}{=} 20$

$4 + 8 \stackrel{?}{=} 12$ $\quad$ $-4 + 24 \stackrel{?}{=} 20$

$12 = 12$ $\quad$ $20 = 20$

Copyright © McDougal Littell Inc.
All rights reserved.

85.
$$\begin{aligned} 2a + 3b &= 17 \\ 3a + 4b &= 24 \\ -6a - 9b &= -51 && \text{Multiply by } -3. \\ 6a + 8b &= 48 && \text{Multiply by } 2. \\ \hline -b &= -3 \\ b &= 3 \\ 2a + 3(3) &= 17 \\ 2a + 9 &= 17 \\ 2a &= 8 \\ a &= 4 \end{aligned}$$

Solution: (4, 3)

Check:

$$\begin{aligned} 2(4) + 3(3) &\stackrel{?}{=} 17 & 3(4) + 4(3) &\stackrel{?}{=} 24 \\ 8 + 9 &\stackrel{?}{=} 17 & 12 + 12 &\stackrel{?}{=} 24 \\ 17 &= 17 & 24 &= 24 \end{aligned}$$

86.
$$\begin{aligned} 2m + 3n &= 7 \\ m + n &= 1 \\ 2m + 3n &= 7 \\ -2m - 2n &= -2 && \text{Multiply by } -2. \\ \hline n &= 5 \\ m + 5 &= 1 \\ m &= -4 \end{aligned}$$

Solution: $(-4, 5)$

Check:

$$\begin{aligned} 2(-4) + 3(5) &\stackrel{?}{=} 7 & -4 + 5 &\stackrel{?}{=} 1 \\ -8 + 15 &\stackrel{?}{=} 7 & 1 &= 1 \\ 7 &= 7 \end{aligned}$$

87.
$$\begin{aligned} x + 10y &= -1 \\ 2x + 9y &= 9 \\ -2x - 20y &= 2 && \text{Multiply by } -2. \\ 2x + 9y &= 9 \\ \hline -11y &= 11 \\ y &= -1 \\ x + 10(-1) &= -1 \\ x - 10 &= -1 \\ x &= 9 \end{aligned}$$

Solution: $(9, -1)$

Check:

$$\begin{aligned} 9 + 10(-1) &\stackrel{?}{=} -1 & 2(9) + 9(-1) &\stackrel{?}{=} 9 \\ 9 - 10 &\stackrel{?}{=} -1 & 18 - 9 &\stackrel{?}{=} 9 \\ -1 &= -1 & 9 &= 9 \end{aligned}$$

88.
$$\begin{aligned} 8r - 3t &= 2 \\ 2r - 2t &= 3 \\ 8r - 3t &= 2 \\ -8r + 8t &= -12 && \text{Multiply by } -4. \\ \hline 5t &= -10 \\ t &= -2 \\ 8r - 3(-2) &= 2 \\ 8r + 6 &= 2 \\ 8r &= -4 \\ r &= -\frac{1}{2} \end{aligned}$$

Solution: $\left(-\frac{1}{2}, -2\right)$

Check:

$$\begin{aligned} 8\left(-\frac{1}{2}\right) - 3(-2) &\stackrel{?}{=} 2 & 2\left(-\frac{1}{2}\right) - 2(-2) &\stackrel{?}{=} 3 \\ -4 + 6 &\stackrel{?}{=} 2 & -1 + 4 &\stackrel{?}{=} 3 \\ 2 &= 2 & 3 &= 3 \end{aligned}$$

8.4 Maintaining Skills (p. 468)

89-94. Estimates may vary.

89. $287 + 165 \approx 200 + 85 + 100 + 65$
$= 300 + 150$
$= 450$

90. $4672 + 1807 \approx 4000 + 700 + 1000 + 800$
$= 5000 + 1500$
$= 6500$

91. $46.18 + 34.42 \approx 40 + 6.2 + 30 + 4.4$
$= 70 + 10.6$
$= 80.6$

92. $172 - 112 \approx 100 + 70 - (100 + 10)$
$= 100 + 70 - 100 - 10$
$= 60$

93. $4882 - 3117 \approx 4800 + 80 - (3100 + 20)$
$= 4800 + 80 - 3100 - 20$
$= 1760$

94. $3.84 - 1.68 \approx 3 + 0.8 - (1 + 0.7)$
$= 3 + 0.8 - 1 - 0.7$
$= 2.1$

Lesson 8.5

8.5 Checkpoint (pp. 469–471)

1. $2.39 \times 10^4 = 23{,}900$

2. $1.045 \times 10^7 = 10{,}450{,}000$

3. $3.7 \times 10^8 = 370{,}000{,}000$

4. $8.4 \times 10^{-6} = 0.0000084$

5. $1.0 \times 10^{-2} = 0.01$

6. $9.2 \times 10^{-8} = 0.000000092$

7. $423 = 4.23 \times 10^2$

8. $2{,}000{,}000 = 2 \times 10^6$

9. $0.0001 = 1 \times 10^{-4}$

10. $0.0098 = 9.8 \times 10^{-3}$

11. $(2.3 \times 10^3)(1.8 \times 10^{-5}) = (2.3 \times 1.8)(10^3 \times 10^{-5})$
$= 4.14 \times 10^{-2}$

12. $\frac{5.2 \times 10^3}{1.3 \times 10^1} = \frac{5.2}{1.3} \times \frac{10^3}{10^1}$
$= 4 \times 10^2$

13. $(5 \times 10^{-4})^2 = 5^2 \times 10^{-8}$
$= 25 \times 10^{-8}$
$= (2.5 \times 10^1) \times 10^{-8}$
$= 2.5 \times 10^{-7}$

14. $(5.1 \times 10^2)(8 \times 10^{-5}) = 4.08 \times 10^{-2}$ or 0.0408

15. $\frac{8.9 \times 10^0}{6.4 \times 10^{-5}} \approx 1.3906 \times 10^5$ or 139,060

Copyright © McDougal Littell Inc.
All rights reserved.

16. $(1.5 \times 10^6)^{-1} \approx 6.6667 \times 10^{-7}$ or 0.00000066667

17. $\frac{5.6 \times 10^{10} \text{ calls}}{3.1 \times 10^7 \text{ people}} \approx 1.806 \times 10^3$ calls/person or 1806 calls per person

8.5 Guided Practice (p. 472)

1. No; the form must be $c \times 10^n$, where $1 \le c < 10$.

2. $9 \times 10^4 = 90{,}000$ **3.** $4.3 \times 10^2 = 430$

4. $8.11 \times 10^3 = 8110$ **5.** $5 \times 10^{-2} = 0.05$

6. $9.4 \times 10^{-5} = 0.000094$ **7.** $2.45 \times 10^{-1} = 0.245$

8. $15 = 1.5 \times 10^1$ **9.** $6{,}900{,}000 = 6.9 \times 10^6$

10. $39.6 = 3.96 \times 10^1$ **11.** $0.99 = 9.9 \times 10^{-1}$

12. $0.0003 = 3 \times 10^{-4}$ **13.** $0.0205 = 2.05 \times 10^{-2}$

14. $(5 \times 10^6)(6 \times 10^{-2}) = (5 \times 6)(10^6 \times 10^{-2})$
$= 30 \times 10^4$
$= (3 \times 10^1) \times 10^4$
$= 3 \times 10^5$

15. $\frac{1.4 \times 10^{-3}}{7 \times 10^7} = \frac{1.4}{7} \times \frac{10^{-3}}{10^7}$
$= 0.2 \times 10^{-10}$
$= (2 \times 10^{-1}) \times 10^{-10}$
$= 2 \times 10^{-11}$

16. $(9 \times 10^{-9})^2 = 9^2 \times 10^{-18}$
$= 81 \times 10^{-18}$
$= (8.1 \times 10^1) \times 10^{-18}$
$= 8.1 \times 10^{-17}$

8.5 Practice and Applications (pp. 472–474)

17. 1.5×10^2; right 2 places

18. 6.89×10^5; right 5 places

19. 9.04×10^{-7}; left 7 places

20. $5 \times 10^5 = 500{,}000$ **21.** $8 \times 10^3 = 8000$

22. $1 \times 10^6 = 1{,}000{,}000$ **23.** $2.1 \times 10^4 = 21{,}000$

24. $7.75 \times 10^0 = 7.75$

25. $4.33 \times 10^8 = 433{,}000{,}000$

26. $3 \times 10^{-4} = 0.0003$ **27.** $9 \times 10^{-3} = 0.009$

28. $4 \times 10^{-5} = 0.00004$ **29.** $9.8 \times 10^{-2} = 0.098$

30. $6.02 \times 10^{-6} = 0.00000602$

31. $1.1 \times 10^{-10} = 0.00000000011$

32. 0.7×10^2 is not in scientific notation; 7×10^1.

33. 2.9×10^5 is in scientific notation.

34. 10×10^{-3} is not in scientific notation; 1×10^{-2}.

35. $900 = 9 \times 10^2$ **36.** $700{,}000{,}000 = 7 \times 10^8$

37. $88{,}000{,}000 = 8.8 \times 10^7$ **38.** $1012 = 1.012 \times 10^3$

39. $95.2 = 9.52 \times 10^1$ **40.** $370.2 = 3.702 \times 10^2$

41. $0.1 = 1 \times 10^{-1}$ **42.** $0.05 = 5 \times 10^{-2}$

43. $0.000006 = 6 \times 10^{-6}$ **44.** $0.0422 = 4.22 \times 10^{-2}$

45. $0.0085 = 8.5 \times 10^{-3}$ **46.** $0.000459 = 4.59 \times 10^{-4}$

47. $(4.1 \times 10^2)(3 \times 10^6) = (4.1 \times 3)(10^2 \times 10^6)$
$= 12.3 \times 10^8$
$= (1.23 \times 10^1) \times 10^8$
$= 1.23 \times 10^9$

48. $(9 \times 10^{-6})(2 \times 10^4) = (9 \times 2)(10^{-6} \times 10^4)$
$= 18 \times 10^{-2}$
$= (1.8 \times 10^1) \times 10^{-2}$
$= 1.8 \times 10^{-1}$

49. $(6 \times 10^5)(2.5 \times 10^{-1}) = (6 \times 2.5)(10^5 \times 10^{-1})$
$= 15 \times 10^4$
$= (1.5 \times 10^1) \times 10^4$
$= 1.5 \times 10^5$

50. $\frac{8 \times 10^{-3}}{4 \times 10^{-5}} = \frac{8}{4} \times \frac{10^{-3}}{10^{-5}} = 2 \times 10^2$

51. $\frac{3.5 \times 10^{-4}}{5 \times 10^{-1}} = \frac{3.5}{5} \times \frac{10^{-4}}{10^{-1}}$
$= 0.7 \times 10^{-3}$
$= (7 \times 10^{-1}) \times 10^{-3}$
$= 7 \times 10^{-4}$

52. $\frac{6.6 \times 10^{-1}}{1.1 \times 10^{-1}} = \frac{6.6}{1.1} \times \frac{10^{-1}}{10^{-1}} = 6 \times 10^0$

53. $(3 \times 10^2)^3 = 3^3 \times 10^6$
$= 27 \times 10^6$
$= (2.7 \times 10^1) \times 10^6$
$= 2.7 \times 10^7$

54. $(2 \times 10^{-3})^4 = 2^4 \times 10^{-12}$
$= 16 \times 10^{-12}$
$= (1.6 \times 10^1) \times 10^{-12}$
$= 1.6 \times 10^{-11}$

55. $(0.5 \times 10)^{-2} = 5^{-2}$
$= \frac{1}{5^2}$
$= \frac{1}{25}$
$= 0.04$
$= 4 \times 10^{-2}$

56. $6{,}000{,}000 \cdot 324{,}000 = 1.944 \times 10^{12}$
$= 1{,}944{,}000{,}000{,}000$

57. $(2.79 \times 10^{-4})(3.94 \times 10^9) = 1.09926 \times 10^6$
$= 1{,}099{,}260$

58. $\frac{3{,}940{,}000}{0.0002} = 1.97 \times 10^{10} = 19{,}700{,}000{,}000$

59. $\frac{6.45 \times 10^{-6}}{4.3 \times 10^5} = 1.5 \times 10^{-11} = 0.000000000015$

60. $(0.000094)^3 = 8.30584 \times 10^{-13}$
$= 0.000000000000830584$

61. $(2.4 \times 10^{-4})^5 \approx 7.9626 \times 10^{-19}$
$= 0.00000000000000000079626$

Copyright © McDougal Littell Inc.
All rights reserved.

62. $9.46 \times 10^{12} = 9{,}460{,}000{,}000{,}000$

63. $9.8 \times 10^{-4} = 0.00098$

64. $6{,}035{,}000{,}000 = 6.035 \times 10^{9}$

65. $0.00000000000000000000002 = 2 \times 10^{-23}$

66. $d = rt$

$d = (3 \times 10^{5})(1.5 \times 10^{4})$
$= (3 \times 1.5)(10^{5} \times 10^{4})$
$= 4.5 \times 10^{9}$ km

67. $\dfrac{\$15{,}000{,}000}{8.28 \times 10^{5}\text{ mi}^2} = \$18.12/\text{mi}^2$

68. $\dfrac{\$10{,}000{,}000}{2.96 \times 10^{4}\text{ mi}^2} = \$337.84/\text{mi}^2$

69. $V = \dfrac{4}{3}\pi r^3$

$V = \dfrac{4}{3}\pi(7.15 \times 10^{4})^3$

$V = \dfrac{4}{3}\pi(7.15^3)(10^{12})$

$V \approx 1.53 \times 10^{15}$ km^3

8.5 Standardized Test Practice (p. 474)

70. D; $12.25 > 10$, therefore it is not in scientific notation.

71. $\dfrac{1.1 \times 10^{-1}}{5.5 \times 10^{-5}} = \dfrac{1.1}{5.5} \times \dfrac{10^{-1}}{10^{-5}}$
$= 0.2 \times 10^{4}$
$= (2 \times 10^{-1}) \times 10^{4}$
$= 2 \times 10^{3}$

H

8.5 Mixed Review (p. 474)

72. $4x + 2y = 12$

$2y = -4x + 12$

$y = -2x + 6; m = -2; b = 6$

$-6x + 3y = 6$

$3y = 6x + 6$

$y = 2x + 2; m = 2; b = 2$

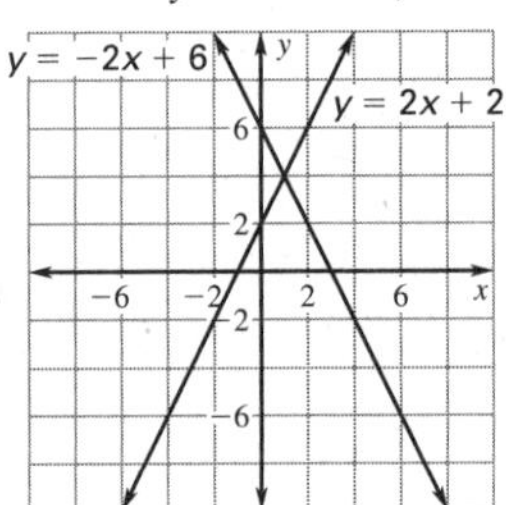

One solution

73. $3x - 2y = 0$

$-2y = -3x$

$y = \dfrac{3}{2}x; m = \dfrac{3}{2}; b = 0$

$3x - 2y = -4$

$-2y = -3x - 4$

$y = \dfrac{3}{2}x + 2; m = \dfrac{3}{2}; b = 2$

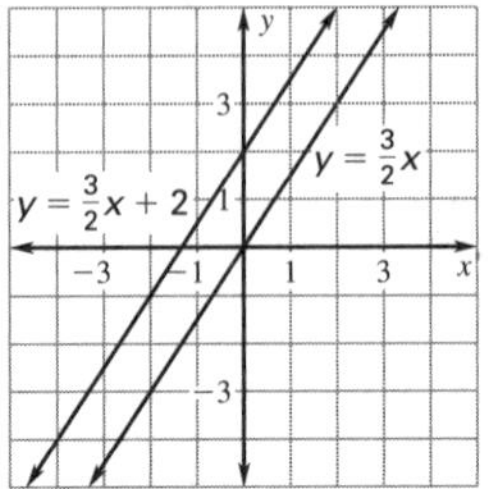

No solution

74. $x - 5y = 8$

$-5y = -x + 8$

$y = \dfrac{1}{5}x - \dfrac{8}{5}; m = \dfrac{1}{5}; b = -1\dfrac{3}{5}$

$-x + 5y = -8$

$5y = x - 8$

$y = \dfrac{1}{5}x - \dfrac{8}{5}; m = \dfrac{1}{5}; b = -1\dfrac{3}{5}$

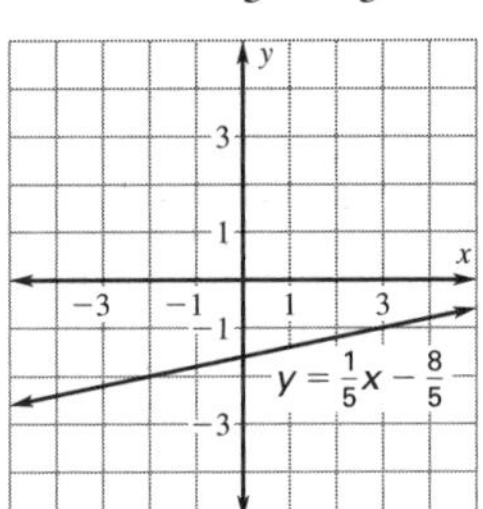

Infinitely many solutions

75. $2x + y \le 1$

$y \le -2x + 1$

$-2x + y \le 1$

$y \le 2x + 1$

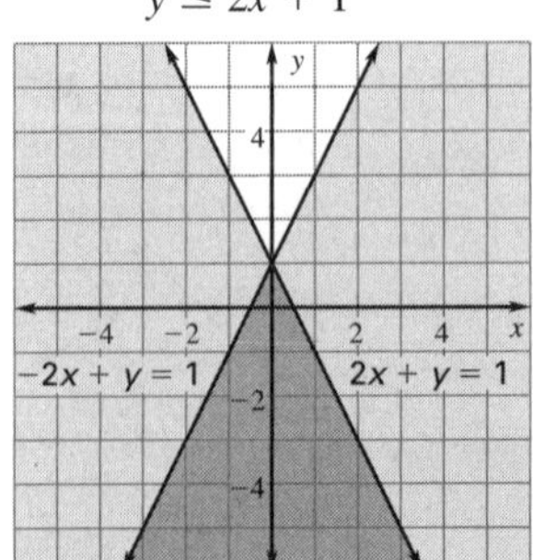

Copyright © McDougal Littell Inc.
All rights reserved.

76. $x + 2y < 3$

$2y < -x + 3$

$y < -\frac{1}{2}x + \frac{3}{2}$

$x - 3y > 1$

$-3y > -x + 1$

$y < \frac{1}{3}x - \frac{1}{3}$

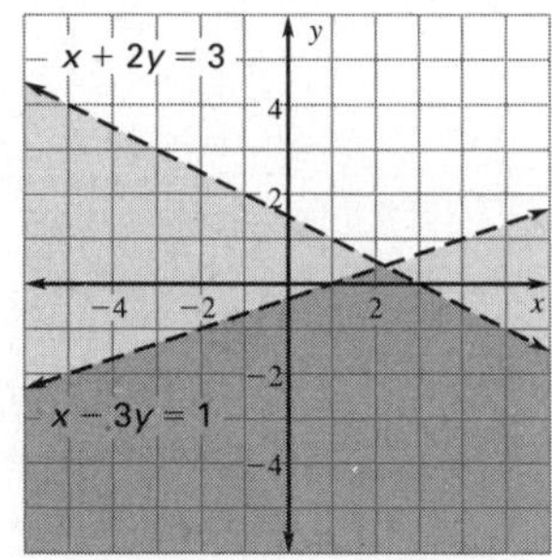

77. $2x + y \geq 2$

$y \geq -2x + 2$

$x < 2$

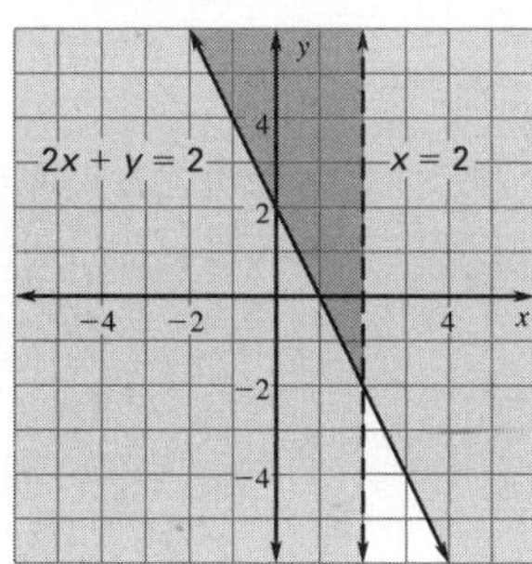

8.5 Maintaining Skills (p. 474)

78. $\frac{1}{3} = 0.3333\ldots$

79. $\frac{53}{25} \times \frac{4}{4} = \frac{212}{100} = 212\%$

80. $1.45 = \frac{145}{100} = \frac{5 \cdot 29}{5 \cdot 20} = \frac{29}{20}$

81. $0.674 = 67.4\%$

82. $15\% = \frac{15}{100} = \frac{3}{20}$

83. $756.7\% = 7.567$

Quiz 2 *(p. 474)*

1. $\frac{6^7}{6^2} = 6^{7-2} = 6^5 = 7776$

2. $\frac{x^9}{x^{11}} = x^{9-11} = x^{-2} = \frac{1}{x^2}$

3. $\left(\frac{-7}{2}\right)^3 = \frac{(-7)^3}{2^3} = -\frac{343}{8}$

4. $\left(\frac{a}{b}\right)^{-5} = \frac{a^{-5}}{b^{-5}} = \frac{b^5}{a^5}$

5. $\frac{3xy^5}{9x^4y^6} \cdot \frac{4x^4}{xy^8} = \frac{x^{-3}y^{-1}}{3} \cdot \frac{4x^3}{y^8}$

$= \frac{4x^0y^{-1}}{3y^8}$

$= \frac{4y^{-9}}{3} = \frac{4}{3y^9}$

6. $\frac{20x^3y}{4xy^2} \cdot \frac{-6xy}{-x} = 5x^2y^{-1} \cdot 6y$

$= 30x^2y^0$

$= 30x^2$

7. $\frac{5ab^3}{-2a^{-1}b^2} \cdot \frac{10a^{-3}b}{a^2b^{-4}} = \frac{5a^2b^1}{-2} \cdot 10a^{-5}b^5$

$= \frac{50a^{-3}b^6}{-2}$

$= -\frac{25b^6}{a^3}$

8. $\left(\frac{-2m^2n}{3mn^2}\right)^4 = \left(\frac{-2mn^{-1}}{3}\right)^4$

$= \frac{(-2)^4m^4n^{-4}}{3^4}$

$= \frac{16m^4}{81n^4}$

9. $\frac{xy^{10}}{5x^3y^6} \cdot \frac{(2x^2y)^4}{4x^3y} = \frac{xy^{10}}{5x^3y^6} \cdot \frac{2^4x^8y^4}{4x^3y}$

$= \frac{16x^9y^{14}}{20x^6y^7}$

$= \frac{4x^3y^7}{5}$

10. $\frac{9wz^{-2}}{w^{-3}z^3} \cdot \left(\frac{w^2z}{3z^{-1}}\right)^{-3} = \frac{9wz^{-2}}{w^{-3}z^3} \cdot \frac{w^{-6}z^{-3}}{3^{-3}z^3}$

$= \frac{9w^{-5}z^{-5}}{3^{-3}w^{-3}z^6}$

$= 9(3^3)w^{-2}z^{-11}$

$= \frac{9(27)}{w^2z^{11}}$

$= \frac{243}{w^2z^{11}}$

11. $5 \times 10^9 = 5{,}000{,}000{,}000$

12. $4.8 \times 10^3 = 4800$

13. $3.35 \times 10^4 = 33{,}500$

14. $7 \times 10^{-6} = 0.000007$

15. $1.1 \times 10^{-2} = 0.011$

16. $2.08 \times 10^{-5} = 0.0000208$

17. $105 = 1.05 \times 10^2$

18. $99{,}000 = 9.9 \times 10^4$

19. $30{,}700{,}000 = 3.07 \times 10^7$

20. $0.25 = 2.5 \times 10^{-1}$

21. $0.0004 = 4 \times 10^{-4}$

22. $0.0000067 = 6.7 \times 10^{-6}$

Copyright © McDougal Littell Inc.
All rights reserved.

Lesson 8.6

8.6 Developing Concepts: Think About It
(p. 475)

1. $y = x + 5$

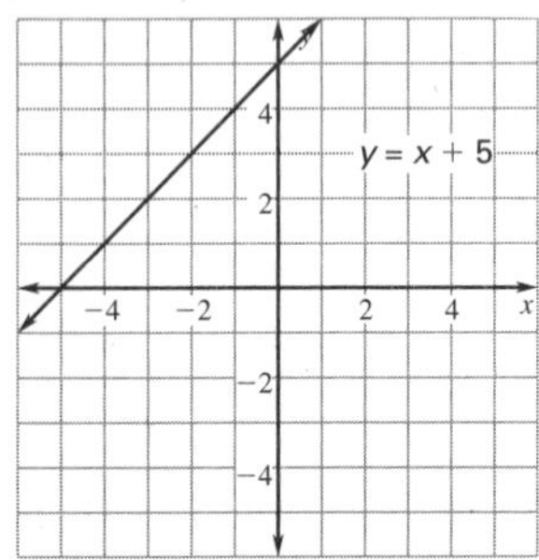

2. $y = 3^x$

x	0	1	2	3	4	5
y	1	3	9	27	81	243

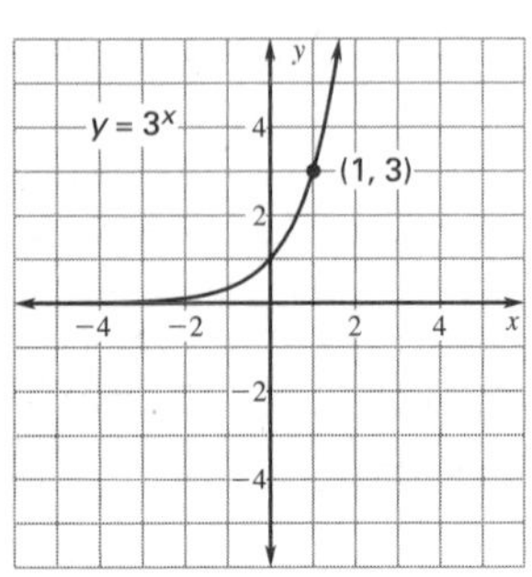

3. $y = 10 + 2x$
   $y = 2x + 10$

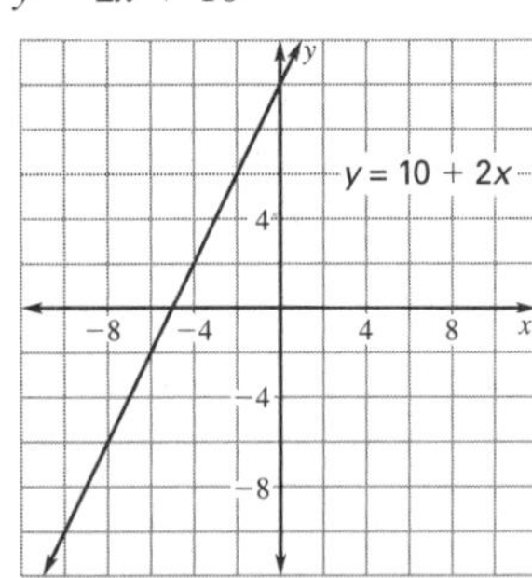

4. $y = -3(2)^x$

x	-1	0	1	2	3	4	5
y	$-\frac{3}{2}$	-3	-6	-12	-24	-48	-96

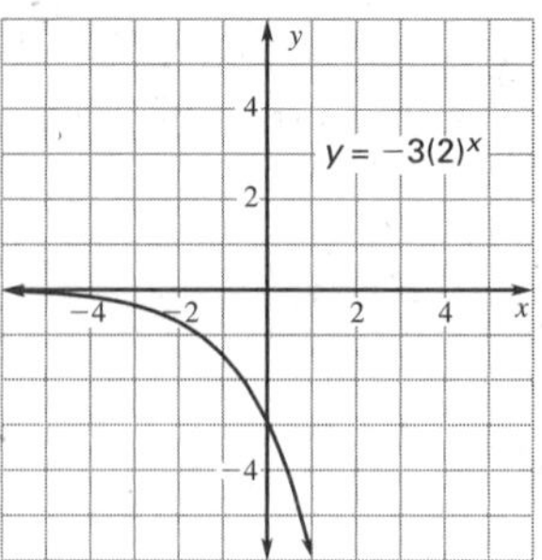

5. $y = 5(4x - 7)$
   $y = 20x - 35$

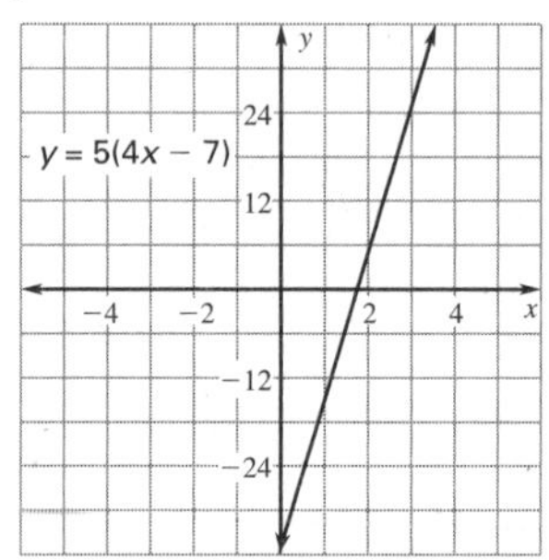

6. $y = 10(1.2)^x$

x	-1	0	1	2	3	4	5
y	8.3	10	12	14.4	17.3	20.7	24.9

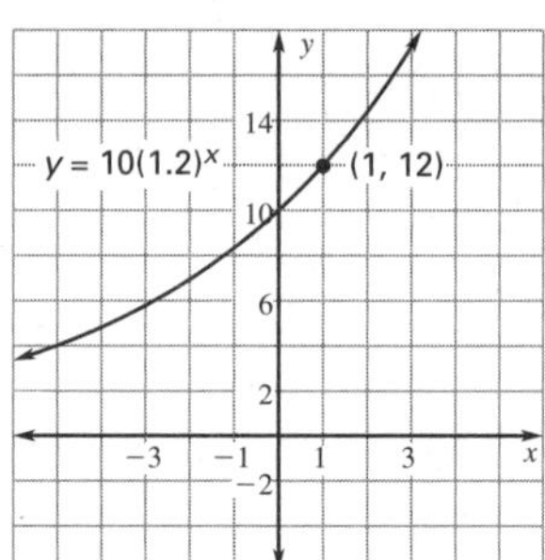

7. same

8. *Sample answer:* The rate of increase increases for each unit on the x-axis. The rate of change is not constant.

9. *Sample answer:* A linear function does not contain an exponent.

8.6 Checkpoint (pp. 476–478)

1. $y = C(1 + r)^t$ — Exponential growth formula
   $v = 50{,}000(1 + 0.02)^t$ — Substitute v for y, 50,000 for C, 0.02 for r.
   $v = 50{,}000(1.02)^t$ — Add.

2. $A = P(1 + r)^t$ — Compound interest formula
   $A = 750(1 + 0.06)^{10}$ — Substitute 750 for P, 0.06 for r, 10 for t.
   $A = 750(1.06)^{10}$ — Add.
   $A \approx \$1343$ — Use a calculator.

Copyright © McDougal Littell Inc.
All rights reserved.

3. $y = C(1 + r)^t$ Exponential growth model
$P = 30(2^6)$ P is population, $C = 30$; 2 is substituted for $1 + r$ (growth factor).
$P = 30(64)$ $t = 6$
$P = 1920$ rabbits

4. Make a table of values:

$P = 30(2)^t$

t	0	1	2	3	4
P	30	60	120	240	480

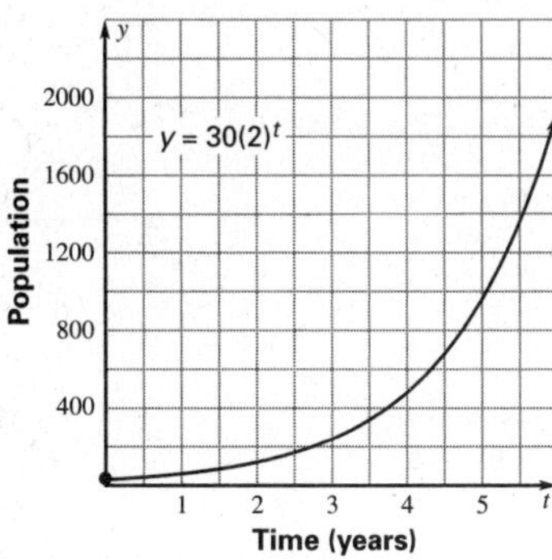

Guided Practice (p. 479)

1. initial amount; growth factor

2. $P = \$500$

3. $r = 4\% = 0.04$

4. $A = 500(1 + 0.04)^t$

5. $A = 500(1.04)^5$
$A \approx \$608$

6. Initial amount: 100 (Choice A or B)
When $t = 1$, $y = 120$
For B, $y = 100(1.2)^1 = 120$
B

8.6 Practice and Applications (pp. 479–481)

7. $y = 100(1 + 0.5)^t$; $C = 100$; $r = 0.5$

8. $y = 12(1 + 2)^t$; $C = 12$; $r = 2$

9. $y = 7.5(1.75)^t = 7.5(1 + 0.75)^t$
$C = 7.5$; $r = 0.75$

10. $y = 25{,}000(1 + 0.07)^t$
$y = 25{,}000(1.07)^t$
y = salary; t = number of years

11. $y = 310{,}000(1 + 0.15)^t$
$y = 310{,}000(1.15)^t$
y = population; t = number of years

12. $y = 10{,}000(1 + 0.05)^t$
$y = 10{,}000(1.05)^t$
y = attendance; t = number of years

13. $y = 10{,}000(1 + 0.25)^t$
$y = 10{,}000(1.25)^t$

14. $y = 20{,}000(1 + 0.20)^t$
$y = 20{,}000(1.2)^t$

15. $y = 15{,}000(1 + 0.30)^t$
$y = 15{,}000(1.3)^t$

16. $A = 1400(1.06)^5$
$A \approx \$1873.52$

17. $A = 1400(1.06)^8$
$A \approx \$2231.39$

18. $A = 1400(1.06)^{12}$
$A \approx \$2817.08$

19. $A = 1400(1.06)^{20}$
$A \approx \$4489.99$

20. $A = 250(1.05)^5$
$A \approx \$319.07$

21. $A = 300(1.05)^5$
$A \approx \$382.88$

22. $A = 350(1.05)^5$
$A \approx \$446.70$

23. $A = 400(1.05)^5$
$A \approx \$510.51$

24. $A = 900(1.04)^{10}$
$A \approx \$1332.22$

25. $A = 900(1.05)^{10}$
$A \approx \$1466.01$

26. $A = 900(1.06)^{10}$
$A \approx \$1611.76$

27. $A = 900(1.07)^{10}$
$A \approx \$1770.44$

28. $y = 50(1 + 1)^t$
growth rate: 1
growth factor: $1 + 1 = 2$

29. $y = 31(4)^t$
$1 + r = 4$
$r = 3$
growth rate: 3
growth factor: 4

30. $y = 5.6(2.3)^t$
$1 + r = 2.3$
$r = 1.3$
growth rate: 1.3
growth factor: 2.3

31. growth factor: 2

32. $P = 1000(2)^t$
$P = 1000(2)^4 = 1000(16) = 16{,}000$
16,000 starfish

33. growth factor: 3

34. $l = 0.006(3)^t$
$l = 0.006(3)^7$
$l = 13.122$
about 13 feet

Copyright © McDougal Littell Inc.
All rights reserved.

35. $b = 6.37(1.11)^s$
$b = 6.37(1.11)^7$
$b \approx 13.2$ L/min
$b = 6.37(1.11)^{19}$
$b \approx 46.3$ L/min
$b = 6.37(1.11)^{25}$
$b \approx 86.5$ L/min

36.

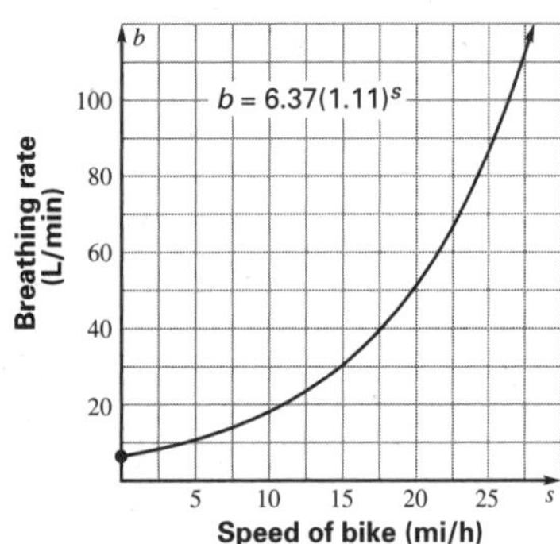

37. $r = 6\%$ (slowest growth rate); C

38. $r = 12\%$ (medium growth rate); A

39. $r = 20\%$ (fastest growth rate); B

40. Make a table of values for Exercises 13, 14, and 15, then graph.
Ex. 13

$y = 10{,}000(1.25)^t$

t	0	2	4	6	8	10
y	10,000	15,625	24,414	38,147	59,605	93,132

Ex. 14

$y = 20{,}000(1.2)^t$

t	0	2	4	6	8	10
y	20,000	28,800	41,472	59,720	85,996	123,835

Ex. 15

$y = 15{,}000(1.3)^t$

t	0	2	4	6	8	10
y	15,000	25,350	42,842	72,402	122,360	206,788

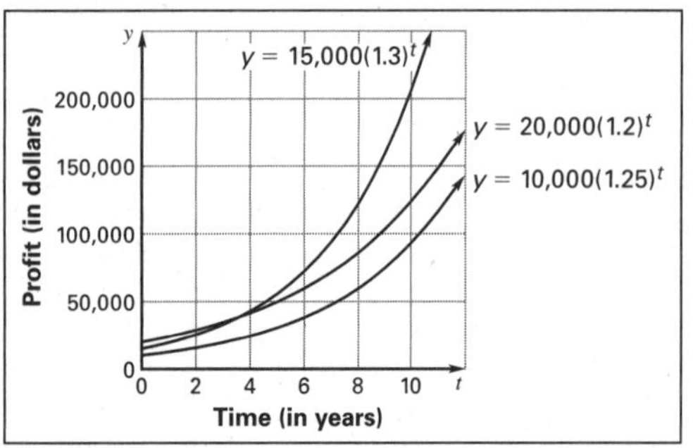

Sample answer: The business in Exercise 15 because it attains an annual profit of about \$206,788 in 10 years versus \$93,132 and \$123,835. Also, the company in Exercise 15 generates a higher percentage of profit and for a longer period of time.

41. $A = P\left(1 + \dfrac{r}{n}\right)^{tn}$
$A = 1000\left(1 + \dfrac{0.06}{4}\right)^{5(4)}$
$A = 1000(1 + 0.015)^{20}$
$A = 1000(1.015)^{20}$
$A \approx \$1346.86$

8.6 Standardized Test Practice (p. 481)

42. $y = 5.00(1 + 0.09)^t$
$y = 5(1.09)^5$
$y \approx \$7.69$
C

43. initial value: 2 (choice H or J)
Test a point to find the rate:
(4, 5.7)
$y = 2(1 - 0.3)^4$
$y = 2(0.7)^4$
$y \approx 0.4802 \neq 5.7$
$y = 2(1.3)^4$
$y = 5.71 \approx 5.7$
J

8.6 Mixed Review (p. 481)

44. $24 + m^2 = 24 + 5^2 = 24 + 25 = 49$

45. $6x - 1 = 6(1) - 1 = 6 - 1 = 5$

46. $3 \cdot 15y = 3 \cdot 15(2) = 45(2) = 90$

47. $1 - \dfrac{a}{3} = 1 - \dfrac{9}{3} = 1 - 3 = -2$

48. $-2(4 - 3x) = 6(2x + 1) + 4$
$-8 + 6x = 12x + 6 + 4$
$-8 + 6x = 12x + 10$
$-8 = 6x + 10$
$-18 = 6x$
$-3 = x$

49. $7x - (4x + 3) = 4(3x + 15)$
$7x - 4x - 3 = 12x + 60$
$3x - 3 = 12x + 60$
$-3 = 9x + 60$
$-63 = 9x$
$-7 = x$

50. $\dfrac{2}{3}(6m - 3) + 10 = -8(m + 2)$
$4m - 2 + 10 = -8m - 16$
$4m + 8 = -8m - 16$
$12m + 8 = -16$
$12m = -24$
$m = -2$

Copyright © McDougal Littell Inc.
All rights reserved.

51. $\frac{1}{4}(12y - 4) - 2y = -3(y - 5)$

$$3y - 1 - 2y = -3y + 15$$
$$y - 1 = -3y + 15$$
$$4y - 1 = 15$$
$$4y = 16$$
$$y = 4$$

52.
$$6b + 8d = 8.60$$
$$3b + 3d = 3.75$$
$$6b + 8d = 8.60$$
$$-6b - 6d = -7.50 \quad \text{Multiply by } -2$$
$$2d = 1.10$$
$$d = 0.55$$
$$3b + 3(0.55) = 3.75$$
$$3b + 1.65 = 3.75$$
$$3b = 2.10$$
$$b = 0.70$$

Doughnuts cost \$0.55 each; bagels cost \$0.70 each.

53. $2^2 \cdot 2^2 = 2^{2+2} = 2^4$

54. $7^6 \cdot 7^2 = 7^{6+2} = 7^8$

55. $3^5 \cdot 3^2 = 3^{5+2} = 3^7$

56. $y^3 \cdot y = y^{3+1} = y^4$

57. $r^2 \cdot r^4 = r^{2+4} = r^6$

58. $a^9 \cdot a^4 = a^{9+4} = a^{13}$

8.6 Maintaining Skills (p. 481)

59. $\frac{25}{100} = \frac{1}{4}$

60. $\frac{215}{645} = \frac{5 \cdot 43}{5 \cdot 129} = \frac{43}{129} = \frac{1 \cdot 43}{3 \cdot 43} = \frac{1}{3}$

61. $\frac{53}{424} = \frac{1 \cdot 53}{8 \cdot 53} = \frac{1}{8}$

62. $\frac{71}{355} = \frac{1 \cdot 71}{5 \cdot 71} = \frac{1}{5}$

Lesson 8.7

8.7 Checkpoint (pp. 482–484)

1. $y = 24{,}000(1 - 0.10)^t$
$y = 24{,}000(0.9)^t$

2. $y = 24{,}000(0.9)^6$
$y \approx \$12{,}755$

3.

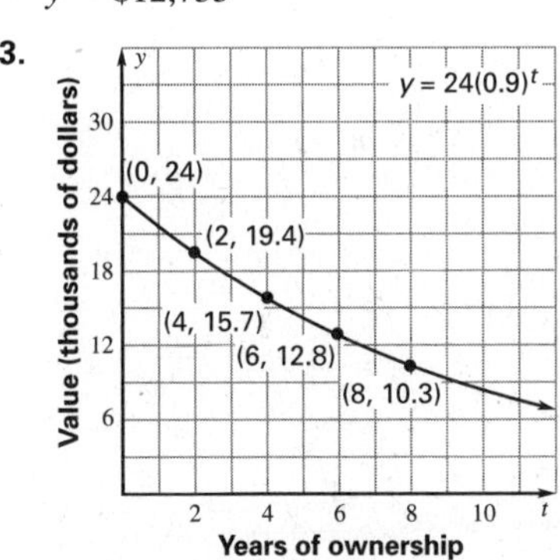

4. about \$14,200

5. $y = (2)^t$
$b = 2 > 1$, growth model
growth factor: 2

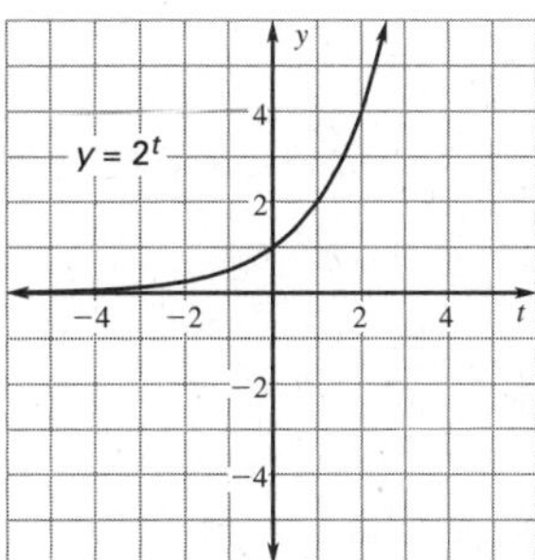

6. $y = (0.5)^t$
$b = 0.5; 0 < 0.5 < 1$; decay model
decay factor: 0.5

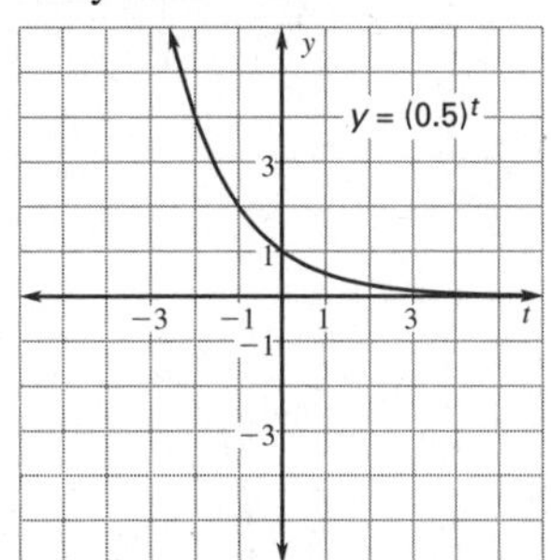

7. $y = 5(0.2)^t$
$b = 0.2; 0 < 0.2 < 1$; decay model
decay factor: 0.2

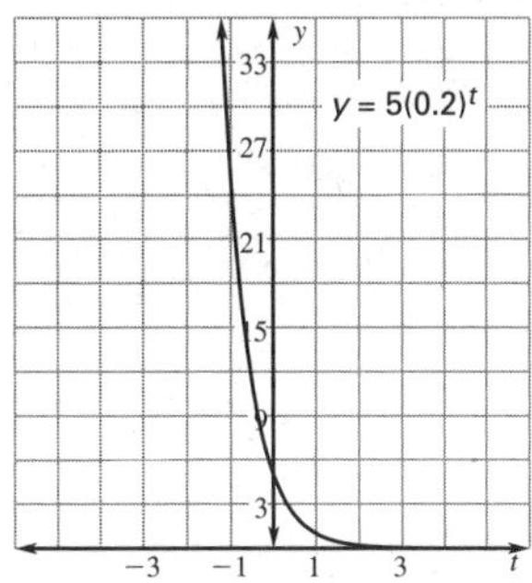

8. $y = 0.7(1.1)^t$
$b = 1.1 > 1$; growth model
growth factor: 1.1

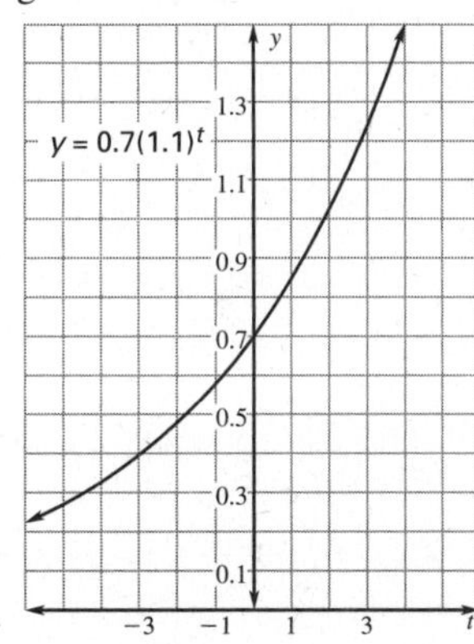

Copyright © McDougal Littell Inc.
All rights reserved.

8.7 Guided Practice (p. 485)

1. $1 - r$

2. $y = 85{,}000(1 - 0.02)^t$
   $y = 85{,}000(0.98)^t$

3. $y = 7000(1 - 0.06)^t$
   $y = 7000(0.94)^2$
   $y = \$6185.20$

4. $y = 7000(1 - 0.06)^t$
   $y = 7000(0.94)^5$
   $y \approx \$5137.33$

5. $y = 7000(1 - 0.06)^t$
   $y = 7000(0.94)^8$
   $y \approx \$4266.98$

6. $y = 7000(1 - 0.06)^t$
   $y = 7000(0.94)^{10}$
   $y \approx \$3770.31$

7. A and C are decay models ($0 < b < 1$); Substitute a point on the graph and test it:
   (2, 10)
   A. $10 \stackrel{?}{=} 60(0.08)^2$
   $10 \neq 0.384$
   C. $10 \stackrel{?}{=} 60(0.40)^2$
   $10 \approx 9.6$
   C

8. $b = 3 > 1$; exponential growth

9. $b = 0.55$; $0 < 0.55 < 1$; exponential decay

10. $b = 3 > 1$; exponential growth

11. $b = 0.3$; $0 < 0.3 < 1$; exponential decay

8.7 Practice and Applications (pp. 485-488)

12. $y = 10(0.2)^t$
    $C = 10$
    decay factor $= 0.2$

13. $y = 18(0.11)^t$
    $C = 18$
    decay factor $= 0.11$

14. $y = 2\left(\frac{1}{4}\right)^t$
    $C = 2$
    decay factor $= \frac{1}{4} = 0.25$

15. $y = 0.5\left(\frac{5}{8}\right)^t$
    $C = 0.5$
    decay factor $= \frac{5}{8} = 0.625$

16. $y = 25{,}000(1 - 0.09)^t$
    $y = 25{,}000(0.91)^t$
    $y =$ value of car; $t =$ number of years

17. $y = 100{,}000(1 - 0.02)^t$
    $y = 100{,}000(0.98)^t$
    $y =$ population; $t =$ number of years

18. $y = 800(1 - 0.10)^t$
    $y = 800(0.9)^t$
    $y =$ value of sound system; $t =$ number of years

19. $y = 100(1 - 0.09)^t$
    $y = 100(0.91)^t$

20. $y = 550(1 - 0.04)^t$
    $y = 550(0.96)^t$

21. $y = 70(1 - 0.01)^t$
    $y = 70(0.99)^t$

22. $y = 20{,}000(1 - 0.07)^t$
    $y = 20{,}000(0.93)^3$
    $y \approx \$16{,}087$

23. $y = 20{,}000(1 - 0.07)^t$
    $y = 20{,}000(0.93)^8$
    $y \approx \$11{,}192$

24. $y = 20{,}000(1 - 0.07)^t$
    $y = 20{,}000(0.93)^{10}$
    $y \approx \$9{,}680$

25. $y = 20{,}000(1 - 0.07)^t$
    $y = 20{,}000(0.93)^{12}$
    $y \approx \$8{,}372$

26. $y = A(0.8)^t$
    $y = 250(0.8)^2$
    $y = 160$ mg

27. $y = A(0.8)^t$
    $y = 500(0.8)^{3.5}$
    $y \approx 229$ mg

28. $y = A(0.8)^t$
    $y = 750(0.8)^5$
    $y = 246$ mg

29. $y = 64(0.5)^t$

30. $y = 64(0.5)^3$
    $y = 8$
    or 8 teams after 3 rounds
    $y = 64(0.5)^4$
    $y = 4$
    or 4 teams after 4 rounds

Copyright © McDougal Littell Inc.
All rights reserved.

31. $y = 15(0.9)^t$

t	0	2	4	6	8	10
y	15	12	10	8	6	5

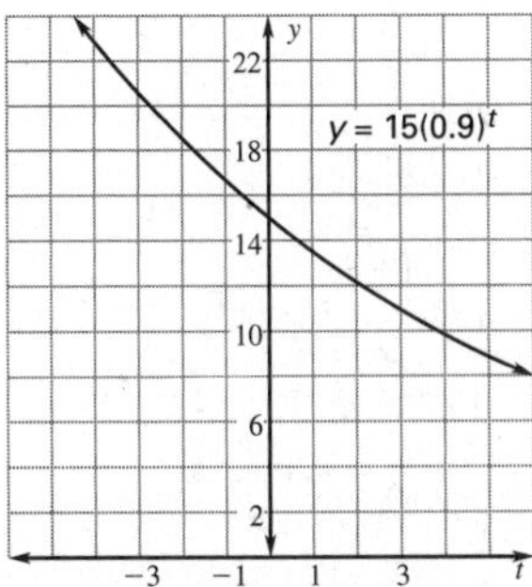

32. $y = 72(0.85)^t$

t	0	2	4	6	8	10
y	72	52	38	27	20	14

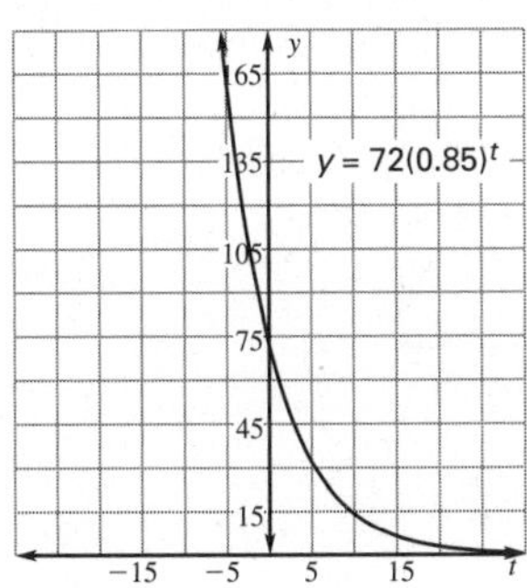

33. $y = 10\left(\frac{1}{2}\right)^t$

t	0	2	4	6	8	10
y	10	2.5	0.63	0.16	0.04	0.01

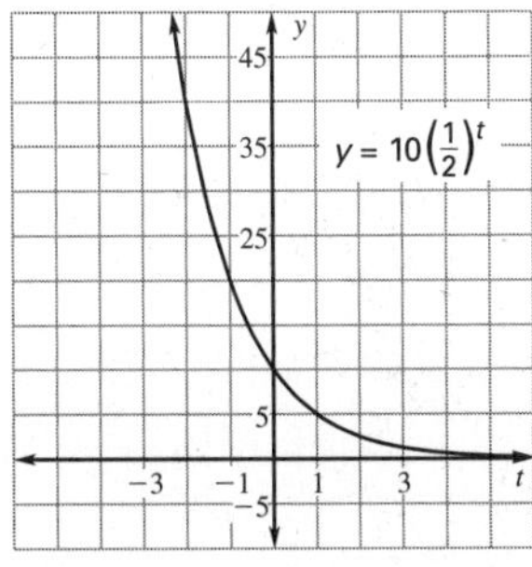

34. $y = 55\left(\frac{3}{4}\right)^t$

t	0	2	4	6	8	10
y	55	30.9	17.4	9.8	5.5	3.1

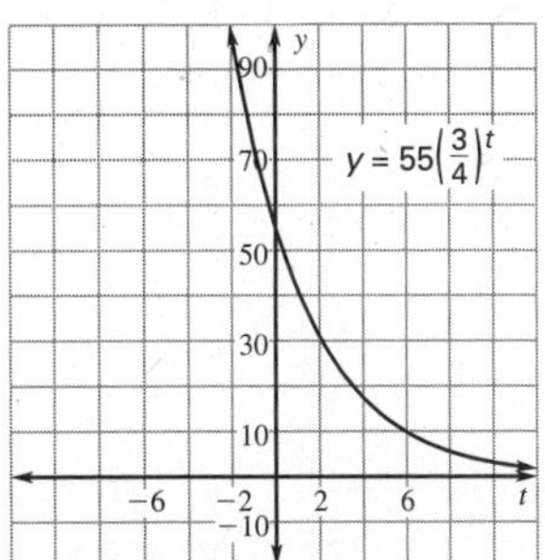

35. $y = 22{,}000(1 - 0.09)^t$
$y = 22{,}000(0.91)^t$

t	0	2	4	6	8
y	22,000	18,218	15,086	12,493	10,346

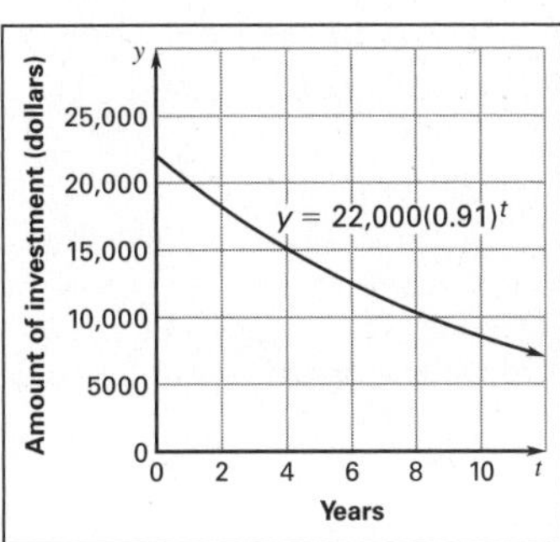

When $t = 8$, $y \approx \$10{,}300$.

36. $y = 2{,}000{,}000(1 - 0.02)^t$
$y = 2{,}000{,}000(0.98)^t$

t	0	4	8	12	16	20
y	2,000,000	1,840,000	1,700,000	1,570,000	1,450,000	1,340,000

About $1,480,000

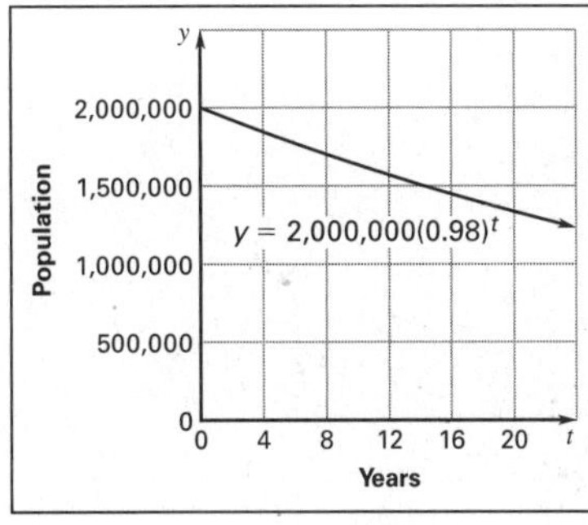

When $t = 15$, $y \approx \$1{,}480{,}000$.

Copyright © McDougal Littell Inc.
All rights reserved.

37. $y = 10{,}500(1 - 0.10)^t$
$y = 10{,}500(0.9)^t$

t	0	2	4	6	8	10
y	10,500	8500	6900	5600	4500	3700

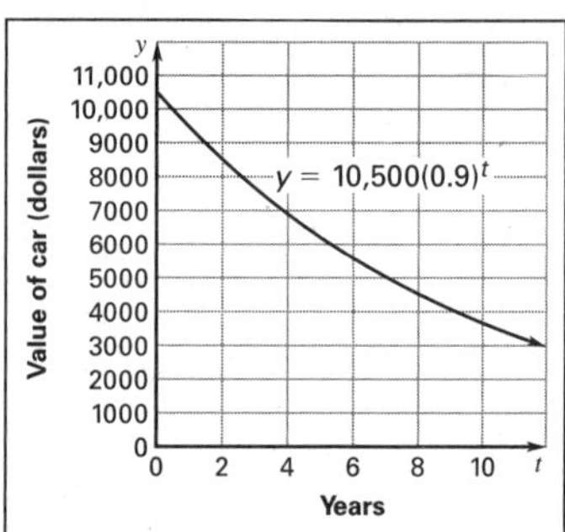

When $t = 10$, $y \approx \$3700$.

38. $y = 302(1 - 0.11)^t$
$y = 302(0.89)^t$

39.

Year	1894 $t = 0$	1896 $t = 2$	1898 $t = 4$	1900 $t = 6$	1902 $t = 8$
Miles of track	302	239	189	150	119

40.

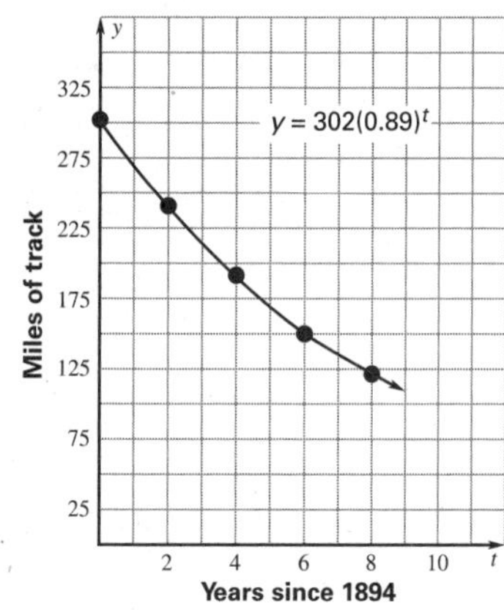

41. About 106 miles

42. $y = 4 - 3t$ (linear); B

43. $y = 4(0.6)^t$ (exponential decay); A

44. $y = 24(1.18)^t$
$b = 1.18 > 1$; exponential growth
growth factor: 1.18

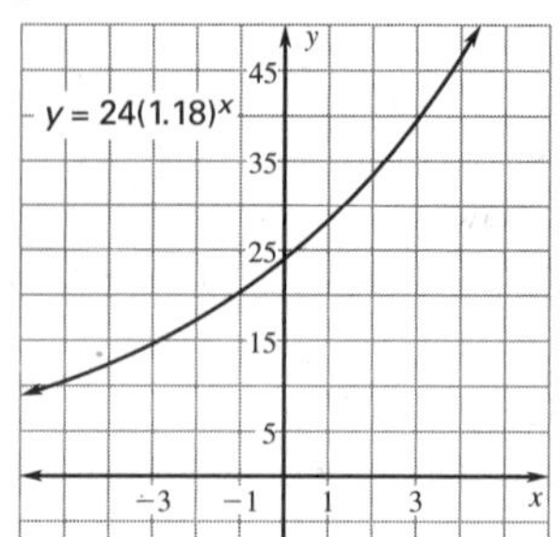

45. $y = 14(0.98)^t$
$b = 0.98$; $0 < 0.98 < 1$; exponential decay
decay factor: 0.98

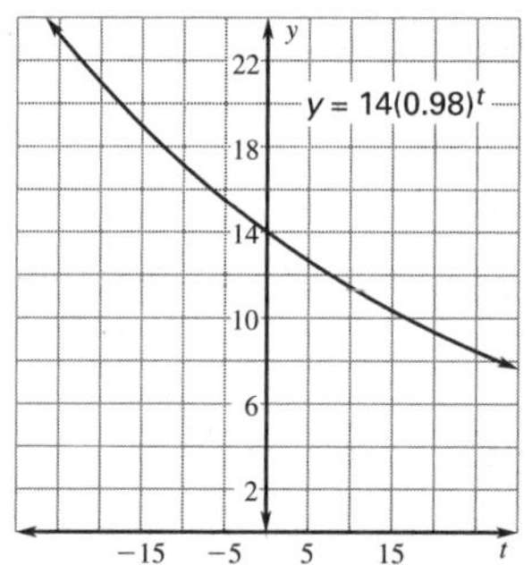

46. $y = 97(1.01)^t$
$b = 1.01 > 1$; exponential growth
growth factor: 1.01

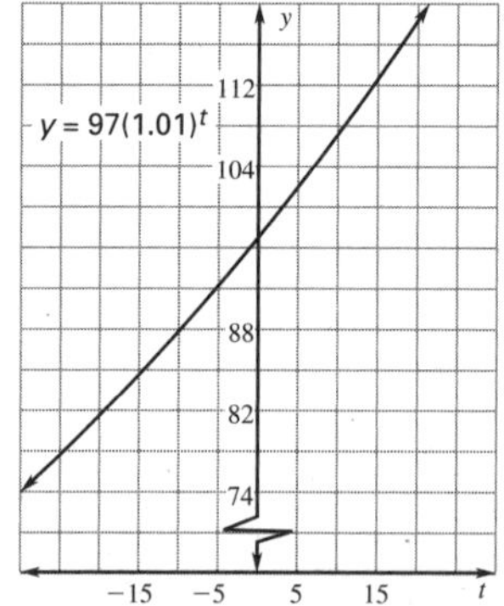

Copyright © McDougal Littell Inc.
All rights reserved.

47. $y = 112\left(\frac{2}{3}\right)^t$

$b = \frac{2}{3}$; $0 < \frac{2}{3} < 1$; exponential decay

decay factor: $\frac{2}{3}$

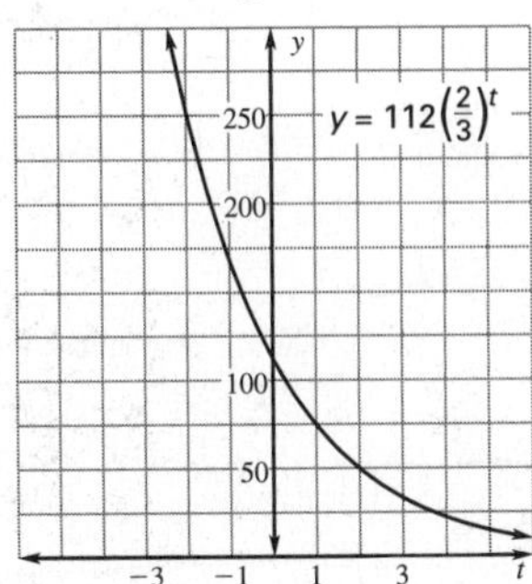

48. $y = 9\left(\frac{2}{5}\right)^t$

$b = \frac{2}{5}$; $0 < \frac{2}{5} < 1$; exponential decay

decay factor: $\frac{2}{5}$

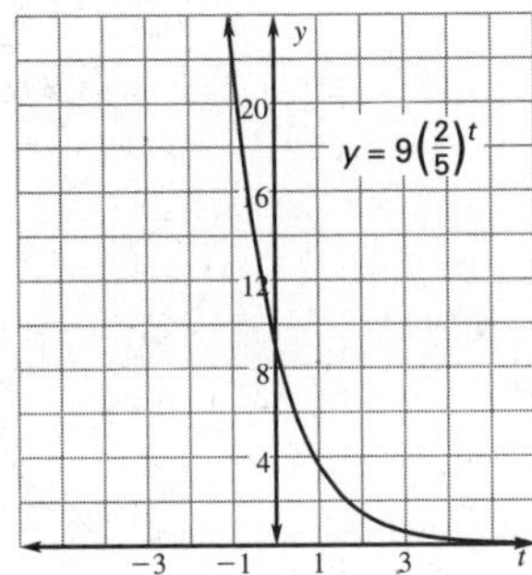

49. $y = 35\left(\frac{5}{4}\right)^t$

$b = \frac{5}{4} > 1$; exponential growth

growth factor: $\frac{5}{4}$

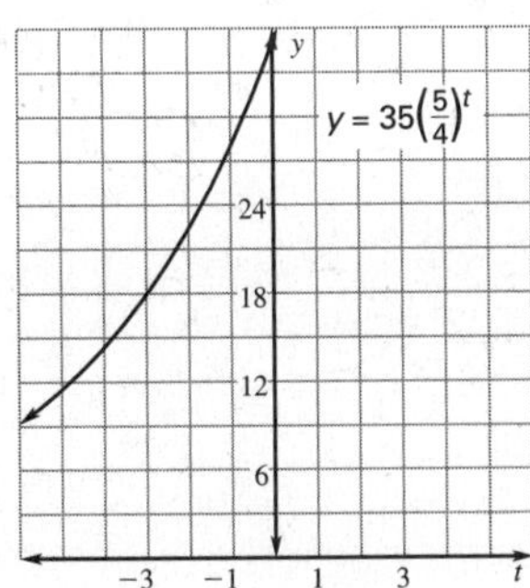

50. *Sample answer:* The greater the value of a, the steeper or more vertical the curve is. Since $2^0 = 1$ and $a(2^0) = a$, as a changes, so does the y-intercept.

51. *Sample answer:* As b increases, the curve becomes steeper or more vertical.

52. *Sample answer:* As b decreases, the curve becomes steeper or more vertical.

53. *Sample answer:* The graphs of $y = b^x$ and $y = \left(\frac{1}{b}\right)^x$ are reflections of each other about the y-axis. For example, the point $(1, b)$ reflects to $(-1, b)$. The graphs share the point $(0, 1)$ as the y-intercept.

54. Let P = initial price of sweaters

$y = P(1 - 0.20)^t$

$y = P(0.8)^t$

On day 5:

$y = P(0.8)^5 \approx 0.33P$

No, the sweaters will not be free. They will be about $\frac{1}{3}$ of the original price.

8.7 Standardized Test Practice (p. 487)

55. $t = 0$ in 1995; $t = 7$ in 2002

$y = 8000(1 - 0.04)^t$

$y = 8000(0.96)^7$

$y \approx \$6012$

C

56. F and G are decay models $(0 < b < 1)$;

Test a point on the graph:

(3, 20)

F. $20 \stackrel{?}{=} 50(0.25)^3$

$20 \neq 0.78$

G. $20 = 50(0.75)^3$

$20 \approx 21$

G

8.7 Mixed Review (p. 488)

57. $x^2 - 12 = 6^2 - 12 = 36 - 12 = 24$

58. $49 - 4w = 49 - 4(2)$

$= 49 - 8$

$= 41$

59. $100 - rs = 100 - 4(7) = 100 - 28 = 72$

60. $b^2 - 4ac = 5^2 - 4(1)(3)$

$= 25 - 4(1)(3)$

$= 25 - 12$

$= 13$

61. $1.29x = 5.22x + 3.61$

$-3.93x = 3.61$

$x \approx -0.92$

62. $1.33x - 7.42 = 5.48x$

$-7.42 = 4.15x$

$-1.79 \approx x$

63. $10.52x + 1.15 = -1.12x - 6.35$

$11.64x + 1.15 = -6.35$

$11.64x = -7.5$

$x \approx -0.64$

Copyright © McDougal Littell Inc.
All rights reserved.

64. $8.75x + 2.16 = 18.28x - 6.59$
$2.16 = 9.53x - 6.59$
$8.75 = 9.53x$
$0.92 = x$

65. $y - 5 = 3(x - 2)$

66. $y - (-3) = 5(x - 0)$
$y + 3 = 5x$

67. $y - (-4) = 4[x - (-1)]$
$y + 4 = 4(x + 1)$

68. $y - 3 = -1(x - 6)$
$y - 3 = -(x - 6)$

69. $y - 7 = -6[x - (-1)]$
$y - 7 = -6(x + 1)$

70. $y - (-5) = -2[x - (-4)]$
$y + 5 = -2(x + 4)$

8.7 Maintaining Skills (p. 488)

71. $0.5 \div 0.2 = 5 \div 2 = 2.5$

72. $4.62 \div 0.4 = 46.2 \div 4 = 11.55$

73. $0.074 \div 0.37 = 7.4 \div 37 = 0.2$

74. $0.084 \div 0.007 = 84 \div 7 = 12$

75. $0.451 \div 0.082 = 451 \div 82 = 5.5$

76. $0.6064 \div 0.758 = 606.4 \div 758 = 0.8$

Quiz 3 *(p. 488)*

1. $y = 250(1 + 0.08)^1$
$y = 250(1.08) = \$270$

2. $y = 250(1 + 0.08)^3$
$y = 250(1.08)^3 \approx \$314.93$

3. $y = 250(1 + 0.08)^5$
$y = 250(1.08)^5 \approx \$367.33$

4. $y = 250(1 + 0.08)^8$
$y = 250(1.08)^8 \approx \$462.73$

5. $y = 50(2)^5$
$y = 1600$ raccoons

6. $y = 15{,}000(1 - 0.09)^t$
$y = 15{,}000(0.91)^2$
$y \approx \$12{,}422$

7. $y = 15{,}000(1 - 0.09)^t$
$y = 15{,}000(0.91)^4$
$y \approx \$10{,}286$

8. $y = 15{,}000(1 - 0.09)^t$
$y = 15{,}000(0.91)^5$
$y \approx \$9{,}360$

9. $y = 15{,}000(1 - 0.09)^t$
$y = 15{,}000(0.91)^{10}$
$y \approx \$5{,}841$

10. $y = 20{,}000(1 - 0.08)^t$
$y = 20{,}000(0.92)^t$

t	0	2	4	6	8
y	20,000	16,900	14,300	12,100	10,300

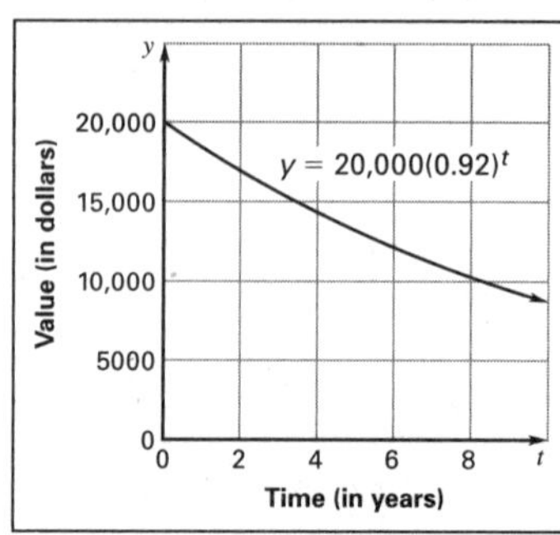

When $t = 5$, $y \approx \$13{,}200$.

11. $y = 6(0.1)^t$
$b = 0.1$; $0 < 0.1 < 1$; exponential decay
decay factor: 0.1

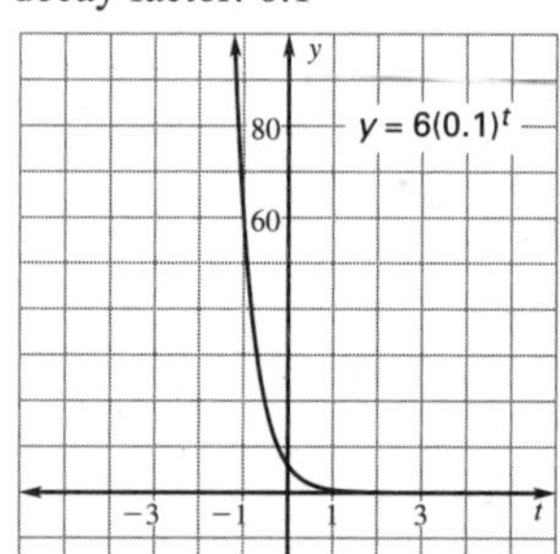

12. $y = 10(1.2)^t$
$b = 1.2 > 1$; exponential growth
growth factor: 1.2

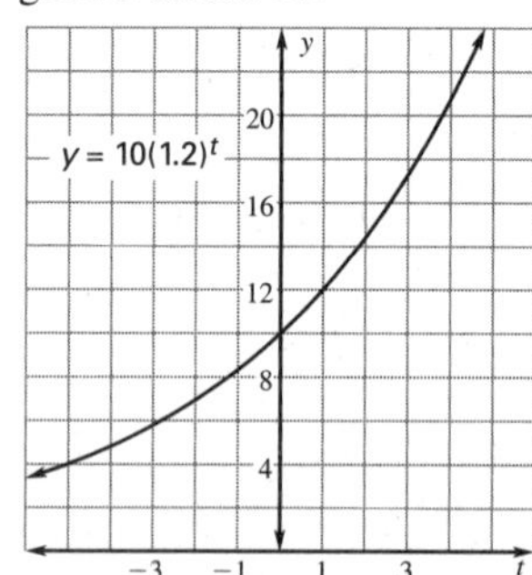

Copyright © McDougal Littell Inc.
All rights reserved.

13. $y = 3\left(\frac{9}{2}\right)^t$

$b = \frac{9}{2} = 4.5 > 1$; exponential growth

growth factor: $\frac{9}{2}$ or 4.5

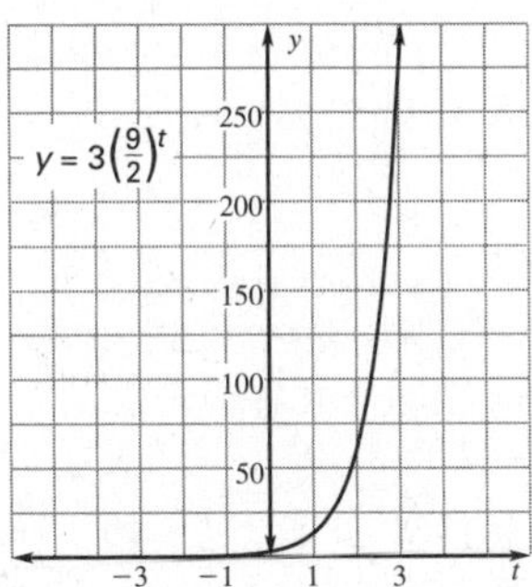

14. $y = 2\left(\frac{1}{10}\right)^t$

$b = \frac{1}{10} = 0.1; 0 < 0.1 < 1$; exponential decay

decay factor: 0.1

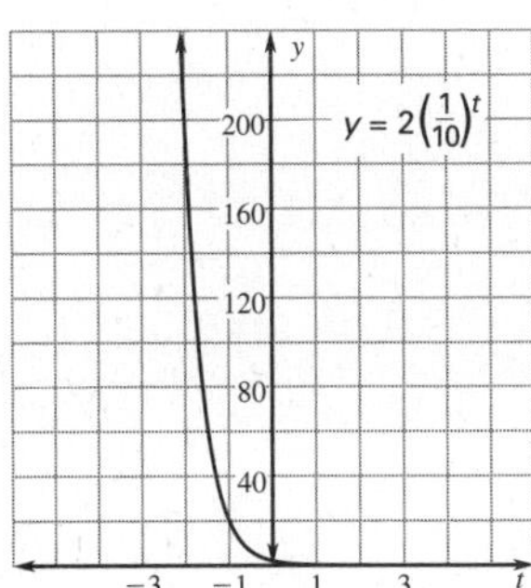

17. $y = 5^x$

x	−2	−1	0	1	2	3
y	$\frac{1}{25}$	$\frac{1}{5}$	1	5	25	125

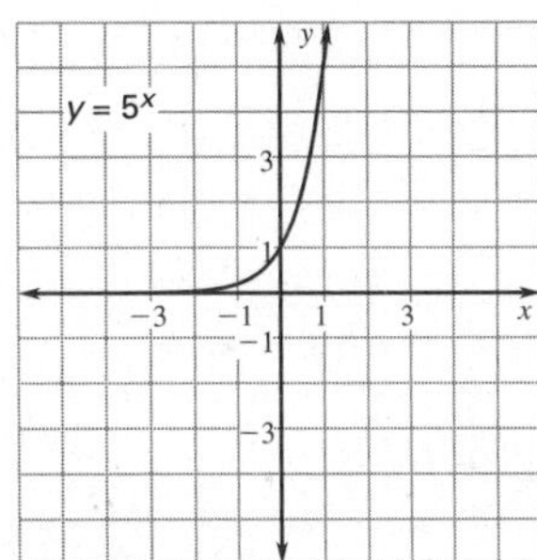

18. $y = 2(3)^x$

x	−2	−1	0	1	2	3
y	$\frac{2}{9}$	$\frac{2}{3}$	2	6	18	54

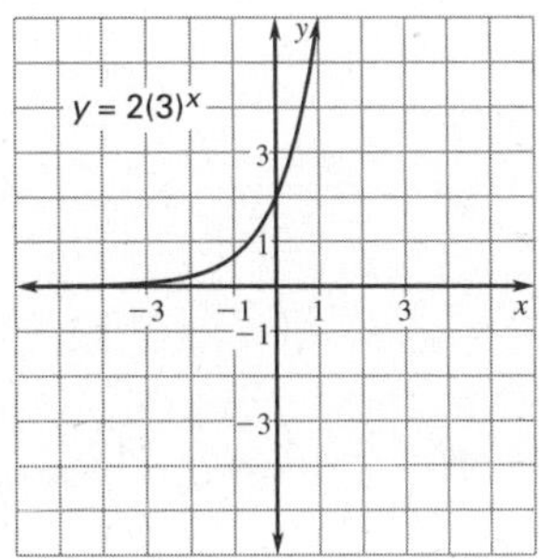

19. $y = \left(\frac{1}{4}\right)^x$

x	−2	−1	0	1	2	3
y	16	4	1	$\frac{1}{4}$	$\frac{1}{16}$	$\frac{1}{64}$

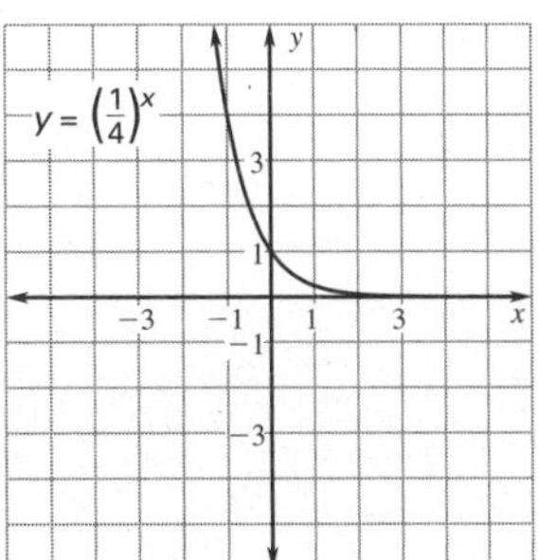

Chapter Summary and Review *(pp. 489–492)*

1. $2^2 \cdot 2^5 = 2^{2+5} = 2^7 = 128$

2. $x^3 \cdot x^3 = x^{3+3} = x^6$

3. $(4^3)^2 = 4^{3 \cdot 2} = 4^6 = 4096$

4. $(n^4)^3 = n^{4 \cdot 3} = n^{12}$

5. $(3x)^4 = 3^4 \cdot x^4 = 81x^4$

6. $(st^2)^2 = s^2t^{2 \cdot 2} = s^2t^4$

7. $p(2p)^3 = p \cdot 2^3 \cdot p^3 = 2^3p^{1+3} = 8p^4$

8. $(3a)^3(2a)^2 = 3^3a^3 \cdot 2^2a^2 = 27 \cdot 4 \cdot a^{3+2} = 108a^5$

9. $2^0 = 1$

10. $5^{-3} = \frac{1}{5^3} = \frac{1}{125}$

11. $(-7)^{-2} = \frac{1}{(-7)^2} = \frac{1}{49}$

12. $\frac{1}{2^{-1}} = 2^1 = 2$

13. $x^6y^{-6} = x^6 \cdot \frac{1}{y^6} = \frac{x^6}{y^6}$

14. $\frac{5}{q^{-3}} = 5q^3$

15. $\frac{a^{-2}}{b^{-5}} = \frac{b^5}{a^2}$

16. $(2y)^{-4} = \frac{1}{(2y)^4} = \frac{1}{2^4y^4} = \frac{1}{16y^4}$

Copyright © McDougal Littell Inc.
All rights reserved.

20. $y = -\left(\frac{3}{2}\right)^x$

x	-2	-1	0	1	2	3
y	$-\frac{4}{9}$	$-\frac{2}{3}$	-1	$-\frac{3}{2}$	$-\frac{9}{4}$	$-\frac{27}{8}$

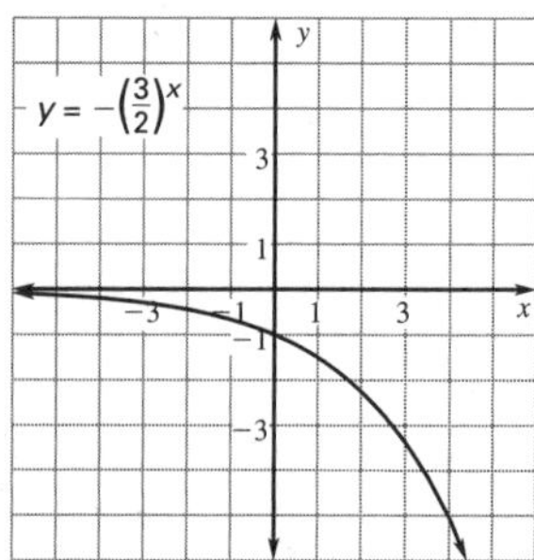

21. $\frac{3^2}{3^3} = 3^{2-3} = 3^{-1} = \frac{1}{3}$

22. $\frac{x^5}{x^2} = x^{5-2} = x^3$

23. $\left(\frac{4}{9}\right)^2 = \frac{4^2}{9^2} = \frac{16}{81}$

24. $\left(\frac{r}{3}\right)^{-3} = \frac{r^{-3}}{3^{-3}} = \frac{3^3}{r^3} = \frac{27}{r^3}$

25. $$\begin{aligned}\frac{9x^6}{y} \cdot \frac{y^2}{x^6} &= \frac{9x^6y^2}{yx^6}\\ &= 9x^{6-6}y^{2-1}\\ &= 9x^0y^1\\ &= 9(1)y\\ &= 9y\end{aligned}$$

26. $$\begin{aligned}\frac{m^7}{3n^4} \cdot \frac{3m^2n^2}{mn} &= \frac{3m^{7+2}n^2}{3mn^{4+1}}\\ &= \frac{m^9n^2}{mn^5}\\ &= m^{9-1}n^{2-5}\\ &= m^8n^{-3}\\ &= \frac{m^8}{n^3}\end{aligned}$$

27. $$\begin{aligned}\left(\frac{2a^4b^5}{5a^2b}\right)^3 &= \left(\frac{2a^{4-2}b^{5-1}}{5}\right)^3\\ &= \left(\frac{2a^2b^4}{5}\right)^3\\ &= \frac{2^3a^{2\cdot 3}b^{4\cdot 3}}{5^3}\\ &= \frac{8a^6b^{12}}{125}\end{aligned}$$

28. $$\begin{aligned}\frac{8s^4t^{-2}}{2s^3t^3} \cdot \frac{3s^2t^7}{2s^{-1}} &= \frac{24s^{4+2}t^{-2+7}}{4s^{3-1}t^3}\\ &= \frac{6s^6t^5}{s^2t^3}\\ &= 6s^{6-2}t^{5-3}\\ &= 6s^4t^2\end{aligned}$$

29. $7 \times 10^1 = 70$

30. $6.7 \times 10^3 = 6700$

31. $2 \times 10^{-4} = 0.0002$

32. $7.68 \times 10^{-5} = 0.0000768$

33. $52{,}000{,}000 = 5.2 \times 10^7$

34. $63.5 = 6.35 \times 10^1$

35. $0.009 = 9 \times 10^{-3}$

36. $0.00000023 = 2.3 \times 10^{-7}$

37. $$\begin{aligned}(5 \times 10^4)(3 \times 10^2) &= (5 \cdot 3) \times (10^4 \times 10^2)\\ &= 15 \times 10^6\\ &= (1.5 \times 10^1) \times 10^6\\ &= 1.5 \times 10^7\end{aligned}$$

38. $$\begin{aligned}(4.1 \times 10^{-1})(6 \times 10^5) &= (4.1 \times 6)(10^{-1} \times 10^5)\\ &= 24.6 \times 10^4\\ &= (2.46 \times 10^1) \times 10^4\\ &= 2.46 \times 10^5\end{aligned}$$

39. $$\begin{aligned}(1.2 \times 10^7)(1.2 \times 10^0) &= (1.2 \times 1.2)(10^7 \times 10^0)\\ &= 1.44 \times 10^7\end{aligned}$$

40. $\frac{9 \times 10^6}{3 \times 10^3} = \frac{9}{3} \times \frac{10^6}{10^3} = 3 \times 10^3$

41. $$\begin{aligned}\frac{4.9 \times 10^1}{7 \times 10^{-8}} &= \frac{4.9}{7} \times \frac{10^1}{10^{-8}}\\ &= 0.7 \times 10^9\\ &= (7 \times 10^{-1}) \times 10^9\\ &= 7 \times 10^8\end{aligned}$$

42. $$\begin{aligned}\frac{3.4 \times 10^{-4}}{6.8 \times 10^{-3}} &= \frac{3.4}{6.8} \times \frac{10^{-4}}{10^{-3}}\\ &= \frac{1}{2} \times 10^{-1}\\ &= 0.5 \times 10^{-1}\\ &= (5 \times 10^{-1}) \times 10^{-1}\\ &= 5 \times 10^{-2}\end{aligned}$$

43. $y = 2(1 + 0.05)^t$
$y = 2(1.05)^t$

44. $y = 2(1.05)^{10} \approx 3.26$ miles

45. $y = 125(1 - 0.03)^t$
$y = 125(0.97)^t$

46. In 2000, $t = 7$; $y = 125(0.97)^7 \approx 101$ people

Chapter Test *(p. 493)*

1. $x^3 \cdot x^4 = x^{3+4} = x^7$

2. $(a^3)^7 = a^{3\cdot 7} = a^{21}$

3. $(2d)^3 = 2^3d^3 = 8d^3$

4. $(mn)^2 \cdot n^4 = m^2n^2 \cdot n^4 = m^2n^{2+4} = m^2n^6$

5. $9^0 = 1$

6. $\frac{1}{5^{-2}} = 5^2 = 25$

7. $8x^2y^{-4} = \frac{8x^2}{y^4}$

8. $\frac{9p^{-3}}{q^{-4}} = \frac{9q^4}{p^3}$

Copyright © McDougal Littell Inc.
All rights reserved.

9. $y = 2^x$

x	-2	-1	0	1	2	3
y	$\frac{1}{4}$	$\frac{1}{2}$	1	2	4	8

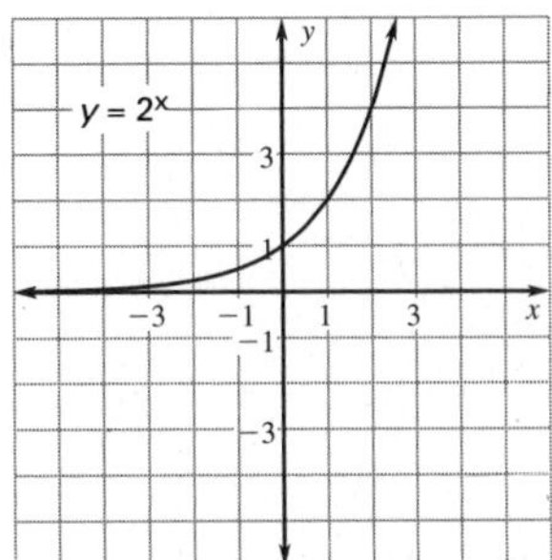

10. $y = -5(3)^x$

x	-2	-1	0	1	2	3
y	$-\frac{5}{9}$	$-\frac{5}{3}$	-5	-15	-45	-135

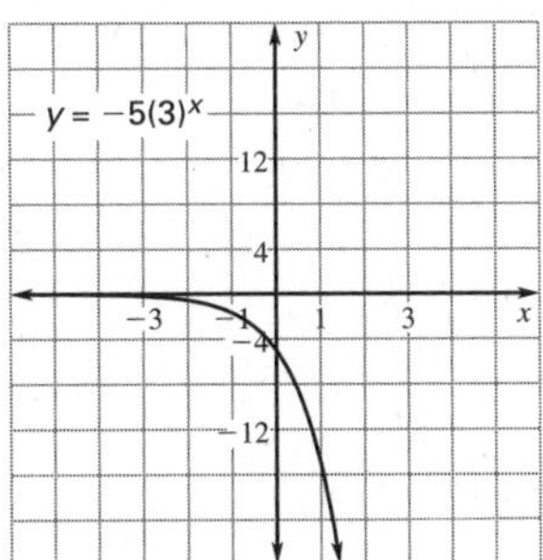

11. $y = \left(\frac{2}{3}\right)^x$

x	-2	-1	0	1	2	3
y	$\frac{9}{4}$	$\frac{3}{2}$	1	$\frac{2}{3}$	$\frac{4}{9}$	$\frac{8}{27}$

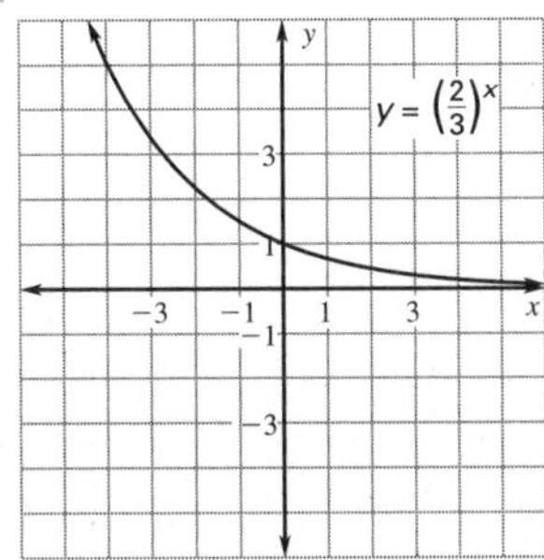

12. $y = 10\left(\frac{1}{4}\right)^x$

x	-2	-1	0	1	2	3
y	160	40	10	2.5	0.6	0.2

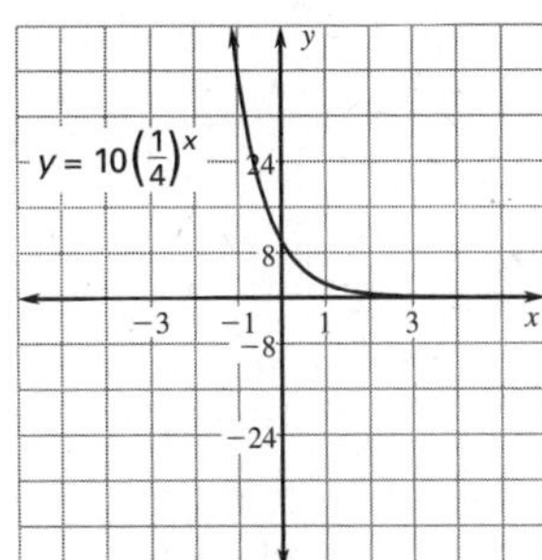

13. $g = 16(0.5)^h$

h	0	1	2	3	4
g	16	8	4	2	1

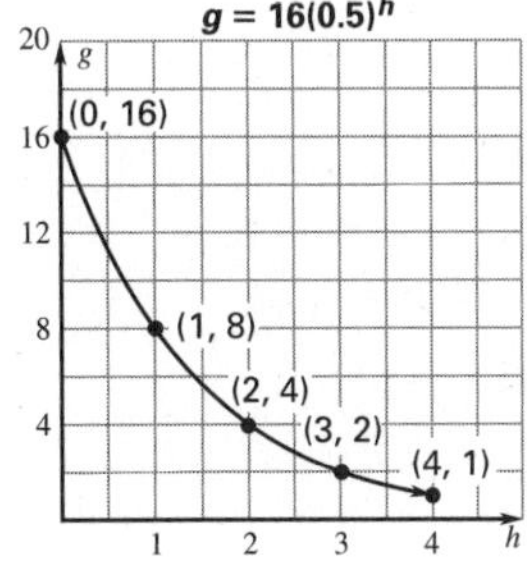

14. $\frac{5^4}{5} = 5^{4-1} = 5^3 = 125$

15. $\left(\frac{3}{4}\right)^3 = \frac{3^3}{4^3} = \frac{27}{64}$

16. $\frac{x^3}{xy^4} \cdot \frac{y^5}{x^5} = \frac{x^3y^5}{x^{1+5}y^4}$
$= \frac{x^3y^5}{x^6y^4}$
$= x^{3-6}y^{5-4}$
$= x^{-3}y^1$
$= \frac{y}{x^3}$

17. $\frac{a^{-1}b^2}{ab} \cdot \frac{a^2b^3}{a^{-2}} = \frac{a^{-1+2}b^{2+3}}{a^{1-2} \cdot b}$
$= \frac{a^1b^5}{a^{-1}b^1}$
$= a^{1-(-1)}b^{5-1}$
$= a^2b^4$

18. $4 \times 10^5 = 400{,}000$

19. $8.56 \times 10^3 = 8560$

20. $5 \times 10^{-2} = 0.05$

21. $6.28 \times 10^{-4} = 0.000628$

22. $9{,}000{,}000 = 9 \times 10^6$

23. $6550 = 6.55 \times 10^3$

24. $0.012 = 1.2 \times 10^{-2}$

Copyright © McDougal Littell Inc.
All rights reserved.

25. $0.0000317 = 3.17 \times 10^{-5}$

26. $(4.2 \times 10^6)(3.2 \times 10^7) = (4.2 \times 3.2)(10^6 \times 10^7)$
$= 13.44 \times 10^{13}$
$= (1.344 \times 10^1) \times 10^{13}$
$\approx 1.3 \times 10^{14}\ \text{ft}^3$

27. $y = 500(1 + 0.07)^t$
$y = 500(1.07)^t$

28. $y = 500(1.07)^7 \approx \$802.89$

29. $y = 88{,}500(1 - 0.10)^t$
$y = 88{,}500(0.9)^t$

30. In 2001, $t = 5$.
$y = 88{,}500(0.9)^5$
$y \approx \$52{,}258$ or $\$52{,}300$

Chapter Standardized Test *(p. 494)*

1. $7^4 \cdot 7^7 = 7^{4+7} = 7^{11}$; A

2. $(a^3)^4 = a^{3 \cdot 4} = a^{12}$; C

3. $(2x^2y^3)^2 = 2^2x^{2 \cdot 2}y^{3 \cdot 2} = 4x^4y^6$; C

4. $\dfrac{2a^{-1}}{b^{-2}c^2} = \dfrac{2b^2}{ac^2}$; C

5. Initial value is 5 for B or D;
Test a point in B and D.
(1, 1.2)
B. $1.2 \stackrel{?}{=} 5(4)^1$
$1.2 \neq 20$
D. $1.2 \stackrel{?}{=} 5\left(\dfrac{1}{4}\right)^1$
$1.2 \approx 1.25$

D

Also, since $b = 4$ in B, it is an exponential growth model, and since $b = \dfrac{1}{4}$ in D, it is an exponential decay model. The graph shown is decreasing (decaying).

6. D; $\dfrac{x^5}{x^2} = x^{5-2} = x^3$

7. $\left(\dfrac{3}{5}\right)^{-2} = \dfrac{3^{-2}}{5^{-2}} = \dfrac{5^2}{3^2} = \dfrac{25}{9}$; B

8. $\dfrac{4x^2y^2}{4xy} \cdot \dfrac{8xy^3}{4y} = \dfrac{32x^{2+1}y^{2+3}}{16xy^{1+1}}$
$= \dfrac{2x^3y^5}{xy^2}$
$= 2x^{3-1}y^{5-2}$
$= 2x^2y^3$

C

9. C; $21.2 > 10$

10. $\dfrac{1.55 \times 10^4}{2.5 \times 10^{-3}} = 0.62 \times 10^{4-(-3)}$
$= (6.2 \times 10^{-1}) \times 10^7$
$= 6.2 \times 10^6$

D

11. $y = 450(1 + 0.06)^6$
$y = 450(1.06)^6 \approx \$638.33$
C

12. $y = 42{,}000(1 - 0.08)^6$
$y = 42{,}000(0.92)^6$
$y \approx \$25{,}467$
D

Maintaining Skills *(p. 495)*

1.
$8 = 2^3$
2×4
$2 \times 2 \times 2$

2.
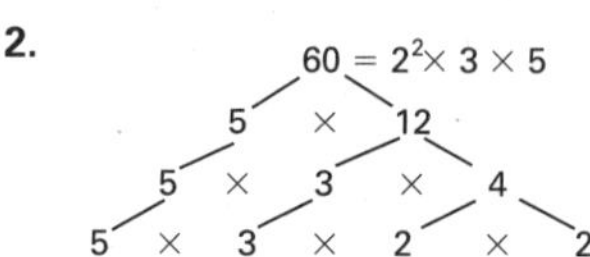

3.
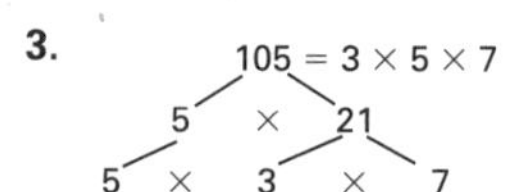

4.
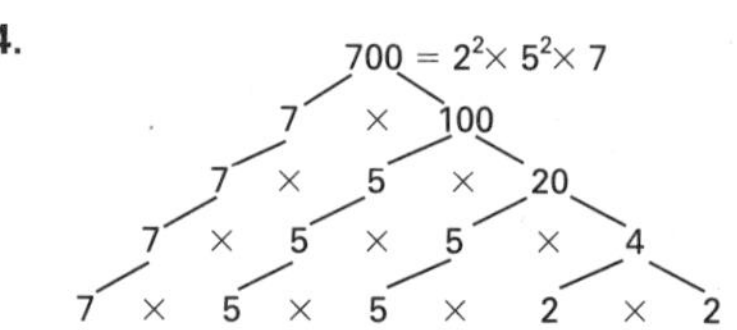

5. $\dfrac{21}{8} = 21 \div 8 = 2$ remainder $5 = 2\dfrac{5}{8}$

6. $\dfrac{42}{5} = 42 \div 5 = 8$ remainder $2 = 8\dfrac{2}{5}$

7. $\dfrac{27}{15} = 27 \div 15 = 1$ remainder $12 = 1\dfrac{12}{15} = 1\dfrac{4}{5}$

8. $\dfrac{75}{9} = 75 \div 9 = 8$ remainder $3 = 8\dfrac{3}{9} = 8\dfrac{1}{3}$

Copyright © McDougal Littell Inc.
All rights reserved.

CHAPTER 9

Chapter Opener *(p. 496)*

Think & Discuss (p. 497)

1. 100 ft

2. 400 ft

Chapter Readiness Quiz (p. 498)

1. x-intercept (B)

2. $3x^2 - 108 = 3(-4)^2 - 108 = 3(16) - 108$
$= 48 - 108 = -60$
(D)

3. C $(-2, 2)$
$3(-2) + 4(2) \stackrel{?}{<} 5$
$-6 + 8 \stackrel{?}{<} 5$
$2 < 5$

Lesson 9.1

9.1 Checkpoint (pp. 499–500)

1. The positive square root of 4 is 2.

2. The positive square root of 25 is 5.

3. The negative square root of 16 is -4.

4. The positive and negative square roots of 36 are 6 and -6.

5. $\pm\sqrt{100} = \pm\sqrt{10^2} = \pm 10$

6. $-\sqrt{25} = -\sqrt{5^2} = -5$

7. $\sqrt{36} = \sqrt{6^2} = 6$

8. $\sqrt{16} = \sqrt{4^2} = 4$

9. $\sqrt{100} = \sqrt{10^2} = 10$

10. $-\sqrt{5} \approx -2.24$

11. $\sqrt{23} \approx 4.80$

12. $-\sqrt{81} = -\sqrt{9^2} = -9$

13. $\sqrt{b^2 - 4ac} = \sqrt{3^2 - 4(2)(-5)}$
$= \sqrt{9 + 40}$
$= \sqrt{49}$
$= 7$

14. $\sqrt{b^2 - 4ac} = \sqrt{8^2 - 4(-1)(20)}$
$= \sqrt{64 + 80}$
$= \sqrt{144}$
$= 12$

15. $6 \pm \sqrt{5} = 8.24$ and 3.76

16. $4 \pm \sqrt{8} = 6.83$ and 1.17

17. $\dfrac{2 \pm \sqrt{3}}{3} = 1.24$ and 0.09

18. $\dfrac{2 \pm 3\sqrt{6}}{4} = 2.34$ and -1.34

9.1 Guided Practice (p. 502)

1. square root

2. positive or principal square root, negative square root, positive and negative square roots

3. 4

4. $\sqrt{81} = \sqrt{9^2} = 9$

5. $\pm\sqrt{121} = \pm\sqrt{11^2} = \pm 11$

6. $-\sqrt{36} = -\sqrt{6^2} = -6$

7. $-\sqrt{4} = -2$

8. $\sqrt{25} = \sqrt{5^2} = 5$, rational

9. $\sqrt{6} \approx 2.45$, irrational

10. $\sqrt{100} = \sqrt{10^2} = 10$, rational

11. $\sqrt{10} \approx 3.16$, irrational

12. $1 \pm \sqrt{2} = 2.41, -0.41$

13. $6 \pm 5\sqrt{3} = 14.66, -2.66$

14. $3 \pm \sqrt{7} = 5.65, 0.35$

15. $2 \pm 4\sqrt{8} = 13.31, -9.31$

9.1 Practice and Applications (pp. 502–504)

16. The positive square root of 625 is 25.

17. The positive and negative square roots of 16 are 4 and -4.

18. The positive and negative square roots of 4 are 2 and -2.

19. The positive square root of 225 is 15.

20. The negative square root of 121 is -11.

21. The negative square root of 289 is -17.

22. The positive square root of 49 is 7.

23. The positive square root of 1 is 1.

24. The positive square root of $\frac{1}{9}$ is $\frac{1}{3}$.

25. $\sqrt{144} = \sqrt{12^2} = 12$

26. $\pm\sqrt{25} = \pm\sqrt{5^2} = \pm 5$

27. $\sqrt{196} = \sqrt{14^2} = 14$

28. $\pm\sqrt{900} = \pm\sqrt{30^2} = \pm 30$

29. $\pm\sqrt{49} = \pm\sqrt{7^2} = \pm 7$

30. $\sqrt{0} = 0$

31. $-\sqrt{256} = -\sqrt{16^2} = -16$

32. $-\sqrt{100} = -\sqrt{10^2} = -10$

33. $\sqrt{400} = \sqrt{20^2} = 20$

34. $-\sqrt{225} = -\sqrt{15^2} = -15$

35. $\sqrt{121} = \sqrt{11^2} = 11$

Copyright © McDougal Littell Inc.
All rights reserved.

Chapter 9 *continued*

36. $\sqrt{289} = \sqrt{17^2} = 17$

37. $-\sqrt{1} = -\sqrt{1^2} = -1$

38. $\pm\sqrt{81} = \pm\sqrt{9^2} = \pm 9$

39. $\sqrt{169} = \sqrt{13^2} = 13$

40. $-\sqrt{625} = -\sqrt{25^2} = -25$

41. no, $\sqrt{10} \approx 3.16$

42. yes, $\sqrt{81} = 9$

43. no, $\sqrt{-5}$ is imaginary

44. no, $\sqrt{120} \approx 10.95$

45. yes, $\sqrt{16} = 4$

46. yes, $\sqrt{1} = 1$

47. no, $\sqrt{111} \approx 10.54$

48. yes, $\sqrt{225} = 15$

49. no, $\sqrt{-4}$ is imaginary

50. yes, $\sqrt{10{,}000} = 100$

51. no, $\sqrt{\frac{9}{4}} = \frac{3}{2}$

52. no, $\sqrt{\frac{1}{2}} \approx 0.71$

53. $\sqrt{5} \approx 2.24$

54. $\sqrt{25} = 5$

55. $\sqrt{13} \approx 3.61$

56. $-\sqrt{125} \approx -11.18$

57. $-\sqrt{49} = -7$

58. $\pm\sqrt{70} \approx \pm 8.37$

59. $\pm\sqrt{1} = \pm 1$

60. $\sqrt{10} \approx 3.16$

61. $\pm\sqrt{15} \approx \pm 3.87$

62. $-\sqrt{400} = -20$

63. $-\sqrt{20} \approx -4.47$

64. $\pm\sqrt{144} = \pm 12$

65. $\sqrt{b^2 - 4ac} = \sqrt{5^2 - 4(4)(1)}$
$= \sqrt{25 - 16}$
$= \sqrt{9}$
$= 3$

66. $\sqrt{b^2 - 4ac} = \sqrt{4^2 - 4(2)(-6)}$
$= \sqrt{16 + 48}$
$= \sqrt{64}$
$= 8$

67. $\sqrt{b^2 - 4ac} = \sqrt{8^2 - 4(-2)(-8)}$
$= \sqrt{64 - 64}$
$= \sqrt{0}$
$= 0$

68. $\sqrt{b^2 - 4ac} = \sqrt{5^2 - 4(-5)(10)}$
$= \sqrt{25 + 200}$
$= \sqrt{225}$
$= 15$

69. $\sqrt{b^2 + 10a} = \sqrt{4^2 + 10(2)}$
$= \sqrt{16 + 20}$
$= \sqrt{36}$
$= 6$

70. $\sqrt{b^2 - 8a} = \sqrt{4^2 - 8(2)}$
$= \sqrt{16 - 16}$
$= \sqrt{0}$
$= 0$

71. $\sqrt{a^2 + 45} = \sqrt{2^2 + 45}$
$= \sqrt{4 + 45}$
$= \sqrt{49}$
$= 7$

72. $\frac{\sqrt{b^2 + 42a}}{a} = \frac{\sqrt{4^2 + 42(2)}}{2}$
$= \frac{\sqrt{16 + 84}}{2}$
$= \frac{\sqrt{100}}{2}$
$= \frac{10}{2} = 5$

73. $\frac{10 + 2\sqrt{b}}{a} = \frac{10 + 2\sqrt{4}}{2}$
$= \frac{10 + 2(2)}{2}$
$= \frac{10 + 4}{2}$
$= \frac{14}{2} = 7$

74. $\frac{36 - \sqrt{8a}}{b} = \frac{36 - \sqrt{8(2)}}{4}$
$= \frac{36 - \sqrt{16}}{4}$
$= \frac{36 - 4}{4}$
$= \frac{32}{4} = 8$

75. $8 \pm \sqrt{5} = 10.24, 5.76$

76. $2 \pm 5\sqrt{3} = 10.66, -6.66$

77. $-6 \pm 4\sqrt{2} = -0.34, -11.66$

78. $\frac{1 \pm 6\sqrt{8}}{6} = 3.00, -2.66$

79. $\frac{7 \pm 3\sqrt{2}}{-1} = -11.24, -2.76$

80. $\frac{4 \pm 7\sqrt{3}}{2} = 8.06, -4.06$

81. $\frac{5 \pm 6\sqrt{3}}{3} = 5.13, -1.80$

82. $\frac{3 \pm 4\sqrt{5}}{4} = 2.99, -1.49$

83. $\frac{7 \pm 3\sqrt{12}}{-6} = -2.90, 0.57$

84. yes, 9 squares on each side.

85. m is a perfect square

86. true; *Sample example:* The square roots of 25 are 5 and -5.

87. false; The square root of 0 is 0.

88. true; Any negative number, for example -12, has no real root.

Copyright © McDougal Littell Inc.
All rights reserved.

89. $3 \pm \sqrt{(-3)^2 - 4(0.5)(-8)}$

$= 3 \pm \sqrt{9 + 16}$

$= 3 \pm \sqrt{25}$

$= 3 \pm 5$

$= 3 + 5 = 8$ and $3 - 5 = -2$

Answer 8, -2

9.1 Standardized Test Practice (p. 504)

90. $\frac{15 \pm 5\sqrt{225}}{3} = \frac{15 \pm 5(15)}{3} = \frac{15 \pm 75}{3}$

$\frac{15 + 75}{3} = \frac{90}{3} = 30$ and $\frac{15 - 75}{3} = \frac{-60}{3} = -20$

Answer: *B*

91. *H*; $\sqrt{121} = \sqrt{11^2} = 11$ (an integer)

92. $14^2 = 196$; $15^2 = 225$

$14 < \sqrt{200} < 15$

14 and 15 (*C*)

93. $b = \sqrt{b^2} = \sqrt{49} = 7$ or -7

$a = \sqrt{a^2} = \sqrt{36} = 6$ or -6

$b - a = (7) - (6) = 1$

$b - a = (-7) - (-6) = -1$

$b - a = 7 - (-6) = 13$

$b - a = (-7) - 6 = -13$

greatest value is 13 (*J*)

9.1 Mixed Review (p. 504)

94. $y = -3$

$x = 4$

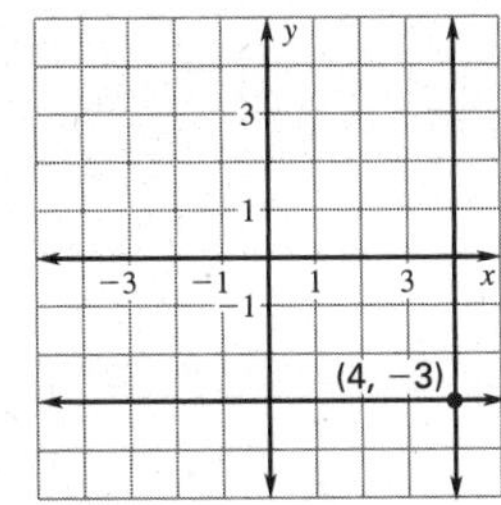

Solution: $(4, -3)$

Check: $-3 = -3$ $\quad 4 = 4$

95. $2x - 4y = 12$

$-4y = -2x + 12$

$y = \frac{1}{2}x - 3$

$m = \frac{1}{2}$; $b = -3$

$y = -2$

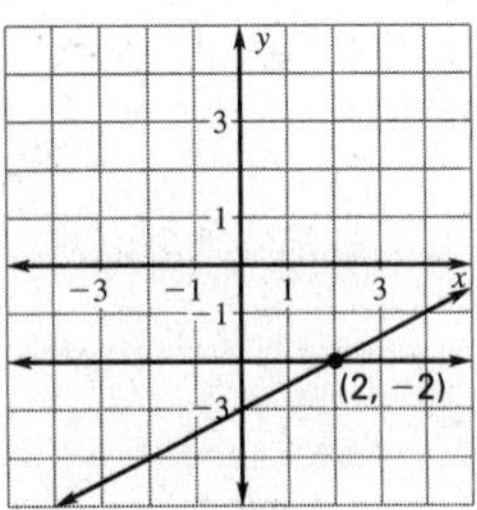

Solution: $(2, -2)$

Check:

$2(2) - 4(-2) \stackrel{?}{=} 12$

$4 + 8 \stackrel{?}{=} 12$

$12 = 12$

$-2 = -2$

96. $2x - y = 10$

$-y = -2x + 10$

$y = 2x - 10$

$m = 2$; $b = -10$

$x + y = 5$

$y = -x + 5$

$m = -1$; $b = 5$

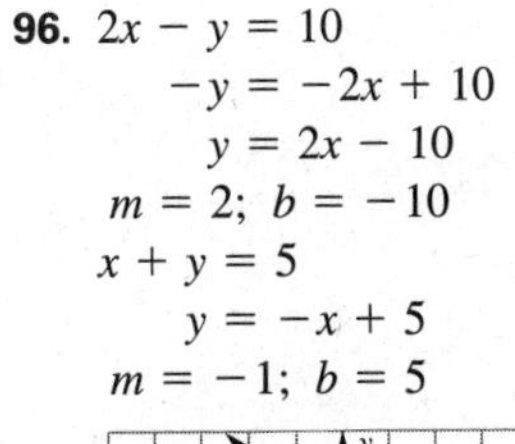

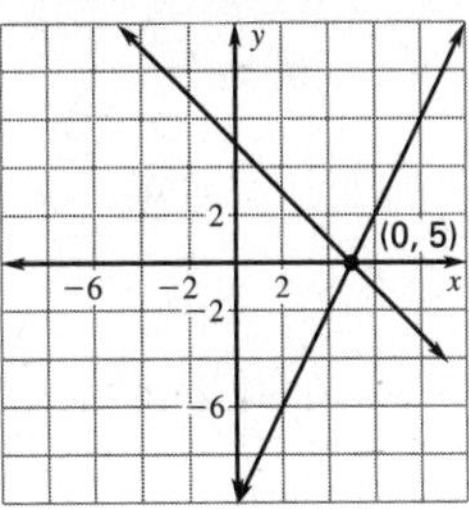

Solution: $(5, 0)$

Check:

$2(5) - 0 \stackrel{?}{=} 10$

$10 = 10$

$5 + 0 \stackrel{?}{=} 5$

$5 = 5$

97.

$s + a = 324$

$2s + 3a = 764$

$-2s - 2a = -648$ $\quad$ Multiply by -2

$+ 2s + 3a = 764$

$a = 116$

$s + 116 = 324$

$s = 208$

116 adult tickets, 208 student tickets

Copyright © McDougal Littell Inc.
All rights reserved.

98. $I + L = 15$

$4I + 3L = 50$

$-4I - 4L = -60$ Multiply by -4.

$+ 4I + 3L = 50$

$-L = -10$

$L = 10$

$I + 10 = 15$

$I = 5$

5 irises and 10 lilies

99. $10x - 3y = 17$

$-7x + y = 9$

Sample answer:

$10x - 3y = 17$

$-21x + 3y = 27$ Multiply by 3.

$-11x = 44$

$x = -4$

$-7(-4) + y = 9$

$28 + y = 9$

$y = -19$

Solution: $(-4, -19)$

100. $12x - 4y = -32$

$x + 3y = 4$

Sample answer:

$12x - 4y = -32$

$-12x - 36y = -48$ Multiply by -12.

$-40y = -80$

$x + 3(2) = 4$

$x = -2$

$y = 2$

Solution: $(-2, 2)$

101. $8x - 5y = 70$

$2x + y = 4$

Sample answer:

$8x - 5y = 70$

$10x + 5y = 20$

$18x = 90$

$x = 5$

$2(5) + y = 4$

$10 + y = 4$

$y = -6$

Solution: $(5, -6)$

9.1 Maintaining Skills (p. 504)

102. $\frac{3}{4} = 0.75$

103. $\frac{8}{15} = 0.5\bar{3}$

104. $\frac{6}{11} = 0.\overline{54}$

105. $\frac{7}{8} = 0.875$

106. $\frac{2}{9} = 0.\bar{2}$

107. $\frac{5}{16} = 0.3125$

108. $\frac{5}{6} = 0.8\bar{3}$

109. $\frac{2}{5} = 0.4$

110. $\frac{5}{8} = 0.625$

111. $\frac{8}{9} = 0.\bar{8}$

112. $\frac{3}{5} = 0.6$

113. $\frac{9}{10} = 0.9$

Lesson 9.2

9.2 Checkpoint (pp. 505–507)

1. $x^2 = 81$

$x = \pm\sqrt{81}$

$x = \pm 9$

Check: $(9)^2 \stackrel{?}{=} 81$

$81 = 81$

$(-9)^2 \stackrel{?}{=} 81$

$81 = 81$

2. $y^2 = 11$

$y = \pm\sqrt{11}$

Check: $(\sqrt{11})^2 \stackrel{?}{=} 11$

$11 = 11$

$(-\sqrt{11})^2 \stackrel{?}{=} 11$

$11 = 11$

3. $n^2 = 25$

$n = \pm\sqrt{25}$

$n = \pm 5$

Check: $(5)^2 \stackrel{?}{=} 25$

$25 = 25$

$(-5)^2 \stackrel{?}{=} 25$

$25 = 25$

4. $x^2 = 10$

$x = \pm\sqrt{10}$

Check: $(\sqrt{10})^2 \stackrel{?}{=} 10$

$10 = 10$

$(-\sqrt{10})^2 \stackrel{?}{=} 10$

$10 = 10$

5. $x^2 - 1 = 0$

$x^2 = 1$

$x = \pm\sqrt{1}$

$x = \pm 1$

6. $2x^2 - 72 = 0$

$2x^2 = 72$

$x^2 = 36$

$x = \pm\sqrt{36}$

$x = \pm 6$

7. $27 - 3y^2 = 0$

$-3y^2 = -27$

$y^2 = 9$

$y = \pm\sqrt{9}$

$y = \pm 3$

8. $h = -16t^2 + s$

$h = -16t^2 + 64$ Substitute 64 for s.

Copyright © McDougal Littell Inc.
All rights reserved.

9. $h = 0$ on the ground,

$$0 = -16t^2 + 64$$
$$-64 = -16t^2$$
$$4 = t^2$$
$$\pm\sqrt{4} = t$$
$$\pm 2 = t$$

Note: negative 2 does not make sense in this situation.
Answer: 2 seconds

9.2 Guided Practice (p. 508)

1. No; There is no x^2 term.

2. $7x^2 - 3x - 12 = 0$; 7

3. $x = \pm\sqrt{6}$; 2 real solutions

4. $x = \pm\sqrt{0}$; 1 real solution

5. $x = \pm\sqrt{-17}$; no real solutions

6. $x^2 = 0$
$x = \pm\sqrt{0}$;
1 real solution

7. $x^2 = 20$
$x = \pm\sqrt{20}$;
2 real solutions

8. $x^2 = -4$
$x = \pm\sqrt{-4}$;
no real solution

9. $y^2 = 49$
$y = \pm\sqrt{49}$
$y = \pm 7$

10. $x^2 = -16$
$x = \pm\sqrt{-16}$;
no real solution

11. $n^2 = 7$
$n = \pm\sqrt{7}$

12. $3x^2 - 20 = -2$
$3x^2 = 18$
$x^2 = 6$
$x = \pm\sqrt{6}$

13. $5x^2 = -25$
$x^2 = -5$
$x = \pm\sqrt{-5}$;
no real solution

14. $2x^2 - 8 = 0$
$2x^2 = 8$
$x^2 = 4$
$x = \pm\sqrt{4}$
$x = \pm 2$

15.

$$h = -16t^2 + s$$
$$0 = -16t^2 + 48$$
$$-48 = -16t^2$$
$$3 = t^2$$
$$\pm\sqrt{3} = t$$
$$\pm 1.7 = t$$

-1.7 seconds does not make sense
Answer: 1.7 sec

16.

$$h = -16t^2 + s$$
$$0 = -16t^2 + 160$$
$$-160 = -16t^2$$
$$10 = t^2$$
$$\pm\sqrt{10} = t$$
$$\pm 3.2 = t$$

-3.2 seconds does not make sense.
Answer: 3.2 sec

17.

$$h = -16t^2 + s$$
$$0 = -16t^2 + 192$$
$$-192 = -16t^2$$
$$12 = t^2$$
$$\pm\sqrt{12} = t$$
$$\pm 3.5 = t$$

-3.5 seconds does not make sense.
Answer: 3.5 sec

9.2 Practice and Applications (pp. 508–510)

18. $x^2 = 9$
$x = \pm\sqrt{9}$
$x = \pm 3$

19. $m^2 = 1$
$m = \pm\sqrt{1}$
$m = \pm 1$

20. $x^2 = 17$
$x = \pm\sqrt{17}$

21. $k^2 = -44$
$k = \pm\sqrt{-44}$;
no real solution

22. $y^2 = 15$
$y = \pm\sqrt{15}$

23. $x^2 = 225$
$x = \pm\sqrt{225}$
$x = \pm 15$

24. $r^2 = -81$
$r = \pm\sqrt{-81}$;
no real solution

25. $x^2 = 121$
$x = \pm\sqrt{121}$
$x = \pm 11$

26. $t^2 = 39$
$t = \pm\sqrt{39}$

27. $x^2 = 256$
$x = \pm 16$

Copyright © McDougal Littell Inc.
All rights reserved.

28. $y^2 = 0$
$y = \pm\sqrt{0}$
$y = 0$

29. $n^2 = 49$
$n = \pm\sqrt{49}$
$n = \pm 7$

30. $y^2 = 400$
$y = \pm\sqrt{400}$
$y = \pm 20$

31. $x^2 = 64$
$x = \pm\sqrt{64}$
$x = \pm 8$

32. $m^2 = -9$
$m = \pm\sqrt{-9}$;
no real solution

33. $x^2 = 16$
$x = \pm\sqrt{16}$
$x = \pm 4$

34. $5x^2 = 500$
$x^2 = 100$
$x = \pm\sqrt{100}$
$x = \pm 10$

35. $3x^2 = 6$
$x^2 = 2$
$x = \pm\sqrt{2}$

36. $5y^2 = 25$
$y^2 = 5$
$y = \pm\sqrt{5}$

37. $a^2 + 3 = 12$
$a^2 = 9$
$a = \pm\sqrt{9}$
$a = \pm 3$

38. $x^2 - 7 = 57$
$x^2 = 64$
$x = \pm\sqrt{64}$
$x = \pm 8$

39. $x^2 + 36 = 0$
$x^2 = -36$
$x = \pm\sqrt{-36}$;
no real solution

40. $2s^2 - 5 = 27$
$2s^2 = 32$
$s^2 = 16$
$s = \pm\sqrt{16}$
$s = \pm 4$

41. $3x^2 - 75 = 0$
$3x^2 = 75$
$x^2 = 25$
$x = \pm\sqrt{25}$
$x = \pm 5$

42. $7x^2 + 30 = 9$
$7x^2 = -21$
$x^2 = -3$
$x = \pm\sqrt{-3}$;
no real solution

43. $5x^2 + 5 = 20$
$5x^2 = 15$
$x^2 = 3$
$x = \pm\sqrt{3}$

44. $5t^2 + 10 = 135$
$5t^2 = 125$
$t^2 = 25$
$t = \pm\sqrt{25}$
$t = \pm 5$

45. $3x^2 - 50 = 58$
$3x^2 = 108$
$x^2 = 36$
$x = \pm\sqrt{36}$
$x = \pm 6$

46. $m^2 - 12 = 52$
$m^2 = 64$
$m = \pm\sqrt{64}$
$m = \pm 8$

47. $2y^2 + 13 = 41$
$2y^2 = 28$
$y^2 = 14$
$y = \pm\sqrt{14}$

48. $20 - x^2 = 4$
$-x^2 = -16$
$x^2 = 16$
$x = \pm\sqrt{16}$
$x = \pm 4$

49. When the equation $x^2 = -36$ was obtained, you should write "no real solution," since negative numbers do not have real square roots.

50. $4x^2 - 3 = 57$
$4x^2 = 60$
$x^2 = 15$
$x = \pm\sqrt{15}$
$x = \pm 3.87$

51. $6y^2 + 22 = 34$
$6y^2 = 12$
$y^2 = 2$
$y = \pm\sqrt{2}$
$y = \pm 1.41$

52. $2x^2 - 4 = 10$
$2x^2 = 14$
$x^2 = 7$
$x = \pm\sqrt{7}$
$x = \pm 2.65$

Copyright © McDougal Littell Inc.
All rights reserved.

53. $3x^2 + 7 = 31$
$3x^2 = 24$
$x^2 = 8$
$x = \pm\sqrt{8}$
$x = \pm 2.83$

54. $7n^2 - 6 = 15$
$7n^2 = 21$
$n^2 = 3$
$n = \pm\sqrt{3}$
$n = \pm 1.73$

55. $5x^2 - 12 = 5$
$5x^2 = 17$
$x^2 = \frac{17}{5} = 3.4$
$x = \pm\sqrt{3.4}$
$x = \pm 1.84$

56. True; *Sample answer:* A negative number has no real square root.

57. True; the solutions of $x^2 = c$ are $\sqrt{c}$ and $-\sqrt{c}$.

58. False; the solution is 0.

59. $h = -16t^2 + s$
$h = -16t^2 + 96$

60. $0 = -16t^2 + 96$
$-96 = -16t^2$
$6 = t^2$
$\pm\sqrt{6} = t$
$\pm 2.4 = t$
2.4 sec

61. $Hd^2 = 1.89$
$12d^2 = 1.89$
$d^2 = 0.1575$
$d = \pm\sqrt{0.1575}$
$d = \pm 0.40$
0.40 mm

62. $Hd^2 = 1.89$
$50d^2 = 1.89$
$d^2 = 0.0378$
$d = \pm\sqrt{0.0378}$
$d = \pm 0.19$
0.19 mm

63. $Hd^2 = 1.89$
$80d^2 = 1.89$
$d^2 = 0.023625$
$d = \pm\sqrt{0.023625}$
$d = \pm 0.15$
0.15 mm

64. $Hd^2 = 1.89$
$125d^2 = 1.89$
$d^2 = 0.01512$
$d = \pm\sqrt{0.01512}$
$d = \pm 0.12$
0.12 mm

65. $Hd^2 = 1.89$
$140d^2 = 1.89$
$d^2 = 0.0135$
$d = \pm\sqrt{0.0135}$
$d = \pm 0.12$
0.12 mm

66. $Hd^2 = 1.89$
$755d^2 = 1.89$
$d^2 = 0.0025$
$d = \pm\sqrt{0.0025}$
$d = \pm 0.05$
0.05 mm

67. In 1800, $t = 0$
$P = 5{,}500{,}400 + 683{,}300t^2$
$P = 5{,}500{,}400 + 683{,}300(0)^2$
$P = 5{,}500{,}400$
In 1850, $t = 5$
$P = 5{,}500{,}400 + 683{,}300(5)^2$
$P = 22{,}582{,}900$
In 1900, $t = 10$
$P = 5{,}500{,}400 + 683{,}300(10)^2$
$P = 73{,}830{,}400$

68. $50{,}000{,}000 = 5{,}500{,}400 + 683{,}300t^2$
$44{,}499{,}600 = 683{,}300t^2$
$65.1245 = t^2$
$\pm\sqrt{65.1245} = t$
$\pm 8.07 = t$
$8 \approx t$ (negative 8 does not make sense)
When $t = 8$, the year is 1880.

9.2 Standardized Test Practice (p. 510)

69. C $5x^2 + 8x - 9 = 0$

70. $3x^2 - 44 = x^2 + 84$
$2x^2 - 44 = 84$
$2x^2 = 128$
$x^2 = 64$
$x = \pm\sqrt{64}$
$x = \pm 8$
two real solutions (G)

9.2 Mixed Review (p. 510)

71. $2x^3 + 2x + 2 = 2(-2)^3 + 2(-2) + 2$
$= 2(-8) + (-4) + 2$
$= -16 - 4 + 2$
$= -20 + 2$
$= -18$

72. $4x^2 + 3x + 5 = 4(-2)^2 + 3(-2) + 5$
$= 4(4) + (-6) + 5$
$= 16 - 6 + 5$
$= 10 + 5$
$= 15$

Copyright © McDougal Littell Inc.
All rights reserved.

73. $3x^2 + 4x + 8 = 3(-2)^2 + 4(-2) + 8$
$= 3(4) + (-8) + 8$
$= 12 + (-8 + 8)$
$= 12 + 0$
$= 12$

74. $x^2 + 7x + 9 = (-2)^2 + 7(-2) + 9$
$= 4 + (-14) + 9$
$= -10 + 9$
$= -1$

75. $y = 5x + 6; m = 5; b = 6$

76. $y = -4x + 5; m = -4; b = 5$

77. $y - 8x = 2$
$y = 8x + 2; m = 8; b = 2$

78. $2x + 3y = 6$
$3y = -2x + 6$
$y = -\frac{2}{3}x + 2;$
$m = -\frac{2}{3};$
$b = 2$

79. $-9 \le x - 7$
$-2 \le x$ or $x \ge -2$

80. $-15 > x - 8$
$-7 > x$ or $x < -7$

81. $2 + x < 4$
$x < 2$

82. $6 \ge x + 1$
$5 \ge x$ or $x \le 5$

83. $0.0000008 = 8 \times 10^{-7}$

84. $564 = 5.64 \times 10^2$

85. $8721 = 8.721 \times 10^3$

86. $23{,}000 = 2.3 \times 10^4$

9.2 Maintaining Skills (p. 510)

87. $\frac{6}{9} = \frac{2}{3}$

88. $\frac{4}{8} = \frac{1}{2}$

89. $\frac{5}{15} = \frac{1}{3}$

90. $\frac{30}{48} = \frac{6 \cdot 5}{6 \cdot 8} = \frac{5}{8}$

91. $\frac{20}{24} = \frac{5 \cdot 4}{6 \cdot 4} = \frac{5}{6}$

92. $\frac{50}{100} = \frac{1}{2}$

93. $\frac{12}{16} = \frac{4 \cdot 3}{4 \cdot 4} = \frac{3}{4}$

94. $\frac{28}{35} = \frac{7 \cdot 4}{7 \cdot 5} = \frac{4}{5}$

Lesson 9.3

9.3 Checkpoint (pp. 511–513)

1. $\sqrt{12} = \sqrt{4 \cdot 3}$
$= \sqrt{4} \cdot \sqrt{3}$
$= 2\sqrt{3}$

2. $\sqrt{32} = \sqrt{16 \cdot 2}$
$= \sqrt{16} \cdot \sqrt{2}$
$= 4\sqrt{2}$

3. $\sqrt{75} = \sqrt{25 \cdot 3}$
$= \sqrt{25} \cdot \sqrt{3}$
$= 5\sqrt{3}$

4. $\sqrt{180} = \sqrt{36 \cdot 5}$
$= \sqrt{36} \cdot \sqrt{5}$
$= 6\sqrt{5}$

5. $\sqrt{\frac{4}{9}} = \frac{\sqrt{4}}{\sqrt{9}} = \frac{2}{3}$

6. $5\sqrt{\frac{1}{25}} = 5 \cdot \frac{\sqrt{1}}{\sqrt{25}} = 5 \cdot \frac{1}{5} = 1$

7. $\sqrt{\frac{1}{3}} = \frac{\sqrt{1}}{\sqrt{3}} = \frac{1}{\sqrt{3}} \cdot \frac{\sqrt{3}}{\sqrt{3}} = \frac{\sqrt{3}}{\sqrt{9}} = \frac{\sqrt{3}}{3}$

8. $\sqrt{\frac{27}{15}} = \sqrt{\frac{3 \cdot 9}{3 \cdot 5}}$
$= \sqrt{\frac{9}{5}}$
$= \frac{\sqrt{9}}{\sqrt{5}}$
$= \frac{3}{\sqrt{5}}$
$= \frac{3}{\sqrt{5}} \cdot \frac{\sqrt{5}}{\sqrt{5}}$
$= \frac{3\sqrt{5}}{\sqrt{25}}$
$= \frac{3\sqrt{5}}{5}$

Copyright © McDougal Littell Inc.
All rights reserved.

9. $s^2 = \frac{16}{9}x$

$s^2 = \frac{16}{9}(50)$

$s = \sqrt{\frac{16}{9} \cdot 50}$

$s = \frac{\sqrt{16}}{\sqrt{9}} \cdot \sqrt{50} = \frac{4}{3}\sqrt{25 \cdot 2}$

$s = \frac{4}{3}\sqrt{25} \cdot \sqrt{2} = \frac{4}{3} \cdot 5\sqrt{2}$

$s = \frac{20\sqrt{2}}{3} \approx 9.4$ knots

9.3 Guided Practice (p. 514)

1. yes; no perfect squares

2. no; fraction under radical

3. no; 4 is a factor of 40 and it is a perfect square

4. no; radical in the denominator

5. $\sqrt{45} = \sqrt{9 \cdot 5} = \sqrt{9} \cdot \sqrt{5} = 3\sqrt{5}$ (D)

6. $\sqrt{98} = \sqrt{49 \cdot 2} = \sqrt{49} \cdot \sqrt{2} = 7\sqrt{2}$ (C)

7. $\sqrt{75} = \sqrt{25 \cdot 3} = \sqrt{25} \cdot \sqrt{3} = 5\sqrt{3}$ (B)

8. $\sqrt{54} = \sqrt{9 \cdot 6} = \sqrt{9} \cdot \sqrt{6} = 3\sqrt{6}$ (A)

9. $\sqrt{36} = 6$

10. $\sqrt{24} = \sqrt{4 \cdot 6} = \sqrt{4} \cdot \sqrt{6} = 2\sqrt{6}$

11. $\sqrt{60} = \sqrt{4 \cdot 15} = \sqrt{4} \cdot \sqrt{15} = 2\sqrt{15}$

12. $\sqrt{\frac{64}{25}} = \frac{\sqrt{64}}{\sqrt{25}} = \frac{8}{5}$

13. $\sqrt{\frac{15}{16}} = \frac{\sqrt{15}}{\sqrt{16}} = \frac{\sqrt{15}}{4}$

14. $\frac{1}{2}\sqrt{20} = \frac{1}{2}\sqrt{4 \cdot 5} = \frac{1}{2}\sqrt{4} \cdot \sqrt{5} = \frac{1}{2} \cdot 2\sqrt{5} = \sqrt{5}$

15. $\sqrt{\frac{2}{5}} = \frac{\sqrt{2}}{\sqrt{5}} = \frac{\sqrt{2}}{\sqrt{5}} \cdot \frac{\sqrt{5}}{\sqrt{5}} = \frac{\sqrt{10}}{5}$

16. $9\sqrt{\frac{1}{3}} = 9 \cdot \frac{\sqrt{1}}{\sqrt{3}}$

$= 9 \cdot \frac{1}{\sqrt{3}}$

$= 9 \cdot \frac{1}{\sqrt{3}} \cdot \frac{\sqrt{3}}{\sqrt{3}}$

$= \frac{9\sqrt{3}}{3}$

$= 3\sqrt{3}$

9.3 Practice and Applications (pp. 514–516)

17. No; there is a radical in the denominator.

18. No; 20 has a factor of 4, and 4 is a perfect square.

19. Yes; there are no perfect square factors of 31 other than 1.

20. No; there is a fraction in the radicand.

21. $\sqrt{44} = \sqrt{4 \cdot 11} = \sqrt{4} \cdot \sqrt{11} = 2\sqrt{11}$

22. $\sqrt{54} = \sqrt{9 \cdot 6} = \sqrt{9} \cdot \sqrt{6} = 3\sqrt{6}$

23. $\sqrt{18} = \sqrt{9 \cdot 2} = \sqrt{9} \cdot \sqrt{2} = 3\sqrt{2}$

24. $\sqrt{56} = \sqrt{4 \cdot 14} = \sqrt{4} \cdot \sqrt{14} = 2\sqrt{14}$

25. $\sqrt{27} = \sqrt{9 \cdot 3} = \sqrt{9} \cdot \sqrt{3} = 3\sqrt{3}$

26. $\sqrt{63} = \sqrt{9 \cdot 7} = \sqrt{9} \cdot \sqrt{7} = 3\sqrt{7}$

27. $\sqrt{200} = \sqrt{100 \cdot 2} = \sqrt{100} \cdot \sqrt{2} = 10\sqrt{2}$

28. $\sqrt{90} = \sqrt{9 \cdot 10} = \sqrt{9} \cdot \sqrt{10} = 3\sqrt{10}$

29. $\sqrt{125} = \sqrt{25 \cdot 5} = \sqrt{25} \cdot \sqrt{5} = 5\sqrt{5}$

30. $\sqrt{132} = \sqrt{4 \cdot 33} = \sqrt{4} \cdot \sqrt{33} = 2\sqrt{33}$

31. $\sqrt{144} = 12$

32. $\sqrt{196} = 14$

33. $\sqrt{\frac{4}{16}} = \sqrt{\frac{1}{4}} = \frac{\sqrt{1}}{\sqrt{4}} = \frac{1}{2}$

34. $\sqrt{\frac{9}{49}} = \frac{\sqrt{9}}{\sqrt{49}} = \frac{3}{7}$

35. $\sqrt{\frac{4}{25}} = \frac{\sqrt{4}}{\sqrt{25}} = \frac{2}{5}$

36. $\sqrt{\frac{81}{100}} = \frac{\sqrt{81}}{\sqrt{100}} = \frac{9}{10}$

37. $\sqrt{\frac{36}{25}} = \frac{\sqrt{36}}{\sqrt{25}} = \frac{6}{5}$

38. $\sqrt{\frac{7}{9}} = \frac{\sqrt{7}}{\sqrt{9}} = \frac{\sqrt{7}}{3}$

39. $\sqrt{\frac{11}{81}} = \frac{\sqrt{11}}{\sqrt{81}} = \frac{\sqrt{11}}{9}$

40. $\sqrt{\frac{5}{4}} = \frac{\sqrt{5}}{\sqrt{4}} = \frac{\sqrt{5}}{2}$

41. $\sqrt{\frac{18}{32}} = \sqrt{\frac{2 \cdot 9}{2 \cdot 16}} = \sqrt{\frac{9}{16}} = \frac{\sqrt{9}}{\sqrt{16}} = \frac{3}{4}$

42. $\sqrt{\frac{27}{36}} = \sqrt{\frac{9 \cdot 3}{9 \cdot 4}} = \frac{\sqrt{3}}{\sqrt{4}} = \frac{\sqrt{3}}{2}$

43. $\sqrt{\frac{10}{162}} = \sqrt{\frac{2 \cdot 5}{2 \cdot 81}} = \frac{\sqrt{5}}{\sqrt{81}} = \frac{\sqrt{5}}{9}$

Copyright © McDougal Littell Inc.
All rights reserved.

44. $\sqrt{\frac{12}{147}} = \sqrt{\frac{3 \cdot 4}{3 \cdot 49}} = \frac{\sqrt{4}}{\sqrt{49}} = \frac{2}{7}$

45. Find a perfect square factor (2 and 10 are not perfect squares).

$\sqrt{20} = \sqrt{4 \cdot 5} = \sqrt{4} \cdot \sqrt{5} = 2\sqrt{5}$

46. Simplify the radical before dividing.

$\frac{\sqrt{9}}{3} = \frac{3}{3} = 1$

47. $\sqrt{\frac{1}{5}} = \frac{\sqrt{1}}{\sqrt{5}} = \frac{1}{\sqrt{5}} \cdot \frac{\sqrt{5}}{\sqrt{5}} = \frac{\sqrt{5}}{5}$

48. $\sqrt{\frac{5}{6}} = \frac{\sqrt{5}}{\sqrt{6}} \cdot \frac{\sqrt{6}}{\sqrt{6}} = \frac{\sqrt{30}}{6}$

49. $\sqrt{\frac{1}{2}} = \frac{\sqrt{1}}{\sqrt{2}} \cdot \frac{\sqrt{2}}{\sqrt{2}} = \frac{\sqrt{2}}{2}$

50. $\sqrt{\frac{3}{5}} = \frac{\sqrt{3}}{\sqrt{5}} \cdot \frac{\sqrt{5}}{\sqrt{5}} = \frac{\sqrt{15}}{5}$

51. $\sqrt{\frac{5}{15}} = \sqrt{\frac{1 \cdot 5}{3 \cdot 5}} = \frac{\sqrt{1}}{\sqrt{3}} \cdot \frac{\sqrt{3}}{\sqrt{3}} = \frac{\sqrt{3}}{3}$

52. $\sqrt{\frac{3}{21}} = \sqrt{\frac{1 \cdot 3}{7 \cdot 3}} = \frac{\sqrt{1}}{\sqrt{7}} = \frac{1}{\sqrt{7}} \cdot \frac{\sqrt{7}}{\sqrt{7}} = \frac{\sqrt{7}}{7}$

53. $\sqrt{\frac{4}{10}} = \sqrt{\frac{2 \cdot 2}{2 \cdot 5}} = \frac{\sqrt{2}}{\sqrt{5}} \cdot \frac{\sqrt{5}}{\sqrt{5}} = \frac{\sqrt{10}}{5}$

54. $\sqrt{\frac{4}{3}} = \frac{\sqrt{4}}{\sqrt{3}} = \frac{2}{\sqrt{3}} \cdot \frac{\sqrt{3}}{\sqrt{3}} = \frac{2\sqrt{3}}{3}$

55. $\sqrt{\frac{1}{11}} = \frac{\sqrt{1}}{\sqrt{11}} = \frac{1}{\sqrt{11}} \cdot \frac{\sqrt{11}}{\sqrt{11}} = \frac{\sqrt{11}}{11}$

56. $\sqrt{\frac{3}{2}} = \frac{\sqrt{3}}{\sqrt{2}} \cdot \frac{\sqrt{2}}{\sqrt{2}} = \frac{\sqrt{6}}{2}$

57. $\sqrt{\frac{25}{3}} = \frac{\sqrt{25}}{\sqrt{3}} = \frac{5}{\sqrt{3}} \cdot \frac{\sqrt{3}}{\sqrt{3}} = \frac{5\sqrt{3}}{3}$

58. $\sqrt{\frac{16}{10}} = \sqrt{\frac{2 \cdot 8}{2 \cdot 5}} = \frac{\sqrt{8}}{\sqrt{5}} = \frac{\sqrt{4 \cdot 2}}{\sqrt{5}} = \frac{\sqrt{4} \cdot \sqrt{2}}{\sqrt{5}}$

$= \frac{2\sqrt{2}}{\sqrt{5}} \cdot \frac{\sqrt{5}}{\sqrt{5}} = \frac{2\sqrt{10}}{5}$

59. $4\sqrt{25} = 4(5) = 20$

60. $9\sqrt{100} = 9(10) = 90$

61. $-2\sqrt{27} = -2\sqrt{9 \cdot 3}$

$= -2\sqrt{9} \cdot \sqrt{3}$

$= -2(3)\sqrt{3}$

$= -6\sqrt{3}$

62. $\frac{1}{3}\sqrt{63} = \frac{1}{3}\sqrt{9 \cdot 7} = \frac{1}{3}\sqrt{9} \cdot \sqrt{7} = \frac{1}{3}(3)\sqrt{7} = \sqrt{7}$

63. $-6\sqrt{4} = -6(2) = -12$

64. $3\sqrt{44} = 3\sqrt{4 \cdot 11}$

$= 3\sqrt{4} \cdot \sqrt{11}$

$= 3(2)\sqrt{11}$

$= 6\sqrt{11}$

65. $-\frac{1}{7}\sqrt{49} = -\frac{1}{7}(7) = -1$

66. $\frac{1}{2}\sqrt{32} = \frac{1}{2}\sqrt{16 \cdot 2}$

$= \frac{1}{2}\sqrt{16} \cdot \sqrt{2}$

$= \frac{1}{2}(4)\sqrt{2}$

$= 2\sqrt{2}$

67. $\frac{3}{2}\sqrt{24} = \frac{3}{2}\sqrt{4 \cdot 6} = \frac{3}{2}\sqrt{4} \cdot \sqrt{6} = \frac{3}{2}(2)\sqrt{6} = 3\sqrt{6}$

68. $\frac{1}{8}\sqrt{56} = \frac{1}{8}\sqrt{14 \cdot 4}$

$= \frac{1}{8}\sqrt{4} \cdot \sqrt{14}$

$= \frac{1}{8}(2)\sqrt{14}$

$= \frac{\sqrt{14}}{4}$

69. $-\frac{1}{2}\sqrt{360} = -\frac{1}{2}\sqrt{36 \cdot 10} = -\frac{1}{2}\sqrt{36} \cdot \sqrt{10}$

$= -\frac{1}{2}(6)\sqrt{10} = -3\sqrt{10}$

70. $\sqrt{\frac{48}{81}} = \frac{\sqrt{48}}{\sqrt{81}} = \frac{\sqrt{16 \cdot 3}}{9} = \frac{\sqrt{16} \cdot \sqrt{3}}{9} = \frac{4\sqrt{3}}{9}$

71. $\sqrt{\frac{21}{35}} = \sqrt{\frac{7 \cdot 3}{7 \cdot 5}} = \sqrt{\frac{3}{5}} = \frac{\sqrt{3}}{\sqrt{5}} \cdot \frac{\sqrt{5}}{\sqrt{5}} = \frac{\sqrt{15}}{5}$

72. $-4\sqrt{\frac{1}{10}} = -4\frac{\sqrt{1}}{\sqrt{10}}$

$= \frac{-4}{\sqrt{10}} \cdot \frac{\sqrt{10}}{\sqrt{10}}$

$= \frac{-4\sqrt{10}}{10}$

$= \frac{-2\sqrt{10}}{5}$

73. $6\sqrt{\frac{5}{9}} = 6\frac{\sqrt{5}}{\sqrt{9}} = \frac{6\sqrt{5}}{3} = 2\sqrt{5}$

74. $2\sqrt{\frac{6}{18}} = 2\sqrt{\frac{1}{3}} = 2\frac{\sqrt{1}}{\sqrt{3}} \cdot \frac{\sqrt{3}}{\sqrt{3}} = \frac{2\sqrt{3}}{3}$

Copyright © McDougal Littell Inc.
All rights reserved.

75. $s = \sqrt{gd}$
$s = \sqrt{(9.8)(1000)}$
$s = \sqrt{9800} = \sqrt{4900 \cdot 2}$
$s = \sqrt{49 \cdot 100 \cdot 2} = \sqrt{49} \cdot \sqrt{100} \cdot \sqrt{2}$
$s = 7(10)\sqrt{2} = 70\sqrt{2}$ m/sec

76. $s = \sqrt{gd}$
$s = \sqrt{(9.8)(4000)}$
$s = \sqrt{39200} = \sqrt{4 \cdot 9800}$
$s = \sqrt{4 \cdot 4900 \cdot 2}\sqrt{4 \cdot 49 \cdot 100 \cdot 2}$
$s = \sqrt{4} \cdot \sqrt{49} \cdot \sqrt{100} \cdot \sqrt{2}$
$s = 2(7)(10)\sqrt{2} = 140\sqrt{2}$ m/sec

77. Speed of tsunami in an ocean region 1000 meters deep is $70\sqrt{2}$ m/sec; Speed of tsunami in an ocean region 4000 meters deep is $140\sqrt{2}$ m/sec.

Ratio: $\frac{140\sqrt{2}}{70\sqrt{2}} = 2$; the speed is twice as fast, not 4 times as fast.

78. $A = l \cdot w$
$A = \sqrt{20} \cdot \sqrt{10}$
$= \sqrt{200}$
$= \sqrt{100 \cdot 2}$
$= \sqrt{100} \cdot \sqrt{2}$
$= 10\sqrt{2}$

79. $A = l \cdot w$
$A = 7\sqrt{2}(7\sqrt{2})$
$= 7(7)\sqrt{2} \cdot \sqrt{2}$
$= 49\sqrt{2 \cdot 2}$
$= 49\sqrt{4}$
$= 49(2)$
$= 98$

80. Area of a square $= s^2$

$s^2 = 12(33)$
$s^2 = 396$
$s = \sqrt{396} = \sqrt{4 \cdot 99}$
$s = \sqrt{4 \cdot 9 \cdot 11} = \sqrt{4} \cdot \sqrt{9} \cdot \sqrt{11}$
$s = 2(3)\sqrt{11}$
$s = 6\sqrt{11}$ cm

81. $\frac{x^2}{4} = 9$ Original Equation.
$x^2 = 36$ Multiplication Property of Equality.
$x = \pm 6$ Definition of square root.

82. $3\sqrt{63} \cdot \sqrt{4} = 3\sqrt{9 \cdot 7(2)}$
$= 6\sqrt{9} \cdot \sqrt{7}$
$= 6(3)\sqrt{7}$
$= 18\sqrt{7}$

83. $-2\sqrt{27} \cdot \sqrt{3} = -2\sqrt{9 \cdot 3} \cdot \sqrt{3}$
$= -2\sqrt{9} \cdot \sqrt{3} \cdot \sqrt{3}$
$= -2(3)(3)$
$= -18$

84. $\sqrt{9} \cdot 4\sqrt{25} = 3 \cdot 4(5) = 60$

85. $\frac{1}{2}\sqrt{32} \cdot \sqrt{2} = \frac{1}{2}\sqrt{16 \cdot 2} \cdot \sqrt{2}$
$= \frac{1}{2}\sqrt{16} \cdot \sqrt{2} \cdot \sqrt{2}$
$= \frac{1}{2}(4)(2)$
$= 4$

86. $-\sqrt{4} \cdot \frac{\sqrt{81}}{\sqrt{36}} = \frac{-2(9)}{6} = \frac{-18}{6} = -3$

87. $-5\sqrt{2} \cdot \sqrt{\frac{9}{50}} = -5\sqrt{2}\frac{\sqrt{9}}{\sqrt{50}}$
$= \frac{-5\sqrt{2}(3)}{\sqrt{25 \cdot 2}}$
$= \frac{-15\sqrt{2}}{\sqrt{25} \cdot \sqrt{2}}$
$= \frac{-15}{5}$
$= -3$

9.3 Standardized Test Practice (p. 516)

88. $\sqrt{80} = \sqrt{16 \cdot 5} = \sqrt{16} \cdot \sqrt{5} = 4\sqrt{5}$ (*B*)

89. $\frac{\sqrt{125}}{\sqrt{25}} = \sqrt{\frac{125}{25}} = \sqrt{\frac{25 \cdot 5}{25}} = \sqrt{5}$ (*F*)

90. $12\sqrt{16} = 12(4) = 48 \neq \sqrt{48}$ (*D*)

91. (*F*) Multiply by $\frac{\sqrt{10}}{\sqrt{10}}$.

9.3 Mixed Review (p. 517)

92. $y = x + 5$
Sample answer:

x	-2	-1	0	1	2
y	3	4	5	6	7

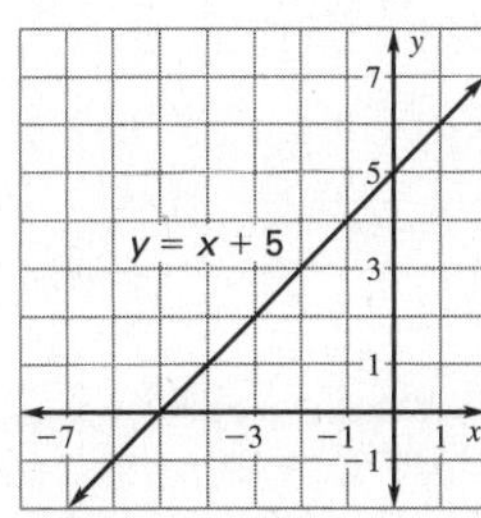

Copyright © McDougal Littell Inc.
All rights reserved.

93. $x + y = -4$

$y = -x - 4$

Sample answer:

x	-2	-1	0	1	2
y	-2	-3	-4	-5	-6

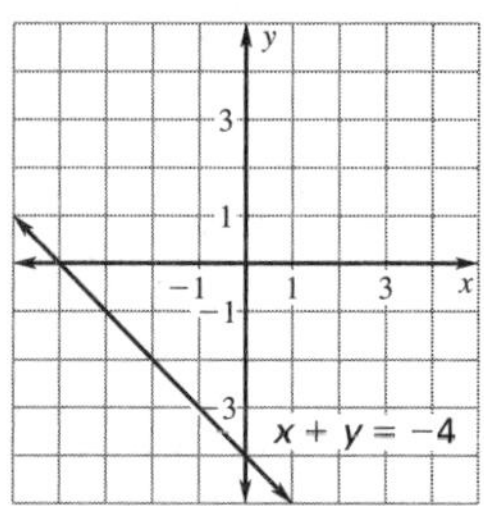

94. $y = 3x - 1$

x	-2	-1	0	1	2
y	-7	-4	-1	2	5

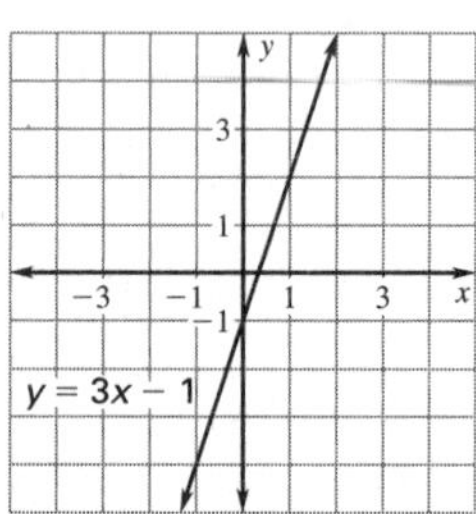

95. $2x + y = 6$

$y = -2x + 6$

Sample answer:

x	-2	-1	0	1	2
y	10	8	6	4	2

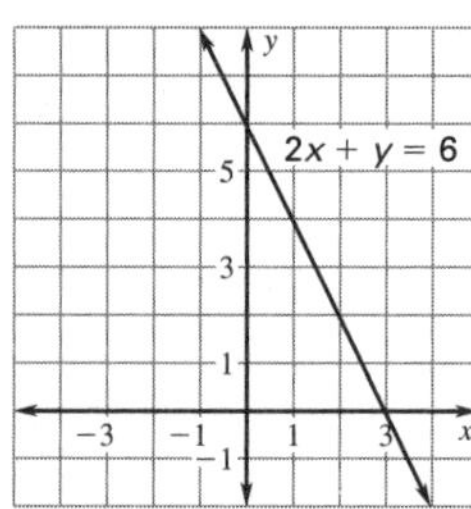

96. $(5 \cdot 2)^5 = (10)^5 = 100{,}000$

97. $(3x)^4 = 3^4x^4 = 81x^4$

98. $(-5x)^3 = (-5)^3x^3 = -125x^3$

99. $(-3 \cdot 4)^2 = (-12)^2 = 144$

100. $(ab)^6 = a^6b^6$

101. $(8xy)^2 = 8^2x^2y^2 = 64x^2y^2$

102. $(-3mn)^4 = (-3)^4m^4n^4 = 81m^4n^4$

103. $(-abc)^3 = (-a)^3b^3c^3 = -a^3b^3c^3$

104. Domain: all real numbers
Range: all positive real numbers

105. Domain: all real numbers
Range: all negative real numbers

9.3 Maintaining Skills (p. 517)

106. $\frac{1}{2} \div 4 = \frac{1}{2} \cdot \frac{1}{4} = \frac{1}{8}$

107. $\frac{3}{4} \div 3 = \frac{3}{4} \cdot \frac{1}{3} = \frac{1}{4}$

108. $\frac{7}{8} \div \frac{3}{4} = \frac{7}{8} \cdot \frac{4}{3} = \frac{7}{6} = 1\frac{1}{6}$

109. $\frac{1}{5} \div \frac{8}{15} = \frac{1}{5} \cdot \frac{15}{8} = \frac{3}{8}$

110. $\frac{4}{5} \div 10 = \frac{4}{5} \cdot \frac{1}{10} = \frac{2}{25}$

111. $\frac{2}{3} \div 63 = \frac{2}{3} \cdot \frac{1}{63} = \frac{2}{189}$

112. $\frac{5}{6} \div \frac{1}{5} = \frac{5}{6} \cdot \frac{5}{1} = \frac{25}{6} = 4\frac{1}{6}$

113. $\frac{7}{10} \div 7 = \frac{7}{10} \cdot \frac{1}{7} = \frac{1}{10}$

Quiz 1 *(p. 517)*

1. $\sqrt{81} = 9$

2. $-\sqrt{25} = -5$

3. $\sqrt{16} = 4$

4. $-\sqrt{4} = -2$

5. $\pm\sqrt{1} = \pm 1$

6. $\sqrt{100} = 10$

7. $\pm\sqrt{49} = \pm 7$

8. $\sqrt{121} = 11$

9. $x^2 = 64$

$x = \pm\sqrt{64}$

$x = \pm 8$

10. $x^2 = 63$

$x = \pm\sqrt{63} = \pm\sqrt{9 \cdot 7} = \pm\sqrt{9} \cdot \sqrt{7}$

$x = \pm 3\sqrt{7}$

11. $-8x^2 = -48$

$x^2 = 6$

$x = \pm\sqrt{6}$

12. $12x^2 = -120$

$x^2 = -10$

$x = \pm\sqrt{-10}$; no real solution

Copyright © McDougal Littell Inc.
All rights reserved.

13. $4x^2 = 64$

$$x^2 = 16$$
$$x = \pm\sqrt{16}$$
$$x = \pm 4$$

14. $5x^2 - 44 = 81$

$$5x^2 = 125$$
$$x^2 = 25$$
$$x = \pm\sqrt{25}$$
$$x = \pm 5$$

15. $\sqrt{18} = \sqrt{9 \cdot 2} = \sqrt{9} \cdot \sqrt{2} = 3\sqrt{2}$

16. $\sqrt{60} = \sqrt{4 \cdot 15} = \sqrt{4} \cdot \sqrt{15} = 2\sqrt{15}$

17. $\frac{1}{5}\sqrt{75} = \frac{1}{5}\sqrt{25 \cdot 3}$

$$= \frac{1}{5}\sqrt{25} \cdot \sqrt{3}$$
$$= \frac{1}{5}(5)\sqrt{3}$$
$$= \sqrt{3}$$

18. $-3\sqrt{9} = -3(3) = -9$

19. $2\sqrt{120} = 2\sqrt{4 \cdot 30}$

$$= 2\sqrt{4} \cdot \sqrt{30}$$
$$= 2(2)\sqrt{30}$$
$$= 4\sqrt{30}$$

20. $\frac{1}{3}\sqrt{12} = \frac{1}{3}\sqrt{4 \cdot 3} = \frac{1}{3}\sqrt{4} \cdot \sqrt{3} = \frac{1}{3}(2)\sqrt{3} = \frac{2\sqrt{3}}{3}$

21. $\frac{\sqrt{45}}{9} = \frac{\sqrt{9 \cdot 5}}{9} = \frac{\sqrt{9} \cdot \sqrt{5}}{9} = \frac{3\sqrt{5}}{9} = \frac{\sqrt{5}}{3}$

22. $\sqrt{\frac{5}{20}} = \frac{\sqrt{5}}{\sqrt{20}} = \frac{\sqrt{5}}{\sqrt{4 \cdot 5}} = \frac{\sqrt{5}}{\sqrt{4} \cdot \sqrt{5}} = \frac{1}{2}$

23. $\sqrt{\frac{5}{16}} = \frac{\sqrt{5}}{\sqrt{16}} = \frac{\sqrt{5}}{4}$

24. $\sqrt{\frac{32}{4}} = \frac{\sqrt{32}}{\sqrt{4}}$

$$= \frac{\sqrt{16 \cdot 2}}{2}$$
$$= \frac{\sqrt{16} \cdot \sqrt{2}}{2}$$
$$= \frac{4\sqrt{2}}{2} = 2\sqrt{2}$$

25. $\sqrt{\frac{2}{3}} = \frac{\sqrt{2}}{\sqrt{3}} \cdot \frac{\sqrt{3}}{\sqrt{3}} = \frac{\sqrt{6}}{3}$

26. $\sqrt{\frac{36}{5}} = \frac{\sqrt{36}}{\sqrt{5}} \cdot \frac{\sqrt{5}}{\sqrt{5}} = \frac{6\sqrt{5}}{5}$

9.4 Developing Concepts: Explore *(p. 518)*

1.

x	-3	-2	-1	0	1	2	3
y	9	4	1	0	1	4	9

2.

x	-3	-2	-1	0	1	2	3
y	-9	-4	-1	0	-1	-4	-9

Think About It (p. 518)

1. $y = x^2$ is a u-shaped graph opening upward; $y = -x^2$ is a u-shaped graph opening downward.
2. up
3. no highest point; lowest point is (0, 0)
4. down
5. no lowest point; highest point is (0, 0)
6. For $y = x^2$, (2, 4), (0, 0), $(-1, 1)$
   For $y = -x^2$, $(2, -4)$, (0, 0), $(-1, -1)$
7. $-k^2$
8. 0

Explore I (p. 519)

1.

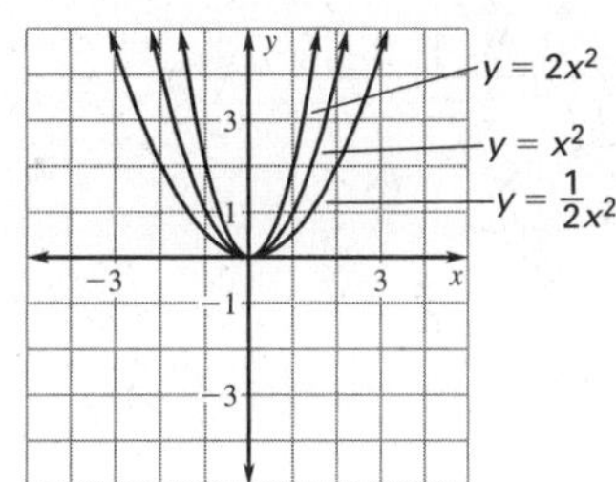

Think About It I (p. 519)

1. up
2. (0, 0), (0, 0), (0, 0)
3. The higher the value of a, the narrower the graph.

Explore II (p. 519)

2.

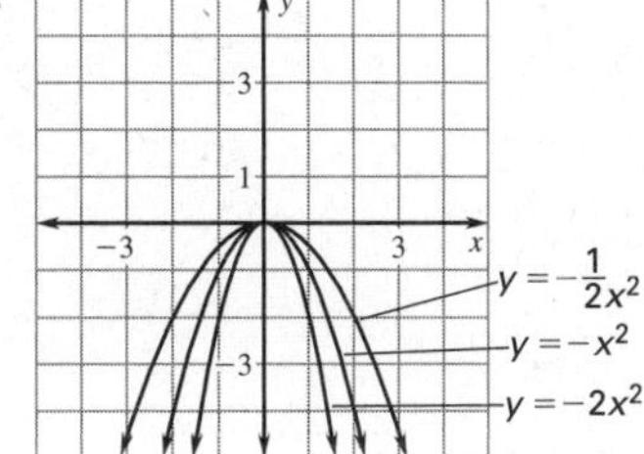

Copyright © McDougal Littell Inc.
All rights reserved.

Chapter 9 *continued*

Think About It II (p. 519)

1. down
2. (0, 0), (0, 0), (0, 0)
3. The higher the value of $|a|$ the narrower the graph.
4. narrower
5. $y = 5x^2$, up, narrower
6. $y = -4x^2$, down, narrower
7. $y = \frac{1}{4}x^2$, up, wider

Lesson 9.4

9.4 Checkpoint (pp. 520–522)

1. $y = -x^2$; down (a is negative)
2. $y = 2x^2 - 4$; up (a is positive)
3. $y = -3x^2 + 5x - 1$; down (a is negative)
4. $y = x^2 + 2$; $a = 1, b = 0, c = 2$

$$x = -\frac{b}{2a} = -\frac{0}{2(1)} = 0$$

x	-2	-1	0	1	2
y	6	3	2	3	6

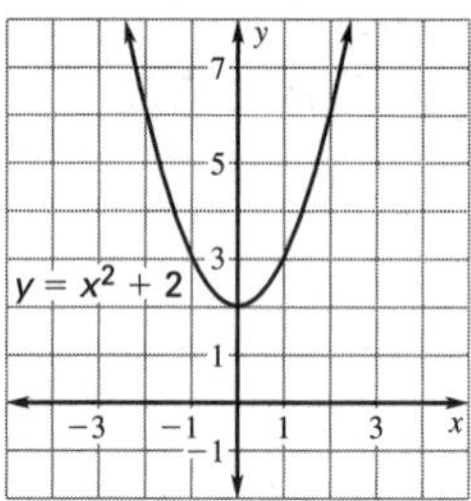

5. $y = 2x^2 - 4x - 1$; $a = 2, b = -4, c = -1$

$$x = -\frac{b}{2a} = -\frac{(-4)}{2(2)} = \frac{4}{4} = 1$$

x	-1	0	1	2	3
y	5	-1	-3	-1	5

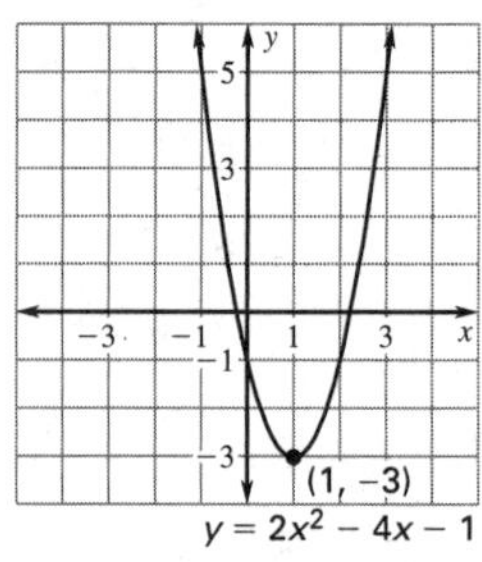

6. $y = x^2 + 2x$; $a = 1, b = 2, c = 0$

$$x = -\frac{b}{2a} = -\frac{2}{2(1)} = -\frac{2}{2} = -1$$

x	-3	-2	-1	0	1
y	3	0	-1	0	3

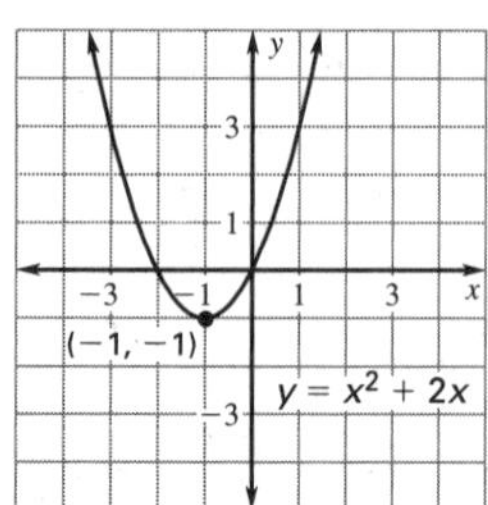

7. $y = -x^2 + 1$; $a = -1, b = 0, c = 1$

$$x = -\frac{b}{2a} = -\frac{0}{2(-1)} = 0$$

x	-2	-1	0	1	2
y	-3	0	1	0	-3

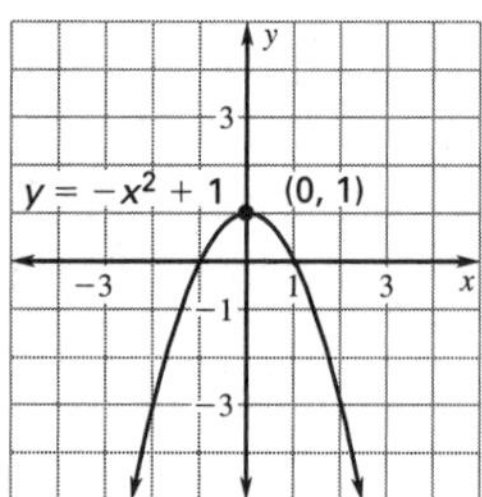

8. $y = -x^2 + 3x$; $a = -1, b = 3, c = 0$

$$x = -\frac{b}{2a} = -\frac{3}{2(-1)} = \frac{3}{2} = 1\frac{1}{2}$$

x	0	1	$1\frac{1}{2}$	2	3
y	0	2	$2\frac{1}{4}$	2	0

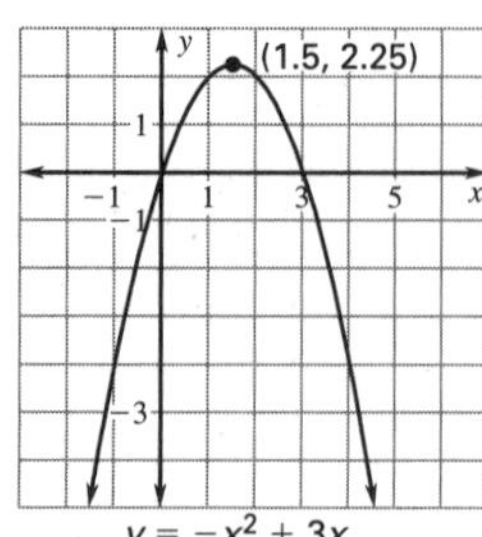

Copyright © McDougal Littell Inc.
All rights reserved.

9. $y = -2x^2 + 4x + 1;\ a = -2,\ b = 4,\ c = 1$

$$x = -\frac{b}{2a} = -\frac{4}{2(-2)} = -\frac{4}{-4} = 1$$

x	−1	0	1	2	3
y	−5	1	3	1	−5

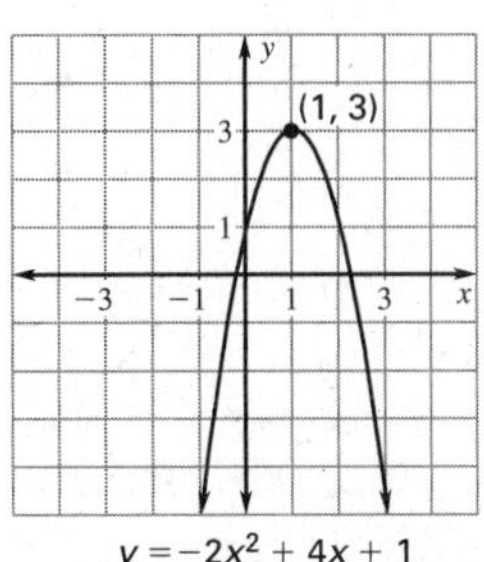

9.4 Guided Practice (p. 523)

1. $a = -5, b = 7, c = -4$

2. a parabola

3. up $(a = 1)$

4. up $(a = 3)$

5. down $(a = -1)$

6. down $(a = -1)$

7. up $(a = 5)$

8. down $(a = -8)$

9. $y = -3x^2;\ a = -3,\ b = 0,\ c = 0$

$$x = -\frac{b}{2a} = -\frac{0}{2(-3)} = 0$$

$x = 0$ (axis)

x	−2	−1	0	1	2
y	−12	−3	0	−3	−12

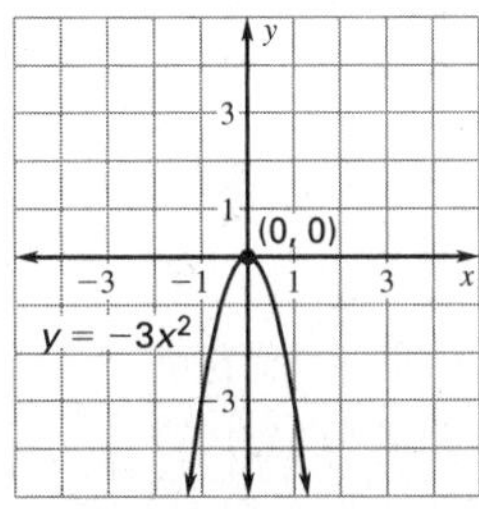

10. $y = -5x^2 + 10;\ a = -5,\ b = 0,\ c = 10$

$$x = -\frac{b}{2a} = -\frac{0}{2(-5)} = 0$$

$x = 0$ (axis)

x	−2	−1	0	1	2
y	−10	5	10	5	−10

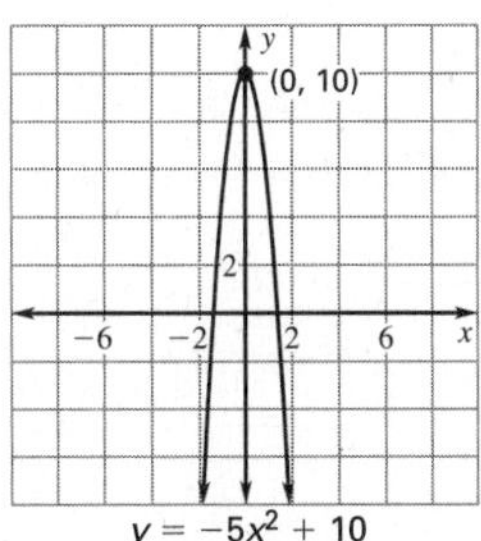

11. $y = x^2 + 4;\ a = 1,\ b = 0,\ c = 4$

$$x = -\frac{b}{2a} = -\frac{0}{2(1)} = 0$$

$x = 0$ (axis)

x	−2	−1	0	1	2
y	8	5	4	5	8

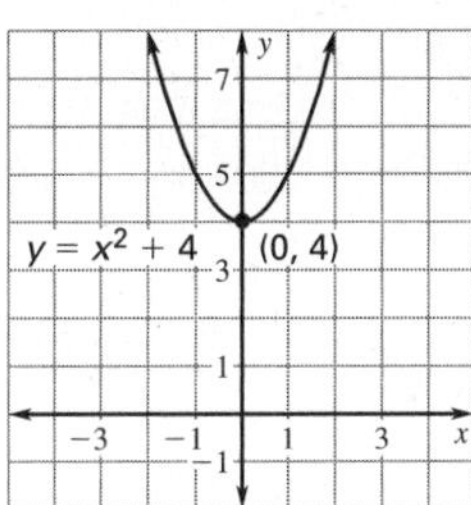

12. $y = x^2 - 6x + 8;\ a = 1,\ b = -6,\ c = 8$

$$x = -\frac{b}{2a} = -\frac{(-6)}{2(1)} = \frac{6}{2} = 3$$

$x = 3$ (axis)

x	1	2	3	4	5
y	3	0	−1	0	3

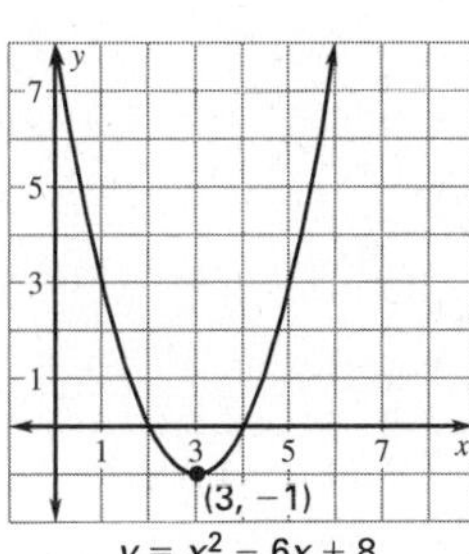

Copyright © McDougal Littell Inc.
All rights reserved.

13. $y = -3x^2 + 6x + 2;\ a = -3, b = 6, c = 2$

$x = -\frac{b}{2a} = -\frac{6}{2(-3)} = -\frac{6}{-6} = 1$

$x = 1$ (axis)

x	-1	0	1	2	3
y	-7	2	5	2	-7

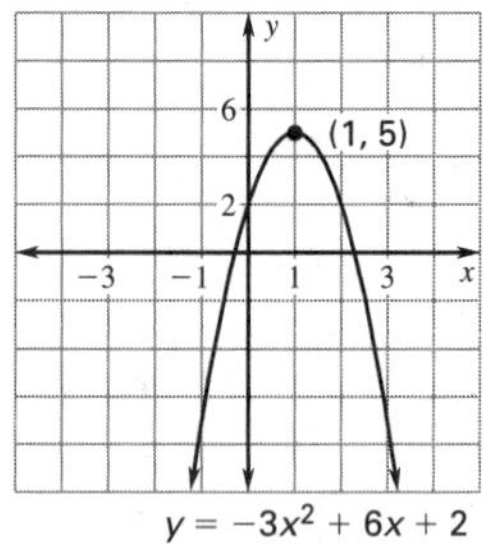

$y = -3x^2 + 6x + 2$

14. $y = 2x^2 - 8x + 3;\ a = 2, b = -8, c = 3$

$x = -\frac{b}{2a} = -\frac{(-8)}{2(2)} = \frac{8}{4} = 2$

$x = 2$ (axis)

x	0	1	2	3	4
y	3	-3	-5	-3	3

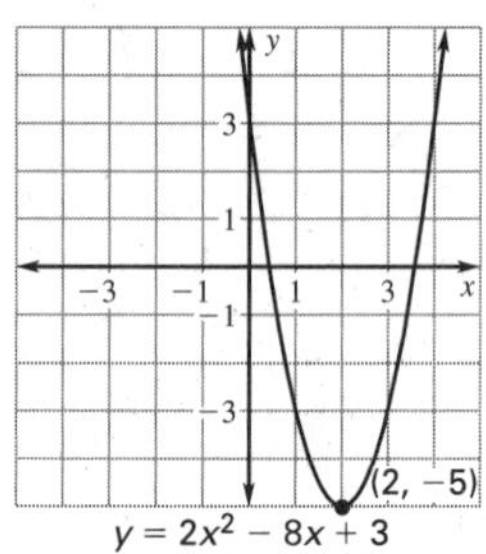

$y = 2x^2 - 8x + 3$

9.4 Practice and Applications (pp. 523–525)

15. $a = 2$, up

16. $a = -5$, down

17. $a = -7$, down

18. $a = 6$, up

19. $a = -8$, down

20. $a = 3$, up

21. $a = -3$, down

22. $a = -6$, down

23. $a = -1$, down

24. $y = 3x^2;\ a = 3, b = 0$

$x = -\frac{b}{2a} = -\frac{0}{2(3)} = 0$

Vertex: (0, 0)

x	-2	-1	0	1	2
y	12	3	0	3	12

25. $y = 6x^2;\ a = 6, b = 0$

$x = -\frac{b}{2a} = -\frac{0}{2(6)} = 0$

Vertex: (0, 0)

x	-2	-1	0	1	2
y	24	6	0	6	24

26. $y = -12x^2;\ a = -12, b = 0$

$x = -\frac{b}{2a} = -\frac{0}{2(-12)} = 0$

Vertex: (0, 0)

x	-2	-1	0	1	2
y	-48	-12	0	-12	-48

27. $y = 2x^2 - 10x;\ a = 2, b = -10$

$x = -\frac{b}{2a} = -\frac{(-10)}{2(2)} = \frac{10}{4} = \frac{5}{2} = 2\frac{1}{2}$

Vertex: $\left(2\frac{1}{2}, -12\frac{1}{2}\right)$

x	1	2	$2\frac{1}{2}$	3	4
y	-8	-12	$-12\frac{1}{2}$	-12	-8

28. $y = -7x^2 + 2x;\ a = -7, b = 2$

$x = -\frac{b}{2a} = -\frac{2}{2(-7)} = \frac{1}{7}$

Vertex: $\left(\frac{1}{7}, \frac{1}{7}\right)$

x	-2	-1	0	$\frac{1}{7}$	1	2	3
y	-32	-9	0	$\frac{1}{7}$	-5	-24	-57

29. $y = 6x^2 + 2x + 4;\ a = 6, b = 2$

$x = -\frac{b}{2a} = -\frac{2}{2(6)} = -\frac{1}{6}$

Vertex: $\left(-\frac{1}{6}, 3\frac{5}{6}\right)$

x	-3	-2	-1	$-\frac{1}{6}$	0	1	2
y	52	24	8	$3\frac{5}{6}$	4	12	32

30. $y = 5x^2 + 10x + 7;\ a = 5, b = 10$

$x = -\frac{b}{2a} = -\frac{10}{2(5)} = -1$

Vertex $(-1, 2)$

x	-3	-2	-1	0	1
y	22	7	2	7	22

Copyright © McDougal Littell Inc.
All rights reserved.

31. $y = -4x^2 - 4x + 8;\ a = -4,\ b = -4$

$x = -\frac{b}{2a} = -\frac{(-4)}{2(-4)} = \frac{4}{-8} = -\frac{1}{2}$

Vertex: $\left(-\frac{1}{2}, 9\right)$

x	-2	-1	$-\frac{1}{2}$	0	1
y	0	8	9	8	0

32. $y = -x^2 + 8x + 32;\ a = -1,\ b = 8$

$x = -\frac{b}{2a} = -\frac{8}{2(-1)} = 4$

Vertex: (4, 48)

x	2	3	4	5	6
y	44	47	48	47	44

33. $y = -x^2 - 3;\ a = -1$ (opens down)

$x = -\frac{b}{2a} = -\frac{0}{2(-1)} = 0$

Vertex: $(0, -3)$; C

34. $y = x^2 - 3;\ a = 1$ (opens up)

$x = -\frac{b}{2a} = -\frac{0}{2(1)} = 0$

Vertex: $(0, -3)$; A

35. $y = x^2 - 3x;\ a = 1$ (opens up), $b = -3$

$x = -\frac{b}{2a} = -\frac{(-3)}{2(1)} = \frac{3}{2} = 1\frac{1}{2}$

Vertex: $\left(1\frac{1}{2}, -2\frac{1}{4}\right)$; B

36. $y = -2x^2;\ a = -2,\ b = 0$

$x = -\frac{b}{2a} = -\frac{0}{2(-2)} = 0$

Vertex: (0, 0)

x	-2	-1	0	1	2
y	-8	-2	0	-2	-8

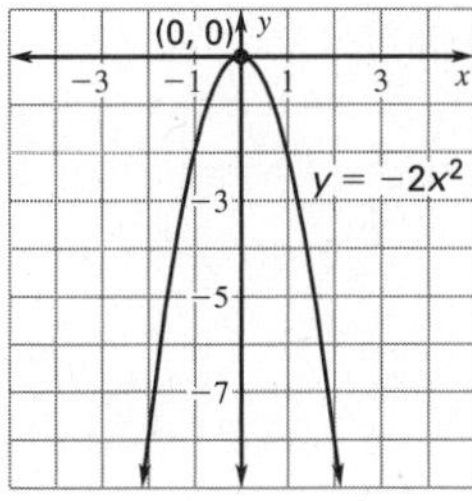

37. $y = 4x^2;\ a = 4,\ b = 0$

$x = -\frac{b}{2a} = -\frac{0}{2(4)} = 0$

Vertex: (0, 0)

x	-2	-1	0	1	2
y	16	4	0	4	16

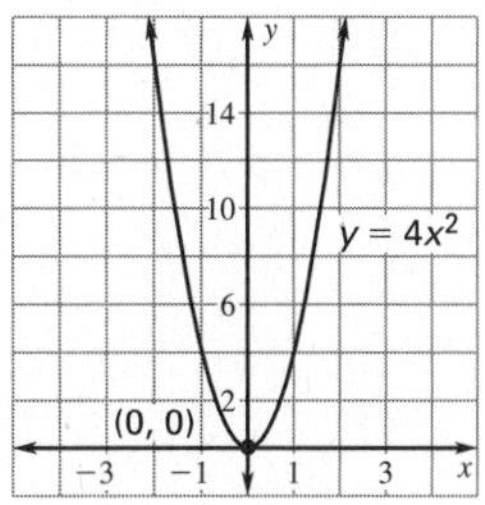

38. $y = x^2 + 4x - 1;\ a = 1,\ b = 4$

$x = -\frac{b}{2a} = -\frac{4}{2(1)} = -2$

Vertex: $(-2, -5)$

x	-4	-3	-2	-1	0
y	-1	-4	-5	-4	-1

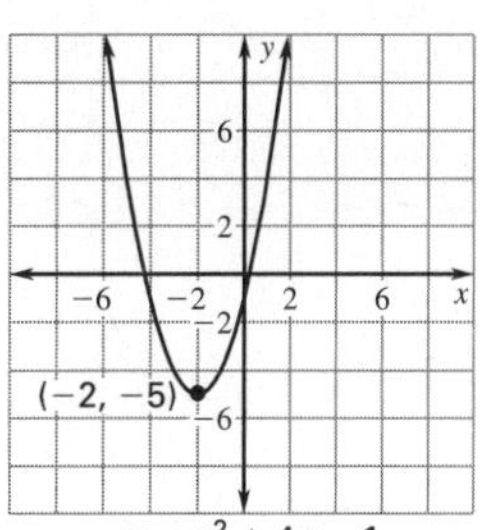

39. $y = 4x^2 + 8x - 3;\ a = 4,\ b = 8$

$x = -\frac{b}{2a} = -\frac{8}{2(4)} = -\frac{8}{8} = -1$

Vertex: $(-1, -7)$

x	-3	-2	-1	0	1
y	9	-3	-7	-3	9

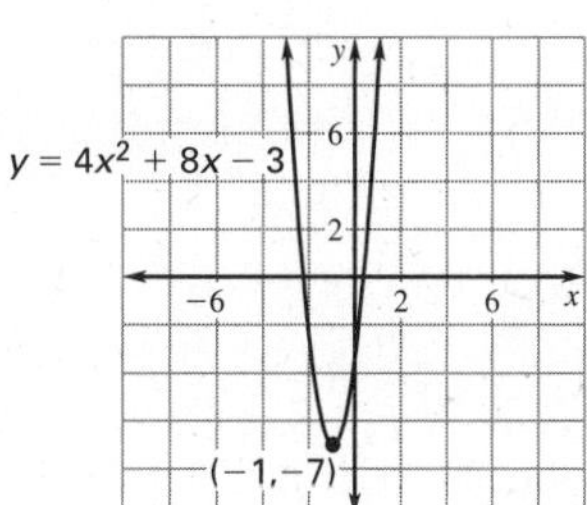

Copyright © McDougal Littell Inc.
All rights reserved.

40. $y = x^2 + x + 4; a = 1, b = 1$

$x = -\frac{b}{2a} = -\frac{1}{2(1)} = -\frac{1}{2}$

Vertex: $\left(-\frac{1}{2}, 3\frac{3}{4}\right)$

x	-2	-1	$-\frac{1}{2}$	0	1
y	6	4	$3\frac{3}{4}$	4	6

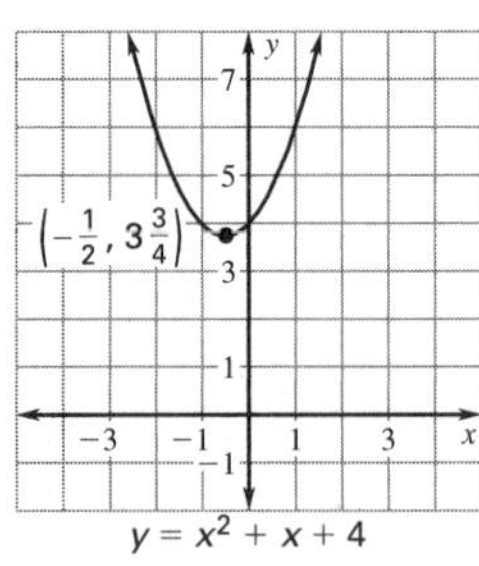

41. $y = 3x^2 - 2x - 1; a = 3, b = -2$

$x = -\frac{b}{2a} = -\frac{(-2)}{2(3)} = \frac{2}{6} = \frac{1}{3}$

Vertex: $\left(\frac{1}{3}, -1\frac{1}{3}\right)$

x	-1	0	$\frac{1}{3}$	1	2
y	4	-1	$-1\frac{1}{3}$	0	7

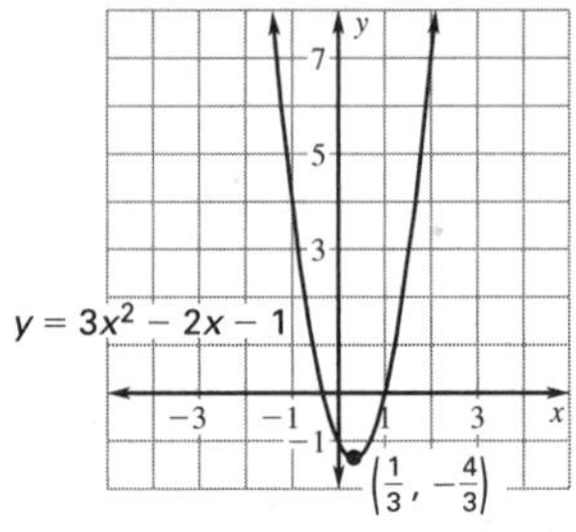

42. $y = 2x^2 + 5x - 3; a = 2, b = 5$

$x = -\frac{b}{2a} = -\frac{5}{2(2)} = -\frac{5}{4} = -1\frac{1}{4}$

Vertex: $\left(-1\frac{1}{4}, -6\frac{1}{8}\right)$

x	-3	-2	$-1\frac{1}{4}$	-1	0
y	0	-5	$-6\frac{1}{8}$	-6	-3

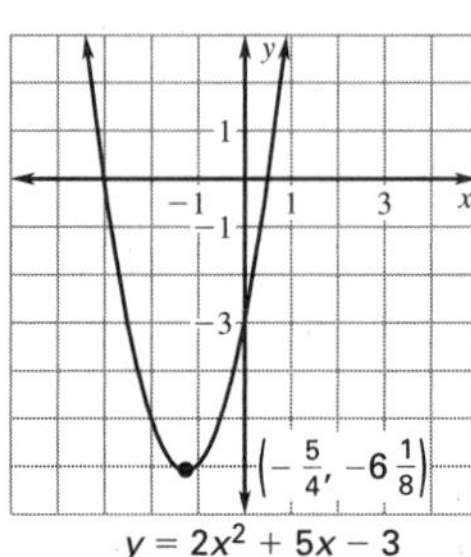

43. $y = -4x^2 + 4x + 7$

$a = -4; b = 4$

$x = -\frac{b}{2a} = -\frac{4}{2(-4)} = \frac{1}{2}$

Vertex: $\left(\frac{1}{2}, 8\right)$

x	-2	-1	0	$\frac{1}{2}$	1	2
y	-17	-1	7	8	7	-1

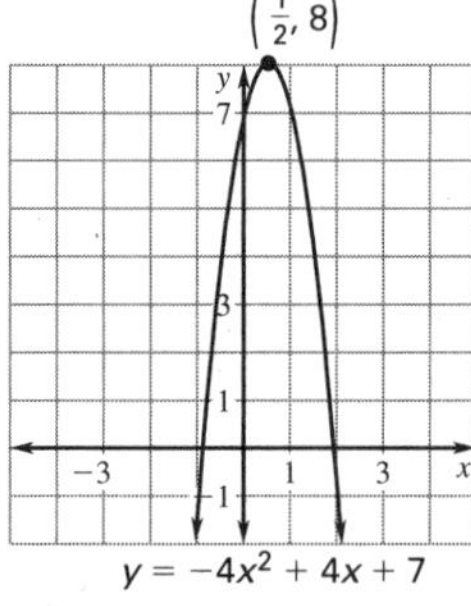

Copyright © McDougal Littell Inc.
All rights reserved.

44. $y = -3x^2 - 3x + 4;\ a = -3,\ b = -3$

$$x = -\frac{b}{2a} = -\frac{-3}{2(-3)} = -\frac{3}{6} = -\frac{1}{2}$$

Vertex: $\left(-\frac{1}{2}, 4\frac{3}{4}\right)$

x	-2	-1	$-\frac{1}{2}$	0	1
y	-2	4	$4\frac{3}{4}$	4	-2

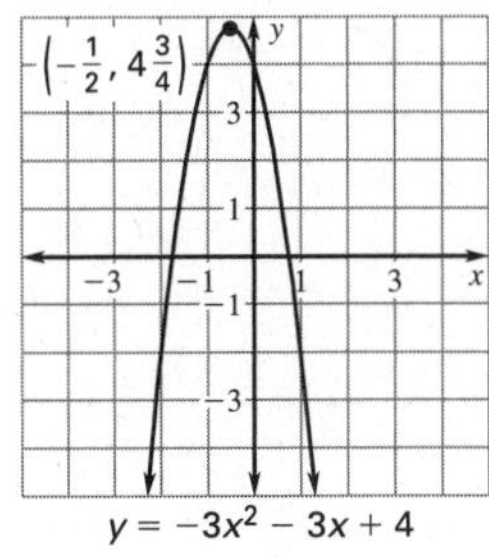

45. $h = -16t^2 + 15t + 6;\ a = -16,\ b = 15$

$$t = -\frac{b}{2a} = -\frac{15}{2(-16)} = \frac{15}{32}$$

$$h = -16\left(\frac{15}{32}\right)^2 + 15\left(\frac{15}{32}\right) + 6$$

$$h = -16\left(\frac{225}{1024}\right) + 15\left(\frac{15}{32}\right) + 6$$

$$h = -\frac{225}{64} + \frac{225}{32} + 6$$

$$h = -\frac{225}{64} + \frac{450}{64} + 6$$

$$h = \frac{225}{64} + 6 = \frac{225}{64} + \frac{384}{64} = \frac{609}{64}$$

$$h = 9\frac{33}{64} \approx 9.52 \text{ ft}$$

Vertex: $\left(\frac{15}{32}, \frac{609}{64}\right)$, this point represents the highest point on the path of the basketball. At $\frac{15}{32} \approx 0.47$ seconds the ball reaches its high point of $\frac{609}{64} \approx 9.52$ ft.

46. $h = -0.2d^2 + 2d;\ a = -0.2,\ b = 2$

$$d = -\frac{b}{2a} = -\frac{2}{2(-0.2)} = \frac{1}{0.2} = 5$$

$h = -0.2(5)^2 + 2(5)$

$h = 5$

Vertex: (5, 5)

The peak of the dolphin's jump is a height of 5 feet and a horizontal distance of 5 feet from where it left the water.

47. 10 ft

48. $h = -0.0137x^2 + 0.9325x + 5.5;\ a = -0.0137,\ b = 0.9325$

$$x = -\frac{b}{2a} = -\frac{0.9325}{2(-0.0137)} \approx 34.03$$

$h = -0.0137(34.03)^2 + 0.9325(34.03) + 5.5$

$h \approx 21.4$ ft (maximum height)

49. *Sample answer:* Each graph has a y-intercept of (0, 1), and all three open down and intersect the x-axis. As the value of $|a|$ gets smaller, the curve gets wider. The graphs nest inside one another and are tangent at (0, 1).

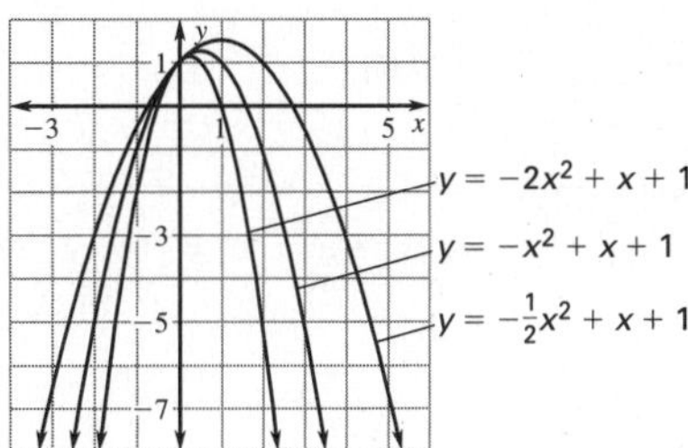

50. *Sample answer:* Each graph has a y-intercept of (0, 1). Each graph is identical in shape, but as b gets larger, the graph moves further down and to the left.

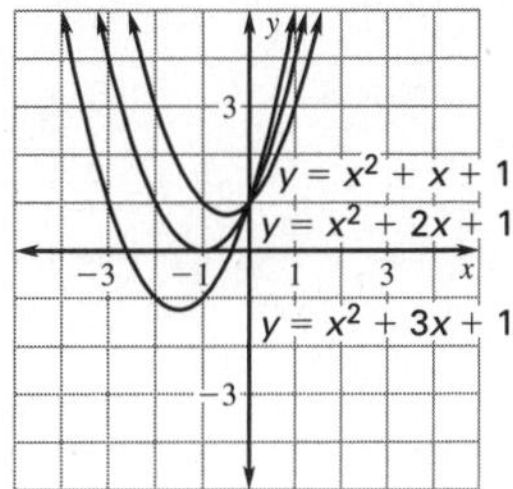

51. *Sample answer:* Each graph has an identical shape, and each has the line $x = \frac{1}{2}$ as its axis of symmetry. They are vertical translations of each other, with the value of c being the y-intercept of each graph.

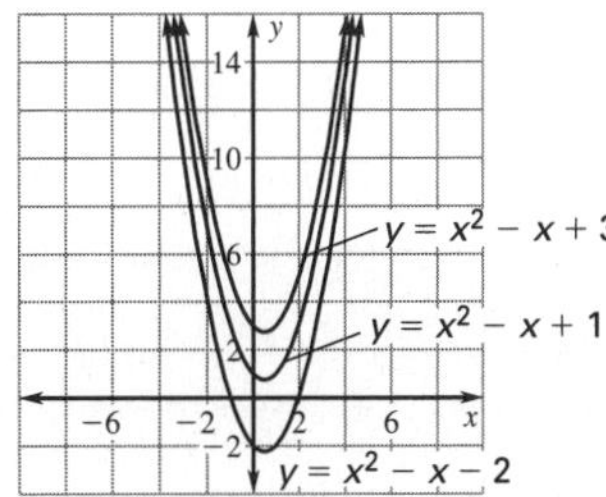

Copyright © McDougal Littell Inc.
All rights reserved.

9.4 Standardized Test Practice (p. 525)

52. B; $x = -\frac{b}{2a} = -\frac{(-2)}{2(-1)} = -\frac{2}{2} = -1$

Vertex: $(-1, 2)$; opens down since $a = -1$.

53. $y = -2x^2 + 8x - 5$

$x = -\frac{b}{2a} = -\frac{8}{2(-2)} = -\frac{8}{-4} = 2$

Vertex: $(2, 3)$; G

54. $y = x^2 + 3x - 2$

$x = -\frac{b}{2a} = -\frac{3}{2(1)} = -\frac{3}{2}$ (B)

9.4 Mixed Review (p. 525)

55. $x - 3y \geq 3$

$-3y \geq -x + 3$

$y \leq \frac{1}{3}x - 1;$

$x - 3y < 12$

$-3y < -x + 12$

$y > \frac{1}{3}x - 4$

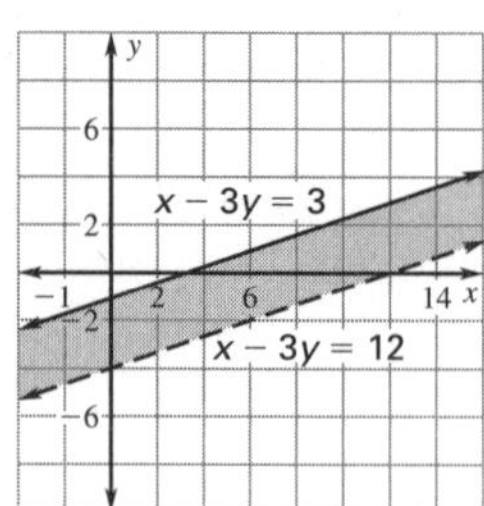

56. $x + y \leq 5$

$y \leq -x + 5;$

$x \geq 2;$

$y \geq 0$

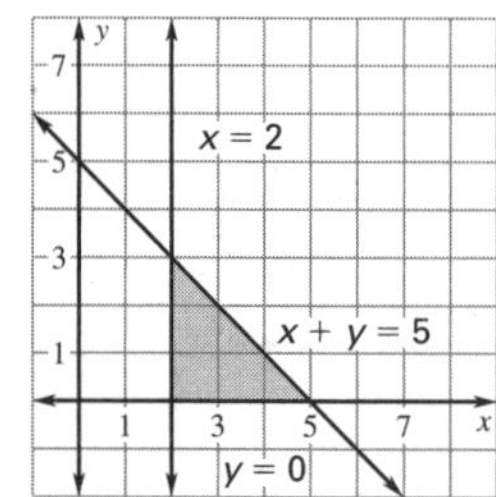

57. $x + y < 10$

$y < -x + 10;$

$2x + y > 10$

$y > -2x + 10;$

$x - y < 2$

$-y < -x + 2$

$y > x - 2$

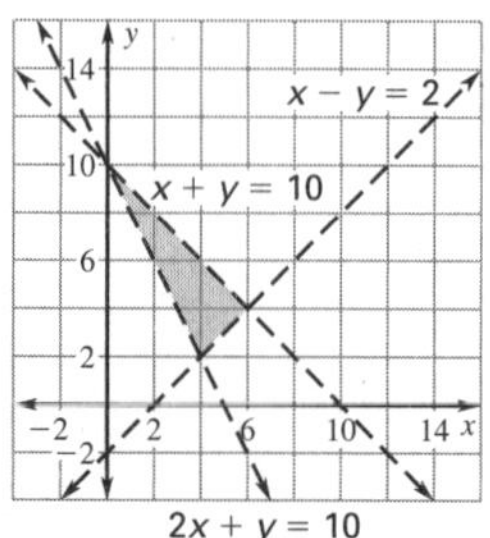

58. $4^2 \cdot 4^5 = 4^7$

59. $(-5) \cdot (-5)^8 = (-5)^9$

60. $x^2 \cdot x^4 \cdot x^6 = x^{2+4+6} = x^{12}$

61. $x^3 \cdot x^5 = x^8$

62. $t \cdot (t^3) = t^4$

63. $m \cdot m^4 \cdot m^3 = m^{1+4+3} = m^8$

64. $5 \cdot 5^2 \cdot 5^3 = 5^{1+2+3} = 5^6$

65. $2(2)^4 = 2^5$

9.4 Maintaining Skills (p. 525)

66. $\frac{5}{12}, \frac{1}{2} = \frac{6}{12}, \frac{2}{3} = \frac{8}{12}$

67. $\frac{4}{15}, \frac{1}{3} = \frac{5}{15}, \frac{2}{5} = \frac{6}{15}$

68. $\frac{5}{15} = \frac{10}{30}, \frac{4}{10} = \frac{12}{30}, \frac{3}{5} = \frac{18}{30}$

69. $\frac{3}{4} = 0.75, \frac{7}{8} = 0.875, \frac{9}{10} = 0.9$

Lesson 9.5

9.5 Checkpoint (pp. 526–528)

1. Estimate: 0, 2

Check:

$y = 2(0)^2 - 4(0)$

$y = 0$

$y = 2(2)^2 - 4(2)$

$y = 2(4) - 8$

$y = 8 - 8 = 0$

Copyright © McDougal Littell Inc.
All rights reserved.

2. $x^2 - x = 6$ Original equation.

$x^2 - x - 6 = 0$ Write in standard form.

$y = x^2 - x - 6$ Related quadratic function.

$x = -\frac{(-1)}{2(1)} = \frac{1}{2}$ Axis of symmetry.

Vertex: $\left(\frac{1}{2}, -6\frac{1}{4}\right)$

x	-1	0	$\frac{1}{2}$	1	2
y	-4	-6	$-6\frac{1}{4}$	-6	-4

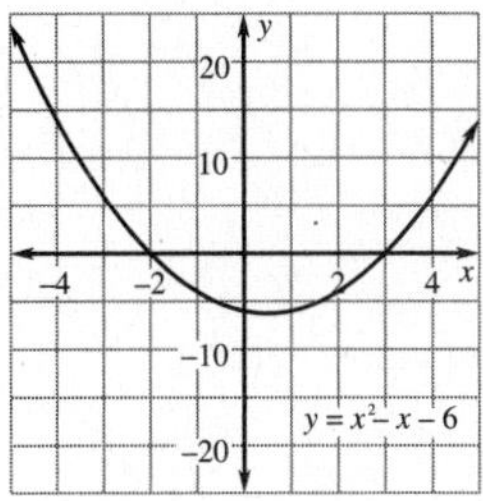

Estimate of x-intercepts (solutions): $3, -2$

3. Check 3 and -2.

$x^2 - x = 6$

$3^2 - 3 \stackrel{?}{=} 6$

$9 - 3 \stackrel{?}{=} 6$

$6 = 6$

$(-2)^2 - (-2) \stackrel{?}{=} 6$

$4 + 2 \stackrel{?}{=} 6$

$6 = 6$

4. $y = 0.0007748x^2$ Original equation.

$150 = 0.0007748x^2$ Substitute 150 for y.

$0 = 0.0007748x^2 - 150$ Subtract 150 from each side.

$y = 0.0007748x^2 - 150$

Use a graphing calculator to sketch the related quadratic function.

From the graphing calculator screen you can see that the x-intercepts are approximately -440 and 440. Each tower is approximately 440 feet from the midpoint. The distance between the towers is $440 + 440 = 880$ feet.

9.5 Guided Practice (p. 529)

1. its solutions

2. *Sample answer:* Write the equation in standard form, and then rewrite it as a quadratic function. Graph the function. The x-intercepts are the roots of the original equation.

3. $y = x^2 - 3$

$x = -\frac{b}{2a} = -\frac{0}{2(1)} = 0$

Vertex: $(0, -3)$; *B*

4. $y = x^2 + x - 4$

$x = -\frac{b}{2a} = -\frac{1}{2(1)} = -\frac{1}{2}$

Vertex: $\left(-\frac{1}{2}, -4\frac{1}{4}\right)$; *C*

5. $y = x^2 - 2x - 1$

$x = -\frac{b}{2a} = -\frac{(-2)}{2(1)} = \frac{2}{2} = 1$

Vertex: $(1, -2)$; *A*

6. $3x^2 - 12 = 0$

$3x^2 = 12$

$x^2 = 4$

$x = \pm 2$

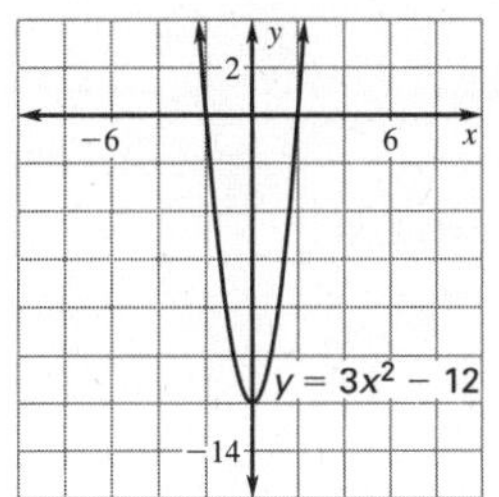

7. $5x^2 - 5 = 0$

$5x^2 = 5$

$x^2 = 1$

$x = \pm 1$

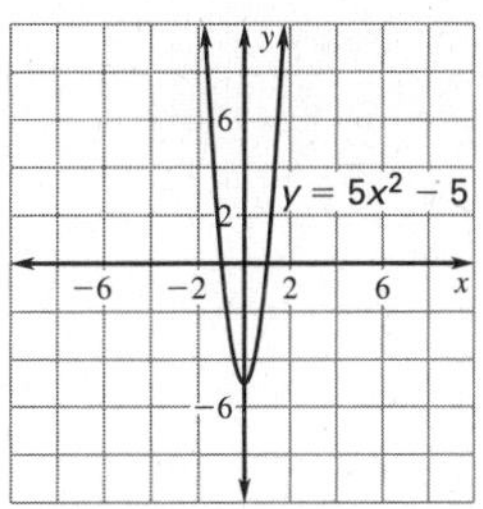

8. $-2x^2 = -18$

$x^2 = 9$

$x = \pm 3$

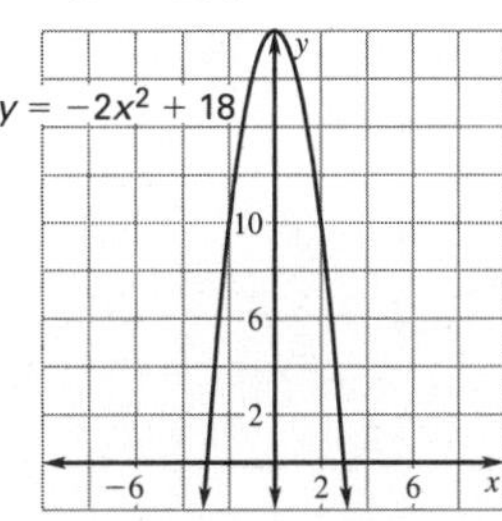

Copyright © McDougal Littell Inc.
All rights reserved.

9. $3x^2 = 48$ Original equation.

$3x^2 - 48 = 0$ Subtract 48 from each side.

$y = 3x^2 - 48$ Related quadratic function.

$x = -\frac{0}{2(3)} = 0$ Axis of symmetry.

Vertex: $(0, -48)$

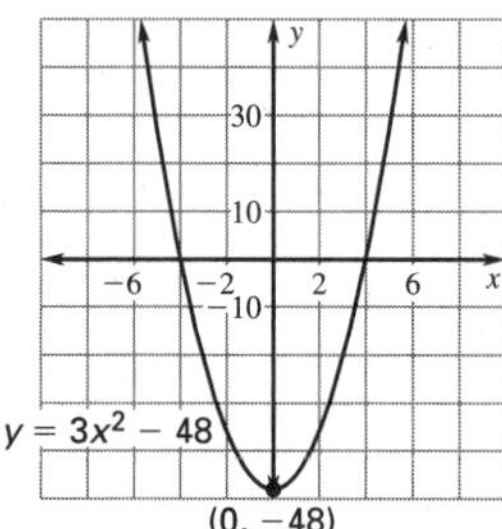

Estimate solutions: $-4, 4$

Check solutions in original equation:

$3(-4)^2 \stackrel{?}{=} 48$

$3(16) \stackrel{?}{=} 48$

$48 = 48$

$3(4)^2 \stackrel{?}{=} 48$

$3(16) \stackrel{?}{=} 48$

$48 = 48$

10. $x^2 - 4 = 5$ Original equation.

$x^2 - 9 = 0$ Subtract 5 from each side.

$y = x^2 - 9$ Related quadratic function.

$x = -\frac{0}{2(1)} = 0$ Axis of symmetry.

Vertex: $(0, -9)$

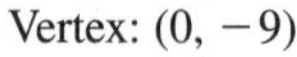

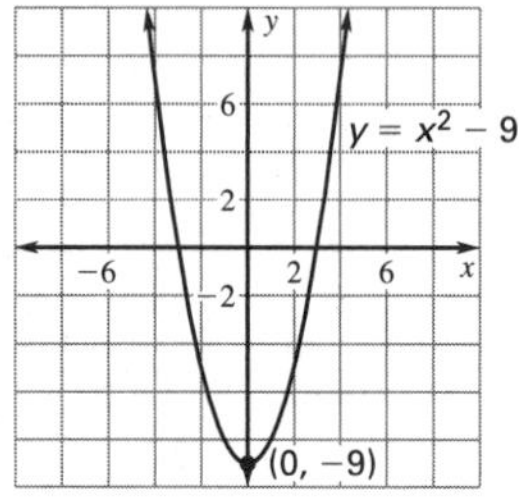

Estimate solutions: $-3, 3$

Check solutions in original equation:

$(-3)^2 - 4 \stackrel{?}{=} 5$

$9 - 4 \stackrel{?}{=} 5$

$5 = 5$

$3^2 - 4 \stackrel{?}{=} 5$

$9 - 4 \stackrel{?}{=} 5$

$5 = 5$

11. $-x^2 + 7x - 10 = 0$ Original equation.

$y = -x^2 + 7x - 10$ Related quadratic function.

$x = -\frac{7}{2(-1)} = \frac{7}{2} = 3\frac{1}{2}$ Axis of symmetry.

Vertex: $\left(3\frac{1}{2}, 2\frac{1}{4}\right)$

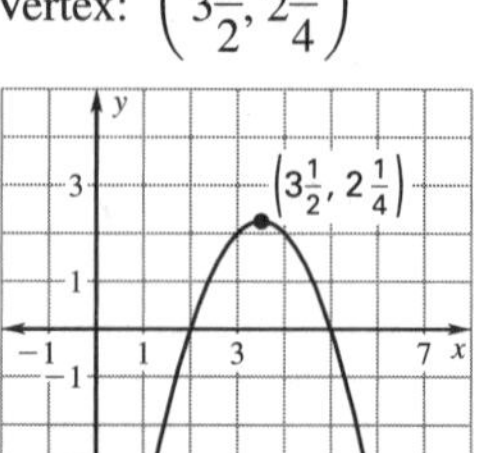

Estimate solutions: 2, 5

Check solutions in original equation.

$-(2)^2 + 7(2) - 10 \stackrel{?}{=} 0$

$-4 + 14 - 10 \stackrel{?}{=} 0$

$0 = 0$

$-(5)^2 + 7(5) - 10 \stackrel{?}{=} 0$

$-25 + 35 - 10 \stackrel{?}{=} 0$

$0 = 0$

9.5 Practice and Applications (pp. 529–530)

12. $4x^2 = 12$

$4x^2 - 12 = 0$

13. $x^2 - 6x = -6$

$x^2 - 6x + 6 = 0$

14. $-x^2 = 15$

$-x^2 - 15 = 0$ or $x^2 + 15 = 0$

15. $5 + x = 3x^2$

$-3x^2 + x + 5 = 0$ or $3x^2 - x - 5 = 0$

16. $2x - x^2 = 1$

$-x^2 + 2x - 1 = 0$ or $x^2 - 2x + 1 = 0$

17. $6x^2 = 12x$

$6x^2 - 12x = 0$

18. Roots: 1, 2

19. Roots: $-3, 1$

20. Roots: $-2, 4$

Copyright © McDougal Littell Inc.
All rights reserved.

21. Ex. 18: $-x^2 + 3x - 2 = 0$

Check 1:

$-(1)^2 + 3(1) - 2 \stackrel{?}{=} 0$

$-1 + 3 - 2 \stackrel{?}{=} 0$

$0 = 0$

Check 2:

$-(2)^2 + 3(2) - 2 \stackrel{?}{=} 0$

$-4 + 6 - 2 \stackrel{?}{=} 0$

$0 = 0$

Ex. 19: $-x^2 - 2x + 3 = 0$

Check -3:

$-(-3)^2 - 2(-3) + 3 \stackrel{?}{=} 0$

$-9 + 6 + 3 \stackrel{?}{=} 0$

$0 = 0$

Check 1:

$-(1)^2 - 2(1) + 3 \stackrel{?}{=} 0$

$-1 - 2 + 3 \stackrel{?}{=} 0$

$0 = 0$

Ex. 20: $x^2 - 2x - 8 = 0$

Check -2:

$(-2)^2 - 2(-2) - 8 \stackrel{?}{=} 0$

$4 + 4 - 8 \stackrel{?}{=} 0$

$0 = 0$

Check 4:

$(4)^2 - 2(4) - 8 \stackrel{?}{=} 0$

$16 - 8 - 8 \stackrel{?}{=} 0$

$0 = 0$

22. $x^2 + 2x = 3$ Original equation.

$x^2 + 2x - 3 = 0$ Standard form.

$y = x^2 + 2x - 3$ Related quadratic function.

$x = -\dfrac{2}{2(1)} = -1$ Axis of symmetry.

Vertex: $(-1, -4)$

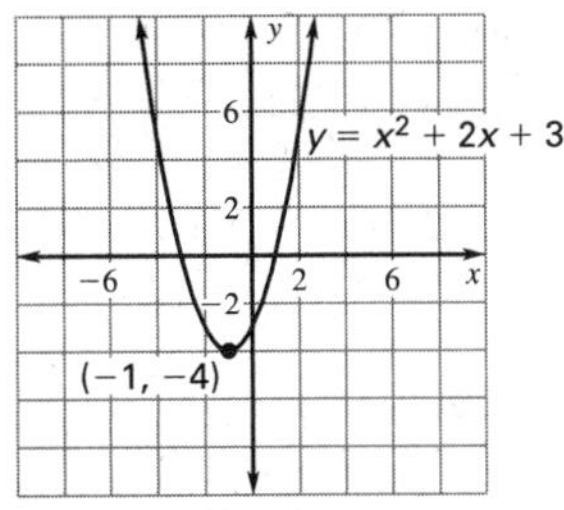

Estimate solutions: -3, 1

Check -3:

$(-3)^2 + 2(-3) \stackrel{?}{=} 3$

$9 - 6 \stackrel{?}{=} 3$

$3 = 3$

Check 1:

$1^2 + 2(1) \stackrel{?}{=} 3$

$1 + 2 \stackrel{?}{=} 3$

$3 = 3$

23. $-4x^2 - 8x = -12$

$-4x^2 - 8x + 12 = 0$

$4x^2 + 8x - 12 = 0$

Related quadratic function: $y = 4x^2 + 8x - 12$

$x = -\dfrac{8}{2(4)} = -1$

Vertex: $(-1, -16)$

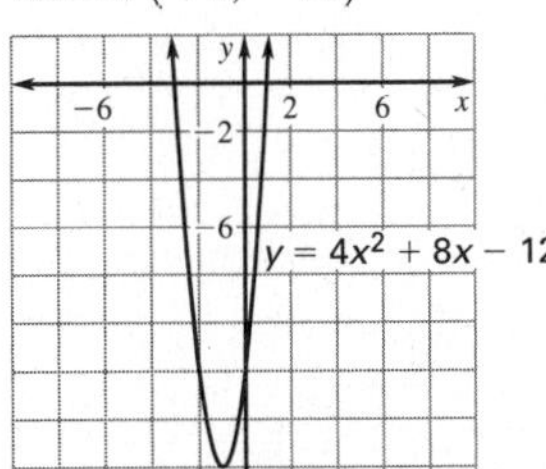

Estimate solutions: -3, 1

Check -3:

$-4(-3)^2 - 8(-3) \stackrel{?}{=} -12$

$-4(9) + 24 \stackrel{?}{=} -12$

$-36 + 24 \stackrel{?}{=} -12$

$-12 = -12$

Check 1:

$-4(1)^2 - 8(1) \stackrel{?}{=} -12$

$-4 - 8 \stackrel{?}{=} -12$

$-12 = -12$

24. $-x^2 + 3x = -4$

$-x^2 + 3x + 4 = 0$

$x^2 - 3x - 4 = 0$

Related quadratic function: $y = x^2 - 3x - 4$

$x = -\dfrac{(-3)}{2(1)} = \dfrac{3}{2} = 1\frac{1}{2}$

Vertex: $\left(1\frac{1}{2}, -6\frac{1}{4}\right)$

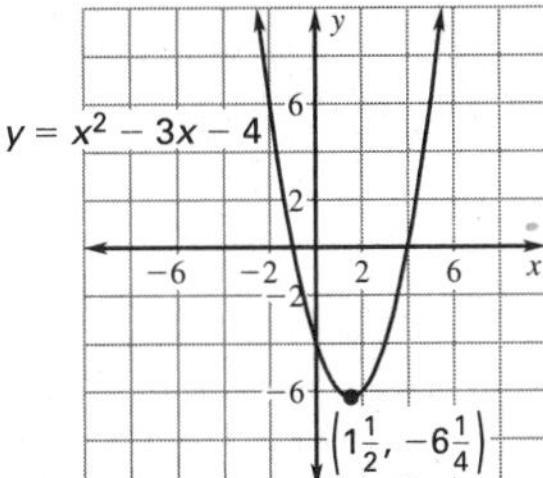

Estimate solutions: -1, 4

Check -1:

$-(-1)^2 + 3(-1) \stackrel{?}{=} -4$

$-(1) - 3 \stackrel{?}{=} -4$

$-4 = -4$

Check 4:

$-(4)^2 + 3(4) \stackrel{?}{=} -4$

$-16 + 12 \stackrel{?}{=} -4$

$-4 = -4$

Copyright © McDougal Littell Inc.
All rights reserved.

25. $2x^2 + 4x = 6$

$2x^2 + 4x - 6 = 0$

Related quadratic function: $y = 2x^2 + 4x - 6$

$x = -\frac{4}{2(2)} = -1$

Vertex: $(-1, -8)$

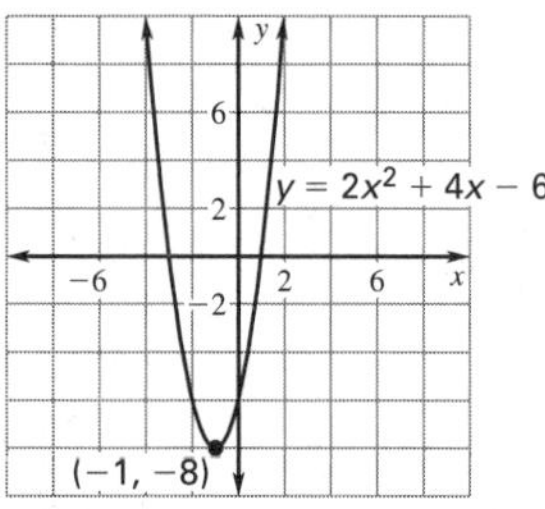

Estimate solutions: $-3, 1$

Check -3:

$2(-3)^2 + 4(-3) \stackrel{?}{=} 6$

$2(9) + (-12) \stackrel{?}{=} 6$

$6 = 6$

Check 1:

$2(1)^2 + 4(1) \stackrel{?}{=} 6$

$2 + 4 \stackrel{?}{=} 6$

$6 = 6$

26. $3x^2 + 3x = 6$

$3x^2 + 3x - 6 = 0$

Related quadratic function: $y = 3x^2 + 3x - 6$

$x = -\frac{3}{2(3)} = -\frac{3}{6} = -\frac{1}{2}$

Vertex: $\left(-\frac{1}{2}, -6\frac{3}{4}\right)$

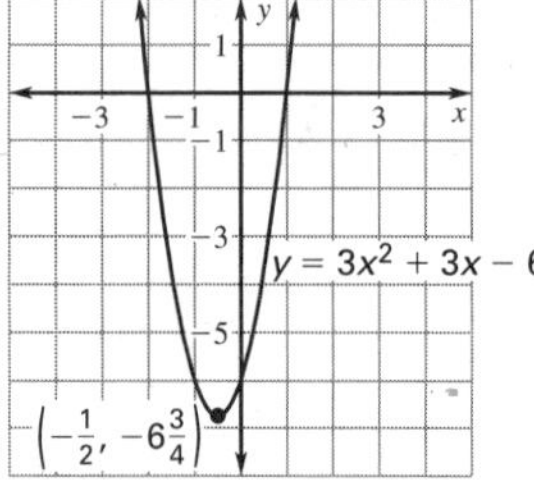

Estimate solutions: $-2, 1$

Check -2:

$3(-2)^2 + 3(-2) \stackrel{?}{=} 6$

$3(4) - 6 \stackrel{?}{=} 6$

$6 = 6$

Check 1:

$3(1)^2 + 3(1) \stackrel{?}{=} 6$

$3 + 3 \stackrel{?}{=} 6$

$6 = 6$

27. $x^2 - 4x - 5 = 0$

Related quadratic function: $y = x^2 - 4x - 5$

$x = -\frac{(-4)}{2(1)} = 2$

Vertex: $(2, -9)$

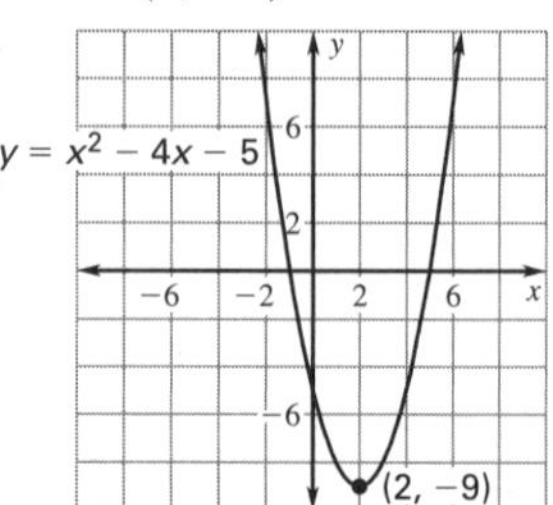

Estimate solutions: $-1, 5$

Check 1:

$(-1)^2 - 4(-1) - 5 \stackrel{?}{=} 0$

$1 + 4 - 5 \stackrel{?}{=} 0$

$0 = 0$

Check 5:

$5^2 - 4(5) - 5 \stackrel{?}{=} 0$

$25 - 20 - 5 \stackrel{?}{=} 0$

$0 = 0$

28. $x^2 - x = 12$

$x^2 - x - 12 = 0$

Related quadratic function: $y = x^2 - x - 12$

$x = -\frac{(-1)}{2(1)} = \frac{1}{2}$

Vertex: $\left(\frac{1}{2}, -12\frac{1}{4}\right)$

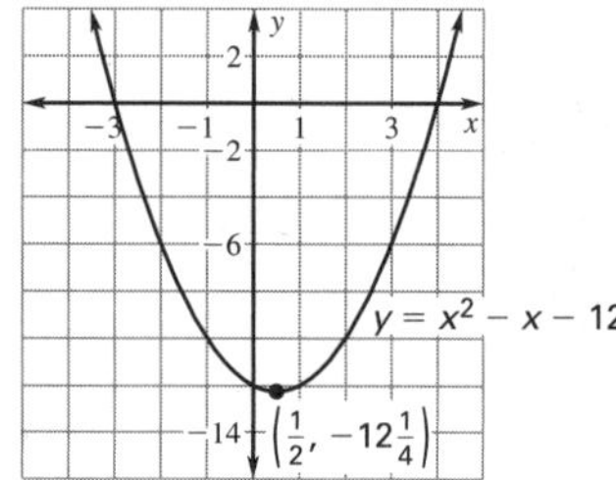

Estimate solutions: $-3, 4$

Check -3:

$(-3)^2 - (-3) \stackrel{?}{=} 12$

$9 + 3 \stackrel{?}{=} 12$

$12 = 12$

Check 4:

$4^2 - 4 \stackrel{?}{=} 12$

$16 - 4 \stackrel{?}{=} 12$

$12 = 12$

Copyright © McDougal Littell Inc.
All rights reserved.

29. $-x^2 - 4x = -5$

$-x^2 - 4x + 5 = 0$

$x^2 + 4x - 5 = 0$

Related quadratic function: $y = x^2 + 4x - 5$

$x = -\dfrac{4}{2(1)} = -2$

Vertex; $(-2, -9)$

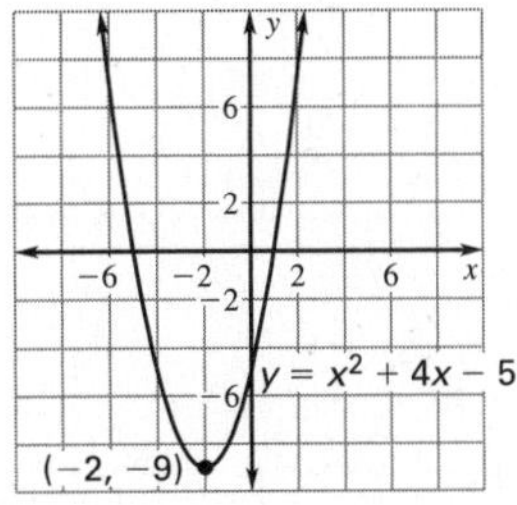

Estimate solutions: $-5, 1$

Check -5:

$-(-5)^2 - 4(-5) \stackrel{?}{=} -5$

$-(25) + 20 \stackrel{?}{=} -5$

$-5 = -5$

Check 1:

$-(1)^2 - 4(1) \stackrel{?}{=} -5$

$-1 - 4 \stackrel{?}{=} -5$

$-5 = -5$

30. $x^2 + x = 2$

$x^2 + x - 2 = 0$

Related quadratic function: $y = x^2 + x - 2$

$x = -\dfrac{1}{2(1)} = -\dfrac{1}{2}$

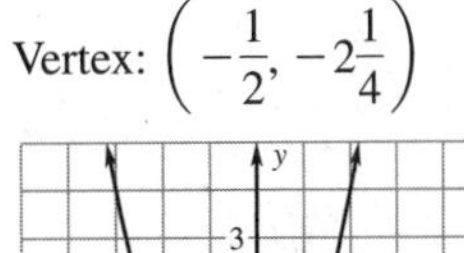

Vertex: $\left(-\dfrac{1}{2}, -2\dfrac{1}{4}\right)$

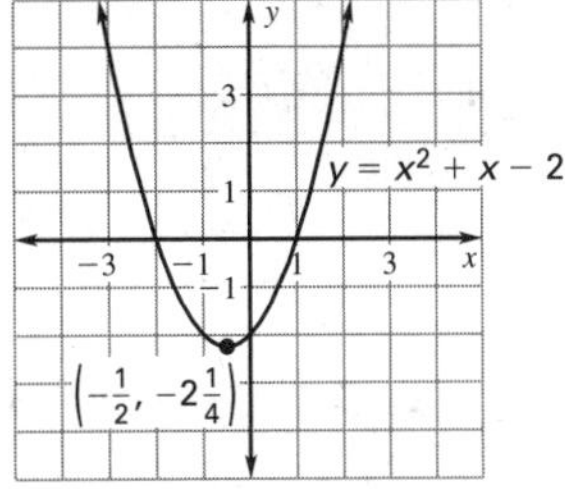

Estimate solutions: $-2, 1$

Check -2:

$(-2)^2 + (-2) \stackrel{?}{=} 2$

$4 - 2 \stackrel{?}{=} 2$

$2 = 2$

Check 1:

$(1)^2 + 1 \stackrel{?}{=} 2$

$1 + 1 \stackrel{?}{=} 2$

$2 = 2$

31. $-x^2 - x + 6 = 0$

Related quadratic function: $y = -x^2 - x + 6$

$x = -\dfrac{(-1)}{2(-1)} = -\dfrac{1}{2}$

Vertex: $\left(-\dfrac{1}{2}, 6\dfrac{1}{4}\right)$

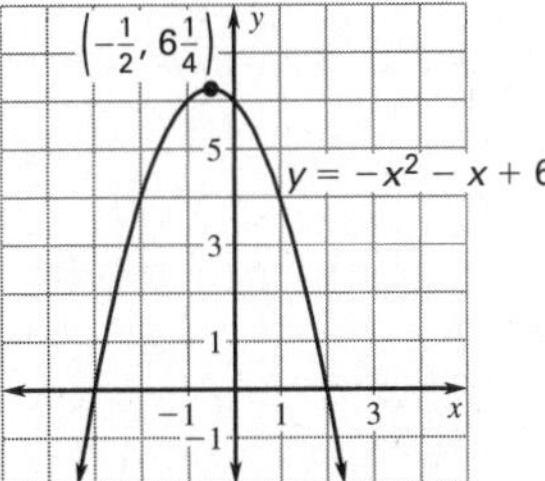

Estimate solutions: $-3, 2$

Check -3:

$-(-3)^2 - (-3) + 6 \stackrel{?}{=} 0$

$-(9) + 3 + 6 \stackrel{?}{=} 0$

$0 = 0$

Check 2:

$-(2)^2 - (2) + 6 \stackrel{?}{=} 0$

$-(4) - 2 + 6 \stackrel{?}{=} 0$

32. $2x^2 - 8x = 10$

$2x^2 - 8x - 10 = 0$

Related quadratic function: $y = 2x^2 - 8x - 10$

$x = -\dfrac{(-8)}{2(2)} = \dfrac{8}{4} = 2$

Vertex: $(2, -18)$

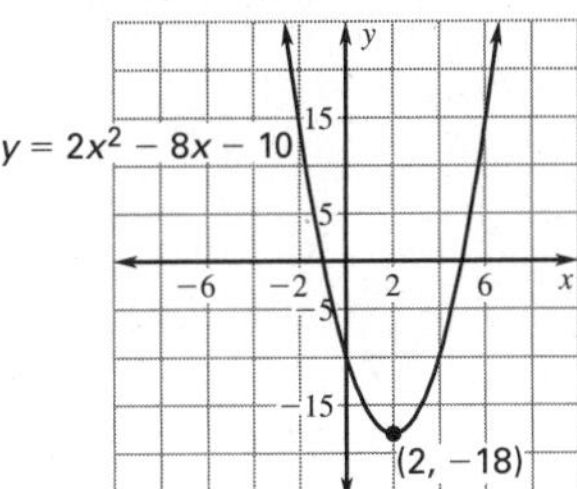

Estimate solutions: $-1, 5$

Check -1:

$2(-1)^2 - 8(-1) \stackrel{?}{=} 10$

$2(1) + 8 \stackrel{?}{=} 10$

$10 = 10$

Check 5:

$2(5)^2 - 8(5) \stackrel{?}{=} 10$

$2(25) - 40 \stackrel{?}{=} 10$

$10 = 10$

Copyright © McDougal Littell Inc.
All rights reserved.

Chapter 9 *continued*

33. $-x^2 + x = -2$

$-x^2 + x + 2 = 0$

Related quadratic function: $y = -x^2 + x + 2$

$x = -\frac{1}{2(-1)} = -\frac{1}{-2} = \frac{1}{2}$

Vertex: $\left(\frac{1}{2}, 2\frac{1}{4}\right)$

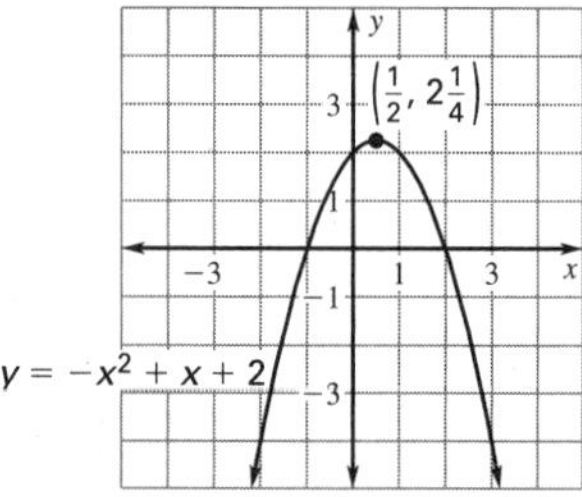

Estimate solutions: −1, 2

Check −1:

$-(-1)^2 + (-1) \stackrel{?}{=} -2$

$-(1) - 1 \stackrel{?}{=} -2$

$-2 = -2$

Check 2:

$-(2)^2 + (2) \stackrel{?}{=} -2$

$-4 + 2 \stackrel{?}{=} -2$

$-2 = -2$

34. $2x^2 = 32$

$x^2 = 16$

$x = \pm 4$

Related quadratic function: $y = 2x^2 - 32$

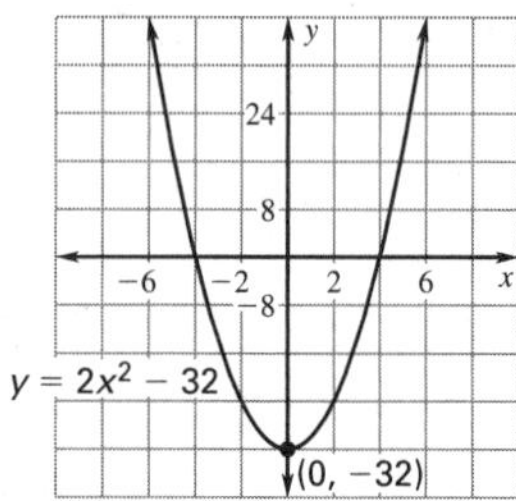

35. $4x^2 = 100$

$x^2 = 25$

$x = \pm 5$

Related quadratic function: $y = 4x^2 - 100$

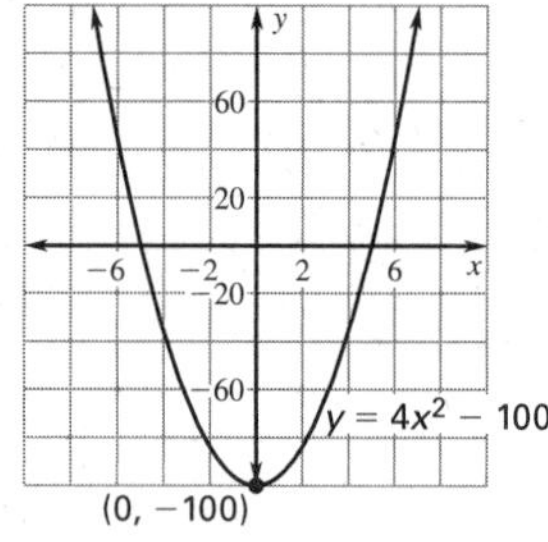

36. $4x^2 = 16$

$x^2 = 4$

$x = \pm 2$

Related quadratic function: $y = 4x^2 - 16$

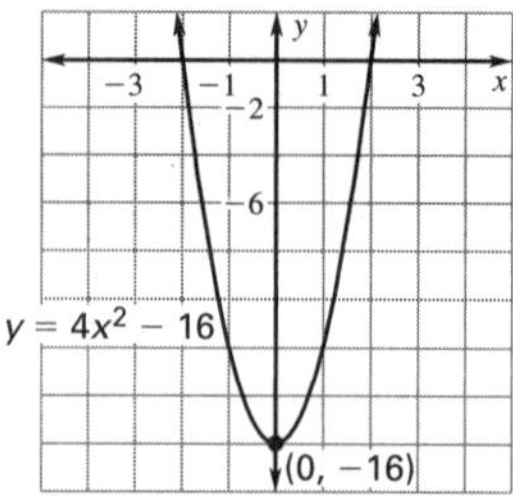

37. $x^2 - 11 = 14$

$x^2 = 25$

$x = \pm 5$

Related quadratic function: $y = x^2 - 25$

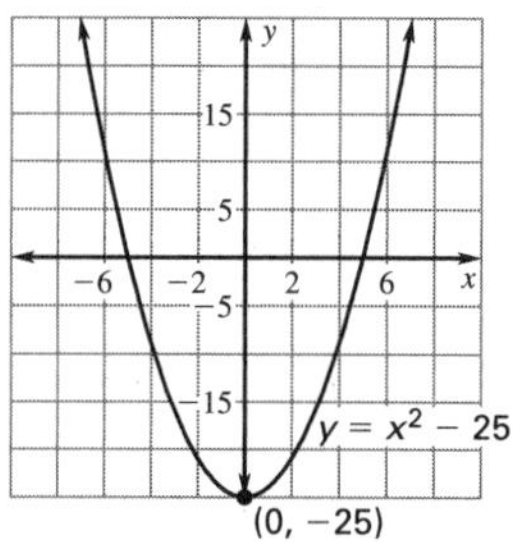

38. $x^2 - 13 = 36$

$x^2 = 49$

$x = \pm 7$

Related quadratic function: $y = x^2 - 49$

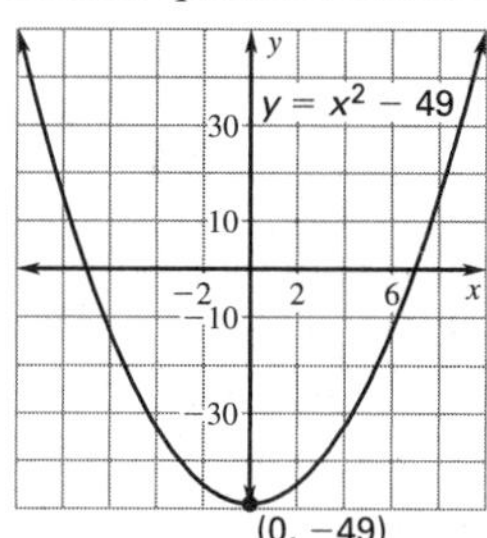

39. $x^2 - 4 = 12$

$x^2 = 16$

$x = \pm 4$

Related quadratic function: $y = x^2 - 16$

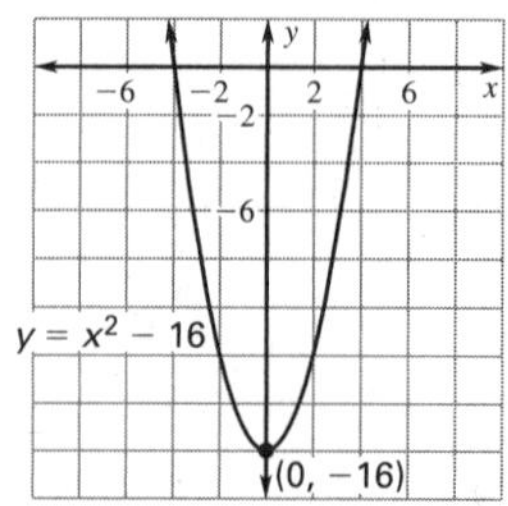

Copyright © McDougal Littell Inc.
All rights reserved.

40. $x^2 - 53 = 11$
$x^2 = 64$
$x = \pm 8$
Related quadratic function: $y = x^2 - 64$

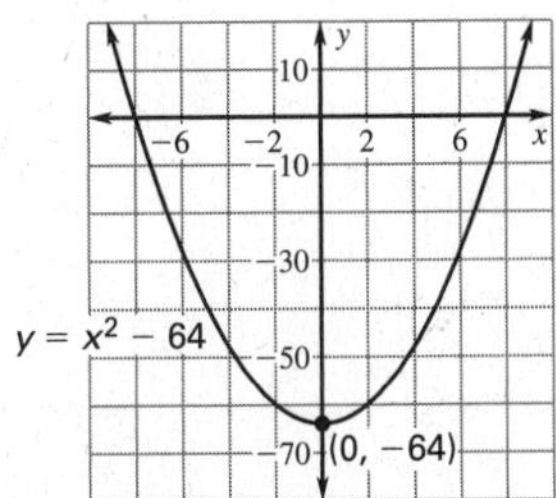

41. $x^2 + 37 = 118$
$x^2 = 81$
$x = \pm 9$
Related quadratic function: $y = x^2 - 81$

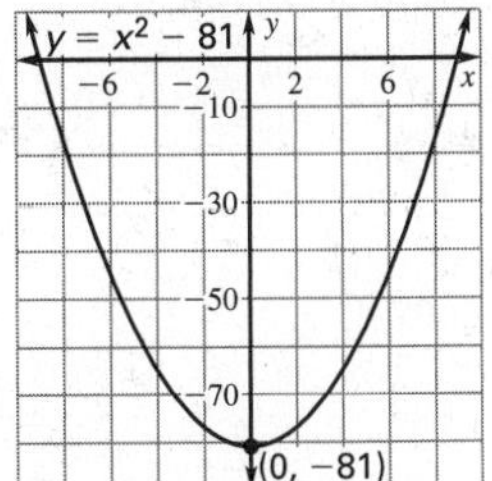

42. $2x^2 - 89 = 9$
$2x^2 = 98$
$x^2 = 49$
$x = \pm 7$
Related quadratic function: $y = 2x^2 - 98$

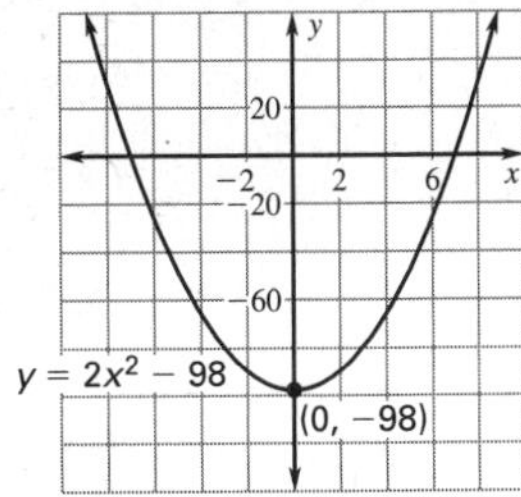

43. $2x^2 + 8 = 16$
$2x^2 = 8$
$x^2 = 4$
$x = \pm 2$
Related quadratic function: $y = 2x^2 - 8$

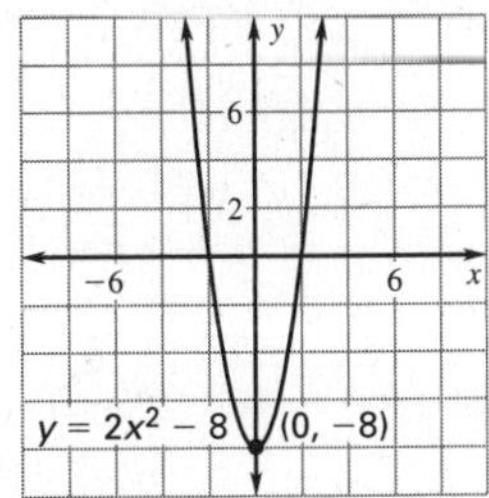

44. $3x^2 + 5 = 32$
$3x^2 = 27$
$x^2 = 9$
$x = \pm 3$
Related quadratic function: $y = 3x^2 - 27$

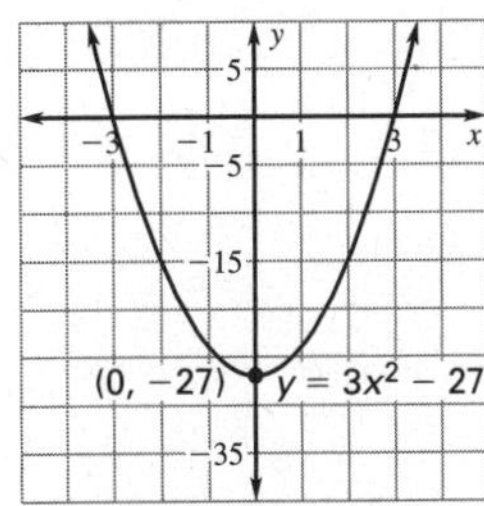

45. $2x^2 - 7 = 11$
$2x^2 = 18$
$x^2 = 9$
$x = \pm 3$
Related quadratic function: $y = 2x^2 - 18$

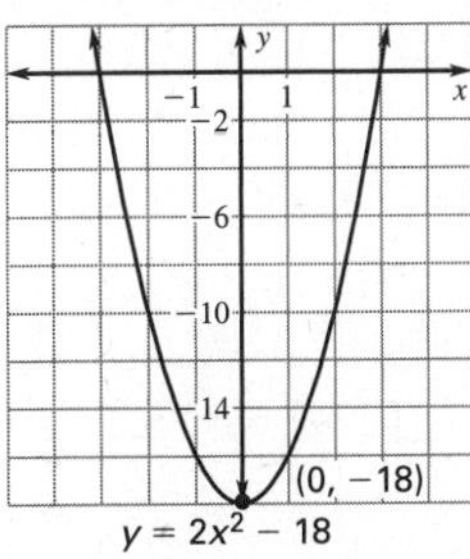

46. According to the graph, $P = 0$ in 39 years, or $1970 + 39 = 2009$. No, this is not a realistic prediction since people will probably still eat Swiss cheese in 2009.

47. $-x^2 - 3x + 4 = 0$
$y = -x^2 - 3x + 4$ (Related quadratic function)

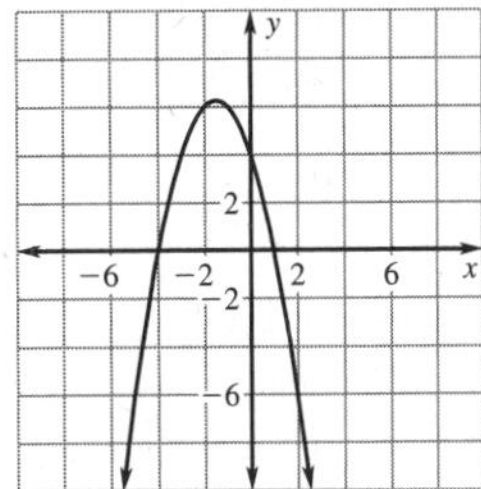

Solutions: $-4, 1$

48. $x^2 + 6x - 7 = 0$
$y = x^2 + 6x - 7$ (Related quadratic function)

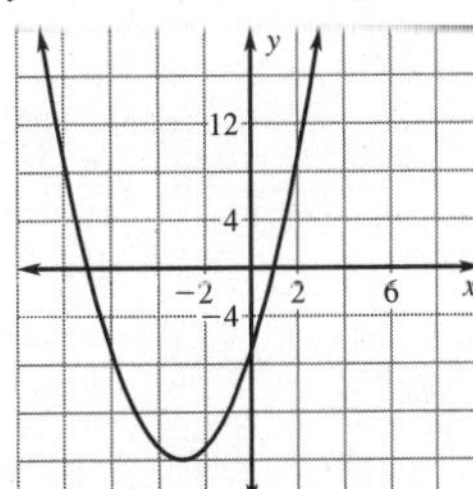

Solutions: $-7, 1$

Copyright © McDougal Littell Inc.
All rights reserved.

49. $-\frac{1}{2}x^2 + 2x + 16 = 0$

$y = -\frac{1}{2}x^2 + 2x + 16$ (Related quadratic function)

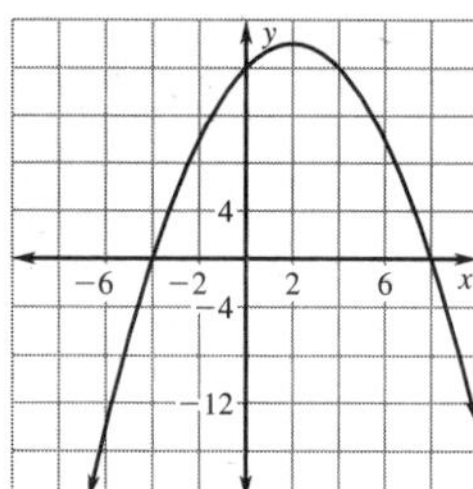

Solutions: 4, 8

50. $\frac{5}{4}x^2 + 15x + 40 = 0$

$y = \frac{5}{4}x^2 + 15x + 40$ (Related quadratic function)

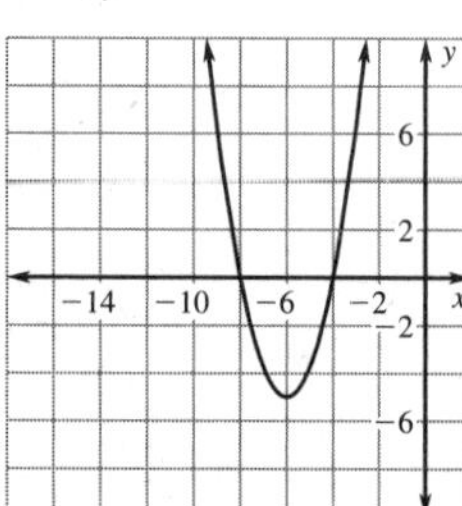

Solutions: $-8, -4$

51. $d = 4.9t^2$
$490 = 4.9t^2$
$100 = t^2$
$10 = t$, 10 sec

52. $y = 4.9x^2 - 490$

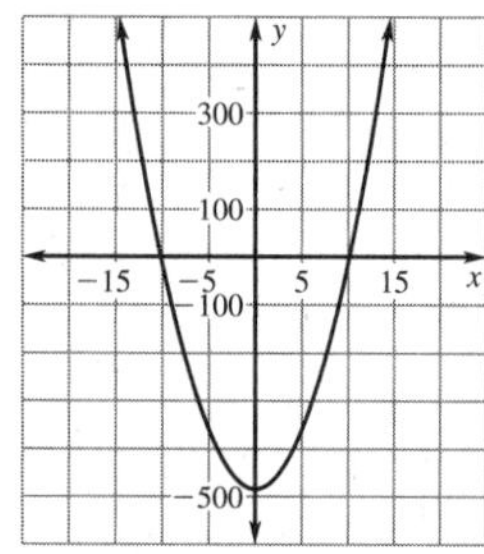

9.5 Practice and Applications (p. 531)

53. *D*;
$0 = x^2 - 2x - 3$
$0 \stackrel{?}{=} (3)^2 - 2(3) - 3$
$0 \stackrel{?}{=} 9 - 6 - 3$
$0 = 0$
$0 \stackrel{?}{=} (-1)^2 - 2(-1) - 3$
$0 \stackrel{?}{=} (1) + 2 - 3$
$0 = 0$

54. *G*; Roots: $-5, 5$
$\frac{1}{5}x^2 - 5 = 0$
$\frac{1}{5}x^2 = 5$
$x^2 = 25$
$x = \pm 5$

9.5 Mixed Review (p. 531)

55. $p + s = 7.90$
$p + 2s = 9.85$
$p + s = 7.90$
$-p - 2s = -9.85$ Multiply by -1
$-s = -1.95$
$s = 1.95$
$p + 1.95 = 7.90$
$p = 5.95$
salad: \$1.95
pasta: \$5.95

56. $x + 6y = 2$
$x = -6y + 2$
$-2(-6y + 2) + 8y = 11$
$12y - 4 + 8y = 11$
$20y - 4 = 11$
$20y = 15$
$y = \frac{3}{4}$
$x = -6\left(\frac{3}{4}\right) + 2$
$x = -\frac{9}{2} + \frac{4}{2} = -\frac{5}{2}$
one solution: $\left(-\frac{5}{2}, \frac{3}{4}\right)$

57. $x + 6y = 15$
$x = -6y + 15$
$-2(-6y + 15) + 8y = 10$
$12y - 30 + 8y = 10$
$20y - 30 = 10$
$20y = 40$
$y = 2$
$x = -6(2) + 15$
$x = 3$
one solution: (3, 2)

Copyright © McDougal Littell Inc.
All rights reserved.

58. $-2x + 2y = 4$
$x - y = -2$
$$\begin{aligned} -2x + 2y &= 4 \\ 2x - 2y &= -4 \quad \text{Multiply by 2.} \\ \hline 0 &= 0 \end{aligned}$$
infinitely many solutions

59. $4x - y = -20$
$$\begin{aligned} 4x + 20 &= y \\ 8x + 4(4x + 20) &= -4 \\ 8x + 16x + 80 &= -4 \\ 24x + 80 &= -4 \\ 24x &= -84 \\ x &= -\frac{7}{2} \end{aligned}$$
$y = 4\left(-\frac{7}{2}\right) + 20$
$y = -14 + 20 = 6$
one solution: $\left(-\frac{7}{2}, 6\right)$

60. $2x - y = -6$
$$\begin{aligned} 2x + 6 &= y \\ 6x + 4(2x + 6) &= -4 \\ 6x + 8x + 24 &= -4 \\ 14x + 24 &= -4 \\ 14x &= -28 \\ x &= -2 \end{aligned}$$
$y = 2(-2) + 6$
$y = 2$
one solution: $(-2, 2)$

61.
$$\begin{aligned} 5x + 4y &= -3 \\ 15x + 12y &= 9 \\ -15x - 12y &= 9 \\ +\ 15x + 12y &= 9 \\ \hline 0 &\neq 18 \end{aligned}$$
no solution

62. $\sqrt{b^2 - 11a} = \sqrt{5^2 - 11(-1)} = \sqrt{25 + 11} = \sqrt{36} = 6$

63. $\sqrt{b^2 + 9a} = \sqrt{5^2 + 9(-1)} = \sqrt{25 - 9} = \sqrt{16} = 4$

64. $\sqrt{a^2 + 8} = \sqrt{(-1)^2 + 8} = \sqrt{1 + 8} = \sqrt{9} = 3$

65. $\sqrt{a^2 - 1} = \sqrt{(-1)^2 - 1} = \sqrt{1 - 1} = \sqrt{0} = 0$

66. $\frac{\sqrt{b^2 + 24a}}{a} = \frac{\sqrt{5^2 + 24(-1)}}{-1} = \frac{\sqrt{25 - 24}}{-1} = \frac{\sqrt{1}}{-1} = \frac{1}{-1} = -1$

67. $\frac{\sqrt{b^2 - 75a}}{b} = \frac{\sqrt{5^2 - 75(-1)}}{5} = \frac{\sqrt{25 + 75}}{5} = \frac{\sqrt{100}}{5} = \frac{10}{5} = 2$

68. $\frac{\sqrt{65 - a^2}}{-a} = \frac{\sqrt{65 - (-1)^2}}{-(-1)} = \frac{\sqrt{65 - 1}}{1} = \frac{\sqrt{64}}{1} = \frac{8}{1} = 8$

69. $\frac{\sqrt{86 + ab}}{a} = \frac{\sqrt{86 + (-1)(5)}}{-1} = \frac{\sqrt{86 - 5}}{-1} = \frac{\sqrt{81}}{-1} = \frac{9}{-1} = -9$

70. $\sqrt{40} = \sqrt{4 \cdot 10} = \sqrt{4} \cdot \sqrt{10} = 2\sqrt{10}$

71. $\sqrt{24} = \sqrt{4 \cdot 6} = \sqrt{4} \cdot \sqrt{6} = 2\sqrt{6}$

72. $\sqrt{60} = \sqrt{4 \cdot 15} = \sqrt{4} \cdot \sqrt{15} = 2\sqrt{15}$

73. $\sqrt{200} = \sqrt{100 \cdot 2} = \sqrt{100} \cdot \sqrt{2} = 10\sqrt{2}$

74. $\frac{1}{2}\sqrt{80} = \frac{1}{2}\sqrt{16 \cdot 5} = \frac{1}{2}\sqrt{16} \cdot \sqrt{5} = \frac{1}{2}(4)\sqrt{5} = 2\sqrt{5}$

75. $\frac{1}{3}\sqrt{27} = \frac{1}{3}\sqrt{9 \cdot 3} = \frac{1}{3}\sqrt{9} \cdot \sqrt{3} = \frac{1}{3}(3)\sqrt{3} = \sqrt{3}$

Copyright © McDougal Littell Inc.
All rights reserved.

76. $\frac{1}{8}\sqrt{32} = \frac{1}{8}\sqrt{16 \cdot 2}$

$= \frac{1}{8}\sqrt{16} \cdot \sqrt{2}$

$= \frac{1}{8}(4)\sqrt{2}$

$= \frac{\sqrt{2}}{2}$

77. $\frac{2}{3}\sqrt{300} = \frac{2}{3}\sqrt{100 \cdot 3}$

$= \frac{2}{3}\sqrt{100} \cdot \sqrt{3}$

$= \frac{2}{3}(10)\sqrt{3}$

$= \frac{20\sqrt{3}}{3}$

9.5 Maintaining Skills (p. 531)

78. $\frac{8}{7} = 1\frac{1}{7}$

79. $\frac{8}{3} = 2\frac{2}{3} > 2\frac{1}{3}$

80. $\frac{17}{5} = 3\frac{2}{5} < 3\frac{4}{5}$

81. $\frac{13}{6} = 2\frac{1}{6} > 1\frac{1}{6}$

82. $\frac{23}{10} = 2\frac{3}{10}$

83. $\frac{100}{9} = 11\frac{1}{9} < 11\frac{2}{9}$

84. $1\frac{7}{17} < 1\frac{22}{17}$

85. $\frac{9}{4} = 2\frac{1}{4} < 2\frac{3}{4}$

9.5 Try These (p. 532)

1. $x^2 - x - 2 = 0$

$y = x^2 - x - 2$ (Related quadratic function)
Solutions: $-1, 2$

2. $6x^2 + 4x - 12 = 0$

$y = 6x^2 + 4x - 12$ (Related quadratic function)
Solutions: $-1.79, 1.12$

3. $-4x^2 + 6x + 7 = 0$

$y = -4x^2 + 6x + 7$ (Related quadratic function)
Solutions: $-0.77, 2.27$

4. $-2x^2 + 3x + 6 = 0$

$y = -2x^2 + 3x + 6$ (Related quadratic function)
Solutions: $-1.14, 2.64$

5. 2

6. 1, 0

Lesson 9.6

9.6 Checkpoint (pp. 533–535)

1. $x^2 - 4x + 3 = 0;\ a = 1,\ b = -4,\ c = 3$

$x = \frac{-(-4) \pm \sqrt{(-4)^2 - 4(1)(3)}}{2(1)}$

$x = \frac{4 \pm \sqrt{16 - 12}}{2}$

$x = \frac{4 \pm \sqrt{4}}{2}$

$x = \frac{4 \pm 2}{2}$

Solutions: $\frac{4 + 2}{2} = \frac{6}{2} = 3$ and $\frac{4 - 2}{2} = \frac{2}{2} = 1$

2. $2x^2 + x - 10 = 0;\ a = 2,\ b = 1,\ c = -10$

$x = \frac{-1 \pm \sqrt{1^2 - 4(2)(-10)}}{2(2)}$

$x = \frac{-1 \pm \sqrt{1 + 80}}{4}$

$x = \frac{-1 \pm \sqrt{81}}{4}$

$x = \frac{-1 \pm 9}{4}$

Solutions: $x = \frac{-1 + 9}{4} = \frac{8}{4} = 2$ and

$x = \frac{-1 - 9}{4} = \frac{-10}{4} = -\frac{5}{2}$

3. $-x^2 + 3x + 4 = 0;\ a = -1,\ b = 3,\ c = 4$

$x = \frac{-3 \pm \sqrt{3^2 - 4(-1)(4)}}{2(-1)}$

$x = \frac{-3 \pm \sqrt{9 + 16}}{-2}$

$x = \frac{-3 \pm \sqrt{25}}{-2}$

$x = \frac{-3 \pm 5}{2}$

Solutions: $x = \frac{-3 + 5}{-2} = \frac{2}{-2} = -1$ and

$x = \frac{-3 - 5}{-2} = \frac{-8}{-2} = 4$

4. $x^2 + x = 1$ Original equation.

$x^2 + x - 1 = 0$ Standard form.

$a = 1,\ b = 1,\ c = -1$

$x = \frac{-1 \pm \sqrt{1^2 - 4(1)(-1)}}{2(1)}$

$x = \frac{-1 \pm \sqrt{1 + 4}}{2} = \frac{-1 \pm \sqrt{5}}{2}$

Solutions: $\frac{-1 + \sqrt{5}}{2} \approx 0.62$ and $\frac{-1 - \sqrt{5}}{2} \approx -1.62$

Copyright © McDougal Littell Inc.
All rights reserved.

5. $-x^2 = 2x - 3$ Original equation.

$-x^2 - 2x + 3 = 0$ Standard form.

$a = -1,\ b = -2,\ c = 3$

$$x = \frac{-(-2) \pm \sqrt{(-2)^2 - 4(-1)(3)}}{2(-1)}$$

$$x = \frac{2 \pm \sqrt{4 + 12}}{-2} = \frac{2 \pm \sqrt{16}}{-2}$$

$$x = \frac{2 \pm 4}{-2}$$

Solutions: $x = \frac{2 + 4}{-2} = \frac{6}{-2} = -3$ and

$$x = \frac{2 - 4}{-2} = \frac{-2}{-2} = 1$$

6. $7x^2 - 1 = -2x$ Original equation.

$7x^2 + 2x - 1 = 0$ Standard form.

$a = 7,\ b = 2,\ c = -1$

$$x = \frac{-2 \pm \sqrt{2^2 - 4(7)(-1)}}{2(7)}$$

$$x = \frac{-2 \pm \sqrt{4 + 28}}{14} = \frac{-2 \pm \sqrt{32}}{14}$$

$$x = \frac{-2 \pm \sqrt{16 \cdot 2}}{14} = \frac{-2 \pm 4\sqrt{2}}{14} = \frac{2(-1 \pm 2\sqrt{2})}{14}$$

$$x = \frac{-1 \pm 2\sqrt{2}}{7}$$

Solutions: $x = 0.26$ and -0.55

7. $h = -16t^2 + vt + s$

$0 = -16t^2 + (-60)t + 200$

$a = -16, b = -60, c = 200$

$$t = \frac{-(-60) \pm \sqrt{(-60)^2 - 4(-16)(200)}}{2(-16)}$$

$$t = \frac{60 \pm \sqrt{3600 + 12800}}{-32}$$

$$t = \frac{60 \pm \sqrt{16400}}{-32}$$

$t = -5.88$ or 2.13

No; it takes about 2.13 seconds (about $\frac{2.13}{2.72} = 0.78$ or 78% of the time when the speed was -30 ft/sec).

9.6 Guided Practice (p. 536)

1. $x = \frac{-b \pm \sqrt{b^2 - 4ac}}{2a}$

2. The solutions of the function will be the x-intercepts of the graph.

3. *Sample answer*: The new model takes into account an initial velocity other than zero.

4. $x^2 = 1$

$x^2 - 1 = 0$

$a = 1, b = 0, c = -1$

5. $16x - 32 = 2x^2$

$2x^2 - 16x + 32 = 0$

$a = 2, b = -16, c = 32$

6. $x^2 - 7x + 42 = 6x$

$x^2 - 13x + 42 = 0$

$a = 1, b = -13, c = 42$

7. $x^2 + 6x - 7 = 0$

$a = 1,\ b = 6,\ c = -7$

$$x = \frac{-6 \pm \sqrt{6^2 - 4(1)(-7)}}{2(1)}$$

$$x = \frac{-6 \pm \sqrt{36 + 28}}{2} = \frac{-6 \pm \sqrt{64}}{2}$$

$$x = \frac{-6 \pm 8}{2}$$

$$x = \frac{-6 + 8}{2} = \frac{2}{2} = 1 \text{ and } x = \frac{-6 - 8}{2} = \frac{-14}{2} = -7$$

8. $x^2 - 2x - 15 = 0$

$a = 1,\ b = -2,\ c = -15$

$$x = \frac{-(-2) \pm \sqrt{(-2)^2 - 4(1)(-15)}}{2(1)}$$

$$x = \frac{2 \pm \sqrt{4 + 60}}{2} = \frac{2 \pm \sqrt{64}}{2}$$

$$x = \frac{2 \pm 8}{2}$$

$$x = \frac{2 + 8}{2} = \frac{10}{2} = 5 \text{ and } x = \frac{2 - 8}{2} = \frac{-6}{2} = -3$$

9. $x^2 + 12x + 36 = 0$

$a = 1,\ b = 12,\ c = 36$

$$x = \frac{-12 \pm \sqrt{12^2 - 4(1)(36)}}{2(1)}$$

$$x = \frac{-12 \pm \sqrt{144 - 144}}{2} = \frac{-12 \pm \sqrt{0}}{2}$$

$$x = \frac{-12}{2} = -6$$

one solution

10. $4x^2 - 8x + 3 = 0$

$a = 4,\ b = -8,\ c = 3$

$$x = \frac{-(-8) \pm \sqrt{(-8)^2 - 4(4)(3)}}{2(4)}$$

$$x = \frac{8 \pm \sqrt{64 - 48}}{8} = \frac{8 \pm \sqrt{16}}{8}$$

$$x = \frac{8 \pm 4}{8}$$

$$x = \frac{8 + 4}{8} = \frac{12}{8} = \frac{3}{2} \text{ and } x = \frac{8 - 4}{8} = \frac{4}{8} = \frac{1}{2}$$

11. $3x^2 + x - 1 = 0$

$a = 3,\ b = 1,\ c = -1$

$$x = \frac{-1 \pm \sqrt{1^2 - 4(3)(-1)}}{2(3)}$$

$$x = \frac{-1 \pm \sqrt{1 + 12}}{6} = \frac{-1 \pm \sqrt{13}}{6}$$

Copyright © McDougal Littell Inc.
All rights reserved.

12. $x^2 + 6x - 3 = 0$

$a = 1,\ b = 6,\ c = -3$

$$x = \frac{-6 \pm \sqrt{6^2 - 4(1)(-3)}}{2(1)}$$

$$x = \frac{-6 \pm \sqrt{36 + 12}}{2} = \frac{-6 \pm \sqrt{48}}{2}$$

$$x = \frac{-6 \pm \sqrt{16 \cdot 3}}{2} = \frac{-6 \pm 4\sqrt{3}}{2} = \frac{2(-3 \pm 2\sqrt{3})}{2}$$

$$x = -3 \pm 2\sqrt{3}$$

13. $2x^2 = -x + 6$

$2x^2 + x - 6 = 0$

$a = 2,\ b = 1,\ c = -6$

$$x = \frac{-1 \pm \sqrt{1^2 - 4(2)(-6)}}{2(2)}$$

$$x = \frac{-1 \pm \sqrt{1 + 48}}{4}$$

$$x = \frac{-1 \pm \sqrt{49}}{4} = \frac{-1 \pm 7}{4}$$

$$x = \frac{-1 + 7}{4} = \frac{6}{4} = \frac{3}{2} \text{ and } x = \frac{-1 - 7}{4} = \frac{-8}{4} = -2$$

14. $-3x = 2x^2 + 1$

$2x^2 + 3x + 1 = 0$

$a = 2,\ b = 3,\ c = 1$

$$x = \frac{-3 \pm \sqrt{3^2 - 4(2)(1)}}{2(2)}$$

$$x = \frac{-3 \pm \sqrt{9 - 8}}{4} = \frac{-3 \pm \sqrt{1}}{4}$$

$$x = \frac{-3 \pm 1}{4}$$

$$x = \frac{-3 + 1}{4} = \frac{-2}{4} = -\frac{1}{2} \text{ and}$$

$$x = \frac{-3 - 1}{4} = \frac{-4}{4} = -1$$

15. $2 = x^2 - x$

$x^2 - x - 2 = 0$

$a = 1,\ b = -1,\ c = -2$

$$x = \frac{-(-1) \pm \sqrt{(-1)^2 - 4(1)(-2)}}{2(1)}$$

$$x = \frac{1 \pm \sqrt{1 + 8}}{2} = \frac{1 \pm \sqrt{9}}{2} = \frac{1 \pm 3}{2}$$

$$x = \frac{1 + 3}{2} = \frac{4}{2} = 2 \text{ and } x = \frac{1 - 3}{2} = \frac{-2}{2} = -1$$

16. $-14x = -2x^2 + 36$

$2x^2 - 14x - 36 = 0$

$a = 2,\ b = -14,\ c = -36$

$$x = \frac{-(-14) \pm \sqrt{(-14)^2 - 4(2)(-36)}}{2(2)}$$

$$x = \frac{14 \pm \sqrt{196 + 288}}{4}$$

$$x = \frac{14 \pm \sqrt{484}}{4} = \frac{14 \pm 22}{4}$$

$$x = \frac{14 + 22}{4} = \frac{36}{4} = 9 \text{ and } x = \frac{14 - 22}{4} = \frac{-8}{4} = -2$$

17. $-x^2 + 4x = 3$

$-x^2 + 4x - 3 = 0$

$a = -1,\ b = 4,\ c = -3$

$$x = \frac{-4 \pm \sqrt{4^2 - 4(-1)(-3)}}{2(-1)}$$

$$x = \frac{-4 \pm \sqrt{16 - 12}}{-2} = \frac{-4 \pm \sqrt{4}}{-2}$$

$$x = \frac{-4 \pm 2}{-2}$$

$$x = \frac{-4 + 2}{-2} = \frac{-2}{-2} = 1 \text{ and } x = \frac{-4 - 2}{-2} = \frac{-6}{-2} = 3$$

18. $4x^2 + 4x = -1$

$4x^2 + 4x + 1 = 0$

$a = 4,\ b = 4,\ c = 1$

$$x = \frac{-4 \pm \sqrt{4^2 - 4(4)(1)}}{2(4)}$$

$$x = \frac{-4 \pm \sqrt{16 - 16}}{8} = \frac{-4 \pm \sqrt{0}}{8} = \frac{-4 \pm 0}{8}$$

$$x = \frac{-4}{8} = -\frac{1}{2}$$

9.6 Practice and Applications (pp. 536–538)

19. $3x^2 = 3x + 6$

$3x^2 - 3x - 6 = 0$

$a = 3, b = -3, c = -6$

20. $-2t^2 = -8$ or $-2t^2 = -8$

$-2t^2 + 8 = 0$ $0 = 2t^2 - 8$

$a = -2, b = 0, c = 8$ $a = 2, b = 0, c = -8$

21. $-x^2 = -5x + 6$

$-x^2 + 5x - 6 = 0$ or $0 = x^2 - 5x + 6$

$a = -1, b = 5, c = -6$ $a = 1, b = -5, c = 6$

22. $3x^2 = 27x$

$3x^2 - 27x = 0$

$a = 3, b = -27, c = 0$

23. $-24x + 45 = -3x^2$

$3x^2 - 24x + 45 = 0$

$a = 3, b = -24, c = 45$

24. $32 - 4m^2 = 28m$

$0 = 4m^2 + 28m - 32$

$a = 4, b = 28, c = -32$

Copyright © McDougal Littell Inc.
All rights reserved.

25. $k^2 = \frac{1}{4}$

$k^2 - \frac{1}{4} = 0$

$a = 1, b = 0, c = -\frac{1}{4}$

26. $2x^2 - \frac{1}{5} = -\frac{2}{5}x$

$2x^2 + \frac{2}{5}x - \frac{1}{5} = 0$

$a = 2, b = \frac{2}{5}, c = -\frac{1}{5}$

27. $\frac{1}{3} - 2x = \frac{2}{3}x^2$

$\frac{2}{3}x^2 + 2x - \frac{1}{3} = 0$

$a = \frac{2}{3}, b = 2, c = -\frac{1}{3}$

28. $x^2 - 3x - 4 = 0$
$a = 1, b = -3, c = -4$
$b^2 - 4ac = (-3)^2 - 4(1)(-4)$
$= 9 + 16 = 25$

29. $4x^2 + 5x + 1 = 0$
$a = 4, b = 5, c = 1$
$b^2 - 4ac = 5^2 - 4(4)(1)$
$= 25 - 16 = 9$

30. $-5w^2 - 3w + 2 = 0$
$a = -5, b = -3, c = 2$
$b^2 - 4ac = (-3)^2 - 4(-5)(2)$
$= 9 + 40 = 49$

31. $r^2 - 11r + 30 = 0$
$a = 1, b = -11, c = 30$
$b^2 - 4ac = (-11)^2 - 4(1)(30)$
$= 121 - 120 = 1$

32. $s^2 - 13s + 42 = 0$
$a = 1, b = -13, c = 42$
$b^2 - 4ac = (-13)^2 - 4(1)(42)$
$= 169 - 168 = 1$

33. $3x^2 - 5x - 12 = 0$
$a = 3, b = -5, c = -12$
$b^2 - 4ac = (-5)^2 - 4(3)(-12)$
$= 25 + 144 = 169$

34. $2x^2 + 4x - 1 = 0$
$a = 2, b = 4, c = -1$
$b^2 - 4ac = (4)^2 - 4(2)(-1)$
$= 16 + 8 = 24$

35. $3t^2 - 8t - 7 = 0$
$a = 3, b = -8, c = -7$
$b^2 - 4ac = (-8)^2 - 4(3)(-7)$
$= 64 + 84 = 148$

36. $-8m^2 - 6m + 3 = 0$
$a = -8, b = -6, c = 3$
$b^2 - 4ac = (-6)^2 - 4(-8)(3)$
$= 36 + 96 = 132$

37. $5x^2 + 5x + \frac{1}{5} = 0$

$a = 5, b = 5, c = \frac{1}{5}$

$b^2 - 4ac = 5^2 - 4(5)\left(\frac{1}{5}\right)$
$= 25 - 4 = 21$

38. $\frac{1}{2}t^2 + 5t - 8 = 0$

$a = \frac{1}{2}, b = 5, c = -8$

$b^2 - 4ac = 5^2 - 4\left(\frac{1}{2}\right)(-8)$
$= 25 + 16 = 41$

39. $\frac{1}{4}v^2 - 6v - 3 = 0$

$a = \frac{1}{4}, b = -6, c = -3$

$b^2 - 4ac = (-6)^2 - 4\left(\frac{1}{4}\right)(-3)$
$= 36 + 3 = 39$

40. $4x^2 - 13x + 3 = 0$
$a = 4, b = -13, c = 3$

$x = \frac{-(-13) \pm \sqrt{(-13)^2 - 4(4)(3)}}{2(4)}$

$x = \frac{13 \pm \sqrt{169 - 48}}{8} = \frac{13 \pm \sqrt{121}}{8}$

$x = \frac{13 \pm 11}{8}$

$x = \frac{13 + 11}{8} = \frac{24}{8} = 3$ and $x = \frac{13 - 11}{8} = \frac{2}{8} = \frac{1}{4}$

41. $y^2 + 11y + 10 = 0$
$a = 1, b = 11, c = 10$

$x = \frac{-11 \pm \sqrt{(11)^2 - 4(1)(10)}}{2(1)} = \frac{11 \pm \sqrt{121 - 40}}{2}$

$x = \frac{-11 \pm \sqrt{81}}{2} = \frac{-11 \pm 9}{2}$

$x = \frac{-11 + 9}{2} = \frac{-2}{2} = -1$ and

$x = \frac{-11 - 9}{2} = \frac{-20}{2} = -10$

42. $7x^2 + 8x + 1 = 0$
$a = 7, b = 8, c = 1$

$x = \frac{-8 \pm \sqrt{8^2 - 4(7)(1)}}{2(7)}$

$x = \frac{-8 \pm \sqrt{64 - 28}}{14} = \frac{-8 \pm \sqrt{36}}{14}$

$x = \frac{-8 \pm 6}{14}$

$x = \frac{-8 + 6}{14} = \frac{-2}{14} = -\frac{1}{7}$ or

$x = \frac{-8 - 6}{14} = \frac{-14}{14} = -1$

Copyright © McDougal Littell Inc.
All rights reserved.

43. $-3y^2 + 2y + 8 = 0$

$a = -3, b = 2, c = 8$

$$y = \frac{-2 \pm \sqrt{2^2 - 4(-3)(8)}}{2(-3)}$$

$$y = \frac{-2 \pm \sqrt{4 + 96}}{-6} = \frac{-2 \pm \sqrt{100}}{-6}$$

$$y = \frac{-2 \pm 10}{-6}$$

$$y = \frac{-2 + 10}{-6} = \frac{8}{-6} = -\frac{4}{3} \text{ or}$$

$$y = \frac{-2 - 10}{-6} = \frac{-12}{-6} = 2$$

44. $6n^2 - 10n + 3 = 0$

$a = 6, b = -10, c = 3$

$$n = \frac{-(-10) \pm \sqrt{(-10)^2 - 4(6)(3)}}{2(6)}$$

$$n = \frac{10 \pm \sqrt{100 - 72}}{12} = \frac{10 \pm \sqrt{28}}{12}$$

$n = 1.27$ or 0.39

45. $9x^2 + 14x + 3 = 0$

$a = 9, b = 14, c = 3$

$$x = \frac{-14 \pm \sqrt{(14)^2 - 4(9)(3)}}{2(9)}$$

$$x = \frac{-14 \pm \sqrt{196 - 108}}{18} = \frac{-14 \pm \sqrt{88}}{18}$$

$x = -0.26$ or -1.30

46. $8m^2 + 6m - 1 = 0$

$a = 8, b = 6, c = -1$

$$m = \frac{-6 \pm \sqrt{6^2 - 4(8)(-1)}}{2(8)}$$

$$m = \frac{-6 \pm \sqrt{36 + 32}}{16} = \frac{-6 \pm \sqrt{68}}{16}$$

$m = 0.14$ or -0.89

47. $-\frac{1}{2}x^2 + 6x + 13 = 0$

$a = -\frac{1}{2}, b = 6, c = 13$

$$x = \frac{-6 \pm \sqrt{6^2 - 4(-\frac{1}{2})(13)}}{2(-\frac{1}{2})}$$

$$x = \frac{-6 \pm \sqrt{36 + 26}}{-1} = \frac{-6 \pm \sqrt{62}}{-1}$$

$x = -1.87$ or 13.87

48. $2x^2 - 3x + 1 = 0$

$a = 2, b = -3, c = 1$

$$x = \frac{-(-3) \pm \sqrt{(-3)^2 - 4(2)(1)}}{2(2)}$$

$$x = \frac{3 \pm \sqrt{9 - 8}}{4} = \frac{3 \pm \sqrt{1}}{4}$$

$$x = \frac{3 \pm 1}{4}$$

$$x = \frac{3 + 1}{4} = \frac{4}{4} = 1 \text{ and } x = \frac{3 - 1}{4} = \frac{2}{4} = \frac{1}{2}$$

49. $2x^2 = 4x + 30$

$2x^2 - 4x - 30 = 0$

$a = 2, b = -4, c = -30$

$$x = \frac{-(-4) \pm \sqrt{(-4)^2 - 4(2)(-30)}}{2(2)}$$

$$x = \frac{4 \pm \sqrt{16 + 240}}{4} = \frac{4 \pm \sqrt{256}}{4}$$

$$x = \frac{4 \pm 16}{4}$$

$$x = \frac{4 + 16}{4} = \frac{20}{4} = 5 \text{ and } x = \frac{4 - 16}{4} = \frac{-12}{4} = -3$$

50. $x^2 + 3x = -2$

$x^2 + 3x + 2 = 0$

$a = 1, b = 3, c = 2$

$$x = \frac{-3 \pm \sqrt{3^2 - 4(1)(2)}}{2(1)} = \frac{-3 \pm \sqrt{9 - 8}}{2}$$

$$x = \frac{-3 \pm \sqrt{1}}{2} = \frac{-3 \pm 1}{2}$$

$$x = \frac{-3 + 1}{2} = \frac{-2}{2} = -1 \text{ and}$$

$$x = \frac{-3 - 1}{2} = \frac{-4}{2} = -2$$

51. $5 = x^2 + 6x$

$x^2 + 6x - 5 = 0$

$a = 1, b = 6, c = -5$

$$x = \frac{-6 \pm \sqrt{6^2 - 4(1)(-5)}}{2(1)}$$

$$x = \frac{-6 \pm \sqrt{36 + 20}}{2} = \frac{-6 \pm \sqrt{56}}{2}$$

$$x = \frac{-6 \pm \sqrt{4 \cdot 14}}{2} = \frac{-6 \pm 2\sqrt{14}}{2}$$

$$x = \frac{2(-3 \pm \sqrt{14})}{2} = -3 \pm \sqrt{14}$$

52. $5x + 2 = 2x^2$

$2x^2 - 5x - 2 = 0$

$a = 2, b = -5, c = -2$

$$x = \frac{-(-5) \pm \sqrt{(-5)^2 - 4(2)(-2)}}{2(2)}$$

$$x = \frac{5 \pm \sqrt{25 + 16}}{4} = \frac{5 \pm \sqrt{41}}{4}$$

Copyright © McDougal Littell Inc.
All rights reserved.

53. $5x - 2x^2 + 15 = 8$

$0 = 2x^2 - 5x - 7$ or $2x^2 - 5x - 7 = 0$

$a = 2, b = -5, c = -7$

$$x = \frac{-(-5) \pm \sqrt{(-5)^2 - 4(2)(-7)}}{2(2)}$$

$$x = \frac{5 \pm \sqrt{25 + 56}}{4} = \frac{5 \pm \sqrt{81}}{4}$$

$$x = \frac{5 + 9}{4} = \frac{14}{4} = \frac{7}{2} \text{ and } x = \frac{5 - 9}{4} = \frac{-4}{4} = -1$$

54. $-2 + x^2 = -x$

$x^2 + x - 2 = 0$

$a = 1, b = 1, c = -2$

$$x = \frac{-1 \pm \sqrt{1^2 - 4(1)(-2)}}{2(1)}$$

$$x = \frac{-1 \pm \sqrt{1 + 8}}{2} = \frac{-1 \pm \sqrt{9}}{2} = \frac{-1 \pm 3}{2}$$

$$x = \frac{-1 + 3}{2} = \frac{2}{2} = 1 \text{ and } x = \frac{-1 - 3}{2} = \frac{-4}{2} = -2$$

55. $x^2 - 2x = 3$

$x^2 - 2x - 3 = 0$

$a = 1, b = -2, c = -3$

$$x = \frac{-(-2) \pm \sqrt{(-2)^2 - 4(1)(-3)}}{2(1)}$$

$$x = \frac{2 \pm \sqrt{4 + 12}}{2} = \frac{2 \pm \sqrt{16}}{2} = \frac{2 \pm 4}{2}$$

$$x = \frac{2 + 4}{2} = \frac{6}{2} = 3 \text{ or } x = \frac{2 - 4}{2} = \frac{-2}{2} = -1$$

56. $2x^2 + 4 = 6x$

$2x^2 - 6x + 4 = 0$

$a = 2, b = -6, c = 4$

$$x = \frac{-(-6) \pm \sqrt{(-6)^2 - 4(2)(4)}}{2(2)}$$

$$x = \frac{6 \pm \sqrt{36 - 32}}{4} = \frac{6 \pm \sqrt{4}}{4} = \frac{6 \pm 2}{4}$$

$$x = \frac{6 + 2}{4} = \frac{8}{4} = 2 \text{ and } x = \frac{6 - 2}{4} = \frac{4}{4} = 1$$

57. $12 = 2x^2 - 2x$

$2x^2 - 2x - 12 = 0$

$a = 2, b = -2, c = -12$

$$x = \frac{-(-2) \pm \sqrt{(-2)^2 - 4(2)(-12)}}{2(2)}$$

$$x = \frac{2 \pm \sqrt{4 + 96}}{4} = \frac{2 \pm \sqrt{100}}{4}$$

$$x = \frac{2 \pm 10}{4}$$

$$x = \frac{2 + 10}{4} = \frac{12}{4} = 3 \text{ and } x = \frac{2 - 10}{4} = \frac{-8}{4} = -2$$

58. $y = -x^2 + x + 6$; let $y = 0$

$0 = -x^2 + x + 6$

$a = -1, b = 1, c = 6$

$$x = \frac{-1 \pm \sqrt{1^2 - 4(-1)(6)}}{2(-1)}$$

$$x = \frac{-1 \pm \sqrt{1 + 24}}{-2} = \frac{-1 \pm \sqrt{25}}{-2}$$

$$x = \frac{-1 \pm 5}{-2}$$

$$x = \frac{-1 + 5}{-2} = \frac{4}{-2} = -2 \text{ and}$$

$$x = \frac{-1 - 5}{-2} = \frac{-6}{-2} = 3$$

59. $y = x^2 + 5x + 6$; let $y = 0$

$0 = x^2 + 5x + 6$

$a = 1, b = 5, c = 6$

$$x = \frac{-5 \pm \sqrt{5^2 - 4(1)(6)}}{2(1)}$$

$$x = \frac{-5 \pm \sqrt{25 - 24}}{2} = \frac{-5 \pm \sqrt{1}}{2}$$

$$x = \frac{-5 \pm 1}{2}$$

$$x = \frac{-5 + 1}{2} = \frac{-4}{2} = -2 \text{ and}$$

$$x = \frac{-5 - 1}{2} = \frac{-6}{2} = -3$$

60. $y = x^2 - 11x + 24$; let $y = 0$

$0 = x^2 - 11x + 24$

$a = 1, b = -11, c = 24$

$$x = \frac{-(-11) \pm \sqrt{(-11)^2 - 4(1)(24)}}{2(1)}$$

$$x = \frac{11 \pm \sqrt{121 - 96}}{2} = \frac{11 \pm \sqrt{25}}{2}$$

$$x = \frac{11 \pm 5}{2}$$

$$x = \frac{11 + 5}{2} = \frac{16}{2} = 8 \text{ and } x = \frac{11 - 5}{2} = \frac{6}{2} = 3$$

61. $y = x^2 + 10x + 16$; let $y = 0$

$0 = x^2 + 10x + 16$

$a = 1, b = 10, c = 16$

$$x = \frac{-10 \pm \sqrt{10^2 - 4(1)(16)}}{2(1)}$$

$$x = \frac{-10 \pm \sqrt{100 - 64}}{2} = \frac{-10 \pm \sqrt{36}}{2}$$

$$x = \frac{-10 \pm 6}{2}$$

$$x = \frac{-10 + 6}{2} = \frac{-4}{2} = -2 \text{ and}$$

$$x = \frac{-10 - 6}{2} = \frac{-16}{2} = -8$$

Copyright © McDougal Littell Inc.
All rights reserved.

62. $y = -x^2 - 4x + 2$; let $y = 0$

$0 = -x^2 - 4x + 2$

$a = -1,\ b = -4,\ c = 2$

$$x = \frac{-(-4) \pm \sqrt{(-4)^2 - 4(-1)(2)}}{2(-1)}$$

$$x = \frac{4 \pm \sqrt{16 + 8}}{-2} = \frac{4 \pm \sqrt{24}}{-2}$$

$$x = \frac{4 \pm \sqrt{4 \cdot 6}}{-2} = \frac{4 \pm 2\sqrt{6}}{-2} = \frac{2(2 \pm \sqrt{6})}{-2}$$

$x = -2 \pm \sqrt{6}$

63. $y = 2x^2 - 6x - 8$; let $y = 0$

$0 = 2x^2 - 6x - 8$

$a = 2, b = -6, c = -8$

$$x = \frac{-(-6) \pm \sqrt{(-6)^2 - 4(2)(-8)}}{2(2)}$$

$$x = \frac{6 \pm \sqrt{36 + 64}}{4} = \frac{6 \pm \sqrt{100}}{4} = \frac{6 \pm 10}{4}$$

$$x = \frac{6 + 10}{4} = \frac{16}{4} = 4 \text{ and } x = \frac{6 - 10}{4} = \frac{-4}{4} = -1$$

64. $y = x^2 - 2x - 2$; let $y = 0$

$0 = x^2 - 2x - 2$

$a = 1, b = -2, c = -2$

$$x = \frac{-(-2) \pm \sqrt{(-2)^2 - 4(1)(-2)}}{2(1)}$$

$$x = \frac{2 \pm \sqrt{4 + 8}}{2} = \frac{2 \pm \sqrt{12}}{2} = \frac{2 \pm \sqrt{4 \cdot 3}}{2}$$

$$x = \frac{2 \pm 2\sqrt{3}}{2} = \frac{2(1 \pm \sqrt{3})}{2} = 1 \pm \sqrt{3}$$

65. $y = 2x^2 + 4x - 6$; let $y = 0$

$0 = 2x^2 + 4x - 6$

$a = 2, b = 4, c = -6$

$$x = \frac{-4 \pm \sqrt{4^2 - 4(2)(-6)}}{2(2)}$$

$$x = \frac{-4 \pm \sqrt{16 + 48}}{4} = \frac{-4 \pm \sqrt{64}}{4}$$

$$x = \frac{-4 \pm 8}{4}$$

$$x = \frac{-4 + 8}{4} = \frac{4}{4} = 1 \text{ and } x = \frac{-4 - 8}{4} = \frac{-12}{4} = -3$$

66. $y = -3x^2 + 17x - 20$; let $y = 0$

$0 = -3x^2 + 17x - 20$

$a = -3, b = 17, c = -20$

$$x = \frac{-17 \pm \sqrt{17^2 - 4(-3)(-20)}}{2(-3)}$$

$$x = \frac{-17 \pm \sqrt{289 - 240}}{-6} = \frac{-17 \pm \sqrt{49}}{-6}$$

$$x = \frac{-17 \pm 7}{-6}$$

$$x = \frac{-17 + 7}{-6} = \frac{-10}{-6} = \frac{5}{3} \text{ and}$$

$$x = \frac{-17 - 7}{-6} = \frac{-24}{-6} = 4$$

67. $h = -16t^2 + vt + s$

$0 = -16t^2 - 50t + 200$

$a = -16, b = -50, c = 200$

$$t = \frac{-(-50) \pm \sqrt{(-50)^2 - 4(-16)(200)}}{2(-16)}$$

$$t = \frac{50 \pm \sqrt{2500 + 12800}}{-32} = \frac{50 \pm \sqrt{15300}}{-32}$$

$$t = \frac{50 \pm 123.69}{-32}$$

$t = -5.43$ and 2.30

$t = 2.30$ sec

68. $h = -16t^2 + vt + s$

$0 = -16t^2 - 25t + 150$

$a = -16, b = -25, c = 150$

$$t = \frac{-(-25) \pm \sqrt{(-25)^2 - 4(-16)(150)}}{2(-16)}$$

$$t = \frac{25 \pm \sqrt{625 + 9600}}{-32} = \frac{25 \pm \sqrt{10225}}{-32}$$

$$t = \frac{25 \pm 101.12}{-32}$$

$t = -3.94$ and 2.38

$t = 2.38$ sec

69. $h = -16t^2 + vt + s$

$0 = -16t^2 - 10t + 100$

$a = -16, b = -10, c = 100$

$$t = \frac{-(-10) \pm \sqrt{(-10)^2 - 4(-16)(100)}}{2(-16)}$$

$$t = \frac{10 \pm \sqrt{100 + 6400}}{-32} = \frac{10 \pm \sqrt{6500}}{-32}$$

$$t = \frac{10 \pm 80.62}{-32}$$

$t = -2.83$ and 2.21

$t = 2.21$ sec

70. $h = -16t^2 + vt + s$

$0 = -16t^2 - 33t + 150$

$a = -16, b = -33, c = 150$

$$t = \frac{-(-33) \pm \sqrt{(-33)^2 - 4(-16)(150)}}{2(-16)}$$

$$t = \frac{33 \pm \sqrt{1089 + 9600}}{-32} = \frac{33 \pm \sqrt{10689}}{-32}$$

$$t = \frac{33 \pm 103.39}{-32}$$

$t = -4.26$ and 2.20

$t = 2.20$ sec

Copyright © McDougal Littell Inc.
All rights reserved.

71. $h = -16t^2 + vt + s$

$0 = -16t^2 - 40t + 50$

$a = -16, b = -40, c = 50$

$$t = \frac{-(-40) \pm \sqrt{(-40)^2 - 4(-16)(50)}}{2(-16)}$$

$$t = \frac{40 \pm \sqrt{1600 + 3200}}{-32} = \frac{40 \pm \sqrt{4800}}{-32}$$

$$t = \frac{40 \pm 69.28}{-32}$$

$t = -3.42$ and 0.92

$t = 0.92$ sec.

72. $h = -16t^2 + vt + s$

$0 = -16t^2 - 20t + 50$

$a = -16, b = -20, c = 50$

$$t = \frac{-(-20) \pm \sqrt{(-20)^2 - 4(-16)(50)}}{2(-16)}$$

$$t = \frac{20 \pm \sqrt{400 + 3200}}{-32} = \frac{20 \pm \sqrt{3600}}{-32}$$

$$t = \frac{20 \pm 60}{-32}$$

$t = -2.5$ and 1.25

$t = 1.25$ sec

73. $h = -16t^2 + vt + s$

$0 = -16t^2 - 220t + 100$

$a = -16, b = -220, c = 100$

$$t = \frac{-(-220) \pm \sqrt{(-220)^2 - 4(-16)(100)}}{2(-16)}$$

$$t = \frac{220 \pm \sqrt{48400 + 6400}}{-32} = \frac{220 \pm \sqrt{54800}}{-32}$$

$$t = \frac{220 \pm 234.09}{-32}$$

$t = -14.19$ and 0.44

The pigeon has 0.4 seconds to escape.

74. $h = -16t^2 + vt + s$

$0 = -16t^2 - 105t + 200$

$a = -16, b = -105, c = 200$

$$t = \frac{-(-105) \pm \sqrt{(-105)^2 - 4(-16)(200)}}{2(-16)}$$

$$t = \frac{105 \pm \sqrt{11025 + 12800}}{-32} = \frac{105 \pm 154.35}{-32}$$

$t = -8.10$ and 1.54

The snake has 1.5 seconds to escape.

75. $h = -16t^2 + s$

$0 = -16t^2 + 30$

$-30 = -16t^2$

$$\frac{15}{8} = t^2$$

$$\pm\sqrt{\frac{15}{8}} = t$$

$t \approx 1.4$ sec

76. $h = -16t^2 + s$

$0 = -16t^2 + 45$

$-45 = -16t^2$

$$\frac{45}{16} = t^2$$

$$\pm\sqrt{\frac{45}{16}} = t$$

$t \approx 1.7$ sec

77. $h = -16t^2 + vt + s$

$0 = -16t^2 + 90t + 7$

$a = -16, b = 90, c = 7$

$$t = \frac{-90 \pm \sqrt{90^2 - 4(-16)(7)}}{2(-16)}$$

$$t = \frac{-90 \pm \sqrt{8100 + 448}}{-32}$$

$$t = \frac{-90 \pm \sqrt{8548}}{-32}$$

$t = -0.08$ or 5.7

$t \approx 5.7$ sec

78. $h = -16t^2 + vt + s$

$0 = -16t^2 - 10t + 20$

$a = -16, b = -10, c = 20$

$$t = \frac{-(-10) \pm \sqrt{(-10)^2 - 4(-16)(20)}}{2(-16)}$$

$$t = \frac{10 \pm \sqrt{100 + 1280}}{-32} = \frac{10 \pm \sqrt{1380}}{-32}$$

$t = -1.5$ or 0.8

$t \approx 0.8$ sec

79. $h = -16t^2 + 80t + 3$; let $h = 0$

$0 = -16t^2 + 80t + 3$

$a = -16, b = 80, c = 3$

$$t = \frac{-80 \pm \sqrt{80^2 - 4(-16)(3)}}{2(-16)}$$

$$t = \frac{-80 \pm \sqrt{6400 + 192}}{-32} = \frac{-80 \pm \sqrt{6592}}{-32}$$

$t = -0.04$ or 5.04

about 5.04 sec

Copyright © McDougal Littell Inc.
All rights reserved.

80. $m = -2.7t^2 + 50t + 6$; let $m = 0$

$0 = -2.7t^2 + 50t + 6$

$a = -2.7, b = 50, c = 6$

$t = \dfrac{-50 \pm \sqrt{50^2 - 4(-2.7)(6)}}{2(-2.7)}$

$t = \dfrac{-50 \pm \sqrt{2500 + 64.8}}{-5.4} = \dfrac{-50 \pm \sqrt{2564.8}}{-5.4}$

$t = \dfrac{-50 \pm 50.64}{-5.4}$

$t = -0.12$ or 18.64

about 18.6 seconds on the moon

$e = -16t^2 + 50t + 6$; let $e = 0$

$0 = -16t^2 + 50t + 6$

$a = -16, b = 50, c = 6$

$t = \dfrac{-50 \pm \sqrt{50^2 - 4(-16)(6)}}{2(-16)}$

$t = \dfrac{-50 \pm \sqrt{2500 + 384}}{-32}$

$t = \dfrac{-50 \pm \sqrt{2884}}{-32} = \dfrac{-50 \pm 53.7}{-32}$

$t = -0.12$ or 3.24

about 3.2 seconds on earth

The rock would hit the ground in less time on earth since it would take about 18.6 seconds on the moon and about 3.2 seconds on the earth.

9.6 Standardized Test Practice (p. 538)

81. $2x^2 - 10 = x$

$2x^2 - x - 10 = 0$

$a = 2, b = -1, c = -10$

$x = \dfrac{-(-1) \pm \sqrt{(-1)^2 - 4(2)(-10)}}{2(2)}$

$x = \dfrac{1 \pm \sqrt{1 - 4(2)(-10)}}{4}$ (*A*)

82. $x = \dfrac{1 \pm \sqrt{1 + 80}}{4} = \dfrac{1 \pm \sqrt{81}}{4} = \dfrac{1 \pm 9}{4}$

$x = \dfrac{1 - 9}{4} = \dfrac{-8}{4} = -2$ and $x = \dfrac{1 + 9}{4} = \dfrac{10}{4} = \dfrac{5}{2}$, (G)

83. $b = 9,\ 4ac = 56$

$ac = 14$

$2(7) = 14$ or $-2(-7) = 14$

(*D*) $2x^2 + 9x + 7 = 0$

84. $h = -16t^2 + vt + s$

$h = -16t^2 - 10t + 100$ (*H*)

9.6 Mixed Review (p. 539)

85. $-3(x) = -3(9) = -27$

86. $-5(-n)(-n) = -5(-n)^2$

$= -5(-2)^2$

$= -5(4)$

$= -20$

87. $4(-6)(m) = -24m = -24(-2) = 48$

88. $2(-1)(-x)^3 = -2(-x)^3$

$= 2x^3$

$= 2(-3)^3$

$= 2(-27)$

$= -54$

89. $-3x + y + 6 = 0$

$y = 3x - 6$

90. $-x + y - 7 = 0$

$y = x + 7$

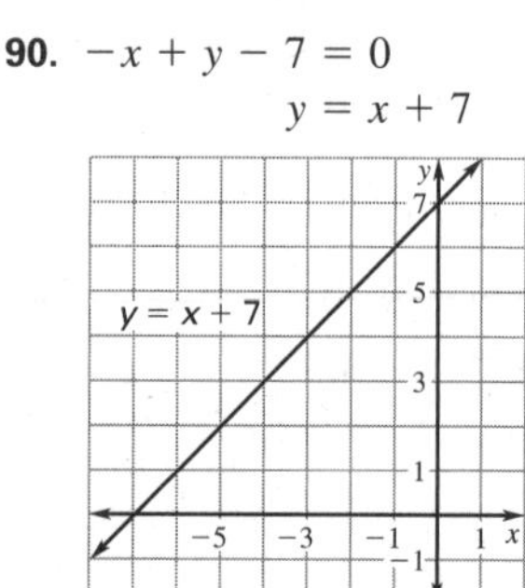

91. $4x + 2y - 12 = 0$

$2y = -4x + 12$

$y = -2x + 6$

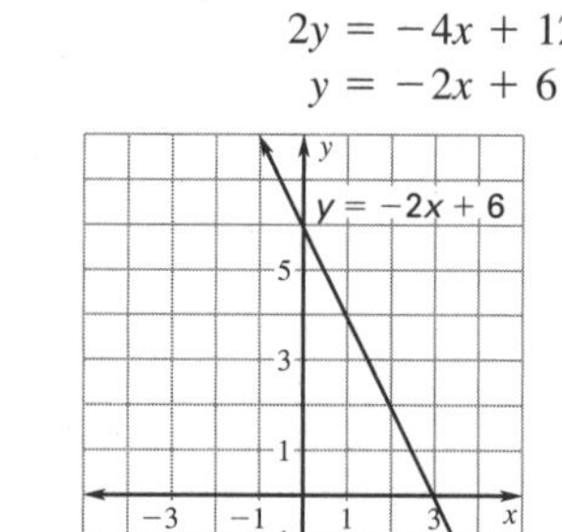

92. $6x \le -2$

$x \le -\dfrac{1}{3}$

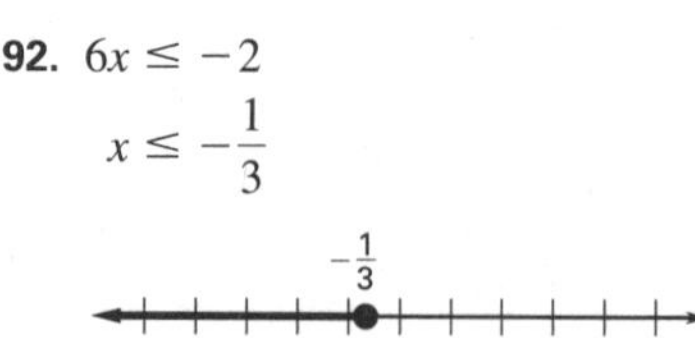

93. $-3x \ge 15$

$x \le -5$

Copyright © McDougal Littell Inc.
All rights reserved.

94. $\frac{3}{4}x > 12$

$x > 12 \cdot \frac{4}{3}$

$x > 16$

95. $\frac{1.4 \times 10^7 \text{ visitors}}{\text{yr}} \times \frac{1 \text{ yr}}{12 \text{ mo}} = \frac{1.4 \times 10^7 \text{ visitors}}{12 \text{ mo}}$

$\approx 1.2 \times 10^6$ visitors/mo

or 1.2 million visitors/mo

9.6 Maintaining Skills (p. 539)

96. $\frac{8}{15} > \frac{2}{15}$

97. $\frac{2}{3} = \frac{4}{6} < \frac{5}{6}$

98. $\frac{1}{4} = 0.25 > \frac{1}{5} = 0.2$

99. $\frac{7}{8} = \frac{21}{24} < \frac{11}{12} = \frac{22}{24}$

100. $4\frac{1}{8} = 4\frac{5}{40} < 4\frac{1}{5} = 4\frac{8}{40}$

101. $2\frac{2}{3} < 3\frac{1}{2}$

Quiz 2 *(p. 539)*

1. $a > 0$, up

2. $a > 0$, up

3. $a < 0$, down

4. $a > 0$, up

5. $a < 0$, down

6. $a < 0$, down

7. $y = -x^2 + 2x - 3$

$x = -\frac{b}{2a} = -\frac{2}{2(-1)} = -\frac{2}{-2} = 1$

Vertex: $(1, -2)$

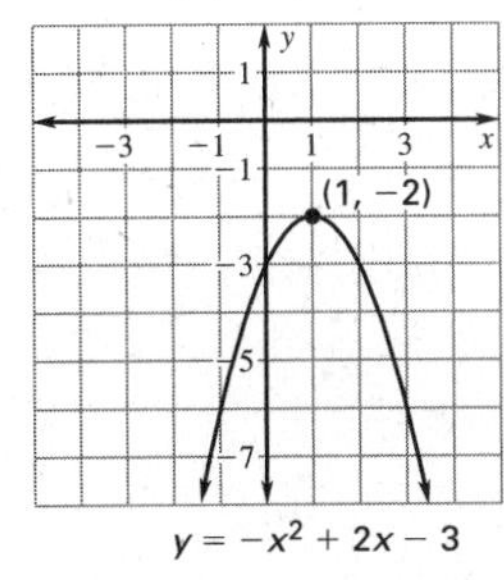

$y = -x^2 + 2x - 3$

8. $y = -3x^2 + 12x - 10$

$x = -\frac{b}{2a} = -\frac{12}{2(-3)} = -\frac{12}{-6} = 2$

Vertex: $(2, 2)$

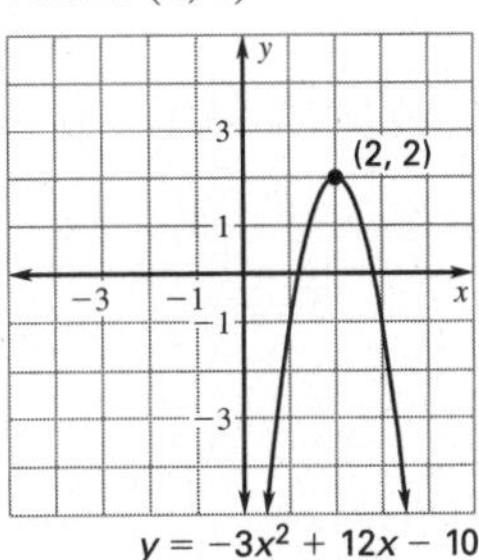

$y = -3x^2 + 12x - 10$

9. $y = 2x^2 - 6x + 7$

$x = -\frac{b}{2a} = -\frac{(-6)}{2(2)} = \frac{6}{4} = \frac{3}{2}$

Vertex: $\left(\frac{3}{2}, \frac{5}{2}\right)$

$y = 2x^2 - 6x + 7$

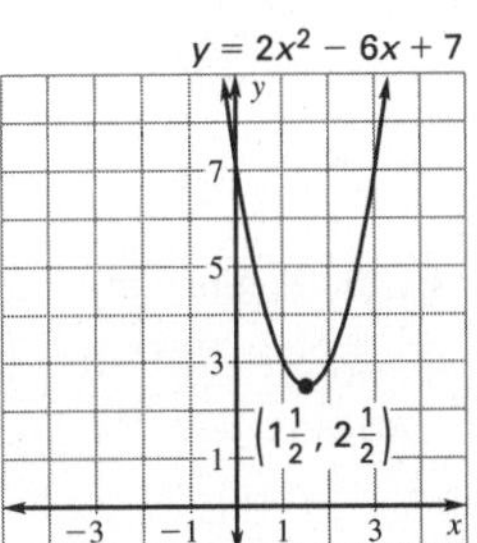

10. $x^2 - 3x = 10$

$x^2 - 3x - 10 = 0$

$y = x^2 - 3x - 10$ (Related quadratic function)

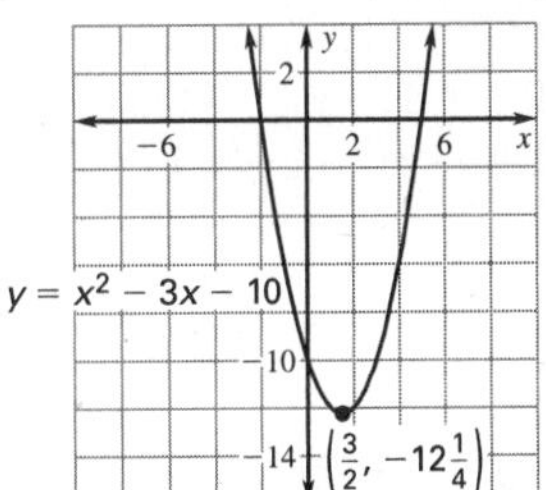

$x = -\frac{(-3)}{2(1)} = \frac{3}{2}$

Vertex: $\left(\frac{3}{2}, -12\frac{1}{4}\right)$

Solutions: $-2, 5$

Check:

$(-2)^2 - 3(-2) \stackrel{?}{=} 10$

$4 + 6 \stackrel{?}{=} 10$

$10 = 10$

$(5)^2 - 3(5) \stackrel{?}{=} 10$

$25 - 15 \stackrel{?}{=} 10$

$10 = 10$

Copyright © McDougal Littell Inc.
All rights reserved.

11. $x^2 - 12x = -36$

$x^2 - 12x + 36 = 0$

$y = x^2 - 12x + 36$ (Related quadratic function)

$x = -\frac{(-12)}{2(1)} = \frac{12}{2} = 6$

Vertex: (6, 0)

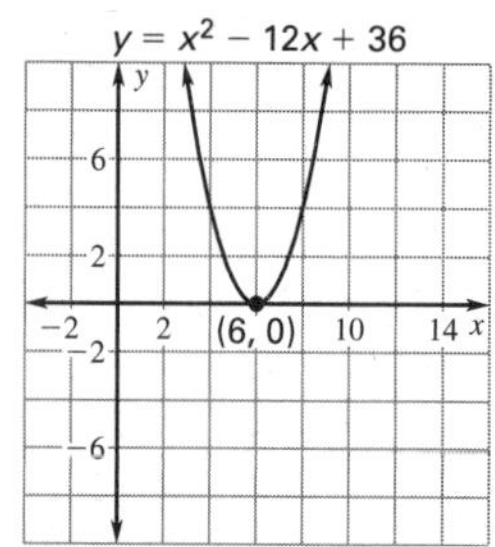

Solution: 6

Check:

$6^2 - 12(6) \stackrel{?}{=} -36$

$36 - 72 \stackrel{?}{=} -36$

$-36 = -36$

12. $3x^2 + 12x = -9$

$3x^2 + 12x + 9 = 0$

$y = 3x^2 + 12x + 9$ (Related quadratic function)

$x = -\frac{12}{2(3)} = -2$

Vertex: $(-2, -3)$

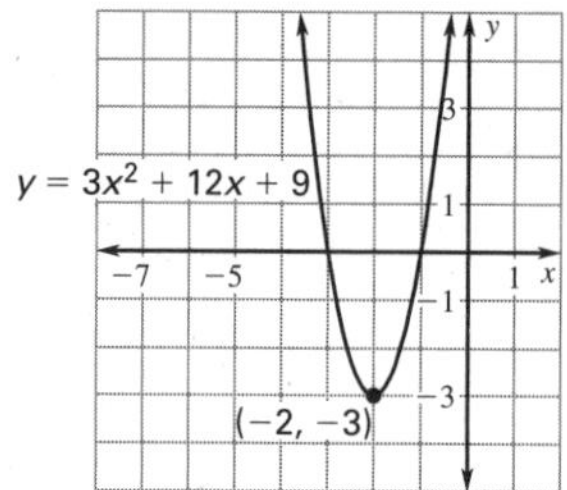

Solutions: $-1, -3$

Check:

$3(-1)^2 + 12(-1) \stackrel{?}{=} -9$

$3(1) - 12 \stackrel{?}{=} -9$

$-9 = -9$

$3(-3)^2 + 12(-3) \stackrel{?}{=} -9$

$3(9) - 36 = -9$

$-9 = -9$

13. $x^2 + 6x + 9 = 0$

$a = 1, b = 6, c = 9$

$x = \frac{-6 \pm \sqrt{6^2 - 4(1)(9)}}{2(1)}$

$x = \frac{-6 \pm \sqrt{36 - 36}}{2} = \frac{-6 \pm \sqrt{0}}{2} = \frac{-6}{2} = -3$

14. $2x^2 + 13x + 6 = 0$

$a = 2, b = 13, c = 6$

$x = \frac{-13 \pm \sqrt{13^2 - 4(2)(6)}}{2(2)}$

$x = \frac{-13 \pm \sqrt{169 - 48}}{4} = \frac{-13 \pm \sqrt{121}}{4}$

$x = \frac{-13 \pm 11}{4}$

$x = \frac{-13 + 11}{4} = \frac{-2}{4} = -\frac{1}{2}$ and

$x = \frac{-13 - 11}{4} = \frac{-24}{4} = -6$

15. $-x^2 + 6x + 16 = 0$

$a = -1, b = 6, c = 16$

$x = \frac{-6 \pm \sqrt{6^2 - 4(-1)(16)}}{2(-1)}$

$x = \frac{-6 \pm \sqrt{36 + 64}}{-2} = \frac{-6 \pm \sqrt{100}}{-2}$

$x = \frac{-6 \pm 10}{-2}$

$x = \frac{-6 + 10}{-2} = \frac{4}{-2} = -2$ and

$x = \frac{-6 - 10}{-2} = \frac{-16}{-2} = 8$

16. $-2x^2 + 7x - 6 = 0$

$a = -2, b = 7, c = -6$

$x = \frac{-7 \pm \sqrt{7^2 - 4(-2)(-6)}}{2(-2)}$

$x = \frac{-7 \pm \sqrt{49 - 48}}{-4} - \frac{-7 \pm \sqrt{1}}{-4}$

$x = \frac{-7 \pm 1}{-4}$

$x = \frac{-7 + 1}{-4} = \frac{-6}{-4} = \frac{3}{2}$ and $x = \frac{-7 - 1}{-4} = \frac{-8}{-4} = 2$

17. $-3x^2 - 5x + 10 = 0$

$a = -3, b = -5, c = 10$

$x = \frac{-(-5) \pm \sqrt{(-5)^2 - 4(-3)(10)}}{2(-3)}$

$x = \frac{5 \pm \sqrt{25 + 120}}{-6} = \frac{5 \pm \sqrt{145}}{-6}$

$x = -2.84$ and 1.17

18. $3x^2 - 4x - 1 = 0$

$a = 3, b = -4, c = -1$

$x = \frac{-(-4) \pm \sqrt{(-4)^2 - 4(3)(-1)}}{2(3)}$

$x = \frac{4 \pm \sqrt{16 + 12}}{6} = \frac{4 \pm \sqrt{28}}{6}$

$x = 1.55$ or -0.22

Copyright © McDougal Littell Inc.
All rights reserved.

Lesson 9.7

9.7 Checkpoint (pp. 541–542)

1. $x^2 - 3x + 4 = 0$
   $a = 1,\ b = -3,\ c = 4$
   $b^2 - 4ac = (-3)^2 - 4(1)(4)$
   $= 9 - 16 = -7$; no real solution

2. $x^2 - 4x + 4 = 0$
   $a = 1,\ b = -4,\ c = 4$
   $b^2 - 4ac = (-4)^2 - 4(1)(4)$
   $= 16 - 16 = 0$; one solution

3. $x^2 - 5x + 4 = 0$
   $a = 1,\ b = -5,\ c = 4$
   $b^2 - 4ac = (-5)^2 - 4(1)(4)$
   $= 25 - 16 = 9$; two solutions

4. $y = x^2 - 4x + 3$; Let $y = 0$.
   $0 = x^2 - 4x + 3$
   $a = 1,\ b = -4,\ c = 3$
   $b^2 - 4ac = (-4)^2 - 4(1)(3)$
   $= 16 - 12 = 4$; two x-intercepts

5. $y = x^2 - 4 + 4$; Let $y = 0$.
   $0 = x^2 - 4x + 4$
   $a = 1,\ b = -4,\ c = 4$
   $b^2 - 4ac = (-4)^2 - 4(1)(4)$
   $= 16 - 16 = 0$; one x-intercept

6. $y = x^2 - 4x + 5 = 0$; Let $y = 0$.
   $0 = x^2 - 4x + 5$
   $a = 1,\ b = -4,\ c = 5$
   $b^2 - 4ac = (-4)^2 - 4(1)(5)$
   $= 16 - 20 = -4$; zero x-intercepts

9.7 Guided Practice (p. 543)

1. $x = \dfrac{-b \pm \sqrt{b^2 - 4ac}}{2a}$

2. the number of solutions

3. *Sample answer*: The graphs will all have the same shape and all open up. The first has one x-intercept, the second none, and the third two. Each has a different y-intercept, 0, 3, and -6 respectively.

4. $3x^2 - 3x + 5 = 0$
   $a = 3,\ b = -3,\ c = 5$
   $b^2 - 4ac = (-3)^2 - 4(3)(5)$
   $= 9 - 60 = -51$; no real solution

5. $-3x^2 + 6x - 3 = 0$
   $a = -3,\ b = 6,\ c = -3$
   $b^2 - 4ac = 6^2 - 4(-3)(-3)$
   $= 36 - 36 = 0$; one solution

6. $x^2 - 5x - 10 = 0$
   $a = 1,\ b = -5,\ c = -10$
   $b^2 - 4ac = (-5)^2 - 4(1)(-10)$
   $= 25 + 40 = 65$; two solutions

7. $b^2 - 4ac = 2$; two solutions; *B*

8. $b^2 - 4ac = 0$; one solution; *C*

9. $b^2 - 4ac = -3$; zero real solutions; *A*

10. $y = x^2 + 2x + 4$
    $0 = x^2 + 2x + 4$
    $a = 1,\ b = 2,\ c = 4$
    $b^2 - 4ac = 2^2 - 4(1)(4)$
    $= 4 - 16 = -12$; zero

11. $y = -x^2 - 3x + 5$
    $0 = -x^2 - 3x + 5$
    $a = -1,\ b = -3,\ c = 5$
    $b^2 - 4ac = (-3)^2 - 4(-1)(5)$
    $= 9 + 20 = 29$; two

12. $y = 6x - 3 - 3x^2$
    $0 = -3x^2 + 6x - 3$
    $a = -3,\ b = 6,\ c = -3$
    $b^2 - 4ac = 6^2 - 4(-3)(-3)$
    $= 36 - 36 = 0$; one

9.7 Practice and Applications (pp. 543–545)

13. $-2x^2 - 5x + 3 = 0$
    $a = -2,\ b = -5,\ c = 3$
    $b^2 - 4ac = (-5)^2 - 4(-2)(3)$
    $= 25 + 24 = 49$

14. $3x^2 + 6x - 8 = 0$
    $a = 3,\ b = 6,\ c = -8$
    $b^2 - 4ac = 6^2 - 4(3)(-8)$
    $= 36 + 96 = 132$

15. $x^2 + 10 = 0$
    $a = 1, b = 0, c = 10$
    $b^2 - 4ac = 0^2 - 4(1)(10) = -40$

16. $5x^2 + 3x = 12$
    $5x^2 + 3x - 12 = 0$
    $a = 5,\ b = 3,\ c = -12$
    $b^2 - 4ac = 3^2 - 4(5)(-12)$
    $= 9 + 240 = 249$

17. $2x^2 + 8x = -8$
    $2x^2 + 8x + 8 = 0$
    $a = 2,\ b = 8,\ c = 8$
    $b^2 - 4ac = 8^2 - 4(2)(8)$
    $= 64 - 64 = 0$

18. $7 - 5x^2 + 9x = x$
    $-5x^2 + 8x + 7 = 0$
    $a = -5,\ b = 8,\ c = 7$
    $b^2 - 4ac = 8^2 - 4(-5)(7)$
    $= 64 + 140 = 204$

19. $-x = 7x^2 + 4$
    $7x^2 + x + 4 = 0$
    $a = 7,\ b = 1,\ c = 4$
    $b^2 - 4ac = 1^2 - 4(7)(4)$
    $= 1 - 112 = -111$

20. $2x = x^2 - x$
    $x^2 - 3x = 0$
    $a = 1,\ b = -3,\ c = 0$
    $b^2 - 4ac = (-3)^2 - 4(1)(0)$
    $= 9 - 0 = 9$

Copyright © McDougal Littell Inc.
All rights reserved.

21. $-2 - x^2 = 4x^2$
$5x^2 + 2 = 0$
$a = 5,\ b = 0,\ c = 2$
$b^2 - 4ac = 0^2 - 4(5)(2)$
$= 0 - 40 = -40$

22. $x^2 - 3x + 2 = 0$
$a = 1,\ b = -3,\ c = 2$
$b^2 - 4ac = (-3)^2 - 4(1)(2)$
$= 9 - 8 = 1$; two solutions

23. $2x^2 - 4x + 3 = 0$
$a = 2,\ b = -4,\ c = 3$
$b^2 - 4ac = (-4)^2 - 4(2)(3)$
$= 16 - 24 = -8$; no real solution

24. $-3x^2 + 5x - 1 = 0$
$a = -3,\ b = 5,\ c = -1$
$b^2 - 4ac = 5^2 - 4(-3)(-1)$
$= 25 - 12 = 13$; two solutions

25. $2x^2 + 3x - 2 = 0$
$a = 2,\ b = 3,\ c = -2$
$b^2 - 4ac = 3^2 - 4(2)(-2)$
$= 9 + 16 - 25$; two solutions

26. $x^2 - 2x + 4 = 0$
$a = 1,\ b = -2,\ c = 4$
$b^2 - 4ac = (-2)^2 - 4(1)(4)$
$= 4 - 16 = -12$; no real solution

27. $6x^2 - 2x + 4 = 0$
$a = 6,\ b = -2,\ c = 4$
$b^2 - 4ac = (-2)^2 - 4(6)(4)$
$= 4 - 96 = -92$; no real solution

28. $3x^2 - 6x + 3 = 0$
$a = 3,\ b = -6,\ c = 3$
$b^2 - 4ac = (-6)^2 - 4(3)(3)$
$= 36 - 36 = 0$; one solution

29. $4x^2 - 5x + 1 = 0$
$a = 4,\ b = -5,\ c = 1$
$b^2 - 4ac = (-5)^2 - 4(4)(1)$
$= 25 - 16 = 9$; two solutions

30. $-5x^2 + 6x - 6 = 0$
$a = -5,\ b = 6,\ c = -6$
$b^2 - 4ac = 6^2 - 4(-5)(-6)$
$= 36 - 120 = -84$; no real solution

31. $-\frac{1}{2}x^2 + x + 3 = 0$
$a = -\frac{1}{2},\ b = 1,\ c = 3$
$b^2 - 4ac = 1^2 - 4\left(-\frac{1}{2}\right)(3)$
$= 1 + 6 = 7$; two solutions

32. $\frac{1}{4}x^2 - 2x + 4 = 0$
$a = \frac{1}{4},\ b = -2,\ c = 4$
$b^2 - 4ac = (-2)^2 - 4\left(\frac{1}{4}\right)(4)$
$= 4 - 4 = 0$; one solution

33. $5x^2 + 4x + \frac{4}{5} = 0$
$a = 5,\ b = 4,\ c = \frac{4}{5}$
$b^2 - 4ac = 4^2 - 4(5)\left(\frac{4}{5}\right)$
$= 16 - 16 = 0$; one solution

34. $3x^2 + 4x - 2 = 0$
$a = 3,\ b = 4,\ c = -2$
$b^2 - 4ac = (4)^2 - 4(3)(-2)$
$= 16 + 24$ (instead of $16 - 24$)
$= 40$

35. $a = 2,\ b = 6,\ c = -3$
$b^2 - 4ac = 6^2 - 4(2)(-3)$
$= 36 + 24 = 60$

36. two

37. It crosses the x-axis at two distinct points.

38. $y = 2x^2 + 3x - 2$; Let $y = 0$.
$0 = 2x^2 + 3x - 2$
$a = 2,\ b = 3,\ c = -2$
$b^2 - 4ac = 3^2 - 4(2)(-2)$
$= 9 + 16 = 25$; two

39. $y = x^2 - 2x + 4$; Let $y = 0$.
$0 = x^2 - 2x + 4$
$a = 1,\ b = -2,\ c = 4$
$b^2 - 4ac = (-2)^2 - 4(1)(4)$
$= 4 - 16 = -12$; zero

40. $y = -2x^2 + 4x - 2$; Let $y = 0$.
$0 = -2x^2 + 4x - 2$
$a = -2,\ b = 4,\ c = -2$
$b^2 - 4ac = 4^2 - 4(-2)(-2)$
$= 16 - 16 = 0$; one

41. $y = 2x^2 + 2x + 6$; Let $y = 0$.
$0 = 2x^2 + 2x + 6$
$a = 2,\ b = 2,\ c = 6$
$b^2 - 4ac = 2^2 - 4(2)(6)$
$= 4 - 48 = -44$; zero

42. $y = 5x^2 + 2x - 3$; Let $y = 0$.
$0 = 5x^2 + 2x - 3$
$a = 5,\ b = 2,\ c = -3$
$b^2 - 4ac = 2^2 - 4(5)(-3)$
$= 4 + 60 = 64$; two

43. $y = 3x^2 - 6x + 3$; Let $y = 0$.
$0 = 3x^2 - 6x + 3$
$a = 3,\ b = -6,\ c = 3$
$b^2 - 4ac = (-6)^2 - 4(3)(3)$
$= 36 - 36 = 0$; one

Copyright © McDougal Littell Inc.
All rights reserved.

Chapter 9 *continued*

44. $a = -1,\ b = -2,\ c = -1$
$b^2 - 4ac = (-2)^2 - 4(-1)(-1)$
$= 4 - 4 = 0$; B (one x-intercept)

45. $a = -1,\ b = -2,\ c = -3$
$b^2 - 4ac = (-2)^2 - 4(-1)(-3)$
$= 4 - 12 = -8$; C (no x-intercept)

46. $a = -1,\ b = -2,\ c = 3$
$b^2 - 4ac = (-2)^2 - 4(-1)(3)$
$= 4 + 12 = 16$; A (2 x-intercepts)

47. domain: $0 \le t \le 5$
range: $9.29 \le P \le 161.49$

48. Yes; the model shows it growing without bound.

49. About 8.5 years

50. $h = -16t^2 + vt + s$
$2.2 = -16t^2 + 12t + 0$
$0 = -16t^2 + 12t - 2.2$
$a = -16,\ b = 12,\ c = -2.2$
$b^2 - 4ac = 12^2 - 4(-16)(-2.2)$
$= 144 - 140.8 = 3.2$;
Yes, there are two solutions. You can dunk the ball.

9.7 Standardized Test Practice (p. 545)

51. A; $a = -3,\ b = 6$
$b^2 - 4ac = 6^2 - 4(-3)c = 36 + 12c$
If $36 + 12c < 0$, there will be no real solution.
$36 + 12c < 0$
$12c < -36$
$c < -3$

52. G; $a = 1,\ b = -10,\ c = 25$
$b^2 - 4ac = (-10)^2 - 4(1)(25)$
$= 100 - 100 = 0$; one

9.7 Mixed Review (p. 545)

53. $2 \le x + 1 < 5$
$1 \le x < 4$

54. $8 > 2x > -4$
$4 > x > -2$

55. $-12 < 2x - 6 < 4$
$-6 < 2x < 10$
$-3 < x < 5$

56. $3x + y \le 9$
$y \le -3x + 9$

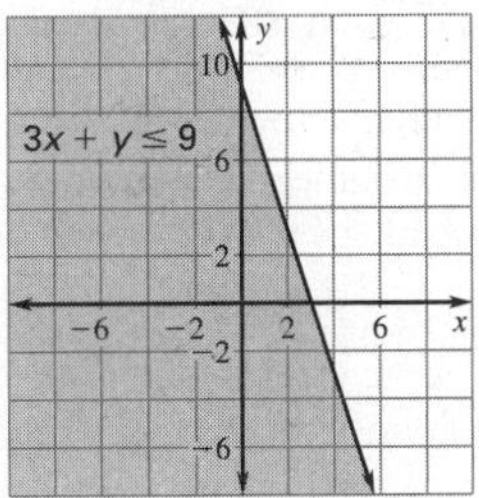

57. $y - 4x < 0$
$y < 4x$

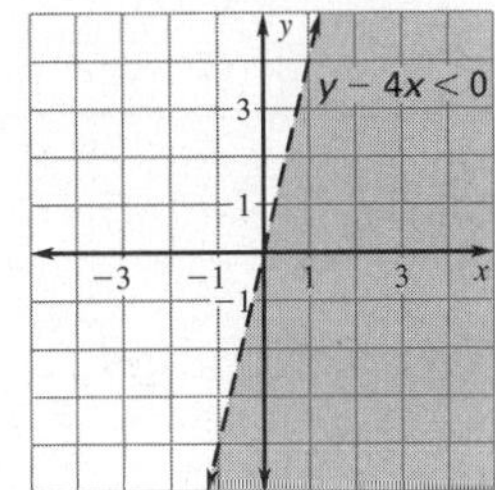

58. $-2x - y \ge 4$
$-y \ge 2x + 4$
$y \le -2x - 4$

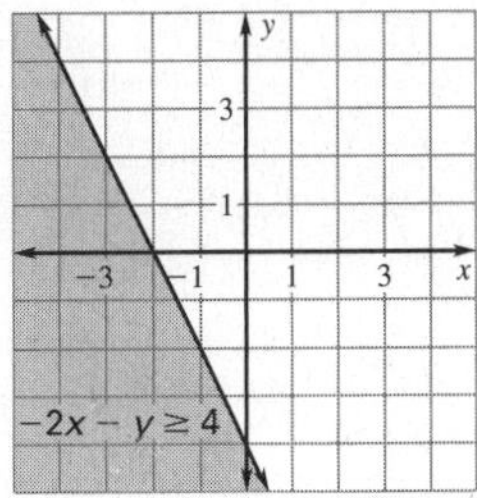

9.7 Maintaining Skills (p. 545)

59. $0.02 \times 3 = 0.06$

60. $0.7 \times 0.8 = 0.56$

61. $0.1 \times 0.1 = 0.01$

62. $0.05 \times 0.003 = 0.00015$

63. $0.09 \times 0.02 = 0.0018$

64. $0.06 \times 0.0004 = 0.000024$

Copyright © McDougal Littell Inc.
All rights reserved.

Chapter 9 *continued*

Lesson 9.8

9.8 Developing Concepts: Think About It *(p. 546)*

1. A; *Sample explanation*: The graph shows a solid curve which is $y = x^2 - 4$, and the origin is not a solution since $0 > -4$, so the area outside of the curve needs to be shaded.
2. C; *Sample explanation*: The curve goes through the origin, and the point (4, 1) is a solution of the inequality.
3. B; *Sample explanation*: The curve shows a single x-intercept at 4 and the origin is a solution.

9.8 Checkpoint (pp. 547–549)

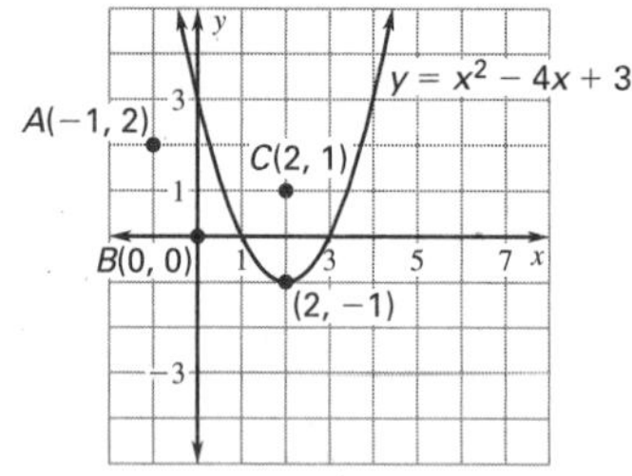

1. A(−1, 2); outside (see graph)
2. B(0, 0); outside (see graph)
3. C(2, 1); inside (see graph)
4. $y < x^2 + 2x + 2$

   $-\frac{b}{2a} = -\frac{2}{2(1)} = -1$

x	−3	−2	−1	0	1
y	5	2	1	2	5

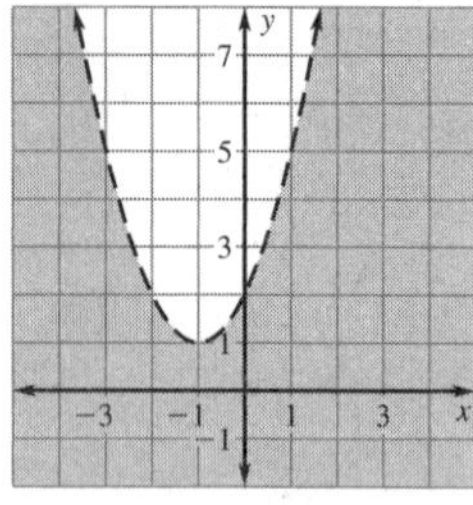

5. $y > -x^2 - 2x + 3$

   $-\frac{b}{2a} = -\frac{(-2)}{2(-1)} = \frac{2}{-2} = -1$

x	−3	−2	−1	0	1
y	0	3	4	3	0

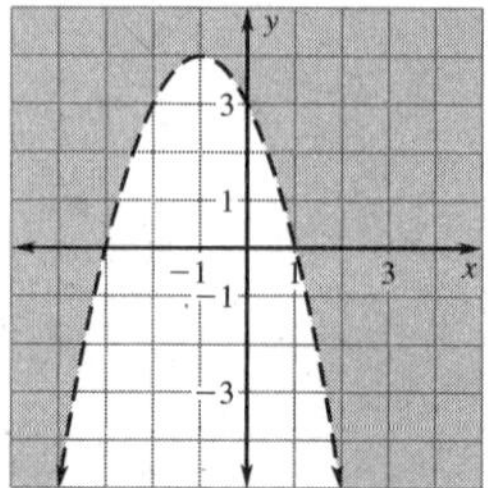

6. $y \geq 2x^2 - 4x + 2$

   $-\frac{b}{2a} = -\frac{(-4)}{2(2)} = \frac{4}{4} = 1$

x	−1	0	1	2	3
y	8	2	0	2	8

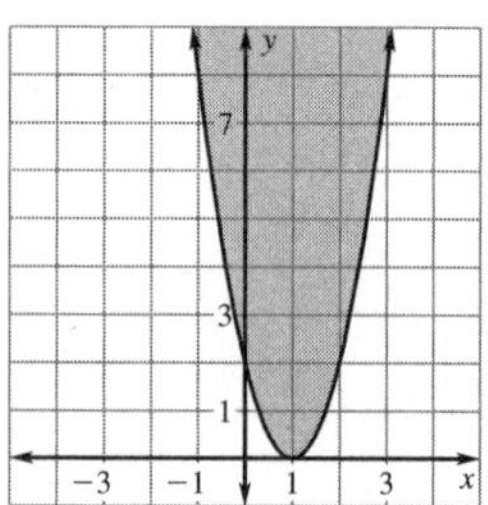

9.8 Guided Practice (p. 550)

1. *Sample answer*: $y < 3x^2 - 2x + 1$; $y \leq -2x^2 + 5x$, $y \geq x^2 - 16$; $y > -x^2 - 3x + 9$
2. false; use a dashed parabola

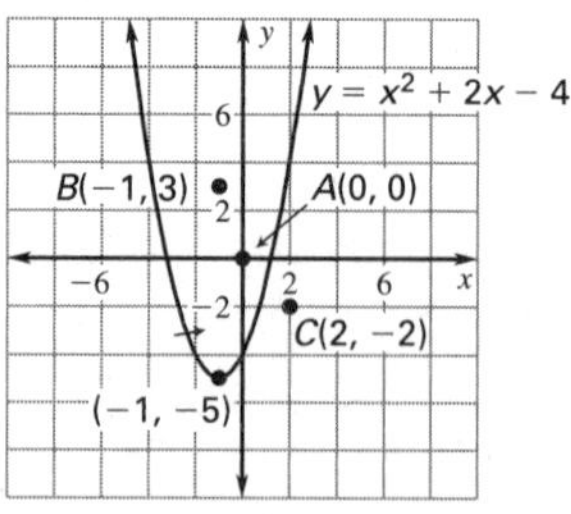

3. A(0, 0); inside (see graph)
4. B(−1, 3); inside (see graph)
5. C(2, −2); outside (see graph)
6. $y < -x^2$

   (1, 1); $1 \quad -(1)^2 = -1$; no

   (0, −4); $-4 < -(0)^2 = 0$; yes
7. $y \geq x^2 - 2$

   (0, 0); $0 \geq 0^2 - 2 = -2$; yes

   (1, −2); $-2 \geq 1^2 - 2 = -1$; no

Copyright © McDougal Littell Inc.
All rights reserved.

8. $y \le 2x^2 + 5x$
$(1, 1); 1 \le 2(1)^2 + 5(1) = 7$; yes
$(-1, 1); 1 \le 2(-1)^2 + 5(-1) = -3$; no

9. $y \le x^2$

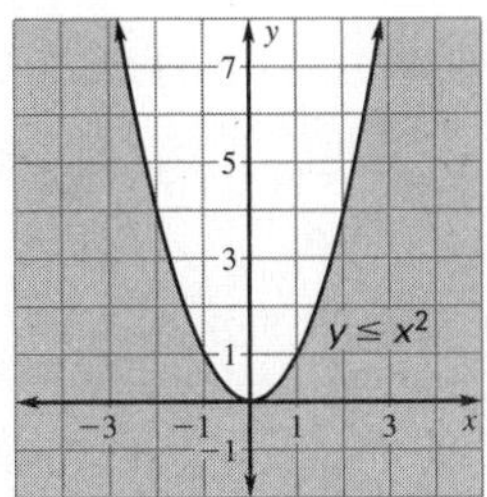

10. $y > -x^2 + 3$

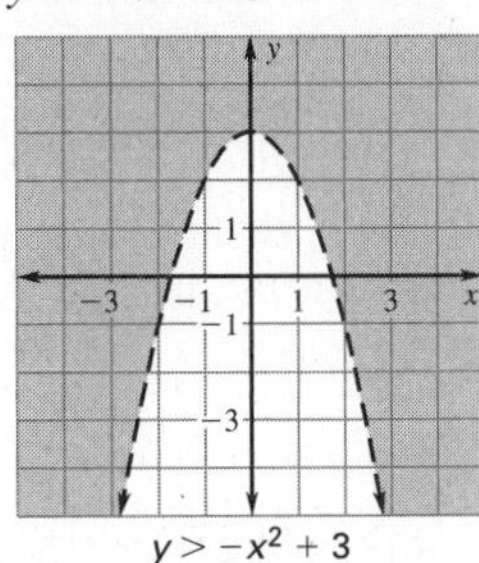
$y > -x^2 + 3$

11. $y < -x^2 + 2x$

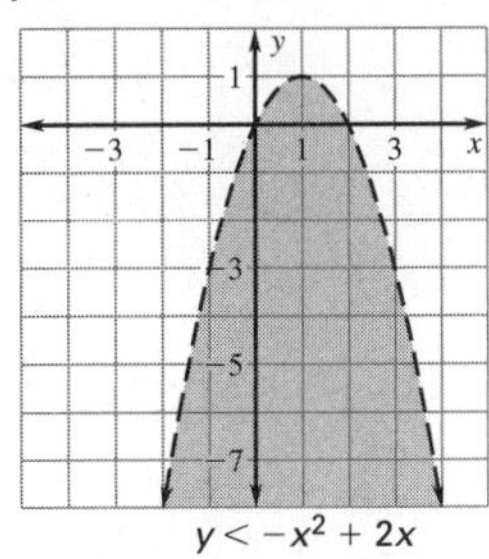
$y < -x^2 + 2x$

12. $y \ge x^2 - 2x$

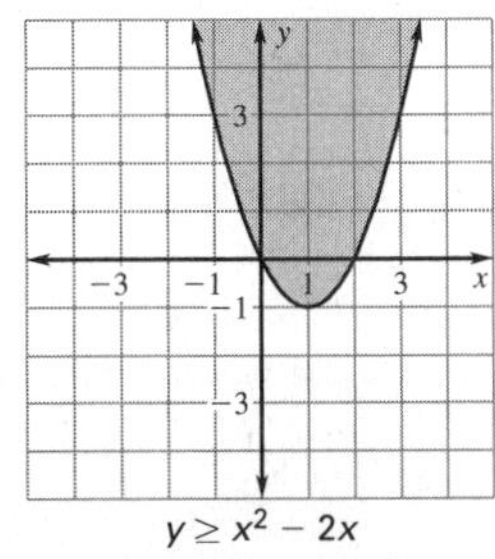
$y \ge x^2 - 2x$

13. $y < -2x^2 + 6x$

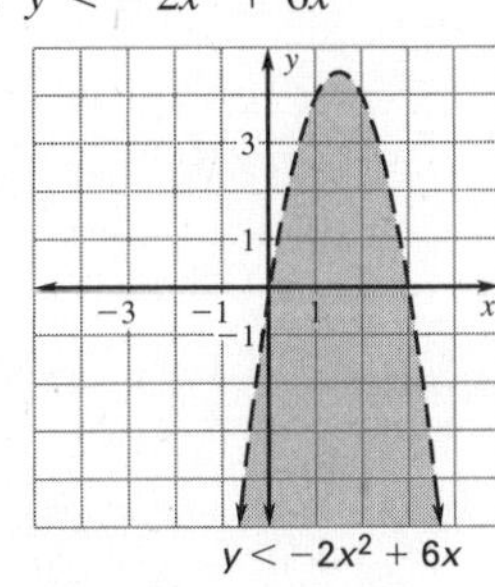
$y < -2x^2 + 6x$

14. $y \le 2x^2 - 4x + 3$

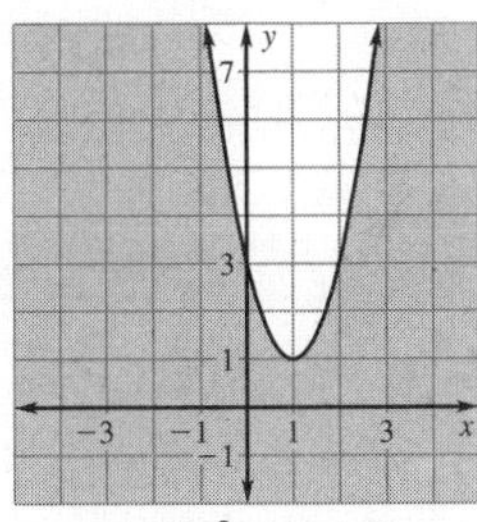
$y \le 2x^2 - 4x + 3$

9.8 Practice and Applications (pp. 550–551)

15. $y \ge 2x^2 - x$; (–2, 10)
$10 \overset{?}{\ge} 2(-2)^2 - (-2)$
$10 \ge 10$, yes

16. $y \le 3x^2 + 7$; (4, 31)
$31 \overset{?}{\le} 3(4)^2 + 7$
$31 \le 55$; yes

17. $y < x^2 + 9x$; (–3, 18)
$18 \overset{?}{<} (-3)^2 + 9(-3)$
$18 \not< -18$; no

18. $y < 5x^2 + 8$; (3, 45)
$45 \overset{?}{<} 5(3)^2 + 8$
$45 < 53$; yes

19. $y > 4x^2 - 7x$; (2, 0)
$0 \overset{?}{>} 4(2)^2 - 7(2)$
$0 \not> 2$; no

20. $y \ge x^2 - 13x$; (–1, 14)
$14 \overset{?}{\ge} (-1)^2 - 13(-1)$
$14 \ge 14$; yes

21. $y = x^2 - 2x + 5$
$$-\frac{b}{2a} = -\frac{(-2)}{2(1)} = 1$$

x	−1	0	1	2	3
y	8	5	4	5	8

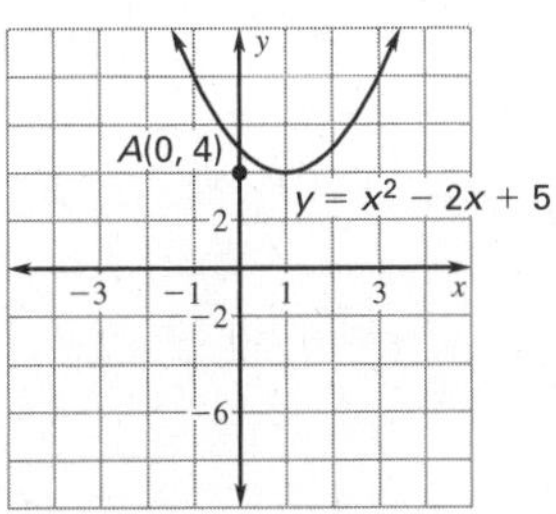

A(0, 4); outside

Copyright © McDougal Littell Inc.
All rights reserved.

22. $y = -x^2 + 4x - 2$

$-\frac{b}{2a} = -\frac{4}{2(-1)} = 2$

x	0	1	2	3	4
y	−2	1	2	1	−2

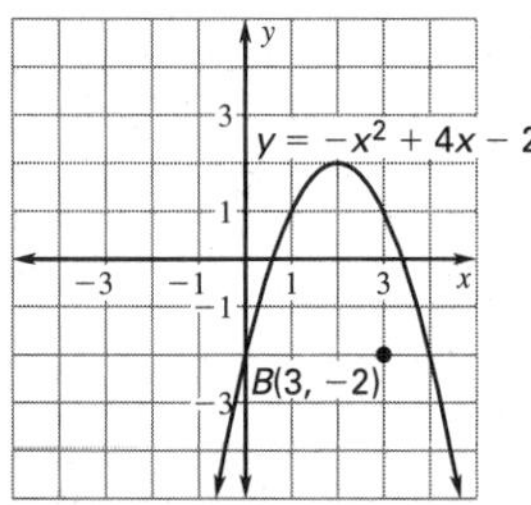

B(3, −2); inside

23. $y = \frac{1}{2}x^2 + x - 4$

$-\frac{b}{2a} = -\frac{1}{2(\frac{1}{2})} = -1$

x	−3	−2	−1	0	1
y	$-2\frac{1}{2}$	−4	$-4\frac{1}{2}$	−4	$-2\frac{1}{2}$

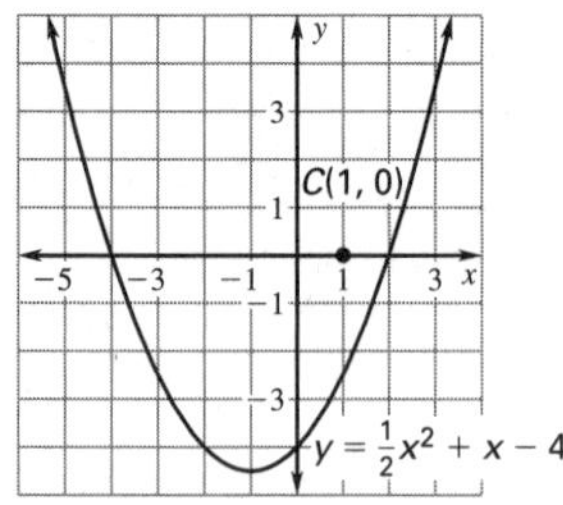

C(1, 0); inside

24. $y = 4x^2 - x + 1$

$-\frac{b}{2a} = -\frac{(-1)}{2(4)} = \frac{1}{8}$

x	−2	−1	0	$\frac{1}{8}$	1	2	3
y	19	6	1	$\frac{15}{16}$	4	15	34

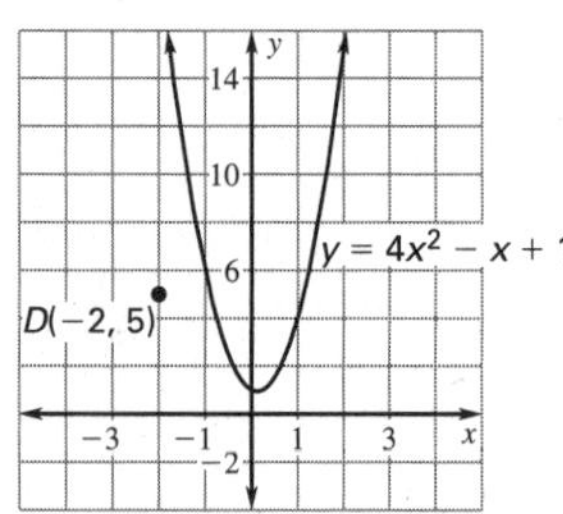

D(−2, 5); outside

25. sometimes; if $a = 4$ and $b = 1$, then $4 > 1, 4^2 = 16, 1^2 = 1$, so $a^2 > b^2$; if $a = -4$ and $b = -5$, then $-4 > -5, (-4)^2 = 16, (-5)^2 = 25$, so $a^2 \not> b^2$.

26. always

27. sometimes; a could be -2 and $a^2 = (-2)^2 = 4$.

28. always

29. $y \geq -2x^2 - 2x + 1$; B
$a = -2$, parabola opens down
$\geq$ means solid parabola and shaded above.

30. $y > -2x^2 + 4x + 3$; C
$a = -2$, parabola opens down
$>$ means dashed parabola and shaded above.

31. $y \leq 2x^2 + x + 1$; A
$a = 2$, parabola opens up
$\leq$ means solid parabola and shaded below

32. $y < -x^2 + x$

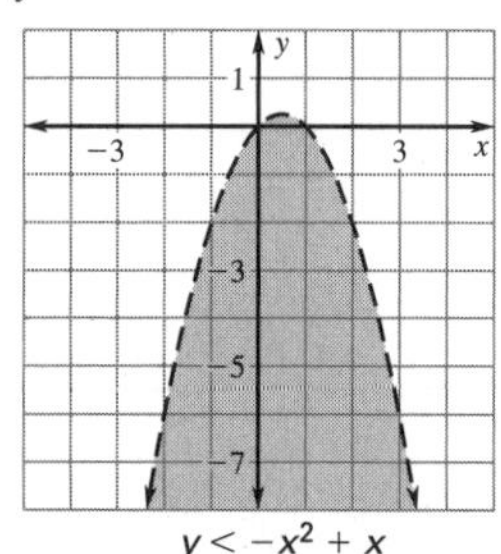

33. $y < x^2 - 4$

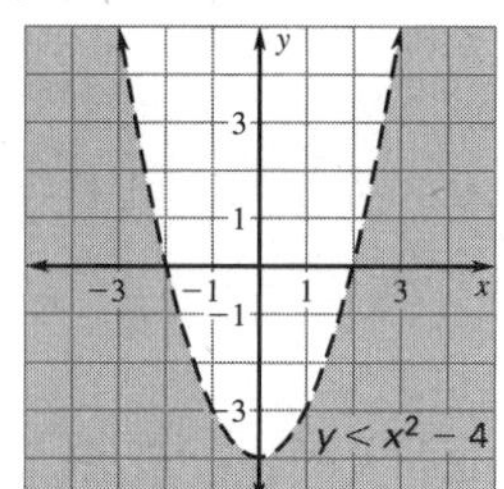

34. $y \geq x^2 - 5x$

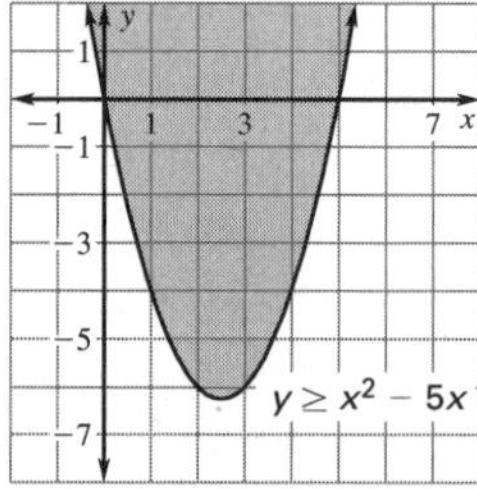

35. $y > -x^2 - 3x - 2$

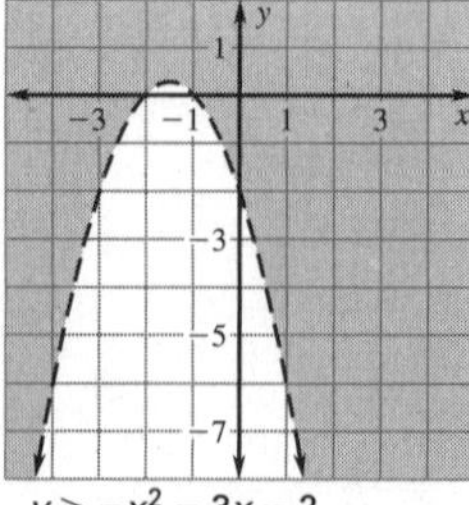

Copyright © McDougal Littell Inc.
All rights reserved.

36. $y \le -x^2 + 3x + 4$

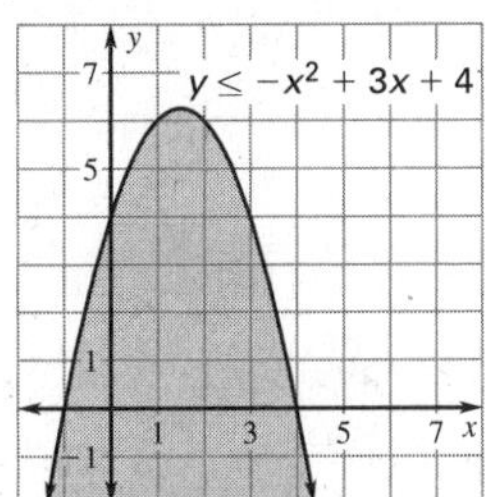

37. $y > -3x^2 - 5x - 1$

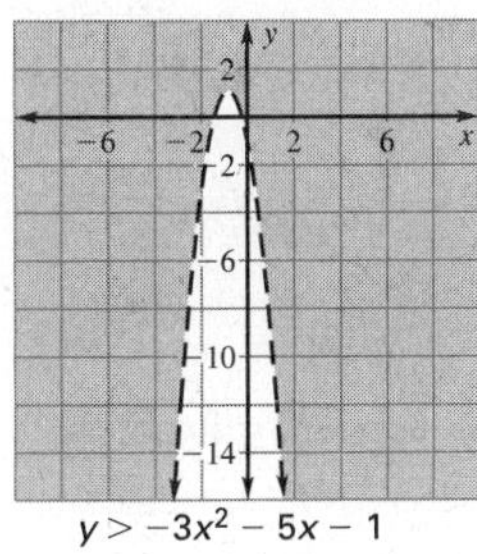

38. B; bulb is above parabola $\left(y > \frac{1}{24}x^2 + 1\right)$

9.8 Standardized Test Practice (p. 551)

39. C; (4, −13)

$$\begin{aligned} y &\ge 2x^2 - 7x - 10 \\ -13 &\overset{?}{\ge} 2(4)^2 - 7(4) - 10 \\ -13 &\overset{?}{\ge} 32 - 28 - 10 \\ -13 &\not\ge -6 \end{aligned}$$

40. B; $y < 5x^2 + 6x + 2$

$$-\frac{b}{2a} = -\frac{6}{2(5)} - \frac{3}{5}$$

Vertex: $\left(-\frac{3}{5}, \frac{1}{5}\right)$

9.8 Mixed Review (p. 552)

41. $$\begin{aligned} y &= rx \\ 42 &= r(6) \\ 7 &= r \\ y &= 7x \end{aligned}$$

42. $$\begin{aligned} y &= rx \\ 54 &= r(-9) \\ -6 &= r \\ y &= -6x \end{aligned}$$

43. $$\begin{aligned} y &= rx \\ 7 &= r(14) \\ \frac{1}{2} &= r \\ y &= \frac{1}{2}x \end{aligned}$$

44. $$\begin{aligned} y &= rx \\ -52 &= r(-13) \\ 4 &= r \\ y &= 4x \end{aligned}$$

45. $$\begin{aligned} y &= rx \\ -6 &= r(3) \\ -2 &= r \\ y &= -2x \end{aligned}$$

46. $$\begin{aligned} y &= rx \\ 60 &= r(-5) \\ -12 &= r \\ y &= -12x \end{aligned}$$

47. $y = 3^x$

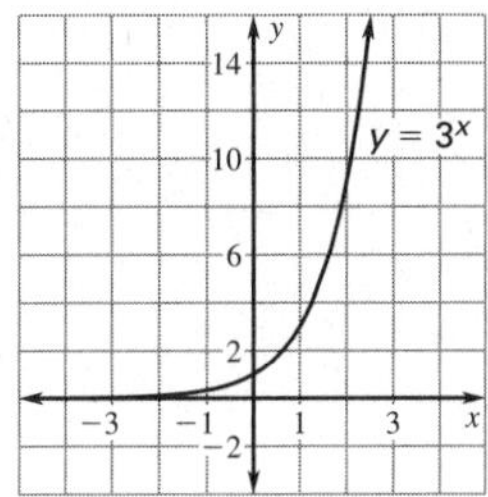

48. $y = 5^x$

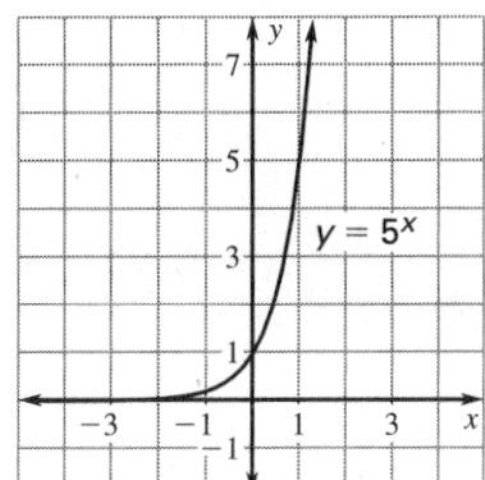

49. $y = 3(2)^x$

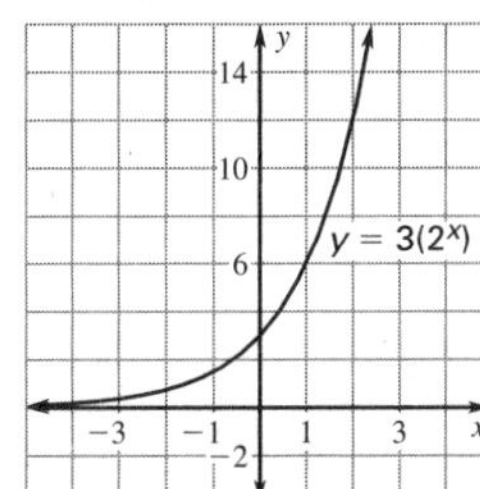

50. $y = \left(\frac{1}{3}\right)^x$

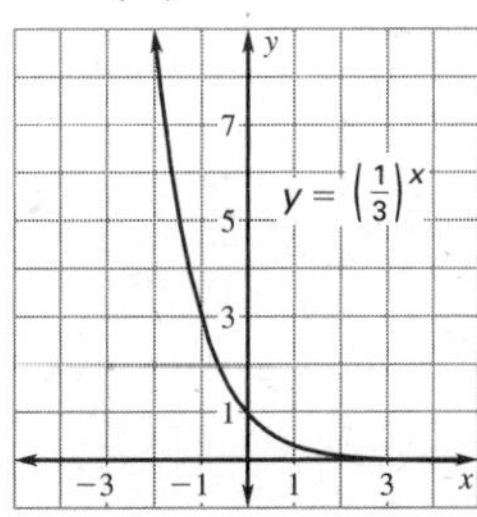

Copyright © McDougal Littell Inc.
All rights reserved.

51. 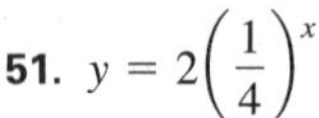
$y = 2\left(\frac{1}{4}\right)^x$

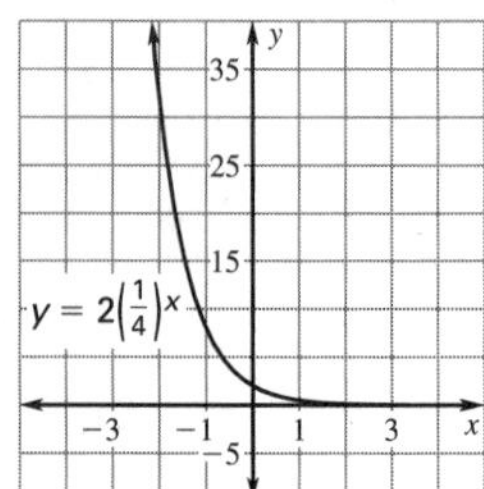

52. $y = \left(\frac{2}{3}\right)^x$

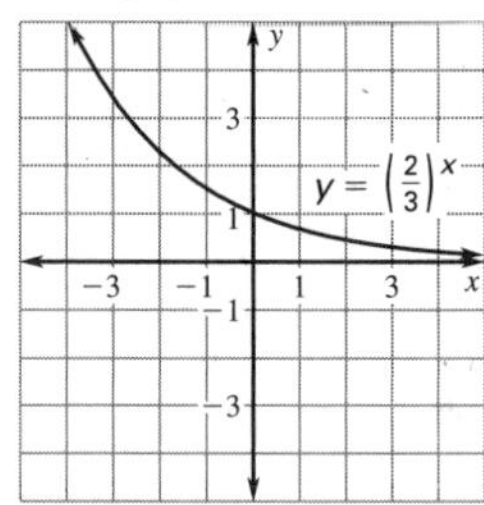

9.8 Maintaining Skills (p. 552)

53. $4\% = \frac{4}{100} = \frac{1}{25}$

54. $392\% = \frac{392}{100} = 3\frac{92}{100} = 3\frac{23}{25}$

55. $45\% = \frac{45}{100} = \frac{9}{20}$

56. $500\% = \frac{500}{100} = 5$

57. $3\% = \frac{3}{100}$

58. $6\% = \frac{6}{100} = \frac{3}{50}$

59. $24\% = \frac{24}{100} = \frac{6}{25}$

60. $10\% = \frac{10}{100} = \frac{1}{10}$

61. $390\% = \frac{390}{100} = 3\frac{90}{100} = 3\frac{9}{10}$

62. $225\% = \frac{225}{100} = 2\frac{25}{100} = 2\frac{1}{4}$

63. $175\% = \frac{175}{100} = 1\frac{75}{100} = 1\frac{3}{4}$

64. $8\% = \frac{8}{100} = \frac{2}{25}$

65. $91\% = \frac{91}{100}$

66. $2\% = \frac{2}{100} = \frac{1}{50}$

67. $25\% = \frac{25}{100} = \frac{1}{4}$

68. $16\% = \frac{16}{100} = \frac{4}{25}$

Quiz 3 *(p. 552)*

1. $a = 1, b = -15, c = 56$
$b^2 - 4ac = (-15)^2 - 4(1)(56)$
$= 225 - 224 = 1$; two solutions

2. $a - 1, b = 8, c = 16$
$b^2 - 4ac = 8^2 - 4(1)(16)$
$= 64 - 64 = 0$; one solution

3. $a = 1, b = -3, c = 4$
$b^2 - 4ac = (-3)^2 - 4(1)(4)$
$= 9 - 16 = -7$; no real solution

4. $h = -16t^2 + vt + s$
No. *Sample answer*: The vertical motion model is $h = -16t^2 + 50t + 5$. If you let $h = 45$ and solve for t you have the quadratic equation $8t^2 - 25t + 20 = 0$. The discriminant has a value of $625 - 640 = -15$, so there are no solutions.

5. $y < -2x^2 + 4x - 2; A$

6. $y \le -2x^2 + 3x + 2; C$

7. $y \ge -2x^2 - 3x + 2; B$

8. $y \ge 2x^2 + 5$

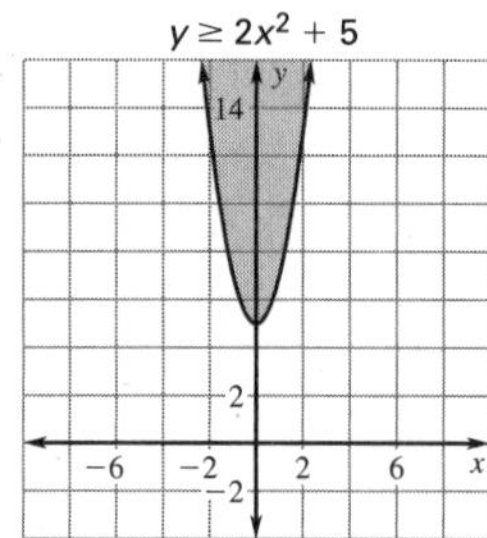

9. $y < x^2 + 3x$

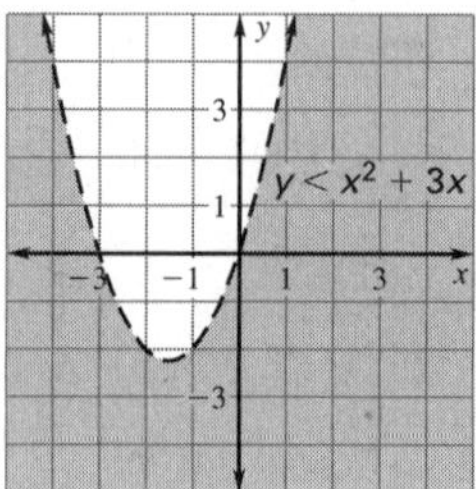

Copyright © McDougal Littell Inc.
All rights reserved.

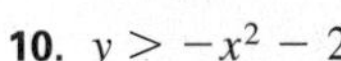

10. $y > -x^2 - 2$

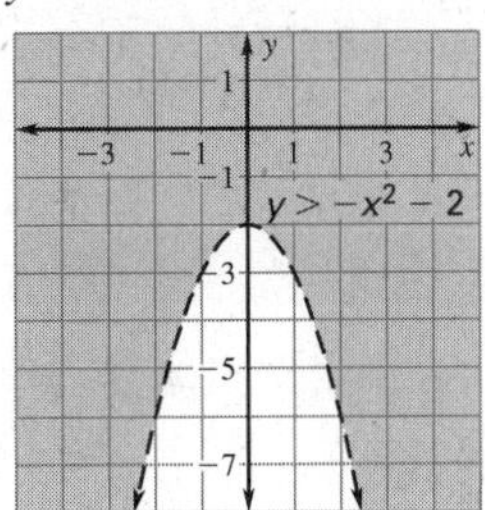

11. $y \le x^2 + 3x - 2$

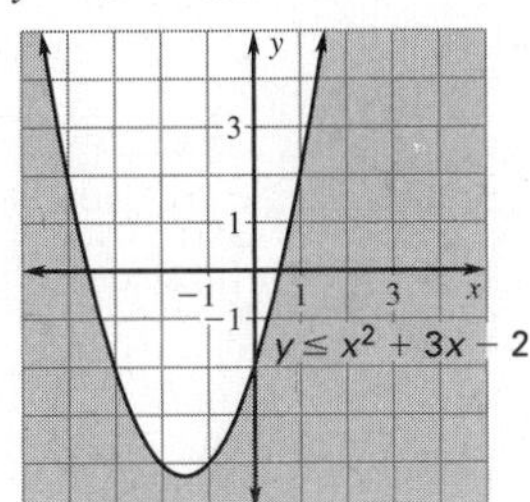

12. $y > x^2 + 2x + 1$

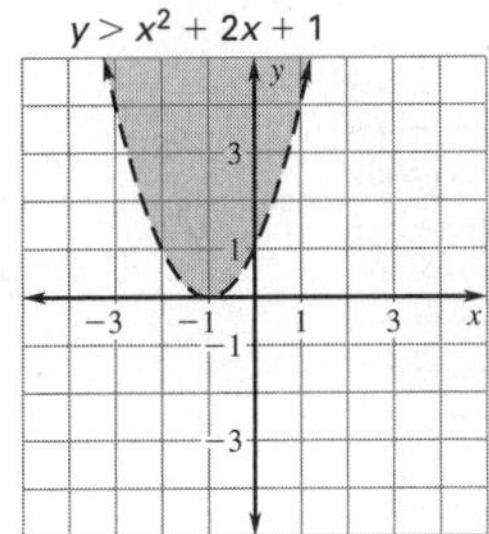

13. $y \le -x^2 + 2x - 3$

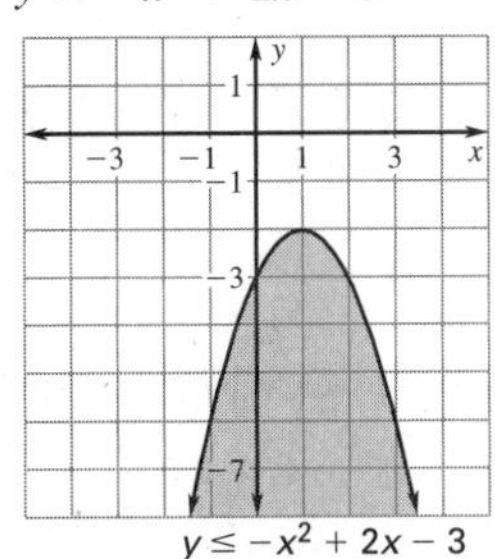

Chapter Summary and Review *(pp. 553–556)*

1. $-\sqrt{4} = -2$

2. $\sqrt{144} = 12$

3. $\sqrt{100} = 10$

4. $-\sqrt{25} = -5$

5. $x^2 = 144$
$x = \pm\sqrt{144}$
$x = \pm 12$

6. $8y^2 = 968$
$y^2 = 121$
$y = \pm\sqrt{121}$
$y = \pm 11$

7. $5y^2 - 80 = 0$
$5y^2 = 80$
$y^2 = 16$
$y = \pm\sqrt{16}$
$y = \pm 4$

8. $3x^2 - 4 = 8$
$3x^2 = 12$
$x^2 = 4$
$x = \pm\sqrt{4}$
$x = \pm 2$

9. $\sqrt{45} = \sqrt{9 \cdot 5}$
$= \sqrt{9} \cdot \sqrt{5}$
$= 3\sqrt{5}$

10. $\sqrt{28} = \sqrt{4 \cdot 7}$
$= \sqrt{4} \cdot \sqrt{7}$
$= 2\sqrt{7}$

11. $\sqrt{\frac{36}{24}} = \frac{\sqrt{36}}{\sqrt{24}} = \frac{6}{\sqrt{4 \cdot 6}} = \frac{6}{\sqrt{4} \cdot \sqrt{6}} = \frac{6}{2\sqrt{6}} \cdot \frac{\sqrt{6}}{\sqrt{6}}$
$= \frac{3\sqrt{6}}{6} = \frac{\sqrt{6}}{2}$

12. $\sqrt{\frac{8}{6}} = \sqrt{\frac{4}{3}} = \frac{\sqrt{4}}{\sqrt{3}} = \frac{2}{\sqrt{3}} \cdot \frac{\sqrt{3}}{\sqrt{3}} = \frac{2\sqrt{3}}{3}$

13. $y = x^2 - 5x + 4$
$a = 1, b = -5, c = 4$
$-\frac{b}{2a} = -\frac{(-5)}{2(1)} = \frac{5}{2} = 2\frac{1}{2}$

x	1	2	$2\frac{1}{2}$	3	4
y	0	−2	$-2\frac{1}{4}$	−2	0

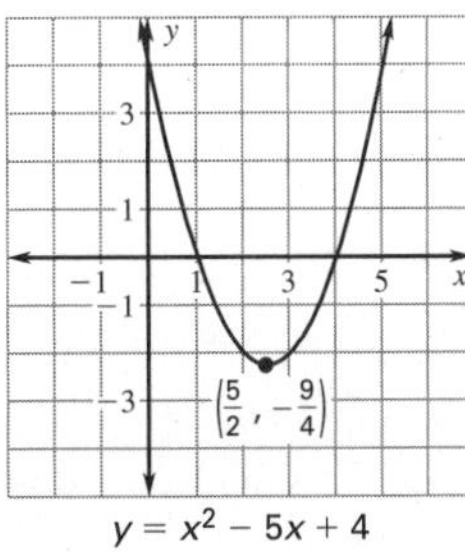

Copyright © McDougal Littell Inc.
All rights reserved.

14. $y = -x^2 + 2x - 1$

$a = -1, b = 2, c = -1$

$-\dfrac{b}{2a} = -\dfrac{2}{2(-1)} = 1$

x	-1	0	1	2	3
y	-4	-1	0	-1	-4

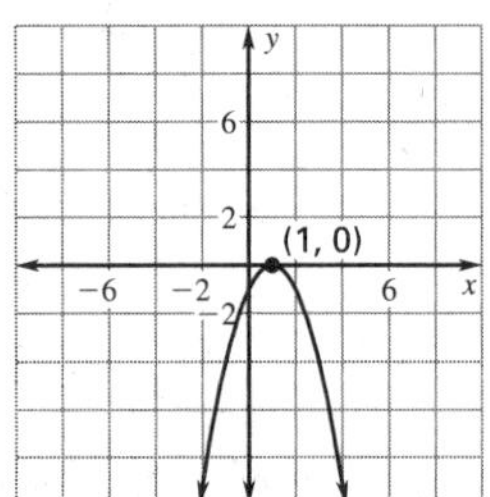

15. $y = 2x^2 - 3x - 2$

$a = 2, b = -3, c = -2$

$-\dfrac{b}{2a} = -\dfrac{(-3)}{2(2)} = \dfrac{3}{4}$

x	-1	0	$\frac{1}{2}$	1	2
y	0	-2	$\frac{1}{4}$	-4	0

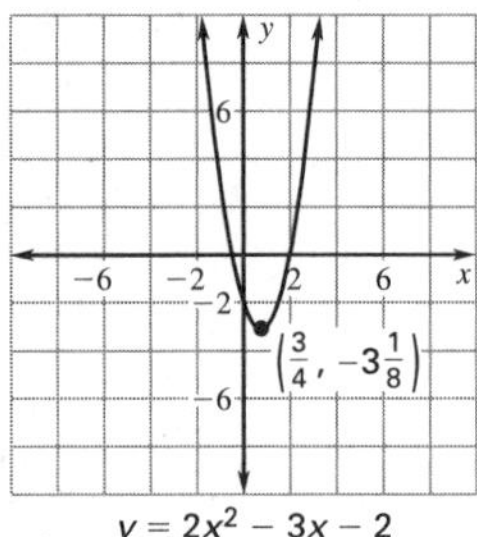

16. $x^2 - 3x = -2$

$x^2 - 3x + 2 = 0$

$y = x^2 - 3x + 2$ (Related quadratic function)

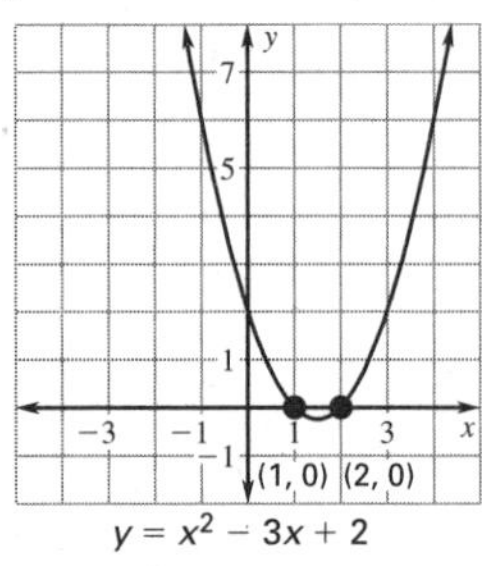

Solutions: 1, 2

Check 1: $(1)^2 - 3(1) \stackrel{?}{=} -2$

$1 - 3 \stackrel{?}{=} -2$

$-2 = -2$

Check 2: $(2)^2 - 3(2) \stackrel{?}{=} -2$

$4 - 6 \stackrel{?}{=} -2$

$-2 = -2$

17. $-x^2 + 6x = 5$

$-x^2 + 6x - 5 = 0$

$y = -x^2 + 6x - 5$ (Related quadratic function)

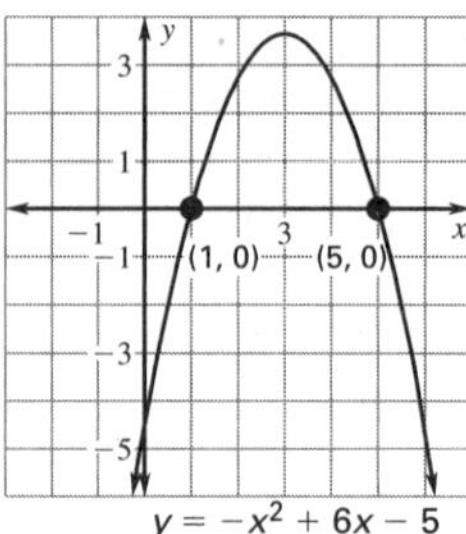

Solutions: 5, 1

Check 5: $-(5)^2 + 6(5) \stackrel{?}{=} 5$

$-25 + 30 \stackrel{?}{=} 5$

$5 = 5$

Check 1: $-(1)^2 + 6(1) = 5$

$-1 + 6 \stackrel{?}{=} 5$

$5 = 5$

18. $x^2 - 2x = 3$

$x^2 - 2x - 3 = 0$

$y = x^2 - 2x - 3$ (Related quadratic function)

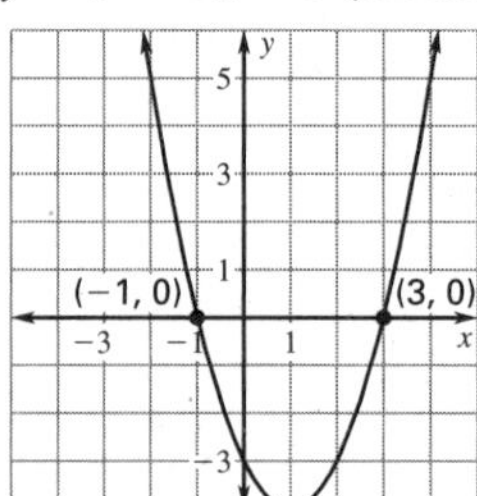

Solutions: 3, -1

Check 3: $(3)^2 - 2(3) \stackrel{?}{=} 3$

$9 - 6 \stackrel{?}{=} 3$

$3 = 3$

Check -1: $(-1)^2 - 2(-1) \stackrel{?}{=} 3$

$1 + 2 \stackrel{?}{=} 3$

$3 = 3$

19. $3x^2 - 4x + 1 = 0$

$a = 3, b = -4, c = 1$

$x = \dfrac{-(-4) \pm \sqrt{(-4)^2 - 4(3)(1)}}{2(3)}$

$x = \dfrac{4 \pm \sqrt{16 - 12}}{6} = \dfrac{4 \pm \sqrt{4}}{6}$

$x = \dfrac{4 \pm 2}{6}$

$x = \dfrac{4 + 2}{6} = \dfrac{6}{6} = 1$ and $x = \dfrac{4 - 2}{6} = \dfrac{2}{6} = \dfrac{1}{3}$

Copyright © McDougal Littell Inc.
All rights reserved.

20. $-2x^2 + x + 6 = 0$
$a = -2, b = 1, c = 6$
$$x = \frac{-1 \pm \sqrt{1^2 - 4(-2)(6)}}{2(-2)}$$
$$x = \frac{-1 \pm \sqrt{1 + 48}}{-4} = \frac{-1 \pm \sqrt{49}}{-4}$$
$$x = \frac{-1 \pm 7}{-4}$$
$$x = \frac{-1 + 7}{-4} = \frac{6}{-4} = -\frac{3}{2} \text{ and } x = \frac{-1 - 7}{-4} = \frac{-8}{-4} = 2$$

21. $10x^2 - 11x + 3 = 0$
$a = 10, b = -11, c = 3$
$$x = \frac{-(-11) \pm \sqrt{(-11)^2 - 4(10)(3)}}{2(10)}$$
$$x = \frac{11 \pm \sqrt{121 - 120}}{20} = \frac{11 \pm \sqrt{1}}{20}$$
$$x = \frac{11 \pm 1}{20}$$
$$x = \frac{11 + 1}{20} = \frac{12}{20} = \frac{3}{5} \text{ and } x = \frac{11 - 1}{20} = \frac{10}{20} = \frac{1}{2}$$

22. $3x^2 - 12x + 12 = 0$
$a = 3, b = -12, c = 12$
$b^2 - 4ac = (-12)^2 - 4(3)(12)$
$= 144 - 144 = 0$; one solution

23. $2x^2 + 10x + 6 = 0$
$a = 2, b = 10, c = 6$
$b^2 - 4ac = 10^2 - 4(2)(6)$
$= 100 - 48 = 52$; two solutions

24. $-x^2 + 3x - 5 = 0$
$a = -1, b = 3, c = -5$
$b^2 - 4ac = 3^2 - 4(-1)(-5)$
$= 9 - 20 = -11$; no real solution

25. $y = 2x^2 - 3x - 1$; Let $y = 0$.
$0 = 2x^2 - 3x - 1$
$a = 2, b = -3, c = -1$
$b^2 - 4ac = (-3)^2 - 4(2)(-1)$
$= 9 + 8 = 17$; two x-intercepts

26. $y = -x^2 - 3x + 3$; Let $y = 0$.
$0 = -x^2 - 3x + 3$
$a = -1, b = -3, c = 3$
$b^2 - 4ac = (-3)^2 - 4(-1)(3)$
$= 9 + 12 = 21$; two x-intercepts

27. $y = x^2 + 2x + 1$; Let $y = 0$.
$0 = x^2 + 2x + 1$
$a = 1, b = 2, c = 1$
$b^2 - 4ac = 2^2 - 4(1)(1)$
$= 4 - 4 = 0$; one x-intercept

28. $y \leq x^2 - 4$
$a = 1, b = 0, c = -4$
$$-\frac{b}{2a} = -\frac{0}{2(1)} = 0$$

x	−2	−1	0	1	2
y	0	−3	−4	−3	0

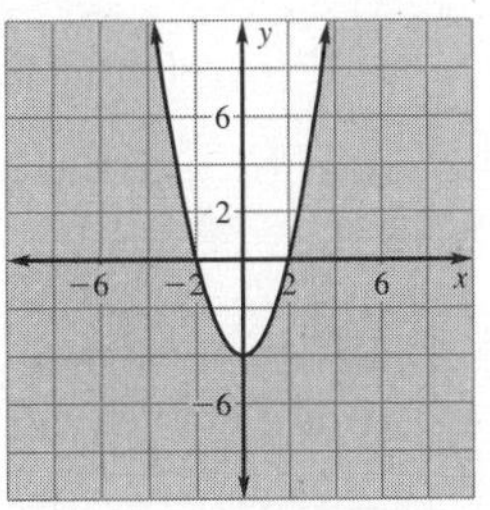

29. $y \geq -x^2 - 2x + 3$
$a = -1, b = -2, c = 3$
$$-\frac{b}{2a} = -\frac{(-2)}{2(-1)} = -1$$

x	−3	−2	−1	0	1
y	0	3	4	3	0

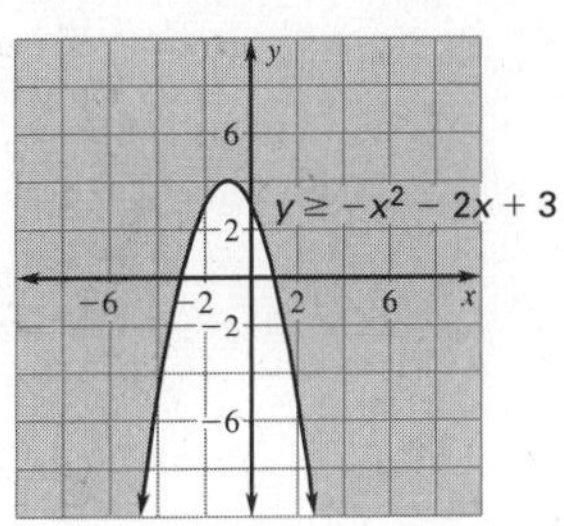

30. $y > 2x^2 - 4x - 6$
$a = 2, b = -2, c = -6$
$$-\frac{b}{2a} = -\frac{(-2)}{2(2)} = \frac{1}{2}$$

x	−1	0	$\frac{1}{2}$	1	2
y	0	−6	$-7\frac{1}{2}$	−8	−6

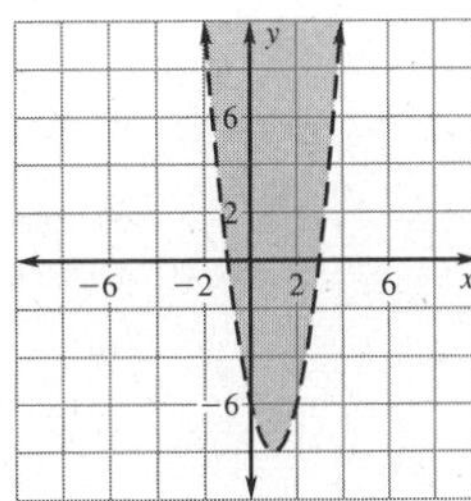

Chapter Test *(p. 557)*

1. $\sqrt{64} = 8$

2. $-\sqrt{25} = -5$

3. $\pm\sqrt{169} = \pm 13$

Copyright © McDougal Littell Inc.
All rights reserved.

Chapter 9 *continued*

4. $-\sqrt{100} = -10$

5. $x^2 = 1$
$x = \pm\sqrt{1}$
$x = \pm 1$

6. $n^2 = 36$
$n = \pm\sqrt{36}$
$n = \pm 6$

7. $4y^2 = 16$
$y^2 = 4$
$y = \pm\sqrt{4}$
$y = \pm 2$

8. $8x^2 = 800$
$x^2 = 100$
$x = \pm\sqrt{100}$
$x = \pm 10$

9. $t^2 - 64 = 0$
$t^2 = 64$
$t = \pm\sqrt{64}$
$t = \pm 8$

10. $5x^2 + 125 = 0$
$5x^2 = -125$
$x^2 = -25$
$x = \pm\sqrt{-25}$; no real solution

11. $2x^2 + 1 = 19$
$2x^2 = 18$
$x^2 = 9$
$x = \pm\sqrt{9}$
$x = \pm 3$

12. $x^2 + 6 = -10$
$x^2 = -16$
$x = \pm\sqrt{-16}$; no real solution

13. $\sqrt{150} = \sqrt{25 \cdot 6} = \sqrt{25} \cdot \sqrt{6} = 5\sqrt{6}$

14. $5\sqrt{\frac{4}{25}} = \frac{5\sqrt{4}}{\sqrt{25}} = \frac{5(2)}{5} = 2$

15. $\sqrt{\frac{27}{45}} = \sqrt{\frac{9 \cdot 3}{9 \cdot 5}} = \sqrt{\frac{3}{5}} = \frac{\sqrt{3}}{\sqrt{5}} \cdot \frac{\sqrt{5}}{\sqrt{5}} = \frac{\sqrt{15}}{5}$

16. $\sqrt{\frac{9}{7}} = \frac{\sqrt{9}}{\sqrt{7}} = \frac{3}{\sqrt{7}} \cdot \frac{\sqrt{7}}{\sqrt{7}} = \frac{3\sqrt{7}}{7}$

17. $y = -x^2 - 2x + 3$; C
$a = -1$
$b = -2$
$\frac{-b}{2a} = -\frac{(-2)}{2(-1)} = -1$

18. $y = -3x^2 - x + 2$; A
$a = -3$; parabola opens down.

19. $y = 2x^2 + x - 3$; B
$a = 2$; parabola opens up.

20. $x^2 - 4 = 5$
$x^2 - 9 = 0$
$y = x^2 - 9$ (Related quadratic function)

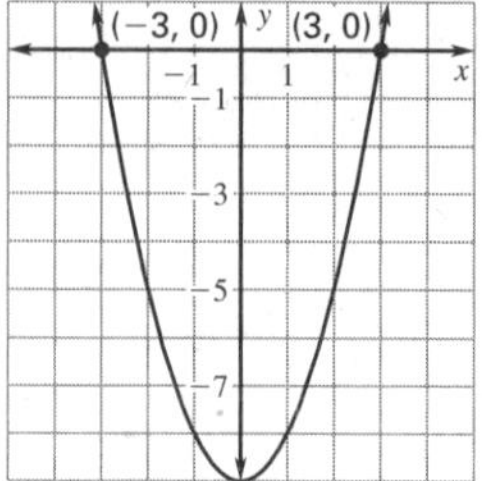

Solutions: ± 3
Check 3: $3^2 - 4 \stackrel{?}{=} 5$
$9 - 4 \stackrel{?}{=} 5$
$5 = 5$
Check −3: $(-3)^2 - 4 \stackrel{?}{=} 5$
$9 - 4 \stackrel{?}{=} 5$
$5 = 5$

21. $-x^2 + 7x - 10 = 0$
$y = -x^2 + 7x - 10$ (Related quadratic function)

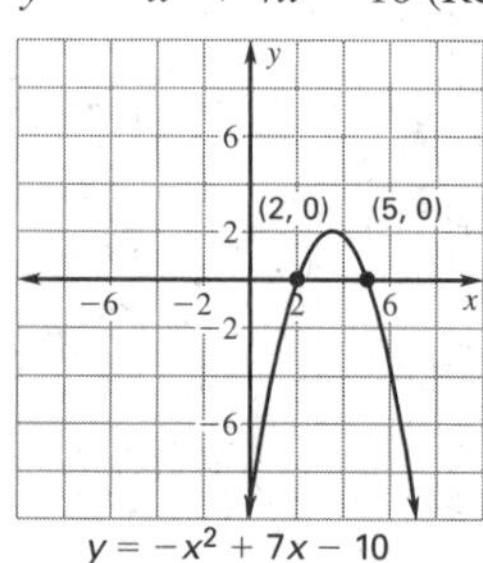

$y = -x^2 + 7x - 10$

Solutions: 5, 2
Check 5: $-(5)^2 + 7(5) - 10 \stackrel{?}{=} 0$
$-25 + 35 - 10 \stackrel{?}{=} 0$
$0 = 0$
Check 2: $-(2)^2 + 7(2) - 10 \stackrel{?}{=} 0$
$-4 + 14 - 10 \stackrel{?}{=} 0$
$0 = 0$

22. $-2x^2 + 4x + 6 = 0$
$y = -2x^2 + 4x + 6$ (Related quadratic function)

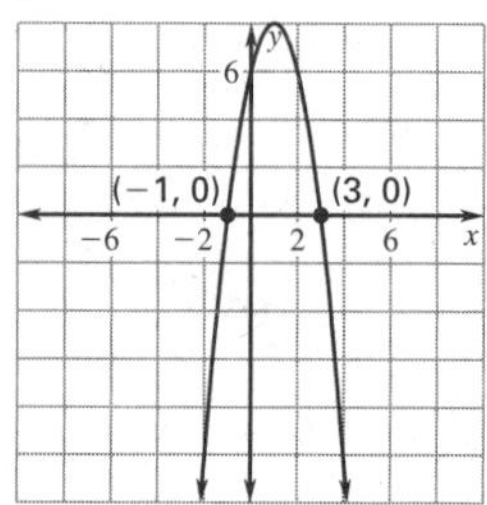

Solutions: 3, −1
Check 3: $-2(3)^2 + 4(3) + 6 \stackrel{?}{=} 0$
$-18 + 12 + 6 \stackrel{?}{=} 0$
$0 = 0$
Check −1: $-2(-1)^2 + 4(-1) + 6 \stackrel{?}{=} 0$
$-2 - 4 + 6 \stackrel{?}{=} 0$
$0 = 0$

Copyright © McDougal Littell Inc.
All rights reserved.

23. $x^2 - 6x - 27 = 0$

$a = 1, b = -6, c = -27$

$$x = \frac{-(-6) \pm \sqrt{(-6)^2 - 4(1)(-27)}}{2(1)}$$

$$x = \frac{6 \pm \sqrt{36 + 108}}{2} = \frac{6 \pm \sqrt{144}}{2}$$

$$x = \frac{6 \pm 12}{2}$$

$$x = \frac{6 + 12}{2} = \frac{18}{2} = 9 \text{ and } x = \frac{6 - 12}{2} = \frac{-6}{2} = -3$$

24. $-x^2 + 3x + 10 = 0$

$a = -1, b = 3, c = 10$

$$x = \frac{-3 \pm \sqrt{3^2 - 4(-1)(10)}}{2(-1)}$$

$$x = \frac{-3 \pm \sqrt{9 + 40}}{-2} = \frac{-3 \pm \sqrt{49}}{-2}$$

$$x = \frac{-3 \pm 7}{-2}$$

$$x = \frac{-3 + 7}{-2} = \frac{4}{-2} = -2 \text{ and } x = \frac{-3 - 7}{-2} = \frac{-10}{-2} = 5$$

25. $3x^2 + 4x - 7 = 0$

$a = 3, b = 4, c = -7$

$$x = \frac{-4 \pm \sqrt{4^2 - 4(3)(-7)}}{2(3)}$$

$$x = \frac{-4 \pm \sqrt{16 + 84}}{6} = \frac{-4 \pm \sqrt{100}}{6}$$

$$x = \frac{-4 \pm 10}{6}$$

$$x = \frac{-4 + 10}{6} = \frac{6}{6} = 1 \text{ and}$$

$$x = \frac{-4 - 10}{6} = \frac{-14}{6} = -\frac{7}{3}$$

26. $-3x^2 + x - 2 = 0$

$a = -3, b = 1, c = -2$

$b^2 - 4ac = 1^2 - 4(-3)(-2)$

$= 1 - 24 = -23$; no solution

27. $x^2 - 4x + 4 = 0$

$a = 1, b = -4, c = 4$

$b^2 - 4ac = (-4)^2 - 4(1)(4)$

$= 16 - 16 = 0$; one solution

28. $5x^2 - 2x - 6 = 0$

$a = 5, b = -2, c = -6$

$b^2 - 4ac = (-2)^2 - 4(5)(-6)$

$= 4 + 120 = 124$; two solutions

29. $y < x^2 + 2x - 3$

$$-\frac{b}{2a} = -\frac{2}{2(1)} = -1$$

x	-3	-2	-1	0	1
y	0	-3	-4	-3	0

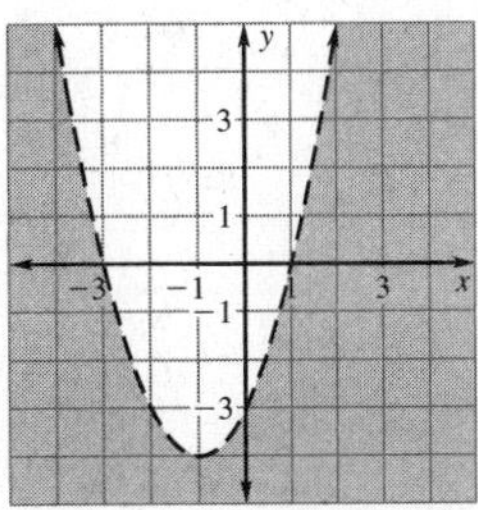

30. $y \le -x^2 + 5x - 4$

$$-\frac{b}{2a} = -\frac{5}{2(-1)} = \frac{5}{2} = 2\frac{1}{2}$$

x	1	2	$2\frac{1}{2}$	3	4
y	0	2	$2\frac{1}{4}$	2	0

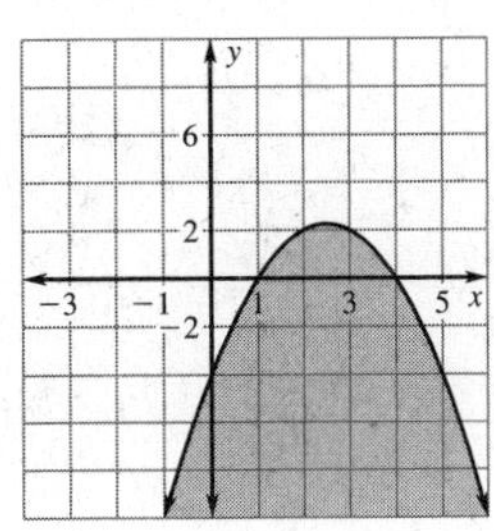

31. $y \ge x^2 + 7x + 6$

$$-\frac{b}{2a} = -\frac{7}{2(1)} = -\frac{7}{2} = -3\frac{1}{2}$$

x	-5	-4	$-3\frac{1}{2}$	-3	-2
y	-4	-6	$-6\frac{1}{4}$	-6	-4

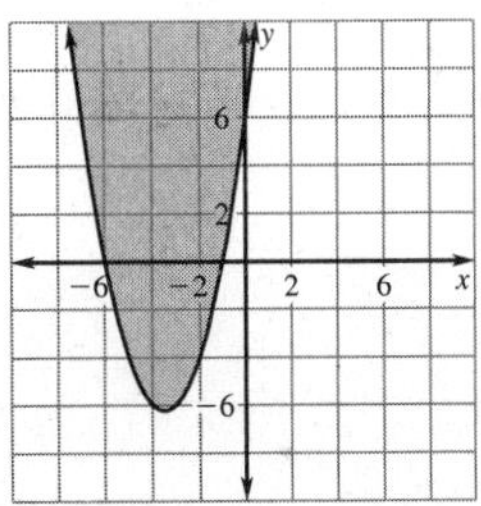

32.

$h = -16t^2 + s$

$0 = -16t^2 + 20$

$-20 = -16t^2$

$\frac{5}{4} = t^2$

$\pm\sqrt{\frac{5}{4}} = t$

$\pm 1.12 \approx t$

about 1.12 sec

Copyright © McDougal Littell Inc.
All rights reserved.

Chapter 9 *continued*

33. $h = -16t^2 + vt + s$

$0 = -16t^2 + 30t + 20$

$a = -16,\ b = 30,\ c = 20$

$$t = \frac{-30 \pm \sqrt{30^2 - 4(-16)(20)}}{2(-16)}$$

$$t = \frac{-30 \pm \sqrt{900 + 1280}}{-32} = \frac{-30 \pm \sqrt{2180}}{-32}$$

$t \approx -0.52$ and 2.40

about 2.40 sec

Chapter Standardized Test *(p. 558)*

1. *D*; $\sqrt{100} = 10$

2. *C*; $-7x + 12 = 0$ does not have an x^2 term.

3. *A*;

$$\begin{aligned} 2(-6)^2 - 21 &\stackrel{?}{=} 51 \\ 2(36) - 21 &\stackrel{?}{=} 51 \\ 51 &= 51 \end{aligned}$$

4. *D*;

$$\begin{aligned} 3x^2 - 78 &= 114 \\ 3x^2 &= 192 \\ x^2 &= 64 \\ x &= \pm\sqrt{64} \\ x &= \pm 8 \end{aligned}$$

5. *E*; None of these.

A and *B* contain a fraction in the radicand;
C contains a radical in the denominator;
D has a perfect square factor in the radicand.

6. *A*;

$$\begin{aligned} A &= l \cdot w \\ A &= \sqrt{20} \cdot \sqrt{12} \\ &= \sqrt{240} \\ &= \sqrt{16 \cdot 15} \\ &= \sqrt{16} \cdot \sqrt{15} \\ &= 4\sqrt{15} \end{aligned}$$

7. *B*; $-\frac{1}{4}$

$y = -2x^2 - x + 8$

$$x = -\frac{b}{2a} = -\frac{(-1)}{2(-2)} = -\frac{1}{4}$$

8. *A*: -10 and 4

$y = -x^2 - 6x + 40$

$a = -1, b = -6, c = 40$

$$x = \frac{-(-6) \pm \sqrt{(-6)^2 - 4(-1)(40)}}{2(-1)}$$

$$x = \frac{6 \pm \sqrt{36 + 160}}{-2} = \frac{6 \pm \sqrt{196}}{-2}$$

$$x = \frac{6 \pm 14}{-2}$$

$$x = \frac{6 + 14}{-2} = \frac{20}{-2} = -10 \text{ and } x = \frac{6 - 14}{-2} = \frac{-8}{-2} = 4$$

9. *C*: $y = 2x^2 + 6$

At the y-intercept, $x = 0$.

$y = 2(0)^2 + 6 = 6$

10. *D*: 144

$$\begin{aligned} b^2 - 4ac &= 2^2 - 4(5)(-7) \\ &= 4 + 140 = 144 \end{aligned}$$

11. A: $y < -4x^2 + 8x - 5$

"$<$" means a dashed parabola with solution below the parabola.

Maintaining Skills *(p. 559)*

1. $8(2x - 12) = 8(2x) - 8(12) = 16x - 96$

2. $4(3x + 2) = 4(3x) + 4(2) = 12x + 8$

3. $-5(13 - m) = -5(13) - (-5)(m) = -65 + 5m$ or $5m - 65$

4. $8(-5 + 6c) = 8(-5) + 8(6c) = -40 + 48c$ or $48c - 40$

5. $10(8 + 3a) = 80 + 30a$ or $30a + 80$

6. $-12(5 + 6t) = -12(5) + (-12)(6t) = -60 - 72t$ or $-72t - 60$

7.
$$\begin{aligned} 8n - 2n + 18m + 3m &= (8 - 2)n + (18 + 3)m \\ &= 6n + 21m \end{aligned}$$

or $21m + 6n$

8.
$$\begin{aligned} 25c - 7d - 10d + 5c &= 25c + 5c - 7d - 10d \\ &= (25 + 5)c + (-7 - 10)d \\ &= 30c - 17d \end{aligned}$$

9. $4 + 2(x + 3) = 4 + 2x + 6 = 10 + 2x$ or $2x + 10$

10.
$$\begin{aligned} 2x + 4(2x - 5) &= 2x + 8x - 20 \\ &= (2 + 8)x - 20 \\ &= 10x - 20 \end{aligned}$$

Chapters 1–9 Cumulative Practice *(pp. 560–561)*

1. No. Each input value can only have one output value. 5 has two output values.

2. Yes. There is only one output for each input.

3. $$\frac{27x - 54}{9} = \frac{9(3x - 6)}{9} = 3x - 6$$

4.
$$\begin{aligned} \frac{66r + 39}{-3} &= \frac{3(22r + 13)}{-3} \\ &= -1(22r + 13) \\ &= -22r - 13 \end{aligned}$$

5.
$$\begin{aligned} \frac{-72 + 16h}{-8} &= \frac{8(-9 + 2h)}{-8} \\ &= -1(-9 + 2h) \\ &= 9 - 2h \end{aligned}$$

6. $$\frac{-28 - 10t}{-2} = \frac{-2(14 + 5t)}{-2} = 14 + 5t$$

Copyright © McDougal Littell Inc.
All rights reserved.

7. $1.25x = 60$
$x = 48$
48 pretzels

8. 75% of 48 $= 0.75 \times 48 = 36$

9. $54 = 15\%(x)$
$54 = 0.15x$
$360 = x$

10. $64 = p(80)$
$0.8 = p$
$80\% = p$

11. $20 = p(5)$
$4 = p$
$400\% = p$

12. $x + 2y = 8$
x-intercept: $x + 2(0) = 8$
y-intercept: $0 + 2y = 8$
$2y = 8$
$y = 4$

13. $x - 6y = -3$
x-intercept: $x - 6(0) = -3$
$x = -3$
y-intercept: $0 - 6y = -3$
$-6y = -3$
$y = \frac{1}{2}$

14. $y = 12x - 2$
x-intercept: $0 = 12x - 2$
$2 = 12x$
$\frac{1}{6} = x$
y-intercept: $y = 12(0) - 2$
$y = -2$

15. $y = -5x + 14$
x-intercept: $0 = -5x + 14$
$-14 = -5x$
$\frac{14}{5} = x$
y-intercept: $y = -5(0) + 14$
$y = 14$

16. $-2x - 7y = 20$
x-intercept: $-2x - 7(0) = 20$
$-2x = 20$
$x = -10$
y-intercept: $-2(0) - 7y = 20$
$-7y = 20$
$y = -\frac{20}{7}$

17. $-14x - y = 28$
x-intercept: $-14x - 0 = 28$
$-14x = 28$
$x = -2$
y-intercept: $-14(0) - y = 28$
$-y = 28$
$y = -28$

18. line a: $y = 2x + 3;\ m = 2$
line b: $y - 3x = 2$
$y = 3x + 2;\ m = 3$
No; different slopes

19. line a: $y - 4x + 1 = 0$
$y = 4x - 1;\ m = 4$
line b: $2y = 8x + 6$
$y = 4x + 3;\ m = 4$
Yes; same slopes

20. line a: $2x - 5y = -30$
$-5y = -2x - 30$
$y = \frac{2}{5}x + 6;\ m = \frac{2}{5}$
line b: $-4x + 10y = -10$
$10y = 4x - 10$
$y = \frac{2}{5}x - 1;\ m = \frac{2}{5}$
Yes; same slopes

21. $m = \frac{4 - 3}{6 - 7} = \frac{1}{-1} = -1$
$y - 3 = -1(x - 7)$
$y - 3 = -x + 7$
$y = -x + 10$

22. $m = \frac{8 - 5}{11 - 2} = \frac{3}{9} = \frac{1}{3}$
$y - 5 = \frac{1}{3}(x - 2)$
$y - 5 = \frac{1}{3}x - \frac{2}{3}$
$y = \frac{1}{3}x - \frac{2}{3} + \frac{15}{3}$
$y = \frac{1}{3}x + \frac{13}{3}$

23. $m = \frac{-8 - 6}{3 - (-4)} = \frac{-14}{7} = -2$
$y - 6 = -2[x - (-4)]$
$y - 6 = -2(x + 4)$
$y - 6 = -2x - 8$
$y = -2x - 2$

24. $m = \frac{3 - (-12)}{3 - 0} = \frac{15}{3} = 5$
$y - 3 = 5(x - 3)$
$y - 3 = 5x - 15$
$y = 5x - 12$

25. $m = \frac{7 - 2}{-5 - 5} = \frac{5}{-10} = -\frac{1}{2}$
$y - 2 = -\frac{1}{2}(x - 5)$
$y - 2 = -\frac{1}{2}x + \frac{5}{2}$
$y = -\frac{1}{2}x + \frac{5}{2} + \frac{4}{2}$
$y = -\frac{1}{2}x + \frac{9}{2}$

Copyright © McDougal Littell Inc.
All rights reserved.

26. $m = \frac{2 - (-10)}{8 - 5} = \frac{12}{3} = 4$

$y - (-10) = 4(x - 5)$

$y + 10 = 4x - 20$

$y = 4x - 30$

27. $3x - 5y + 6 = 0$

$3x - 5y = -6$

28. $6y = 2x + 4$

$3y = x + 2$

$x - 3y = -2$

29. $-2x + 7y - 15 = 0$

$-2x + 7y = 15$

30. $y = \frac{2}{3}x - 1$

$3y = 2x - 3$

$2x - 3y = 3$

31. $y = -\frac{1}{4}x + 6$

$4y = -x + 24$

$x + 4y = 24$

32. $y = \frac{4}{5}x + 5$

$5y = 4x + 25$

$-4x + 5y = 25$

33. $m + 5 \le -4$

$m \le -9$

34. $8 > c - 3$

$11 > c$ or $c < 11$

35. $-5t \ge 40$

$t \le -8$

36. $\frac{2}{3}x < 9$

$x < \frac{27}{2}$

37. $-\frac{1}{2}y \le -7$

$y \ge 14$

38. $-\frac{x}{5} \ge 2$

$x \le -10$

39. $5y + 6 > -14$

$5y > -20$

$y > -4$

40. $4(a - 1) < 8$

$4a - 4 < 8$

$4a < 12$

$a < 3$

41. $6 + 2k \le 3k - 1$

$6 \le k - 1$

$7 \le k$ or $k \ge 7$

42. $x + 4y = 0$

$x = 12$

$12 + 4y = 0$

$4y = -12$

$y = -3$

Solution: $(12, -3)$

43. $x + y = 8$

$2x + y = 10$

$-x - y = -8$

$\underline{2x + y = 10}$

$x = 2$

$2 + y = 8$

$y = 6$

Solution: $(2, 6)$

44. $10x - 3y = -1$

$\underline{-5x + 3y = 2}$

$5x = 1$

$x = \frac{1}{5}$

$10\left(\frac{1}{5}\right) - 3y = -1$

$2 - 3y = -1$

$-3y = -3$

$y = 1$

Solution: $\left(\frac{1}{5}, 1\right)$

45. $3x + y = -19$

$-32x + 4y = 144$

$y = -3x - 19$

$-32x + 4(-3x - 19) = 144$

$-32x - 12x - 76 = 144$

$-44x - 76 = 144$

$-44x = 220$

$x = -5$

$y - 3(-5) - 19$

$y = -4$

Solution: $(-5, -4)$

46. $-2x + 20y = 10$

$x - 5y = -5$

$-x + 10y = 5$ Multiply by 1/2.

$\underline{x - 5y = -5}$

$5y = 0$

$y = 0$

$x - 5(0) = -5$

$x = -5$

Solution: $(-5, 0)$

Copyright © McDougal Littell Inc.
All rights reserved.

47. $4x + 2y = 3$

$3x - 4y = 5$

$8x + 4y = 6$ Multiply by 2.

$\underline{3x - 4y = 5}$

$11x = 11$

$x = 1$

$3(1) - 4y = 5$

$3 - 4y = 5$

$-4y = 2$

$y = -\frac{1}{2}$

Solution: $\left(1, -\frac{1}{2}\right)$

48. $g + r = 13$

$1.2g + 1.5r = 18$

$g = -r + 13$

$1.2(-r + 13) + 1.5r = 18$

$-1.2r + 15.6 + 1.5r = 18$

$15.6 + 0.3r = 18$

$0.3r = 2.4$

$r = 8$

$g = -8 + 13$

$g = 5$

Solution: 5 green peppers and 8 red peppers

49. $x \geq 0$

$y \geq 0$

$x < 5$

$y < 2$

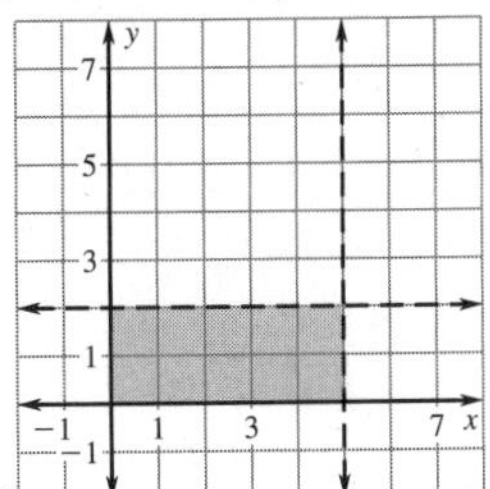

50. $x > 2$

$x - y \leq 2$ or $-y \leq -x + 2$, $y \geq x - 2$

$x + 2y \leq 6$ or $2y \leq -x + 6$, $y \leq -\frac{1}{2}x + 3$

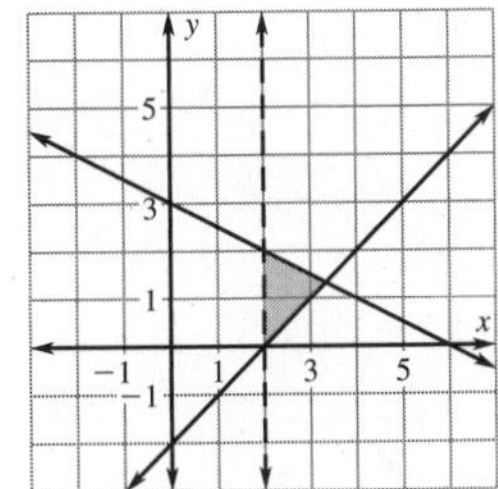

51. $3x + 5y \geq 15$ or $5y \geq -3x + 15$

$y \geq -\frac{3}{5}x + 3;$

$x - 2y < 10$ or $-2y < -x + 10$

$y > \frac{1}{2}x - 5;$

$x > 1$

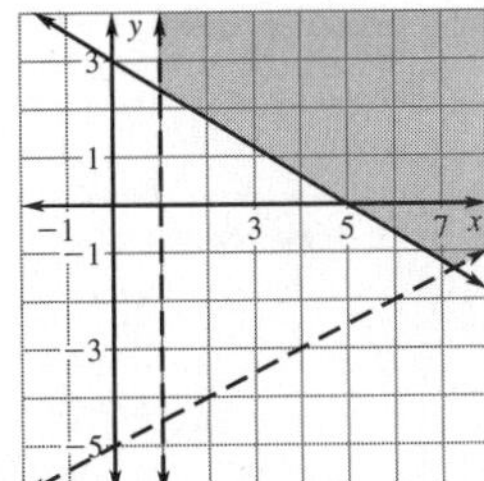

52. $-x + 4y \leq 8$ or $4y \leq x + 8$

$y \leq \frac{1}{4}x + 2;$

$-4x + y \geq -4$ or $y \geq 4x - 4;$

$2x + y \geq -4$ or $y \geq -2x - 4$

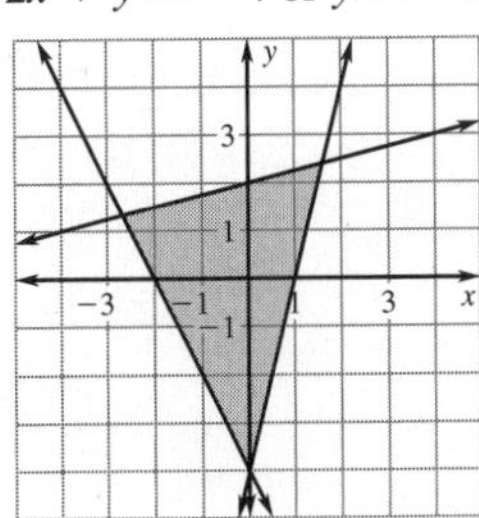

53. $x^3 \cdot x^6 = x^9$

54. $(c^5)^4 = c^{20}$

55. $(8t)^2 = 8^2t^2 = 64t^2$

56. $-3(-5)^2 = -3(25) = -75$

57. $3^2 \cdot 3^3 = 3^5 = 243$

58. $3x^5y^{-3} = \frac{3x^5}{y^3}$

59. $4^{-2} \cdot 4^0 = 4^{-2} = \frac{1}{4^2} = \frac{1}{16}$

60. $\left(\frac{2}{3}\right)^{-4} = \frac{3^4}{2^4} = \frac{81}{16}$

61. $\frac{1}{4x^{-4}y^{-8}} = \frac{x^4y^8}{4}$

62. $\frac{x^8}{x^3} = x^5$

63. $\frac{3x^2y}{y^3} \cdot \frac{6xy^2}{2y} = \frac{18x^3y^3}{2y^4} = 9x^3y^{-1} = \frac{9x^3}{y}$

64. $\frac{2x^4}{y^{-3}} \cdot \left(\frac{x^3}{y^2}\right)^{-2} = \frac{2x^4}{y^{-3}} \cdot \frac{x^{-6}}{y^{-4}} = \frac{2x^{-2}}{y^{-7}} = \frac{2y^7}{x^2}$

Copyright © McDougal Littell Inc.
All rights reserved.

65. $(5 \times 10^{-2})(3 \times 10^{4}) = (5 \times 3)(10^{-2} \times 10^{4})$
$= 15 \times 10^{2}$
$= (1.5 \times 10^{1}) \times 10^{2}$
$= 1.5 \times 10^{3}$

66. $(6 \times 10^{-8})(7 \times 10^{5}) = (6 \times 7)(10^{-8} \times 10^{5})$
$= 42 \times 10^{-3}$
$= (4.2 \times 10^{1}) \times 10^{-3}$
$= 4.2 \times 10^{-2}$

67. $(20 \times 10^{6})(3 \times 10^{3}) = (20 \times 3)(10^{6} \times 10^{3})$
$= 60 \times 10^{9}$
$= (6 \times 10^{1}) \times 10^{9}$
$= 6 \times 10^{10}$

68. $(7 \times 10^{3})^{-3} = 7^{-3} \times 10^{-9}$
$= \frac{1}{7^3} \times 10^{-9}$
$\approx 0.00292 \times 10^{-9}$
$= (2.92 \times 10^{-3}) \times 10^{-9}$
$= 2.92 \times 10^{-12}$

69. $\frac{8.8 \times 10^{-1}}{1.1 \times 10^{-1}} = 8 \times 10^{0}$

70. $(2.8 \times 10^{-2})^{3} = 2.8^{3} \times 10^{-6}$
$= 21.952 \times 10^{-6}$
$= (2.1952 \times 10^{1}) \times 10^{-6}$
$= 2.1952 \times 10^{-5}$

71. $\sqrt{40} = \sqrt{4 \cdot 10} = 2\sqrt{10}$

72. $\sqrt{52} = \sqrt{4 \cdot 13} = 2\sqrt{13}$

73. $\sqrt{72} = \sqrt{36 \cdot 2} = 6\sqrt{2}$

74. $\sqrt{96} = \sqrt{16 \cdot 6} = 4\sqrt{6}$

75. $\frac{1}{4}\sqrt{84} = \frac{1}{4}\sqrt{4 \cdot 21} = \frac{2\sqrt{21}}{4} = \frac{\sqrt{21}}{2}$

76. $\sqrt{\frac{28}{36}} = \frac{\sqrt{4 \cdot 7}}{6} = \frac{2\sqrt{7}}{6} = \frac{\sqrt{7}}{3}$

77. $3\sqrt{\frac{18}{9}} = 3\sqrt{2}$

78. $\sqrt{\frac{12}{75}} = \sqrt{\frac{3 \cdot 4}{3 \cdot 25}} = \sqrt{\frac{4}{25}} = \frac{2}{5}$

79. $\frac{1}{\sqrt{10}} \cdot \frac{\sqrt{10}}{\sqrt{10}} = \frac{\sqrt{10}}{10}$

80. $-2\sqrt{\frac{1}{6}} = \frac{-2\sqrt{1}}{\sqrt{6}} \cdot \frac{\sqrt{6}}{\sqrt{6}} = \frac{-2\sqrt{6}}{6} = -\frac{\sqrt{6}}{3}$

81. $\sqrt{\frac{14}{21}} = \sqrt{\frac{7 \cdot 2}{7 \cdot 3}} = \frac{\sqrt{2}}{\sqrt{3}} \cdot \frac{\sqrt{3}}{\sqrt{3}} = \frac{\sqrt{6}}{3}$

82. $\sqrt{\frac{1}{27}} = \frac{\sqrt{1}}{\sqrt{9 \cdot 3}} = \frac{1}{3\sqrt{3}} \cdot \frac{\sqrt{3}}{\sqrt{3}} = \frac{\sqrt{3}}{3 \cdot 3} = \frac{\sqrt{3}}{9}$

83. $y = -3x^2 + 6x - 1$

$-\frac{b}{2a} = -\frac{6}{2(-3)} = 1$

x	-1	0	1	2	3
y	-10	-1	2	-1	-10

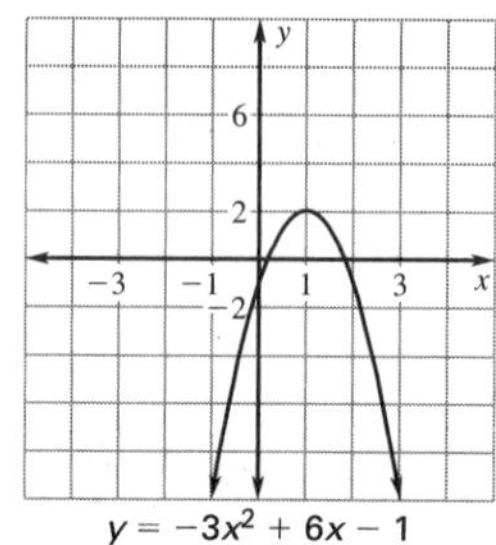

$y = -3x^2 + 6x - 1$

84. $y \geq 5x^2 + 20x + 15$

$-\frac{b}{2a} = -\frac{20}{2(5)} = -2$

x	-4	-3	-2	-1	0
y	15	0	-5	0	15

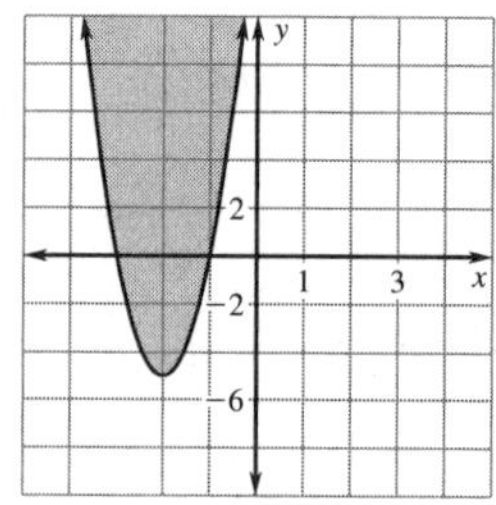

85. $y < 2x^2 - 5x + 2$

$-\frac{b}{2a} = -\frac{(-5)}{2(2)} = \frac{5}{4} = 1\frac{1}{4}$

x	0	1	$1\frac{1}{4}$	2	3
y	2	-1	$-1\frac{1}{8}$	0	5

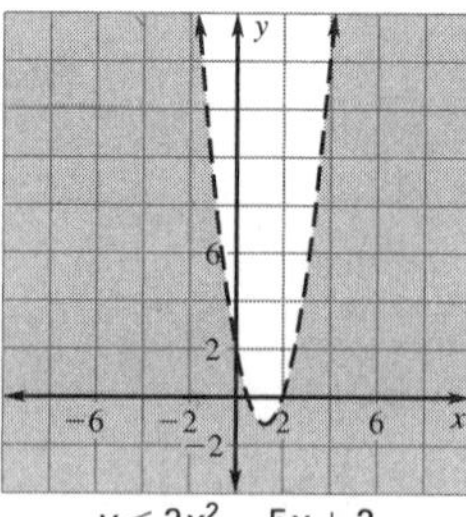

$y < 2x^2 - 5x + 2$

Copyright © McDougal Littell Inc.
All rights reserved.

86. $h = -16t^2 + vt + s$
$150 = -16t^2 + 100t + 0$
$0 = -16t^2 + 100t - 150$
$a = -16,\ b = 100,\ c = -150$

$$t = \frac{-100 \pm \sqrt{100^2 - 4(-16)(-150)}}{2(-16)}$$

$$t = \frac{-100 \pm \sqrt{10000 - 9600}}{-32}$$

$$t = \frac{-100 \pm \sqrt{400}}{-32} = \frac{-100 \pm 20}{-32}$$

$$t = \frac{-100 + 20}{-32} = \frac{-80}{-32} = 2.5$$

$$\text{and } t = \frac{-100 - 20}{-32} = \frac{-120}{-32} = 3.75$$

The flare first reaches a height of 150 feet after 2.5 seconds.

87. $h = -16t^2 + vt + s$
$180 = -16t^2 + 100t + 0$
$0 = -16t^2 + 100t - 180$
$b^2 - 4ac = 100^2 - 4(-16)(-180)$
$= 10{,}000 - 11{,}520 = -1520$; no real solution
The flare does not reach a height of 180 feet.

Chapters 7–9 Project *(p. 562)*

1.

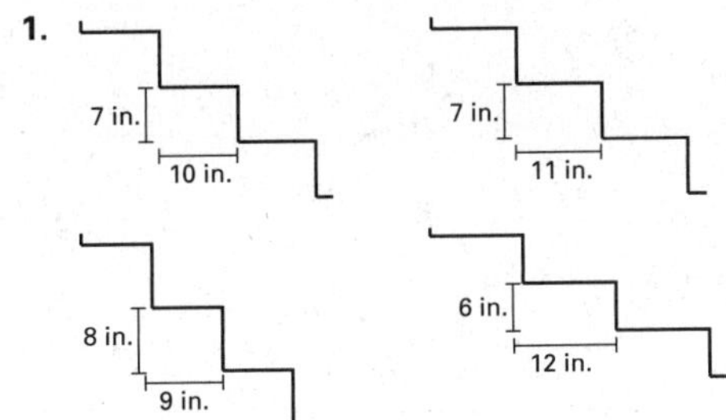

2. Stairway C is steepest. Stairway D gives the most foot space.

3. A: $\frac{7}{10} = 0.7$

B: $\frac{7}{11} \approx 0.6$

C: $\frac{8}{9} \approx 0.9$

D: $\frac{6}{12} = 0.5$

These ratios describe the slope of the stairway.

4. $t + 2r \geq 24,\ t + 2r \leq 25$
A: $10 + 2(7) = 24$;
B: $11 + 2(7) = 25$;
C: $9 + 2(8) = 25$;
D: $12 + 2(6) = 24$

5.

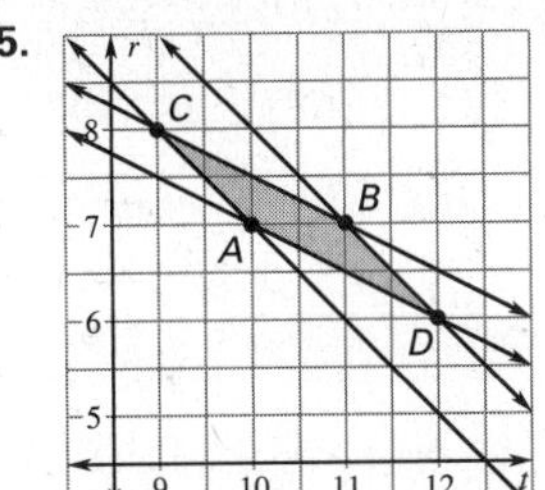

Each solution to the system represents a set of stair measurements that satisfies all four inequalities.

6. *Sample answer*: (11, 6.5); Tread = 11 in.,
riser = $6\frac{1}{2}$ in.

Copyright © McDougal Littell Inc.
All rights reserved.

CHAPTER 10

Chapter Opener

Think and Discuss (p. 565)

1. x-intercepts: (40, 0), (−40, 0)
The distance from one edge of the dish (or one x-intercept) to the other is 80 feet, which represents the diameter.

2. The distance from (0, 0) on the diameter to the center of the dish at approximately (0, −13) is about 13 feet.

Chapter Readiness Quiz (p. 566)

1. B; $3x(x + 6) = 3x \cdot x + 3x \cdot 6 = 3x^2 + 18x$
2. C; $(x^6)^2 = x^{6 \cdot 2} = x^{12}$
3. D; The discriminant, $(-4)^2 - 4(3)(6) = -56 < 0$, so there are no solutions.

Lesson 10.1

10.1 Developing Concepts: Think About It (p. 567)

1. 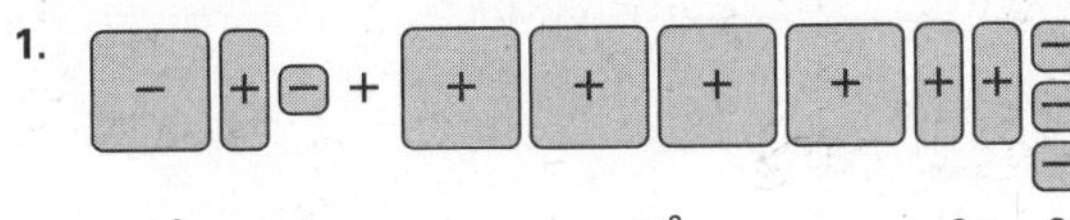

$-x^2 + x - 1$ $4x^2 + 2x - 3$

Combine like terms:

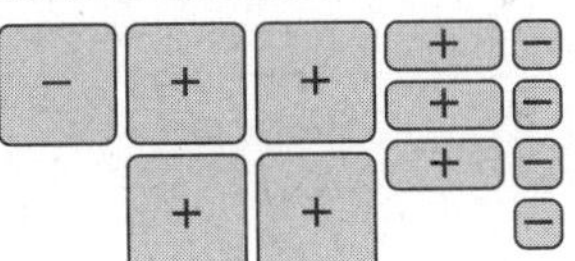

Remove the zero pairs:

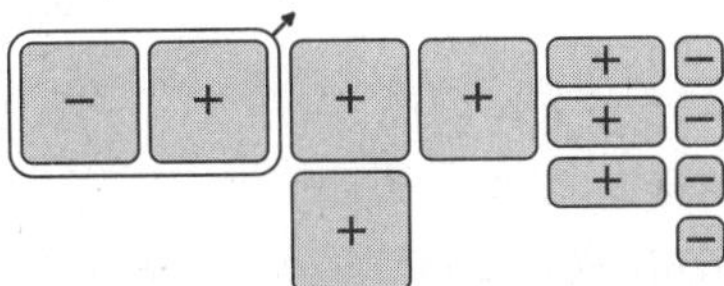

The sum is $3x^2 + 3x - 4$.

2. 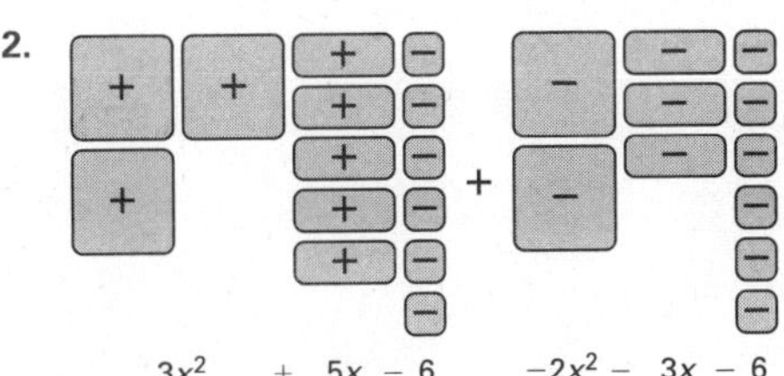

$3x^2 + 5x - 6$ $-2x^2 - 3x - 6$

Combine like terms:

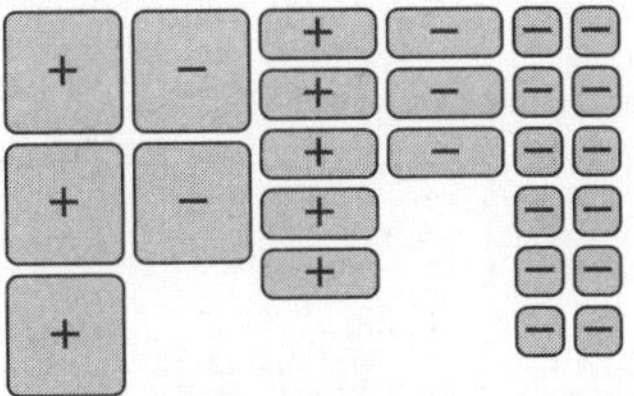

Remove the zero pairs:

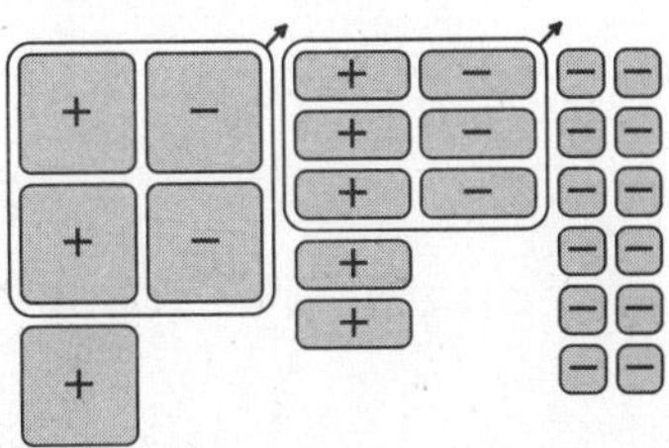

The sum is $x^2 + 2x - 12$.

3. 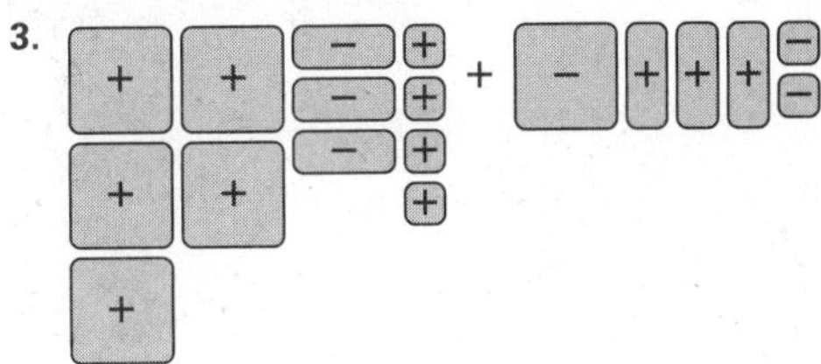

$5x^2 - 3x + 4$ $-x^2 + 3x - 2$

Combine like terms:

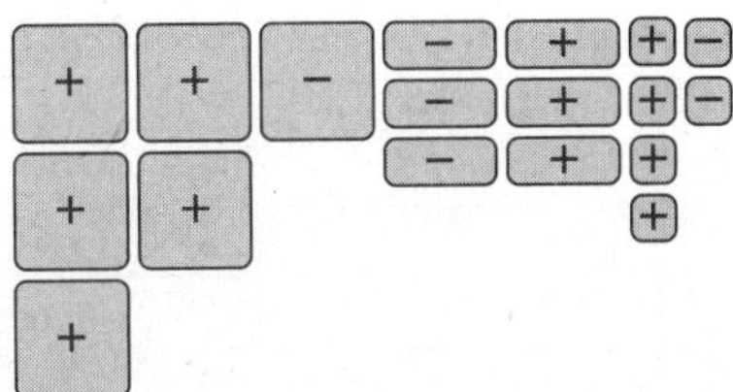

Remove the zero pairs:

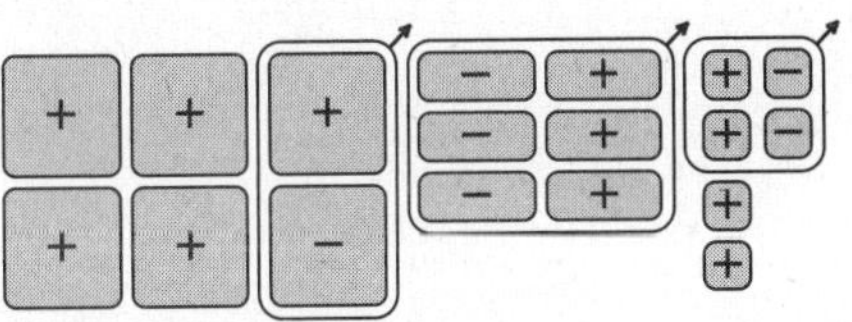

The sum is $4x^2 + 2$.

Copyright © McDougal Littell Inc.
All rights reserved.

4. 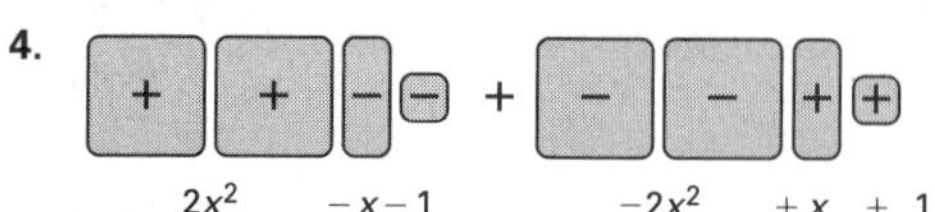

$2x^2 \quad -x-1 \quad -2x^2 \quad +x \quad +1$

Combine like terms:

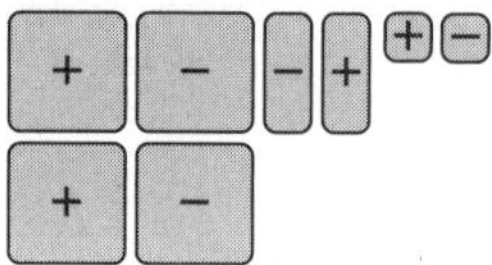

Remove the zero pairs:

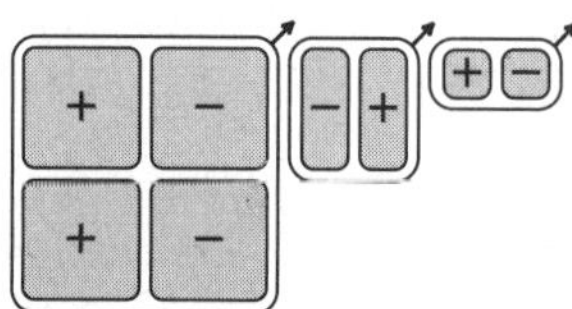

The sum is 0.

5. 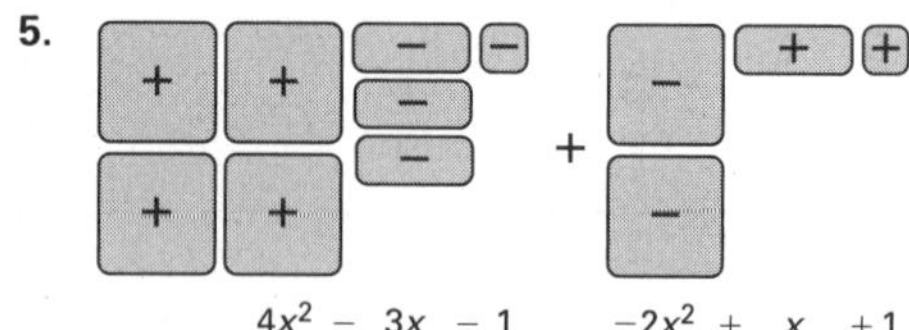

$4x^2 - 3x - 1 \quad -2x^2 + x + 1$

Combine like terms:

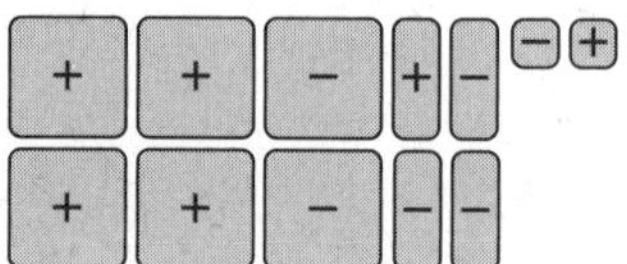

Remove the zero pairs:

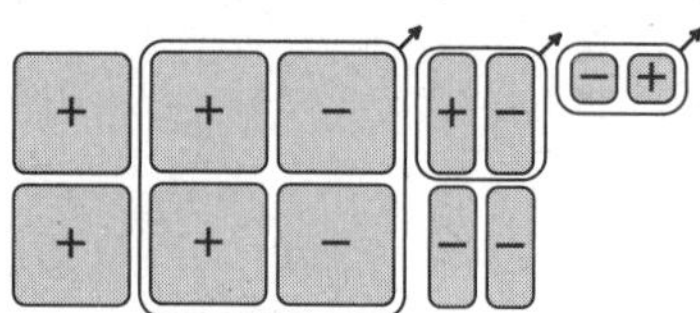

The sum is $2x^2 - 2x$.

6. 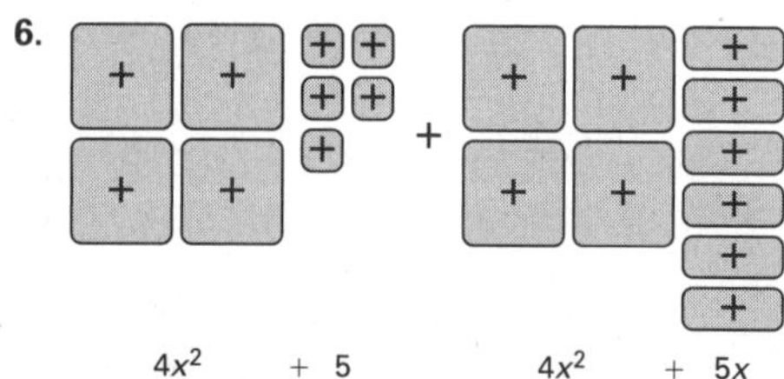

$4x^2 \quad + 5 \quad 4x^2 \quad + 5x$

Combine like terms:

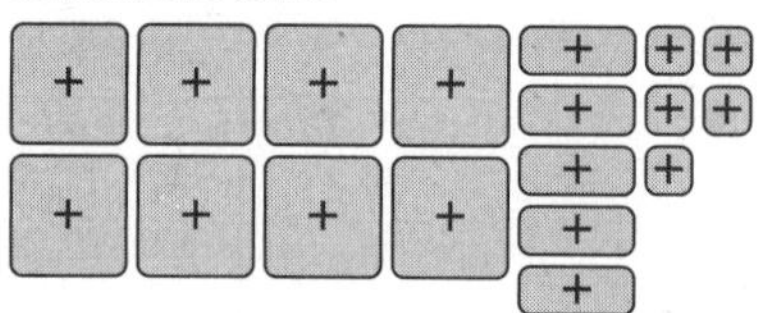

Since there are no zero pairs to remove, the sum is $8x^2 + 5x + 5$.

7. Add the opposite value of each term or multiply each term by -1 and then add.

8. 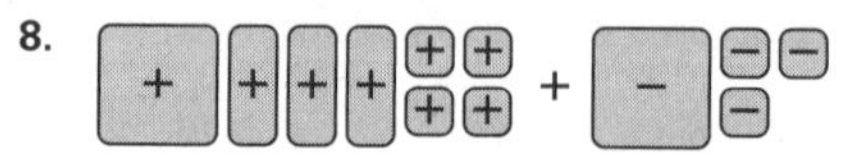

$x^2 + 3x + 4 \quad -x^2 - 3$

Combine like terms:

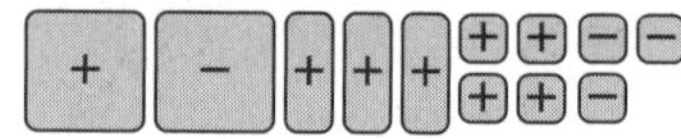

Remove the zero pairs:

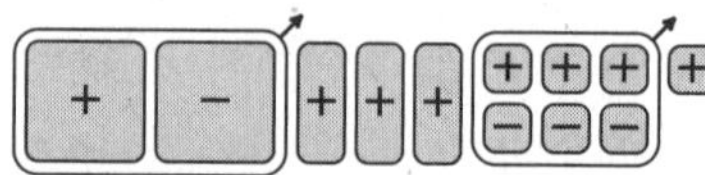

The sum is $3x + 1$.

9. 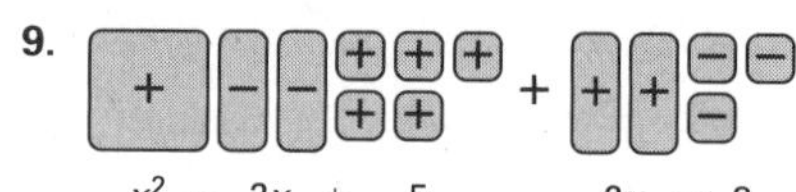

$x^2 - 2x + 5 \quad 2x - 3$

Combine like terms:

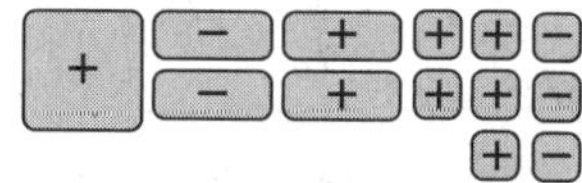

Remove the zero pairs:

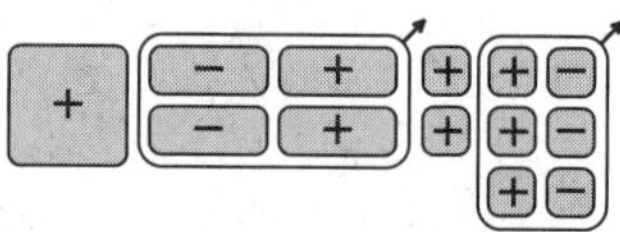

The sum is $x^2 + 2$.

10.1 Checkpoint (p. 568–570)

1. The exponent of x is 3, so the degree is 3.

2. The exponent of p is 1, so the degree is 1.

3. There is no variable, so the degree is 0.

4. The exponent of a is 5, so the degree is 5.

5. The degree of $8x$ is 1 and this is one term, so $8x$ is linear and is a monomial.

6. This polynomial has two terms and the degree is 1, so $10x - 5$ is linear and is a binomial.

7. This polynomial has three terms and the degree is 2, so $x^2 - 4x + 4$ is quadratic and is a trinomial.

8. This polynomial has two terms and the degree is 3, so $-24 - x^3$ is cubic and is a binomial.

9. $(x^2 + 2x^2) + (3x - 4x) + (2 + 2) = 3x^2 - x + 4$

10. $(2x^2 + x^2) + (-4x - 4x) + (3 - 4) = 3x^2 - 8x - 1$

11. $2x^2 + 3x - 5 - 2x - 8 - x^2$
$= (2x^2 - x^2) + (3x - 2x) + (-5 - 8)$
$= x^2 + x - 13$

12. $4x^3 + 4x^2 - x - 2 - 3x^3 + 2x^2 - 1$
$= (4x^3 - 3x^3) + (4x^2 + 2x^2) - x + (-2 - 1)$
$= x^3 + 6x^2 - x - 3$

Copyright © McDougal Littell Inc.
All rights reserved.

10.1 Guided Practice (p. 571)

1. No; the terms are not arranged in descending order.
2. No; the degree is 3 because $-4x^3$ has the largest exponent.
3. Two terms, degree = 1; this is a linear binomial
4. One term, degree = 3; $6x^3$ is a cubic monomial
5. Two terms, degree = 2; $12x^2 + 7x$ is a quadratic binomial.
6. Three terms, degree = 3; $4w^3 - 8w + 9$ is a cubic trinomial
7. Three terms, degree = 3; $7y + 2y^3 - y^2$ is a cubic trinomial
8. One term, degree = 0; -15 is a constant monomial
9. $-3x^2$ and $-5x$ are not like terms; $9x^3 - 3x^2 - 5x - 2$
10. distribute the negative sign to get $(-9x - 3x) + 7$; $12x^2 - 12x + 7$
11. $(2x + x) + (-9 - 7) = 3x - 16$
12. $7x - 3 - 9x + 2 = (7x - 9x) + (-3 + 2)$ $= -2x - 1$
13. $(x^2 + 3x^2) + (-4x - 3x) + (3 - 5) = 4x^2 - 7x - 2$
14. $3x^2 + 2x - 4 - 2x^2 - x + 1$ $= (3x^2 - 2x^2) + (2x - x) + (-4 + 1)$ $= x^2 + x - 3$

10.1 Practice and Applications (p. 571–572)

15. always
16. sometimes
17. sometimes
18. sometimes
19. always
20. 1
21. 4
22. 3
23. 4
24. $2x$; one term, degree = 1; linear monomial
25. $20m^3$; one term, degree = 3; cubic monomial
26. $7 - 3w$; two terms, degree = 1; linear binomial
27. -16; one term, degree = 0; constant monomial
28. $5y^2 - 3y + 8$; three terms, degree = 2; quadratic trinomial
29. $11y^3 - 14$; two terms, degree = 3; cubic binomial
30. $5x^3 - 2x - 6$; three terms, degree = 3; cubic trinomial
31. $7b^3 - 4b^2$; two terms, degree = 3, cubic binomial
32. $9w^3 + 14w^2$; two terms, degree = 3; cubic binomial
33. $\begin{array}{r} (12x^3 + x^2 \qquad) \\ -(18x^3 - 3x^2 + 6) \\ \hline \end{array}$ $\qquad \begin{array}{r} 12x^3 + x^2 \qquad \\ -18x^3 + 3x^2 - 6 \\ \hline -6x^3 + 4x^2 - 6 \end{array}$
34. $\begin{array}{r} (2a^3 + 3a^2 + a) \\ -(-a^3 + a^2 \qquad) \\ \hline \end{array}$ $\qquad \begin{array}{r} 2a^3 + 3a^2 + a \\ +a^3 - a^2 \qquad \\ \hline 3a^3 + 2a^2 + a \end{array}$
35. $\begin{array}{r} -8m^2 + 2m - 3 \\ + m^2 + 5m \qquad \\ \hline -7m^2 + 7m - 3 \end{array}$
36. $\begin{array}{r} 8y^2 + 2 \\ + -3y^2 + 5 \\ \hline 5y^2 + 7 \end{array}$
37. $\begin{array}{r} (3x^2 + 7x - 6) \\ -(3x^2 + 7x \qquad) \\ \hline \end{array}$ $\qquad \begin{array}{r} 3x^2 + 7x - 6 \\ -3x^2 - 7x \qquad \\ \hline -6 \end{array}$
38. $\begin{array}{r} 4x^2 - 7x + 2 \\ -x^2 + x - 2 \\ \hline 3x^2 - 6x \qquad \end{array}$
39. $(x^2 + 2x^2) + (-7 + 2) = 3x^2 - 5$
40. $(-3a^2 - a^2) + 4a + (5 - 6) = -4a^2 + 4a - 1$
41. $z^3 + (z^2 - z^2) + 1 = z^3 + 1$
42. $12 - y^3 - 10y - 16 = -y^3 - 10y + (12 - 16)$ $= -y^3 - 10y - 4$
43. $3n^2 + 2n - 7 - n^3 + n + 2$ $= -n^3 + 3n^2 + (2n + n) + (-7 + 2)$ $= -n^3 + 3n^2 + 3n - 5$
44. $3a^3 - 4a^2 + 3 - a^3 - 3a^2 + a + 4$ $= (3a^3 - a^3) + (-4a^2 - 3a^2) + a + (3 + 4)$ $= 2a^3 - 7a^2 + a + 7$
45. $\begin{array}{r} 9x^3 + 12x \qquad \\ +16x^3 - 4x + 2 \\ \hline 25x^3 + 8x + 2 \end{array}$
46. $-2t^4 + 6t^2 + 5 + 2t^4 - 5t^2 - 1$ $= (-2t^4 + 2t^4) + (6t^2 - 5t^2) + (5 - 1)$ $= t^2 + 4$
47. $\begin{array}{r} (2x^2 + 3x - 4) \\ -(x^2 + x - 6) \\ \hline \end{array}$ $\qquad \begin{array}{r} 2x^2 + 3x - 4 \\ -x^2 - x + 6 \\ \hline x^2 + 2x + 2 \end{array}$
48. $u^3 - u - u^2 - 5 = u^3 - u^2 - u - 5$
49. $-7x^2 + 12 - 6 + 4x^2 = (-7x^2 + 4x^2) + (12 - 6)$ $= -3x^2 + 6$
50. $\begin{array}{r} 10x^3 + 2x^2 \qquad\quad -11 \\ + \qquad 9x^2 + 2x - 1 \\ \hline 10x^3 + 11x^2 + 2x - 12 \end{array}$
51. Area of land $= 3x(x + 20) - 1.5x(x)$ $= 3x \cdot x + 3x \cdot 20 - 1.5x \cdot x$ $= 3x^2 + 60x - 1.5x^2$ $= 1.5x^2 + 60x$
52. Area of house $= 1.5x(x) = 1.5x^2$. If $x = 30$, the area of the house is $1.5(30)^2 = 1350$ ft². The area of the entire property when $x = 30$ is $3(30)^2 + 60(30) = 4500$ ft².
53. Add the polynomials for N and E:

$$\begin{array}{r} 1.488t^2 - 3.403t + 65.590 \\ + -0.107t^2 + 6.897t + 169.735 \\ \hline 1.381t^2 + 3.494t + 235.325 \end{array}$$

So, $A = 1.381t^2 + 3.494t + 235.325$

Copyright © McDougal Littell Inc.
All rights reserved.

54. In 2020, $t = 31$. Compare the values of N and E when $t = 31$.
$N = 1.488(31)^2 - 3.403(31) + 65.590 \approx 1390$
$E = -0.107(31)^2 + 6.897(31) + 169.735 \approx 281$
Therefore, according to the models more money will be spent on natural gas in 2020.

10.1 Standardized Test Practice (p. 573)

55. B; it should be $3y^3 - y^2 + 4y - 15$

56. F; 4 since the exponent of x is 4

57. D; there is only one term

10.1 Mixed Review (p. 573)

58. $-3(x + 1) - 2 = -3x - 3 - 2 = -3x - 5$

59. $(2x - 1)(2) + x = 4x - 2 + x = 5x - 2$

60. $11x + 3(8 - x) = 11x + 24 - 3x$
$= 8x + 24$

61. $(5x - 1)(-3) + 6 = -15x + 3 + 6 = -15x + 9$

62. $-4(1 - x) + 7 = -4 + 4x + 7 = 4x + 3$

63. $-12x - 5(11 - x) = -12x - 55 + 5x = -7x - 55$

64.

miles/gallon	24.0	24.1	23.9	24.1	24.0	24.0

65. $2^2 \cdot 2^3 = 2^{2+3} = 2^5 = 32$

66. $(3^2 \cdot 1^3)^2 = (3^2)^2 = 3^4 = 81$

67. $[(-1)^8 \cdot 2^4]^2 = (1 \cdot 2^4)^2$
$= (2^4)^2$
$= 2^{4 \cdot 2}$
$= 2^8 = 256$

68. $(-1 \cdot 3^2)^3 = (-3^2)^3 = (-9)^3 = -729$

69. $(2^2 \cdot 2^2) = (2^{2+2})^2$
$= (2^4)^2$
$= 2^{4 \cdot 2}$
$= 2^8 = 256$

70. $(3^2 \cdot 2^3)^3 = (9 \cdot 8)^3 = (72)^3 = 373{,}248$

71. Population in 2025:
$P(30) = 4227(1.0104)^{30} \approx 5765$
Population in 2000:
$P(5) = 4227(1.0104)^5 \approx 4451$
The ratio of the population in 2025 to the population in 2000 is $\frac{5765}{4451} \approx 1.295$. The ratio of the population in 2000 to the population in 1995 is $\frac{4451}{4227} \approx 1.053$.

10.1 Maintaining Skills (p. 573)

72. $\frac{12}{11} + 1\frac{3}{11} = 1\frac{1}{11} + 1\frac{3}{11} = 2\frac{4}{11}$

73. $\frac{2}{5} + 3\frac{3}{5} = 3\frac{5}{5} = 4$

74. $1\frac{2}{3} + \frac{1}{6} = 1\frac{4}{6} + \frac{1}{6} = 1\frac{5}{6}$

75. $\frac{1}{8} + 1\frac{1}{2} = \frac{1}{8} + 1\frac{4}{8} = 1\frac{5}{8}$

76. $\frac{11}{3} + 5\frac{5}{6} = \frac{22}{6} + 5\frac{5}{6}$
$= 3\frac{4}{6} + 5\frac{5}{6}$
$= 8\frac{9}{6} = 9\frac{3}{6} = 9\frac{1}{2}$

77. $2\frac{3}{4} + \frac{19}{20} = 2\frac{15}{20} + \frac{19}{20} = 2\frac{34}{20} = 3\frac{14}{20} = 3\frac{7}{10}$

78. $5\frac{1}{2} + 4\frac{5}{16} = 5\frac{8}{16} + 4\frac{5}{16} = 9\frac{13}{16}$

79. $9\frac{2}{7} + 3\frac{11}{28} = 9\frac{8}{28} + 3\frac{11}{28} = 12\frac{19}{28}$

80. $2\frac{1}{2} + \frac{4}{3} = 2\frac{3}{6} + \frac{8}{6} = 2\frac{3}{6} + 1\frac{2}{6} = 3\frac{5}{6}$

81. $2\frac{1}{2} + \frac{5}{7} = 2\frac{7}{14} + \frac{10}{14} = 2\frac{17}{14} = 3\frac{3}{14}$

82. $12\frac{7}{12} + 8\frac{9}{32} = 12\frac{56}{96} + 8\frac{27}{96} = 20\frac{83}{96}$

83. $9\frac{7}{24} + 6\frac{5}{36} = 9\frac{21}{72} + 6\frac{10}{72} = 15\frac{31}{72}$

Lesson 10.2

10.2 Developing Concepts: Try These *(p. 574)*

1.
$$\begin{array}{r} x + 3 \\ \times\ x + 7 \\ \hline 7x + 21 \\ x^2 + 3x \\ \hline x^2 + 10x + 21 \end{array}$$

2.
$$\begin{array}{r} 2x + 5 \\ \times\ 3x + 4 \\ \hline 8x + 20 \\ 6x^2 + 15x \\ \hline 6x^2 + 23x + 20 \end{array}$$

3.
$$\begin{array}{r} x - 5 \\ \times\ x + 7 \\ \hline 7x - 35 \\ x^2 - 5x \\ \hline x^2 + 2x - 35 \end{array}$$

4.
$$\begin{array}{r} 4x + 1 \\ \times\ 5x + 2 \\ \hline 8x + 2 \\ 20x^2 + 5x \\ \hline 20x^2 + 13x + 2 \end{array}$$

Copyright © McDougal Littell Inc.
All rights reserved.

5.
$$\begin{array}{r} 3x - 1 \\ \times\ 5x - 2 \\ \hline -6x + 2 \\ 15x^2 - 5x \quad \\ \hline 15x^2 - 11x + 2 \end{array}$$

6.
$$\begin{array}{r} 3x + 7 \\ \times\ 2x + 9 \\ \hline 27x + 63 \\ 6x^2 + 14x \quad\quad \\ \hline 6x^2 + 41x + 63 \end{array}$$

7.
$$\begin{array}{r} x^2 + 2x + 3 \\ \times\ x + 4 \\ \hline 4x^2 + 8x + 12 \\ x^3 + 2x^2 + 3x \quad\quad \\ \hline x^3 + 6x^2 + 11x + 12 \end{array}$$

8.
$$\begin{array}{r} x^2 - 4x + 6 \\ \times\ x - 2 \\ \hline -2x^2 + 8x - 12 \\ x^3 - 4x^2 + 6x \quad\quad \\ \hline x^3 - 6x^2 + 14x - 12 \end{array}$$

9.
$$\begin{array}{r} x^2 + 3x + 5 \\ \times\ 3x + 1 \\ \hline x^2 + 3x + 5 \\ 3x^3 + 9x^2 + 15x \quad\quad \\ \hline 3x^3 + 10x^2 + 18x + 5 \end{array}$$

10.
$$\begin{array}{r} x^2 + 5x - 7 \\ \times\ 4x - 1 \\ \hline -x^2 - 5x + 7 \\ 4x^3 + 20x^2 - 28x \quad\quad \\ \hline 4x^3 + 19x^2 - 33x + 7 \end{array}$$

11. Answers may vary. Sample: Distribute the x and the 4 across $(3x + 2)$ to get
$3x^2 + 2x + 12x + 8 = 3x^2 + 14x + 8$.

10.2 Checkpoint (p. 575–577)

1. $(x + 1)(x + 2) = x(x + 2) + 1(x + 2)$
$= x(x) + x(2) + 1(x) + 1(2)$
$= x^2 + 2x + x + 2$
$= x^2 + 3x + 2$

2. $(x - 2)(x + 4) = x(x + 4) - 2(x + 4)$
$= x(x) + x(4) - 2(x) - 2(4)$
$= x^2 + 4x - 2x - 8$
$= x^2 + 2x - 8$

3. $(2x + 1)(x + 2) = 2x(x + 2) + 1(x + 2)$
$= 2x(x) + 2x(2) + 1(x) + 1(2)$
$= 2x^2 + 4x + 1x + 2$
$= 2x^2 + 5x + 2$

4. $(x + 1)(x - 4) = \overset{F}{x^2} - \overset{O}{4x} + \overset{I}{1x} - \overset{L}{4} = x^2 - 3x - 4$

5. $(2x - 3)(x - 1) = \overset{F}{2x^2} - \overset{O}{2x} - \overset{I}{3x} + \overset{L}{3} = 2x^2 - 5x + 3$

6. $(x - 2)(2x + 1) = \overset{F}{2x^2} + \overset{O}{1x} - \overset{I}{4x} - \overset{L}{2} = 2x^2 - 3x - 2$

7.
$$\begin{array}{r} x^2 + 3x - 2 \\ \times\ x + 1 \\ \hline x^2 + 3x - 2 \\ x^3 + 3x^2 - 2x \quad\quad \\ \hline x^3 + 4x^2 + x - 2 \end{array}$$

8.
$$\begin{array}{r} 2x^2 + x - 3 \\ \times\ 2x - 1 \\ \hline -2x^2 - x + 3 \\ 4x^3 + 2x^2 - 6x \quad\quad \\ \hline 4x^3 \quad\quad - 7x + 3 \end{array}$$

9.
$$\begin{array}{r} 3x^2 + x - 4 \\ \times\ 2x - 3 \\ \hline -9x^2 - 3x + 12 \\ 6x^3 + 2x^2 - 8x \quad\quad \\ \hline 6x^3 - 7x^2 - 11x + 12 \end{array}$$

10. $(x - 4)(x^2 + x + 1)$
$= x(x^2 + x + 1) - 4(x^2 + x + 1)$
$= x(x^2) + x(x) + x(1) - 4(x^2) - 4(x) - 4(1)$
$= x^3 + x^2 + x - 4x^2 - 4x - 4$
$= x^3 - 3x^2 - 3x - 4$

11. $(x + 5)(x^2 - x - 3)$
$= x(x^2 - x - 3) + 5(x^2 - x - 3)$
$= x(x^2) + x(-x) + x(-3) + 5(x^2)$
$+ 5(-x) + 5(-3)$
$= x^3 - x^2 - 3x + 5x^2 - 5x - 15$
$= x^3 + 4x^2 - 8x - 15$

12. $(2x + 1)(3x^2 + x - 1)$
$= 2x(3x^2 + x - 1) + 1(3x^2 + x - 1)$
$= 2x(3x^2) + 2x(x) + 2x(-1)$
$+ 1(3x^2) + 1(x) + 1(-1)$
$= 6x^3 + 2x^2 - 2x + 3x^2 + x - 1$
$= 6x^3 + 5x^2 - x - 1$

13. Glass has a height of $5x$ and a width of $3x$, so the total area of the window will be $(5x + 10)(3x + 6)$.
$A = (5x + 10)(3x + 6)$
$= 5x(3x) + 5x(6) + 10(3x) + 10(6)$
$= 15x^2 + 30x + 30x + 60$
$= 15x^2 + 60x + 60$

10.2 Guided Practice (p. 578)

1. FOIL describes a pattern for multiplying two binomials. It stands for First, Outside, Inside, and Last.

2. Answers may vary. Sample: $3x$; $2x - 5$; $3x^2 + x - 2$

3. $x\underline{(x + 3)} - 2\underline{(x + 3)}$

4. $3x\underline{(2x - 1)} + 4\underline{(2x - 1)}$

5. $x^2 - 2x - \underline{3}$

6. $x^2 + \underline{8x} + 12$

7. $x^2 - 9x + \underline{20}$

8. $\underline{2x^2} + 5x + 2$

9. $-2x(4x) - 2x(7) = -8x^2 - 14x$

10. $2x(x^2) + 2x(x) + 2x(-5) = 2x^3 + 2x^2 - 10x$

11. $-4x^2(3x^2) - 4x^2(2x) - 4x^2(-6)$
$= -12x^4 - 8x^3 + 24x^2$

12. $a(a + 5) + 4(a + 5)$
$= a(a) + a(5) + 4(a) + 4(5)$
$= a^2 + 5a + 4a + 20$
$= a^2 + 9a + 20$

Copyright © McDougal Littell Inc.
All rights reserved.

13. $y(y + 8) - 2(y + 8)$
$= y(y) + y(8) - 2(y) - 2(8)$
$= y^2 + 8y - 2y - 16$
$= y^2 + 6y - 16$

14. $2x(4x + 1) + 3(4x + 1)$
$= 2x(4x) + 2x(1) + 3(4x) + 3(1)$
$= 8x^2 + 2x + 12x + 3$
$= 8x^2 + 14x + 3$

15. $\overset{F}{w^2} + \overset{O}{5w} - \overset{I}{3w} - \overset{L}{15} = w^2 + 2w - 15$

16. $\overset{F}{x^2} + \overset{O}{9x} + \overset{I}{6x} + \overset{L}{54} = x^2 + 15x + 54$

17. $\overset{F}{8x^2} + \overset{O}{3x} - \overset{I}{32x} - \overset{L}{12} = 8x^2 - 29x - 12$

18. $\overset{F}{x^2} + \overset{O}{4x} - \overset{I}{3x} - \overset{L}{12} = x^2 + x - 12$

19. $\overset{F}{x^2} - \overset{O}{7x} + \overset{I}{8x} - \overset{L}{56} = x^2 + x - 56$

20. $\overset{F}{6x^2} - \overset{O}{3x} - \overset{I}{8x} + \overset{L}{4} = 6x^2 - 11x + 4$

10.2 Practice and Applications (p. 578–580)

21. $-4x(2x) - 4x(-5) = -8x^2 + 20x$

22. $3t^2(-t^3 + 7t - 3) = 3t^2(-t^3) + 3t^2(7t) + 3t^2(-3)$
$= -3t^5 + 21t^3 - 9t^2$

23. $2x(x^2) + 2x(-8x) + 2x(1) = 2x^3 - 16x^2 + 2x$

24. $-y(6y^2) - y(5y) = -6y^3 - 5y^2$

25. $4w^2(3w^3) + 4w^2(-2w^2) + 4w^2(-w)$
$= 12w^5 - 8w^4 - 4w^3$

26. $-b^2(6b^3) - b^2(-16b) - b^2(11)$
$= -6b^5 + 16b^3 - 11b^2$

27. $t^2 + 5t + 8t + 40 = t^2 + 13t + 40$

28. $x^2 - 2x + 6x - 12 = x^2 + 4x - 12$

29. $d^2 + 3d - 5d - 15 = d^2 - 2d - 15$

30. $a^2 - 3a + 8a - 24 = a^2 + 5a - 24$

31. $2y^2 + y + 4y + 2 = 2y^2 + 5y + 2$

32. $4m^2 + 3m - 8m - 6 = 4m^2 - 5m - 6$

33. $3s^2 + 6s - s - 2 = 3s^2 + 5s - 2$

34. $6d^2 + 2d + 9d + 3 = 6d^2 + 11d + 3$

35. $8y^2 - 4y - 14y + 7 = 8y^2 - 18y + 7$

36. $a^2 + 7a + 6a + 42 = a^2 + 13a + 42$

37. $y^2 - 8y + 5y - 40 = y^2 - 3y - 40$

38. $x^2 - 6x + 6x - 36 = x^2 - 36$

39. $2w^2 + 10w - 5w - 25 = 2w^2 + 5w - 25$

40. $4b^2 - 24b - b + 6 = 4b^2 - 25b + 6$

41. $2x^2 + 15x - 18x - 135 = 2x^2 - 3x - 135$

42. $3a^2 - 27a - a + 9 = 3a^2 - 28a + 9$

43. $6z^2 + 4z + 21z + 14 = 6z^2 + 25z + 14$

44. $12q^2 + 32q - 3q - 8 = 12q^2 + 29q - 8$

45. $10t^2 + 15t - 6t - 9 = 10t^2 + 9t - 9$

46. $16x^2 - 12x + 20x - 15 = 16x^2 + 8x - 15$

47. $63w^2 - 108w - 35w + 60 = 63w^2 - 143w + 60$

48.
$$\begin{array}{r} x^2 + 3x + 5 \\ \times\ x + 2 \\ \hline 2x^2 + 6x + 10 \\ x^3 + 3x^2 + 5x \\ \hline x^3 + 5x^2 + 11x + 10 \end{array}$$

49.
$$\begin{array}{r} d^2 - 2d - 6 \\ \times\ d - 5 \\ \hline -5d^2 + 10d + 30 \\ d^3 - 2d^2 - 6d \\ \hline d^3 - 7d^2 + 4d + 30 \end{array}$$

50.
$$\begin{array}{r} a^2 - 4a - 6 \\ \times\ a - 3 \\ \hline -3a^2 + 12a + 18 \\ a^3 - 4a^2 - 6a \\ \hline a^3 - 7a^2 + 6a + 18 \end{array}$$

51.
$$\begin{array}{r} 3x^2 - 4x + 2 \\ \times\ 2x + 3 \\ \hline 9x^2 - 12x + 6 \\ 6x^3 - 8x^2 + 4x \\ \hline 6x^3 + x^2 - 8x + 6 \end{array}$$

52. $x^3 - 2x^2 + 3x + 4x^2 - 8x + 12$
$= x^3 + 2x^2 - 5x + 12$

53. $a^3 + 6a^2 - 7a - 2a^2 - 12a + 14$
$= a^3 + 4a^2 - 19a + 14$

54. $(m - 4)(m^2 + 2m - 9)$
$= m^3 + 2m^2 - 9m - 4m^2 - 8m + 36$
$= m^3 - 2m^2 - 17m + 36$

55. $(y + 12)(4y^2 - 3y - 2)$
$= 4y^3 - 3y^2 - 2y + 48y^2 - 36y - 24$
$= 4y^3 + 45y^2 - 38y - 24$

56. $(3x + 4)(2x + 4) = 6x^2 + 12x + 8x + 16$
$= 6x^2 + 20x + 16$

57. $(7x + 10)(3x + 10) = 21x^2 + 70x + 30x + 100$
$= 21x^2 + 100x + 100$

58. $3x + 10 = 160$
$3x = 150$
$x = 50$
$7x + 10 = 360$
$7x = 350$
$x = 50$

59. $R = (15t + 281)(-0.21t + 3.52)$
$= -3.15t^2 + 52.8t - 59.01t + 989.12$
$= -3.15t^2 - 6.21t + 989.12$

60. Sample answer: The revenue will decrease over time.

61. $(2x + 1)(x + 3) = 2x(x + 3) + 1(x + 3)$
$= 2x(x) + 2x(3) + 1(x) + 1(3)$
$= 2x^2 + 6x + x + 3$
$= 2x^2 + 7x + 3$

Sample answer: The second application of the distributive property results in four terms, which are the product of the First, Outer, Inner, and Last terms of the two original binomials.

Copyright © McDougal Littell Inc.
All rights reserved.

Chapter 10 *continued*

10.2 Standardized Test Practice (p. 580)

62. D; $2a^4 - 6a^3 + 2a^2$

63. F; $x^2 - 2x + 9x - 18 = x^2 + 7x - 18$

64. C; $2x^3 + x^2 + x - 2x^2 - x - 1 = 2x^3 - x^2 - 1$

10.2 Mixed Review (p. 580)

65. $(7x)(7x) = 49x^2$

66. $\left(\frac{1}{3}m\right)\left(\frac{1}{3}m\right) = \frac{1}{9}m^2$

67. $\left(\frac{2}{5}y\right)\left(\frac{2}{5}y\right) = \frac{4}{25}y^2$

68. $(0.5w)(0.5w) = 0.25w^2$

69. $9^{3+5} = 9^8$ **70.** $4^{2 \cdot 4} = 4^8$ **71.** $b^{2+5} = b^7$

72. $4^4c^{2 \cdot 4} = 4^4c^8 = 256c^8$

73. $2^4t^4 \cdot 3^3 = 16t^4 \cdot 81 = 432t^4$

74. $(-1)^3w^{4 \cdot 3} = -w^{12}$

75. $(-3)^3x^3y^3 2^2y^2 = -27x^3y^3 \cdot 4y^2 = -108x^3y^5$

76. $8^3x^{2 \cdot 3}y^{8 \cdot 3} = 512x^6y^{24}$

77. $(-5)^2 - 4(1)(6) = 1 > 0$, two solutions

78. $7^2 - 4(1)(12) = 1 > 0$, two solutions

79. $(-2)^2 - 4(1)(-24) = 100 > 0$, two solutions

80. $(-3)^2 - 4(2)(-1) = 17 > 0$, two solutions

81. $4^2 - 4(4)(1) = 0$, one solution

82. $(-7)^2 - 4(3)(5) = -11 < 0$, no real solution

83. $(-8)^2 - 4(7)(-6) = 232 > 0$, two solutions

84. $(-13)^2 - 4(10)(-9) = 529 > 0$, two solutions

85. $(-12)^2 - 4(6)(-6) = 288 > 0$, two solutions

86.

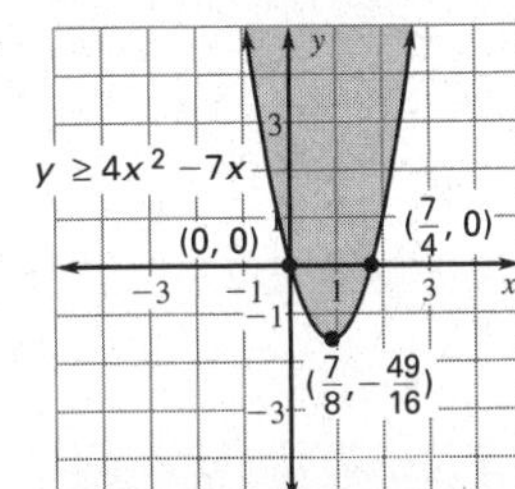

87.

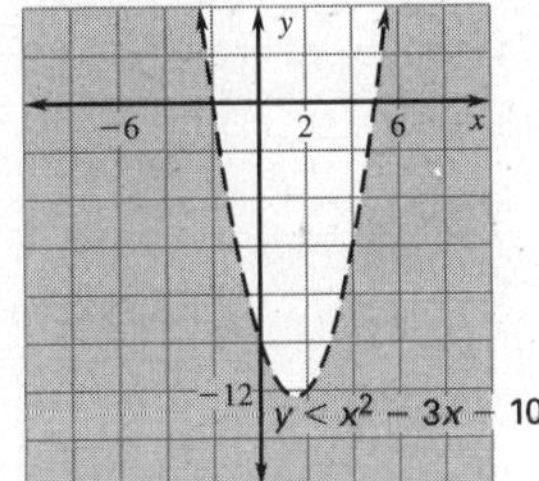

88.

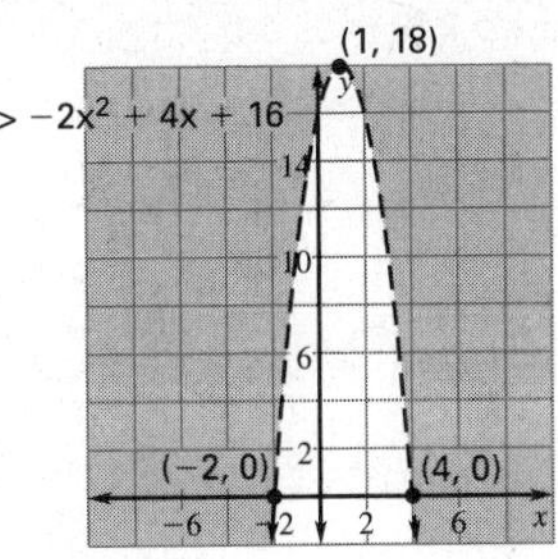

89. $\frac{1.5 \times 10^8}{4.5 \times 10^9} = 0.\overline{3} \times 10^{-1} = 0.0\overline{3}$

10.2 Maintaining Skills (p. 580)

90. $\frac{1}{6} \times \frac{3}{2} = \frac{3}{12} = \frac{1}{4}$

91. $\frac{3}{4} \times \frac{24}{9} = \frac{72}{36} = 2$

92. $\frac{7}{8} \times \frac{2}{5} = \frac{14}{40} = \frac{7}{20}$

93. $\frac{3}{4} \times \frac{9}{2} = \frac{27}{8}$

94. $\frac{13}{15} \times \frac{10}{7} = \frac{130}{105} = \frac{26}{21}$

95. $\frac{29}{32} \times \frac{24}{23} = \frac{696}{736} = \frac{87}{92}$

96. $\frac{11}{16} \times \frac{12}{11} = \frac{132}{176} = \frac{3}{4}$

97. $\frac{3}{2} \times \frac{4}{3} = \frac{12}{6} = 2$

98. $\frac{7}{3} \times \frac{27}{7} = \frac{189}{21} = 9$

Lesson 10.3

10.3 Checkpoint (p. 582–584)

1. $x^2 - 2^2 = x^2 - 4$

2. $n^2 - 3^2 = n^2 - 9$

3. $p^2 - 8^2 = p^2 - 64$

4. $(2x)^2 - 1^2 = 4x^2 - 1$

5. $(3x)^2 - 2^2 = 9x^2 - 4$

6. $(2x)^2 - 5^2 = 4x^2 - 25$

7. $x^2 + 2(x)(1) + 1^2 = x^2 + 2x + 1$

8. $t^2 - 2(t)(3) + 3^2 = t^2 - 6t + 9$

9. $a^2 - 2(a)(7) + 7^2 = a^2 - 14a + 49$

10. $(2x)^2 + 2(2x)(1) + 1^2 = 4x^2 + 4x + 1$

11. $(4x)^2 - 2(4x)(1) + 1^2 = 16x^2 - 8x + 1$

12. $(3a)^2 - 2(3a)(4) + 4^2 = 9a^2 - 24a + 16$

13. $A = (x + 2)^2 = x^2 + 4x + 4$; square of a binomial

14. a. $(0.5C + 0.5c)^2$
$= (0.5C)^2 + 2(0.5C)(0.5c) + (0.5c)^2$
$= 0.25C^2 + 0.5Cc + 0.25c^2$

b. Since $\frac{3}{4}$ of the square is made up of *CC* or *Cc*, and $\frac{1}{4}$ is made up of *cc*, 75% will have normal coloring and 25% will be white.

10.3 Guided Practice (p. 585)

1. $(a + b)(a - b) = a^2 - b^2$

2. Square of a binomial

3. $(x - 6)^2 = x^2 - 2(x)(6) + 6^2$
$= x^2 - 12x + 36$

Copyright © McDougal Littell Inc.
All rights reserved.

4. $(w + 11)(w - 11) = w^2 - 11^2 = w^2 - 121$

5. $(6 + p)^2 = (p + 6)^2$
$= p^2 + 2p(6) + 6^2$
$= p^2 + 12p + 36$

6. $(3y - 1)^2 = (3y)^2 - 2(3y)(1) + 1^2$
$= 9y^2 - 6y + 1$

7. $(t - 6)(t + 6) = t^2 - 6^2 = t^2 - 36$

8. $(a - 2)(a + 2) = a^2 - 2^2 = a^2 - 4$

9. false; $9x^2 + 24x + 16$ **10.** true

11. true **12.** false; $4x^2 - 36$

10.3 Practice and Applications (p. 585–587)

13. yes **14.** yes **15.** no **16.** no

17. yes **18.** no **19.** yes **20.** no

21. yes **22.** yes

23. $x^2 - 5^2 = x^2 - 25$ **24.** $y^2 - 1^2 = y^2 - 1$

25. $(2m)^2 - 2^2 = 4m^2 - 4$ **26.** $(3b)^2 - 1^2 = 9b^2 - 1$

27. $3^2 - (2x)^2 = 9 - 4x^2$ **28.** $6^2 - (5n)^2 = 36 - 25n^2$

29. $x^2 + 2x(5) + 5^2 = x^2 + 10x + 25$

30. $a^2 + 2a(8) + 8^2 = a^2 + 16a + 64$

31. $(3x)^2 + 2(3x)(1) + 1^2 = 9x^2 + 6x + 1$

32. $(2y)^2 - 2(2y)(4) + 4^2 = 4y^2 - 16y + 16$

33. $(4b)^2 - 2(4b)(3) + 3^2 = 16b^2 - 24b + 9$

34. $x^2 - 2x(7) + 7^2 = x^2 - 14x + 49$

35. $x^2 - 4^2 = x^2 - 16$

36. $x^2 - 3^2 = x^2 - 9$

37. $(3x)^2 - 2(3x)(1) + 1^2 = 9x^2 - 6x + 1$

38. $(4 - n)^2 = (n - 4)^2$
$= n^2 - 2n(4) + 4^2$
$= n^2 - 8n + 16$

39. $(2y)^2 - 5^2 = 4y^2 - 25$

40. $(4n)^2 - 2(4n)(3) + 3^2 = 16n^2 - 24n + 9$

41. $a^2 - (2b)^2 = a^2 - 4b^2$

42. $(4x)^2 + 2(4x)(5) + 5^2 = 16x^2 + 40x + 25$

43. $(3x)^2 - (4y)^2 = 9x^2 - 16y^2$

44. $(3y)^2 + 2(3y)(8) + 8^2 = 9y^2 + 48y + 64$

45. $9^2 - (4t)^2 = 81 - 16t^2$

46. $a^2 - 2(a)(2b) + (2b)^2 = a^2 - 4ab + 4b^2$

47. false; $a^2 + 4ab + 4b^2$ **48.** false; $9s^2 - 4t^2$

49. true **50.** false; $36y^2 - 84wy + 49w^2$

51. $(x + 3)^2 = x^2 + 6x + 9$; square of a binomial

52. $(2x + 2)^2 = (2x)^2 + 2(2x)(2) + 2^2$
$= 4x^2 + 8x + 4$; square of a binomial

53. $(2x + 4)^2 = (2x)^2 + 2(2x)(4) + 4^2$
$= 4x^2 + 16x + 16$; square of a binomial

54. If $A = 4x^2 - 20x + 25$, then $A = (2x - 5)^2$. So, $P = 4(2x - 5) = 8x - 20$.

55. $A = (3x - 4)^2$
$= (3x)^2 - 2(3x)(4) + 4^2$
$= (9x^2 - 24x + 16)$ square inches

56. $(0.5F + 0.5N)^2 = (0.5F)^2 + 2(0.5F)(0.5N) + (0.5N)^2$
$= 0.25F^2 + 0.5FN + 0.25N^2$

57. Since $\frac{1}{4}$ of the square is NN, there are 25% normal feathers. Since $\frac{1}{2}$ of the square is NF, there are 50% mildly frizzled. Since $\frac{1}{4}$ of the square is FF, there are 25% extremely frizzled.

10.3 Standardized Test Practice (p. 587)

58. B; $(2x)^2 - 3^2 = 4x^2 - 9$

59. J; $(3x)^2 + 2(3x)(5) + 5^2 = 9x^2 + 30x + 25$

10.3 Mixed Review (p. 587)

60. $\frac{6^2}{x^2} = \frac{36}{x^2}$ **61.** $x^{3-2} = x^1 = x$

62. $\frac{x^7}{x^4} = x^{7-4} = x^3$

63. $\frac{45x^{4+1}y^{1+1}}{3x^{1+2}y^{2+1}} = \frac{45x^5y^2}{3x^3y^3} = \frac{15x^{5-3}}{y^{3-2}} = \frac{15x^2}{y}$

64.

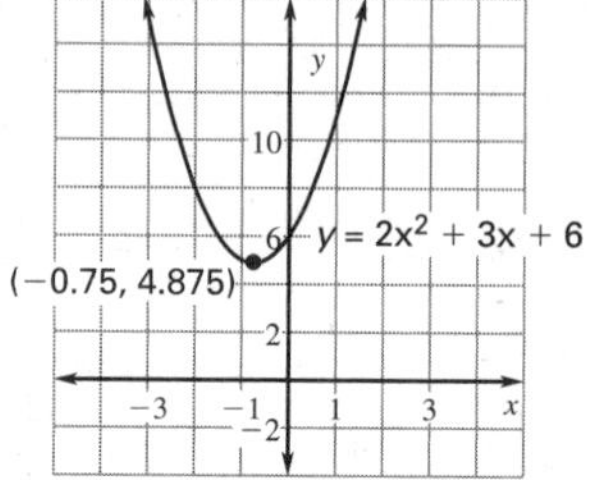

65.

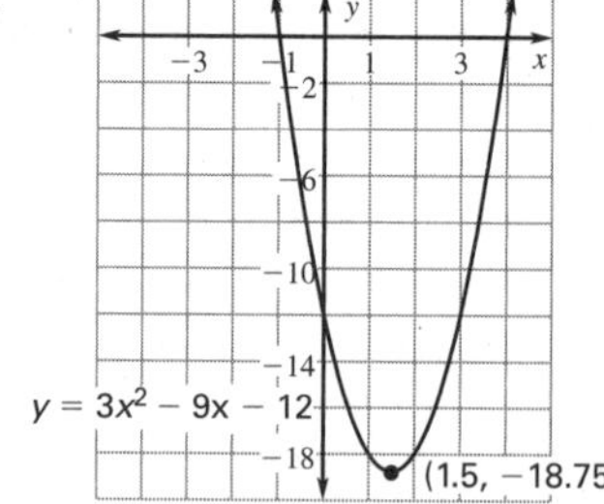

66.

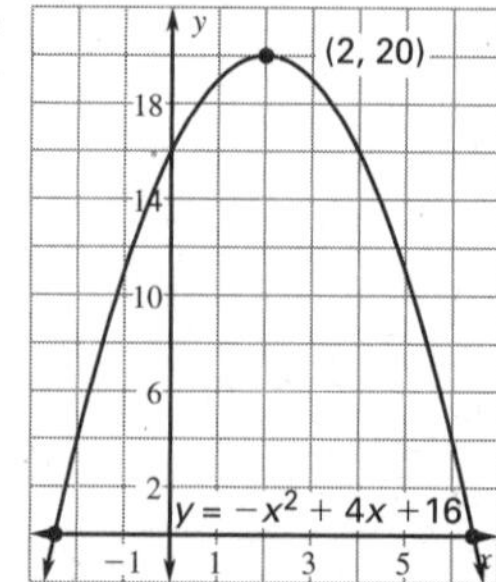

Copyright © McDougal Littell Inc.
All rights reserved.

10.3 Maintaining Skills (p. 587)

67. $\frac{1^2}{2^2} = \frac{1}{4}$ **68.** $\frac{1}{4^2} = \frac{1}{16}$ **69.** $\frac{2^2}{3^2} = \frac{4}{9}$ **70.** $\frac{4^2}{9^2} = \frac{16}{81}$

71. $\frac{1^3}{3^3} = \frac{1}{27}$ **72.** $\frac{2^3}{5^3} = \frac{8}{125}$

73. $\frac{3^3}{4^3} = \frac{27}{64}$ **74.** $\frac{5^3}{8^3} = \frac{125}{512}$

Quiz 1 *(p. 587)*

1. 2 **2.** 0 **3.** 3 **4.** 5

5. $(2x^2 + x^2) + (7x - 2x) + (1 + 8) = 3x^2 + 5x + 9$

6. $-4x^3 - 5x^2 + 2x - 2x^3 - 9x^2 - 2$
$= (-4x^3 - 2x^3) + (-5x^2 - 9x^2) + 2x - 2$
$= -6x^3 - 14x^2 + 2x - 2$

7. $7t^2 - 3t + 5 - 4t^2 - 10t + 9$
$= (7t^2 - 4t^2) + (-3t - 10t) + (5 + 9)$
$= 3t^2 - 13t + 14$

8. $(5x^3 + x^3) + (-x^2 + 4x^2) + (3x + x) + 3$
$= 6x^3 + 3x^2 + 4x + 3$

9. $x^2 - x + 8x - 8 = x^2 + 7x - 8$

10. $y^2 + 9y + 2y + 18 = y^2 + 11y + 18$

11. $-x^2(12x^3) - x^2(-11x^2) - x^2(3)$
$= -12x^5 + 11x^4 - 3x^2$

12. $6x^2 + 15xy - 2xy - 5y^2$
$= 6x^2 + 13xy - 5y^2$

13. $(4n)^2 - 7^2 = 16n^2 - 49$

14. $(x - 2)(2x^2 + x - 4)$
$= x(2x^2 + x - 4) - 2(2x^2 + x - 4)$
$= x(2x^2) + x(x) + x(-4) - 2(2x^2) - 2(x) - 2(-4)$
$= 2x^3 + x^2 - 4x - 4x^2 - 2x + 8$
$= 2x^3 - 3x^2 - 6x + 8$

15. $x^2 - 6^2 = x^2 - 36$ **16.** $(4x)^2 - 3^2 = 16x^2 - 9$

17. $5^2 - (3b)^2 = 25 - 9b^2$

18. $(2x)^2 - (7y)^2 = 4x^2 - 49y^2$

19. $(3x)^2 + 2(3x)(6) + 6^2 = 9x^2 + 36x + 36$

20. $(-8x - 6)^2 = (-8x)^2 - 2(-8x)(6) + 6^2$
$= 64x^2 + 96x + 36$

Lesson 10.4

10.4 Checkpoint (p. 588–590)

1. $x + 1 = 0$ or $x - 3 = 0$
$x = -1$ $x = 3$

2. $x = 0$ or $x - 2 = 0$
$x = 2$

3. $x - 5 = 0$ or $x + 7 = 0$
$x = 5$ $x = -7$

4. $x - 4 = 0$
$x = 4$

5. $x + 6 = 0$
$x = -6$

6. $2x - 5 = 0$
$2x = 5$
$x = \frac{5}{2}$

7. $x - 4 = 0$ or $x + 6 = 0$
$x = 4$ $x = -6$
or
$4x + 3 = 0$
$4x = -3$
$x = -\frac{3}{4}$

8. $x - 3 = 0$ or $x + 6 = 0$
$x = 3$ $x = -6$
or
$3x + 2 = 0$
$3x = -2$
$x = -\frac{2}{3}$

9. $2x + 1 = 0$ or $x - 8 = 0$
$2x = -1$ $x = 8$
$x = -\frac{1}{2}$

10. $y - 3 = 0$ or $3y - 2 = 0$
$y = 3$ $3y = 2$
$y = \frac{2}{3}$

11. $x = 0$ or $x + 2 = 0$
$x = -2$

The x-intercepts are $(0, 0)$ and $(-2, 0)$. The x-coordinate of the vertex is $x = \frac{0 + (-2)}{2} = -1$. Substitute -1 for x into $y = x(x + 2)$ to find the y-coordinate of the vertex:
$y = -1(-1 + 2) = -1$
So the vertex is $(-1, -1)$.

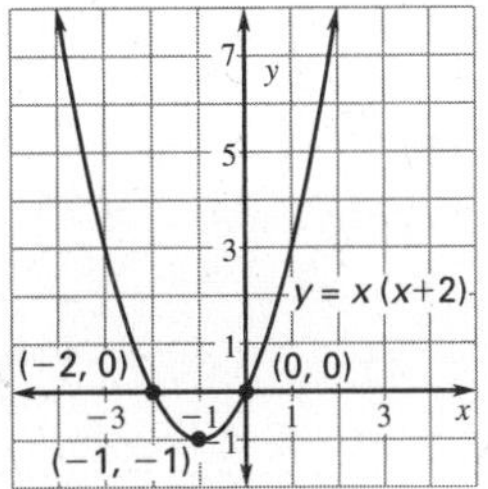

12. $x + 4 = 0$ or $x - 5 = 0$
$x = -4$ $x = 5$

The x-intercepts are $(-4, 0)$ and $(5, 0)$. The x-coordinate of the vertex is $x = \frac{-4 + 5}{2} = 0.5$. Substitute 0.5 for x into $y = (x + 4)(x - 5)$ to find the y-coordinate of the vertex; $y = (0.5 + 4)(0.5 - 5) = -20.25$.
So, the vertex is $(0.5, -20.25)$.

Copyright © McDougal Littell Inc.
All rights reserved.

Chapter 10 *continued*

12. ***continued***

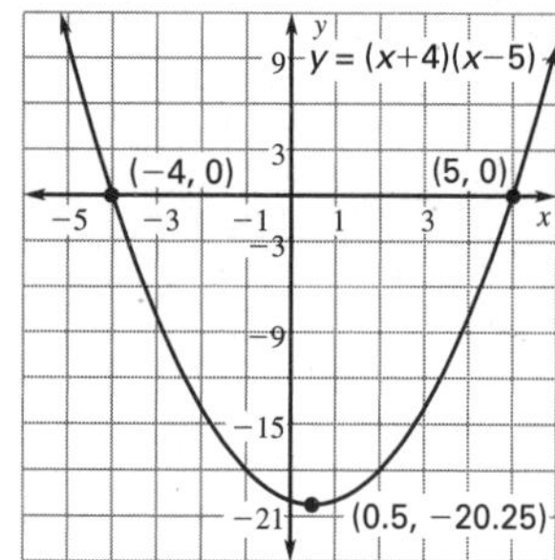

13. $x - 1 = 0$ or $x - 6 = 0$
$x = 1$ $x = 6$

The x-intercepts are (1, 0) and (6, 0). The x-coordinate of the vertex is $x = \frac{1 + 6}{2} = 3.5$. Substitute 3.5 for x into $y = (x - 1)(x - 6)$ to find the y-coordinate of the vertex:

$y = (3.5 - 1)(3.5 - 6) = -6.25.$
So, the vertex is $(3.5, -6.25)$.

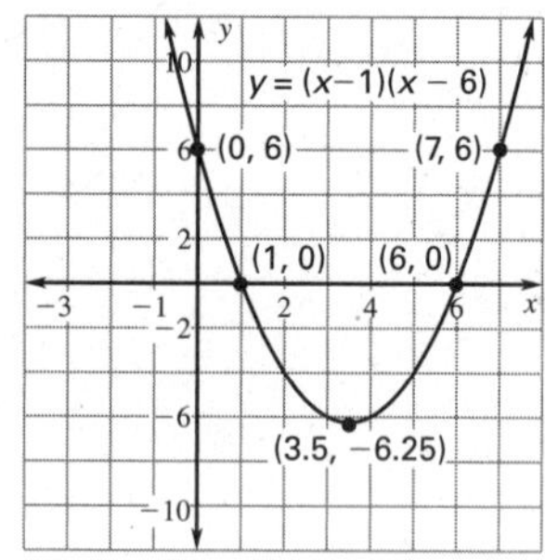

10.4 Guided Practice (p. 591)

1. If $ab = 0$, then $a = 0$ or $b = 0$.
2. No; $x^2 - 9 = (x - 3)(x + 3)$.
3. No; 2 and -5 are solutions, 3 is not.
4. Subtract 4 from each side of $2x + 4 = 0$ so that $2x = -4$; $x = -2$.

5. no **6.** no **7.** yes **8.** yes

9. $b + 1 = 0$ or $b + 3 = 0$
$b = -1$ $b = -3$

10. $t - 3 = 0$ or $t - 5 = 0$
$t = 3$ $t = 5$

11. $x - 7 = 0$
$x = 7$

12. $y + 9 = 0$ or $y - 2 = 0$
$y = -9$ $y = 2$
or
$y - 5 = 0$
$y = 5$

13.

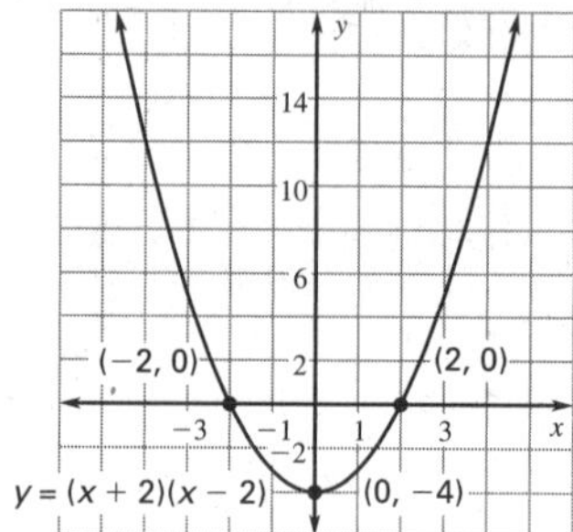

10.4 Practice and Applications (p. 591–593)

14. $x + 4 = 0$ or $x + 1 = 0$
$x = -4$ $x = -1$

15. $t + 8 = 0$ or $t - 6 = 0$
$t = -8$ $t = 6$

16. $x = 0$ or $x + 8 = 0$
$x = -8$

17. $y + 3 = 0$
$y = -3$

18. $b - 9 = 0$ or $b + 8 = 0$
$b = 9$ $b = -8$

19. $d + 7 = 0$
$d = -7$

20. $y - 2 = 0$ or $y + 1 = 0$
$y = 2$ $y = -1$

21. $z + 2 = 0$ or $z + 3 = 0$
$z = -2$ $z = -3$

22. $y - 7 = 0$ or $y - 5 = 0$
$y = 7$ $y = 5$

23. $w - 17 = 0$
$w = 17$

24. $p = 0$ or $2p + 1 = 0$
$2p = -1$
$p = -\frac{1}{2}$

25. $c + 9 = 0$
$c = -9$

26. $z + 9 = 0$ or $z - 11 = 0$
$z = -9$ $z = 11$

27. $a - 20 = 0$ or $a + 15 = 0$
$a = 20$ $a = -15$

28. $d + 6 = 0$ or $3d - 4 = 0$
$d = -6$ $3d = 4$
$d = \frac{4}{3}$

29. $x + 1 = 0$ or $x + 2 = 0$
$x = -1$ $x = -2$
or
$x - 4 = 0$
$x = 4$

Copyright © McDougal Littell Inc.
All rights reserved.

30. $y = 0$ or $y - 4 = 0$
$y = 4$

or
$y - 8 = 0$
$y = 8$

31. $a + 5 = 0$ or $a - 6 = 0$
$a = -5$ $a = 6$

32. $r = 0$ or $r - 12 = 0$
$r = 12$

33. $d + 8 = 0$ or $d - 12 = 0$
$d = -8$ $d = 12$

or
$d + 9 = 0$
$d = -9$

34. $n + 9 = 0$ or $n - 9 = 0$
$n = -9$ $n = 9$

or
$n + 12 = 0$
$n = -12$

35. $b - 8 = 0$ or $2b + 1 = 0$
$b = 8$ $2b = -1$
$b = -\frac{1}{2}$

or
$b + 2 = 0$
$b = -2$

36. $y - 5 = 0$ or $y - 6 = 0$
$y = 5$ $y = 6$

or
$3y - 2 = 0$
$3y = 2$
$y = \frac{2}{3}$

37. C **38.** B **39.** A

40. $x - 4 = 0$ or $x + 2 = 0$
$x = 4$ $x = -2$

The x-intercepts are (4, 0) and $(-2, 0)$. The x-coordinate of the vertex is $x = \frac{4 + (-2)}{2} = 1$. Substitute 1 for x into $y = (x - 4)(x + 2)$ to find the y-coordinate of the vertex: $y = (1 - 4)(1 + 2) = -9$.

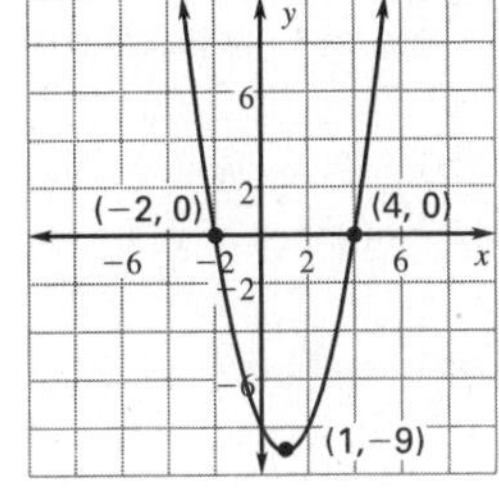

41. $x + 5 = 0$ or $x + 3 = 0$
$x = -5$ $x = -3$

The x-intercepts are $(-5, 0)$ and $(-3, 0)$. The x-coordinate of the vertex is $x = \frac{-5 + (-3)}{2} = -4$. Substitute -4 for x into $y = (x + 5)(x + 3)$ to find the y-coordinate of the vertex: $y = (-4 + 5)(-4 + 3) = -1$. So, the vertex is $(-4, -1)$.

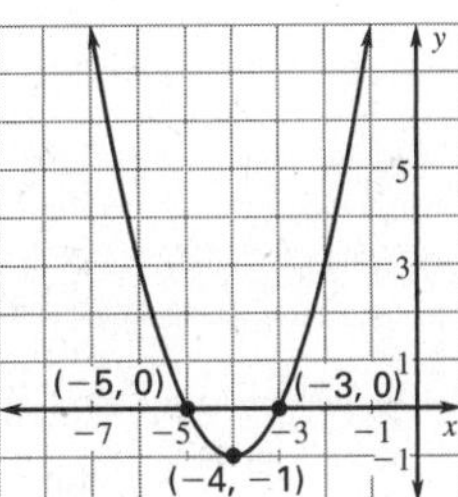

42. $x - 3 = 0$ or $x + 3 = 0$
$x = 3$ $x = -3$

The x-intercepts are (3, 0) and $(-3, 0)$. The x-coordinate of the vertex is $x = \frac{3 + (-3)}{2} = 0$. Substitute 0 for x into $y = (x - 3)(x + 3)$ to find the y-coordinate of the vertex: $y = (0 - 3)(0 + 3) = -9$. So, the vertex is $(0, -9)$.

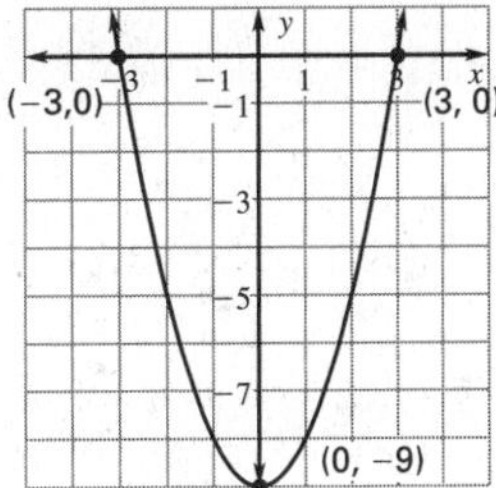

43. $x - 1 = 0$ or $x + 7 = 0$
$x = 1$ $x = -7$

The x-intercepts are (1, 0) and $(-7, 0)$. The x-coordinate of the vertex is $x = \frac{1 + (-7)}{2} = -3$. Substitute -3 for x into $y = (x - 1)(x + 7)$ to find the y-coordinate of the vertex: $y = (-3 - 1)(-3 + 7) - 16$. So, the vertex is $(-3, -16)$.

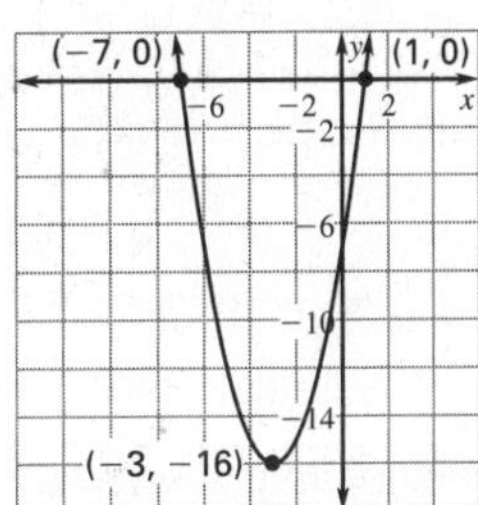

Copyright © McDougal Littell Inc.
All rights reserved.

44. $x - 2 = 0$ or $x - 6 = 0$

$x = 2$ $\quad x = 6$

The x-intercepts are (2, 0) and (6, 0). The x-coordinate of the vertex is $x = \dfrac{2 + 6}{2} = 4$. Substitute 4 for x into $y = (x - 2)(x - 6)$ to find the y-coordinate of the vertex: $y = (4 - 2)(4 - 6) = -4$. So, the vertex is $(4, -4)$.

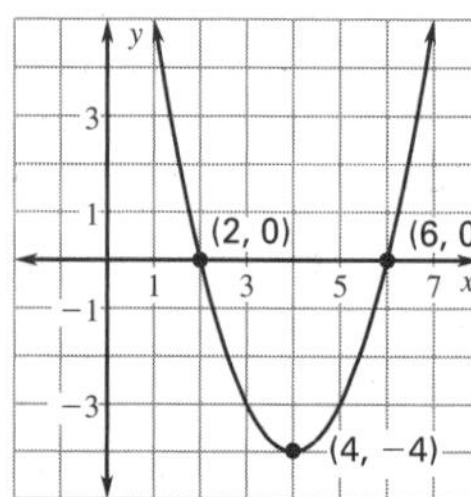

45. $x + 4 = 0$ or $x + 3 = 0$

$x = -4$ $\quad x = -3$

The x-intercepts are $(-4, 0)$ and $(-3, 0)$. The x-coordinate of the vertex is $x = \dfrac{-4 + (-3)}{2} = -3.5$.

Substitute -3.5 for x into $y = (x + 4)(x + 3)$ to find the y-coordinate of the vertex:

$y = (-3.5 + 4)(-3.5 + 3) = -0.25$. So, the vertex is $(-3.5, \ -0.25)$.

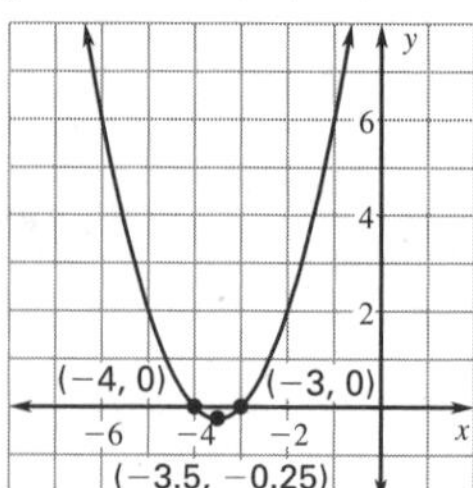

46. Since the x-intercepts are $(-41, 0)$ and $(41, 0)$, the distance between the edges of the dish is 82 feet, which is the width of the dish.

47. The center of the dish is the vertex of the function. The x-coordinate of the vertex is $x = \dfrac{-41 + 41}{2} = 0$.

Substitute 0 for x into the function to find the y-coordinate of the vertex: $y = \dfrac{14}{41^2}(0 + 41)(0 - 41) = -14$.

So, the vertex is $(0, -14)$, which is the center of the dish.

48. Since the x-intercepts are $(-300, 0)$ and $(300, 0)$, the distance between the legs of the arch at the base is 600 feet.

49. Find the vertex of the function. The x-coordinate of the vertex is $x = \dfrac{-300 + 300}{2} = 0$. Substitute 0 for x into the function to find the y-coordinate of the vertex:

$y = -\dfrac{7}{1000}(0 + 300)(0 - 300) = 630$. So, the vertex is (0, 630). The arch is, therefore, 630 feet high.

50. Since the x-intercepts are (600, 0) and $(-600, 0)$, the width of the crater is 1200 meters.

51. Find the vertex. The x-coordinate of the vertex is $x = \dfrac{600 + (-600)}{2} = 0$. Substitute 0 for x into the function to find the y-coordinate of the vertex:

$y = \dfrac{1}{1800}(0 - 600)(0 + 600) = -200$. So, the vertex is $(0, -200)$. Therefore, the depth of the crater is 200 meters.

10.4 Standardized Test Practice (p. 593)

52. B;

$x - 3 = 0$ or $x + 5 = 0$

$x = 3$ $\quad x = -5$

or

$x - 9 = 0$

$x = 9$

53. H; the x-intercepts of $y = (x - 2)(x - 4)$ are (2, 0) and (4, 0).

10.4 Mixed Review (p. 593)

54. 210,000

55. 0.04443

56. 857,000,000

57. 1,250,000

58. 0.00371

59. 9,960,000

60. 0.000722

61. 81,700,000

62. $x^2 - 7x - 2x + 14 = x^2 - 9x + 14$

63. $x^2 - 8^2 = x^2 - 64$

64. $x^2 + 5x - 4x - 20 = x^2 + x - 20$

65. $6x^2 - 2x + 21x - 7 = 6x^2 + 19x - 7$

66. $25x^2 + 10x - 5x - 2 = 25x^2 + 5x - 2$

67. $24x^2 - 9x + 8x - 3 = 24x^2 - x - 3$

68. $8x^2 - 4x - 16x + 8 = 8x^2 - 20x + 8$

69. $x^2 + 2x(10) + 10^2 = x^2 + 20x + 100$

70. $6x^2 - 9x + 10x - 15 = 6x^2 + x - 15$

71. Exponential decay; $y = P(0.84)^t$ where P is the average price of the computer in 1996, and t is the number of years since 1996.

72. Exponential growth; $y = N(1.23)^t$ where N is the number of CD's sold in 1995 and t is the number of years since 1995.

73. Exponential decay; $y = N(0.97)^t$ where N is the number of members in 1996 and t is the number of years since 1996.

74. Exponential growth; $y = R(2.37)^t$ where R is total revenue in 1993 and t is the number of years since 1993.

Copyright © McDougal Littell Inc.
All rights reserved.

10.4 Maintaining Skills (p. 593)

75. 1, 2, 3, 4, 6, 12

76. 1, 2, 4, 5, 10, 20

77. 1, 2, 3, 6, 9, 18

78. 1, 5, 7, 35

79. 1, 3, 17, 51

80. 1, 2, 3, 4, 6, 8, 12, 24

81. 1, 2, 3, 4, 6, 9, 12, 18, 36

82. 1, 2, 3, 4, 6, 8, 12, 16, 24, 48

83. 1, 2, 4, 8, 16, 32, 64

84. 1, 2, 3, 5, 6, 9, 10, 15, 18, 30, 45, 90

85. 1, 2, 3, 4, 6, 7, 12, 14, 21, 28, 42, 84

86. 1, 2, 4, 7, 8, 14, 16, 28, 56, 112

Lesson 10.5

10.5 Developing Concepts: Explore *(p. 594)*

3. $x + 2,\ x + 3;\ (x + 2)(x + 3)$

Think About It (p. 594)

1. $x^2 + 8x + 12 = (x + 6)(x + 2)$

2. $x^2 + 10x + 21 = (x + 7)(x + 3)$

3.

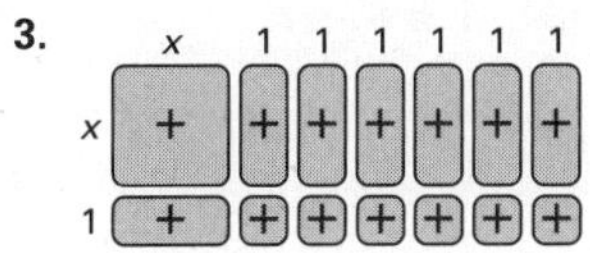

$(x + 6)(x + 1)$

4.

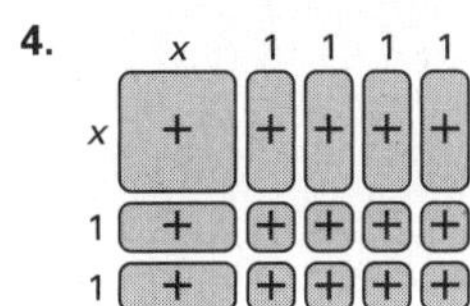

$(x + 2)(x + 4)$

5.

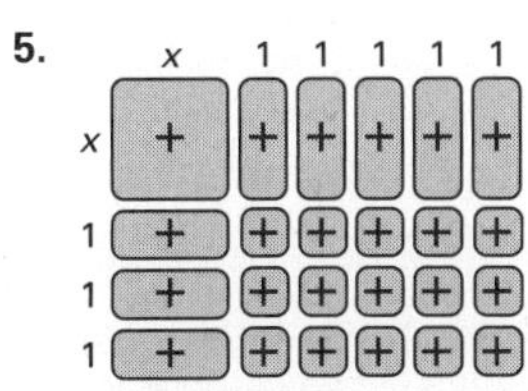

$(x + 3)(x + 5)$

6.

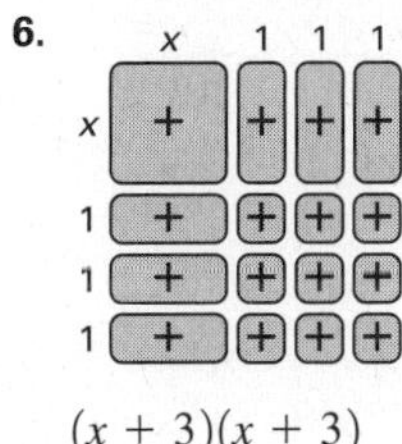

$(x + 3)(x + 3)$

7.

$(x + 2)(x + 2)$

8.

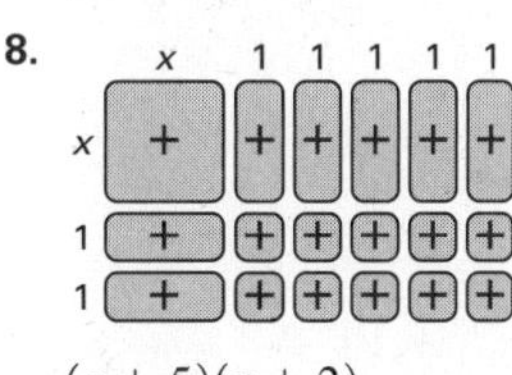

$(x + 5)(x + 2)$

9. Sample: Two units are left outside of the rectangle. It is not possible to include all the tiles into one rectangle. When this happens, the trinomial cannot be factored.

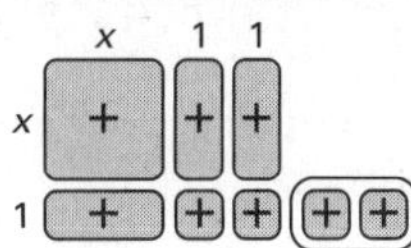

10.5 Checkpoint (p. 595–598)

1. $(x + 1)(x + 3)$

2. $(x + 2)(x + 3)$

3. $(x + 1)(x + 7)$

4. $(x + 1)(x + 6)$

5. $(x - 1)(x - 4)$

6. $(x - 2)(x - 2)$

7. $(x - 7)(x - 1)$

8. $(x - 3)(x - 4)$

9. $(x - 6)(x + 1)$

10. $(x - 5)(x + 2)$

11. $(x - 14)(x + 1)$

12. $(x - 7)(x + 1)$

13. $(x + 3)(x - 2)$

14. $(x + 4)(x - 2)$

15. $(x + 10)(x - 2)$

16. $(x + 5)(x - 2)$

17. $0 = (x + 3)(x + 1)$

$x + 3 = 0$ or $x + 1 = 0$

$x = -3$ $\quad$ $x = -1$

18. $0 = (x - 4)(x - 1)$

$x - 4 = 0$ or $x - 1 = 0$

$x = 4$ $\quad$ $x = 1$

19. $0 = (x + 1)(x - 6)$

$x + 1 = 0$ or $x - 6 = 0$

$x = -1$ $\quad$ $x = 6$

20. $66 = (x + 7)(x + 12) - (7)(12)$

$66 = x^2 + 19x + 84 - 84$

$66 = x^2 + 19x$

$0 = x^2 + 19x - 66$

$0 = (x + 22)(x - 3)$

$x + 22 = 0$ or $x - 3 = 0$

$x = -22$ $\quad$ $x = 3$

Only $x = 3$ is a reasonable solution, so the border should be 3 yards wide.

Copyright © McDougal Littell Inc.
All rights reserved.

10.5 Guided Practice (p. 599)

1. To factor a trinomial of the form $x^2 + bx + c$ means to find 2 binomials whose product equals the original trinomial.

2. D; $(x + 4)(x - 5)$ **3.** A; $(x + 5)(x - 4)$

4. B; $(x + 4)(x + 5)$ **5.** C; $(x - 4)(x - 5)$

6. $0 = (x - 2)(x - 2)$
$x - 2 = 0$
$x = 2$

7. $0 = (x - 5)(x + 1)$
$x - 5 = 0$ or $x + 1 = 0$
$x = 5$ $x = -1$

8. $0 = (x - 2)(x + 3)$
$x - 2 = 0$ or $x + 3 = 0$
$x = 2$ $x = -3$

9. always **10.** always **11.** never

10.5 Practice and Applications (p. 599–601)

12. B; $(x + 4)(x + 3)$ **13.** B; $(x - 8)(x - 2)$

14. B; $(x + 13)(x - 2)$ **15.** $(z + 1)(z + 5)$

16. $(x + 9)(x - 1)$ **17.** $(b + 8)(b - 3)$

18. $(a - 5)(a + 4)$ **19.** $(r + 4)(r + 4)$

20. $(y - 6)(y + 3)$ **21.** $(m - 10)(m + 3)$

22. $(w + 9)(w + 4)$ **23.** $(b + 8)(b - 5)$

24. $(x + 2)(x + 5) = 0$
$x + 2 = 0$ or $x + 5 = 0$
$x = -2$ $x = -5$

25. $(x - 2)(x + 7) = 0$
$x - 2 = 0$ or $x + 7 = 0$
$x = 2$ $x = -7$

26. $(x + 3)(x + 3) = 0$
$x + 3 = 0$
$x = -3$

27. $(x + 1)(x + 15) = 0$
$x + 1 = 0$ or $x + 15 = 0$
$x = -1$ $x = -15$

28. $x^2 - 9x + 14 = 0$
$(x - 2)(x - 7) = 0$
$x - 2 = 0$ or $x - 7 = 0$
$x = 2$ $x = 7$

29. $x^2 + 3x - 54 = 0$
$(x - 6)(x + 9) = 0$
$x - 6 = 0$ or $x + 9 = 0$
$x = 6$ $x = -9$

30. $x^2 - 20x + 100 = 0$
$(x - 10)(x - 10) = 0$
$x - 10 = 0$
$x = 10$

31. $(x - 4)(x - 11) = 0$
$x - 4 = 0$ or $x - 11 = 0$
$x = 4$ $x = 11$

32. $x^2 - 20x + 51 = 0$
$(x - 3)(x - 17) = 0$
$x - 3 = 0$ or $x - 17 = 0$
$x = 3$ $x = 17$

33. $x^2 + 8x - 65 = 0$
$(x - 5)(x + 13) = 0$
$x - 5 = 0$ or $x + 13 = 0$
$x = 5$ $x = -13$

34. $x^2 - 13x + 42 = 0$
$(x - 6)(x - 7) = 0$
$x - 6 = 0$ or $x - 7 = 0$
$x = 6$ $x = 7$

35. $x^2 - x - 56 = 0$
$(x + 7)(x - 8) = 0$
$x + 7 = 0$ or $x - 8 = 0$
$x = -7$ $x = 8$

36. $x^2 - x - 8 - 82 = 0$
$x^2 - x - 90 = 0$
$(x + 9)(x - 10) = 0$
$x + 9 = 0$ or $x - 10 = 0$
$x = -9$ $x = 10$

37. $n^2 + 8n + 32 + 4n = 0$
$n^2 + 12n + 32 = 0$
$(n + 4)(n + 8) = 0$
$n + 4 = 0$ or $n + 8 = 0$
$n = -4$ $n = -8$

38. $c^2 + 10c - 48 - 12c = 0$
$c^2 - 2c - 48 = 0$
$(c - 8)(c + 6) = 0$
$c - 8 = 0$ or $c + 6 = 0$
$c = 8$ $c = -6$

39. $(x - 2)(x - 15) = 0$
$x - 2 = 0$ or $x - 15 = 0$
$x = 2$ $x = 15$

40. $(x - 19)(x - 1) = 0$
$x - 19 = 0$ or $x - 1 = 0$
$x = 19$ $x = 1$

41. $(x - 3)(x + 6) = 0$
$x - 3 = 0$ or $x + 6 = 0$
$x = 3$ $x = -6$

42. Area $= \frac{1}{2}$base $\cdot$ height

The base of the sign is $2h - 2$. Since the surface area of the sign can be no more than 20 square feet, the inequality is:

$$\frac{1}{2}(2h - 2)(h) \le 20$$
$$\frac{1}{2} \cdot 2(h - 1)(h) \le 20$$
$$(h - 1)(h) \le 20$$
$$h^2 - h \le 20$$
$$h^2 - h - 20 \le 0$$

Copyright © McDougal Littell Inc.
All rights reserved.

43. $h^2 - h - 20 \le 0$

$(h - 5)(h + 4) \le 0$

$h - 5 \le 0$ or $h + 4 \le 0$

$h \le 5$ $\quad h \le -4$

Only $h \le 5$ is the reasonable height. When $h = 5$, the base is $2h - 2 = 2(5) - 2 = 8$. The largest sign that meets the zoning ordinance has a base of 8 feet and a height of 5 feet.

44. Since the platform is a square, the sides are the same width. Since the area of the platform is 9025 square meters, each side is 95 meters. Therefore, the platform has dimensions 95 m × 95 m. Because the platform is 38 meters wider than the main building and $95 - 38 = 57$, the dimensions of the main building are 57 m × 57 m.

45. Since area = length × width and we know the area is 167,750 and the length is 245 meters longer than it is wide, then $w(w + 245) = 167{,}750$. Solving for w, find that

$w(w + 245) = 167{,}750$

$w^2 + 245w = 167{,}750$

$w^2 + 245w - 167{,}750 = 0$

$(w - 305)(w + 550) = 0$

$w - 305 = 0$ or $w + 550 = 0$

$w = 305$ $\quad w = -550$

Only $w = 305$ is the reasonable solution, so when $w = 305$, length is $305 + 245 = 550$. Therefore, the dimensions of the Taj Mahal are 305 m by 550 m.

10.5 Standardized Test Practice (p. 601)

46. C; $(x + 2)(x - 12)$

47. F;

$x^2 - 9x = 36$

$x^2 - 9x - 36 = 0$

$(x - 12)(x + 3) = 0$

$x - 12 = 0$ or $x + 3 = 0$

$x = 12$ $\quad x = -3$

48. C;

Area of unpaved part = Area of Plot − Area of Paved Part

$880 = w(w + 24) - 8(12)$

$880 = w^2 + 24w - 96$

49. G;

$\text{Area} = \frac{1}{2}\text{base} \cdot \text{height}$

$48 = \frac{1}{2}(2h - 16)(h)$

$48 = \frac{1}{2} \cdot 2(h - 8)(h)$

$48 = (h - 8)(h)$

$48 = h^2 - 8h$

10.5 Mixed Review (p. 601)

50. Factors of 12: 1, 2, 3, 4, 6, 12
Factors of 36: 1, 2, 3, 4, 6, 9, 12, 18, 36
GCF: 12

51. Factors of 30: 1, 2, 3, 5, 6, 10, 15, 30
Factors of 45: 1, 3, 5, 9, 15, 45
GCF: 15

52. Factors of 24: 1, 2, 3, 4, 6, 8, 12, 24
Factors of 72: 1, 2, 3, 4, 6, 8, 9, 12, 18, 24, 36, 72
GCF: 24

53. Factors of 49: 1, 7, 49
Factors of 64: 1, 2, 4, 8, 16, 32, 64
GCF: 1

54. Factors of 20: 1, 2, 4, 5, 10, 20
Factors of 32: 1, 2, 4, 8, 16, 32
Factors of 40: 1, 4, 5, 8, 10, 40
GCF: 4

55. Factors of 36: 1, 2, 3, 4, 6, 9, 12, 18, 36
Factors of 54: 1, 2, 3, 6, 9, 18, 27, 54
Factors of 90: 1, 2, 3, 5, 6, 9, 10, 15, 18, 30, 45, 90
GCF: 18

56. $3q^4 - 15q^3 + 18q$

57. $y^2 - 4y + 9y - 36 = y^2 + 5y - 36$

58. $(7x)^2 - 2(7x)(11) + 11^2 = 49x^2 - 154x + 121$

59. $60 + 15w - 12w - 3w^2 = 60 + 3w - 3w^2$

$= -3w^2 + 3w + 60$

60. $12a^2 + 18a - 8a - 12 = 12a^2 + 10a - 12$

61. $20t^2 - 50t - 12t + 30 = 20t^2 - 62t + 30$

62. $(x + 12)(x + 7) = 0$

$x + 12 = 0$ or $x + 7 = 0$

$x = -12$ $\quad x = -7$

63. $(z + 2)(z + 3) = 0$

$z + 2 = 0$ or $z + 3 = 0$

$z = -2$ $\quad z = -3$

64. $(t - 19)^2 = 0$

$t - 19 = 0$

$t = 19$

65. $5(x - 9)(x - 6) = 0$

$x - 9 = 0$ or $x - 6 = 0$

$x = 9$ $\quad x = 6$

66. $(y + 47)(y - 27) = 0$

$y + 47 = 0$ or $y - 27 = 0$

$y = -47$ $\quad y = 27$

67. $(z - 1)(4z + 2) = 0$

$(z - 1)(2)(2z + 1) = 0$

$z - 1 = 0$ or $2z + 1 = 0$

$z = 1$ $\quad 2z = -1$

$z = -\frac{1}{2}$

Copyright © McDougal Littell Inc.
All rights reserved.

68. $(a - 3)(a + 5)^2 = 0$

$a - 3 = 0$ or $a + 5 = 0$

$a = 3$ $\quad a = -5$

69. $(b + 4)(b - 3)(2b - 1) = 0$

$b + 4 = 0$ or $b - 3 = 0$

$b = -4$ $\quad b = 3$

or

$2b - 1 = 0$

$2b = 1$

$b = \frac{1}{2}$

10.5 Maintaining Skills (p. 601)

70. $$\begin{array}{r} 3.7 \\ 1.04 \\ +\ 5.2 \\ \hline 9.94 \end{array}$$

71. $$\begin{array}{r} 6.7 \\ 0.356 \\ +\ 4 \\ \hline 11.056 \end{array}$$

72. $$\begin{array}{r} 7.421 \\ 5 \\ +\ 8.09 \\ \hline 20.511 \end{array}$$

73. $$\begin{array}{r} 8.1 \\ 0.2 \\ +\ 3.56 \\ \hline 11.86 \end{array}$$

74. $$\begin{array}{r} 6.012 \\ 2.9 \\ +\ 5.6314 \\ \hline 14.5434 \end{array}$$

75. $$\begin{array}{r} 7.9 \\ 3.0204 \\ +\ 10 \\ \hline 20.9204 \end{array}$$

76. $$\begin{array}{r} 3.2 \\ 5.013 \\ +\ 0.0021 \\ \hline 8.2151 \end{array}$$

77. $$\begin{array}{r} 100 \\ 9.81 \\ +\ 5.0006 \\ \hline 114.8106 \end{array}$$

Lesson 10.6

10.6 Developing Concepts: Think About It *(p. 602)*

1.

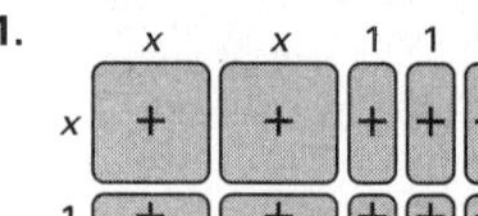

$(2x + 3)(x + 3)$

2.

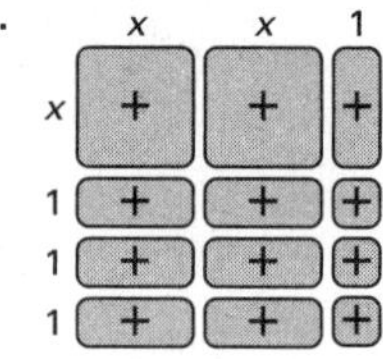

$(2x + 1)(x + 3)$

3.

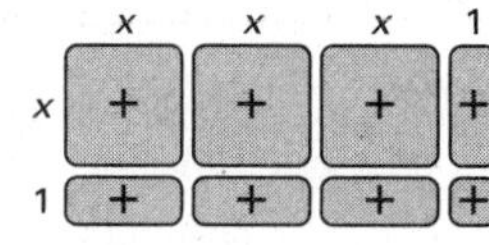

$(3x + 1)(x + 1)$

4.

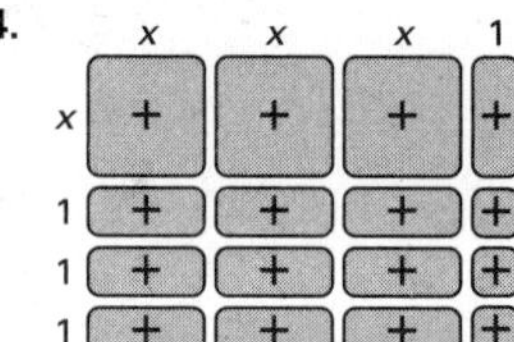

$(3x + 1)(x + 3)$

5.

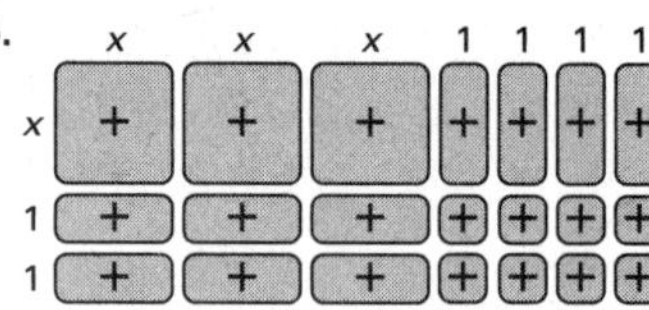

$(3x + 4)(x + 2)$

6.

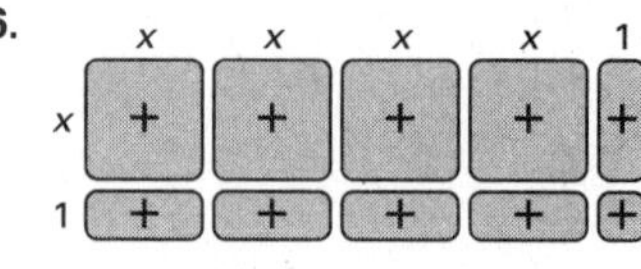

$(4x + 1)(x + 1)$

7.

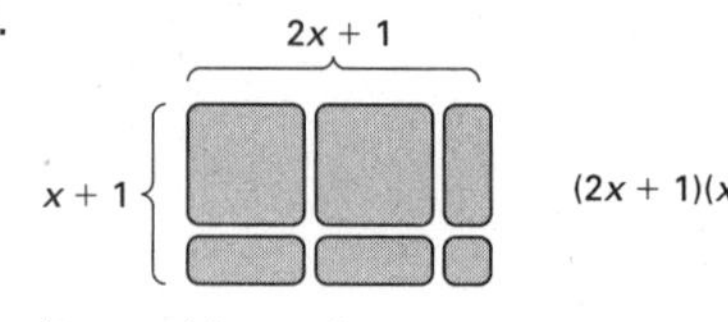

$(2x + 1)(x + 1)$

Copyright © McDougal Littell Inc.
All rights reserved.

8.

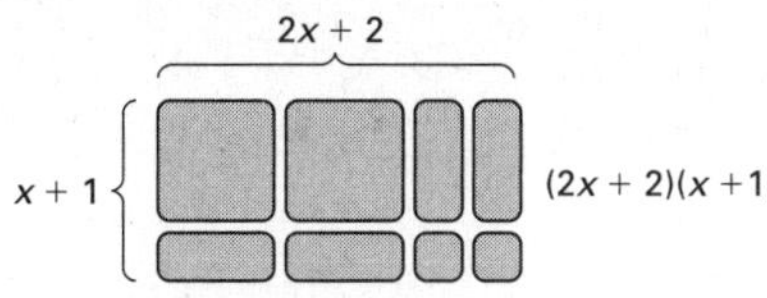

$(2x + 2)(x + 1)$

9.

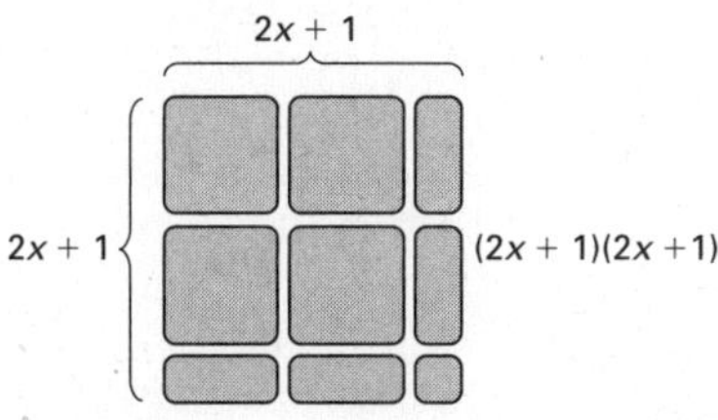

$(2x + 1)(2x + 1)$

10.6 Checkpoint (p. 603–605)

1. $(2x + 1)(x + 3)$ **2.** $(2x + 3)(x + 1)$

3. $(3x + 1)(x + 3)$ **4.** $(2x + 1)(x + 2)$

5. $(5x - 2)(x - 1)$ **6.** $(2x + 1)(2x + 3)$

7. $(2r - 3)(4r + 3)$ **8.** $2(3x - 1)(x - 2)$

9. $5(4x - 3)(x + 1)$

10. $2x^2 + 7x + 3 = 0$
$(2x + 1)(x + 3) = 0$
$2x + 1 = 0$ or $x + 3 = 0$
$2x = -1$ $x = -3$
$x = -\frac{1}{2}$

11. $2x^2 - x - 3 = 0$
$(2x - 3)(x + 1) = 0$
$2x - 3 = 0$ or $x + 1 = 0$
$2x = 3$ $x = -1$
$x = \frac{3}{2}$

12. $4x^2 - 16x + 15 = 0$
$(2x - 3)(2x - 5) = 0$
$2x - 3 = 0$ or $2x - 5 = 0$
$2x = 3$ $2x = 5$
$x = \frac{3}{2}$ $x = \frac{5}{2}$

10.6 Guided Practice (p. 606)

1. To factor a trinomial of the type $ax^2 + bx + c$, one must find factors of a and c in such a way that the product of the binomials results in the original trinomial.

2. $(2x + 1)(x + 1) = 2x^2 + 2x + x + 1$
$= \underline{2x^2 + 3x} + 1$

3. $(3x + 2)(x - 3) = 3x^2 - 9x + 2x - 6$
$= 3x^2 - 7x \underline{- 6}$

4. $(3x - 4)(x - 5) = 3x^2 - 15x - 4x + 20$
$= 3x^2 \underline{- 19x} + 20$

5. $(5x + 2)(2x + 1) = 10x^2 + 5x + 4x + 2$
$= \underline{10x^2} + 9x + 2$

6. B; $(3x + 1)(x - 6)$ **7.** D; $(3x - 2)(x + 3)$

8. A; $(3x + 2)(x + 3)$ **9.** C; $(3x - 1)(x + 6)$

10. $(2x + 3)(x + 7)$ **11.** $(2x + 1)(x - 2)$

12. $(6t + 5)(t - 1)$ **13.** $(3x - 4)(4x - 1)$

14. $(2x + 5)(3x - 4)$ **15.** $(3x - 4)(x + 2)$

16. $3b^2 + 26b + 35 = 0$
$(3b + 5)(b + 7) = 0$
$3b + 5 = 0$ or $b + 7 = 0$
$3b = -5$ $b = -7$
$b = -\frac{5}{3}$

17. $2z^2 + 15z - 8 = 0$
$(2z - 1)(z + 8) = 0$
$2z - 1 = 0$ or $z + 8 = 0$
$2z = 1$ $z = -8$
$z = \frac{1}{2}$

18. $-7n^2 - 40n + 12 = 0$
$(-7n + 2)(n + 6) = 0$
$-7n + 2 = 0$ or $n + 6 = 0$
$-7n = -2$ $n = -6$
$n = \frac{-2}{-7} = \frac{2}{7}$

10.6 Practice and Applications (p. 606–608)

19. A; $(3x - 4)(x + 2)$ **20.** neither, $(6y + 1)(y - 5)$

21. A; $(2w + 3)(2w - 10)$ **22.** $(2x - 3)(x + 1)$

23. $(3t + 1)(t + 5)$ **24.** $(5x - 3)(x + 1)$

25. $(2a + 1)(3a + 1)$ **26.** $(5w + 1)(w - 2)$

27. $(6b + 1)(b - 2)$ **28.** $(2b - 1)(4b + 3)$

29. $3(x + 1)(2x - 5)$ **30.** $4(y - 1)(3y - 2)$

31. $(2z - 1)(z + 10)$ **32.** $(2y - 5)(3y + 2)$

33. $(4x + 7)(x + 5)$ **34.** $2(n - 7)(2n + 3)$

35. $(3c - 4)(c - 11)$ **36.** $3(2r - 3)(4r + 5)$

37. $(2t + 7)(3t - 10)$ **38.** $(7y - 4)(2y - 1)$

39. $(2y - 5)(4y - 3)$

40. Subtract 10 from each side of the equation to yield $2x^2 - 3x - 9 = 0$; then factor.
$(2x + 3)(x - 3) = 0$
$2x + 3 = 0$ or $x - 3 = 0$
$2x = -3$ $x = 3$
$x = -\frac{3}{2}$

Copyright © McDougal Littell Inc.
All rights reserved.

Chapter 10 *continued*

41. Incorrectly factored:

$3y^2 - 16y - 35 = 0$

$(3y + 5)(y - 7) = 0$

$3y + 5 = 0$ or $y - 7 = 0$

$3y = -5$ $\quad$ $y = 7$

$y = -\frac{5}{3}$

42. $2x^2 - 9x - 35 = 0$

$(2x + 5)(x - 7) = 0$

$2x + 5 = 0$ or $x - 7 = 0$

$2x = -5$ $\quad$ $x = 7$

$x = -\frac{5}{2}$

43. $7x^2 - 10x + 3 = 0$

$(7x - 3)(x - 1) = 0$

$7x - 3 = 0$ or $x - 1 = 0$

$7x = 3$ $\quad$ $x = 1$

$x = \frac{3}{7}$

44. $3x^2 + 34x + 11 = 0$

$(3x + 1)(x + 11) = 0$

$3x + 1 = 0$ or $x + 11 = 0$

$3x = -1$ $\quad$ $x = -11$

$x = -\frac{1}{3}$

45. $4x^2 - 21x + 5 = 0$

$(4x - 1)(x - 5) = 0$

$4x - 1 = 0$ or $x - 5 = 0$

$4x = 1$ $\quad$ $x = 5$

$x = \frac{1}{4}$

46. $2x^2 - 17x - 19 = 0$

$(2x - 19)(x + 1) = 0$

$2x - 19 = 0$ or $x + 1 = 0$

$2x = 19$ $\quad$ $x = -1$

$x = \frac{19}{2}$

47. $5x^2 - 3x - 26 = 0$

$(5x - 13)(x + 2) = 0$

$5x - 13 = 0$ or $x + 2 = 0$

$5x = 13$ $\quad$ $x = -2$

$x = \frac{13}{5}$

48. $2x^2 + 19x + 24 = 0$

$(2x + 3)(x + 8) = 0$

$2x + 3 = 0$ or $x + 8 = 0$

$2x = -3$ $\quad$ $x = -8$

$x = -\frac{3}{2}$

49. $4x^2 - 8x + 3 = 0$

$(2x - 1)(2x - 3) = 0$

$2x - 1 = 0$ or $2x - 3 = 0$

$2x = 1$ $\quad$ $2x = 3$

$x = \frac{1}{2}$ $\quad$ $x = \frac{3}{2}$

50. $6x^2 - 23x - 18 = 0$

$(2x - 9)(3x + 2) = 0$

$2x - 9 = 0$ or $3x + 2 = 0$

$2x = 9$ $\quad$ $3x = -2$

$x = \frac{9}{2}$ $\quad$ $x = -\frac{2}{3}$

51. $8x^2 - 34x + 35 = 0$

$(2x - 5)(4x - 7) = 0$

$2x - 5 = 0$ or $4x - 7 = 0$

$2x = 5$ $\quad$ $4x = 7$

$x = \frac{5}{2}$ $\quad$ $x = \frac{7}{4}$

52. $6x^2 + 19x + 10 = 0$

$(2x + 5)(3x + 2) = 0$

$2x + 5 = 0$ or $3x + 2 = 0$

$2x = -5$ $\quad$ $3x = -2$

$x = -\frac{5}{2}$ $\quad$ $x = -\frac{2}{3}$

53. $28x^2 - 5x - 3 = 0$

$(7x - 3)(4x + 1) = 0$

$7x - 3 = 0$ or $4x + 1 = 0$

$7x = 3$ $\quad$ $4x = -1$

$x = \frac{3}{7}$ $\quad$ $x = -\frac{1}{4}$

54. $10x^2 + 3x - 18 = 0$

$(2x + 3)(5x - 6) = 0$

$2x + 3 = 0$ or $5x - 6 = 0$

$2x = -3$ $\quad$ $5x = 6$

$x = -\frac{3}{2}$ $\quad$ $x = \frac{6}{5}$

55. a. $h = -16t^2 + 8t + 8$

b. Let $h = 0$ and solve for t.

$0 = -16t^2 + 8t + 8$

$0 = -8(2t^2 - t - 1)$

$0 = 2t^2 - t - 1$

$0 = (2t + 1)(t - 1)$

$2t + 1 = 0$ or $t - 1 = 0$

$2t = -1$ $\quad$ $t = 1$

$t = -\frac{1}{2}$

Only $t = 1$ is the reasonable solution, so it takes 1 second for the gymnast to reach the ground.

56. a. $10 = -16t^2 + 50t + 4$

b. $10 = -16t^2 + 50t + 4$

$0 = -16t^2 + 50t - 6$

$0 = -2(8t^2 - 25t + 3)$

$0 = 8t^2 - 25t + 3$

$0 = (8t - 1)(t - 3)$

$8t - 1 = 0$ or $t - 3 = 0$

$8t = 1$ $\quad$ $t = 3$

$t = \frac{1}{8}$

Therefore, it takes 3 seconds for her to reach the net. The other solution of $\frac{1}{8}$ second is the time it takes her to go from the cannon to 10 feet on her way up.

Copyright © McDougal Littell Inc.
All rights reserved.

Chapter 10 *continued*

57. Use a vertical motion model.

$h = -16t^2 + 44t + 6$

Let $h = 30$ and solve for t.

$30 = -16t^2 + 44t + 6$

$0 = -16t^2 + 44t - 24$

$0 = -4(4t^2 - 11t + 6)$

$0 = 4t^2 - 11t + 6$

$0 = (4t - 3)(t - 2)$

$4t - 3 = 0$ or $t - 2 = 0$

$4t = 3$ $\quad t = 2$

$t = \frac{3}{4}$

Therefore, the T-shirt was in the air for 2 seconds before it was caught. The other solution of $\frac{3}{4}$ second is the time it takes for the T-shirt to leave the cannon and go up to a height of 30 feet. You would probably catch the T-shirt as it fell.

10.6 Standardized Test Practice (p. 608)

58. B; $(3x + 5)(3x - 7)$

59. F;

$2x^2 + 5x + 3 = 0$

$(2x + 3)(x + 1) = 0$

$2x + 3 = 0$ or $x + 1 = 0$

$2x = -3$ $\quad x = -1$

$x = -\frac{3}{2}$

10.6 Mixed Review (p. 608)

60.

$4x + 5y = 7$ (1)

$6x - 2y = -18$ (2)

$-12x - 15y = -21$ Multiply (1) by -3

$12x - 4y = -36$ Multiply (2) by 3

$-19y = -57$

$y = 3$

Substitute 3 for y into $4x + 5y = 7$:

$4x + 5(3) = 7$

$4x + 15 = 7$

$4x = -8$

$x = -2$

Solution: $(-2, 3)$

61.

$6x - 5y = 3$ (1)

$-12x + 8y = 5$ (2)

$12x - 10y = 6$ Multiply (1) by 2

$-12x + 8y = 5$

$-2y = 11$

$y = -\frac{11}{2}$

Substitute $-\frac{11}{2}$ for y into $6x - 5y = 3$:

$6x - 5\left(-\frac{11}{2}\right) = 3$

$6x + \frac{55}{2} = 3$

$6x = -\frac{49}{2}$

$x = -\frac{49}{2} \cdot \frac{1}{6}$

$x = -\frac{49}{12}$

Solution: $\left(-\frac{49}{12}, -\frac{11}{2}\right)$

62.

$2x + y = 120$ (1)

$x + 2y = 120$ (2)

$2x + y = 120$

$-2x - 4y = -240$ Multiply (2) by -2

$-3y = -120$

$y = 40$

Substitute 40 for y into $2x + y = 120$:

$2x + 40 = 120$

$2x = 80$

$x = 40$

Solution: $(40, 40)$

63. $(4t)^2 - 2(4t)(1) + 1^2 = 16t^2 - 8t + 1$

64. $b^2 - 9^2 = b^2 - 81$

65. $(3x)^2 + 2(3x)(5) + 5^2 = 9x^2 + 30x + 25$

66. $(2a)^2 - 7^2 = 4a^2 - 49$

67. $(11)^2 - 2(11)(6x) + (6x)^2 = 121 - 132x + 36x^2$

68. $100^2 + 2(100)(27x) + (27x)^2$

$= 10{,}000 + 5400x + 729x^2$

$= 729x^2 + 5400x + 10{,}000$

10.6 Maintaining Skills (p. 608)

69. $\frac{2}{3} \cdot \frac{6}{9} = \frac{12}{27} \cdot \frac{3}{11} = \frac{36}{297} = \frac{4}{33}$

70. $\frac{1}{2} \cdot \frac{9}{1} = \frac{9}{2} \cdot \frac{2}{3} = \frac{18}{6} = 3$

71. $\frac{1}{2} \cdot \frac{4}{9} = \frac{4}{18} \cdot \frac{5}{6} = \frac{20}{108} = \frac{5}{27}$

72. $\frac{8}{9} \cdot \frac{8}{9} = \frac{64}{81} \cdot \frac{8}{9} = \frac{512}{729}$

73. $\frac{2}{3} \cdot \frac{4}{5} = \frac{8}{15} \cdot \frac{6}{7} = \frac{48}{105} = \frac{16}{35}$

74. $\frac{12}{15} \cdot \frac{3}{4} = \frac{36}{60} \cdot \frac{7}{1} = \frac{252}{60} = \frac{21}{5}$

75. $\frac{5}{6} \cdot \frac{9}{4} = \frac{45}{24} \cdot \frac{1}{3} = \frac{45}{72} \cdot \frac{2}{1} = \frac{90}{72} = \frac{5}{4}$

76. $\frac{1}{2} \cdot \frac{1}{3} = \frac{1}{6} \cdot \frac{4}{1} = \frac{4}{6} \cdot \frac{1}{5} = \frac{4}{30} = \frac{2}{15}$

Copyright © McDougal Littell Inc.
All rights reserved.

Quiz 2 *(p. 608)*

1. $(x + 5)(2x + 10) = 0$
$x + 5 = 0$
$x = -5$
or
$2x + 10 = 0$
$2x = -10$
$x = -\frac{10}{2} = -5$

2. $(2x + 8)^2 = 0$
$2x + 8 = 0$
$2x = -8$
$x = -4$

3. $(2x + 7)(3x - 12) = 0$
$2x + 7 = 0$ or $3x - 12 = 0$
$2x = -7$ $\quad$ $3x = 12$
$x = -\frac{7}{2}$ $\quad$ $x = \frac{12}{3} = 4$

4. $x(5x - 2) = 0$
$x = 0$ or $5x - 2 = 0$
$5x = 2$
$x = \frac{2}{5}$

5. $3(x - 5)(2x + 1) = 0$
$x - 5 = 0$ or $2x + 1 = 0$
$x = 5$ $\quad$ $2x = -1$
$x = -\frac{1}{2}$

6. $x(x + 4)(x - 7)^2 = 0$
$x = 0$ or $x + 4 = 0$
$x = -4$
or
$x - 7 = 0$
$x = 7$

7. Let $y = 0$ and solve for x:
$0 = (x - 2)(x + 2)$
$x - 2 = 0$ or $x + 2 = 0$
$x = 2$ $\quad$ $x = -2$

The x-intercepts are $(2, 0)$ and $(-2, 0)$. The x-coordinate of the vertex is $x = \frac{2 + (-2)}{2} = 0$. Substitute 0 for x into $y = (x - 2)(x + 2)$ to find the y-coordinate of the vertex:

$y = (0 - 2)(0 + 2) = -4$
The vertex is $(0, -4)$.

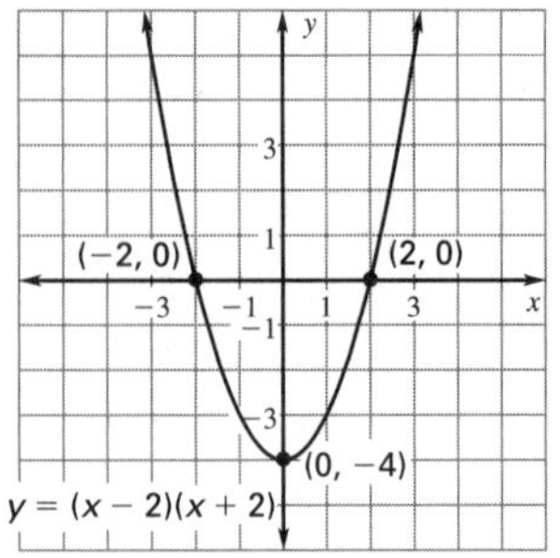

8. Let $y = 0$ and solve for x:
$0 = (x + 3)(x + 5)$
$x + 3 = 0$ or $x + 5 = 0$
$x = -3$ $\quad$ $x = -5$

The x-intercepts are $(-3, 0)$ and $(-5, 0)$. The x-coordinate of the vertex is $x = \frac{-3 + (-5)}{2} = -4$. Substitute -4 for x into $y = (x + 3)(x + 5)$ to find the y-coordinate of the vertex:

$y = (-4 + 3)(-4 + 5) = -1$

The vertex is $(-4, -1)$.

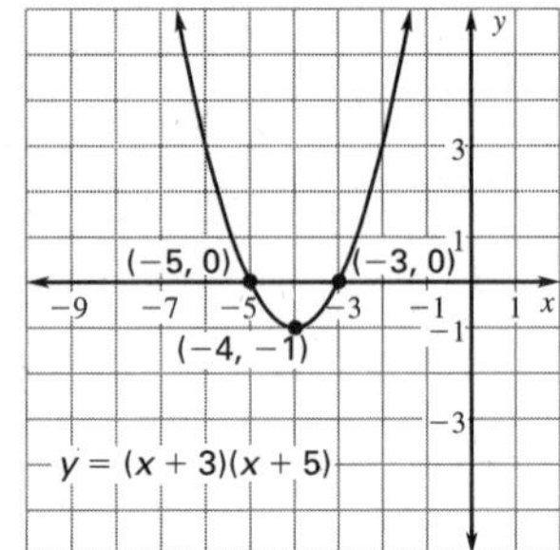

9. Let $y = 0$ and solve for x:
$0 = (x - 1)(x + 3)$
$x - 1 = 0$ or $x + 3 = 0$
$x = 1$ $\quad$ $x = -3$

The x-intercepts are $(1, 0)$ and $(-3, 0)$. The x-coordinate of the vertex is $x = \frac{1 + (-3)}{2} = -1$. Substitute -1 for x into $y = (x - 1)(x + 3)$ to find the y-coordinate of the vertex:

$y = (-1 - 1)(-1 + 3) = -4$

The vertex is $(-1, -4)$.

Copyright © McDougal Littell Inc.
All rights reserved.

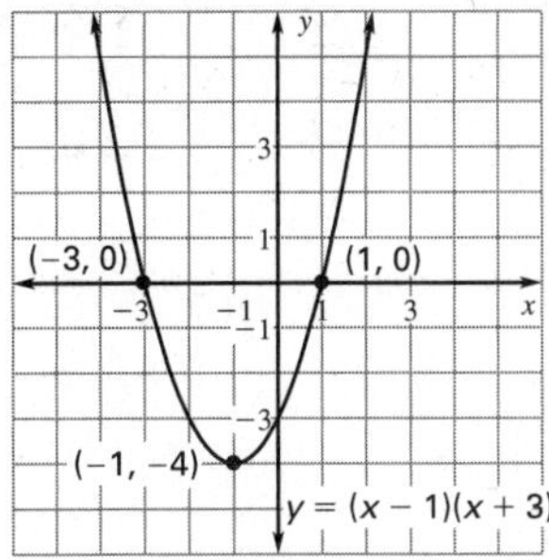

10. $(y + 4)(y - 1)$

11. $(w + 11)(w + 2)$

12. $(n + 19)(n - 3)$

13. not factorable using integers; $x^2 + 7x + 24$

14. $(b - 8)(b + 2)$

15. $(r - 7)(r + 4)$

16. $(m - 9)(m + 5)$

17. $(x + 6)(x + 11)$

18. $(r - 43)(r + 2)$

19. $y^2 + 5y - 6 = 0$
$(y + 6)(y - 1) = 0$
$y + 6 = 0$ or $y - 1 = 0$
$y = -6$ $\quad$ $y = 1$

20. $n^2 + 26n + 25 = 0$
$(n + 1)(n + 25) = 0$
$n + 1 = 0$ or $n + 25 = 0$
$n = -1$ $\quad$ $n = -25$

21. $z^2 - 14z + 45 = 0$
$(z - 9)(z - 5) = 0$
$z - 9 = 0$ or $z - 5 = 0$
$z = 9$ $\quad$ $z = 5$

22. $t^2 + 11t + 18 = 0$
$(t + 9)(t + 2) = 0$
$t + 9 = 0$ or $t + 2 = 0$
$t = -9$ $\quad$ $t = -2$

23. $2a^2 + 11a + 5 = 0$
$(2a + 1)(a + 5) = 0$
$2a + 1 = 0$ or $a + 5 = 0$
$2a = -1$ $\quad$ $a = -5$
$a = -\frac{1}{2}$

24. $3p^2 - 4p + 1 = 0$
$(3p - 1)(p - 1) = 0$
$3p - 1 = 0$ or $p - 1 = 0$
$3p = 1$ $\quad$ $p = 1$
$p = \frac{1}{3}$

25. $3b^2 - 10b - 8 = 0$
$(3b + 2)(b - 4) = 0$
$3b + 2 = 0$ or $b - 4 = 0$
$3b = -2$ $\quad$ $b = 4$
$b = -\frac{2}{3}$

26. $4c^2 + 12c + 9 = 0$
$(2c + 3)(2c + 3) = 0$
$2c + 3 = 0$
$2c = -3$
$c = -\frac{3}{2}$

27. $15b^2 + 41b + 14 = 0$
$(3b + 7)(5b + 2) = 0$
$3b + 7 = 0$ or $5b + 2 = 0$
$3b = -7$ $\quad$ $5b = -2$
$b = -\frac{7}{3}$ $\quad$ $b = -\frac{2}{5}$

Lesson 10.7

10.7 Checkpoint (p. 610–612)

1. $x^2 - 16 = x^2 - 4^2 = (x + 4)(x - 4)$

2. $n^2 - 36 = n^2 - 6^2 = (n + 6)(n - 6)$

3. $r^2 - 20$ cannot be factored using integers

4. $m^2 - 100 = m^2 - 10^2 = (m + 10)(m - 10)$

5. $8y^2 - 1$ cannot be factored using integers

6. $4y^2 - 49 = (2y)^2 - 7^2 = (2y + 7)(2y - 7)$

7. $9x^2 - 25 = (3x)^2 - 5^2 = (3x + 5)(3x - 5)$

8. $16q^2 - 45$ cannot be factored using integers

9. $x^2 + 6x + 9 = x^2 + 2(x)(3) + 3^2$
$= (x + 3)^2$

10. $n^2 - 8n + 16 = n^2 + 2(n)(4) + 4^2$
$= (n - 4)^2$

11. $a^2 + 18a + 81 = a^2 + 2(a)(9) + 9^2$
$= (a + 9)^2$

12. $4b^2 - 4b + 1 = (2b)^2 - 2(2b)(1) + 1^2$
$= (2b - 1)^2$

13. $25m^2 + 10m + 1 = (5m)^2 + 2(5m)(1) + 1^2$
$= (5m + 1)^2$

14. $9a^2 - 30a + 25 = (3a)^2 - 2(3a)(5) + 5^2$
$= (3a - 5)^2$

15. $2x^2 - 32 = 2(x^2 - 16)$
$= 2(x^2 - 4^2)$
$= 2(x + 4)(x - 4)$

16. $3p^2 + 36p + 108 = 3(p^2 + 12p + 36)$
$= 3[p^2 + 2(p)(6) + 6^2]$
$= 3(p + 6)^2$

17. $3b^2 - 48 = 3(b^2 - 16)$
$= 3(b^2 - 4^2)$
$= 3(b + 4)(b - 4)$

18. $8n^2 - 24n + 18 = 2(4n^2 - 12n + 9)$
$= 2[(2n)^2 - 2(2n)(3) + 3^2]$
$= 2(2n - 3)^2$

Copyright © McDougal Littell Inc.
All rights reserved.

19. $1000 - 10m^2 = 10(100 - m^2)$
$= 10(10^2 - m^2)$
$= -10(m^2 - 10^2)$
$= -10(m + 10)(m - 10)$

20. $2a^2 + 28a + 98 = 2(a^2 + 14a + 49)$
$= 2[a^2 + 2(a)(7) + 7^2]$
$= 2(a + 7)^2$

21. $x^2 - 81 = 0$
$x^2 - 9^2 = 0$
$(x + 9)(x - 9) = 0$
$x + 9 = 0$ or $x - 9 = 0$
$x = -9$ $x = 9$

22. $m^2 - 4m + 4 = 0$
$m^2 - 2(m)(2) + 2^2 = 0$
$(m - 2)^2 = 0$
$m - 2 = 0$
$m = 2$

23. $2n^2 - 288 = 0$
$2(n^2 - 144) = 0$
$2(n^2 - 12^2) = 0$
$2(n + 12)(n - 12) = 0$
$n + 12 = 0$ or $n - 12 = 0$
$n = -12$ $n = 12$

10.7 Guided Practice (p. 613)

1. Difference of two squares:

$a^2 - b^2 = (a - b)(a + b)$; Perfect square trinomials: $a^2 + 2ab + b^2 = (a + b)^2$, $a^2 - 2ab + b^2 = (a - b)^2$
Sample examples: $x^2 - 81 = (x - 9)(x + 9)$; $x^2 + 6x + 9 = (x + 3)^2$; $4x^2 - 12x + 9 = (2x - 3)^2$

2. $x^2 - 9 = x^2 - 3^2 = (x - 3)(x + 3)$

3. $b^2 + 10b + 25 = b^2 + 2(b)(5) + 5^2$
$= (b + 5)^2$

4. $p^2 + 25$ cannot be factored using integers

5. $w^2 - 16w + 64 = w^2 - 2(w)(8) + 8^2$
$= (w - 8)^2$

6. $16 - c^2 = 4^2 - c^2 = (4 - c)(4 + c)$

7. $6y^2 - 24 = 6(y^2 - 4)$
$= 6(y^2 - 2^2)$
$= 6(y - 2)(y + 2)$

8. $18 - 2b^2 = 2(9 - b^2)$
$= 2(3^2 - b^2)$
$= 2(3 - b)(3 + b)$

9. $4x^2 - 4x + 1 = (2x)^2 - 2(x)(1) + 1^2$
$= (2x - 1)^2$

10. $4a^2 - b^2 = (2a)^2 - b^2$
$= (2a - b)(2a + b)$

11. $x^2 + 6x + 9 = 0$
$(x + 3)^2 = 0$
$x + 3 = 0$
$x = -3$

12. $144 - y^2 = 0$
$(12 - y)(12 + y) = 0$
$12 - y = 0$ or $12 + y = 0$
$y = 12$ $y = -12$

13. $s^2 - 14s + 49 = 0$
$(s - 7)^2 = 0$
$s - 7 = 0$
$s = 7$

14. $x^2 - 25 = 0$
$(x - 5)(x + 5) = 0$
$x - 5 = 0$ or $x + 5 = 0$
$x = 5$ $x = -5$

15. $4y^2 - 24y + 36 = 0$
$4(y^2 - 6y + 9) = 0$
$4(y - 3)^2 = 0$
$y - 3 = 0$
$y = 3$

16. $7x^2 + 28x + 28 = 0$
$7(x^2 + 4x + 4) = 0$
$7(x + 2)^2 = 0$
$x + 2 = 0$
$x = -2$

17. $144 = -16t^2 + 96t$
$0 = -16t^2 + 96t - 144$
$0 = -16(t^2 - 6t + 9)$
$0 = t^2 - 6t + 9$
$0 = (t - 3)^2$
$t - 3 = 0$
$t = 3$
If will take the ball 3 seconds to reach a height of 144 feet.

10.7 Practice and Applications (p. 613–615)

18. $(n - 4)(n + 4)$

19. $(q - 8)(q + 8)$

20. $b^2 - 48$ is not factorable using integers

21. $(3c - 1)(3c + 1)$

22. $(7 - a)(7 + a)$

23. $(9 - x)(9 + x)$

24. $36x^2 + 25$ is not factorable using integers

25. $(w - 3y)(w + 3y)$

26. $(5s - 4t)(5s + 4t)$

27. $(x + 4)^2$

28. $(x - 10)^2$

29. $(b - 7)^2$

30. $(y + 15)^2$

31. $(3x + 1)^2$

32. $(2r + 3)^2$

33. $(5n - 2)^2$

34. $2(3x + 1)^2$

35. $4(2w - 5)^2$

36. $(6m - 7)^2$

37. $(a - 2b)^2$

38. $(x + 6y)^2$

39. $4(n^2 - 9) = 4(n - 3)(n + 3)$

40. $18x^2 - 32 = 2(9x^2 - 16)$
$= 2(3x - 4)(3x + 4)$

41. $5(c^2 + 4c + 4) = 5(c + 2)^2$

42. $6(b^2 - 9) = 6(b - 3)(b + 3)$

Copyright © McDougal Littell Inc.
All rights reserved.

43. $9(3t^2 + 2t + 1)$

44. $7(4y^2 - 1) = 7(2y - 1)(2y + 1)$

45. $3(k^2 - 13k + 30) = 3(k - 10)(k - 3)$

46. $24a^2 - 54 = 6(2a - 3)(2a + 3)$

47. $4(b^2 - 10b + 25) = 4(b - 5)^2$

48. $2(16x^2 - 24x + 9) = 2(4x - 3)^2$

49. $4(4w^2 + 20w + 25) = 4(2w + 5)^2$

50. $2(x^2 + 14xy + 49y^2) = 2(x + 7y)^2$

51. $(2x + 1)^2 = 0$
$2x + 1 = 0$
$2x = -1$
$x = -\frac{1}{2}$

52. $(5x - 2)(5x + 2) = 0$
$5x - 2 = 0$ or $5x + 2 = 0$
$5x = 2$ $\quad$ $5x = -2$
$x = \frac{2}{5}$ $\quad$ $x = -\frac{2}{5}$

53. $3(x^2 - 8x + 16) = 0$
$x^2 - 8x + 16 = 0$
$(x - 4)^2 = 0$
$x - 4 = 0$
$x = 4$

54. $3x^2 - 27 = 0$
$3(x^2 - 9) = 0$
$x^2 - 9 = 0$
$(x - 3)(x + 3) = 0$
$x - 3 = 0$ or $x + 3 = 0$
$x = 3$ $\quad$ $x = -3$

55. $6(b^2 - 12b + 36) = 0$
$b^2 - 12b + 36 = 0$
$(b - 6)^2 = 0$
$b - 6 = 0$
$b = 6$

56. $10(9x^2 - 12x + 4) = 0$
$9x^2 - 12x + 4 = 0$
$(3x - 2)^2 = 0$
$3x - 2 = 0$
$3x = 2$
$x = \frac{2}{3}$

57. $(4x - 7)^2 = 0$
$4x - 7 = 0$
$4x = 7$
$x = \frac{7}{4}$

58. $2(25x^2 + 30x + 9) = 0$
$25x^2 + 30x + 9 = 0$
$(5x + 3)^2 = 0$
$5x + 3 = 0$
$5x = -3$
$x = -\frac{3}{5}$

59. $400 = -16t^2 + 160t$
$0 = -16t^2 + 160t - 400$
$0 = -16(t^2 - 10t + 25)$
$0 = t^2 - 10t + 25$
$0 = (t - 5)^2$
$t - 5 = 0$
$t = 5$; 5 sec

60. $4 \cdot D^2 = 9$
$D^2 = 2.25$
$D = \pm 1.5$
The reasonable solution is 1.5 inches for the diameter.

61. $S = 4 \cdot \frac{D^2}{2} = 2D^2$; When $S = 9, 9 = 2D^2, D^2 = 4.5$ and $D \approx \pm 2.12$. The reasonable solution is about 2.12 inches for the diameter.

62. $1 = 4t^2$
$t^2 = \frac{1}{4}$
$t = \pm\frac{1}{2}$
The reasonable solution is $t = \frac{1}{2}$, so the hang time is 0.5 seconds.

63. $4 = 4t^2$
$t^2 = 1$
$t = \pm 1$
The reasonable solution is $t = 1$, so the hang time is 1 second.

64. $9 = \frac{v^2}{2g}$ where $g = 32$
$9 = \frac{v^2}{2(32)}$
$9 = \frac{v^2}{64}$
$v^2 = 576$
$v = \pm 24$
The reasonable solution is $v = 24$, so the velocity is 24 feet per second.

65. $h = \frac{32^2}{2g}$ where $g = 32$
$h = \frac{32^2}{2(32)} = 16$
The height is 16 feet when the velocity is 32 feet per second.

Copyright © McDougal Littell Inc.
All rights reserved.

10.7 Standardized Test Practice (p. 615)

66. D; $-3(2x - 7)(2x + 7)$

67. G; $2(36x^2 - 12x + 1) = 2(6x - 1)^2$

68. C;

$$9x^2 - 12x + 4 = 0$$
$$(3x - 2)^2 = 0$$
$$3x - 2 = 0$$
$$3x = 2$$
$$x = \frac{2}{3}$$

10.7 Mixed Review (p. 615)

69. Substitute 7 for x and -2 for y into the equations:

$$x + 9y = -11$$
$$7 + 9(-2) \stackrel{?}{=} -11$$
$$-11 = 11$$
$$-4x + y = -30$$
$$-4(7) + (-2) \stackrel{?}{=} -30$$
$$-30 = -30$$

$(7, -2)$ is a solution.

70. Substitute -5 for x and -2 for y into the equations:

$$2x + 6y = 22$$
$$2(-5) + 6(-2) \stackrel{?}{=} 22$$
$$-22 \neq 22$$
$$-x - 4y = -13$$
$$-(-5) - 4(-2) \stackrel{?}{=} -13$$
$$13 = 13$$

$(-5, -2)$ is not a solution.

71. Substitute -10 for x and 3 for y into the equations:

$$-2x + 7y = -41$$
$$-2(-10) + 7(3) \stackrel{?}{=} -41$$
$$41 \neq -41$$
$$3x + 5y = 15$$
$$3(-10) + 5(3) \stackrel{?}{=} 15$$
$$-15 \neq 15$$

$(-10, 3)$ is not a solution.

72. Substitute 4 for x and -6 for y into the equations:

$$-5x - 8y = 28$$
$$-5(4) - 8(-6) \stackrel{?}{=} 28$$
$$28 = 28$$
$$9x - 2y = 48$$
$$9(4) - 2(-6) \stackrel{?}{=} 48$$
$$48 = 48$$

$(4, -6)$ is a solution.

73. Since $x - y = 2$, $x = y + 2$. Substitute $y + 2$ for x into $2x + y = 1$ to solve for y:

$$2(y + 2) + y = 1$$
$$2y + 4 + y = 1$$
$$3y + 4 = 1$$
$$3y = -3$$
$$y = -1$$

Substitute -1 for y into $x - y = 2$:

$$x - (-1) = 2$$
$$x + 1 = 2$$
$$x = 1$$

The solution is $(1, -1)$.

74. Since $x - 2y = 10$, $x = 2y + 10$. Substitute $2y + 10$ for x into $3x - y = 0$ and solve for y:

$$3(2y + 10) - y = 0$$
$$6y + 30 - y = 0$$
$$5y + 30 = 0$$
$$3y = -30$$
$$y = -6$$

Substitute -6 for y into

$$x - 2y = 10$$
$$x - 2(-6) = 10$$
$$x + 12 = 10$$
$$x = -2$$

The solution is $(-2, -6)$.

75. Since $-x + y = 0$, $y = x$. Substitute y for x into $2x + y = 0$ and solve for y.

$$2(y) + y = 0$$
$$3y = 0$$
$$y = 0$$

Since $y = x$, $x = 0$. The solution is $(0, 0)$.

76. Since $x - 2y = 4$, $x = 2y + 4$. Substitute $2y + 4$ for x into $2x + y = 3$:

$$2(2y + 4) + y = 3$$
$$4y + 8 + y = 3$$
$$5y + 8 = 3$$
$$5y = -5$$
$$y = -1$$

Substitute -1 for y into

$$x - 2y = 4$$
$$x - 2(-1) = 4$$
$$x + 2 = 4$$
$$x = 2$$

The solution is $(2, -1)$.

77. Since $x - y = 0$, $x = y$. Substitute y for x into $3x + 4y = 14$ and solve for y:

$$3(y) + 4y = 14$$
$$7y = 14$$
$$y = 2$$

Since $x = y$, $x = 2$. The solution is $(2, 2)$.

78. Since $x - 2y = -6$, $x = 2y - 6$. Substitute $2y - 6$ for x into $2x + 3y = -5$ and solve for y:

$$2(2y - 6) + 3y = -5$$
$$4y - 12 + 3y = -5$$
$$7y - 12 = -5$$
$$7y = 7$$
$$y = 1$$

Substitute 1 for y into

$$x - 2y = -6$$
$$x - 2(1) = -6$$
$$x - 2 = -6$$
$$x = -4$$

The solution is $(-4, 1)$.

Copyright © McDougal Littell Inc.
All rights reserved.

Chapter 10 *continued*

79. $\sqrt{216} = \sqrt{36 \cdot 6} = \sqrt{6 \cdot 6 \cdot 6} = 6\sqrt{6}$

80. $\sqrt{5} \cdot \sqrt{15} = \sqrt{5} \cdot \sqrt{5 \cdot 3} = \sqrt{5 \cdot 5 \cdot 3} = 5\sqrt{3}$

81. $\sqrt{10} \cdot \sqrt{20} = \sqrt{10} \cdot \sqrt{10 \cdot 2}$
$= \sqrt{10 \cdot 10 \cdot 2}$
$= 10\sqrt{2}$

82. $\sqrt{4} \cdot 3\sqrt{9} = \sqrt{2 \cdot 2} \cdot 3\sqrt{3 \cdot 3} = 2 \cdot 9 = 18$

83. $\sqrt{\frac{28}{49}} = \sqrt{\frac{4 \cdot 7}{7 \cdot 7}} = \sqrt{\frac{4}{7}} = \frac{2}{\sqrt{7}} = \frac{2}{\sqrt{7}} \cdot \frac{\sqrt{7}}{\sqrt{7}} = \frac{2\sqrt{7}}{7}$

84. $\frac{10\sqrt{8}}{\sqrt{25}} = \frac{10\sqrt{4 \cdot 2}}{5} = 2\sqrt{4 \cdot 2} = 4\sqrt{2}$

85. $\frac{12\sqrt{4}}{\sqrt{9}} = \frac{12 \cdot 2}{3} = 8$

86. $-\frac{6\sqrt{12}}{\sqrt{4}} = -6\sqrt{\frac{12}{4}} = -6\sqrt{3}$

87. $x = \frac{-(-14) \pm \sqrt{(-14)^2 - 4(9)(-7)}}{2(9)}$
$= \frac{14 \pm \sqrt{448}}{18}$
$= \frac{14 \pm 8\sqrt{7}}{18}$
$= \frac{2(7 \pm 4\sqrt{7})}{18}$
$= \frac{7 \pm 4\sqrt{7}}{9}$
$= \frac{1}{9}(7 \pm 4\sqrt{7})$

88. $x = \frac{-(-58) \pm \sqrt{(-58)^2 - 4(9)(24)}}{2(9)}$
$= \frac{58 \pm \sqrt{2500}}{18}$
$= \frac{58 \pm 50}{18}$
$x = \frac{108}{18} = 6 \text{ or } x = \frac{8}{18} = \frac{4}{9}$

89. $y = \frac{-(-9) \pm \sqrt{(-9)^2 - 4(7)(-17)}}{2(7)}$
$= \frac{9 \pm \sqrt{557}}{14}$

10.7 Maintaining Skills (p. 615)

90. $8 = 2 \cdot 2 \cdot 2 = 2^3$

91. $20 = 2 \cdot 2 \cdot 5 = 2^2 \cdot 5$

92. $45 = 3 \cdot 3 \cdot 5 = 3^2 \cdot 5$

93. $57 = 3 \cdot 19$

94. $96 = 2 \cdot 2 \cdot 2 \cdot 2 \cdot 2 \cdot 3 = 2^5 \cdot 3$

95. $80 = 2 \cdot 2 \cdot 2 \cdot 2 \cdot 5 = 2^4 \cdot 5$

96. 101 is prime

97. $120 = 2 \cdot 2 \cdot 2 \cdot 3 \cdot 5 = 2^3 \cdot 3 \cdot 5$

98. $244 = 2 \cdot 2 \cdot 61 = 2^2 \cdot 61$

99. $345 = 3 \cdot 5 \cdot 23$

100. $250 = 2 \cdot 5 \cdot 5 \cdot 5 = 2 \cdot 5^3$

101. $600 = 2 \cdot 2 \cdot 2 \cdot 3 \cdot 5 \cdot 5 = 2^3 \cdot 3 \cdot 5^2$

Lesson 10.8

10.8 Checkpoint (p. 616–618)

1. $11x - 22 = 11(x - 2)$

2. $6x^2 + 12x + 18 = 6(x^2 + 2x + 3)$

3. $8x^3 - 16x = 8x(x^2 - 2)$

4. $3n^3 - 36n^2 + 12n = 3n(n^2 - 12n + 4)$

5. $4y^3 - 10y^2 = 2y^2(2y - 5)$

6. $9x^3 + 6x^2 + 18x = 3x(3x^2 + 2x + 6)$

7. $2n^3 + 4n^2 + 2n = 2n(n^2 + 2n + 1) = 2n(n + 1)^2$

8. $3x^3 - 12x = 3x(x^2 - 4) = 3x(x - 2)(x + 2)$

9. $5m^3 - 45m = 5m(m^2 - 9) = 5m(m - 3)(m + 3)$

10. $x(x^2 + 4x + 4) = x(x + 2)^2$

11. $2x^3 - 10x^2 + 8x = 2x(x^2 - 5x + 4)$
$= 2x(x - 4)(x - 1)$

12. $6p^3 + 21p^2 + 9p = 3p(2p^2 + 7p + 3)$
$= 3p(2p + 1)(p + 3)$

13. $2x^3 - 8x^2 + 3x - 12 = (2x^3 - 8x^2) + (3x - 12)$
$= 2x^2(x - 4) + 3(x - 4)$
$= (2x^2 + 3)(x - 4)$

14. $x^3 + 5x^2 - 4x - 20 = (x^3 + 5x^2) - (4x + 20)$
$= x^2(x + 5) - 4(x + 5)$
$= (x + 5)(x^2 - 4)$
$= (x + 5)(x - 2)(x + 2)$

15. $x^3 - 4x^2 - 9x + 36 = (x^3 - 4x^2) - (9x - 36)$
$= x^2(x - 4) - 9(x - 4)$
$= (x^2 - 9)(x - 4)$
$= (x - 3)(x + 3)(x - 4)$

16. $x^3 + 125 = x^3 + 5^3 = (x + 5)(x^2 - 5x + 25)$

17. $n^3 + 8 = n^3 + 2^3 = (n + 2)(n^2 - 2n + 4)$

18. $2m^3 + 2 = 2(m^3 + 1) = 2(m + 1)(m^2 - m + 1)$

19. $4x^3 + 32 = 4(x^3 + 8)$
$= 4(x^3 + 2^3)$
$= 4(x + 2)(x^2 - 2x + 4)$

20. $x^3 - 27 = x^3 - 3^3 = (x - 3)(x^2 + 3x + 9)$

21. $p^3 - 216 = p^3 - 6^3 = (p - 6)(p^2 + 6p + 36)$

22. $2n^3 - 250 = 2(n^3 - 125)$
$= 2(n^3 - 5^3)$
$= 2(n - 5)(n^2 + 5n + 25)$

23. $4z^3 - 32 = 4(z^3 - 8)$
$= 4(z^3 - 2^3)$
$= 4(z - 2)(z^2 + 2z + 4)$

Copyright © McDougal Littell Inc.
All rights reserved.

10.8 Guided Practice (p. 620)

1. A polynomial is prime if it cannot be factored using integer coefficients.

2. $x^2 + 9$ is a prime factor; $4x(x^2 + 9)$

3. When factoring out $-2b$, the remaining factor is $(b^2 - 6b + 7)$; answer: $-2b(b - 7)(b + 1)$

4. $5n(n^2 - 4)$

5. $6x^2 + 3x^4 = 3x^2(2 + x^2)$

6. $2y^2(3y^2 + 7y - 5)$

7. $x^3 - 1^3 = (x - 1)(x^2 + x + 1)$

8. $x^3 + 64 = x^3 + 4^3 = (x + 4)(x^2 - 4x + 16)$

9. $(3x)^3 + 1^3 = (3x + 1)(9x^2 - 3x + 1)$

10. $(5x)^3 - 1^3 = (5x - 1)(25x^2 + 5x + 1)$

11. $2b(b^2 - 9) = 2b(b - 3)(b + 3)$

12. $7a(a^2 - 2a - 3) = 7a(a - 3)(a + 1)$

13. $3t(t^2 + 6t + 9) = 3t(t + 3)^2$

14. $y(y^2 - 6y + 5) = y(y - 5)(y - 1)$

15. $x(x^2 - 16) = x(x - 4)(x + 4)$

16. $5b(b^2 - 5b - 14) = 5b(b - 7)(b + 2)$

10.8 Practice and Applications (p. 620–622)

17. $6v(v^2 - 3)$

18. $4q(q^3 + 3)$

19. $3x(1 - 3x)$

20. $5x^2(2 + 3x)$

21. $4a^2(1 - 2a^3)$

22. $6t^3(4t^2 + 1)$

23. $5x(3x^2 - x - 2)$

24. $2a^2(2a^3 + 4a - 1)$

25. $3d(6d^5 - 2d + 1)$

26. $(x^2 + 2x) + (xy + 2y) = x(x + 2) + y(x + 2)$
$= (x + y)(x + 2)$

27. $(a^2 + 3a) + (ab + 3b) = a(a + 3) + b(a + 3)$
$= (a + b)(a + 3)$

28. $(2x^3 - 3x^2) - (4x - 6) = x^2(2x - 3) - 2(2x - 3)$
$= (x^2 - 2)(2x - 3)$

29. $(10x^2 - 15x) + (2x - 3) = 5x(2x - 3) + 1(2x - 3)$
$= (5x + 1)(2x - 3)$

30. $(8x^2 - 3x) - (8x - 3) = x(8x - 3) - 1(8x - 3)$
$= (x - 1)(8x - 3)$

31. $(10x^2 - 7x) - (10x - 7) = x(10x - 7) - 1(10x - 7)$
$= (x - 1)(10x - 7)$

32. $m^3 + 1^3 = (m + 1)(m^2 - m + 1)$

33. $c^3 - 2^3 = (c - 2)(c^2 + 2c + 4)$

34. $r^3 + 4^3 = (r + 4)(r^2 - 4r + 16)$

35. $m^3 - 5^3 = (m - 5)(m^2 + 5m + 25)$

36. $6x^2(4x + 3)$

37. $2y(y^2 - 5y - 6) = 2y(y - 6)(y + 1)$

38. $5s(s^2 + 6s + 8) = 5s(s + 2)(s + 4)$

39. $4t(t^3 - 36) = 4t(t - 6)(t + 6)$

40. $-3z^2(4z - 1)$

41. $(c^4 + c^3) - (12c + 12) = c^3(c + 1) - 12(c + 1)$
$= (c^3 - 12)(c + 1)$

42. $(x^3 - 3x^2) + (x - 3) = x^2(x - 3) + 1(x - 3)$
$= (x^2 + 1)(x - 3)$

43. $3(x^3 + 1000) = 3(x^3 + 10^3)$
$= 3(x + 10)(x^2 - 10x + 100)$

44. $2(x^3 - 3375) = 2(x^3 - 15^3)$
$= 2(x - 15)(x^2 + 15x + 225)$

45. $(y + 3)(y + 4) = 0$
$y + 3 = 0$ or $y + 4 = 0$
$y = -3$ $\quad y = -4$

46. $(x - 4)(x + 1) = 0$
$x - 4 = 0$ or $x + 1 = 0$
$x = 4$ $\quad x = -1$

47.
$$-w^2 + 6w + 27 = 0$$
$$-1(w^2 - 6w - 27) = 0$$
$$w^2 - 6w - 27 = 0$$
$$(w + 3)(w - 9) = 0$$
$w + 3 = 0$ or $w - 9 = 0$
$w = -3$ $\quad w = 9$

48. $5x^2(x^2 - 16) = 0$
$5x^2 = 0$ or $x^2 - 16 = 0$
$x^2 = 0$ $\quad x^2 = 16$
$x = 0$ $\quad x = \pm 4$

49. $-4x(4x^2 - 1) = 0$
$-4x = 0$ or $4x^2 - 1 = 0$
$x = 0$ $\quad 4x^2 = 1$
$x^2 = \frac{1}{4}$
$x = \pm\frac{1}{2}$

50. $10x(x^2 - 29x + 62) = 0$
$10x = 0$
$x = 0$

or
$x^2 - 29x + 62 = 0$
$$x = \frac{-(-29) \pm \sqrt{(-29)^2 - 4(1)(62)}}{2(1)}$$
$$= \frac{29 \pm \sqrt{593}}{2}$$
$$= \frac{29 \pm 24.35}{2}$$
$x = 0$ or $x = \frac{29 + 24.352}{2}$ or $x = \frac{29 - 24.352}{2}$
$x = 0$ or $x \approx 26.68$ or $x \approx 2.32$

Copyright © McDougal Littell Inc.
All rights reserved.

51. $4x^2 - 9x - 9 = (4x + 3)(x - 3)$

$4x + 3 = 0$ or $x - 3 = 0$

$4x = -3$ $\quad x = 3$

$x = -\frac{3}{4}$

52. $5x^2 + 2x - 3 = (5x - 3)(x + 1)$

$5x - 3 = 0$ or $x + 1 = 0$

$5x = 3$ $\quad x = -1$

$x = \frac{3}{5}$

53. $2x^2 + 5x + 1$

$a = 2 \; b = 5 \; c = 1$

$$x = \frac{-5 \pm \sqrt{5^2 - 4(2)(1)}}{2(2)}$$

$$= \frac{-5 \pm \sqrt{17}}{4}$$

54. $3x^2 - 4x + 1 = (3x - 1)(x - 1)$

$3x - 1 = 0$ or $x - 1 = 0$

$3x = 1$ $\quad x = 1$

$x = \frac{1}{3}$

55. $6x^2 - 2x - 7$

$a = 6 \; b = -2 \; c = -7$

$$x = \frac{-(-2) \pm \sqrt{(-2)^2 - 4(6)(-7)}}{2(6)}$$

$$= \frac{2 \pm \sqrt{172}}{12} = \frac{2 \pm 2\sqrt{43}}{12} = \frac{1 \pm \sqrt{43}}{6}$$

56. $3x^2 + 8x - 2$

$a = 3 \; b = 8 \; c = -2$

$$x = \frac{-8 \pm \sqrt{8^2 - 4(3)(-2)}}{2(3)} = \frac{-8 \pm \sqrt{88}}{6}$$

$$= \frac{-8 \pm 2\sqrt{22}}{6} = \frac{-4 \pm \sqrt{22}}{3}$$

57. $96 = 16t^2 - 16t$

$0 = 16t^2 - 16t - 96$

$0 = 16(t^2 - t - 6)$

$0 = t^2 - t - 6$

$0 = (t - 3)(t + 2)$

$t - 3 = 0$ or $t + 2 = 0$

$t = 3$ $\quad t = -2$

Only $t = 3$ is a reasonable solution, so it will take 3 seconds for the tennis ball to reach the ground.

58. $96 = \frac{16}{6}t^2 - 16t$

$0 = \frac{8}{3}t^2 - 16t - 96$

$0 = \frac{8}{3}(t^2 - 6t - 36)$

$0 = t^2 - 6t - 36$

$$t = \frac{-(-6) \pm \sqrt{(-6)^2 - 4(1)(-36)}}{2(1)}$$

$$t = \frac{6 \pm \sqrt{180}}{2}$$

$$t = \frac{6 \pm 6\sqrt{5}}{2}$$

$$t = \frac{6(1 \pm \sqrt{5})}{2}$$

$t = 3(1 \pm \sqrt{5})$

$t = 3 + 3\sqrt{5}$ or $t = 3 - 3\sqrt{5}$

$t \approx 9.7$ $\quad t \approx -3.7$

Only $t = 9.7$ is a reasonable solution, so it will take the ball about 9.7 seconds to reach the surface of the moon.

59.

60. $h(h - 3)(h - 9) = 324$

61.

$h(h - 3)(h - 9) = 324$

$(h^2 - 3h)(h - 9) = 324$

$h^3 - 12h^2 + 27h = 324$

$h^3 - 12h^2 + 27h - 324 = 0$

$(h^3 - 12h^2) + (27h - 324) = 0$

$h^2(h - 12) + 27(h - 12) = 0$

$(h^2 + 27)(h - 12) = 0$

$h^2 + 27 = 0$ or $h - 12 = 0$

$h^2 = -27$ $\quad h = 12$

Since the square root of a negative number is not real, there is no solution for h when $h^2 = -27$. Therefore, the height is 12 inches. The width, $h - 9$, is 3 inches and the length, $h - 3$, is 9 inches.

10.8 Standardized Test Practice (p. 622)

62. C;

$x^3 - 5x^2 + 4x - 20 = (x^3 - 5x^2) + (4x - 20)$

$= x^2(x - 5) + 4(x - 5)$

$= (x^2 + 4)(x - 5)$

63. G

$x^3 - 4x = 0$

$x(x^2 - 4) = 0$

$x = 0$ or $x^2 - 4 = 0$

$x^2 = 4$

$x = \pm 2$

Copyright © McDougal Littell Inc.
All rights reserved.

Chapter 10 *continued*

10.8 Mixed Review (p. 622)

64. $7 + x \leq -9$

$x \leq -16$

65. $-3 > 2x - 5$

$2 > 2x$

$1 > x$

$x < 1$

66. $-x + 6 \leq 12$

$-x \leq 6$

$x \geq -6$

67. $x = \pm 3$

68. $|x - 5| = 7$

$x - 5 = 7$ or $x - 5 = -7$

$x = 12$ $\quad$ $x = -2$

69. $|x + 6| = 13$

$x + 6 = 13$ or $x + 6 = -13$

$x = 7$ $\quad$ $x = -19$

70. $|4x + 3| = 9$

$4x + 3 = 9$

$4x = 6$

$x = \frac{6}{4} = \frac{3}{2}$

or

$4x + 3 = -9$

$4x = -12$

$x = -3$

71. $y < -x + 9$

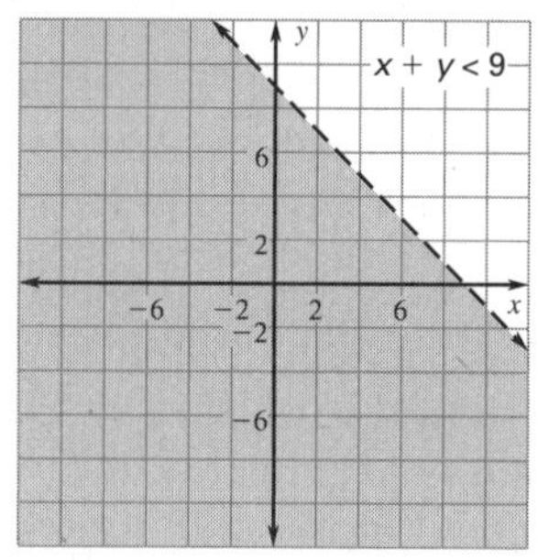

72. $y \geq 3x + 2$

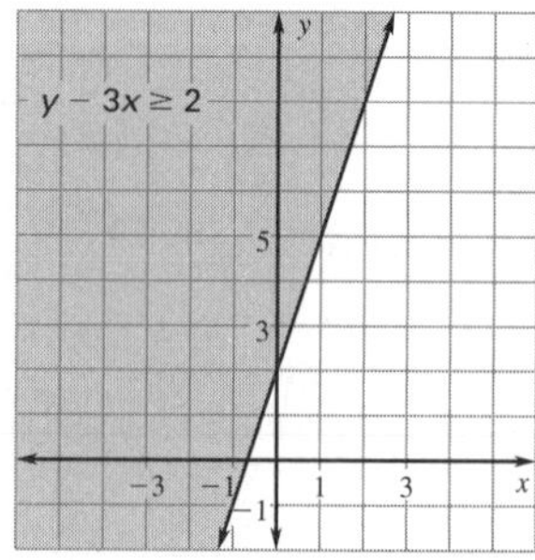

73. $y \leq 4x + 10$

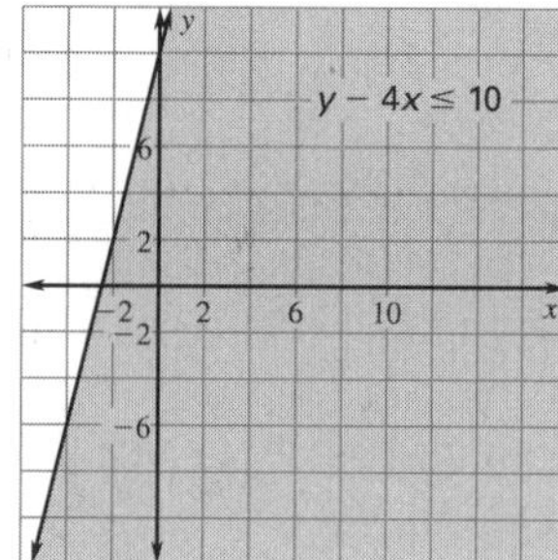

10.8 Maintaining Skills (p. 622)

74. $\frac{1}{18}$ **75.** $-\frac{1}{7}$ **76.** $\frac{9}{2}$ **77.** $\frac{4}{7}$

78. $\frac{6}{5}$ **79.** $-\frac{8}{21}$ **80.** $\frac{10}{97}$ **81.** $-\frac{4}{35}$

Quiz 3 ***(p. 622)***

1. $(7x)^2 - 8^2 = (7x - 8)(7x + 8)$;
difference of squares

2. $11^2 - (3x)^2 = (11 - 3x)(11 + 3x)$;
difference of squares

3. $(2t)^2 + 2(2t)(5) + 5^2 = (2t + 5)^2$;
perfect square trinomial

4. $2(36 - 25y^2) = 2[6^2 - (5y)^2]$

$= 2(6 - 5y)(6 + 5y)$

difference of squares

5. $(3y)^2 + 2(3y)(7) + 7^2 = (3y + 7)^2$;
perfect square trinomial

6. $3(n^2 - 12n + 36) = 3[n^2 - 2n(6) + 6^2]$

$= 3(n - 6)^2$

perfect square trinomial

7. $(x - 4)^2 = 0$

$x - 4 = 0$

$x = 4$

8. $4(x^2 + 8x + 16) = 0$

$4(x + 4)^2 = 0$

$x + 4 = 0$

$x = -4$

9. $x(x^2 + 9x - 36) = 0$

$x(x + 12)(x - 3) = 0$

$x = 0$ or $x + 12 = 0$

$x = -12$

or

$x - 3 = 0$

$x = 3$

10. $3x^2(x + 4)$ **11.** $3x(2x + 1)$

12. $9x^3(2x - 1)$ **13.** $2x(4x^4 + 2x - 1)$

Copyright © McDougal Littell Inc.
All rights reserved.

14. $2x(x^2 - 3x + 2) = 2x(x - 2)(x - 1)$

15. $(x^3 + 3x^2) + (4x + 12) = x^2(x + 3) + 4(x + 3)$
$= (x^2 + 4)(x + 3)$

16. $4(x^3 - 125) = 4(x^3 - 5^3)$
$= 4(x - 5)(x^2 + 5x + 25)$

17. $3y(36y^2 - 25) = 0$
$3y[(6y)^2 - 5^2] = 0$
$3y(6y - 5)(6y + 5) = 0$
$3y = 0$
$y = 0$
or
$6y - 5 = 0$ or $6y + 5 = 0$
$6y = 5$ $\quad 6y = -5$
$y = \frac{5}{6}$ $\quad y = -\frac{5}{6}$

18. $3x^3 - 6x^2 + 5x - 10 = 0$
$(3x^3 - 6x^2) + (5x - 10) = 0$
$3x^2(x - 2) + 5(x - 2) = 0$
$(3x^2 + 5)(x - 2) = 0$
$3x^2 + 5 = 0$ or $x - 2 = 0$
$3x^2 = -5$ $\quad x = 2$
$x^2 = -\frac{5}{3}$

Since the square root of a negative number is not real, there is no real number solution for $x^2 = -\frac{5}{3}$, so $x = 2$ is the only solution.

Chapter 10 Summary and Review *(p. 623)*

1. $5x - 12 - 2x + 7 = 3x - 5$

2. $24m - 13 - 18m - 7 + 6m - 4 = 12m - 24$

3. $-x^2 + x + 2 + 3x^2 + 4x + 5 = 2x^2 + 5x + 7$

4. $x^2 + 3x - 1 - 4x^2 + 5x - 6 = -3x^2 + 8x - 7$

5. $x^3 + 5x^2 - 4x - 3x^2 + 6x - 2 = x^3 + 2x^2 + 2x - 2$

6. $4x^3 + x^2 - 1 + 2 - x - x^2 = 4x^3 - x + 1$

7. $6a^3 - 15a^2 + 3a$

8. $-4x^5 - 8x^4 + 28x^3$

9. $a^2 + 8a - 5a - 40 = a^2 + 3a - 40$

10. $20x^2 + 8x - 5x - 2 = 20x^2 + 3x - 2$

11. $d^3 - 3d^2 - 10d + 2d^2 - 6d - 20$
$= d^3 - d^2 - 16d - 20$

12. $6b^3 + 10b^2 + 8b - 3b^2 - 5b - 4$
$= 6b^3 + 7b^2 + 3b - 4$

13. $x^2 - 15^2 = x^2 - 225$

14. $(5x)^2 - 2^2 = 25x^2 - 4$

15. $x^2 + 2(x)(2) + 2^2 = x^2 + 4x + 4$

16. $(7m)^2 - 2(7m)(6) + 6^2 = 49m^2 - 84m + 36$

17. $(2x + 2)^2 = (2x)^2 + 2(2x)(2) + 2^2$
$= 4x^2 + 8x + 4$
square of a binomial

18. $x + 1 = 0$ or $x + 10 = 0$
$x = -1$ $\quad x = -10$

19. $x - 3 = 0$ or $x - 2 = 0$
$x = 3$ $\quad x = 2$

20. $y - 7 = 0$
$y = 7$

21. $b = 0$ or $5b - 3 = 0$
$5b = 3$
$b = \frac{3}{5}$

22. $5a - 1 = 0$ or $3a + 1 = 0$
$5a = 1$ $\quad 3a = -1$
$a = \frac{1}{5}$ $\quad a = -\frac{1}{3}$

23. $n = 0$
or
$n + 9 = 0$ or $n - 12 = 0$
$n = -9$ $\quad n = 12$

24. $c + 5 = 0$
$c = -5$
or
$2c - 1 = 0$ or $3c + 2 = 0$
$2c = 1$ $\quad 3c = -2$
$c = \frac{1}{2}$ $\quad c = -\frac{2}{3}$

25. $3x + 1 = 0$ or $x - 4 = 0$
$3x = -1$ $\quad x = 4$
$x = -\frac{1}{3}$

26. $2c = 0$ or $4c + 3 = 0$
$c = 0$ $\quad 4c = -3$
$c = -\frac{3}{4}$

27. $(x + 6)(x + 4)$

28. $(a - 8)(a + 2)$

29. $(m - 10)(m + 2)$

30. $(b - 4)(b - 7) = 0$
$b - 4 = 0$ or $b - 7 = 0$
$b = 4$ $\quad b = 7$

Copyright © McDougal Littell Inc.
All rights reserved.

Chapter 10 *continued*

31. $(y + 8)(y - 4) = 0$
$y + 8 = 0$ or $y - 4 = 0$
$y = -8$ $\quad y = 4$

32. $(a - 10)(a + 4) = 0$
$a - 10 = 0$ or $a + 4 = 0$
$a = 10$ $\quad a = -4$

33. $(3x + 1)(4x + 1)$ **34.** $(3x - 2)(x - 2)$

35. $(4r - 3)(r + 2)$ **36.** $(5c + 2)(c - 7)$

37. $(2p + 1)(p - 1) = 0$
$2p + 1 = 0$ or $p - 1 = 0$
$2p = -1$ $\quad p = 1$
$p = -\frac{1}{2}$

38. $(4x + 1)(x - 1) = 0$
$4x + 1 = 0$ or $x - 1 = 0$
$4x = -1$ $\quad x = 1$
$x = -\frac{1}{4}$

39. $2a^2 + 7a - 4 = 0$
$(2a - 1)(a + 4) = 0$
$2a - 1 = 0$ or $a + 4 = 0$
$2a = 1$ $\quad a = -4$
$a = \frac{1}{2}$

40. $(b - 7)(b + 7) = 0$
$b - 7 = 0$ or $b + 7 = 0$
$b = 7$ $\quad b = -7$

41. $(4a)^2 - 1^2 = 0$
$(4a - 1)(4a + 1) = 0$
$4a - 1 = 0$ or $4a + 1 = 0$
$4a = 1$ $\quad 4a = -1$
$a = \frac{1}{4}$ $\quad a = -\frac{1}{4}$

42. $(3d)^2 - 2(3d)(1) + 1^2 = 0$
$(3d - 1)^2 = 0$
$3d - 1 = 0$
$3d = 1$
$d = \frac{1}{3}$

43. $m^2 - 10^2 = 0$
$(m - 10)(m + 10) = 0$
$m - 10 = 0$ or $m + 10 = 0$
$m = 10$ $\quad m = -10$

44. $(2b)^2 - 2(2b)(3) + 3^2 = 0$
$(2b - 3)^2 = 0$
$2b - 3 = 0$
$2b = 3$
$b = \frac{3}{2}$

45. $(5x)^2 + 2(5x)(2) + 2^2 = 0$
$(5x + 2)^2 = 0$
$5x + 2 = 0$
$5x = -2$
$x = -\frac{2}{5}$

46. $-2x(x^2 - 3x + 7)$ **47.** $5y^2(y^2 - 4y + 2)$

48. $(x^3 + 3x^2) - (4x + 12) = x^2(x + 3) - 4(x + 3)$
$= (x^2 - 4)(x + 3)$
$= (x - 2)(x + 2)(x + 3)$

49. $(3y^3 - 4y^2) - (6y - 8) = y^2(3y - 4) - 2(3y - 4)$
$= (y^2 - 2)(3y - 4)$

50. $x^3 - 4^3 = (x - 4)(x^2 + 4x + 16)$

51. $(3b)^3 + 1^3 = (3b + 1)(9b^2 - 3b + 1)$

52. $(x - 5)(x - 1) = 0$
$x - 5 = 0$ or $x - 1 = 0$
$x = 5$ $\quad x = 1$

53. $2(x^2 - 25) = 0$
$2(x - 5)(x + 5) = 0$
$x - 5 = 0$ or $x + 5 = 0$
$x = 5$ $\quad x = -5$

54. $8x^3 - 30x^2 + 25x = 0$
$x(8x^2 - 15x + 25) = 0$
$x(2x - 5)(4x - 5) = 0$
$x = 0$
or
$2x - 5 = 0$ or $4x - 5 = 0$
$2x = 5$ $\quad 4x = 5$
$x = \frac{5}{2}$ $\quad x = \frac{5}{4}$

Chapter Test *(p. 627)*

1. $x^2 + 4x - 1 + 5x^2 + 2 = 6x^2 + 4x + 1$

2. $5t^2 - 9t + 1 - 8t - 13 = 5t^2 - 17t - 12$

3. $7n^3 + 2n^2 - n - 4 - 4n^3 + 3n^2 - 8$
$= 3n^3 + 5n^2 - n - 12$

4. $x^4 + 6x^2 + 7 + 2x^4 - 3x^2 + 1$
$= 3x^4 + 3x^2 + 8$

5. $2x^2 + 3x + 6x + 9 = 2x^2 + 9x + 9$

6. $15x^2 + 3x - 5x - 1 = 15x^2 - 2x - 1$

7. $4w^3 + w^2 - 7w - 24w^2 - 6w + 42$
$= 4w^3 - 23w^2 - 13w + 42$

8. $20t^3 + 40t^2 - 35t + 8t^2 + 16t - 14$
$= 20t^3 + 48t^2 - 19t - 14$

9. $3z^4 + 6z^3 - 5z^3 - 10z^2 + 8z + 16$
$= 3z^4 + z^3 - 10z^2 + 8z + 16$

10. $16x^2 - 12x + 4x - 3 = 16x^2 - 8x - 3$

11. $x^2 - 2(x)(12) + 12^2 = x^2 - 24x + 144$

12. $(7x)^2 + 2(7x)(2) + 2^2 = 49x^2 + 28x + 4$

13. $(8x)^2 - 3^2 = 64x^2 - 9$

Copyright © McDougal Littell Inc.
All rights reserved.

14. $6x - 5 = 0$ or $x + 2 = 0$
$6x = 5$ $x = -2$
$x = \frac{5}{6}$

15. $x + 8 = 0$
$x = -8$

16. $x + 3 = 0$ or $x - 1 = 0$
$x = -3$ $x = 1$

or
$3x + 2 = 0$
$3x = -2$
$x = -\frac{2}{3}$

17. Solve for x when $y = 0$:
$0 = (x + 1)(x - 5)$
$x + 1 = 0$ or $x - 5 = 0$
$x = -1$ $x = 5$

The x-intercepts are $(-1, 0)$ and $(5, 0)$. The x-coordinate of the vertex is $x = \frac{-1 + 5}{2} = 2$. Substitute 2 for x into $y = (x + 1)(x - 5)$ to find the y-coordinate of the vertex:

$y = (2 + 1)(2 - 5) = -9$
The vertex is $(2, -9)$.

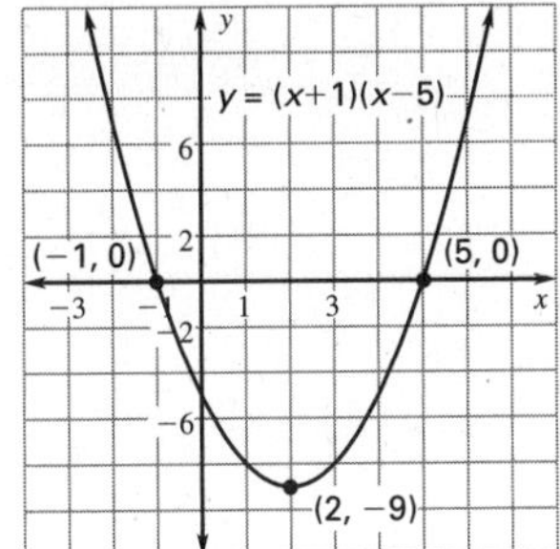

18. Solve for x when $y = 0$:
$0 = (x - 4)(x + 4)$
$x - 4 = 0$ or $x + 4 = 0$
$x = 4$ $x = -4$

The x-intercepts are $(4, 0)$ and $(-4, 0)$. The x-coordinate of the vertex is $x = \frac{-4 + 4}{2} = 0$. Substitute 0 for x into $y = (x - 4)(x + 4)$ to find the y-coordinate of the vertex.

$y = (0 - 4)(0 + 4) = -16$. So, the vertex is $(0, -16)$.

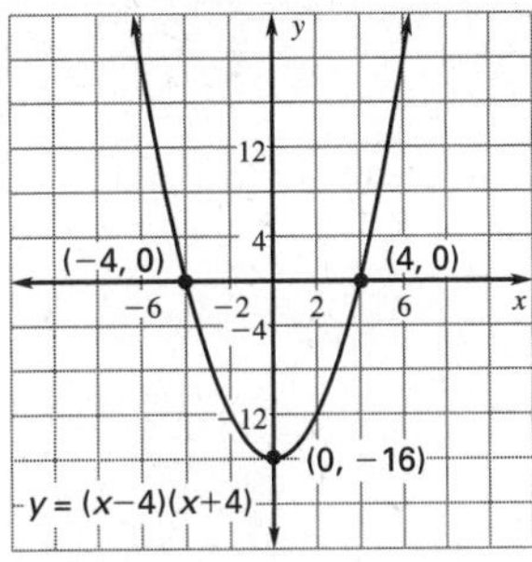

19. Solve for x when $y = 0$:
$0 = (x + 2)(x + 6)$
$x + 2 = 0$ or $x + 6 = 0$
$x = -2$ $x = -6$

The x-intercepts are $(-2, 0)$ and $(-6, 0)$. The x-coordinate of the vertex is $x = \frac{-2 + (-6)}{2} = -4$. Substitute -4 for x into $y = (x + 2)(x + 6)$ to find the y-coordinate of the vertex.

$y = (-4 + 2)(-4 + 6) = -4$. So, the vertex is $(-4, -4)$.

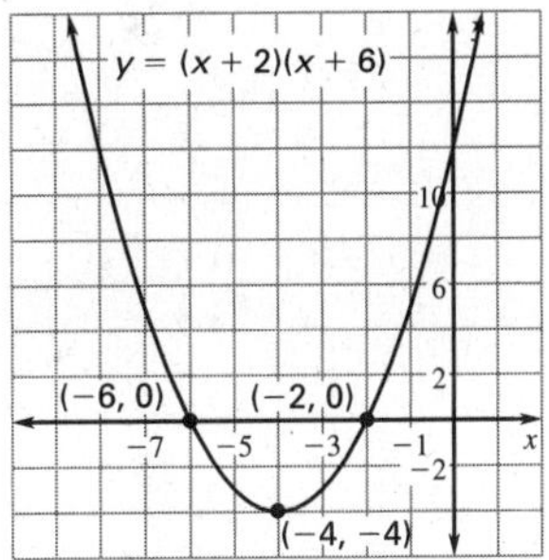

20. $(x + 10)(x + 3) = 0$
$x + 10 = 0$ or $x + 3 = 0$
$x = -10$ $x = -3$

21. $(x - 7)(x - 12) = 0$
$x - 7 = 0$ or $x - 12 = 0$
$x = 7$ $x = 12$

22. $(x - 40)(x + 6) = 0$
$x - 40 = 0$ or $x + 6 = 0$
$x = 40$ $x = -6$

23. $(2x - 9)(x + 12) = 0$
$2x - 9 = 0$ or $x + 12 = 0$
$2x = 9$ $x = -12$
$x = \frac{9}{2}$

24. $9x^2 - 9x - 28 = 0$
$(3x + 4)(3x - 7) = 0$
$3x + 4 = 0$ or $3x - 7 = 0$
$3x = -4$ $3x = 7$
$x = -\frac{4}{3}$ $x = \frac{7}{3}$

Copyright © McDougal Littell Inc.
All rights reserved.

25. $18x^2 - 57x + 35 = 0$

$(3x - 7)(6x - 5) = 0$

$3x - 7 = 0$ or $6x - 5 = 0$

$3x = 7$ $\quad 6x = 5$

$x = \frac{7}{3}$ $\quad x = \frac{5}{6}$

26. $x^2 - 14^2 = (x - 14)(x + 14)$

27. $4(4x^2 - 9) = 4[(2x)^2 - 3^2] = 4(2x - 3)(2x + 3)$

28. $-2(25x^2 - 64) = -2[(5x)^2 - 8^2]$

$= -2(5x - 8)(5x + 8)$

29. $x^2 - 2x(3) + 3^2 = (x - 3)^2$

30. $(2x)^2 + 2(2x)(11) + 11^2 = (2x + 11)^2$

31. $-3x(2x^2 + x - 15) = -3x(x + 3)(2x - 5)$

32. $9(t^2 - 6)$

33. $(x^3 + 2x^2) - (16x + 32) = x^2(x + 2) - 16(x + 2)$

$= (x^2 - 16)(x + 2)$

$= (x - 4)(x + 4)(x + 2)$

34. $2x(x^2 - 81) = 2x(x - 9)(x + 9)$

35. $x^2 - 60 + 11 = 0$

$x^2 - 49 = 0$

$(x - 7)(x + 7) = 0$

$x - 7 = 0$ or $x + 7 = 0$

$x = 7$ $\quad x = -7$

36. $(2x - 1)(x + 8) = 0$

$2x - 1 = 0$ or $x + 8 = 0$

$2x = 1$ $\quad x = -8$

$x = \frac{1}{2}$

37. $x^2 - 13x + 40 = 0$

$(x - 5)(x - 8) = 0$

$x - 5 = 0$ or $x - 8 = 0$

$x = 5$ $\quad x = 8$

38. $x = 0$ or $x - 16 = 0$

$x = 16$

39. $3x(4x + 1) = 0$

$3x = 0$ or $4x + 1 = 0$

$x = 0$ $\quad 4x = -1$

$x = -\frac{1}{4}$

40. $(x^4 + 7x^3) - (8x + 56) = 0$

$x^3(x + 7) - 8(x + 7) = 0$

$(x^3 - 8)(x + 7) = 0$

$x^3 - 8 = 0$ or $x + 7 = 0$

$x^3 = 8$ $\quad x = -7$

$x = 2$

41. $5x(x^2 - 121) = 0$

$5x = 0$ or $x^2 - 121 = 0$

$x = 0$ $\quad x^2 = 121$

$x = \pm 11$

42. $4x(x^2 + 6x + 9) = 0$

$4x(x + 3)^2 = 0$

$4x = 0$ or $x + 3 = 0$

$x = 0$ $\quad x = -3$

43. $(2x - 5)(8x + 3) = 0$

$2x - 5 = 0$ or $8x + 3 = 0$

$2x = 5$ $\quad 8x = -3$

$x = \frac{5}{2}$ $\quad x = -\frac{3}{8}$

44. $135 = w(2w - 3)$

$135 = 2w^2 - 3w$

$0 = 2w^2 - 3w - 135$

$0 = (2w + 15)(w - 9)$

$2w + 15 = 0$ or $w - 9 = 0$

$2w = -15$ $\quad w = 9$

$w = -\frac{15}{2}$

Only $w = 9$ is the reasonable solution, so the width is 9 feet. The length, $2w - 3$, is 15 feet. The dimensions are 9 ft by 15 ft.

45. The rug covers 20 square feet of the room floor, which is $\frac{2}{3}$ of the floor area. Therefore, the entire floor area is 30 square meters. From the diagram below we find that the area of the floor can be described by $30 = 5(2x + 4)$ where x is the width of the strip of floor not covered by the rug.

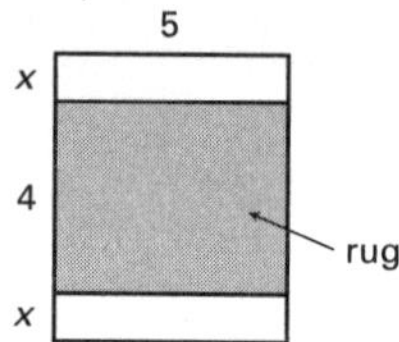

Solve for x:

$30 = 5(2x + 4)$

$30 = 10x + 20$

$10 = 10x$

$x = 1$

Therefore, the strip is 1 foot wide.

Chapter Standardized Test *(p. 628)*

1. B, cubic polynomial

2. A;

$(-x^2 - 7x^2) + (-5x + 5x) + (7 + (-2))$

$= -8x^2 + 5$

3. D;

$5x^3 + 3x^2 - x + 1 - 2x^3 - x + 5$

$= (5x^3 - 2x^3) + (3x^2) + (-x - x) + (1 + 5)$

$= 3x^3 + 3x^2 - 2x + 6$

4. B; $20x^2 - 8x - 5x + 2 = 20x^2 - 13x + 2$

5. D; $(2x)^2 - 2(2x)(9) + 9^2 = 4x^2 - 36x + 81$

Copyright © McDougal Littell Inc.
All rights reserved.

6. B;

$$x^2 - 2x - 120 = 0$$
$$(x + 10)(x - 12) = 0$$
$$x + 10 = 0 \quad \text{or} \quad x - 12 = 0$$
$$x = -10 \qquad\qquad x = 12$$

7. C; $-5(9x^2 - 30x - 25) = -5(3x - 5)^2$

8. D;

$$(x^3 - 2x^2) - (11x - 22) = x^2(x - 2) - 11(x - 2)$$
$$= (x^2 - 11)(x - 2)$$

9. B; $x^3 + 4^3 = (x + 4)(x^2 - 4x + 16)$

Maintaining Skills *(p. 629)*

1. LCD: 20

$\frac{1}{4} = \frac{1 \cdot 5}{4 \cdot 5} = \frac{5}{20}; \frac{2}{5} = \frac{2 \cdot 4}{5 \cdot 4} = \frac{8}{20}$

$5 < 8$, so $\frac{1}{4} < \frac{2}{5}$

order: $\frac{1}{4}, \frac{2}{5}$

2. LCD: 56

$\frac{4}{7} = \frac{4 \cdot 8}{7 \cdot 8} = \frac{32}{56}; \frac{3}{8} = \frac{3 \cdot 7}{8 \cdot 7} = \frac{21}{56}$

$21 < 32$, so $\frac{3}{8} < \frac{4}{7}$

order: $\frac{3}{8}, \frac{4}{7}$

3. LCD: 6

$\frac{1}{3} = \frac{1 \cdot 2}{3 \cdot 2} = \frac{2}{6}; \frac{5}{6} = \frac{5}{6}; \frac{1}{2} = \frac{1 \cdot 3}{2 \cdot 3} = \frac{3}{6}$

$2 < 3 < 5$, so $\frac{1}{3} < \frac{1}{2} < \frac{5}{6}$

order: $\frac{1}{3}, \frac{1}{2}, \frac{5}{6}$

4. LCD: 12

$\frac{3}{4} = \frac{3 \cdot 3}{4 \cdot 3} = \frac{9}{12}; \frac{1}{6} = \frac{1 \cdot 2}{6 \cdot 2} = \frac{2}{12}; \frac{1}{2} = \frac{1 \cdot 6}{2 \cdot 6} = \frac{6}{12}$

$2 < 6 < 9$, so $\frac{1}{6} < \frac{1}{2} < \frac{3}{4}$

order: $\frac{1}{6}, \frac{1}{2}, \frac{3}{4}$

5. LCD: 20

$\frac{3}{10} = \frac{3 \cdot 2}{10 \cdot 2} = \frac{6}{20}; \frac{3}{4} = \frac{3 \cdot 5}{4 \cdot 5} = \frac{15}{20}; \frac{13}{20} = \frac{13}{20}$

$6 < 13 < 15$, so $\frac{3}{10} \le \frac{13}{20} \le \frac{3}{4}$

order: $\frac{3}{10}, \frac{13}{20}, \frac{3}{4}$

6. LCD: 24

$\frac{7}{8} = \frac{7 \cdot 3}{8 \cdot 3} = \frac{21}{24}; \frac{5}{4} = \frac{5 \cdot 6}{4 \cdot 6} = \frac{30}{24}; \frac{7}{24} = \frac{7}{24}$

$7 < 21 < 30$, so $\frac{7}{24} < \frac{7}{8} < \frac{5}{4}$

order: $\frac{7}{24}, \frac{7}{8}, \frac{5}{4}$

7. LCD: 12

$1\frac{1}{3} = \frac{4}{3} = \frac{4 \cdot 4}{3 \cdot 4} = \frac{16}{12}; \frac{5}{4} = \frac{5 \cdot 3}{4 \cdot 3} = \frac{15}{12};$

$\frac{5}{6} = \frac{5 \cdot 2}{6 \cdot 2} = \frac{10}{12}$

$10 < 15 < 16$, so $\frac{5}{6} < \frac{5}{4} < 1\frac{1}{3}$

order: $\frac{5}{6}, \frac{5}{4}, 1\frac{1}{3}$

8. LCD: 12

$2\frac{1}{4} = \frac{9}{4} = \frac{9 \cdot 3}{4 \cdot 3} = \frac{27}{12}; 1\frac{2}{3} = \frac{5}{3} = \frac{5 \cdot 4}{3 \cdot 4} = \frac{20}{12}$

$\frac{5}{6} = \frac{5 \cdot 2}{6 \cdot 2} = \frac{10}{12}$

$10 < 20 < 27$, so $\frac{5}{6} < 1\frac{2}{3} < 2\frac{1}{4}$

order: $\frac{5}{6}, 1\frac{2}{3}, 2\frac{1}{4}$

9. $\frac{2}{3} + \frac{5}{12} = \frac{8}{12} + \frac{5}{12} = \frac{13}{12} = 1\frac{1}{12}$

10. $\frac{1}{6} - \frac{3}{4} = \frac{2}{12} - \frac{9}{12} = -\frac{7}{12}$

11. $\frac{2}{5} + \frac{3}{7} = \frac{14}{35} + \frac{15}{35} = \frac{29}{35}$

12. $\frac{7}{8} - \frac{5}{12} = \frac{21}{24} - \frac{10}{24} = \frac{11}{24}$

13. $\frac{7}{10} - \frac{1}{3} = \frac{21}{30} - \frac{10}{30} = \frac{11}{30}$

14. $\frac{5}{9} + \frac{11}{12} = \frac{20}{36} + \frac{33}{36} = \frac{53}{36} = 1\frac{17}{36}$

15. $1\frac{1}{2} + 3\frac{5}{6} = \frac{3}{2} + \frac{23}{6} = \frac{9}{6} + \frac{23}{6} = \frac{32}{6} = \frac{16}{3} = 5\frac{1}{3}$

16. $2\frac{3}{4} - \frac{17}{20} = \frac{11}{4} - \frac{17}{20} = \frac{55}{20} - \frac{17}{20} = \frac{38}{20} = \frac{19}{10} = 1\frac{9}{10}$

Copyright © McDougal Littell Inc.
All rights reserved.

CHAPTER 11

Chapter Opener *(p. 631)*

Think and Discuss (p. 631)

1. length: 1 inch $\times \dfrac{14 \text{ feet}}{1 \text{ inch}} = 14$ feet in length

2. width: $\dfrac{1}{2}$ inch $\times \dfrac{14 \text{ feet}}{1 \text{ inch}} = 7$ feet in width

3.
$$\frac{3}{1} = \frac{x}{14}$$
$$14(3) = x$$
$$42 = x$$
42 feet

Chapter Readiness Quiz (p. 632)

1. B;
$$y = (x - 5)(x + 1)$$
$$y = x^2 - 5x + x - 5$$
$$y = x^2 - 4x - 5$$
and
$$y - x^2 = -4x - 5$$
$$y = x^2 - 4x - 5$$

2. B;
$$49x^2 \div -\frac{7x}{3} = 49x^2 \cdot \frac{3}{-7x}$$
$$= \frac{49(3)x^2}{-7x}$$
$$= -7(3)x$$
$$= -21x$$

3. D;
$$4x^2 - 10x + 6 = 0$$
$$2(2x^2 - 5x + 3) = 0$$
$$2x^2 - 5x + 3 = 0$$
$$(2x - 3)(x - 1) = 0$$
$2x - 3 = 0$ or $x - 1 = 0$

$2x = 3$ $\quad x = 1$

$x = \dfrac{3}{2}$

Lesson 11.1

11.1 Checkpoint (p. 634)

1.

$\frac{2}{b} = \frac{5}{2}$	Original proportion
$2 \cdot 2 = b \cdot 5$	Cross product property
$4 = 5b$	Simplify.
$\frac{4}{5} = b$	Divide each side by 5.

Check: Substitute $\frac{4}{5}$ for b.
$$\frac{2}{\frac{4}{5}} \stackrel{?}{=} \frac{5}{2}$$
$$2 \div \frac{4}{5} \stackrel{?}{=} \frac{5}{2}$$
$$2 \cdot \frac{5}{4} \stackrel{?}{=} \frac{5}{2}$$
$$\frac{5}{2} = \frac{5}{2}$$

2.

$\frac{25}{n} = \frac{n}{4}$	Original proportion
$25(4) = n \cdot n$	Cross product property
$100 = n^2$	Simplify
$\pm\sqrt{100} = n$	
$\pm 10 = n$	

Check both solutions:
$$\frac{25}{10} \stackrel{?}{=} \frac{10}{4}$$
$$\frac{5}{2} = \frac{5}{2}$$
$$\frac{25}{-10} \stackrel{?}{=} -\frac{10}{4}$$
$$-\frac{5}{2} = -\frac{5}{2}$$

3.

$-\frac{3}{x} = \frac{x + 6}{3}$	Original proportion
$-3(3) = x(x + 6)$	Cross product property
$-9 = x^2 + 6x$	Multiply.
$0 = x^2 + 6x + 9$	Collect terms on one side.
$0 = (x + 3)(x + 3)$	Factor.
$x = -3$	Solve.

Check:
$$\frac{-3}{-3} \stackrel{?}{=} \frac{-3 + 6}{3}$$
$$1 \stackrel{?}{=} \frac{3}{3}$$
$$1 = 1$$

Copyright © McDougal Littell Inc.
All rights reserved.

4. $\frac{x}{4} = \frac{x-1}{x}$ Original proportion

$x(x) = 4(x - 1)$ Cross product property.

$x^2 = 4x - 4$ Multiply.

$x^2 - 4x + 4 = 0$ Collect terms on one side.

$(x - 2)(x - 2) = 0$ Factor.

$x = 2$ Solve.

Check:

$\frac{2}{4} \stackrel{?}{=} \frac{2-1}{2}$

$\frac{1}{2} = \frac{1}{2}$

11.1 Guided Practice (p. 636)

1. a. $\frac{3}{4} = \frac{9}{12}$; extremes: 3 and 12; means: 4 and 9

b. $\frac{9}{12} = \frac{3}{4}$; extremes: 9 and 4; means: 12 and 3

2. $\frac{2}{x} = \frac{16}{40}$

$2(40) = x(16)$

$80 = 16x$

$5 = x$

Check:

$\frac{2}{5} \stackrel{?}{=} \frac{16}{40}$

$\frac{2}{5} \stackrel{?}{=} \frac{8 \cdot 2}{8 \cdot 5}$

$\frac{2}{5} = \frac{2}{5}$

3. $\frac{72}{96} = \frac{x}{4}$

$72(4) = 96x$

$288 = 96x$

$3 = x$

Check:

$\frac{79}{96} \stackrel{?}{=} \frac{3}{4}$

$\frac{3 \cdot 24}{4 \cdot 24} \stackrel{?}{=} \frac{3}{4}$

$\frac{3}{4} = \frac{3}{4}$

4. $\frac{x}{3} = \frac{2}{7}$

$x(7) = 3(2)$

$7x = 6$

$x = \frac{6}{7}$

Check:

$\frac{\frac{6}{7}}{3} \stackrel{?}{=} \frac{2}{7}$

$\frac{6}{7} \div 3 \stackrel{?}{=} \frac{2}{7}$

$\frac{6}{7} \cdot \frac{1}{3} \stackrel{?}{=} \frac{2}{7}$

$\frac{2}{7} = \frac{2}{7}$

5. $\frac{4}{x+1} = \frac{7}{2}$

$4(2) = (x + 1)7$

$8 = 7x + 7$

$1 = 7x$

$\frac{1}{7} = x$

Check:

$\frac{4}{\frac{1}{7} + 1} \stackrel{?}{=} \frac{7}{2}$

$\frac{4}{\frac{1}{7} + \frac{7}{7}} \stackrel{?}{=} \frac{7}{2}$

$\frac{4}{\frac{8}{7}} \stackrel{?}{=} \frac{7}{2}$

$4 \div \frac{8}{7} \stackrel{?}{=} \frac{7}{2}$

$4 \cdot \frac{7}{8} \stackrel{?}{=} \frac{7}{2}$

$\frac{7}{2} = \frac{7}{2}$

6. $\frac{2}{2x+1} = \frac{1}{5}$

$2(5) = (2x + 1)(1)$

$10 = 2x + 1$

$9 = 2x$

$4.5 = \frac{9}{2} = x$

Check:

$\frac{2}{2(4.5) + 1} \stackrel{?}{=} \frac{1}{5}$

$\frac{2}{10} \stackrel{?}{=} \frac{1}{5}$

$\frac{1}{5} = \frac{1}{5}$

Copyright © McDougal Littell Inc.
All rights reserved.

7. $\frac{x-2}{x} = \frac{2}{3}$

$3(x-2) = x(2)$

$3x - 6 = 2x$

$-6 = -x$

$6 = x$

Check:

$\frac{6-2}{6} \stackrel{?}{=} \frac{2}{3}$

$\frac{4}{6} \stackrel{?}{=} \frac{2}{3}$

$\frac{2}{3} = \frac{2}{3}$

8. $ad = bc$; yes (cross product)

9. $ba = dc$; no (did not cross multiply)

10. $\frac{a}{d} = \frac{b}{c}$; no (did not cross multiply)

11. $\frac{b}{a} = \frac{d}{c}$; yes assuming $a, c \neq 0$ (reciprocal property)

11.1 Practice and Applications (pp. 636–638)

12. $\frac{3}{x} = \frac{1}{2}$

$\frac{x}{3} = \frac{2}{1}$

$x = 6$

Check:

$\frac{3}{6} \stackrel{?}{=} \frac{1}{2}$

$\frac{1}{2} = \frac{1}{2}$

13. $\frac{3}{4} = \frac{8}{3c}$

$\frac{4}{3} = \frac{3c}{8}$

$\frac{32}{3} = 3c$

$\frac{32}{9} = c$

Check:

$\frac{3}{4} \stackrel{?}{=} \frac{8}{3(\frac{32}{9})}$

$\frac{3}{4} \stackrel{?}{=} \frac{8}{(\frac{32}{3})}$

$\frac{3}{4} \stackrel{?}{=} 8 \div \frac{32}{3}$

$\frac{3}{4} \stackrel{?}{=} 8 \cdot \frac{3}{32}$

$\frac{3}{4} = \frac{3}{4}$

14. $\frac{13}{z} = \frac{1}{3}$

$\frac{z}{13} = \frac{3}{1}$

$z = 39$

Check:

$\frac{13}{39} \stackrel{?}{=} \frac{1}{3}$

$\frac{1}{3} = \frac{1}{3}$

15. $\frac{5}{8} = \frac{c}{56}$

$5(56) = 8c$

$280 = 8c$

$35 = c$

Check:

$\frac{5}{8} \stackrel{?}{=} \frac{35}{56}$

$\frac{5}{8} = \frac{5}{8}$

16. $\frac{x}{3} = \frac{7}{3}$

$x(3) = 3(7)$

$3x = 21$

$x = 7$

Check: $\frac{7}{3} = \frac{7}{3}$

17. $\frac{16}{4} = \frac{12}{z}$

$16z = 4(12)$

$16z = 48$

$z = 3$

Check:

$\frac{16}{4} \stackrel{?}{=} \frac{12}{3}$

$4 = 4$

18. $\frac{42}{28} = \frac{3}{x}$

$42x = 28(3)$

$42x = 84$

$x = 2$

Check:

$\frac{42}{28} \stackrel{?}{=} \frac{3}{2}$

$\frac{14 \cdot 3}{14 \cdot 2} \stackrel{?}{=} \frac{3}{2}$

$\frac{3}{2} = \frac{3}{2}$

Copyright © McDougal Littell Inc.
All rights reserved.

19. $\frac{5}{y} = \frac{8}{9}$

$5(9) = y(8)$

$45 = 8y$

$\frac{45}{8} = y$

Check:

$\frac{5}{\left(\frac{45}{8}\right)} \stackrel{?}{=} \frac{8}{9}$

$5 \div \frac{45}{8} \stackrel{?}{=} \frac{8}{9}$

$5 \cdot \frac{8}{45} \stackrel{?}{=} \frac{8}{9}$

$\frac{8}{9} = \frac{8}{9}$

20. $\frac{4}{2w} = \frac{7}{3}$

$4(3) = 2w(7)$

$12 = 14w$

$\frac{12}{14} = w$

$\frac{6}{7} = w$

Check:

$\frac{4}{2\left(\frac{6}{7}\right)} \stackrel{?}{=} \frac{7}{3}$

$\frac{4}{\left(\frac{12}{7}\right)} \stackrel{?}{=} \frac{7}{3}$

$4 \div \frac{12}{7} \stackrel{?}{=} \frac{7}{3}$

$4 \cdot \frac{7}{12} \stackrel{?}{=} \frac{7}{3}$

$\frac{7}{3} = \frac{7}{3}$

21. $\frac{5}{3d} = \frac{2}{3}$

$5(3) = 3d(2)$

$15 = 6d$

$\frac{5}{2} = \frac{15}{6} = d$

$2.5 = d$

Check:

$\frac{5}{3(2.5)} \stackrel{?}{=} \frac{2}{3}$

$\frac{5}{7.5} \stackrel{?}{=} \frac{2}{3}$

$5 \div \frac{15}{2} \stackrel{?}{=} \frac{2}{3}$

$5 \cdot \frac{2}{15} \stackrel{?}{=} \frac{2}{3}$

$\frac{2}{3} = \frac{2}{3}$

22. $\frac{14}{3} = \frac{7b}{2}$

$14(2) = 3(7b)$

$28 = 21b$

$\frac{28}{21} = b$

$\frac{4}{3} = b$

Check:

$\frac{14}{3} \stackrel{?}{=} \frac{7\left(\frac{4}{3}\right)}{2}$

$\frac{14}{3} \stackrel{?}{=} \frac{28}{3} \div 2$

$\frac{14}{3} \stackrel{?}{=} \frac{28}{3} \cdot \frac{1}{2}$

$\frac{14}{3} = \frac{14}{3}$

23. $\frac{3}{10} = \frac{1}{10a}$

$3(10a) = 10(1)$

$30a = 10$

$a = \frac{1}{3}$

Check:

$\frac{3}{10} \stackrel{?}{=} \frac{1}{10\left(\frac{1}{3}\right)}$

$\frac{3}{10} \stackrel{?}{=} \frac{1}{\left(\frac{10}{3}\right)}$

$\frac{3}{10} \stackrel{?}{=} 1 \div \frac{10}{3}$

$\frac{3}{10} \stackrel{?}{=} 1 \cdot \frac{3}{10}$

$\frac{3}{10} = \frac{3}{10}$

24. $\frac{z}{9} = \frac{4}{z}$

$z(z) = 9(4)$

$z^2 = 36$

$z = \pm\sqrt{36}$

$z = \pm 6$

Check:

$\frac{6}{9} \stackrel{?}{=} \frac{4}{6}$

$\frac{2}{3} = \frac{2}{3}$

$-\frac{6}{9} \stackrel{?}{=} -\frac{4}{6}$

$-\frac{2}{3} = -\frac{2}{3}$

Copyright © McDougal Littell Inc.
All rights reserved.

25. $\frac{4}{p} = \frac{p}{16}$

$4(16) = p(p)$

$64 = p^2$

$\pm\sqrt{64} = p$

$\pm 8 = p$

Check both solutions:

$\frac{4}{8} \stackrel{?}{=} \frac{8}{16}$

$\frac{1}{2} = \frac{1}{2}$

$-\frac{4}{8} \stackrel{?}{=} -\frac{8}{16}$

$-\frac{1}{2} = -\frac{1}{2}$

26. $\frac{x+6}{3} = \frac{x-5}{2}$

$(x+6)2 = 3(x-5)$

$2x + 12 = 3x - 15$

$12 = x - 15$

$27 = x$

Check:

$\frac{27+6}{3} \stackrel{?}{=} \frac{27-5}{2}$

$\frac{33}{3} \stackrel{?}{=} \frac{22}{2}$

$11 = 11$

27. $\frac{x-2}{4} = \frac{x+10}{10}$

$(x-2)10 = 4(x+10)$

$10x - 20 = 4x + 40$

$6x - 20 = 40$

$6x = 60$

$x = 10$

Check:

$\frac{10-2}{4} \stackrel{?}{=} \frac{10+10}{10}$

$\frac{8}{4} \stackrel{?}{=} \frac{20}{10}$

$2 = 2$

28. $\frac{r+4}{3} = \frac{r}{5}$

$(r+4)5 = 3r$

$5r + 20 = 3r$

$2r = -20$

$r = -10$

Check:

$\frac{-10+4}{3} \stackrel{?}{=} \frac{-10}{5}$

$-\frac{6}{3} \stackrel{?}{=} -2$

$-2 = -2$

29. $\frac{5}{2y} = \frac{7}{y-3}$

$5(y-3) = 2y(7)$

$5y - 15 = 14y$

$-15 = 9y$

$-\frac{5}{3} = y$

Check:

$\frac{5}{2(-\frac{5}{3})} \stackrel{?}{=} \frac{7}{(-\frac{5}{3}) - 3}$

$\frac{5}{(-\frac{10}{3})} \stackrel{?}{=} \frac{7}{(-\frac{5}{3} - \frac{9}{3})}$

$5 \div \left(-\frac{10}{3}\right) \stackrel{?}{=} 7 \div \left(-\frac{14}{3}\right)$

$5 \cdot \left(-\frac{3}{10}\right) \stackrel{?}{=} 7 \cdot \left(-\frac{3}{14}\right)$

$-\frac{3}{2} = -\frac{3}{2}$

30. $\frac{2}{3t} = \frac{t-1}{t}$

$2(t) = 3t(t-1)$

$2t = 3t^2 - 3t$

$0 = 3t^2 - 5t$

$0 = t(3t-5)$

$t = 0$ or $3t - 5 = 0$

$3t = 5$

$t = \frac{5}{3}$

Check both answers:

$\frac{2}{3(0)} \stackrel{?}{=} \frac{0-1}{0}$; undefined, so 0 is not a solution

$\frac{2}{3(\frac{5}{3})} \stackrel{?}{=} \frac{(\frac{5}{3}) - 1}{(\frac{5}{3})}$

$\frac{2}{5} \stackrel{?}{=} \frac{(\frac{5}{3} - \frac{3}{3})}{\frac{5}{3}}$

$\frac{2}{5} \stackrel{?}{=} \frac{2}{3} \div \frac{5}{3}$

$\frac{2}{5} \stackrel{?}{=} \frac{2}{3} \cdot \frac{3}{5}$

$\frac{2}{5} = \frac{2}{5}$

Copyright © McDougal Littell Inc.
All rights reserved.

31. $\frac{x}{2} = \frac{5}{x+3}$

$x(x+3) = 2(5)$

$x^2 + 3x = 10$

$x^2 + 3x - 10 = 0$

$(x-2)(x+5) = 0$

$x = 2, -5$

Check both solutions:

$\frac{2}{2} \stackrel{?}{=} \frac{5}{2+3}$

$1 = 1$

$-\frac{5}{2} \stackrel{?}{=} \frac{5}{-5+3}$

$-\frac{5}{2} = -\frac{5}{2}$

32. $\frac{x-3}{18} = \frac{3}{x}$

$(x-3)x = 18(3)$

$x^2 - 3x = 54$

$x^2 - 3x - 54 = 0$

$(x-9)(x+6) = 0$

$x = 9, -6$

Check both solutions:

$\frac{9-3}{18} \stackrel{?}{=} \frac{3}{9}$

$\frac{1}{3} = \frac{1}{3}$

$\frac{-6-3}{18} \stackrel{?}{=} \frac{3}{-6}$

$-\frac{1}{2} = -\frac{1}{2}$

33. $\frac{-2}{a-7} = \frac{a}{5}$

$-2(5) = (a-7)a$

$-10 = a^2 - 7a$

$0 = a^2 - 7a + 10$

$0 = (a-2)(a-5)$

$a = 2, 5$

$\frac{-2}{2-7} \stackrel{?}{=} \frac{2}{5}$

$\frac{2}{5} = \frac{2}{5}$

$\frac{-2}{5-7} \stackrel{?}{=} \frac{5}{5}$

$1 = 1$

34. $\frac{x-3}{x} = \frac{x}{x+6}$

$(x-3)(x+6) = x(x)$

$x^2 + 3x - 18 = x^2$

$3x - 18 = 0$

$3x = 18$

$x = 6$

Check:

$\frac{6-3}{6} \stackrel{?}{=} \frac{6}{6+6}$

$\frac{1}{2} = \frac{1}{2}$

35. $\frac{9-x}{x+4} = \frac{5}{2x}$

$(9-x)(2x) = (x+4)(5)$

$18x - 2x^2 = 5x + 20$

$0 = 2x^2 - 13x + 20$

$0 = (2x-5)(x-4)$

$2x - 5 = 0$ or $x - 4 = 0$

$2x = 5$ $x = 4$

$x = \frac{5}{2}$

Check both solutions:

$\frac{9-\left(\frac{5}{2}\right)}{\left(\frac{5}{2}\right)+4} \stackrel{?}{=} \frac{5}{2\left(\frac{5}{2}\right)}$

$\frac{\left(\frac{13}{2}\right)}{\left(\frac{13}{2}\right)} \stackrel{?}{=} \frac{5}{5}$

$1 = 1$

$\frac{9-4}{4+4} \stackrel{?}{=} \frac{5}{2(4)}$

$\frac{5}{8} = \frac{5}{8}$

36. $\frac{15}{30} = \frac{60}{x}$

$15x = 30(60)$

$15x = 1800$

$x = 120$ clay pots

37. $\frac{9 \text{ inches}}{x} = \frac{1}{10}$

$90 = x$

$90 \text{ inches} \times \frac{1 \text{ foot}}{12 \text{ inches}} = 7.5 \text{ feet}$

$\frac{6.5 \text{ inches}}{x} = \frac{1}{10}$

$6.5(10) = x$

$65 = x$

$65 \text{ inches} \times \frac{1 \text{ foot}}{12 \text{ inches}} = 5.41\overline{6} \text{ feet}$

Copyright © McDougal Littell Inc.
All rights reserved.

38. Convert feet to inches:

$4 \text{ ft} \times \frac{12 \text{ inches}}{1 \text{ ft}} = 48 \text{ inches}$

$8 \text{ ft} \times \frac{12 \text{ inches}}{1 \text{ ft}} = 96 \text{ inches}$

$$\frac{\text{Length of plywood}}{\text{Width of plywood}} = \frac{\text{Length of drawing}}{\text{width of drawing}}$$

$$\frac{96}{48} = \frac{x}{11}$$

$$1056 = 48x$$

$$22 = x$$

Length of drawing needed to be 22 inches.

39. Convert: $2\frac{1}{2} \text{ feet} \times \frac{12 \text{ inch}}{1 \text{ ft}} = 30 \text{ inches}$

$$\frac{\text{height on panel}}{\text{height of panel}} = \frac{\text{height on drawing}}{\text{height of paper}}$$

$$\frac{30}{96} = \frac{x}{22}$$

$$30(22) = 96x$$

$$660 = 96x$$

$$6.875 = x$$

6.875 inches

40. Sample answer: By rewriting 1 ft as 12 inches, you can set up the proportion $\frac{\frac{1}{16} \text{ in.}}{12 \text{ in.}} = \frac{1 \text{ in.}}{192 \text{ in.}}$. Now that all the units are the same, you can use the cross product property. This gives $12 = 12$, which shows that the proportion is correct.

11.1 Standardized Test Practice (p. 638)

41. D; extremes of $\frac{1}{3} = \frac{x}{18}$ are 1, 18; extremes of $\frac{x}{18} = \frac{1}{3}$ are x, 3

42. J;

$$\frac{x-2}{x+5} = \frac{x-5}{x+2}$$

$$(x-2)(x+2) = (x+5)(x-5)$$

$$x^2 - 4 = x^2 - 25$$

$-4 \neq -25$; no solution

43. B;

$$\frac{c}{c-4} = \frac{8}{c-10}$$

$$c(c-10) = (c-4)(8)$$

$$c^2 - 10c = 8c - 32$$

$$c^2 - 18c + 32 = 0$$

$$(c-16)(c-2) = 0$$

$$c = 16, 2$$

11.1 Mixed Review (p. 638)

44. $y - (-2) = 2[x - (-1)]$

$y + 2 = 2(x + 1)$

45. $y - (-3) = -4(x - 5)$

$y + 3 = -4(x - 5)$

46. $y - 8 = -1[x - (-8)]$

$y - 8 = -1(x + 8)$

47. $y - 6 = -2(x - 10)$

$y - 6 = -2x + 20$

$2x + y = 26$

48. $y - (-7) = \frac{1}{2}[x - (-7)]$

$y + 7 = \frac{1}{2}(x + 7)$

$y + 7 = \frac{1}{2}x + \frac{7}{2}$

$2y + 14 = x + 7$

$-x + 2y = -7$ or $x - 2y = 7$

49. $y - 8 = \frac{3}{4}(x - 1)$

$y - 8 = \frac{3}{4}x - \frac{3}{4}$

$4y - 32 = 3x - 3$

$-3x + 4y = 29$ or $3x - 4y = -29$

50. $y - 5 = 3(x - 0)$

$y - 5 = 3x$

$-3x + y = 5$ or $3x - y = -5$

51. $y - 12 = -12(x - 6)$

$y - 12 = -12x + 72$

$12x + y = 84$

52. $y - (-1) = 0(x - 6)$

$y + 1 = 0$

$y = -1$

53. $\sqrt{64} = 8$

54. $-\sqrt{9} = -3$

55. $\sqrt{10{,}000} = 100$

56. $\pm\sqrt{169} = \pm 13$

57. $\sqrt{18} = \sqrt{9 \cdot 2} = 3\sqrt{2}$

58. $\sqrt{20} = \sqrt{4 \cdot 5} = 2\sqrt{5}$

59. $\sqrt{80} = \sqrt{16 \cdot 5} = 4\sqrt{5}$

60. $\sqrt{162} = \sqrt{81 \cdot 2} = 9\sqrt{2}$

61. $9\sqrt{36} = 9 \cdot 6 = 54$

62. $\sqrt{\frac{11}{9}} = \frac{\sqrt{11}}{3}$

63. $\frac{1}{2}\sqrt{28} = \frac{1}{2}\sqrt{4 \cdot 7} = \frac{1}{2}(2)\sqrt{7} = \sqrt{7}$

64. $\sqrt{\frac{5}{8}} = \frac{\sqrt{5}}{\sqrt{4 \cdot 2}} = \frac{\sqrt{5}}{2\sqrt{2}} \cdot \frac{\sqrt{2}}{\sqrt{2}} = \frac{\sqrt{10}}{2 \cdot 2} = \frac{\sqrt{10}}{4}$

Copyright © McDougal Littell Inc.
All rights reserved.

11.1 Maintaining Skills (p. 638)

65.

Decimal	0.78	0.2	$0.\overline{66}$	0.073	0.03	0.48
Percent	78%	20%	$66\frac{2}{3}\%$	7.3%	3%	48%
Fraction	$\frac{78}{100} = \frac{39}{50}$	$\frac{20}{100} = \frac{1}{5}$	$\frac{2}{3}$	$\frac{73}{1000}$	$\frac{3}{100}$	$\frac{12}{25}$

Lesson 11.2

11.2 Checkpoint (pp. 640–641)

1. a. $\frac{y}{x} = k$ direct variation model

Substitute 6 for y, 2 for x.

$\frac{6}{2} = k$ Simplify.

$3 = k$

$\frac{y}{x} = 3$ or $y = 3x$

b. $xy = k$ model for inverse variation

$2(6) = k$ Substitute 2 for x, 6 for y.

$12 = k$ Simplify.

$xy = 12$ or $y = \frac{12}{x}$

x-value	−4	−3	−2	−1	1	2	3	4
Direct, $y = 3x$	−12	−9	−6	−3	3	6	9	12
Inverse, $y = \frac{12}{x}$	−3	−4	−6	−12	12	6	4	3

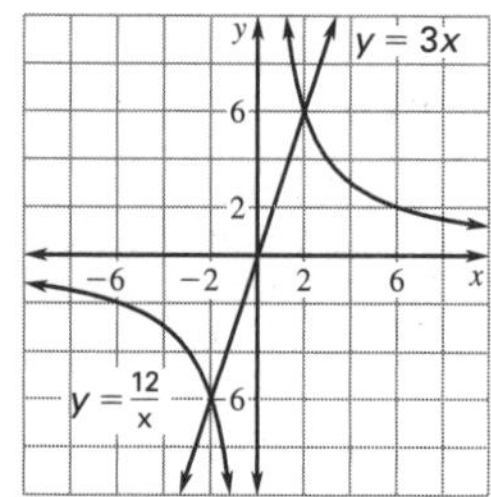

3. $B = \frac{112}{8} = 14°$

4. The model does not apply when $r = 1$. According to the model, $B = 112°$ when $r = 1$. B cannot be greater than 90°.

11.2 Guided Practice (p. 642)

1. The quantities x and y vary directly if there is a non-zero constant k such that $y = kx$.

2. The quantities x and y vary inversely if there is a non-zero constant k such that $y = \frac{k}{x}$.

3. Direct variation; The graph is a line passing through the origin.

4. Neither; The graph is a parabola.

5. Inverse variation; The graph is a hyperbola.

6. inverse variation

7. Neither; the line does not pass through the origin.

8. direct variation

9. inverse variation

10. $y = kx$

$6 = k(4)$

$\frac{3}{2} = k$

$y = \frac{3}{2}x$

11. $y = \frac{k}{x}$

$6 = \frac{k}{4}$

$24 = k$

$y = \frac{24}{x}$

11.2 Practice and Applications (pp. 642–644)

12. $y = kx$

$9 = k(3)$

$3 = k$

$y = 3x$

13. $y = kx$

$8 = k(2)$

$4 = k$

$y = 4x$

14. $y = kx$

$6 = k(18)$

$\frac{1}{3} = k$

$y = \frac{1}{3}x$

15. $y = kx$

$24 = k(8)$

$3 = k$

$y = 3x$

16. $y = kx$

$12 = k(36)$

$\frac{1}{3} = k$

$y = \frac{1}{3}x$

Copyright © McDougal Littell Inc.
All rights reserved.

17. $y = kx$

$3 = k(27)$

$\frac{1}{9} = k$

$y = \frac{1}{9}x$

18. $y = \frac{k}{x}$

$5 = \frac{k}{2}$

$10 = k$

$y = \frac{10}{x}$

19. $y = \frac{k}{x}$

$7 = \frac{k}{3}$

$21 = k$

$y = \frac{21}{x}$

20. $y = \frac{k}{x}$

$1 = \frac{k}{16}$

$16 = k$

$y = \frac{16}{x}$

21. $y = \frac{k}{x}$

$2 = \frac{k}{11}$

$22 = k$

$y = \frac{22}{x}$

22. $y = \frac{k}{x}$

$8 = \frac{k}{\frac{1}{2}}$

$4 = k$

$y = \frac{4}{x}$

23. $y = \frac{k}{x}$

$\frac{13}{5} = \frac{k}{5}$

$13 = k$

$y = \frac{13}{x}$

24. $y = \frac{k}{x}$

$50 = \frac{k}{1.5}$

$75 = k$

$y = \frac{75}{x}$

25. $y = \frac{k}{x}$

$0.6 = \frac{k}{45}$

$27 = k$

$y = \frac{27}{x}$

26. $y = \frac{k}{x}$

$7 = \frac{k}{10.5}$

$73.5 = k$

$y = \frac{73.5}{x}$

27. $y = \frac{4}{x}$

x	−4	−3	−2	−1	1	2	3	4
y	−1	$-\frac{4}{3}$	−2	−4	4	2	$\frac{4}{3}$	1

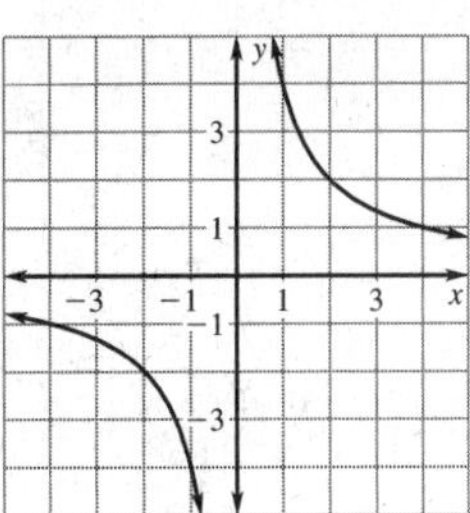

inversely

Copyright © McDougal Littell Inc.
All rights reserved.

28. $y = \frac{3x}{2}$

x	-4	-3	-2	-1	1	2	3	4
y	-6	$-\frac{9}{2}$	-3	$-\frac{3}{2}$	$\frac{3}{2}$	3	$\frac{9}{2}$	6

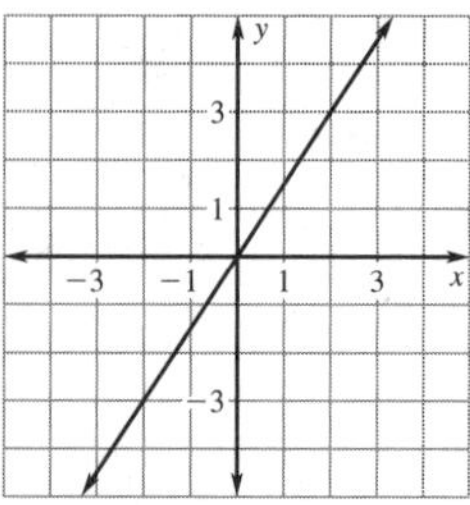

directly

29. $y = 3x$

x	-4	-3	-2	-1	1	2	3	4
y	-12	-9	-6	-3	3	6	9	12

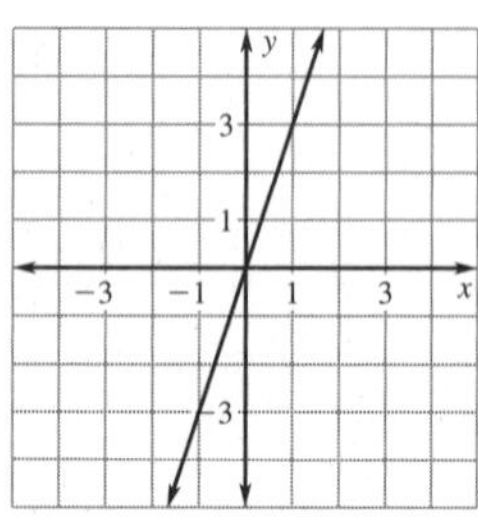

directly

30. $y = \frac{6}{x}$

x	-4	-3	-2	-1	1	2	3	4
y	$-\frac{3}{2}$	-2	-3	-6	6	3	2	$\frac{3}{2}$

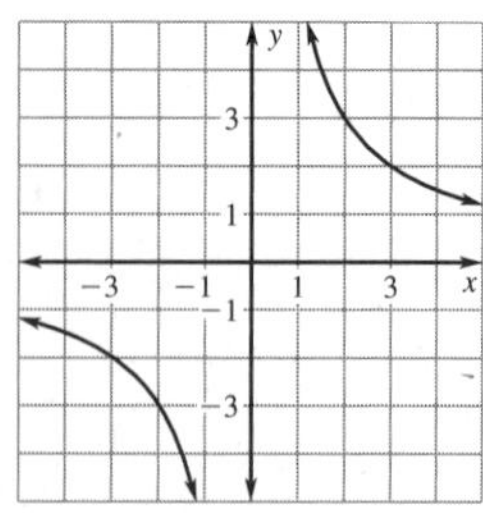

inversely

31. inverse variation

32. direct variation

33. inverse variation

34. C; a line through origin

35.
$$P = \frac{k}{A}$$
$$\frac{4 \text{ lbs}}{\text{in}^2} = \frac{k}{29 \text{ in}^2}$$
$$\frac{4 \text{ lbs}}{\text{in}^2} \times 29 \text{ in}^2 = k$$
$$116 \text{ lbs} = k$$

36. $P = \frac{116}{A}$

37. $P = \frac{116}{319}$

$P \approx 0.36$ lbs per in^2

38.
$$T = \frac{k}{d}$$
$$1.2 = \frac{k}{3700}$$
$$4440 = k$$
$$T = \frac{4440}{d}$$

39. $T = \frac{4440}{2000} = 2.2°\text{C}$

40. $\frac{1 \text{ gal}}{26 \text{ miles}} = \frac{1}{26}$ gal/mi ≈ 0.04 gal/mi

41. $g = 12 - \frac{1}{26}m$

42. Neither; the equation cannot be written either in the form $g = km$ or $g = \frac{k}{m}$ for any constant k.

11.2 Standardized Test Practice (p. 644)

43. B
$$y = kx$$
$$14 = k(6)$$
$$\frac{7}{3} = k$$
$$y = \frac{7}{3}k$$

44. F
$$y = \frac{k}{x}$$
$$9 = \frac{k}{10}$$
$$90 = k$$
$$y = \frac{90}{x} \text{ or } xy = 90$$

Copyright © McDougal Littell Inc.
All rights reserved.

11.2 Mixed Review (p. 644)

45. $0.45(10) = 4.5$

46. $0.30(42) = 12.6$

47. $0.005(200) = 1$

48. $1.50(300) = 450$

49. $0.11(50) = 5.5$

50. $0.99(10{,}000) = 9900$

51. yes;
$4 \overset{?}{<} (-1)^2 + 6(-1) + 12$
$4 \overset{?}{<} 1 - 6 + 12$
$4 < 7$

52. yes;
$2 \overset{?}{\leq} (-1)^2 - 7(-1) + 9$
$2 \overset{?}{\leq} 1 + 7 + 9$
$2 \leq 17$

53. yes;
$5 \overset{?}{\geq} 5^2 - 25$
$5 \geq 0$

54. no;
$-7 \overset{?}{>} 1^2 - 2(1) + 5$
$-7 \not> 4$

55. $x^2 + 5x - 14 = (x + 7)(x - 2)$

56. $7x^2 + 8x + 1 = (7x + 1)(x + 1)$

57. $5x^2 - 51x + 54 = (5x - 6)(x - 9)$

58. $36x^3 - 9x = 9x(4x^2 - 1) = 9x(2x + 1)(2x - 1)$

59. $15x^4 - 50x^3 - 40x^2 = 5x^2(3x^2 - 10x - 8)$
$= 5x^2(3x + 2)(x - 4)$

60. $6x^2 + 16x = 2x(3x + 8)$

61. For 2025, $t = 30$; For 2000, $t = 5$
$\dfrac{18{,}870(1.0124)^{30}}{18{,}870(1.0124)^5} = \dfrac{(1.0124)^{25}}{1}$
or about 1.36 to 1

11.2 Maintaining Skills (p. 644)

62. $2\frac{7}{8} - \frac{7}{8} = 2$

63. $\frac{16}{9} - 1\frac{1}{9} = \frac{16}{9} - \frac{10}{9} = \frac{6}{9} = \frac{2}{3}$

64. $4\frac{1}{2} - \frac{20}{8} = \frac{9}{2} - \frac{20}{8} = \frac{36}{8} - \frac{20}{8} = \frac{16}{8} = 2$

65. $3\frac{1}{3} - \frac{4}{3} = \frac{10}{3} - \frac{4}{3} = \frac{6}{3} = 2$

66. $\frac{10}{4} - \frac{1}{2} = \frac{10}{4} - \frac{2}{4} = \frac{8}{4} = 2$

67. $\frac{41}{3} - 4\frac{1}{5} = \frac{205}{15} - \frac{63}{15} = \frac{142}{15} = 9\frac{7}{15}$

68. $12\frac{5}{6} - \frac{50}{7} = 12\frac{5}{6} - 7\frac{1}{7} = 12\frac{35}{42} - 7\frac{6}{42} = 5\frac{29}{42}$

69. $\frac{43}{11} - 2\frac{2}{5} = 3\frac{10}{11} - 2\frac{2}{5} = 3\frac{50}{55} - 2\frac{22}{55} = 1\frac{28}{55}$

11.2 Using a Graphing Calculator: Try These *(p. 645)*

1. directly; 0.825; $y = 0.825x$

2. inversely; 25; $y = \dfrac{25}{x}$

Lesson 11.3

11.3 Checkpoint (pp. 647–648)

1. $\dfrac{3x^3}{6x^2} = \dfrac{3 \cdot x \cdot x \cdot x}{3 \cdot 2 \cdot x \cdot x} = \dfrac{x}{2}$

2. $\dfrac{3m}{3(m - 4)} = \dfrac{m}{m - 4}$

3. $\dfrac{x^2(x + 3)}{x} = \dfrac{x \cdot x(x + 3)}{x} = x(x + 3)$

4. $\dfrac{5}{n + 5}$; already in simplest form

5. $\dfrac{2x - 6}{4} = \dfrac{2(x - 3)}{2 \cdot 2} = \dfrac{x - 3}{2}$

6. $\dfrac{5x}{10x^2 - 5x} = \dfrac{5x}{5x(2x - 1)} = \dfrac{1}{2x - 1}$

7. $\dfrac{4m^3}{2m^3 + 8m^2} = \dfrac{2 \cdot 2 \cdot m \cdot m \cdot m}{2m^2(m + 4)} = \dfrac{2m}{m + 4}$

8. $\dfrac{p^3 - p^2}{p^2} = \dfrac{p^2(p - 1)}{p^2} = p - 1$

9. $\dfrac{3(4 - m)}{3(m - 4)} = \dfrac{4 - m}{m - 4} = \dfrac{-(m - 4)}{(m - 4)} = -1$

10. $\dfrac{3 - x}{x^2 - 9} = \dfrac{-(x - 3)}{(x + 3)(x - 3)} = -\dfrac{1}{x + 3}$

11. $\dfrac{4(1 - m)}{m^2 - 2m + 1} = \dfrac{-4(m - 1)}{(m - 1)(m - 1)} = -\dfrac{4}{m - 1}$

12. $\dfrac{2x - 5}{20 - 8x} = \dfrac{2x - 5}{4(5 - 2x)} = \dfrac{2x - 5}{-4(2x - 5)} = -\dfrac{1}{4}$

13. $\dfrac{y^2 + 3y - 28}{16 - y^2} = \dfrac{(y + 7)(y - 4)}{-(y^2 - 16)}$
$= \dfrac{(y + 7)(y - 4)}{-(y + 4)(y - 4)}$
$= -\dfrac{y + 7}{y + 4}$

14. $\dfrac{10x - 5}{1 - 2x} = \dfrac{5(2x - 1)}{-(2x - 1)} = -5$

15. $\dfrac{x^2 - 4}{x + 2} = \dfrac{(x + 2)(x - 2)}{(x + 2)} = x - 2$

16. $\dfrac{(2n^2 - 8n + 8)}{(n - 2)} = \dfrac{(2n - 4)(n - 2)}{(n - 2)} = 2n - 4$

17. $\dfrac{(m^2 - 4m + 3)}{(m - 1)} = \dfrac{(m - 3)(m - 1)}{(m - 1)} = m - 3$

18. $\dfrac{(x^2 - 2x - 8)}{(x - 4)} = \dfrac{(x + 2)(x - 4)}{(x - 4)} = x + 2$

Copyright © McDougal Littell Inc.
All rights reserved.

Chapter 11 *continued*

11.3 Guided Practice (p. 649)

1. a number that can be written as the quotient of two integers;
$5 = \frac{5}{1}$; $\frac{2}{3}$; $-\frac{17}{2}$; $1.45 = \frac{145}{100}$; $0 = \frac{0}{n}$
(where n is any integer)

2. a fraction whose numerator and denominator are nonzero polynomials; example: $\frac{x^2}{x+2}$

3. a rational expression whose numerator and denominator have no common factors except ± 1; example: $\frac{3n}{n+4}$

4. $\frac{28y}{4} = 7y$ **5.** $\frac{16}{128c} = \frac{1}{8c}$ **6.** $\frac{12x^2}{6x} = 2x$

7. $\frac{a-8}{4}$; already in simplest form

8. $\frac{t^4}{t^2(t+2)} = \frac{t^2}{t+2}$

9. $\frac{8n^3}{12n^4 + 40n^2} = \frac{8n^3}{4n^2(3n^2+10)} = \frac{2n}{3n^2+10}$

10. $\frac{18}{2x+4} = \frac{18}{2(x+2)} = \frac{9}{x+2}$

11. $\frac{y^7 - y^3}{y^3} = \frac{y^3(y^4-1)}{y^3} = y^4 - 1$

12. $\frac{7-m}{m^2-49} = \frac{-(m-7)}{(m-7)(m+7)} = -\frac{1}{m+7}$

13. $\frac{3y^2+22y+7}{y+7} = \frac{(3y+1)(y+7)}{y+7} = 3y+1$

14. $\frac{x^2+5x+6}{x+3} = \frac{(x+2)(x+3)}{x+3} = x+2$

15. $\frac{2x^2-5x-7}{2x-7} = \frac{(2x-7)(x+1)}{2x-7} = x+1$

11.3 Practice and Applications (pp. 649–650)

16. $\frac{4x}{20} = \frac{x}{5}$ **17.** $\frac{45x}{15} = 3x$

18. $-\frac{18x^2}{12x} = -\frac{3x}{2}$ **19.** $\frac{14x^2}{50x^4} = \frac{7}{25x^2}$

20. $\frac{10x^5}{16x^3} = \frac{5x^2}{8}$ **21.** $\frac{36x}{27x} = \frac{4}{3}$

22. $\frac{x-14}{x}$; already in simplest form

23. $\frac{t^4}{t^2(t+2)} = \frac{t^2}{t+2}$ **24.** $\frac{10(r-6)}{10r} = \frac{r-6}{r}$

25. $\frac{7x}{12x+x^2} = \frac{7x}{x(12+x)} = \frac{7}{12+x}$

26. $\frac{3x^2-18x}{-9x^2} = \frac{3x(x-6)}{-3 \cdot 3x \cdot x} = -\frac{x-6}{3x}$ or $\frac{6-x}{3x}$

27. $\frac{42x-6x^3}{36x} = \frac{6x(7-x^2)}{6 \cdot 6x} = \frac{7-x^2}{6}$

28. $\frac{x^2+25}{2x+10}$; already in simplest form

29. $\frac{2(5-d)}{2(d-5)} = -\frac{d-5}{d-5} = -1$

30. $\frac{x^2+8x+16}{3x+12} = \frac{(x+4)(x+4)}{3(x+4)} = \frac{x+4}{3}$

31. $\frac{x^2+x-20}{x^2+2x-15} = \frac{(x-4)(x+5)}{(x-3)(x+5)} = \frac{x-4}{x-3}$

32. $\frac{x^3+9x^2+14x}{x^2-4} = \frac{x(x^2+9x+14)}{(x+2)(x-2)}$
$= \frac{x(x+7)(x+2)}{(x+2)(x-2)}$
$= \frac{x(x+7)}{(x-2)}$

33. $\frac{x^3-x}{x^3+5x^2-6x} = \frac{x(x^2-1)}{x(x^2+5x-6)}$
$= \frac{(x+1)(x-1)}{(x-1)(x+6)}$
$= \frac{x+1}{x+6}$

34. $\frac{x^2-9}{x^2-5x-6} = \frac{(x+3)(x-3)}{(x+1)(x-6)}$;
already in simplest form

35. $\frac{2x^2+11x-6}{x+6} = \frac{(2x-1)(x+6)}{x+6} = 2x-1$

36. $\frac{121-x^2}{x^2+15x+44} = \frac{-(x^2-121)}{(x+4)(x+11)}$
$= -\frac{(x+11)(x-11)}{(x+4)(x+11)}$
$= -\frac{x-11}{x+4}$

37. $\frac{1-x}{x^2-x} = \frac{-(x-1)}{x(x-1)} = -\frac{1}{x}$

38. $\frac{12-5x}{10x^2-24x} = \frac{-(5x-12)}{2x(5x-12)} = -\frac{1}{2x}$

39. $\frac{8y^2-7y}{14y^2-16y^3} = \frac{y(8y-7)}{-2y^2(8y-7)} = -\frac{1}{2y}$

40. $\frac{5-x}{x^2-8x+15} = \frac{-(x-5)}{(x-3)(x-5)} = -\frac{1}{x-3}$

41. $\frac{9-2y}{2y^2-3y-27} = \frac{-(2y-9)}{(2y-9)(y+3)} = -\frac{1}{y+3}$

42. $\frac{3x-5}{25-30x+9x^2} = \frac{3x-5}{9x^2-30x+25}$
$= \frac{3x-5}{(3x-5)(3x-5)}$
$= \frac{1}{3x-5}$

Copyright © McDougal Littell Inc.
All rights reserved.

43. $\dfrac{a^2 - 3a + 2}{a - 1} = \dfrac{(a - 2)(a - 1)}{a - 1} = a - 2$

44. $\dfrac{5g^2 + 13g - 6}{g + 3} = \dfrac{(5g - 2)(g + 3)}{g + 3} = 5g - 2$

45. $\dfrac{x^2 - 6x - 16}{x + 2} = \dfrac{(x + 2)(x - 8)}{x + 2} = x - 8$

46. $\dfrac{-5m^2 + 25m}{5m} = \dfrac{5m(-m + 5)}{5m} = -m + 5$

47. $P = \dfrac{2952x - 44x^2}{200x + 5x^2}$

$P = \dfrac{4x(738 - 11x)}{5x(40 + x)} = \dfrac{-0.8(11x - 738)}{x + 40}$

At 36,000 ft:

$P = \dfrac{-0.8[11(36) - 738]}{36 + 40}$

$P = 3.6$ lb per in^2

48. $\dfrac{ac}{bc} = \dfrac{a}{b} \cdot \dfrac{c}{c}$

$\dfrac{ac}{bc} = \dfrac{a}{b} \cdot 1$

$\dfrac{ac}{bc} = \dfrac{a}{b}$

11.3 Standardized Test Practice (p. 650)

49. $\dfrac{6 + 2x}{x^2 + 5x + 6} = \dfrac{2(x + 3)}{(x + 2)(x + 3)} = \dfrac{2}{x + 2}$; A

50. $\dfrac{3 - x}{x^2 - 5x + 6} = \dfrac{-(x - 3)}{(x - 2)(x - 3)} = -\dfrac{1}{x - 2}$; J

11.3 Mixed Review (p. 651)

51. $\left(-\dfrac{1}{2}\right)\left(\dfrac{2}{3}\right) = -\dfrac{1}{3}$

52. $-15\left(-\dfrac{5}{6}\right) = \dfrac{25}{2}$

53. $\dfrac{2}{7} \div \dfrac{14}{24} = \dfrac{2}{7} \cdot \dfrac{24}{14} = \dfrac{24}{49}$

54. $\dfrac{4}{9} \div (-36) = \dfrac{4}{9} \cdot -\dfrac{1}{36} = -\dfrac{1}{81}$

55. $\left(-\dfrac{3}{4}\right)\left(-\dfrac{3y}{5}\right) = \dfrac{9y}{20}$

56. $-(-5)^2(2j) = -(25)(2j) = -50j$

57. $\dfrac{2m}{3} \cdot 6m^2 = 4m^3$

58. $\dfrac{36}{45a} \div \dfrac{-9a}{5} = \dfrac{36}{45a} \cdot -\dfrac{5}{9a} = -\dfrac{4}{9a^2}$

59. $18c^3 \div \dfrac{-27c}{-4} = 18c^3 \cdot \dfrac{4}{27c} = \dfrac{9 \cdot 2 \cdot 4c^3}{9 \cdot 3c} = \dfrac{8c^2}{3}$

60. $A = \dfrac{1}{2}bh$

$192 = \dfrac{1}{2}(3x + 3x)(4x)$

$192 = \dfrac{1}{2}(6x)(4x)$

$192 = \dfrac{1}{2}(24x^2)$

$192 = 12x^2$

$16 = x^2$

$4 = x$

Perimeter $= 5x + 5x + 3x + 3x$

$= 16x$

$= 16(4) = 64$ m

61. $y = x^2$

x	-2	-1	0	1	2
y	4	1	0	1	4

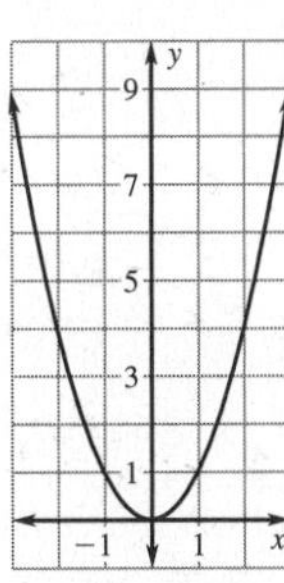

62. $y = 4 - x^2$

$y = -x^2 + 4$

$-\dfrac{b}{2a} = -\dfrac{0}{2a} = 0$

x	-2	-1	0	1	2
y	0	3	4	3	0

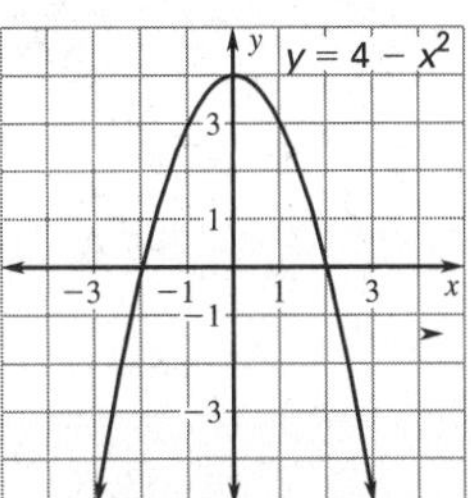

Copyright © McDougal Littell Inc.
All rights reserved.

63. $y = \frac{1}{2}x^2$

x	−2	−1	0	1	2
y	2	$\frac{1}{2}$	0	$\frac{1}{2}$	2

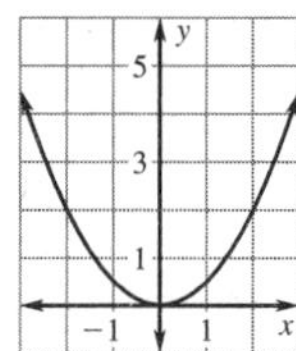

64. $$y = 5x^2 + 4x - 5$$
$$-\frac{b}{2a} = \frac{-4}{2(5)} = \frac{-4}{10} = -\frac{2}{5}$$

x	−2	−1	$-\frac{2}{5}$	0	1
y	7	−4	$-5\frac{4}{5}$	−5	4

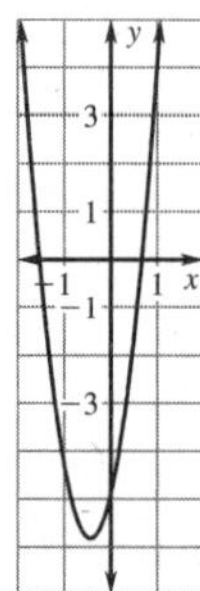

65. $$y = 4x^2 - x + 6$$
$$-\frac{b}{2a} = \frac{-(-1)}{2(4)} = \frac{1}{8}$$

x	−1	0	$\frac{1}{8}$	1	2
y	11	6	$5\frac{15}{16}$	9	20

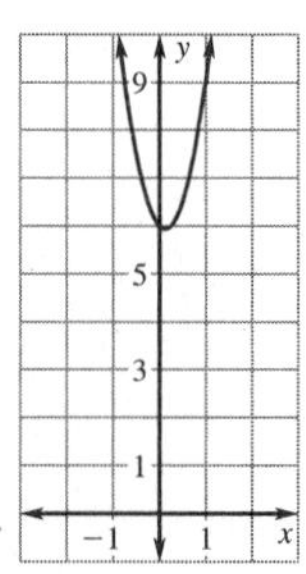

66. $$y = -3x^2 - x + 7$$
$$-\frac{b}{2a} = \frac{-(-1)}{2(-3)} = -\frac{1}{6}$$

x	−2	−1	$-\frac{1}{6}$	0	1
y	−3	5	$7\frac{1}{12}$	7	3

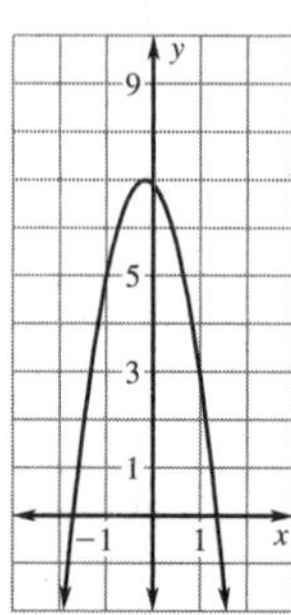

11.3 Maintaining Skills (p. 651)

67. $0.987 + 1.4 = 2.387$

68. $0.009 + 9 = 9.009$

69. $75.6 + 35.8 = 111.4$

70. $1.23 + 0.45 = 1.68$

71. $0.01 + 0.01 = 0.02$

72. $100.02 + 10 = 110.02$

Quiz 1 *(p. 651)*

1. $$\frac{x}{10} = \frac{4}{5}$$
$$5x = 40$$
$$x = 8$$

2. $$\frac{3}{x} = \frac{7}{9}$$
$$27 = 7x$$
$$\frac{27}{7} = x$$

3. $$\frac{x}{4x - 8} = \frac{2}{x}$$
$$x^2 = 2(4x - 8)$$
$$x^2 = 8x - 16$$
$$x^2 - 8x + 16 = 0$$
$$(x - 4)(x - 4) = 0$$
$$x = 4$$

4. $$\frac{6x + 4}{5} = \frac{2}{x}$$
$$(6x + 4)x = 10$$
$$6x^2 + 4x = 10$$
$$6x^2 + 4x - 10 = 0$$
$$3x^2 + 2x - 5 = 0$$
$$(3x + 5)(x - 1) = 0$$
$$3x + 5 = 0 \qquad x - 1 = 0$$
$$3x = -5 \qquad x = 1$$
$$x = -\frac{5}{3}$$

Copyright © McDougal Littell Inc.
All rights reserved.

5. $y = kx$
$32 = k(8)$
$4 = k$
$y = 4x$

6. $y = kx$
$3 = k(5)$
$\frac{3}{5} = k$
$y = \frac{3}{5}x$

7. $y = kx$
$15 = k(10)$
$\frac{3}{2} = k$
$y = \frac{3}{2}x$

8. $y = \frac{k}{x}$
$2 = \frac{k}{12}$
$24 = k$
$y = \frac{24}{x}$

9. $y = \frac{k}{x}$
$4 = \frac{k}{4}$
$16 = k$
$y = \frac{16}{x}$

10. $y = \frac{k}{x}$
$2.5 = \frac{k}{3}$
$7.5 = k$
$y = \frac{7.5}{x}$

11. $\frac{15x^2}{10x} = \frac{3x}{2}$

12. $\frac{x^2 - 7x + 12}{x^2 + 3x - 18} = \frac{(x - 3)(x - 4)}{(x + 6)(x - 3)} = \frac{x - 4}{x + 6}$

13. $\frac{3 - x}{x^2 + x - 12} = \frac{-(x - 3)}{(x - 3)(x + 4)} = -\frac{1}{x + 4}$

14. $\frac{5x}{11x + x^2} = \frac{5x}{x(11 + x)} = \frac{5}{11 + x}$

15. $\frac{x^2 - 3x - 28}{x - 7} = \frac{(x + 4)(x - 7)}{x - 7} = x + 4$

16. $\frac{6x^2 + 11x + 3}{3x + 1} = \frac{(3x + 1)(2x + 3)}{3x + 1} = 2x + 3$

Copyright © McDougal Littell Inc.
All rights reserved.

Chapter 11 *continued*

Lesson 11.4

11.4 Checkpoint (pp. 653–654)

1. $\frac{y^3}{2y^2} \cdot \frac{4y^2}{6}$ Original expression.

$= \frac{4y^5}{12y^2}$ Multiply numerators and denominators.

$= \frac{2 \cdot 2 \cdot y \cdot y \cdot y \cdot y \cdot y}{2 \cdot 2 \cdot 3 \cdot y \cdot y}$ Factor and divide out common factors.

$= \frac{y^3}{3}$ Simplify.

2. $\frac{5x + 10}{x - 3} \cdot \frac{x^2 - 9}{5}$ Original expression.

$= \frac{5(x + 2)}{(x - 3)} \cdot \frac{(x + 3)(x - 3)}{5}$ Factor numerators and denominators.

$= \frac{5(x + 2)(x + 3)(x - 3)}{(x - 3)(5)}$ Multiply numerators and denominators; divide out common factors.

$= (x + 2)(x + 3)$ Simplify.

3. $\frac{4x^2}{(x + 2)^2} \cdot \frac{(x^2 + 3x + 2)}{x^2 + 1}$ Original expression.

$= \frac{4x^2}{(x + 2)(x + 2)} \cdot \frac{(x + 2)(x + 1)}{(x^2 + 1)}$ Factor numerators and denominators.

$= \frac{4x^2(x + 2)(x + 1)}{(x + 2)(x + 2)(x^2 + 1)}$ Multiply numerators and denominators; divide out common factors.

$= \frac{4x^2(x + 1)}{(x + 2)(x^2 + 1)}$ Simplify.

4. $\frac{3}{x + 1} \cdot \frac{(2x + 2)}{1}$ Write $2x + 2$ as $\frac{2x + 2}{1}$.

$= \frac{3}{x + 1} \cdot \frac{2(x + 1)}{1}$ Factor numerators and denominators.

$= \frac{6(x + 1)}{(x + 1)}$ Multiply numerators and denominators; divide out common factors.

$= 6$ Simplify.

5. $\frac{x}{2x + 4} \cdot \frac{x^2 + 2x}{1}$ Write $x^2 + 2x$ as $\frac{x^2 + 2x}{1}$.

$= \frac{x}{2(x + 2)} \cdot \frac{x(x + 2)}{1}$ Factor numerators and denominators.

$= \frac{x^2(x + 2)}{2(x + 2)}$ Multiply numerators and denominators; divide out common factors.

$= \frac{x^2}{2}$ Simplify.

6. $\frac{(x - 3)}{1} \cdot \frac{x + 3}{x^2 - 9}$ Write $x - 3$ as $\frac{x - 3}{1}$.

$= \frac{(x - 3)}{1} \cdot \frac{(x + 3)}{(x + 3)(x - 3)}$ Factor numerators and denominators.

$= \frac{(x - 3)(x + 3)}{(x + 3)(x - 3)}$ Multiply numerators and denominators; divide out common factors.

$= 1$ Simplify.

Copyright © McDougal Littell Inc.
All rights reserved.

7. $\frac{4}{x+2} \div \frac{3}{x+2}$ Original problem.

$= \frac{4}{x+2} \cdot \frac{x+2}{3}$ Multiply by reciprocal.

$= \frac{4(x+2)}{(x+2)(3)}$ Multiply numerators and denominators; divide out common factors.

$= \frac{4}{3}$ Simplify.

8. $\frac{x+3}{4} \div \frac{2x+6}{3}$ Original problem.

$= \frac{x+3}{4} \cdot \frac{3}{2x+6}$ Multiply by reciprocal.

$= \frac{x+3}{4} \cdot \frac{3}{2(x+3)}$ Factor numerators and denominators.

$= \frac{(x+3)(3)}{8(x+3)}$ Multiply numerator and denominators; divide out common factors.

$= \frac{3}{8}$ Simplify.

9. $\frac{3x}{2x-4} \div \frac{6x^2}{x-2}$ Original problem.

$= \frac{3x}{2(x-2)} \cdot \frac{(x-2)}{2 \cdot 3x \cdot x}$ Multiply by reciprocal; factor numerators and denominators.

$= \frac{3x(x-2)}{2 \cdot 2 \cdot 3(x-2)x \cdot x}$ Multiply numerators and denominators; divide out common factors.

$= \frac{1}{4x}$ Simplify.

10. $\frac{x+1}{x+2} \div (2x+2)$ Original problem.

$= \frac{x+1}{x+2} \cdot \frac{1}{2x+2}$ Multiply by reciprocal.

$= \frac{x+1}{x+2} \cdot \frac{1}{2(x+1)}$ Factor numerators and denominators.

$= \frac{x+1}{(x+2)(2)(x+1)}$ Multiply numerators and denominators; divide out common factors.

$= \frac{1}{2(x+2)}$ Simplify.

11. $\frac{x+2}{x-1} \div (x^2+2x)$ Original problem.

$= \frac{x+2}{x-1} \cdot \frac{1}{(x^2+2x)}$ Multiply by reciprocal.

$= \frac{x+2}{x-1} \cdot \frac{1}{x(x+2)}$ Factor numerators and denominators.

$= \frac{x+2}{(x-1)(x)(x+2)}$ Multiply numerators and denominators; divide out common factors.

$= \frac{1}{x(x-1)}$ Simplify.

Copyright © McDougal Littell Inc.
All rights reserved.

12. $\frac{x^2 - 4}{x + 2} \div (4x - 8)$ Original problem.

$= \frac{x^2 - 4}{x + 2} \cdot \frac{1}{4x - 8}$ Multiply by reciprocal.

$= \frac{(x + 2)(x - 2)}{(x + 2)} \cdot \frac{1}{4(x - 2)}$ Factor numerators and denominators.

$= \frac{(x + 2)(x - 2)}{(x + 2)(4)(x - 2)}$ Multiply numerators and denominators; divide out common factors.

$= \frac{1}{4}$ Simplify.

11.4 Guided Practice (p. 655)

1. numerators; denominators

2. reciprocal, divisor

3. $\frac{3x}{8x^2} \cdot \frac{4x^3}{3x^4} = \frac{3 \cdot 2 \cdot 2 \cdot x \cdot x \cdot x \cdot x}{2 \cdot 2 \cdot 2 \cdot 3 \cdot x \cdot x \cdot x \cdot x \cdot x \cdot x} = \frac{1}{2x^2}$

4. $\frac{x^2 - 1}{x} \cdot \frac{2x}{3x - 3} = \frac{(x + 1)(x - 1)}{x} \cdot \frac{2x}{3(x - 1)}$

$= \frac{(x + 1)(x - 1)(2x)}{3x(x - 1)}$

$= \frac{2(x + 1)}{3}$

5. $\frac{x}{x^2 - 25} \cdot \frac{x - 5}{x + 5} = \frac{x}{(x + 5)(x - 5)} \cdot \frac{x - 5}{x + 5}$

$= \frac{x(x - 5)}{(x + 5)(x - 5)(x + 5)}$

$= \frac{x}{(x + 5)(x + 5)}$

$= \frac{x}{(x + 5)^2}$

6. $\frac{3x}{x^2 - 2x - 15} \cdot (x + 3) = \frac{3x}{(x + 3)(x - 5)} \cdot \frac{(x + 3)}{1}$

$= \frac{3x(x + 3)}{(x + 3)(x - 5)}$

$= \frac{3x}{x - 5}$

7. $\frac{x}{8 - 2x} \div \frac{2x}{4 - x} = \frac{x}{8 - 2x} \cdot \frac{4 - x}{2x}$

$= \frac{x}{2(4 - x)} \cdot \frac{4 - x}{2x}$

$= \frac{x(4 - x)}{2(4 - x)(2x)}$

$= \frac{1}{4}$

8. $\frac{4x^2 - 25}{4x} \div (2x - 5) = \frac{4x^2 - 25}{4x} \cdot \frac{1}{(2x - 5)}$

$= \frac{(2x + 5)(2x - 5)}{4x} \cdot \frac{1}{2x - 5}$

$= \frac{(2x + 5)(2x - 5)}{4x(2x - 5)}$

$= \frac{2x + 5}{4x}$

Copyright © McDougal Littell Inc.
All rights reserved.

9. The solver should have multiplied the first expression by the reciprocal of the second expression.

$$\frac{x+3}{x-3} \div \frac{4x}{x^2-9} = \frac{x+3}{x+3} \cdot \frac{x^2-9}{4x}$$
$$= \frac{(x+3)}{(x-3)} \cdot \frac{(x+3)(x-3)}{4x}$$
$$= \frac{(x+3)(x+3)(x-3)}{(x-3)(4x)}$$
$$= \frac{(x+3)^2}{4x}$$

11.4 Practice and Applications (pp. 655–657)

10. $\frac{4x}{3} \cdot \frac{1}{x} = \frac{4x}{3x} = \frac{4}{3}$

11. $\frac{9x^2}{4} \cdot \frac{8}{18x} = \frac{3 \cdot 3 \cdot 2 \cdot 2 \cdot 2 \cdot x \cdot x}{2 \cdot 2 \cdot 2 \cdot 3 \cdot 3 \cdot x} = x$

12. $\frac{7d^2}{6d} \cdot \frac{12d^2}{2d} = \frac{7 \cdot 2 \cdot 2 \cdot 3 \cdot d \cdot d \cdot d \cdot d}{2 \cdot 3 \cdot 2 \cdot d \cdot d} = 7d^2$

13. $\frac{6x}{14} \cdot \frac{2x^3}{5x^5} = \frac{2 \cdot 3 \cdot 2 \cdot x \cdot x \cdot x \cdot x}{2 \cdot 7 \cdot 5 \cdot x \cdot x \cdot x \cdot x \cdot x} = \frac{6}{35x}$

14. $\frac{y}{16} \cdot \frac{4y^4}{y^2} = \frac{2 \cdot 2 \cdot y \cdot y \cdot y \cdot y \cdot y}{2 \cdot 2 \cdot 2 \cdot 2 \cdot y \cdot y} = \frac{y^3}{4}$

15.
$$-\frac{3}{x-4} \cdot \frac{x-4}{12(x-7)} = \frac{-3(x-4)}{(x-4)(2 \cdot 2 \cdot 3)(x-7)}$$
$$= -\frac{1}{4(x-7)}$$

16.
$$\frac{3x}{x^2-2x-24} \cdot \frac{x-6}{6x^2} = \frac{3x}{(x-6)(x+4)} \cdot \frac{x-6}{6x^2}$$
$$= \frac{1}{(x+4)(2x)}$$

17.
$$\frac{z^2+8z+7}{10z} \cdot \frac{z^2}{z^2-49} = \frac{(z+7)(z+1)}{10z} \cdot \frac{z \cdot z}{(z+7)(z-7)}$$
$$= \frac{z(z+1)}{10(z-7)}$$

18.
$$\frac{5-2x}{6} \cdot \frac{24}{10-4x} = \frac{5-2x}{6} \cdot \frac{6 \cdot 2 \cdot 2}{2(5-2x)}$$
$$= 2$$

19.
$$\frac{3a}{a+4} \cdot \frac{a^2+5a+4}{a^2+a} = \frac{3a}{a+4} \cdot \frac{(a+1)(a+4)}{a(a+1)}$$
$$= \frac{3a(a+4)}{(a+4)(a)}$$
$$= 3$$

20.
$$\frac{3x^2-6x}{2x+1} \cdot \frac{4x+2}{x-2} = \frac{3x(x-2)}{2x+1} \cdot \frac{2(2x+1)}{x-2}$$
$$= \frac{3x(x-2)(2)(2x+1)}{(2x+1)(x-2)}$$
$$= 6x$$

21.
$$\frac{x}{x-2} \cdot \frac{x^2-3x+2}{x-1} = \frac{x}{x-2} \cdot \frac{(x-2)(x-1)}{(x-1)}$$
$$= \frac{x(x-2)}{x-2}$$
$$= x$$

Copyright © McDougal Littell Inc.
All rights reserved.

22. $$\frac{45x^3 - 9x^2}{x} \cdot \frac{2}{6(x-5)} = \frac{9x^2(5x-1)}{x} \cdot \frac{2}{2 \cdot 3(x-5)}$$
$$= \frac{3 \cdot 3 \cdot x \cdot x(5x-1)(2)}{x \cdot 2 \cdot 3(x-5)}$$
$$= \frac{3x(5x-1)}{x-5}$$

23. $$\frac{c^2 - 64}{4c^3} \cdot \frac{c}{c^2 + 9c + 8} = \frac{(c+8)(c-8)}{2 \cdot 2 \cdot c \cdot c \cdot c} \cdot \frac{c}{(c+8)(c+1)}$$
$$= \frac{(c+8)(c-8)(c)}{2 \cdot 2 \cdot c \cdot c \cdot c \cdot (c+8)(c+1)}$$
$$= \frac{c-8}{4c^2(c+1)}$$

24. $$\frac{3}{x^2 - 5x + 6} \cdot \frac{x-3}{x-2} = \frac{3}{(x-2)(x-3)} \cdot \frac{x-3}{x-2}$$
$$= \frac{3(x-3)}{(x-2)(x-3)(x-2)}$$
$$= \frac{3}{(x-2)^2}$$

25. $$\frac{3x}{x+4} \cdot (3x+12) = \frac{3x}{x+4} \cdot \frac{3(x+4)}{1}$$
$$= \frac{3x \cdot 3(x+4)}{(x+4)}$$
$$= 9x$$

26. $$\frac{7x - 15}{11x + 121} \cdot (x+11) = \frac{7x-15}{11(x+11)} \cdot \frac{x+11}{1}$$
$$= \frac{(7x-15)(x+11)}{11(x+11)}$$
$$= \frac{7x-15}{11}$$

27. $$(y-3)^2 \cdot \frac{2y-2}{y^2 - 4y + 3} = \frac{(y-3)^2}{1} \cdot \frac{2(y-1)}{(y-3)(y-1)}$$
$$= \frac{(y-3)(y-3)(2)(y-1)}{(y-3)(y-1)}$$
$$= 2(y-3)$$

28. $$(x^2 + 2x + 1) \cdot \frac{x+2}{(x^2 + 3x + 2)} = \frac{(x+1)(x+1)}{1} \cdot \frac{(x+2)}{(x+2)(x+1)}$$
$$= \frac{(x+1)(x+1)}{(x+1)}$$
$$= x + 1$$

29. $$\frac{2x+3}{2x^2 - 3x - 9} \cdot (x^2 - 9) = \frac{(2x+3)}{(2x+3)(x-3)} \cdot \frac{(x+3)(x-3)}{1}$$
$$= \frac{(x+3)(x-3)}{(x-3)}$$
$$= x + 3$$

30. $$3z^2 + 10z + 3 \cdot \frac{(z+3)}{3z^2 + 4z + 1} = \frac{(3z+1)(z+3)}{1} \cdot \frac{(z+3)}{(3z+1)(z+1)}$$
$$= \frac{(3z+1)(z+3)(z+3)}{(3z+1)(z+1)}$$
$$= \frac{(z+3)^2}{z+1}$$

Copyright © McDougal Littell Inc.
All rights reserved.

31. $\frac{25x^2}{10x} \div \frac{5x}{10x} = \frac{5 \cdot 5 \cdot x \cdot x}{2 \cdot 5 \cdot x} \cdot \frac{5 \cdot 2 \cdot x}{5 \cdot x}$

$= \frac{5 \cdot x \cdot 2}{2}$

$= 5x$

32. $\frac{16x^2}{8x} \div \frac{4x^2}{16x} = \frac{2 \cdot 2 \cdot 2 \cdot 2 \cdot x \cdot x}{2 \cdot 2 \cdot 2 \cdot x} \cdot \frac{2 \cdot 2 \cdot 2 \cdot 2 \cdot x}{2 \cdot 2 \cdot x \cdot x}$

$= \frac{2 \cdot x \cdot 2 \cdot 2}{1 \cdot x}$

$= 8$

33. $\frac{3x^2}{10} \div \frac{9x^3}{25} = \frac{3x^2}{10} \cdot \frac{25}{9x^3}$

$= \frac{3 \cdot x \cdot x}{2 \cdot 5} \cdot \frac{5 \cdot 5}{3 \cdot 3 \cdot x \cdot x \cdot x}$

$= \frac{3 \cdot x \cdot x \cdot 5 \cdot 5}{2 \cdot 5 \cdot 3 \cdot 3 \cdot x \cdot x \cdot x}$

$= \frac{5}{6x}$

34. $\frac{x}{x+2} \div \frac{x+5}{x+2} = \frac{x}{x+2} \cdot \frac{x+2}{x+5}$

$= \frac{x(x+2)}{(x+2)(x+5)}$

$= \frac{x}{x+5}$

35. $\frac{2(x+2)}{5(x-3)} \div \frac{4(x-2)}{5x-15} = \frac{2(x+2)}{5(x-3)} \cdot \frac{5(x-3)}{4(x-2)}$

$= \frac{2(x+2)(5)(x-3)}{5(x-3)(2 \cdot 2)(x-2)}$

$= \frac{x+2}{2(x-2)}$

36. $\frac{x}{x-2} \div \frac{2x-2}{x^2-3x+2} = \frac{x}{x-2} \cdot \frac{x^2-3x+2}{2x-2}$

$= \frac{x}{x-2} \cdot \frac{(x-1)(x-2)}{2(x-1)}$

$= \frac{x(x-2)}{(x-2)(2)}$

$= \frac{x}{2}$

37. $\frac{x}{x+6} \div \frac{x+3}{x^2-36} = \frac{x}{x+6} \cdot \frac{x^2-36}{x+3}$

$= \frac{x}{x+6} \cdot \frac{(x+6)(x-6)}{(x+3)}$

$= \frac{x(x+6)(x-6)}{(x+6)(x+3)}$

$= \frac{x(x-6)}{x+3}$

38. $\frac{3x+12}{4x} \div \frac{x+4}{2x} = \frac{3(x+4)}{4x} \cdot \frac{2x}{x+4}$

$= \frac{3(x+4)(2x)}{2 \cdot 2x \cdot (x+4)}$

$= \frac{3}{2}$

Copyright © McDougal Littell Inc.
All rights reserved.

39. $\dfrac{2x^2 + 3x + 1}{12x - 12} \div \dfrac{x^2 - 1}{6x} = \dfrac{2x^2 + 3x + 1}{12x - 12} \cdot \dfrac{6x}{x^2 - 1}$

$= \dfrac{(2x + 1)(x + 1)}{12(x - 1)} \cdot \dfrac{6x}{(x + 1)(x - 1)}$

$= \dfrac{x(2x + 1)}{2(x - 1)^2}$

40. $\dfrac{x + 5}{2 + 3x} \div (x^2 - 25) = \dfrac{x + 5}{2 + 3x} \cdot \dfrac{1}{x^2 - 25}$

$= \dfrac{(x + 5)}{(2 + 3x)} \cdot \dfrac{1}{(x + 5)(x - 5)}$

$= \dfrac{x + 5}{(2 + 3x)(x + 5)(x - 5)}$

$= \dfrac{1}{(2 + 3x)(x - 5)}$

41. $\dfrac{x^2 - 36}{-5x^2} \div (x - 6) = \dfrac{x^2 - 36}{-5x^2} \cdot \dfrac{1}{x - 6}$

$= \dfrac{(x + 6)(x - 6)}{-5x^2} \cdot \dfrac{1}{x - 6}$

$= \dfrac{(x + 6)(x - 6)}{-5x^2(x - 6)}$

$= -\dfrac{x + 6}{5x^2}$

42. $\dfrac{x^2 + 19x - 20}{x^2} \div (x^2 - 1) = \dfrac{x^2 + 19x - 20}{x^2} \cdot \dfrac{1}{x^2 - 1}$

$= \dfrac{(x + 20)(x - 1)}{x^2} \cdot \dfrac{1}{(x + 1)(x - 1)}$

$= \dfrac{(x + 20)(x - 1)}{x^2(x + 1)(x - 1)}$

$= \dfrac{x + 20}{x^2(x + 1)}$

43. $\dfrac{y - 12}{2y + 3} \div (y^2 - 14y + 24) = \dfrac{y - 12}{2y + 3} \cdot \dfrac{1}{y^2 - 14y + 24}$

$= \dfrac{y - 12}{2y + 3} \cdot \dfrac{1}{(y - 12)(y - 2)}$

$= \dfrac{y - 12}{(2y + 3)(y - 12)(y - 2)}$

$= \dfrac{1}{(2y + 3)(y - 2)}$

44. $\dfrac{3x^2 + 2x - 8}{3x} \div (3x - 4) = \dfrac{(3x - 4)(x + 2)}{3x} \cdot \dfrac{1}{(3x - 4)}$

$= \dfrac{(3x - 4)(x + 2)}{3x(3x - 4)}$

$= \dfrac{x + 2}{3x}$

45. $\dfrac{4x + 3}{x - 1} \div (4x^2 + x - 3) = \dfrac{4x + 3}{x - 1} \cdot \dfrac{1}{4x^2 + x - 3}$

$= \dfrac{4x + 3}{x - 1} \cdot \dfrac{1}{(4x - 3)(x + 1)}$

$= \dfrac{4x + 3}{(x - 1)(4x - 3)(x + 1)}$

Copyright © McDougal Littell Inc.
All rights reserved.

46. $P_1 = \dfrac{100x^2}{x+1}, P_2 = \dfrac{100x^2}{x+3}$

x	1	2	3	4	5	6	7	8	9	10
P_1	50	133	225	320	417	514	613	711	810	909
P_2	25	80	150	229	313	400	490	582	675	769

47. $$\frac{P_1}{P_2} = \frac{100x^2}{x+1} \div \frac{100x^2}{x+3} = \frac{100x^2}{x+1} \cdot \frac{x+3}{100x^2} = \frac{x+3}{x+1}$$

48.

$\frac{P_1}{P_2}$	2	$1\frac{2}{3}$	$1\frac{1}{2}$	$1\frac{2}{5}$	$1\frac{1}{3}$	$1\frac{2}{7}$	$1\frac{1}{4}$	$1\frac{2}{9}$	$1\frac{1}{5}$	$1\frac{2}{11}$

49. The ratios decrease steadily from 2. If the value of x gets very large, $\frac{P_1}{P_2}$ gets close to 1. Sample answer: First, I evaluated $\frac{P_1}{P_2}$ for $x = 100{,}000$ and found that $\frac{P_1}{P_2} = 1.00002$. Then, I reasoned that as x gets very large, $x + 3 \approx x + 1$, so $\frac{P_1}{P_2} = \frac{x+3}{x+1} \approx 1$.

50. Area of smaller $= \dfrac{(x+4)}{2x} \cdot \dfrac{(x+1)}{2x^2} = \dfrac{(x+4)(x+1)}{4x^3}$

$$\text{Area of larger} = \frac{(x^2-16)}{x^2-x-6} \cdot \frac{(x-3)}{x^2-3x-4} = \frac{(x+4)(x-4)}{(x+2)(x-3)} \cdot \frac{(x-3)}{(x-4)(x+1)} = \frac{(x+4)(x-4)(x-3)}{(x+2)(x-3)(x-4)(x+1)} = \frac{(x+4)}{(x+2)(x+1)}$$

$$\frac{\text{Area of smaller}}{\text{Area of larger}} = \frac{(x+4)(x+1)}{4x^3} \div \frac{(x+4)}{(x+2)(x+1)} = \frac{(x+4)(x+1)}{4x^3} \cdot \frac{(x+2)(x+1)}{(x+4)} = \frac{(x+4)(x+1)(x+2)(x+1)}{4x^3(x+4)} = \frac{(x+1)^2(x+2)}{4x^3}$$

Copyright © McDougal Littell Inc.
All rights reserved.

51. Divide the first two expressions; simplify as much as possible.

$$\frac{x^2 + 11x + 18}{x^2 - 25} \div \frac{14x^3}{x^2 - x - 20} = \frac{(x^2 + 11x + 18)}{(x^2 - 25)} \cdot \frac{(x^2 - x - 20)}{14x^3}$$
$$= \frac{(x + 9)(x + 2)}{(x + 5)(x - 5)} \cdot \frac{(x - 5)(x + 4)}{14x^3}$$
$$= \frac{(x + 9)(x + 2)(x + 4)}{(x + 5)(14x^3)}$$

Multiply the quotient of the first two expressions by the third expression.

$$\frac{(x + 9)(x + 2)(x + 4)}{(x + 5)(14x^3)} \cdot \frac{x}{(x + 4)} = \frac{(x + 9)(x + 2)}{(x + 5)(14x^2)}$$

Find the quotient of the previous product and the fourth expression.

$$\frac{(x + 9)(x + 2)}{(x + 5)(14x^2)} \div \frac{(2x - 1)}{6x} = \frac{(x + 9)(x + 2)}{(x + 5)(14x^2)} \cdot \frac{(6x)}{(2x - 1)}$$
$$= \frac{(x + 9)(x + 2)(3)}{(x + 5)(7x)(2x - 1)}$$

Multiply the previous quotient by the fifth expression.

$$\frac{(x + 9)(x + 2)(3)}{(x + 5)(7x)(2x - 1)} \cdot \frac{2x^2 + 9x - 5}{x^2 + 3x + 2} = \frac{(x + 9)(x + 2)(3)}{(x + 5)(7x)(2x - 1)} \cdot \frac{(2x - 1)(x + 5)}{(x + 2)(x + 1)}$$
$$= \frac{3(x + 9)}{7x(x + 1)}$$

11.4 Standardized Test Practice (p. 657)

52. C;

$$\frac{x^2 - 3x}{x^2 - 5x + 6} \cdot \frac{(x - 2)^2}{2x} = \frac{x(x - 3)}{(x - 2)(x - 3)} \cdot \frac{(x - 2)(x - 2)}{2x}$$
$$= \frac{x(x - 2)(x - 2)}{(x - 2)2x}$$
$$= \frac{x - 2}{2}$$

53. J; $(2x + 2) \div \frac{x^2 + x}{4} = \frac{(2x + 2)}{1} \cdot \frac{4}{(x^2 + x)}$

11.4 Mixed Review (p. 657)

54. Sample answer: When $x = 2$, $y = 11$; When $x = 4$, $y = 13$; and when $x = 6$, $y = 15$.

55.

x	2	4	6
y	11	13	15

56. domain: $2 \le x \le 6$; range: $11 \le y \le 15$

57. $|x + 7| < 12$
$-12 < x + 7 < 12$
$-19 < x < 5$

58. $|2x - 15| \le 15$
$-15 \le 2x - 15 \le 15$
$0 \le 2x \le 30$
$0 \le x \le 15$

59. $|x + 13| \ge 33$
$x + 13 \ge 33$ or $x + 13 \le -33$
$x \ge 20$ $x \le -46$

Copyright © McDougal Littell Inc.
All rights reserved.

60. $|3x - 10| < 4$

$-4 < 3x - 10 < 4$

$6 < 3x < 14$

$2 < x < \frac{14}{3}$

61. $|x + 5| > 17$

$x + 5 > 17$ or $x + 5 < -17$

$x > 12$ $\quad x < -22$

62. $|5x - 1| \leq 0$

$0 \leq 5x - 1 \leq 0$

$1 \leq 5x \leq 1$

$\frac{1}{5} \leq x \leq \frac{1}{5}$

$x = \frac{1}{5}$

63. $2x^2 + 12x - 6 = 0$

$a = 2, b = 12, c = -6$

$x = \frac{-12 \pm \sqrt{12^2 - 4(2)(-6)}}{2(2)}$

$x = \frac{-12 \pm \sqrt{144 + 48}}{4} = \frac{-12 \pm \sqrt{192}}{4}$

$x = \frac{-12 \pm \sqrt{64 \cdot 3}}{4} = \frac{-12 \pm 8\sqrt{3}}{4}$

$x = \frac{4(-3 \pm 2\sqrt{3})}{4} = -3 \pm 2\sqrt{3}$

64. $x^2 - 6x + 7 = 0$

$a = 1, b = -6, c = 7$

$x = \frac{-(-6) \pm \sqrt{(-6)^2 - 4(1)(7)}}{2(1)}$

$x = \frac{6 \pm \sqrt{36 - 28}}{2} = \frac{6 \pm \sqrt{8}}{2} = \frac{6 \pm \sqrt{4 \cdot 2}}{2}$

$x = \frac{6 \pm 2\sqrt{2}}{2} = \frac{2(3 \pm \sqrt{2})}{2} = 3 \pm \sqrt{2}$

65. $3x^2 + 11x + 10 = 0$

$a = 3, b = 11, c = 10$

$x = \frac{-11 \pm \sqrt{11^2 - 4(3)(10)}}{2(3)}$

$x = \frac{-11 \pm \sqrt{121 - 120}}{6} = \frac{-11 \pm \sqrt{1}}{6}$

$x = \frac{-11 \pm 1}{6}$

$x = \frac{-11 + 1}{6} = -\frac{10}{6} = -\frac{5}{3}$ or

$x = \frac{-11 - 1}{6} = -\frac{12}{6} = -2$

66. $6x^2 = 130$

$x^2 = \frac{65}{3}$

$x = \pm\sqrt{\frac{65}{3}} = \pm\frac{\sqrt{65}}{\sqrt{3}} \cdot \frac{\sqrt{3}}{\sqrt{3}} = \pm\frac{\sqrt{195}}{3}$

67. $5 = 6x^2 + 7x$

$0 = 6x^2 + 7x - 5$

$a = 6, b = 7, c = -5$

$x = \frac{-7 \pm \sqrt{7^2 - 4(6)(-5)}}{2(6)}$

$x = \frac{-7 \pm \sqrt{49 + 120}}{12} = \frac{-7 \pm \sqrt{169}}{12}$

$x = \frac{-7 \pm 13}{12}$

$x = \frac{-7 + 13}{12} = \frac{6}{12} = \frac{1}{2}$ or

$x = \frac{-7 - 13}{12} = -\frac{20}{12} = -\frac{5}{3}$

68. $2x^2 + 4x = 7$

$2x^2 + 4x - 7 = 0$

$a = 2, b = 4, c = -7$

$x = \frac{-4 \pm \sqrt{4^2 - 4(2)(-7)}}{2(2)}$

$x = \frac{-4 \pm \sqrt{16 + 56}}{4} = \frac{-4 \pm \sqrt{72}}{4}$

$x = \frac{-4 \pm \sqrt{36 \cdot 2}}{4} = \frac{-4 \pm 6\sqrt{2}}{4} = \frac{2(-2 \pm 3\sqrt{2})}{4}$

$x = \frac{-2 \pm 3\sqrt{2}}{2}$

69. $(-5x^2 + 2x - 12) - (6 - 9x - 7x^2)$

$= -5x^2 + 2x - 12 - 6 + 9x + 7x^2$

$= 2x^2 + 11x - 18$

70. $(a^4 - 12a) + (4a^3 + 11a - 1)$

$= a^4 + 4a^3 - a - 1$

71. $(16p^3 - p^2 + 24) + (12p^2 - 8p - 16)$

$= 16p^3 + 11p^2 - 8p + 8$

72. $(4t^2 + 5t + 2) - (t^2 - 3t - 8)$

$= 4t^2 + 5t + 2 - t^2 + 3t + 8$

$= 3t^2 + 8t + 10$

11.4 Maintaining Skills (p. 657)

73. $0.35 + \frac{1}{2} = 0.35 + 0.5 = 0.85$

74. $0.58 + \frac{2}{5} = 0.58 + 0.4 = 0.98$

75. $0.99 + \frac{3}{4} = 0.99 + 0.75 = 1.74$

76. $0.06 + \frac{1}{8} = 0.06 + 0.125 = 0.185$

77. $\frac{7}{8} + 0.25 = 0.875 + 0.25 = 1.125$

78. $\frac{3}{5} + 0.4 = 0.6 + 0.4 = 1.0$

Copyright © McDougal Littell Inc.
All rights reserved.

79. $\frac{12}{12} + 0.12 = 1 + 0.12 = 1.12$

80. $\frac{3}{10} + 0.45 = 0.3 + 0.45 = 0.75$

Lesson 11.5

11.5 Checkpoint (p. 659)

1. $\frac{x+2}{x} + \frac{3x-2}{x}$ Original expression.

$= \frac{(x+2)+(3x-2)}{x}$ Add numerators.

$= \frac{4x}{x}$ Combine like terms.

$= 4$ Simplify.

2. $\frac{x+2}{x^2+5} - \frac{3x+2}{x^2+5}$ Original expression.

$= \frac{(x+2)-(3x+2)}{x^2+5}$ Subtract numerators.

$= \frac{x+2-3x-2}{x^2+5}$ Distribute the negative.

$= \frac{-2x}{x^2+5}$ Simplify.

3. $\frac{3x-4}{x-4} - \frac{2x}{x-4}$ Original expression.

$= \frac{3x-4-2x}{x-4}$ Subtract numerators.

$= \frac{x-4}{x-4}$ Combine like terms.

$= 1$ Divide out common factor.

4. $\frac{2x}{x^2+2x+1} + \frac{2}{x^2+2x+1}$ Original expression.

$= \frac{2x+2}{x^2+2x+1}$ Add numerators.

$= \frac{2(x+1)}{(x+1)(x+1)}$ Factor.

$= \frac{2}{x+1}$ Divide out common factor.

5. $\frac{2x-4}{x^2+3x} - \frac{x-7}{x^2+3x}$ Original expression.

$= \frac{(2x-4)-(x-7)}{x^2+3x}$ Subtract numerators.

$= \frac{2x-4-x+7}{x^2+3x}$ Distribute the negative.

$= \frac{x+3}{x^2+3x}$ Combine like terms.

$= \frac{x+3}{x(x+3)}$ Factor.

$= \frac{1}{x}$ Divide out common factor.

11.5 Guided Practice (p. 660)

1. common denominator

2. $\frac{1}{3x} + \frac{5}{3x} = \frac{1+5}{3x} = \frac{6}{3x} = \frac{2}{x}$

3. $\frac{8y}{y+3} + \frac{10-3y}{y+3} = \frac{8y+10-3y}{y+3}$

$= \frac{5y+10}{y+3}$

$= \frac{5(y+2)}{y+3}$

4. $\frac{x}{x^2-9} + \frac{3x+1}{x^2-9} = \frac{x+3x+1}{x^2-9}$

$= \frac{4x+1}{x^2-9}$

$= \frac{4x+1}{(x+3)(x-3)}$

5. $\frac{8}{3r} - \frac{1}{3r} = \frac{8-1}{3r} = \frac{7}{3r}$

6. $\frac{12k}{k^2} - \frac{3k+7}{k^2} = \frac{12k-(3k+7)}{k^2}$

$= \frac{12k-3k-7}{k^2}$

$= \frac{9k-7}{k^2}$

7. $\frac{c+1}{c^2-4} - \frac{c+6}{c^2-4} = \frac{c+1-(c+6)}{c^2-4}$

$= \frac{c+1-c-6}{c^2-4}$

$= -\frac{5}{c^2-4}$

8. $\frac{5x}{x+4} + \frac{20}{4+x} = \frac{5x+20}{x+4} = \frac{5(x+4)}{x+4} = 5$

9. $\frac{-12y}{y^2-9y+14} + \frac{84}{y^2-9y+14} = \frac{-12y+84}{y^2-9y+14}$

$= \frac{-12(y-7)}{(y-7)(y-2)}$

$= -\frac{12}{y-2}$

10. $\frac{2y+3}{y^2-4y} - \frac{-y+15}{y^2-4y} = \frac{2y+3-(-y+15)}{y^2-4y}$

$= \frac{2y+3+y-15}{y^2-4y}$

$= \frac{3y-12}{y^2-4y}$

$= \frac{3(y-4)}{y(y-4)}$

$= \frac{3}{y}$

Copyright © McDougal Littell Inc.
All rights reserved.

11. $\frac{10}{r^2 + 9r + 20} - \frac{-2r}{r^2 + 9r + 20} = \frac{10 - (-2r)}{r^2 + 9r + 20}$
$= \frac{10 + 2r}{r^2 + 9r + 20}$
$= \frac{2(5 + r)}{(r + 5)(r + 4)}$
$= \frac{2}{r + 4}$

11.5 Practice and Applications (pp. 660–661)

12. $\frac{7}{2x} + \frac{x + 2}{2x} = \frac{7 + x + 2}{2x} = \frac{x + 9}{2x}$

13. $\frac{2}{x + 7} + \frac{5}{x + 7} = \frac{2 + 5}{x + 7} = \frac{7}{x + 7}$

14. $\frac{4t - 1}{1 - 4t} + \frac{2t + 3}{1 - 4t} = \frac{4t - 1 + 2t + 3}{1 - 4t}$
$= \frac{6t + 2}{1 - 4t}$

15. $\frac{4}{x + 1} + \frac{2x - 2}{x + 1} = \frac{4 + 2x - 2}{x + 1}$
$= \frac{2x + 2}{x + 1}$
$= \frac{2(x + 1)}{x + 1}$
$= 2$

16. $\frac{a + 1}{15a} + \frac{2a - 1}{15a} = \frac{a + 1 + 2a - 1}{15a}$
$= \frac{3a}{15a}$
$= \frac{1}{5}$

17. $\frac{2x}{4x + 6} + \frac{3}{4x + 6} = \frac{2x + 3}{4x + 6}$
$= \frac{2x + 3}{2(2x + 3)}$
$= \frac{1}{2}$

18. $\frac{7x}{x^3} - \frac{6x}{x^3} = \frac{7x - 6x}{x^3} = \frac{x}{x^3} = \frac{1}{x^2}$

19. $\frac{8 + 6t}{3t} - \frac{5t - 6}{3t} = \frac{8 + 6t - (5t - 6)}{3t}$
$= \frac{8 + 6t - 5t + 6}{3t}$
$= \frac{t + 14}{3t}$

20. $\frac{2x}{x + 2} - \frac{2x + 1}{x + 2} = \frac{2x - (2x + 1)}{x + 2}$
$= \frac{2x - 2x - 1}{x + 2}$
$= -\frac{1}{x + 2}$

21. $\frac{2}{3x - 1} - \frac{5x}{3x - 1} = \frac{2 - 5x}{3x - 1}$

22. $\frac{4x}{2x + 6} - \frac{16}{2x + 6} = \frac{4x - 16}{2x + 6}$
$= \frac{4(x - 4)}{2(x + 3)}$
$= \frac{2(x - 4)}{x + 3}$

23. $\frac{4m}{m - 2} - \frac{2m + 4}{m - 2} = \frac{4m - (2m + 4)}{m - 2}$
$= \frac{4m - 2m - 4}{m - 2}$
$= \frac{2m - 4}{m - 2}$
$= \frac{2(m - 2)}{m - 2}$
$= 2$

24. $\frac{x}{x^2 + 5x - 24} + \frac{8}{x^2 + 5x - 24} = \frac{x + 8}{x^2 + 5x - 24}$
$= \frac{x + 8}{(x + 8)(x - 3)}$
$= \frac{1}{x - 3}$

25. $\frac{a^2 - 2}{a^2 - 25} + \frac{4a - 3}{a^2 - 25} = \frac{a^2 - 2 + 4a - 3}{a^2 - 25}$
$= \frac{a^2 + 4a - 5}{a^2 - 25}$
$= \frac{(a + 5)(a - 1)}{(a + 5)(a - 5)}$
$= \frac{a - 1}{a - 5}$

26. $\frac{2x}{x^2 + 5x + 4} + \frac{8}{x^2 + 5x + 4} = \frac{2x + 8}{x^2 + 5x + 4}$
$= \frac{2(x + 4)}{(x + 4)(x + 1)}$
$= \frac{2}{x + 1}$

27. $\frac{x^2 - 10}{x^2 - 4} + \frac{3x}{x^2 - 4} = \frac{x^2 - 10 + 3x}{x^2 - 4}$
$= \frac{x^2 + 3x - 10}{x^2 - 4}$
$= \frac{(x - 2)(x + 5)}{(x + 2)(x - 2)}$
$= \frac{x + 5}{x + 2}$

28. $\frac{2x}{x^2 + 5x} - \frac{x}{x^2 + 5x} = \frac{2x - x}{x^2 + 5x}$
$= \frac{x}{x(x + 5)}$
$= \frac{1}{x + 5}$

Copyright © McDougal Littell Inc.
All rights reserved.

29. $\dfrac{2x(x+4)}{(x+1)^2} - \dfrac{3x-3}{(x+1)^2} = \dfrac{2x^2+8x-(3x-3)}{(x+1)^2}$
$= \dfrac{2x^2+8x-3x+3}{(x+1)^2}$
$= \dfrac{2x^2+5x+3}{(x+1)^2}$
$= \dfrac{(2x+3)(x+1)}{(x+1)(x+1)}$
$= \dfrac{2x+3}{x+1}$

30. $\dfrac{y^2-2y}{y^2-7y-18} - \dfrac{9(y-2)}{y^2-7y-18} = \dfrac{y^2-2y-(9y-18)}{y^2-7y-18}$
$= \dfrac{y^2-2y-9y+18}{y^2-7y-18}$
$= \dfrac{y^2-11y+18}{y^2-7y-18}$
$= \dfrac{(y-9)(y-2)}{(y-9)(y+2)}$
$= \dfrac{y-2}{y+2}$

31. $\dfrac{y^2}{y^2-3y-28} - \dfrac{12-y}{y^2-3y-28} = \dfrac{y^2-(12-y)}{y^2-3y-28}$
$= \dfrac{y^2-12+y}{y^2-3y-28}$
$= \dfrac{y^2+y-12}{y^2-3y-28}$
$= \dfrac{(y-3)(y+4)}{(y-7)(y+4)}$
$= \dfrac{y-3}{y-7}$

32. $n^2 - 144$ is factored incorrectly.
$\dfrac{3n^2}{n^2-144} - \dfrac{36n}{n^2-144} = \dfrac{3n^2-36n}{n^2-144}$
$= \dfrac{3n(n-12)}{(n+12)(n-12)}$
$= \dfrac{3n}{n+12}$

33. The solver multiplied the rational expressions rather than adding them.
$\dfrac{y+2}{y+3} + \dfrac{y-4}{y+3} = \dfrac{y+2+y-4}{y+3} = \dfrac{2y-2}{y+3}$

34. $\dfrac{11x-5}{2x+5} + \dfrac{11x+12}{2x+5} + \dfrac{3x-100}{2x+5}$
$= \dfrac{11x-5+11x+12+3x-100}{2x+5}$
$= \dfrac{25x-93}{2x+5}$

35. $\dfrac{4+x}{x-9} + \dfrac{6+x}{x-9} - \dfrac{1-x}{x-9} = \dfrac{4+x+6+x-(1-x)}{x-9}$
$= \dfrac{10+2x-1+x}{x-9}$
$= \dfrac{3x+9}{x-9}$

36. $\dfrac{c-15}{2c+6} - \dfrac{2c}{2c+6} + \dfrac{12}{2c+6} = \dfrac{c-15-(2c)+12}{2c+6}$
$= \dfrac{-c-3}{2c+6}$
$= \dfrac{-(c+3)}{2(c+3)} = -\dfrac{1}{2}$

37. $\dfrac{2x}{x^2-9} - \dfrac{4x+2}{x^2-9} - \dfrac{4}{x^2-9} = \dfrac{2x-(4x+2)-4}{x^2-9}$
$= \dfrac{2x-4x-2-4}{x^2-9}$
$= \dfrac{-2x-6}{x^2-9}$
$= \dfrac{-2(x+3)}{(x+3)(x-3)}$
$= \dfrac{-2}{x-3}$

38. $\dfrac{3x^2}{56}\left(\dfrac{3}{x} + \dfrac{5}{x}\right) = \dfrac{3x^2}{56}\left(\dfrac{8}{x}\right) = \dfrac{3x}{7}$

39. $\left(\dfrac{3x-5}{x} + \dfrac{1}{x}\right) \div \left(\dfrac{x}{6x-8}\right) = \dfrac{3x-5+1}{x} \cdot \dfrac{6x-8}{x}$
$= \dfrac{3x-4}{x} \cdot \dfrac{6x-8}{x}$
$= \dfrac{(3x-4)(2)(3x-4)}{x \cdot x}$
$= \dfrac{2(3x-4)^2}{x^2}$

40. $2\left(\dfrac{x^2-3}{x-2}\right) + 2\left(\dfrac{2x-5}{x-2}\right) = \dfrac{2x^2-6}{x-2} + \dfrac{4x-10}{x-2}$
$= \dfrac{2x^2-6+4x-10}{x-2}$
$= \dfrac{2x^2+4x-16}{x-2}$
$= \dfrac{(2x+8)(x-2)}{x-2}$
$= 2x+8 = 2(x+4)$

41. $\dfrac{4x}{x+1} + \dfrac{5x}{x+1} + \dfrac{5x}{x+1} = \dfrac{4x+5x+5x}{x+1}$
$= \dfrac{14x}{x+1}$

42. K_2: $\dfrac{9}{x}$; K_1: $\dfrac{7}{x}$; Work: $\dfrac{9-7}{x} = \dfrac{2}{x}$ Joules

43. K_2: $\dfrac{5}{a}$; K_1: $\dfrac{5-a}{a}$; Work: $\dfrac{5-(5-a)}{a} = \dfrac{a}{a} = 1$ Joule

44. K_2: $\dfrac{2t}{t-1}$; K_1: $\dfrac{t+4}{t-1}$;
Work: $\dfrac{2t-(t+4)}{t-1} = \dfrac{t-4}{t-1}$ Joules

45. K_2: $\dfrac{x^2-7}{x^2-100}$; K_1: $\dfrac{-10x-7}{x^2-100}$;
Work: $\dfrac{x^2+10x}{x^2-100} = \dfrac{x}{x-10}$ Joules
$\dfrac{x^2+10x}{x^2-100} = \dfrac{x(x+10)}{(x+10)(x-10)}$

Copyright © McDougal Littell Inc.
All rights reserved.

11.5 Standardized Test Practice (p. 662)

46. B;

$$\frac{x^2}{x-7} - \frac{4x+21}{x-7} = \frac{x^2-4x-21}{x-7} = \frac{(x-7)(x+3)}{x-7} = x+3$$

47. H;

$$\frac{x^2}{x+5} - \frac{25}{x+5} = \frac{x^2-25}{x+5} = \frac{(x+5)(x-5)}{x+5} = x-5$$

48. D;

$$\frac{24y^2+24}{8y-3} - \frac{73y}{8y-3} = \frac{24y^2-73y+24}{8y-3} = \frac{(8y-3)(3y-8)}{8y-3} = 3y-8$$

11.5 Mixed Review (p. 662)

49. $x^5y^{-6} = \frac{x^5}{y^6}$

50. $8x^{-1}y^{-3} = \frac{8}{xy^3}$

51. $\frac{1}{2x^8y^{-5}} = \frac{y^5}{2x^8}$

52. $\frac{3}{10t^{-3}r^{-1}} = \frac{3t^3r}{10}$

53. $(-6c)^{-4} = \frac{1}{(-6c)^4} = \frac{1}{(-6)^4c^4} = -\frac{1}{1296c^4}$

54. $(-y)^0n = 1n = n$

55. $\frac{d}{c^{-2}} = c^2d$

56. $\frac{1}{(-7m)^{-3}} = (-7m)^3 = -343m^3$

57. $\frac{p^6}{p^8} = p^{-2} = \frac{1}{p^2}$

58. $x^5 \cdot \frac{1}{x^4} = x$

59. $\left(\frac{a^8}{a^3}\right)^{-1} = (a^5)^{-1} = a^{-5} = \frac{1}{a^5}$

60. $\left(\frac{y^5}{y^7}\right)^{-2} = (y^{-2})^{-2} = y^4$

61. $\frac{m^8 \cdot m^{10}}{m^2} = \frac{m^{18}}{m^2} = m^{16}$

62. $\frac{(a^3)^4}{(a^3)^8} = \frac{a^{12}}{a^{24}} = a^{-12} = \frac{1}{a^{12}}$

63.
$$\left(\frac{-2u^2v}{uv^4}\right)^{-3} = (-2uv^{-3})^{-3} = (-2)^{-3}u^{-3}v^9 = \frac{v^9}{(-2)^3u^3} = -\frac{v^9}{8u^3}$$

64.
$$\left(\frac{42a^3b^{-4}}{6ab}\right)^3 = (7a^2b^{-5})^3 = 7^3a^6b^{-15} = \frac{343a^6}{b^{15}}$$

65. $\frac{8 \times 10^{-3}}{5 \times 10^{-5}} = 1.6 \times 10^2$

66. $\frac{1.4 \times 10^{-1}}{3.5 \times 10^{-4}} = 0.4 \times 10^3 = (4 \times 10^{-1}) \times 10^3 = 4 \times 10^2$

67.
$$(3 \times 10^{-2})^4 = 81 \times 10^{-8} = (8.1 \times 10^1) \times 10^{-8} = 8.1 \times 10^{-7}$$

68.
$$2 \times 10^3 + 3 \times 10^2 = 2000 + 300 = 2300 = 2.3 \times 10^3$$

69.
$$(2.5 \times 10)^{-2} = (2.5^{-2})(10^{-2}) = \frac{1}{(2.5)^2} \times 10^{-2} = 0.16 \times 10^{-2} = (1.6 \times 10^{-1}) \times 10^{-2} = 1.6 \times 10^{-3}$$

70.
$$3.2 \times 10 + 5.8 \times 10 = 32 + 58 = 90 = 9 \times 10^1$$

11.5 Maintaining Skills (p. 662)

71. 9, 11, 13

72. 15, 21, 28

73. 42, 35, 27

74. $\frac{5}{6}, \frac{6}{7}, \frac{7}{8}$

75. $8, \frac{19}{2}, 11$

76. 36, 25, 16

Lesson 11.6

11.6 Checkpoint (pp. 663–666)

1. Factor the denominators:
$5 = 5$
$6 = 2 \cdot 3$
Find the highest power of each factor that appears in either denominator.
5, 2, 3
Multiply these to find LCD.
$5 \cdot 2 \cdot 3 = 30$

Copyright © McDougal Littell Inc.
All rights reserved.

2. Factor the denominators.
$36x = 2^2 \cdot 3^2 \cdot x$
$9x^5 = 3^2x^5$
Find the highest power of each factor that appears in either denominator.
$2^2, 3^2, x^5$
Multiply these to find the LCD.
$2^2 \cdot 3^2 \cdot x^5 = 4 \cdot 9 \cdot x^5 = 36x^5$

3. Factor the denominators.
$16x^3 = 2^4x^3$
$24x^2 = 2^3 \cdot 3x^2$
Find the highest power of each factor that appears in either denominator.
$2^4, 3, x^3$
Multiply these to find the LCD.
$2^4 \cdot 3 \cdot x^3 = 16 \cdot 3 \cdot x^3 = 48x^3$

4. The denominators are already simplified.
$(x - 5), (x + 7)$
Multiply these to find the LCD.
$(x - 5)(x + 7)$

5. The denominators are already simplified.
$(x + 1), (x - 1)$
Multiply these to find the LCD.
$(x + 1)(x - 1)$

6. Factor the denominators.
$30x^5 = 2 \cdot 3 \cdot 5 \cdot x^5$
$8x = 2^3 \cdot x$
Find the highest power of each factor that appears in either denominator.
$2^3, 3, 5, x^5$
Multiply these to find the LCD.
$2^3 \cdot 3 \cdot 5 \cdot x^5 = 8 \cdot 3 \cdot 5 \cdot x^5 = 120x^5$

7. Multiply $5x$ by $6x^4$ to get $30x^5$.
Multiply 9 by $6x^4$ to get $54x^4$.

8. Multiply y by $13y$ to get $13y^2$.
Multiply $(y - 1)$ by $13y$ to get $13y^2 - 13y$.

9. Multiply $(c + 1)$ by $(c - 3)$ to get $(c + 1)(c - 3)$.
Multiply c by $(c - 3)$ to get $c^2 - 3c$.

10. $\frac{1}{x^2} + \frac{2}{x}$ The LCD is x^2.
$= \frac{1}{x^2} + \frac{2x}{x^2}$ Rewrite using LCD.
$= \frac{1 + 2x}{x^2}$ Add.

11. $\frac{2}{3m} + \frac{3 - 2m}{m^2}$ The LCD is $3m^2$.
$= \frac{2m}{3m^2} + \frac{3(3 - 2m)}{3m^2}$ Rewrite using LCD.
$= \frac{2m + 9 - 6m}{3m^2}$ Distribute; Add.
$= \frac{9 - 4m}{3m^2}$ Combine like terms.

12. $\frac{3}{15x^2} + \frac{1}{9x^3}$ The LCD is $45x^3$.
$= \frac{9x}{45x^3} + \frac{5}{45x^3}$ Rewrite using LCD.
$= \frac{9x + 5}{45x^3}$ Add.

13. $\frac{3}{x^2} - \frac{2}{3x}$ The LCD is $3x^2$.
$= \frac{9}{3x^2} - \frac{2x}{3x^2}$ Rewrite using LCD.
$= \frac{9 - 2x}{3x^2}$ Subtract.

14. $\frac{2}{p} - \frac{3 - 10p}{5p^2}$ The LCD is $5p^2$.
$= \frac{10p}{5p^2} - \frac{3 - 10p}{5p^2}$ Rewrite using LCD.
$= \frac{10p - 3 + 10p}{5p^2}$ Subtract.
$= \frac{20p - 3}{5p^2}$ Combine like terms.

15. $\frac{3 + 4x}{4x^3} - \frac{1}{10x^2}$ The LCD is $20x^3$.
$= \frac{15 + 20x}{20x^3} - \frac{2x}{20x^3}$ Rewrite using LCD.
$= \frac{15 + 20x - 2x}{20x^3}$ Subtract.
$= \frac{15 + 18x}{20x^3}$ Combine like terms.
$= \frac{3(6x + 5)}{20x^2}$ Factor.

16. $\frac{1}{x + 1} + \frac{1}{x - 1}$ The LCD is $(x + 1)(x - 1)$.
$= \frac{x - 1}{x + 1} + \frac{x + 1}{x - 1}$ Rewrite using LCD.
$= \frac{x - 1 + x + 1}{(x + 1)(x - 1)}$ Add.
$= \frac{2x}{(x + 1)(x - 1)}$ Combine like terms.

17. $\frac{3}{x - 6} + \frac{1}{x}$ The LCD is $x(x - 6)$.
$= \frac{3x}{x(x - 6)} + \frac{x - 6}{x(x - 6)}$ Rewrite using LCD.
$= \frac{3x + x - 6}{x(x - 6)}$ Add.
$= \frac{4x - 6}{x(x - 6)}$ Combine like terms.
$= \frac{2(2x - 3)}{x(x - 6)}$ Factor.

Copyright © McDougal Littell Inc.
All rights reserved.

18. $\frac{x-5}{x+5} - \frac{x+2}{x-2}$ The LCD is $(x+5)(x-2)$.

$= \frac{(x-5)(x-2)}{(x+5)(x-2)} - \frac{(x+2)(x+5)}{(x+5)(x-2)}$ Rewrite using LCD.

$= \frac{x^2-7x+10}{(x+5)(x-2)} - \frac{x^2+7x+10}{(x+5)(x-2)}$ Multiply.

$= \frac{x^2-7x+10-x^2-7x-10}{(x+5)(x-2)}$ Subtract.

$= \frac{-14x}{(x+5)(x-2)}$ Combine like terms.

19. $T = \frac{x+600}{120}$

Distance (country), x	0	60	120	180	240	300
Total time, T	5	5.5	6	6.5	7	7.5

11.6 Guided Practice (p. 667)

1. The least common multiple of the denominators of the two rational expressions.

2. When subtracting the binomial $2x - 2$, the solver did not distribute the negative sign.

$\frac{3}{x-1} - \frac{2}{x} = \frac{3x}{x(x-1)} - \frac{2(x-1)}{x(x-1)}$

$= \frac{3x}{x(x-1)} - \frac{2x-2}{x(x-1)}$

$= \frac{3x-2x+2}{x(x-1)}$

$= \frac{x+2}{x(x-1)}$

3. $\frac{x}{12} + \frac{x}{4} = \frac{x}{12} + \frac{3x}{12} = \frac{4x}{12} = \frac{x}{3}$

4. $\frac{3}{10x} - \frac{1}{4x^2} = \frac{6x}{20x^2} - \frac{5}{20x^2} = \frac{6x-5}{20x^2}$

5. $\frac{x+6}{x+1} - \frac{4}{2x+3}$

$= \frac{(x+6)(2x+3)}{(x+1)(2x+3)} - \frac{4(x+1)}{(x+1)(2x+3)}$

$= \frac{2x^2+15x+18}{(x+1)(2x+3)} - \frac{4x+4}{(x+1)(2x+3)}$

$= \frac{2x^2+15x+18-4x-4}{(x+1)(2x+3)}$

$= \frac{2x^2+11x+14}{(x+1)(2x+3)}$

$= \frac{(2x+7)(x+2)}{(x+1)(2x+3)}$

6. $\frac{x-2}{2x-10} + \frac{x+3}{x-5} = \frac{x-2}{2(x-5)} + \frac{2(x+3)}{2(x-5)}$

$= \frac{x-2}{2(x-5)} + \frac{2x+6}{2(x-5)}$

$= \frac{x-2+2x+6}{2(x-5)}$

$= \frac{3x+4}{2(x-5)}$

7. -1

11.6 Practice and Applications (pp. 667–668)

8. $3x = 3x$
$9x^3 = 3^2x^3$
$\text{LCD} = 3^2 \cdot x^3 = 9x^3$

9. $15 = 3 \cdot 5$
$5 = 5$
$\text{LCD} = 3 \cdot 5 = 15$

10. $\text{LCD} = z^2 \cdot 3y = 3yz^2$

11. $\text{LCD} = 7c^5$

12. $\text{LCD} = 3 \cdot 13 \cdot v^7 = 39v^7$

13. $\text{LCD} = 5b$

14. $\text{LCD} = (x-2)(x-4)$

15. $15x = 3 \cdot 5 \cdot x$
$18x^3 = 2 \cdot 3^2 \cdot x^3$
$\text{LCD} = 2 \cdot 3^2 \cdot 5 \cdot x^3 = 90x^3$

16. $3x \cdot 4x^2 = 12x^3$
$11 \cdot 4x^2 = 44x^2$

17. $5 \cdot 3y^2 = 15y^2$
$8 \cdot 3y^2 = 24y^2$

18. $2 \cdot 14x = 28x$
$(x-3) \cdot 14x = 14x^2 - 42x$

19. $9a^5 \cdot 7a^6 = 63a^{11}$
$(3a+1) \cdot 7a^6 = 21a^7 + 7a^6$

20. $(2x+3) \cdot x = x(2x+3)$
$(x-9) \cdot x = x^2 - 9x$

21. $35a^2 \cdot 4a^3 = 140a^5$
$(2a-3) \cdot 4a^3 = 8a^4 - 12a^3$

22. $\frac{3}{2z} + \frac{1}{z} = \frac{3}{2z} + \frac{2}{2z} = \frac{5}{2z}$

23. $\frac{11}{6x} + \frac{2}{13x} = \frac{143}{78x} + \frac{12}{78x} = \frac{155}{78x}$

24. $\frac{9}{4x} + \frac{7}{-5x} = \frac{-45}{-20x} + \frac{28}{-20x} = \frac{-17}{-20x} = \frac{17}{20x}$

Copyright © McDougal Littell Inc.
All rights reserved.

25. $\frac{2x+3}{4}+\frac{x+1}{2}=\frac{2x+3}{4}+\frac{2(x+1)}{4}$
$=\frac{2x+3}{4}+\frac{2x+2}{4}$
$=\frac{2x+3+2x+2}{4}$
$=\frac{4x+5}{4}$

26. $\frac{3}{12m^3}+\frac{m+1}{4m^3}=\frac{1}{4m^3}+\frac{m+1}{4m^3}$
$=\frac{1+m+1}{4m^3}$
$=\frac{m+2}{4m^3}$

27. $\frac{3n}{15}+\frac{n^2+1}{30n}=\frac{6n^2}{30n}+\frac{n^2+1}{30n}$
$=\frac{6n^2+n^2+1}{30n}$
$=\frac{7n^2+1}{30n}$

28. $\frac{2x}{5}-\frac{x+1}{4}=\frac{4(2x)}{20}-\frac{5(x+1)}{20}$
$=\frac{8x}{20}-\frac{5x+5}{20}$
$=\frac{8x-5x-5}{20}$
$=\frac{3x-5}{20}$

29. $\frac{9}{2x}-\frac{2}{7x^2}=\frac{7x(9)}{14x^2}-\frac{2(2)}{14x^2}=\frac{63x-4}{14x^2}$

30. $\frac{3}{6b^2}-\frac{1}{4b}=\frac{1}{2b^2}-\frac{1}{4b}=\frac{2}{4b^2}-\frac{b}{4b^2}=\frac{2-b}{4b^2}$

31. $\frac{x-1}{6x^2}-\frac{2}{3x}=\frac{x-1}{6x^2}-\frac{2(2x)}{6x^2}$
$=\frac{x-1}{6x^2}-\frac{4x}{6x^2}$
$=\frac{-3x-1}{6x^2}$

32. $\frac{5c}{15}-\frac{2+c}{25c}=\frac{c}{3}-\frac{2+c}{25c}$
$=\frac{25c^2}{75c}-\frac{3(2+c)}{75c}$
$=\frac{25c^2-6-3c}{75c}$
$=\frac{25c^2-3c-6}{75c}$

33. $\frac{2x-1}{3x}-\frac{1}{11}=\frac{11(2x-1)}{33x}-\frac{3x}{33x}$
$=\frac{22x-11}{33x}-\frac{3x}{33x}$
$=\frac{19x-11}{33x}$

34. $\frac{2}{x+1}+\frac{3}{x-2}=\frac{2(x-2)}{(x+1)(x-2)}+\frac{3(x+1)}{(x+1)(x-2)}$
$=\frac{2x-4}{(x+1)(x-2)}+\frac{3x+3}{(x+1)(x-2)}$
$=\frac{2x-4+3x+3}{(x+1)(x-2)}$
$=\frac{5x-1}{(x+1)(x-2)}$

35. $\frac{x}{x-10}+\frac{x+4}{x+6}$
$=\frac{x(x+6)}{(x-10)(x+6)}+\frac{(x+4)(x-10)}{(x-10)(x+6)}$
$=\frac{x^2+6x}{(x-10)(x+6)}+\frac{x^2-6x-40}{(x-10)(x+6)}$
$=\frac{x^2+6x+x^2-6x-40}{(x-10)(x+6)}$
$=\frac{2x^2-40}{(x-10)(x+6)}$
$=\frac{2(x^2-20)}{(x-10)(x+6)}$

36. $\frac{x-3}{x+3}+\frac{x+9}{x-3}=\frac{(x-3)(x-3)}{(x+3)(x-3)}+\frac{(x+9)(x+3)}{(x+3)(x-3)}$
$=\frac{x^2-6x+9}{(x+3)(x-3)}+\frac{x^2+12x+27}{(x+3)(x-3)}$
$=\frac{2x^2+6x+36}{(x+3)(x-3)}$
$=\frac{2(x^2+3x+18)}{(x+3)(x-3)}$

37. $\frac{x+8}{3x-1}+\frac{x+3}{x+1}$
$=\frac{(x+8)(x+1)}{(3x-1)(x+1)}+\frac{(x+3)(3x-1)}{(3x-1)(x+1)}$
$=\frac{x^2+9x+8}{(3x-1)(x+1)}+\frac{3x^2+8x-3}{(3x-1)(x+1)}$
$=\frac{4x^2+17x+5}{(3x-1)(x+1)}$

38. $\frac{4}{x+4}-\frac{7}{5x}=\frac{4(5x)}{5x(x+4)}-\frac{7(x+4)}{5x(x+4)}$
$=\frac{20x}{5x(x+4)}-\frac{7x+28}{5x(x+4)}$
$=\frac{20x-7x-28}{5x(x+4)}$
$=\frac{13x-28}{5x(x+4)}$

39. $\frac{2x+1}{3x-1}-\frac{x+4}{x-2}$
$=\frac{(2x+1)(x-2)}{(3x-1)(x-2)}-\frac{(x+4)(3x-1)}{(3x-1)(x-2)}$
$=\frac{2x^2-3x-2}{(3x-1)(x-2)}-\frac{3x^2+11x-4}{(3x-1)(x-2)}$
$=\frac{2x^2-3x-2-3x^2-11x+4}{(3x-1)(x-2)}$
$=\frac{-x^2-14x+2}{(3x-1)(x-2)}$

Copyright © McDougal Littell Inc.
All rights reserved.

40. $\frac{4x}{5x-2} - \frac{2x}{5x+1}$

$= \frac{4x(5x+1)}{(5x-2)(5x+1)} - \frac{2x(5x-2)}{(5x-2)(5x+1)}$

$= \frac{20x^2+4x}{(5x-2)(5x+1)} - \frac{10x^2-4x}{(5x-2)(5x+1)}$

$= \frac{20x^2+4x-10x^2+4x}{(5x-2)(5x+1)}$

$= \frac{10x^2+8x}{(5x-2)(5x+1)}$

$= \frac{2x(5x+4)}{(5x-2)(5x+1)}$

41. $\frac{2x}{x-1} - \frac{7x}{x+4} = \frac{2x(x+4)}{(x-1)(x+4)} - \frac{7x(x-1)}{(x-1)(x+4)}$

$= \frac{2x^2+8x}{(x-1)(x+4)} - \frac{7x^2-7x}{(x-1)(x+4)}$

$= \frac{2x^2+8x-7x^2+7x}{(x-1)(x+4)}$

$= \frac{-5x^2+15x}{(x-1)(x+4)}$

$= \frac{-5x(x-3)}{(x-1)(x+4)}$

42. $\frac{3x+10}{7x-4} - \frac{x}{4x+3}$

$= \frac{(3x+10)(4x+3)}{(7x-4)(4x+3)} - \frac{x(7x-4)}{(7x-4)(4x+3)}$

$= \frac{12x^2+49x+30}{(7x-4)(4x+3)} - \frac{7x^2-4x}{(7x-4)(4x+3)}$

$= \frac{12x^2+49x+30-7x^2+4x}{(7x-4)(4x+3)}$

$= \frac{5x^2+53x+30}{(7x-4)(4x+3)}$

$= \frac{(x+10)(5x+3)}{(7x-4)(4x+3)}$

43. Let x = number of miles in the woods, and T = total time

$T = \frac{x}{10} + \frac{8-x}{20}$

44. $T = \frac{x \cdot 2}{10 \cdot 2} + \frac{8-x}{20}$

$= \frac{2x}{20} + \frac{8-x}{20} = \frac{x+8}{20}$

45.

Distance (woods), x	0	2	4	6	8
Total time, T	0.4	0.5	0.6	0.7	0.8

46. $T = \frac{24 \text{ km}}{(x-2) \text{ km/h}} + \frac{24 \text{ km}}{(x+2) \text{ km/h}}$

$T = \frac{24}{x-2} + \frac{24}{x+2}$

47. $T = \frac{24(x+2)}{(x-2)(x+2)} + \frac{24(x-2)}{(x-2)(x+2)}$

$T = \frac{24x+48}{(x-2)(x+2)} + \frac{24x-48}{(x-2)(x+2)}$

$T = \frac{24x+48+24x-48}{(x-2)(x+2)}$

$T = \frac{48x}{(x-2)(x+2)}$

48. $T = \frac{48(10)}{(10-2)(10+2)} = \frac{48(10)}{8(12)} = 5$ hours

49. $\left(\frac{x}{2x+1} + \frac{x}{2x+1}\right) + \left(\frac{1}{2x-1} + \frac{1}{2x-1}\right)$

$= \frac{2x}{2x+1} + \frac{2}{2x-1}$

$= \frac{2x(2x-1)}{(2x+1)(2x-1)} + \frac{2(2x+1)}{(2x+1)(2x-1)}$

$= \frac{4x^2-2x}{(2x+1)(2x-1)} + \frac{4x+2}{(2x+1)(2x-1)}$

$= \frac{4x^2-2x+4x+2}{(2x+1)(2x-1)}$

$= \frac{4x^2+2x+2}{(2x+1)(2x-1)}$

$= \frac{2(2x^2+x+1)}{(2x+1)(2x-1)}$

50. $P = \frac{2[2(3)^2+(3)+1]}{[2(3)+1][2(3)-1]}$

$P = \frac{2[2(9)+3+1]}{[6+1][6-1]}$

$P = \frac{2(22)}{(7)(5)} = \frac{44}{35}$

51. $A = l \cdot w$

$A = \left(\frac{x}{2x+1}\right)\left(\frac{1}{2x-1}\right)$

$A = \left(\frac{3}{2(3)+1}\right)\left(\frac{1}{2(3)-1}\right) = \frac{3}{7} \cdot \frac{1}{5}$

$A = \frac{3}{35}$

11.6 Standardized Test Practice (p. 669)

52. LCD $= 3 \cdot 2 \cdot t^6 = 6t^6$; C

53. $\frac{5x+6}{8x^2} = \frac{?}{48x^3}$

$8x^2$ multiplied by $6x$ is $48x^3$.

$(5x+6)$ multiplied by $6x$ is $30x^2 + 36x$; H

54. C;

$\frac{x(2x+1)}{(x-1)(2x+1)} - \frac{1(x-1)}{(x-1)(2x+1)}$

$= \frac{2x^2+x}{(x-1)(2x+1)} - \frac{x-1}{(x-1)(2x+1)}$

$= \frac{2x^2+x-x+1}{(x-1)(2x+1)}$

$= \frac{2x^2+1}{(x-1)(2x+1)}$

Copyright © McDougal Littell Inc.
All rights reserved.

11.6 Mixed Review (p. 669)

55. $y - (-2) = 2[x - (-3)]$
$y + 2 = 2(x + 3)$

56. $y - 5 = -1(x - 0)$
$y - 5 = -x$

57. $y - 6 = \frac{1}{2}[x - (-3)]$
$y - 6 = \frac{1}{2}(x + 3)$

58. $y - 5 = 5(x - 5)$

59. $y - 0 = \frac{3}{7}(x - 7)$
$y = \frac{3}{7}(x - 7)$

60. $y - (-3) = \frac{1}{3}(x - 14)$
$y + 3 = \frac{1}{3}(x - 14)$

61. $\frac{5}{10x} = \frac{1}{2x}$

62. $\frac{4m^2}{6m} = \frac{2m}{3}$

63. $\frac{16x^4}{32x^8} = \frac{x^{-4}}{2} = \frac{1}{2x^4}$

64. $\frac{42x^4y^3}{6x^3y^9} = 7xy^{-6} = \frac{7x}{y^6}$

65. $\frac{12x}{144x^2} = \frac{1}{12x}$

66. $\frac{2x^2y^3z^4}{5x^4y^3z^2} = \frac{2x^{-2}y^0z^2}{5} = \frac{2z^2}{5x^2}$

67. $\frac{33p^4}{44p^2q} = \frac{3p^2}{4q}$

68. $\frac{15w^2}{9w^5} = \frac{5w^{-3}}{3} = \frac{5}{3w^3}$

69. $6x^2 = 5x - 7$
$6x^2 - 5x + 7 = 0$

70. $9 - 6x = 2x^2$
$2x^2 + 6x - 9 = 0$

71. $-4 + 3y^2 = y$
$3y^2 - y - 4 = 0$

72. $12x = x^2 + 25$
$x^2 - 12x + 25 = 0$

73. $7 - 12x^2 = 5x$
$12x^2 + 5x - 7 = 0$

74. $8 = 5x^2 - 4x$
$5x^2 - 4x - 8 = 0$

75. Let x = contestant's guess
$|x - 8500| \leq 1000$

11.6 Maintaining Skills (p. 669)

76. $\frac{47}{99} = 0.475$

77. $\frac{63}{200} = 0.315$

78. $\frac{32}{155} = 0.206$

79. $\frac{59}{199} = 0.296$

80. $-\frac{115}{144} = -0.799$

81. $-\frac{63}{89} = -0.708$

82. $-\frac{12}{43} = -0.279$

83. $-\frac{79}{145} = -0.545$

84. $-\frac{23}{25} = -0.920$

85. $\frac{8}{77} = 0.104$

86. $\frac{12}{7} = 1.714$

87. $-\frac{18}{35} = -0.514$

Lesson 11.7

11.7 Checkpoint (pp. 670–673)

1. $\frac{x}{2} = \frac{x + 2}{6}$
$x(6) = (x + 2)(2)$
$6x = 2x + 4$
$4x = 4$
$x = 1$
Check:
$\frac{1}{2} \stackrel{?}{=} \frac{1 + 2}{6}$
$\frac{1}{2} = \frac{1}{2}$

Copyright © McDougal Littell Inc.
All rights reserved.

2. $\frac{3}{2m} = \frac{m+1}{4m}$

$3(4m) = 2m(m+1)$

$12m = 2m^2 + 2m$

$0 = 2m^2 - 10m$

$0 = 2m(m-5)$

$m = 0, 5$

Check:

If $m = 0$, the denominators are zero; zero is not a solution.

$\frac{3}{2(5)} \stackrel{?}{=} \frac{5+1}{4(5)}$

$\frac{3}{10} \stackrel{?}{=} \frac{6}{20}$

$\frac{3}{10} = \frac{3}{10}$

3. $\frac{y}{5} = \frac{6}{y+7}$

$y(y+7) = 5(6)$

$y^2 + 7y = 30$

$y^2 + 7y - 30 = 0$

$(y-3)(y+10) = 0$

$y = 3, -10$

Check:

$\frac{3}{5} \stackrel{?}{=} \frac{6}{3+7}$

$\frac{3}{5} \stackrel{?}{=} \frac{6}{10}$

$\frac{3}{5} = \frac{3}{5}$

$-\frac{10}{5} \stackrel{?}{=} \frac{6}{-10+7}$

$-2 \stackrel{?}{=} \frac{6}{-3}$

$-2 = -2$

4. LCD is $4x$.

$4x\left(\frac{3}{x}\right) + 4x\left(\frac{1}{4}\right) = 4x\left(\frac{4}{x}\right)$ Multiply each side by the LCD.

$12 + x = 16$ Simplify.

$x = 4$ Solve.

Check:

$\frac{3}{4} + \frac{1}{4} \stackrel{?}{=} \frac{4}{4}$

$\frac{4}{4} = \frac{4}{4}$

5. $\frac{1}{n+1} + \frac{1}{n} = \frac{11}{n^2+n}$ Factor

$\frac{1}{n+1} + \frac{1}{n} = \frac{11}{n(n+1)}$ LCD is $n(n+1)$.

$n(n+1) \cdot \frac{1}{n+1} + n(n+1) \cdot \frac{1}{n} = n(n+1) \cdot \frac{11}{n(n+1)}$ Multiply each side by LCD and simplify.

$n + (n+1) = 11$ Combine like terms.

$2n + 1 = 11$

$2n = 10$

$n = 5$

Check:

$\frac{1}{5+1} + \frac{1}{5} \stackrel{?}{=} \frac{11}{5^2+5}$

$\frac{1}{6} + \frac{1}{5} \stackrel{?}{=} \frac{11}{30}$

$\frac{5+6}{30} \stackrel{?}{=} \frac{11}{30}$

$\frac{11}{30} = \frac{11}{30}$

Copyright © McDougal Littell Inc.
All rights reserved.

6.

$$\frac{4}{x-3} + \frac{x}{x+3} = 1$$ LCD is $(x-3)(x+3)$.

$$(x-3)(x+3) \cdot \frac{4}{x-3} + (x-3)(x+3)\frac{x}{x+3} = (x-3)(x+3)(1)$$ Multiply each side by LCD.

$$(x+3)4 + (x-3)x = (x-3)(x+3)$$ Simplify.

$$4x + 12 + x^2 - 3x = x^2 - 9$$ Multiply.

$$x^2 + x + 12 = x^2 - 9$$ Combine like terms.

$$x + 12 = -9$$

$$x = -21$$

Check:

$$\frac{4}{-21-3} + \frac{-21}{-21+3} \stackrel{?}{=} 1$$

$$\frac{4}{-24} + \frac{-21}{-18} \stackrel{?}{=} 1$$

$$-\frac{1}{6} + \frac{7}{6} \stackrel{?}{=} 1$$

$$1 = 1$$

7. Part you do in one hour · Time you spend cleaning + Part sister does in one hour · Time sister spends cleaning = 1(whole job)

$$\frac{1}{4} \cdot t + \frac{1}{6} \cdot t = 1$$

$$\frac{t}{4} + \frac{t}{6} = 1$$

Multiply by the LCD, which is 12.

$$12 \cdot \left(\frac{t}{4}\right) + 12\left(\frac{t}{6}\right) = 12(1)$$

$$3t + 2t = 12$$

$$5t = 12$$

$$t = \frac{12}{5} = 2\frac{2}{5} = 2.4 \text{ hours}$$

or $\frac{2}{5}$ of an hour $= \frac{2}{5} \cdot 60$ min $= 24$ min,

2 hours and 24 minutes

8. Part contractor does in one hour · time spent + Part assistant does in one hour · time spent = 1 (whole job)

$$\frac{1}{20}t + \frac{1}{30}t = 1$$ Multiply by the LCD which is 60.

$$60 \cdot \frac{t}{20} \cdot 60 \cdot \frac{t}{30} = 60 \cdot 1$$

$$3t + 2t = 60$$

$$5t = 60$$

$$t = 12 \text{ hours}$$

9.

	Number of kg ×	*Price per kg* =	*Cost*
Apples	x	6.00	$6x$
Apricots	$10 - x$	8.00	$8(10 - x)$
Mixture	10	7.20	72

$$6x + 8(10 - x) = 72$$

$$6x + 80 - 8x = 72$$

$$80 - 2x = 72$$

$$-2x = -8$$

$$x = 4$$

4 kg of apples; 6 kg of apricots

11.7 Guided Practice (p. 674)

1. Use the cross product property or multiply each side by the LCD.
2. Using the cross product property
3. $3x$
4. $4x = 2^2x$
   $6x^2 = 2 \cdot 3x^2$
   $8x^2 = 2^3 \cdot x^2$
   LCD $= 2^3 \cdot 3 \cdot x^2 = 24x^2$
5. $3x^3$

Copyright © McDougal Littell Inc.
All rights reserved.

6.
$$\begin{aligned}\frac{3}{x} &= \frac{x}{12}\\ 3(12) &= x \cdot x\\ 36 &= x^2\\ \pm\sqrt{36} &= x\\ \pm 6 &= x\end{aligned}$$

Check:

$$\frac{3}{6} \stackrel{?}{=} \frac{6}{12}$$
$$\frac{1}{2} \stackrel{?}{=} \frac{1}{2}$$
$$\frac{3}{-6} \stackrel{?}{=} \frac{-6}{12}$$
$$-\frac{1}{2} = -\frac{1}{2}$$

7.
$$\begin{aligned}\frac{x}{x+2} &= \frac{3}{x-2}\\ x(x-2) &= 3(x+2)\\ x^2 - 2x &= 3x + 6\\ x^2 - 2x - 3x - 6 &= 0\\ x^2 - 5x - 6 &= 0\\ (x-6)(x+1) &= 0\\ x &= 6, -1\end{aligned}$$

Check:

$$\frac{6}{6+2} \stackrel{?}{=} \frac{3}{6-2}$$
$$\frac{3}{4} = \frac{3}{4}$$
$$\frac{-1}{-1+2} \stackrel{?}{=} \frac{3}{-1-2}$$
$$-1 = -1$$

8.
$$\begin{aligned}\frac{3}{u+2} &= \frac{1}{u-2}\\ 3(u-2) &= (u+2)1\\ 3u - 6 &= u + 2\\ 2u - 6 &= 2\\ 2u &= 8\\ u &= 4\end{aligned}$$

Check:

$$\frac{3}{4+2} \stackrel{?}{=} \frac{1}{4-2}$$
$$\frac{1}{2} = \frac{1}{2}$$

9.
$$\begin{aligned}\frac{1}{5} - \frac{2}{5x} &= \frac{1}{x}\\ 5x \cdot \frac{1}{5} - 5x \cdot \frac{2}{5x} &= 5x \cdot \frac{1}{x}\\ x - 2 &= 5\\ x &= 7\end{aligned}$$

Check:

$$\frac{1}{5} - \frac{2}{5(7)} \stackrel{?}{=} \frac{1}{7}$$
$$\frac{1}{5} - \frac{2}{35} \stackrel{?}{=} \frac{1}{7}$$
$$\frac{7}{35} - \frac{2}{35} \stackrel{?}{=} \frac{1}{7}$$
$$\frac{5}{35} \stackrel{?}{=} \frac{1}{7}$$
$$\frac{1}{7} = \frac{1}{7}$$

10.
$$\begin{aligned}\frac{2}{x} + \frac{1}{4} &= \frac{1}{x}\\ 4x \cdot \frac{2}{x} + 4x \cdot \frac{1}{4} &= 4x \cdot \frac{1}{x}\\ 8 + x &= 4\\ x &= -4\end{aligned}$$

Check:

$$\frac{2}{-4} + \frac{1}{4} \stackrel{?}{=} \frac{1}{-4}$$
$$-\frac{1}{4} = -\frac{1}{4}$$

11.
$$\begin{aligned}\frac{1}{x} + \frac{x}{x+2} &= 1\\ x(x+2) \cdot \frac{1}{x} + x(x+2) \cdot \frac{x}{x+2} &= x(x+2) \cdot 1\\ (x+2) + x^2 &= x(x+2)\\ x^2 + x + 2 &= x^2 + 2x\\ x + 2 &= 2x\\ 2 &= x\end{aligned}$$

Check:

$$\frac{1}{2} + \frac{2}{2+2} \stackrel{?}{=} 1$$
$$\frac{1}{2} + \frac{2}{4} \stackrel{?}{=} 1$$
$$\frac{1}{2} + \frac{1}{2} \stackrel{?}{=} 1$$
$$1 = 1$$

Copyright © McDougal Littell Inc.
All rights reserved.

11.7 Practice and Applications (pp. 674–676)

12. $\frac{x}{5} = \frac{7}{3}$

$x(3) = 5(7)$

$3x = 35$

$x = \frac{35}{3}$

Check:

$\frac{35}{3} \div 5 \stackrel{?}{=} \frac{7}{3}$

$\frac{35}{3} \cdot \frac{1}{5} \stackrel{?}{=} \frac{7}{3}$

$\frac{7}{3} = \frac{7}{3}$

13. $\frac{x}{10} = \frac{14}{5}$

$x(5) = 10(14)$

$5x = 140$

$x = 28$

Check:

$\frac{28}{10} \stackrel{?}{=} \frac{14}{5}$

$\frac{14}{5} = \frac{14}{5}$

14. $\frac{4}{x} = \frac{12}{5(x + 2)}$

$4(5)(x + 2) = x(12)$

$20(x + 2) = 12x$

$20x + 40 = 12x$

$8x + 40 = 0$

$8x = -40$

$x = -5$

Check:

$\frac{4}{-5} \stackrel{?}{=} \frac{12}{5(-5 + 2)}$

$-\frac{4}{5} \stackrel{?}{=} \frac{12}{-15}$

$-\frac{4}{5} = -\frac{4}{5}$

15. $\frac{7}{x + 1} = \frac{5}{x - 3}$

$7(x - 3) = (x + 1) \cdot 5$

$7x - 21 = 5x + 5$

$2x - 21 = 5$

$2x = 26$

$x = 13$

Check:

$\frac{7}{13 + 1} \stackrel{?}{=} \frac{5}{13 - 3}$

$\frac{7}{14} \stackrel{?}{=} \frac{5}{10}$

$\frac{1}{2} = \frac{1}{2}$

16. $\frac{6}{x + 2} = \frac{x}{4}$

$6(4) = (x + 2)x$

$24 = x^2 + 2x$

$0 = x^2 + 2x - 24$

$0 = (x + 6)(x - 4)$

$x = -6, 4$

Check:

$\frac{6}{-6 + 2} \stackrel{?}{=} \frac{-6}{4}$

$-\frac{3}{2} = -\frac{3}{2}$

$\frac{6}{4 + 2} \stackrel{?}{=} \frac{4}{4}$

$1 = 1$

17. $\frac{5}{x + 4} = \frac{5}{3(x + 1)}$

$5(3)(x + 1) = (x + 4)5$

$15(x + 1) = 5x + 20$

$15x + 15 = 5x + 20$

$10x + 15 = 20$

$10x = 5$

$x = \frac{1}{2}$

Check:

$\frac{5}{\frac{1}{2} + 4} \stackrel{?}{=} \frac{5}{3(\frac{1}{2} + 1)}$

$\frac{5}{4.5} \stackrel{?}{=} \frac{5}{3(1.5)}$

$\frac{5}{4.5} = \frac{5}{4.5}$

18. $\frac{1}{y} = \frac{2}{y - 3}$

$1(y - 3) = y(2)$

$y - 3 = 2y$

$-3 = y$

Check:

$\frac{1}{-3} \stackrel{?}{=} \frac{2}{-3 - 3}$

$-\frac{1}{3} = -\frac{1}{3}$

Copyright © McDougal Littell Inc.
All rights reserved.

19. $\dfrac{3(t^2+1)}{6t^2-t-1} = \dfrac{1}{2}$

$2(3)(t^2+1) = (6t^2-t-1)(1)$

$6(t^2+1) = 6t^2-t-1$

$6t^2+6 = 6t^2-t-1$

$6 = -t-1$

$7 = -t$

$-7 = t$

Check:

$\dfrac{3[(-7)^2+1]}{6(-7)^2-(-7)-1} \stackrel{?}{=} \dfrac{1}{2}$

$\dfrac{3[49+1]}{6(49)+7-1} \stackrel{?}{=} \dfrac{1}{2}$

$\dfrac{150}{300} \stackrel{?}{=} \dfrac{1}{2}$

$\dfrac{1}{2} = \dfrac{1}{2}$

20. $\dfrac{(x+1)^2}{(x-3)^2} = \dfrac{1}{1}$

$(x+1)^2(1) = (x-3)^2(1)$

$x^2+2x+1 = x^2-6x+9$

$2x+1 = -6x+9$

$8x+1 = 9$

$8x = 8$

$x = 1$

Check:

$\dfrac{(1+1)^2}{(1-3)^2} \stackrel{?}{=} 1$

$\dfrac{4}{4} \stackrel{?}{=} 1$

$1 = 1$

21. $\dfrac{5}{x} + 2 = \dfrac{x}{4}$

$4x \cdot \dfrac{5}{x} + 4x \cdot 2 = 4x \cdot \dfrac{x}{4}$

$20 + 8x = x^2$

$0 = x^2 - 8x - 20$

$0 = (x-10)(x+2)$

$x = 10, -2$

Check:

$\dfrac{5}{10} + 2 \stackrel{?}{=} \dfrac{10}{4}$

$2\frac{1}{2} = 2\frac{1}{2}$

$\dfrac{5}{-2} + 2 \stackrel{?}{=} \dfrac{-2}{4}$

$-2\frac{1}{2} + 2 \stackrel{?}{=} -\dfrac{1}{2}$

$-\dfrac{1}{2} = -\dfrac{1}{2}$

22. $\dfrac{x}{x+9} = \dfrac{9}{x+9} + 4$

$(x+9) \cdot \dfrac{x}{x+9} = (x+9) \cdot \dfrac{9}{x+9} + (x+9) \cdot 4$

$x = 9 + 4x + 36$

$-3x = 45$

$x = -15$

Check:

$\dfrac{-15}{-15+9} \stackrel{?}{=} \dfrac{9}{-15+9} + 4$

$\dfrac{-15}{-6} \stackrel{?}{=} \dfrac{9}{-6} + 4$

$\dfrac{5}{2} \stackrel{?}{=} -\dfrac{3}{2} + \dfrac{8}{2}$

$\dfrac{5}{2} = \dfrac{5}{2}$

23. $\dfrac{3x}{x-1} = \dfrac{x}{5}$

$5(x-1) \cdot \dfrac{3x}{x-1} = 5(x-1) \cdot \dfrac{x}{5}$

$15x = x^2 - x$

$0 = x^2 - 16x$

$0 = x(x-16)$

$x = 0, 16$

Check:

$\dfrac{3(0)}{0-1} \stackrel{?}{=} \dfrac{0}{5}$

$0 = 0$

$\dfrac{3(16)}{16-1} \stackrel{?}{=} \dfrac{16}{5}$

$\dfrac{48}{15} \stackrel{?}{=} \dfrac{16}{5}$

$\dfrac{16}{5} = \dfrac{16}{5}$

24. $\dfrac{3}{t} - \dfrac{1}{3t} = \dfrac{2}{3}$

$3t \cdot \dfrac{3}{t} - 3t \cdot \dfrac{1}{3t} = 3t \cdot \dfrac{2}{3}$

$9 - 1 = 2t$

$8 = 2t$

$4 = t$

Check:

$\dfrac{3}{4} - \dfrac{1}{3(4)} \stackrel{?}{=} \dfrac{2}{3}$

$\dfrac{3}{4} - \dfrac{1}{12} \stackrel{?}{=} \dfrac{2}{3}$

$\dfrac{9-1}{12} \stackrel{?}{=} \dfrac{2}{3}$

$\dfrac{2}{3} = \dfrac{2}{3}$

Copyright © McDougal Littell Inc.
All rights reserved.

25.

$$\frac{4}{x(x+1)} = \frac{3}{x}$$

$$x(x+1)\cdot\frac{4}{x(x+1)} = x(x+1)\cdot\frac{3}{x}$$

$$4 = 3x + 3$$

$$1 = 3x$$

$$\frac{1}{3} = x$$

Check:

$$\frac{4}{\frac{1}{3}(\frac{1}{3}+1)} \stackrel{?}{=} 3 \div \frac{1}{3}$$

$$4 \div \left(\frac{1}{9}+\frac{1}{3}\right) \stackrel{?}{=} 3\cdot\frac{3}{1}$$

$$4 \div \left(\frac{1}{9}+\frac{3}{9}\right) \stackrel{?}{=} 9$$

$$4\cdot\frac{9}{4} \stackrel{?}{=} 9$$

$$9 = 9$$

26.

$$\frac{x}{x+3} + \frac{1}{x-3} = 1$$

$$(x+3)(x-3)\cdot\frac{x}{x+3} + (x+3)(x-3)\cdot\frac{1}{x-3} = (x+3)(x-3)$$

$$(x-3)x + (x+3) = (x+3)(x-3)$$

$$x^2 - 3x + x + 3 = x^2 - 9$$

$$-2x + 3 = -9$$

$$-2x = -12$$

$$x = 6$$

Check:

$$\frac{6}{6+3} + \frac{1}{6-3} \stackrel{?}{=} 1$$

$$\frac{2}{3} + \frac{1}{3} \stackrel{?}{=} 1$$

$$1 = 1$$

27.

$$\frac{1}{s} + \frac{s}{s+2} = 1$$

$$s(s+2)\cdot\frac{1}{s} + s(s+2)\frac{s}{s+2} = s(s+2)(1)$$

$$(s+2) + s^2 = s^2 + 2s$$

$$s + 2 = 2s$$

$$2 = s$$

Check:

$$\frac{1}{2} + \frac{2}{2+2} \stackrel{?}{=} 1$$

$$\frac{1}{2} + \frac{1}{2} \stackrel{?}{=} 1$$

$$1 = 1$$

Copyright © McDougal Littell Inc.
All rights reserved.

28.

$$\frac{2}{3x+1} + 2 = \frac{2}{3}$$

$$3(3x+1) \cdot \frac{2}{3x+1} + 3(3x+1)(2) = 3(3x+1) \cdot \frac{2}{3}$$

$$6 + 6(3x+1) = (3x+1)2$$

$$6 + 18x + 6 = 6x + 2$$

$$18x + 12 = 6x + 2$$

$$12x + 12 = 2$$

$$12x = -10$$

$$x = -\frac{5}{6}$$

Check:

$$\frac{2}{3(-\frac{5}{6}) + 1} + 2 \stackrel{?}{=} \frac{2}{3}$$

$$\frac{2}{-\frac{5}{2} + 1} + 2 \stackrel{?}{=} \frac{2}{3}$$

$$\frac{2}{-\frac{3}{2}} + 2 \stackrel{?}{=} \frac{2}{3}$$

$$2 \cdot \left(-\frac{2}{3}\right) + 2 \stackrel{?}{=} \frac{2}{3}$$

$$-\frac{4}{3} + \frac{6}{3} \stackrel{?}{=} \frac{2}{3}$$

$$\frac{2}{3} = \frac{2}{3}$$

29.

$$\frac{5}{2r+1} - \frac{3}{2r-1} = 0$$

$$(2r+1)(2r-1) \cdot \frac{5}{2r+1} - (2r+1)(2r-1) \cdot \frac{3}{2r-1} = 0$$

$$(2r-1)5 - (2r+1)3 = 0$$

$$10r - 5 - (6r + 3) = 0$$

$$10r - 5 - 6r - 3 = 0$$

$$4r - 8 = 0$$

$$4r = 8$$

$$r = 2$$

Check:

$$\frac{5}{2(2)+1} - \frac{3}{2(2)-1} \stackrel{?}{=} 0$$

$$\frac{5}{5} - \frac{3}{3} \stackrel{?}{=} 0$$

$$1 - 1 \stackrel{?}{=} 0$$

$$0 = 0$$

Copyright © McDougal Littell Inc.
All rights reserved.

30.

$$u = \frac{2}{5} - \frac{u}{2}$$
$$10(u) = 10\left(\frac{2}{5}\right) - 10\left(\frac{u}{2}\right)$$
$$10u = 4 - 5u$$
$$15u = 4$$
$$u = \frac{4}{15}$$

Check:

$$\frac{4}{15} \stackrel{?}{=} \frac{2}{5} - \left(\frac{4}{15} \div 2\right)$$
$$\frac{4}{15} \stackrel{?}{=} \frac{2}{5} - \left(\frac{4}{15} \cdot \frac{1}{2}\right)$$
$$\frac{4}{15} \stackrel{?}{=} \frac{2}{5} - \left(\frac{2}{15}\right)$$
$$\frac{4}{15} \stackrel{?}{=} \frac{6}{15} - \frac{2}{15}$$
$$\frac{4}{15} = \frac{4}{15}$$

31.

$$\frac{5}{x+1} - \frac{7}{x+1} = \frac{12}{x}$$
$$x(x+1)\left(\frac{5}{x+1}\right) - x(x+1)\left(\frac{7}{x+1}\right) = x(x+1)\left(\frac{12}{x}\right)$$
$$5x - 7x = 12x + 12$$
$$-2x = 12x + 12$$
$$-14x = 12$$
$$x = -\frac{6}{7}$$

Check:

$$\frac{5}{-\frac{6}{7}+1} - \frac{7}{-\frac{6}{7}+1} \stackrel{?}{=} \frac{12}{-\frac{6}{7}}$$
$$\frac{5}{\frac{1}{7}} - \frac{7}{\frac{1}{7}} \stackrel{?}{=} 12 \cdot \left(-\frac{7}{6}\right)$$
$$5\left(\frac{7}{1}\right) - 7\left(\frac{7}{1}\right) \stackrel{?}{=} -14$$
$$35 - 49 \stackrel{?}{=} -14$$
$$-14 = -14$$

Copyright © McDougal Littell Inc.
All rights reserved.

32.
$$\frac{5}{3} + \frac{250}{9r} = \frac{r}{9}$$
$$9r\left(\frac{5}{3}\right) + 9r\left(\frac{250}{9r}\right) = 9r\left(\frac{r}{9}\right)$$
$$15r + 250 = r^2$$
$$0 = r^2 - 15r - 250$$
$$0 = (r - 25)(r + 10)$$
$$r = 25, -10$$

Check:
$$\frac{5}{3} + \frac{250}{9(25)} \stackrel{?}{=} \frac{25}{9}$$
$$\frac{15}{9} + \frac{10}{9} \stackrel{?}{=} \frac{25}{9}$$
$$\frac{25}{9} = \frac{25}{9}$$
$$\frac{5}{3} + \frac{250}{9(-10)} \stackrel{?}{=} -\frac{10}{9}$$
$$\frac{15}{9} + \frac{-25}{9} \stackrel{?}{=} -\frac{10}{9}$$
$$-\frac{10}{9} = -\frac{10}{9}$$

33.
$$\frac{2}{y-2} + \frac{1}{y+2} = \frac{4}{y^2 - 4}$$
$$\frac{2}{y-2} + \frac{1}{y+2} = \frac{4}{(y+2)(y-2)}$$
$$(y+2)(y-2)\left(\frac{2}{y-2}\right) + (y+2)(y-2)\left(\frac{1}{y+2}\right) = (y+2)(y-2)\frac{4}{(y+2)(y-2)}$$
$$2y + 4 + y - 2 = 4$$
$$3y + 2 = 4$$
$$3y = 2$$
$$y = \frac{2}{3}$$

Check:
$$\frac{2}{\frac{2}{3} - 2} + \frac{1}{\frac{2}{3} + 2} \stackrel{?}{=} \frac{4}{(\frac{2}{3})^2 - 4}$$
$$\frac{2}{-\frac{4}{3}} + \frac{1}{\frac{8}{3}} \stackrel{?}{=} \frac{4}{\frac{4}{9} - \frac{36}{9}}$$
$$2\left(-\frac{3}{4}\right) + 1\left(\frac{3}{8}\right) \stackrel{?}{=} \frac{4}{-\frac{32}{9}}$$
$$-\frac{3}{2} + \frac{3}{8} \stackrel{?}{=} 4\left(-\frac{9}{32}\right)$$
$$-\frac{9}{8} = -\frac{9}{8}$$

Copyright © McDougal Littell Inc.
All rights reserved.

34.

$$\frac{3}{x+1} - \frac{1}{x-2} = \frac{1}{x^2 - x - 2}$$
$$\frac{3}{x+1} - \frac{1}{x-2} = \frac{1}{(x-2)(x+1)}$$
$$(x-2)(x+1)\frac{3}{x+1} - (x-2)(x+1)\frac{1}{x-2} = \frac{(x-2)(x+1)(1)}{(x-2)(x+1)}$$
$$3x - 6 - (x+1) = 1$$
$$3x - 6 - x - 1 = 1$$
$$2x - 7 = 1$$
$$2x = 8$$
$$x = 4$$

Check:

$$\frac{3}{4+1} - \frac{1}{4-2} \stackrel{?}{=} \frac{1}{4^2 - 4 - 2}$$
$$\frac{3}{5} - \frac{1}{2} \stackrel{?}{=} \frac{1}{10}$$
$$\frac{6}{10} - \frac{5}{10} \stackrel{?}{=} \frac{1}{10}$$
$$\frac{1}{10} = \frac{1}{10}$$

35.

$$\frac{3}{x-1} + \frac{10}{x^2 - 2x + 1} = 4$$
$$\frac{3}{x-1} + \frac{10}{(x-1)(x-1)} = 4$$
$$(x-1)^2\left(\frac{3}{x-1}\right) + (x-1)^2\frac{10}{(x-1)^2} = (x-1)^2 \cdot 4$$
$$(x-1)(3) + 10 = (x^2 - 2x + 1)4$$
$$3x - 3 + 10 = 4x^2 - 8x + 4$$
$$3x + 7 = 4x^2 - 8x + 4$$
$$0 = 4x^2 - 11x - 3$$
$$0 = (x-3)(4x+1)$$
$$x = 3, -\frac{1}{4}$$

Check:

$$\frac{3}{3-1} + \frac{10}{3^2 - 2(3) + 1} \stackrel{?}{=} 4$$
$$\frac{3}{2} + \frac{10}{4} \stackrel{?}{=} 4$$
$$\frac{3}{2} + \frac{5}{2} \stackrel{?}{=} 4$$
$$4 = 4$$

$$\frac{3}{-\frac{1}{4} - 1} + \frac{10}{(-\frac{1}{4})^2 - 2(-\frac{1}{4}) + 1} \stackrel{?}{=} 4$$
$$\frac{3}{-\frac{5}{4}} + \frac{10}{\frac{1}{16} + \frac{1}{2} + 1} \stackrel{?}{=} 4$$
$$3\left(-\frac{4}{5}\right) + \frac{10}{\frac{25}{16}} \stackrel{?}{=} 4$$
$$-\frac{12}{5} + 10\left(\frac{16}{25}\right) \stackrel{?}{=} 4$$
$$-\frac{12}{5} + \frac{32}{5} \stackrel{?}{=} 4$$
$$4 = 4$$

Copyright © McDougal Littell Inc.
All rights reserved.

36.

$$\frac{x}{x+3} + \frac{1}{x-1} = \frac{4}{x^2+2x-3}$$

$$\frac{x}{x+3} + \frac{1}{x-1} = \frac{4}{(x+3)(x-1)}$$

$$(x+3)(x-1)\left(\frac{x}{x+3}\right) + (x+3)(x-1)\left(\frac{1}{x-1}\right) = (x+3)(x-1)\frac{4}{(x+3)(x-1)}$$

$$x^2 - x + x + 3 = 4$$

$$x^2 + 3 = 4$$

$$x^2 = 1$$

$$x = \pm\sqrt{1}$$

$$x = \pm 1$$

Check:

$$\frac{1}{1+3} + \frac{1}{1-1} \stackrel{?}{=} \frac{4}{1^2 + 2(1) - 3}$$

$$\frac{1}{4} + \frac{1}{0} \stackrel{?}{=} \frac{4}{0}\text{; undefined}$$

so 1 is not a solution.

$$\frac{-1}{-1+3} + \frac{1}{-1-1} \stackrel{?}{=} \frac{4}{(-1)^2 + 2(-1) - 3}$$

$$-\frac{1}{2} + -\frac{1}{2} \stackrel{?}{=} \frac{4}{-4}$$

$$-1 = -1$$

37.

$$\frac{2}{x-1} - \frac{x}{x+3} = \frac{6}{x^2+2x-3}$$

$$\frac{2}{x-1} - \frac{x}{x+3} = \frac{6}{(x+3)(x-1)}$$

$$(x-1)(x+3)\frac{2}{x-1}$$

$$-(x-1)(x+3)\frac{x}{(x+3)} = (x-1)(x+3)\frac{6}{(x+3)(x-1)}$$

$$2x + 6 - (x^2 - x) = 6$$

$$2x + 6 - x^2 + x = 6$$

$$-x^2 + 3x + 6 = 6$$

$$-x^2 + 3x = 0$$

$$-x(x-3) = 0$$

$$x = 0, 3$$

Check:

$$\frac{2}{0-1} - \frac{0}{0+3} \stackrel{?}{=} \frac{6}{0^2 + 2(0) - 3}$$

$$-2 - 0 \stackrel{?}{=} \frac{6}{-3}$$

$$-2 = -2$$

$$\frac{2}{3-1} - \frac{3}{3+3} \stackrel{?}{=} \frac{6}{3^2 + 2(3) - 3}$$

$$1 - \frac{1}{2} \stackrel{?}{=} \frac{6}{12}$$

$$\frac{1}{2} = \frac{1}{2}$$

Copyright © McDougal Littell Inc.
All rights reserved.

38.

$$\frac{1}{y^2 - 16} - \frac{2}{y + 4} = \frac{2}{y - 4}$$

$$\frac{1}{(y + 4)(y - 4)} - \frac{2}{y + 4} = \frac{2}{y - 4}$$

$$\frac{(y + 4)(y - 4)}{(y + 4)(y - 4)} - \frac{(y + 4)(y - 4)(2)}{y + 4} = \frac{(y + 4)(y - 4)(2)}{(y - 4)}$$

$$1 - (2y - 8) = 2y + 8$$

$$1 - 2y + 8 = 2y + 8$$

$$-2y + 9 = 2y + 8$$

$$-4y = -1$$

$$y = \frac{1}{4}$$

Check:

$$\frac{1}{(\frac{1}{4})^2 - 16} - \frac{2}{(\frac{1}{4}) + 4} \stackrel{?}{=} \frac{2}{(\frac{1}{4}) - 4}$$

$$\frac{1}{\frac{1}{16} - 16} - \frac{2}{\frac{17}{4}} \stackrel{?}{=} \frac{2}{-\frac{15}{4}}$$

$$\frac{1}{-\frac{255}{16}} - 2\left(\frac{4}{17}\right) \stackrel{?}{=} 2\left(-\frac{4}{15}\right)$$

$$-\frac{16}{255} - \frac{8}{17} \stackrel{?}{=} -\frac{8}{15}$$

$$-\frac{16}{255} - \frac{8(15)}{17(15)} \stackrel{?}{=} -\frac{8}{15}$$

$$\frac{-16 - 120}{255} \stackrel{?}{=} -\frac{8}{15}$$

$$-\frac{136}{255} \stackrel{?}{=} -\frac{8}{15}$$

$$-\frac{8}{15} = -\frac{8}{15}$$

39.

$$\frac{1}{4} + \frac{4}{x} = \frac{1}{x}$$

$$4x\left(\frac{1}{4}\right) + 4x\left(\frac{4}{x}\right) = 4x\left(\frac{1}{x}\right)$$

$$x + 16 = 4$$

$$x = -12$$

Check:

$$\frac{1}{4} + \frac{4}{-12} \stackrel{?}{=} \frac{1}{-12}$$

$$\frac{3}{12} - \frac{4}{12} \stackrel{?}{=} -\frac{1}{12}$$

$$-\frac{1}{12} = -\frac{1}{12}$$

Copyright © McDougal Littell Inc.
All rights reserved.

40.
$$\frac{-3x}{x+1} = \frac{-2}{x-1}$$
$$-3x(x-1) = (x+1)(-2)$$
$$-3x^2 + 3x = -2x - 2$$
$$-3x^2 + 5x + 2 = 0$$
$$3x^2 - 5x - 2 = 0$$
$$a = 3, b = -5, c = -2$$
$$x = \frac{-(-5) \pm \sqrt{(-5)^2 - 4(3)(-2)}}{2(3)}$$
$$x = \frac{5 \pm \sqrt{25 + 24}}{6}$$
$$= \frac{5 \pm \sqrt{49}}{6}$$
$$= \frac{5 \pm 7}{6}$$
$$x = \frac{5+7}{6} = 2 \text{ or } x = \frac{5-7}{6} = -\frac{1}{3}$$

Check:
$$\frac{-3(2)}{2+1} \stackrel{?}{=} \frac{-2}{2-1}$$
$$-2 = -2$$
$$\frac{-3(-\frac{1}{3})}{(-\frac{1}{3}) + 1} \stackrel{?}{=} \frac{-2}{(-\frac{1}{3}) - 1}$$
$$\frac{1}{\frac{2}{3}} \stackrel{?}{=} \frac{-2}{-\frac{4}{3}}$$
$$\frac{3}{2} \stackrel{?}{=} -2\left(-\frac{3}{4}\right)$$
$$\frac{3}{2} = \frac{3}{2}$$

41.
$$\frac{x}{6} - \frac{1}{x} = \frac{1}{6}$$
$$6x\left(\frac{x}{6}\right) - 6x\left(\frac{1}{x}\right) = 6x\left(\frac{1}{6}\right)$$
$$x^2 - 6 = x$$
$$x^2 - x - 6 = 0$$
$$(x+2)(x-3) = 0$$
$$x = -2, 3$$

Check:
$$\frac{-2}{6} - \frac{1}{-2} \stackrel{?}{=} \frac{1}{6}$$
$$\frac{-2}{6} + \frac{3}{6} \stackrel{?}{=} \frac{1}{6}$$
$$\frac{1}{6} = \frac{1}{6}$$
$$\frac{3}{6} - \frac{1}{3} \stackrel{?}{=} \frac{1}{6}$$
$$\frac{3}{6} - \frac{2}{6} \stackrel{?}{=} \frac{1}{6}$$
$$\frac{1}{6} = \frac{1}{6}$$

42.
$$\frac{x}{9} - \frac{8}{x} = \frac{1}{9}$$
$$9x\left(\frac{x}{9}\right) - 9x\left(\frac{8}{x}\right) = 9x\left(\frac{1}{9}\right)$$
$$x^2 - 72 = x$$
$$x^2 - x - 72 = 0$$
$$(x-9)(x+8) = 0$$
$$x = 9, -8$$

Check:
$$\frac{9}{9} - \frac{8}{9} \stackrel{?}{=} \frac{1}{9}$$
$$\frac{1}{9} = \frac{1}{9}$$
$$-\frac{8}{9} - \frac{8}{-8} \stackrel{?}{=} \frac{1}{9}$$
$$-\frac{8}{9} + 1 \stackrel{?}{=} \frac{1}{9}$$
$$\frac{1}{9} = \frac{1}{9}$$

43.
$$\frac{x+42}{x} = x$$
$$x + 42 = x^2$$
$$0 = x^2 - x - 42$$
$$0 = (x-7)(x+6)$$
$$x = 7, -6$$

Check:
$$\frac{7+42}{7} \stackrel{?}{=} 7$$
$$\frac{49}{7} \stackrel{?}{=} 7$$
$$7 = 7$$
$$\frac{-6+42}{-6} \stackrel{?}{=} -6$$
$$\frac{36}{-6} \stackrel{?}{=} -6$$
$$-6 = -6$$

Copyright © McDougal Littell Inc.
All rights reserved.

44.
$$\frac{2}{x}-\frac{x}{8}=\frac{3}{4}$$
$$8x\left(\frac{2}{x}\right)-8x\left(\frac{x}{8}\right)=8x\left(\frac{3}{4}\right)$$
$$16-x^2=6x$$
$$0=x^2+6x-16$$
$$0=(x+8)(x-2)$$
$$x=-8,2$$

Check:
$$\frac{2}{-8}-\frac{-8}{8}\stackrel{?}{=}\frac{3}{4}$$
$$-\frac{1}{4}+1\stackrel{?}{=}\frac{3}{4}$$
$$\frac{3}{4}=\frac{3}{4}$$
$$\frac{2}{2}-\frac{2}{8}\stackrel{?}{=}\frac{3}{4}$$
$$1-\frac{1}{4}\stackrel{?}{=}\frac{3}{4}$$
$$\frac{3}{4}=\frac{3}{4}$$

45.
$$\frac{-3}{x+7}=\frac{2}{x+2}$$
$$-3(x+2)=(x+7)2$$
$$-3x-6=2x+14$$
$$-5x-6=14$$
$$-5x=20$$
$$x=-4$$

Check:
$$\frac{-3}{-4+7}\stackrel{?}{=}\frac{2}{-4+2}$$
$$-1=-1$$

46.
$$\frac{2}{x+3}+\frac{1}{x}=\frac{4}{3x}$$
$$3x(x+3)\left(\frac{2}{x+3}\right)+3x(x+3)\left(\frac{1}{x}\right)=3x(x+3)\frac{4}{3x}$$
$$6x+3x+9=4x+12$$
$$9x+9=4x+12$$
$$5x+9=12$$
$$5x=3$$
$$x=\frac{3}{5}$$

Check:
$$\frac{2}{\frac{3}{5}+3}+\frac{1}{\frac{3}{5}}\stackrel{?}{=}\frac{4}{3(\frac{3}{5})}$$
$$\frac{2}{\frac{18}{5}}+\frac{5}{3}\stackrel{?}{=}\frac{4}{\frac{9}{5}}$$
$$2\left(\frac{5}{18}\right)+\frac{5}{3}\stackrel{?}{=}4\left(\frac{5}{9}\right)$$
$$\frac{5}{9}+\frac{15}{9}\stackrel{?}{=}\frac{20}{9}$$
$$\frac{20}{9}=\frac{20}{9}$$

47.
$$\frac{1}{x}-\frac{2}{x^2}=\frac{1}{9}$$
$$9x^2\left(\frac{1}{x}\right)-9x^2\left(\frac{2}{x^2}\right)=9x^2\left(\frac{1}{9}\right)$$
$$9x-18=x^2$$
$$0=x^2-9x+18$$
$$0=(x-3)(x-6)$$
$$x=3,6$$

Check:
$$\frac{1}{3}-\frac{2}{(3)^2}\stackrel{?}{=}\frac{1}{9}$$
$$\frac{3}{9}-\frac{2}{9}\stackrel{?}{=}\frac{1}{9}$$
$$\frac{1}{9}=\frac{1}{9}$$
$$\frac{1}{6}-\frac{2}{6^2}\stackrel{?}{=}\frac{1}{9}$$
$$\frac{1}{6}-\frac{2}{36}\stackrel{?}{=}\frac{1}{9}$$
$$\frac{6}{36}-\frac{2}{36}\stackrel{?}{=}\frac{1}{9}$$
$$\frac{4}{36}\stackrel{?}{=}\frac{1}{9}$$
$$\frac{1}{9}=\frac{1}{9}$$

48.
$$\frac{x}{4}+\frac{x}{5}=1$$
$$5x+4x=20$$
$$9x=20$$
$$x=\frac{20}{9}\approx 2.22 \text{ hours}$$

or about 2 hours and 13 minutes

49.
$$\frac{x}{10}+\frac{x}{18}=1$$
$$90\left(\frac{x}{10}\right)+90\left(\frac{x}{18}\right)=90(1)$$
$$9x+5x=90$$
$$14x=90$$
$$x=\frac{45}{7}\approx 6.43 \text{ hours}$$

or 6 hours and 26 minutes for 1 mile

For 20 miles: $\dfrac{\frac{45}{7}\text{ hours}}{1\text{ miles}}\times 20\text{ miles}=128.57\text{ hours}$

or 128 hours 34 minutes

50.
$$\frac{x}{30}+\frac{x}{40}+\frac{x}{60}=1$$
$$120\left(\frac{x}{30}\right)+120\left(\frac{x}{40}\right)+120\left(\frac{x}{60}\right)=120(1)$$
$$4x+3x+2x=120$$
$$9x=120$$
$$x=\frac{120}{9}$$
$$x=13\frac{1}{3}$$

or 13 min and 20 seconds

Copyright © McDougal Littell Inc.
All rights reserved.

51.

	Number of pounds ×	*Price per pound* =	*Cost*
egg noodles	5	0.80	4.00
spinach noodles	2	1.50	3.00
mixture	7	x	7.00

$7x = 7.00$

$x = 1$

\$1.00 per pound

52.

	Number of liters ×	*Price per liter* =	*Cost*
apple juice	8	0.45	3.60
cranberry juice	10	1.08	10.80
mixture	18	x	14.40

$18x = 14.40$

$x = \$0.80$ per liter

53.

	Number of coins ×	*Value per coin* =	*total value*
dimes	x	\$0.10	$0.10x$
quarters	$12 - x$	\$0.25	$0.25(12 - x)$
mixture	12		1.95

$$0.10x + 0.25(12 - x) = 1.95$$
$$10x + 25(12 - x) = 195$$
$$10x + 300 - 25x = 195$$
$$-15x = -105$$
$$x = 7$$

7 dimes, 5 quarters

54. $\dfrac{35 + x}{140 + x} = 0.300$

$$35 + x = 0.300(140 + x)$$
$$35 + x = 42 + 0.3x$$
$$35 + 0.7x = 42$$
$$0.7x = 7$$

$x = 10$ consecutive hits

55.

	Number of liters ×	*% acid* =	*liters of acid*
original solution	50	0.30	15
water added	x	0	0
new solution	$50 + x$	0.20	15

$$(50 + x)(0.20) = 15$$
$$10 + 0.2x = 15$$
$$0.2x = 5$$

$x = 25$ liters of water

11.7 Standardized Test Practice (p. 676)

56. B;

$$2x = 2x$$
$$7x^2 = 7x^2$$
$$4x = 2^2 \cdot x$$
$$\text{LCD} = 2^2 \cdot 7 \cdot x^2 = 28x^2$$

57. G;

$$\frac{10r}{r + 1} + \frac{1}{r + 1} = 2$$
$$\frac{10r + 1}{r + 1} = 2$$
$$10r + 1 = 2(r + 1)$$
$$10r + 1 = 2r + 2$$
$$8r + 1 = 2$$
$$8r = 1$$
$$r = \frac{1}{8}$$

58. A;

$$\frac{x}{6} - \frac{6}{x} = 0$$
$$6x\left(\frac{x}{6}\right) - 6x\left(\frac{6}{x}\right) = 6x(0)$$
$$x^2 - 36 = 0$$
$$x^2 = 36$$
$$x = \pm 6$$

59. J;

$$\frac{5}{x + 1} + \frac{x}{x^2 - 1} = \frac{1}{x - 1}$$
$$\frac{5}{x + 1} + \frac{x}{(x + 1)(x - 1)} = \frac{1}{x - 1}$$
$$5(x - 1) + x = x + 1$$
$$5x - 5 + x = x + 1$$
$$6x - 5 = x + 1$$
$$5x - 5 = 1$$
$$5x = 6$$
$$x = \frac{6}{5}$$

11.7 Mixed Review (p. 676)

60. $f(x) = 4x$

x	0	1	2	3	4
$f(x)$	0	4	8	12	16

61. $f(x) = -x + 9$

x	0	1	2	3	4
$f(x)$	9	8	7	6	5

62. $f(x) = 3x + 1$

x	0	1	2	3	4
$f(x)$	1	4	7	10	13

63. $f(x) = -x^2$

x	0	1	2	3	4
$f(x)$	0	−1	−4	−9	−16

Copyright © McDougal Littell Inc.
All rights reserved.

Chapter 11 *continued*

64. $f(x) = x^2 - 1$

x	0	1	2	3	4
$f(x)$	-1	0	3	8	15

65. $f(x) = \frac{x^2}{2}$

x	0	1	2	3	4
$f(x)$	0	$\frac{1}{2}$	2	$\frac{9}{2}$	8

66. $2^4 \cdot 2^3 = 2^7 = 128$

67. $6^3 \cdot 6^{-1} = 6^2 = 36$

68. $(3^3)^2 = 3^6 = 729$

69. $(4^5)^0 = 4^0 = 1$

70. $12^{-5} \cdot 12^3 = 12^{-2} = \frac{1}{12^2} = \frac{1}{144}$

71. $5^2 \cdot 5^1 = 5^3 = 125$

72. $\sqrt{50} = \sqrt{25 \cdot 2} = 5\sqrt{2}$

73. $\sqrt{72} = \sqrt{36 \cdot 2} = 6\sqrt{2}$

74. $\frac{1}{4}\sqrt{112} = \frac{1}{4}\sqrt{16 \cdot 7} = \frac{1}{4} \cdot 4\sqrt{7} = \sqrt{7}$

75. $\frac{1}{2}\sqrt{52} = \frac{1}{2}\sqrt{4 \cdot 13} = \frac{1}{2} \cdot 2\sqrt{13} = \sqrt{13}$

76. $\sqrt{128} = \sqrt{64 \cdot 2} = 8\sqrt{2}$

77. $\frac{1}{4}\sqrt{90} = \frac{1}{4}\sqrt{9 \cdot 10} = \frac{1}{4} \cdot 3\sqrt{10} = \frac{3}{4}\sqrt{10}$

78. $3\sqrt{63} = 3\sqrt{9 \cdot 7} = 3 \cdot 3\sqrt{7} = 9\sqrt{7}$

79. $\frac{7}{8}\sqrt{153} = \frac{7}{8}\sqrt{9 \cdot 17} = \frac{7}{8} \cdot 3\sqrt{17} = \frac{21}{8}\sqrt{17}$

80. $\frac{2}{3}\sqrt{18} = \frac{2}{3}\sqrt{9 \cdot 2} = \frac{2}{3} \cdot 3\sqrt{2} = 2\sqrt{2}$

81. $\sqrt{27} = \sqrt{9 \cdot 3} = 3\sqrt{3}$

82. $\frac{1}{5}\sqrt{500} = \frac{1}{5}\sqrt{100 \cdot 5} = \frac{1}{5} \cdot 10\sqrt{5} = 2\sqrt{5}$

83. $\frac{3}{7}\sqrt{147} = \frac{3}{7}\sqrt{49 \cdot 3} = \frac{3}{7} \cdot 7\sqrt{3} = 3\sqrt{3}$

11.7 Maintaining Skills (p. 677)

84. $\frac{2}{3} + \frac{1}{6} - \frac{1}{3} = \frac{4}{6} + \frac{1}{6} - \frac{2}{6} = \frac{3}{6} = \frac{1}{2}$

85. $\frac{3}{4} + \frac{5}{8} - \frac{1}{2} = \frac{6}{8} + \frac{5}{8} - \frac{4}{8} = \frac{7}{8}$

86. $\frac{2}{5} + \frac{3}{8} - \frac{1}{4} = \frac{16}{40} + \frac{15}{40} - \frac{10}{40} = \frac{21}{40}$

87. $\frac{2}{9} - \frac{1}{3} + \frac{4}{5} = \frac{10}{45} - \frac{15}{45} + \frac{36}{45} = \frac{31}{45}$

88. $\frac{1}{10} + \frac{1}{5} - \frac{3}{10} + \frac{2}{5} = \frac{1}{10} + \frac{2}{10} - \frac{3}{10} + \frac{4}{10} = \frac{4}{10} = \frac{2}{5}$

89. $\frac{1}{4} + \frac{2}{4} - \frac{3}{4} + \frac{4}{4} = \frac{4}{4} = 1$

90. $\frac{3}{17} - \frac{3}{34} + \frac{1}{2} = \frac{6}{34} - \frac{3}{34} + \frac{17}{34} = \frac{20}{34} = \frac{10}{17}$

91. $\frac{1}{2} - \frac{3}{4} + \frac{5}{6} - \frac{7}{8} = \frac{12}{24} - \frac{18}{24} + \frac{20}{24} - \frac{21}{24} = -\frac{7}{24}$

92. $\frac{12}{13} + \frac{7}{26} - \frac{1}{2} = \frac{24}{26} + \frac{7}{26} - \frac{13}{26} = \frac{18}{26} = \frac{9}{13}$

93. $\frac{103}{202} + \frac{1}{2} - \frac{1}{101} = \frac{103}{202} + \frac{101}{202} - \frac{2}{202} = \frac{202}{202} = 1$

94. $\frac{7}{3} + \frac{1}{5} - \frac{2}{15} = \frac{35}{15} + \frac{3}{15} - \frac{2}{15} = \frac{36}{15} = \frac{12}{5} = 2\frac{2}{5}$

95. $\frac{5}{11} - \frac{4}{5} + \frac{3}{4} = \frac{100}{220} - \frac{176}{220} + \frac{165}{220} = \frac{89}{220}$

Quiz 2 *(p. 677)*

1. $\frac{5x^2}{2x} \cdot \frac{14x^2}{10x} = \frac{70x^4}{20x^2} = \frac{7x^2}{2}$

2. $\frac{5}{10 + 4x} \cdot (20 + 8x) = \frac{5}{2(5 + 2x)} \cdot \frac{4(5 + 2x)}{1} = 10$

3. $\frac{3x + 12}{4x} \div \frac{x + 4}{2x} = \frac{3x + 12}{4x} \cdot \frac{2x}{x + 4}$

$= \frac{3(x + 4)}{4x} \cdot \frac{2x}{(x + 4)}$

$= \frac{3}{2}$

Copyright © McDougal Littell Inc.
All rights reserved.

4. $\frac{5x^2 - 30x + 45}{x + 2} \cdot \frac{1}{5x - 15} = \frac{5(x^2 - 6x + 9)}{(x + 2)} \cdot \frac{1}{5(x - 3)}$

$= \frac{5(x - 3)(x - 3)}{(x + 2)} \cdot \frac{1}{5(x - 3)}$

$= \frac{x - 3}{x + 2}$

5. $\frac{x}{x^2 - 2x - 35} + \frac{5}{x^2 - 2x - 35} = \frac{x + 5}{(x + 5)(x - 7)}$

$= \frac{1}{x - 7}$

6. $\frac{4x - 1}{3x^2 + 8x + 5} - \frac{x - 6}{3x^2 + 8x + 5} = \frac{4x - 1 - x + 6}{(3x + 5)(x + 1)}$

$= \frac{3x + 5}{(3x + 5)(x + 1)}$

$= \frac{1}{x + 1}$

7. $\frac{6}{x^2 - 1} + \frac{7x}{x + 1} = \frac{6}{(x + 1)(x - 1)} + \frac{7x(x - 1)}{(x + 1)(x - 1)}$

$= \frac{6 + 7x^2 - 7x}{(x + 1)(x - 1)}$

$= \frac{7x^2 - 7x + 6}{(x + 1)(x - 1)}$

8. $\frac{3x^2}{3x - 9} - \frac{2x}{x^2 - x - 6} = \frac{3x^2}{3(x - 3)} - \frac{2x}{(x + 2)(x - 3)}$

$= \frac{3x^2(x + 2)}{3(x - 3)(x + 2)} - \frac{2x(3)}{(3)(x + 2)(x - 3)}$

$= \frac{3x^3 + 6x^2 - 6x}{3(x - 3)(x + 2)}$

$= \frac{3x(x^2 + 2x - 2)}{3(x - 3)(x + 2)}$

$= \frac{x(x^2 + 2x - 2)}{(x - 3)(x + 2)}$

9. $\frac{3}{x} = \frac{9}{2(x + 2)}$

$3(2)(x + 2) = x(9)$

$6x + 12 = 9x$

$12 = 3x$

$4 = x$

Check:

$\frac{3}{4} \stackrel{?}{=} \frac{9}{2(4 + 2)}$

$\frac{3}{4} \stackrel{?}{=} \frac{9}{12}$

$\frac{3}{4} = \frac{3}{4}$

Copyright © McDougal Littell Inc.
All rights reserved.

10. $\frac{1}{2} + \frac{2}{t} = \frac{1}{t}$

$2t \cdot \frac{1}{2} + 2t \cdot \frac{2}{t} = 2t \cdot \frac{1}{t}$

$t + 4 = 2$

$t = -2$

Check:

$\frac{1}{2} + \frac{2}{-2} \stackrel{?}{=} \frac{1}{-2}$

$\frac{1}{2} + -1 \stackrel{?}{=} -\frac{1}{2}$

$-\frac{1}{2} = -\frac{1}{2}$

11. $\frac{1}{x-5} + \frac{1}{x+5} = \frac{x+3}{x^2-25}$

$\frac{1}{x-5} + \frac{1}{x+5} = \frac{x+3}{(x+5)(x-5)}$

$(x+5) + (x-5) = (x+3)$

$2x = x + 3$

$x = 3$

Check:

$\frac{1}{3-5} + \frac{1}{3+5} \stackrel{?}{=} \frac{3+3}{3^2-25}$

$\frac{1}{-2} + \frac{1}{8} \stackrel{?}{=} \frac{6}{-16}$

$-\frac{4}{8} + \frac{1}{8} \stackrel{?}{=} -\frac{3}{8}$

$-\frac{3}{8} = -\frac{3}{8}$

12. $\frac{7}{8} - \frac{16}{x-2} = \frac{3}{4}$

$8(x-2) \cdot \frac{7}{8} - 8(x-2) \cdot \frac{16}{(x-2)} = 8(x-2) \cdot \frac{3}{4}$

$7x - 14 - 128 = 6x - 12$

$7x - 142 = 6x - 12$

$x - 142 = -12$

$x = 130$

Check:

$\frac{7}{8} - \frac{16}{130-2} \stackrel{?}{=} \frac{3}{4}$

$\frac{7}{8} - \frac{16}{128} \stackrel{?}{=} \frac{3}{4}$

$\frac{7}{8} - \frac{1}{8} \stackrel{?}{=} \frac{3}{4}$

$\frac{6}{8} \stackrel{?}{=} \frac{3}{4}$

$\frac{3}{4} = \frac{3}{4}$

13. downstream: $\frac{15}{x+2}$

upstream: $\frac{15}{x-2}$

14. $\frac{15}{x+2} + \frac{15}{x-2} = \frac{15(x-2)}{(x+2)(x-2)} + \frac{15(x+2)}{(x+2)(x-2)}$

$= \frac{15x - 30 + 15x + 30}{(x+2)(x-2)}$

$= \frac{30x}{(x+2)(x-2)}$

15. $\frac{30(3)}{(3+2)(3-2)} = \frac{90}{(5)(1)} = 18$ hours

16. $\frac{x}{3} + \frac{x}{4} = 1$

$4x + 3x = 12$

$7x = 12$

$x = \frac{12}{7} \approx 1.71$ hours

or 1 hour and 43 minutes

Chapter 11 Extension

Checkpoint (pp. 678–679)

1. $(f+g)(x) = f(x) + g(x)$

$= \frac{x+1}{x} + \frac{1}{x}$

$= \frac{x+2}{x}$

2. $(f+g)(x) = f(x) + g(x)$

$= \frac{1}{x-3} + \frac{1}{x+3}$

$= \frac{(x+3) + (x-3)}{(x-3)(x+3)}$

$= \frac{2x}{(x-3)(x+3)}$

3. $(f-g)(x) = f(x) - g(x)$

$= \frac{x+1}{x} - \frac{1}{x}$

$= \frac{x}{x}$

$= 1$

4. $(f-g)(x) = f(x) - g(x)$

$= \frac{1}{x-3} - \frac{1}{x+3}$

$= \frac{(x+3) - (x-3)}{(x-3)(x+3)}$

$= \frac{x + 3 - x + 3}{(x-3)(x+3)}$

$= \frac{6}{(x-3)(x+3)}$

5. $(f \cdot g)(x) = f(x) \cdot g(x)$

$= \frac{x}{x+7} \cdot \frac{2x+14}{8}$

$= \frac{x}{x+7} \cdot \frac{2(x+7)}{8}$

$= \frac{x}{4}$

Copyright © McDougal Littell Inc.
All rights reserved.

6. $(f \div g)(x) = f(x) \div g(x)$

$= \frac{1-x}{x} \div \frac{x-1}{x^2}$

$= \frac{-(x-1)}{x} \cdot \frac{x^2}{(x-1)}$

$= -x$

Exercises (p. 680)

1. $(f+g)(x) = \frac{1}{x-9} + \frac{9}{x-9}$

$= \frac{10}{x-9}$

2. $(f+g)(x) = \frac{x}{x^2-25} + \frac{5}{x^2-25}$

$= \frac{x+5}{(x+5)(x-5)}$

$= \frac{1}{x-5}$

3. $(f+g)(x) = \frac{x-1}{x^2} + \frac{1}{x}$

$= \frac{x-1}{x^2} + \frac{x}{x^2}$

$= \frac{2x-1}{x^2}$

4. $(f+g)(x) = \frac{2}{x-3} + \frac{7}{3-x}$

$= \frac{2}{x-3} + \frac{-7}{x-3}$

$= \frac{-5}{x-3}$

5. $(f+g)(x) = \frac{6x}{x-7} + \frac{5x}{x+7}$

$= \frac{6x(x+7) + 5x(x-7)}{(x-7)(x+7)}$

$= \frac{6x^2 + 42x + 5x^2 - 35x}{(x-7)(x+7)}$

$= \frac{11x^2 + 7x}{(x-7)(x+7)}$

$= \frac{x(11x+7)}{(x-7)(x+7)}$

6. $(f+g)(x) = \frac{x-3}{20x} + \frac{x+4}{15x}$

$= \frac{3(x-3)}{60x} + \frac{4(x+4)}{60x}$

$= \frac{3x - 9 + 4x + 16}{60x}$

$= \frac{7x+7}{60x}$

$= \frac{7(x+1)}{60x}$

7. $(f-g)(x) = \frac{4x}{3x+7} - \frac{x-5}{3x+7}$

$= \frac{4x - x + 5}{3x+7}$

$= \frac{3x+5}{3x+7}$

8. $(f-g)(x) = \frac{x}{x^2-36} - \frac{6}{x^2-36}$

$= \frac{x-6}{(x+6)(x-6)}$

$= \frac{1}{x+6}$

9. $(f-g)(x) = \frac{1}{x} - \frac{2x+3}{x^2}$

$= \frac{x}{x^2} - \frac{2x+3}{x^2}$

$= \frac{x - 2x - 3}{x^2}$

$= \frac{-x-3}{x^2}$

10. $(f-g)(x) = \frac{3}{x+4} - \frac{4}{x-2}$

$= \frac{3(x-2)}{(x+4)(x-2)} - \frac{4(x+4)}{(x+4)(x-2)}$

$= \frac{3x - 6 - 4x - 16}{(x+4)(x-2)}$

$= \frac{-x-22}{(x+4)(x-2)}$

11. $(f-g)(x) = \frac{1}{x+9} - \frac{1}{x-9}$

$= \frac{x-9}{(x+9)(x-9)} - \frac{x+9}{(x+9)(x-9)}$

$= \frac{x - 9 - (x+9)}{(x+9)(x-9)}$

$= \frac{x - 9 - x - 9}{(x+9)(x-9)}$

$= \frac{-18}{(x+9)(x-9)}$

12. $(f-g)(x) = \frac{2x}{x-3} - \frac{3}{2x-6}$

$= \frac{2x}{x-3} - \frac{3}{2(x-3)}$

$= \frac{2(2x)}{2(x-3)} - \frac{3}{2(x-3)}$

$= \frac{4x-3}{2(x-3)}$

13. $(f \cdot g)(x) = \frac{1}{2x} \cdot \frac{6}{x+15}$

$= \frac{6}{2x(x+15)}$

$= \frac{3}{x(x+15)}$

Copyright © McDougal Littell Inc.
All rights reserved.

14. $(f \cdot g)(x) = \frac{4}{3x + 6} \cdot \frac{x + 2}{x}$
$= \frac{4}{3(x + 2)} \cdot \frac{x + 2}{x}$
$= \frac{4(x + 2)}{3x(x + 2)}$
$= \frac{4}{3x}$

15. $(f \cdot g)(x) = \frac{x^2 - 5x + 6}{2x} \cdot \frac{3x - 6}{x - 3}$
$= \frac{(x - 2)(x - 3)}{2x} \cdot \frac{3(x - 2)}{(x - 3)}$
$= \frac{3(x - 2)^2}{2x}$

16. $(f \cdot g)(x) = \frac{x + 2}{x^2} \cdot \frac{8x}{4x^2 - 16}$
$= \frac{(x + 2)}{x^2} \cdot \frac{8x}{4(x^2 - 4)}$
$= \frac{x + 2}{x^2} \cdot \frac{8x}{4(x + 2)(x - 2)}$
$= \frac{2}{x(x - 2)}$

17. $(f \cdot g)(x) = \frac{x^2 + 3x - 10}{x + 2} \cdot \frac{x^2 - 4}{x + 5}$
$= \frac{(x - 2)(x + 5)}{x + 2} \cdot \frac{(x + 2)(x - 2)}{x + 5}$
$= (x - 2)^2$

18. $(f \cdot g)(x) = \frac{x^2 - 3x + 2}{x^2 + 3x + 2} \cdot \frac{8x + 8}{4x + 8}$
$= \frac{(x - 2)(x - 1)}{(x + 2)(x + 1)} \cdot \frac{8(x + 1)}{4(x + 2)}$
$= \frac{2(x - 2)(x - 1)}{(x + 2)^2}$

19. $(f \div g)(x) = \frac{x + 3}{x^2} \div \frac{x + 1}{x^3}$
$= \frac{x + 3}{x^2} \cdot \frac{x^3}{x + 1}$
$= \frac{x(x + 3)}{x + 1}$

20. $(f \div g)(x) = \frac{2}{3x} \div \frac{1}{4x}$
$= \frac{2}{3x} \cdot \frac{4x}{1}$
$= \frac{8}{3}$

21. $(f \div g)(x) = \frac{x}{2x + 1} \div \frac{2x + 1}{x}$
$= \frac{x}{2x + 1} \cdot \frac{x}{2x + 1}$
$= \frac{x^2}{(2x + 1)^2}$

22. $(f \div g)(x) = \frac{2x}{x^3 - 5x^2} \div \frac{10}{x^2 - 5x}$
$= \frac{2x}{x^2(x - 5)} \cdot \frac{x(x - 5)}{10}$
$= \frac{1}{5}$

23. $(f \div g)(x) = \frac{x^2 + 3x - 10}{x + 2} \div \frac{x^2 - 4}{x + 5}$
$= \frac{(x - 2)(x + 5)}{x + 2} \cdot \frac{x + 5}{(x + 2)(x - 2)}$
$= \frac{(x + 5)^2}{(x + 2)^2}$

24. $(f \div g)(x) = \frac{x^2 - x - 20}{5x - 25} \div \frac{x - 1}{x^2 - 25}$
$= \frac{(x + 4)(x - 5)}{5(x - 5)} \cdot \frac{(x + 5)(x - 5)}{(x - 1)}$
$= \frac{(x + 4)(x - 5)(x + 5)}{5(x - 1)}$

25. $f(x) = y = \frac{1}{x - 9}$

x	-3	-2	-1	0	1	2	3	6	9
y	$-\frac{1}{12}$	$-\frac{1}{11}$	$-\frac{1}{10}$	$-\frac{1}{9}$	$-\frac{1}{8}$	$-\frac{1}{7}$	$-\frac{1}{6}$	$-\frac{1}{3}$	undef

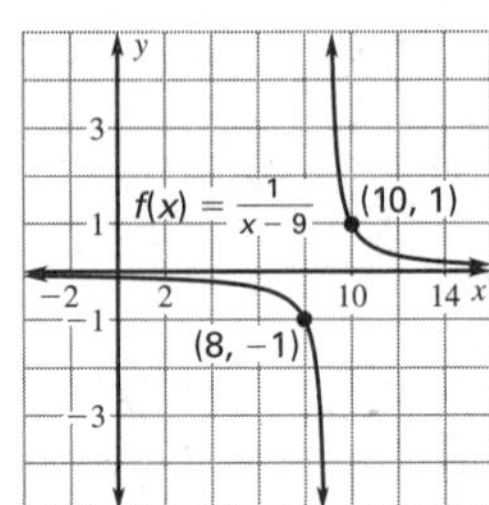

26. $f(x) = y = \frac{1}{2x} - 3$

x	-3	-2	-1	0	1	2	3
y	$-3\frac{1}{6}$	$-3\frac{1}{4}$	$-3\frac{1}{2}$	undef	$-2\frac{1}{2}$	$-2\frac{3}{4}$	$-2\frac{5}{6}$

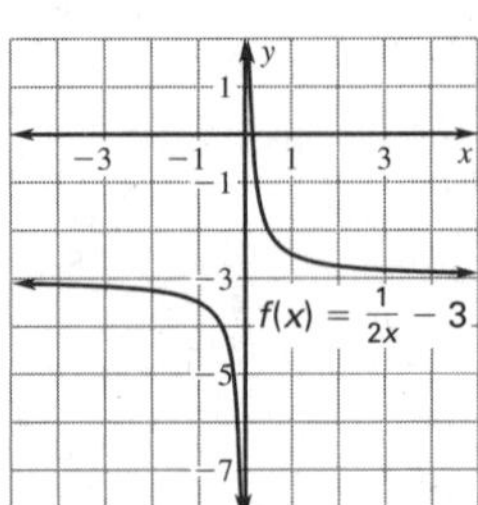

Copyright © McDougal Littell Inc.
All rights reserved.

27. $g(x) = y = \dfrac{x}{2x + 3}$

x	−3	−2	−1	0	1	2	3
y	1	2	1	0	$\frac{1}{5}$	$\frac{2}{7}$	$\frac{1}{3}$

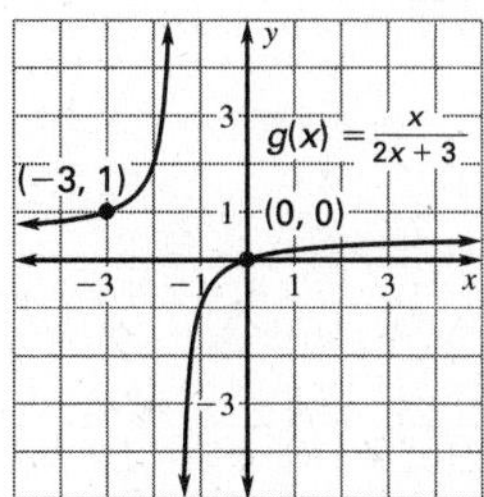

28. $g(x) = y = \dfrac{-1}{x + 2} + 1$

x	−3	−2	−1	0	1	2	3
y	2	undef	0	$\frac{1}{2}$	$\frac{2}{3}$	$\frac{3}{4}$	$\frac{4}{5}$

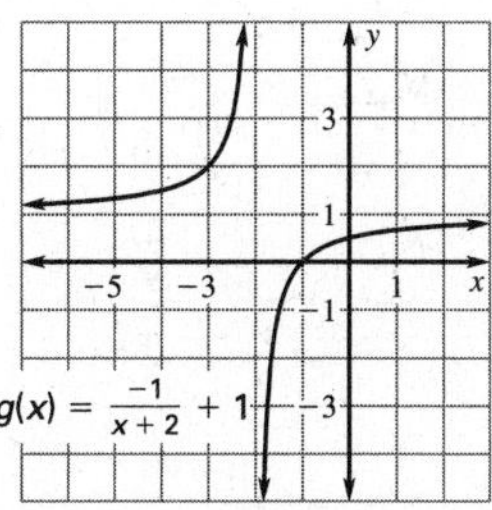

Chapter Summary and Review ***(pp. 681–684)***

1. $\dfrac{x}{2} = \dfrac{4}{7}$

$7x = 8$

$x = \dfrac{8}{7}$

Check:

$\dfrac{\frac{8}{7}}{2} \stackrel{?}{=} \dfrac{4}{7}$

$\dfrac{8}{7} \div 2 \stackrel{?}{=} \dfrac{4}{7}$

$\dfrac{8}{7} \cdot \dfrac{1}{2} \stackrel{?}{=} \dfrac{4}{7}$

$\dfrac{4}{7} = \dfrac{4}{7}$

2. $\dfrac{7}{10} = \dfrac{9 + x}{x}$

$7x = 10(9 + x)$

$7x = 90 + 10x$

$-3x = 90$

$x = -30$

Check:

$\dfrac{7}{10} \stackrel{?}{=} \dfrac{9 + (-30)}{-30}$

$\dfrac{7}{10} \stackrel{?}{=} \dfrac{-21}{-30}$

$\dfrac{7}{10} = \dfrac{7}{10}$

3. $\dfrac{x^2 - 16}{x + 4} = \dfrac{x - 4}{3}$

$3(x^2 - 16) = (x + 4)(x - 4)$

$3x^2 - 48 = x^2 - 16$

$2x^2 - 48 = -16$

$2x^2 = 32$

$x^2 = 16$

$x = \pm 4$

Check:

$\dfrac{4^2 - 16}{4 + 4} \stackrel{?}{=} \dfrac{4 - 4}{3}$

$0 = 0$

$\dfrac{(-4)^2 - 16}{(-4) + 4} \stackrel{?}{=} \dfrac{(-4) - 4}{3}$

$\dfrac{0}{0} \stackrel{?}{=}$ undefined

-4 is not a solution

4. $\dfrac{5}{x + 6} = \dfrac{x - 6}{x}$

$5x = (x + 6)(x - 6)$

$5x = x^2 - 36$

$0 = x^2 - 5x - 36$

$0 = (x - 9)(x + 4)$

$x = 9, -4$

Check:

$\dfrac{5}{9 + 6} \stackrel{?}{=} \dfrac{9 - 6}{9}$

$\dfrac{5}{15} \stackrel{?}{=} \dfrac{3}{9}$

$\dfrac{1}{3} = \dfrac{1}{3}$

$\dfrac{5}{-4 + 6} \stackrel{?}{=} \dfrac{-4 - 6}{-4}$

$\dfrac{5}{2} \stackrel{?}{=} \dfrac{-10}{-4}$

$\dfrac{5}{2} = \dfrac{5}{2}$

5. $50 = k(10)$

$5 = k$

$y = 5x$

Copyright © McDougal Littell Inc.
All rights reserved.

6. $6 = k(24)$

$\frac{1}{4} = k$

$y = \frac{1}{4}x$

7. $36 = k(45)$

$\frac{4}{5} = k$

$y = \frac{4}{5}x$

8. $20 = k(2)$

$10 = k$

$y = 10x$

9. $7 = k\left(\frac{1}{2}\right)$

$14 = k$

$y = 14x$

10. $132 = k(66)$

$2 = k$

$y = 2x$

11. $3 = \frac{k}{12}$

$36 = k$

$y = \frac{36}{x}$

12. $10 = \frac{k}{20}$

$200 = k$

$y = \frac{200}{x}$

13. $5 = \frac{k}{90}$

$450 = k$

$y = \frac{450}{x}$

14. $3 = \frac{k}{\frac{2}{3}}$

$2 = k$

$y = \frac{2}{x}$

15. $\frac{11}{2} = \frac{k}{4}$

$22 = k$

$y = \frac{22}{x}$

16. $\frac{1}{4} = \frac{k}{24}$

$6 = k$

$y = \frac{6}{x}$

17. $\frac{3x}{9x^2 + 3} = \frac{3x}{3(3x^2 + 1)} = \frac{x}{3x^2 + 1}$

18. $\frac{6x^2}{12x^4 + 18x^2} = \frac{6x^2}{6x^2(2x^2 + 3)} = \frac{1}{2x^2 + 3}$

19. $\frac{7x^3 - 28x}{3x^2 + 8x + 4} = \frac{7x(x^2 - 4)}{(3x + 2)(x + 2)}$

$= \frac{7x(x + 2)(x - 2)}{(3x + 2)(x + 2)}$

$= \frac{7x(x - 2)}{(3x + 2)}$

20. $\frac{5x^2 + 21x + 4}{25x + 100} = \frac{(5x + 1)(x + 4)}{25(x + 4)} = \frac{5x + 1}{25}$

21. $\frac{x^2 + 4x + 4}{x^2 + 9x + 14} = \frac{(x + 2)(x + 2)}{(x + 7)(x + 2)} = \frac{x + 2}{x + 7}$

22. $\frac{6x^2 - 19x + 10}{2x^2 - 5x} = \frac{(3x - 2)(2x - 5)}{x(2x - 5)} = \frac{3x - 2}{x}$

23. $\frac{2x^2 + 17x + 21}{2x^2 + x - 3} = \frac{(2x + 3)(x + 7)}{(2x + 3)(x - 1)} = \frac{x + 7}{x - 1}$

24. $\frac{13x^2 - 39x}{3x^2 - 8x - 3} = \frac{13x(x - 3)}{(3x + 1)(x - 3)} = \frac{13x}{3x + 1}$

25. $\frac{y^2 - 2y - 48}{2y^2 + 9y - 18} = \frac{(y + 6)(y - 8)}{(2y - 3)(y + 6)} = \frac{y - 8}{2y - 3}$

26. $\frac{x(2)(x + 1)}{3x(4)(x + 3)} = \frac{x + 1}{6(x + 3)}$

27. $\frac{12x^2}{5x^3} \cdot \frac{25x^4}{3x} = 20x^2$

28. $\frac{a^2 - 7a - 18}{4a^2 + 8a} \cdot \frac{12}{a^2 - 81}$

$= \frac{(a - 9)(a + 2)}{4a(a + 2)} \cdot \frac{12}{(a + 9)(a - 9)}$

$= \frac{3}{a(a + 9)}$

29. $\frac{2x^2 + 9x + 7}{2x} \cdot \frac{16x^2}{x^3 - x} = \frac{(2x + 7)(x + 1)}{2x} \cdot \frac{16x^2}{x(x^2 - 1)}$

$= \frac{8(2x + 7)(x + 1)}{(x + 1)(x - 1)}$

$= \frac{8(2x + 7)}{x - 1}$

30. $\frac{6y^2}{y + 3} \div \frac{9y}{(y + 3)^2} = \frac{6y^2}{y + 3} \cdot \frac{(y + 3)^2}{9y}$

$= \frac{2y(y + 3)}{3}$

31. $\frac{9x^3}{x^3 - x^2} \div \frac{x - 8}{x^2 - 9x + 8} = \frac{9x^3}{x^2(x - 1)} \cdot \frac{(x - 8)(x - 1)}{(x - 8)}$

$= 9x$

32. $\frac{x^2 + 3x + 2}{x^2 + 7x + 12} \div \frac{x^2 + 5x + 4}{x^2 + 5x + 6}$

$= \frac{(x + 1)(x + 2)}{(x + 3)(x + 4)} \cdot \frac{(x + 2)(x + 3)}{(x + 4)(x + 1)}$

$= \frac{(x + 2)^2}{(x + 4)^2}$

Copyright © McDougal Littell Inc.
All rights reserved.

33. $\dfrac{2x+1}{3x}+\dfrac{x+5}{3x}=\dfrac{3x+6}{3x}$

$=\dfrac{3(x+2)}{3x}$

$=\dfrac{x+2}{x}$

34. $\dfrac{-2b-5}{b^2}+\dfrac{5}{b^2}=\dfrac{-2b}{b^2}=-\dfrac{2}{b}$

35. $\dfrac{6x}{x+4}-\dfrac{5x-4}{x+4}=\dfrac{6x-5x+4}{x+4}=\dfrac{x+4}{x+4}=1$

36. $\dfrac{x(x+1)}{(x-3)^2}-\dfrac{12}{(x-3)^2}=\dfrac{x^2+x-12}{(x-3)^2}$

$=\dfrac{(x-3)(x+4)}{(x-3)^2}$

$=\dfrac{x+4}{x-3}$

37. $2\left(\dfrac{x+1}{16}\right)+2\left(\dfrac{x+3}{16}\right)=\dfrac{x+1}{8}+\dfrac{x+3}{8}$

$=\dfrac{2x+4}{8}$

$=\dfrac{2(x+2)}{8}$

$=\dfrac{x+2}{4}$

38. $\dfrac{x+3}{3x-1}+\dfrac{4}{x-3}$

$=\dfrac{(x+3)(x-3)}{(3x-1)(x-3)}+\dfrac{4(3x-1)}{(3x-1)(x-3)}$

$=\dfrac{x^2-9+12x-4}{(3x-1)(x-3)}$

$=\dfrac{x^2+12x-13}{(3x-1)(x-3)}$

$=\dfrac{(x+13)(x-1)}{(3x-1)(x-3)}$

39. $\dfrac{-5x-10}{x^2-4}+\dfrac{4x}{x-2}=\dfrac{-5(x+2)}{(x+2)(x-2)}+\dfrac{4x}{x-2}$

$=\dfrac{-5}{x-2}+\dfrac{4x}{x-2}$

$=\dfrac{-5+4x}{x-2}$

40. $\dfrac{p}{p-1}-\dfrac{p}{p+1}=\dfrac{p(p+1)}{(p-1)(p+1)}-\dfrac{p(p-1)}{(p-1)(p+1)}$

$=\dfrac{p^2+p-p^2+p}{(p-1)(p+1)}$

$=\dfrac{2p}{(p-1)(p+1)}$

41. $\dfrac{x-4}{2x}-\dfrac{x-6}{3x}=\dfrac{3(x-4)}{6x}-\dfrac{2(x-6)}{6x}$

$=\dfrac{3x-12-2x+12}{6x}$

$=\dfrac{x}{6x}=\dfrac{1}{6}$

42. $2\left(\dfrac{x+3}{x-2}\right)+2\left(\dfrac{6}{x+4}\right)$

$=\dfrac{2x+6}{x-2}+\dfrac{12}{x+4}$

$=\dfrac{(2x+6)(x+4)}{(x-2)(x+4)}+\dfrac{12(x-2)}{(x-2)(x+4)}$

$=\dfrac{2x^2+14x+24+12x-24}{(x-2)(x+4)}$

$=\dfrac{2x^2+26x}{(x-2)(x+4)}$

$=\dfrac{2x(x+13)}{(x-2)(x+4)}$

43. $\dfrac{x+2}{2}=\dfrac{4}{x}$

$x(x+2)=2(4)$

$x^2+2x=8$

$x^2+2x-8=0$

$(x+4)(x-2)=0$

$x=-4, 2$

Check:

$\dfrac{-4+2}{2}\stackrel{?}{=}\dfrac{4}{-4}$

$-1=-1$

$\dfrac{2+2}{2}\stackrel{?}{=}\dfrac{4}{2}$

$\dfrac{4}{2}=\dfrac{4}{2}$

44. $\dfrac{1}{s}+\dfrac{s}{s+2}=1$

$s(s+2)\dfrac{1}{s}+s(s+2)\dfrac{s}{s+2}=s(s+2)(1)$

$s+2+s^2=s(s+2)$

$s^2+s+2=s^2+2s$

$s+2=2s$

$2=s$

Check:

$\dfrac{1}{2}+\dfrac{2}{2+2}\stackrel{?}{=}1$

$\dfrac{1}{2}+\dfrac{1}{2}\stackrel{?}{=}1$

$1=1$

Copyright © McDougal Littell Inc.
All rights reserved.

Chapter 11 *continued*

45.

$$\frac{1}{x-1}+\frac{1}{x+2}=\frac{3}{x^2+x-2}$$

$$\frac{1}{x-1}+\frac{1}{x+2}=\frac{3}{(x+2)(x-1)}$$

$$\frac{(x+2)(x-1)}{x-1}+\frac{(x+2)(x-1)}{x+2}=\frac{(x+2)(x-1)(3)}{(x+2)(x-1)}$$

$$x+2+x-1=3$$

$$2x+1=3$$

$$2x=2$$

$$x=1$$

Check:

$$\frac{1}{1-1}+\frac{1}{1+2}\stackrel{?}{=}\frac{3}{1^2+1-2}$$

$\frac{1}{0}$ is undefined; no solution

Chapter Test *(p. 685)*

1. $\frac{6}{x}=\frac{17}{5}$

$30=17x$

$\frac{30}{17}=x$

Check:

$6\div\frac{30}{17}\stackrel{?}{=}\frac{17}{5}$

$6\cdot\frac{17}{30}\stackrel{?}{=}\frac{17}{5}$

$\frac{17}{5}=\frac{17}{5}$

2.

$$\frac{x}{4}=\frac{x+8}{x}$$

$$x^2=4x+32$$

$$x^2-4x-32=0$$

$$(x-8)(x+4)=0$$

$$x=8,-4$$

Check:

$\frac{8}{4}\stackrel{?}{=}\frac{8+8}{8}$

$2=2$

$\frac{-4}{4}\stackrel{?}{=}\frac{-4+8}{-4}$

$-1=-1$

3.

$$\frac{x}{-3}=\frac{7}{x-10}$$

$$x(x-10)=-21$$

$$x^2-10x=-21$$

$$x^2-10x+21=0$$

$$(x-7)(x-3)=0$$

$$x=7,3$$

Check:

$\frac{7}{-3}\stackrel{?}{=}\frac{7}{7-10}$

$-\frac{7}{3}=-\frac{7}{3}$

$\frac{3}{-3}=\frac{7}{3-10}$

4. $\frac{x}{x^2+4}=\frac{4}{5x}$

$5x^2=4x^2+16$

$x^2=16$

$x=\pm4$

Check:

$\frac{4}{4^2+4}\stackrel{?}{=}\frac{4}{5(4)}$

$\frac{4}{20}=\frac{4}{20}$

$\frac{-4}{(-4)^2+4}\stackrel{?}{=}\frac{4}{5(-4)}$

$-\frac{4}{20}=-\frac{4}{20}$

5. $y=4x$; directly

x	1	2	3	4
y	4	8	12	16

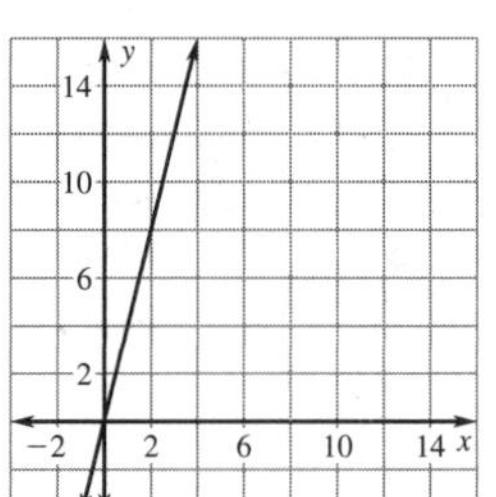

Copyright © McDougal Littell Inc.
All rights reserved.

6. $y = \dfrac{50}{x}$; inversely

x	1	2	3	4
y	50	25	$16\frac{2}{3}$	$12\frac{1}{2}$

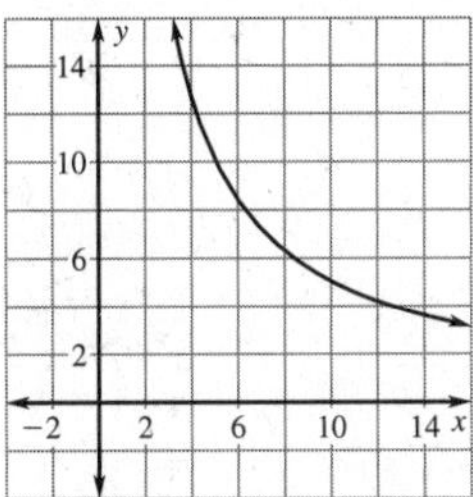

7. $y = \dfrac{9}{2}x$; directly

x	1	2	3	4
y	4.5	9	13.5	18

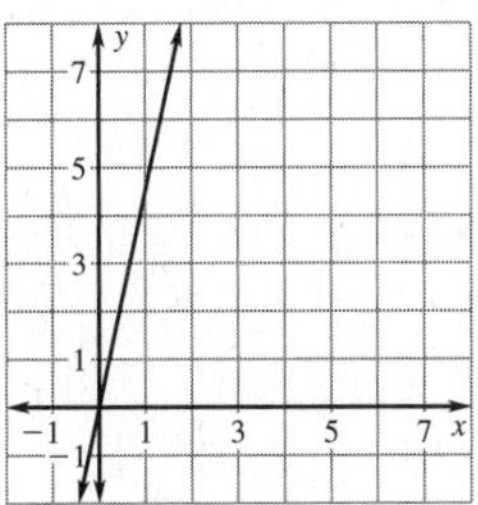

8. $y = \dfrac{15}{2x}$; inversely

x	1	2	3	4
y	7.5	3.75	2.5	1.875

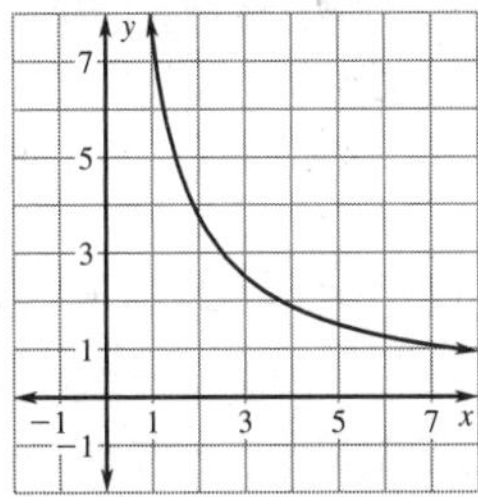

9. $\dfrac{56x^6}{4x^4} = 14x^2$

10. $\dfrac{5x^2 - 15x}{15x^4} = \dfrac{5x(x-3)}{15x^4} = \dfrac{x-3}{3x^3}$

11. $\dfrac{x^2 - x - 6}{x^2 - 4} = \dfrac{(x+2)(x-3)}{(x+2)(x-2)} = \dfrac{x-3}{x-2}$

12. $\dfrac{2x - 14}{3x^2 - 21x} = \dfrac{2(x-7)}{3x(x-7)} = \dfrac{2}{3x}$

13. $\dfrac{x^2 - 1}{2x^2 + x - 1} = \dfrac{(x+1)(x-1)}{(2x-1)(x+1)} = \dfrac{x-1}{2x-1}$

14. $\dfrac{2x^2 + 12x + 18}{x^2 - x - 12} = \dfrac{2(x^2 + 6x + 9)}{(x+3)(x-4)}$

$= \dfrac{2(x+3)(x+3)}{(x+3)(x-4)}$

$= \dfrac{2(x+3)}{x-4}$

15. $\dfrac{6x^2}{8x} \cdot \dfrac{-4x^3}{2x^2} = \dfrac{2 \cdot 3 \cdot -2 \cdot 2 \cdot x^5}{2 \cdot 2 \cdot 2 \cdot 2 \cdot x^3} = -\dfrac{3x^2}{2}$

16. $\dfrac{x^3 + x^2}{x^2 - 16} \cdot \dfrac{x + 4}{3x^4 + x^3 - 2x^2}$

$= \dfrac{x^2(x+1)}{(x+4)(x-4)} \cdot \dfrac{x+4}{x^2(3x^2 + x - 2)}$

$= \dfrac{x+1}{(x-4)(3x-2)(x+1)}$

17. $\dfrac{3x^2 - 6x}{x^2 - 6x + 9} \cdot \dfrac{x^2 - x - 6}{x^2 - 4}$

$= \dfrac{3x(x-2)}{(x-3)(x-3)} \cdot \dfrac{(x-3)(x+2)}{(x+2)(x-2)}$

$= \dfrac{3x}{x-3}$

18. $\dfrac{3x^2 + 6x}{4x} \div \dfrac{15}{8x^2} = \dfrac{3x(x+2)}{4x} \cdot \dfrac{8x^2}{15}$

$= \dfrac{2x^2(x+2)}{5}$

19. $\dfrac{x+3}{x^3 - x^2 - 6x} \div \dfrac{x^2 - 9}{x}$

$= \dfrac{x+3}{x(x^2 - x - 6)} \cdot \dfrac{x}{(x+3)(x-3)}$

$= \dfrac{(x+3)}{x(x+2)(x-3)} \cdot \dfrac{x}{(x+3)(x-3)}$

$= \dfrac{1}{(x+2)(x-3)^2}$

20. $\dfrac{x^2}{x-1} \div \dfrac{x}{x^2 + x - 2} = \dfrac{x^2}{x-1} \cdot \dfrac{(x+2)(x-1)}{x}$

$= x(x+2)$

21. $\dfrac{12x - 4}{x-1} + \dfrac{4x}{x-1} = \dfrac{16x - 4}{x-1}$

$= \dfrac{4(4x-1)}{x-1}$

22. $\dfrac{6(2y+1)}{y^2 - 100} - \dfrac{2(5y-7)}{y^2 - 100} = \dfrac{12y + 6 - 10y + 14}{y^2 - 100}$

$= \dfrac{2y + 20}{y^2 - 100}$

$= \dfrac{2(y+10)}{(y+10)(y-10)}$

$= \dfrac{2}{y-10}$

Copyright © McDougal Littell Inc.
All rights reserved.

23. $\frac{5}{2x^2} + \frac{4}{3x} = \frac{15}{6x^2} + \frac{8x}{6x^2}$

$= \frac{15 + 8x}{6x^2}$

$= \frac{8x + 15}{6x^2}$

24. $\frac{4}{x+3} + \frac{3x}{x-2} = \frac{4(x-2)}{(x+3)(x-2)} + \frac{3x(x+3)}{(x+3)(x-2)}$

$= \frac{4x - 8 + 3x^2 + 9x}{(x+3)(x-2)}$

$= \frac{3x^2 + 13x - 8}{(x+3)(x-2)}$

25. $\frac{8}{5x} - \frac{4}{x^2} = \frac{8x}{5x^2} - \frac{20}{5x^2}$

$= \frac{8x - 20}{5x^2}$

$= \frac{4(2x-5)}{5x^2}$

26. $\frac{5x+1}{x-3} - \frac{2x}{x-1} = \frac{(5x+1)(x-1) - 2x(x-3)}{(x-3)(x-1)}$

$= \frac{5x^2 - 4x - 1 - 2x^2 + 6x}{(x-3)(x-1)}$

$= \frac{3x^2 + 2x - 1}{(x-3)(x-1)}$

$= \frac{(3x-1)(x+1)}{(x-3)(x-1)}$

27. $\frac{3}{4x-9} = \frac{x}{3}$

$9 = x(4x - 9)$

$9 = 4x^2 - 9x$

$0 = 4x^2 - 9x - 9$

$a = 4, b = -9, c = -9$

$x = \frac{-(-9) \pm \sqrt{(-9)^2 - 4(4)(-9)}}{2(4)}$

$= \frac{9 \pm \sqrt{81 + 144}}{8}$

$= \frac{9 \pm \sqrt{225}}{8}$

$= \frac{9 \pm 15}{8}$

$x = \frac{9 + 15}{8} = 3$ or $x = \frac{9 - 15}{8} = \frac{-6}{8} = -\frac{3}{4}$

Check:

$\frac{3}{4(3) - 9} \stackrel{?}{=} \frac{3}{3}$

$1 = 1$

$\frac{3}{4(-\frac{3}{4}) - 9} \stackrel{?}{=} -\frac{3}{4} \div 3$

$-\frac{3}{12} \stackrel{?}{=} -\frac{3}{4} \cdot \frac{1}{3}$

$-\frac{1}{4} = -\frac{1}{4}$

28. $\frac{5}{9} + \frac{2}{9x} = \frac{3}{x}$

$\frac{9x(5)}{9} + \frac{9x(2)}{9x} = \frac{3(9x)}{x}$

$5x + 2 = 27$

$5x = 25$

$x = 5$

Check:

$\frac{5}{9} + \frac{2}{9(5)} \stackrel{?}{=} \frac{3}{5}$

$\frac{25}{45} + \frac{2}{45} \stackrel{?}{=} \frac{3}{5}$

$\frac{27}{45} \stackrel{?}{=} \frac{3}{5}$

$\frac{3}{5} = \frac{3}{5}$

29. $\frac{x}{7} - \frac{6}{x} = -\frac{1}{7}$

$7x\left(\frac{x}{7}\right) - 7x\left(\frac{6}{x}\right) = 7x\left(\frac{1}{7}\right)$

$x^2 - 42 = x$

$x^2 - x - 42 = 0$

$(x + 6)(x - 7) = 0$

$x = -6, 7$

Check:

$-\frac{6}{7} - \frac{6}{-6} \stackrel{?}{=} \frac{1}{7}$

$-\frac{6}{7} + 1 \stackrel{?}{=} \frac{1}{7}$

$\frac{1}{7} = \frac{1}{7}$

$\frac{7}{7} - \frac{6}{7} \stackrel{?}{=} \frac{1}{7}$

$\frac{1}{7} = \frac{1}{7}$

30. $\frac{3}{u+2} = \frac{1}{u-2}$

$3(u - 2) = u + 2$

$3u - 6 = u + 2$

$2u - 6 = 2$

$2u = 8$

$u = 4$

Check:

$\frac{3}{4+2} \stackrel{?}{=} \frac{1}{4-2}$

$\frac{1}{2} = \frac{1}{2}$

Copyright © McDougal Littell Inc.
All rights reserved.

31.
$$\frac{1}{4} - \frac{6}{x} = \frac{3}{x}$$
$$4x\left(\frac{1}{4}\right) - 4x\left(\frac{6}{x}\right) = 4x\left(\frac{3}{x}\right)$$
$$x - 24 = 12$$
$$x = 36$$

Check:
$$\frac{1}{4} - \frac{6}{36} \stackrel{?}{=} \frac{3}{36}$$
$$\frac{1}{4} - \frac{1}{6} \stackrel{?}{=} \frac{1}{12}$$
$$\frac{3}{12} - \frac{2}{12} \stackrel{?}{=} \frac{1}{12}$$
$$\frac{1}{12} = \frac{1}{12}$$

32.
$$\frac{x}{x+1} + \frac{x}{x-2} = 2$$
$$\frac{(x+1)(x-2)(x)}{x+1} + \frac{(x+1)(x-2)(x)}{x-2} = (x+1)(x-2)(2)$$
$$x(x-2) + x(x+1) = (x^2 - x - 2)(2)$$
$$x^2 - 2x + x^2 + x = 2x^2 - 2x - 4$$
$$2x^2 - 2x + x = 2x^2 - 2x - 4$$
$$-2x + x = -2x - 4$$
$$-x = -2x - 4$$
$$x = -4$$

Check:
$$\frac{-4}{-4+1} + \frac{-4}{-4-2} \stackrel{?}{=} 2$$
$$\frac{-4}{-3} + \frac{-4}{-6} \stackrel{?}{=} 2$$
$$\frac{4}{3} + \frac{2}{3} \stackrel{?}{=} 2$$
$$2 = 2$$

33. inverse variation

34.
$$\frac{x}{60} + \frac{x}{20} = 1$$
$$\frac{x}{60} + \frac{3x}{60} = 1$$
$$\frac{x + 3x}{60} = 1$$
$$\frac{4x}{60} = 1$$
$$\frac{x}{15} = 1$$
$$x = 15 \text{ hours}$$

Chapter Standardized Test (p. 686)

1. B
$$\frac{4}{y+9} = \frac{6}{y-7}$$
$$4(y-7) = 6(y+9)$$
$$4y - 28 = 6y + 54$$
$$-2y = 82$$
$$y = -41$$

Copyright © McDougal Littell Inc.
All rights reserved.

2. C;

$$\begin{aligned} xy &= k \\ 9(36) &= k \\ 324 &= k \\ 3y &= 324 \\ y &= 108 \end{aligned}$$

3. D;

$$\begin{aligned} \frac{x^3 - 10x^2 + 9x}{x^2 + 5x - 6} &= \frac{x(x^2 - 10x + 9)}{(x + 6)(x - 1)} \\ &= \frac{x(x - 9)(x - 1)}{(x + 6)(x - 1)} \\ &= \frac{x(x - 9)}{x + 6} \end{aligned}$$

4. C; $\frac{9x^2}{4x} \cdot \frac{16x^3}{x^5} = \frac{36}{x}$

5. A;

$$\begin{aligned} \frac{x^2 - 64}{3x^2} \div (x - 8) &= \frac{(x + 8)(x - 8)}{3x^2} \cdot \frac{1}{x - 8} \\ &= \frac{x + 8}{3x^2} \end{aligned}$$

6. D;

$$\begin{aligned} \frac{x + 2}{(x + 5)(x - 5)} + \frac{3}{(x + 5)(x - 5)} &= \frac{x + 5}{(x + 5)(x - 5)} \\ &= \frac{1}{x - 5} \end{aligned}$$

7. D;

$$\begin{aligned} \frac{2x + 9}{x + 5} - \frac{x - 4}{x - 2} &= \frac{(x - 2)(2x + 9)}{(x + 5)(x - 2)} - \frac{(x + 5)(x - 4)}{(x + 5)(x - 2)} \\ &= \frac{2x^2 + 5x - 18 - (x^2 + x - 20)}{(x + 5)(x - 2)} \\ &= \frac{2x^2 + 5x - 18 - x^2 - x + 20}{(x + 5)(x - 2)} \\ &= \frac{x^2 + 4x + 2}{(x + 5)(x - 2)} \end{aligned}$$

8. D;

$$\begin{aligned} \frac{4}{x + 2} + \frac{3}{x} &= 1 \\ x(x + 2)\frac{4}{x + 2} + x(x + 2)\frac{3}{x} &= x(x + 2)(1) \\ 4x + 3(x + 2) &= x^2 + 2x \\ 4x + 3x + 6 &= x^2 + 2x \\ 7x + 6 &= x^2 + 2x \\ 0 &= x^2 - 5x - 6 = 0 \\ 0 &= (x - 6)(x + 1) \\ x &= 6, -1 \end{aligned}$$

9. B; $\frac{x(x + 7)}{2x(3x + 21)} = \frac{x + 7}{2 \cdot 3(x + 7)} = \frac{1}{6}$

Maintaining Skills *(p. 687)*

1. $\sqrt{\frac{32}{49}} = \frac{\sqrt{16 \cdot 2}}{7} = \frac{4\sqrt{2}}{7}$

2. $\sqrt{\frac{32}{64}} = \frac{\sqrt{16 \cdot 2}}{8} = \frac{4\sqrt{2}}{8} = \frac{\sqrt{2}}{2}$

3. $\sqrt{\frac{125}{225}} = \sqrt{\frac{25 \cdot 5}{25 \cdot 9}} = \sqrt{\frac{5}{9}} = \frac{\sqrt{5}}{3}$

4. $\sqrt{\frac{162}{4}} = \frac{\sqrt{81 \cdot 2}}{2} = \frac{9\sqrt{2}}{2}$

5. $\sqrt{\frac{363}{144}} = \frac{\sqrt{121 \cdot 3}}{12} = \frac{11\sqrt{3}}{12}$

6. $\sqrt{\frac{288}{400}} = \frac{\sqrt{144 \cdot 2}}{20} = \frac{12\sqrt{2}}{20} = \frac{3\sqrt{2}}{5}$

7. $\sqrt{\frac{72}{9}} = \sqrt{8} = \sqrt{4 \cdot 2} = 2\sqrt{2}$

8. $\sqrt{\frac{14}{200}} = \sqrt{\frac{7}{100}} = \frac{\sqrt{7}}{10}$

9. $a^2 - 18a + 81 = (a - 9)^2$

10. $x^2 + 6x + 9 = (x + 3)^2$

11. $y^2 - 22y + 121 = (y - 11)^2$

12. $169 + 26m + m^2 = (13 + m)^2$ or $(m + 13)^2$

13. $225 + 30r + r^2 = (15 + r)^2$ or $(r + 15)^2$

14. $100 - 20t + t^2 = (10 - t)^2$ or $(t - 10)^2$

15. $4x^2 + 20x + 25 = (2x + 5)^2$

16. $9b^2 - 6b + 1 = (3b - 1)^2$

17. $16 - 56x + 49x^2 = (4 - 7x)^2$ or $(7x - 4)^2$

Copyright © McDougal Littell Inc.
All rights reserved.

Chapter 12

Chapter Opener

Think & Discuss (p. 689)

1. No; for a height (input) of 44.3 feet there are two different revolutions per minute (outputs).
2. Sample answer: a range of 12 to 17

Chapter Readiness Quiz (p. 690)

1. D; $\frac{\sqrt{36}}{\sqrt{9}} = \frac{6}{3} = 2$
2. A; $\sqrt{140} = \sqrt{4 \cdot 35} = 2\sqrt{35}$
3. B; $x^2 - 3x - 18 = (x - 6)(x + 3)$

12.1 Developing Concepts: Explore *(p. 691)*

x	−2	−1	0	1	2	3	4	5
y	und.	und.	0	1	1.4	1.7	2	2.2

$\sqrt{x}$ is not defined for $x = -2$ or $x = -1$.

Think About It *(p. 691)*

1. $\sqrt{x+1}$ is defined if and only if $x + 1 \geq 0$. So, $x \geq -1$ and the domain is all real numbers greater than or equal to -1. Since $y = \sqrt{x+1}$, $y \geq 0$, and the range is all non-negative real numbers.
2. $\sqrt{x}$ is defined if and only if $x \geq 0$, so the domain is all nonnegative real numbers. Since $y = 2 + \sqrt{x} \geq 2$ for all x in the domain, the range is all real numbers greater than or equal to 2.

Lesson 12.1

12.1 Checkpoint (pp. 692–694)

1. $y = \sqrt{x}$
domain: all nonnegative real numbers

x	y
0	$y = \sqrt{0} = 0$
1	$y = \sqrt{1} = 1$
2	$y = \sqrt{2} \approx 1.41$
3	$y = \sqrt{3} \approx 1.73$
4	$y = \sqrt{4} = 2$
5	$y = \sqrt{5} \approx 2.24$

2. $y = 3\sqrt{x}$
domain: all nonnegative real numbers

x	y
0	$y = 3\sqrt{0} = 0$
1	$y = 3\sqrt{1} = 3$
2	$y = 3\sqrt{2} \approx 4.24$
3	$y = 3\sqrt{3} \approx 5.20$
4	$y = 3\sqrt{4} = 6$
5	$y = 3\sqrt{5} \approx 6.71$

3. $y = \sqrt{2x}$
domain: all nonnegative real numbers

x	y
0	$y = \sqrt{2 \cdot 0} = 0$
1	$y = \sqrt{2 \cdot 1} \approx 1.41$
2	$y = \sqrt{2 \cdot 2} = 2$
3	$y = \sqrt{2 \cdot 3} \approx 2.45$
4	$y = \sqrt{2 \cdot 4} \approx 2.83$
5	$y = \sqrt{2 \cdot 5} \approx 3.16$

4. $y = \sqrt{x} - 1$
domain: all nonnegative real numbers

x	y
0	$y = \sqrt{0} - 1 = -1$
1	$y = \sqrt{1} - 1 = 0$
2	$y = \sqrt{2} - 1 \approx 0.41$
3	$y = \sqrt{3} - 1 \approx 0.73$
4	$y = \sqrt{4} - 1 = 1$
5	$y = \sqrt{5} - 1 \approx 1.24$

5. $y = -3\sqrt{x}$
domain: all nonnegative real numbers

x	y
0	$y = -3\sqrt{0} = 0$
1	$y = -3\sqrt{1} = -3$
2	$y = -3\sqrt{2} \approx -4.24$
3	$y = -3\sqrt{3} \approx -5.20$
4	$y = -3\sqrt{4} = -6$
5	$y = -3\sqrt{5} \approx -6.71$

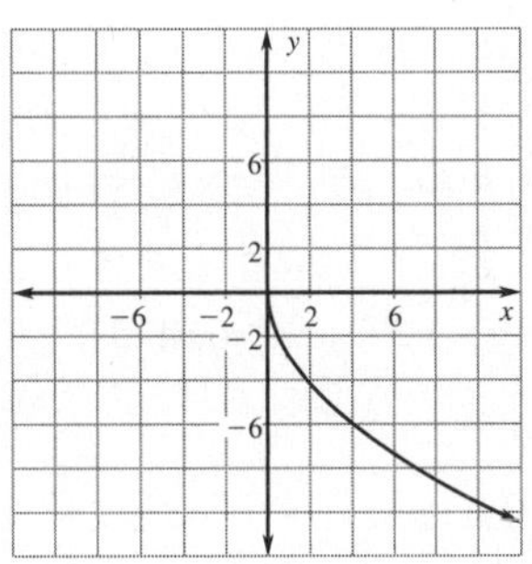

range: all nonpositive real numbers

Copyright © McDougal Littell Inc.
All rights reserved.

6. $y = -2\sqrt{x}$

domain: all nonnegative real numbers

x	y
0	$y = -2\sqrt{0} = 0$
1	$y = -2\sqrt{1} = -2$
2	$y = -2\sqrt{2} \approx -2.83$
3	$y = -2\sqrt{3} \approx -3.46$
4	$y = -2\sqrt{4} = -4$
5	$y = -2\sqrt{5} \approx -4.47$

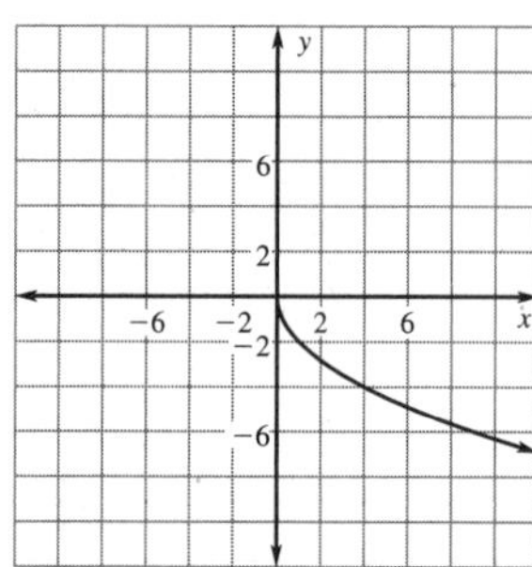

range: all real numbers less than or equal to zero

7. $y = \sqrt{x} + 2$

domain: all nonnegative real numbers

x	y
0	$y = \sqrt{0} + 2 = 2$
1	$y = \sqrt{1} + 2 = 3$
2	$y = \sqrt{2} + 2 \approx 3.41$
3	$y = \sqrt{3} + 2 \approx 3.73$
4	$y = \sqrt{4} + 2 = 4$
5	$y = \sqrt{5} + 2 \approx 4.24$

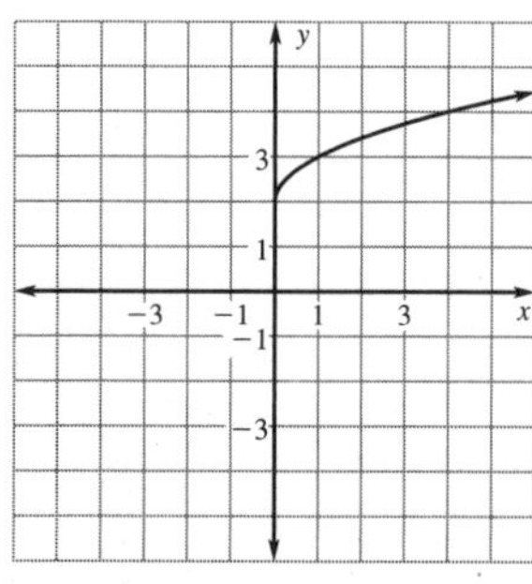

range: all real numbers greater than or equal to 2

8. $y = \sqrt{x} - 2$

domain: all nonnegative real numbers

x	y
0	$y = \sqrt{0} - 2 = -2$
1	$y = \sqrt{1} - 2 = -1$
2	$y = \sqrt{2} - 2 \approx -0.59$
3	$y = \sqrt{3} - 2 \approx -0.27$
4	$y = \sqrt{4} - 2 = 0$
5	$y = \sqrt{5} - 2 \approx 0.24$

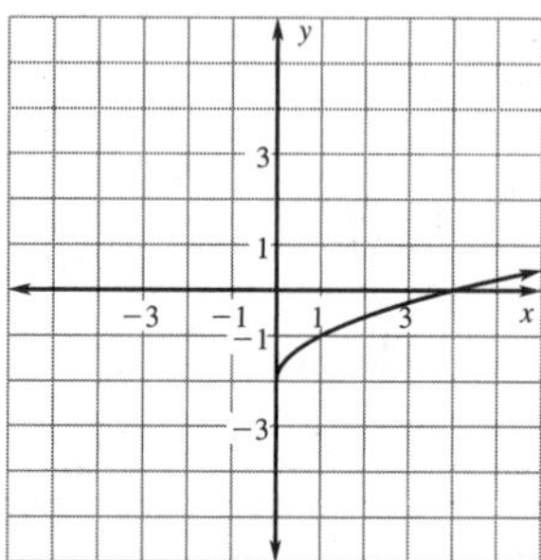

range: all real numbers greater than or equal to -2

9. $y = 3 - \sqrt{x}$

domain: all nonnegative real numbers

x	y
0	$y = 3 - \sqrt{0} = 3$
1	$y = 3 - \sqrt{1} = 2$
2	$y = 3 - \sqrt{2} \approx 1.59$
3	$y = 3 - \sqrt{3} \approx 1.27$
4	$y = 3 - \sqrt{4} = 1$
5	$y = 3 - \sqrt{5} \approx 0.76$

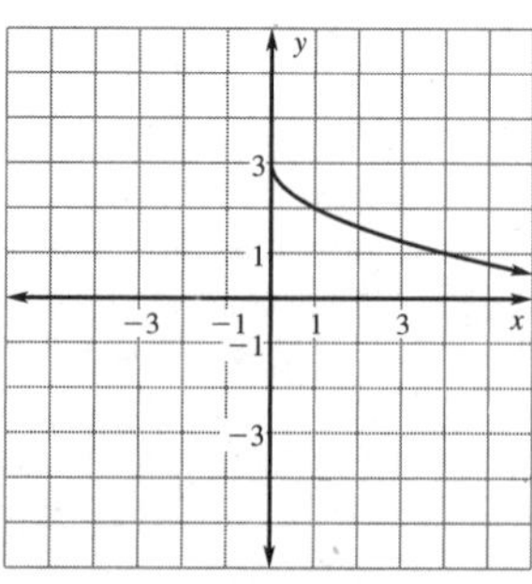

range: all real numbers less than or equal to 3

Copyright © McDougal Littell Inc.
All rights reserved.

10. $y = 2\sqrt{x} + 1$

domain: all nonnegative real numbers

x	y
0	$y = 2\sqrt{0} + 1 = 1$
1	$y = 2\sqrt{1} + 1 = 3$
2	$y = 2\sqrt{2} + 1 \approx 3.83$
3	$y = 2\sqrt{3} + 1 \approx 4.64$
4	$y = 2\sqrt{4} + 1 = 5$
5	$y = 2\sqrt{5} + 1 \approx 5.47$

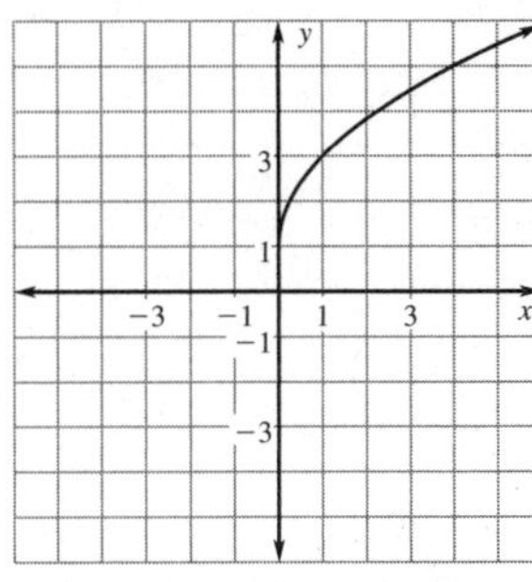

range: all real numbers greater than or equal to 1

11. $h = \sqrt{0.6A}$

$0.6A \geq 0$

$A \geq 0$

domain: all nonnegative real numbers

A	h
0	$h = \sqrt{0.6 \cdot 0} = 0$
1	$h = \sqrt{0.6 \cdot 1} \approx 0.77$
2	$h = \sqrt{0.6 \cdot 2} \approx 1.10$
3	$h = \sqrt{0.6 \cdot 3} \approx 1.34$
4	$h = \sqrt{0.6 \cdot 4} \approx 1.55$
5	$h = \sqrt{0.6 \cdot 5} \approx 1.73$

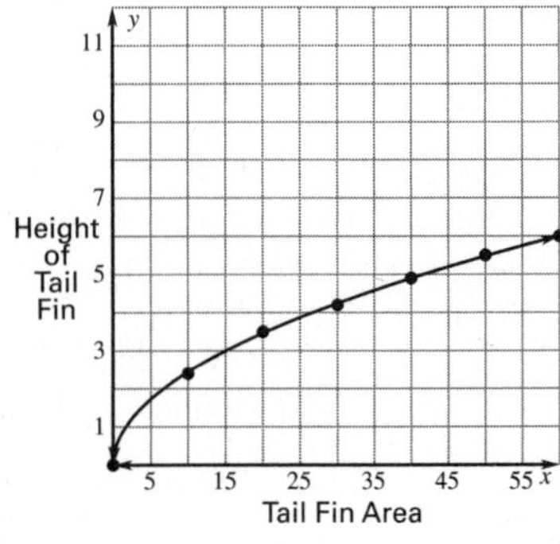

12.1 Guided Practice (p. 695)

1. A square root function has the form of $y = \sqrt{x}$.

2. domain

3. $y = 4\sqrt{x}$

x	0	1	2	3	4
y	0	4	5.7	6.9	8

4. $y = -\sqrt{x}$

x	0	1	2	3	4
y	0	−1	−1.4	−1.7	−2

5. $y = \sqrt{x} + 4$

x	0	1	2	3	4
y	4	7	8.2	9.2	10

6. $y = 6\sqrt{x} - 3$

x	0	1	2	3	4
y	−3	3	5.5	7.4	9

7. $y = \sqrt{x + 2}$

x	0	1	2	3	4
y	1.4	1.7	2	2.2	2.4

8. $y = \sqrt{4x - 1}$

x	0	1	2	3	4
y	undefined	1.7	2.6	3.3	3.9

9. $y = 5\sqrt{x}$

domain: all nonnegative real numbers

range: all nonnegative real numbers

10. $y = \sqrt{x}$

domain: all nonnegative real numbers

range: all nonnegative real numbers

11. $y = \sqrt{x} - 10$

domain: all nonnegative real numbers

range: all real numbers ≥ -10

12. $y = \sqrt{x} + 6$

domain: all nonnegative real numbers

range: all real numbers ≥ 6

13. $y = \sqrt{x + 5}$

domain: all real numbers ≥ -5

range: all nonnegative real numbers

14. $y = \sqrt{x - 10}$

domain: all real numbers ≥ 10

range: all nonnegative real numbers

Copyright © McDougal Littell Inc.
All rights reserved.

15. $y = 4\sqrt{x}$

domain: all nonnegative real numbers

x	y
0	$y = 4\sqrt{0} = 0$
1	$y = 4\sqrt{1} = 4$
2	$y = 4\sqrt{2} \approx 5.7$
3	$y = 4\sqrt{3} \approx 6.9$
4	$y = 4\sqrt{4} = 8$
5	$y = 4\sqrt{5} \approx 8.9$

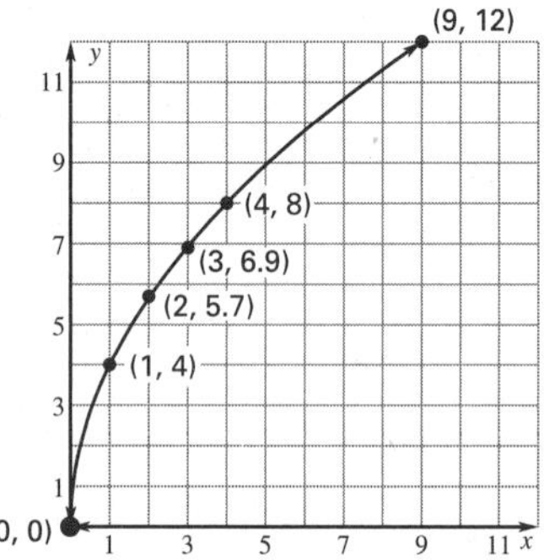

16. $y = \sqrt{x} + 5$

domain: all nonnegative real numbers

x	y
0	$y = \sqrt{0} + 5 = 5$
1	$y = \sqrt{1} + 5 = 6$
2	$y = \sqrt{2} + 5 = 6.4$
3	$y = \sqrt{3} + 5 = 6.7$
4	$y = \sqrt{4} + 5 = 7$
5	$y = \sqrt{5} + 5 = 7.2$

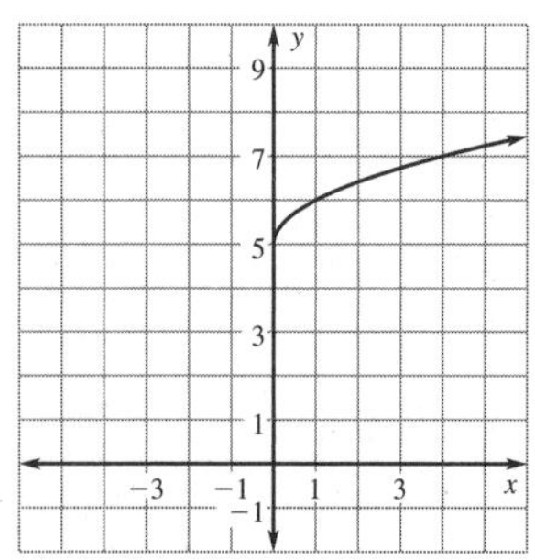

17. $y = 3\sqrt{x + 1}$

domain: all real numbers ≥ -1

x	y
-1	$y = 3\sqrt{-1 + 1} = 0$
0	$y = 3\sqrt{0 + 1} = 3$
1	$y = 3\sqrt{1 + 1} \approx 4.2$
2	$y = 3\sqrt{2 + 1} \approx 5.2$
3	$y = 3\sqrt{3 + 1} = 6$
4	$y = 3\sqrt{4 + 1} \approx 6.7$

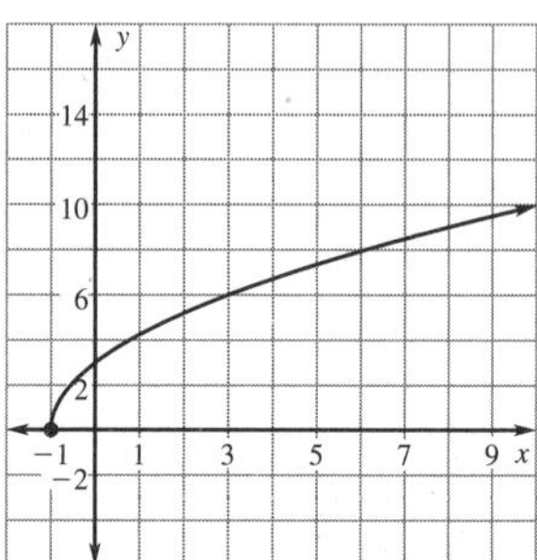

18. $f = 120\sqrt{p}$

domain: all nonnegative real numbers

p	f
0	$f = 120\sqrt{0} = 0$
1	$f = 120\sqrt{1} = 120$
2	$f = 120\sqrt{2} \approx 169.7$
3	$f = 120\sqrt{3} \approx 207.8$
4	$f = 120\sqrt{4} = 240$
5	$f = 120\sqrt{5} \approx 268.3$

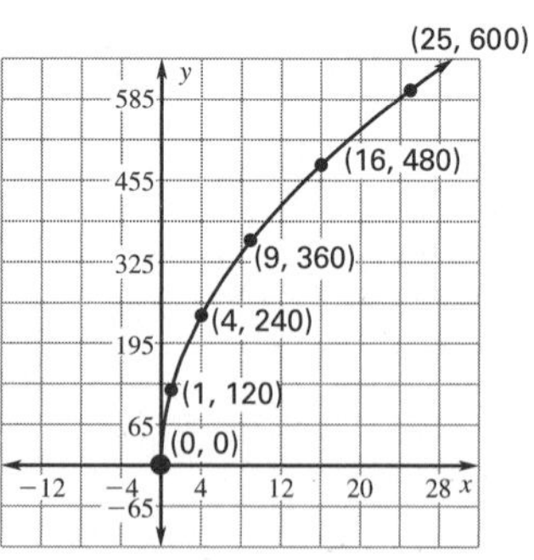

19. $f = 120\sqrt{100} = 120(10) = 1200$ gal/min

Copyright © McDougal Littell Inc.
All rights reserved.

12.1 Practice and Applications (pp. 695–697)

20. $y = 2\sqrt{x}$
$y = 2\sqrt{9} = 2(3) = 6$

21. $y = -2\sqrt{x}$
$y = -2\sqrt{25} = -2(5) = -10$

22. $y = \sqrt{32x}$
$y = \sqrt{32(2)} = \sqrt{64} = 8$

23. $y = \sqrt{3x} = \sqrt{3(12)} = \sqrt{36} = 6$

24. $y = \sqrt{x} + 4$
$y = \sqrt{4} + 4 = 2 + 4 = 6$

25. $y = 10 - \sqrt{x}$
$y = 10 - \sqrt{16} = 10 - 4 = 6$

26. $y = \sqrt{x - 7}$
$y = \sqrt{56 - 7} = \sqrt{49} = 7$

27. $y = \sqrt{3x - 5}$
$y = \sqrt{3(7) - 5} = \sqrt{16} = 4$

28. $y = \sqrt{21 - 2x}$
$y = \sqrt{21 - 2(-2)} = \sqrt{25} = 5$

29. $y = 6\sqrt{x}$
domain: all nonnegative real numbers

x	y
0	$y = 6\sqrt{0} = 0$
1	$y = 6\sqrt{1} = 6$
2	$y = 6\sqrt{2} \approx 8.5$
3	$y = 6\sqrt{3} \approx 10.4$
4	$y = 6\sqrt{4} = 12$
5	$y = 6\sqrt{5} \approx 13.4$

30. $y = \sqrt{x - 17}$
domain: all real numbers ≥ 17

x	y
17	$y = \sqrt{17 - 17} = 0$
18	$y = \sqrt{18 - 17} = 1$
19	$y = \sqrt{19 - 17} \approx 1.4$
20	$y = \sqrt{20 - 17} \approx 1.7$
21	$y = \sqrt{21 - 17} = 2$
22	$y = \sqrt{22 - 17} \approx 2.2$

31. $y = \sqrt{3x - 10}$

$3x - 10 \geq 0$
$3x \geq 10$
$x \geq \frac{10}{3} = 3\frac{1}{3}$

domain: all real numbers $\geq 3\frac{1}{3}$

x	y
$3\frac{1}{3}$	$y = \sqrt{3\left(3\frac{1}{3}\right) - 10} = 0$
4	$y = \sqrt{3(4) - 10} \approx 1.4$
5	$y = \sqrt{3(5) - 10} \approx 2.2$
6	$y = \sqrt{3(6) - 10} \approx 2.8$
7	$y = \sqrt{3(7) - 10} \approx 3.3$
8	$y = \sqrt{3(8) - 10} \approx 3.7$

32. $y = \sqrt{x + 1}$
domain: all real numbers ≥ -1

x	y
-1	$y = \sqrt{-1 + 1} = 0$
0	$y = \sqrt{0 + 1} = 1$
1	$y = \sqrt{1 + 1} \approx 1.4$
2	$y = \sqrt{2 + 1} \approx 1.7$
3	$y = \sqrt{3 + 1} \approx 2$
4	$y = \sqrt{4 + 1} \approx 2.2$

33. $y = 4 + \sqrt{x}$
domain: all nonnegative real numbers

x	y
0	$y = 4 + \sqrt{0} = 4$
1	$y = 4 + \sqrt{1} = 5$
2	$y = 4 + \sqrt{2} \approx 5.4$
3	$y = 4 + \sqrt{3} \approx 5.7$
4	$y = 4 + \sqrt{4} = 6$
5	$y = 4 + \sqrt{5} \approx 6.2$

34. $y = \sqrt{x} - 3$
domain: all nonnegative real numbers

x	y
0	$y = \sqrt{0} - 3 = -3$
1	$y = \sqrt{1} - 3 = -2$
2	$y = \sqrt{2} - 3 \approx -1.6$
3	$y = \sqrt{3} - 3 \approx -1.3$
4	$y = \sqrt{4} - 3 = -1$

Copyright © McDougal Littell Inc.
All rights reserved.

35. $y = \sqrt{x + 9}$
domain: all real numbers ≥ -9

x	y
-9	$y = \sqrt{-9 + 9} = 0$
-8	$y = \sqrt{-8 + 9} = 1$
-7	$y = \sqrt{-7 + 9} \approx 1.4$
-6	$y = \sqrt{-6 + 9} \approx 1.7$
-5	$y = \sqrt{-5 + 9} = 2$
-4	$y = \sqrt{-4 + 9} \approx 2.2$

36. $y = 2\sqrt{4x} = 2(2)\sqrt{x} = 4\sqrt{x}$
domain: all nonnegative real numbers

x	y
0	$y = 4\sqrt{0} = 0$
1	$y = 4\sqrt{1} = 4$
2	$y = 4\sqrt{2} \approx 5.7$
3	$y = 4\sqrt{3} \approx 6.9$
4	$y = 4\sqrt{4} = 8$
5	$y = 4\sqrt{5} \approx 8.9$

37. $y = x\sqrt{x}$
domain: all nonnegative real numbers

x	y
0	$y = 0\sqrt{0} = 0$
1	$y = 1\sqrt{1} = 1$
2	$y = 2\sqrt{2} \approx 2.8$
3	$y = 3\sqrt{3} \approx 5.2$
4	$y = 4\sqrt{4} = 8$
5	$y = 5\sqrt{5} \approx 11.2$

38. $S = \sqrt{30(120)(1.0)} = \sqrt{3600} = 60$ mph

39. $S = \sqrt{30(147)(0.4)} = \sqrt{1764} = 42$ mph
Incorrect statement; the driver was going at about 42 mph.

40. $y = 7\sqrt{x}$
domain: all nonnegative real numbers

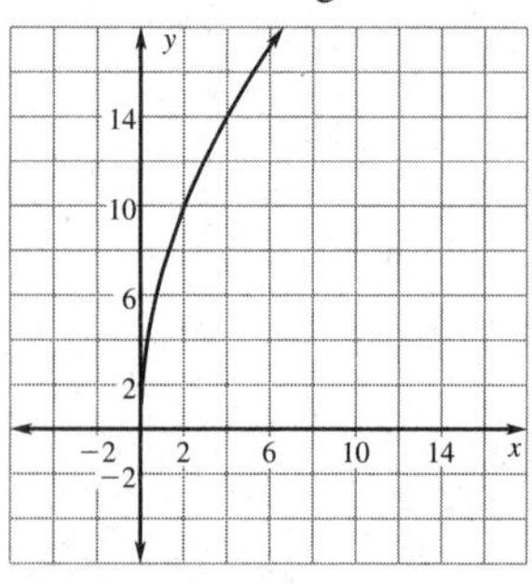

range: all nonnegative real numbers

41. $y = 4\sqrt{x}$
domain: all nonnegative real numbers

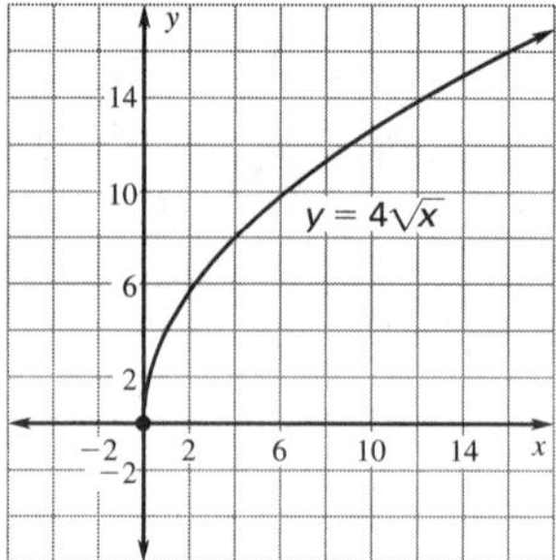

range: all nonnegative real numbers

42. $y = 5\sqrt{x}$
domain: all nonnegative real numbers

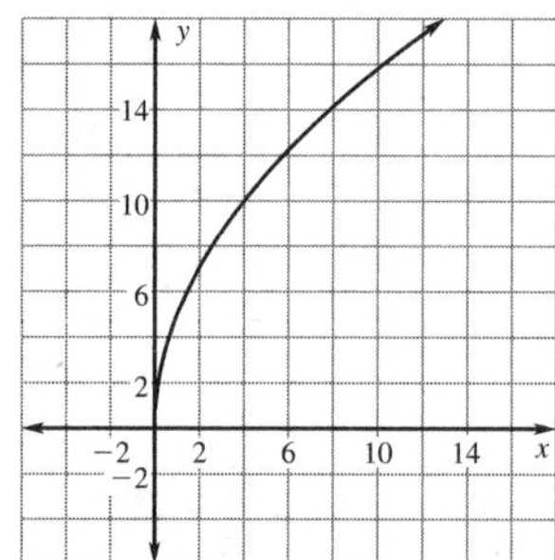

range: all nonnegative real numbers

43. $y = 6\sqrt{x}$
domain: all nonnegative real numbers

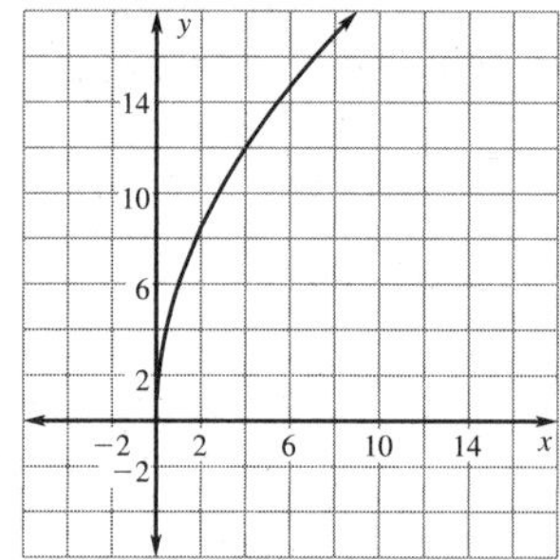

range: all nonnegative real numbers

44. $y = \sqrt{3x}$
domain: all nonnegative real numbers

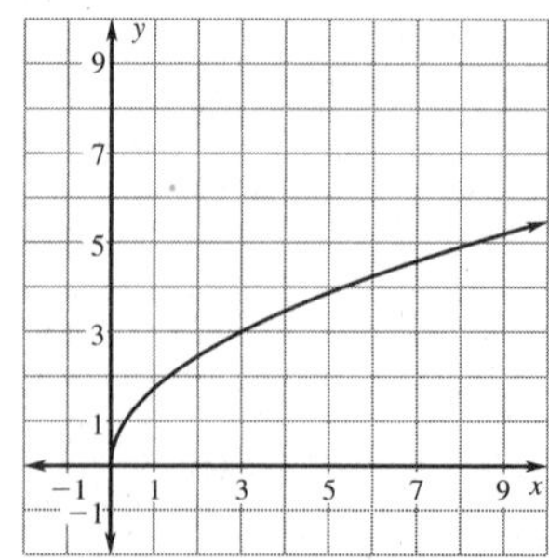

range: all nonnegative real numbers

Copyright © McDougal Littell Inc.
All rights reserved.

45. $y = -\sqrt{2x}$
domain: all nonnegative real numbers

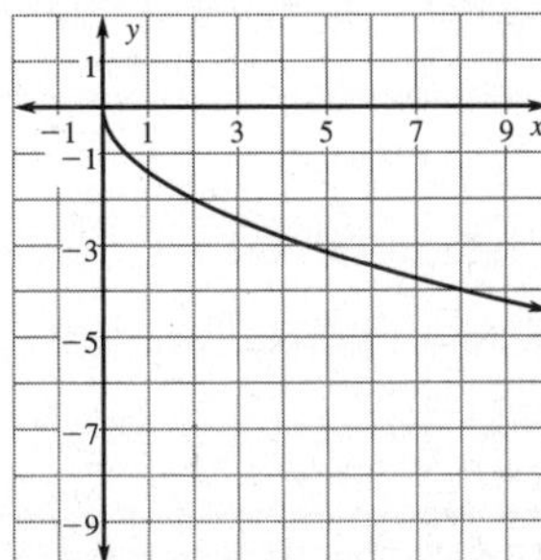

range: all real numbers ≤ 0

46. $y = \sqrt{x} + 4$
domain: all nonnegative real numbers

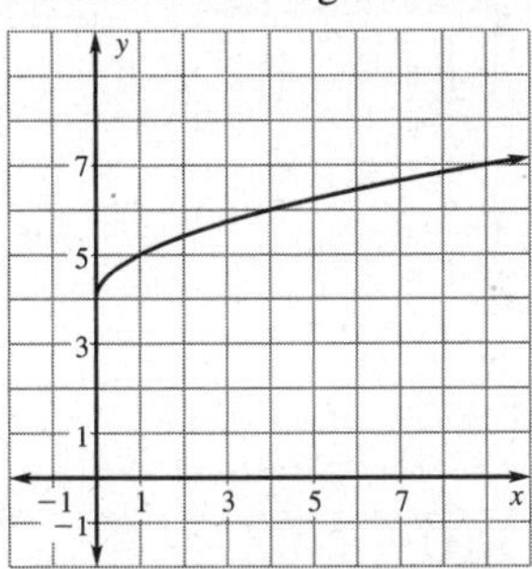

range: all real numbers ≥ 4

47. $y = \sqrt{x} - 3$
domain: all nonnegative real numbers

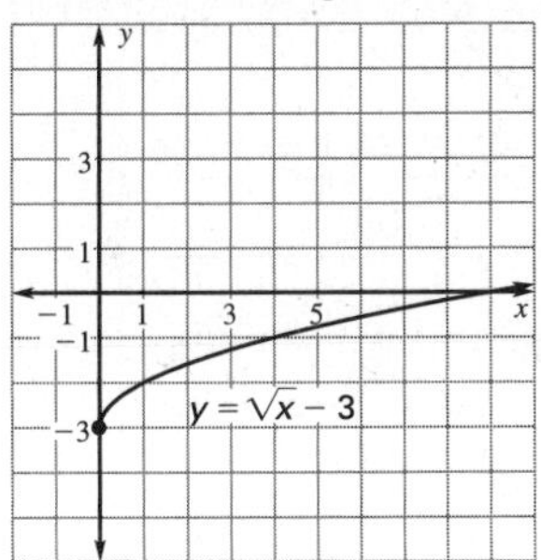

range: all real numbers ≥ -3

48. $y = 5 - \sqrt{x}$
domain: all nonnegative real numbers

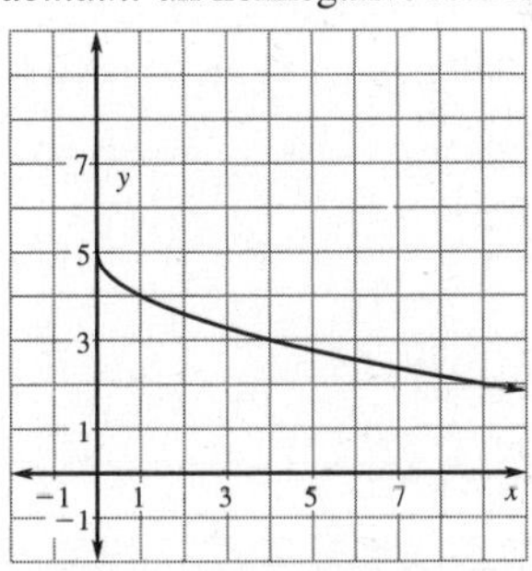

range: all real numbers ≤ 5

49. $y = 6 - \sqrt{x}$
domain: all nonnegative real numbers

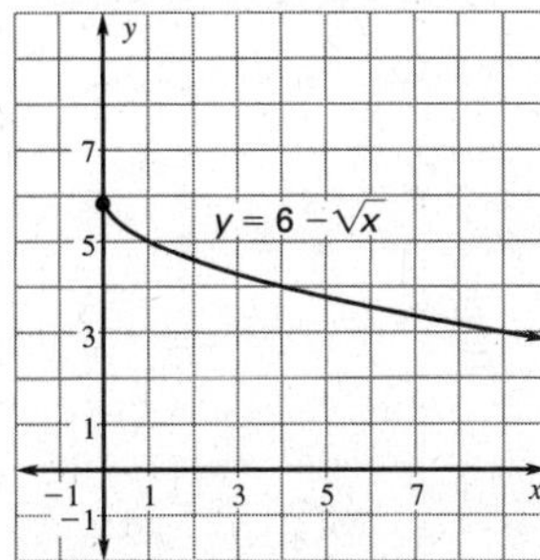

range: all real numbers ≤ 6

50. $y = 2\sqrt{x} + 3$
domain: all nonnegative real numbers

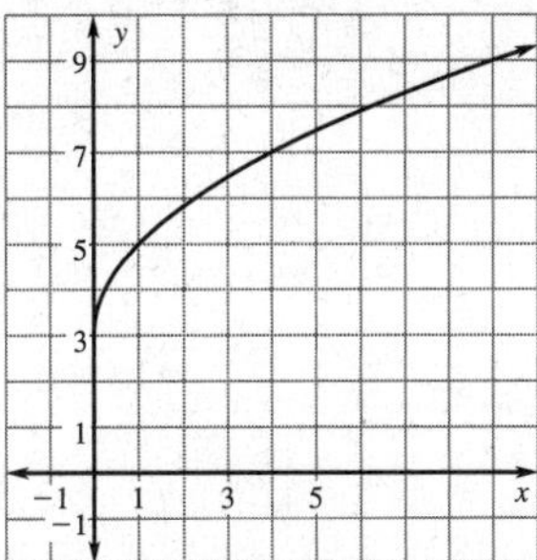

range: all real numbers ≥ 3

51. $y = 5\sqrt{x} - 2$
domain: all nonnegative real numbers

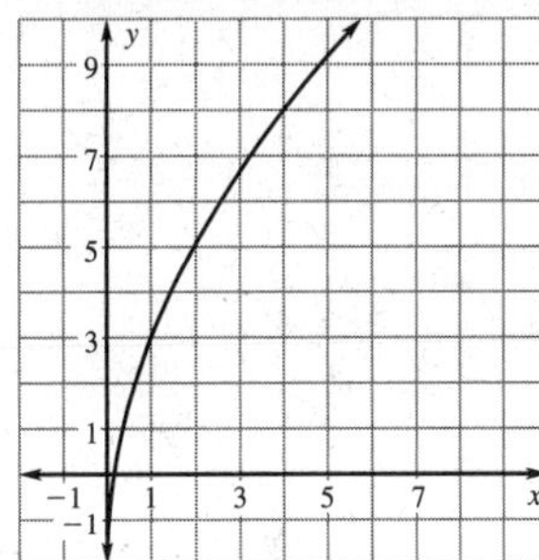

range: all real numbers ≥ -2

52. $y = \sqrt{x - 4}$
domain: all real numbers ≥ 4

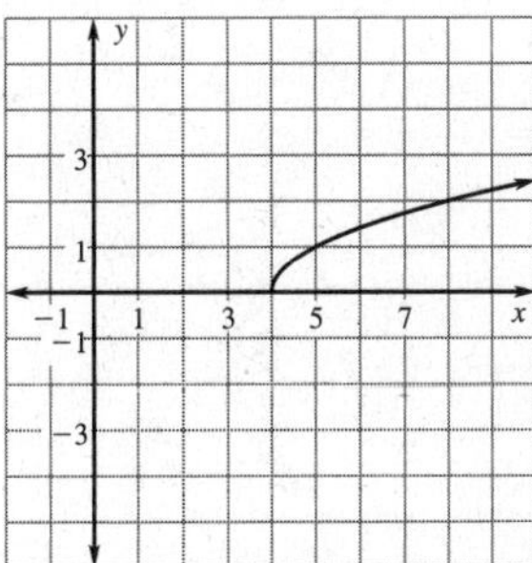

range: all nonnegative real numbers

Copyright © McDougal Littell Inc.
All rights reserved.

53. $y = \sqrt{x + 1}$

domain: all real numbers ≥ -1

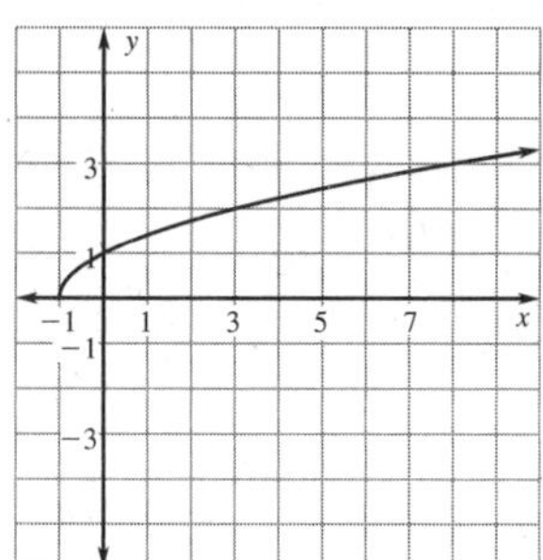

range: all nonnegative real numbers

54. $y = \sqrt{3x + 1}$

$3x + 1 \geq 0$

$3x \geq -1$

$x \geq -\frac{1}{3}$

domain: all real numbers $\geq -\frac{1}{3}$

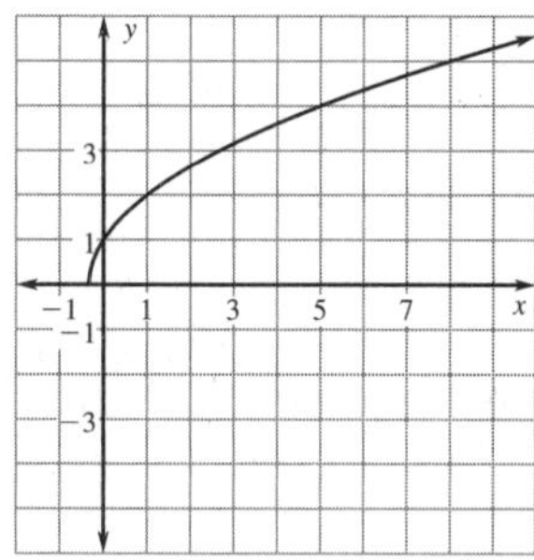

range: all nonnegative real numbers

55. $y = 2\sqrt{4x + 10}$

$4x + 10 \geq 0$

$4x \geq -10$

$x \geq -2\frac{1}{2}$

domain: all real numbers $\geq -2\frac{1}{2}$

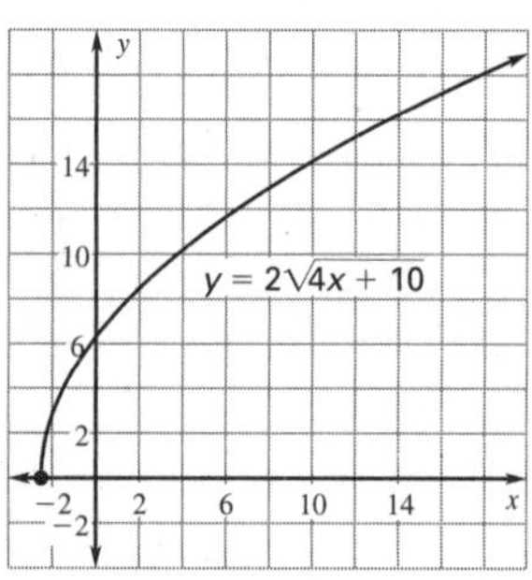

range: all nonnegative real numbers

56. $S = \sqrt{32L}$

domain: all nonnegative real numbers

L	*S*
0	$S = \sqrt{32(0)} = 0$
1	$S = \sqrt{32(1)} \approx 5.7$
2	$S = \sqrt{32(2)} = 8$
3	$S = \sqrt{32(3)} \approx 9.8$
4	$S = \sqrt{32(4)} \approx 11.3$
5	$S = \sqrt{32(5)} \approx 12.6$

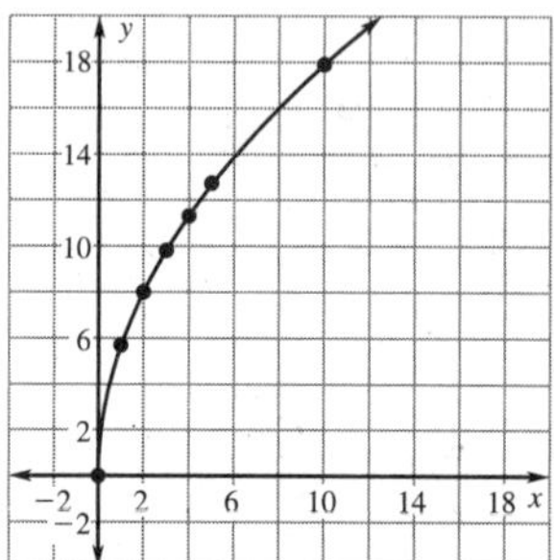

57. Shorter dinosaur: $S = \sqrt{32(1)} = \sqrt{32}$

Taller dinosaur: $S = \sqrt{32(4)} = 2\sqrt{32}$

$\frac{2\sqrt{32}}{1\sqrt{32}} = \frac{2}{1}$; taller dinosaur walks twice as fast.

58. $S = \pi(14)\sqrt{14^2 + h^2}$

h	*S*
0	$S = 14\pi\sqrt{14^2 + 0^2} = 14^2\pi \approx 615.8$
1	$S = 14\pi\sqrt{14^2 + 1^2} \approx 617.3$
2	$S = 14\pi\sqrt{14^2 + 2^2} \approx 622.0$
3	$S = 14\pi\sqrt{14^2 + 3^2} \approx 629.7$
4	$S = 14\pi\sqrt{14^2 + 4^2} \approx 640.4$
5	$S = 14\pi\sqrt{14^2 + 5^2} \approx 653.8$

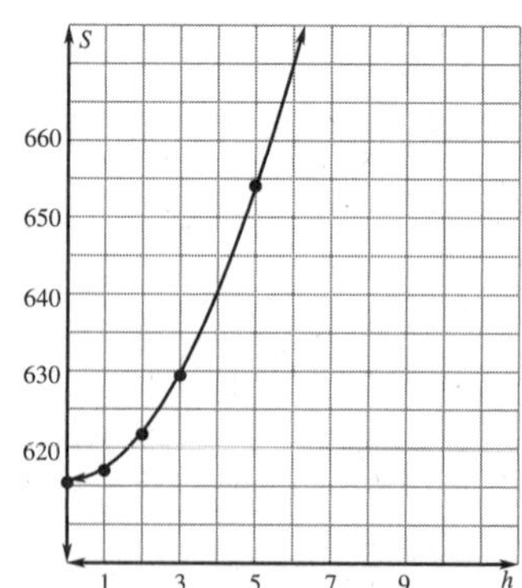

59. $S = \pi(14)\sqrt{14^2 + 30^2}$

$S \approx 1456 \text{ cm}^2$

Copyright © McDougal Littell Inc.
All rights reserved.

60. denominator cannot equal zero, so $\sqrt{x}$ cannot equal 2, therefore x cannot equal 4; also, radicand cannot be less than zero, so x must be non-negative; all non-negative numbers except 4

12.1 Standardized Test Practice (p. 697)

61. D; substitute (0, −3), (1, −1) and (4, 1) to test the function.

$-3 \stackrel{?}{=} 2\sqrt{0} - 3$

$-3 = -3$

$-1 \stackrel{?}{=} 2\sqrt{1} - 3$

$-1 = -1$

$1 \stackrel{?}{=} 2\sqrt{4} - 3$

$1 = 1$

12.1 Mixed Review (p. 697)

62. $\sqrt{24} = \sqrt{4 \cdot 6} = 2\sqrt{6}$

63. $\sqrt{60} = \sqrt{4 \cdot 15} = 2\sqrt{15}$

64. $\sqrt{175} = \sqrt{25 \cdot 7} = 5\sqrt{7}$

65. $\sqrt{360} = \sqrt{36 \cdot 10} = 6\sqrt{10}$

66. $\sqrt{\frac{20}{25}} = \frac{\sqrt{4 \cdot 5}}{5} = \frac{2\sqrt{5}}{5}$

67. $\frac{1}{2}\sqrt{80} = \frac{1}{2}\sqrt{16 \cdot 5} = \frac{1}{2}(4)\sqrt{5} = 2\sqrt{5}$

68. $\frac{3\sqrt{7}}{\sqrt{9}} = \frac{3\sqrt{7}}{3} = \sqrt{7}$

69. $4 \cdot \sqrt{\frac{11}{16}} = \frac{4\sqrt{11}}{4} = \sqrt{11}$

70. $x^2 + 4x - 8 = 0$

$a = 1, b = 4, c = -8$

$x = \frac{-4 \pm \sqrt{4^2 - 4(1)(-8)}}{2(1)}$

$= \frac{-4 \pm \sqrt{16 + 32}}{2}$

$= \frac{-4 \pm \sqrt{48}}{2}$

$x \approx 1.46, -5.46$

71. $x^2 - 2x - 4 = 0$

$a = 1, b = -2, c = -4$

$x = \frac{-(-2) \pm \sqrt{(-2)^2 - 4(1)(-4)}}{2(1)}$

$= \frac{2 \pm \sqrt{4 + 16}}{2}$

$= \frac{2 \pm \sqrt{20}}{2}$

$x \approx 3.24, -1.24$

72. $x^2 - 6x + 1 = 0$

$a = 1, b = -6, c = 1$

$x = \frac{-(-6) \pm \sqrt{(-6)^2 - 4(1)(1)}}{2(1)}$

$= \frac{6 \pm \sqrt{36 - 4}}{2}$

$= \frac{6 \pm \sqrt{32}}{2}$

$x \approx 5.83, 0.17$

73. $x^2 + 3x - 1 = 0$

$a = 1, b = 3, c = -1$

$x = \frac{-3 \pm \sqrt{3^2 - 4(1)(-1)}}{2(1)}$

$= \frac{-3 \pm \sqrt{9 + 4}}{2}$

$= \frac{-3 \pm \sqrt{13}}{2}$

$x \approx 0.30, -3.30$

74. $2x^2 + x - 3 = 0$

$a = 2, b = 1, c = -3$

$x = \frac{-1 \pm \sqrt{1^2 - 4(2)(-3)}}{2(2)}$

$= \frac{-1 \pm \sqrt{1 + 24}}{4}$

$= \frac{-1 \pm \sqrt{25}}{4}$

$x = \frac{-1 \pm 5}{4}$

$x = 1, -\frac{3}{2} = -1.5$

75. $4x^2 - 6x + 1 = 0$

$a = 4, b = -6, c = 1$

$x = \frac{-(-6) \pm \sqrt{(-6)^2 - 4(4)(1)}}{2(4)}$

$= \frac{6 \pm \sqrt{36 - 16}}{8}$

$= \frac{6 \pm \sqrt{20}}{8}$

$x \approx 1.31, 0.19$

76. $(x - 2)(x + 11) = x^2 + 9x - 22$

77. $(x + 4)(3x - 7) = 3x^2 + 5x - 28$

78. $(x - 5)(x - 4) = x^2 - 9x + 20$

79. $(2x - 3)(5x - 9) = 10x^2 - 33x + 27$

80. $(6x + 2)(x^2 - x - 1)$

$= 6x^3 - 6x^2 - 6x + 2x^2 - 2x - 2$

$= 6x^3 - 4x^2 - 8x - 2$

81. $(2x - 1)(x^2 + x + 1)$

$= 2x^3 + 2x^2 + 2x - x^2 - x - 1$

$= 2x^3 + x^2 + x - 1$

Copyright © McDougal Littell Inc.
All rights reserved.

82. $\frac{x}{5} = \frac{12}{1}$
$x = 60$ ft

83. $\frac{8x}{3} \cdot \frac{1}{x} = \frac{8}{3}$

84. $\frac{8x^2}{3} \cdot \frac{9}{16x} = \frac{3x}{2}$

85. $\frac{x}{x+6} \cdot \frac{x+6}{x+1} = \frac{x}{x+1}$

12.1 Maintaining Skills (p. 697)

86. $A = \frac{1}{2}(4)(9) = 18$

87. $A = \frac{1}{2}(1)(1) = \frac{1}{2}$

88. $A = \frac{1}{2}(12)(9) = 54$

89. $A = \frac{1}{2}(6)(8) = 24$

90. $A = \frac{1}{2}(8)(3) = 12$

91. $A = \frac{1}{2}(10)(7) = 35$

92. $A = \frac{1}{2}(0.75)(4) = 1.5$

93. $A = \frac{1}{2}(0.85)(0.62) = 0.2635$

94. $A = \frac{1}{2}(0.25)(1.75) = 0.21875$

Lesson 12.2

12.2 Checkpoint (pp. 698–700)

1. $\sqrt{3} + 2\sqrt{3} = 3\sqrt{3}$

2. $3\sqrt{5} - 2\sqrt{5} = \sqrt{5}$

3. $\sqrt{7} + \sqrt{2} + 3\sqrt{7} = (\sqrt{7} + 3\sqrt{7}) + \sqrt{2}$
$= 4\sqrt{7} + 2$

4. $\sqrt{8} - \sqrt{2} = \sqrt{4 \cdot 2} - \sqrt{2} = 2\sqrt{2} - \sqrt{2} = \sqrt{2}$

5. $\sqrt{18} + \sqrt{2} = \sqrt{9 \cdot 2} + \sqrt{2} = 3\sqrt{2} + \sqrt{2} = 4\sqrt{2}$

6. $5\sqrt{3} - \sqrt{12} = 5\sqrt{3} - \sqrt{4 \cdot 3}$
$= 5\sqrt{3} - 2\sqrt{3}$
$= 3\sqrt{3}$

7. $\sqrt{3} \cdot \sqrt{12} = \sqrt{36} = 6$

8. $\sqrt{5}(\sqrt{2} + 1) = \sqrt{10} + \sqrt{5}$

9. $(\sqrt{2} + 1)(\sqrt{2} - 1) = \sqrt{4} - \sqrt{2} + \sqrt{2} - 1$
$= 2 - 1$
$= 1$

10. $\frac{1}{\sqrt{2}} \cdot \frac{\sqrt{2}}{\sqrt{2}} = \frac{\sqrt{2}}{2}$

11. $\frac{\sqrt{18}}{\sqrt{2}} \cdot \frac{\sqrt{2}}{\sqrt{2}} = \frac{\sqrt{36}}{2} = \frac{6}{2} = 3$

12. $\frac{7}{3 - \sqrt{2}} \cdot \frac{3 + \sqrt{2}}{3 + \sqrt{2}} = \frac{21 + 7\sqrt{2}}{9 - \sqrt{4}}$
$= \frac{21 + 7\sqrt{2}}{9 - 2}$
$= \frac{7(3 + \sqrt{2})}{7}$
$= 3 + \sqrt{2}$

13. $\frac{11}{5 + \sqrt{3}} \cdot \frac{5 - \sqrt{3}}{5 - \sqrt{3}} = \frac{11(5 - \sqrt{3})}{25 - \sqrt{9}}$
$= \frac{11(5 - \sqrt{3})}{25 - 3}$
$= \frac{11(5 - \sqrt{3})}{22}$
$= \frac{5 - \sqrt{3}}{2}$

14. Difference in distances = Friend's distance − Your distance
$D = \sqrt{\frac{3(20)}{2}} - \sqrt{\frac{3(16)}{2}}$
$= \sqrt{30} - \sqrt{24}$
$= \sqrt{30} - \sqrt{4 \cdot 6}$
$= \sqrt{30} - 2\sqrt{6} \approx 0.58$
Your friend can see 0.58 times further than you.

12.2 Guided Practice (p. 701)

1. radicand

2. B; $\frac{4}{\sqrt{3}} \cdot \frac{\sqrt{3}}{\sqrt{3}} = \frac{4\sqrt{3}}{3}$

3. $4 + (\sqrt{5} + 5\sqrt{5}) = 4 + 6\sqrt{5}$

4. $3\sqrt{7} - 2\sqrt{7} = \sqrt{7}$

5. $3\sqrt{6} + \sqrt{24} = 3\sqrt{6} + \sqrt{4 \cdot 6}$
$= 3\sqrt{6} + 2\sqrt{6}$
$= 5\sqrt{6}$

6. $\sqrt{3} \cdot \sqrt{4 \cdot 2} = \sqrt{3} \cdot 2\sqrt{2} = 2\sqrt{6}$

7. $(3 + \sqrt{7})^2 = 3^2 + 2(3\sqrt{7}) + (\sqrt{7})^2$
$= 9 + 6\sqrt{7} + 7$
$= 16 + 6\sqrt{7}$

Copyright © McDougal Littell Inc.
All rights reserved.

8. $\sqrt{3}(5\sqrt{3} - 2\sqrt{6}) = 5\sqrt{9} - 2\sqrt{18}$
$= 5(3) - 2\sqrt{9 \cdot 2}$
$= 15 - 2(3)\sqrt{2}$
$= 15 - 6\sqrt{2}$

9. $\frac{4}{\sqrt{13}} \cdot \frac{\sqrt{13}}{\sqrt{13}} = \frac{4\sqrt{13}}{13}$

10. $\frac{3}{8 - \sqrt{10}} \cdot \frac{8 + \sqrt{10}}{8 + \sqrt{10}} = \frac{3(8 + \sqrt{10})}{64 - 10}$
$= \frac{3(8 + \sqrt{10})}{54}$
$= \frac{8 + \sqrt{10}}{18}$

11. $\frac{6}{\sqrt{10}} \cdot \frac{\sqrt{10}}{\sqrt{10}} = \frac{6\sqrt{10}}{10} = \frac{3\sqrt{10}}{5}$

12. $D = \sqrt{\frac{3(24)}{2}} - \sqrt{\frac{3(12)}{2}}$
$= \sqrt{36} - \sqrt{18}$
$= 6 - \sqrt{9 \cdot 2}$
$= 6 - 3\sqrt{2}$
$\approx$ 1.8 miles farther than your friend.

12.2 Practice and Applications (pp. 701–702)

13. $5\sqrt{7} + 2\sqrt{7} = 7\sqrt{7}$

14. $\sqrt{3} + 5\sqrt{3} = 6\sqrt{3}$

15. $11\sqrt{3} - 12\sqrt{3} = -\sqrt{3}$

16. $2\sqrt{6} - \sqrt{6} = \sqrt{6}$

17. $4\sqrt{5} + \sqrt{3} + \sqrt{5} = (4\sqrt{5} + \sqrt{5}) + \sqrt{3}$
$= 5\sqrt{5} + \sqrt{3}$

18. $3\sqrt{11} - \sqrt{5} + \sqrt{11} = (3\sqrt{11} + \sqrt{11}) - \sqrt{5}$
$= 4\sqrt{11} - \sqrt{5}$

19. $\sqrt{32} + \sqrt{2} = \sqrt{16 \cdot 2} + \sqrt{2}$
$= 4\sqrt{2} + \sqrt{2}$
$= 5\sqrt{2}$

20. $\sqrt{75} + \sqrt{3} = \sqrt{25 \cdot 3} + \sqrt{3}$
$= 5\sqrt{3} + \sqrt{3}$
$= 6\sqrt{3}$

21. $\sqrt{80} - \sqrt{45} = \sqrt{16 \cdot 5} - \sqrt{9 \cdot 5}$
$= 4\sqrt{5} - 3\sqrt{5}$
$= \sqrt{5}$

22. $\sqrt{72} - \sqrt{18} = \sqrt{36 \cdot 2} - \sqrt{9 \cdot 2}$
$= 6\sqrt{2} - 3\sqrt{2}$
$= 3\sqrt{2}$

23. $4\sqrt{5} + \sqrt{125} + \sqrt{45} = 4\sqrt{5} + \sqrt{25 \cdot 5} + \sqrt{9 \cdot 5}$
$= 4\sqrt{5} + 5\sqrt{5} + 3\sqrt{5}$
$= 12\sqrt{5}$

24. $\sqrt{24} - \sqrt{96} + \sqrt{6} = \sqrt{4 \cdot 6} - \sqrt{16 \cdot 6} + \sqrt{6}$
$= 2\sqrt{6} - 4\sqrt{6} + \sqrt{6}$
$= -\sqrt{6}$

25. $\sqrt{3} \cdot \sqrt{75} = \sqrt{225} = 15$

26. $\sqrt{16} \cdot \sqrt{4} = 4 \cdot 2 = 8$

27. $\sqrt{18} \cdot \sqrt{5} = \sqrt{9 \cdot 2} \cdot \sqrt{5} = 3\sqrt{2} \cdot \sqrt{5} = 3\sqrt{10}$

28. $\sqrt{5} \cdot \sqrt{8} = \sqrt{40} = \sqrt{4 \cdot 10} = 2\sqrt{10}$

29. $\sqrt{6}(\sqrt{6} - 1) = \sqrt{36} - \sqrt{6} = 6 - \sqrt{6}$

30. $\sqrt{6}(7\sqrt{3} + 6) = 7\sqrt{18} + 6\sqrt{6}$
$= 7\sqrt{9 \cdot 2} + 6\sqrt{6}$
$= 7(3)\sqrt{2} + 6\sqrt{6}$
$= 21\sqrt{2} + 6\sqrt{6}$

31. $\sqrt{5}(4 + \sqrt{5}) = 4\sqrt{5} + \sqrt{25} = 4\sqrt{5} + 5$

32. $\sqrt{2}(\sqrt{8} - 4) = \sqrt{16} - 4\sqrt{2} = 4 - 4\sqrt{2}$

33. $\sqrt{3}(5\sqrt{2} + \sqrt{3}) = 5\sqrt{6} + \sqrt{9} = 5\sqrt{6} + 3$

34. $(\sqrt{2} + 6)(\sqrt{2} - 6) = 2 - 36 = -34$

35. $(1 + \sqrt{13})(1 - \sqrt{13}) = 1 - 13 = -12$

36. $(\sqrt{2} + \sqrt{3})(\sqrt{2} - \sqrt{3}) = 2 - 3 = -1$

37. $(\sqrt{7} + \sqrt{2})(\sqrt{7} - \sqrt{2}) = 7 - 2 = 5$

38. $\sqrt{68} \cdot \sqrt{17} = \sqrt{1156} = 34$

39. $\frac{1}{2}(\sqrt{44})(\sqrt{99}) = \frac{1}{2}\sqrt{4 \cdot 11}\sqrt{9 \cdot 11}$
$= \frac{1}{2}(2)\sqrt{11} \cdot (3)\sqrt{11}$
$= 3(\sqrt{11})^2$
$= 3 \cdot 11$
$= 33$

40. $\frac{1}{2}(\sqrt{25} + 4)(\sqrt{75} + 10)$
$= \frac{1}{2}(5 + 4)(\sqrt{25 \cdot 3} + 10)$
$= \frac{1}{2}(9)(5\sqrt{3} + 10)$
$= \frac{9}{2}(5\sqrt{3}) + \frac{9}{2}(10)$
$= \frac{45}{2}\sqrt{3} + 45$
$= 45\left(\frac{\sqrt{3}}{2} + 1\right)$ or $\frac{45}{2}(\sqrt{3} + 2)$

Copyright © McDougal Littell Inc.
All rights reserved.

41. $\frac{5}{\sqrt{7}} \cdot \frac{\sqrt{7}}{\sqrt{7}} = \frac{5\sqrt{7}}{7}$

42. $\frac{2}{\sqrt{2}} \cdot \frac{\sqrt{2}}{\sqrt{2}} = \frac{2\sqrt{2}}{2} = \sqrt{2}$

43. $\frac{3}{\sqrt{48}} = \frac{3}{\sqrt{16 \cdot 3}} = \frac{3}{4\sqrt{3}} \cdot \frac{\sqrt{3}}{\sqrt{3}} = \frac{3\sqrt{3}}{4 \cdot 3} = \frac{\sqrt{3}}{4}$

44. $\frac{5}{\sqrt{13}} \cdot \frac{\sqrt{13}}{\sqrt{13}} = \frac{5\sqrt{13}}{13}$

45. $\frac{\sqrt{10}}{\sqrt{3}} \cdot \frac{\sqrt{3}}{\sqrt{3}} = \frac{\sqrt{30}}{3}$

46. $\frac{\sqrt{3}}{\sqrt{7}} \cdot \frac{\sqrt{7}}{\sqrt{7}} = \frac{\sqrt{21}}{7}$

47. $\frac{6}{6 + \sqrt{3}} \cdot \frac{6 - \sqrt{3}}{6 - \sqrt{3}} = \frac{6(6 - \sqrt{3})}{36 - 3}$

$= \frac{6(6 - \sqrt{3})}{33}$

$= \frac{2(6 - \sqrt{3})}{11}$

$= \frac{12 - 2\sqrt{3}}{11}$

48. $\frac{9}{5 - \sqrt{7}} \cdot \frac{5 + \sqrt{7}}{5 + \sqrt{7}} = \frac{9(5 + \sqrt{7})}{25 - 7}$

$= \frac{9(5 + \sqrt{7})}{18}$

$= \frac{5 + \sqrt{7}}{2}$

49. $\frac{1}{2 + \sqrt{2}} \cdot \frac{2 - \sqrt{2}}{2 - \sqrt{2}} = \frac{2 - \sqrt{2}}{4 - 2}$

$= \frac{2 - \sqrt{2}}{2}$

50. $\frac{6}{10 + \sqrt{2}} \cdot \frac{10 - \sqrt{2}}{10 - \sqrt{2}} = \frac{6(10 - \sqrt{2})}{100 - 2}$

$= \frac{6(10 - \sqrt{2})}{98}$

$= \frac{3(10 - \sqrt{2})}{49}$

$= \frac{30 - 3\sqrt{2}}{49}$

51. $\frac{\sqrt{5}}{3 - \sqrt{5}} \cdot \frac{3 + \sqrt{5}}{3 + \sqrt{5}} = \frac{3\sqrt{5} + 5}{9 - 5}$

$= \frac{3\sqrt{5} + 5}{4}$

52. $\frac{\sqrt{3}}{\sqrt{3} - 1} \cdot \frac{\sqrt{3} + 1}{\sqrt{3} + 1} = \frac{3 + \sqrt{3}}{3 - 1}$

$= \frac{3 + \sqrt{3}}{2}$

53. $\sqrt{12}$ and $\sqrt{13}$ are not like terms;
$\sqrt{12} + \sqrt{13} = 2\sqrt{3} + \sqrt{13}$

54. multiplying $(1 + \sqrt{3})(1 - \sqrt{3})$ in the denominator yields -2, not 4;

$\frac{5}{1 + \sqrt{3}} = \frac{5(1 - \sqrt{3})}{(1 + \sqrt{3})(1 - \sqrt{3})}$

$= \frac{5 - 5\sqrt{3}}{1 - 3}$

$= \frac{5 - 5\sqrt{3}}{-2}$

55. $V = 8\sqrt{20} - 8\sqrt{16}$
$V = 8\sqrt{4(5)} - 8(4)$
$V = 8(2)\sqrt{5} - 32 = 16\sqrt{5} - 32$
$V \approx 3.78$ ft/sec faster

56. $T = \frac{\sqrt{50}}{4} - \frac{\sqrt{32}}{4}$
$T = \frac{\sqrt{25 \cdot 2}}{4} - \frac{\sqrt{16 \cdot 2}}{4}$
$T = \frac{5\sqrt{2}}{4} - \frac{4\sqrt{2}}{4}$
$T = \frac{\sqrt{2}}{4}(5 - 4) = \frac{\sqrt{2}}{4}(1) = \frac{\sqrt{2}}{4}$
$T \approx 0.35$ seconds

12.2 Standardized Test Practice (p. 703)

57. C; $\sqrt{5}(6 + \sqrt{5}) = 6\sqrt{5} + 5$

58. F; $\sqrt{3} - 5\sqrt{9} = \sqrt{3} - 5(3) = \sqrt{3} - 15$

59. A;

$\frac{3}{5 - \sqrt{2}} \cdot \frac{5 + \sqrt{2}}{5 + \sqrt{2}} = \frac{3(5 + \sqrt{2})}{25 - 2}$

$= \frac{3(5 + \sqrt{2})}{23}$

$= \frac{15 + 3\sqrt{2}}{23}$

12.2 Mixed Review (p. 703)

60. $x = 0.3(160) = 48$

61. $105 = p(240)$
$0.4375 = p$
$43.75\% = p$

Copyright © McDougal Littell Inc.
All rights reserved.

62. $203 = p(406)$
$0.5 = p$
$50\% = p$

63. $x = 0.7(210)$
$x = 147$

64. $x^2 - 25 = 0$
$(x + 5)(x - 5) = 0$
$x = -5, 5$

65. $x^2 + 2x - 15 = 0$
$(x - 3)(x + 5) = 0$
$x = 3, -5$

66. $x^2 - 13x = -42$
$x^2 - 13x + 42 = 0$
$(x - 6)(x - 7) = 0$
$x = 6, 7$

67. $x^2 - 26 = 11x$
$x^2 - 11x - 26 = 0$
$(x - 13)(x + 2) = 0$
$x = 13, -2$

68. $-9x + 4 = -2x^2$
$2x^2 - 9x + 4 = 0$
$(2x - 1)(x - 4) = 0$
$2x - 1 = 0$
$2x = 1$
$x = \frac{1}{2}$ or $x = 4$

69. $2 + 3x^2 = -5x$
$3x^2 + 5x + 2 = 0$
$(3x + 2)(x + 1) = 0$
$3x + 2 = 0$
$3x = -2$
$x = -\frac{2}{3}$ or $x = -1$

70. $\frac{2}{x + 3} = \frac{1}{x - 6}$
$2(x - 6) = x + 3$
$2x - 12 = x + 3$
$x - 12 = 3$
$x = 15$
Check:
$\frac{2}{15 + 3} \stackrel{?}{=} \frac{1}{15 - 6}$
$\frac{2}{18} \stackrel{?}{=} \frac{1}{9}$
$\frac{1}{9} = \frac{1}{9}$

71. $\frac{6}{x} = \frac{7}{x - 5}$
$6(x - 5) = 7x$
$6x - 30 = 7x$
$-30 = x$
Check:
$\frac{6}{-30} \stackrel{?}{=} \frac{7}{-30 - 5}$
$-\frac{1}{5} \stackrel{?}{=} \frac{7}{-35}$
$-\frac{1}{5} = -\frac{1}{5}$

72. $\frac{7}{x + 4} = \frac{2}{x - 6}$
$7(x - 6) = 2(x + 4)$
$7x - 42 = 2x + 8$
$5x - 42 = 8$
$5x = 50$
$x = 10$
Check:
$\frac{7}{10 + 4} \stackrel{?}{=} \frac{2}{10 - 6}$
$\frac{1}{2} = \frac{1}{2}$

73. $y = \sqrt{x} - 3$
domain: all nonnegative real numbers

x	y
0	$y = \sqrt{0} - 3 = -3$
1	$y = \sqrt{1} - 3 = -2$
2	$y = \sqrt{2} - 3 \approx -1.6$
3	$y = \sqrt{3} - 3 \approx -1.3$
4	$y = \sqrt{4} - 3 = -1$
5	$y = \sqrt{5} - 3 \approx -0.8$

74. $y = \sqrt{x} + 4$
domain: all nonnegative real numbers

x	y
0	$y = \sqrt{0} + 4 = 4$
1	$y = \sqrt{1} + 4 = 5$
2	$y = \sqrt{2} + 4 \approx 5.4$
3	$y = \sqrt{3} + 4 \approx 5.7$
4	$y = \sqrt{4} + 4 = 6$
5	$y = \sqrt{5} + 4 \approx 6.2$

Copyright © McDougal Littell Inc.
All rights reserved.

75. $y = 6\sqrt{x}$
domain: all nonnegative real numbers

x	y
0	$y = 6\sqrt{0} = 0$
1	$y = 6\sqrt{1} = 6$
2	$y = 6\sqrt{2} \approx 8.5$
3	$y = 6\sqrt{3} \approx 10.4$
4	$y = 6\sqrt{4} = 12$
5	$y = 6\sqrt{5} \approx 13.4$

76. $y = 11\sqrt{x}$
domain: all nonnegative real numbers

x	y
0	$y = 11\sqrt{0} = 0$
1	$y = 11\sqrt{1} = 11$
2	$y = 11\sqrt{2} \approx 15.6$
3	$y = 11\sqrt{3} \approx 19.1$
4	$y = 11\sqrt{4} = 22$
5	$y = 11\sqrt{5} \approx 24.6$

77. $y = \sqrt{x + 3}$
domain: all real numbers ≥ -3

x	y
-3	$y = \sqrt{-3 + 3} = 0$
-2	$y = \sqrt{-2 + 3} = 1$
-1	$y = \sqrt{-1 + 3} \approx 1.4$
0	$y = \sqrt{0 + 3} \approx 1.7$
1	$y = \sqrt{1 + 3} = 2$
2	$y = \sqrt{2 + 3} \approx 2.2$

78. $y = \sqrt{x - 8}$
domain: all real numbers ≥ 8

x	y
8	$y = \sqrt{8 - 8} = 0$
9	$y = \sqrt{9 - 8} = 1$
10	$y = \sqrt{10 - 8} \approx 1.4$
11	$y = \sqrt{11 - 8} \approx 1.7$
12	$y = \sqrt{12 - 8} = 2$
13	$y = \sqrt{13 - 8} \approx 2.2$

12.2 Maintaining Skills (p. 703)

79. $40\% = 0.40 > 0.35$ **80.** $110\% = 1.10 < 110$

81. $1.8 = 180\%$ **82.** $0.22 = 22\% > 20\%$

83. $200\% = 2 > 1.0$ **84.** $12\% = 0.12 < 1$

85. $0.3 = 30\% < 33\%$ **86.** $0.75 = 75\% < 85\%$

87. $1\% = 0.01 < 0.1$ **88.** $5\% = 0.05 < 0.5$

89. $1.5 = 150\%$ **90.** $0.9 = 90\% > 89\%$

91. $101\% = 1.01 < 1.1$ **92.** $20\% = 0.20 < 0.25$

93. $0.66 = 66\% > 60\%$ **94.** $2.25 = 225\% < 250\%$

95. $80\% = 0.8 < 1.8$ **96.** $100\% = 1.0$

Lesson 12.3

12.3 Checkpoint (pp. 705–706)

1. $\sqrt{x} = 3$ Original equation.
$x = 9$ Square each side of the equation.

2. $\sqrt{m} - 4 = 0$ Original equation.
$\sqrt{m} = 4$ Add 4 to each side.
$m = 16$ Square each side.

3. $\sqrt{x - 6} = 4$ Original equation.
$x - 6 = 16$ Square each side.
$x = 22$ Add 6 to each side.

4. $\sqrt{n + 1} = 1$ Original equation.
$n + 1 = 1$ Square each side.
$n = 0$ Subtract 1 from each side.

5. $\sqrt{x - 4} + 5 = 11$ Original equation.
$\sqrt{x - 4} = 6$ Subtract 5 from each side.
$x - 4 = 36$ Square each side.
$x = 40$ Add 4 to each side.

6. $\sqrt{3n + 1} - 3 = 1$ Original equation.
$\sqrt{3n + 1} = 4$ Add 3 to each side.
$3n + 1 = 16$ Square each side.
$3n = 15$ Subtract 1 from each side.
$n = 5$ Divide.

7. $\sqrt{x + 6} = x$ Original equation.
$x + 6 = x^2$ Square each side.
$x^2 - x - 6 = 0$ Write equation in standard form.
$(x + 2)(x - 3) = 0$ Factor.
$x = -2, 3$ Check both solutions.

$\sqrt{-2 + 6} \stackrel{?}{=} -2$
$\sqrt{4} \stackrel{?}{=} -2$
$2 \neq -2$
$\sqrt{3 + 6} \stackrel{?}{=} 3$
$\sqrt{9} \stackrel{?}{=} 3$
$3 = 3$

-2 is extraneous

Copyright © McDougal Littell Inc.
All rights reserved.

8.
$$\begin{aligned} x &= \sqrt{8-2x} && \text{Original equation.}\\ x^2 &= 8-2x && \text{Square each side.}\\ x^2+2x-8 &= 0 && \text{Write in standard form.}\\ (x+4)(x-2) &= 0 && \text{Factor.}\\ x &= -4, 2 && \text{Check both solutions.}\\ -4 &\stackrel{?}{=} \sqrt{8-2(-4)}\\ -4 &\stackrel{?}{=} \sqrt{16}\\ -4 &\neq 4\\ 2 &\stackrel{?}{=} \sqrt{8-2(2)}\\ 2 &\stackrel{?}{=} \sqrt{4}\\ 2 &= 2 \end{aligned}$$

-4 is extraneous

9. $\sqrt{n}+4=0$ Original equation.
$\sqrt{n}=-4$ No solution since the positive square root of any number is positive.

10.
$$\begin{aligned} t &= \sqrt{\frac{1620\pi^2}{F}} && \text{Model for centripetal force.}\\ 11^2 &= \left(\sqrt{\frac{1620\pi^2}{F}}\right)^2 && \text{Substitute 11 for } t \text{ and square each side.}\\ 121 &= \frac{1620\pi^2}{F} && \text{Simplify.}\\ F &= \frac{1620\pi^2}{121} \approx 132 \text{ Newtons} && \text{Solve for } F. \end{aligned}$$

12.3 Guided Practice (p. 707)

1. An equation in which the variable is in a radical is called a radical equation.

2. An extraneous solution is an answer that is generated when solving a radical equation, however, it is not a solution to the original equation.

3. $8=\sqrt{x}$
$64=x$
Check:
$8 \stackrel{?}{=} \sqrt{64}$
$8=8$

4. $\sqrt{x}=11$
$x=121$
Check:
$\sqrt{121} \stackrel{?}{=} 11$
$11=11$

5. $14=\sqrt{x}$
$196=x$
Check:
$14 \stackrel{?}{=} \sqrt{196}$
$14=14$

6. $\sqrt{x}=-7$
No solution since the positive square root of any number is positive.

7. $6=\sqrt{x}$
$36=x$
Check:
$6 \stackrel{?}{=} \sqrt{36}$
$6=6$

8. $\sqrt{x}=1$
$x=1$
Check:
$\sqrt{1} \stackrel{?}{=} 1$
$1=1$

9. $\sqrt{x}+6=0$
$\sqrt{x}=-6$
$x=36$
Check:
$\sqrt{36}+6 \stackrel{?}{=} 0$
$6+6\neq 0$; No solution

10. $\sqrt{x}-20=0$
$\sqrt{x}=20$
$x=400$
Check:
$\sqrt{400}-20 \stackrel{?}{=} 0$
$20-20 \stackrel{?}{=} 0$
$0=0$

11. $\sqrt{4x}-1=3$
$\sqrt{4x}=4$
$4x=16$
$x=4$
Check:
$\sqrt{4(4)}-1 \stackrel{?}{=} 3$
$4-1 \stackrel{?}{=} 3$
$3=3$

Copyright © McDougal Littell Inc.
All rights reserved.

12.
$$x = \sqrt{x + 12}$$
$$x^2 = x + 12$$
$$x^2 - x - 12 = 0$$
$$(x - 4)(x + 3) = 0$$
$$x = 4, -3$$

Check:

$4 \stackrel{?}{=} \sqrt{4 + 12}$

$4 \stackrel{?}{=} \sqrt{16}$

$4 = 4$

$-3 = \sqrt{-3 + 12}$

$-3 = \sqrt{9}$

$-3 \neq 3$; extraneous

13. $-5 + \sqrt{x} = 0$
$$(-5)^2 = (-\sqrt{x})^2$$
$$25 = x$$

Check:

$-5 + \sqrt{25} \stackrel{?}{=} 0$

$-5 + 5 \stackrel{?}{=} 0$

$0 = 0$

14.
$$x = \sqrt{5x + 24}$$
$$x^2 = 5x + 24$$
$$x^2 - 5x - 24 = 0$$
$$(x - 8)(x + 3) = 0$$
$$x = 8, -3$$

Check:

$8 \stackrel{?}{=} \sqrt{5(8) + 24}$

$8 \stackrel{?}{=} \sqrt{64}$

$8 = 8$

$-3 \stackrel{?}{=} \sqrt{5(-3) + 24}$

$-3 \stackrel{?}{=} \sqrt{9}$

$-3 \neq 3$; extraneous

15. $\sqrt{5x + 1} + 8 = 12$
$$\sqrt{5x + 1} = 4$$
$$5x + 1 = 16$$
$$5x = 15$$
$$x = 3$$

Check:

$\sqrt{5(3) + 1} + 8 \stackrel{?}{=} 12$

$\sqrt{16} + 8 \stackrel{?}{=} 12$

$4 + 8 \stackrel{?}{=} 12$

$12 = 12$

16. $\sqrt{4x + 5} = x$
$$4x + 5 = x^2$$
$$0 = x^2 - 4x - 5$$
$$0 = (x - 5)(x + 1)$$
$$x = 5, -1$$

Check:

$\sqrt{4(5) + 5} \stackrel{?}{=} 5$

$\sqrt{25} \stackrel{?}{=} 5$

$5 = 5$

$\sqrt{4(-1) + 5} \stackrel{?}{=} -1$

$\sqrt{1} \stackrel{?}{=} -1$

$1 \neq -1$; extraneous

17. $\sqrt{x + 6} = x$
$$x + 6 = x^2$$
$$0 = x^2 - x - 6$$
$$0 = (x + 2)(x - 3)$$
$$x = -2, 3$$

Check:

$\sqrt{-2 + 6} \stackrel{?}{=} -2$

$\sqrt{4} \stackrel{?}{=} -2$

$2 \neq -2$; extraneous

$\sqrt{3 + 6} \stackrel{?}{=} 3$

$\sqrt{9} \stackrel{?}{=} 3$

$3 = 3$

12.3 Practice and Applications (pp. 707–709)

18. $\sqrt{x} - 9 = 0$
$$\sqrt{x} = 9$$
$$x = 81$$

19. $\sqrt{x} - 1 = 0$
$$\sqrt{x} = 1$$
$$x = 1$$

20. $\sqrt{x} - 5 = 0$
$$\sqrt{x} = 5$$
$$x = 25$$

21. $\sqrt{x} - 10 = 0$
$$\sqrt{x} = 10$$
$$x = 100$$

22. $\sqrt{x} - 15 = 0$
$$\sqrt{x} = 15$$
$$x = 225$$

23. $\sqrt{x} - 16 = 0$
$$\sqrt{x} = 16$$
$$x = 256$$

Copyright © McDougal Littell Inc.
All rights reserved.

24. $\sqrt{6x} - 13 = 23$
$\sqrt{6x} = 36$
$6x = 1296$
$x = 216$

25. $\sqrt{4x + 1} + 5 = 10$
$\sqrt{4x + 1} = 5$
$4x + 1 = 25$
$4x = 24$
$x = 6$

26. $\sqrt{9 - x} - 10 = 14$
$\sqrt{9 - x} = 24$
$9 - x = 576$
$-x = 567$
$x = -567$

27. $\sqrt{5x + 1} + 2 = 6$
$\sqrt{5x + 1} = 4$
$5x + 1 = 16$
$5x = 15$
$x = 3$

28. $\sqrt{6x - 2} - 3 = 7$
$\sqrt{6x - 2} = 10$
$6x - 2 = 100$
$6x = 102$
$x = 17$

29. $4 = 7 - \sqrt{33x - 2}$
$(-3)^2 = (-\sqrt{33x - 2})^2$
$9 = 33x - 2$
$11 = 33x$
$\frac{1}{3} = x$

30. $4\sqrt{3x + 3} = 24$
$\sqrt{3x + 3} = 6$
$3x + 3 = 36$
$3x = 33$
$x = 11$

31. $\sqrt{2x + 4} + 1 = 11$
$\sqrt{2x + 4} = 10$
$2x + 4 = 100$
$2x = 96$
$x = 48$

32. $8\sqrt{x + 3} = 64$
$\sqrt{x + 3} = 8$
$x + 3 = 64$
$x = 61$

33. In line 2, do not put a radical over 7.
$\sqrt{x} = 7$
$(\sqrt{x})^2 = 7^2$
$x = 49$

34. $15^2 = 225$, not -225.
$\sqrt{x} - 15 = 0$
$\sqrt{x} = 15$
$(\sqrt{x})^2 = (15)^2$
$x = 225$

35. $2(6) + 2\sqrt{x + 6} = 30$
$12 + 2\sqrt{x + 6} = 30$
$2\sqrt{x + 6} = 18$
$\sqrt{x + 6} = 9$
$x + 6 = 81$
$x = 75$

36. $\frac{1}{2}(11)(\sqrt{3x} - 2) = 88$
$\sqrt{3x} - 2 = 88\left(\frac{2}{11}\right)$
$\sqrt{3x} - 2 = 16$
$\sqrt{3x} = 18$
$3x = 324$
$x = 108$

37. $r = 30d^2\sqrt{P}$
$250 = 30(1.25)^2\sqrt{P}$
$5.\bar{3} = \sqrt{P}$
$28.\bar{4} = P$; 28.4 lbs/in^2

38. $250 = 30(1.75)^2\sqrt{P}$
$2.72 = \sqrt{P}$
$7.4 = P$; 7.4 lbs/in^2

39. *Sample answer:* $\sqrt{(2x - 20)} = 4$

40. $\sqrt{x} - 3 = 4$
$\sqrt{x} = 7$
$x = 49$

Check:
$\sqrt{49} - 3 \stackrel{?}{=} 4$
$7 - 3 \stackrel{?}{=} 4$
$4 = 4$

Copyright © McDougal Littell Inc.
All rights reserved.

41. $\sqrt{x} - 6 = 0$

$\sqrt{x} = 6$

$x = 36$

Check:

$\sqrt{36} - 6 \stackrel{?}{=} 0$

$6 - 6 \stackrel{?}{=} 0$

$0 = 0$

42. $\sqrt{x} + 5 = 1$

$\sqrt{x} = -4$

$x = 16$

Check:

$\sqrt{16} + 5 \stackrel{?}{=} 1$

$4 + 5 \stackrel{?}{=} 1$

$9 \neq 1$; no solution

43. $6 + \sqrt{3x} = -3$

$\sqrt{3x} = -9$

$3x = 81$

$x = 27$

Check:

$6 + \sqrt{3(27)} \stackrel{?}{=} -3$

$6 + 9 \stackrel{?}{=} -3$

$15 \neq -3$; no solution

44. $\sqrt{x + 5} = 7$

$x + 5 = 49$

$x = 44$

Check:

$\sqrt{44 + 5} \stackrel{?}{=} 7$

$7 = 7$

45. $\sqrt{5x + 10} = -5$

$5x + 10 = 25$

$5x = 15$

$x = 3$

Check:

$\sqrt{5(3) + 10} \stackrel{?}{=} -5$

$\sqrt{25} \stackrel{?}{=} -5$

$5 \neq -5$; no solution

46. $\sqrt{x} + 11 = 1$

$\sqrt{x} = -10$

$x = 100$

Check:

$\sqrt{100} + 11 \stackrel{?}{=} 1$

$10 + 11 \stackrel{?}{=} 1$

$21 \neq 1$; no solution

47. $x = \sqrt{x + 42}$

$x^2 = x + 42$

$x^2 - x - 42 = 0$

$(x + 6)(x - 7) = 0$

$x = -6, 7$

Check:

$-6 \stackrel{?}{=} \sqrt{-6 + 42}$

$-6 \stackrel{?}{=} \sqrt{36}$

$-6 \neq 6$; extraneous

$7 \stackrel{?}{=} \sqrt{7 + 42}$

$7 = 7$

48. $\sqrt{x} - 5 = 20$

$\sqrt{x} = 25$

$x = 625$

Check:

$\sqrt{625} - 5 \stackrel{?}{=} 20$

$25 - 5 \stackrel{?}{=} 20$

$20 = 20$

49. $\sqrt{x - 10} = -1$

$x - 10 = 1$

$x = 11$

Check:

$\sqrt{11 - 10} \stackrel{?}{=} -1$

$1 \neq -1$; no solution

50. $3\sqrt{x} = -21$

$\sqrt{x} = -7$

$x = 49$

Check:

$3\sqrt{49} \stackrel{?}{=} -21$

$21 \neq -21$; no solution

51. $x = \sqrt{2x + 3}$

$x^2 = 2x + 3$

$x^2 - 2x - 3 = 0$

$(x - 3)(x + 1) = 0$

$x = 3, -1$

Check:

$3 \stackrel{?}{=} \sqrt{2(3) + 3}$

$3 = 3$

$-1 \stackrel{?}{=} \sqrt{2(-1) + 3}$

$-1 \neq 1$; extraneous

Copyright © McDougal Littell Inc.
All rights reserved.

52. $2\sqrt{x} = -18$

$\sqrt{x} = -9$

$x = 81$

Check:

$2\sqrt{81} \stackrel{?}{=} -18$

$18 \neq -18$; no solution

53. $x = \sqrt{-x + 12}$

$x^2 = -x + 12$

$x^2 + x - 12 = 0$

$(x - 3)(x + 4) = 0$

$x = 3, -4$

Check:

$3 \stackrel{?}{=} \sqrt{-3 + 12}$

$3 = 3$

$-4 \stackrel{?}{=} \sqrt{4 + 12}$

$-4 \neq 4$; extraneous

54. $2\sqrt{x} + 7 = 19$

$2\sqrt{x} = 12$

$\sqrt{x} = 6$

$x = 36$

Check:

$2\sqrt{36} + 7 \stackrel{?}{=} 19$

$19 = 19$

55. $s = \sqrt{1.2a}$

$18 = \sqrt{1.2a}$

$324 = 1.2a$

$270 = a$; 270 m/sec^2

56. $24 = \sqrt{1.2a}$

$576 = 1.2a$

$480 = a$; 480 m/sec^2

57. $\sqrt{x} \stackrel{?}{=} -6$

$\sqrt{36} \stackrel{?}{=} -6$

$6 \neq -6$; false

12.3 Standardized Test Practice (p. 709)

58. C;

$5 \stackrel{?}{=} \sqrt{30 - 5}$

$5 \stackrel{?}{=} \sqrt{25}$

$5 = 5$

59. J;

$5 \stackrel{?}{=} \sqrt{5 + 20}$

$5 \stackrel{?}{=} \sqrt{25}$

$5 = 5$

12.3 Mixed Review (p. 709)

60. $x^2 = 36$

$x = \pm 6$

61. $x^2 = 11$

$x = \pm\sqrt{11}$

62. $7x^2 = 700$

$x^2 = 100$

$x = \pm 10$

63. $25x^2 - 9 = 91$

$25x^2 = 100$

$x^2 = 4$

$x = \pm 2$

64. $x^2 - 16 = -7$

$x^2 = 9$

$x = \pm 3$

65. $-16x^2 + 48 = 0$

$-16x^2 = -48$

$x^2 = 3$

$x = \pm\sqrt{3}$

66. $(x + 5)^2 = x^2 + 2(5x) + 5^2$

$= x^2 + 10x + 25$

67. $(2x - 3)^2 = (2x)^2 + 2(-3)(2x) + (-3)^2$

$= 4x^2 - 12x + 9$

68. $(6y - 4)(6y + 4) = (6y)^2 - 4^2$

$= 36y^2 - 16$

69. $(3x + 5y)(3x - 5y) = (3x)^2 - (5y)^2$

$= 9x^2 - 25y^2$

70. $(x + 7y)^2 = x^2 + 2(7y)(x) + (7y)^2$

$= x^2 + 14xy + 49y^2$

71. $(2a - 9b)^2 = (2a)^2 + 2(2a)(-9b) + (-9b)^2$

$= 4a^2 - 36ab + 81b^2$

72. $x^2 + 18x + 81 = (x)^2 + 2(9x) + (9)^2$

$= (x + 9)^2$

73. $x^2 - 12x + 36 = (x)^2 + 2(-6x) + (-6)^2$

$= (x - 6)^2$

74. $4x^2 + 28x + 49 = (2x)^2 + 2(7)(2x) + (7)^2$

$= (2x + 7)^2$

12.3 Maintaining Skills (p. 709)

75. $2\frac{1}{9} = \frac{19}{9}; \frac{9}{19}$

76. $4\frac{2}{5} = \frac{22}{5}; \frac{5}{22}$

77. $1\frac{3}{10} = \frac{13}{10}; \frac{10}{13}$

78. $6\frac{1}{2} = \frac{13}{2}; \frac{2}{13}$

79. $1\frac{7}{50} = \frac{57}{50}; \frac{50}{57}$

Copyright © McDougal Littell Inc.
All rights reserved.

80. $8\frac{1}{6} = \frac{49}{6}; \frac{6}{49}$

81. $3\frac{7}{9} = \frac{34}{9}; \frac{9}{34}$

82. $5\frac{8}{25} = \frac{133}{25}; \frac{25}{133}$

Quiz 1 *(p. 709)*

1. $y = 10\sqrt{x}$

domain: all nonnegative real numbers

x	y
0	$y = 10\sqrt{0} = 0$
1	$y = 10\sqrt{1} = 10$
2	$y = 10\sqrt{2} \approx 14.1$
3	$y = 10\sqrt{3} \approx 17.3$
4	$y = 10\sqrt{4} = 20$
5	$y = 10\sqrt{5} \approx 22.4$

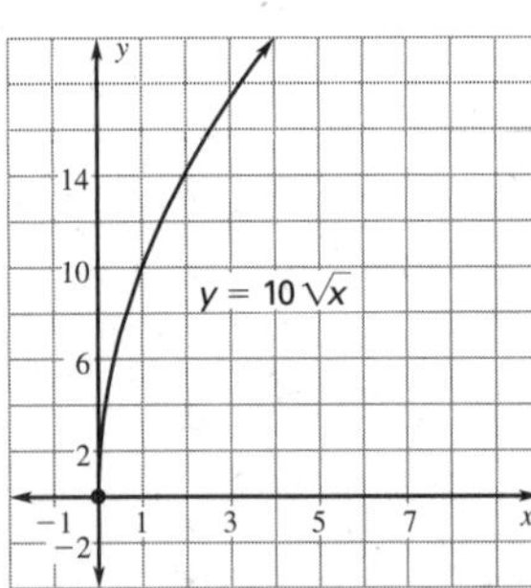

range: all nonnegative real numbers

2. $y = \sqrt{x - 9}$

domain: all real numbers ≥ 9

x	y
9	$y = \sqrt{9 - 9} = 0$
10	$y = \sqrt{10 - 9} = 1$
11	$y = \sqrt{11 - 9} \approx 1.4$
12	$y = \sqrt{12 - 9} \approx 1.7$
13	$y = \sqrt{13 - 9} = 2$
14	$y = \sqrt{14 - 9} \approx 2.2$

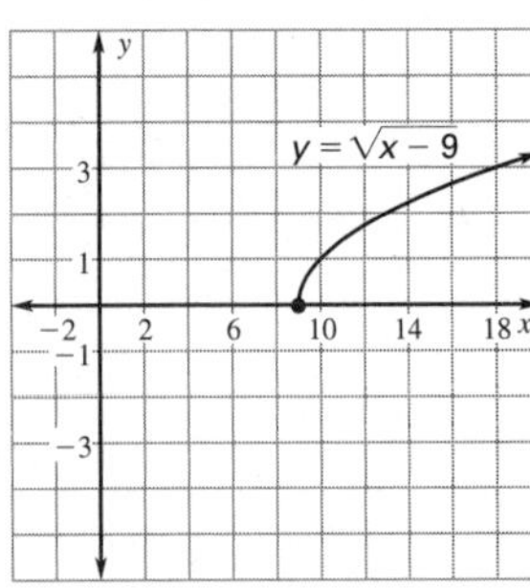

range: all nonnegative real numbers

3. $y = \sqrt{2x - 1}$

$2x - 1 \geq 0$

$2x \geq 1$

$x \geq \frac{1}{2}$

domain: all real numbers $\geq \frac{1}{2}$

x	y
$\frac{1}{2}$	$y = \sqrt{2\left(\frac{1}{2}\right) - 1} = 0$
1	$y = \sqrt{2(1) - 1} = 1$
2	$y = \sqrt{2(2) - 1} \approx 1.7$
3	$y = \sqrt{2(3) - 1} \approx 2.2$
4	$y = \sqrt{2(4) - 1} \approx 2.6$
5	$y = \sqrt{2(5) - 1} = 3$

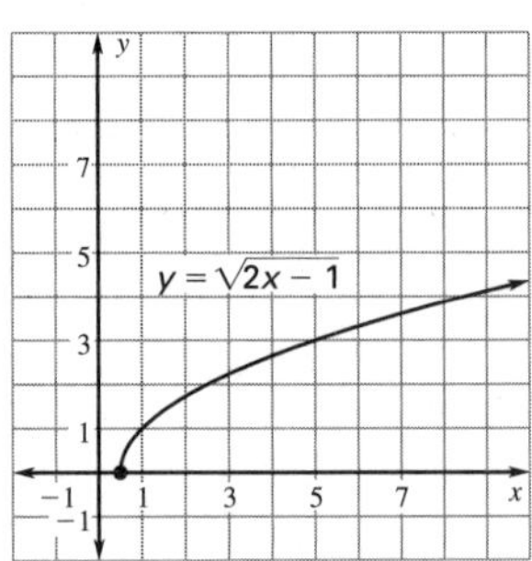

range: all nonnegative real numbers

4. $y = \sqrt{x} - 2$

domain: all nonnegative real numbers

x	y
0	$y = \sqrt{0} - 2 = -2$
1	$y = \sqrt{1} - 2 = -1$
2	$y = \sqrt{2} - 2 \approx -0.6$
3	$y = \sqrt{3} - 2 \approx -0.3$
4	$y = \sqrt{4} - 2 = 0$
5	$y = \sqrt{5} - 2 \approx 0.2$

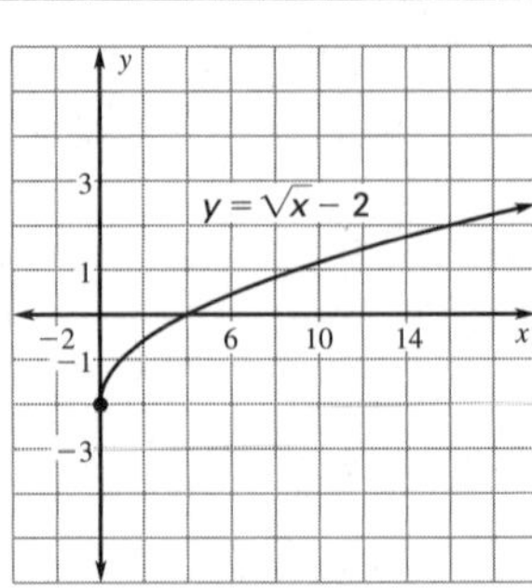

range: all real numbers ≥ -2

Copyright © McDougal Littell Inc.
All rights reserved.

5. $7\sqrt{10} + 11\sqrt{10} = 18\sqrt{10}$

6. $\sqrt{3}(3\sqrt{2} + \sqrt{3}) = 3\sqrt{6} + 3$

7. $4\sqrt{7} + \sqrt{125} - \sqrt{80}$
$= 4\sqrt{7} + \sqrt{25 \cdot 5} - \sqrt{16 \cdot 5}$
$= 4\sqrt{7} + 5\sqrt{5} - 4\sqrt{5}$
$= 4\sqrt{7} + \sqrt{5}$

8. $\sqrt{x} - 2 = 0$
$\sqrt{x} = 2$
$x = 4$

Check:
$\sqrt{4} - 2 \stackrel{?}{=} 0$
$0 = 0$

9. $\sqrt{x} - 8 \stackrel{?}{=} 0$
$\sqrt{x} \stackrel{?}{=} 8$
$x = 64$

Check:
$\sqrt{64} - 8 \stackrel{?}{=} 0$
$0 = 0$

10. $\sqrt{3x + 2} + 2 = 3$
$\sqrt{3x + 2} = 1$
$3x + 2 = 1$
$3x = -1$
$x = -\frac{1}{3}$

Check:
$\sqrt{3\left(-\frac{1}{3}\right) + 2} + 2 \stackrel{?}{=} 3$
$\sqrt{1} + 2 \stackrel{?}{=} 3$
$3 = 3$

11. $\sqrt{3x - 2} + 3 = 7$
$\sqrt{3x - 2} = 4$
$3x - 2 = 16$
$3x = 18$
$x = 6$

Check:
$\sqrt{3(6) - 2} + 3 \stackrel{?}{=} 7$
$4 + 3 \stackrel{?}{=} 7$
$7 = 7$

12. $\sqrt{77 - 4x} = x$
$77 - 4x = x^2$
$0 = x^2 + 4x - 77$
$0 = (x - 7)(x + 11)$
$x = 7, -11$

Check:
$\sqrt{77 - 4(7)} \stackrel{?}{=} 7$
$\sqrt{49} \stackrel{?}{=} 7$
$7 = 7$
$\sqrt{77 - 4(-11)} \stackrel{?}{=} -11$
$\sqrt{121} \stackrel{?}{=} -11$
$11 \neq -11$; extraneous

13. $x = \sqrt{2x + 3}$
$x^2 = 2x + 3$
$x^2 - 2x - 3 = 0$
$(x - 3)(x + 1) = 0$
$x = 3, -1$

Check:
$3 \stackrel{?}{=} \sqrt{2(3) + 3}$
$3 = 3$
$-1 \stackrel{?}{=} \sqrt{2(-1) + 3}$
$-1 \neq 1$; extraneous

14. $r = 30d^2\sqrt{P}$
$250 = 30(2.5)^2\sqrt{P}$
$1.\bar{3} = \sqrt{P}$
$1.78 = P$; 1.78 lbs/in^2

Lesson 12.4

12.4 Checkpoint (pp. 711–712)

1. $\sqrt[3]{64} = 4$

2. $625^{1/2} = 25$

3. $225^{1/2} = 15$

4. $216^{1/3} = 6$

5. $64^{3/2} = (64^{1/2})^3 = 8^3 = 512$

6. $(\sqrt[3]{27})^2 = 3^2 = 9$

7. $(\sqrt{4})^5 = 2^5 = 32$

8. $1000^{2/3} = (1000^{1/3})^2 = 10^2 = 100$

9. $(8^{1/3})^2 = 2^2 = 4$

Copyright © McDougal Littell Inc.
All rights reserved.

10. $(4 \cdot 16)^{1/2} = 4^{1/2} \cdot 16^{1/2} = 2 \cdot 4 = 8$

11. $4^{1/2} \cdot 4^{3/2} = 4^{1/2+3/2} = 4^2 = 16$

12. $(3^{1/2})^2 = 3^1 = 3$

13. $(27 \cdot 64)^{1/3} = 27^{1/3} \cdot 64^{1/3} = 3 \cdot 4 = 12$

14. $2^{5/2} \cdot 2^{1/2} = 2^{5/2+1/2} = 2^3 = 8$

15. $(6^{2/3})^{3/2} = 6^{2/3 \cdot (3/2)} = 6^1 = 6$

16. $(64 \cdot 81)^{1/2} = 64^{1/2} \cdot 81^{1/2} = 8 \cdot 9 = 72$

17. $(x \cdot y^{1/2})^4 x = x^{4+1} + y^{1/2 \cdot (4)} = x^5y^2$

18. $(x^{3/2} \cdot y)^2 = x^{(3/2) \cdot 2}y^2 = x^3y^2$

19. $(y^3)^{1/6} = y^{3/6} = y^{1/2} = \sqrt{y}$

20. $(x^{1/3} \cdot x^{5/3})^{1/2} = (x^{1/3+5/3})^{1/2}$
$= (x^{6/3})^{1/2}$
$= (x^2)^{1/2}$
$= x^1$
$= x$

21. $(x^{1/2} \cdot y^{1/3})^6 = x^{6/2} \cdot y^{6/3} = x^3y^2$

22. $\sqrt[3]{x}(x^3 \cdot y^2)^{1/3} = x^{1/3}(x^{3/3}y^{2/3})$
$= x^{1/3} \cdot x \cdot y^{2/3}$
$= x \cdot x^{1/3} \cdot y^{2/3}$
$= x(xy^2)^{1/3}$
$= x\sqrt[3]{xy^2}$

12.4 Guided Practice (p. 713)

1. $\sqrt[3]{27}, 27^{1/3}$

2. $\sqrt[3]{125} = 5$

3. $49^{1/2} = 7$

4. $(\sqrt[3]{8})^5 = (2)^5 = 32$

5. $25^{3/2} = (25^{1/2})^3 = 5^3 = 125$

6. $121^{1/2} = 11$

7. $9^{3/2} = (9^{1/2})^3 = 3^3 = 27$

8. $\sqrt[3]{343} = 7$

9. $(\sqrt{81})^3 = 9^3 = 729$

12.4 Practice and Applications (pp. 713–714)

10. $\sqrt{14} = 14^{1/2}$

11. $\sqrt[3]{11} = 11^{1/3}$

12. $(\sqrt[3]{5})^2 = 5^{2/3}$

13. $(\sqrt{16})^5 = 16^{5/2}$

14. $6^{1/3} = \sqrt[3]{6}$

15. $7^{1/2} = \sqrt{7}$

16. $10^{3/2} = (\sqrt{10})^3$

17. $8^{7/3} = (\sqrt[3]{8})^7$

18. $\sqrt[3]{8} = 2$

19. $\sqrt{10{,}000} = 100$

20. $512^{1/3} = 8$

21. $4^{1/2} = 2$

22. $1^{1/3} = 1$

23. $256^{1/2} = 16$

24. $(\sqrt{16})^4 = (4)^4 = 256$

25. $(\sqrt[3]{27})^4 = 3^4 = 81$

26. $4^{3/2} = (\sqrt{4})^3 = 2^3 = 8$

27. $125^{2/3} = (\sqrt[3]{125})^2 = 5^2 = 25$

28. $(\sqrt{100})^3 = 10^3 = 1000$

29. $(\sqrt[3]{64})^4 = 4^4 = 256$

30. $3^{5/3} \cdot 3^{1/3} = 3^{5/3+(1/3)} = 3^{6/3} = 3^2 = 9$

31. $4^{3/2} \cdot 4^{1/2} = 4^{3/2+(1/2)} = 4^{4/2} = 4^2 = 16$

32. $(8^{2/3})^{1/2} = 8^{(2/3) \cdot (1/2)} = 8^{1/3} = 2$

33. $(6^{1/3})^6 = 6^{6/3} = 6^2 = 36$

34. $(8 \cdot 27)^{1/3} = 8^{1/3} \cdot 27^{1/3} = 2 \cdot 3 = 6$

35. $(16 \cdot 25)^{1/2} = 16^{1/2} \cdot 25^{1/2} = 4 \cdot 5 = 20$

36. $(2^3 \cdot 3^3)^{1/3} = 2^{3/3}3^{3/3} = 2^1 \cdot 3^1 = 6$

37. $(2^{2/3} \cdot 2^{1/3})^6 = (2^{2/3+(1/3)})^6 = (2^1)^6 = 2^6 = 64$

38. $(4^2 \cdot 5^2)^{1/2} = 4^{2/2} \cdot 5^{2/2} = 4^1 \cdot 5^1 = 20$

39. $x^{1/3} \cdot x^{1/2} = x^{1/3+(1/2)} = x^{5/6} = (\sqrt[6]{x})^5$

40. $x \cdot \sqrt[3]{y^6} + y^2 \cdot \sqrt[3]{x^3} = x \cdot y^{6/3} + y^2 \cdot x^{3/3}$
$= x \cdot y^2 + y^2 \cdot x$
$= xy^2 + xy^2$
$= 2xy^2$

41. $(y^{1/6})^3 \cdot \sqrt{x} = y^{3/6} \cdot x^{1/2} = y^{1/2}x^{1/2} = \sqrt{xy}$

42. $(36x^3)^{1/2} = 36^{1/2}x^{3/2} = 6x^{3/2} = 6(\sqrt{x})^3$

43. $(y \cdot y^{1/3})^{3/2} = (y^{4/3})^{3/2} = y^{4/3 \cdot (3/2)} = y^2$

44. $(x^{1/3} \cdot y^{1/2})^6 \cdot \sqrt{x} = x^{6/3} \cdot y^{6/2} \cdot x^{1/2}$
$= x^2y^3x^{1/2}$
$= x^2y^3\sqrt{x}$

45. sometimes, if *a* and *b* are both zero.

46. $$V = \frac{4}{3}\pi r^3$$
$$524 = \frac{4}{3}\pi r^3$$
$$\left(\frac{3}{4} \cdot \frac{524}{1}\right) = \pi r^3$$
$$393 = \pi r^2$$
$$125.096 \approx r^3$$
$$5 \approx r; \text{5 cm}$$

12.4 Standardized Test Practice (p. 714)

47. C; $100^{3/2} = (\sqrt{100})^3 = 10^3 = 1000$

Copyright © McDougal Littell Inc.
All rights reserved.

12.4 Mixed Review (p. 714)

48. $16 + x^2 = 64$
$x^2 = 48$
$x = \pm\sqrt{48} = \pm\sqrt{16 \cdot 3} = \pm 4\sqrt{3}$

49. $x^2 + 25 = 81$
$x^2 = 56$
$x = \pm\sqrt{56} = \pm\sqrt{4 \cdot 14} = \pm 2\sqrt{14}$

50. $x^2 + 81 = 144$
$x^2 = 63$
$x = \pm\sqrt{63} = \pm\sqrt{9 \cdot 7} = \pm 3\sqrt{7}$

51. $4x^2 - 144 = 0$
$4x^2 = 144$
$x^2 = 36$
$x = \pm 6$

52. $x^2 - 30 = -3$
$x^2 = 27$
$x = \pm\sqrt{27} = \pm\sqrt{9 \cdot 3} = \pm 3\sqrt{3}$

53. $x^2 = \frac{20}{25}$
$x^2 = \frac{4}{5}$
$x = \pm\sqrt{\frac{4}{5}} = \pm\frac{2}{\sqrt{5}} \cdot \frac{\sqrt{5}}{\sqrt{5}} = \pm\frac{2\sqrt{5}}{5}$

54. $(x + 4)^2 = 0$
$x = -4$

55. $(x + 4)(x - 8) = 0$
$x = -4, 8$

56. $x(x - 14)^2 = 0$
$x = 0, 14$

12.4 Maintaining Skills (p. 714)

57. 13 prime

58. $28 = 2^2 \cdot 7$; composite

59. $75 = 3 \cdot 5^2$; composite

60. $99 = 3^2 \cdot 11$; composite

61. $18 = 2 \cdot 3^2$; composite

62. $33 = 3 \cdot 11$; composite

63. $69 = 3 \cdot 23$; composite

64. $80 = 2^4 \cdot 5$; composite

12.5 Developing Concepts: Think About It *(p. 715)*

1.

Expression	*Number of tiles to complete the square*	*Number of tiles as a perfect square*
$x^2 + 6x$	9	3^2
$x^2 + 4x$	4	2^2
$x^2 + 2x$	1	1^2

2. It is the square of one half the coefficient of x.

3. The coefficient of x is 8. One row of x-tiles contains half of 8 which is 4. $4^2 = 16$; 16 tiles should be added.

Lesson 12.5

12.5 Checkpoint (pp. 716–718)

1. $\left(\frac{2}{2}\right)^2 = 1^2 = 1$

2. $\left(-\frac{4}{2}\right)^2 = (-2)^2 = 4$

3. $\left(\frac{6}{2}\right)^2 = 3^2 = 9$

4. $\left(-\frac{10}{2}\right)^2 = (-5)^2 = 25$

5.

$x^2 - 2x - 3 = 0$	Original equation.
$x^2 - 2x = 3$	Add 3 to each side.
$x^2 - 2x + 1^2 = 3 + 1^2$	Add $(-\frac{2}{2})^2 = (-1)^2$ to each side.
$(x - 1)^2 = 4$	Write left side as a perfect square.
$x - 1 = \pm 2$	Find square root of each side.
$x = 1 \pm 2$	Add 1 to each side.
$x = 3$ or $x = -1$	Simplify.

6.

$x^2 - 12x + 4 = 0$	Original equation.
$x^2 - 12x = -4$	Subtract 4 from each side.
$x^2 - 12x + 6^2 = -4 + 6^2$	Add $(-\frac{12}{2})^2$ to each side.
$(x - 6)^2 = 32$	Write left side as a perfect square.
$x - 6 = \pm\sqrt{32}$	Find square root of each side.
$x = 6 \pm \sqrt{32}$	Add 6 to each side.
$x = 6 \pm \sqrt{16 \cdot 2} = 6 \pm 4\sqrt{2}$	Simplify.

7.

$x^2 + 16x + 4 = 0$	Original equation.
$x^2 + 16x = -4$	Subtract 4 from each side.
$x^2 + 16x + 8^2 = -4 + 8^2$	Add $(\frac{16}{2})^2$ to each side.
$(x + 8)^2 = 60$	Write left side as a perfect square.
$x + 8 = \pm\sqrt{60}$	Find square root of each side.
$x = -8 \pm \sqrt{4 \cdot 15}$	Subtract 8 from each side.
$x = -8 \pm 2\sqrt{15}$	Simplify.

Copyright © McDougal Littell Inc.
All rights reserved.

Sample answers given for methods in 8–10.

8. $x^2 - 3 = 0$ find square root
$x^2 = 3$
$x = \pm\sqrt{3}$

9. $2x^2 = 8$ find square root
$x^2 = 4$
$x = \pm 2$

10. $x^2 + 3x + 4 = 6$ quadratic formula
$x^2 + 3x - 2 = 0$
$a = 1, b = 3, c = -2$
$$x = \frac{-3 \pm \sqrt{3^2 - 4(1)(-2)}}{2(1)} = \frac{-3 \pm \sqrt{9 + 8}}{2} = \frac{-3 \pm \sqrt{17}}{2}$$

12.5 Guided Practice (p. 719)

1. add $\left(\frac{b}{2}\right)^2$

2. false; add $\left(\frac{6}{2}\right)^2 = (3)^2 = 9$ to both sides

3. $\left(\frac{20}{2}\right)^2 = 10^2 = 100$

4. $\left(\frac{30}{2}\right)^2 = 15^2 = 225$

5. $\left(-\frac{10}{2}\right)^2 = (-5)^2 = 25$

6. $\left(-\frac{14}{2}\right)^2 = (-7)^2 = 49$

7. $\left(-\frac{22}{2}\right)^2 = (-11)^2 = 121$

8. $\left(\frac{24}{2}\right)^2 = (12)^2 = 144$

9. $x^2 - 3x = 8$ complete the square
$$x^2 - 3x + \left(\frac{3}{2}\right)^2 = 8 + \left(\frac{3}{2}\right)^2$$
$$\left(x - \frac{3}{2}\right)^2 = 8 + \frac{9}{4} = \frac{32}{4} + \frac{9}{4} = \frac{41}{4}$$
$$x - \frac{3}{2} = \pm\sqrt{\frac{41}{4}} = \pm\frac{\sqrt{41}}{2}$$
$$x = \frac{3}{2} \pm \frac{\sqrt{41}}{2} = \frac{3 \pm \sqrt{41}}{2}$$

$x^2 - 3x = 8$ quadratic formula
$x^2 - 3x - 8 = 0$
$a = 1, b = -3, c = -8$
$$x = \frac{-(-3) \pm \sqrt{(-3)^2 - 4(1)(-8)}}{2(1)} = \frac{3 \pm \sqrt{9 + 32}}{2} = \frac{3 \pm \sqrt{41}}{2}$$

10. $x^2 - 2x - 18 = 0$
$x^2 - 2x = 18$
$x^2 - 2x + (1)^2 = 18 + 1^2$
$(x - 1)^2 = 19$
$x - 1 = \pm\sqrt{19}$
$x = 1 \pm \sqrt{19}$

11. $x^2 + 10x - 10 = 0$
$x^2 + 10x = 10$
$x^2 + 10x + 5^2 = 10 + 5^2$
$(x + 5)^2 = 35$
$x + 5 = \pm\sqrt{35}$
$x = -5 \pm \sqrt{35}$

12. $x^2 + 8x = -3$
$x^2 + 8x + 4^2 = -3 + 4^2$
$(x + 4)^2 = 13$
$x + 4 = \pm\sqrt{13}$
$x = -4 \pm \sqrt{13}$

13. $x^2 + 14x = -13$
$x^2 + 14x + 7^2 = -13 + 7^2$
$(x + 7)^2 = 36$
$x + 7 = \pm 6$
$x = -7 \pm 6$
$x = -1$ or $x = -13$

Sample answers given for methods in 14–19.

14. $x^2 - x - 2 = 0$; factor
$(x + 1)(x - 2) = 0$
$x = -1, 2$

Copyright © McDougal Littell Inc.
All rights reserved.

15. $3x^2 + 17x + 10 = 0$; factor
$(3x + 2)(x + 5) = 0$
$x = -\frac{2}{3}, 5$

16. $x^2 - 9 = 0$; find the square root
$x^2 = 9$
$x = \pm 3$

17. $-3x^2 + 5x + 5 = 0$; quadratic formula
$a = -3, b = 5, c = 5$

$$x = \frac{-5 \pm \sqrt{5^2 - 4(-3)(5)}}{2(-3)}$$
$$= \frac{-5 \pm \sqrt{25 + 60}}{-6}$$
$$= \frac{-5 \pm \sqrt{85}}{-6}$$

18. $x^2 + 2x - 14 = 0$ complete the square
$x^2 + 2x = 14$
$x^2 + 2x + 1^2 = 14 + 1^2$
$(x + 1)^2 = 15$
$x + 1 = \pm\sqrt{15}$
$x = -1 \pm \sqrt{15}$

19. $3x^2 - 2 = 0$ find square root
$3x^2 = 2$
$x^2 = \frac{2}{3}$
$x = \pm\sqrt{\frac{2}{3}} = \pm\frac{\sqrt{2}}{\sqrt{3}} \cdot \frac{\sqrt{3}}{\sqrt{3}} = \pm\frac{\sqrt{6}}{3}$

12.5 Practice and Applications (pp. 719–721)

20. $\left(-\frac{12}{2}\right)^2 = 36$

21. $\left(\frac{8}{2}\right)^2 = 16$

22. $\left(\frac{10}{2}\right)^2 = 25$

23. $\left(\frac{22}{2}\right)^2 = 121$

24. $\left(\frac{14}{2}\right)^2 = 49$

25. $\left(-\frac{40}{2}\right)^2 = 400$

26. $\left(\frac{4}{2}\right)^2 = 4$

27. $\left(-\frac{6}{2}\right)^2 = 9$

28. $\left(\frac{16}{2}\right)^2 = 64$

29. $x^2 - 8x + 12 = 0$
$x^2 - 8x = -12$
$x^2 - 8x + 4^2 = -12 + 4^2$
$(x - 4)^2 = 4$
$x - 4 = \pm 2$
$x = 4 \pm 2$
$x = 6, 2$

30. $x^2 - 2x = 3$
$x^2 - 2x + 1^2 = 3 + 1^2$
$(x - 1)^2 = 4$
$x - 1 = \pm 2$
$x = 1 \pm 2$
$x = 3, -1$

31. $x^2 + 6x - 16 = 0$
$x^2 + 6x = 16$
$x^2 + 6x + 3^2 = 16 + 3^2$
$(x + 3)^2 = 25$
$x + 3 = \pm 5$
$x = -3 \pm 5$
$x = 2, -8$

32. $x^2 + 4x = 12$
$x^2 + 4x + 2^2 = 12 + 2^2$
$(x + 2)^2 = 16$
$x + 2 = \pm 4$
$x = -2 \pm 4$
$x = 2, -6$

33. $x^2 + 10x = 12$
$x^2 + 10x + 5^2 = 12 + 5^2$
$(x + 5)^2 = 37$
$x + 5 = \pm\sqrt{37}$
$x = -5 \pm \sqrt{37}$

34. $x^2 + 8x = 15$
$x^2 + 8x + 4^2 = 15 + 4^2$
$(x + 4)^2 = 31$
$x + 4 = \pm\sqrt{31}$
$x = -4 \pm \sqrt{31}$

35. $x^2 + 10x = 39$
$x^2 + 10x + 5^2 = 39 + 5^2$
$(x + 5)^2 = 64$
$x + 5 = \pm 8$
$x = -5 \pm 8$
$x = 3, -13$

36. $x^2 + 16x = 17$
$x^2 + 16x + 8^2 = 17 + 8^2$
$(x + 8)^2 = 81$
$x + 8 = \pm 9$
$x = -8 \pm 9$
$x = 1, -17$

37. $x^2 - 24x = -44$
$x^2 - 24x + 12^2 = -44 + 12^2$
$(x - 12)^2 = 100$
$x - 12 = \pm 10$
$x = 12 \pm 10$
$x = 22, 2$

Copyright © McDougal Littell Inc.
All rights reserved.

38. $x^2 - 6x - 11 = 0$
$$x^2 - 6x = 11$$
$$x^2 - 6x + 3^2 = 11 + 3^2$$
$$(x - 3)^2 = 20$$
$$x - 3 = \pm\sqrt{20}$$
$$x = 3 \pm \sqrt{4 \cdot 5}$$
$$= 3 \pm 2\sqrt{5}$$

39. $x^2 - 2x = 5$
$$x^2 - 2x + 1^2 = 5 + 1^2$$
$$(x - 1)^2 = 6$$
$$x - 1 = \pm\sqrt{6}$$
$$x = 1 \pm \sqrt{6}$$

40. $x^2 + 30x - 7 = 0$
$$x^2 + 30x = 7$$
$$x^2 + 30x + 15^2 = 7 + 15^2$$
$$(x + 15)^2 = 232$$
$$x + 15 = \pm\sqrt{232} = \pm\sqrt{4 \cdot 58}$$
$$x = -15 \pm 2\sqrt{58}$$

41. $x^2 - 4x - 1 = 0$
$$x^2 - 4x = 1$$
$$x^2 - 4x + 2^2 = 1 + 2^2$$
$$(x - 2)^2 = 5$$
$$x - 2 = \pm\sqrt{5}$$
$$x = 2 \pm \sqrt{5}$$

42. $x^2 + 20x + 3 = 0$
$$x^2 + 20x = -3$$
$$x^2 + 20x + 10^2 = -3 + 10^2$$
$$(x + 10)^2 = 97$$
$$x + 10 = \pm\sqrt{97}$$
$$x = -10 \pm \sqrt{97}$$

43. $x^2 + 14x - 2 = 0$
$$x^2 + 14x = 2$$
$$x^2 + 14x + 7^2 = 2 + 7^2$$
$$(x + 7)^2 = 51$$
$$x + 7 = \pm\sqrt{51}$$
$$x = -7 \pm \sqrt{51}$$

44. $x^2 + 4x + 5 = 0$
$$x = \frac{-4 \pm \sqrt{4^2 - 4(1)(5)}}{2(1)}$$
$$x = \frac{-4 \pm \sqrt{-4}}{2}$$

Since there is a negative number in the radicand, there are no real solutions.

45. $x^2 + 10x - 3 = 0$
$$x^2 + 10x = 3$$
$$x^2 + 10x + 5^2 = 3 + 5^2$$
$$(x + 5)^2 = 28$$
$$x + 5 = \pm\sqrt{28}$$
$$x = -5 \pm \sqrt{4 \cdot 7} = -5 \pm 2\sqrt{7}$$

46. $x^2 + 16x + 9 = 0$
$$x^2 + 16x = -9$$
$$x^2 + 16x + 8^2 = -9 + 8^2$$
$$(x + 8)^2 = 55$$
$$x + 8 = \pm\sqrt{55}$$
$$x = -8 \pm \sqrt{55}$$

47. $x^2 + 22x + 1 = 0$
$$x^2 + 22x = -1$$
$$x^2 + 22x + 11^2 = -1 + 11^2$$
$$(x + 11)^2 = 120$$
$$x + 11 = \pm\sqrt{120}$$
$$x = -11 \pm \sqrt{4 \cdot 30} = -11 \pm 2\sqrt{30}$$

48. $x^2 + 2x - 11 = 0$
$$x^2 + 2x = 11$$
$$x^2 + 2x + 1^2 = 11 + 1^2$$
$$(x + 1)^2 = 12$$
$$x + 1 = \pm\sqrt{12}$$
$$x = -1 \pm \sqrt{4 \cdot 3} = -1 \pm 2\sqrt{3}$$

49. $x^2 + 8x - 6 = 0$
$$x^2 + 8x = 6$$
$$x^2 + 8x + 4^2 = 6 + 4^2$$
$$(x + 4)^2 = 22$$
$$x + 4 = \pm\sqrt{22}$$
$$x = -4 \pm \sqrt{22}$$

50. $x^2 + 14x - 7 = 0$
$$x^2 + 14x = 7$$
$$x^2 + 14x + 7^2 = 7 + 7^2$$
$$(x + 7)^2 = 56$$
$$x + 7 = \pm\sqrt{56}$$
$$x = -7 \pm \sqrt{4 \cdot 14}$$
$$x = -7 \pm 2\sqrt{14}$$

51. $x^2 + 20x + 2 = 0$
$$x^2 + 20x = -2$$
$$x^2 + 20x + 10^2 = -2 + 10^2$$
$$(x + 10)^2 = 98$$
$$x + 10 = \pm\sqrt{98}$$
$$x = -10 \pm \sqrt{49 \cdot 2}$$
$$x = -10 \pm 7\sqrt{2}$$

52. $x^2 - 6x - 10 = 0$
$$x^2 - 6x = 10$$
$$x^2 - 6x + 3^2 = 10 + 3^2$$
$$(x - 3)^2 = 19$$
$$x - 3 = \pm\sqrt{19}$$
$$x = 3 \pm \sqrt{19}$$

53. $x^2 - 12x - 3 = 0$
$$x^2 - 12x = 3$$
$$x^2 - 12x + 6^2 = 3 + 6^2$$
$$(x - 6)^2 = 39$$
$$x - 6 = \pm\sqrt{39}$$
$$x = 6 \pm \sqrt{39}$$

Copyright © McDougal Littell Inc.
All rights reserved.

54. $x^2 - 18x + 5 = 0$
$x^2 - 18x = -5$
$x^2 - 18x + 9^2 = -5 + 9^2$
$(x - 9)^2 = 76$
$x - 9 = \pm\sqrt{76}$
$x = 9 \pm \sqrt{4 \cdot 19}$
$x = 9 \pm 2\sqrt{19}$

55. $x^2 - 2x - 4 = 0$
$x^2 - 2x = 4$
$x^2 - 2x + 1^2 = 4 + 1^2$
$(x - 1)^2 = 5$
$x - 1 = \pm\sqrt{5}$
$x = 1 \pm \sqrt{5}$

56. Since the formula has $2a$ in the denominator, $2a \neq 0$, which implies $a \neq 0$. Since $b^2 - 4ac$ is the radicand, it must be a non-negative number to yield a solution.

57. $\sqrt{150} = 12.25$; 12.25 ft by 12.25 ft

58. $2x(x + 5) = 600$
$2x^2 + 10x = 600$
$x^2 + 5x = 300$
$x^2 + 5x - 300 = 0$
$$x = \frac{-5 \pm \sqrt{5^2 - 4(1)(-300)}}{2(1)}$$
$$= \frac{-5 \pm \sqrt{1225}}{2}$$
$$= \frac{-5 \pm 35}{2}$$
$x = 15, -20$ (does not make sense)
length $= 2x = 2(15) = 30$ ft
width $= x + 5 = 15 + 5 = 20$ ft

59. $\frac{1}{2}(x)(4 + 2x) = 60$
$x(4 + 2x) = 120$
$4x + 2x^2 = 120$
$2x + x^2 = 60$
$x^2 + 2x - 60 = 0$
$$x = \frac{-2 \pm \sqrt{2^2 - 4(1)(-60)}}{2(1)}$$
$$= \frac{-2 \pm \sqrt{244}}{2}$$
$x = 6.81, -8.81$ (does not make sense)
base $= x = 6.8$ ft
height $= 4 + 2x = 4 + 2(6.8) = 17.6$ ft

Sample answers given for methods in 60–74.

60. $x^2 - x - 12 = 0$; factor
$(x - 4)(x + 3) = 0$
$x = 4, -3$

61. $x^2 - 9 = 0$; find square root
$x^2 = 9$
$x = \pm 3$

62. $x^2 - 4x = 8$; complete the square
$x^2 - 4x + 2^2 = 8 + 2^2$
$(x - 2)^2 = 12$
$x - 2 = \pm\sqrt{12}$
$x = 2 \pm \sqrt{4 \cdot 3} = 2 \pm 2\sqrt{3}$

63. $x^3 + 5x - 14 = 0$; factor
$(x + 7)(x - 2) = 0$
$x = -7, 2$

64. $x^2 - 2x = 2$; complete the square
$x^2 - 2x + 1^2 = 2 + 1^2$
$(x - 1)^2 = 3$
$x - 1 = \pm\sqrt{3}$
$x = 1 \pm \sqrt{3}$

65. $3x^2 + 5x - 12 = 0$; factor
$(3x - 4)(x + 3) = 0$
$x = \frac{4}{3}, -3$

66. $x^2 + 5x - 6 = 0$; factor
$(x + 6)(x - 1) = 0$
$x = -6, 1$

67. $x^2 - 6x + 7 = 0$; complete the square
$x^2 - 6x = -7$
$x^2 - 6x + 3^2 = -7 + 3^2$
$(x - 3)^2 = 2$
$x - 3 = \pm\sqrt{2}$
$x = 3 \pm \sqrt{2}$

68. $x^2 + 2 = 6$; find square root
$x^2 = 4$
$x = \pm 2$

69. $2x^2 + 7x + 3 = 0$; quadratic formula
$$x = \frac{-7 \pm \sqrt{7^2 - 4(2)(3)}}{2(2)}$$
$$x = \frac{-7 \pm \sqrt{25}}{4} = \frac{-7 \pm 5}{4}$$
$$x = -\frac{1}{2}, -3$$

70. $2x^2 - 200 = 0$; find square root
$2x^2 = 200$
$x^2 = 100$
$x = \pm 10$

71. $x^2 - 24x = 6$; complete the square
$x^2 - 24x + 12^2 = 6 + 12^2$
$(x - 12)^2 = 150$
$x - 12 = \pm\sqrt{150}$
$x = 12 \pm \sqrt{25 \cdot 6} = 12 \pm 5\sqrt{6}$

72. $3x^2 - 48 = 0$; find square root
$3x^2 = 48$
$x^2 = 16$
$x = \pm 4$

Copyright © McDougal Littell Inc.
All rights reserved.

Chapter 12 *continued*

73. $x^2 + 3x + 4 = 1$; quadratic formula

$$x^2 + 3x + 3 = 0$$

$$x = \frac{-3 \pm \sqrt{3^2 - 4(1)(3)}}{2(1)}$$

$$= \frac{-3 \pm \sqrt{-3}}{2}\text{; no solution}$$

74. $3x^2 + 7x + 2 = 0$; factor

$$(3x + 1)(x + 2) = 0$$

$$x = -\frac{1}{3}, -2$$

75. $h = -0.44x^2 + 2.61x + 10$

$$0 = -0.44x^2 + 2.61x + 10$$

$$x = \frac{-2.61 \pm \sqrt{(2.61)^2 - 4(-0.44)(10)}}{2(-0.44)}$$

$$= \frac{-2.61 \pm 4.94}{-0.88}$$

$$x = -2.65, 8.58$$

about 8.6 feet

76. $h = -16t^2 + 15t + 5$

$$0 = -16t^2 + 15t + 5$$

$$t = \frac{-15 \pm \sqrt{15^2 - 4(-16)(5)}}{2(-16)}$$

$$= \frac{-15 \pm 23.35}{-32}$$

$$t = -0.26, 1.20$$

about 1.2 seconds

12.5 Standardized Test Practice (p. 721)

77. A;

$$2x^2 + 8x - 25 = 5$$

$$2x^2 + 8x - 30 = 0$$

$$x^2 + 4x - 15 = 0$$

$$x = \frac{-4 \pm \sqrt{4^2 - 4(1)(-15)}}{2(1)}$$

$$x = \frac{-4 \pm \sqrt{76}}{2} = \frac{-4 \pm \sqrt{4 \cdot 19}}{2}$$

$$x = \frac{-4 \pm 2\sqrt{19}}{2} = \frac{2(-2 \pm \sqrt{19})}{2}$$

$$x = -2 \pm \sqrt{19}$$

78. H; $\left(-\frac{1}{2} \div 2\right)^2 = \left(-\frac{1}{2} \cdot \frac{1}{2}\right)^2 = \left(-\frac{1}{4}\right)^2 = \frac{1}{16}$

79. A;

$$x^2 + 8x - 2 = 0$$

$$x^2 + 8x = 2$$

$$x^2 + 8x + 4^2 = 2 + 4^2$$

$$(x + 4)^2 = 18$$

$$x + 4 = \pm\sqrt{18}$$

$$x = -4 \pm \sqrt{9 \cdot 2}$$

$$x = -4 \pm 3\sqrt{2}$$

12.5 Mixed Review (p. 721)

80.

$$y = 4x$$

$$x + (4x) = 10$$

$$5x = 10$$

$$x = 2$$

$$y = 4(2) = 8$$

(2, 8)

81.

$$3x + y = 12$$

$$\underline{9x - y = 36}$$

$$12x = 48$$

$$x = 4$$

$$3(4) + y = 12$$

$$y = 0$$

(4, 0)

82.

$$2x - y = 8$$

$$\underline{-2x - 2y = -2}$$

$$-3y = 6$$

$$y = -2$$

$$2x - (-2) = 8$$

$$2x = 6$$

$$x = 3$$

(3, −2)

83. $3x^2 - 147 = 0$

$$3x^2 = 147$$

$$x^2 = 49$$

$$x = \pm 7$$

84. $x^2 - 5 = 20$

$$x^2 = 25$$

$$x = \pm 5$$

85. $x^2 + 2 = 83$

$$x^2 = 81$$

$$x = \pm 9$$

86. $9 + x^2 = 49$

$$x^2 = 40$$

$$x = \pm\sqrt{40}$$

$$x = \pm\sqrt{4 \cdot 10} = \pm 2\sqrt{10}$$

87. $x^2 - 16 = 144$

$$x^2 = 160$$

$$x = \pm\sqrt{160} = \pm\sqrt{16 \cdot 10} = \pm 4\sqrt{10}$$

88. $x^2 + 64 = 169$

$$x^2 = 105$$

$$x = \pm\sqrt{105}$$

Copyright © McDougal Littell Inc.
All rights reserved.

89. graph $y = x^2 + x + 2$

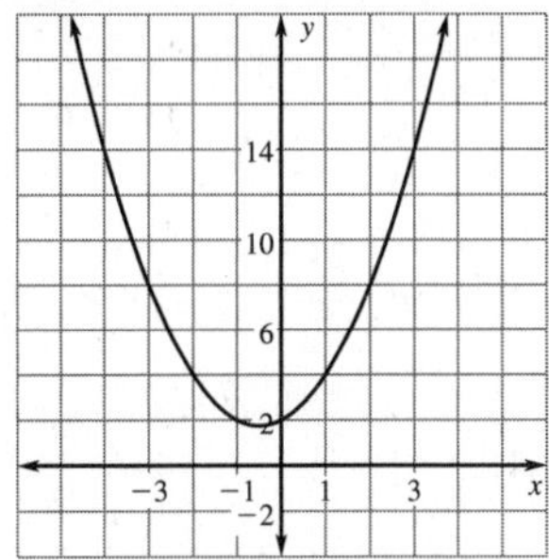

No solution

90. graph $y = -3x^2 - x - 4$

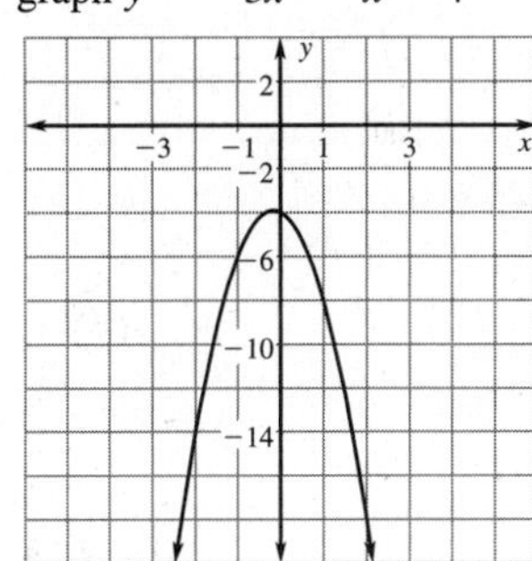

No solution

91. graph $y = 2x^2 - 3x + 4$

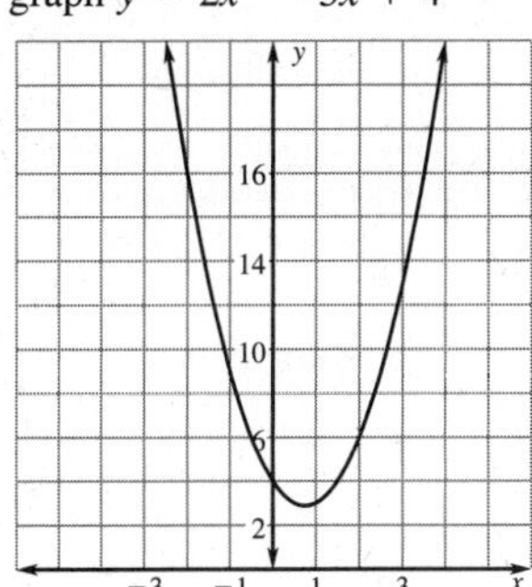

No solution

92. graph $y = x^2 - x - 12$

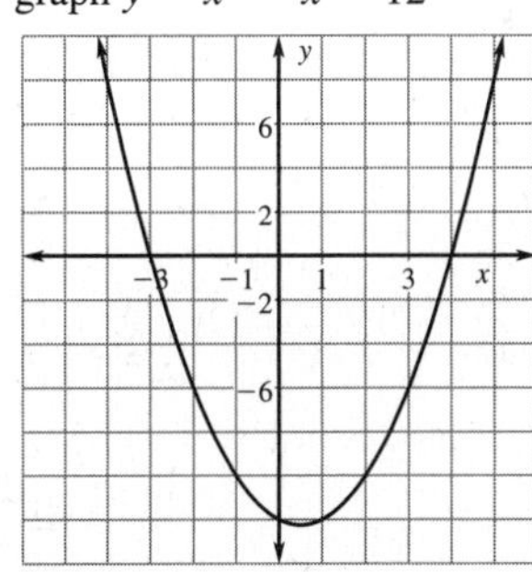

Solutions: 4, -3

Check:

$$4^2 - 4 - 12 \stackrel{?}{=} 0$$
$$0 = 0$$
$$(-3)^2 - (-3) - 12 \stackrel{?}{=} 0$$
$$0 = 0$$

93. graph $y = x^2 - 2x - 3$

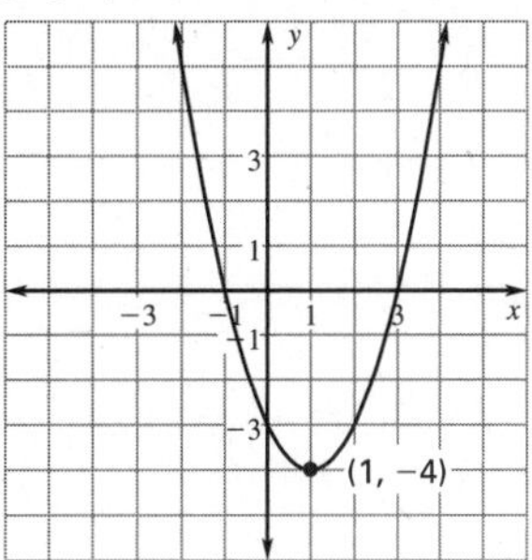

Solutions: 3, -1

Check:

$$3^2 - 2(3) - 3 \stackrel{?}{=} 0$$
$$0 = 0$$
$$(-1)^2 - 2(-1) - 3 \stackrel{?}{=} 0$$
$$0 = 0$$

94. graph $y = 2x^2 + 10x + 12$

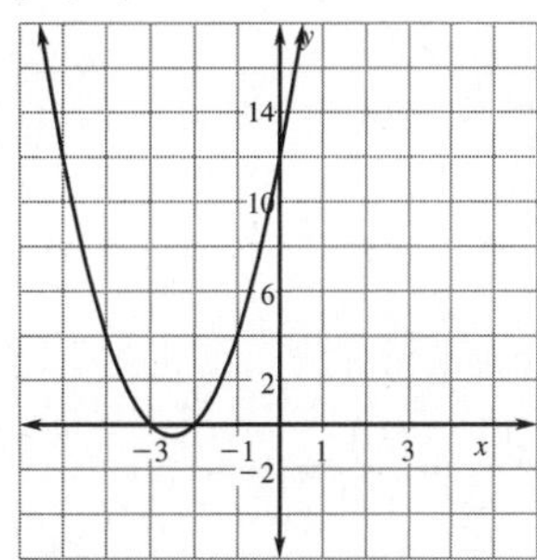

Solutions: -3, -2

Check:

$$2(-3)^2 + 10(-3) + 12 \stackrel{?}{=} 0$$
$$0 = 0$$
$$2(-2)^2 + 10(-2) + 12 \stackrel{?}{=} 0$$
$$0 = 0$$

95. $(x + 4)(x - 8) = 0$

$x = -4, 8$

96. $(x - 3)(x - 2) = 0$

$x = 3, 2$

97. $(x + 5)(x + 6) = 0$

$x = -5, -6$

98. $(x + 4)^2 = 0$

$x = -4$

99. $(x - 3)^2 = 0$

$x = 3$

100. $6(x - 14)^2 = 0$

$x = 14$

101. $x^2 + x - 20 = (x - 4)(x + 5)$

102. $x^2 - 10x + 24 = (x - 6)(x - 4)$

103. $x^2 + 4x + 4 = (x + 2)(x + 2) = (x + 2)^2$

104. $3x^2 - 15x + 18 = 3(x^2 - 5x + 6) = 3(x - 2)(x - 3)$

105. $2x^2 - x - 3 = (2x - 3)(x + 1)$

106. $14x^2 - 19x - 3 = (2x - 3)(7x + 1)$

Copyright © McDougal Littell Inc.
All rights reserved.

12.5 Maintaing Skills (p. 721)

107. $\frac{3}{4} - 15\% = \frac{3}{4} - \frac{15}{100}$
$= \frac{3}{4} - \frac{3}{20}$
$= \frac{15}{20} - \frac{3}{20}$
$= \frac{12}{20}$
$= \frac{3}{5}$

108. $\frac{7}{8} - 80\% = \frac{7}{8} - \frac{80}{100} = \frac{7}{8} - \frac{4}{5} = \frac{35}{40} - \frac{32}{40} = \frac{3}{40}$

109. $\frac{1}{2} - 39\% = \frac{50}{100} - \frac{39}{100} = \frac{11}{100}$

110. $\frac{4}{5} - 45\% = \frac{80}{100} - \frac{45}{100} = \frac{35}{100} = \frac{7}{20}$

111. $26\% - \frac{1}{4} = \frac{26}{100} - \frac{25}{100} = \frac{1}{100}$

112. $75\% - \frac{3}{4} = \frac{75}{100} - \frac{75}{100} = 0$

113. $8\% - \frac{1}{20} = \frac{8}{100} - \frac{5}{100} = \frac{3}{100}$

114. $100\% - \frac{2}{5} = \frac{100}{100} - \frac{40}{100} = \frac{60}{100} = \frac{3}{5}$

115. $50\% - \frac{1}{8} = \frac{50}{100} - \frac{1}{8} = \frac{1}{2} - \frac{1}{8} = \frac{4}{8} - \frac{1}{8} = \frac{3}{8}$

12.6 Developing Concepts: Explore *(p. 722)*

5. $<$; right, 169, $=$, 169; acute, 113, $>$, 100

Think About It *(p. 722)*

1. Answers may vary.

2. $<$; $=$; $>$

12.6 Developing Concepts: Think About It *(p. 723)*

1. Answers may vary.

2. right; obtuse; acute

Lesson 12.6

12.6 Checkpoint (pp. 725–726)

1. $12^2 + 5^2 = c^2$
$144 + 25 = c^2$
$169 = c^2$
$13 = c$

2. $3^2 + 4^2 = c^2$
$9 + 16 = c^2$
$25 = c^2$
$5 = c$

3. $12^2 + 16^2 = c^2$
$144 + 256 = c^2$
$400 = c^2$
$20 = c$

4. $x^2 + x^2 = 2^2$
$2x^2 = 4$
$x^2 = 2$
$x = \sqrt{2} \approx 1.41$

5. $x^2 + (x + 1)^2 = (x + 2)^2$
$x^2 + x^2 + 2x + 1 = x^2 + 4x + 4$
$2x^2 + 2x + 1 = x^2 + 4x + 4$
$x^2 - 2x - 3 = 0$
$(x - 3)(x + 1) = 0$
$x = 3, -1$ (does not make sense)
sides are 3, 4, 5

6. $12^2 + (x - 3)^2 = (x + 3)^2$
$144 + x^2 - 6x + 9 = x^2 + 6x + 9$
$x^2 - 6x + 153 = x^2 + 6x + 9$
$-6x + 153 = 6x + 9$
$-12x + 153 = 9$
$-12x = -144$
$x = 12$
sides: 12, 9, 15

7. $5^2 + 11^2 \stackrel{?}{=} 12^2$
$25 + 121 \stackrel{?}{=} 144$
$146 \neq 144$; not a right triangle

8. $5^2 + 12^2 \stackrel{?}{=} 13^2$
$25 + 144 \stackrel{?}{=} 169$
$169 = 169$; a right triangle

9. $11.9^2 + 12^2 \stackrel{?}{=} 16.9^2$
$141.61 + 144 \stackrel{?}{=} 285.61$
$285.61 = 285.61$; a right triangle

12.6 Guided Practice (p. 727)

1. legs

2. hypothesis: x is an even number;
conclusion: x^2 is an even number

3. $7^2 + 24^2 = c^2$
$49 + 576 = c^2$
$625 = c^2$
$25 = c$

4. $5^2 + b^2 = 13^2$
$25 + b^2 = 169$
$b^2 = 144$
$b = 12$

5. $a^2 + 15^2 = 17^2$
$a^2 + 225 = 289$
$a^2 = 64$
$a = 8$

6. $9^2 + b^2 = 41^2$
$81 + b^2 = 1681$
$b^2 = 1600$
$b = 40$

Copyright © McDougal Littell Inc.
All rights reserved.

7. $a^2 + 11^2 = 61^2$
$a^2 + 121 = 3721$
$a^2 = 3600$
$a = 60$

8. $12^2 + 35^2 = c^2$
$144 + 1225 = c^2$
$1369 = c^2$
$37 = c$

9. $12^2 + b^2 = 20^2$
$144 + b^2 = 400$
$b^2 = 256$
$b = 16$

10. $20^2 + 21^2 = c^2$
$400 + 441 = c^2$
$841 = c^2$
$29 = c$

11. $x^2 + (x + 2)^2 = 10^2$
$x^2 + x^2 + 4x + 4 = 10^2$
$2x^2 + 4x + 4 = 100$
$x^2 + 2x + 2 = 50$
$x^2 + 2x + 1^2 = 48 + 1^2$
$(x + 1)^2 = 49$
$x + 1 = \pm 7$
$x = -1 \pm 7$
$x = 6, -8$
Length is positive, so the solution $x = -8$ is extraneous.
legs: 6, 8

12. If $a^2 + b^2 = c^2$, then the sides a, b, and c form a right triangle.

12.6 Practice and Applications (pp. 727–729)

13. $3^2 + b^2 = 4^2$
$9 + b^2 = 16$
$b^2 = 7$
$b = \sqrt{7} \approx 2.65$

14. $10^2 + 24^2 = c^2$
$100 + 576 = c^2$
$676 = c^2$
$26 = c$

15. $a^2 + 3^2 = 7^2$
$a^2 + 9 = 49$
$a^2 = 40$
$a = \sqrt{40} = \sqrt{4 \cdot 10} = 2\sqrt{10} \approx 6.32$

16. $a^2 + 9^2 = 16^2$
$a^2 + 81 = 256$
$a^2 = 175$
$a = \sqrt{25 \cdot 7} = 5\sqrt{7} \approx 13.23$

17. $5^2 + b^2 = 10^2$
$25 + b^2 = 100$
$b^2 = 75$
$b = \sqrt{75} = \sqrt{25 \cdot 3} = 5\sqrt{3} \approx 8.66$

18. $14^2 + b^2 = 21^2$
$196 + b^2 = 441$
$b^2 = 245$
$b = \sqrt{49 \cdot 5} = 7\sqrt{5} \approx 15.65$

19. $2^2 + 8^2 = c^2$
$4 + 64 = c^2$
$68 = c^2$
$\sqrt{4 \cdot 17} = c$
$8.25 \approx 2\sqrt{17} = c$

20. $11^2 + 15^2 = c^2$
$121 + 225 = c^2$
$346 = c^2$
$18.60 \approx c$

21. $a^2 + 3^2 = 10^2$
$a^2 + 9 = 100$
$a^2 = 91$
$a = \sqrt{91} \approx 9.54$

22. $a^2 + 1^2 = 3^2$
$a^2 + 1 = 9$
$a^2 = 8$
$a = \sqrt{4 \cdot 2} = 2\sqrt{2} \approx 2.83$

23. $4^2 + b^2 = 7^2$
$16 + b^2 = 49$
$b^2 = 33$
$b = \sqrt{33} \approx 5.74$

24. $8^2 + b^2 = 10^2$
$64 + b^2 = 100$
$b^2 = 36$
$b = 6$

25. $x^2 + (x - 6)^2 = 30^2$
$x^2 + x^2 - 12x + 36 = 900$
$2x^2 - 12x - 864 = 0$
$x^2 - 6x - 432 = 0$
$$x = \frac{6 \pm \sqrt{36 - 4(1)(-432)}}{2(1)}$$
$$= \frac{6 \pm 42}{2}$$
$x = 24, -18$
legs: 24, 18

26. $x^2 + (x + 1)^2 = (\sqrt{61})^2$
$x^2 + x^2 + 2x + 1 = 61$
$2x^2 + 2x + 1 = 61$
$2x^2 + 2x - 60 = 0$
$x^2 + x - 30 = 0$
$$x = \frac{-1 \pm \sqrt{1^2 - 4(1)(-30)}}{2(1)}$$
$$= \frac{-1 \pm \sqrt{121}}{2}$$
$$= \frac{-1 \pm 11}{2}$$
$x = 5, -6$
legs: 5, 6

Copyright © McDougal Littell Inc.
All rights reserved.

27.
$$\begin{aligned}(x+5)^2+x^2&=(5\sqrt{5})^2\\ x^2+10x+25+x^2&=25(5)\\ 2x^2+10x+25&=125\\ 2x^2+10x-100&=0\\ x^2+5x-50&=0\\ x&=\frac{-5\pm\sqrt{25-4(1)(-50)}}{2(1)}\\ &=\frac{-5\pm\sqrt{225}}{2}\\ &=\frac{-5\pm 15}{2}\\ x&=5,-10\end{aligned}$$
legs: 5, 10

28.
$$\begin{aligned}(2x-1)^2+x^2&=(2x+1)^2\\ 4x^2-4x+1+x^2&=4x^2+4x+1\\ 5x^2-4x+1&=4x^2+4x+1\\ x^2-8x&=0\\ x(x-8)&=0\\ x&=0,8\end{aligned}$$
legs: 8, 15; hypotenuse: 17

29.
$$\begin{aligned}x^2+1^2&=(\sqrt{2x})^2\\ x^2+1&=2x\\ x^2-2x+1&=0\\ (x-1)(x-1)&=0\\ x&=1\end{aligned}$$
leg: 1, hypotenuse: $\sqrt{2}$

30.
$$\begin{aligned}x^2+(x+6)^2&=(2\sqrt{17})^2\\ x^2+x^2+12x+36&=4(17)\\ 2x^2+12x+36&=68\\ 2x^2+12x-32&=0\\ x^2+6x-16&=0\\ x&=\frac{-6\pm\sqrt{36-4(1)(-16)}}{2(1)}\\ &=\frac{-6\pm\sqrt{100}}{2}\\ &=\frac{-6\pm 10}{2}\\ x&=2,-8\end{aligned}$$
legs: 2, 8

31.
$$\begin{aligned}90^2+90^2&=c^2\\ 2(90)^2&=c^2\\ 2(8100)&=c^2\\ 16200&=c^2\\ 127.3&\approx c\end{aligned}$$
about 127.3 ft

32.
$$\begin{aligned}60^2+100^2&=c^2\\ 3600+10000&=c^2\\ 13600&=c^2\\ 116.6&\approx c;\ \text{about 116.6 yd}\end{aligned}$$

33.
$$\begin{aligned}10^2+7^2&=d^2\\ 100+49&=d^2\\ 149&=d^2\\ 12.2&\approx d;\ \text{about 12.2 in.}\end{aligned}$$

34. Horizontal distance of staircase: (10 in.)(6) = 60 in.
Vertical distance of staircase: (7 in.)(6) = 42 in.
Length of handrail (c)
$$\begin{aligned}60^2+42^2&=c^2\\ 3600+1764&=c^2\\ 5364&=c^2\\ 73.2&\approx c;\ \text{about 73.2 in.}\end{aligned}$$

35.
$$\begin{aligned}5^2+x^2&=7^2\\ 25+x^2&=49\\ x^2&=24\\ x&\approx 4.9\text{ ft}\end{aligned}$$

36.
$$\begin{aligned}2^2+10^2&\stackrel{?}{=}11^2\\ 4+100&\stackrel{?}{=}121\\ 104&\neq 121;\ \text{not a right triangle}\end{aligned}$$

37.
$$\begin{aligned}5^2+12^2&\stackrel{?}{=}13^2\\ 25+144&\stackrel{?}{=}169\\ 169&=169;\ \text{a right triangle}\end{aligned}$$

38.
$$\begin{aligned}12^2+16^2&\stackrel{?}{=}20^2\\ 144+256&\stackrel{?}{=}400\\ 400&=400;\ \text{a right triangle}\end{aligned}$$

39.
$$\begin{aligned}11^2+60^2&\stackrel{?}{=}61^2\\ 121+3600&\stackrel{?}{=}3721\\ 3721&=3721;\ \text{a right triangle}\end{aligned}$$

40.
$$\begin{aligned}7^2+24^2&\stackrel{?}{=}26^2\\ 49+576&\stackrel{?}{=}676\\ 625&\neq 676;\ \text{not a right triangle}\end{aligned}$$

41.
$$\begin{aligned}3^2+9^2&\stackrel{?}{=}10^2\\ 9+81&\stackrel{?}{=}100\\ 90&\neq 100;\ \text{not a right triangle}\end{aligned}$$

42.
$$\begin{aligned}12^2+9^2&\stackrel{?}{=}15^2\\ 144+81&\stackrel{?}{=}225\\ 225&=225;\ \text{a right triangle}\end{aligned}$$

43.
$$\begin{aligned}6^2+9^2&\stackrel{?}{=}11^2\\ 36+81&\stackrel{?}{=}121\\ 117&\neq 121;\ \text{not a right triangle}\end{aligned}$$

44.
$$\begin{aligned}8^2+10^2&\stackrel{?}{=}13^2\\ 64+100&\stackrel{?}{=}169\\ 164&\neq 169;\ \text{not a right triangle}\end{aligned}$$

45. 6 knots, 8 knots, 10 knots; the side lengths are a 3-4-5 triangle multiplied by 2.
$$\begin{aligned}6^2+8^2&\stackrel{?}{=}10^2\\ 36+64&\stackrel{?}{=}100\\ 100&=100;\ \text{a right triangle}\end{aligned}$$
Since you know the rope forms a right triangle you can use the right angle to check a corner.

12.6 Standardized Test Practice (p. 729)

46. D;
$$\begin{aligned}10^2+49^2&\stackrel{?}{=}50^2\\ 100+2401&\stackrel{?}{=}2500\\ 2501&\neq 2500\end{aligned}$$

Copyright © McDougal Littell Inc.
All rights reserved.

12.6 Mixed Review (p. 729)

47.

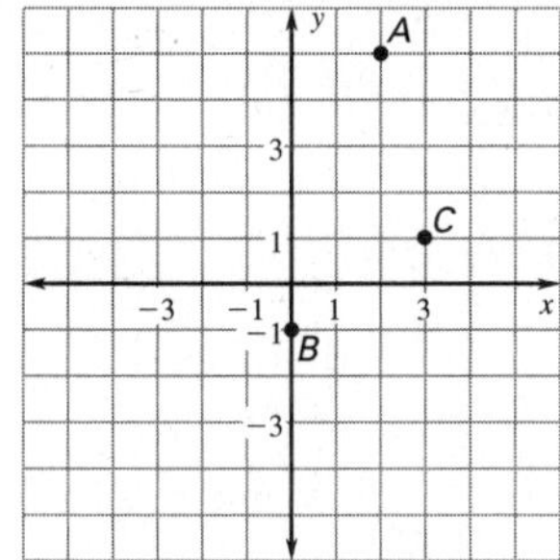

48.

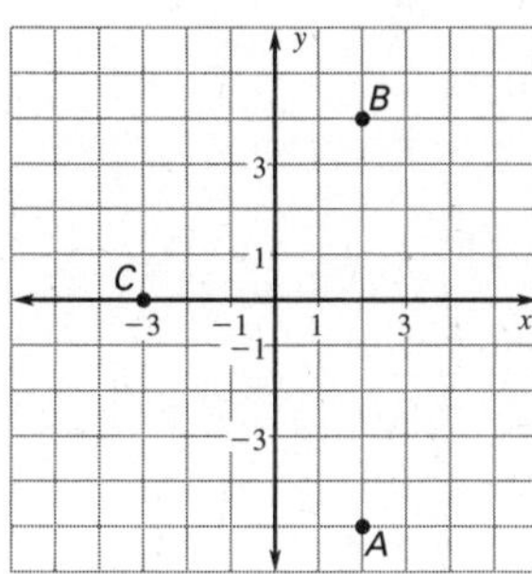

49.

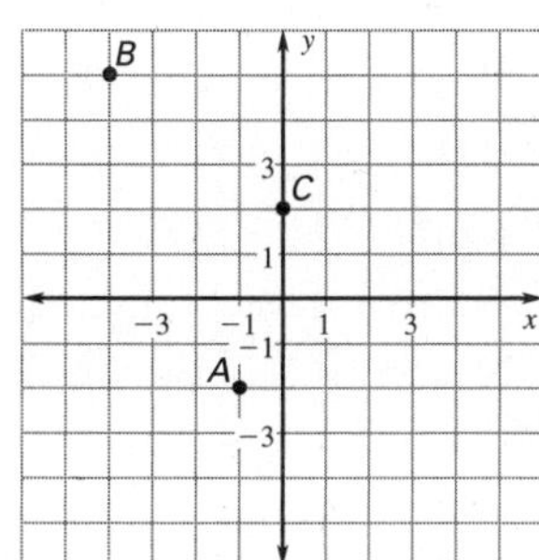

50.

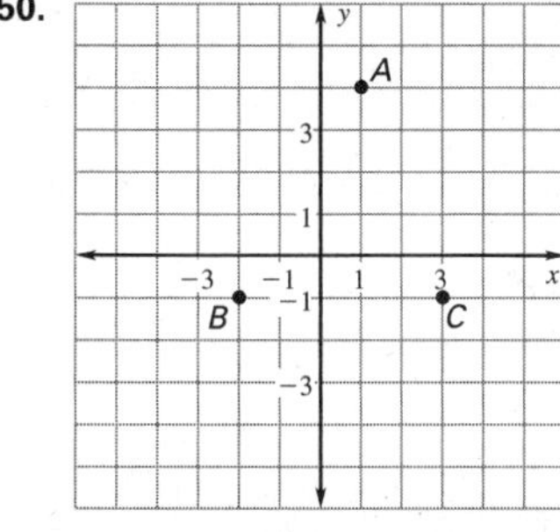

51. $b^2 - 4ac = 2^2 - 4(1)(15) = -56$; zero

52. $b^2 - 4ac = 8^2 - 4(1)(12) = 16$; two

53. $b^2 - 4ac = 1^2 - 4(1)(-10) = 41$; two

54. $b^2 - 4ac = 8^2 - 4(1)(16) = 0$; one

55. $b^2 - 4ac = 3^2 - 4(1)(1) = 5$; two

56. $b^2 - 4ac = (-8)^2 - 4(1)(-11) = 108$; two

12.6 Maintaining Skills (p. 729)

57. 5.1 by 7.2
$5 \times 7 = 35$

58. 10.6 by 17.3
$11 \times 17 = 187$

59. 5.1 by 9.9
$5 \times 10 = 50$

60. 100.4 by 7.0
$100 \times 7 = 700$

61. 17.3 by 2.8
$17 \times 3 = 51$

62. 20.5 by 1.5
$21 \times 2 = 42$

Quiz 2 *(p. 729)*

1. $2^{1/3} \cdot 2^{2/3} = 2^{3/3} = 2$

2. $(36 \cdot 49)^{1/2} = 36^{1/2} \cdot 49^{1/2} = 6 \cdot 7 = 42$

3. $(3^{1/2})^4 = 3^{4/2} = 3^2 = 9$

4.
$$x^2 - 6x + 7 = 0$$
$$x^2 - 6x = -7$$
$$x^2 - 6x + 3^2 = -7 + 3^2$$
$$(x - 3)^2 = 2$$
$$x - 3 = \pm\sqrt{2}$$
$$x = 3 \pm \sqrt{2}$$

5.
$$x^2 + 4x - 1 = 0$$
$$x^2 + 4x = 1$$
$$x^2 + 4x + 2^2 = 1 + 2^2$$
$$(x + 2)^2 = 5$$
$$x + 2 = \pm\sqrt{5}$$
$$x = -2 \pm \sqrt{5}$$

6.
$$x^2 + 2x = 2$$
$$x^2 + 2x + 1^2 = 2 + 1^2$$
$$(x + 1)^2 = 3$$
$$x + 1 = \pm\sqrt{3}$$
$$x = -1 \pm \sqrt{3}$$

7. $6^2 + 9^2 \stackrel{?}{=} 11^2$
$36 + 81 \stackrel{?}{=} 121$
$117 \neq 121$; not a right triangle

8. $12^2 + 35^2 \stackrel{?}{=} 37^2$
$144 + 1225 \stackrel{?}{=} 1369$
$1369 = 1369$; a right triangle

9. $1^2 + 1^2 \stackrel{?}{=} (\sqrt{2})^2$
$2 = 2$; a right triangle

10.
$$1500^2 + b^2 = 2500^2$$
$$2{,}250{,}000 + b^2 = 6{,}250{,}000$$
$$b^2 = 4{,}000{,}000$$
$$b = 2000 \text{ ft}$$

Copyright © McDougal Littell Inc.
All rights reserved.

Lesson 12.7

12.7 Checkpoint (pp. 731–732)

1. $d = \sqrt{(0-2)^2 + (4-5)^2}$
   $d = \sqrt{4+1} = \sqrt{5} \approx 2.24$

2. $d = \sqrt{[2-(-3)]^2 + (-2-2)^2}$
   $d = \sqrt{25+16} = \sqrt{41} \approx 6.40$

3. $d = \sqrt{(0-8)^2 + (6-0)^2}$
   $d = \sqrt{64+36} = \sqrt{100} = 10$

4. $d = \sqrt{[-1-(-4)]^2 + (3-2)^2}$
   $d = \sqrt{9+1} = \sqrt{10} \approx 3.16$

5. $d_1 = \sqrt{(5-1)^2 + (5-2)^2}$
   $= \sqrt{16+9} = \sqrt{25} = 5$
   $d_2 = \sqrt{(5-5)^2 + (5-2)^2}$
   $= \sqrt{0+9} = \sqrt{9} = 3$
   $d_3 = \sqrt{(5-1)^2 + (2-2)^2}$
   $= \sqrt{16+0} = \sqrt{16} = 4$
   $3^2 + 4^2 \stackrel{?}{=} 5^2$
   $9 + 16 \stackrel{?}{=} 25$
   $25 = 25$; a right triangle

6. $d_1 = \sqrt{(3-0)^2 + (5-2)^2}$
   $= \sqrt{9+9} = \sqrt{18} = \sqrt{9 \cdot 2} = 3\sqrt{2} \approx 4.2$
   $d_2 = \sqrt{(5-0)^2 + (3-2)^2}$
   $= \sqrt{25+1} = \sqrt{26} \approx 5.1$
   $d_3 = \sqrt{(3-5)^2 + (5-3)^2}$
   $= \sqrt{4+4} = \sqrt{8} = \sqrt{4 \cdot 2} = 2\sqrt{2} \approx 2.8$
   $(\sqrt{18})^2 + (\sqrt{8})^2 \stackrel{?}{=} (\sqrt{26})^2$
   $18 + 8 \stackrel{?}{=} 26$
   $26 = 26$; a right triangle

7. $d_1 = \sqrt{(3-1)^2 + (6-1)^2}$
   $= \sqrt{4+25} = \sqrt{29}$
   $d_2 = \sqrt{(3-5)^2 + (6-3)^2}$
   $= \sqrt{4+9} = \sqrt{13}$
   $d_3 = \sqrt{(5-1)^2 + (3-1)^2}$
   $= \sqrt{16+4} = \sqrt{20}$
   $(\sqrt{13})^2 + (\sqrt{20})^2 \stackrel{?}{=} (\sqrt{29})^2$
   $13 + 20 \stackrel{?}{=} 29$
   $33 \neq 29$; not a right triangle

8. (15, 25), (30, 65)
   $d = \sqrt{(30-15)^2 + (65-25)^2}$
   $d = \sqrt{225+1600} = \sqrt{1825} \approx 42.7$ yards

12.7 Guided Practice (p. 733)

1. Pythagorean theorem

2. $d = \sqrt{(-3-1)^2 + (1-5)^2}$
   $= \sqrt{16+16} = \sqrt{32} \approx 5.66$

3. $d = \sqrt{[4-(-3)]^2 + [1-(-2)]^2}$
   $= \sqrt{49+9} = \sqrt{58} \approx 7.62$

4. $d = \sqrt{(-1-5)^2 + [1-(-2)]^2}$
   $= \sqrt{36+9} = \sqrt{45} \approx 6.71$

5. $d_1 = \sqrt{(20-0)^2 + (0-0)^2} = \sqrt{20^2} = 20$
   $d_2 = \sqrt{(20-0)^2 + (21-0)^2} = \sqrt{400+441}$
   $= \sqrt{841} = 29$
   $d_3 = \sqrt{(20-20)^2 + (21-0)^2} = \sqrt{21^2} = 21$
   $21^2 + 20^2 \stackrel{?}{=} 29^2$
   $441 + 400 \stackrel{?}{=} 841$
   $841 = 841$; a right triangle

6. $d_1 = \sqrt{(4-4)^2 + (-4-0)^2} = \sqrt{16} = 4$
   $d_2 = \sqrt{(10-4)^2 + (-4-0)^2} = \sqrt{36+16} = \sqrt{52}$
   $d_2 \approx 7.2$
   $d_3 = \sqrt{(10-4)^2 + [-4-(-4)]^2} = \sqrt{36} = 6$
   $4^2 + 6^2 \stackrel{?}{=} (7.2)^2$
   $16 + 36 \stackrel{?}{=} 52$
   $52 = 52$; a right triangle

7. $d_1 = \sqrt{[-1-(-2)]^2 + (0-0)^2} = \sqrt{1^2} = 1$
   $d_2 = \sqrt{[1-(-2)]^2 + (7-0)^2} = \sqrt{9+49} = \sqrt{58}$
   ≈ 7.6
   $d_3 = \sqrt{[1-(-1)]^2 + (7-0)^2} = \sqrt{4+49} = \sqrt{53}$
   ≈ 7.3
   $1^2 + (7.3)^2 \stackrel{?}{=} (7.6)^2$
   $1 + 53 \stackrel{?}{=} 58$
   $54 \neq 58$; not a right triangle

8. $d_1 = \sqrt{(-2-2)^2 + (2-0)^2} = \sqrt{16+4} = \sqrt{20}$
   ≈ 4.5
   $d_2 = \sqrt{(-3-2)^2 + (-5-0)^2}$
   $= \sqrt{25+25} = \sqrt{50}$
   ≈ 7.1
   $d_3 = \sqrt{[-3-(-2)]^2 + (-5-2)^2}$
   $= \sqrt{1+49} = \sqrt{50}$
   ≈ 7.1
   $4.5^2 + 7.1^2 \stackrel{?}{=} 7.1^2$
   $20 + 50 \stackrel{?}{=} 50$
   $70 \neq 50$; not a right triangle

9. (10, 5), (25, 25)
   $d = \sqrt{(25-10)^2 + (25-5)^2}$
   $= \sqrt{225+400} = \sqrt{625} = 25$ yd

Copyright © McDougal Littell Inc.
All rights reserved.

12.7 Practice and Applications (pp. 733–735)

10. $d = \sqrt{(8 - 2)^2 + (-3 - 0)^2}$
$= \sqrt{36 + 9} = \sqrt{45} \approx 6.71$

11. $d = \sqrt{(-3 - 2)^2 + [3 - (-8)]^2}$
$= \sqrt{25 + 121}$
$= \sqrt{146} \approx 12.08$

12. $d = \sqrt{(0 - 3)^2 + [3 - (-2)]^2}$
$= \sqrt{9 + 25} = \sqrt{34} \approx 5.83$

13. $d = \sqrt{(-2 - 5)^2 + (3 - 8)^2}$
$= \sqrt{49 + 25} = \sqrt{74} \approx 8.60$

14. $d = \sqrt{[2 - (-3)]^2 + (6 - 1)^2}$
$= \sqrt{25 + 25} = \sqrt{50} \approx 7.07$

15. $d = \sqrt{[-3 - (-6)]^2 + [-5 - (-2)]^2}$
$= \sqrt{9 + 9}$
$= \sqrt{18} \approx 4.24$

16. $d = \sqrt{(-1 - 4)^2 + (3 - 5)^2}$
$= \sqrt{25 + 4} = \sqrt{29} \approx 5.39$

17. $d = \sqrt{[3 - (-6)]^2 + (1 - 1)^2}$
$= \sqrt{81 + 0} = \sqrt{81} = 9$

18. $d = \sqrt{[3 - (-2)]^2 + [-3 - (-1)]^2}$
$= \sqrt{25 + 4}$
$= \sqrt{29} \approx 5.39$

19. $d = \sqrt{(-7 - 7)^2 + (-4 - 12)^2}$
$= \sqrt{196 + 256}$
$= \sqrt{452} \approx 21.26$

20. $d = \sqrt{(8 - 2)^2 + (4 - 1)^2}$
$= \sqrt{36 + 9} = \sqrt{45} \approx 6.71$

21. $d = \sqrt{(-4 - 2)^2 + (16 - 1)^2}$
$= \sqrt{36 + 225}$
$= \sqrt{261} \approx 16.16$

22. $d = \sqrt{[0 - (-1)]^2 + (7 - 9)^2}$
$= \sqrt{1 + 4} = \sqrt{5} \approx 2.24$

23. $d = \sqrt{(-5 - 4)^2 + (2 - 11)^2}$
$= \sqrt{81 + 81}$
$= \sqrt{162} \approx 12.73$

24. $d = \sqrt{[1 - (-10)]^2 + [7 - (-2)]^2}$
$= \sqrt{121 + 81}$
$= \sqrt{202} \approx 14.21$

25. $d_1 = \sqrt{(2 - 4)^2 + (1 - 0)^2} = \sqrt{4 + 1} = \sqrt{5}$
≈ 2.24
$d_2 = \sqrt{(-1 - 4)^2 + (-5 - 0)^2}$
$= \sqrt{25 + 25}$
$= \sqrt{50}$
≈ 7.07
$d_3 = \sqrt{(-1 - 2)^2 + (-5 - 1)^2} = \sqrt{9 + 36} = \sqrt{45}$
≈ 6.71
$2.24^2 + 6.71^2 \stackrel{?}{=} 7.07^2$
$5 + 45 \stackrel{?}{=} 50$
$50 = 50$; a right triangle

26. $d_1 = \sqrt{(2 - 5)^2 + (1 - 4)^2} = \sqrt{9 + 9} = \sqrt{18}$
≈ 4.24
$d_2 = \sqrt{(-3 - 5)^2 + (2 - 4)^2} = \sqrt{64 + 4} = \sqrt{68}$
≈ 8.25
$d_3 = \sqrt{(-3 - 2)^2 + (2 - 1)^2} = \sqrt{25 + 1} = \sqrt{26}$
≈ 5.10
$4.24^2 + 5.10^2 \stackrel{?}{=} 8.25^2$
$18 + 26 \stackrel{?}{=} 68$
$44 \neq 68$; not a right triangle

27. $d_1 = \sqrt{(2 - 1)^2 + [3 - (-5)]^2} = \sqrt{1 + 64} = \sqrt{65}$
≈ 8.06
$d_2 = \sqrt{(-3 - 1)^2 + [4 - (-5)]^2}$
$= \sqrt{16 + 81}$
$= \sqrt{97}$
≈ 9.85
$d_3 = \sqrt{(-3 - 2)^2 + (4 - 3)^2} = \sqrt{25 + 1} = \sqrt{26}$
≈ 5.10
$5.10^2 + 8.06^2 \stackrel{?}{=} 9.85^2$
$26 + 65 \stackrel{?}{=} 97$
$91 \neq 97$; not a right triangle

28. $d_1 = \sqrt{[-3 - (-1)]^2 + (3 - 1)^2}$
$= \sqrt{4 + 4} = \sqrt{8} \approx 2.83$
$d_2 = \sqrt{[-7 - (-1)]^2 + (-1 - 1)^2}$
$= \sqrt{36 + 4} = \sqrt{40} \approx 6.32$
$d_3 = \sqrt{[-7 - (-3)]^2 + (-1 - 3)^2}$
$= \sqrt{16 + 16} = \sqrt{32} \approx 5.66$
$2.83^2 + 5.66^2 \stackrel{?}{=} 6.32^2$
$8 + 32 \stackrel{?}{=} 40$
$40 = 40$; a right triangle

Copyright © McDougal Littell Inc.
All rights reserved.

Chapter 12 *continued*

29. $d_1 = \sqrt{[-3-(-3)]^2 + (5-2)^2}$
$= \sqrt{0+9} = \sqrt{9} = 3$
$d_2 = \sqrt{[0-(-3)]^2 + (2-2)^2}$
$= \sqrt{9+0} = \sqrt{9} = 3$
$d_3 = \sqrt{[0-(-3)]^2 + (2-5)^2}$
$= \sqrt{9+9} = \sqrt{18} \approx 4.24$
$3^2 + 3^2 \stackrel{?}{=} 4.24^2$
$9 + 9 \stackrel{?}{=} 18$
$18 = 18$; a right triangle

30. $d_1 = \sqrt{(2-3)^2 + [4-(-1)]^2}$
$= \sqrt{1+25} = \sqrt{26} \approx 5.10$
$d_2 = \sqrt{(-3-3)^2 + [0-(-1)]^2}$
$= \sqrt{36+1} = \sqrt{37} \approx 6.08$
$d_3 = \sqrt{(-3-2)^2 + (0-4)^2}$
$= \sqrt{25+16} = \sqrt{41} \approx 6.40$
$5.10^2 + 6.08^2 \stackrel{?}{=} 6.40^2$
$26 + 37 \stackrel{?}{=} 41$
$63 \neq 41$; not a right triangle

31. $A(-3, -2), B(1, 2); C(2, -2)$
$AB = \sqrt{[1-(-3)]^2 + [2-(-2)]^2}$
$= \sqrt{16+16} = \sqrt{32} = 4\sqrt{2} \approx 5.66$
$CA = \sqrt{[2-(-3)]^2 + [-2-(-2)]^2}$
$= \sqrt{25+0} = \sqrt{25} = 5$
$BC = \sqrt{(2-1)^2 + (-2-2)^2}$
$= \sqrt{1+16} = \sqrt{17} \approx 4.12$

32. $P = 5.66 + 5 + 4.12 = 14.78$ units

33. $d = \sqrt{(100-0)^2 + (250-0)^2}$
$= \sqrt{10{,}000 + 62{,}500} = \sqrt{72{,}500}$
$d \approx 269.25$; about 269 miles

34. Home to amusement park: 269 miles
Amusement park to beach: 403 miles
$d = \sqrt{(450-100)^2 + (450-250)^2}$
$= \sqrt{122{,}500 + 40{,}000}$
$= \sqrt{162{,}500} \approx 403.11$
Beach to home: 636 miles
$d = \sqrt{(450-0)^2 + (450-0)^2}$
$= \sqrt{202{,}500 + 202{,}500} = \sqrt{405{,}000}$
≈ 636.40
Distance traveled:
$269.25 + 403.11 + 636.40 \approx 1309$ miles

35. $d = \sqrt{[30-(-305)]^2 + [420-(-160)]^2}$
$= \sqrt{112{,}225 + 336{,}400}$
$= \sqrt{448{,}625} \approx 670$ miles

36. $d = \sqrt{[170-(-305)]^2 + [-15-(-160)]^2}$
$= \sqrt{225{,}625 + 21{,}025}$
≈ 497 miles

37. $d = \sqrt{(30-170)^2 + [420-(-15)]^2}$
$= \sqrt{19{,}600 + 189{,}225}$
≈ 457 miles

38. $d_1 = \sqrt{(2-0)^2 + (6-0)^2} = \sqrt{4+36}$
$= \sqrt{40} \approx 6.32$
$d_2 = \sqrt{(8-2)^2 + (8-6)^2} = \sqrt{36+4}$
$= \sqrt{40} \approx 6.32$
$d_3 = \sqrt{(8-14)^2 + (8-0)^2}$
$= \sqrt{36+64} = \sqrt{100} = 10$
$d_4 = 14$
$P = 6.32 + 6.32 + 10 + 14 = 36.65$ units

39. $d_1 = \sqrt{[-8-(-6)]^2 + [-6-(-2)]^2}$
$= \sqrt{4+16} = \sqrt{20} \approx 4.47$
$d_2 = \sqrt{(-6-4)^2 + (-2-4)^2}$
$= \sqrt{100+36} = \sqrt{136} \approx 11.66$
$d_3 = \sqrt{(6-4)^2 + (0-4)^2}$
$= \sqrt{4+16} = \sqrt{20} \approx 4.47$
$d_4 = \sqrt{(6-0)^2 + [0-(-8)]^2}$
$= \sqrt{36+64} = \sqrt{100} = 10$
$d_5 = \sqrt{(-8-0)^2 + [-6-(-8)]^2}$
$= \sqrt{64+4} = \sqrt{68} \approx 8.25$
$P = 4.47 + 11.66 + 4.47 + 10 + 8.25 = 38.85$ units

12.7 Standardized Test Practice (p. 735)

40. C;
$d = \sqrt{[2-(-6)]^2 + [4-(-2)]^2}$
$= \sqrt{64+36} = \sqrt{100} = 10$

41. G;
$d = \sqrt{(0-6)^2 + (6-0)^2}$
$= \sqrt{36+36}$
$= \sqrt{72} = \sqrt{36 \cdot 2} = 6\sqrt{2}$

12.7 Mixed Review (p. 735)

42. $m^2 - 25 = (m+5)(m-5)$

43. $81x^2 - 144 = 9(9x^2 - 16) = 9(3x+4)(3x-4)$

44. $16t^2 - 49 = (4t+7)(4t-7)$

45. $x^2 + 12x + 36 = (x+6)^2$

46. $c^2 - 22c + 121 = (c-11)^2$

Copyright © McDougal Littell Inc.
All rights reserved.

47. $9s^2 + 6s + 1 = (3s + 1)^2$

48. $4n^2 - 64 = 4(n^2 - 16) = 4(n + 4)(n - 4)$

49. $72 - 50p^2 = 2(36 - 25p^2) = 2(6 + 5p)(6 - 5p)$

50. $60y^2 - 240 = 60(y^2 - 4) = 60(y + 2)(y - 2)$

51. $3y^3 + 15y^2 - 18y = 3y(y^2 + 5y - 6)$
$= 3y(y + 6)(y - 1)$

52. $2t^3 - 98t = 2t(t^2 - 49) = 2t(t + 7)(t - 7)$

53. $2x^4 - 8x^2 = 2x^2(x^2 - 4) = 2x^2(x + 2)(x - 2)$

54. $c^3 + 2c^2 - 8c - 16 = c^2(c + 2) - 8(c + 2)$
$= (c + 2)(c^2 - 8)$

55. $\dfrac{4x}{28} = \dfrac{x}{7}$

56. $\dfrac{15x}{75} = \dfrac{x}{5}$

57. $\dfrac{-48x^3}{-12x^2} = 4x$

58. $\dfrac{18x^3}{56x^7} = \dfrac{9}{28x^4}$

59. $\dfrac{-3x^2 + 21x}{12x^2} = \dfrac{3x(-x + 7)}{12x^2} = \dfrac{7 - x}{4x}$

60. $\dfrac{35x - 7x^3}{49x} = \dfrac{7x(5 - x^2)}{49x} = \dfrac{5 - x^2}{7}$

61. $\dfrac{-4x^2 - 24x}{-4x} = \dfrac{-4x(x + 6)}{-4x} = x + 6$

62. $\dfrac{7p^5 + 18p^4}{p^4} = \dfrac{p^4(7p + 18)}{p^4} = 7p + 18$

63. $\dfrac{9a^2 - 27a - 36}{a + 1} = \dfrac{9(a^2 - 3a - 4)}{a + 1}$
$= \dfrac{9(a - 4)(a + 1)}{a + 1}$
$= 9(a - 4)$
$= 9a - 36$

64. $\dfrac{4n^2 - 41n + 45}{4n - 5} = \dfrac{(4n - 5)(n - 9)}{4n - 5} = n - 9$

65. $\dfrac{3}{x} + \dfrac{x + 9}{x} = \dfrac{3 + x + 9}{x} = \dfrac{x + 12}{x}$

66. $\dfrac{8}{4a + 1} + \dfrac{5}{4a + 1} = \dfrac{13}{4a + 1}$

67. $\dfrac{2}{2x} + \dfrac{12}{x} = \dfrac{1}{x} + \dfrac{12}{x} = \dfrac{13}{x}$

68. $\dfrac{2x}{x + 1} + \dfrac{5}{x + 3} = \dfrac{2x(x + 3)}{(x + 1)(x + 3)} + \dfrac{5(x + 1)}{(x + 1)(x + 3)}$
$= \dfrac{2x^2 + 6x + 5x + 5}{(x + 1)(x + 3)}$
$= \dfrac{2x^2 + 11x + 5}{(x + 1)(x + 3)}$
$= \dfrac{(2x + 1)(x + 5)}{(x + 1)(x + 3)}$
or $\dfrac{2x^2 + 11x + 5}{x^2 + 4x + 3}$

69. $\dfrac{5}{4x} + \dfrac{7}{3x} = \dfrac{5(3)}{12x} + \dfrac{7(4)}{12x}$
$= \dfrac{15 + 28}{12x}$
$= \dfrac{43}{12x}$

70. $\dfrac{6x}{x + 1} + \dfrac{2x + 4}{x + 1} = \dfrac{6x + 2x + 4}{x + 1} = \dfrac{8x + 4}{x + 1}$

12.7 Maintaining Skills (p. 735)

71. $\dfrac{2}{5} = 0.40 = 40\%$

72. $\dfrac{4}{5} = 0.80 = 80\%$

73. $\dfrac{1}{3} = 0.33\overline{3} = 33.\overline{3}\%$

74. $\dfrac{9}{10} = 0.9 = 90\%$

75. $\dfrac{5}{8} = 0.625 = 62.5\%$

76. $\dfrac{11}{20} = 0.55 = 55\%$

77. $\dfrac{4}{100} = 0.04 = 4\%$

78. $\dfrac{9}{25} = 0.36 = 36\%$

Lesson 12.8

12.8 Checkpoint (pp. 736–737)

1. $\left(\dfrac{-2 + 4}{2}, \dfrac{3 + 1}{2}\right) = (1, 2)$

2. $\left(\dfrac{2 + 2}{2}, \dfrac{5 + (-1)}{2}\right) = (2, 2)$

3. $\left(\dfrac{0 + 4}{2}, \dfrac{0 + 6}{2}\right) = (2, 3)$

4. $\left(\dfrac{1 + 2}{2}, \dfrac{2 + (-2)}{2}\right) = \left(\dfrac{3}{2}, 0\right)$

5. $\left(\dfrac{25 + 112.5}{2}, \dfrac{175 + 125}{2}\right) = (68.75, 150)$

12.8 Guided Practice (p. 738)

1. It is the point on the line segment that is halfway between the endpoints or that is equidistant from each endpoint.

2. Use a graph or use the distance formula.

3. $\left(\dfrac{4 + (-1)}{2}, \dfrac{4 + 2}{2}\right) = \left(\dfrac{3}{2}, 3\right)$

4. $\left(\dfrac{6 + 2}{2}, \dfrac{2 + (-3)}{2}\right) = \left(4, -\dfrac{1}{2}\right)$

Copyright © McDougal Littell Inc.
All rights reserved.

5. $\left(\frac{-5+(-3)}{2}, \frac{3+(-3)}{2}\right) = (-4, 0)$

6. $\left(\frac{-4+2}{2}, \frac{4+0}{2}\right) = (-1, 2)$

7. $\left(\frac{0+0}{2}, \frac{0+10}{2}\right) = (0, 5)$

8. $\left(\frac{2+14}{2}, \frac{1+6}{2}\right) = \left(8, \frac{7}{2}\right)$

9. $\left(\frac{-2+6}{2}, \frac{0+2}{2}\right) = (2, 1)$

$d_1 = \sqrt{[2-(-2)]^2 + (1-0)^2}$
$= \sqrt{16+1} = \sqrt{17} \approx 4.12$
$d_2 = \sqrt{(2-6)^2 + (1-2)^2}$
$= \sqrt{16+1} = \sqrt{17} \approx 4.12$

10. $\left(\frac{-2+2}{2}, \frac{2+(-10)}{2}\right) = (0, -4)$

$d_1 = \sqrt{[0-(-2)]^2 + (-4-2)^2}$
$= \sqrt{4+36} = \sqrt{40} \approx 6.32$
$d_2 = \sqrt{(0-2)^2 + [-4-(-10)]^2}$
$= \sqrt{4+36} = \sqrt{40} \approx 6.32$

11. $\left(\frac{2+4}{2}, \frac{6+2}{2}\right) = (3, 4)$

$d_1 = \sqrt{(2-3)^2 + (6-4)^2}$
$= \sqrt{1+4} = \sqrt{5} \approx 2.24$
$d_2 = \sqrt{(4-3)^2 + (2-4)^2}$
$= \sqrt{1+4} = \sqrt{5} \approx 2.24$

12. $\left(\frac{-6+(-10)}{2}, \frac{0+(-2)}{2}\right) = (-8, -1)$

$d_1 = \sqrt{[-8-(-6)]^2 + (-1-0)^2}$
$= \sqrt{4+1} = \sqrt{5} \approx 2.24$
$d_2 = \sqrt{[-10-(-8)]^2 + [-2-(-1)]^2}$
$= \sqrt{4+1} = \sqrt{5} \approx 2.24$

13. $\left(\frac{-3+1}{2}, \frac{6+8}{2}\right) = (-1, 7)$

$d_1 = \sqrt{[-1-(-3)]^2 + (7-6)^2}$
$= \sqrt{4+1} = \sqrt{5} \approx 2.24$
$d_2 = \sqrt{(-1-1)^2 + (7-8)^2}$
$= \sqrt{4+1} = \sqrt{5} \approx 2.24$

14. $\left(\frac{0+(-8)}{2}, \frac{0+12}{2}\right) = (-4, 6)$

$d_1 = \sqrt{(-4-0)^2 + (6-0)^2}$
$= \sqrt{16+36} = \sqrt{52} \approx 7.21$
$d_2 = \sqrt{[-4-(-8)]^2 + (6-12)^2}$
$= \sqrt{16+36} = \sqrt{52} \approx 7.21$

12.8 Practice and Applications (pp. 738–739)

15. $\left(\frac{1+5}{2}, \frac{2+4}{2}\right) = (3, 3)$

16. $\left(\frac{0+0}{2}, \frac{0+8}{2}\right) = (0, 4)$

17. $\left(\frac{-1+7}{2}, \frac{2+4}{2}\right) = (3, 3)$

18. $\left(\frac{0+(-4)}{2}, \frac{-3+2}{2}\right) = \left(-2, -\frac{1}{2}\right)$

19. $\left(\frac{-3+2}{2}, \frac{3+(-2)}{2}\right) = \left(-\frac{1}{2}, \frac{1}{2}\right)$

20. $\left(\frac{5+(-5)}{2}, \frac{-5+1}{2}\right) = (0, -2)$

21. $\left(\frac{-1+(-4)}{2}, \frac{1+(-4)}{2}\right) = \left(-\frac{5}{2}, -\frac{3}{2}\right)$

22. $\left(\frac{-4+(-1)}{2}, \frac{0+(-5)}{2}\right) = \left(-\frac{5}{2}, -\frac{5}{2}\right)$

23. $\left(\frac{-4+(-1)}{2}, \frac{-3+(-5)}{2}\right) = \left(-\frac{5}{2}, -4\right)$

24. $\left(\frac{7+(-1)}{2}, \frac{-3+(-9)}{2}\right) = (3, -6)$

$d_1 = \sqrt{(3-7)^2 + [-6-(-3)]^2}$
$= \sqrt{16+9} = \sqrt{25} = 5$
$d_2 = \sqrt{[3-(-1)]^2 + [-6-(-9)]^2}$
$= \sqrt{16+9} = \sqrt{25} = 5$

25. $\left(\frac{1+0}{2}, \frac{2+0}{2}\right) = \left(\frac{1}{2}, 1\right)$

$d_1 = \sqrt{\left(\frac{1}{2}-1\right)^2 + (1-2)^2}$
$= \sqrt{\frac{1}{4}+1} = \sqrt{\frac{5}{4}} = \frac{\sqrt{5}}{2}$
$d_2 = \sqrt{\left(\frac{1}{2}-0\right)^2 + (1-0)^2}$
$= \sqrt{\frac{1}{4}+1} = \sqrt{\frac{5}{4}} = \frac{\sqrt{5}}{2}$

26. $\left(\frac{3+(-5)}{2}, \frac{0+4}{2}\right) = (-1, 2)$

$d_1 = \sqrt{(-1-3)^2 + (2-0)^2}$
$= \sqrt{16+4} = \sqrt{20} = 2\sqrt{5}$
$d_2 = \sqrt{[-1-(-5)]^2 + (2-4)^2}$
$= \sqrt{16+4} = \sqrt{20} = 2\sqrt{5}$

27. $\left(\frac{5+1}{2}, \frac{1+(-5)}{2}\right) = (3, -2)$

$d_1 = \sqrt{(3-5)^2 + (-2-1)^2}$
$= \sqrt{4+9} = \sqrt{13}$
$d_2 = \sqrt{(3-1)^2 + [-2-(-5)]^2}$
$= \sqrt{4+9} = \sqrt{13}$

Copyright © McDougal Littell Inc.
All rights reserved.

28. $\left(\frac{2+4}{2}, \frac{7+3}{2}\right) = (3, 5)$

$d_1 = \sqrt{(3-2)^2 + (5-7)^2}$
$= \sqrt{1+4} = \sqrt{5}$
$d_2 = \sqrt{(3-4)^2 + (5-3)^2}$
$= \sqrt{1+4} = \sqrt{5}$

29. $\left(\frac{-3+1}{2}, \frac{-2+7}{2}\right) = \left(-1, \frac{5}{2}\right)$

$d_1 = \sqrt{[-1-(-3)]^2 + \left[\frac{5}{2}-(-2)\right]^2}$
$= \sqrt{4 + \left(\frac{9}{2}\right)^2} = \sqrt{4 + \frac{81}{4}}$
$= \sqrt{\frac{16+81}{4}} = \frac{\sqrt{97}}{2}$
$d_2 = \sqrt{(-1-1)^2 + \left(\frac{5}{2}-7\right)^2}$
$= \sqrt{4 + \left(-\frac{9}{2}\right)^2} = \sqrt{4 + \frac{81}{4}}$
$= \sqrt{\frac{16+81}{4}} = \frac{\sqrt{97}}{2}$

30. $\left(\frac{-3+6}{2}, \frac{-3+7}{2}\right) = \left(\frac{3}{2}, 2\right)$

$d_1 = \sqrt{\left[\frac{3}{2}-(-3)\right]^2 + [2-(-3)]^2}$
$= \sqrt{\left(-\frac{9}{2}\right)^2 + 25} = \sqrt{\frac{81}{4} + \frac{100}{4}} = \frac{\sqrt{181}}{2}$
$d_2 = \sqrt{\left[\frac{3}{2}-6\right]^2 + [2-7]^2}$
$= \sqrt{\left(-\frac{9}{2}\right)^2 + 25} = \sqrt{\frac{81}{4} + \frac{100}{4}} = \frac{\sqrt{181}}{2}$

31. $\left(\frac{-9+5}{2}, \frac{17+(-7)}{2}\right) = (-2, 5)$

$d_1 = \sqrt{[-2-(-9)]^2 + (5-17)^2}$
$= \sqrt{49+144} = \sqrt{193}$
$d_2 = \sqrt{(-2-5)^2 + [5-(-7)]^2}$
$= \sqrt{49+144} = \sqrt{193}$

32. $\left(\frac{-4+10}{2}, \frac{-2+(-6)}{2}\right) = (3, -4)$

$d_1 = \sqrt{(-4-3)^2 + [-2-(-4)]^2}$
$= \sqrt{49+4} = \sqrt{53}$
$d_2 = \sqrt{(3-10)^2 + [-4-(-6)]^2}$
$= \sqrt{49+4} = \sqrt{53}$

33. $\left(\frac{-13+(-4)}{2}, \frac{8+(-6)}{2}\right) = \left(-\frac{17}{2}, 1\right)$

$\left(\frac{-13+18}{2}, \frac{8+8}{2}\right) = \left(\frac{5}{2}, 8\right)$

$\left(\frac{18+(-4)}{2}, \frac{8+(-6)}{2}\right) = (7, 1)$

34. $d_1 = \sqrt{\left(-\frac{17}{2}-\frac{5}{2}\right)^2 + (1-8)^2}$
$= \sqrt{\left(-\frac{22}{2}\right)^2 + 49} = \sqrt{11^2 + 49}$
$= \sqrt{121+49} = \sqrt{170} \approx 13.04$ units
$d_2 = \sqrt{\left(\frac{5}{2}-7\right)^2 + (8-1)^2}$
$= \sqrt{\left(\frac{5-14}{2}\right)^2 + 49}$
$= \sqrt{\left(-\frac{9}{2}\right)^2 + 49} = \sqrt{\frac{81}{4} + 49}$
$= \sqrt{\frac{81+196}{4}} = \frac{\sqrt{277}}{2} \approx 8.32$ units
$d_3 = \sqrt{\left(-\frac{17}{2}-7\right)^2 + (1-1)^2}$
$= \sqrt{\left(-\frac{31}{2}\right)^2 + 0} = \frac{31}{2} = 15.5$ units

35. $\left(\frac{40.0+39.9}{2}, \frac{115.5+115.2}{2}\right) = (39.95, 115.35)$
$= (39.95°\text{N}, 115.35°\text{W})$

36.

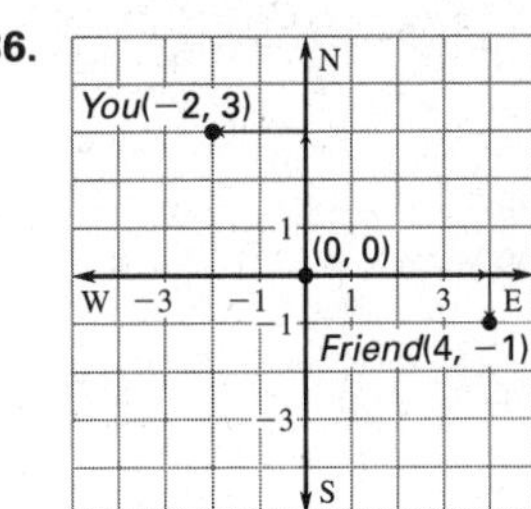

$d = \sqrt{[4-(-2)]^2 + (-1-3)^2}$
$= \sqrt{36+16} = \sqrt{52} \approx 7.21$ miles

37. Find midpoint from Exercise 36.
$\left(\frac{-2+4}{2}, \frac{3+(-1)}{2}\right) = (1, 1);$
1 mi east and 1 mi north of the starting point. To reach meeting place, you go 3 mi east and 2 mi south;
$d = \sqrt{(-2-1)^2 + (3-1)^2} = \sqrt{(-3)^2 + (2)^2} =$
$\sqrt{9+4} = \sqrt{13} \approx 3.61$ mi.

12.8 Standardized Test Practice (p. 739)

38. B; $\left(\frac{-2+1}{2}, \frac{-3+7}{2}\right) = \left(-\frac{1}{2}, 2\right)$

Copyright © McDougal Littell Inc.
All rights reserved.

12.8 Mixed Review (p. 739)

39. $4x + 3y = 1$

$$\begin{aligned} 2x - 3y &= 1 \\ \hline 6x &= 2 \\ x &= \frac{1}{3} \end{aligned}$$

$$4\left(\frac{1}{3}\right) + 3y = 1$$

$$3y = 1 - \frac{4}{3}$$

$$3y = -\frac{1}{3}$$

$$y = -\frac{1}{9}$$

Solution: $\left(\frac{1}{3}, -\frac{1}{9}\right)$

Check:

$$2\left(\frac{1}{3}\right) - 3\left(-\frac{1}{9}\right) \stackrel{?}{=} 1$$

$$\frac{2}{3} + \frac{1}{3} \stackrel{?}{=} 1$$

$$1 = 1$$

Check:

$$3\left(-\frac{1}{2}\right) + 5\left(\frac{3}{2}\right) \stackrel{?}{=} 6$$

$$-\frac{3}{2} + \frac{15}{2} \stackrel{?}{=} 6$$

$$\frac{12}{2} \stackrel{?}{=} 6$$

$$6 = 6$$

40. *Sample answer:*

$3x + 5y = 6$ multiply by 2

$-4x + 2y = 5$ multiply by -5

$$\begin{aligned} 6x + 10y &= 12 \\ 20x - 10y &= -25 \\ \hline 26x &= -13 \\ x &= -\frac{1}{2} \end{aligned}$$

$$-4\left(-\frac{1}{2}\right) + 2y = 5$$

$$2 + 2y = 5$$

$$2y = 3$$

$$y = \frac{3}{2}$$

Solution: $\left(-\frac{1}{2}, \frac{3}{2}\right)$

Check:

$$3\left(-\frac{1}{2}\right) + 5\left(\frac{3}{2}\right) \stackrel{?}{=} 6$$

$$-\frac{3}{2} + \frac{15}{2} \stackrel{?}{=} 6$$

$$\frac{12}{2} \stackrel{?}{=} 6$$

$$6 = 6$$

41. $2x + 3y = 1$ multiply by 5

$5x - 4y = 14$ multiply by -2

$$\begin{aligned} 10x + 15y &= 5 \\ -10x + 8y &= -28 \\ \hline 23y &= -23 \\ y &= -1 \end{aligned}$$

$$\begin{aligned} 2x + 3(-1) &= 1 \\ 2x - 3 &= 1 \\ 2x &= 4 \\ x &= 2 \end{aligned}$$

Solution: $(2, -1)$

Check:

$$2(2) + 3(-1) \stackrel{?}{=} 1$$

$$4 - 3 \stackrel{?}{=} 1$$

$$1 = 1$$

42. $2x + y = 3$

$$\begin{aligned} y &= -2x + 3 \\ 4x + 2(-2x + 3) &= 8 \\ 4x - 4x + 6 &= 8 \end{aligned}$$

$6 \neq 8$; no solution

43. $2x + 2y = 3$

$-4x - 2y = -6$ (multiplied by -1)

$$\begin{aligned} -2x &= -3 \\ x &= \frac{3}{2} \end{aligned}$$

$$2\left(\frac{3}{2}\right) + 2y = 3$$

$$\begin{aligned} 3 + 2y &= 3 \\ 2y &= 0 \\ y &= 0 \end{aligned}$$

Solution: $\left(\frac{3}{2}, 0\right)$

44. $2x + y = -4$

$$\begin{aligned} y &= -2x - 4 \\ (-2x - 4) + 2x &= 8 \end{aligned}$$

$-4 \neq 8$; no solution

12.8 Maintaining Skills (p. 739)

45. $54\% = 0.54$

46. $\frac{2}{3} \approx 66.7\% > 6\left(\frac{2}{3}\right)\%$

47. $\frac{3}{1000} = 0.003 < 0.03$

48. $0.23 = \frac{23}{100}$

Copyright © McDougal Littell Inc.
All rights reserved.

Lesson 12.9

12.9 Checkpoint (pp. 741–743)

1. $(a + b) + c = a + (b + c)$ Associative property
$= (b + c) + a$ Commutative property

2. Since the client commutes 45 minutes to work, she left her house at 8:30 a.m. By 9 a.m. the time when the violation occurred, she would have been closer to work than home. Thus, she could not have been at the place where the violation occurred at 9 a.m.

12.9 Guided Practice (p. 743)

1. An axiom is a mathematical rule accepted without proof. A theorem is a statement that can be proven true, based on the axioms.

2. You assume the statement is false.

3. $y(1) = y$; Identify property of multiplication

4. $2x + 3 = 3 + 2x$; commutative property of addition

5. $5(x + y) = 5x + 5y$; distributive property

6. $(4x)y = 4(xy)$; associative property of multiplication

7. $y + 0 = y$; identity property of addition

8. $x + (-x) = 0$; inverse property of addition

12.9 Practice and Applications (pp. 744–746)

9. $(a + b) - b = (a + b) + (-b)$ Def. of subtraction
$= a + [b + (-b)]$ Associative property of addition
$= a + 0$ Inverse property of addition
$= a$ Identity property of addition

10. $a - b = a + (-b)$ Def. of subtraction
$= -b + a$ Commutative property of addition

11. $(a - b)c = [a + (-b)]c$ Def. of subtraction
$= ac + (-b)c$ Distributive property
$= ac - bc$ Def. of subtraction

12. No, this does not prove that it is true for all cases. It seems to be true.

13. Sample answer: Let $a = 3, b = 4$
$(3 + 4)^2 \stackrel{?}{=} 3^2 + 4^2$
$7^2 \stackrel{?}{=} 9 + 16$
$49 \neq 25$

14. Sample answer: Let $a = 15, b = 3, c = 3$
$(15 \div 3) \div 3 \stackrel{?}{=} 15 \div (3 \div 3)$
$5 \div 3 \stackrel{?}{=} 15 \div 1$
$\frac{5}{3} \neq 15$

15. Sample answer: Let $a = 3, b = 2$. Then $a \div b = 3 \div 2 = 1.5$, which is not an integer.

16. Sample answer: Let $a = 16$. Then $\sqrt{a} = 4$, which is a rational number.

17. Yes, the map is a counterexample to the proposal. Only one counterexample is needed to show a conjecture is false.

18. The figures show 1, 1 + 3, 1 + 3 + 5, 1 + 3 + 5 + 7, 1 + 3 + 5 + 7 + 9. With each arrangement, a perfect square is formed. The sum of the odd integers is a square number.

19. For the bus to travel 45 miles at 60 mph, it will take 45 minutes. 45 minutes past 4:30 p.m. is 5:15 p.m., which is 15 minutes after dinner is served.

20. Suppose $a + c \geq b + c$.
$a \geq b$ Subtract c from both sides.
This contradicts the assumption that $a < b$.
So $a + c < b + c$.

21. Suppose $a \leq b$
$ac \leq bc$ Multiply both sides by $c(> 0)$.
This contradicts the assumption that $ac > bc$. So $a > b$.

22.
$$D = \left(\frac{0 + x}{2}, \frac{y + 0}{2}\right) = \left(\frac{x}{2}, \frac{y}{2}\right)$$
$$AD = \sqrt{\left(0 - \frac{x}{2}\right)^2 + \left(0 - \frac{y}{2}\right)^2}$$
$$= \sqrt{\frac{x^2}{4} + \frac{y^2}{4}}$$
$$= \sqrt{\frac{x^2 + y^2}{4}}$$
$$= \frac{\sqrt{x^2 + y^2}}{2}$$
$$= \frac{1}{2}\sqrt{x^2 + y^2} = BD = CD$$

23. The middle diagram shows that
$(a + b)^2 = a^2 + b^2 + 2ab$
The third diagram shows that
$(a + b)^2 = c^2 + 4 \cdot \frac{1}{2}ab$
$= c^2 + 2ab.$
Then by substitution
$a^2 + b^2 + 2ab = c^2 + 2ab$
so $a^2 + b^2 = c^2$.

12.9 Standardized Test Practice (p. 745)

24. C; $(x + a) - a = b - a$

25. H; $4(x + 1) = 4x + 4$

12.9 Mixed Review (p. 746)

26. $0.15(15) = \$2.25$

27. $100 = 0.01x$
$10{,}000 = x$

28. $6 = p(3)$
$2 = p$
$200\% = p$

29. $5 = 0.25x$
$20 = x$

30. $b^2 - 4ac = (-2)^2 - 4(1)(4)$
$= -12$; no real solution

Copyright © McDougal Littell Inc.
All rights reserved.

31. $b^2 - 4ac = 4^2 - 4(2)(-2)$
$= 32$; two solutions

32. $b^2 - 4ac = (-8)^2 - 4(8)(2)$
$= 0$; one solution

33. $b^2 - 4ac = (-14)^2 - 4(1)(49)$
$= 0$; one solution

34. $b^2 - 4ac = (-5)^2 - 4(3)(1)$
$= 13$; two solutions

35. $b^2 - 4ac = (-1)^2 - 4(6)(5)$
$= -119$; no real solutions

36. $1 \overset{?}{>} 1^2 - 2(1) - 5$
$1 > -6$; true; a solution

37. $-2 \overset{?}{\geq} 2(3)^2 - 8(3) + 8$
$-2 \ngeq 2$; not a solution

38. $20 \overset{?}{\leq} 2(-2)^2 - 3(-2) + 10$
$20 \leq 24$; true; a solution

39. $17 \overset{?}{\geq} 4(1)^2 - 48(1) + 61$
$17 \geq 17$; true; a solution

12.9 Maintaining Skills (p. 746)

40. $\frac{2}{3} \cdot \frac{2}{5} + \frac{1}{5} = \frac{4}{15} + \frac{3}{15} = \frac{7}{15}$

41. $\frac{2}{7} \div \frac{1}{14} - \frac{5}{4} = \frac{2}{7} \cdot \frac{14}{1} - \frac{5}{4} = 4 - \frac{5}{4} = \frac{16}{4} - \frac{5}{4} = \frac{11}{4}$

42. $\frac{11}{2}\left(\frac{1}{10} - \frac{1}{4}\right) = \frac{11}{2}\left(\frac{4}{40} - \frac{10}{40}\right) = \frac{11}{2}\left(-\frac{6}{40}\right) = -\frac{33}{40}$

43. $\frac{5}{3} - \left(\frac{2}{9} \cdot \frac{3}{4} + \frac{7}{12}\right) = \frac{5}{3} - \left(\frac{2}{12} + \frac{7}{12}\right)$
$= \frac{5}{3} - \frac{9}{12}$
$= \frac{20}{12} - \frac{9}{12}$
$= \frac{11}{12}$

44. $\frac{1}{2} + \frac{2}{3} - \frac{3}{4} \cdot \frac{4}{5} = \frac{1}{2} + \frac{2}{3} - \frac{3}{5} = \frac{15}{30} + \frac{20}{30} - \frac{18}{30} = \frac{17}{30}$

45. $\left(\frac{3}{8} - \frac{2}{3}\right) \div \frac{1}{3} = \left(\frac{9}{24} - \frac{16}{24}\right) \cdot \frac{3}{1}$
$= -\frac{7}{24} \cdot \frac{3}{1}$
$= -\frac{7}{8}$

Quiz 3 ***(p. 746)***

1. $d_1 = \sqrt{(2-2)^2 + (7-0)^2} = \sqrt{7^2} = 7$
$d_2 = \sqrt{(2-14)^2 + (7-0)^2}$
$= \sqrt{144 + 49} = \sqrt{193} \approx 13.9$
$d_3 = \sqrt{(14-2)^2 + (0-0)^2} = \sqrt{12^2} = 12$
$7^2 + 12^2 \overset{?}{=} 13.9^2$
$49 + 144 \overset{?}{=} 193$
$193 = 193$; a right triangle

2. $d_1 = \sqrt{(12-0)^2 + (0-5)^2}$
$= \sqrt{144 + 25} = \sqrt{169} = 13$
$d_2 = 12$
$d_3 = 5$
$5^2 + 12^2 \overset{?}{=} 13^2$
$25 + 144 \overset{?}{=} 169$
$169 = 169$; a right triangle

3. $d = \sqrt{(7-1)^2 + (-9-3)^2}$
$= \sqrt{36 + 144} = \sqrt{180} \approx 13.42$
$\left(\frac{1+7}{2}, \frac{3+(-9)}{2}\right) = (4, -3)$

4. $d = \sqrt{(6-2)^2 + [-11-(-5)]^2}$
$= \sqrt{16 + 36} = \sqrt{52} \approx 7.21$
$\left(\frac{2+6}{2}, \frac{-5+(-11)}{2}\right) = (4, -8)$

5. $d = \sqrt{(8-0)^2 + (-14-0)^2}$
$= \sqrt{64 + 196} = \sqrt{260} \approx 16.12$
$\left(\frac{8+0}{2}, \frac{-14+0}{2}\right) = (4, -7)$

6. $d = \sqrt{[-8-(-8)]^2 + [8-(-8)]^2}$
$= \sqrt{0 + 256} = 16$
$\left(\frac{-8+(-8)}{2}, \frac{-8+8}{2}\right) = (-8, 0)$

7. $d = \sqrt{(-3-3)^2 + (4-4)^2}$
$= \sqrt{36 + 0} = 6$
$\left(\frac{3+(-3)}{2}, \frac{4+4}{2}\right) = (0, 4)$

8. $d = \sqrt{(-4-1)^2 + (-2-7)^2}$
$= \sqrt{25 + 81} = \sqrt{106} \approx 10.30$
$\left(\frac{-4+1}{2}, \frac{-2+7}{2}\right) = \left(-\frac{3}{2}, \frac{5}{2}\right)$

9. Let $a = 2$, $b = 3$, $c = -5$. Then $2 < 3$, but $2(-5) > 3(-5)$, that is $-10 > -15$.

10. Let $a = 2$, $b = 3$. Then $-(a + b) = -(2 + 3) = -5$. And $(-a) - (-b) = (-2) - (-3) = -2 + 3 = 1$. $-5 \neq 1$

Copyright © McDougal Littell Inc.
All rights reserved.

Chapter Summary and Review *(pp. 747–750)*

1. *domain:* all nonnegative real numbers

x	y
0	$y = 11\sqrt{0} = 0$
1	$y = 11\sqrt{1} = 11$
2	$y = 11\sqrt{2} \approx 15.6$
3	$y = 11\sqrt{3} \approx 19.1$
4	$y = 11\sqrt{4} = 22$

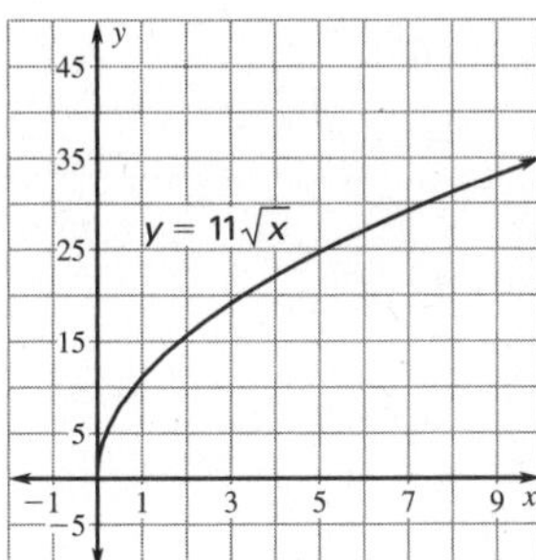

range: all nonnegative real numbers

2. *domain:* all real numbers ≥ 5

x	y
5	$y = 2\sqrt{5-5} = 0$
6	$y = 2\sqrt{6-5} = 2$
7	$y = 2\sqrt{7-5} \approx 2.8$
8	$y = 2\sqrt{8-5} \approx 3.5$
9	$y = 2\sqrt{9-5} = 4$

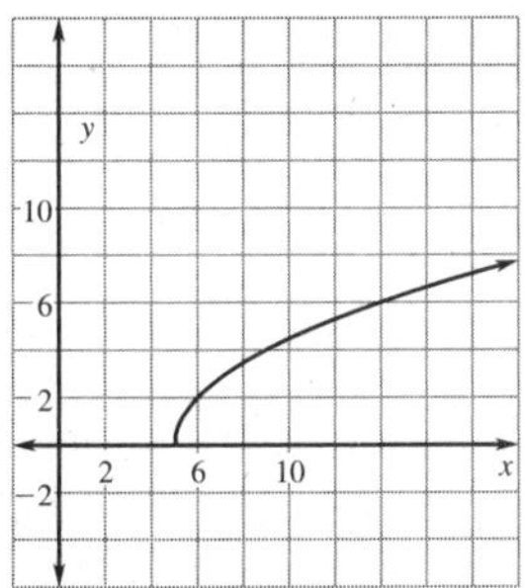

range: all nonnegative real numbers

3. *domain:* all nonnegative real numbers

x	y
0	$y = \sqrt{0} + 3 = 3$
1	$y = \sqrt{1} + 3 = 4$
2	$y = \sqrt{2} + 3 \approx 4.4$
3	$y = \sqrt{3} + 3 \approx 4.7$
4	$y = \sqrt{4} + 3 = 5$

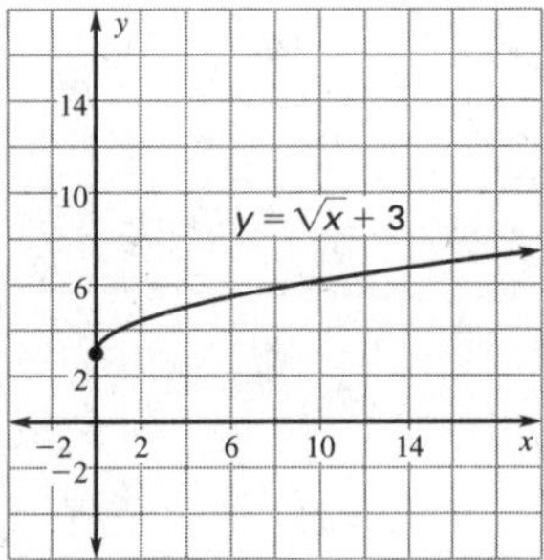

range: all real numbers ≥ 3

4. $6\sqrt{2} - \sqrt{2} = 5\sqrt{2}$

5. $\sqrt{5} + \sqrt{20} - \sqrt{3} = \sqrt{5} + \sqrt{4 \cdot 5} - \sqrt{3}$
$= \sqrt{5} + 2\sqrt{5} - \sqrt{3}$
$= 3\sqrt{5} - \sqrt{3}$

6. $(3 - \sqrt{10})(3 + \sqrt{10}) = 9 - 10 = -1$

7. $\sqrt{6}(2\sqrt{3} - 4\sqrt{2}) = 2\sqrt{18} - 4\sqrt{12}$
$= 2\sqrt{9 \cdot 2} - 4\sqrt{4 \cdot 3}$
$= 2 \cdot 3\sqrt{2} - 4 \cdot 2\sqrt{3}$
$= 6\sqrt{2} - 8\sqrt{3}$

8. $\dfrac{21}{\sqrt{3}} \cdot \dfrac{\sqrt{3}}{\sqrt{3}} = \dfrac{21\sqrt{3}}{3} = 7\sqrt{3}$

9. $\dfrac{8}{6 - \sqrt{7}} \cdot \dfrac{6 + \sqrt{7}}{6 + \sqrt{7}} = \dfrac{8(6 + \sqrt{7})}{36 - 7}$
$= \dfrac{48 + 8\sqrt{7}}{29}$

10. $2\sqrt{x} - 4 = 0$
$2\sqrt{x} = 4$
$\sqrt{x} = 2$
$x = 4$

Check:

$2\sqrt{4} - 4 \stackrel{?}{=} 0$
$4 - 4 \stackrel{?}{=} 0$
$0 = 0$

Copyright © McDougal Littell Inc.
All rights reserved.

11. $\sqrt{-4x - 4} = x$

$-4x - 4 = x^2$

$0 = x^2 + 4x + 4$

$0 = (x + 2)(x + 2)$

$x = -2$

Check:

$\sqrt{-4(-2) - 4} \stackrel{?}{=} -2$

$\sqrt{4} \stackrel{?}{=} -2$

$2 \neq -2$; no solution

12. $\sqrt{x - 3} + 2 = 8$

$\sqrt{x - 3} = 6$

$x - 3 = 36$

$x = 39$

Check:

$\sqrt{39 - 3} + 2 \stackrel{?}{=} 8$

$6 + 2 \stackrel{?}{=} 8$

$8 = 8$

13. $\sqrt{x - 1} = 5$

$x - 1 = 25$

$x = 26$

Check:

$\sqrt{26 - 1} \stackrel{?}{=} 5$

$5 = 5$

14. $8\sqrt{x} - 16 = 0$

$8\sqrt{x} = 16$

$\sqrt{x} = 2$

$x = 4$

Check:

$8\sqrt{4} - 16 \stackrel{?}{=} 0$

$16 - 16 \stackrel{?}{=} 0$

$0 = 0$

15. $\sqrt{5x + 36} = x$

$5x + 36 = x^2$

$0 = x^2 - 5x - 36$

$0 = (x - 9)(x + 4)$

$x = 9, -4$

Check:

$\sqrt{5(9) + 36} \stackrel{?}{=} 9$

$9 = 9$

$\sqrt{5(-4) + 36} \stackrel{?}{=} -4$

$4 \neq -4$; extraneous

16. $27^{2/3} = (27^{1/3})^2 = (3)^2 = 9$

17. $(\sqrt[3]{64})^2 = 4^2 = 16$

18. $121^{3/2} = (121^{1/2})^3 = 11^3 = 1331$

19. $(\sqrt{4})^4 = (4^{1/2})^4 = 4^{4/2} = 4^2 = 16$

20. $5^{1/3} \cdot 5^{5/3} = 5^{6/3} = 5^2 = 25$

21. $(4 \cdot 121)^{1/2} = 4^{1/2} \cdot 121^{1/2} = 2 \cdot 11 = 22$

22. $(125^{2/3})^{1/2} = 125^{1/3} = 5$

23. $x^2 - 4x = 8$

$x^2 - 4x + 2^2 = 8 + 2^2$

$(x - 2)^2 = 12$

$x - 2 = \pm\sqrt{12}$

$x = 2 \pm \sqrt{4 \cdot 3}$

$x = 2 \pm 2\sqrt{3}$

24. $x^2 + 20x + 19 = 0$

$x^2 + 20x = -19$

$x^2 + 20x + 10^2 = -19 + 10^2$

$(x + 10)^2 = 81$

$x + 10 = \pm 9$

$x = -10 \pm 9$

$x = -1, -19$

25. $x^2 - 16x + 8 = 0$

$x^2 - 16x = -8$

$x^2 - 16x + 8^2 = -8 + 8^2$

$(x - 8)^2 = 56$

$x - 8 = \pm\sqrt{56}$

$x = 8 \pm \sqrt{4 \cdot 14}$

$x = 8 \pm 2\sqrt{14}$

26. $4x^2 + 8x + 8 = 0$ complete the square

$4(x^2 + 2x + 2) = 0$

$x^2 + 2x + 2 = 0$

$x^2 + 2x + 1^2 = -2 + 1^2$

$(x + 1)^2 = -1$

$x + 1 = \pm\sqrt{-1}$; no solution

27. $x^2 - x - 3 = 0$; quadratic formula

$a = 1, b = -1, c = -3$

$$x = \frac{-(-1) \pm \sqrt{(-1)^2 - 4(1)(-3)}}{2(1)}$$

$$= \frac{1 \pm \sqrt{13}}{2}$$

28. $3x^2 - x + 2 = 0$; quadratic formula

$a = 3, b = -1, c = 2$

$$x = \frac{-(-1) \pm \sqrt{(-1)^2 - 4(3)(2)}}{2(3)}$$

$$= \frac{1 \pm \sqrt{-23}}{6}\text{; no solution}$$

29. $4^2 + 6^2 = c^2$

$16 + 36 = c^2$

$52 = c^2$

$\sqrt{4 \cdot 13} = \sqrt{52} = c$

$2\sqrt{13} = c$

Copyright © McDougal Littell Inc.
All rights reserved.

30. $(\sqrt{2})^2 + b^2 = (\sqrt{3})^2$

$2 + b^2 = 3$

$b^2 = 1$

$b = 1$

31. $b^2 + (2b + 2)^2 = 13^2$

$b^2 + 4b^2 + 8b + 4 = 169$

$5b^2 + 8b + 4 = 169$

$5b^2 + 8b - 165 = 0$

$b = \dfrac{-8 \pm \sqrt{8^2 - 4(5)(-165)}}{2(5)}$

$= \dfrac{-8 \pm 58}{10}$

$b = 5, -6.6$ (not applicable)

$b = 5, 2b + 2 = 12$

32. $18^2 + 24^2 \stackrel{?}{=} 30^2$

$324 + 576 \stackrel{?}{=} 900$

$900 = 900$; a right triangle

33. $10^2 + 14^2 \stackrel{?}{=} 17^2$

$100 + 196 \stackrel{?}{=} 289$

$296 \neq 289$; not a right triangle

34. $24^2 + 32^2 \stackrel{?}{=} 40^2$

$576 + 1024 \stackrel{?}{=} 1600$

$1600 = 1600$; a right triangle

35. $d = \sqrt{(11 - 8)^2 + (-4 - 5)^2}$

$= \sqrt{9 + 81} = \sqrt{90} \approx 9.49$

36. $d = \sqrt{(-3 - 1)^2 + (6 - 7)^2}$

$= \sqrt{16 + 1} = \sqrt{17} \approx 4.12$

37. $d = \sqrt{(-2 - 2)^2 + (-2 - 8)^2}$

$= \sqrt{16 + 100} = \sqrt{116} \approx 10.77$

38. $d_1 = \sqrt{(-4 - 0)^2 + [1 - (-2)]^2}$

$= \sqrt{16 + 9} = 5$

$d_2 = \sqrt{(-4 - 0)^2 + [-2 - (-2)]^2}$

$= \sqrt{16 + 0} = 4$

$d_3 = \sqrt{[-4 - (-4)]^2 + [1 - (-2)]^2}$

$= \sqrt{0 + 9} = 3$

$3^2 + 4^2 = 5^2$

$9 + 16 = 25$

$25 = 25$; a right triangle

39. $\left(\dfrac{-1 + 5}{2}, \dfrac{-3 + 1}{2}\right) = (2, -1)$

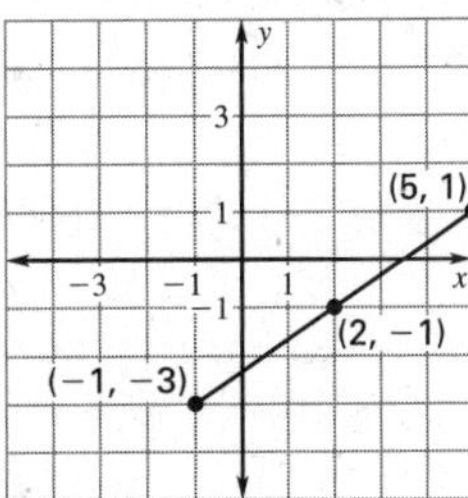

40. $\left(\dfrac{0 + (-2)}{2}, \dfrac{4 + 4}{2}\right) = (-1, 4)$

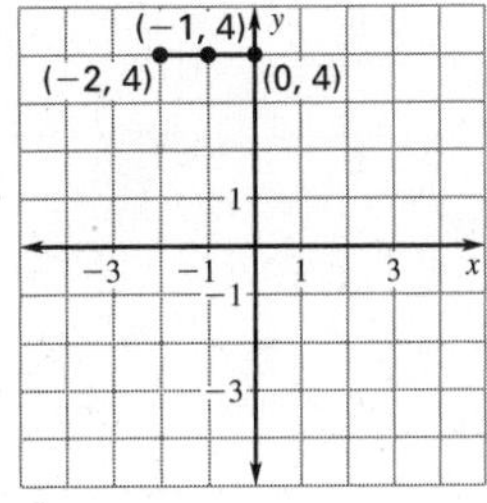

41. $\left(\dfrac{9 + (-10)}{2}, \dfrac{-5 + (-8)}{2}\right) = \left(-\dfrac{1}{2}, -\dfrac{13}{2}\right)$

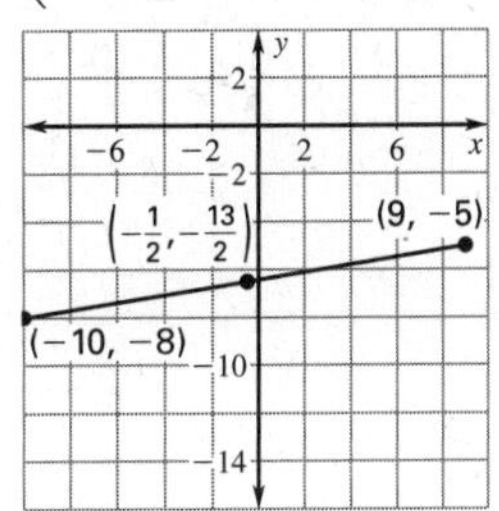

42. commutative property of multiplication

43.

$(c)(-b) = c(-1 \cdot b)$	Multiplication property of −1.
$= (c \cdot -1)b$	Associative property of mult.
$= (-1 \cdot c) \cdot b$	Commutative property of mult.
$= -cb$	Multiplication property of −1.

Copyright © McDougal Littell Inc.
All rights reserved.

Chapter Test *(p. 751)*

1. *domain:* all nonnegative real numbers

x	y
0	$y = 12\sqrt{0} = 0$
1	$y = 12\sqrt{1} = 12$
2	$y = 12\sqrt{2} \approx 17$
3	$y = 12\sqrt{3} \approx 20.8$
4	$y = 12\sqrt{4} = 24$

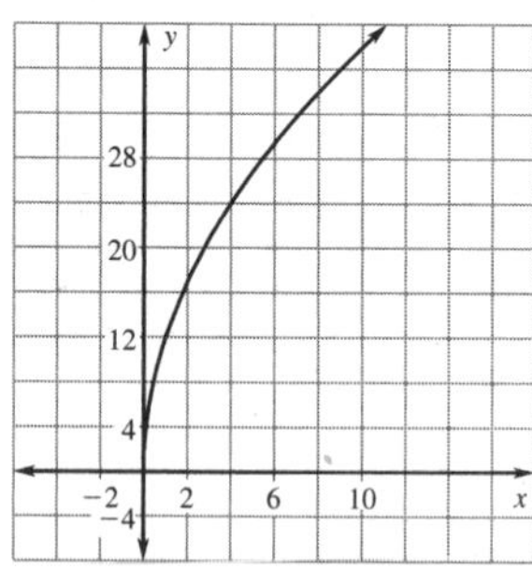

range: all nonnegative real numbers

2. *domain:*

$2x + 7 \geq 0$

$2x \geq -7$

$x \geq -\frac{7}{2} = -3\frac{1}{2}$

all real numbers $\geq -3\frac{1}{2}$

x	y
$-3\frac{1}{2}$	$y = \sqrt{2\left(-3\frac{1}{2}\right) + 7} = 0$
-3	$y = \sqrt{2(-3) + 7} = 1$
-2	$y = \sqrt{2(-2) + 7} \approx 1.7$
-1	$y = \sqrt{2(-1) + 7} \approx 2.2$
0	$y = \sqrt{2(0) + 7} \approx 2.6$

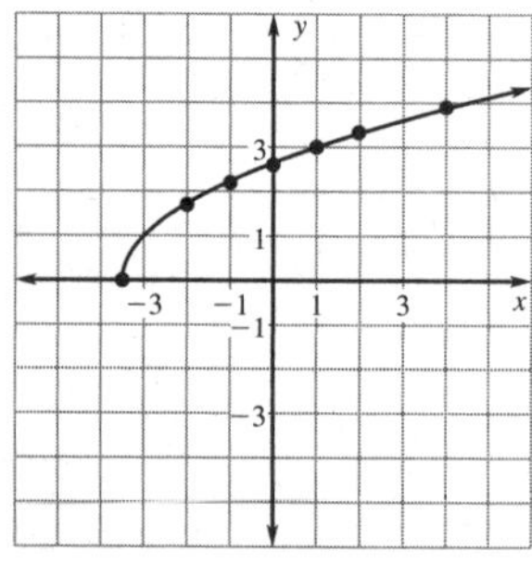

range: all nonnegative real numbers

3. *domain:* all nonnegative real numbers

x	y
0	$y = \sqrt{3 \cdot 0} - 3 = -3$
1	$y = \sqrt{3 \cdot 1} - 3 \approx -1.3$
2	$y = \sqrt{3 \cdot 2} - 3 \approx -0.6$
3	$y = \sqrt{3 \cdot 3} - 3 = 0$
4	$y = \sqrt{3 \cdot 4} - 3 \approx 0.5$

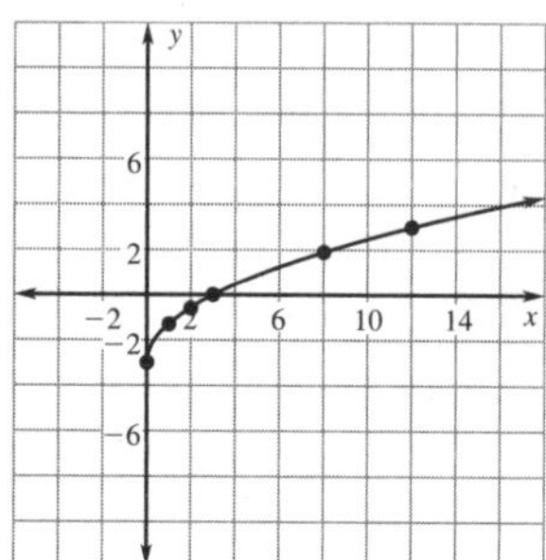

range: all real numbers ≥ -3

4. *domain:* all real numbers ≥ 5

x	y
5	$y = \sqrt{5 - 5} = 0$
6	$y = \sqrt{6 - 5} = 1$
7	$y = \sqrt{7 - 5} \approx 1.4$
8	$y = \sqrt{8 - 5} \approx 1.7$
9	$y = \sqrt{9 - 5} = 2$

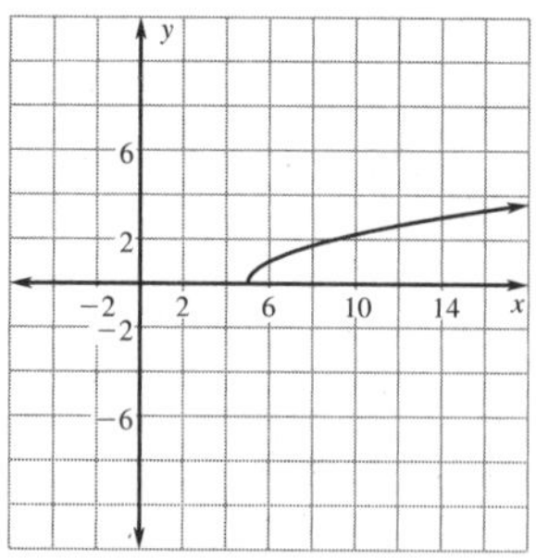

range: all nonnegative real numbers

5. $3\sqrt{2} - \sqrt{2} = 2\sqrt{2}$

6. $(4 + \sqrt{7})(4 - \sqrt{7}) = 16 - 7 = 9$

7. $\frac{4}{\sqrt{10}} \cdot \frac{\sqrt{10}}{\sqrt{10}} = \frac{4\sqrt{10}}{10} = \frac{2\sqrt{10}}{5}$

Copyright © McDougal Littell Inc.
All rights reserved.

8. $\frac{8}{3-\sqrt{5}} \cdot \frac{3+\sqrt{5}}{3+\sqrt{5}} = \frac{8(3+\sqrt{5})}{9-5}$

$= \frac{8(3+\sqrt{5})}{4}$

$= 2(3+\sqrt{5})$

$= 6 + 2\sqrt{5}$

9. $\frac{1}{\sqrt{6}} \cdot \frac{\sqrt{6}}{\sqrt{6}} = \frac{\sqrt{6}}{6}$

10. $\frac{\sqrt{11}}{2-\sqrt{11}} \cdot \frac{2+\sqrt{11}}{2+\sqrt{11}} = \frac{2\sqrt{11}+11}{4-11}$

$= \frac{2\sqrt{11}+11}{-7}$

11. $(8-\sqrt{5})(8+\sqrt{5}) = 64 - 5 = 59$

12. $\sqrt{3}(\sqrt{12}+4) = \sqrt{36} + 4\sqrt{3} = 6 + 4\sqrt{3}$

13. $\sqrt{y} + 6 = 10$

$\sqrt{y} = 4$

$y = 16$

Check:

$\sqrt{16} + 6 \stackrel{?}{=} 10$

$10 = 10$

14. $\sqrt{2m+3} - 6 = 4$

$\sqrt{2m+3} = 10$

$2m + 3 = 100$

$2m = 97$

$m = \frac{97}{2}$

Check:

$\sqrt{2\left(\frac{97}{2}\right) + 3} - 6 \stackrel{?}{=} 4$

$10 - 6 \stackrel{?}{=} 4$

$4 = 4$

15. $n = \sqrt{9n - 18}$

$n^2 = 9n - 18$

$n^2 - 9n + 18 = 0$

$(n-3)(n-6) = 0$

$n = 3, 6$

Check:

$3 \stackrel{?}{=} \sqrt{9(3) - 18}$

$3 = 3$

$6 \stackrel{?}{=} \sqrt{9(6) - 18}$

$6 = 6$

16. $p = \sqrt{-3p + 18}$

$p^2 = -3p + 18$

$p^2 + 3p - 18 = 0$

$(p+6)(p-3) = 0$

$p = -6, 3$

Check:

$-6 \stackrel{?}{=} \sqrt{-3(-6) + 18}$

$-6 \neq 6$; extraneous

$3 \stackrel{?}{=} \sqrt{-3(3) + 18}$

$3 = 3$

17. $x^{1/2} \cdot x^{3/2} = x^{4/2} = x^2$

18. $\sqrt{25x^3} = (25x^3)^{1/2}$

$= 25^{1/2}x^{3/2}$

$= 5x^{2/2} \cdot x^{1/2}$

$= 5x\sqrt{x}$

19. $(x^{1/3})^2 \cdot \sqrt{y} = (\sqrt[3]{x})^2\sqrt{y}$

20. $(x^2 \cdot x^{1/3})^{3/2} = x^3 \cdot x^{1/2} = x^3\sqrt{x}$

21. $x^2 - 6x = -5$

$x^2 - 6x + 3^2 = -5 + 3^2$

$(x-3)^2 = 4$

$x - 3 = \pm 2$

$x = 3 \pm 2$

$x = 5, 1$

22. $x^2 - 2x = 2$

$x^2 - 2x + 1^2 = 2 + 1^2$

$(x-1)^2 = 3$

$x - 1 = \pm\sqrt{3}$

$x = 1 \pm \sqrt{3}$

23. $x^2 + 16x - 1 = 0$

$x^2 + 16x = 1$

$x^2 + 16x + 8^2 = 1 + 8^2$

$(x+8)^2 = 65$

$x + 8 = \pm\sqrt{65}$

$x = -8 \pm \sqrt{65}$

24. $7^2 + 24^2 = c^2$

$49 + 576 = c^2$

$625 = c^2$

$25 = c$

25. $5^2 + b^2 = 13^2$

$25 + b^2 = 169$

$b^2 = 144$

$b = 12$

26. $a^2 + 15^2 = 17^2$

$a^2 + 225 = 289$

$a^2 = 64$

$a = 8$

Copyright © McDougal Littell Inc.
All rights reserved.

27. $30^2 + 40^2 = c^2$
$900 + 1600 = c^2$
$2500 = c^2$
$50 = c$

28. $6^2 + b^2 = 10^2$
$36 + b^2 = 100$
$b^2 = 64$
$b = 8$

29. $a^2 + 12^2 = 15^2$
$a^2 + 144 = 225$
$a^2 = 81$
$a = 9$

30. $8^2 + 15^2 \stackrel{?}{=} 17^2$
$64 + 225 \stackrel{?}{=} 289$
$289 = 289$; a right triangle

30. $8^2 + 15^2 \stackrel{?}{=} 17^2$
$64 + 225 \stackrel{?}{=} 289$
$289 = 289$; a right triangle

31. $20^2 + 20^2 \stackrel{?}{=} 29^2$
$400 + 400 \stackrel{?}{=} 841$
$800 \neq 841$; not a right triangle

32. $5^2 + 12^2 \stackrel{?}{=} 13^2$
$25 + 144 \stackrel{?}{=} 169$
$169 = 169$; a right triangle

33. vertical sides:
$d = \sqrt{[-3 - (-3)]^2 + (5 - 1)^2} = \sqrt{4^2} = 4$ units
other sides:
$d = \sqrt{(-3 - 2)^2 + (5 - 7)^2}$
$d = \sqrt{25 + 4} = \sqrt{29} \approx 5.39$ units

34. $P = 2(4) + 2\sqrt{29} = 8 + 2\sqrt{29} \approx 18.77$

35. $\left(\frac{-3 + -3}{2}, \frac{5 + 1}{2}\right) = (-3, 3)$
$\left(\frac{-3 + 2}{2}, \frac{5 + 7}{2}\right) = \left(\frac{-1}{2}, 6\right)$
$\left(\frac{2 + 2}{2}, \frac{7 + 3}{2}\right) = (2, 5)$
$\left(\frac{-3 + 2}{2}, \frac{1 + 3}{2}\right) = \left(-\frac{1}{2}, 2\right)$

36.

$a + c = b + c$	Given
$(a + c) + (-c) = (b + c) + (-c)$	Add. prop. of equality
$a + (c + -c) = b + (c + -c)$	Assoc. prop. of add.
$a + 0 = b + 0$	Inverse prop. of add.
$a = b$	Identity prop. of add.

Chapter Standardized Test *(pp. 752–753)*

1. C;
$y = \frac{8\sqrt{8^2 - 1}}{8^2 + 8} = \frac{8\sqrt{63}}{72} = \frac{\sqrt{9 \cdot 7}}{9} = \frac{3\sqrt{7}}{9} = \frac{\sqrt{7}}{3}$

2. C; all numbers ≥ 7

3. A;
$5\sqrt{7} + \sqrt{448} + \sqrt{175} - \sqrt{63}$
$= 5\sqrt{7} + \sqrt{64 \cdot 7} + \sqrt{25 \cdot 7} - \sqrt{9 \cdot 7}$
$= 5\sqrt{7} + 8\sqrt{7} + 5\sqrt{7} - 3\sqrt{7}$
$= 15\sqrt{7}$

4. B;
$\frac{2}{3 - \sqrt{6}} \cdot \frac{3 + \sqrt{6}}{3 + \sqrt{6}} = \frac{2(3 + \sqrt{6})}{9 - 6}$
$= \frac{2(3 + \sqrt{6})}{3}$
$= \frac{6 + 2\sqrt{6}}{3}$

5. C;
$22 \stackrel{?}{=} \sqrt{880 - 18(22)}$
$22 \stackrel{?}{=} \sqrt{484}$
$22 = 22$

6. C; $x^3y^{3/3}x^2 = x^5y$

7. $\left(-\frac{18}{2}\right)^2 = (-9)^2 = 81$; D

8. D;
$9^2 + x^2 = (5\sqrt{10})^2$
$81 + x^2 = 25(10)$
$x^2 = 250 - 81 = 169$
$x = 13$

9. B;
$d = \sqrt{(-5 - 2)^2 + (6 - 2)^2}$
$d = \sqrt{49 + 16} = \sqrt{65}$

10. A; $\left(\frac{-5 + 2}{2}, \frac{6 + 2}{2}\right) = \left(-\frac{3}{2}, 4\right)$

11. D; Distributive property

12. C; Substitute $(0, -2)$ and $(1, 1)$ to test.
$-2 \stackrel{?}{=} 3\sqrt{0} - 2$
$-2 = -2$
$1 \stackrel{?}{=} 3\sqrt{1} - 2$
$1 = 1$

13. C;
$9^2 + 12^2 \stackrel{?}{=} 15^2$
$81 + 144 \stackrel{?}{=} 225$
$225 = 225$

Cumulative Practice *(pp. 754–755)*

1. $\frac{m}{7} \geq 16$; $m \geq 112$

2. $4 + b^2 = 104$; $b = \pm 10$

3. $t = 3d$
$t = 3(3) = 9$ miles

4. $3 + 5 + (-4) = 4$

5. $2(9) + 12 - 5 = 25$

6. $3.5 - (-1.5) = 3.5 + 1.5 = 5$

7. $-(-3)^2(7) = -63$

8. $6(2)(2 + 2) = 48$

9. $[8(1) + 1](-3) = -27$

Copyright © McDougal Littell Inc.
All rights reserved.

10. $\frac{1}{4}|(4)(4)(-4)| = \frac{1}{4}(64) = 16$

11. $\frac{8^2 + 4}{6} = \frac{68}{6} = 11\frac{1}{3}$ or $\frac{34}{3}$

12. $(-5)\left(-\frac{3}{4}x\right) = (-5)\left(-\frac{3}{4} \cdot 6\right) = \frac{45}{2}$

13. $-\frac{2}{9}(x - 5) = 12$

$x - 5 = -\frac{9}{2}(12)$

$x - 5 = -54$

$x = -49$

14. $7x - (3x - 2) = 38$

$4x + 2 = 38$

$4x = 36$

$x = 9$

15. $\frac{1}{3}x + 7 = -7x - 5$

$x + 21 = -21x - 15$

$22x + 21 = -15$

$22x = -36$

$x = -1.64$

16. $8(x + 3) - 2x = 4(x - 8)$

$8x + 24 - 2x = 4x - 32$

$6x + 24 = 4x - 32$

$2x + 24 = -32$

$2x = -56$

$x = -28$

17. $11 + 6.23x = 7 + 5.51x$

$4 + 6.23x = 5.51x$

$4 = -0.72x$

$-5.56 = x$

18. $-3(2.9 - 4.1x) = 9.2x + 6$

$-8.7 + 12.3x = 9.2x + 6$

$3.1x = 14.7$

$x = 4.74$

19. $m = \frac{-3 - 1}{-3 - 3} = \frac{-4}{-6} = \frac{2}{3}$

$y - (-2) = \frac{2}{3}(x - 2)$

$y + 2 = \frac{2}{3}x - \frac{4}{3}$

$y = \frac{2}{3}x - \frac{10}{3}$

20. $m = -\frac{3}{2}$ of perpendicular line

$y - 2 = -\frac{3}{2}[x - (-4)]$

$y - 2 = -\frac{3}{2}(x + 4)$

$y - 2 = -\frac{3}{2}x - 6$

$y = -\frac{3}{2}x - 4$

21. a function; one output for each input
domain: $-1, 1, 3, 5$
range: $-1, 1, 3$

22. not a function; two outputs for -1 and 0

23. a function; one output for each input
domain: $-2, -1, 0, 1, 2$
range: $-2, -1, 0, 1$

24. not a function; does not pass vertical line test

25. $y = \frac{4}{5}x - 3$

$5y = 4x - 15$

$4x - 5y = 15$

26. $y - 2 = \frac{1}{3}[x - (-1)]$

$y - 2 = \frac{1}{3}(x + 1)$

$y - 2 = \frac{1}{3}x + \frac{1}{3}$

$y = \frac{1}{3}x + \frac{7}{3}$

$3y = x + 7$

$x - 3y = -7$

27. $-3 < -4x + 9 \le 14$

$-12 < -4x \le 5$

$3 > x \ge -\frac{5}{4}$ or

$-\frac{5}{4} \le x < 3$

−2 −1 0 1 2 3 4

28. $|3x + 16| + 2 < 10$

$|3x + 16| < 8$

$-8 < 3x + 16 < 8$

$-24 < 3x < -8$

$-8 < x < -\frac{8}{3}$

−9 −7 −5 −3 −1 0 1

29. $3x - 4 > 5$ or $5x + 1 < 11$

$3x > 9$ $\quad$ $5x < 10$

$x > 3$ $\quad$ $x < 2$

−1 0 1 2 3 4 5

Copyright © McDougal Littell Inc.
All rights reserved.

30.
$$\begin{aligned} 4y &= 8x + 16 \\ 2y &= 11x - 7 \quad \text{multiply by } -2 \\ 4y &= 8x + 16 \\ -4y &= -22x + 14 \\ 0 &= -14x + 30 \\ -30 &= -14x \\ \frac{15}{7} &= x \\ 4y &= 8\left(\frac{15}{7}\right) + 16 \\ 4y &= \frac{120}{7} + \frac{112}{7} \\ 4y &= \frac{232}{7} \\ y &= \frac{232}{4 \cdot 7} = \frac{58}{7} \end{aligned}$$

Solution: $\left(\frac{15}{7}, \frac{58}{7}\right)$

31.
$$\begin{aligned} -2x + 3y &= 15 \quad \text{multiply by 5} \\ -10x + 15y &= 75 \\ 10x - 11y &= 9 \\ 4y &= 84 \\ y &= 21 \\ -2x + 3(21) &= 15 \\ -2x + 63 &= 15 \\ -2x &= -48 \\ x &= 24 \end{aligned}$$

Solution: (24, 21)

32. $y = 5x - 2$
$$\begin{aligned} 3x + 7(5x - 2) &= 5 \\ 3x + 35x - 14 &= 5 \\ 38x - 14 &= 5 \\ 38x &= 19 \\ x &= \frac{1}{2} \\ y &= 5\left(\frac{1}{2}\right) - 2 \\ y &= \frac{5}{2} - \frac{4}{2} = \frac{1}{2} \end{aligned}$$

Solution: $\left(\frac{1}{2}, \frac{1}{2}\right)$

33. $\frac{b^8}{b^2} = b^6; 2^6 = 64$

34. $3a^4 \cdot a^{-3} = 3a = 3(1) = 3$

35. $(-a^3)(2b^2)^3 = (-a^3)(2^3b^6) = -8a^3b^6;$
$$\begin{aligned} (-1^3)(2^3 \cdot 2^6) &= (-1)(2^9) \\ &= (-1)(2^9) \\ &= -512 \end{aligned}$$

36. $4b^3 \cdot (2 + b)^2 = 4b^3(4 + 4b + b^2)$
$$= 16b^3 + 16b^4 + 4b^5;$$
$16(2)^3 + 16(2)^4 + 4(2)^5 = 512$

37. $\frac{4a^{-3}b^3}{ab^{-2}} = 4a^{-4}b^5 = \frac{4b^5}{a^4};$

$\frac{4(2)^2}{1^4} = 4(32) = 128$

38.
$$\begin{aligned} \frac{(5ab^2)^{-2}}{a^{-3}b} &= \frac{a^3}{(5ab^2)^2b} \\ &= \frac{a^3}{25a^2b^4b} \\ &= \frac{a}{25b^5}; \\ \frac{1}{25(2)^5} &= \frac{1}{25(32)} \\ &= \frac{1}{800} \end{aligned}$$

39. $6x^2 = 26$ two real solutions
$$x^2 = \frac{13}{3}$$
$$x = \pm\sqrt{\frac{13}{3}} \cdot \frac{\sqrt{3}}{\sqrt{3}} = \frac{\pm\sqrt{39}}{3}$$

40. $4x^2 - 9x + 5 = 0$

$b^2 - 4ac = (-9)^2 - 4(4)(5) = 81 - 80 = 1$; two solutions
$$x = \frac{-(-9) \pm \sqrt{1}}{2(4)} = \frac{9 \pm 1}{8}$$
$$x = \frac{5}{4}, 1$$

41. $3x^2 + 6x + 3 = 0$

$b^2 - 4ac = 6^2 - 4(3)(3) = 36 - 36 = 0$; one solution
$$x = \frac{-6 \pm \sqrt{0}}{2(3)} = \frac{-6}{6} = -1$$

42. $x^2 + 6x + 8 = (x + 4)(x + 2)$

43. $x^2 - 24x - 112 = (x - 28)(x + 4)$

44. $3x^2 + 17x - 6 = (3x - 1)(x + 6)$

45. $4x^2 + 12x + 9 = (2x + 3)(2x + 3) = (2x + 3)^2$

46. $x^2 + 10x + 25 = (x + 5)^2$

47. $x^2 - 14x + 49 = (x - 7)^2$

48. $(3x + 1)(2x + 7) = 0$
$$\begin{aligned} 3x + 1 &= 0 \\ 3x &= -1 \\ x &= -\frac{1}{3} \\ 2x + 7 &= 0 \\ 2x &= -7 \\ x &= -\frac{7}{2} \end{aligned}$$

Copyright © McDougal Littell Inc.
All rights reserved.

49. $6x^2 - x - 7 = 8$

$6x^2 - x - 15 = 0$

$$x = \frac{-(-1) \pm \sqrt{(-1)^2 - 4(6)(-15)}}{2(6)}$$

$$= \frac{1 \pm \sqrt{1 + 360}}{12}$$

$$= \frac{1 \pm \sqrt{361}}{12}$$

$$= \frac{1 \pm 19}{12}$$

$$x = \frac{5}{3}, -\frac{3}{2}$$

50. $x^2 - 4x + 4 = 0$

$(x - 2)(x - 2) = 0$

$x = 2$

51. $4x^2 + 16x + 16 = 0$

$4(x^2 + 4x + 4) = 0$

$x^2 + 4x + 4 = 0$

$(x + 2)^2 = 0$

$x = -2$

52. $(x^3 + 5x^2) - 4x - 20 = 0$

$(x^3 + 5x^2) - 4(x + 5) = 0$

$x^2(x + 5) - 4(x + 5) = 0$

$(x^2 - 4)(x + 5) = 0$

$(x + 2)(x - 2)(x + 5) = 0$

$x = -2, 2, -5$

53. $x^4 + 9x^3 + 18x^2 = 0$

$x^2(x^2 + 9x + 18) = 0$

$x^2(x + 6)(x + 3) = 0$

$x = 0, -6, -3$

54. $\frac{4x}{12x^2} = \frac{1}{3x}$

55. $\frac{2x + 6}{x^2 - 9} = \frac{2(x + 3)}{(x + 3)(x - 3)} = \frac{2}{x - 3}$

56. $\frac{3x}{x^2 - 2x - 24} \cdot \frac{x - 6}{6x^2 + 9x}$

$$= \frac{3x(x - 6)}{(x - 6)(x + 4)(3x)(2x + 3)}$$

$$= \frac{1}{(x + 4)(2x + 3)}$$

$$= \frac{1}{2x^2 + 11x + 12}$$

57. $\frac{x^2 - 6x + 8}{x^2 - 2x} \div (3x - 12)$

$$= \frac{(x - 4)(x - 2)}{x(x - 2)} \cdot \frac{1}{3(x - 4)}$$

$$= \frac{1}{3x}$$

58. $\frac{4}{x + 2} + \frac{15x}{3x + 6} = \frac{4}{x + 2} + \frac{15x}{3(x + 2)}$

$$= \frac{4}{x + 2} + \frac{5x}{x + 2}$$

$$= \frac{4 + 5x}{x + 2}$$

$$= \frac{5x + 4}{x + 2}$$

59. $\frac{3x}{x + 4} - \frac{x}{x - 1} = \frac{3x(x - 1)}{(x + 4)(x - 1)} - \frac{x(x + 4)}{(x + 4)(x - 1)}$

$$= \frac{3x^2 - 3x - x^2 - 4x}{(x + 4)(x - 1)}$$

$$= \frac{2x^2 - 7x}{(x + 4)(x - 1)}$$

$$= \frac{2x^2 - 7x}{x^2 + 3x - 4}$$

60. $4\sqrt{7} + 3\sqrt{7} = 7\sqrt{7}$

61. $9\sqrt{2} - 12\sqrt{8} = 9\sqrt{2} - 12\sqrt{4 \cdot 2}$

$= 9\sqrt{2} - 12(2)\sqrt{2}$

$= 9\sqrt{2} - 24\sqrt{2}$

$= -15\sqrt{2}$

62. $\sqrt{6}(5\sqrt{3} + 6) = 5\sqrt{18} + 6\sqrt{6}$

$= 5\sqrt{9 \cdot 2} + 6\sqrt{6}$

$= 5(3)\sqrt{2} + 6\sqrt{6}$

$= 15\sqrt{2} + 6\sqrt{6}$

63. $\frac{11}{(7 - \sqrt{3})} \cdot \frac{(7 + \sqrt{3})}{(7 + \sqrt{3})} = \frac{11(7 + \sqrt{3})}{49 - 3}$

$$= \frac{11(7 + \sqrt{3})}{46}$$

$$= \frac{77 + 11\sqrt{3}}{46}$$

64. $x^2 + 24x = -3$

$x^2 + 24x + 12^2 = -3 + 12^2$

$(x + 12)^2 = 141$

$x + 12 = \pm\sqrt{141}$

$x = -12 \pm \sqrt{141}$

65. $x^2 - 12x = 19$

$x^2 - 12x + 6^2 = 19 + 6^2$

$(x - 6)^2 = 55$

$x - 6 = \pm\sqrt{55}$

$x = 6 \pm \sqrt{55}$

66. $x^2 + 20x = -7$

$x^2 + 20x + 10^2 = -7 + 10^2$

$(x + 10)^2 = 93$

$x + 10 = \pm\sqrt{93}$

$x = -10 \pm \sqrt{93}$

Copyright © McDougal Littell Inc.
All rights reserved.

67.
$$x^2 - 6x = 13$$
$$x^2 - 6x + 3^2 = 13 + 3^2$$
$$(x - 3)^2 = 22$$
$$x - 3 = \pm\sqrt{22}$$
$$x = 3 \pm \sqrt{22}$$

68.
$$x^2 + 16x = 1$$
$$x^2 + 16x + 8^2 = 1 + 8^2$$
$$(x + 8)^2 = 65$$
$$x + 8 = \pm\sqrt{65}$$
$$x = -8 \pm \sqrt{65}$$

69.
$$x^2 + 22x + 5 = 0$$
$$x^2 + 22x = -5$$
$$x^2 + 22x + 11^2 = -5 + 11^2$$
$$(x + 11)^2 = 116$$
$$x + 11 = \pm\sqrt{116}$$
$$x = -11 \pm 2\sqrt{29}$$

70. $d = \sqrt{(-5 - 3)^2 + (4 - 0)^2}$
$= \sqrt{64 + 16} = \sqrt{80} = 4\sqrt{5} \approx 8.94$
$\left(\frac{3 + (-5)}{2}, \frac{0 + 4}{2}\right) = (-1, 2)$

71. $d = \sqrt{(2 - 4)^2 + (7 - 3)^2}$
$= \sqrt{4 + 16} = \sqrt{20} = 2\sqrt{5} \approx 4.47$
$\left(\frac{2 + 4}{2}, \frac{7 + 3}{2}\right) = (3, 5)$

72. $d = \sqrt{(5 - 1)^2 + [1 - (-5)]^2}$
$= \sqrt{16 + 36} = \sqrt{52} = 2\sqrt{13} \approx 7.21$
$\left(\frac{5 + 1}{2}, \frac{1 + (-5)}{2}\right) = (3, -2)$

73. $d = \sqrt{(-2 - 6)^2 + (-3 - 2)^2}$
$= \sqrt{64 + 25} = \sqrt{89} \approx 9.43$
$\left(\frac{-2 + 6}{2}, \frac{-3 + 2}{2}\right) = \left(2, -\frac{1}{2}\right)$

74. $d = \sqrt{(-1 - 6)^2 + (2 - 9)^2}$
$= \sqrt{49 + 49} = \sqrt{98} \approx 9.90$
$\left(\frac{-1 + 6}{2}, \frac{2 + 9}{2}\right) = \left(\frac{5}{2}, \frac{11}{2}\right)$

75. $d = \sqrt{(0 - 10)^2 + (4 - 11)^2}$
$= \sqrt{100 + 49} = \sqrt{149} \approx 12.21$
$\left(\frac{10 + 0}{2}, \frac{11 + 4}{2}\right) = \left(5, \frac{15}{2}\right)$

76. $d = \sqrt{(-5 - 5)^2 + (-7 - 7)^2}$
$= \sqrt{100 + 196} = \sqrt{296}$
$= \sqrt{4 \cdot 74} = 2\sqrt{74} \approx 17.20$
$\left(\frac{-5 + 5}{2}, \frac{-7 + 7}{2}\right) = (0, 0)$

77. $d = \sqrt{(1 - 3)^2 + (-1 - 10)^2}$
$= \sqrt{4 + 121} = \sqrt{125} = \sqrt{25 \cdot 5} = 5\sqrt{5} \approx 11.18$
$\left(\frac{1 + 3}{2}, \frac{-1 + 10}{2}\right) = \left(2, \frac{9}{2}\right)$

Chapters 10–12 Project *(pp. 756–757)*

1. Check students' work.
2.

length b	3	5	8	13	21	34
width a	2	3	5	8	13	21
$\frac{b}{a}$	1.5	1.6667	1.6	1.625	1.6154	1.6190

3. The ratios in the table get closer to the golden ratio as you move to the right in the table.

Copyright © McDougal Littell Inc.
All rights reserved.

Skills Review Handbook

Decimals *(p. 760)*

1. 7.92
+6.50
14.42

2. 12.36
+9.00
21.36

3. 28.012
+94.300
122.312

4. 19.900
93.800
+5.992
119.692

5. 9.02
8.00
+8.70
25.72

6. 2.250
7.789
+4.320
14.359

7. 3.42
− 2.40
1.02

8. 0.88
− 0.39
0.49

9. 2.910
−0.452
2.458

10. 15.00
−6.32
8.68

8.68
−1.44
7.24

11. 10.24
−3.10
7.14

7.14
−0.07
7.07

12. 94.48
−16.70
77.78

77.780
−42.902
34.878

13. 6.25
× 6.5
3125
37500
40.625

14. 0.26
× 9.58
208
1300
23400
2.4908

15. 0.15
× 24
60
300
3.60

16. 3.51
× 64
1404
21060
224.64

17. 183.62
× 2.834
73448
550860
14689600
36724000
520.37908

18. 510.375
× 80.2
1020750
408300000
40,932.0750

19. 16.7
8)133.6
8
53
48
5 6
5 6
0

20. 19100
3)57300
3
27
27
03
3
00

21. 18.4
126)2318.4
126
1058
1008
50 4
50 4
0

22. 4.78
21)100.38
84
16 3
14 7
1 68
1 68
0

23. 4220
2)8440
8
04
4
04
4
00

24. 77.49
35)2712.15
245
262
245
17 1
14 0
3 15
3 15
0

25. 24.00
25.99
12.45
62.44
spent \$62.44

70.00
−62.44
7.56
change: \$7.56

Factors and Multiples *(p. 762)*

1. 18: 1, 2, 3, 6, 9, 18

2. 10: 1, 2, 5, 10

3. 77: 1, 7, 11, 77

4. 35: 1, 5, 7, 35

5. 27: 1, 3, 9, 27

6. 100: 1, 2, 4, 5, 10, 20, 25, 50, 100

7. 42: 1, 2, 3, 6, 7, 14, 21, 42

8. 49: 1, 7, 49

9. $27 = 3^3$

10. $24 = 2^3 \cdot 3$

11. $32 = 2^5$

Copyright © McDougal Littell Inc.
All rights reserved.

12. 61, prime

13. $55 = 5 \cdot 11$

14. $68 = 2^2 \cdot 17$

15. $148 = 2^2 \cdot 37$

16. $225 = 3^2 \cdot 5^2$

17. 15: 1, 3, 5, 15
22: 1, 2, 11, 22
Common factor: 1

18. 36: 1, 2, 3, 4, 6, 9, 12, 18, 36
54: 1, 2, 3, 6, 9, 18, 27, 54
Common factors: 1, 2, 3, 6, 9, 18

19. 5: 1, 5
20: 1, 2, 4, 5, 10, 20
Common factors: 1, 5

20. 14: 1, 2, 7, 14
21: 1, 3, 7, 21
Common factors: 1, 7

21. 9: 1, 3, 9
36: 1, 2, 3, 4, 6, 9, 12, 18, 36
Common factors: 1, 3, 9

22. 24: 1, 2, 3, 4, 6, 8, 12, 24
25: 1, 5, 25
Common factor: 1

23. 20: 1, 2, 4, 5, 10, 20
55: 1, 5, 11, 55
Common factors: 1, 5

24. 12: 1, 2, 3, 4, 6, 12
30: 1, 2, 3, 5, 6, 10, 15, 30
Common factors: 1, 2, 3, 6

25. $25 = 5^2$
$30 = 2 \cdot 3 \cdot 5$
GCF = 5

26. $32 = 2^5$
$40 = 2^3 \cdot 5$
$\text{GCF} = 2^3 = 8$

27. 17, prime
$24 = 2^3 \cdot 3$
GCF: 1

28. $35 = 5 \cdot 7$
$150 = 2 \cdot 3 \cdot 5^2$
GCF = 5

29. $14 = 2 \cdot 7$
$28 = 2^2 \cdot 7$
$\text{GCF} = 2 \cdot 7 = 14$

30. $65 = 5 \cdot 13$
$39 = 3 \cdot 13$
GCF = 13

31. $102 = 2 \cdot 3 \cdot 17$
$51 = 3 \cdot 17$
$\text{GCF} = 3 \cdot 17 = 51$

32. $128 = 2^7$
$104 = 2^3 \cdot 13$
$\text{GCF} = 2^3 = 8$

33. 5, prime
7, prime
$\text{LCM} = 5 \cdot 7 = 35$

34. 7, prime
$12 = 2^2 \cdot 3$
$\text{LCM} = 7 \cdot 2^2 \cdot 3 = 84$

35. $16 = 2^4$
$26 = 2 \cdot 13$
$\text{LCM} = 2^4 \cdot 13 = 208$

36. 5, prime
$10 = 2 \cdot 5$
$\text{LCM} = 2 \cdot 5 = 10$

37. $9 = 3^2$
$15 = 3 \cdot 5$
$\text{LCM} = 3^2 \cdot 5 = 45$

38. $12 = 2^2 \cdot 3$
$35 = 5 \cdot 7$
$\text{LCM} = 2^2 \cdot 3 \cdot 5 \cdot 7 = 420$

39. $6 = 2 \cdot 3$
$14 = 2 \cdot 7$
$\text{LCM} = 2 \cdot 3 \cdot 7 = 42$

40. $20 = 2^2 \cdot 5$
$25 = 5^2$
$\text{LCM} = 2^2 \cdot 5^2 = 100$

41. 3, prime
$12 = 2^2 \cdot 3$
$\text{LCD} = 2^2 \cdot 3 = 12$

42. $9 = 3^2$
$12 = 2^2 \cdot 3$
$\text{LCD} = 2^2 \cdot 3^2 = 36$

43. $6 = 2 \cdot 3$
$10 = 2 \cdot 5$
$\text{LCD} = 2 \cdot 3 \cdot 5 = 30$

44. $8 = 2^3$
$14 = 2 \cdot 7$
$\text{LCD} = 2^3 \cdot 7 = 56$

45. $4 = 2^2$
$70 = 2 \cdot 5 \cdot 7$
$\text{LCD} = 2^2 \cdot 5 \cdot 7 = 140$

46. $10 = 2 \cdot 5$
$24 = 2^3 \cdot 3$
$\text{LCD} = 2^3 \cdot 3 \cdot 5 = 120$

47. 3, prime
17, prime
$\text{LCD} = 3 \cdot 17 = 51$

48. $15 = 3 \cdot 5$
$40 = 2^3 \cdot 5$
$\text{LCD} = 2^3 \cdot 3 \cdot 5 = 120$

Fractions *(p. 766)*

1. $7, \frac{1}{7}$

2. $\frac{1}{14}, 14$

Copyright © McDougal Littell Inc.
All rights reserved.

Skills Review Handbook *continued*

3. $\frac{7}{12}, \frac{12}{7}$ or $1\frac{5}{7}$

4. $\frac{5}{8}, \frac{8}{5}$ or $1\frac{3}{5}$

5. $\frac{1}{20}$, 20

6. 100, $\frac{1}{100}$

7. $\frac{5}{13}, \frac{13}{5}$ or $2\frac{3}{5}$

8. $\frac{6}{7}, \frac{7}{6}$ or $1\frac{1}{6}$

9. $1\frac{1}{5} = \frac{6}{5}, \frac{5}{6}$

10. $2\frac{3}{5} = \frac{13}{5}, \frac{5}{13}$

11. $\frac{3}{9} = \frac{1}{3}, 3$

12. $\frac{12}{17}, \frac{17}{12}$ or $1\frac{5}{12}$

13. $6\frac{2}{5} = \frac{32}{5}, \frac{5}{32}$

14. $10\frac{1}{3} = \frac{31}{3}, \frac{3}{31}$

15. $\frac{2}{7}, \frac{7}{2}$ or $3\frac{1}{2}$

16. $4\frac{3}{4} = \frac{19}{4}, \frac{4}{19}$

17. $\frac{1}{6} + \frac{4}{6} = \frac{5}{6}$

18. $\frac{5}{8} - \frac{3}{8} = \frac{2}{8} = \frac{1}{4}$

19. $\frac{4}{9} - \frac{1}{9} = \frac{3}{9} = \frac{1}{3}$

20. $\frac{5}{12} + \frac{3}{12} = \frac{8}{12} = \frac{2}{3}$

21. $\frac{1}{2} + \frac{1}{8} = \frac{4}{8} + \frac{1}{8} = \frac{5}{8}$

22. $\frac{3}{5} - \frac{1}{10} = \frac{6}{10} - \frac{1}{10} = \frac{5}{10} = \frac{1}{2}$

23. $\frac{7}{10} + \frac{1}{3} = \frac{21}{30} + \frac{10}{30} = \frac{31}{30} = 1\frac{1}{30}$

24. $\frac{15}{24} - \frac{7}{12} = \frac{15}{24} - \frac{14}{24} = \frac{1}{24}$

25. $5\frac{1}{8} - 2\frac{3}{4} = \frac{41}{8} - \frac{11}{4} = \frac{41}{8} - \frac{22}{4} = \frac{19}{8} = 2\frac{3}{8}$

26. $1\frac{3}{7} + \frac{1}{2} = \frac{10}{7} + \frac{1}{2} = \frac{20}{14} + \frac{7}{14} = \frac{27}{14} = 1\frac{13}{14}$

27. $4\frac{3}{8} - 2\frac{5}{6} = \frac{35}{8} - \frac{17}{6} = \frac{105}{24} - \frac{68}{24} = \frac{37}{24} = 1\frac{13}{24}$

28. $\frac{3}{7} + \frac{3}{4} = \frac{12}{28} + \frac{21}{28} = \frac{33}{28} = 1\frac{5}{28}$

29. $7\frac{1}{2} + \frac{7}{10} = \frac{15}{2} + \frac{7}{10} = \frac{75}{10} + \frac{7}{10} = \frac{82}{10} = 8\frac{2}{10} = 8\frac{1}{5}$

30. $5\frac{5}{9} - 2\frac{1}{3} = 5\frac{5}{9} - 2\frac{3}{9} = 3\frac{2}{9}$

31. $4\frac{5}{8} - 1\frac{3}{16} = 4\frac{10}{16} - 1\frac{3}{16} = 3\frac{7}{16}$

32. $9\frac{2}{5} + 3\frac{1}{3} = 9\frac{6}{15} + 3\frac{5}{15} = 12\frac{11}{15}$

33. $\frac{1}{2} \times \frac{1}{2} = \frac{1}{4}$

34. $\frac{2}{3} \times \frac{4}{5} = \frac{8}{15}$

35. $\frac{5}{8} \times \frac{4}{15} = \frac{5 \cdot 2 \cdot 2}{2 \cdot 2 \cdot 2 \cdot 3 \cdot 5} = \frac{1}{6}$

36. $\frac{3}{7} \times \frac{7}{9} = \frac{1}{3}$

37. $\frac{3}{4} \times \frac{8}{9} = \frac{2}{3}$

38. $1\frac{2}{3} \times \frac{3}{5} = \frac{5}{3} \times \frac{3}{5} = 1$

39. $\frac{3}{1} \times 2\frac{5}{9} = \frac{3}{1} \times \frac{23}{9} = \frac{23}{3} = 7\frac{2}{3}$

40. $5\frac{1}{4} \times 1\frac{1}{7} = \frac{21}{4} \times \frac{8}{7} = 6$

41. $\frac{7}{8} \div \frac{3}{4} = \frac{7}{8} \cdot \frac{4}{3} = \frac{7}{6} = 1\frac{1}{6}$

42. $\frac{5}{12} \div \frac{1}{2} = \frac{5}{12} \cdot \frac{2}{1} = \frac{5}{6}$

43. $\frac{4}{5} \div \frac{2}{3} = \frac{4}{5} \cdot \frac{3}{2} = \frac{6}{5} = 1\frac{1}{5}$

44. $\frac{11}{16} \div 1\frac{1}{2} = \frac{11}{16} \div \frac{3}{2} = \frac{11}{16} \cdot \frac{2}{3} = \frac{11}{24}$

45. $4\frac{1}{2} \div \frac{3}{4} = \frac{9}{2} \cdot \frac{4}{3} = 6$

46. $2\frac{1}{4} \div 1\frac{1}{3} = \frac{9}{4} \div \frac{4}{3} = \frac{9}{4} \cdot \frac{3}{4} = \frac{27}{16} = 1\frac{11}{16}$

47. $3\frac{2}{5} \div 4 = \frac{17}{5} \div \frac{4}{1} = \frac{17}{5} \cdot \frac{1}{4} = \frac{17}{20}$

48. $7\frac{1}{5} \div 2\frac{1}{4} = \frac{36}{5} \div \frac{9}{4} = \frac{36}{5} \cdot \frac{4}{9} = \frac{16}{5} = 3\frac{1}{5}$

49. $\frac{15}{16} - \frac{1}{8} = \frac{15}{16} - \frac{2}{16} = \frac{13}{16}$

50. $\frac{5}{9} \times 1\frac{1}{2} = \frac{5}{9} \times \frac{3}{2} = \frac{5}{6}$

51. $\frac{12}{13} \div \frac{12}{13} = \frac{12}{13} \cdot \frac{13}{12} = 1$

52. $\frac{24}{25} + \frac{1}{5} = \frac{24}{25} + \frac{5}{25} = \frac{29}{25} = 1\frac{4}{25}$

53. $5\frac{1}{2} - \frac{1}{8} = \frac{11}{2} - \frac{1}{8} = \frac{44}{8} - \frac{1}{8} = \frac{43}{8} = 5\frac{3}{8}$

54. $\frac{3}{10} \div \frac{1}{5} = \frac{3}{10} \cdot \frac{5}{1} = \frac{3}{2} = 1\frac{1}{2}$

55. $\frac{7}{8} \times \frac{4}{9} = \frac{7}{18}$

56. $\frac{1}{3} + \frac{1}{6} = \frac{2}{6} + \frac{1}{6} = \frac{3}{6} = \frac{1}{2}$

57. $4\frac{1}{4} \times \frac{2}{3} = \frac{17}{4} \times \frac{2}{3} = \frac{17}{6} = 2\frac{5}{6}$

58. $9\frac{2}{5} + 3\frac{1}{2} = 9\frac{4}{10} + 3\frac{5}{10} = 12\frac{9}{10}$

59. $\frac{4}{5} \div \frac{1}{2} = \frac{4}{5} \cdot \frac{2}{1} = \frac{8}{5} = 1\frac{3}{5}$

60. $6\frac{5}{7} - 2\frac{1}{5} = 6\frac{25}{35} - 2\frac{7}{35} = 4\frac{18}{35}$

61. $\frac{9}{10} + \frac{3}{8} = \frac{36}{40} + \frac{15}{40} = \frac{51}{40} = 1\frac{11}{40}$

62. $8\frac{1}{2} \times \frac{1}{4} = \frac{17}{2} \cdot \frac{1}{4} = \frac{17}{8} = 2\frac{1}{8}$

Copyright © McDougal Littell Inc.
All rights reserved.

63. $\frac{11}{15} \cdot \frac{3}{8} = \frac{11}{40}$

64. $\frac{4}{7} \div \frac{4}{5} = \frac{4}{7} \cdot \frac{5}{4} = \frac{5}{7}$

Writing Fractions and Decimals *(p. 768)*

1. $\frac{1}{4} = \frac{25}{100} = 0.25$

2. $\frac{7}{10} = \frac{70}{100} = 0.70 = 0.7$

3. $\frac{2}{25} = \frac{8}{100} = 0.08$

4. $\frac{41}{50} = \frac{82}{100} = 0.82$

5. $\frac{1}{3} = 0.\overline{3}$

$$\begin{array}{r} 0.3\overline{3} \\ 3\overline{)1.0} \\ \underline{9} \\ 10 \end{array}$$

$0.\overline{3}$

6. $\frac{4}{9} = 0.\overline{4}$

$$\begin{array}{r} 0.\overline{4} \\ 9\overline{)4.0} \\ \underline{36} \\ 4 \end{array}$$

$0.\overline{4}$

7. $\frac{10}{11} = 0.\overline{90}$

$$\begin{array}{r} 0.909 \\ 11\overline{)10.0} \\ \underline{99} \\ 100 \\ \underline{99} \\ 1 \end{array}$$

$0.\overline{90}$

8. $\frac{27}{37} = 0.\overline{729}$

$$\begin{array}{r} 0.729 \\ 37\overline{)27.0} \\ \underline{25\ 9} \\ 1\ 10 \\ \underline{74} \\ 360 \\ \underline{333} \\ 27 \end{array}$$

$0.\overline{729}$

9. $0.5 = \frac{5}{10} = \frac{1}{2}$

10. $0.16 = \frac{16}{100} = \frac{4}{25}$

11. $0.289 = \frac{289}{1000}$

12. $0.1234 = \frac{1234}{10000} = \frac{617}{5000}$

13. $0.\overline{7}$; Let $x = 0.\overline{7}$

$$\begin{aligned} 10x &= 7.\overline{7} \\ -x &= -0.\overline{7} \\ \hline 9x &= 7 \\ x &= \frac{7}{9} \end{aligned}$$

14. $0.\overline{15}$; Let $x = 0.\overline{15}$

$$\begin{aligned} 100x &= 15.\overline{15} \\ -\ x &= -0.\overline{15} \\ \hline 99x &= 15 \\ x &= \frac{15}{99} = \frac{5}{33} \end{aligned}$$

15. $0.\overline{613}$; Let $x = 0.\overline{613}$

$$\begin{aligned} 1000x &= 613.\overline{613} \\ -\ x &= -0.\overline{613} \\ \hline 999x &= 613 \\ x &= \frac{613}{999} \end{aligned}$$

16. $0.\overline{5840}$; Let $x = 0.\overline{5840}$

$$\begin{aligned} 10000x &= 5840.\overline{5840} \\ -\ x &= -0.\overline{5840} \\ \hline 9999x &= 5840 \\ x &= \frac{5840}{9999} \end{aligned}$$

Fractions, Decimals, and Percents *(p. 769)*

1. $63\% = 0.63 = \frac{63}{100}$

2. $7\% = 0.07 = \frac{7}{100}$

3. $24\% = 0.24 = \frac{24}{100} = \frac{6}{25}$

4. $35\% = 0.35 = \frac{35}{100} = \frac{7}{20}$

5. $17\% = 0.17 = \frac{17}{100}$

6. $125\% = 1.25 = \frac{125}{100} = \frac{5}{4} = 1\frac{1}{4}$

7. $45\% = 0.45 = \frac{45}{100} = \frac{9}{20}$

8. $250\% = 2.5 = \frac{250}{100} = \frac{5}{2} = 2\frac{1}{2}$

9. $33.\overline{3}\% = 0.\overline{3} = \frac{1}{3}$

10. $96\% = 0.96 = \frac{96}{100} = \frac{24}{25}$

11. $62.5\% = 0.625 = \frac{625}{1000} = \frac{5}{8}$

12. $725\% = 7.25 = \frac{725}{100} = \frac{29}{4} = 7\frac{1}{4}$

13. $5.2\% = 0.052 = \frac{52}{1000} = \frac{13}{250}$

14. $0.8\% = 0.008 = \frac{8}{1000} = \frac{1}{125}$

15. $0.12\% = 0.0012 = \frac{12}{10000} = \frac{3}{2500}$

16. $0.39 = 39\% = \frac{39}{100}$

17. $0.08 = 8\% = \frac{8}{100} = \frac{2}{25}$

18. $0.12 = 12\% = \frac{12}{100} = \frac{3}{25}$

19. $1.5 = 150\% = \frac{150}{100} = \frac{3}{2}$

20. $0.72 = 72\% = \frac{72}{100} = \frac{18}{25}$

21. $0.05 = 5\% = \frac{5}{100} = \frac{1}{20}$

Copyright © McDougal Littell Inc.
All rights reserved.

22. $2.08 = 208\% = \frac{208}{100} = 2\frac{8}{100} = 2\frac{2}{25}$

23. $4.8 = 480\% = \frac{480}{100} = 4\frac{8}{10} = 4\frac{4}{5}$

24. $0.02 = 2\% = \frac{2}{100} = \frac{1}{50}$

25. $3.75 = 375\% = \frac{375}{100} = 3\frac{75}{100} = 3\frac{3}{4}$

26. $0.85 = 85\% = \frac{85}{100} = \frac{17}{20}$

27. $0.52 = 52\% = \frac{52}{100} = \frac{13}{25}$

28. $0.9 = 90\% = \frac{9}{10}$

29. $0.005 = 0.5\% = \frac{5}{1000} = \frac{1}{200}$

30. $2.01 = 201\% = \frac{201}{100} = 2\frac{1}{100}$

31. $\frac{7}{10} = 0.7 = 70\%$

32. $\frac{13}{20} = \frac{65}{100} = 0.65 = 65\%$

33. $\frac{11}{25} = \frac{44}{100} = 0.44 = 44\%$

34. $\frac{3}{10} = 0.3 = 30\%$

35. $\frac{3}{8} = 3 \div 8 = 0.375 = 37.5\%$

36. $2\frac{3}{4} = 2\frac{75}{100} = 2.75 = 275\%$

37. $5\frac{1}{8} = 5 + (1 \div 8) = 5.125 = 512.5\%$

38. $\frac{19}{20} = \frac{95}{100} = 0.95 = 95\%$

39. $\frac{7}{8} = 7 \div 8 = 0.875 = 87.5\%$

40. $3\frac{7}{25} = 3\frac{28}{100} = 3.28 = 328\%$

Comparing and Ordering Numbers *(p. 771)*

1. $12{,}428 < 15{,}116$
2. $905 < 961$
3. $-140{,}999 > -142{,}109$
4. $-16.82 < -14.09$
5. $0.40506 > 0.00456$
6. $23.03 < 23.3$
7. $1005.2 < 1050.7$
8. $932{,}778 < 934{,}112$
9. $-0.058 > -0.102$
10. $\frac{7}{13} > \frac{3}{13}$
11. $17\frac{1}{4} = 17\frac{2}{8}$
12. $\frac{7}{10} = \frac{14}{20}, \frac{3}{4} = \frac{15}{20}$
    $\frac{14}{20} < \frac{15}{20}$
13. $-\frac{5}{9} = -\frac{15}{27}$
14. $-\frac{1}{2} = -\frac{4}{8}$
    $-\frac{4}{8} < -\frac{3}{8}$
15. $\frac{1}{8} = \frac{9}{72}, \frac{1}{9} = \frac{8}{72}$
    $\frac{9}{72} > \frac{8}{72}$
16. $\frac{4}{5} = \frac{12}{15}, \frac{2}{3} = \frac{10}{15}$
    $\frac{12}{15} > \frac{10}{15}$
17. $42\frac{1}{5} > 41\frac{7}{8}$
18. $508.881 > 508.793$
19. $32{,}227 > 32{,}226.5$
20. $\frac{5}{8} = \frac{15}{24}, \frac{2}{3} = \frac{16}{24}$
    $\frac{15}{24} < \frac{16}{24}$
21. $-17\frac{5}{6} < -17\frac{5}{7}$
22. 1207, 1220, 1702, 1772
23. −45,617; −45,242; −40,099; −40,071
24. −24.01, −24.0, −23.5, −23.12, −23.08
25. 9.003, 9.027, 9.10, 9.27, 9.3
26. 4.01, 4.07, 4.22, 4.5
27. $\frac{1}{3} = \frac{8}{24}, \frac{3}{8} = \frac{9}{24}, \frac{5}{6} = \frac{20}{24}, \frac{5}{4} = \frac{30}{24}$
28. $\frac{3}{10}, \frac{3}{7}, \frac{3}{5}, \frac{3}{4}, \frac{3}{2}$
29. $\frac{15}{16}, 1\frac{1}{8} = 1.125, 1\frac{2}{5} = 1.4, \frac{5}{3} = 1.\overline{6}, \frac{7}{4} = 1.75$
30. $-15\frac{1}{3} = -15.\overline{3}, -15\frac{1}{4} = -15.25, -14\frac{5}{6} = -14.8\overline{3},$
    $-14\frac{7}{9} = -14.\overline{7}$
31. $-1\frac{1}{3} = -1\frac{32}{96}, -\frac{5}{4} = -1\frac{24}{96}, -\frac{7}{8} = -\frac{84}{96}, -\frac{5}{12} = -\frac{40}{96}$
32. yes; $6\frac{3}{4} = 6.75,\ 6\frac{5}{8} = 6.625,\ 6.75 > 6.625$

Perimeter, Area, and Volume *(p. 773)*

1. $2(10) + 2(7) = 20 + 14 = 34$ units
2. $2(0.5) + 2(0.75) = 1 + 1.5 = 2.5$ in.

Copyright © McDougal Littell Inc.
All rights reserved.

3. $21 + 35 + 28 = 84$ ft

4. $3.5(4) = 14$ m

5. $18(4) = 72$ ft

6. $2(6) + 2(7) = 12 + 14 = 26$ m

7. $29^2 = 841$ yd^2

8. $7 \cdot 4 = 28$ km^2

9. $3.5^2 = 12.25$ in.^{2}

10. $24 \cdot 6 = 144$ ft^2

11. $\frac{1}{2}(8)(5) = 20$ in.^{2}

12. $\frac{1}{2}(7.2)(5.3) = 19.08$ cm^2

13. $25^3 = 15{,}625$ ft^3

14. $4.2^3 = 74.088$ cm^3

15. $15 \cdot 7 \cdot 4 = 420$ yd^3

16. $(7.3)(5)(3.2) = 116.8$ cm^3

17. $(5.3)(4)(10) = 212$ in.^{3}

Estimation *(p. 776)*

1. $40 + 10 = 50$

2. $200 + 800 = 1000$

3. $1600 + 800 = 2400$

4. $20 + 20 + 70 = 110$

5. $100 + 100 + 300 = 500$

6. $1000 + 5100 + 3900 = 10{,}000$

7. $60 - 40 = 20$

8. $1400 - 900 = 500$

9. $2000 - 400 = 1600$

10. $70 - 40 - 10 = 20$

11. $1100 - 200 - 100 = 800$

12. $8400 - 3800 - 1200 = 3400$

13. $15 + 6 = 21$
$0.98 \approx 1$
$0.46 \approx 0.5$
$21 + 1 + 0.5 = 22.5$

14. $62 + 44 = 106$
$0.36 + 0.68 \approx 1$
$106 + 1 = 107$

15. $156 + 324 = 480$
$0.22 + 0.72 \approx 1$
$480 + 1 = 481$

16. $533 + 37 = 570$
$0.2 + 0.2 \approx 0.0$
$570 + 0.0 = 570$

17. $912 + 428 = 1340$
$0.14 + 0.13 \approx 0.0$
$1340 + 0.0 = 1340$

18. $588 + 120 = 708$
$0.61 + 0.37 \approx 1$
$708 + 1 = 709$

19. $24 + 4 + 12 = 40$
$0.22 + 0.53 + 0.31 \approx 1$
$40 + 1 = 41$

20. $16 + 34 + 25 = 75$
$0.1 + 0.2 + 0.2 \approx 1$
$75 + 1 = 76$

21. $59 + 71 + 78 = 208$
$0.31 + 0.21 + 0.47 \approx 1$
$208 + 1 = 209$

22. $113 + 97 + 65 = 275$
$0.73 + 0.1 + 0.18 \approx 1$
$275 + 1 = 276$

23. $88 + 86 + 92 = 266$
$0.9 + 0.19 + 0.14 \approx 1$
$266 + 1 = 267$

24. $0 + 120 + 584 = 704$
$0.4 + 0.46 + 0.53 \approx 1$
$704 + 1 = 705$

25. $50 \times 50 = 2500$

26. $30 \times 400 = 12{,}000$

27. $600 \times 50 = 30{,}000$

28. $40 \times 6 = 240$

29. $10 \times 3 = 30$

30. $100 \times 400 = 40{,}000$

31. $600 \div 200 = 3$

32. $120 \div 60 = 2$

33. $800 \div 20 = 40$

34. $80 \div 4 = 20$

35. $60 \div 15 = 4$

36. $40 \div 1 = 40$

37. $75 \times 10 = 750$

38. $400 \times 40 = 16{,}000$

39. $4000 \times 20 = 80{,}000$

40. $500 \times 20 = 10{,}000$

41. $500 \times 14 = 7000$

42. $2000 \times 70 = 140{,}000$

43. $70 \div 3 = 23.\overline{3} \approx 23$

44. $1000 \div 100 = 10$

45. $500 \div 50 = 10$

46. $900 \div 45 = 20$

47. $1500 \div 30 = 50$

48. $150 \div 15 = 10$

49. 9 whole squares + $\frac{1}{2}$(14 partially shaded squares)

$= 9 + 7 = 16$ square units

50. 7 whole squares + $\frac{1}{2}$(25 partially shaded squares)

$= 7 + 12.5 = 19.5 \approx 20$ units^2

51. 13 mostly shaded and completely shaded squares

+ $\frac{1}{2}$(12 partially shaded squares)

$= 13 + 6 = 19$ units^2

52. 13 whole squares + $\frac{1}{2}$(13 partially shaded squares)

$= 13 + 6.5 = 19.5 \approx 20$ units^2

53. 8 whole squares + $\frac{1}{2}$(20 partially shaded squares)

$= 8 + 10 = 18$ units^2

54. 8 whole squares + $\frac{1}{2}$(15 partially shaded squares)

$= 8 + 7.5 = 15.5 \approx 16$ units^2

Data Displays *(p. 779)*

1. 0 to 25 by fives

Copyright © McDougal Littell Inc.
All rights reserved.

2.

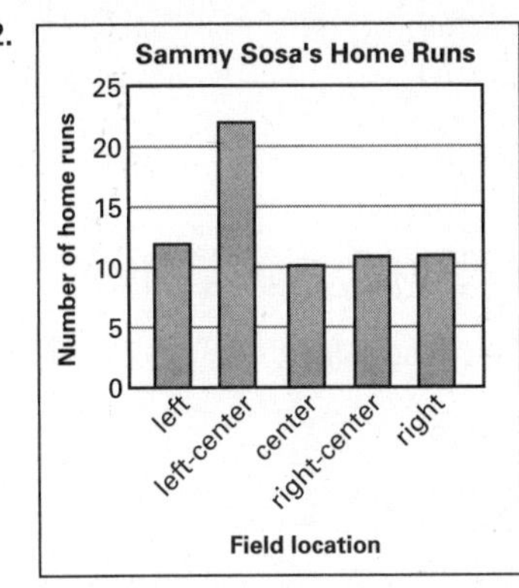

3. 0 to 20 by fives

4.

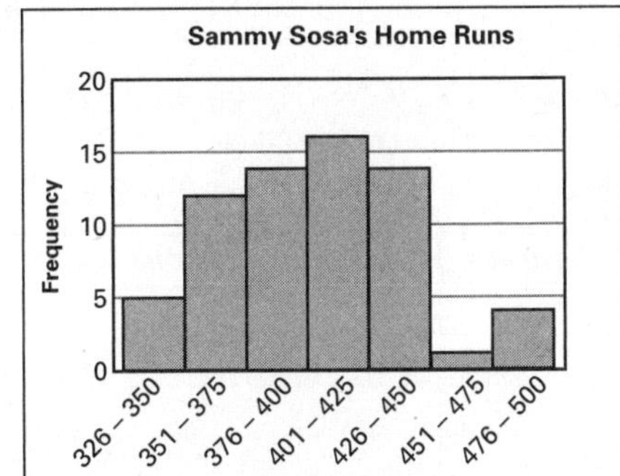

5.

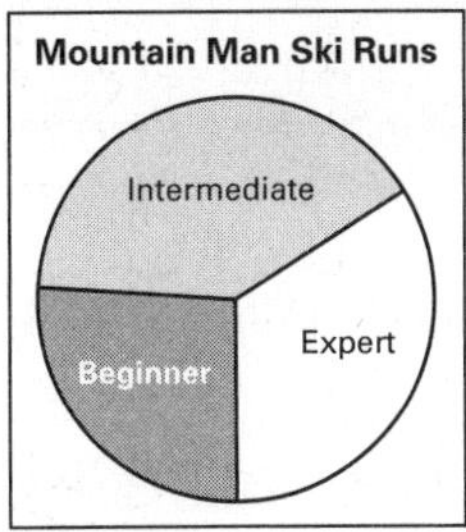

Find the degree measure for each sector of the circle:

$\frac{51}{150} \cdot 360° = 122.4°$

$\frac{60}{150} \cdot 360° = 144°$

$\frac{39}{150} \cdot 360° = 93.6°$

6.

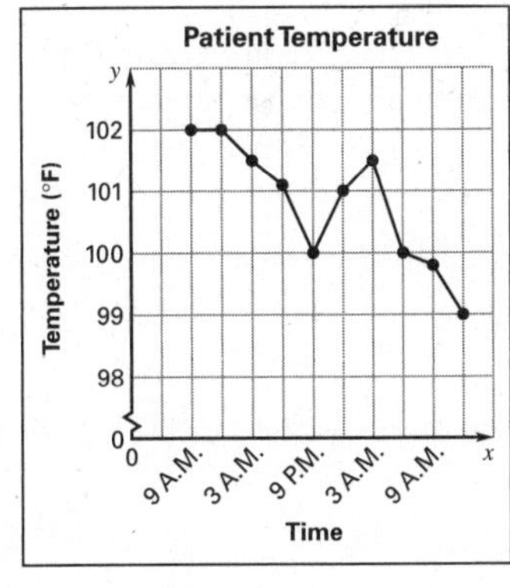

7.

8.

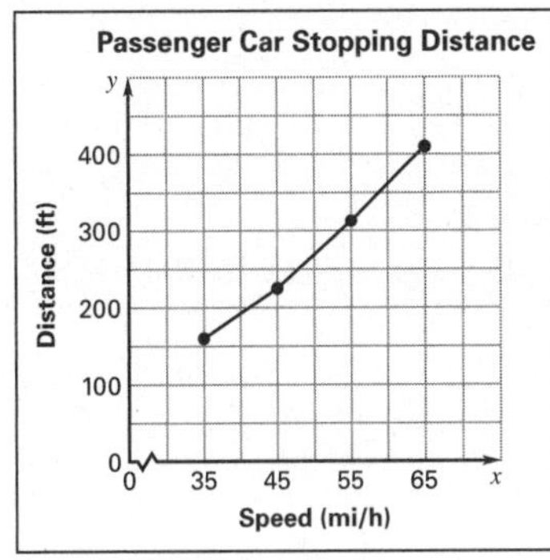

9.

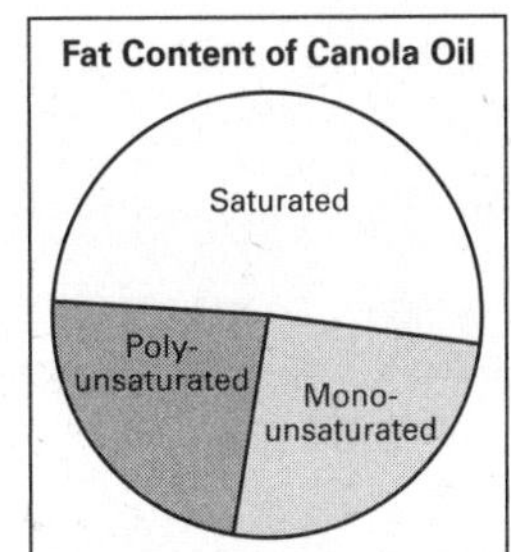

Find the degree measure for each sector of the circle.

$\frac{22}{43} \cdot 360° \approx 184°$

$\frac{10}{43} \cdot 360° \approx 84°$

$\frac{11}{43} \cdot 360° \approx 92°$

10.

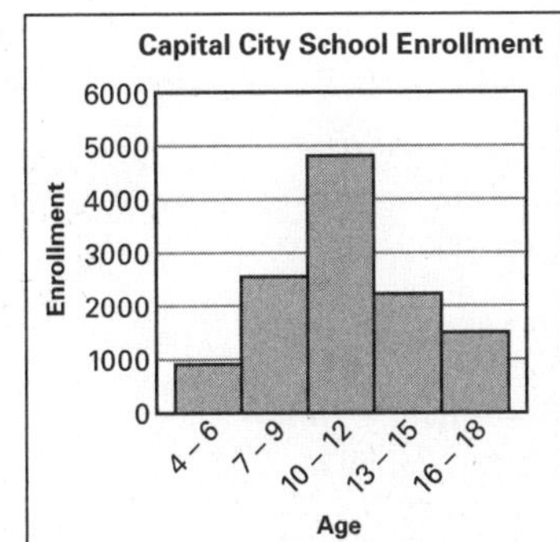

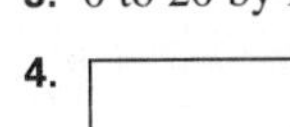

Copyright © McDougal Littell Inc.
All rights reserved.

Skills Review Handbook *continued*

Measures of Central Tendency *(p. 780)*

1. mean:
$(0 + 0 + 0 + 0 + 0 + 1 + 2 + 2 + 4 + 4) \div 10$
$= 13 \div 10$
$= 1.3$
median: $\frac{0 + 1}{2} = \frac{1}{2} = 0.5$
mode: 0

2. mean:
$(1 + 1 + 1 + 2 + 3 + 3 + 3 + 5 + 8) \div 9$
$= 27 \div 9$
$= 3$
median: 3
modes: 1, 3

3. mean:
$(10 + 15 + 20 + 25 + 30 + 35 + 40 + 45 + 50) \div 9$
$= 270 \div 9$
$= 30$
median: 30
mode: none

4. mean:
$(10 + 14 + 14 + 23 + 35 + 38 + 45 + 50 + 60 + 68) \div 10$
$= 357 \div 10$
$= 35.7$
median: $\frac{35 + 38}{2} = 36.5$
mode: 14

5. mean:
$(376 + 376 + 386 + 393 + 487 + 598 + 737 + 745 + 853) \div 9$
$= 4951 \div 9$
about 550.1
median: 487
mode: 376

6. mean:
$(7 + 13 + 26 + 50 + 52 + 76 + 101 + 1000) \div 8$
$= 1325 \div 8$
$= 165.625$
median: $\frac{50 + 52}{2} = 51$
mode: none

Problem Solving *(p. 782)*

1. $275s + 0.8m = 16.15$
Guess: 5 salads, 5 cartons of milk
$5(2.75) + 5(0.80) = 17.75 > 16.15$
Guess: 5 salads, 3 cartons of milk
$5(2.75) + 3(0.80) = 16.15$
Answer: 5 salads, 3 cartons of milk

2. $45 + 45 + w + w = 150$
$90 + 2w = 150$
$2w = 60$
$w = 30$
Area $= 45(30) = 1350$ ft^2

3. $\frac{\$18.75}{5 \text{ sandwiches}} = \frac{\$3.75}{\text{sandwich}}$
$7(3.75) = \$26.25$ for 7 sandwiches

4.

9 diagonals

5. Time to get ready:
$25 + 15 + 20 = 60$ minutes = 1 hour
He needs to get out of bed no later than 6:25 A.M.

6.

Number of players	*Number of games needed*
2	1
3	2
4	3
5	4
...	...
x	$x - 1$
32	31
...	...

31 games

7. A, B, J, K, and P are starters. The possible combinations are:
ABJ AJK AKP ABP AJP
ABK BJK BJP BKP JKP
10 groups are possible.

8. Let x be the number of weeks.
$135 + 5x = 90 + 10x$
$45 = 5x$
$9 = x$
9 weeks

9. $18(15) = 270$ ft^2; 270 tiles are needed;
We don't know how many tiles are in a carton. The problem cannot be solved; not enough information is given.

Copyright © McDougal Littell Inc.
All rights reserved.

EXTRA PRACTICE FOR CHAPTERS 1–12

Chapter 1 *(p. 783)*

1. $15(7) = 105$
2. $7 + 15 = 22$
3. $\frac{32}{4} = 8$
4. $3(5)^2 = 75$
5. $(4 \cdot 2)^3 = 8^3 = 512$
6. $6(4)^4 = 1536$
7. $3^4 - 5 = 76$
8. $(4 + 2)^3 = 6^3 = 216$
9. $(10 - 3)^2 = 7^2 = 49$
10. $33 - 12 \div 4 = 33 - 3 = 30$
11. $10^2 \div 4 + 6 = 100 \div 4 + 6 = 25 + 6 = 31$
12. $10^2 \div (4 + 6) = 100 \div 10 = 10$
13. $2 + 21 \div 3 - 6 = 2 + 7 - 6 = 9 - 6 = 3$
14. $3 + 7 \cdot 35 \div 5 = 3 + 245 \div 5 = 3 + 49 = 52$
15. $15 \div (6 - 1) - 2 = 15 \div 5 - 2 = 3 - 2 = 1$
16. $[(5 \cdot 8) + 8] \div 16 = [40 + 8] \div 16 = 48 \div 16 = 3$
17. $\frac{9 \cdot 7^2}{5 + 8^2 - 6} = \frac{9 \cdot 49}{5 + 64 - 6} = \frac{441}{63} = 7$
18. $x + 7 = 13$
    $x = 6$
19. $n - 4 = 8$
    $n = 12$
20. $3y = 21$
    $y = 7$
21. $\frac{m}{4} = 6$
    $m = 24$
22. $12 + 10 \not< 22$; not a solution
23. $6(5) \overset{?}{\geq} 25$
    $30 \geq 25$
    a solution
24. $3(4) \overset{?}{\leq} 12$
    $12 \leq 12$
    a solution
25. $4 + 6 \overset{?}{\geq} 11$
    $10 \not\geq 11$
    not a solution
26. $48 \div 16 \overset{?}{<} 4$
    $3 < 4$
    a solution
27. $9 - 5 \overset{?}{>} 3$
    $4 > 3$
    a solution
28. $4x \leq 36$
29. $16 = 20 - x$
30. your friend's score $= 2 \cdot$ your score
    $48 = 2x$
    $24 = x$
    your score: 24
31.

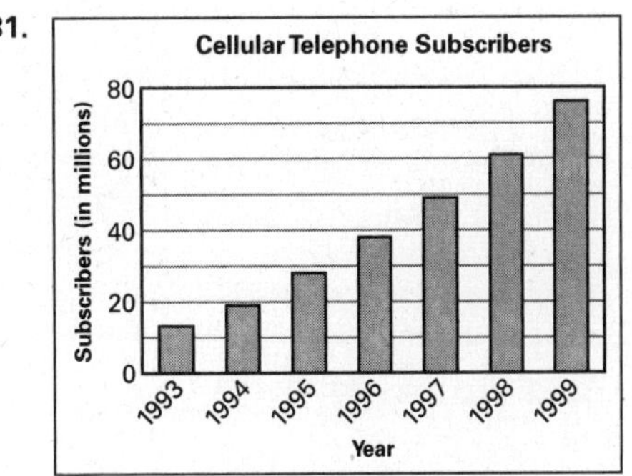

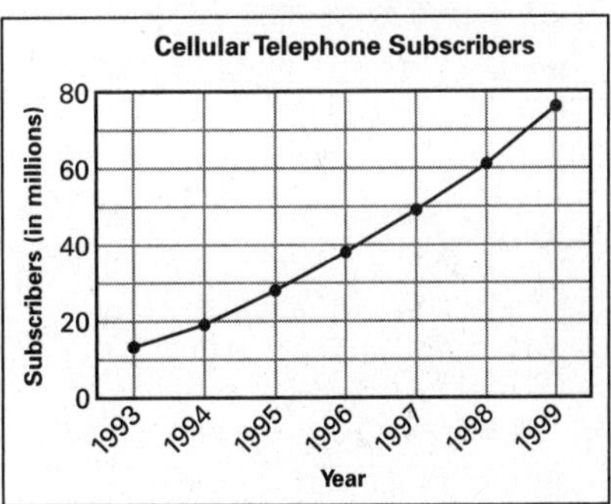

32. $y = 8 - 2x$

x	0	1	2	3	4	5
y	8	6	4	2	0	−2

33. $y = 7x + 1$

x	0	1	2	3	4	5
y	1	8	15	22	29	36

34. $y = 3(x - 4)$

x	0	1	2	3	4	5
y	−12	−9	−6	−3	0	3

Chapter 2 *(p. 784)*

1.

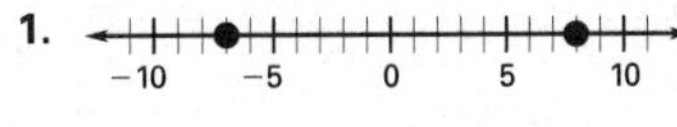

$-7 < 8, 8 > -7$

2. $3 > -5, -5 < 3$

3. $-4 > -7, -7 < -4$

Copyright © McDougal Littell Inc.
All rights reserved.

Extra Practice *continued*

4. 

$0 > -3, -3 < 0$

5. $|-3| = 3$

6. $-|4| = -(4) = -4$

7. $|8.5| = 8.5$

8. $\left|-\frac{3}{4}\right| = \frac{3}{4}$

9. $-3 + 8 = 5$

10. $18 + 27 = 45$

11. $5 + (-7) = -2$

12. $-4 + (-11) = -15$

13. $-4 + 13 + (-6) = 3$

14. $15 + (-12) + (-4) = -1$

15. $-2 + (-9) + 8 = -3$

16. $17 + (-5) + 15 = 27$

17. $-8 - 5 = -8 + (-5) = -13$

18. $-3 - (-7) = -3 + 7 = 4$

19. $4.1 - 6.3 = 4.1 + (-6.3) = -2.2$

20. $-\frac{2}{5} - \frac{3}{5} = -\frac{2}{5} + \left(-\frac{3}{5}\right) = -\frac{5}{5} = -1$

21. $6 - 13 = 6 + (-13) = -7$

22. $5 - (-2) = 5 + 2 = 7$

23. $-10 - (-3.5) = -10 + 3.5 = -6.5$

24. $-2 - 14 = -16$

25. $-6 - (-3) - 4 = -6 + 3 + (-4) = -7$

26. $-15 - 4 - 12 = -15 + (-4) + (-12) = -31$

27. $2 - 5 - (-18) = 2 + (-5) + 18 = 15$

28. $(-6)(-7) = 42$

29. $-5(90) = -450$

30. $4(-1.5) = -6$

31. $-14\left(-\frac{3}{7}\right) = 6$

32. $(-4)^3 = -64$

33. $-(3)^4 = -81$

34. $-(-2)^5 = -(-32) = 32$

35. $3(-8)(-2) = 48$

36. $d = -6t$

37. $d = -6(15) = -90$ ft

38. $6(y + 5) = 6y + 6(5) = 6y + 30$

39. $4(a - 6) = 4a - 4(6) = 4a - 24$

40. $(3 + w)2 = 3(2) + w(2) = 6 + 2w$

41. $(4x + 3)2 = 4x(2) + 3(2) = 8x + 6$

42. $-3(r - 5) = -3r - (-3)(5) = -3r + 15$

43. $-(2 + t) = -2 - t$

44. $(x + 4)(-6) = x(-6) + 4(-6) = -6x - 24$

45. $(y - 3)1.5 = y(1.5) - 3(1.5) = 1.5y - 4.5$

46. $3x + 7x = (3 + 7)x = 10x$

47. $8r - r^2$; already simplified

48. $6 + 2y - 3 = 2y + 3$

49. $w + 2w + 4w - 4 = 7w - 4$

50. $7 + 5r - 6 + 4r = 7 - 6 + 5r + 4r$
$= 1 + 9r$
$= 9r + 1$

51. $m^2 + 3m - 2m^2 - m = m^2 - 2m^2 + 3m - m$
$= -m^2 + 2m$

52. $18 \div (-2) = -9$

53. $-48 \div 12 = -4$

54. $16 \div \left(-\frac{4}{5}\right) = 16 \cdot -\frac{5}{4} = -20$

55. $\frac{-22}{\left(-\frac{1}{3}\right)} = -22 \cdot -\frac{3}{1} = 66$

Chapter 3 *(p. 785)*

1. $y - 6 = 8$
$y = 14$

2. $5 + n = -10$
$n = -15$

3. $3 = r - 14$
$17 = r$

4. $-4 = 5 + q$
$-9 = q$

5. $8 = x - (-1)$
$8 = x + 1$
$7 = x$

6. $t - 4 = -7$
$t = -3$

7. $m + 6 = 9$
$m = 3$

8. $-2 = r - (-5)$
$-2 = r + 5$
$-7 = r$

9. $7x = 35$
$x = 5$

10. $-15m = 150$
$m = -10$

11. $6a = 3$
$a = \frac{1}{2}$

12. $-144 = -12t$
$12 = t$

13. $\frac{x}{5} = -4$
$x = -20$

14. $\frac{y}{10} = -\frac{2}{5}$
$y = -\frac{2}{5} \cdot 10$
$y = -4$

Copyright © McDougal Littell Inc.
All rights reserved.

Extra Practice *continued*

15. $-\frac{g}{6} = -14$

$g = 84$

16. $\frac{t}{-8} = -\frac{3}{8}$

$t = -\frac{3}{8} \cdot (-8)$

$t = 3$

17. $6x + 8 = 32$

$6x = 24$

$x = 4$

18. $2x - 1 = 11$

$2x = 12$

$x = 6$

19. $4m + 8m - 2 = 22$

$12m - 2 = 22$

$12m = 24$

$m = 2$

20. $2x - 3(x + 4) = -1$

$2x - 3x - 12 = -1$

$-x - 12 = -1$

$-x = 11$

$x = -11$

21. $\frac{1}{3}(m - 1) = -5$

$m - 1 = -5(3)$

$m - 1 = -15$

$m = -14$

22. $\frac{2}{5}(n + 3) = 4$

$n + 3 = 4\left(\frac{5}{2}\right)$

$n + 3 = 10$

$n = 7$

23. $-6 + 5x = 8x - 9$

$-6 = 3x - 9$

$3 = 3x$

$1 = x$

24. $8r + 1 = 23 - 3r$

$11r + 1 = 23$

$11r = 22$

$r = 2$

25. $2w + 3 = 3w + 1$

$3 = w + 1$

$2 = w$

26. $3a + 12 = 4a - 2a + 1$

$3a + 12 = 2a + 1$

$a + 12 = 1$

$a = -11$

27. $5x + 6 = 2x + x + 2$

$5x + 6 = 3x + 2$

$2x + 6 = 2$

$2x = -4$

$x = -2$

28. $6d - 2d = 10d + 6$

$4d = 10d + 6$

$-6d = 6$

$d = -1$

29. $4(a + 3) = 3(a + 5)$

$4a + 12 = 3a + 15$

$a + 12 = 15$

$a = 3$

30. $8(r - 2) + 6 = 2(r + 1)$

$8r - 16 + 6 = 2r + 2$

$8r - 10 = 2r + 2$

$6r - 10 = 2$

$6r = 12$

$r = 2$

31. $6(x - 1) = 5(2x + 3) - 15$

$6x - 6 = 10x + 15 - 15$

$6x - 6 = 10x$

$-6 = 4x$

$-\frac{6}{4} = x$

$x = -\frac{3}{2}$ or $-1\frac{1}{2}$

32. $\frac{1}{2}(4q + 12) = 2 + 3(6 - q)$

$2q + 6 = 2 + 18 - 3q$

$2q + 6 = 20 - 3q$

$5q + 6 = 20$

$5q = 14$

$q = \frac{14}{5}$ or $2\frac{4}{5}$

33. $-26x - 59 = 135$

$-26x = 194$

$x = -7.46$

34. $18.25d - 4.15 = 2.75d$

$-4.15 = -15.5d$

$0.27 = d$

35. $2.3 - 4.8w = 8.2w + 5.6$

$2.3 - 13w = 5.6$

$-13w = 3.3$

$w = -0.25$

36. $d = rt$

$\frac{d}{t} = r$

37. $r = \frac{36 \text{ mi}}{3 \text{ h}} = 12 \text{ mi/h}$

38. $\frac{33 \text{ oz}}{6 \text{ cans}} = 5.5 \text{ oz/can}$

Copyright © McDougal Littell Inc.
All rights reserved.

39. $\frac{\$50.75}{7 \text{ hr}} = \$7.25/\text{h}$

40. $\frac{10.5 \text{ mi}}{3 \text{ hr}} = 3.5 \text{ mi/h}$

41. $\frac{16 \text{ g}}{8 \text{ bars}} = 2 \text{ g/bar}$

42. $x = (.40)(800)$
$x = \$320$

43. $(0.15)(320) = x$
$48 \text{ m} = x$

44. $24 = p(60)$
$40\% = 0.4 = p$

45. $x = (0.30)(150)$
$x = 45$

Chapter 4 *(p. 786)*

1.

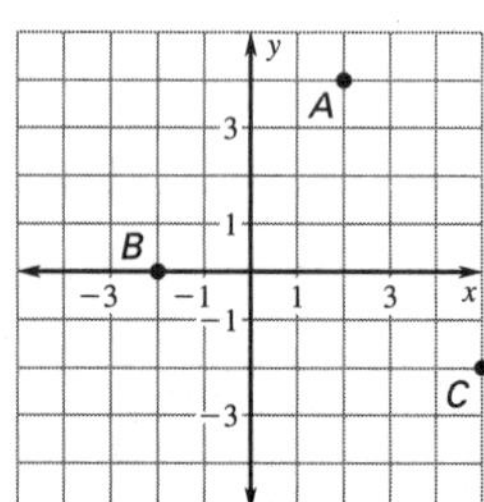

2.

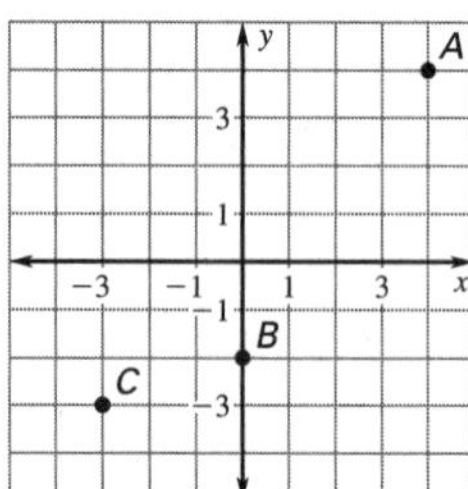

3.

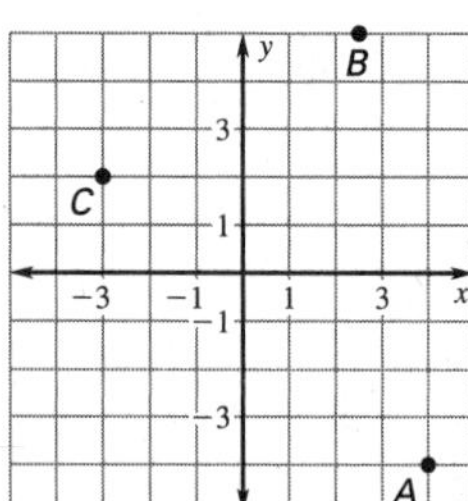

4.

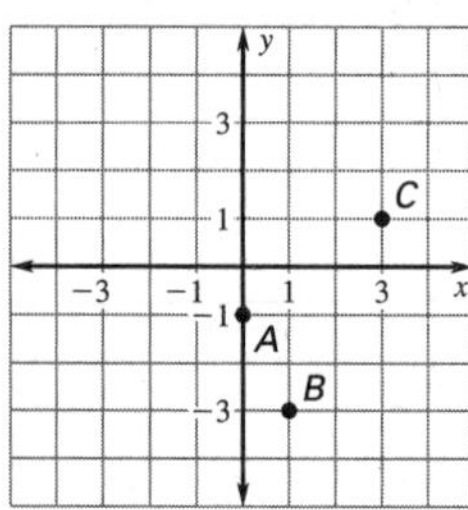

5.

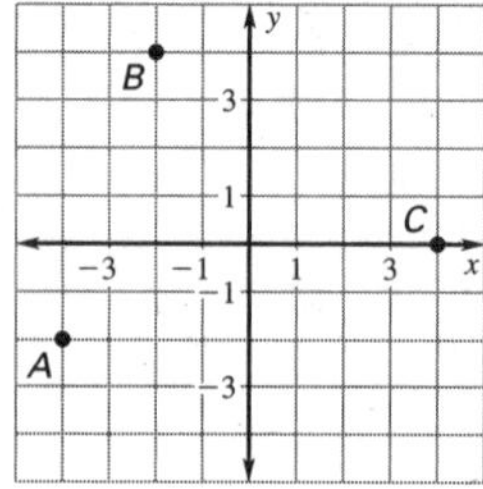

6.

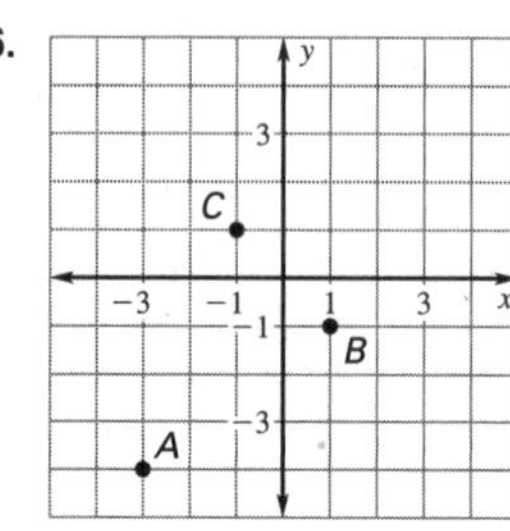

7. $y = 5x + 1$

x	-2	-1	0	1	2
y	-9	-4	1	6	11

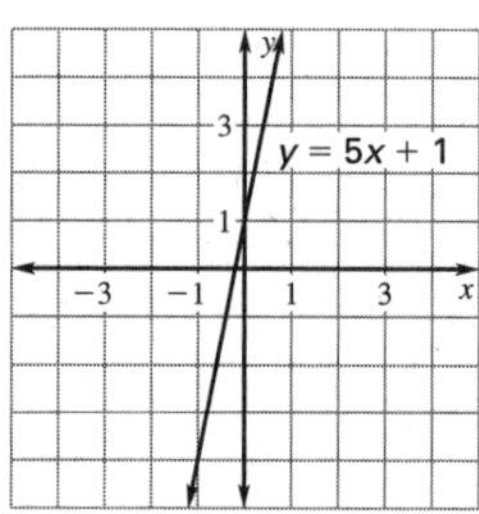

8. $y = -2x + 4$

x	-2	-1	0	1	2
y	8	6	4	2	0

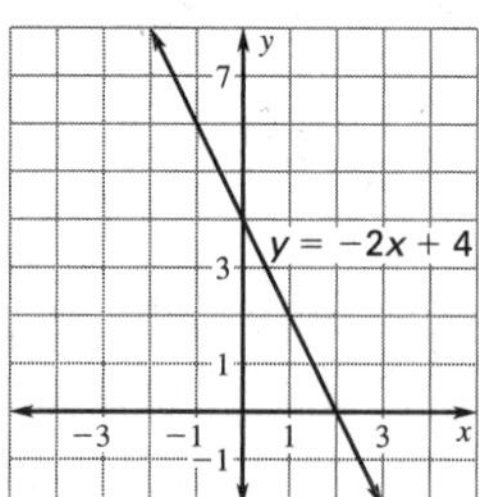

Copyright © McDougal Littell Inc.
All rights reserved.

Extra Practice *continued*

9. $4x + y = -8; y = -4x - 8$

x	-2	-1	0	1	2
y	0	-4	-8	-12	-16

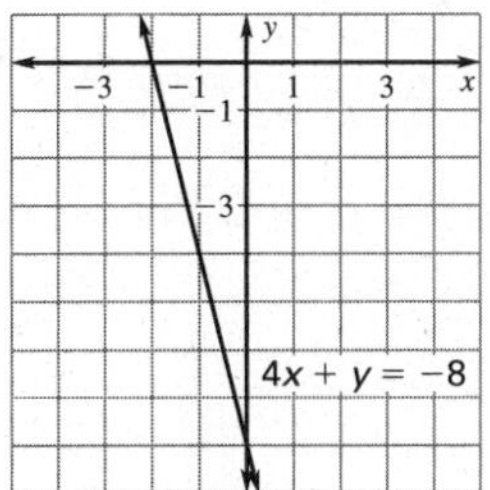

10. $2y - x = -1$

$2y = x - 1$

$y = \frac{1}{2}x - \frac{1}{2}$

x	-2	-1	0	1	2
y	$-1\frac{1}{2}$	-1	$-\frac{1}{2}$	0	$\frac{1}{2}$

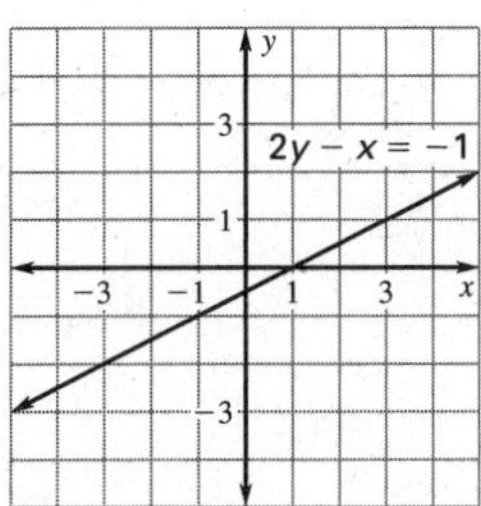

11. $y - 2x = -5$

$y = 2x - 5$

x	-2	-1	0	1	2
y	-9	-7	-5	-3	-1

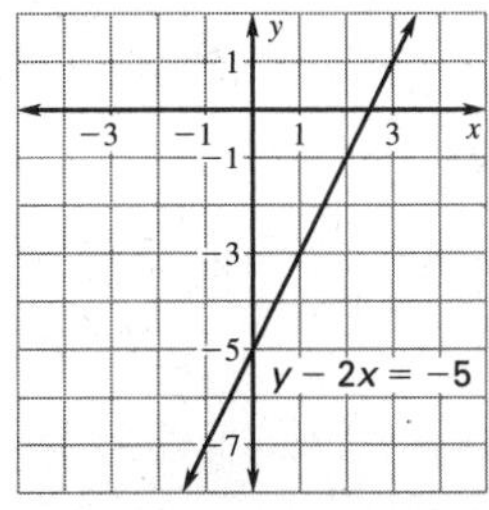

12. $y = 3x - 1$

x	-2	-1	0	1	2
y	-7	-4	-1	2	5

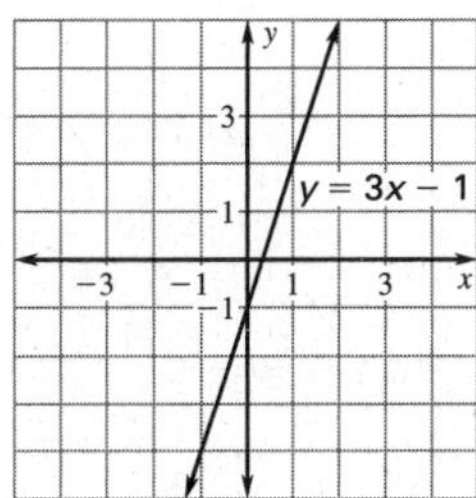

13. $y = -2x + 1$

x	-2	-1	0	1	2
y	5	3	1	-1	-3

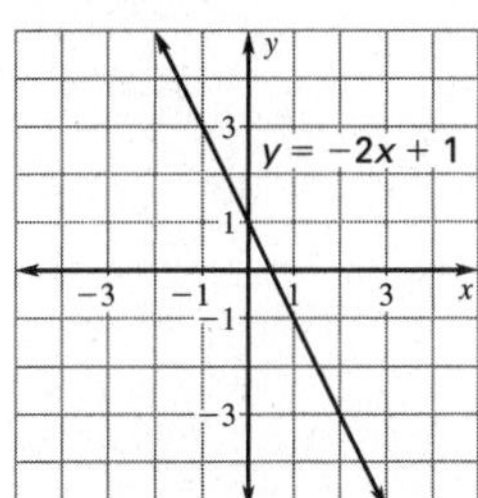

14. $5y - 10x = 20$

$5y = 10x + 20$

$y = 2x + 4$

x	-2	-1	0	1	2
y	0	2	4	6	8

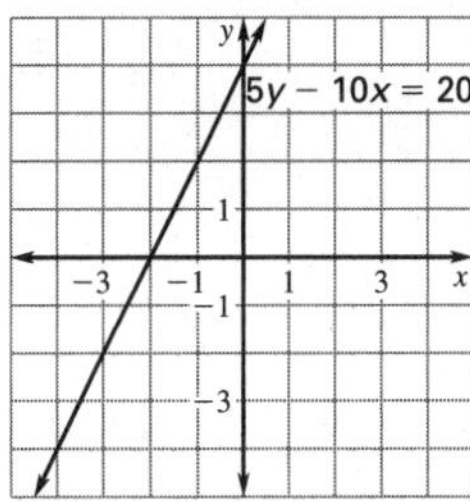

15.

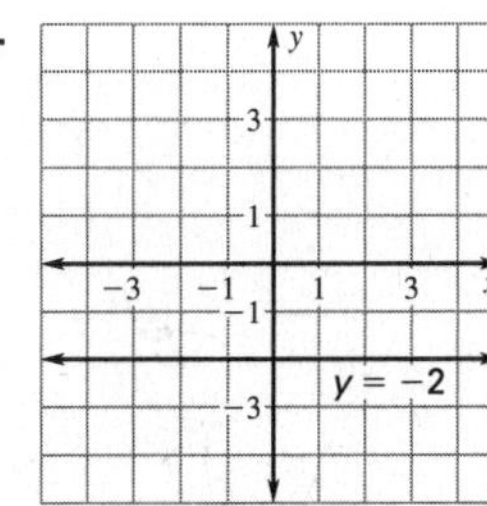

Copyright © McDougal Littell Inc.
All rights reserved.

16.

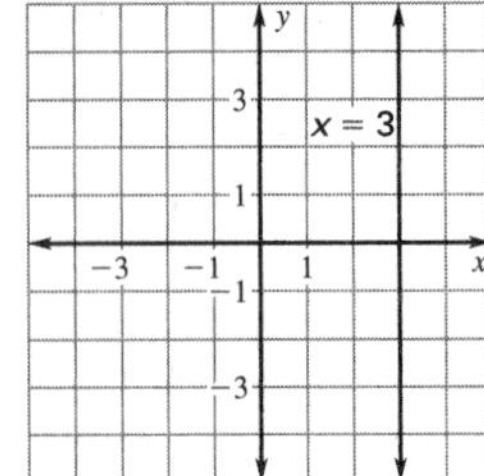

17.

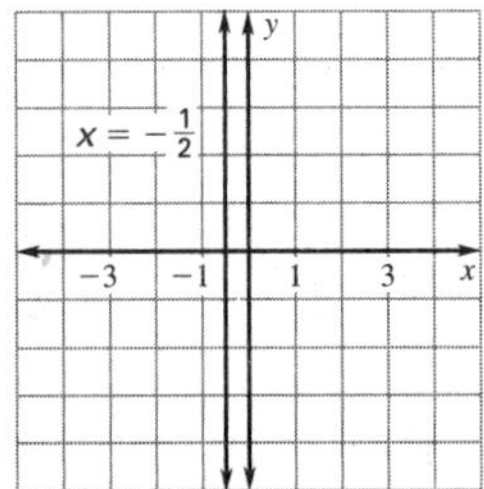

18.

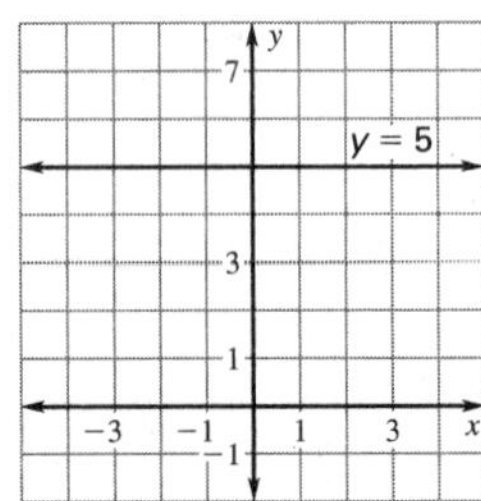

19. Let $y = 0$;
$5x + 0 = -5$
$5x = -5$
$x = -1$ (x-intercept)

20. Let $y = 0$;
$2x - 0 = 6$
$2x = 6$
$x = 3$ (x-intercept)

21. Let $y = 0$;
$6(0) + 2x = 12$
$2x = 12$
$x = 6$ (x-intercept)

22. Let $y = 0$;
$8x + 2(0) = -16$
$8x = -16$
$x = -2$ (x-intercept)

23. Let $x = 0$;
$y = 2(0) - 5$
$y = -5$ (y-intercept)

24. Let $x = 0$;
$y = 2(0) + 14$
$y = 14$ (y-intercept)

25. Let $x = 0$;
$y = 6 - 3(0)$
$y = 6$ (y-intercept)

26. Let $x = 0$;
$10(0) - 15y = 30$
$-15y = 30$
$y = -2$ (y-intercept)

27. $m = \frac{1 - 1}{-4 - 6} = 0$

28. $m = \frac{4 - 2}{-1 - 2} = \frac{2}{-3} = -\frac{2}{3}$

29. $m = \frac{-5 - 2}{-3 - (-4)} = \frac{-7}{1} = -7$

30. $m = \frac{2 - 5}{2 - 4} = \frac{-3}{-2} = \frac{3}{2}$

31. $m = \frac{-1 - 6}{3 - 3}$; undefined

32. $m = \frac{0 - 6}{3 - 0} = \frac{-6}{3} = -2$

33. $y = kx$
$18 = k(6)$
$3 = k$
$y = 3x$

34. $y = kx$
$1 = k(4)$
$\frac{1}{4} = k$
$y = \frac{1}{4}x$

35. $y = kx$
$-7 = k(8)$
$-\frac{7}{8} = k$
$y = -\frac{7}{8}x$

36. $y = kx$
$-20 = k(-1)$
$20 = k$
$y = 20x$

37. $y = kx$
$-2 = k(-2)$
$1 = k$
$y = x$

38. $y = kx$
$-4 = k(8)$
$-\frac{1}{2} = k$
$y = -\frac{1}{2}x$

39. $y = kx$
$-6 = k(2)$
$-3 = k$
$y = -3x$

Copyright © McDougal Littell Inc.
All rights reserved.

Extra Practice *continued*

40. $y = kx$
$2 = k(5)$
$\frac{2}{5} = k$
$y = \frac{2}{5}x$

41. $x - y = 1$
$-y = -x + 1$
$y = x - 1$

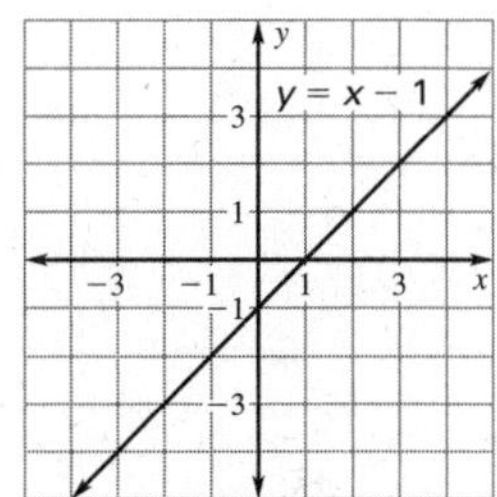

42. $-3x + 2y = 6$
$2y = 3x + 6$
$y = \frac{3}{2}x + 3$

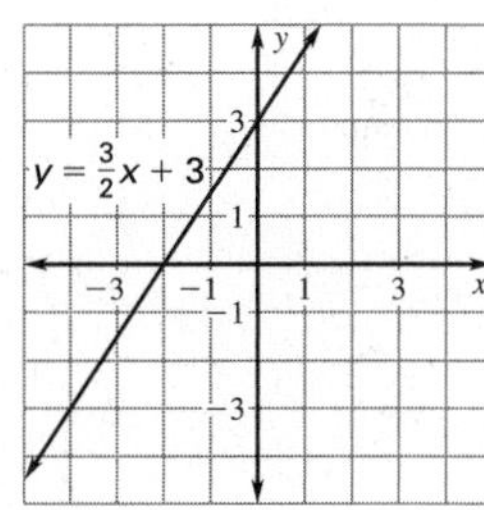

43. $x + y + 4 = 0$
$y = -x - 4$

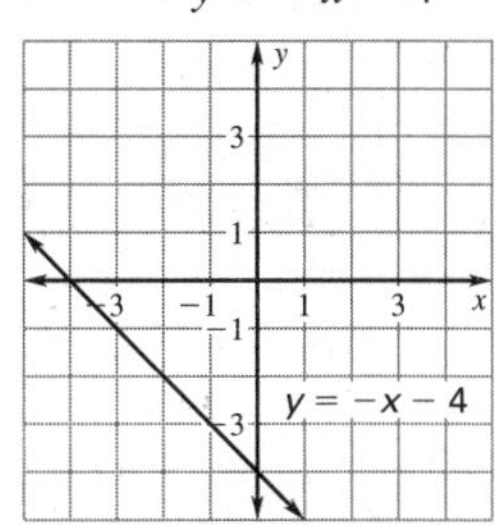

44. $2x - 4y + 6 = 0$
$-4y = -2x - 6$
$y = \frac{1}{2}x + \frac{3}{2}$

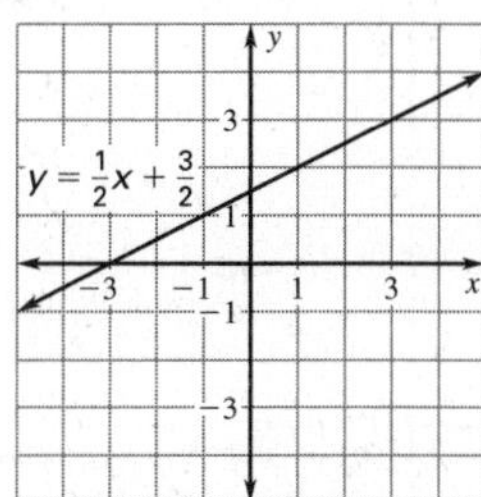

45. $2x + 2y + 2 = 4y$
$2x + 2 = 2y$
$y = x + 1$

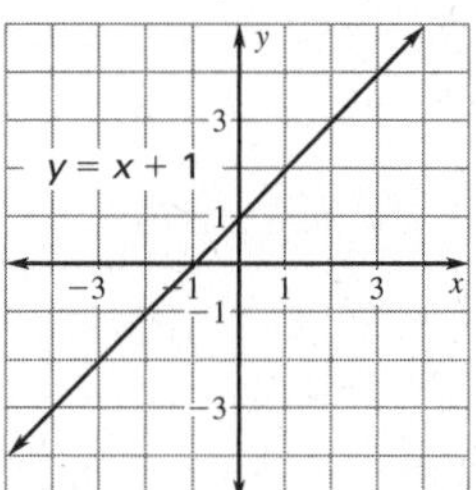

46. $5x - 3y + 2 = 14 - 4x$
$-3y + 2 = 14 - 9x$
$-3y = -9x + 12$
$y = 3x - 4$

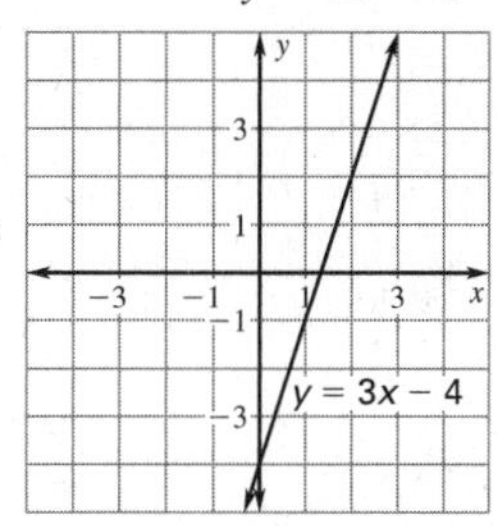

47. function; domain is 1, 3, 5, 7 and range is 1, 2, 3

48. not a function; 3 has two outputs

49. not a function; 4 has two outputs

Chapter 5 *(p. 787)*

1. $y = 2x + 1$

2. $y = -3x - 2$

3. $y = \frac{1}{2}x - 3$

4. $y = -4x$

5. $y - 0 = 3[x - (-1))$
$y = 3(x + 1)$

6. $y - 2 = -2(x - 5)$

7. $y - 6 = 0(x - 3)$

8. $y - 1 = -5[x - (-2))$
$y - 1 = -5(x + 2)$

9. $y - (-1) = 4[x - (-3))$
$y + 1 = 4(x + 3)$

10. $y - 5 = 8(x - 1)$

11. $y - (-1) = \frac{1}{2}(x - 2)$
$y + 1 = \frac{1}{2}(x - 2)$

12. $y - 3 = -\frac{1}{3}[x - (-4))$
$y - 3 = -\frac{1}{3}(x + 4)$

Copyright © McDougal Littell Inc.
All rights reserved.

13. $m = \frac{4 - (-2)}{5 - 3} = \frac{6}{2} = 3$

$y - 4 = 3(x - 5)$
$y - 4 = 3x - 15$
$y = 3x - 11$

14. $m = \frac{-6 - 1}{0 - 5} = \frac{-7}{-5} = \frac{7}{5}$

$y - 1 = \frac{7}{5}(x - 5)$
$y - 1 = \frac{7}{5}x - 7$
$y = \frac{7}{5}x - 6$

15. $m = \frac{-4 - (-1)}{4 - (-2)} = \frac{-3}{6} = -\frac{1}{2}$

$y - (-1) = -\frac{1}{2}[x - (-2))$
$y + 1 = -\frac{1}{2}(x + 2)$
$y + 1 = -\frac{1}{2}x - 1$
$y = -\frac{1}{2}x - 2$

16. $m = \frac{7 - 7}{5 - (-1)} = 0$

$y - 7 = 0[x - (-1))$
$y - 7 = 0$
$y = 7$

17. $m = \frac{8 - 5}{-6 - (-3)} = \frac{3}{-3} = -1$

$y - 5 = -1[x - (-3))$
$y - 5 = -1(x + 3)$
$y - 5 = -x - 3$
$y = -x + 2$

18. $m = \frac{4 - 2}{1 - 5} = \frac{2}{-4} = -\frac{1}{2}$

$y - 2 = -\frac{1}{2}(x - 5)$
$y - 2 = -\frac{1}{2}x + \frac{5}{2}$
$y = -\frac{1}{2}x + \frac{5}{2} + \frac{4}{2}$
$y = -\frac{1}{2}x + \frac{9}{2}$

19. $y - (-2) = 3(x - 5)$
$y + 2 = 3x - 15$
$-3x + y = -17$
$3x - y = 17$

20. $y - 5 = 5[x - (-2))$
$y - 5 = 5(x + 2)$
$y - 5 = 5x + 10$
$-5x + y = 15$
$5x - y = -15$

21. $y - 3 = -\frac{5}{6}[x - (-4))$
$y - 3 = -\frac{5}{6}(x + 4)$
$y - 3 = -\frac{5}{6}x - \frac{10}{3}$
$y = -\frac{5}{6}x - \frac{10}{3} + \frac{9}{3}$
$y = -\frac{5}{6}x - \frac{1}{3}$
$6y = -5x - 2$
$5x + 6y = -2$

22. $y - 7 = \frac{3}{4}(x - 5)$
$y - 7 = \frac{3}{4}x - \frac{15}{4}$
$y = \frac{3}{4}x - \frac{15}{4} + \frac{28}{4}$
$y = \frac{3}{4}x + \frac{13}{4}$
$4y = 3x + 13$
$-3x + 4y = 13$
$3x - 4y = -13$

23. $y - 8 = -7(x - 0)$
$y - 8 = -7x$
$7x + y = 8$

24. $y - (-7) = 4[x - (-1))$
$y + 7 = 4(x + 1)$
$y + 7 = 4x + 4$
$-4x + y = -3$
$4x - y = 3$

25. $y - 6 = -2(x - 3)$
$y - 6 = -2x + 6$
$2x + y = 12$

26. $y - 5 = -5(x - 4)$
$y - 5 = -5x + 20$
$5x + y = 25$

27. $0.80A + 1.00R = 10.00$

28.

Pounds of apples, A	0	1	2	3	4	5
Pounds of oranges, R	10	9.2	8.4	7.6	6.8	6

29.

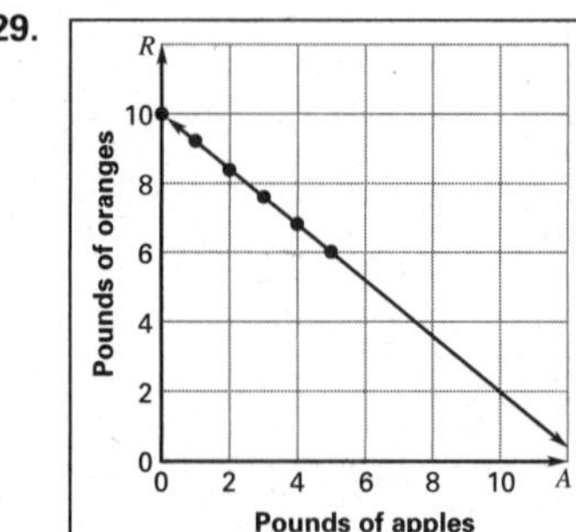

Copyright © McDougal Littell Inc.
All rights reserved.

30. $m_1 = 1; m_2 = -1$
yes, $1(-1) = -1$

31. $m_1 = \frac{1}{4}, m_2 = -\frac{1}{4}$
no, $\frac{1}{4}\left(-\frac{1}{4}\right) \neq -1$

32. $m_1 = \frac{1}{2}, m_2 = -2$
yes, $\frac{1}{2}(-2) = -1$

33. $m_1 = -\frac{2}{3}, m_2 = -\frac{3}{2};$
no, $-\frac{2}{3}\left(-\frac{3}{2}\right) \neq -1$

34. $m_1 = 1, m_2 = -1$
$y - 2 = -1(x - 1)$
$y - 2 = -x + 1$
$y = -x + 3$

35. $m_1 = \frac{3}{4}, m_2 = -\frac{4}{3}$
$y - 4 = -\frac{4}{3}[x - (-1))$
$y - 4 = -\frac{4}{3}(x + 1)$
$y - 4 = -\frac{4}{3}x - \frac{4}{3}$
$y = -\frac{4}{3}x - \frac{4}{3} + \frac{12}{3}$
$y = -\frac{4}{3}x + \frac{8}{3}$

36. $m_1 = 0$; horizontal line
m_2 is undefined; vertical line
$x = 3$

Chapter 6 *(p. 788)*

1. $x < 1$

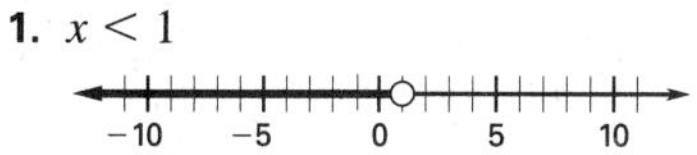

2. $r > -9$

3. $7 \geq y$

4. $t \leq -10$

5. $x \geq 4$

6. $w < -3$

7. $k \leq 18$

8. $n < 4 \cdot \left(\frac{3}{2}\right)$
$n < -6$

9. $2x + 5 > 3$
$2x > -2$
$x > -1$

10. $-3x - 7 < 2$
$-3x < 9$
$x > -3$

11. $4(x + 5) \geq 10$
$4x + 20 \geq 10$
$4x \geq -10$
$x \geq -\frac{5}{2}$ or $-2\frac{1}{2}$

12. $3x + 8 \geq -2x + 3$
$5x + 8 \geq 3$
$5x \geq -5$
$x \geq -1$

13. $4(x - 2) \leq 3x + 1$
$4x - 8 \leq 3x + 1$
$x - 8 \leq 1$
$x \leq 9$

14. $-(x + 5) < -4x - 11$
$-x - 5 < -4x - 11$
$3x - 5 < -11$
$3x < -6$
$x < -2$

15. $-5 < x < 2$

16. $4 \leq x < 6$

17. $-3 < x \leq 5$

18. $-1 \leq x < 6$

19. $3 \leq x + 4 < 8$
$-1 \leq x < 4$

20. $-36 < 6x < 12$
$-6 < x < 2$

Copyright © McDougal Littell Inc.
All rights reserved.

Extra Practice *continued*

21. $-2 < 2x - 4 \leq 10$
$2 < 2x \leq 14$
$1 < x \leq 7$

22. $0 \leq 5x - 6 < 9$
$6 \leq 5x < 15$
$1\frac{1}{5} \leq x < 3$

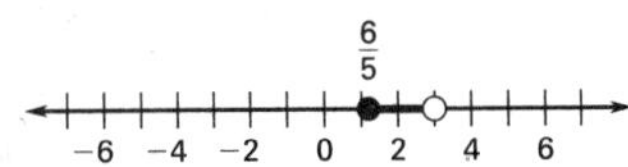

23. $x - 3 \leq -2$ or $x + 2 > 6$
$x \leq 1$ $\quad$ $x > 4$

24. $x + 1 > 4$ or $2x + 3 \leq 5$
$x > 3$ $\quad$ $2x \leq 2$
$x \leq 1$

25. $2x + 1 > 9$ or $3x - 5 < 4$
$2x > 8$ $\quad$ $3x < 9$
$x > 4$ $\quad$ $x < 3$

26. $-4x + 1 \geq 17$ or $5x - 4 > 6$
$-4x \geq 16$ $\quad$ $5x > 10$
$x \leq -4$ $\quad$ $x > 2$

27. $|x| = 14$
$x = 14, -14$

28. $|x| = -10$; no solution

29. $|x| = 12$; $x = 12, -12$

30. $|5x| = 15$
$5x = 15$ or $5x = -15$
$x = 3$ $\quad$ $x = -3$

31. $|10 + x| = 4$
$10 + x = 4$ or $10 + x = -4$
$x = -6$ $\quad$ $x = -14$

32. $|x - 8| = 2$
$x - 8 = 2$ or $x - 8 = -2$
$x = 10$ $\quad$ $x = 6$

33. $|5x - 3| = 2$
$5x - 3 = 2$ or $5x - 3 = -2$
$5x = 5$ $\quad$ $5x = 1$
$x = 1$ $\quad$ $x = \frac{1}{5}$

34. $|2x + 3| = 9$
$2x + 3 = 9$ or $2x + 3 = -9$
$2x = 6$ $\quad$ $2x = -12$
$x = 3$ $\quad$ $x = -6$

35. $|x - 4| + 4 = 7$
$|x - 4| = 3$
$x - 4 = 3$ or $x - 4 = -3$
$x = 7$ $\quad$ $x = 1$

36. $|x| \geq 2$
$x \geq 2$ or $x \leq -2$

37. $|x| \leq 8$
$-8 \leq x \leq 8$

38. $|x - 5| < 10$
$-10 < x - 5 < 10$
$-5 < x < 15$

39. $|6x| \leq 30$
$-30 \leq 6x \leq 30$
$-5 \leq x \leq 5$

40. $|4 + x| > 8$
$4 + x > 8$ or $4 + x < -8$
$x > 4$ $\quad$ $x < -12$

41. $|4x + 5| \geq 3$
$4x + 5 \geq 3$ or $4x + 5 \leq -3$
$4x \geq -2$ $\quad$ $4x \leq -8$
$x \geq -\frac{1}{2}$ $\quad$ $x \leq -2$

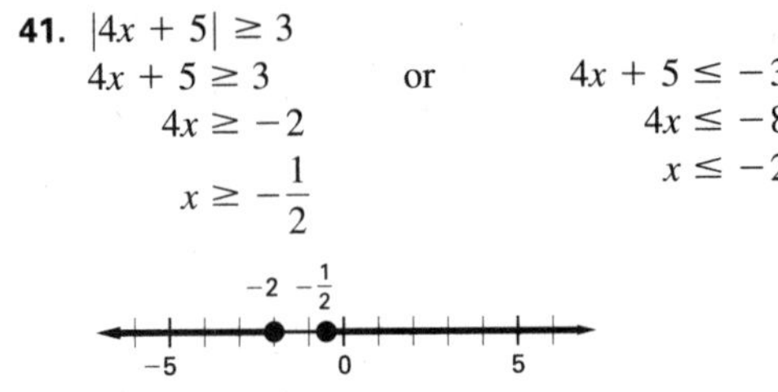

42. $|10 - 4x| \leq 2$
$-2 \leq 10 - 4x \leq 2$
$-12 \leq -4x \leq -8$
$3 \geq x \geq 2$
$2 \leq x \leq 3$

43. $|6x - 5| + 1 < 8$
$|6x - 5| < 7$
$-7 < 6x - 5 < 7$
$-2 < 6x < 12$
$-\frac{1}{3} < x < 2$

Copyright © McDougal Littell Inc.
All rights reserved.

44. $|3x + 4| - 6 \geq 14$

$|3x + 4| \geq 20$

$3x + 4 \geq 20$ or $3x + 4 \leq -20$

$3x \geq 16$ $\qquad 3x \leq -24$

$x \geq 5\frac{1}{3}$ $\qquad x \leq -8$

$\frac{16}{3}$

−10 −5 0 5 10

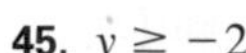

45. $y \geq -2$

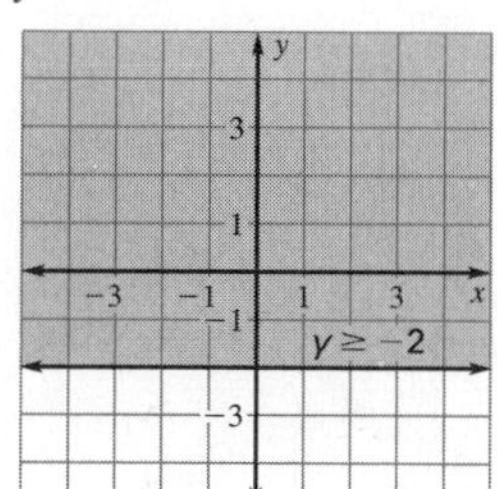

46. $x - y \leq 0$

$-y \leq -x$

$y \geq x$

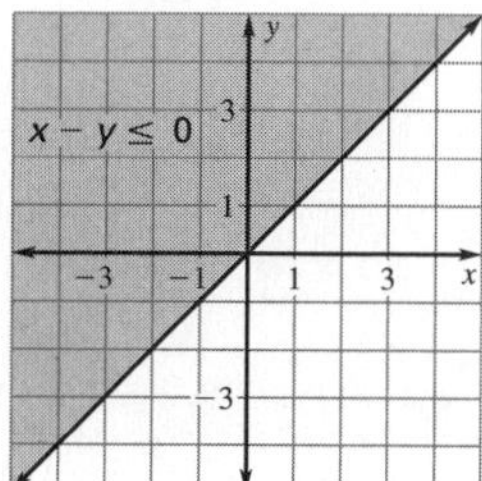

47. $x + y \geq 5$

$y \geq -x + 5$

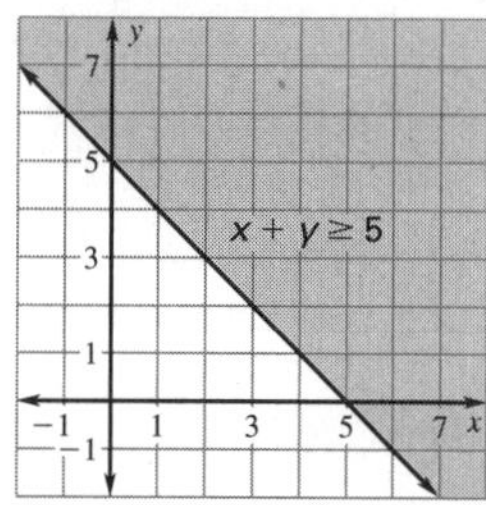

48. $4y + x < 4$

$4y < -x + 4$

$y < -\frac{1}{4}x + 1$

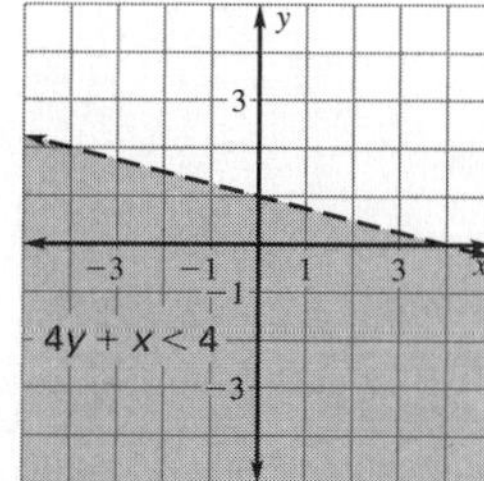

49. $x - 3y \leq 0$

$-3y \leq -x$

$y \geq \frac{1}{3}x$

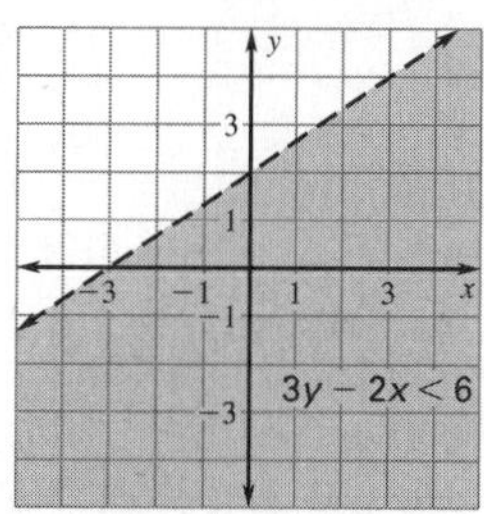

50. $3y - 2x < 6$

$3y < 2x + 6$

$y < \frac{2}{3}x + 2$

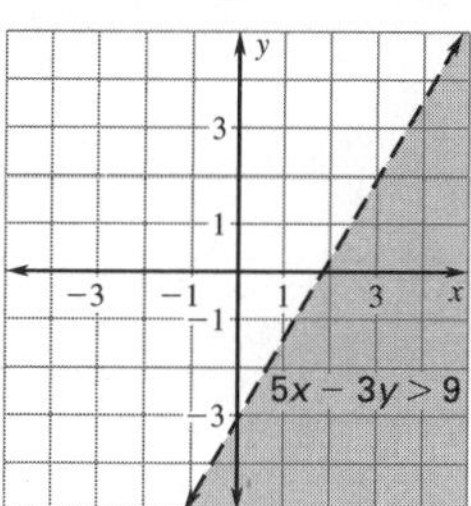

51. $5x - 3y > 9$

$-3y > -5x + 9$

$y < \frac{5}{3}x - 3$

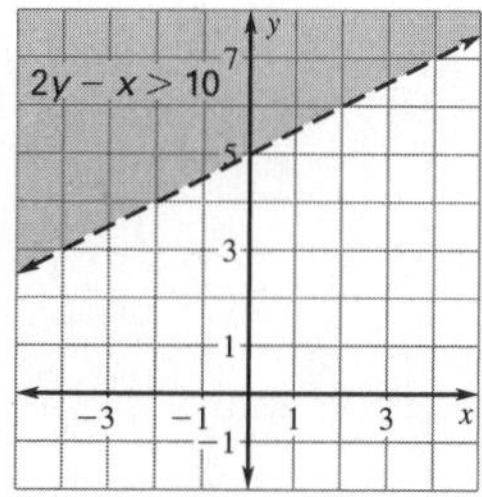

52. $2y - x > 10$

$2y > x + 10$

$y > \frac{1}{2}x + 5$

Copyright © McDougal Littell Inc.
All rights reserved.

Extra Practice *continued*

Chapter 7 *(p. 789)*

1.

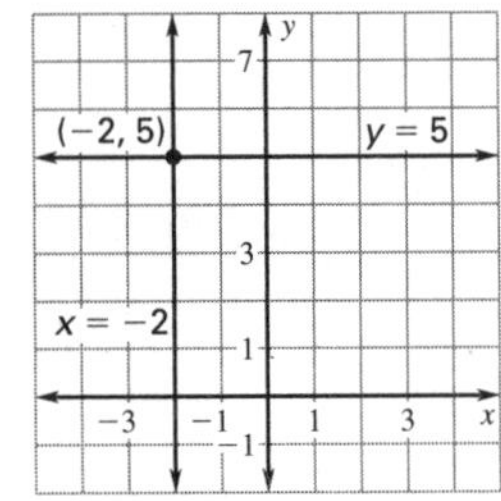

Solution: $(-2, 5)$
Check: $5 = 5, -2 = -2$

2.

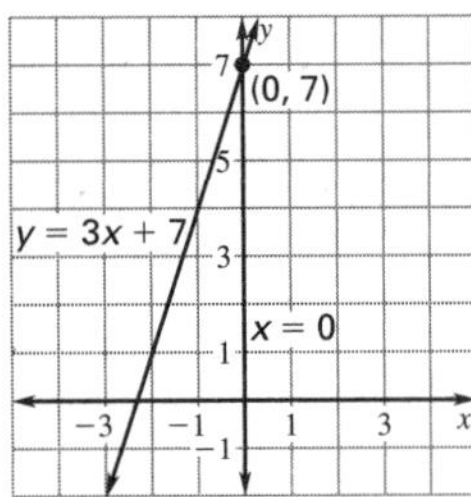

Solution: $(0, 7)$
Check: $0 = 0$
$7 \stackrel{?}{=} 3(0) + 7$
$7 = 7$

3.
$$x + y = 10$$
$$y = -x + 10$$
$$x - y = -2$$
$$-y = -x - 2$$
$$y = x + 2$$

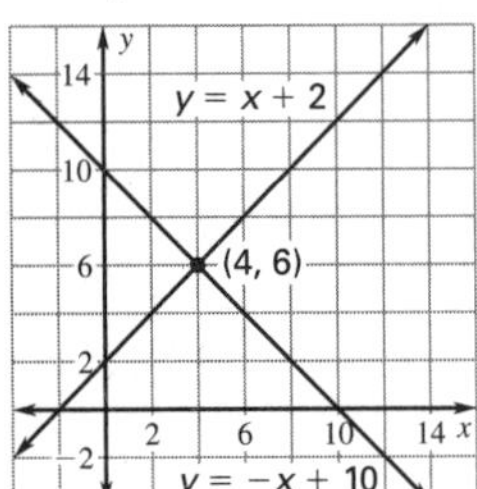

Check:
$4 + 6 \stackrel{?}{=} 10$
$10 = 10$
$4 - 6 \stackrel{?}{=} -2$
$-2 = -2$

4.
$$-2x + 4y = 12$$
$$4y = 2x + 12$$
$$y = \frac{1}{2}x + 3$$
$$5x - 2y = 10$$
$$-2y = -5x + 10$$
$$y = \frac{5}{2}x - 5$$

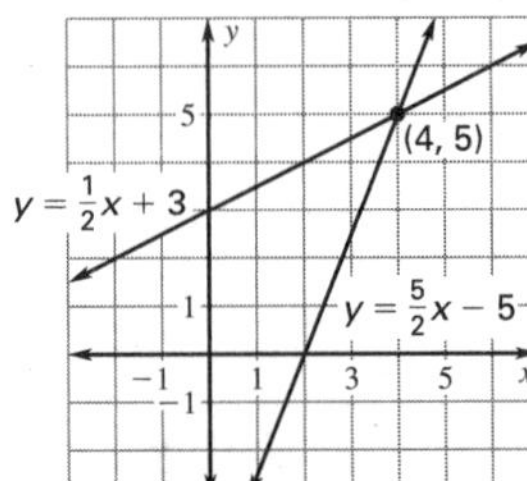

Solution: $(4, 5)$
Check:
$-2(4) + 4(5) \stackrel{?}{=} 12$
$12 = 12$
$5(4) - 2(5) \stackrel{?}{=} 10$
$10 = 10$

5.
$$x = 5y$$
$$2(5y) + 3y = -13$$
$$10y + 3y = -13$$
$$13y = -13$$
$$y = -1$$
$$x = 5(-1) = -5$$
Solution: $(-5, -1)$

6.
$$y = -2x$$
$$x + (-2x) = 7$$
$$-x = 7$$
$$x = -7$$
$$y = -2(-7) = 14$$
Solution: $(-7, 14)$

7.
$$x + y = 9$$
$$y = -x + 9$$
$$x - (-x + 9) = 3$$
$$x + x - 9 = 3$$
$$2x = 12$$
$$x = 6$$
$$y = -(6) + 9 = 3$$
Solution: $(6, 3)$

8.
$$a - 6b = -6$$
$$a = 6b - 6$$
$$2(6b - 6) + 3b = 3$$
$$12b - 12 + 3b = 3$$
$$15b - 12 = 3$$
$$15b = 15$$
$$b = 1$$
$$a = 6(1) - 6 = 0$$
Solution: $(0, 1)$

Copyright © McDougal Littell Inc.
All rights reserved.

9.
$$-s - t = -5$$
$$-s = t - 5$$
$$s = -t + 5$$
$$3(-t + 5) + 4t = 16$$
$$-3t + 15 + 4t = 16$$
$$t = 1$$
$$s = -(1) + 5 = 4$$
Solution: (4, 1)

10.
$$3x - y = 5$$
$$-y = -3x + 5$$
$$y = 3x - 5$$
$$5x - 8(3x - 5) = -17$$
$$5x - 24x + 40 = -17$$
$$-19x + 40 = -17$$
$$-19x = -57$$
$$x = 3$$
$$y = 3(3) - 5 = 4$$
Solution: (3, 4)

11.
$$2m + n = 7$$
$$n = -2m + 7$$
$$4m + 3(-2m + 7) = -1$$
$$4m - 6m + 21 = -1$$
$$-2m = -22$$
$$m = 11$$
$$n = -2(11) + 7 = -15$$
Solution: (11, −15)

12.
$$5a + b = 4$$
$$b = -5a + 4$$
$$7a + 5(-5a + 4) = 11$$
$$7a - 25a + 20 = 11$$
$$-18a + 20 = 11$$
$$-18a = -9$$
$$a = \frac{1}{2}$$
$$b = -5\left(\frac{1}{2}\right) + 4 = 1\frac{1}{2}$$
Solution: $\left(\frac{1}{2}, 1\frac{1}{2}\right)$

13.
$$x + y = 6$$
$$\underline{x - y = 2}$$
$$2x = 8$$
$$x = 4$$
$$4 + y = 6$$
$$y = 2$$
Solution: (4, 2)
Check:
$$4 + 2 \stackrel{?}{=} 6$$
$$6 = 6$$
$$4 - 2 \stackrel{?}{=} 2$$
$$2 = 2$$

14.
$$3x + 3y = 6$$
$$\underline{2x - 3y = 4}$$
$$5x = 10$$
$$x = 2$$
$$2(2) - 3y = 4$$
$$4 - 3y = 4$$
$$-3y = 0$$
$$y = 0$$
Solution: (2, 0)
Check:
$$3(2) + 3(0) \stackrel{?}{=} 6$$
$$6 = 6$$
$$2(2) - 3(0) \stackrel{?}{=} 4$$
$$4 = 4$$

15.
$$4x - 5y = 10$$
$$\underline{2x + 5y = -10}$$
$$6x = 0$$
$$x = 0$$
$$4(0) - 5y = 10$$
$$y = -2$$
Solution: (0, −2)
Check:
$$4(0) - 5(-2) \stackrel{?}{=} 10$$
$$10 = 10$$
$$2(0) + 5(-2) \stackrel{?}{=} -10$$
$$-10 = -10$$

16.
$$2x + 8y = 9$$
$$\underline{-2x + 2y = 0} \quad \text{(multiply by } -2\text{)}$$
$$10y = 9$$
$$y = \frac{9}{10}$$
$$x - \frac{9}{10} = 0$$
$$x = \frac{9}{10}$$
Solution: $\left(\frac{9}{10}, \frac{9}{10}\right)$
Check:
$$2\left(\frac{9}{10}\right) + 8\left(\frac{9}{10}\right) \stackrel{?}{=} 9$$
$$\frac{9}{5} + \frac{36}{5} \stackrel{?}{=} 9$$
$$\frac{45}{5} \stackrel{?}{=} 9$$
$$9 = 9$$
$$\frac{9}{10} - \frac{9}{10} \stackrel{?}{=} 0$$
$$0 = 0$$

Copyright © McDougal Littell Inc.
All rights reserved.

Extra Practice *continued*

17. $-x + y = -15$
$x + 4y = 5$
$5y = -10$
$y = -2$
$x + 4(-2) = 5$
$x - 8 = 5$
$x = 13$
Solution: $(13, -2)$
Check:
$-(13) + (-2) \stackrel{?}{=} -15$
$-15 = -15$
$13 + 4(-2) \stackrel{?}{=} 5$
$5 = 5$

18. $2x + 3y = 15$
$-5x - 3y = -12$ (multiply by -1 and re-order)
$-3x = 3$
$x = -1$
$2(-1) + 3y = 15$
$-2 + 3y = 15$
$3y = 17$
$y = 5\frac{2}{3}$
Solution: $\left(-1, 5\frac{2}{3}\right)$
Check:
$2(-1) + 3\left(\frac{17}{3}\right) \stackrel{?}{=} 15$
$15 = 15$
$3\left(\frac{17}{3}\right) + 5(-1) \stackrel{?}{=} 12$
$12 = 12$

19. $y = 2x - 3$
$3x - 5(2x - 3) = 1$
$3x - 10x + 15 = 1$
$-7x + 15 = 1$
$-7x = -14$
$x = 2$
$y = 2(2) - 3 = 1$
Solution: $(2, 1)$
Check:
$1 \stackrel{?}{=} 2(2) - 3$
$1 = 1$
$3(2) - 5(1) \stackrel{?}{=} 1$
$1 = 1$

20. $-4x - 15 = 5y; -4x - 5y = 15$
$2y = 11 - 5x; 5x + 2y = 11$
$-20x - 25y = 75$
$20x + 8y = 44$
$-17y = 119$
$y = -7$
$-4x - 15 = 5(-7)$
$-4x - 15 = -35$
$-4x = -20$
$x = 5$
Solution: $(5, -7)$
Check:
$-4(5) - 15 \stackrel{?}{=} 5(-7)$
$-35 = -35$
$2(-7) \stackrel{?}{=} 11 - 5(5)$
$-14 = -14$

21. *Sample answer:* substitution; it is easy to solve for x.
$x = 2y - 10$
$3(2y - 10) + y = 5$
$6y - 30 + y = 5$
$7y = 35$
$y = 5$
$x = 2(5) - 10 = 0$
Solution: $(0, 5)$

22. *Sample answer:* linear combinations; it is easy to eliminate y.
$5x + 3y = 15$
$4x - 3y = 12$
$9x = 27$
$x = 3$
$5(3) + 3y = 15$
$15 + 3y = 15$
$3y = 0$
$y = 0$
Solution: $(3, 0)$

23. *Sample answer:* substitution; y is already isolated
$y = -4$
$y = -2x - 6$
$-4 = -2x - 6$
$2 = -2x$
$-1 = x$
Solution: $(-1, -4)$

24. *Sample answer:* linear combinations; it is easy to eliminate y.
$x + y = 8$
$x - y = 4$
$2x = 12$
$x = 6$
$6 + y = 8$
$y = 2$
Solution: $(6, 2)$

Copyright © McDougal Littell Inc.
All rights reserved.

25. *Sample answer:* linear combinations; it is easy to eliminate y.

$$\begin{aligned} 2x - 3y &= 6 \\ 3x + 3y &= 9 \quad \text{(Multiply by 3)} \\ \hline 5x &= 15 \\ x &= 3 \\ 3 + y &= 3 \\ y &= 0 \end{aligned}$$

Solution: (3, 0)

26. *Sample answer:* linear combinations; it is easy to eliminate y

$$\begin{aligned} 2x + y &= -8 \\ -6x - y &= 2 \quad \text{(multiply by } -1) \\ \hline -4x &= -6 \\ x &= \frac{3}{2} \\ 2\left(\frac{3}{2}\right) + y &= -8 \\ 3 + y &= -8 \\ y &= -11 \end{aligned}$$

Solution: $\left(\frac{3}{2}, -11\right)$

27. *Sample answer:* linear combinations; it is easy to eliminate y

$$\begin{aligned} 5x - y &= 10 \\ 2x + y &= 4 \\ \hline 7x &= 14 \\ x &= 2 \\ 5(2) - y &= 10 \\ -y &= 0 \\ y &= 0 \end{aligned}$$

Solution: (2, 0)

28. *Sample answer:* linear combinations; it is easy to eliminate x.

$$\begin{aligned} 8x - 6y &= -2 \quad \text{(multiply by } -2) \\ -8x + 4y &= -4 \\ \hline -2y &= -6 \\ y &= 3 \\ -4x + 3(3) &= 1 \\ -4x + 9 &= 1 \\ -4x &= -8 \\ x &= 2 \end{aligned}$$

Solution: (2, 3)

29.

$$\begin{aligned} a + s &= 20 \\ a &= -s + 20 \\ 6a + 4s &= 104 \\ 6(-s + 20) + 4s &= 104 \\ -6s + 120 + 4s &= 104 \\ -2s + 120 &= 104 \\ -2s &= -16 \\ s &= 8 \\ a + 8 &= 20 \\ a &= 12 \end{aligned}$$

12 adult tickets; 8 student tickets

30.

$$\begin{aligned} y &= -x + 4 \\ 3y &= -2x + 9 \\ y &= -\frac{2}{3}x + 3 \end{aligned}$$

one solution

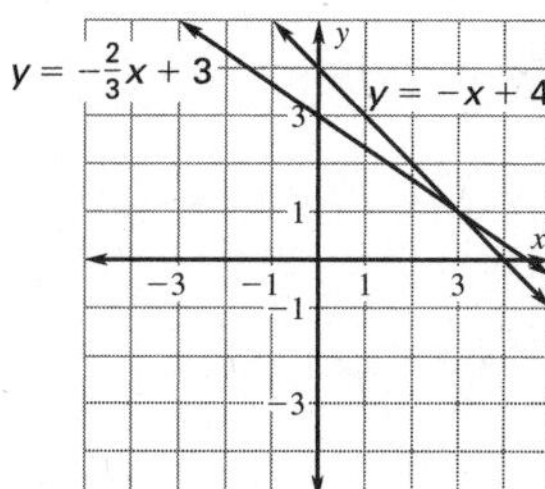

31.

$$\begin{aligned} y &= -x + 6 \\ 3y &= -3x + 3 \\ y &= -x + 1 \end{aligned}$$

none

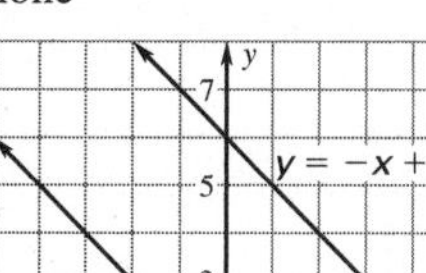
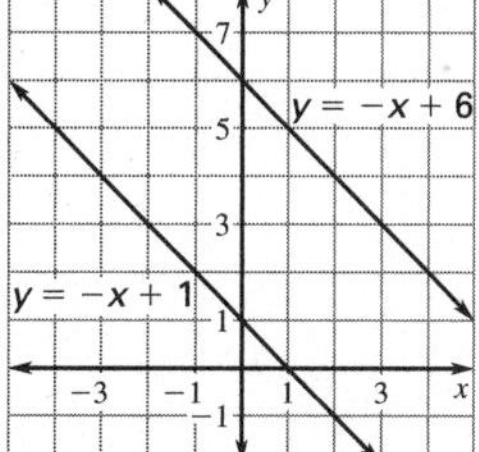

32.

$$\begin{aligned} 2y &= -x + 5 \\ y &= -\frac{1}{2}x + \frac{5}{2} \\ -6y &= 3x - 15 \\ y &= -\frac{1}{2}x + \frac{5}{2} \end{aligned}$$

infinitely many (same line)

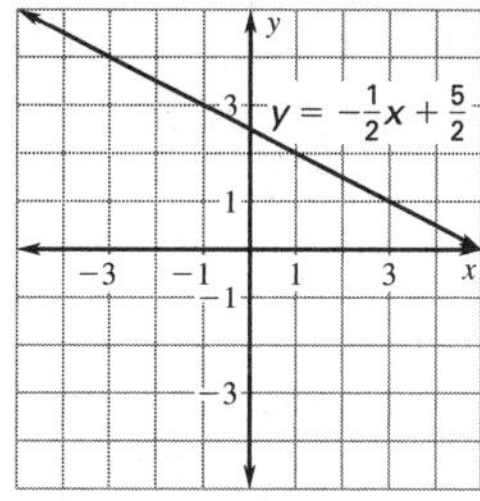

33.

$$\begin{aligned} -y &= -12x + 5 \\ y &= 12x - 5 \\ y &= 8x - 5 \end{aligned}$$

one

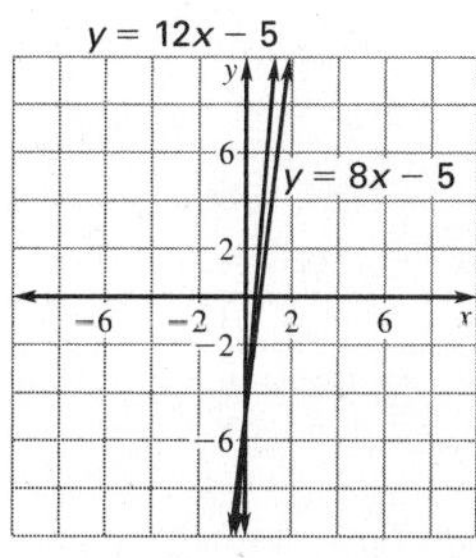

Copyright © McDougal Littell Inc.
All rights reserved.

Extra Practice *continued*

34. $y = -3x$
$6y = x + 38$
$y = \frac{1}{6}x + 6\frac{1}{3}$
one

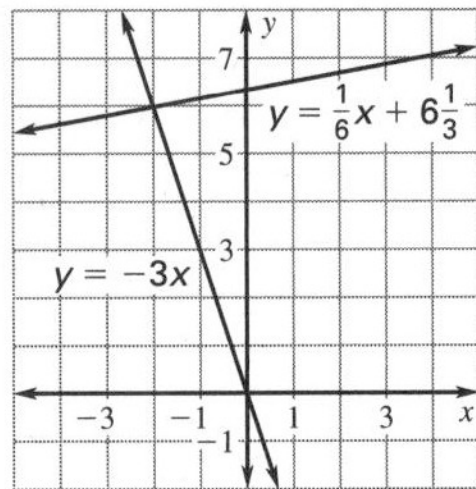

35. $-3y = -2x + 3; y = \frac{2}{3}x - 1$
$-9y = -6x + 9; y = \frac{2}{3}x - 1$
infinitely many (same line)

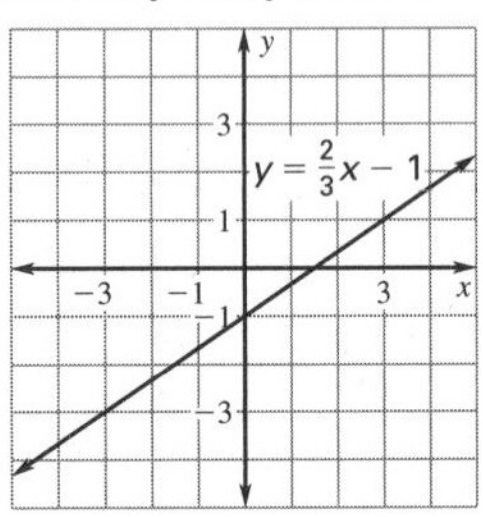

36. $7y = 3x + 6; y = \frac{3}{7}x + \frac{6}{7}$
$2y = -x + 11; y = -\frac{1}{2}x + \frac{11}{2}$
one

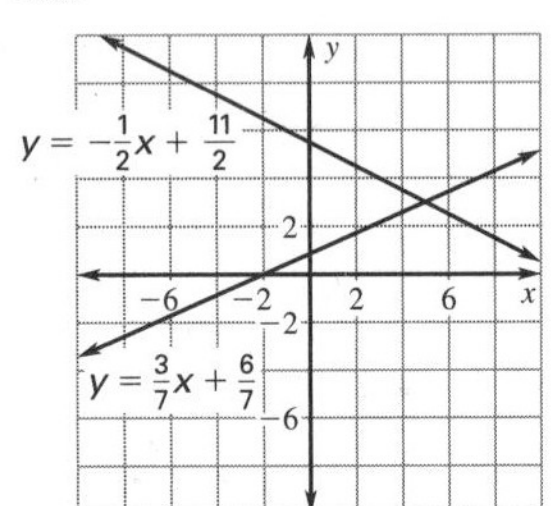

37. $-8y = -3x + 4; y = \frac{3}{8}x - \frac{1}{2}$
$16y = 6x - 42; y = \frac{3}{8}x - \frac{21}{8}$
none

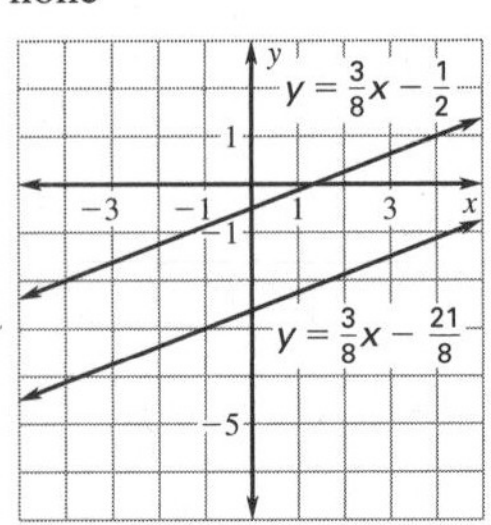

38.

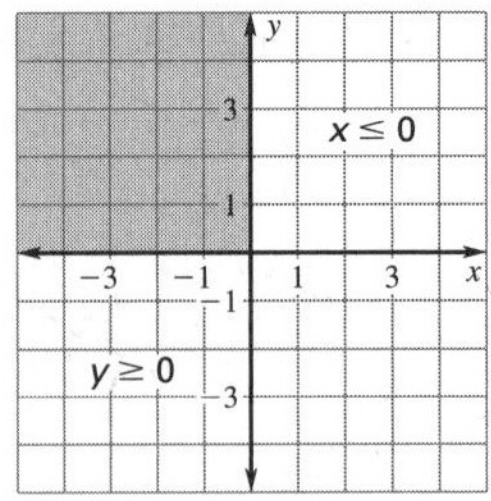

39.

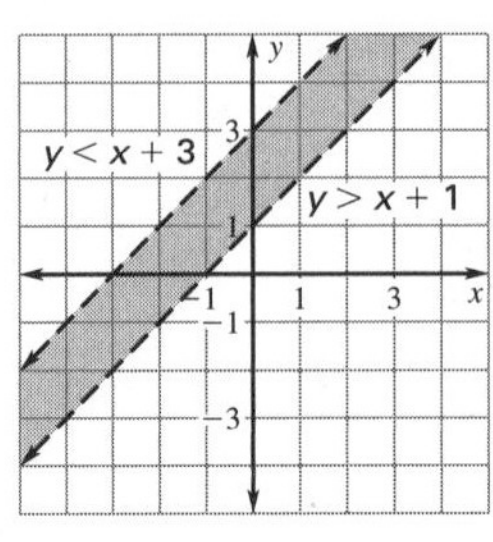

40. $x \ge 1$
$y + x \le 5$
$y \le -x + 5$

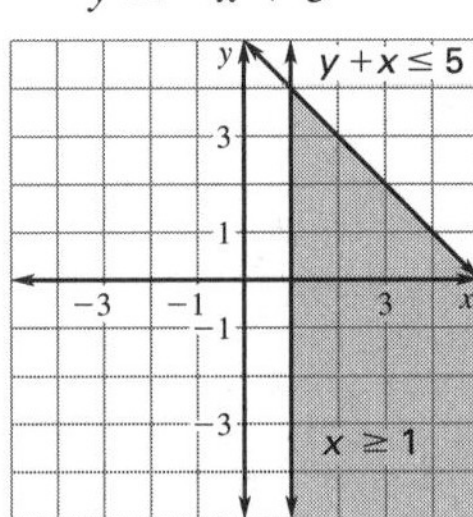

41. $y < -x - 2$
$2y > 3x + 4$
$y > \frac{3}{2}x + 2$

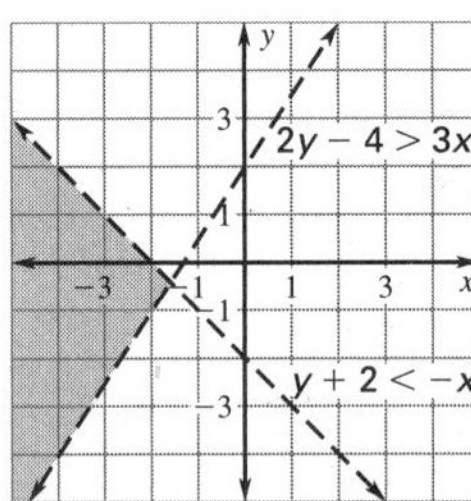

42.

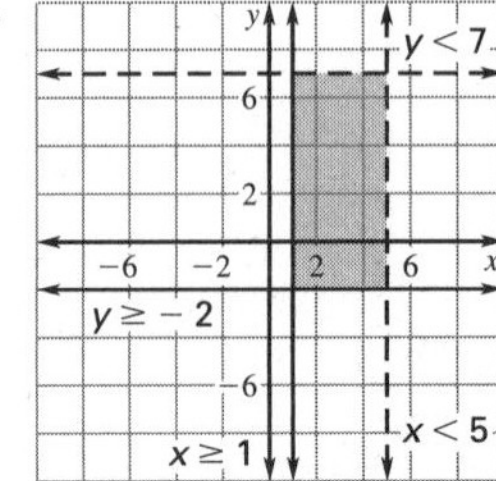

Copyright © McDougal Littell Inc.
All rights reserved.

43.

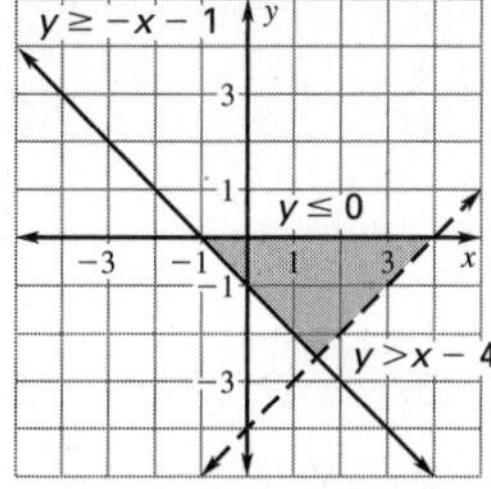

44.

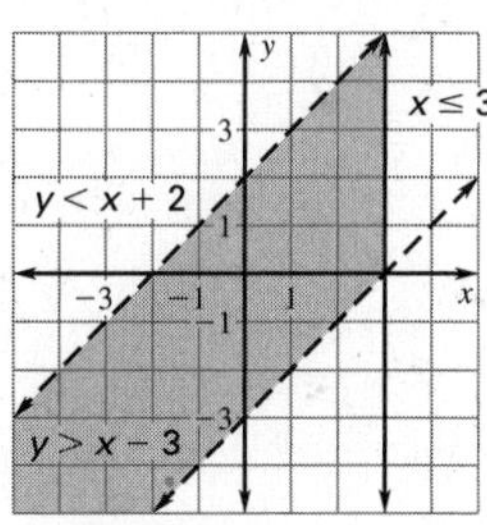

45. $3x < 6$
$x < 2$
$y \le x + 10$
$-5x < 10;\ x > -2$

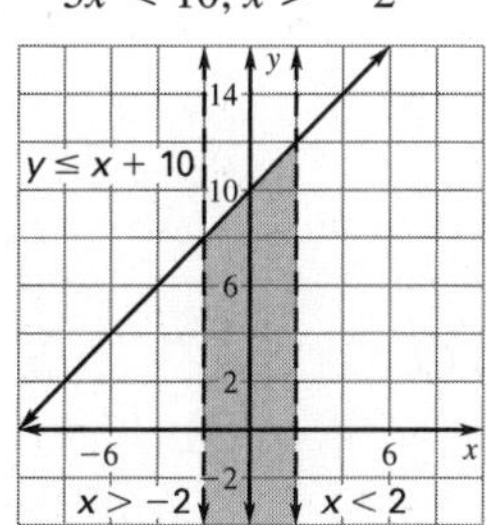

Chapter 8 *(p. 790)*

1. $7^2 \cdot 7^3 = 7^5 = 16807$

2. $(2^3)^4 = 12^{12} = 4096$

3. $(12x)^3 = 12^3x^3 = 1728x^3$

4. $(-3cd)^4 = (-3)^4c^4d^4 = 81c^4d^4$

5. $(m^3)^2 = m^6$

6. $(4r)^2 \cdot r = 4^2r^2 \cdot r = 16r^3$

7. $$\begin{aligned}(7x^2)^2 \cdot 2x^3 &= 7^2x^4 \cdot 2x^3\\ &= 49x^4 \cdot 2 \cdot x^3\\ &= (49 \cdot 2) \cdot x^{4+3}\\ &= 98x^7\end{aligned}$$

8. $$\begin{aligned}(3x)^3(-5y)^2 &= 3^3x^3(-5)^2y^2\\ &= 27x^3(25)y^2\\ &= 675x^3y^2\end{aligned}$$

9. $x^{-4} = \dfrac{1}{x^4}$

10. $2x^{-2} = \dfrac{2}{x^2}$

11. $x^{-3}y^{-2} = \dfrac{1}{x^3y^2}$

12. $\dfrac{2}{x^{-2}} = 2x^2$

13. $\dfrac{4x}{y^{-5}} = 4xy^5$

14. $\dfrac{3y^{-3}}{x^{-1}} = \dfrac{3x}{y^3}$

15. $(4y^{-2})^2 = \left(\dfrac{4}{y^2}\right)^2 = \dfrac{4^2}{y^4} = \dfrac{16}{y^4}$

16. $\dfrac{2}{(5x)^{-2}} = 2(5x)^2 = 2 \cdot 5^2 \cdot x^2 = 50x^2$

17. $y = 5^x$

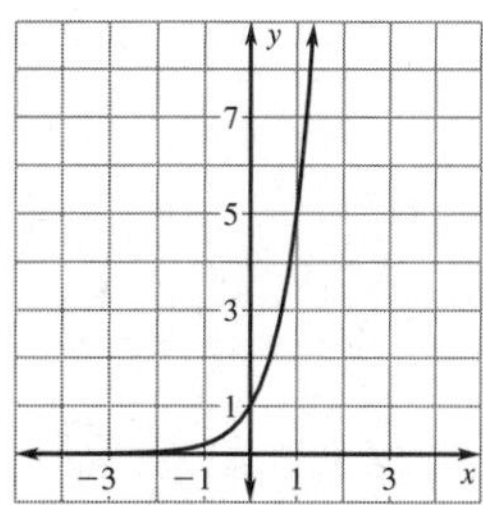

18. $y = -3^x$

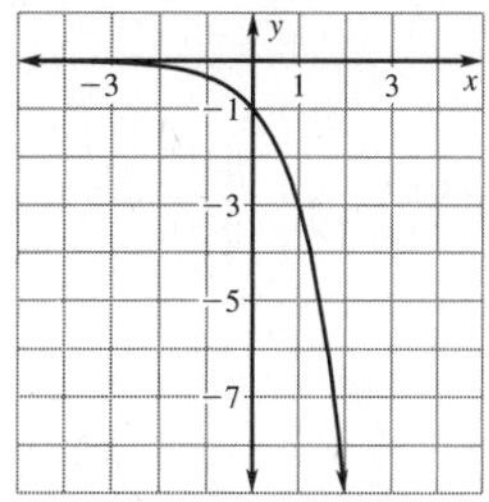

19. $y = \left(\dfrac{1}{4}\right)^x$

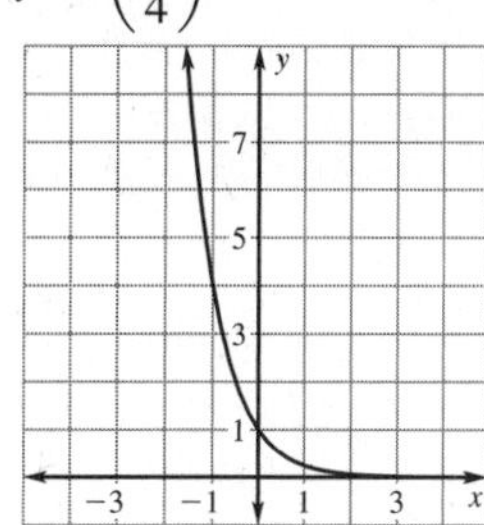

20. $y = 2\left(\dfrac{1}{3}\right)^x$

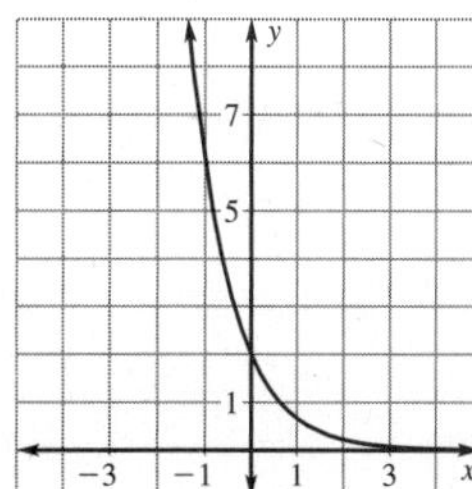

21. $\dfrac{2^{11}}{2^8} = 2^3$

22. $x^5 \cdot \dfrac{1}{x^4} = x$

23. $\left(\dfrac{2}{3}\right)^4 = \dfrac{2^4}{3^4} = \dfrac{16}{81}$

24. $\left(\dfrac{x}{4}\right)^{-2} = \dfrac{x^{-2}}{4^{-2}} = \dfrac{4^2}{x^2} = \dfrac{16}{x^2}$

Copyright © McDougal Littell Inc.
All rights reserved.

25. $\dfrac{(-4)^2}{(-4)^5} = (-4)^{-3} = \dfrac{1}{(-4)^3} = -\dfrac{1}{64}$

26. $\dfrac{a^3}{a^4} = \dfrac{1}{a}$

27. $\left(\dfrac{3}{8}\right)^{-1} = \dfrac{3^{-1}}{8^{-1}} = \dfrac{8}{3}$

28. $\left(\dfrac{4}{x}\right)^3 = \dfrac{4^3}{x^3} = \dfrac{64}{x^3}$

29. $\dfrac{2x^4y^2}{xy} \cdot \dfrac{3x^2y}{4x} = \dfrac{6x^6y^3}{4x^2y} = \dfrac{3x^4y^2}{2}$

30. $\dfrac{16r^5s^9}{-2rs^2} \cdot \dfrac{r^2s}{-8} = \dfrac{r^7s^{10}}{rs^2} = r^6s^8$

31. $\left(\dfrac{3x^2z^4}{2xz}\right)^3 = \left(\dfrac{3xz^3}{2}\right)^3 = \dfrac{27x^3z^9}{8}$

32. $\dfrac{3x^2y}{2x} \cdot \dfrac{2y^2}{x^2y} = \dfrac{6x^2y^3}{2x^3y} = \dfrac{3y^2}{x}$

33. $\dfrac{4a^{-1}b^3}{a^4b^{-2}} \cdot \left(\dfrac{3a}{ab}\right)^{-2} = 4a^{-5}b^5\left(\dfrac{3}{b}\right)^{-2} = \dfrac{4b^5}{a^5} \cdot \dfrac{b^2}{3^2} = \dfrac{4b^7}{9a^5}$

34. $\dfrac{(a^2)^4}{(a^5)^4} = \dfrac{a^8}{a^{20}} = a^{-12} = \dfrac{1}{a^{12}}$

35. $4.813 \times 10^{-6} = 0.000004813$

36. $3.11 \times 10^4 = 31{,}100$

37. $8.4162 \times 10^{-2} = 0.084162$

38. $9.43 \times 10^0 = 9.43$

39. $5.0645 \times 10^1 = 50.645$

40. $1.2468 \times 10^{-3} = 0.0012468$

41. $2.34 \times 10^{-8} = 0.0000000234$

42. $6.09013 \times 10^{10} = 60{,}901{,}300{,}000$

43. 5.28×10^3

44. 3.78×10^{-2}

45. 1.138×10^1

46. 3.3×10^7

47. 8.2766×10^2

48. 2.08054×10^{-1}

49. 1.6354×10^1

50. 8.91×10^{-4}

51. 3.95×10^0

52. 7.84×10^1

53. 8×10^{-3}

54. 6.7×10^4

55. $A = P(1 + r)^t$
$A = 1100(1 + 0.05)^1$
$A = 1100(1.05) = \$1155$

56. $A = 1100(1.05)^{10} = \$1791.78$

57. $A = 1100(1.05)^{15} = \$2286.82$

58. $A = 1100(1.05)^{25} = \$3724.99$

59. $A = P(1 + r)^t$
$A = 120{,}000(1 - 0.10)^t$
$A = 120{,}000(0.90)^t$

Chapter 9 *(p. 791)*

1. 1.73

2. 25

3. -10

4. ± 26

5. 3.87

6. -11.18

7. 14.83

8. ± 9.49

9. $x = \pm 5$

10. $4x^2 - 8 = 0$
$4x^2 = 8$
$x^2 = 2$
$x = \pm\sqrt{2}$

11. no solution

12. $x^2 + 1 = 1$
$x^2 = 0$
$x = 0$

13. $3x^2 - 48 = 0$
$3x^2 = 48$
$x^2 = 16$
$x = \pm 4$

14. $6x^2 + 6 = 4$
$6x^2 = -2$
$x^2 = -\dfrac{1}{3}$; no solution

15. $2x^2 - 6 = 0$
$2x^2 = 6$
$x^2 = 3$
$x = \pm\sqrt{3}$

16. $x^2 - 4 = -3$
$x^2 = 1$
$x = \pm 1$

17. $h = -16t^2 + 80$
$0 = -16t^2 + 80$
$-80 = -16t^2$
$5 = t^2$
$\pm\sqrt{5} = t$
$\pm 2.2 \approx t$
about 2.2 seconds

18. $\sqrt{60} = \sqrt{4 \cdot 15} = 2\sqrt{15}$

19. $\sqrt{88} = \sqrt{4 \cdot 22} = 2\sqrt{22}$

20. $\sqrt{250} = \sqrt{25 \cdot 10} = 5\sqrt{10}$

21. $\sqrt{112} = \sqrt{16 \cdot 7} = 4\sqrt{7}$

22. $\sqrt{\dfrac{11}{16}} = \dfrac{\sqrt{11}}{4}$

23. $\dfrac{\sqrt{20}}{\sqrt{5}} = \dfrac{\sqrt{4 \cdot 5}}{\sqrt{5}} = \dfrac{2\sqrt{5}}{\sqrt{5}} = 2$

24. $2\sqrt{\dfrac{9}{2}} = \dfrac{2\sqrt{9}}{\sqrt{2}} \cdot \dfrac{\sqrt{2}}{\sqrt{2}} = \dfrac{2(3)\sqrt{2}}{2} = 3\sqrt{2}$

Copyright © McDougal Littell Inc.
All rights reserved.

Extra Practice *continued*

25. $\frac{1}{3}\sqrt{27} = \frac{1}{3}\sqrt{9 \cdot 3} = \frac{1}{3}(3)\sqrt{3} = \sqrt{3}$

26. vertex: $x = -\frac{b}{2a} = \frac{0}{2(3)} = 0$; $(0, 0)$

$y = 3x^2$

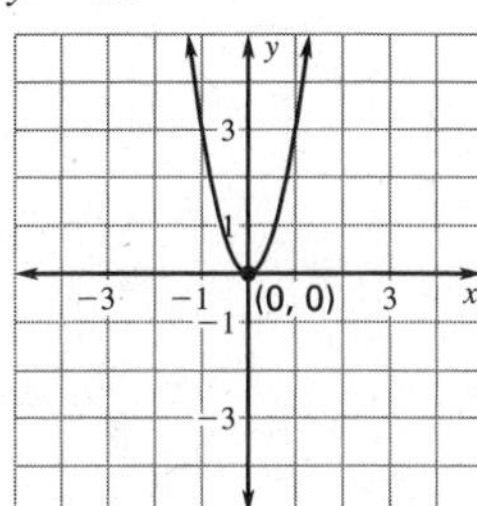

27. vertex: $x = \frac{-b}{2a} = \frac{0}{2(1)} = 0$; $(0, -4)$

$y = x^2 - 4$

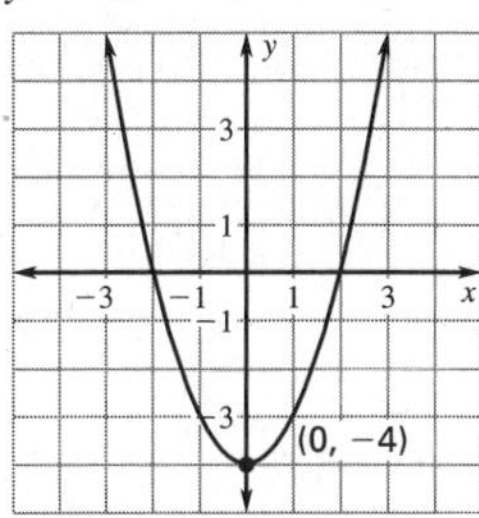

28. vertex: $x = \frac{-b}{2a} = \frac{-(-2)}{2(-1)} = -1$; $(-1, 1)$

$y = -x^2 - 2x$

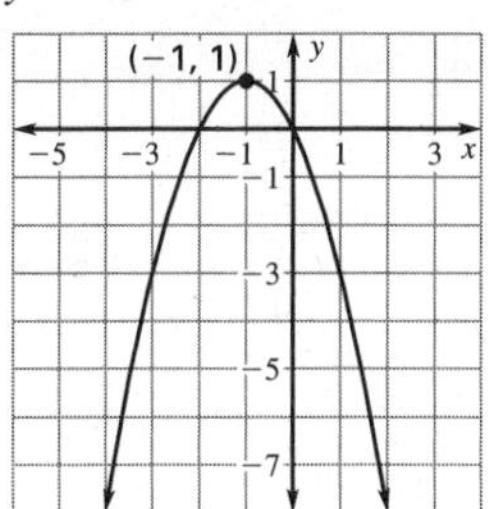

29. vertex: $x = \frac{-b}{2a} = \frac{-(-6)}{2(1)} = 3$; $(3, -1)$

$y = x^2 - 6x + 8$

30. vertex: $x = \frac{-b}{2a} = \frac{-4}{2(4)} = -\frac{1}{2}$; $\left(-\frac{1}{2}, -6\right)$

$y = 4x^2 + 4x - 5$

31. vertex: $x = \frac{-b}{2a} = \frac{-(-2)}{2(1)} = 1$; $(1, 2)$

$y = x^2 - 2x + 3$

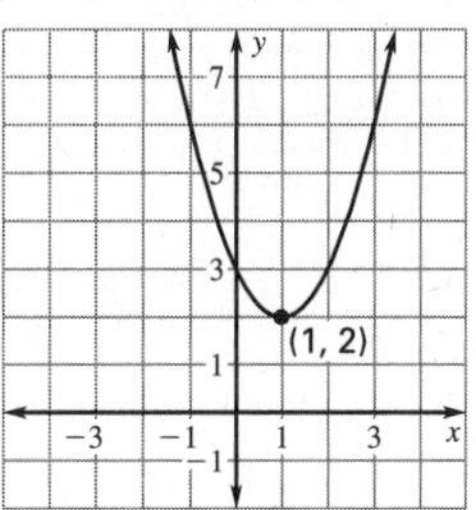

32. vertex: $\frac{-b}{2a} = \frac{-3}{2(-1)} = \frac{3}{2}$; $\left(\frac{3}{2}, 8.75\right)$

$y = -x^2 + 3x + 2$

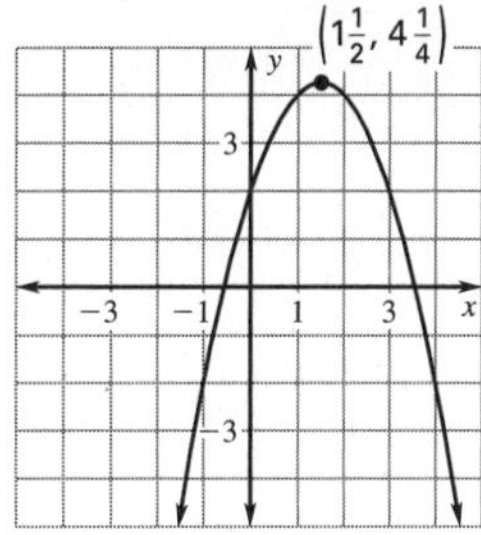

33. vertex: $x = \frac{-b}{2a} = \frac{-12}{2(-3)} = 2$; $(2, 11)$

$y = -3x^2 + 12x - 1$

Copyright © McDougal Littell Inc.
All rights reserved.

Extra Practice *continued*

34. $x^2 - 6x = -5x$
$x^2 - x = 0$
$x(x - 1) = 0$
$x = 0, 1$
graph: $y = x^2 - x$

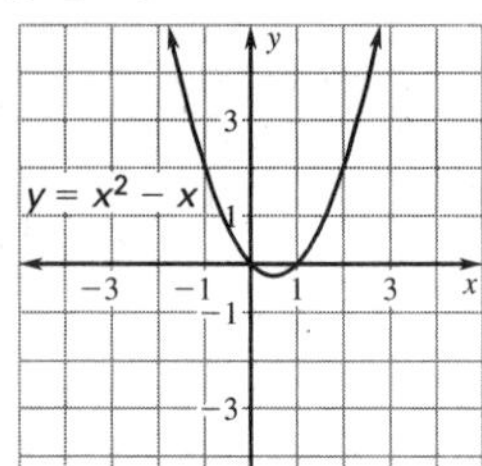

35. $x^2 + 5x = -6$
$x^2 + 5x + 6 = 0$
$(x + 2)(x + 3) = 0$
$x = -2, -3$
graph: $y = x^2 + 5x + 6$

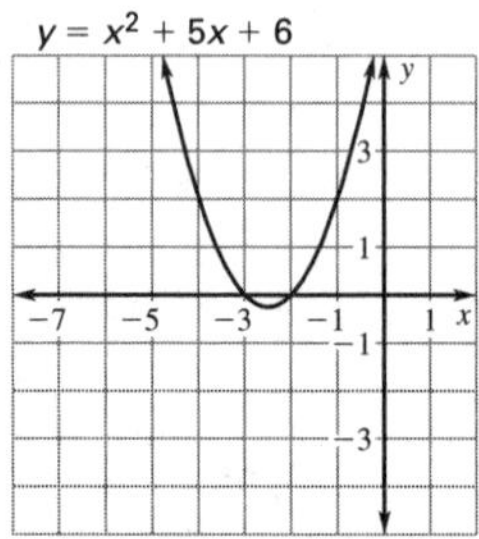

36. $x^2 - 3x = 4$
$x^2 - 3x - 4 = 0$
$(x - 4)(x + 1) = 0$
$x = 4, -1$
graph: $y = x^2 - 3x - 4$

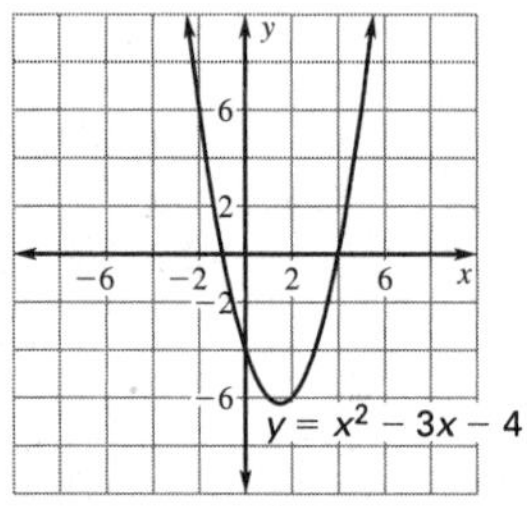

37. $x^2 + 3x = 10$
$x^2 + 3x - 10 = 0$
$(x - 2)(x + 5) = 0$
$x = 2, -5$
graph: $y = x^2 + 3x - 10$

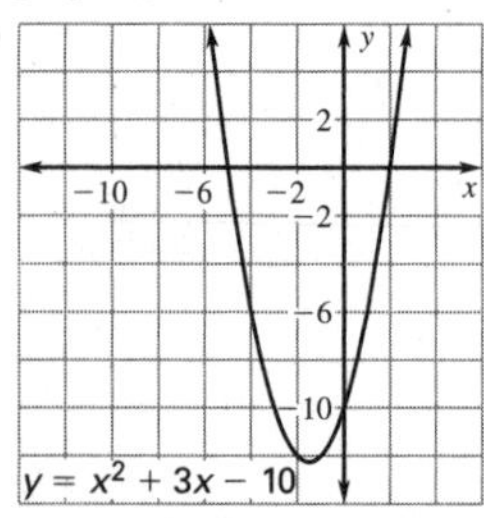

38. $x^2 - 9 = 0$
$x^2 = 9$
$x = \pm 3$
graph: $y = x^2 - 9$

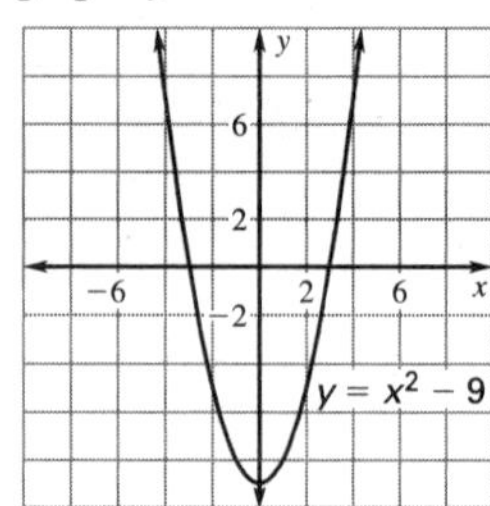

39. $-2x^2 + 4x + 6 = 0$
$x^2 - 2x - 3 = 0$
$(x - 3)(x + 1) = 0$
$x = 3, -1$
graph: $y = -2x^2 + 4x + 6$

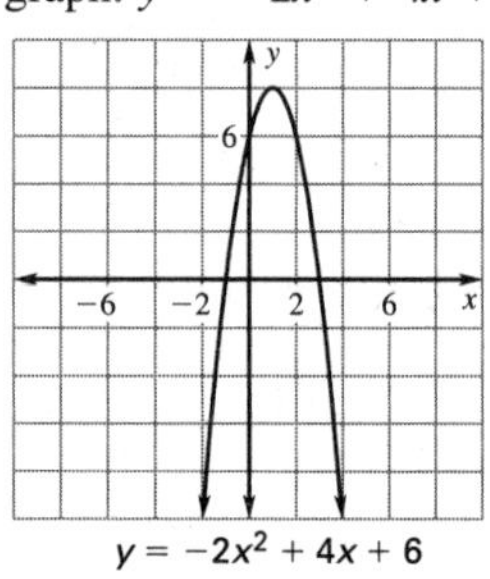

40. $x^2 + x - 12 = 0$
$a = 1, b = 1, c = -12$
$$x = \frac{-1 \pm \sqrt{1^2 - 4(1)(-12)}}{2(1)}$$
$$x = \frac{-1 \pm \sqrt{49}}{2} = \frac{-1 \pm 7}{2}$$
$x = 3, -4$

41. $x^2 - 4x - 12 = 0$
$a = 1, b = -4, c = -12$
$$x = \frac{-(-4) \pm \sqrt{(-4)^2 - 4(1)(-12)}}{2(1)}$$
$$x = \frac{4 \pm \sqrt{64}}{2} = \frac{4 \pm 8}{2}$$
$x = 6, -2$

42. $3x^2 + 11x - 4 = 0$
$a = 3, b = 11, c = -4$
$$x = \frac{-11 \pm \sqrt{11^2 - 4(3)(-4)}}{2(3)}$$
$$x = \frac{-11 \pm \sqrt{169}}{6} = \frac{-11 \pm 13}{6}$$
$x = \frac{1}{3}, -4$

Copyright © McDougal Littell Inc.
All rights reserved.

Extra Practice *continued*

43. $-x^2 + 5x - 4 = 0$

$a = -1, b = 5, c = -4$

$$x = \frac{-5 \pm \sqrt{5^2 - 4(-1)(-4)}}{2(-1)}$$

$$x = \frac{-5 \pm \sqrt{9}}{2} = \frac{-5 \pm 3}{-2}$$

$x = 1, 4$

44. $x^2 - 3x + 2 = 0$

$a = 1, b = -3, c = 2$

$$x = \frac{-(-3) \pm \sqrt{(-3)^2 - 4(1)(2)}}{2(1)}$$

$$x = \frac{3 \pm \sqrt{1}}{2} = \frac{3 \pm 1}{2}$$

$x = 2, 1$

45. $-x^2 - 5x - 6 = 0$

$a = -1, b = -5, c = -6$

$$x = \frac{-(-5) \pm \sqrt{(-5)^2 - 4(-1)(-6)}}{2(-1)}$$

$$x = \frac{5 \pm \sqrt{1}}{-2} = \frac{5 \pm 1}{-2}$$

$x = -3, -2$

46. $x^2 - 7x - 8 = 0$

$a = 1, b = -7, c = -8$

$$x = \frac{-(-7) \pm \sqrt{(-7)^2 - 4(1)(-8)}}{2(1)}$$

$$x = \frac{7 \pm \sqrt{49 + 32}}{2} = \frac{7 \pm \sqrt{81}}{2}$$

$$x = \frac{7 \pm 9}{2}$$

$x = 8, -1$

47. $-2x^2 + x + 10 = 0$

$a = -2, b = 1, c = 10$

$$x = \frac{-1 \pm \sqrt{1^2 - 4(-2)(10)}}{2(-2)}$$

$$x = \frac{-1 \pm \sqrt{81}}{-4} = \frac{-1 \pm 9}{-4}$$

$$x = -2, \frac{5}{2}$$

48. $b^2 - 4ac = 14^2 - 4(3)(-5) = 256$; two solutions

49. $b^2 - 4ac = 12^2 - 4(4)(9) = 0$; one solution

50. $b^2 - 4ac = 10^2 - 4(1)(9) = 64$; two solutions

51. $b^2 - 4ac = 8^2 - 4(2)(8) = 0$; one solution

52. $b^2 - 4ac = 0 - 4(5)(125) = -2500$; no real solution

53. $b^2 - 4ac = (-2)^2 - 4(1)(35) = -136$; no real solution

54. $b^2 - 4ac = (-1)^2 - 4(2)(-3) = 25$; two solutions

55. $b^2 - 4ac = 5^2 - 4(-3)(-6) = -47$; no real solution

56.

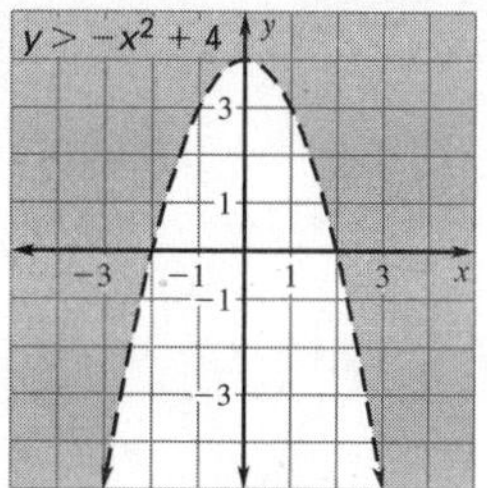

57.

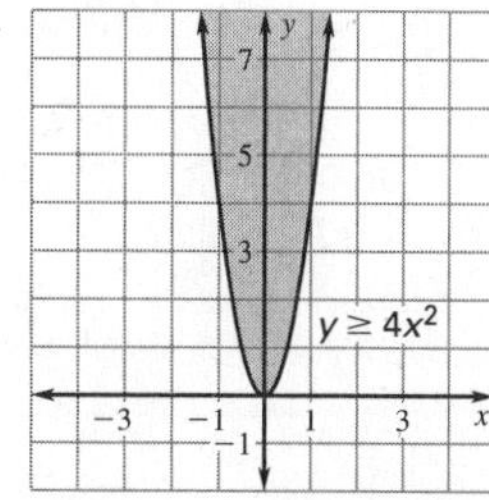

58.

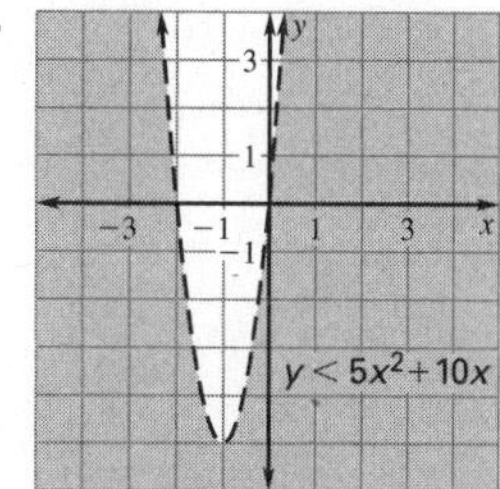

59.

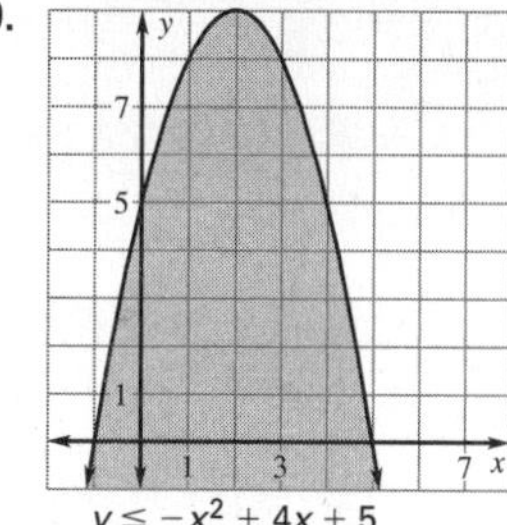

$y \le -x^2 + 4x + 5$

Chapter 10 *(p. 792)*

1.
$$\begin{array}{r} 7x^2 - 4 \\ +\ x^2 + 5 \\ \hline 8x^2 + 1 \end{array}$$

2.
$$\begin{array}{r} 3x^2 + 0x - 2 \\ +\ 6x^2 - 2x + 0 \\ \hline 9x^2 - 2x - 2 \end{array}$$

3.
$$\begin{array}{r} 8x^2 - 3x + 7 \\ +\ 6x^2 - 4x + 1 \\ \hline 14x^2 - 7x + 8 \end{array}$$

4.
$$\begin{array}{r} -z^3 + 0z^2 + 3z + 0 \\ -\ z^2 - 4z - 6 \\ \hline -z^3 - z^2 - z - 6 \end{array}$$

5.
$$\begin{array}{r} 5x^2 + 7x - 4 \\ -4x^2 + 2x + 0 \\ \hline x^2 + 9x - 4 \end{array}$$

Copyright © McDougal Littell Inc.
All rights reserved.

Extra Practice *continued*

6. $$\begin{array}{r} 2a^4 + 0a^3 + 0a^2 + 3a - 5 \\ -2a^4 - a^3 + 0a^2 - 5a + 0 \\ \hline -a^3 - 2a - 5 \end{array}$$

7. $x(4x^2 - 8x + 7) = 4x^3 - 8x^2 + 7x$

8. $-3x(x^2 + 5x - 5) = -3x^3 - 15x^2 + 15x$

9. $5b^2(3b^3 - 2b^2 + 1) = 15b^5 - 10b^4 + 5b^2$

10. $(t + 9)(2t + 1) = 2t^2 + t + 18t + 9$
    $= 2t^2 + 19t + 9$

11. $(d - 1)(d + 5) = d^2 + 5d - d - 5$
    $= d^2 + 4d - 5$

12. $(3z + 4)(5z - 8) = 15z^2 - 24z + 20z - 32$
    $= 15z^2 - 4z - 32$

13. $(x + 3)(x^2 - 2x + 6)$
    $$\begin{array}{l} x^3 - 2x^2 + 6x \\ + \quad 3x^2 - 6x + 18 \\ \hline x^3 + x^2 \qquad + 18 \end{array}$$

14. $(3 + 2s - s^2)(s - 1) = 3s - 3 + 2s^2 - 2s - s^3 + s^2$
    $= -s^3 + 3s^2 + s - 3$

15. $x^2 + 18x + 81$

16. $c^2 + 2cd + d^2$

17. $a^2 - 4$

18. $-m^2 + 49$

19. $16x^2 + 40x + 25$

20. $25p^2 - 60pq + 36q^2$

21. $4a^2 - 9b^2$

22. $100x^2 - 25y^2$

23. $x = -3, x = -6$

24. $x = 11$

25. $z = 1, -5$

26. $w = 0, 4$

27. $6n - 9 = 0$
    $6n = 9$
    $n = \frac{3}{2}$ or $n = 7$

28. $x = -2$

29. $2d - 2 = 0$ or $4d - 8 = 0$
    $2d = 2$ $\quad$ $4d = 8$
    $d = 1$ $\quad$ $d = 2$

30. $x = 0$ or $3x + 1 = 0$
    $3x = -1$
    $x = -\frac{1}{3}$

31. 6, 8; (7, −1)
    $y = (x - 8)(x - 6)$

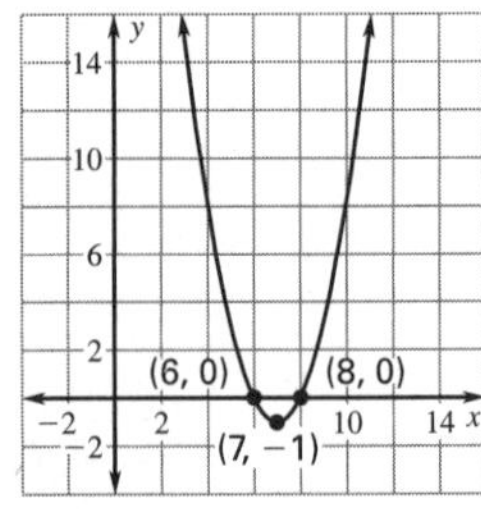

32. −4, 4; (0, −16)
    $y = (x + 4)(x - 4)$

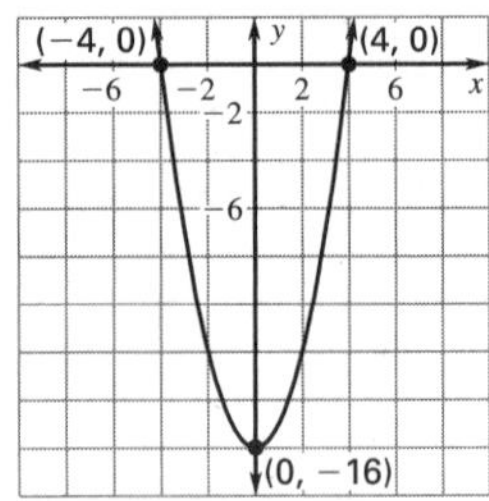

33. 5, 7; (6, −1)
    $y = (x - 5)(x - 7)$

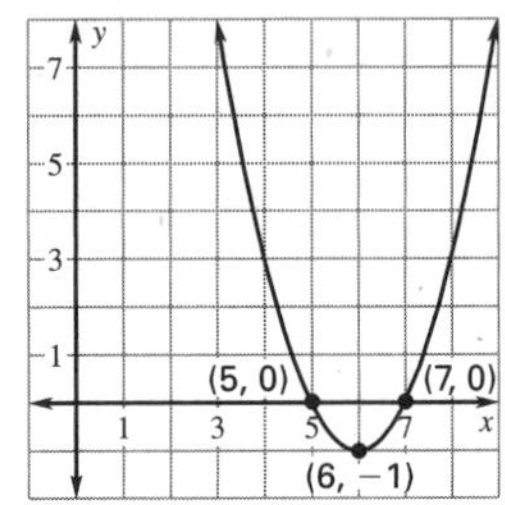

34. −6, −1; (−3.5, −6.25)
    $y = (x + 1)(x + 6)$

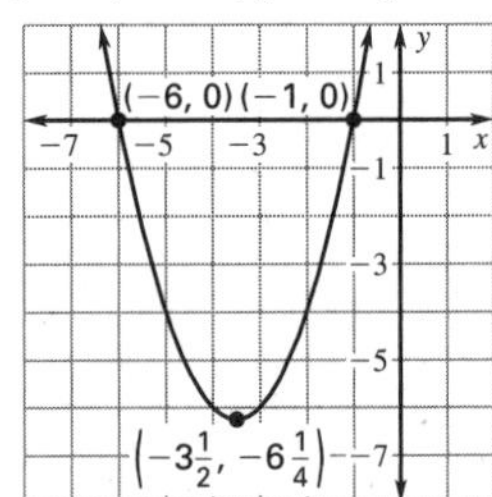

35. 5, 9; (7, 4)
    $y = (-x + 5)(x - 9)$

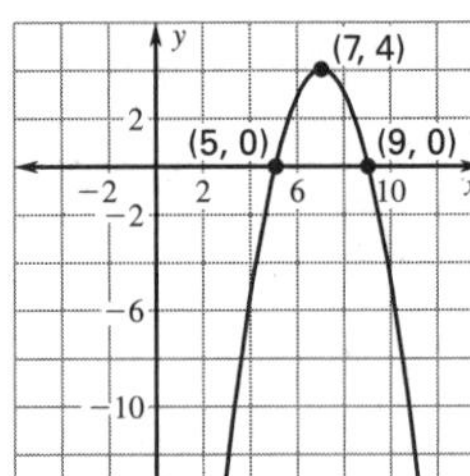

36. −5, 1; (−2, 9)
    $y = (-x + 1)(x + 5)$

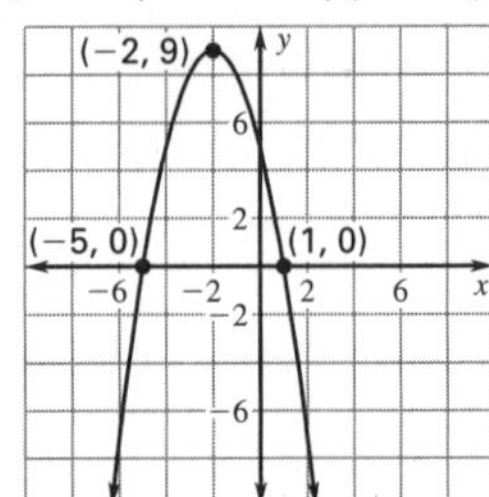

Copyright © McDougal Littell Inc.
All rights reserved.

Extra Practice *continued*

37. $-1, 3; (1, -4)$

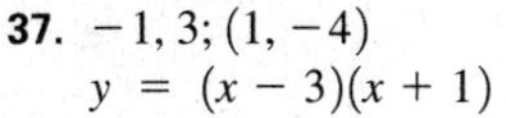

$y = (x - 3)(x + 1)$

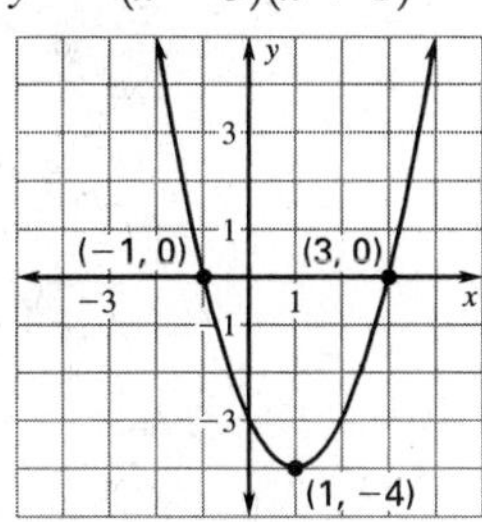

38. $-7, -3; (-5, 4)$

$y = (-x - 3)(x + 7)$

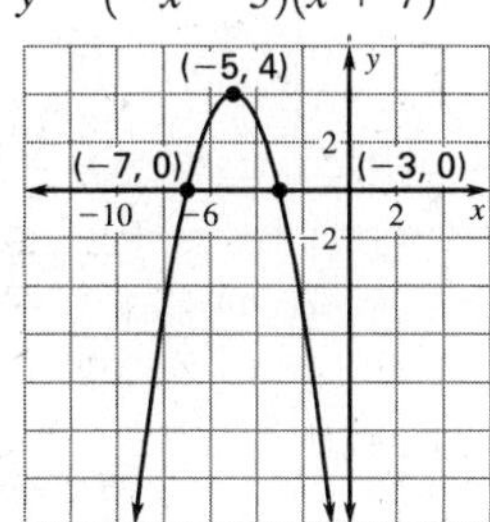

39.
$$\begin{aligned} x^2 + 6x + 9 &= 0 \\ (x + 3)(x + 3) &= 0 \\ x &= -3 \end{aligned}$$

40.
$$\begin{aligned} x^2 + 2x - 35 &= 0 \\ (x - 5)(x + 7) &= 0 \\ x &= 5, -7 \end{aligned}$$

41.
$$\begin{aligned} x^2 - 12x + 36 &= 0 \\ (x - 6)^2 &= 0 \\ x &= 6 \end{aligned}$$

42.
$$\begin{aligned} -x^2 - 4x - 3 &= 0 \\ x^2 + 4x + 3 &= 0 \\ (x + 3)(x + 1) &= 0 \\ x &= -3, -1 \end{aligned}$$

43.
$$\begin{aligned} x^2 - 15x + 54 &= 0 \\ (x - 9)(x - 6) &= 0 \\ x &= 9, 6 \end{aligned}$$

44.
$$\begin{aligned} -x^2 + 14x - 48 &= 0 \\ x^2 - 14x + 48 &= 0 \\ (x - 6)(x - 8) &= 0 \\ x &= 6, 8 \end{aligned}$$

45.
$$\begin{aligned} x^2 - 2x - 24 &= 0 \\ (x - 6)(x + 4) &= 0 \\ x &= 6, -4 \end{aligned}$$

46.
$$\begin{aligned} x^2 - 5x + 4 &= 0 \\ (x - 4)(x - 1) &= 0 \\ x &= 4, 1 \end{aligned}$$

47.
$$\begin{aligned} 2x^2 + x - 6 &= 0 \\ (2x - 3)(x + 2) &= 0 \end{aligned}$$
$2x - 3 = 0$ or $x = -2$
$$\begin{aligned} 2x &= 3 \\ x &= \frac{3}{2} \end{aligned}$$

48.
$$\begin{aligned} 2x^2 + 7x + 3 &= 0 \\ (2x + 1)(x + 3) &= 0 \end{aligned}$$
$2x + 1 = 0$ or $x = -3$
$$\begin{aligned} 2x &= -1 \\ x &= -\frac{1}{2} \end{aligned}$$

49.
$$\begin{aligned} 9x^2 + 24x + 16 &= 0 \\ 3^2x^2 + 2(3)(4)x + 4^2 &= 0 \\ (3x + 4)^2 &= 0 \\ 3x + 4 &= 0 \\ 3x &= -4 \\ x &= -\frac{4}{3} \end{aligned}$$

50.
$$\begin{aligned} 20x^2 + 23x + 6 &= 0 \\ (5x + 2)(4x + 3) &= 0 \end{aligned}$$
$5x + 2 = 0$ or $4x + 3 = 0$
$5x = -2$ $\quad 4x = -3$
$x = -\frac{2}{5}$ $\quad x = -\frac{3}{4}$

51.
$$\begin{aligned} 4x^2 - 5x - 6 &= 0 \\ (x - 2)(4x + 3) &= 0 \end{aligned}$$
$x = 2$ or $4x + 3 = 0$
$$\begin{aligned} 4x &= -3 \\ x &= -\frac{3}{4} \end{aligned}$$

52.
$$\begin{aligned} 3x^2 - 5 &= -14x \\ 3x^2 + 14x - 5 &= 0 \\ (x + 5)(3x - 1) &= 0 \end{aligned}$$
$x = -5$ or $3x - 1 = 0$
$$\begin{aligned} 3x &= 1 \\ x &= \frac{1}{3} \end{aligned}$$

53.
$$\begin{aligned} 3x^2 - 17x - 56 &= 0 \\ (x - 8)(3x + 7) &= 0 \end{aligned}$$
$x = 8$ or $3x + 7 = 0$
$$\begin{aligned} 3x &= -7 \\ x &= -\frac{7}{3} \end{aligned}$$

54.
$$\begin{aligned} 12x^2 + 46x - 36 &= 0 \\ 2(6x^2 + 23x - 18) &= 0 \\ 6x^2 + 23x - 18 &= 0 \\ (2x + 9)(3x - 2) &= 0 \end{aligned}$$
$2x + 9 = 0$ or $3x - 2 = 0$
$2x = -9$ $\quad 3x = 2$
$x = -\frac{9}{2}$ $\quad x = \frac{2}{3}$

55. $x^2 - 1 = (x + 1)(x - 1)$

56. $9b^2 - 81 = 9(b^2 - 9) = 9(b + 3)(b - 3)$

57. $121 - x^2 = (11 + x)(11 - x)$

58. $12 - 27x^2 = 3(4 - 9x^2) = 3(2 + 3x)(2 - 3x)$

59. $t^2 + 2t + 1 = (t + 1)^2$

60. $x^2 + 20x + 100 = x^2 + 2(10x) + 10^2 = (x + 10)^2$

61. $64y^2 + 48y + 9 = 8^2y^2 + 2(8)(3)y + 3^2 = (8y + 3)^2$

Copyright © McDougal Littell Inc.
All rights reserved.

62. $20x^2 - 100x + 125 = 5(4x^2 - 20x + 25)$
$= 5(2^2x^2 - 2(2)(5)x + 5^2)$
$= 5(2x - 5)^2$

63. $x^4 - 9x^2 = x^2(x^2 - 9)$
$= x^4(x + 3)(x - 3)$

64. $m^3 + 11m^2 + 28m = m(m^2 + 11m + 28)$
$= m(m + 7)(m + 4)$

65. $x^4 + 4x^3 - 45x^2 = x^2(x^2 + 4x - 45)$
$= x^2(x + 9)(x - 5)$

66. $x^3 + 2x^2 - 4x - 8 = (x^3 + 2x^2) + [-4x + (-8))$
$= x^2(x + 2) - 4(x + 2)$
$= (x^2 - 4)(x + 2)$
$= (x + 2)(x - 2)(x + 2)$
$= (x + 2)^2(x - 2)$

67. $-3y^3 - 15y^2 - 12y = -3y(y^2 + 5y + 4)$
$= -3y(y + 4)(y + 1)$

68. $x^3 - x^2 + 4x - 4 = (x^3 - x^2) + (4x - 4)$
$= x^2(x - 1) + 4(x - 1)$
$= (x - 1)(x^2 + 4)$

69. $7x^6 - 21x^4 = 7x^4(x^2 - 3)$

70. $8t^3 - 3t^2 + 16t - 6 = t^2(8t - 3) + 2(8t - 3)$
$= (t^2 + 2)(8t - 3)$

71. $w = l - 2$
$h = l + 8$
$V = l \cdot w \cdot h$
$96 = l(l - 2)(l + 8)$
$96 = (l^2 - 2l)(l + 8)$
$96 = l^3 + 8l^2 - 2l^2 - 16l$
$96 = l^3 + 6l^2 - 16l$
$0 = l^3 + 6l^2 - 16l - 96$
$0 = l^2(l + 6) - 16(l + 6)$
$0 = (l^2 - 16)(l + 6)$
$0 = (l + 4)(l - 4)(l + 6)$
$l = 4, -4, \text{ or } -6$
Since -4 and -6 are not legitimate measurements, the length l is 4 ft. $w = 4 - 2 = 2$ ft; $h = 4 + 8 = 12$ ft.

Chapter 11 *(p. 793)*

1. $\frac{9}{m} = \frac{15}{10}$
$90 = 15m$
$6 = m$
Check:
$\frac{9}{6} \stackrel{?}{=} \frac{15}{10}$
$\frac{3}{2} = \frac{3}{2}$

2. $\frac{x}{2} = \frac{8}{x}$
$x^2 = 16$
$x = \pm 4$
Check:
$\frac{4}{2} \stackrel{?}{=} \frac{8}{4}$
$2 = 2$
$\frac{-4}{2} \stackrel{?}{=} \frac{8}{-4}$
$-2 = -2$

3. $\frac{3}{5} = \frac{x + 2}{6}$
$5(x + 2) = 18$
$5x + 10 = 18$
$5x = 8$
$x = \frac{8}{5}$
Check:
$\frac{3}{5} \stackrel{?}{=} \frac{\frac{8}{5} + 2}{6}$
$\frac{3}{5} \stackrel{?}{=} \frac{\left(\frac{18}{5}\right)}{6}$
$\frac{3}{5} \stackrel{?}{=} \frac{18}{5} \cdot \frac{1}{6} = \frac{18}{30}$
$\frac{3}{5} = \frac{3}{5}$

4. $\frac{12}{8} = \frac{5 + t}{t - 3}$
$12(t - 3) = 8(5 + t)$
$12t - 36 = 40 + 8t$
$4t = 76$
$t = 19$
Check:
$\frac{12}{8} \stackrel{?}{=} \frac{5 + 19}{19 - 3}$
$\frac{3}{2} \stackrel{?}{=} \frac{24}{16}$
$\frac{3}{2} = \frac{3}{2}$

5. $\frac{c^2 - 16}{c + 4} = \frac{c - 4}{3}$
$3(c^2 - 16) = (c + 4)(c - 4)$
$3c^2 - 48 = c^2 - 16$
$2c^2 = 32$
$c^2 = 16$
$c = \pm 4$
Check:
$\frac{4^2 - 16}{4 + 4} \stackrel{?}{=} \frac{4 - 4}{3}$
$0 = 0$
$\frac{(-4)^2 - 16}{-4 + 4} \stackrel{?}{=} \frac{-4 - 4}{3}$
undefined; -4 is not a solution; $c = 4$

Copyright © McDougal Littell Inc.
All rights reserved.

6. $$\frac{x+15}{16} = \frac{-9}{x-10}$$
$$(x+15)(x-10) = -144$$
$$x^2 + 5x - 150 = -144$$
$$x^2 + 5x - 6 = 0$$
$$(x+6)(x-1) = 0$$
$$x = -6, 1$$

Check:
$$\frac{-6+15}{16} \stackrel{?}{=} \frac{-9}{-6-10}$$
$$\frac{9}{16} = \frac{9}{16}$$
$$\frac{1+15}{16} \stackrel{?}{=} \frac{-9}{1-10}$$
$$1 = 1$$

7. $y = kx$
$12 = k(4)$
$3 = k$
$y = 3x$

8. $y = kx$
$10 = k(5)$
$2 = k$
$y = 2x$

9. $y = kx$
$4 = k(16)$
$\frac{1}{4} = k$
$y = \frac{1}{4}x$

10. $y = kx$
$7 = k(21)$
$\frac{1}{3} = k$
$y = \frac{1}{3}x$

11. $y = \frac{k}{x}$
$5 = \frac{k}{3}$
$15 = k$
$y = \frac{15}{x}$

12. $y = \frac{k}{x}$
$1 = \frac{k}{7}$
$7 = k$
$y = \frac{7}{x}$

13. $y = \frac{k}{x}$
$\frac{1}{2} = \frac{k}{4}$
$2 = k$
$y = \frac{2}{x}$

14. $y = \frac{k}{x}$
$6 = \frac{k}{5.5}$
$33 = k$
$y = \frac{33}{x}$

15. $\frac{12x^4}{42x} = \frac{2x^3}{7}$

16. $\frac{5x^2 - 15x^3}{10x} = \frac{5x^2(1-3x)}{10x}$
$= \frac{x(1-3x)}{2}$
$= \frac{x - 3x^2}{2}$

17. $\frac{x+6}{x^2+7x+6} = \frac{x+6}{(x+6)(x+1)} = \frac{1}{x+1}$

18. $\frac{x^2 - 8x + 15}{x-3} = \frac{(x-3)(x-5)}{x-3} = x - 5$

19. $\frac{8x^2}{12x^3} = \frac{2}{3x}$

20. $\frac{6}{x+2}$; already in simplest form

21. $\frac{4-y}{y^2-16} = \frac{-(y-4)}{(y+4)(y-4)} = -\frac{1}{y+4}$

22. $\frac{x^2-9x+18}{x^2-4x-12} = \frac{(x-3)(x-6)}{(x-6)(x+2)} = \frac{x-3}{x-2}$

23. $\frac{3x}{5} \cdot \frac{15}{18x} = \frac{3}{6} = \frac{1}{2}$

24. $\frac{z^2+5z+6}{z^2+z} \cdot \frac{z}{z+3} = \frac{(z+3)(z+2)}{z(z+1)} \cdot \frac{z}{z+3}$
$= \frac{z+2}{z+1}$

25. $\frac{10x^2}{x^2-25} \cdot (x-5) = \frac{10x^2(x-5)}{(x+5)(x-5)} = \frac{10x^2}{x+5}$

26. $\frac{1}{4x} \div \frac{6x}{16} = \frac{1}{4x} \cdot \frac{16}{6x} = \frac{4}{6x^2} = \frac{2}{3x^2}$

27. $\frac{5x}{x^2-6x+9} \div \frac{x}{x-3} = \frac{5x}{(x-3)^2} \cdot \frac{x-3}{x} = \frac{5}{x-3}$

28. $\frac{x^2+5x-36}{x^2-81} \cdot \frac{1}{x^2-16} = \frac{(x+9)(x-4)}{(x-9)(x+9)} \cdot$
$\frac{1}{(x+4)(x-4)} = \frac{1}{(x-9)(x+4)}$

Copyright © McDougal Littell Inc.
All rights reserved.

Extra Practice *continued*

29. $\frac{3}{5x} + \frac{2}{5x} = \frac{5}{5x} = \frac{1}{x}$

30. $\frac{3x}{x+2} + \frac{4x-1}{x+2} = \frac{7x-1}{x+2}$

31. $\frac{x}{x-1} - \frac{3x+2}{x-1} = \frac{x-3x-2}{x-1}$

$= \frac{-2x-2}{x-1}$

$= \frac{-2(x+1)}{x-1}$

32. $\frac{6x}{2x-1} - \frac{3}{2x-1} = \frac{6x-3}{2x-1}$

$= \frac{3(2x-1)}{2x-1}$

$= 3$

33. $\frac{5}{x^2} - \frac{3}{x} = \frac{5}{x^2} - \frac{3x}{x^2} = \frac{5-3x}{x^2}$

34. $\frac{8}{3x} - \frac{x+2}{9x^2} = \frac{24x}{9x^2} - \frac{x+2}{9x^2}$

$= \frac{24x-x-2}{9x^2}$

$= \frac{23x-2}{9x^2}$

35. $\frac{x-1}{x+8} + \frac{4}{x-3} = \frac{(x-1)(x-3)}{(x+8)(x-3)} + \frac{4(x+8)}{(x+8)(x-3)}$

$= \frac{x^2-4x+3}{(x+8)(x-3)} + \frac{4x+32}{(x+8)(x-3)}$

$= \frac{x^2+35}{(x+8)(x-3)}$

36. $\frac{x+1}{3x^2} + \frac{3}{4x} = \frac{(x+1)(4)}{12x^2} + \frac{3(3x)}{12x^2}$

$= \frac{4x+4+9x}{12x^2}$

$= \frac{13x+4}{12x^2}$

37. $\frac{5x+3}{x^2-25} + \frac{5}{x-5} = \frac{5x+3}{(x+5)(x-5)} + \frac{5(x+5)}{(x+5)(x-5)}$

$= \frac{5x+3+5x+25}{(x+5)(x-5)}$

$= \frac{10x+28}{(x+5)(x-5)}$

$= \frac{2(5x+14)}{(x+5)(x-5)}$

38. $\frac{4x-1}{3x+2} - \frac{3x}{x-4}$

$= \frac{(4x-1)(x-4)}{(3x+2)(x-4)} - \frac{3x(3x+2)}{(3x+2)(x-4)}$

$= \frac{4x^2-17x+4-9x^2-6x}{(3x+2)(x-4)}$

$= \frac{-5x^2-23x+4}{(3x+2)(x-4)}$

39. $\frac{4}{x} = \frac{3}{25}$

$100 = 3x$

$33\frac{1}{3} = x$

Check:

$\frac{4}{33\frac{1}{3}} \stackrel{?}{=} \frac{3}{25}$

$4 \div \frac{100}{3} \stackrel{?}{=} \frac{3}{25}$

$4 \cdot \frac{3}{100} \stackrel{?}{=} \frac{3}{25}$

$\frac{3}{25} = \frac{3}{25}$

40. $\frac{1}{x-3} = \frac{5}{x+9}$

$x + 9 = 5x - 15$

$-4x = -24$

$x = 6$

Check:

$\frac{1}{6-3} \stackrel{?}{=} \frac{5}{6+9}$

$\frac{1}{3} = \frac{1}{3}$

41. $\frac{-2}{3x} = \frac{4+x}{6}$

$-12 = 12x + 3x^2$

$0 = 12x + 3x^2 + 12$

$0 = 3x^2 + 12x + 12$

$0 = x^2 + 4x + 4$

$0 = (x+2)^2$

$x = -2$

Check:

$\frac{-2}{3(-2)} \stackrel{?}{=} \frac{4+(-2)}{6}$

$\frac{1}{3} = \frac{1}{3}$

Copyright © McDougal Littell Inc.
All rights reserved.

Extra Practice *continued*

42.
$$\frac{4}{x} + \frac{2}{3} = \frac{6}{x}$$
$$3x\left(\frac{4}{x}\right) + 3x\left(\frac{2}{3}\right) = 3x\left(\frac{6}{x}\right)$$
$$12 + 2x = 18$$
$$2x = 6$$
$$x = 3$$

Check:
$$\frac{4}{3} + \frac{2}{3} \stackrel{?}{=} \frac{6}{3}$$
$$\frac{6}{3} = \frac{6}{3}$$

43.
$$\frac{x}{x-5} - \frac{11}{x-5} = 7$$
$$\frac{x-11}{x-5} = \frac{7}{1}$$
$$x - 11 = 7(x-5)$$
$$x - 11 = 7x - 35$$
$$-6x = -24$$
$$x = 4$$

Check:
$$\frac{4}{4-5} - \frac{11}{4-5} \stackrel{?}{=} 7$$
$$-4 + 11 \stackrel{?}{=} 7$$
$$7 = 7$$

44.
$$\frac{5}{x-1} + 1 = \frac{4}{x^2 + 3x - 4}$$
$$\frac{5}{x-1} + 1 = \frac{4}{(x+4)(x-1)}$$
$$\frac{(x+4)(x-1)(5)}{(x-1)} + (x+4)(x-1)(1) = \frac{4(x+4)(x-1)}{(x+4)(x-1)}$$
$$5x + 20 + x^2 + 3x - 4 = 4$$
$$x^2 + 8x + 16 = 4$$
$$x^2 + 8x + 12 = 0$$
$$(x+6)(x+2) = 0$$
$$x = -6, -2$$

Check:
$$\frac{5}{-6-1} + 1 \stackrel{?}{=} \frac{4}{(-6)^2 + 3(-6) - 4}$$
$$-\frac{5}{7} + \frac{7}{7} \stackrel{?}{=} \frac{4}{14}$$
$$\frac{2}{7} = \frac{2}{7}$$

$$\frac{5}{-2-1} + 1 \stackrel{?}{=} \frac{4}{(-2)^2 + 3(-2) - 4}$$
$$-\frac{5}{3} + \frac{3}{3} \stackrel{?}{=} \frac{4}{-6}$$
$$-\frac{2}{3} = -\frac{2}{3}$$

Copyright © McDougal Littell Inc.
All rights reserved.

Extra Practice *continued*

Chapter 12 *(p. 794)*

1. domain: all nonnegative real numbers

x	y
0	$y = 8\sqrt{0} = 0$
1	$y = 8\sqrt{1} = 8$
2	$y = 8\sqrt{2} \approx 11.3$
3	$y = 8\sqrt{3} \approx 13.9$
4	$y = 8\sqrt{4} = 16$
5	$y = 8\sqrt{5} \approx 17.9$

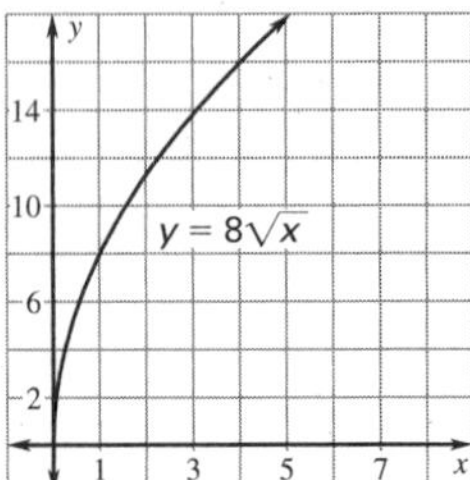

range: all nonnegative real numbers

2. domain: all nonnegative real numbers

x	y
0	$y = \sqrt{5 \cdot 0} = 0$
1	$y = \sqrt{5 \cdot 1} \approx 2.2$
2	$y = \sqrt{5 \cdot 2} \approx 3.2$
3	$y = \sqrt{5 \cdot 3} \approx 3.9$
4	$y = \sqrt{5 \cdot 4} \approx 4.5$
5	$y = \sqrt{5 \cdot 5} = 5$

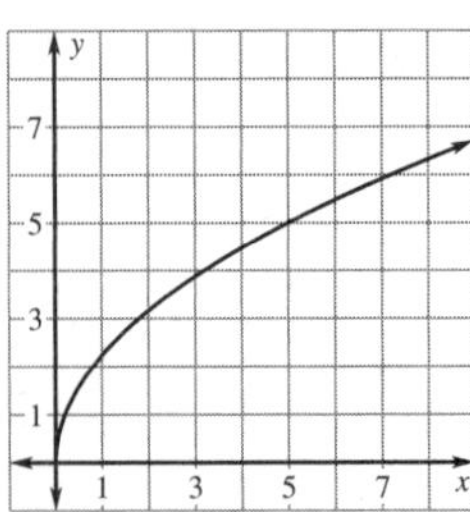

range: all nonnegative real numbers

3. domain: all nonnegative real numbers

x	y
0	$y = \sqrt{0} - 5 = -5$
1	$y = \sqrt{1} - 5 = -4$
2	$y = \sqrt{2} - 5 \approx -3.6$
3	$y = \sqrt{3} - 5 \approx -3.3$
4	$y = \sqrt{4} - 5 = -3$
5	$y = \sqrt{5} - 5 \approx -2.8$

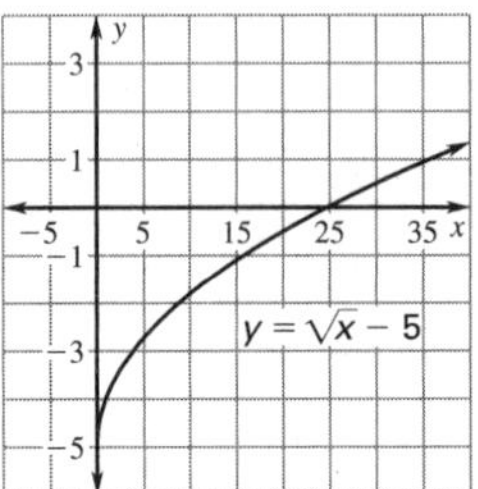

range: all real numbers ≥ -5

4. domain: all nonnegative real numbers

x	y
0	$y = \sqrt{0} + 1 = 1$
1	$y = \sqrt{1} + 1 = 2$
2	$y = \sqrt{2} + 1 \approx 2.4$
3	$y = \sqrt{3} + 1 \approx 2.7$
4	$y = \sqrt{4} + 1 = 3$
5	$y = \sqrt{5} + 1 \approx 3.2$

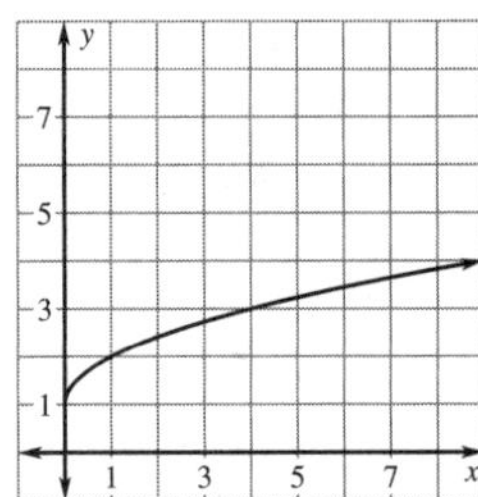

range: all real numbers ≥ 1

Copyright © McDougal Littell Inc.
All rights reserved.

Extra Practice *continued*

5. domain: all real numbers ≥ 2

x	y
2	$y = \sqrt{2 - 2} = 0$
3	$y = \sqrt{3 - 2} = 1$
4	$y = \sqrt{4 - 2} \approx 1.4$
5	$y = \sqrt{5 - 2} \approx 1.7$
6	$y = \sqrt{6 - 2} = 2$
7	$y = \sqrt{7 - 2} \approx 2.2$

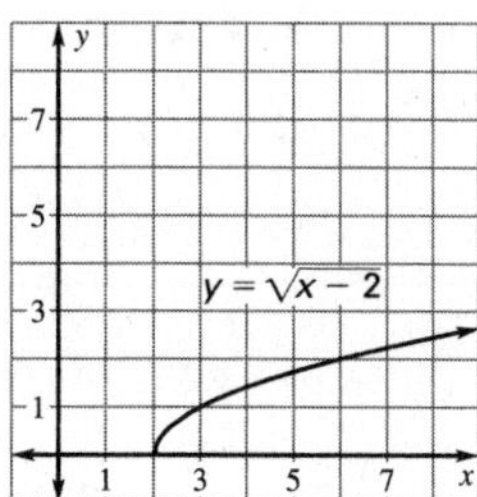

range: all nonnegative real numbers

6. domain: all real numbers ≥ -3

x	y
-3	$y = \sqrt{-3 + 3} = 0$
-2	$y = \sqrt{-2 + 3} = 1$
-1	$y = \sqrt{-1 + 3} \approx 1.4$
0	$y = \sqrt{0 + 3} \approx 1.7$
1	$y = \sqrt{1 + 3} = 2$
2	$y = \sqrt{2 + 3} \approx 2.2$

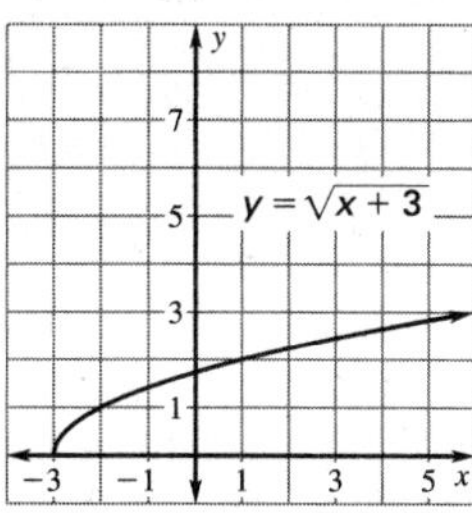

range: all nonnegative real numbers

7. domain:

$$3x + 2 \geq 0$$
$$3x \geq -2$$
$$x \geq -\frac{2}{3}$$

all real numbers $\geq -\frac{2}{3}$

x	y
$-\frac{2}{3}$	$y = \sqrt{3\left(-\frac{2}{3}\right) + 2} = 0$
0	$y = \sqrt{3(0) + 2} \approx 1.4$
1	$y = \sqrt{3(1) + 2} \approx 2.2$
2	$y = \sqrt{3(2) + 2} \approx 2.8$
3	$y = \sqrt{3(3) + 2} \approx 3.3$
4	$y = \sqrt{3(4) + 2} \approx 3.7$

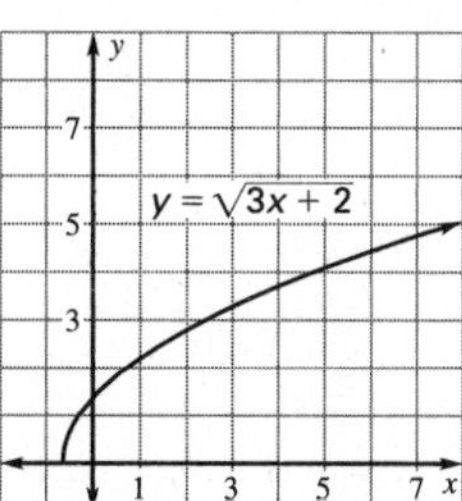

range: all nonnegative real numbers

Copyright © McDougal Littell Inc.
All rights reserved.

Extra Practice *continued*

8. domain:

$$4x - 3 \geq 0$$
$$4x \geq 3$$
$$x \geq \frac{3}{4}$$

all real numbers $\geq \frac{3}{4}$

x	y
$\frac{3}{4}$	$y = \sqrt{4\left(\frac{3}{4}\right) - 3} = 0$
1	$y = \sqrt{4(1) - 3} = 1$
2	$y = \sqrt{4(2) - 3} \approx 2.2$
3	$y = \sqrt{4(3) - 3} = 3$
4	$y = \sqrt{4(4) - 3} \approx 3.6$
5	$y = \sqrt{4(5) - 3} \approx 4.1$

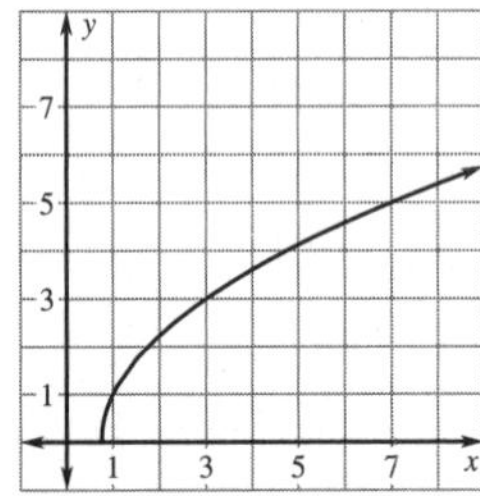

range: all real numbers ≥ 0

9. $3\sqrt{5} + 2\sqrt{5} = 5\sqrt{5}$

10. $8\sqrt{7} - 15\sqrt{7} = -7\sqrt{7}$

11. $2\sqrt{8} + 3\sqrt{32} = 2\sqrt{4 \cdot 2} + 3\sqrt{16 \cdot 2}$
$= 2(2)\sqrt{2} + 3(4)\sqrt{2}$
$= 4\sqrt{2} + 12\sqrt{2}$
$= 16\sqrt{2}$

12. $\sqrt{20} - \sqrt{45} + \sqrt{80}$
$= \sqrt{4 \cdot 5} - \sqrt{9 \cdot 5} + \sqrt{16 \cdot 5}$
$= 2\sqrt{5} - 3\sqrt{5} + 4\sqrt{5}$
$= 3\sqrt{5}$

13. $\sqrt{3}(7 - \sqrt{6}) = 7\sqrt{3} - \sqrt{18}$
$= 7\sqrt{3} - \sqrt{9 \cdot 2}$
$= 7\sqrt{3} - 3\sqrt{2}$

14. $(4 + \sqrt{10})^2 = 16 + 8\sqrt{10} + 10$
$= 26 + 8\sqrt{10}$

15. $\frac{4}{\sqrt{24}} = \frac{4}{\sqrt{4 \cdot 6}}$
$= \frac{4}{2\sqrt{6}} \cdot \frac{\sqrt{6}}{\sqrt{6}}$
$= \frac{2\sqrt{6}}{6} = \frac{\sqrt{6}}{3}$

16. $\frac{3}{5 - \sqrt{2}} \cdot \frac{5 + \sqrt{2}}{5 + \sqrt{2}} = \frac{3(5 + \sqrt{2})}{25 - 2} = \frac{15 + 3\sqrt{2}}{23}$

17. $\sqrt{x} - 11 = 0$
$\sqrt{x} = 11$
$x = 121$

Check:
$\sqrt{121} - 11 \stackrel{?}{=} 0$
$0 = 0$

18. $\sqrt{2x - 1} + 4 = 7$
$\sqrt{2x - 1} = 3$
$2x - 1 = 9$
$2x = 10$
$x = 5$

Check:
$\sqrt{2(5) - 1} + 4 \stackrel{?}{=} 7$
$7 = 7$

19. $\sqrt{x} + 10 = 2$
$\sqrt{x} = -8$; no solution

20. $12 = \sqrt{3x + 1} + 7$
$5 = \sqrt{3x + 1}$
$25 = 3x + 1$
$24 = 3x$
$8 = x$

Check:
$12 \stackrel{?}{=} \sqrt{3(8) + 1} + 7$
$12 = 12$

21. $x = \sqrt{4x - 3}$
$x^2 = 4x - 3$
$x^2 - 4x + 3 = 0$
$(x - 3)(x - 1) = 0$
$x = 3, 1$

Check:
$3 \stackrel{?}{=} \sqrt{4(3) - 3}$
$3 \stackrel{?}{=} \sqrt{9}$
$3 = 3$
$1 \stackrel{?}{=} \sqrt{4(1) - 3}$
$1 \stackrel{?}{=} \sqrt{1}$
$1 = 1$

Copyright © McDougal Littell Inc.
All rights reserved.

22. $4\sqrt{x} + 5 = 21$

$4\sqrt{x} = 16$

$\sqrt{x} = 4$

$x = 16$

Check:

$4\sqrt{16} + 5 \stackrel{?}{=} 21$

$21 = 21$

23. $4^{2/3} \cdot 4^{4/3} = 4^{6/3} = 4^2 = 16$

24. $(27^{1/2})^{2/3} = 27^{1/3} = 3$

25. $(8^{1/4})^8 = 8^{8/4} = 8^2 = 64$

26. $(2^2 \cdot 3^2)^{1/2} = 2^1 \cdot 3^1 = 6$

27. $x^{1/4} \cdot x^{1/2} = x^{3/4}$

28. $(x^2)^{1/4} = x^{1/2}$

29. $(x \cdot y^{1/3})^6 \cdot \sqrt{y} = x^6y^2 \cdot y^{1/2} = x^6y^{5/2}$

30. $(x \cdot x^{1/3})^{3/4} = x^{3/4} \cdot x^{1/4} = x^{4/4} = x$

31. $x^2 + 10x = 56$

$x^2 + 10x + 5^2 = 56 + 5^2$

$(x + 5)^2 = 81$

$x + 5 = \pm 9$

$x = -5 \pm 9$

$x = 4, -14$

32. $x^2 + 2x = 3$

$x^2 + 2x + 1^2 = 3 + 1^2$

$(x + 1)^2 = 4$

$x + 1 = \pm 2$

$x = -1 \pm 2$

$x = 1, -3$

33. $x^2 + 6x + 8 = 0$

$x^2 + 6x + 3^2 = -8 + 3^2$

$(x + 3)^2 = 1$

$x + 3 = \pm 1$

$x = -3 \pm 1$

$x = -2, -4$

34. $x^2 - 12x = 13$

$x^2 - 12x + 6^2 = 13 + 6^2$

$(x - 6)^2 = 49$

$x - 6 = \pm 7$

$x = 6 \pm 7$

$x = 13, -1$

35. $x^2 - 6x = 16$

$x^2 - 6x + 3^2 = 16 + 3^2$

$(x - 3)^2 = 25$

$x - 3 = \pm 5$

$x = 3 \pm 5$

$x = 8, -2$

36. $x^2 - 10x - 39 = 0$

$x^2 - 10x + 5^2 = 39 + 5^2$

$(x - 5)^2 = 64$

$x - 5 = \pm 8$

$x = 5 \pm 8$

$x = 13, -3$

37. $1^2 + 1^2 = c^2$

$2 = c^2$

$\sqrt{2} = c$

38. $1^2 + b^2 = 2^2$

$b^2 = 4 - 1 = 3$

$b = \sqrt{3}$

39. $a^2 + 6^2 = 10^2$

$a^2 = 100 - 36 = 64$

$a = 8$

40. $7^2 + 10^2 = c^2$

$149 = c^2$

$\sqrt{149} = c$

41. $a^2 + 15^2 = 25^2$

$a^2 = 625 - 225 = 400$

$a = 20$

42. $30^2 + b^2 = 50^2$

$b^2 = 2500 - 900 = 1600$

$b = 40$

43. $d = \sqrt{(-1 - 7)^2 + [-6 - (-6)]^2}$

$d = \sqrt{64 + 0} = 8$

44. $d = \sqrt{(5 - 5)^2 + [2 - (-4)]^2}$

$d = \sqrt{0 + 36} = 6$

45. $d = \sqrt{[12 - (-4)]^2 + (-7 - 2)^2}$

$d = \sqrt{256 + 81} = \sqrt{337} \approx 18.36$

46. $d = \sqrt{[-4 - (-8)]^2 + (-5 - 9)^2}$

$d = \sqrt{16 + 196} = \sqrt{212} \approx 14.56$

47. $d = \sqrt{(5 - 0)^2 + [8 - (-3)]^2}$

$d = \sqrt{25 + 121} = \sqrt{146} \approx 12.08$

48. $d = \sqrt{(10 - 4)^2 + (-1 - 11)^2}$

$d = \sqrt{36 + 144} = \sqrt{180} \approx 13.42$

49. $d = \sqrt{[-1 - (-3)]^2 + [-4 - (-8)]^2}$

$d = \sqrt{4 + 16} = \sqrt{20} \approx 4.47$

50. $d = \sqrt{(12 - 9)^2 + (11 - 15)^2}$

$d = \sqrt{9 + 16} = \sqrt{25} = 5$

51. $\left(\frac{0 + 4}{2}, \frac{4 + 5}{2}\right) = \left(2, \frac{9}{2}\right) = (2, 4.5)$

$d_1 = \sqrt{(2 - 0)^2 + (4.5 - 4)^2}$

$d_1 = \sqrt{4 + .25} = \sqrt{4.25} \approx 2.06$

$d_2 = \sqrt{(2 - 4)^2 + (4.5 - 5)^2}$

$d_2 = \sqrt{4 + .25} = \sqrt{4.25} \approx 2.06$

Copyright © McDougal Littell Inc.
All rights reserved.

52. $\left(\frac{-3+6}{2}, \frac{3+(-1)}{2}\right) = \left(\frac{3}{2}, 1\right)$

$d_1 = \sqrt{\left[\frac{3}{2} - (-3)\right]^2 + (1-3)^2}$

$d_1 = \sqrt{20.25 + 4} = \sqrt{24.25} \approx 4.92$

$d_2 = \sqrt{\left(\frac{3}{2} - 6\right)^2 + [1-(-1)]^2}$

$d_2 = \sqrt{20.25 + 4} = \sqrt{24.25} \approx 4.92$

53. $\left(\frac{1+4}{2}, \frac{0+(-4)}{2}\right) = \left(\frac{5}{2}, -2\right)$

$d_1 = \sqrt{\left(\frac{5}{2} - 1\right)^2 + (-2-0)^2}$

$d_1 = \sqrt{2.25 + 4} = \sqrt{6.25} = 2.5$

$d_2 = \sqrt{\left(\frac{5}{2} - 4\right)^2 + [-2-(-4)]^2}$

$d_2 = \sqrt{2.25 + 4} = \sqrt{6.25} = 2.5$

54. $\left(\frac{0+3}{2}, \frac{0+(-2)}{2}\right) = \left(\frac{3}{2}, -1\right)$

$d_1 = \sqrt{\left(\frac{3}{2} - 0\right)^2 + (-1-0)^2}$

$d_1 = \sqrt{2.25 + 1} = \sqrt{3.25} \approx 1.80$

$d_2 = \sqrt{\left(\frac{3}{2} - 3\right)^2 + [-1-(-2)]^2}$

$d_2 = \sqrt{2.25 + 1} = \sqrt{3.25} \approx 1.80$

55. $\left(\frac{-2+2}{2}, \frac{0+8}{2}\right) = (0, 4)$

$d_1 = \sqrt{[0-(-2)]^2 + (4-0)^2}$

$d_1 = \sqrt{4 + 16} = \sqrt{20} = 2\sqrt{5} \approx 4.47$

$d_2 = \sqrt{(0-2)^2 + (4-8)^2}$

$d_2 = \sqrt{4 + 16} = \sqrt{20} = 2\sqrt{5} \approx 4.47$

56. $\left(\frac{3+(-5)}{2}, \frac{7+(-9)}{2}\right) = (-1, -1)$

$d_1 = \sqrt{(-1-3)^2 + (-1-7)^2}$

$d_1 = \sqrt{16 + 64} = \sqrt{80} = 4\sqrt{5} \approx 8.94$

$d_2 = \sqrt{[-1-(-5)]^2 + [-1-(-9)]^2}$

$d_2 = \sqrt{16 + 64} = \sqrt{80} = 4\sqrt{5} \approx 8.94$

57. $\left(\frac{6+4}{2}, \frac{2+10}{2}\right) = (5, 6)$

$d_1 = \sqrt{(5-6)^2 + (6-2)^2}$

$d_1 = \sqrt{1 + 16} = \sqrt{17} \approx 4.12$

$d_2 = \sqrt{(5-4)^2 + (6-10)^2}$

$d_2 = \sqrt{1 + 16} = \sqrt{17} \approx 4.12$

58. $\left(\frac{4+(-8)}{2}, \frac{-6+3}{2}\right) = \left(-2, -\frac{3}{2}\right)$

$d_1 = \sqrt{(-2-4)^2 + \left[-\frac{3}{2} - (-6)\right]^2}$

$d_1 = \sqrt{36 + 20.25} = \sqrt{56.25} = 7.5$

$d_2 = \sqrt{[-2-(-8)]^2 + \left(-\frac{3}{2} - 3\right)^2}$

$d_2 = \sqrt{36 + 20.25} = \sqrt{56.25} = 7.5$

59. Assume $xy = 0$, and both $x \neq 0$ and $y \neq 0$. If $xy = 0$ and $x \neq 0$, then $y = \frac{0}{x} = 0$, but this is impossible since $y \neq 0$. Therefore if $xy = 0$, either $x = 0$ or $y = 0$.

Copyright © McDougal Littell Inc.
All rights reserved.

END-OF-COURSE TEST

End of Course Test *(p. 795)*

1. $(7)^2 - 3(2) + (2)(-4) = 49 - 6 + (-8)$
   $= 35$

2. $|-4 + 1| = |-3| = 3$

3. $-(1) - [-(-4)] = -1 - (4) = -5$

4. $-6\left(\frac{2}{3}\right)(1) = -4$

5. $\dfrac{2 - (-4)}{1} = 2 + 4 = 6$

6. $7[2 + 2(1)] = 7(4) = 28$

7. $(-4)^3(1) = -64$

8. $5(2^{-4}) = \frac{5}{2^4} = \frac{5}{16}$

9. $-ab + ba = -ab + ab$ commutative property of multiplication
   $= 0$ inverse property of addition

10. $0 + \sqrt{2} = \sqrt{2}$ identity property of addition

11. $5(x + 4) = 5x + 20$ distributive property

12. $-1 \cdot n + 0 \cdot n = -n + 0$ multiplicative property of negative one; multiplicative property of zero
    $= -n$ identity property of addition

13. $7^{-3} \cdot 7^5 \cdot 7^3 = 7^5 = 16{,}807$ product of powers property

14. $(2y^2)^4 = 2^4y^8 = 16y^8$ Power of a product property and power of a power property

15. $\frac{a^6}{a^9} = \frac{1}{a^3}$ quotient of powers property

16. $\left(\frac{3}{x}\right)^{-3} = \frac{3^{-3}}{x^{-3}}$ power of a quotient property
    $= \frac{x^3}{3^3}$
    $= \frac{x^3}{27}$

17. $4s - 6 = 18$
    $4s = 24$
    $s = 6$

18. $0.2b - 1.3 \geq 6.7$
    $0.2b \geq 8$
    $b \geq 40$

19. $\frac{1}{3}p - 1 < 11$
    $\frac{1}{3}p < 12$
    $p < 36$

20. $4m - 2(5 - m) = 14$
    $4m - 10 + 2m = 14$
    $6m - 10 = 14$
    $6m = 24$
    $m = 4$

21. $9 + \frac{1}{2}k = 14$
    $\frac{1}{2}k = 5$
    $k = 10$

22. $7(a + 5) = -(2a + 1)$
    $7a + 35 = -2a - 1$
    $9a = -36$
    $a = -4$

23. $0.15x + 5.01 = 1.44$
    $0.15x = -3.57$
    $x = -23.8$

24. $-7 > 5 - 2y$
    $-12 > -2y$
    $6 < y$ or $y > 6$

25. $0 \leq 1 - c \leq \frac{2}{3}$
    $-1 \leq -c \leq -\frac{1}{3}$
    $1 \geq c \geq \frac{1}{3}$ or
    $\frac{1}{3} \leq c \leq 1$

26. $4t < -12$ or $-t < -4$
    $t < -3$ $\quad t > 4$

27. $|2 - x| = 1$
    $2 - x = 1$ or $2 - x = -1$
    $-x = -1$ $\quad -x = -3$
    $x = 1$ $\quad x = 3$

28. $|2n + 5| > 3$
    $2n + 5 > 3$ or $2n + 5 < -3$
    $2n > -2$ $\quad 2n < -8$
    $n > -1$ $\quad n < -4$

Copyright © McDougal Littell Inc.
All rights reserved.

End-of-Course Test *continued*

29. $4x - y = 6$

$x + 3y = 8$

$x = -3y + 8$

$4(-3y + 8) - y = 6$

$-12y + 32 - y = 6$

$-13y + 32 = 6$

$-13y = -26$

$y = 2$

$x = -3(2) + 8$

$x = 2$

Solution: (2, 2)

Check:

$4(2) - 2 \stackrel{?}{=} 6$

$6 = 6$

$2 + 3(2) \stackrel{?}{=} 8$

$8 = 8$

30. $5p + 3q = 4$ (multiply by 2)

$7p + 2q = 21$ (multiply by -3)

$10p + 6q = 8$

$-21p - 6q = -63$

$-11p = -55$

$p = 5$

$7(5) + 2q = 21$

$35 + 2q = 21$

$2q = -14$

$q = -7$

Solution: $(5, -7)$

Check:

$5(5) + 3(-7) \stackrel{?}{=} 4$

$4 = 4$

$7(5) + 2(-7) \stackrel{?}{=} 21$

$21 = 21$

31. $6a - 9b = 18$

$b = \frac{2}{3}a + 2$

$6a - 9\left(\frac{2}{3}a + 2\right) = 18$

$6a - 6a - 18 = 18$

$-18 \neq 18$; no solution

32. $2x + 3y > -6$

$3y > -2x - 6$

$y > -\frac{2}{3}x - 2$

$y \geq 3x - 13$

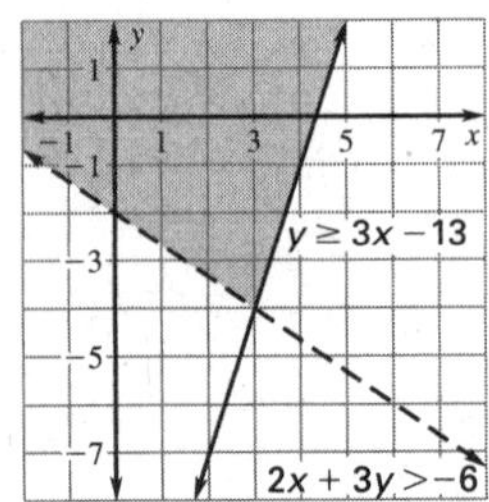

33. $x + 4y > 0$

$4y > -x$

$y > -\frac{1}{4}x$

$y \geq 0$

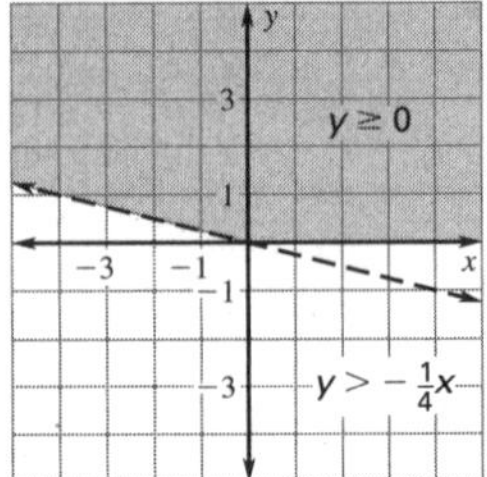

34. $3x - y \geq 1$

$-y \geq -3x + 1$

$y \leq 3x - 1$

$y \geq x$

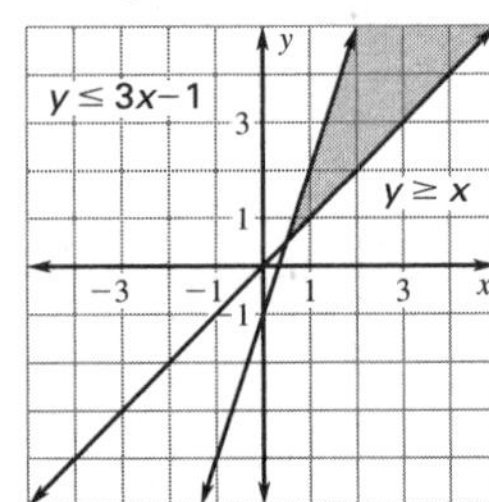

35. $a^2 + 5 = 37$

$a^2 = 32$

$a = \pm\sqrt{32} = \pm\sqrt{16 \cdot 2} = \pm 4\sqrt{2}$

36. $x^2 + 2x = 35$

$x^2 + 2x - 35 = 0$

$(x - 5)(x + 7) = 0$

$x = 5, -7$

37. $2v^2 - 6v - 9 = 0$

$a = 2, b = -6, c = -9$

$$v = \frac{-(-6) \pm \sqrt{(-6)^2 - 4(2)(-9)}}{2(2)}$$

$$v = \frac{6 \pm \sqrt{36 + 72}}{4} = \frac{6 \pm \sqrt{108}}{4}$$

$$v = \frac{6 \pm \sqrt{36 \cdot 3}}{4} = \frac{6 \pm 6\sqrt{3}}{4}$$

$$v = \frac{2(3 \pm 3\sqrt{3})}{2 \cdot 2} = \frac{3 \pm 3\sqrt{3}}{2}$$

Copyright © McDougal Littell Inc.
All rights reserved.

End-of-Course Test *continued*

38.

x	-3	-2	$-\frac{3}{2}$	-1	0
y	0	-2	$-2\frac{1}{4}$	-2	0

vertex: $x = -\frac{b}{2a} = \frac{-3}{2(1)} = -\frac{3}{2}$

$\left(-\frac{3}{2}, -2\frac{1}{4}\right)$

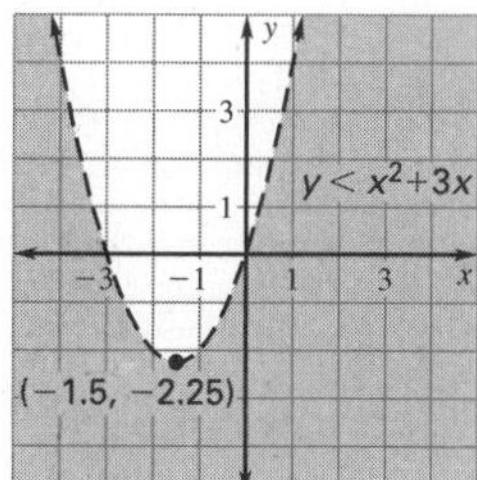

39. $t^2 + 3t - 2 - t - 6 = t^2 + 2t - 8$

40. $x + 2 + x^2 - 6x - 1 = x^2 - 5x + 1$

41. $(x + 2)(x^2 - 6x - 1)$

$$\begin{array}{r} x^3 - 6x^2 - x \phantom{{}-2} \\ +\ \ 2x^2 - 12x - 2 \\ \hline x^3 - 4x^2 - 13x - 2 \end{array}$$

42. $(9c - 5)(9c + 5) = 81c^2 - 25$

43. $y^2 + y - 30 = (y - 5)(y + 6)$

44. $z^3 - 3z^2 + 2z = z(z^2 - 3z + 2)$
$= z(z - 2)(z - 1)$

45. $8 + 27n^3 = 2^3 + 3^3n^3$
$= 3^3n^3 + 2^3$
$= (3n + 2)(9n^2 - 6n + 4)$

46. $\frac{x^2 - 6x + 9}{4x - 12} = \frac{(x - 3)^2}{4(x - 3)} = \frac{x - 3}{4}$

47. $\frac{x^2 - 7x + 6}{2x - 12} \cdot \frac{4x}{3x - 3} = \frac{(x - 6)(x - 1)}{2(x - 6)} \cdot \frac{4x}{3(x - 1)}$
$= \frac{2x}{3}$

48. $\frac{6k^2}{4k + 8} \div \frac{4k^3}{k^2 - 4} = \frac{6k^2}{4(k + 2)} \cdot \frac{(k + 2)(k - 2)}{4k^3}$
$= \frac{3(k - 2)}{8k}$

49. $\frac{3x}{x^2 - 3x} - \frac{9}{x^2 - 3x} = \frac{3x - 9}{x^2 - 3x}$
$= \frac{3(x - 3)}{x(x - 3)}$
$= \frac{3}{x}$

50. $\frac{4}{9z} - \frac{z + 1}{6z^2} = \frac{8z}{18z^2} - \frac{3(z + 1)}{18z^2}$
$= \frac{8z - 3z - 3}{18z^2}$
$= \frac{5z - 3}{18z^2}$

51. $\frac{x}{x - 2} + \frac{x - 2}{x - 1} = \frac{x(x - 1)}{(x - 2)(x - 1)} + \frac{(x - 2)(x - 2)}{(x - 2)(x - 1)}$
$= \frac{x^2 - x + x^2 - 4x + 4}{(x - 2)(x - 1)}$
$= \frac{2x^2 - 5x + 4}{(x - 2)(x - 1)}$

52. $\frac{d}{d + 4} = \frac{d - 5}{d + 1}$
$d(d + 1) = (d + 4)(d - 5)$
$d^2 + d = d^2 - d - 20$
$d = -d - 20$
$2d = -20$
$d = -10$

53. $\frac{1}{2} + \frac{2}{s} = \frac{15}{4s}$
$4s\left(\frac{1}{2}\right) + 4s\left(\frac{2}{s}\right) = 4s\left(\frac{15}{4s}\right)$
$2s + 8 = 15$
$2s = 7$
$s = \frac{7}{2} = 3.5$

54. $\frac{n}{n - 1} + \frac{2}{n + 1} = 2$
$(n - 1)(n + 1)\frac{n}{n - 1}$
$+ (n - 1)(n + 1)\frac{2}{(n + 1)} = (n - 1)(n + 1)(2)$
$(n + 1)(n) + (n - 1)(2) = (n - 1)(n + 1)(2)$
$n^2 + n + 2n - 2 = (n^2 - 1)(2)$
$n^2 + 3n - 2 = 2n^2 - 2$
$-n^2 + 3n = 0$
$n^2 - 3n = 0$
$n(n - 3) = 0$
$n = 0, 3$

55. $\sqrt{18} \cdot \sqrt{2} = \sqrt{36} = 6$

56. $\sqrt{98} \cdot \sqrt{8} = \sqrt{784} = 28$

57. $2\sqrt{6}(5 - \sqrt{6}) = 10\sqrt{6} - 2\sqrt{36}$
$= 10\sqrt{6} - 2(6)$
$= 10\sqrt{6} - 12$

58. $\frac{8}{2 + \sqrt{3}} \cdot \frac{2 - \sqrt{3}}{2 - \sqrt{3}} = \frac{8(2 - \sqrt{3})}{4 - 3}$
$= 8(2 - \sqrt{3})$
$= 16 - 8\sqrt{3}$

59. $4^{5/2} \cdot 4^{1/2} = 4^{6/2} = 4^3 = 64$

60. $(100^2)^{1/4} = 100^{2/4} = 100^{1/2} = 10$

Copyright © McDougal Littell Inc.
All rights reserved.

61. $\sqrt{x} + 4 = 0$

$\sqrt{x} = -4$; no solution

62. $\sqrt{4x - 3} = 3$

$4x - 3 = 9$

$4x = 12$

$x = 3$

Check:

$\sqrt{4(3) - 3} \stackrel{?}{=} 3$

$3 = 3$

63. $\sqrt{x + 2} = x$

$x + 2 = x^2$

$x^2 - x - 2 = 0$

$(x - 2)(x + 1) = 0$

$x = 2, -1$

Check:

$\sqrt{2 + 2} \stackrel{?}{=} 2$

$2 = 2$

$\sqrt{-1 + 2} \stackrel{?}{=} -1$

$1 \neq -1$; extraneous

$x = 2$

Copyright © McDougal Littell Inc.
All rights reserved.